GOETHE

A Psychoanalytic Study
1775–1786

GOETHE

A Psychoanalytic Study
1775–1786

by K. R. Eissler

Volume II

DETROIT / WAYNE STATE UNIVERSITY PRESS / 1963

mar. 1968

Contents / *Volume I*

		page
Introduction		*xvii*

Part I. Goethe's Attempt at Psychotherapy

Chapter 1. The Plessing Episode — 3
Chapter 2. Jacob Michael Reinhold Lenz — 17
Chapter 3. Cornelia — 32

Part II. Goethe's Proto-Psychoanalysis

A. *From the Arrival in Weimar (November, 1775) to the Second Swiss Journey (September, 1779)* — *135*

Introduction — *137*
Chapter 1. The Protagonist — *140*
Chapter 2. The Dynamics of the Initial Situation — *148*
  a. First Meeting — *148*
  b. Acute Reality Problems — *155*
Chapter 3. Goethe's Work-Disturbance — *170*
Chapter 4. Transference — *179*
Chapter 5. *The Siblings* (1776) — *207*
Chapter 6. *Lila* (1777) — *230*
Chapter 7. Cornelia's Death (June 8, 1777) — *248*
Chapter 8. *Iphigenia* (1779) — *292*
Chapter 9. Supplement to *Iphigenia*. The Duke and Corona Schröter — *339*
Chapter 10. The Jacobi Incident (August, 1779) — *358*
Chapter 11. The Second Swiss Journey (September, 1779—January, 1780) — *368*

B. *From the Return from Switzerland (January, 1780) to the Neuenheiligen Episode (March 7–15, 1781)* — *405*

Introduction — *407*
Chapter 1. From the Return from Switzerland (January, 1780) to the Writing of *The Birds* (Early Summer, 1780) — *408*

	page
Chapter 2. From Summer, 1780, to March 23, 1781	450
a. The Masochistic Phase	450
b. The Branconi Episode (August–September, 1780)	460
c. Further Remarks Concerning the Masochistic Phase	485
d. The Neuenheiligen Episode (March 7–15, 1781)	495
C. From March, 1781, to the Death of Goethe's Father (May 25, 1782)	529
Introduction	531
Chapter 1. Further Remarks Concerning the Introduction of the *Du*	532
Chapter 2. Projective Tendencies and Automorphism	536
Chapter 3. Freedom and Thralldom	581
Chapter 4. The Cure of a Symptom	604
Chapter 5. Charity and Homosexuality	620
Chapter 6. The Emotion of Amorousness and the Principle of Repetition	656
Chapter 7. Fate and Infantile Wishes	669

Contents/*Volume II*

page

D. *From the Death of Goethe's Father (1782) to the Preparations for the Italian Journey (1786)*   685

    Chapter 1. Immediate Effects   687

    Chapter 2. Problems of Early Childhood in Book I of *Wilhelm Meisters Theatralische Sendung*   701

    Chapter 3. *Wilhelm Meister*, Book II (Until August, 1782)   722

    Chapter 4. *Wilhelm Meister*, Book III (Until November 12, 1782)   728

    Chapter 5. *Wilhelm Meister*, Book IV (Until November 12, 1783)   751

    Chapter 6. *Wilhelm Meister*, Book V (Until October 16, 1784)   839

Part III. **Solutions and New Problems**

A. *The Italian Journey (September 3, 1786—June 18, 1788)*   899

    Chapter 1. Preliminary Solutions   901
      a. Wilhelm Meister, Book VI, and the Fetish   901
      b. Wilhelm Meister, Book VI, and Hamlet   920
      c. Spinoza   930

    Chapter 2. Hic Rhodus, hic salta   952
      a. Charlotte von Stein's Mistake   952
      b. Progress in the Detachment from the Love-Object   960
      c. Male Friendships and the Court   977
      d. Hypomanic Interlude and the Dethronement of Psychology   984

    Chapter 3. Italy   994
      a. Last Days in Carlsbad   994
      b. Rome, Sicily and the Father Identification   1003

    Chapter 4. Goethe's Sexual Life   1019
      a. First Cohabitation   1019
      b. The Delay in Goethe's Sexual Maturation   1032
      c. Goethe's Sexual Impediment and his Attitude towards Emotions   1053
      d. Recovery   1076

    Chapter 5. General Remarks   1095
      a. Historical Deliberations   1095
      b. The Joseph Identification   1099

	page
B. *Goethe and Science*	1107
Chapter 1. The History of a Partial Psychosis	1109
Chapter 2. Finale to an Experiment in Love	1149
Chapter 3. The End of Self-Cognition	1155

Part IV. **Appendices**

A. *Remarks Upon the Problem of the Relationship Between Psychosis and Artistic Creativity* — 1169

B. *Bibliographical Remarks Concerning Goethe's Correspondence with Charlotte von Stein* — 1183

C. *Further Remarks Concerning Goethe's Attitude Towards Work* — 1186

D. *Remarks Concerning a Cover Memory of the Aging Goethe Ridiculing Castration Fear* — 1203

E. *Further Psychoanalytic Remarks about* A Midsummer Night's Dream — 1207

F. *Further Examples of the Blood Myth in* Iphigenia — 1209

G. *Anna Amalia's Letter to Fritsch of May 13, 1776* — 1211

H. *Supplementary Notes Concerning Goethe's Second Swiss Journey* — 1214

I. *Commentary on the Psychology of Goethe's Drawing* — 1221

J. *Distribution of* Du *and* Sie *in Goethe's Letters to Charlotte von Stein in the Spring of 1781* — 1226

K. *Further Remarks Concerning the Gretchen Episode* — 1228

L. *Remarks on Engel's Novel* Herr Lorenz Stark — 1238

M. *Goethe's Letter of December 26, 1784, to Karl August* — 1240

N. *Notes on an Aspect of Goethe's Relationship to Music* — 1244

O. *Additional Remarks Concerning Goethe's* Roman Elegies — 1266

P. *Goethe's Pheasant Dream* — 1273

Q. *Notes on Goethe's Relationship with Christiane Vulpius and the General Problem of Morality in the Life of the Genius* — 1286

R. *Supplementary Notes on the Relationship of Goethe and Karl August* — 1315

S. *Remarks Concerning Goethe's Erotic Poetry and a Translation by Professor Moses Hadas of Two Latin Essays by Goethe* — 1331

T. *Tentative Notes on the Psychology of Genius* — 1353

U. *Remarks on the Problem of the Transformation of Instinctual Energy* — 1406

V. *Further Remarks Concerning Goethe's* Wilhelm Meister — 1438

W. *Relevant Chronology of Goethe's Life* — 1458

X. *Paternal Genealogy of Johann Wolfgang Goethe* — 1469

Y. *Genealogy of Karl August, Duke of Weimar* — 1470

Bibliography of Works Cited — 1471

Index — 1497

References to Letters to Charlotte von Stein — 1535

Bibliographic References

Documentation is given in the text and notes in the form of a reference number, followed, where relevant, by volume number (in italics) and/or page number(s). The reference number is to the *Bibliography of Works Cited* at the end of Volume II.

References to the writings of Goethe are usually, but with some exceptions specifically indicated, to *Goethes Werke,* herausgegeben im Auftrage der Grossherzogin Sophie von Sachsen. This edition is usually referred to as the *Sophienausgabe* and is abbreviated *Soph.* in this text. (See *Bibliography of Works Cited,* no. 247)

The letters of Goethe have been identified by the dates attributed to them by the editors of the *Sophienausgabe.*

No attempt has been made to modernize Goethe's spelling of words.

Part II
D

*From the Death of Goethe's Father (1782) to the
Preparations for the Italian Journey (1786)*

Chapter 1

Immediate Effects

Goethe's father is now struck off and his mother can at last catch her breath. Malicious tongues accuse you of being capable, even in the face of this misfortune, of claiming that this decampment may well have been the only smart stroke the old man ever brought off.[1] Thus wrote Duke Karl August to Merck, one of Goethe's best friends, after Goethe's father passed away. The particular cynicism of the letter may not come through in the translation as forcefully as in the original. Even granting that the refined subtleness in interpersonal relations about death and death customs that gradually developed in Europe during the nineteenth and early twentieth century was still in the making, the Duke's cruel words about the death of a close relative of one of his most intimate friends must nevertheless strike one as strange. It must be kept in mind that an unpleasant scene had occurred between the Duke and Goethe's father at Frankfurt. Sickness and old age had reduced him to a totally incapacitated burden on those around him; already in 1781 Goethe's mother characterized his existence as "a veritable vegetable life."[2] Thus the Duke's cruel words contained an undeniable truth. However, what prompted him to make such a tactless remark at all?

[1] [Goethens Vater ist ja nun abgestrichen und die Mutter kann nun endlich Luft schöpfen. Die bösen Zungen geben Ihnen Schuld, dass sie wohl gar bey diesem Unglück imstande wären zu behaupten, dass dieser Abmarsch wohl der einzige gescheute Streich wäre, den der Alte je gemacht hätte.] (10, p. 550)

The letter is dated March 30, 1782, in the original publication (540). This date is patently wrong since Goethe's father died on May 25. Willy Andreas gives May 30 as the date. It would be important to ascertain the correct date of this letter because it might help answer the question on what day Goethe was apprised of the loss.

[2] [ein wahres Pflantzenleben.] To Lavater, August 20, 1781, in 340, *1*:103.

The reasons that favor the development of friendship between men are various. Often in two close friends one can observe that they complement each other: what is lacking in one is profusely present in the other. This is of course only one type of friendship formation; more common perhaps is that based on similarity. In the case of Goethe and Karl August it must be remembered that Karl August had lost his father as an infant and that the fact that his brother was posthumously born made the idea of "father" even more mysterious. Boys who have never gone through the experience of an adequate father-relationship often envy others their fathers. Thus one reason for the Duke's attachment to Goethe may have been a secret envy that Goethe still had a father. In this context, a father-relationship may well appear like a valuable possession. The Duke may, by identification with Goethe, have caught up with the privilege fate had denied him. If so, he would, as a consequence, also have relived the ambivalence that is necessarily a part of a son's feeling for his father. Also, quite apart from what Goethe's father may have meant to him, these words may have expressed a kind of triumph that now he and his friend were, in this respect at least, even. How far the Duke was reacting, in this letter to Merck, to things he had observed in Goethe is not known, but that this accounted for the tone he took seems highly improbable, although he may have sensed Goethe's own ambivalence. Yet one may also assume that Goethe, at least unconsciously, felt what his princely friend (and with him perhaps others) thought of his father and his father's death in particular.

But what did Goethe himself think or feel in those days? The material on which to base a sound approach is lacking. Only one direct reference to his father during this period is preserved. On October 25, 1780, a year and a half before his father's death, he wrote to Charlotte von Stein (cf. above, p. 632): "My father is very sick." The sentence was stuck into an alien context, between quite different thoughts. The preceding sentence was: "Farewell, [my] best, keep your love for me." The following sentence reported his having met his friend Merck. It sounds as if he had had to work against great resistance to give this sentence any written form at all, as if he had had to slip it in on the spur of the moment without paying too much attention to it. He was under great pressure at that moment, not only with respect to his father but from various other quarters. He had heard that Charlotte von Stein was sick; he himself did not feel well; Merck had annoyed him (the reference to Psyche will be recalled); there was no hope of an early meeting with the beloved woman. Apparently all these additional pressures were necessary to bring forth this one short comment. One gets the impression that he may have been constantly haunted by thoughts about his father but tried stubbornly to keep them out of the interpersonal context. The barrier that is otherwise impenetrable, at least in his letters and diaries (there is no entry that refers to his father or mother and only two entries referring to his sister in his diaries from 1775 to 1782), could be pierced for a second when his attention was drawn to other worries.[3]

On April 10, 1782, that is to say, six weeks before his father's death, he wrote to Charlotte von Stein from an official trip that took him in the direction of Frankfurt:

At last [I am] at the $\begin{cases} \text{aphelion} \\ \text{most} \end{cases}$ distant point of my trip, as close to my native country as to you, and nevertheless in my thoughts a hundred miles away from the former and as close to *you* as if hand reached hand.[4]

Here his native city appeared in the manifest context and in a significant reference to distance. He must have wrestled with the idea of seeing his father once more, but as if to counteract the thought *in statu nascendi,* his closeness to the beloved woman was exaggerated. The assumption is inescapable that a feeling of guilt arose in such a situation, but that feeling was shifted to his relationship with Charlotte von Stein. It was in this letter that he wrote of the Countess who remarked, "Pour celui-là, on vous le pardonne," that he promised behavior she would be proud of, and that he mentioned a Philippic against Lavater that he declaimed on his way (cf. above, p. 601). Thus the aggression against a friend and the feeling of guilt towards the beloved woman were the derivatives of a profound feeling of guilt about, and probably an equally profound aggression against, his father.

If some of these facts are taken at their face value one may get the erroneous impression of a regression to an archaic preoedipal level (see 209; 71). Yet an ego that tries to act as if a father were not a part of the world is for this reason alone not truly regressed to a preoedipal level. If

---

[3] Prof. Carl Schreiber, as he kindly informed me in a personal communication, believes that this barrier was based on pride. Notwithstanding this factor I think of how enormous the conflict involved in the situation must have been to make it impossible for Goethe to approach it directly. But his silence in his written records still leaves open the question whether he talked with Charlotte von Stein about this topic.

[4] [Endlich am $\begin{cases} \textit{Aphelio} \\ \text{weitsten} \end{cases}$ Punckt meiner Reise, so nah meinem Vaterlande als dir, und doch von ienem hundert Meilen in Gedancken entfernt und *d i r* so nah als wenn Hand zu Hand reichte.] [Goethe's italics]

Goethe's dreams of that time were known, presumably a constant preoccupation with the conflicts about his father could be demonstrated. In his letters one can only perceive some of the mechanisms with which he tried to master the conflict. One must conclude that at this point his tie to a female love-object served mainly a gigantic denial of the subterranean struggle, as if he wanted to say: "I am not concerned with whether my father lives or dies, but exclusively with you." Since Charlotte von Stein functioned also and foremost as a representative of the superego, the shift from his father to her and the efficacy of denial were immeasurably facilitated.

There is a factor of psychic economy that has to be considered in all these deliberations, namely the possibility that Goethe's personality would not have been able to withstand the emotional concussion to which the psychic apparatus is exposed at the sight of a father who does not recognize his son, whose speech is confused, and whom nature has degraded to a vegetable existence. The remark in the letter about the equal distance that separated him from his father and the beloved woman gives, despite its shortness, a momentary glimpse into abysses of conflicts, which were, however, superbly warded off.

To what extent his ego was subterraneously embroiled in the father-conflict can be seen from two effects his father's death had: the discontinuance of the diary and the writing of *Wilhelm Meisters theatralische Sendung*. It may sound strange to name these two effects in the same breath.[5] The one was quite personal, perhaps scarcely noticed by Goethe; the other was a novel of the greatest beauty and extraordinary psychological depth.[6]

There is no statement by Goethe to guide us in the interpretation of his discontinuance of the diary. It stopped abruptly. A few words about its history may be in place. He tended in general throughout his life to keep diaries when traveling and his earliest known diary, which stems from his journey to Switzerland in 1775 and covers a few days of June, was started in such circumstances. He then wrote a short diary in October, 1775, covering just one day, when he left Frankfurt without knowing whether his way would take him to Italy or to Weimar. He called it a travel diary and important conclusions were drawn from it earlier (see

[5] Cf. Freud's analysis of Leonardo's parapraxia found in an entry in his diary recording his father's death (170, pp. 119–21).

[6] Unfortunately, the original version of the novel was lost until its accidental rediscovery in 1910. In the meantime, the final version had won world fame under the title *Wilhelm Meisters Lehrjahre,* and the original version has never won the attention it deserves.

above, p. 222). It is really the arsis of the extensive diary that covers the Weimarian years up to his father's death. After an interval of four years, a new period of diary-writing set in, with the beginning of the famous trip to Italy. The Italian diary is the most extensive he ever wrote. Written for the beloved woman, it was the great gift he sent her to reconcile her with his secret departure. Psychologically it was a kind of chronicle substituting for his (or her) absence. In view of this function I raise the question whether his Weimarian diary may not have served a similar purpose in his relationship with his father. I do not think that he had his father in mind as he did Charlotte von Stein when he wrote the Italian diary, but one of the functions of the Weimarian diary may have been to give an account of his achievements in Weimar.[7] His father had been skeptical of his future and had predicted the worst for the commoner in the princely environment. A feeling of guilt, anxiety about the future, a doubt as to his capacities, may have played a great role in prompting him to keep a record of the tasks of the day and how he spent his time.

The diary was unevenly written. Sometimes long periods passed without entries, sometimes only catchword references to broad topics are found. With the exception of January and February, 1782, the entries became sparser from August, 1781, on. Goethe's diary would be an excellent object for statistical examination. I have not found the key to the law underlying the distribution of entries.[8] I have the impression that the months of January and August provided a stimulus for occupation with the diary. In accordance with the compulsive features of his personality, January would have a particular symbolic meaning as the first month of the year (what a person does at the begining of the year he will continue doing) and August, as the month of his birth, usually offered a challenge to self-justification and accounting.

The two concluding months of this diary deserve, I believe, particular attention. In May there are in all thirteen entries (covering May 3 to 19). The first entry (May 3) lists a few titles apparently referring to literature read. The next twelve consist, except for one entry, of the names of towns Goethe visited on the respective days. This series ends with the entry for Weimar on May 19, the day he returned there. This degeneration into a mere enumeration of localities suggests that Goethe might possibly have given up the diary anyhow even if his father had not died.

In June, entries were made on six days. I wish to mention the items that

---

[7] See Freud's statement about Leonardo da Vinci's diary (170).

[8] See Bernfeld's penetrating study of diaries of juveniles (26).

I think are of importance. He moved from his garden house into the city (June 2). A week later, sleeping one night in the garden (I assume of the house from which he had moved away), he finished putting things to order in the house; he called this day a beautiful day. On June 10, he noted that Kalb, the former President of the Chamber who was dismissed and replaced by Goethe, visited him "for the first time since his removal" from office. On the following day he remarked that he and Schnauss were alone at the State Council, that is to say, the Duke and the chairman of the State Council, von Fritsch, were absent. Since Schnauss was a timid man with little prestige, the full responsibility was implicitly entrusted to Goethe.[9] The two other entries refer mainly to a conversation with the Prince of Dessau, and his departure.

The June entries are noteworthy because they refer principally to matters that formed pleasures and victories, small or great, for Goethe. One cannot call these entries boastful; they are subdued, but nevertheless they are devoid of the expression of conflict; they sound like secret pleasure and gratification at the idea of how far he has got in life. Bernfeld writes, in connection with a girl's diary that consisted principally of reports of her amorous successes: "A presentiment of danger has to be added to an experience of happiness which is not itself fully satisfying, if the urge is to arise to hold tight and to concretize [it in a diary]. This leading theme: 'it will not be wrested from you' sounds like consolation in the presence of considerable danger of being deprived" (26, p. 21), or of fear lest such deprivation will occur. Bernfeld is, I think, quite right in holding that the desire for protection against loss or deprivation may furnish important motives for writing a diary and I can well imagine that this at times also played a part in Goethe's motivation. The soft announcement of victory in the coda of Goethe's pre-Italian diary, however, was born out of the feeling "it has become mine and cannot be taken away from me." Also it is so contradictory to what we officially expect from a son mourning his father's death; it was a derivative of the son's triumph in the face of the father's grave, as if he felt that there was now less need for fear because an enemy was gone. As he was bound to, Goethe must have reacted ambivalently to his progenitor's passing away, and the diary's concluding words: "Ate at home. Occupied with a matter of accounting"[10]—written nineteen days after his father's demise—sound like a symbol of the main process that

---

[9] It had happened only four times before that Goethe had with Schnauss alone constituted the State Council. One of these incidents (August, 1780) was noted in the diary, which tends to prove that it was an event important to Goethe.

[10] [Zu Hause gessen. beschäfftigt mit Rechnungssache.]

took place in Goethe at that time. After all, the last remnant of the infantile source of the superego had vanished and no mental accounting was necessary any more.[11]

A diary such as Goethe kept must, of course, have served a variety of purposes. His keeping a diary may, to a certain extent, be compared to a resistance some patients evolve towards undergoing an analytic treatment. It was perhaps an artificial barrier to the free tapping, in his relationship with Charlotte von Stein, of all the problems that were dormant in him. It may have been a kind of island to which the love-object had no access, a kind of privacy to which no other soul was admitted, a kind of personal mirror.[12] The fear of the intruder was expressed by the secret code in which the principal actors on the stage of Weimar were referred to.

Whether what we find in the diary was actually material Goethe did not confide to the beloved woman, is, of course, not known. Yet in another more formal aspect the diary needs evaluation.[13]

There are patients who count the number of treatment hours and hold their steady accumulation as a reproach against the analyst, thus betraying their lack of feeling for the timelessness of the unconscious. The time experience that forms the background of the writing of a diary is likewise opposed to one that would imply an acknowledgment of the timelessness of the unconscious. As Bernfeld so subtly described it (26, pp. 29–44), the diary, unless it becomes an autobiography, aims at the actual, the most important of the particular moment, at that which in the feeling of the writer signifies most characteristically the momentary or acute situation. It is an aggregate of momentary impressionistic cross sections, even if this cross section contains references to future and past. In an autobiography the writer gains distance from the course of his life, and the integrative synthetic elements prevail. Bernfeld worked out succinctly in what way these integrative functions may bear upon a diary. I believe they are of minor import in Goethe's diary, which shows, more often than not, the typical pattern of a diary in the meaning of an aggregate of impressionistic cross sections, as described above.

On June 21, 1782, that is to say a week after he had stopped keeping a diary, Goethe wrote to Charlotte von Stein:

[11] See 170, p. 102, n., where Freud suggests that Leonardo tried to make a diary take the place of someone to whom he made daily confession.

[12] Cf. Platen's remark "a man without a diary is like a woman without a mirror," quoted after Bernfeld (26, p. 36).

[13] The diary may be superficially compared with another manifestation of resistance, namely the practice of some patients in writing down their dreams. Cf. 174, p. 96; 1.

My first chapters of Wilhelm Meister will now soon be in order and then I hope the desire to continue will arise.[14]

Evidently Goethe himself noticed a more or less sudden change in his attitude towards the novel. The diary had released him from its clutches and left him free to write his autobiography in the form of a novel. Since this novel will be the guide rope for the major part of the following inquiry, it is necessary to give a brief history of Goethe's writing of it.[15]

Unfortunately, it is not known exactly what shape the manuscript was in at the time of his father's death. Book I was certainly finished and the larger part of Book II written. Yet whether Book I was written as we find it today in the early version is also unknown. Goethe made changes after his father's death but there is no information available as to their extent.

Prior to his father's death, the direct references in Goethe's diary and correspondence to his actually working on the manuscript are as follows:

1777:	4 (plus one quite probable one)	1780:	2
1778:	4	1781:	0
1779:	0	1782:	1

For the rest of the year 1782 (June to December) the number of references grows to twenty-one. Thus there can be no doubt that his father's demise marked a statistical breaking point. From this moment on he worked consistently and with great self-discipline until his departure to Italy, when Book VI was finished. The change of outlook towards the novel occurred almost abruptly, and already on June 24 in a letter to Charlotte von Stein he called Wilhelm Meister "my beloved dramatic likeness."[16] With the death of his father and the ensuing discontinuance of a compulsive checking and accounting—as adumbrated in the diary—the way became free to turn towards the active shaping and molding of the projective image of himself.

We are dealing here with a more or less sudden turn from one literary form to another. Evidently the diary did not fulfill its function any more. The day-to-day jotting down of the day's impressions did not permit the concentration and artistic elaboration upon the basic problems of this one individual life form which was represented in Goethe.

[14] [Meine ersten Capitel von Wilhelm Meister sind nun bald in der Ordnung und dann hoff ich soll die Lust kommen fortzufahren.]

[15] For the biographical details see 261, 2:705–34.

References from here on to *Wilhelm Meister*, unless otherwise indicated, always mean the earlier *Wilhelm Meisters theatralische Sendung*, rather than the final version, *Wilhelm Meisters Lehrjahre.*

[16] [mein geliebtes dramatisches Ebenbild]

A sentence from Bernfeld's study points out one of the many limitations inherent in a diary: "I have not become acquainted with one diary of a juvenile that occupied itself with the parents even approximately to the extent that would reflect the true importance parents have for the conflicts of puberty" (26, pp. 47–48). I wonder whether something of that sort is not also true of the diary of the adult. A paradox is often encountered when letters and diaries are compared as to their psychological relevance. Common sense would tell one that a diary is the more important source of information, since its writer, free of the restraints imposed by the need to consider the implicit requirements of the recipient, will reveal his innermost secrets withheld from the communication to others.[17] However, it seems that frequently the diarist, being in a situation conducive to surrender to the free interplay of forces prevailing upon his mind at the moment of writing, easily succumbs to repression and denial which are not always accessible to the same degree when the letter writer addressing the recipient must be regardful of communicability and logic.[18] As a matter of fact, Goethe's letters to Cornelia and Behrisch (which Bernfeld rightly recognized as a concealed diary) reveal more about Goethe than his later diaries. The greater urge for communication prevailing during puberty does not of itself account for this fact. Also, for the ten pre-Italian years, if I had to make a choice between Goethe's letters and Goethe's diaries as biographical sources I should select the former, even though his diaries are probably preserved in their totality and a considerable part of his letters has perhaps been lost. This becomes particularly significant when it is considered that his main channel of communication during that time was his conversations with the beloved woman.

The diary is also a letter, but a letter to oneself (26, p. 46). This basic function of a diary may seldom or never become explicit, but can never be eliminated completely. The implied recipient may be a harsh taskmaster demanding complete honesty; he may be a lenient benevolent despot that lets confession and forgiveness coincide—but he can always be cheated. The recipient of a letter can also be cheated, and regularly is, but the discipline required for the sake of intelligible communication with a *you* enforces elaborations that the diary writer is at leave to omit at will. Just these elaborations (comparable to the secondary revision in dream formation) (see 158, 5:514–15) often permit far-reaching interpretations. There-

---

[17] See the chapter on "Registers of sins and virtues" ("Sünden- und Tugendregister") in diaries (26, pp. 55–63).

[18] For a view differing from the one I have presented here see 427, p. 2.

fore I feel inclined to compare the diary with a dream. Very often the manifest content of a dream, without the dreamer's associations, does not reveal very much about the dreamer, yet occasionally it may contain a deeply repressed content almost undisguised. *Mutatis mutandis* I believe this to be true of diaries in general. An elaborate correspondence will often, when carefully scrutinized, furnish contents that can to a certain extent be likened to the free associations during a treatment hour.[19] One may feel inclined to suggest as the points of differentiation between diary and letter, if such broad categories can be signified at all by specific psychological statements, that the diary may contain in general more id derivatives and a letter will tend rather to show the operation and functioning of the ego. Notwithstanding that the reverse will often take place, it could be expected that the examination of a large number of samples would show that diaries more often permit the reconstruction of an id process and letters more often that of an ego or superego process. The question would need exploration in a statistically significant number. Since conclusions regarding id-contents can very often be drawn from the character of the defense, the superiority of letters as psychological source material may become evident.[20]

Be this as it may, Goethe felt the urge to go beyond the confines of a diary and to create in a novel a hero who would be himself. Although most of his principal characters, such as Werther, Faust, Tasso, are also a projection of one of the many aspects of his personality, in none of the others was this process so direct as in *Wilhelm Meisters theatralische Sendung*. Whatever the autobiographical value of Goethe's other works may be, the autobiographical intent is not noticeable in them. (I omit here *Dichtung und Wahrheit,* where the autobiographical intent is explicit. Nowhere in *Wilhelm Meister* is the autobiographical function explicitly stated.) From Goethe's correspondence and from many details in the novel, however, it can be proved that Wilhelm Meister stood for Wolfgang Goethe. Yet not all the details and events in the novel are realistic descriptions of true-to-fact occurrences in Goethe's life. To cite only a few: Mignon was a product of Goethe's fantasy; none of his plays was ever performed in such circumstances as are described in the novel; and the harpist probably is a symbolization of an aspect or ideology of his. Many more such details could be adduced. Thus it is reasonable to ask what is the autobiographical value of the early version of *Wilhelm Meister.*

[19] In this situation the associations are of course not really free either, and only under exceptional circumstances does a subject succeed in living up to the requirements of the psychoanalytic basic rule. Cf. 153, p. 13.

[20] It seems that Allport is inclined toward a similar view. See 8, pp. 95–110.

This question is particularly important with respect to the peculiar childhood history of Wilhelm Meister, as presented in this first version. I doubt that a master touchstone can be found with which to separate truth from fiction in *Wilhelm Meisters theatralische Sendung,* because every element contains both. The right procedure would be to investigate in each particular situation what the underlying truth was and why the specific element of concealment was used. Aside from the impossibility of achieving this goal because of our irremediable ignorance, even the presentation of the little that can be reconstructed would greatly exceed the scope of this study. I shall limit myself to the general trends that are discernible and that permit conclusions regarding the principal processes characteristic of the respective period.

The question of whether in this instance Goethe pursued what Bernfeld called a pseudo-autobiography (26, p. 41) can be answered in the negative. At many points in the book Goethe could not call a spade a spade. Transformations had to be made for the sake of creating a novel that would be publishable at all. In other respects we shall encounter in it a self that was equivalent not to the author's real self but rather to his potential self [virtuelle Selbst] (26, p. 40), a self closer to the author's wishes and dreams and aspirations and illusions than to the personality that acted and succeeded in reality. Yet this potential self presented in the novel as real was also a real part of the real personality. These remarks refer principally to the original version of the novel. Goethe himself spoke of the final version as a pseudo confession in his letter to Herder of May, 1794 (*Soph.* IV, *10*:158), and, indeed, as I will try to show later (Appendix V), the writing of the two versions fulfilled quite different functions in Goethe's life.[21]

The seriousness of Goethe's effort at self-presentation cannot be doubted. I believe Goethe was at no other time so strongly motivated

[21] The following clinical observation which I made in a schizophrenic woman since this paragraph was written may lead to a partial correction of my previous view of the psychological function of Goethe's writing *Wilhelm Meister.* The patient had lost her father after a protracted illness without experiencing any grief. A half year later she developed a schizophrenic episode of moderate severity that led to a long phase of daydreaming in which extended periods of the past were recapitulated. These recalled periods of the past were not imagined exactly true to fact; many details were changed in accordance with her wishes at the time of daydreaming. Any daydreaming about the death of her father was avoided. I consider this kind of daydreaming rigidly concerned with the past to be a miscarried mourning, since mourning per se would have been too painful to the patient and therefore had to be replaced by preoccupation with her own past. It is easy to determine the differences and similarities of this process with mourning, and the applicability of this clinical observation to Goethe's concentration on *Wilhelm Meister* is evident.

and driven towards self-recognition within the automorphic process.[22] Despite all distortions, the novel is characterized by a surprising realism that can be found only rarely in his other works, and this urge towards realistic representation is, I believe, an indication of his determination to know and face what had happened to him in the past.

Psychologically it is important to take notice of the possibility that the main process of Goethe's work upon the clarification of self slipped back into his artistic creation, away from his relationship to Charlotte von Stein. The fact that this took place immediately after his father's death shows how much of narcissistic-homosexual libido had been absorbed in the relationship with Charlotte von Stein. As soon as his father was dead this amount of libido was set free and became invested in the artistic process. It seems as though Goethe had used the love-object as a protection against the effect of the dread event. His father's death had been expected for several years, and, perhaps unconsciously, he was tense about not being able to know beforehand what the effect would be. Now, too, the seeming equilibrium must have been labile, since his father's death was not re-marked by any direct reference either in communications or in conversations reported by others except for four lines at the beginning of a poem he gave Charlotte von Stein when she was leaving Weimar but had originally sent her once before after Cornelia's death. They appear in his letter to Charlotte of the middle of September, 1782 (*Soph.* IV, 6:56):

> Orphaned on more than one side,
> I here lament over your taking leave.
> Not only my love goes on a journey,
> My virtue goes on a journey with you.[23]

His resort here to snatching back verses from the past and repeating them—which is most unusual in Goethe's creative pattern—shows how acute and unmanageable the conflict must have been behind the surface of composure and unconcern.

The temporary suspension of poetic intuition was noticed before on the occasions of Cornelia's wedding and death. We encounter it here again when the death of his father could not find direct representation in his creative work. We shall later encounter a similar inhibition in Goethe

---

[22] See above, p. 261 for Goethe's remark regarding the vividness of childhood recollections when he wrote the original version as compared with later periods when writing the final one.

[23] [Von mehr als einer Seite verwaist,/ Klag' ich um deinen Abschied hier/ Nicht allein meine Liebe verreist/ Meine Tugend verreist mit dir.]

when a son was born to Karl August and there was the arrival of a crown prince to celebrate. This artistic inhibition in the face of certain kinds of problems, in a man who with stupendous ease responded creatively to the artistic challenges of the present (the day residue, so to speak) is most remarkable.

I wish to refer in passing to Dr. Ernst Kris's theory of artistic creation by regression controlled by the ego or in the service of the ego (346, *passim*). In applying this theory to the instances under consideration the conclusion must be drawn that in such instances the regression necessary for artistic creation may have gotten out of bounds and overwhelmed the ego. In other words, when an acute conflict went beyond a certain optimal intensity, regression, instead of helping the personality by leading to creation, might cause destruction. This possibility is of far-reaching consequences. It warns us to be extremely cautious in drawing conclusions from the content of works of art as to processes in the creative artist. All such conclusions require a reservation, depending on the answer to the question: What conflicts, although intensely activated, did not reach the realm of artistic elaboration because they were too dangerous? Consequently when the psychologist enumerates the problems, conflicts, and experiences that can be unraveled by the analysis of works of art, the resultant list needs to be supplemented by one showing those conflicts that had to remain outside the artistic realm. To be sure, in many instances, perhaps even in most, the second list would remain blank. But as long as this alternative has not been investigated we cannot be certain from what quarter an artistic process obtained its momentum. It behooves the psychologist of art not only to demonstrate positively the psychic contents that were the raw material of the final work of art but also those contents that did not achieve artistic elaboration, if they were intensely cathected at the time of creation. It is possible that the contents that impress the investigator so strongly as the roots of works of art acquire their importance from the fact that they serve the function of defense against overwhelming conflicts that can be kept in isolation by turning the creative impulse towards a conflict of secondary importance. It may be that great art comes into being only when the work of art performs just such a function. We are moving here in terra incognita and dealing with problems that will have to wait a long time for their solution, since only rarely do biographical data concerning those who have created the greatest works of art flow so profusely as to permit such subtle conclusions. Yet I want to repeat that a comprehensive investigation of the psychological roots of a created work of art must not rest with answering the question of what contents found their way into it but must also deal with that of what contents did *not,* although they were highly charged at that time.

Returning to Goethe's four lines, which evidently refer indirectly to his father's demise, we discover that love and virtue, that is to say, id and superego, are represented by the same person, namely the living love-object. Why should Goethe have stressed this identity after Cornelia's death as well as after his father's?

First, both Cornelia and his father had probably actually played such a double role, and in a state of deprivation of these infantile love-objects the existence of a substitute had speedily to be made sure.

Secondly, every loss of a beloved object leaves for the bereaved a break in external reality. As long as the mourning process has not come to rest there is a contradiction in external reality in the eyes of the mourning person, since so many facets of reality remind the bereaved one of just that which reality does not contain any more. This contradiction is, of course, the result of an inner conflict regarding the gulf between a wish and its impossible fulfillment. This conflict will often rage predominantly between the id and the ego (and the superego). The id cannot fathom the permanent absence of a beloved object, and in so far as the ego is dominated by the id or its derivatives it struggles against the acceptance of the truth that a love-object has vanished forever. Yet in most instances the superego and parts of the ego cooperating with it will insist that reality ought to be perceived in its true shape and form.[24] Thus the synthesis of id and superego into one representative who is alive and part of external reality (my love and my virtue went on a journey) serves the purpose of closing a rent which divides not only the personality of the mourner but also the mode in which external reality presents itself to him.

Thus the verses indicate the mourner's attempt at escaping the hardship of mourning. Instead of accepting the torn-asunder reality, he extols the unity that is the product of his own synthesis. However, Goethe did this in a situation of deprivation, when Charlotte von Stein (that is to say, the love-object of the present) was actually absent, thus indicating indirectly the aspect of the underlying situation. Also, the rest of the poem, as written in September of 1782, described a restless person who tried to obtain pleasure by throwing himself into adventures but was prevented from enjoying them, which may reflect Goethe's actual mode of behavior at that time in his—evidently unsuccessful—attempt to evade the pangs of acute mourning.

[24] Without wanting to discuss the far-reaching question of the superego's bearing upon reality-testing (cf. 413, p. 148) I mention its twofold function in mourning: (1) the demand not to give up the love and affection for the deceased person, (2) the prohibition against indulging in the pleasurable illusion that the deceased person is still alive.

Chapter 2

Problems of Early Childhood in Book I of *Wilhelm Meisters Theatralische Sendung*

W HEN WE OPEN the novel, the writing of which was to cover the next three or four years of Goethe's life, we find right at the beginning a full account of the father conflict. The first chapter starts with Wilhelm's father's hesitation about going home because his wife did not make life very pleasant for him. Instead, he drops in at his mother's. She is just preparing puppets for a Christmas show planned as a surprise for her grandchildren, particularly for Wilhelm. And then follows a description of the grandmother with all her understanding of children and willingness to make their childhood enjoyable, in contrast to the grouchy remarks of Wilhelm's father, who protests against the effort she invests in the puppet show. In the second chapter the sweetness of that Christmas Eve when Wilhelm witnessed the puppet show is described.

Undoubtedly this event played a great role in Goethe's life. It became a point of crystallization for fantasies about the processes of procreation, as pointed out earlier (see above, pp. 261–62). In the third chapter the sobering effect of the ensuing Christmas Day is reported. Wilhelm begged his mother to let him repeat the show, but he

> received from her a harsh answer, since she could not enjoy the fun the grandmother provided for her grandchildren because this seemed to reproach her for her unmotherliness.[1]

[1] [Er bat seine Mutter, sie möchte es ihn doch wieder spielen lassen, von der er eine harte Antwort bekam, weil sie keine Freude an dem Spasse, den die Grossmutter ihren

And Goethe then went on with a statement that must be regarded as extraneous, from the standpoint of a comprehensive view of the novel's plot, because it did not refer to facts which would carry significant consequences:

> I regret to say, but it is true, that this woman, who had five children from her husband, two sons and three daughters, of whom Wilhelm was the oldest, developed already in her older years a passion for a silly man, which when her husband became aware of it, he could not put up with, so that negligence, vexation, and discord crept into the household; had the husband not been an upright, faithful citizen and his mother a well-disposed and reasonable woman the family would have been dishonored by a disgraced marriage and divorce suit.[2]

This is an amazing statement in view of Goethe's repeated assertions of his great affection for his mother. His official relationship to her has historically become a symbol and ideal of filial attitudes for a whole nation. Since Wilhelm Meister's childhood is definitely written in an autobiographical vein one cannot escape the conclusion that Goethe was here describing an experience, but was it an objective experience or a product of fantasy? In one respect he seems to have been in error in his account of his family: He says that the old Meister had two sons and three daughters; in reality Goethe's father had three sons and three daughters. (There was one stillbirth when Goethe was seven years old which I do not count.) It is not known whether Goethe remembered the number of his siblings. In *Dichtung und Wahrheit,* in which his sister Cornelia takes a prominent place, the other siblings are only sketchily mentioned; he makes a short remark about a brother three years younger than he and speaks of several siblings born after him, of whom he remembers only

> a very beautiful and agreeable girl, who, however, also soon vanished. Thus we, I and my sister, saw ourselves alone left after the passing of a few years and we joined together in an all the more fond and tender fashion.[3]

Enkeln machte, haben konnte, da dieses ihr einen Vorwurf ihrer Unmütterlichkeit zu machen schien.] (*Soph.* I, 51:11)

[2] [Es ist mir leid, dass ich es sagen muss, indess ist es wahr, dass diese Frau, die von ihrem Manne fünf Kinder hatte, zwei Söhne und drei Töchter, wovon Wilhelm der Älteste war, noch in ihren ältern Jahren eine Leidenschaft für einen abgeschmackten Menschen kriegte, die ihr Mann gewahr wurde, nicht ausstehen konnte, und worüber Nachlässigkeit, Verdruss und Hader sich in den Haushalt einschlich; dass, wäre der Mann nicht ein redlicher treuer Bürger und seine Mutter eine gutdenkende billige Frau gewesen, schimpflicher Ehe- und Scheidungsprocess die Familie entehrt hätte.] (*Soph.* I, 51:11–12) Part of this paragraph has been quoted before; see p. 269.

[3] [. . . erinnere ich mich nur eines sehr schönen und angenehmen Mädchens, die aber auch bald verschwand, da wir denn nach Verlauf einiger Jahre, ich und meine Schwester, uns allein übrig sahen, und nur um so inniger und liebevoller verbanden.] (*Soph.* I, 26:54)

Here an important reference is made to the connection between love and death. If the years are noted in which a sibling was either born or died one gets the following series: 1750, 1752, 1754, 1755, 1756, 1757, 1759 (in this year two siblings died), 1760, 1761. Indeed, there was a steady coming and going of children and six pregnancies up to Goethe's eleventh year of life. It is hard to suppose that the adult Goethe consciously remembered the number and sex of his siblings. His childhood was typical of those who, as patients in analysis, gradually and after a long period of steady analytic work establish the exact sequence of siblings. What makes Goethe's statement that old Meister had two sons and three daughters so very remarkable is the coincidence of that description with an aspect of the historical truth regarding Goethe's siblings. The truth is that while old Goethe did not have two sons and three daughters, Goethe did have two brothers and three sisters. I surmise that when Goethe gave the exact number of Meister's children he was not pursuing a strict artistic intention, but determined the number of children given in the novel according to a flash of thought. By recording the number of siblings he betrayed an important unconscious relation, namely the fantasy or the unconscious wish that these might have been his own children. One often hears a child give, when asked the number of children his parents have, the number of his siblings. This error is deeply rooted in the child's narcissism, but it also betrays an act of denying that the child is one among many. By assigning to himself a position outside of the group, he partly preserves his elevated importance as in early narcissistic phases.

It is impressive that in the situation of artistic production an unconscious, repressed recollection remained accessible that apparently became inaccessible when Goethe later with explicit intent tried to write his autobiography. However, aside from the difference in age at the time of writing the two works, which must be taken into account, in the phase of the early version of *Wilhelm Meister* Goethe was actively engaged in tracing his basic conflicts and therefore the sibling problem must have had a different emotional acuity from what it had later. Goethe was quite close to his childhood during those years, as mentioned before. However, there may in addition have been a change not so much of ability to recollect as of attitude, which made childhood material less relevant. Several conditions (some of them mentioned earlier) conspired to facilitate the return of early childhood memories in the 1780s. One was his father's death. A temporary regression precipitated by the process of mourning takes the bereaved person back to childhood. Moreover, those passages quoted from the early chapters of the novel reinstated his father at the expense of his mother. His father was described as a stern man who did not sympathize with children, but the gloom and tense atmosphere in the parental home was not attributed to him—as it was later in *Dichtung und Wahrheit*—but to his mother's unfaithfulness, levity, and even recklessness. It may be significant that even under the pressure of the recent loss Goethe did not fall into an idealization and glorification of his father but stayed within the framework of reality.[4] Old Meister is sketched in realistic and critical terms, but the center of gravity of guilt is shifted to Goethe's mother—and an unnamed, silly outsider.

I surmise that this outsider was Goethe himself. It is not probable that Goethe's mother could have carried on an affair over years with the tacit consent of her husband and without leaving any record in the voluminous correspondence of the family and their friends. But it is highly probable—perhaps even certain—that she did not love her husband, in the true meaning of the term, but had an attitude characterized by respect or awe, thus rather resembling a father-daughter relationship. She took care of her husband, she respected him, and she worried about him. Bettina von Arnim wrote Goethe about this subject:

> Of your father she [the mother] told me also many nice things; he was in his person a handsome man; she married him without a distinct inclination; she knew how in all sorts of ways to steer him to the advantage of the children, upon whom he was hard with a certain strictness in matters of learning; yet he must also have been very friendly to you for he talked for hours with you about future travels and painted your future for you as resplendent as possible.[5]

His mother's libidinal interest and her admiration were on her son's side.[6] There were evidently instances of the two of them conniving against the father, with the mother trying to persuade him to fulfill the son's wishes. If Bettina von Arnim's reports can be trusted, Goethe, in turn, at an early age felt rather like his mother's master than like her son. Assertedly the mother told Bettina how fussy Goethe was about his clothes as a

---

[4] This holds true, of course, only if we can assume that this part was written after his father's death. Cf. above, p. 694.

[5] [Von Deinem Vater erzählte sie mir auch viel Schönes; er selbst war ein schöner Mann, sie heiratete ihn ohne bestimmte Neigung, sie wusste ihn auf mancherlei Weise zum Vorteil der Kinder zu lenken, denen er mit einer gewissen Strenge im Lernen zusetzte, doch muss er auch sehr freundlich gegen Dich gewesen sein, da er stundenlang mit Dir von zukünftigen Reisen sprach und Dir Deine Zukunft so glanzvoll wie möglich ausmalte.] (11, 2:181)

[6] Cf. also the passage in *Dichtung und Wahrheit*, Book VI, where Goethe describes his mother as having been almost a child who only matured in the process of her children's growing up. (*Soph.* I, 27:21)

young boy. Every day she had to prepare three suits of clothes for him. Once when she shook his vest some little pebbles he had collected hit her in the face. She reproached him and said the stones could easily have injured an eye. His only answer was that they hadn't after all, and that she should help him to gather up the stones, which he needed (11, 2:168). If this story is credible then we actually see here an irresponsible boy who did not hesitate to disturb the peaceful atmosphere of a household and who behaved in such a way as constantly needed his mother's covering up for him. It would also explain the reduction of the number of old Meister's children by one—who in the same breath apparently returns as the mother's lover. It is a belated atonement for oedipal guilt. In Goethe's life the unconscious wish for his mother found partial gratification in reality since his mother became completely absorbed in him, and Goethe may rightly have felt that his father was neglected, at least with respect to affection and tenderness, in favor of an unbounded devotion to and affection for her only son. The words he wrote her (August 11, 1781; see above, p. 581) regarding his father's sickness must also be read in this light.

> May I always hear from you that your cheerfulness never deserts you over father's present condition. Continue to provide yourself with as much diversion as the social life around you offers.[7]

Rarely, I suppose, has a son written in such vein to a mother who had to tend a stricken father. The words sound imperious. They suggest partly a doubt whether his mother was really suffering because of the father's fatal sickness and partly an unwillingness to see her deprived because of her responsibilities for his father. This letter closes with explanations for his delay in coming to Frankfurt. Goethe's persistent efforts at staying away from his native city as much as possible have been noticed by many and much commented upon. There must have been special reasons for it during his father's sickness.

An unresolved Oedipus conflict may lead to particular aggressiveness against the father or to excessive anxiety concerning him. The weakened, sick—that is to say castrated—father arouses different reactions in the aggressive and the anxiety type. As far as I have been able to observe, the person with aggressive reactions is prone to reconcile himself when he beholds his father's weakness; the perception of the father's inferiority makes all the expense of aggression unnecessary. In the anxiety type, however, the danger of a breakthrough of aggression becomes quite great

---

[7] [Möge ich doch immer von Ihnen hören, dass Ihre Munterkeit Sie, bey dem gegenwärtigen Zustande des Vaters, nie verlässt. Fahren Sie fort Sich so viel Veränderung zu verschaffen, als Ihnen das gesellige Leben um Sie herum anbietet.]

when the father is found out to be weak. Suddenly anxiety becomes un-necessary, and the aggression, which has been kept in abeyance up to then, mounts because of the relief of anxiety. Goethe's horror of the defective is well-known, and where would defect become most intolerable if not in the one person who had once served as the model of all perfection? There-fore a meeting with his father would have reactivated the whole ambiva-lence conflict which seemed in the process of healing at that time.

But let us see how Goethe went on to report Wilhelm Meister's child-hood.

> The poor children were the worst off thereby, for, as such a helpless crea-ture can usually, when the father is unfriendly, run to the mother, they were in this instance doubly ill received on the other side; for the mother in her frustration was also in bad spirits most of the time; and when she was not, she at least reviled the old man and was glad to find an occasion to bring forward his hardness, his roughness, his annoying behavior. Wilhelm sometimes felt hurt by this; he only wanted protection against his father and consolation if he found him bad;[8] but he could not bear that he should be belittled, that his complaints should be misinterpreted as a testi-mony against a man of whom he was really fond from the bottom of his heart. He thus acquired an estrangement against his mother and therefore was particularly bad off because his father was also a hard man; thus there remained for him nothing else to do but to crawl inside himself, a fate which in children and old ones is of great consequence.[9]

Here a most intimate mode of a child's experience of the Oedipus complex and his defense against it are described. Reduced to a simpler formula, it says: "I loved both father and mother, but I was not loved by them. Mother used me as a pawn in her struggle against father." The libidinal longing

---

[8] In reporting, in *Dichtung und Wahrheit,* the later quoted incidents (see p. 707) of the father's adopting frightening disguises in contrast with the mother's kindness, was Goethe giving actuality to what was described in the early version as a childhood wish?

[9] [Die armen Kinder waren am übelsten dran; denn wie sonst so ein hülfloses Geschöpf, wenn der Vater unfreundlich ist, sich zu der Mutter flüchtet, so kamen sie hier von der andern Seite doppelt übel an, denn die Mutter hatte in ihrer Unbefriedigung meistens auch üble Launen, und wenn sie die nicht hatte, so schimpfte sie doch wenigstens auf den Alten und freute sich eine Gelegenheit zu finden, wo sie seine Härte, seine Rauhigkeit, sein übles Betragen heraussetzen konnte. Wilhelm schmerzte das etlichemal, er verlangte nur Schutz gegen seinen Vater und Trost, wenn er ihm übel begegnet war; aber dass man ihn verklei-nerte, konnte er nicht leiden, dass man seine Klagen als Zeugnisse gegen einen Mann missdeutete, den er im Grunde des Herzens recht lieb hatte. Er kriegte dadurch eine Ent-fremdung gegen seine Mutter und war daher recht übel dran, weil sein Vater auch ein harter Mann war; dass ihm also nichts übrig blieb, als sich in sich selbst zu verkriechen, ein Schicksal, das bei Kindern und Alten von grossen Folgen ist.] (*Soph.* I, 51:12)

for both parents is admitted, its fulfillment is denied, the aggression is reduced to a mere reaction to frustration, which the child complains of having been unjustifiably burdened with.[10] The resultant of the conflicting components is a narcissistic withdrawal. But laying this withdrawal on the mother's doorstep is like belatedly asking father for pardon.

In *Dichtung und Wahrheit* the whole process is reported in reverse and the roles of father and mother are exchanged. In Book I Goethe describes an equivalent withdrawal but relates it to a different set of circumstances. He describes the beautiful view he had as a child from the window he favored most, over an enchanting expanse:

Yet since I simultaneously saw the neighbors walking in their gardens [for the other details see later] . . . this early excited in me a feeling of solitariness, and, arising from this, a longing, which, in accordance with the seriousness and restlessness[11] that nature had implanted in me, soon—and later even more markedly—showed its influence.[12]

Immediately following this account of his early withdrawal Goethe reports the anxieties the children suffered at night because of the gloom of the old house. His father insisted the children should sleep alone in their bedrooms, but they would try to sneak to the servants at nighttime. His father, however, frightened them in disguise back into their room. "Everyone," Goethe wrote,

can imagine the evil effect of such behavior. How is a person to get rid of his terror whom one squeezes between a double terror? My mother, always cheerful and merry and wishing others the same, hit upon a better pedagogical measure. She knew how to achieve her purpose by rewards. At that time peaches were in season; she promised us our fill of them each morning if we had during the night conquered our fear. It succeeded, and both parties were content.[13]

---

[10] Into the account of this specific childhood constellation the fabric of rationalization and defense is interwoven, as it is on the clinical level in the analyses of neurotic patients.

[11] I have translated "das Ahnungsvolle" as "restlessness," but the German word covers a large area. Paul Fischer (146) attributes three meanings to Goethe's use of the word, of which I think the second finds application in this context, namely "arousing inquisitiveness through the agitation of emotions."

[12] [Da ich aber zu gleicher Zeit die Nachbarn in ihren Gärten wandeln . . . sah, . . . : so erregte diess frühzeitig in mir ein Gefühl der Einsamkeit und einer daraus entspringenden Sehnsucht, das, dem von der Natur in mich gelegten Ernsten und Ahnungsvollen entsprechend, seinen Einfluss gar bald und in der Folge noch deutlicher zeigte.] (*Soph.* I, 26:16)

[13] [Die daraus entspringende üble Wirkung denkt sich jedermann. Wie soll derjenige die Furcht loswerden, den man zwischen ein doppeltes Furchtbare einklemmt? Meine Mutter, stets heiter und froh, und andern das Gleiche gönnend, erfand eine bessere pädagogische

This is how Goethe introduced his parents in *Dichtung und Wahrheit*. But his first reference to the writing of this work is found in his diary for 1809 and Goethe's mother had died at the end of 1808. Apparently, one of the motives that led him at sixty to write an autobiography was the desire to reinstate his mother, much as, twenty-seven years earlier, his father's reinstatement had been one of the leading impulses. But in the meantime, in all probability, a new wave of repression had again gone over the oedipal material. Cornelia became the central incestuous figure in *Dichtung und Wahrheit* and the account of his relationship to his parents was stripped of passion.

A more detailed comparison of the episodes in *Wilhelm Meister* and in *Dichtung und Wahrheit* shows another interesting problem. When I quoted above Goethe's description of the view he beheld from his window I left out the details which he observed and which aroused feelings of solitude and longing in him. These included: (1) neighbors walking; (2) neighbors tending flowers; (3) children playing; (4) parties amusing themselves; (5) seeing skittleballs rolling; (6) hearing skittlepins fall. At first sight it is surprising and not quite understandable why such observations in the surrounding gardens should have had such far-reaching consequences for Goethe. Yet closer scrutiny reveals that these six items may be considered as symbols for processes of propagation.[14] Goethe evidently referred here to observation of sexual intercourse. Hence the version in *Dichtung und Wahrheit* must be understood to intimate the following sequence: "I made an observation regarding my parents. I was puzzled and was preoccupied with the problems of propagation. This made me feel isolated. I became anxious at night. Anxiety made me disobedient. Father made things worse by frightening me. Yet I felt better when my mother met me with affection."

In the early version of *Wilhelm Meister* the sequence is just the reverse. First his anger at his father and his disappointment by his mother are described. In Chapter IV, which is scarcely longer than a printed page and really only an appendage to the one in which the oedipal conflict was described, Goethe returns to his account of the second puppet show and reports his discovery of the mechanism of the show, which had puzzled him so much. Because of its importance I must repeat the passage here:

Auskunft. Sie wusste ihren Zweck durch Belohnungen zu erreichen. Es war die Zeit der Pfirsichen, deren reichlichen Genuss sie uns jeden Morgen versprach, wenn wir Nachts die Furcht überwunden hätten. Es gelang, und beide Theile waren zufrieden.] (*Soph.* I, 26:17)

[14] I am indebted to Dr. William G. Niederland for the information that *Kegel stossen* (lit.: to push skittleballs) is in southern Germany a widespread term for sexual intercourse.

As at certain times children's attention is drawn towards the difference between the sexes and their glimpses through the coverings that conceal these secrets produce in their nature stirrings most strange, so it befell with Wilhelm with this discovery [about the mechanism of the puppet show]; he was quieter and more disquieted than before. . . .[15]

In this version the connection between watching the puppet show and sexual curiosity was still known, whereas in *Dichtung und Wahrheit* the connection between infantile sexual curiosity and anxiety was no longer known, or, at least, not expressed. More important, it seems that when he was writing *Wilhelm Meister* Goethe was faintly aware that the child's sexual curiosity derived from the oedipal situation. I get this impression from the sequence in which he presents the material, namely the closeness of his account of his sexual curiosity to his account of his feelings about his parents. This must be regarded as a particularly free approach towards the childhood material. In the vast majority of analyses in which one has occasion to study the relationship of the child to his parents, infantile sexual activity is held strictly separate from the relationship to the parents. The greatest resistances oppose the analytic attempt at making the patient accept the interrelationship between the two. From *Wilhelm Meister* one gets the impression that Goethe's defensive apparatus was sufficiently loosened to permit access to his own childhood development as it had actually occurred.[16] In the autobiography written by the aging Goethe conflicts are toned down, infantile passion is reduced to naughtiness, and charm is spread where once bitter conflicts raged. Freud compared the ego's rationalizations of its own history with the historiography great nations develop in order to embellish and adorn their own history (see 170, p. 83). In the early *Wilhelm Meister,* the nation was still fighting for its place in the sun; defeat, although no longer probable, was still possible,

---

[15] [So wie in gewissen Zeiten die Kinder auf den Unterschied der Geschlechter aufmerksam werden und ihre Blicke durch die Hüllen, die diese Geheimnisse verbergen, gar wunderbare Bewegungen in ihrer Natur hervorbringen, so war's Wilhelmen mit dieser Entdeckung; er war ruhiger und unruhiger als vorher. . . .] (*Soph.* I, 51:14)

[16] I owe to Professor Meyer Schapiro the important observation that the impression that artists give as to the kind of relationship they had to their parents, particularly to their mothers, may be deeply influenced by the prevailing preconceptions of the historical period in which they create. Thus if an author describes a highly erotic relationship to his mother this cannot be accepted without question as historical truth or even as a *bona fide* childhood recollection but may easily be the product of the fashion of the day. To what extent this historical observation decreases the validity of my conclusions I am not prepared to decide. The fact that Goethe did not include his early account of his childhood in the final version of *Wilhelm Meister* makes me feel that its value as an authentic document may be regarded as high.

but the knowledge of the truth at that time promised the sublimest accomplishments for the future, whereas concealment harbored dangers, and the impetuous young nation indulged in self-criticism in order to mobilize the last ounce of still-untapped vigor. At the age of sixty the nation had reached its peak. The cruel truth of the past was now an annoyance rather than a stimulus to change and reorganization. The ego had lost its resiliency, and mythology could take over where the search for truth had left off.

As Freud has so beautifully put it: "What released the spirit of enquiry in man was not the intellectual enigma, and not every death, but the conflict of feeling at the death of loved yet alien and hated persons. Of this conflict of feeling psychology was the first offspring" (182, pp. 293–94). The conflict of ambivalence in this situation gave birth to the conception or image of a soul. It is of utmost importance to consider that ambivalence of a certain kind may, in a certain situation, provide the indispensable stimulus for a creative process. If the conflict concerns ambivalence towards a living person the ego usually has other channels of finding a solution. However, the discrepancy between the inner feeling that a certain person was still alive, or the wish that this person might still be alive, and the perceived or otherwise established certainty that he was dead apparently made it impossible to find a satisfactory inner solution but required the evolvement of a theory. The fear of one's own death, the temporary identification with the dead, all these factors also favor introspection in our times. Every autobiography is a preparation for death, or, at least, is an attempt to set down such an account of what has gone before as shall, to the extent possible, rid the author of it, free him from the past as if it were dead, and release him for a future that is supposed to be the future of a new self. Thus the writing of *Wilhelm Meister* stood in place of a long and drawn-out period of mourning. The ego offered itself symbolically as a sacrificial victim and thus compensated for and evaded the feeling of guilt that inescapably arises in a son upon his father's death. I have probably restricted all too much the area from which the autobiographical impulse derives its momentum; it is questionable whether the motives of that impulse when investigated in a large number of instances would show a common denominator. However, it is striking to find in Freud's book on the interpretation of dreams a constellation similar to Goethe's. In writing *The Interpretation of Dreams,* Freud not only gave play to his scientific interest but also to an autobiographical impulse, predominantly in the service of settling the Oedipus conflict.

I owe thanks to Mme. Marie Bonaparte for the information (and her subsequent permission to publish it) that Freud succeeded in interpreting his first dream (which later became famous as the dream of Irma's injection; see 158, *4*), of July 23, 1895, upon being told that his eighty-year-old father was suffering from a fatal disease. It is of importance to take note that the first harbinger of the tragic event that will later shed its full effect upon the genius already spurs toward creative action. Therefore—and in analogy to the initiating event that, in Freud's instance, culminated in the writing of *The Interpretation of Dreams*—I feel more certain about my assumption that the first spurt in Goethe's writing of *Wilhelm Meister* in 1777 was initiated or precipitated by news from home that meant to Goethe that his father was a dying man (cf. above, p. 270). Thus the fact that the beginnings of *Wilhelm Meister* precede the death of Goethe's father by five years does not necessarily disprove my main thesis.

Furthermore the enhanced preoccupation with the self—no longer in the form of a story of an imaginary hero but in direct reference to his own self—made the day-to-day details unimportant for Goethe, and this takes us back to his discontinuing his diary. Goethe's behavior is here reminiscent of patients in certain phases of their analyses when the unconscious starts to respond vigorously to the psychoanalytic process. Such a patient may, after reporting a dream, hurry quickly through some day residues and fling himself upon deep unconscious material. He is fascinated by the revelations he obtains about times long past and there is a particularly free communication with the repressed parts of the personality. Freud described such a state in a patient whose treatment he had decided to discontinue at a predetermined time. When the patient became convinced that Freud meant his decision seriously, his resistance ceased temporarily and he showed an unusually high degree of sensitivity to his unconscious processes (188). Significantly, this period of heightened lucidity occurred under the stress of the patient's impending separation from his analyst, which suggests a connection with the problem of separation and thus again of death. Goethe may have been in a state of heightened lucidity when he wrote the early *Wilhelm Meister.* His ear seems to have been geared to the slightest messages it could obtain from the repressed. Of course, the Oedipus conflict and the pregenital phases were not revealed in their original crudeness, but the distortion took place on a level on which the defenses were far more softened than twenty-seven years later. In other words, if someone did not know of the Oedipus complex he could not deduce its existence from reading *Dichtung und Wahrheit,* but in the early *Wilhelm*

711

Meister the defenses are so close to the repressed that the repressed can be seen as through a thin veil.[17]

On December 19, 1781, Goethe wrote to Charlotte von Stein:

With Cook's death I close the book and send it to you. It is a great catastrophe of a great life, and [it is] beautiful that he perished in this way. A man who is deified can no longer live, and ought not to, for his own sake and that of others.[18]

Goethe's reference is to the account of the voyages of James Cook (1728–79), written by J. G. Forster, who accompanied him. Cook was killed in Hawaii on his third great expedition by natives who believed he was a god. Goethe read a German translation of Forster's book (151).

On the following day (December 20, 1781):

I cannot get Cook's death out of my head; may destiny only give to everyone whom it loves a death that corresponds so much with his life as this death did. It is in all respects beautiful, and it is also beautiful that the wild majesty has asserted mankind's claim on him.[19]

The meaning of this last sentence is not definite and therefore not liable to interpretation. I have not translated it literally and I shall return to a discussion of it presently.

Goethe's reference to Cook's death was written only a few months before his father's passing away, at a time when he must have been preoccupied with his sickness. Thus this remark about the kind of death a person may suffer must be understood as an expression of his feelings regarding his own father's sickness.

The two remarks I have quoted from the letters of December 19 and 20 contain, as I understand them, two different viewpoints regarding Cook's death. In the first letter deification of a man and his continuing to live are declared incompatible. Apparently Goethe was very deeply impressed by the report of a deification of a contemporary. I can well imagine that such an idea fanned his ambitious fantasies. In the second letter

---

[17] The comparison of the *theatralische Sendung* and *Dichtung und Wahrheit* leads to the interesting problem of the twice-occurring autobiographical impulse. Its appearance when the sting of old age makes itself noticeable is obvious enough; it is far more difficult to account for its appearance during Goethe's fourth decade.

[18] [Ich schliese mit Coocks Todt das Buch und schick es dir. Es ist eine grose Catastrophe eines grosen Lebens, und schön dass er so umkam. Ein Mensch, der vergöttert wird, kann nicht länger leben, und soll nicht, um seint und andrer willen.]

[19] [Coocks Todt kommt mir nicht aus dem Sinne, möge doch das Schicksaal iedem den es liebt einen Todt geben der so analog zu seinem Leben sey wie dieser war. Er ist in allem Betracht schön und auch schön dass die wilde Majestät ihre Rechte der Menschheit auf ihn behauptet hat.]

the relationship between the form of the death a person suffers and the form of his preceding life is mentioned. Death is viewed as a foreign body carried into man's life by a superior power. By "the wild majesty" Goethe referred, I believe, to destiny, as if possibly the act of deification might have prevented destiny from subjecting Cook to the iron law of a limited lifetime. It sounds to me as if Goethe had been toying, at that juncture, with the idea or fantasy that under special circumstances a human being could acquire a limitless span of life. It sounds further like surprise or awe that destiny should have felled this man too after he was declared a god by mortals. These few sentences probably stood for a maze of fantasies, of which the one that impresses me as the most important is that the future of a man may depend on what his contemporaries believe of him. This fantasy may be a key to Goethe's indomitable impulse to woo fame and strive for eternal glory. But it must also have heightened the conflict about his father's impending death.

His father had become a child, had lost his memory, and did not die like a hero or as a god. The whole ambivalence of the little boy against the father is contained all at once in his remark that a deified man ought to die. At the peak of the oedipal rivalry and shortly thereafter the father is deified by the little boy, but the ambivalence lurking behind the deification is also at its peak. It sounds almost like saying: "I respect father so much I wish him to be in heaven and to take God's place." But this was probably not Goethe's problem at that time, since his father was dying an ignominious death of senile weakness. Perhaps his preoccupation with Cook's death was connected with a wish of the following sort: "If my father had been a great man and were dying the death of a hero, his passing away could be borne by me with greater ease than when I must bear the inescapable ambivalence that arises from his miserably becoming a child."

It is remarkable that after his death virtually all references to the elder Goethe disappeared from the letters of Goethe's mother. To be sure, not all letters are preserved (see 340). But I surmise that it cannot be a mere coincidence that such references are missing in those that are extant.[20]

Impressive here are the only two extensive references to his father that

---

[20] A similar behavior was noted earlier after Cornelia's death. But if this glaring omission in his mother's letters indicated that she did not really mourn her husband's death, then one may surmise that this lack of a mourning reaction increased hostile fantasies in Goethe against his mother. Here may be an additional source of the harsh accusations against her in the early *Wilhelm Meister.* The difference in evaluating Goethe's silence after a bereavement and that of his mother may appear like a sign of partiality. However, whoever is familiar with Elisabeth's character structure will very probably agree with me that the two instances of silence deserve opposite interpretations.

can be found in Goethe's letters after Johann Caspar Goethe's death.[21] On December 3, 1812, he wrote to his friend Zelter (whose stepson[22] had shot himself a short time before). After an introductory paragraph of general consolation, he went on:

About the deed or misdeed itself I can say nothing. When the *taedium vitae* seizes man, then he is to be pitied, not scolded. That all the symptoms of this strange disease, as natural as unnatural, once raced through my inmost [soul] too, of this indeed *Werther,* I believe, leaves no one in doubt. I know all too well what decisions and efforts it cost me to escape the waves of death at that time, just as, wearily, I rescued myself and with difficulty recovered from several later shipwrecks. . . . When one sees how people in general and particularly the young not only surrender to their lusts and passions, but how also at the same time the higher and the better qualities in them are displaced and contorted by the serious follies of the times, so that for them everything that ought to lead to bliss, becomes doom—to say nothing of unspeakable external distress—then one is not surprised at the misdeeds with which man rages against himself and others. I make bold to write a new *Werther* over which people's hair should stand on end more than over the first one. Let me add still a remark. Most of the young people who feel some merit in themselves demand more from themselves than is fair. Yet they are urged and compelled to it by the gigantic environment. . . . No one takes into consideration that we are given reason and a brave will power so that we should refrain not only from the evil but also from the excess of good.[23]

[21] I think it is not incorrect to neglect the other passages which mention his father. For completeness' sake they are enumerated here: 1794 to C. G. Voigt, to whom he gave in trust his father's collections; 1809 to Schlosser, regarding a tax matter; 1811 about a misprint in connection with the publication of his father's doctoral thesis; 1825 referring to a drawing that was part of his father's collection.

[22] Karl Ludwig Flöricke (1784–1812), issue of the first marriage of Zelter's first wife. He was particularly adored by his stepfather. In the letter quoted above Goethe addressed Zelter for the first time with the intimate *Du.* "Zelter had lost a son, but he was to win a brother," commented Schottländer (479, pp. xx–xxi).

[23] [Über die That oder Unthat selbst weiss ich nichts zu sagen. Wenn das *taedium vitae* den Menschen ergreift, so ist er nur zu bedauern, nicht zu schelten. Dass alle Symptome dieser wunderlichen, so natürlichen als unnatürlichen Krankheit auch einmal mein Innerstes durchrast haben, daran lässt Werther wohl niemand zweifeln. Ich weiss recht gut, was es mich für Entschlüsse und Anstrengungen kostete, damals den Wellen des Todes zu entkommen, sowie ich mich aus manchem spätern Schiffbruch auch mühsam rettete und mühselig erholte. . . . Wenn man sieht, wie die Welt überhaupt und besonders die junge, nicht allein ihren Lüsten und Leidenschaften hingegeben ist, sondern wie zugleich das Höhere und Bessere an ihnen durch die ernsten Thorheiten der Zeit verschoben und verfratzt wird, so dass ihnen alles, was zur Seligkeit führen sollte, zur Verdammniss wird, unsäglichen äussern Drang nicht gerechnet, so wundert man sich nicht über Unthaten, durch welche der Mensch gegen sich selbst und andere wüthet. Ich getraute mir, einen neuen Werther zu schreiben, über den dem Volke die Haare noch mehr zu Berge stehn sollten als über den ersten. Lass

I have quoted so extensively from this letter not only because it shows Goethe in a strong identification with the young generation (which, to the misfortune of August von Goethe, Goethe was unable to apply to his own progeny), but also because in the same communication—and this was perhaps more than a coincidence—he explicitly speaks of his relationship to his own father. He had sent Zelter part of the manuscript of *Dichtung und Wahrheit,* about which Zelter had expressed his views. Goethe continues:

> I am glad that the depiction of my father has produced a favorable effect in you. I do not wish to deny that I am weary to the bone of those German patresfamilias, those Lorenz Starks[24] or whatever their names may be, who with comical lugubriousness give full play to their Philistinism, and by indecisively countering the wishes of their kind-heartedness destroy it and the happiness around them. In the following two volumes the character of the father is more fully developed; and if from his side as well as from the son's a grain of awareness had entered this precious family relation, both would have been spared a great deal. Yet this was not to happen and does not seem to belong at all to this world. The best itinerary is upset by a foolish accident and one never goes farther than when he does not know whither he goes.[25]

Here Goethe in unmistakable words turns against the misconception that the conflict between him and his father could be interpreted as a chain of misunderstandings between a well-meaning father who had a rough exterior and an unbridled son. Goethe perceived the necessity of conflict within the nature of a father-son relationship. It is not clear to me what

---

mich noch eine Bemerkung hinzufügen. Die meisten jungen Leute, die ein Verdienst in sich fühlen, fordern mehr von sich als billig. Dazu werden sie aber durch die gigantische Umgebung gedrängt und genöthigt. . . . Niemand bedenkt leicht, dass uns Vernunft und ein tapferes Wollen gegeben sind, damit wir uns nicht allein vom Bösen, sondern auch vom Übermaass des Guten zurückhalten.]

[24] *Herr Lorenz Stark* (1795), a novel written by Johann Jakob Engel (1741–1802) was accepted with great enthusiasm by the German public for its appeal to middle-class sentimentality. For a further discussion of Engel's novel see Appendix L.

[25] [Ich freue mich, dass die Schilderung meines Vaters eine gute Wirkung auf dich hervorgebracht. Ich will nicht leugnen, dass ich die deutschen Hausväter, diese Lorenz Starke, und wie sie heissen mögen, herzlich müde bin, die in humoristischer Trübe ihrem Philisterwesen freyes Spiel lassen, und den Wünschen ihrer Gutmüthigkeit unsicher in den Weg treten, sie und das Glück um sich her zerstören. In den folgenden zwey Bänden bildet sich die Gestalt des Vaters noch völlig aus; und wäre sowohl von seiner Seite als von der Seite des Sohns ein Gran von Bewusstseyn in diess schätzbare Familienverhältniss getreten, so wäre beyden vieles erspart worden. Das sollte nun aber nicht seyn und scheint überhaupt nicht für diese Welt zu gehören. Der beste Reiseplan wird durch einen albernen Zufall gestört und man geht nie weiter, als wenn man nicht weiss, wohin man geht.]

Goethe meant exactly by "a grain of awareness," but it remains of second-ary importance, for Goethe does not in any case put much stock in its beneficial effect upon this family relationship. He acknowledges the shared responsibility. In the case of Zelter's stepson, he seems to side with the younger generation against the world, which, by its follies, crushes the not yet fully developed. In evaluating his own upbringing he was more moderate in judgment. Was this possible only after he had expressed him-self so strongly in the antecedent part of the letter? In any case one gets the impression that the whole problem was on the verge of becoming more a matter of thought and intellectual elaboration to him than of true passion or partisanship. The whole question was lifted to the level of adolescent or postadolescent clashes, and the infantile root—so impres-sively presented in *Wilhelm Meister*—was omitted. But one can still sense in this passage the last ripple of an emotional wave that had been sharply expressed in a letter of November 10, 1772, to Lotte's fiancé, Kestner:

> Dear God, when once I am old shall I also then be so [like father]? Will my soul no longer hang on that which is worthy of love and is good? Strange, for one would believe that the older man grows the freer he should become of what is earthly and small. He [father] becomes always earthlier and smaller.[26]

This deep despair about his father's earthliness and smallness, which weighed heavily upon him during the years before and just after his fa-ther's death, can barely be heard when he wrote to Zelter about his own father, yet was still audible with some shrillness when he tried to explain young Flöricke's suicide.

It was gone in the other passage which the aged Goethe wrote about his father. This is in a draft of a letter (September 19, 1816) to his son August (1789–1830), who was legitimated at the age of eleven. I have not been able to find out about the events leading to this letter, but apparently August had informed Goethe of his intention to vouch for a loan a friend of his wanted to negotiate.

> Without wanting to go into the particulars of the instance submitted to me by you, of a security to be pledged, I must [ask you], my dear son [Goethe wrote], to take the following to heart.
>
> When my late father set me up in some measure, there was, among other good precepts he gave me at the same time, one that was like an order,

[26] [. . . lieber Gott wenn ich einmal alt werde, soll ich dann auch so werden. Soll meine Seele nicht mehr hängen an dem was liebenswerth und gut ist. Sonderbar, dass da man glauben sollte ie älter der Mensch wird, desto freyer er werden sollte von dem was irrdisch und klein ist. Er wird immer irrdischer und kleiner.]

namely that during his lifetime I should not pledge security and also should always heed this warning after his death.

"For," he said, "when you have cash, then may you also lend it to a friend without great security. Nor, if you want to give it away as a gift, is there anything to say against it; if you borrow it then you will be prepared to pay interest and to clear off the principal; yet if you pledge yourself, then you put yourself into a disturbed condition which is all the more embarrassing since you must behave in an inactive, even passive way." Nobody pledges himself lightly unless he believes that he runs no risk; yet as soon as a person has pledged himself, then he feels himself, particularly in worrisome moments, threatened by an evil that shows itself from afar, yet appears all the more terrible inasmuch as he feels he will not be equal to it when it comes closer.

To stake one's life for a friend as for yourself is commendable, since the moment decides; but to cause yourself worries for an uncertain period, or even perhaps for your whole life, and to undermine your certain property, at least in your imagination, is by no means advisable; for our physical states and the course of events cause us quite a few hypochondriacal hours, and then worry calls forth all the specters that a merry day chases away.

This was my father's conviction and mine too has remained the same. In my lifetime I have done much for others, perhaps more than was sensible, and forgot in so doing me and mine; this I can tell you without boasting since you know something of it; but I have never given a guarantee and in my estate you will not find such an act. Therefore have the old adage before you and remember me.[27]

[27] [Ohne in den besondern Fall einer zu übernehmenden Bürgschaft, den du mir, mein lieber Sohn, vorlegtest, einzugehen, muss ich dir Nachstehendes zu Herzen geben.

Als mich mein seliger Vater einigermassen ausstattete, war unter andern guten Lehren, die er mir zugleich ertheilte, eine, die einem Befehl glich, dass ich bey seinem Leben keine Bürgschaft eingehen und auch nach seinem Tode diese Warnung immer bedenken solle.

Denn sagte er: wenn du baares Geld hast, so magst du es einem Freunde auch ohne grosse Sicherheit leihen. Willst du es verschenken, so ist auch nichts dagegen zu sagen, borgst du, so wirst du dich einrichten Interessen zu bezahlen und das Capital abzutragen; verbürgst du dich aber, so versetzest du dich in einen unruhigen Zustand, der desto peinlicher ist, als du dich unthätig ja leidend verhalten musst. Niemand verbürgt sich leicht, ausser wenn er glaubt, er laufe keine Gefahr, ist aber die Verbürgung geschehen, so fühlt er sich gar bald, besonders in sorglichen Augenblicken, von einem in der Ferne sich zeigenden Übel bedroht, welches um so fürchterlicher erscheint, als er fühlt, dass er ihm nicht gewachsen sey, wenn es näher treten sollte.

Das Leben für einen Freund zu wagen wie für dich selbst, ist löblich, denn der Augenblick entscheidet; aber dir auf unbestimmte Zeit, oder wohl gar auf's ganze Leben Sorge zu bereiten, und deinen sichern Besitz wenigstens in der Einbildungskraft zu untergraben, ist keineswegs räthlich: denn unsere körperlichen Zustände und der Lauf der Dinge bereiten uns manche hypochondrische Stunde, und die Sorge ruft alsdann alle Gespenster hervor, die ein heiterer Tag verscheucht.

Here the voice of Goethe's father reaching his grandson from the nether world sounds like that of a lawgiver whose wisdom must not be disputed, and Goethe has made it, or professed to have made it, his own. But this occurred in a typical situation. The grandfather is played off against the son. The whole ambivalence that once upon a time was directed against the father is now transferred against the son. What Goethe is really saying is that the reason he must deprive the son of something is that his father told him to do so. There may also be the implication of channelizing the frustrated son's aggression away from himself to the grandfather, as if the son should now develop the same aggression against his grandfather that the father once felt against his own father.[28] This letter shows that a significant internal change must have occurred in Goethe's relationship to his father. The father had become deified after all, had lost "the earthly and small," and had become what historically he had always been, the fountainhead of law and wisdom.

But it will take a long time and a hard struggle before this inner deification of the father will be accomplished, and we must return—where we left off—to the beginning of this process, when Goethe was evolving his poetic likeness. The first book of the novel goes on to set forth the father-conflict beyond the infantile period. Wilhelm's father is a merchant and Wilhelm must work in his store. The good which the boy, without possessing the "true spirit" of a merchant, accomplished for his father's enterprise is reported in detail. At heart, however, the boy was fascinated only by the theater.

The old disagreement between Goethe and his father regarding his career as a lawyer is here transposed into a different milieu. In the novel the main dispute between father and son rages about Wilhelm's contempt for money.

Wilhelm's mind had been above those low needs for a long time, particularly since he lacked for nothing in his father's house, and he was much too vivacious and candid not to let his contempt for trade show occasionally, even to his father. He regarded it as an oppressive load on his soul, as tar that limed the wings of his spirit, as ropes that fettered his soul's high

---

So war die Gesinnung meines Vaters und so ist auch die meinige geblieben. Ich habe in meinem Leben viel, vielleicht mehr als billig, für andere gethan, und mich und die Meinigen dabei vergessen; diess kann ich dir ohne Ruhmredigkeit sagen, da du manches weisst; aber ich habe mich nie verbürgt, und unter meinem Nachlass findest du keinen solchen Act. Habe daher das alte Sprichwort vor Augen und gedenke mein.]

[28] Heinrich Meyer (391, p. 51) reports an instance that shows Goethe in a full father-identification in his dealings with his son.

flight, towards which he felt his growth from nature. Sometimes a quarrel broke out between father and son over such a remark. It ended most of the time in old Meister's being angry and the young man's being moved, and the matter was made no better by the fact that each party seemed only to become surer of his own opinion, and Wilhelm, who loved his father, did not like to be rebuked either, and shut himself away by himself the more. His feelings, which became warmer and stronger, his imagination, which soared, were turned unchecked towards the theater, and small wonder.[29]

Then follows a description of the dreariness of bourgeois life, which is devoid of the heroic, devoid of contact with and love for nature, but oppressive in its monotony and dreariness.

Here belatedly a feeling of guilt seems to be settled. The longing to leave bourgeois society and to join the world of the theater, which plays the central role in *Wilhelm Meister,* corresponds to Goethe's swing from bourgeois society to the nobility. This swing was justified by the assertion that bourgeois culture stifles the young, the romantic, the passionate, and the adventurous. Yet in the novel the alternatives between which Wilhelm has to choose are not bourgeoisie and nobility, but bourgeoisie and the ill-famed world of the theater. The last vestige of selfishness, which may be suspected when a person forsakes his own social group, was eradicated, and Wilhelm was drawn towards an outside group that was deprived of security, held inferior, and discriminated against. At the same time, however, the theater was endowed with the quality of a mission.

Where is there a citadel against boredom like the theater, where is society more pleasantly joined together, where would people sooner have to confess that they are brethren, than when firmly attached to the figure and the words of one person, all of them uplifted, suspended, in the same feeling? What are paintings and statues to the living flesh of my flesh, to the other I who suffers, is elated, and directly touches in me each nerve identically tuned? And where may one suppose there is more virtue, in the debased bourgeois who scrapes together his livelihood in fearful filthy trade, or in

[29] [Wilhelms Geist war lang über diese niedre Bedürfnisse weg, besonders da ihm in seines Vaters Haus nichts abging, und er war viel zu lebhaft und aufrichtig, als dass nicht manchmal, selbst gegen seinen Vater, die Verachtung des Gewerbes durchgeblickt hätte. Er hielt es für eine drückende Seelenlast, für Pech, das die Flügel seines Geistes verleimte, für Stricke, die den hohen Schwung der Seele fesselten, zu dem er sich von Natur das Wachsthum fühlte. Manchmal gab's über irgend eine solche Äusserung Streit zwischen Vater und Sohn, an dessen Ende der Alte meist erzürnt, der Junge bewegt und die Sache dadurch nichts besser ward, indem jede Partei nur ihrer Meinung gewisser zu werden schien, und Wilhelm, der seinen Vater liebte, auch nicht gerne angefahren war, sich mehr in sich selbst verschloss. Sein Gefühl, das wärmer und stärker ward, seine Einbildung, die sich erhöhte, waren unverrückt gegen das Theater gewendet, und was Wunder?] (*Soph.* I, 51:42)

him whose art which gives him bread simultaneously penetrates to the noblest and highest feelings of mankind, who daily studies and presents virtue and vice in their nakedness and must feel beauty and ugliness most livelily before he can make others feel them with equal liveliness?[30]

These are the words with which Wilhelm glorifies and idealizes the theatrical world. Among those who listen to his enraptured words there is also Mariane, an actress, with whom Wilhelm has fallen in love, but to whom as yet his "bourgeois timidity" [bürgerliche Schüchternheit] has prevented him from confessing his feelings.

In trying to reconstruct the motives that drew Wilhelm so intensely towards the theater, three groups must be considered.

(1) *The historical motive.* The puppet show had left an indelible trace in Wilhelm. Having become in early years a substitute and outlet for sexual curiosity there came to be attached to it various cover memories referring to archaic sexual experiences, and, in accordance with the principle of repetitious compulsion, Wilhelm has his first and only sexual relationship with the just-mentioned Mariane. Yet it would be wrong to believe that only happy, pleasurable (or potentially pleasurable) feelings were attached to Wilhelm's early experiences with the theater. When he himself staged a puppet show before a crowd of invited children everything went fine with the exception

> . . . that Wilhelm in the fire of action let his Jonathan fall and was compelled to reach down his hand and fetch it, which sharply shattered the illusion, caused great laughter, and humiliated him unspeakably.[31]

Jonathan, of course, was one of the puppets in a Biblical play, but the wording strongly suggests a sexual humiliation. Jonathan, that purest of Biblical heroes, the symbol of sublimated male friendship, who was killed in battle, could well serve as a penis symbol. The passage may then indi-

---

[30] [Wo ist ein Sicherplatz gegen die Langeweile wie das Schauspielhaus, wo verbindet sich die Gesellschaft angenehmer, wo müssen die Menschen eher gestehen, dass sie Brüder sind, als wenn sie an der Gestalt, an dem Munde eines Einzigen hangend alle in Einer Empfindung schwebend empor getragen werden? Was sind Gemählde und Statuen gegen das lebendige Fleisch von meinem Fleisch, gegen das andre Ich, das leidet, fröhlich ist und jede gleichgestimmte Nerve in mir unmittelbar berührt? Und wo lässt sich mehr Tugend vermuthen, bei dem gedrückten Bürger, der in ängstlich schmutzigem Gewerb seine Nahrung zusammen schleppt, oder bei dem, dessen Kunst, die ihm Brot gibt, zugleich die edelsten grössten Gefühle der Menschheit durchdringt, der Tugend und Laster täglich in seiner Blösse studirt und darstellt und die Schönheit und Hässlichkeit am lebhaftesten fühlen muss, eh' er sie andre so lebhaft empfinden lassen kann.] (*Soph.* I, *51*:50–51)

[31] [dass Wilhelm in dem Feuer der Action seinen Jonathan fallen liess und er genöthigt war, mit der Hand hinunter zu greifen und ihn zu holen, das denn die Illusion sehr unterbrach, ein grosses Gelächter verursachte und ihn unsäglich kränkte.] (*Soph.* I, *51*:23)

cate a humiliating experience of impotence in the adult projected back into a childhood screen memory (cf. 157), or a childhood attempt at intercourse or its equivalent.[32] Again in conformity with the repetitious compulsion, Mariane is unfaithful to Wilhelm. Although she is made pregnant by him (without his knowing it) and he wants to marry her, she continues to carry on an affair with a wealthy man. Wilhelm accidentally finds out about it shortly after he has decided to suggest an elopement to her. The shock throws him into a serious illness.

(2) *The id motive.* From the first book of the early *Wilhelm Meister* it becomes abundantly clear that, as in all instances of this kind, exhibitionism and voyeurism are the leading pregenital impulses that tie Wilhelm inexorably to the theater. No further quotations are necessary. It must be remembered, too, that the boy's first contact with the splendor and magnificence of the nobility occurred in circumstances that must greatly have aroused his exhibitionistic and voyeuristic impulses, namely on the occasion of the crowning of the emperors at Frankfurt. Here a crowd kept their eyes glued to one or two persons who moved around with majestic calmness taking their exhibition for granted. The fact that in both worlds, that of the theater as well as that of the upper nobility, the same pregenital impulses could find gratification, must be kept in mind in order to grasp the background meaning of *Wilhelm Meister.*

(3) *The ego motive.* In Wilhelm's lengthy apologia, quoted above, for the actor and the theater, he reveals an important expectation which we shall encounter again at a crucial juncture. He describes a situation in which all the members of a group are united by the same simultaneous emotion. The isolation of the individual group member is put an end to; actor and audience are pervaded by the same emotion, and, although activity and passivity are unequally distributed, the whole group becomes a psychological unit by the spontaneous surrender of all participants to the identical emotional experience. The fulfillment of a superego demand was also included in Wilhelm's apologia. This would not need discussion were it not for the strange insistence that the highest virtues existed in the theater, where actually vice, superficiality, and vanity prevailed, in Goethe's time perhaps even more than in modern times. Such naive idealism was quite alien to Goethe, as far as we know him from the written record. He set forth here an aspect of his adolescent idealism he had to pay a higher price to correct than did Wilhelm, the hero he created.

[32] Other humiliating experiences in connection with the theater, or with playing theater, are recorded in *Wilhelm Meister.*

Chapter 3

Wilhelm Meister, Book II
(Until August, 1782)

Book II of the early *Wilhelm Meister* was partly written before Goethe's father died, but the bulk of it fell within the first few months thereafter.[1] Book II deals with Wilhelm's recovery from the disease which set in when he learned of Mariane's unfaithfulness, and, further, with the influence his brother-in-law Werner gained over him, his early endeavors as a writer of plays, and his leaving on a business trip at Werner's suggestion. Goethe's account of Wilhelm's illness and recovery is a masterpiece that could almost be included in a textbook of so-called psychosomatic medicine. In *Dichtung und Wahrheit* Goethe reported that he responded with physical sickness to the great excitement of his first infatuation, when the episode with the enigmatic Gretchen ended abruptly and with humiliation, and the reader will recall the frightful condition in which he returned from Leipzig.[2] The account of Wilhelm's disease requires detailed scrutiny. Here I wish only to mention the strong masochis-

---

[1] It is unfortunately impossible to ascertain the exact date when Goethe finished Book II. On July 27, 1782, he wrote Knebel as if he had finished it and Knebel would soon receive it. On August 23 he wrote Charlotte von Stein that he had read it to the Duke and the Duchess, but added that he was hurrying to finish it before Charlotte von Stein's return. A direct reference to Book III occurs in a letter of October 18, 1782, to Charlotte von Stein. I shall dispose the biographical material on the assumption that Goethe finished Book II in August, or at least was from that month on preoccupied with Book III.

[2] Recently an author has pointed out that Goethe's serious disorder (a pulmonary hemorrhage) two weeks after receiving information of his son's death (November 25, 1830) was probably the aftereffect of that tragedy. Interestingly enough, Goethe as a young man in Leipzig also suffered a pulmonary hemorrhage.

tic coloring, which is also noticeable in his description of the early disease in *Dichtung und Wahrheit*. There he wrote:

> Thus I spent day and night in great restlessness, in raving and exhaustion, so that in the end I felt glad when a physical disease set in with considerable severity.[3]

Goethe recognized the positive effect of disease and apparently was aware that at times the only means available for the solution of a conflict is the rearrangement and reorganization of the biological matrix. He described the physical effect of Wilhelm's disease in the following way:

> With the wisdom of a judicious taskmaster it [the disease] took energetic measures, seized each evil at its root, turned everything topsy-turvy, cast out what was too crude, devoured the more refined, and a few times mercilessly brought our friend by its relentless effects to the gates of death. Yet also its healing was basic; everything alien and false was expelled and the well-built body was restored in its inmost relations to its future happiness.[4]

It is not known when Goethe wrote this account. It is noteworthy that Book II of *Wilhelm Meister* is replete with the problem of separation from a beloved person and the reaction to it. Whether it was written before or after his father's death, it was certainly written at a time when he knew that a separation of the greatest importance would soon occur or had occurred, that is to say, at a time when his mind was forced by external pressures to be preoccupied with an irrevocable separation. Is it possible that this masterly description of a disease was born of the impulse to avert its real occurrence, when the separation in fantasy would become reality?

Wilhelm's father steps into the background as the narrative progresses. We hear that he falls sick, and Wilhelm's brother-in-law Werner takes over a moderately paternal role. He has a better understanding of Wilhelm's problem-beset personality than the father and he tries to assist him without insisting on his own principles. Werner bears some earmarks of Goethe's brother-in-law Schlosser, particularly from the early phase of their relationship when he came to Leipzig to look after the young student

---

[3] [So verbrachte ich Tag und Nacht in grosser Unruhe, in Rasen und Ermattung, so dass ich mich zuletzt glücklich fühlte, als eine körperliche Krankheit mit ziemlicher Heftigkeit eintrat.] (*Soph*. I, 26:341.)

[4] [Mit der Weisheit einer verständigen Zuchtmeisterin griff sie durch, fasste jedes Übel in der Wurzel, kehrte das Oberste zu unterst, warf aus was zu grob war, verzehrte das Feinere, und unbarmherzig in ihren unaufhaltsamen Wirkungen brachte sie unseren Freund etlichemale an die Pforten des Todes. Aber auch ihre Cur war aus dem Grunde; alles Fremde und Falsche ward vertrieben, und der wohlgebaute Körper zu seinem künftigen Glücke in seinen innersten Verhältnissen wieder hergestellt.] (*Soph*. I, 51:103–04)

who worried his parents in distant Frankfurt. A most remarkable deviation from reality, however, can be seen in the minor importance that Amelia, Wilhelm's sister, plays in the whole framework of the novel: Aside from her interest in Wilhelm's poetical products and the constant encouragement she imparts, she remains a colorless figure in the background.

The moderately quiet interval of Wilhelm's convalescence gives opportunity for discussions about literary matters between the sanguine and matter-of-fact Werner and the idealistic Wilhelm, absorbed in the theatrical arts beyond anything else. A series of five fragmentary essays (*Soph.* I, 51:148–52) written by one of Wilhelm's friends on the subject of why man finds enjoyment in drama, particularly in tragedy, seems of great psychological importance. The subject seems abstract, yet it touches upon one of the nerve centers of the novel, namely the problem of human emotionality. The spell that tragedy casts over the human mind has puzzled philosophers since antiquity, for when a man watches a tragedy he voluntarily exposes himself to experiencing events he would in no circumstances want to witness, or even want to have happen, in objective reality.

The ideas of the five essays can be reproduced in the following way by using terms of modern psychology:

(1) A principle of human nature is described which Freud (following Fechner) introduced into psychoanalysis as *the constancy principle,* the tendency of the psychic apparatus to keep the quantity of psychic excitement to an optimal minimum. This idea, of course, is expressed in the novel in unscientific language.

(2) *The pleasure principle* is described, which disturbs the fulfillment of the constancy principle. Goethe's illustration is noteworthy. He refers to masochism and speaks of "a kind of lustful passion for the bad and a dark longing towards the enjoyment of pain . . . related to other feelings, concealed in other symptoms."[5] The state of indifference is the most detestable for man. The avidity to be excited is so strong that the seemingly moderate person although "he does not end each day of his life in a drunken state, nevertheless consumes the sum total of his existence earlier than it was destined."[6]

(3) Yet the external world also intrudes constantly, arouses man and does not let him come to rest. "Man is deeply stirred by everything un-

---

[5] [eine Art Lüsternheit nach dem Übel und eine dunkle Sehnsucht nach dem Genusse des Schmerzens . . . mit andern Gefühlen verwandt, unter andern Symptomen verhüllt.]

[6] [der Mässigscheinende zwar nicht jeden Tag seines Lebens betrunken schliesst, doch aber die ganze Summe seines Daseins früher als es bestimmt war aufzehrt.]

usual that he encounters. An evil that has passed becomes for him a treasured recollection for the rest of his life."[7] Among all the stimulation that
reaches man from the outside, visual stimulation holds a special place.
What is seen becomes rooted more deeply than what we learn from descriptions. And Goethe proceeds to describe the connection between vision and sadism.

How many thousands are irresistibly drawn to an execution which they
abhor, how fearful is the crowd at heart for the evildoer, and how many
would go home unsatisfied if he were pardoned and his head were to stay
on? The gushing blood that stains the pale neck of the guilty, sprinkles the
imagination of the spectator with irremovable spots; shuddering, lustful,
the soul years after looks up again to the scaffold, summons all the terrible circumstances to reappear before it, and is reluctant to confess to itself
that it enjoys the horrible spectacle. Much more welcome are those executions that the poet contrives.[8]

(4) In this essay the divided nature of man's personality is adumbrated. What may be horrible for one part may be enticing for another,
and this enticement may in the end engulf the whole personality. Goethe
writes:

The healthy man cannot be stirred by anything without there being agitated simultaneously those chords of his nature from which the enchanting
harmonies of pleasure pour down. And even gruesome destructive longings at which one is horrified in children too, and which one tries to dis-
pel by punishments, have secret ways and hiding places through which they
pass over into pleasures that are the sweetest of all. All these internal paths
and ways are violently agitated with electric sparks through theatrical per-

---

[7] [Von jedem was dem Menschen Sonderbares begegnet, wird er innig gerührt. Ein
Übel, das vorüber ist, wird ihm zu einem Schatze der Erinnerung für sein ganzes Leben.]
    Here Goethe blended the pleasure and reality principles in a masterly way by showing
that present displeasure may contain the promise of pleasure to be derived later from the
corresponding memory.

[8] [Wie viel Tausende werden unwiderstehlich nach einer Execution, die sie verabscheuen,
hingerissen, wie ängstet sich die Brust der Menge für den Übelthäter, und wie viele würden
unbefriedigt nach Hause gehen, wenn er begnadigt würde und ihm der Kopf sitzen bliebe?
Das sprudelnde Blut, das den bleichen Nacken des Schuldigen färbt, besprengt die Einbildungskraft der Zuschauer mit unauslöschlichen Flecken; schaudernd, lüstern blickt die Seele
wieder nach Jahren zu dem Gerüste hinauf, lässt alle fürchterliche Umstände wieder vor sich
erscheinen und scheut es sich selbst zu gestehen, dass sie sich an dem grässlichen Schauspiele
weidet. Viel willkommener sind jene Executionen, welche der Dichter veranstaltet.]
    A corresponding passage can be found in Diderot's *Jacques le Fataliste et son Maître*
(100, p. 182). Although the book was first published in 1796, the manuscript was well
known to Goethe before that date. He referred to it in his letters from 1780 on.

formances, particularly through tragedy, and an excitation seizes man; the darker it is the greater becomes the pleasure.[9]

(5) In this essay Goethe declares the moral purification of the theater to be a deathblow to the essential effect the theater is supposed to have. He compares the theater to a pond, which must contain not only clear water but also mud and insects if fish are to thrive in it.

In these essays, sadism is discovered as the infantile root of man's pleasure in tragedy, a forward step from the view taken in the first book of the novel, where voyeurism and exhibitionism were emphasized. Sadism prepossesses the onlooker and the playwright, but both are exculpated, for without tragedy where would man's sadism drive him?

From Goethe himself we know that by the just punishment he meted out to evil characters whom he put on the stage, he tried to obtain self-redemption. With remarks about the sadistic impulse involved in writing great tragedy he was more parsimonious. Furthermore, in the essays the existence of the evil is declared to be rooted in man's nature, and tragedy, with its presentation of the evil, is heralded as one of the necessary accouterments of culture. It is understandable that Goethe did not have Wilhelm write these essays, but an unnamed outsider, for they are contrary to Wilhelm's pure, naive, Parzival-like nature. Yet they show how deeply the author of *Wilhelm Meister* was entangled in feelings of guilt about his literary creativity in general, an additional reason why he felt drawn over and over again towards the pictorial arts, within which he preferred landscapes, a province which, to be sure, is likely to afford only minimal occasions for feelings of guilt. But the writing of *Wilhelm Meister,* or at least of this chapter, served the need to clarify this dark, enigmatic feeling of guilt, which probably had had an inhibiting effect on his dramatic creativity. Was *Wilhelm Meister* intended to prove that great tragedy can be written in all purity and sinlessness of soul?

The third essay, with its description of the feelings of the crowd during an execution, takes on even greater importance when one considers that there were public executions by decapitation in Frankfurt, while Goethe was living there, of two women convicted of infanticide, one when

[9] [Der gesunde Mensch kann durch nichts gerührt werden, dass nicht zugleich die Saiten seines Wesens erschüttert werden sollten, von denen die entzückenden Harmonien des Vergnügens auf ihn herabströmen. Und selbst grausame zerstörende Begierden, worüber man sich auch bei Kindern entsetzt, die man durch Strafen zu vertreiben sucht, haben geheime Wege und Schlupfwinkel, wodurch sie zu den allersüssesten Vergnügungen hinübergehen. Alle diese innerlichen Gänge und Wege werden durch Schauspiele, besonders durch Tragödie mit elektrischen Funken durchschüttert, und ein Reiz ergreift den Menschen; je dunkler er ist, je grösser wird das Vergnügen.]

he was nine and the other when he was twenty-three years old (see 28). The enjoyment of the tragedy by an audience, therefore, meant to Goethe the admission of the sadistic impulse. Man apparently cannot live without some channel for the infantile sadomasochistic drives. From Goethe's description, one is compelled to assume that sadomasochistic daydreams must have been frequent in him, and heavily loaded with guilt, to boot.[10] Goethe here discovered a medium that offered gratification and also the diversion of a forbidden impulse to an acceptable goal. The writing of a tragedy, then, meant: "I do not enjoy the slaying of a woman, but I create a play that will absorb the bad instincts of man and draw them towards the good."

The closeness of the writing of tragedy to infantile sadomasochism may have been an important root of the inhibition he had to overcome in writing plays and may help to explain why so many dramatic plans remained unfulfilled. The themes of rescuing a woman, or of restoring her honor, or of redeeming her after she had been destroyed, appear often in his dramatic creations, the most outstanding example being Gretchen in *Faust,* who suffers the same fate as the poor woman executed when Goethe was twenty-three and whom he then as an old man restored to divine beatitude in the finale of Part II of the tragedy.

---

[10] The strength of the infantile sadism in Goethe can be judged from an early phobia. As a child, he could not stand the sight of raw meat. "Thus I also remember that I always took flight with horror from the . . . narrow and ugly butcher stalls." [So erinnere ich mich auch, dass ich immer mit Entsetzen vor den . . . engen und hässlichen Fleischbänken geflohen bin.] (*Soph.* I, 26:23)

Chapter 4

Wilhelm Meister, Book III (Until November 12, 1782)

Book III of *Wilhelm Meister* was written between August (?) and November 12, 1782. In it there are described Wilhelm Meister's opening adventures on the trip undertaken at the suggestion of his brother-in-law in order to collect debts for his father's firm. At first Wilhelm faithfully and successfully carries out the orders. Yet quite early in his journey he is taken, by his driver's mistake, to a town where he has no business to transact, but where a theatrical group is performing. He meets a couple, Melina and his wife, whom Goethe had introduced in Book II. Melina is an actor whom Wilhelm knows from the time of his acquaintance with Mariane. He fell in love with the daughter of a respectable family and eloped with her, but they were apprehended and returned like criminals. Wilhelm had met them on their humiliating journey home, and, taking pity on them, interceded with the girl's parents, and obtained their consent to the marriage, but on condition that they should not live in the parental town. Melina, who had wanted to quit being an actor, was thus forced to return to the stage and his wife also became an actress. Wilhelm becomes acquainted with the whole troupe, of whom two are important: Madame Reti, who is the principal of the outfit, a mannish woman of above average talent as an actress; her lover, Bendel, a drunkard and utterly incompetent as an actor. Here too Wilhelm meets Mignon, the most problematic figure created by Goethe. Under the pressure, first of the Melinas, then of Madame Reti and the rest of the troupe, and using various excuses, Wilhelm postpones his departure and becomes more and more involved in their doings. Not the least of the effects that Mignon

728

has upon him is to make it increasingly difficult for him to extricate himself from among his new friends. When he recites to the group *Belsazar,* a tragedy he had written in earlier years,[1] it is decided that the company will stage his play. Wilhelm had already contributed some of his money earlier to help the troupe financially. Now that his own play is at stake he advances considerable sums. He studies and directs the play with the greatest fervor and the performance promises to be superb except for Bendel, who acts atrociously in one of the leading roles. On the evening of the first performance he is in a condition that makes his appearance on the stage impossible. Reti and Madame Melina implore Wilhelm to substitute for him. Wilhelm considers this utterly impossible, but when word comes that the audience is frantically demanding that the performance begin, and when he senses that the fulfillment of his age-old wish will be thwarted unless he bows to the necessity of the moment, he conquers the distaste he shares with his time for the actor's job and agrees to perform. The book closes with Wilhelm standing in his costume on the stage giving final instructions for the performance and stepping into the side scene as the curtain rises.

On August 10, 1782, Goethe wrote to Charlotte von Stein:

> This morning I finished the chapter in *Wilhelm* the beginning of which I dictated to you. It gave me a good hour. After all, I was born to be a writer. When I have written well something that is in accordance with my thoughts, it yields me a purer joy than ever. Farewell. Preserve me the soul of my life, of my doing, and of my writing.[2]

This remark of Goethe's that he has decided he was born to be a writer is most remarkable in many aspects. It is surprising that it struck him as a kind of revelation although it had long been quite clear to those around him. Also striking is how deep seated it shows Goethe's doubts as to his literary creativity to have been. The German word *eigentlich,* which I have translated "after all," indicates the resistance he had to work against in order to reach this conclusion. But his relationship to Charlotte von Stein had at last brought him to the point where he felt at one with an objective social function that was, so to speak, inborn (rather than ac-

---

[1] Goethe actually wrote a tragedy of that name in his youth, but destroyed it later.

[2] [Heute früh habe ich das Capitel im Wilhelm geendigt, wovon ich dir den Anfang dicktirte. Es machte mir eine gute Stunde. Eigentlich bin ich zum Schrifsteller gebohren. Es gewährt mir eine reinere Freude als iemals wenn ich etwas nach meinen Gedancken gut geschrieben habe. Lebe Wohl. Erhalte mir die Seele meines Lebens, Treibens und Schreibens.]

quired like most of those he was then engaged in) and identified himself totally with it.

Yet the surprising observation can be made here that this development in the author was parallel to that of his hero in the novel. The love-object may have played only a secondary role in this discovery, and Goethe's determination to be, or to become, a writer coincided with his composition of the scene in which Wilhelm Meister breaks with his bourgeois past, and publicly declares himself as a poet and appears as an actor on the stage.[3]

A kind of recoil from the creation to the creator is here noticed. First the imaginary hero, that is to say Goethe's self-projection, reaches a consequential conclusion, and then the author himself limpingly reaches the level at which his own shadow has left off. Perhaps we are dealing here with a phenomenon that occurs far more frequently than is known. How many dreams have inspired great deeds because the dreamer took them as messages from a god; how many visions have led man to enter on a certain course—and were not dream and vision projections of the man's self? In Goethe's case, of course, there are two peculiarities: first, he did not doubt that Wilhelm was his own creation, and he never supposed he had created the character by divine inspiration; and, secondly, he had for some years now obtained his main momentum for action from his love for Charlotte von Stein.

How are we to account for the fact that Goethe was motivated in that important moment less by the living object of his love than by the actions of an imaginary hero who was a projection of his self? Was it that the death of the threatening father, the exhilarating experience of mastering the situation despite the trauma suffered, the coincidental rise almost to the top of the principality, the elevation to hereditary nobility—did all these things provide the ego with such a sense of security and power that it became capable of lifting itself out of thralldom to a beloved person and blossoming forth in a state theretofore repressed? Was the father's death necessary before the ego could find itself and declare boldly what it really wanted? But how many fears and forebodings must have been attached

---

[3] However, it must be added that Wilhelm traveled this leg of his journey under a pseudonym (as his creator more than once did). Since he despairs of ever being a master in any field, he gives his name as *Geselle*. (The German word *Meister*, meaning "master" of a craft, is in contrast with *Geselle*, which means "journeyman.") Melina promises that no one will know his true identity and this is also one of the reasons why Wilhelm can bring himself to the point of appearing as an actor. But, unquestionably, Goethe meant to describe a moment when the hero broke with his past and declared himself, at least temporarily, in favor of his inner calling. One cannot help wondering at this point whether the act of nobilitation also amounted for Goethe to a changing of his name.

to this craving to be a poet, and author, if so many reassurances were needed. To understand this we must look at Wilhelm. To make writing the mainstay of his career apparently meant for Goethe as profound a break, the smashing of as profound a taboo, as for Wilhelm to be an actor.[4] As far as acting goes, Goethe had made his highborn companions act on Weimar's amateur stage, and when Book III of *Wilhelm Meister* was written the opprobrium of the stage was gradually vanishing. And as for the status of an author, Goethe's literary creations were his pride and he almost never published his masterpieces under a pseudonym. But apparently writing was acceptable only as an avocation; to make a vocation of it was, I think, not customary. Wieland, Herder, Lessing, had vocations that took them far afield from writing, though these vocations may have been of secondary importance to them. But in that letter of August 10, 1782, which I am inclined to call fateful, I have the impression that Goethe envisioned a form of existence in which, materially and spiritually, everything would be subordinated to that one function. And this idea may have been felt by Goethe to take him out of the confines of that section of society of which he was bound to remain the greatest representative (see 377).

Goethe in discovering his true function in society benefited again from the progress he had derived from his relationship to Charlotte von Stein. Whereas up to then his strides had been experienced by him as (and probably actually were) improvements within this relationship, he here took a stand that was divorced from any entanglements with the beloved woman and concerned his position in the world independent of her. One would like to know more about this process in the course of which the beloved woman's grip on his life started to slip out of her hands, apparently without either her or Goethe's noticing it. The equivalent process can be observed in the psychoanalytic process when the energy that is bound up in a symptom is loosened up and can then flow towards the world. In the analytic process, the analyst is the first object in which the freed libido is invested. If this object were not at hand the libido could not be drawn out of the symptom at all. The further shift of the patient's libido, from the analyst to the world at large, requires further therapeutic steps. Thus in Goethe too we noticed the flow of the freed libido towards the love-object, and now we observe the partial turn of this freed libido away from that love-object.

Yet when Goethe—after years of struggling, hesitating, and procrasti-

[4] For the man of the twentieth century it is somewhat difficult to identify with such conflicts, although their equivalents bear upon contemporaries, of course, in a different shape.

nation, after having created the greatest literary works but having been compelled nevertheless incessantly to escape into drawing or other fields of art, or into a number of other activities completely unrelated to art—at last wrote these fateful words regarding his true mission in life, he had not made this discovery, as might well have been expected, under the guidance of his all-comprising love-object but under the guidance of a self-created image that represented his own self. This process does not find its equivalent in a psychoanalytic treatment. It reminds me remotely of a puzzling incident in the history of a schizophrenic patient. At a time when she was possessed by delusions, she wrote a novel in which the heroine was the victim of delusions. She herself, of course, had no insight into the delusional nature of her own ideas of that time, but in the novel she created a person who she knew suffered from mental disease. The created picture was her mirror image without her being aware of this uncanny relationship. Here it could be observed within the realm of psychopathology that the person was wiser in the process of artistic creation than outside of it. To a certain extent the psychological process underlying the myth of Pygmalion may be similar. The woman Pygmalion created is probably the image of the artist's own femininity. By falling in love with the created image of himself, the sculptor achieved something he could not otherwise have done. This is significantly different from the myth of Narcissus, whose love for his own image proves fatal. Narcissus, however, is the uncreative person who merely gets absorbed in the beauty of his own image and is the victim of the accretion of self-love. The therapeutic effect observed in Goethe's writing of *Wilhelm Meister* and in the myth of Pygmalion are in the last analysis rooted in a biological law, which Freud described in the self-curative effect of anxiety dreams in traumatic neuroses (see also 83, pp. 392–93).

There were other little signs that, despite all the assurances of love, the idea of Charlotte von Stein's exclusiveness had started to give way to possibilities of substitution. There seems to be a hint of irony when Goethe writes (July 8, 1782) that starting a day without having heard from her makes him feel like a coffee drinker without breakfast, but on August 9, 1782, he even wrote: "Cervantes holds me now above the [legal] papers as a cork jacket does the swimmer."[5] This same simile had once upon a time been used by him to describe how much he needed and depended on Charlotte von Stein; now Cervantes will serve his turn. And on Sep-

[5] [Cervantes hält mich iezo über den Ackten wie ein Korckwamms den Schwimmenden.]

tember 8, 1782,[6] he let Charlotte von Stein know that he felt unable, after all, to sell the garden he owned outside the city, although he had agreed to do so. "I had seen you all the time for two, three days and therefore I thought I needed nothing else. But do I always have you?"[7] Here the garden is declared to be a necessary substitute for the love-object when she is not present. Yet this passage also admits that substitutes for the love-object have become possible.

On the following day, after having decided to keep the property for emotional reasons (ownership of a large city dwelling made the country home superfluous for practical purposes) he wrote: "I went to bed early, my usual means when the world becomes uncanny for me, and read and dozed and thought of you."[8] Goethe's habit, mentioned before, of withdrawing to his bed when the world appeared uncanny is a device used by many. Although it is to be assumed that its meaning varies from person to person, one feels inclined to assert that when it occurs it nearly always signifies a short-lasting, partial preoedipal regression. The world becomes uncanny when an old childhood fear raises its head, and the place of retreat—bed or a hot bath, for example—is a substitute for the place where all of us once upon a time felt safest and happiest, namely, the mother's womb, so to speak. The simultaneous and uniform stimulation of the whole body surface reduces the vastness of the universe in which the adult ego is compelled to live while awake to the smallest possible compass. The narrow shell of warmth and comfortable coziness is an impenetrable armor against the world's turmoil. In the ensuing half-dream Goethe dreamt of the beloved woman, but at the same time he maintained a psychic position in which it was possible for him to dispense with the real presence of the real object. Indeed, there was a certain psychological similarity between taking refuge in the garden which he was disinclined to sell and the withdrawal into bed. The loss of the garden was accepted for a short while when its owner was close to the love-object but immediately repudiated when the idea of even a transitory separation struck him; the withdrawal to the bed may have become necessary under the impact of the idea that he might have to live without either the love-object or the garden. A new substitute, endowed with the advantage of being always available and therefore reliable, and probably the most secure (as the most

---

[6] According to some, Goethe wrote this letter two months earlier.

[7] [Ich hatte dich zwey drey Tage immer gesehn und so glaubt ich mir das übrige nicht nothwendig. Hab ich dich denn immer?]

[8] [Ich legte mich zeitig zu Bette, mein gewöhnlich Mittel wenn mir's in der Welt unheimlich wird, und las und schlummerte und dachte an dich.]

archaic) appeared at a moment when awareness arose that the ego could be subjected to the strain of severe frustrations. What impresses again is the ease with which regressive mechanisms were interpolated without interfering with reality-adequate behavior.[9] The ego had acquired a series of mechanisms that served efficiently to unburden it of pressures put upon it, without destructive effect. These mechanisms became independent of the object and gave the ego a wide range of freedom.

Yet around the time of his thirty-third birthday Goethe seems to have come close to a relapse. This was his first birthday after his father's death. On August 26, 1782, when Charlotte von Stein was out of town, he wrote her:

> When I have worked for a day without finding you in the evening then I do not know what all this hardship is for. . . . I am so accustomed to give you all the details, to tell you everything I am thinking, that it becomes difficult for me to write you. Everything presents itself before me all at once and I should like to tell you everything.[10]

And the following day: "Dear Lotte, come back! Soon I will no longer know why I get up."[11] The last sentence sounds as if Goethe had returned to a full object tie.[12] In the letter of the twenty-sixth, however, Goethe had claimed that it was the abundance of the material he wished to convey to her that prevented him from writing. This is reminiscent of the resistance some patients show in the form of having two thoughts simultaneously and therefore not being able to say either of them.

The gradual process of getting on his own feet showed up quite strongly outside of the private realm of his relationship with Charlotte von Stein. On July 27, 1782, he wrote to his friend Knebel discussing his new financial duties in the principality. He was fully aware that the new appointment meant a sacrifice of the next two years. He was also aware of the great risk he had assumed. Yet he firmly declared that in two years it would become evident whether "I can stay with honor or put in my resignation." However, he rejoiced at the idea of carrying full responsibility. Now was the moment when he carried the responsibility alone.

---

[9] How necessary the ability to do this is has repeatedly been stressed by H. Hartmann, E. Kris, *et al.*

[10] [Wenn ich einen Tag gearbeitet habe, ohne dich Abends zu finden, so weis ich eben nicht wozu alle die Mühseeligkeit soll. . . . Ich bin so gewohnt ausführlich gegen dich zu seyn, dir alles zu sagen was ich dencke, dass mir es schwer wird dir zu schreiben. Es stellt sich mir alles auf einmal vor und ich mögte dir alles sagen.]

[11] [Liebe Lotte komm zurück! Ich weis bald nicht mehr warum ich aufstehe.]

[12] The beautiful Countess who was loved by Karl August was again in Weimar, as Goethe reported, and her presence perhaps created a temptation.

Herein I am more cheerful than ever, for now I do not—at least in this area—have to wish the good and accomplish [only] half, and to abhor the evil, but to suffer it entire. What happens now I must ascribe to myself, and nothing appears dark through the third or fourth, but bright just through me.[13]

If the state finances were to degenerate still more—and most people were not aware how badly off they were—Goethe would be held responsible. Since his training did not seem to have prepared him as a financial expert at all, the reproach of personal ambition and intrigue would inevitably have been leveled against him, and his stay at Weimar would have ended in catastrophe. The courage with which he eyed a dangerous future and the relief he felt at shouldering the responsibility alone, betray the awakening of a new attitude that is striking in its strong masculinity.

The exhibitionistic element in his letter to Knebel carries the earmark of the phallic pride. Indeed, there was perhaps an acute rivalry in this matter with his friend Merck, one of the few Goethe held—as I believe—superior in some respects, and whom he called his Mephisto, probably on false grounds (see 429, p. 210). The reader may remember that Goethe had met him in October of 1780—it was to be their last meeting[14]—and that Goethe became annoyed at their conversation. A few months earlier (June, 1780), a political event had taken place that made a great stir in Germany and in which Merck may have taken a leading role, or so it appeared at least to his contemporaries,[15] and thus also to Goethe. This event was the sudden sensational fall of the all-powerful Carl Friedrich Moser (1723–1798), Chancellor at the court of Darmstadt. Moser was famous throughout Germany for the far-reaching reforms he had introduced and still planned to carry out as well as for the absolute and independent power he held at court. When his resignation, after eight years of service as chancellor, was accepted by Ludwig IX, it created a veritable sensation. The ensuing years were filled with mutual recriminations, lawsuits, and the exile of the erstwhile chancellor, until, in 1790, under the new monarch, Ludwig X, a reconciliation took place. What Merck's real role in Moser's overthrow was has, so far as I know, not been definitely established, but

---

[13] [Nun hab' ich . . . zwey volle Jahre aufzuopfern . . . dass ich mit Ehren bleiben oder abdancken kann. . . . Dabey bin ich vergnügter als iemals denn nun hab ich nicht mehr, wenigstens in diesem Fache das Gute zu wünschen und halb zu thun und das Böse zu verabscheuen und ganz zu leiden. Was nun geschieht muss ich mir selbst zu schreiben, und es würckt nichts dunkel durch den dritten und vierten, sondern hell gleich grade auf mich.]

[14] Some authors assert a meeting between Goethe and Merck in 1784. I have been unable to confirm this.

[15] See Herder's letter to Hamann of December 18, 1780, in 429, pp. 206–07.

from his letters (see 262) it is evident that he was uncompromisingly hostile to Moser, accused him of the worst and—as is now known—exaggerated and falsified the picture into the bargain.[16] The eternal difficulty in Darmstadt as well as in Weimar was the state debt, and Moser was said to have freed the country of any encumbrance, which Merck disputed. It strikes me that Goethe drew a picture of his predecessor in the Treasury, Kalb, that sounds quite similar to that which Merck drew of Moser. The real quality of Kalb's performance cannot be objectively evaluated for the necessary documentary evidence has not been published. In the letter to Knebel already quoted from, Goethe wrote of him: "As a businessman he behaved mediocrely, as a political man badly, and as a human being abominably."[17] I believe that Goethe here was acting out an identification with Merck. In so often calling him his Mephisto he probably expressed a deep psychological (though probably not objective) truth.

Goethe, thus, was also able to overthrow powerful state ministers, as he probably thought Merck capable of doing, but he was more than a tool of political intrigue, he was a candidate for a position of power that was vacant. He was brief in his announcement to Merck himself, but the impulse to brag is unmistakable. In his letter of July 16, 1782, he compared himself to Truefriend, the character in his quasi-translation of Aristophanes' *Birds* upon whom one part of the empire after another is bestowed (see above, p. 444). Though in the letter to Knebel the masculine attitude of enjoying the new and grave responsibility sounds refreshing, one would have thought it wiser, nevertheless, in view of the great risk involved, if he had been able to report to his friend that he had found a reliable expert to assist him in managing the gigantic problems involved in such a position.

In this area of Goethe's character development one is reminded of a phase in the treatment of homosexuals described by Anna Freud in an unpublished paper. When, after having overcome their heterosexual anxieties or inhibitions, they take up intercourse with women, a phase sets in typified by overemphasized penis pride. Similarly Goethe seemed so fascinated by the acquisition of a sense of responsibility that he could not get enough of it and had to plunge into the most risky situations in order to show that he could do better than any of his friends. The fact that he succeeded in managing such situations does not disprove the pathology lurking behind the acceptance of the responsibilities. He made a witty (and

[16] No advantage accrued to Merck from Moser's resignation; he continued in his subaltern position, though Herder in his afore-mentioned letter to Hamann expressed the belief that Merck would succeed Moser.

[17] [Als Geschäfftsmann hat er sich mittelmäsig, als politischer Mensch schlecht, und als Mensch abscheulich aufgeführt.]

probably correct) remark about the Duke during this period. On August 27, 1782, he wrote to Charlotte von Stein:

> The Duke is brave and one could love him wholeheartedly if he did not curdle conviviality through his mischievousness and force his friends through his impetuous foolhardiness to become indifferent about his weal and woe.

> It is a curious sensation daily to behold your best friend, the one most closely related through fate, half lose his neck and arms and legs and to set oneself at ease [about that possibility] without becoming indifferent. Perhaps he will become old and gray while many who are cautious take their departure.[18]

Here Goethe seemed to rationalize the abatement of his erstwhile intense feelings of friendship for his princely friend. But the passage is so important because Goethe here describes a pathological mechanism that, though used by the Duke in an empty and unconstructive way, was almost identical with that underlying Goethe's most constructive and socially significant activities of that time. Some of Goethe's friends, seeing him voluntarily submitting to the most hazardous undertaking, may have felt about him much as he did when he watched the Duke risk his life for a trifle. Thus again Goethe came close to his own pathology by studying his friend and master. And one is also reminded of the vicissitudes of Wilhelm Meister, which found artistic presentation around that time.

In a composition of July, 1782, entitled, "A word about the author of *Pilatus*" (meaning Lavater) (225, pp. 201–02), Goethe elaborated further on the subject of erroneous self-evaluation:

> I have often noticed in living persons with whom I have had intercourse, [and] in departed ones whose writings I have read, that man rarely knows what in him is the greatest and the choicest, let alone sets store by these virtues. What he possesses he looks upon as the one born wealthy looks upon his wealth, as something that belongs to him, as something that he takes for granted, as a thing from which he sets out. But that for which his wishes yearn, that which he lacks, that which he believes he needs in order to enlarge and to complete his existence, that is what interests him most strongly, over which he forgets everything else and for which he would give up everything else; a feeling that a third-[person] onlooker cannot

---

[18] [. . . der Herzog ist wacker und man könnte ihn recht lieben, wenn er nicht durch seine Unarten das Gesellige Leben gerinnen machte, und seine Freunde durch unaufhaltsame Waghalsigkeit nötigte über sein Wohl und Weh gleichgültig zu werden.

Es ist eine kuriose Empfindung, seines nächsten Freundes und Schicksaals Verwandten Hals und Arm und Beine täglich als halb verloren anzusehen und sich darüber zu beruhigen ohne gleichgültig zu werden. Vielleicht wird er alt und grau, indess viele sorgliche abgehn.]

comprehend. When this feeling seizes highly and richly endowed minds, then they forsake the wide inner circle of their existence and swarm about those boundaries that are imposed upon them as well as upon others. If they then speak or write about it, something foolish is usually the result, something that makes us meditate over and lament the narrow boundaries of mankind, at the very instant when they believe they have felt for themselves and revealed to others that which is most essential, sublime, and truest in their whole existence.[19]

Here again Goethe perceived, rightly or wrongly, a state of affairs that he could have studied so much better in himself, in view of his longing to escape into painting and drawing and financial administration and what not. And Goethe continued a little farther on:

> I should like to compare him [Lavater] with a man who does not value property, money, possessions, wife, children, friends, and neglects all of them in order to satisfy an irresistible drive towards the mechanical arts and to invent a flying machine.[20]

Yet, like his great predecessor Leonardo da Vinci, Goethe too became interested in flying machines. As an old man he wrote in 1821, when sketching the development of science during his lifetime and his own involvement in it:

> Air balloons have been invented.
> How close I was to this invention.
> Some annoyance at not having invented it myself.
> Prompt consolation.[21]

[19] [Ich habe öfters an Lebenden mit denen ich umgegangen bin, an Abgeschiedenen, deren Schriften ich gelesen habe, bemerkt, dass der Mensch das, was an ihm das grösste und treflichste ist selten kennt, noch auch diesen Vorzügen einen Werth beylegt. Was er hat sieht er an wie ein reichgebohrner seinen Reichthum, als etwas, das zu ihm gehört, als etwas das sich von selbst versteht, als eine Sache von der er ausgehet. Aber das wohin seine Wünsche sich sehnen, was ihm abgehet, was er, sein Daseyn zu erweitern und zu ergänzen nöthig glaubt, das ist es was ihn auf's stärkste interessiret, worüber er alles andere vergisst, worum er alles andere hingäbe; Eine Empfindung die der dritte Zuschauer nicht begreifen kann. Wenn diese Empfindung hoch- und viel begabte Seelen ergreift, dann verlassen sie den innern weiten Krais ihres Daseyns und schwärmen an denen Gränzen herum, die ihnen so gut wie andern gesezt sind. Sprechen sie alsdann davon, schreiben sie davon, so giebt es meistentheils etwas albernes, etwas das uns über die engen Gränzen der Menschheit nachdenken und trauren lässt, eben in dem Augenblicke, da sie glauben das innigste, höchste, treflichste, lezte ihres ganzen Daseyns für sich gefühlet und andern offenbart zu haben.]

[20] [Ich mögte ihn einem Manne vergleichen, der Güter, Geld, Besizthümer, Weib, Kinder, Freunde, alles nicht achtete und vernachlässigte um einen unwiderstehlichen Trieb nach mechanischen Künsten zu befriedigen und eine Maschine zum fliegen zu erfinden.]

[21] [Die Luftballone werden entdeckt./ Wie nah ich dieser Entdeckung gewesen./ Einiger Verdruss es nicht selbst entdeckt zu haben./ Baldige Tröstung.] (See *Naturwissenschaftlicher Entwicklungsgang*, in *Soph.* II, *11*:301)

It is historically possible that when Goethe wrote the above comparison about Lavater his interest in flying machines had already been aroused,[22] but he certainly became deeply interested in them later. The words of the seventy-two-year-old man still reveal the intensity with which he must have longed for the realization of that old dream of mankind, to acquire the ability to fly. Goethe's desire was not based on intellectual curiosity but sprang from the old Promethean urge to conquer the universe. It is touching to read the concluding remark of the paragraph in which the old man bemoaned the fact that he had not invented the balloon: "[I] believe in the kinship of magnetic and electrical phenomena."[23] How close did he come to the greatest discoveries in basic research![24]

Thus his comparing Lavater with a man who sacrifices everything to invent a flying machine was not arbitrary or incidental but sounds like a warning, as if he meant to say to himself: "Flying machines are again a subject that will fascinate you and for which you will sacrifice the very best that is in you. Look at Lavater, who does not know where his real strength lies and who is off on a wild goose chase." Again he was using a friend as a screen upon which to project a fragment of what he may have perceived in himself.

In his correspondence with Lavater, this process of acquiring independence—the initial step of which was faintly heard in his relationship with Charlotte von Stein—is quite conspicuous. In his letter of July 29, 1782, one finds the concise and cutting statement in which Goethe characterizes his position in the Christian world by saying that he is "not anti-Christian, or un-Christian, but nevertheless a decided non-Christian."[25] This succinct statement was probably the peak of what Lavater had in mind when he wrote to Goethe on July 28, 1782: "I see a foreign spirit moving around you! . . . Dear, when I am still exactly what I was nine years ago—why are not you so any longer?"[26] He undoubtedly sensed the tremendous change that had taken place in his friend during the nine years of their acquaintance and he surely was not aware that his claim that he was still the same now as nine years earlier spelled a devastating

---

[22] See 378. The brothers Montgolfier started their public experiments with balloons in 1782 and Goethe started equivalent experiments in 1783.

[23] [Glaube an die Verwandtschaft magnetischer und elektrischer Phänomene.]

[24] I owe thanks to Mr. Seymour A. Copstein for having called my attention to the fact that Goethe was not the only one who harbored this idea around that time.

[25] [Da ich zwar kein Widerkrist, kein Unkrist aber doch ein dezidirter Nichtkrist binn.]
Goethe seems to have written Lavater prior to their personal acquaintance that he was no Christian. See 225, p. 9.

[26] [Ich sehe einen fremden Geist um dich schweben! . . . Lieber, wenn ich genau noch bin, was ich vor 9 Jahren war—warum bist du es nicht mehr?] (225, p. 208)

criticism against himself. Goethe uncompromisingly rejected Lavater's book.[27] He tried to cut through all the differences that separated them in the field of theology, exegetics, and what not, and to reach Lavater the human being, divorced from all sectarian trappings. "Therefore," he wrote on July 29, 1782, "let me hear your human voice so that we may remain connected on that side, since the other will not work."[28]

In the letters of August 9 and October 4, 1782, which were the last of Goethe's "great" letters to Lavater, he once more made an attempt, with all the intensity at his command, in favor of tolerance. The divinity of the Gospels he repudiated:

> I should never be convinced [even] by an audible voice from Heaven that water burns and fire quenches, that a woman gives birth without a man, and that a dead man rises up. Rather I consider this blasphemy against the great God and his revelation in nature.[29]

Lavater thought the Gospels the most beautiful, but Goethe finds other works equally beautiful and "indispensable." He admits that as far as his feelings are concerned he is as intolerant as Lavater,

> that if I had to speak publicly I should speak and write for the aristocracy, installed according to my conviction by God, with the same zeal as you do for the exclusive Kingdom of God.

And further:

> Yes, I admit to you if I were a teacher of my religion perhaps you would have more reason to scold me for lack of tolerance than I have now regarding you. Breathe on me with good words and put away the foreign spirit. The foreign one blows from all the corners of the world and the spirit of love and friendship only from one.[30]

[27] *Pontius Pilatus oder der Mensch in allen Gestalten,* published in 4 vols., 1782–85. Goethe wrote Lavater that he started to write a parody on his book but he was too fond of him to spend more than an hour on it. Cf. Goethe's earlier behavior towards Jacobi's novel *Woldemar.*

[28] [Drum lass mich deine Menschen Stimme hören damit wir von der Seite verbunden bleiben, da es von der andern nicht geht.]

[29] [. . . mich würde eine vernehmliche Stimme vom Himmel nicht überzeugen, dass das Wasser brennt und das Feuer löscht, dass ein Weib ohne Mann gebiert, und dass ein Todter aufersteht; vielmehr halte ich dieses für Lästerungen gegen den grossen Gott und seine Offenbarung in der Natur.]

[30] [dass ich, wenn ich öffentlich zu reden hätte, für die nach meiner Überzeugung von Gott eingesetzte Aristokratie mit eben dem Eifer sprechen und schreiben würde, als du für das Einreich Christi schreibst; . . .

Ja ich gestehe dir, wäre ich Lehrer meiner Religion, vielleicht hättest du eher Ursach mich der Toleranz mangelnd zu schelten, als ich jetzo dich. Hauche mich mit guten Worten an und entferne den fremden Geist. Der fremde weht von allen Enden der Welt her, und der Geist der Liebe und Freundschaft nur von einer.]

Was Goethe here prolonging a situation which he knew was impossible and was bound to lead to a break? He made a gesture of tolerance and insight by distinguishing between Lavater in his relationship to his fellow men and Lavater as a teacher of religion. The one is tolerant, tender, and forbearing; the other intolerant. The reproach of intolerance seemed too hard, and therefore he added the admission that he himself would also be intolerant, but implied, by the conditional, that his intolerance was actually mastered and not let loose upon mankind.

It is not clear from the record and difficult to decide how far Goethe was in earnest in wanting to preserve his friendship with Lavater. After the break he adamantly refused any occasion of reconciliation that was offered. It seems to me, though I cannot prove it, that he well knew that Lavater the man was so intricately interwoven with Lavater the theologian that his suggestion that the two be kept apart was utterly impossible. Goethe's words on this subject sound to me like an effort to make sure beyond a doubt that he should seem to have done everything in his power to preserve the friendship so that if the break came the burden of responsibility for it should be on the other party. Since at the same time, as will presently be seen, he was striving to pick up an old but discontinued friendship, I do not draw the conclusion that his dealings with Lavater were the outgrowth of a general aversion to male friendship. The specific character of the friendship to which he here did express an aversion was that it smacked of a superego relationship. After all, Lavater had become famous before Goethe; he was an authority, and acted like one. With his father's death Goethe became manifestly antipathetic to the voice of authority (at least in intellectual matters), that is to say, to the acceptance of intellectual authority unsupported by merit. It was this, I think, that made it a matter of necessity for Goethe to rid himself of this friend.

The simultaneous tendency to effect a reconciliation with a friend is unmistakable during this period. When he wrote to F. H. Jacobi on October 2, 1782, he put an end to an old enmity that was hanging over him. (The episode that had led to discord was related earlier on p. 359.) Goethe wrote:

Dear Fritz, let me call you so once more, and, if you wish, for the last time, so that at least we part in peace. . . . When one becomes older and the world narrower he then thinks often indeed with grief of the times when he trifled away friends as a kind of pastime and could neither feel the wounds he inflicted in flippant cockiness nor bestir himself to heal them.[31]

[31] [Lieber Fritz Lass mich dich noch einmal und wenn du dann willst zum letzten mal so nennen, damit wir wenigstens in Friede scheiden. . . . Wenn man älter und die Welt

In the same letter he settled a nearly forgotten debt he had owed Jacobi for many years and admitted that their discord had prevented him from corresponding with him. Goethe succeeded, Jacobi was reconciled, and their former friendship resumed.

Yet another liability of the past was met. A letter of July 26, 1782, to Plessing began:

> My behavior to you I do not want to pass off as virtue, [but] necessary it was. If you had thought then as you do now we would have been closer.[32]

Again his own problem is projected onto his vis-à-vis when he continues:

> Yet man has to throw off many skins before he becomes in some measure certain of himself and of worldly things. You have experienced more and thought more; may you obtain a fulcrum and find a sphere of action.[33]

And then he turned to himself in a way that made it clear to Plessing too that his own problem was involved:

> Thus much I can assure you, that in the midst of good fortune I live in constant self-denial and daily see that, with all toil and labor, not my will but the will of a higher power comes to pass, whose ideas are not my ideas.[34]

Goethe here introduces an important problem, which has to be considered with great attention: his feelings of activity and passivity. It is noteworthy that his confession that he experiences himself as totally passive in the midst of the maximum activity appears not only unexpectedly but at a place where one would hardly expect it. Goethe was writing here to a person who manifestly played a very subordinate role in his life, whom he had not seen for a long time; nevertheless, he slipped in a confession that one would seek in vain at many places that seem more appropriate. Was this passage perhaps brought forth for some educational purpose? How far was it a matter of Goethe's wanting to make an example of himself, as if he still held himself responsible for Plessing's welfare? I do not

---

enger wird denckt man denn freylich manchmal mit Wunden an die Zeiten wo man sich zum Zeitvertreibe Freunde verschertzt, und in leichtsinnigem Übermuth die Wunden die man schlägt nicht fühlen kann, noch zu heilen bemüht ist.]

[32] [Mein Betragen gegen Sie will ich nicht für Tugend ausgeben, nothwendig war es. Hätten Sie damals gedacht wie Sie iezt dencken so wären wir näher.]

[33] [Doch der Mensch hat viel Häute abzuwerfen biss er seiner selbst und der weltlichen Dinge nur einigermasen sicher wird. Sie haben mehr erfahren, mehr gedacht, mögten Sie einen Ruhepunckt treffen und einen Würckungskreis finden.]

[34] [So viel kann ich Sie versichern dass ich mitten im Glück in einem anhaltenden Entsagen lebe, und täglich bey aller Mühe und Arbeit sehe dass nicht mein Wille, sondern der Wille einer höhern Macht geschieht, deren Gedancken nicht meine Gedancken sind.]

wish to deny the possibility of such a tendency in his letter, but on the other hand it is quite possible that the particulars of this occasion made it one in which he could confess something very intimate. The relationship to Plessing apparently still contained at this point a feeling of guilt, mild thought it may have been. Five years after his mystification at Goethe's hands had occurred, Plessing still looked to Goethe as someone whom he unhesitatingly accepted as superior and sought as a counselor or kind of mentor, that is to say, as a superego-substitute. With his friends Goethe was not in such a position, since they had witnessed his growth and knew his foibles.

The questionable passage in Goethe's letter has two aspects. On the one hand, Goethe stepped down from the pedestal of ideal onto which Plessing had placed him, by his warning against the notion that his life in Weimar was one of narcissistic sovereignty and autonomy, when indeed it was a life of resignation and he was merely the instrument of a superior power, so that his achievements were not his but those of a source beyond him. On the other hand, who would not like to be the chosen vessel of a superior power? By declaring himself to be such an instrument he put himself in a position that might be regarded as even loftier than the one he would have held if he had claimed that his achievements were the result of his own efforts and wisdom.

Yet on September 17, 1782, Goethe wrote to Charlotte von Stein:

> I was clearly created to be a private person, and I do not comprehend how fate could have stuck me into a public administration and a princely family.[35]

In this passage too Goethe presents himself as a pawn, the plaything of fate, precisely in a context in which he had shown the greatest effort to obtain the very position he occupied. Was this repudiation of activity a compensatory mechanism against a feeling of guilt at having been so successful? Was he trying to forestall criticism for anticipated failure in the future? Goethe here gives us a glimpse into a deep problem that usually remains unverbalized and goes far deeper than the feeling of guilt expressed by the humble who feels embarrassed at being singled out to receive so much good, or other motives of that order. We are not dealing here with the situation mentioned several times earlier in which the ego repudiates responsibility because it acted under the guidance of the unconscious (see 346 *passim*). Goethe here went a step further and almost

---

[35] [Ich binn recht zu einem Privatmenschen erschaffen und begreiffe nicht wie mich das Schicksal in eine Staatsverwaltung und eine fürstliche Familie hat einflicken mögen.]

claimed that his thoughts were in general not his thoughts, and that even that which he did with great effort was not the result of his own volition. Such passages may easily be interpreted as the product of reflection and not based on a phenomenological description of an actual mode of experience. The literal wording of the passage, however, permits both interpretations. My personal feeling is that such occasional remarks—and we shall report later more of the same sort—have to be taken as descriptions of the most intimate way in which a human being experiences the world. Most people slur over such experiences and do not become aware that they have taken place. They belong to the experiential modes of activity and passivity, a range of problems about which we as yet know very little.

The problem of activity and passivity required discussion on earlier pages. Yet there are so many facets to it that in each new phase it requires discussion anew even at the risk of repetitiousness. As in so many other instances the study of schizophrenic modes of experiencing the world may get us closer to the problem. But the schizophrenic too has great difficulty in talking openly about this subject, which often is shadowed in him by a feeling of guilt for his alleged hypocrisy in not showing the world the full and true state of his personality. In certain phases of the disorder the discrepancy between what is contained in the feelings that the patient shows to the world and what he feels behind them is experienced with inordinate intensity. What he presents to the world, he often claims, is not connected at all with his true self, and what he considers to be his true self no one must know, for reasons of his own, which he usually justifies in an irrational way. Strangely enough, those attitudes that the patient presents to the world, and in which objectively an inordinate amount of energy is invested, are just the ones he denies truly belong to him and just the ones he claims have been created by the world at large or his social environment.

What problems of this type may have played a role in the life of a genius like Goethe cannot be known. The short letter to Plessing opens a large vista, but the gap in our knowledge can be filled only by speculation. Two facts can be accepted with certainty, namely, first, that the genius is driven from one creation to another, although this drive may at times, under the impact of circumstances, be inhibited in manifesting itself, and, secondly, that no great artist can really put into a work of art the full content he wants to pour into it. It is this unfulfilled remainder, which never lets the creative genius relent, and, further, the discrepancy between the internal truth and the external form into which the genius tries to mold it, that constitute points of similarity between the structure of the genius's personality and that of some schizophrenics. However, most creative artists, and Goethe too, complain that because of external circumstances they have not been able to give their best to the world, and this complaint was and still is only all too well founded in reality. Goethe said to Eckermann:

> Could mind and higher education become a common good, the poet would have easy sport; he could always and throughout be honest and would not need to be reluctant to say the best. Yet, as it is, he has to maintain himself on a certain level; he has to take into consideration that his works will come into the hands of a mixed world and he therefore has cause to take care lest he annoy the majority of good people by too great a frankness. And then, time is a curious thing. It is a tyrant, who has his moods and who shows a different face in each century to whatever someone says or does. What it was permitted to the ancient Greeks to say, will no longer be suitable for us to say, and what thoroughly appealed to Shakespeare's strong contemporaries the Englishman of 1820 cannot tolerate any more, so that in the most recent times a *Family Shakespeare* has become a much-felt need.[36]

The plight of the genius in his relationship to society is really one of the most tragic features of human civilization and if an artist wants to live in happiness and peace it is better for him if nature gives him only mediocre talents.

Despite the reasonableness of the genius's complaint one wonders how far this also was a rationalization on Goethe's part. Although Goethe complained here that consideration for the society in which he lived restricted his artistic activity, and that society prevented him from externalizing the full force of his feelings and thoughts, he was aware at times of an inner urge that compelled him to conceal, as can be seen from two passages in a letter to Schiller of July 9, 1796. There he wrote:

---

[36] [Könnten Geist und höhere Bildung, sagte er, ein Gemeingut werden, so hätte der Dichter ein gutes Spiel; er könnte immer durchaus wahr seyn und brauchte sich nicht zu scheuen, das Beste zu sagen. So aber muss er sich immer in einem gewissen Niveau halten; er hat zu bedenken, dass seine Werke in die Hände einer gemischten Welt kommen und er hat daher Ursache sich in Acht zu nehmen, dass er der Mehrzahl guter Menschen durch eine zu grosse Offenheit kein Ärgerniss gebe. Und dann ist die Zeit ein wunderlich Ding. Sie ist ein Tyrann, der seine Launen hat, und der zu dem, was einer sagt und thut, in jedem Jahrhundert ein ander Gesicht macht. Was den alten Griechen zu sagen erlaubt war, will uns zu sagen nicht mehr anstehen, und was Shakspeare's kräftigen Mitmenschen durchaus anmuthete, kann der Engländer von 1820 nicht mehr ertragen, so dass in der neuesten Zeit ein Family-Shakespeare ein gefühltes Bedürfniss wird.] (119, pp. 70–71)

Thomas Bowdler's famous *Family Shakespeare* had been published in 1818.

The fault, which you rightly observe, stems from my innermost nature, from a certain veritable tic through which I find it convenient to remove my existence, my actions, my writings, from the sight of people. Thus I shall always like to travel incognito, to choose the inferior garment rather than the better one, and in conversation with strangers or half-acquaintances to favor the unimportant subject or, at least, the less weighty formulations, to behave less responsibly than I am, and thus, I might say, to place myself between myself and my own appearance. . . . I seem to myself like one who, having placed many large numbers one upon another, finally deliberately made mistakes in adding them together in order to reduce, God knows for what whim, the final sum.[37]

If a person tries to conceal the painful recollection of experiences related to forbidden gratifications we understand this by direct empathy. Yet it is less clear what aspect of the activity-passivity problem could warrant a serious effort at concealment. Clinical observation proves over and over again that intense resistances are mobilized against early recollections related to narcissistic experiences of omnipotence.[38] As a matter of fact patients have the greatest difficulty in talking of narcissistic fantasies that can be characterized as megalomanic. Even after they have admitted sexually offensive material a strong resistance must be overcome to obtain access to those fantasies, which are close derivatives of early childhood attitudes dating back to a time when the ego still believed that the world was created for its pleasure and benefit. I believe that a considerable part of the problems revolving around activity and passivity are genetically connected with conflicts that have their roots in early infantile omnipotence. Since Plessing, as far as I know, was one of the first to approach Goethe as a leader who was to restore him to happiness by his advice, it is understandable that Goethe should in a letter to him have come close to early infantile material in his associations. These remarks to Plessing adumbrate a problem that was acute at that time but about which Goethe evidently did not want to be too specific. He was far more specific when

[37] [Der Fehler, den Sie mit Recht bemerken, kommt aus meiner innersten Natur, aus einem gewissen realistischen Tic, durch den ich meine Existenz, meine Handlungen, meine Schriften den Menschen aus den Augen zu rücken behaglich finde. So werde ich immer gerne incognito reisen, das geringere Kleid vor dem bessern wählen, und, in der Unterredung mit Fremden oder Halbbekannten, den unbedeutendern Gegenstand oder doch den weniger bedeutenden Ausdruck vorziehen, mich leichtsinniger betragen als ich bin und mich so, ich möchte sagen, zwischen mich selbst und zwischen meine eigne Erscheinung stellen. . . . ich komme mir vor wie einer, der, nachdem er viele und grosse Zahlen über einander gestellt, endlich muthwillig selbst Additionsfehler machte, um die letzte Summe aus Gott weiss was für einer Grille zu verringern.]

[38] The above quotation from Goethe's letter to Schiller is easily recognizable as the derivative of early narcissistic attitudes.

he wrote to Lavater (October 4, 1782) of the healing power of religion, thus again denying the effectiveness of the ego's own activity:

> Nature deserves great thanks that she has placed so much healing power in the existence of each living creature that, when it tears itself asunder at one end or the other, it will patch itself together again; and what else are the thousandfold religions but thousandfold manifestations of this healing power?[39]

Out of his own sense of being in the process of healing a gaping wound, he discovered the synthetic function of religion of establishing harmony where his ego was severely rent by a conflict about his father (see 412). Just in the very year when he lost him he wrote to the beloved woman on his birthday:

> Reluctantly I quit a year of my life that has given me so much bliss and that will become unforgettable for me through the assurance of your love. I have few wishes for the next.[40]

This sounds exaggerated,[41] like bragging that even a tragedy in the part of the world closest to him could not touch him—a real triumph of the healing power that nature had placed in him, yet it was not the healing power of religion that triumphed here but the healing power of love, mobilizing all there was in him of object-directed energy and thus offering him the opportunity of shifting away from the point of catastrophe onto the beatified and exalted ideal woman. He ended his birthday letter thus: "Why are you absent just now so that I cannot receive the blessing from your lips?"[42] One must think of the Old Testament to fathom the imagery concealed behind the word "blessing." The sentence may easily have covered a thought about his father: "Why are you absent just now so that I cannot receive the blessing from your hands?" It was his first birthday without the representative of a restraining tradition onto which a share of the responsibility could be shifted; now he had to bear it alone. He must have been deeply moved that day, since he wrote Charlotte von Stein three separate letters. In the evening he avoided company and pre-

---

[39] [Grossen Dank verdient die Natur dass sie in die Existenz eines ieden lebendigen Wesens auch so viel Heilungskraft gelegt hat, dass es sich, wenn es an dem einen oder dem andern Ende zerrissen wird, selbst wieder zusammenflicken kann; und was sind die tausendfältigen Religionen anders als tausendfache Äusserungen dieser Heilungskraft.]

[40] [Ungern trete ich aus einem Jahre meines Lebens das mir so viel Glück gegeben hat, und das mir durch die Versicherung deiner Liebe unvergesslich werden wird. Ich habe für das nächste wenig Wünsche.]

[41] See above, p. 250 for a similar contrast in a letter written after Cornelia's death.

[42] [Warum bist du eben abwesend dass ich den Segen nicht von deinen Lippen erhalten kann.]

ferred "to crawl under my old shingle roof and to live for me and you in silence."[43] Then he read one of Plutarch's *Lives*.[44] Goethe ended his letter to Charlotte with: "Oh, you best! What a splendor of love and faith your letters have; how I see your heart so gently and beautifully opened up for me!"[45] Here the spring of a new active flow becomes visible. He became the observer and the beloved woman the object to be observed. It was not he that revealed himself to her, but Charlotte von Stein that was the passive object; he became spiritually the giving party and she the receiving.

This dawn of a new activity does not pervade the whole relationship and on October 2, 1782, he wrote to her: "As long as I have you both [mother and Charlotte] I cannot lack for anything."[46] Much as such a remark may indicate feelings of—at least temporary—dependence, it is remarkable that the mother and the love-object are here named separately, in contrast to earlier times when Goethe professed that all other women he had ever known had retreated into the background. This remark possibly indicated that the transference character of his relationship to Charlotte von Stein was on the downgrade.

On November 7, 1782, the seventh anniversary of his arrival at Weimar, he wrote to Charlotte von Stein:

Today it is seven years since I came here; may I yet also with this day start a new epoch of my life and being by which I would become always more agreeable to you. A thousand thoughts go to and from you. Oh my beloved, the destinies of man are wondrous.

Herewith I send you the map of the world that you have missed for some time. There is not the smallest place marked on it or contained in it where I would not be thinking of you with love and faithfulness. Farewell, and be and remain to me what you are all in all.[47]

---

[43] [Darauf entschloss ich mich . . . unter mein altes Schindeldach zu kriechen und im Stillen mir und dir zu leben.]

[44] That Goethe retreated to the lives of ancient heroes must be understood as an expression of his longing for a father. It reveals that his usual attitude as shown in the communications of that time served the denial of what was really occurring in him. Many a seemingly contradictory passage referring to activity and passivity may have served the purpose of denying guilt.

[45] [O du beste! was deine Briefe einen Glanz von Liebe und Treue haben, wie ich mir dein Herz so sachte und schön geöffnet sehe!]

[46] [So lang ich euch beyde habe kann mir's an nichts fehlen.]

[47] [Heute sind es sieben Jahre dass ich herkam, mögte ich doch auch mit heute eine neue Epoche meines Lebens und Wesens anfangen wodurch ich dir immer gefälliger würde. Tausend Gedancken gehen zu und von dir. O meine Geliebte die Schicksale der Menschen sind wunderlich.

Hier schick ich dir die Weltkarte die du einige Zeit vermissest, es ist kein Pläzgen darauf

And the following day:

> Today I have thanked you already for a long time in silence for your love and faithfulness; I got up an hour earlier than usual and I will continue [doing] so. My *Wilhelm* runs to the end of the third book. When I am writing, I think it may be for your delight too. Farewell. Fear not the eighth year and no definite or indefinite time. Farewell and love me as yesterday and always.[48]

These two specimens—and many more could be quoted—show that the broad stream of the love relation flowed undisturbed, and nevertheless even in these two beautiful assurances of most tender love and affection one senses some change worthy of examination.

In the first communication Goethe expressed the idea that his relationship to the beloved woman continued on a maximum level of intensity. "You are my all" certainly leaves nothing to be sought for. But by this very fact it may betoken a slackening of that urgent sense of something beyond, that always, in acute love, drives the lover relentlessly on, and that contains the seed of potential, if not actual, suffering. Nor can I take his expressed desire to render himself more agreeable to her as a sign of something significantly dynamic in his love. When such expressions arise from a surging need to extend love, to make it more complete, they commonly are joined with some attempt, however groping, to specify the respects in which the speaker hopes to change himself in accordance with what he supposes to be his sweetheart's wishes. This had indeed been the case with Goethe in an earlier period. This time, the expression may be taken as a *façon de parler;* it probably no more appeared to Goethe than it can to us how he could have done more for her than he had, or how he could have been more devoted or loyal. As a matter of fact, the very words that early in their relationship no doubt meant: "Show me how I may be more agreeable to you, so that you will love me more and I may have more ways of loving you," may at this stage have come close to hinting: "I have exhausted my resources. If you have anything further to propose, I will do it, but I can initiate nothing myself." In the second communication the "for your delight too" sounds suspiciously like an afterthought. *Wilhelm*

---

gezeichnet oder drinn enthalten wo ich nicht dein mit Liebe und Treue gedencken würde. Lebe wohl und sey und bleibe mir was du bist alles und alles.]

[48] [Heute hab ich dir schon lange im Stillen für deine Liebe und Treue gedanckt, ich stieg eine Stunde früher auf als gewöhnlich und werde es so fortsetzen. Mein Wilhelm läuft zum Ende seines dritten Buchs. Wenn ich schreibe dencke ich es sey auch dir zur Freude. Lebe wohl fürchte das achte Jahr nicht und keine bestimmte noch unbestimmte Zeit. Lebe wohl und liebe mich wie gestern und immer.]

Meister was in reality written for reasons that were selfish and no longer in any way connected with problems that grew out of his relationship to Charlotte von Stein. It was apparently this feeling of being preoccupied with work divorced from the direct object-relationship that necessitated this sentence. His reassurance to Charlotte von Stein that she had nothing to fear from the eighth year of their friendship definitely shows that the tables had been turned. Usually it was he who had to fear for the future. Also, the request that Charlotte von Stein continue to love him as she did shows that the relationship had reached a maximum and no longer contained that bottom of unfulfilled desire that is so important, particularly for the poet, in order to obtain from life that spark that over and over again ignites the creative process. Yet all this is not meant to indicate that the intensity of Goethe's feelings for the beloved woman had actually weakened. My remarks refer rather to the repercussions which these feelings caused in his personality.

A few days later, on November 12, another day worthy of commemoration occurred: Goethe finished Book III of *Wilhelm Meister*. By his own doing he created an additional day of celebration,[49] which superseded the accident of birth or the historical event of his arrival at Weimar, that is to say, of meeting Charlotte von Stein, and in subsequent years this type of anniversary was to become increasingly important. The increasing importance of his artistic work thus also found outward manifestation. This creation of a personal holiday based on his own doing reminds me remotely of a problem that I have so far encountered only in schizophrenic patients, namely, the regret over not having borne oneself, or resentment at the idea that one should have to owe one's existence to parents.[50] For some very sensitive schizophrenics this is an almost unbearable blow to their narcissism. I wonder how far Goethe here was making an attempt at solving this problem by reducing the importance of his birthday and substituting for it a self-created red-letter day.[51]

[49] By so acting Goethe reminds one of the English sovereign, who has the right arbitrarily to declare a day as his official birthday and thus has the power to create a holiday.

[50] However, cf. Freud, who reports the same conflict in neurotic patients, on the occasion of the analysis of the fantasy of rescuing one's parents: "All his [the son's] instincts, those of tenderness, gratitude, lustfulness, defiance, and independence, find satisfaction in the single wish *to be his own father.*" (Freud's italics) (171, p. 173)

[51] We have bowed to Goethe's narcissism and followed his example in ordering the biographical material in accordance with the periods in which he wrote the several books of his novel.

Chapter 5

Wilhelm Meister, Book IV (Until November 12, 1783)

Book IV was written between November 12, 1782, and the same date in 1783. Since I shall have to present a few episodes in great detail in accordance with their psychological importance, I wish to give first an outline of how the plot develops in that book.

The performance of Wilhelm's play proves a great success in all respects. But the hero's enjoyment is disturbed the following day by Melina's insistence that he should urge Madame Reti to pay him back her debt out of her great profits from the opening night. Wilhelm reluctantly complies but he is only partially successful. The rumor of the splendid show attracts a great crowd to the second performance, in which Bendel is to substitute for Wilhelm. The latter stays at home that evening. Mignon intrudes into his room and without bidding performs a dance that arouses Wilhelm's affection for her even more. Hardly has she ended the dance when Bendel returns in rage and distress. His acting has been so bad that the crowd was aroused, attacked him, and well-nigh destroyed the theater. The troupe is desolate, for all their hopes are gone. Madame Reti must hide Bendel away at night, for otherwise the crowd would attack him anew. The group elects Melina as their new director and it is decided that whoever wants to continue his connection with the company will move to another city where it is hoped the troupe will be successful again. Wilhelm's funds are greatly reduced through these misfortunes. As they proceed on their way, war breaks out, and they are forced to idle in a small town. A Count and a Countess who are passing through the town engage them to perform in their near-by castle for the entertainment of a prince who will be their guest. The evening before the troupe is to move to the Count's estate, Mignon enters Wilhelm's room and has what looks like a hysterical attack. His affection for the child makes him decide to continue his association with the actors. Two new characters are introduced in this book: Philine, an actress, the prototype of the impulse-ridden, charming, easy-living, seductive, sexually uninhibited female; and the aged harpist, the mythological musician who creates orphic songs, and whose art has moving and soothing power over Wilhelm.

It is of interest to record the content of Wilhelm's play, which, as mentioned before, Goethe originally wrote when he was a boy.[1] Darius, King of the Medes (acted by Wilhelm), stops unrecognized at the court of Belsazar, King of Babylon. A plot to kill Belsazar on his birthday is in process of being organized. Darius tries to delay the deed because he is in love with the Queen of Babylon, but the conspirators go ahead and kill the King. They want to elevate a young princess, daughter of a king who was defeated by Belsazar's father, to the throne, and marry her to King Darius. Darius, however, refuses to marry the princess, but leaves her a part of the wealth that comes into his possession. His affection for the Queen continues and his consolation of the widow is of such a sort that the spectator may rightly assume she will agree to marry him.

The tragedy elaborates on the oedipal problem. In the light of Goethe's biography, the two women of the play are recognizable as mother- and sister-substitutes. The two guilt-arousing factors in the oedipal situation are denied, for Darius tries to delay the consummation of the plot, and his marrying the Queen is not directly declared but left to the spectator's imagination.

The narcissistic gain derived from the composition of this episode in the novel must have been particularly great to the author, since Goethe was deeply disappointed by the tragedy in reality and destroyed it together with many other early writings in Leipzig. In the novel he retrieved a pleasure that fate had denied him. In Goethe's real life, his initial dramatic attempts had been failures, but Wilhelm wins success even with those same plays, although he himself judges them in the novel as deplorable aberrations of his youthful and immature mind, just as Goethe judged his own youthful productions.[2]

---

[1] See Goethe's letters of October 30, December 6, 1766; May 11, October 12, 1767.

[2] Another function of *Wilhelm Meister* becomes evident here. As a cardsharp knows how to *corriger la fortune,* so the poet has the privilege of undoing some of the hardship he has had to bear and substitute for it delightful experiences. To give an example, the erotic sexual bliss Wilhelm experiences in Mariane's arms is, as cited earlier, an episode invented by Goethe, without parallel in his real life, for the purpose of replacing the recollection of a past unpleasant reality by a far more pleasing one.

The plot as set forth in the novel is significant for the delicacy with which the oedipal implication is handled. All the prerequisites of the oedipal conflict are given, but the hero is kept out of the throes of a conflict. His counterpart, Belsazar, is drawn as a sensitive young man who "wants the good, has a feeling for righteousness and virtue."[3] This shows that Goethe did not resort to a black-white technique even in his early dramatic attempts. Yet a black-white technique found its way into the novel under a clever disguise. After Wilhelm has proved himself to be a perfect actor despite his being an amateur, the professional actor who replaces him in the second performance is a complete failure. He has a speech defect and is awkward; the audience hisses and becomes so aroused by his ridiculous acting that a riot results and the theater is destroyed. Since this actor is the lover of the manager, Madame Reti, it is easy to recognize in him the image of the degraded father, an identification which is strengthened by the fact that Bendel originally is cast for the part that Wilhelm plays on opening night. His name is Bendel, but—as Goethe wrote—one could easily have called him Bengel (an idiomatic word for a rude person) if the pun had not been in poor taste (*Soph.* I, *51*:250). If I am not mistaken, the word *Bengel* is also used in some parts of Germany for the penis. Thus in Bendel Goethe derides his father. There is no end to all the poor and laughable qualities he attributes to him, no end to all the harm Mr. Bendel causes. Contrary to his usual delicacy, Goethe here really lays it on thick and freely indulges in crass and almost bizarre exaggeration.

In German there is a vulgar saying for the situation of a neophyte's attempting to do better than the master: to teach one's father how to fuck. This is the very situation behind Goethe's caricature. It is the bragging, boastful enjoyment of the little boy who tears the mask from one who pretends to be superior, and the boy cannot revel enough in his own asserted superiority. The rescue motive, which plays such a great role in Goethe's literary work (see 275), steps into the background on this occasion. The evening before Bendel's ludicrous inefficiency wrecked Madame Reti's theatrical company, when Bendel was in a stupor and Madame Reti pleaded with Wilhelm to save the day by acting the role of Darius, the rescue fantasy was still in full force. Of course, the rescue motive despite its altruistic purpose may also still carry a feeling of guilt, and in the novel Wilhelm's decision to act on the stage is described as one that was not reached spontaneously but under irresistible external pressure. The fulfill-

[3] [Er will das Gute, hat ein Gefühl für Rechtschaffenheit und Tugend.] (*Soph.* I, *51*:142)

ment of Wilhelm's childhood wish to act on the stage is even made to appear as a sacrifice, for by doing so he endangers his standing in bourgeois society.[4] Yet all his good deeds of so great cost—or at least risk—came to naught, for the group was wrecked by the miserable Bendel.

The underlying conflict reflected in this section of the novel centers in the identification with the father. Wilhelm's situation on the day of the performance of his tragedy, when his dearest wishes are to be fulfilled, is described as follows:

> Hundreds of times it has been observed that when a man's fondest wish is at last wholly fulfilled, it is yet spoiled through some mundane admixture, and thereby the most pleasurable enjoyment often becomes a torture. Our friend now saw the day appear that as a boy he had so often wished were here.

> We see that children let themselves be affected first by the external form of the occupation that their fathers pursue, or that they are otherwise tempted to choose. They take sticks and make themselves mustaches in order to look like soldiers . . . ; so also was it with our young poet.[5]

Goethe here seems aware of the importance of his father-identification, and he goes on to describe how the boy expected to feel when his boyish wishes should one day be fulfilled: "And for whom would it not be so who saw others resplendent in wealth, rank, title, position, and honors above himself?"[6] Yet in the way in which the boy aspired to enjoy the envied privileges of the father, the simultaneous rejection of the father-identification is also indicated. In the novel as well as in real life what was involved was the choice of a career, which, though it yielded great public prestige, ran counter to bourgeois respectability, his father's wishes, and quite generally against what his father stood for. In the novel this discrepancy is made even stronger than had been the case in real life. To be sure, Goethe's father opposed many phases of Goethe's career, but none

---

[4] In this way the aggressive component that is regularly contained in rescue fantasies is intimated. Cf. 509.

[5] [Wie hundertmal ist es bemerkt worden, dass der schönste Wunsch des Menschen, wenn er sich ihm endlich in seinem ganzen Umfange erfüllt, doch meist durch eine irdische Zugabe verdorben und der angenehmste Genuss dadurch oft zur Marter wird. Unser Freund sah nunmehr den Tag erschienen, den er sich als Knabe so manchmal herbei gewünscht hatte.

Wir sehen, dass Kinder zuerst durch die äussere Form eines Metiers, das ihr Vater treibt oder das sie sonst zu ergreifen gelockt werden, sich rühren lassen. Sie nehmen Stecken und machen sich Schnurrbärte, um Soldaten . . . zu scheinen; so war es unserm jungen Dichter auch gegangen.] (*Soph.* I, 51:269–70)

[6] [Und wem geht es nicht so, der andere in Reichthum, Rang, Titel, Ämtern und Ehren über sich glänzen sieht?]

of them was so objectionable as that of an actor in a wandering theatrical troupe. The fact that Goethe chose this profession in the novel indicates one of the aspects of his father-identification. There was not to be the shadow of a doubt that he might want to imitate or compete with his father by this professional choice. Yet the Bendel episode proves in the negative that he did not succeed in disentangling himself from a secret competition with his father.

Some features of the riotous events connected with the second stage performance when Bendel publicly makes a fool of himself, suggest that a copulation scene was being worked into this episode. It seems that the underlying fantasy was: "Father was impotent with Mother and therefore he was derided, beaten, and thrown out by her." Since Bendel fails in what Wilhelm had done so splendidly and to such general satisfaction the night before, the attempt to conquer fear and humiliation by a reversal of historical truth becomes evident.

The situation in which Wilhelm finds himself when he is surprised by the news of Bendel's abysmal defeat may be significant. It happens shortly after Mignon has performed the egg-dance for him. First the meaning of the Mignon character must be discussed.[7] Mignon is of androgynous nature. Although her feminine character prevails, she is also a boy. Goethe repeatedly wrote of her as *he,* and this cannot have been due to oversight by the copyist of the manuscript.[8] As a matter of fact, when Wilhelm meets Mignon for the first time he is not sure whether he is facing a boy or a girl.

Mignon is the only woman to whom Wilhelm is devoted with his whole personality and whom he accepts in her totality without reservation or compromise. Whereas his love for Mariane is based on sexual attraction, without real grasp of who and what Mariane really is, his love for Mignon leads to a deep understanding of and empathy with her enigmatic soul.

---

[7] See Philipp Sarasin (464) for a profound and excellent study not only of the meaning of Mignon and the harpist but for a variety of problems that I here discuss. The few points of disagreement between Sarasin's interpretation and mine I shall currently mention.

[8] The manuscript, which by a lucky accident has reached posterity, was a copy written by Barbara Schulthess, Goethe's Swiss friend mentioned earlier, and her daughter. This was copied from a copy made by Goethe's amanuensis Christian Georg Karl Vogel (1760–1819), who, in turn, copied it from a draft that Goethe had dictated. Thus the sources of error are manifold. Philologic research has traced errors caused by auditory mistakes due to Goethe's dictation, etc. See *Soph.* I, 51:283–96. The switch from *sie* to *er* in the text can well be explained psychologically by the particular occasion and is not due to the mechanical circumstances of the various transcriptions. In the course of the *Wanderjahre* Goethe speaks of Mignon as "boy-girl" [Knaben-Mädchen] and "sham boy" [Scheinknabe]. (*Soph.* I, 24: 354, 355)

Eros participates on both sides, but the taboo prevents Wilhelm from ever satisfying Mignon's passion for him. Wilhelm justifies his aversion against women by the deep disappointment he suffered through Mariane's unfaithfulness. This, however, must be considered a rationalization, like Goethe's equivalent complaints that his first adult sweetheart in Leipzig did not marry him. Wilhelm's love for Mignon betrays the root of what must be called his misogyny. An instance of Goethe's writing of Mignon in the masculine gender discloses this root. It happens at the beginning of Book IV, when the famous poem "Know you the land where the lemon trees bloom?" is recited. This was the song that most impressed Wilhelm, of those that Mignon sang. Since the land meant is Italy, to which Mignon wants to travel with her master, the poem has been interpreted as an expression of Goethe's longing for that country. Sarasin has linked it with his father's death, which removed an unconscious barrier that kept him away from Italy (464, p. 392). Without objecting to this interpretation I nevertheless believe that another problem comes forth in the second stanza, the first four lines of which I wish to translate literally:

> Know you the house? On columns rests its roof,
> The hall is bright and the chamber shines,
> And marble statues stand and look at me:
> What have they done to you, you poor child?[9]

In the second sentence after this song (the first occasion for a pronoun) Mignon becomes "he": "He [Wilhelm] demanded it [the song] of him [Mignon]." [Er verlangte es von ihm.]

I believe that the psychological hub of the poem lies in the meaning of the fourth line: "What have they done to you, you poor child?", which is quite puzzling in the context of the poem. Considering the marvelous description of the beauty and peacefulness and happiness in nature expressed in the first stanza, and the beauty and quiet repose of the palace and sculpture in the first three lines of the second stanza, in contrast to something that has happened to the girl, I am compelled to conclude that the question refers to castration.[10] The poem grew out of the profound pity

[9] [Kennst du das Haus, auf Säulen ruht sein Dach,/ Es glänzt der Saal, es schimmert das Gemach,/ Und Marmor-Bilder stehn und sehn mich an:/ Was hat man dir, du armes Kind, gethan?] (*Soph.* I, 52:3)

[10] As Sarasin astutely points out, the third stanza repeats impressions that Goethe obtained during his first journey to Switzerland. He shows that Goethe in that stanza uses terms identical with those used in *Dichtung und Wahrheit* to characterize that which came most to his attention during that journey. Yet this sudden switch from Italy to Switzerland makes me feel more certain about my interpretation. Cf. my earlier interpretations of the connection between Switzerland and homosexuality in Goethe's associations (p. 370).

the boy Goethe felt for the poor, injured sister, Cornelia. Sarasin explains Mignon's androgynous nature by connecting it with Cornelia's pathological inhibition of her femininity and with a synthesis of Goethe's younger siblings (particularly of Hermann Jakob) into the one figure of Mignon (464, pp. 389–90). When Sarasin describes Mignon as fixated to the anal-sadistic level and as never having reached the genital phase, I feel inclined to disagree. As will be shown later, I believe that Mignon shows the earmarks of early infantile passion, that she is not a pregenitally fixated girl but a girl who tries to fight against her genital cravings. Mignon's androgynous appearance in my opinion is the result of the way in which the boy Goethe experienced his sister's body at a certain level of his psychosexual development—as a boy in whom something was missing. And Wilhelm is constantly haunted by the feeling that there is something wrong with Mignon, something that he cannot put into words and that she cannot describe.

The image of the androgynous being which is female also serves man's wish that the female nature of a human being may not be a permanent "stigma" but change one day toward masculine completeness. Up to this point, almost all the female characters in *Wilhelm Meister* are objectionable, if not wicked: Wilhelm's mother is cruel, Melina's wife superficial, Madame Reti mannish, Philine psychopathic, the Countess indiscreet, and Mariane unfaithful. Only Mignon is good, but her sex does not yet seem to have been definitely established.[11]

The quick change of gender in Mignon after the afore-mentioned song strikes me as an inadvertent anodyne quickly administered to soothe the acute mental pain Goethe may have suffered while writing those lines. Furthermore, in the early *Wilhelm Meister* Mignon's origin remains mysterious and unexplained. In the final version the reader is informed that she is the offspring of an incestuous relationship between a brother (the harpist) and a sister.[12] Yet in the early version at least Mignon was in my opinion the product of recollections and fantasies Goethe had about his sister Cornelia.

When one gathers all the details that are dispersed throughout *Dichtung und Wahrheit* regarding Cornelia and compares them with the account Goethe gave of Mignon then the resemblance becomes even clearer:

[11] There are, in addition, two women about whom nothing unfavorable is said in the novel: the grandmother, who is, however, beyond the biological phase of sexual conflict, and Wilhelm's sister, who is a background character drawn in noncommittal terms about whom we hear hardly anything.

[12] Whether the incestuous origin of Mignon was already in Goethe's mind when he wrote the first version or only crystallized later, is not known.

the mystery in the character of both; the complete devotion and obedience to the brother and Wilhelm respectively; Mignon's stubbornness in her relationship to unsympathetic masters and the grave conflict between Cornelia and her father, her using her brother as a refuge and Goethe's promise to rescue her from their father's tyranny, which he described exaggeratedly in *Dichtung und Wahrheit*. Yet there is one notable difference between Mignon in *Wilhelm Meister* and Cornelia in *Dichtung und Wahrheit*. In the latter the relationship to Cornelia is described as a twin relationship, which it apparently was for the longest time. In *Wilhelm Meister,* however, there is nothing of the twin aspect, despite Mignon's being an image of Cornelia. Mignon is the helpless, poor, injured, neglected, naive, childlike, mysterious creature who, nevertheless, is a strong and self-willed personality to whom Wilhelm is incessantly drawn in a fatherly, superior way. The difference between the two is strongly emphasized. I believe that in Mignon Goethe depicted the very early sister-relationship, before the twin relationship had been established.[13]

There are two problems of early childhood worked into Mignon that can occasionally be observed in the relationship of an older brother to his younger sister. The girl is regarded as injured, maimed, on the basis of the boy's observations of her genital. The pity he feels is often partly compensatory to the envy he feels of her privileged status as capable of gratifications denied to him. Yet the older brother may also have the fantasy that the younger sibling is in danger, because of general helplessness and because of dependence on the mother, of whom the boy forms an ambivalent picture of unreliability. In a fashion similar to that quite commonly encountered in the fantasies of women (see 204, p. 254) the boy also evolves the preconscious or unconscious conviction that the mother was responsible for the little sister's injury. The conclusion the boy then often draws is that the baby would have been safer, and would be also safer now, if he took care of her, a theme that played a paramount role in Goethe's relationship to Cornelia.

The other conflict is a purely sexual one and is based on a difference between the sexual development of male and female children. A significant number of female patients report strong, orgasmlike, and truly orgastic experiences in early childhood. Boys generally experience a full orgasm only at or shortly before a time when maturation reaches the stage of emission. (This, however, is not a strict rule and orgasms are occasionally,

[13] The dating of the period when the twin relationship came into existence will be considered further later.

though rarely, reported before the phase of genital maturation.[14]) Since orgasm can arise from stimulation of the clitoris without the requirement of a biologically matured genital apparatus, an orgastic experience is, in general, possible much earlier in girls than in boys.[15] The clitoris seems to be capable of yielding an orgasm from the earliest developmental stages on, whereas the penis as a rule lacks this capacity. One can therefore often observe a greater decisiveness and energy in the pursuit of sexual gratifications in girls than in boys, who in addition early feel the impact of the castration complex.

In *Wilhelm Meister* Goethe describes a seizure in Mignon that I wish to discuss in detail. Eugen Wolff, who for his interpretation of Mignon had only the final version of the novel at his disposal, described this attack as "cardiac cramps and epileptic twitchings" (555, p. 130). Sarasin sees in the attack something more than hysteria can produce. He surmises that Goethe's siblings died from tuberculosis and that the miliary type of the disease, with meningeal irritation, may have led to convulsions observed by the boy. In agreement with Freud, he suggests that the recollection of such a sight may have entered Goethe's description of Mignon's attack (464, pp. 389–90).

My impression of the episode runs in a different direction. But first I wish to give the details. The attack occurred at a time when Mignon rightly thought that Wilhelm would soon depart leaving her with the rest of the company.[16]

Nothing is more touching than when a love that has nourished itself in silence, a faithfulness that has grown strong in secret, at the right time comes forward and reveals itself at last to him who has not been worthy of it until then. The bud long and strictly closed was ripe and Wilhelm's heart could not have been more susceptible. She stood before him and saw

[14] See 329, pp. 175–78. In my limited clinical experience prepubertal orgasm in the male is a bad prognostic sign and the harbinger of severe psychopathology, in contrast to female development where it does not seem correlated with any degree or type of psychopathology. My clinical material is numerically so small that it does not warrant a generalization. However, theoretical deliberations, not to be discussed here, seem to me to provide such a warrant.

[15] The question of early vaginal orgasm is not considered here. It makes no difference in this context whether the early orgastic experiences of girls stem from the clitoris or the vagina. For a discussion of the early vaginal contribution to female sexual development see 136.

[16] The episode takes place when the actors' group has received the invitation to join the Count at his castle and Wilhelm is torn between leaving and staying with his newly won friends when Mignon enters his room.

his disquietude. "Master!" she exclaimed, "if you are unhappy what is to become of Mignon?"—"Dear creature," he said as he took her hands, "you too are among my griefs." She looked into his eyes, which glistened with unshed tears, and impetuously knelt before him; he held onto her hands, she laid her head on his knee and was quite still. He played with her hair and was gentle. She remained calm for a long time. At last he felt a kind of twitching through all her limbs that started quite softly and spread more vigorously. "What is the matter with you, Mignon?" he exclaimed, "what is it?" She raised her little head and looked at him; suddenly she put her hand to her heart as with a gesture that stifles pain. He raised her up and she fell on his lap; he pressed her to him and kissed her. She answered with no squeeze of the hand nor any motion. She held fast to her heart and suddenly she gave a cry that was accompanied with convulsive movements of the body. She started up and at once fell down again before him as if broken in all her joints. It was a frightful sight. "My child," he cried, as he lifted her up and held her fast, "my child, what is the matter?" The twitching persisted, which communicated itself from her heart to her shaking limbs; she just hung in his arms. He locked her to his heart and dampened her with his tears. Suddenly she seemed again strained and more strained, like one who bears the greatest physical pain; and soon, with renewed vehemence, all her limbs came alive again and, like a spring that snaps shut, she threw herself around his neck, while in her inmost [soul something] like an immense rent occurred, and in that moment a stream of tears flowed from her closed eyes onto his bosom. He held her tight. She wept and wept and no tongue [can] tell the power of those tears. Her long hair had come loose and hung down from the weeping [girl] and her whole being seemed unrestrainedly to melt away in a rivulet of tears. Her rigid limbs softened; her innermost [soul] poured forth, and in the aberration[17] of the moment Wilhelm feared she would melt away in his arms and nothing of her should remain to him! He held her all the tighter and tighter. "My child," he cried, "my child, you are indeed mine! If the word can console you, you are mine! I will hold onto you! I will not forsake you!" Her tears still flowed. At last she raised herself. A soft cheerfulness radiated from her face. "My father," she cried, "you do not want to forsake me! You do want to be my father! I am your child!" . . . [Wilhelm] . . . who was holding his child ever tighter in his arms, enjoyed the purest, most indescribable, bliss.[18]

[17] I thought at first that the German word *Verirrung* (aberration) was mistakenly written by the copyist instead of *Verwirrung* (confusion), but the final version of the novel uses the same word.

[18] [Nichts ist rührender, als wenn eine Liebe, die sich im Stillen genährt, eine Treue, die sich im Verborgenen befestiget hat, endlich dem, der ihrer bisher nicht werth gewesen, zur rechten Stunde nahe kömmt und offenbar wird. Die lang und streng verschlossene Knospe war reif, und Wilhelms Herz konnte nicht empfänglicher sein. Sie stand vor ihm und sah

In my opinion this episode admits of only one interpretation, namely, that it is a masterly description, realistic down to the smallest detail, of a girl having an orgasm.[19] Since Mignon stood for Cornelia, this account was probably based on Goethe's observation of an orgasm in his sister. Further, if we try to determine when this event took place in reality, we have to consider Cornelia's frigidity as an adult and her severe emotional disorder, which must have had an early inception. Clinical observation shows that patients who suffer from such a disorder as Cornelia's often are persons who had the experience of an early orgasm with a traumatic effect. The vehemence of the sensation, its unfamiliarity, its seizing the whole body, arouse extreme fright. Even the fear that in the course of the

seine Unruhe. Herr! rief sie aus, wenn du unglücklich bist, was soll aus Mignon werden?— Liebes Geschöpf, sagte er, indem er ihre Hände nahm, du bist auch mit unter meinen Schmerzen. Sie sah ihm in die Augen, die von verhaltenen Thränen blinkten, und kniete mit Heftigkeit vor ihm nieder; er behielt ihre Hände, sie legte ihr Haupt auf seine Knie und war ganz stille. Er spielte mit ihren Haaren und war freundlich. Sie blieb lange ruhig. Endlich fühlte er eine Art Zucken durch alle ihre Glieder, das ganz sachte anfing und sich stärker verbreitete. Was ist dir, Mignon? rief er aus, was ist dir? Sie richtete ihr Köpfchen auf und sah ihn an, fuhr auf einmal nach dem Herzen, wie mit einer Geberde, die Schmerzen verbeisst. Er hub sie auf, und sie fiel auf seinen Schoss, er druckte sie an sich und küsste sie. Sie antwortete durch keinen Händedruck, durch keine Bewegung. Sie hielt ihr Herz fest, und auf einmal that sie einen Schrei, der mit krampfigen Bewegungen des Körpers begleitet war. Sie fuhr auf und fiel auch sogleich wie an allen Gelenken gebrochen vor ihm nieder. Es war ein grässlicher Anblick. Mein Kind! rief er aus, indem er sie aufhob und fest umarmte, mein Kind, was ist dir? Die Zuckung dauerte fort, die vom Herzen sich den schlotternden Gliedern mittheilte, sie hing nur in seinen Armen. Er schloss sie an sein Herz und benetzte sie mit seinen Thränen. Auf einmal schien sie wieder angespannt und angespannter, wie eins, das den höchsten körperlichen Schmerz erträgt; und bald, mit einer neuen Heftigkeit, wurden alle ihre Glieder wieder lebendig, und sie warf sich ihm, wie ein Ressort das zuschlägt, um den Hals, indem in ihrem Innersten wie ein gewaltiger Riss geschah, und in dem Augenblicke floss ein Strom von Thränen aus ihren geschlossenen Augen in seinen Busen. Er hielt sie fest. Sie weinte und weinte und keine Zunge spricht die Gewalt dieser Thränen aus. Ihre langen Haare waren aufgegangen und hingen von der Weinenden nieder, und ihr ganzes Wesen schien in einen Bach von Thränen unaufhaltsam dahin zu schmelzen. Ihre starren Glieder wurden gelinder, es ergoss sich ihr Innerstes, und in der Verirrung des Augenblickes fürchtete Wilhelm, sie werde in seinen Armen zerschmelzen und er nichts von ihr übrig behalten. Er hielt sie nur fester und fester. Mein Kind! rief er aus, mein Kind! du bist ja mein! wenn dich das Wort trösten kann! du bist mein! ich werde dich behalten! dich nicht verlassen! Ihre Thränen flossen noch immer. Endlich richtete sie sich auf. Eine weiche Heiterkeit glänzte von ihrem Gesichte. Mein Vater! rief sie, du willst mich nicht verlassen! Willst mein Vater sein! Ich bin dein Kind! . . . [Wilhelm] . . . der sein Kind immer fester in den Armen haltend, des reinsten unbeschreiblichsten Glückes genoss.] (*Soph.* I, 52:96–98)

[19] At least if a patient told me of such observations in a girl I should not hesitate to conclude that an orgastic experience was being reported. It may have been this that gave Sarasin the impression that Mignon's behavior goes beyond that which hysteria can produce (cf. above, p. 759). Wilhelm responds to the seizure as to a declaration of love, for it induces him to accept Mignon as his permanent ward.

experience one has caused irreparable damage to one's body (the inner-most rent in Goethe's description, with its ambiguous implication) is not the gravest consequence. It is a specific peculiarity of the situation that the child loses its time orientation and actually experiences this first sensation of orgasm as if it would never end, as if it were lasting for an eternity. Further, it is questionable whether a sensation that is really and essentially new can be experienced as pleasurable at all, whether such sensations must not rather be learned by repetition to be potentially pleasurable. All these factors taken together cause the first such orgasm to be so severely associated or identified with annihilation that a repetition is out of the question, and even a drawn-out analysis may not induce such a patient ever to risk a second exposure to this situation, which was experienced as abysmally horrible.

In view of the foregoing one must conclude that Cornelia suffered the trauma not in the latency period or at early puberty, but at an earlier age. The little boy, of course, was bound to interpret the whole event as a terrible suffering to which his poor sister was being exposed. The experience had to be repressed[20] by the boy, but returned in all its detail in an adult context under the favorable conditions of his voyage into the unconscious —under Charlotte von Stein's guidance—and the impact that the undertaking of an artistic presentation of his past automatically had. The fact that Mignon's (Cornelia's) sexual experience unfolds in two phases admits of different explanations. Wilhelm plays with her hair and Mignon holds still for a long time before the twitching sets in. Her gesture of stifling pain corresponds to the attempt at suppressing the sensation that was in process of forming under Wilhelm's tender play. Thereupon Wilhelm provides new stimulation by kissing her. Then the cry occurs, followed by a collapse. The subsequent, renewed convulsive movements suggest to me that she had come to the verge of a second orgasm, which either did not surge up to the previous pitch or was dispelled by her effort. There is, however, also the possibility that the author reversed the sequence and put the cry at the beginning whereas in reality it occurred at the end, prior to the phase of complete relaxation accompanied by unrestrainable tears. The sequence of events must have given the boy the impression that his sister was going to die, and that her limp, paralyzed body would never again show the tension of life.[21] Yet we know how quickly children, even

[20] It is not probable that Goethe would consciously and intentionally have described an undisguised and crude sexual event.

[21] In the dramatic fragment *Prometheus,* written during the *Sturm und Drang* period, Goethe openly equated orgasm, in the female at least, with death (cf. above, pp. 477–78).

when experiencing traumata that will destroy their happiness as adults, can be diverted on the spur of the moment. The "soft cheerfulness" radiating from the girl's face and the boy's "indescribable bliss" sound credible and like the end phase of such a bliss as can be experienced only by the child, the traumatic effects being quickly surrendered to the unconscious, as befits this period of life. After all, at *that* time Cornelia became alive again and she was permitted to embrace her beloved brother.

In the report of Mignon's orgasm the wealth of references to the girl's motor system is remarkable. A scrutiny of this description shows that the most important impressions Wilhelm received were not conveyed by the visual sense but by the effect that changes in the muscular apparatus of the girl's body had on his own kinesthetic sense or that of touch. Since in the early *Wilhelm Meister* as well as in *Dichtung und Wahrheit* Goethe referred to experiences in the dark corners of the large parental building, it is quite conceivable that some of his most important psychosexual experiences were relatively without visual stimuli but depended chiefly on kinesthetic sensations. If this hypothesis is correct it would help to explain one root of Goethe's strong visual endowment. The strong kinesthetic stimulation must have compelled him to form the concomitant visual imagery. In clinical experience one usually finds that the primal scene (of copulation)[22] is experienced either visually or in the auditory sphere, rather than kinesthetically. Which perceptive organ is excited by these early observations has an important bearing on the affinity of the personality to the various sense organs. Yet it is, I surmise, a rather rare occurrence that the early sexual stimulation is conveyed by the kinesthetic system. It is an open question whether this factor may have had a generally stimulating effect on the boy's urge to create. In other words, I raise the question whether this hypothesized mode of early sexual experiences had constructive consequences. One of the shattering effects of the primal scene is related to the helpless child's extraneousness to the whole situation. He is overwhelmed by a tremendous emotional upsurge that does not fit into the context of his own stream of experiences. If Goethe's early psychosexual experiences unfolded in such a way as I have tried to reconstruct, then it may be deduced that this particular traumatic effect was excluded. Despite the terror the experience may have elicited, the source from which the excitation derived was within the boy's reach and not beyond the sphere of his muscular apparatus, as almost always happens when the primal scene produces an early trauma.

[22] For a discussion of the concept of the primal scene see 188, pp. 29–47; 139, pp. 543–46; 413, pp. 74, 256–57.

The closeness of the love-object, the constant physical contact by touch, admitted at least a minimum of control, which is absent in the usual primal scene. The muscular apparatus may thus have been the main pathway over which the little boy learned of a strange passion of which he was not yet capable. Now the muscular apparatus is closer to the sphere of volition than any other ego apparatus. I wonder how far this was one of the roots of the eminently constructive responses Goethe showed from an early age to what so easily results in psychopathology in others. Conceivably, the fact—if this was the fact—that the experience of the primal scene left traces predominantly in the kinesthetic system and, further, occurred in connection with a human being that was partly reachable by the child's empathy, created a particularly favorable starting situation. The reader will, I hope, forgive the speculative nature of these comments, but in view of our present ignorance regarding the subject matter speculation may be welcome.

I mentioned earlier the egg-dance that Mignon performed for Wilhelm shortly before Bendel appeared on the scene in most humiliating circumstances (cf. p. 755). A few of the introductory circumstances must be sketched. Mignon enters Wilhelm's room. There is no sound in the building. The child carries a light although it is still daytime and fastens the shutters, thus making it quite dark in the room. (The light just mentioned is forgotten in the further course of the narration.) For the next few sentences Mignon again becomes a "he." "He" brings some eggs, which are spread out over a rug. Then "she" (once more female) starts her dance like a wound-up clock (*Soph.* I, 52:18, 19). The essential feature of the dance is that, although Mignon is blindfolded, she does not crush a single egg under her heels.[23]

This fantasy is significant: danger and possible destruction due to Mignon's movements, and nevertheless, in the event, absolute reliability. What may have been the underlying repressed recollections? Was it a fantasy compensating for a grave trauma belonging to the castration complex, or was it the derivative of a situation in which such trauma was only feared in prospect, but averted in actuality, through the sister's skill? Goethe relates the following processes in Wilhelm while he watches Mignon:

> In this moment he felt all at once all he had ever felt for Mignon. He longed to incorporate this forlorn creature in his heart in place of a child,

---

[23] Sarasin (464, p. 388) connects the egg-dance with a rope-dancing boy who appears in the autobiographical novel, and connects him in turn with Goethe's younger brother, who died early.

to take her into his arms and to awake the joy of life in her with the love of a father.[24]

The full psychological meaning of this reaction in Wilhelm will become clear only at the end of the novel. Here I wish only to point out that the episode of the egg-dance and Wilhelm's subsequent longing to achieve the greatest closeness to the girl seems to me to reflect another aspect of the castration complex. The girl had been castrated, but survived; therefore, nothing can happen to her, and she acquires maximum physical preciseness (that is to say fearlessness). Mignon actually never walked up and down stairs but jumped, often sat on wardrobes, and sometimes was seen walking about on the roof edges of the building. Gratitude and indebtedness towards her for having taken castration upon herself and thus having saved him from that fate probably was his underlying response when she exhibited herself to Wilhelm. The appearance of the threatening father in the shape of Bendel immediately following Mignon's egg-dance points in the same direction. Since Bendel is a degraded father-substitute it is significant that he enters the picture shortly after Wilhelm has decided to annex Mignon to his heart. One can easily imagine how often the father successfully interfered with the two children when they tried to get off by themselves and escape parental supervision in the darkness of secluded corners.

Having discussed this aspect of Wilhelm Meister's object-relationship I shall turn now to an important phenomenon of ego-psychology. Goethe describes Wilhelm's mood during the first performance of his play as follows:

He [Wilhelm] wholly relished the delightful impression of being the center upon which a crowd of assembled people directed their attention, and, if we may speak metaphorically, of feeling himself to be the keystone of a huge vault, upon which a thousand stones press without disturbing it, and which holds them together without labor and effort merely through its position, whereas they would otherwise quickly tumble down into confused rubble.[25]

[24] [Er empfand, was er alles für Mignon gefühlt, in diesem Augenblicke auf einmal. Er sehnte sich, dieses verlassene Wesen an Kindesstatt seinem Herzen einzuverleiben, es in seine Arme zu nehmen und mit der Liebe eines Vaters Freude des Lebens in ihm zu erwecken.] (*Soph.* I, 52:19–20)

[25] [Er genoss ganz den köstlichen Eindruck, der Mittelpunct zu sein, worauf eine Masse versammelter Menschen ihre Aufmerksamkeit richtet, und wenn wir gleichnissweise reden dürfen, sich als der Schlusstein eines grossen Gewölbes zu fühlen, wohin tausend Steine, ohne ihn zu belästigen, drucken, und der sie ohne Arbeit und Gewalt bloss durch seine Lage zusammenhält, da sie sonst schnell in einen verworrenen Schutt zusammenstürzen würden.] (*Soph.* I, 52:5)

I wish with Goethe to call the feeling here described the "keystone" feeling.[26]

If we look, for example, at those marvelous statues of the Pharaohs in their remoteness and aloofness from mankind, their extreme security centered in themselves, their solemn quietness which needs no gesture or word to enforce their will, then we can grasp by empathy the keystone feeling. Democratization of life has deprived Western man of ever experiencing this feeling in its full reality. Even the president of a powerful republic must ingratiate himself with the voters if he wants to be reelected when his term is over; the industrial magnate must glance occasionally at the stock market; the surviving monarchs are restrained by constitutions, and even dictators are all too aware of the precariousness of their position to expect that their power will be hereditary. No modern power position can provide a feeling such as is reflected in the statues of the Pharaohs. But in every human being there is the germ of such an experience in the form of an infantile wish for it. Wilhelm, as author, actor, director in one, comes as close to it as can be in our times. It was a Pharaonic world created and acted by his own effort, and held together solely by his own presence. Almost like God above the clouds, exerting no effort in order to maintain the harmonious coordination of nature's laws, so Wilhelm, the keystone, had complete power over the people present in the theater. But the craving for this kind of extreme feeling of omnipotence may be the compensatory derivative of an equally extreme childhood fear, when children were born and died around him and the beloved mother's powerlessness to prevent this simultaneously permitted the fulfillment of the child's ever-present longing to be the only loved child in the family.

The keystone feeling belongs to a group of emotions one of which was described by Freud (following a suggestion by Romain Rolland) as oceanic feeling, "a sensation of eternity, a feeling as of something limitless," "a feeling of an indissoluble connection, of belonging inseparably to the external world as a whole" (208, pp. 64–65). Whereas in the oceanic feeling the ego extends to the most distant borders of reality, in the keystone feeling, I believe, reality converges towards the ego and the ego feels itself in full possession of reality because the latter is rushing towards its borders. I therefore surmise that the oceanic and the keystone feelings are different only in directional index. In the oceanic feeling the ego widens to engulf

---

[26] Goethe is really going on here with the discussion of an idea he had broached in the five essays about the psychology of tragedy (see above, p. 724 f.). Though the feeling as described here is far more intense, and also different in quality from the emotional sphere analyzed in the essays it nevertheless belongs in the same category.

reality, and in the keystone feeling the ego may even shrink, but reality is absorbed within its confines, however narrow.

To whatever type this feeling may belong, which Goethe described by this keystone metaphor, its great effect of holding together, harmonizing and integrating by mere position, is perhaps related to the feeling of the infant when healthy and loved. Death and sickness and mother's pregnancies are some of the childhood catastrophes that tragically disturb the early feeling of omnipotent harmony. But art is one of the media through which the ego may, if only temporarily, taste again something of that bliss of the past. At least the situation in which Goethe imputes to Wilhelm the keystone feeling is an exquisitely narcissistic one in three respects: all the events on the stage are the results of his daydreams; he himself is standing on the stage and all the psychic processes of all the people present are coordinated and correlated to him, that is to say, the minds of all the people within the space of which he is spiritual master are completely occupied with the effect of his doing; all those present forget themselves and are replenished by his person. The theatrical performance becomes a celebration in the service of Wilhelm's ego; it is a camouflaged resurgence of early childhood, when the world seems to be nothing but a place in which services are permanently held for the celebration of the infantile ego (see 143).

How close this matter was to Goethe's conscious mind can be seen from a short remark he made to Charlotte von Stein in a letter of September 18, 1782, after the performance of *The Fisherwoman,* one of his minor musical comedies:

> They played badly and committed a hundred grossnesses; finally, to be sure, the play was over, as when someone shoots at a deer, misses it, and by chance hits a hare. So is it with the effect! The best effect is that which two like souls have upon each other, which cannot miss even at a distance, and which does not depend on any third person, actors or musicians.[27]

In this passage Goethe complains that he has not been able to obtain the keystone feeling from a performance of his dramatic work but claims that it is obtainable only within a personal relationship. To be sure, the time of his great dramatic creations had passed. He no longer wrote great plays. *The Fisherwoman's* principal impact consisted of some effects of illumina-

---

[27] [Sie haben schlecht gespielt, und hundert Schweinereyen gemacht, am Ende war freylich das Stück vorüber, wie wenn einer nach einem Reh schösse es fehlte und durch ein ohngefähr einen Hasen träfe. So ists mit dem Effeckt! pp Der beste Effeckt ist den zwey gleiche Seelen auf einander machen. Der auch in der Entfernung nicht fehlen kann und der von keinen dritten, Ackteurs oder Instrumentalisten abhängt.]

tion. It was staged in the open, and in the course of the short play a large
number of torchlights shone up along the river, an effect there was not
really much reason to be proud of.[28] But did Goethe write less outstanding
plays because he was now getting the keystone feeling in his relationship
with Charlotte von Stein, or did he seek it in his relationship to her because he could not create great art during this period?

Hypothetically one must assume, as said before, that the keystone feeling is connected with early experiences related to the mother. Genetically
it may go back to a period when the mother did not yet appear as a discrete
entity and was identical with the world. Once the fateful step has occurred,
and a certain configuration within the world becomes discernible as
mother separated from the rest of the world, the keystone feeling, if it ever
develops to a significant extent, still remains connected with the mother.
In the further course of development the conscious association between
the two wanes more and more, and the feeling may eventually become
completely dissociated from its original object. It certainly is subjected to
variation and modification in accordance with the psychosexual development. Goethe made a remark about it in later years in reference to the
genital level. In the story *The Man of Fifty Years,* included in the *Wanderjahre,* he writes of a man who just at the time when he wants to court a
young woman and remarry loses a front tooth. "He feels as if the keystone
of his organic existence were alienated and the rest of the vault now also
threatened gradually to collapse."[29] Here the keystone feeling is attributed
to the well-functioning of the penis and potential incapacity is experienced
as a deprivation of the very emotional quality. Indeed, during adequate
orgasm the world shrinks to the boundaries of the sensation and the
world exists for the subject only inasmuch as it is contained in the orgastic
sensation. Without conflict, without regret on the part of the subject, everything beyond it vanishes and the subject experiences the shrinkage of the
world to these narrow boundaries as one of the greatest enrichments of
his existence.[30]

Thus in the course of development the circumstances that may be apt

[28] The play started with the *Erlkönig,* one of Goethe's most beautiful ballads, but he had
to take four ballads from Herder's collection of folk poetry for the rest of the play. See
261, part 2, 2:612.

[29] [Es ist ihm, als wenn der Schlussstein seines organischen Wesens entfremdet wäre und
das übrige Gewölbe nun auch nach und nach zusammenzustürzen drohte.] (*Soph.* I, 24:
339)

[30] Another context in which Goethe used the word *Schlussstein* will be found on p. 849
in his letter to Herder, in which he announces the discovery of the intermaxillary bone,
which Goethe called a "keystone to man."

to produce the keystone feeling change in many respects and seem in Goethe's instance to have become correlated with certain feelings of activity and passivity or their combinations, and thus we return again to that ever-puzzling problem.

The metaphor that Goethe uses suggests a combination of both activity and passivity by mere position. In his relationship with Charlotte von Stein one technique which promised attainment was to arouse love by devoted service, which again is based upon the combination of both, namely to arouse a passive gratification by activity. As far as can be reconstructed, he never fell into an overtly passive attitude towards Charlotte von Stein, although behind the exaggerated overt activity many passive feelings may have been hidden, since Charlotte von Stein functioned for long periods as his counselor. The whole adjustment to the protocol of court life was, after all, one of the first demands she imposed on him, and it cannot be determined to what extent he felt himself a mere tool despite his impressive show of activity. In the particular period under consideration Goethe again made an extreme remark regarding passivity in a letter to a man, as he had done to Plessing four months earlier. On November 17, 1782, he wrote to his recently reconciled friend Jacobi:

Of my situation I may report nothing. Here too I remain consecrated to my old fate and suffer where others enjoy, enjoy where they suffer. I have endured ineffably. . . . Let me use a metaphor. When you see a glowing mass of iron on the hearth you do not think that so much slag clings in it as will reveal itself only when it comes under the big hammer. Then there is separated the dross that the fire itself did not set apart . . . and the pure metal remains in the tongs of the workmen.

It seems as if such a powerful hammer was needed to free my nature of its manifold slag and to make my heart pure.

And how much, much mischief still can lurk there.[31]

[31] [Von meiner Lage darf ich nichts melden. Auch hier bleibe ich meinem alten Schicksale geweiht und leide wo andere geniessen, geniesse wo sie leiden. Ich habe unsäglich ausgestanden. . . . Lass mich ein Gleichniss brauchen. Wenn du eine glühende Masse Eisen auf dem Heerde siehst, so denkst du nicht dass soviel Schlacken drinn stecken als sich erst offenbaren wenn es unter den grossen Hammer kommt. Dann scheidet sich der Unrath den das Feuer selbst nicht absonderte . . . und das gediegne Erz bleibt dem Arbeiter in der Zange.

Es scheint als wenn es eines so gewaltigen Hammers bedurft habe um meine Natur von den vielen Schlacken zu befreyen, und mein Herz gediegen zu machen.

Und wieviel, wieviel Unart weis sich auch noch da zu verstecken.]

In the last sentence Goethe makes a pun that cannot be translated: *Unrat*—dross, *Unart*—mischief.

Here the metaphoric description of the passive experience contains particularly strong terms. To be sure, this letter was written to a friend towards whom Goethe was feeling guilty, a factor that also played a role in Goethe's letter to Plessing. A way to appease anger in another person is to present oneself as suffering. Notwithstanding this external factor I am certain that Goethe was expressing a truth in both letters. It was not a pose he adopted in order to impress a friend. The external factor may perhaps explain why it was just to Jacobi that the remark was made and not to some friend who was closer to him.

The seriousness of his expression of pain can be seen from the fact that he sent the letter to Charlotte von Stein before posting it on to his friend,[32] and this fact, I think, also confirms the suggestion that follows. The extent of renunciation accomplished during his stay in Weimar was excessive. And it should not be forgotten that Goethe probably also experienced the decrease in artistic output as an act of renunciation—in the service of the beloved woman as well as of the principality. But first of all he had almost certainly renounced any kind of sexual gratification and lived without any prospect of it. And this was indeed a sacrifice of unbelievable magnitude, particularly when his age and temperament are considered. He was, therefore, right when he said that he suffered where others enjoyed. The only remaining sources of pleasure were service to others, the fulfillment of duties and self-denial, and therefore he was right when he said that he enjoyed where others suffered. Since complaining was no longer part of his relationship to the beloved woman, he probably would not have been able to tell her this directly. But by letting her read the letter he apparently wanted to remind her of what unspeakable pain he had to suffer in order to give his existence its present form. And truly, if the total picture is carefully reviewed one must feel respect—even awe—for Goethe's capacity to endure pain, the price almost every genius must pay for being exempted from the fate of all other mortals, namely to end in eternal oblivion.

Since the colossal reorganization of his personality was performed in the state of transference, without clear awareness that what was happening was exclusively for his benefit and was, in the last analysis, primarily the effect of his own unconscious wishes and needs, he was bound to experience the progress of those seven years as something imposed upon him. With a feeling of full freedom he probably would not have been able to endure the pain involved. Yet all this demonstrates that the keystone feeling, which it was apparently of great importance to him to feel now

[32] See letter to Charlotte von Stein of the same day.

and then, was more and more lacking in his present existence. Goethe, to be sure, tried to obtain the keystone feeling in his relationship to Charlotte von Stein. He may from time to time have achieved it, but the relationship was of such a kind that it soon evaporated and had to be achieved anew if at all.

The danger in that relationship was probably that at times it might have led to a kind of surrender or to complete passivity in Goethe, which would have been most dangerous to his personality development. Apparently in order to counteract that danger Goethe, as was remarked earlier, arrogated functions that might by rights have been considered to belong to Charlotte von Stein. He behaved in a maternal way and provided her with food, sent food for her children, and admonished her to take proper care of them. In the period we are now discussing he took a step that was as consequential as it was characteristic. I believe that that step concerned significant problems that were openly or tacitly pending in his relationship to Charlotte von Stein, that is to say, that were genetically related to his father, mother, sister, and the perennial antagonism between activity and passivity. I refer to his taking practically full responsibility for Charlotte von Stein's youngest and favorite son, Fritz, who moved to Goethe's house shortly after the middle of May, 1783.

I wish now to go into the history of Goethe's relationship to Charlotte von Stein's three sons, Karl (1765–1837), Ernst (1767–1787) and Friedrich, that is, Fritz (1771–1844).

A remark that is perhaps the earliest record of Goethe's about any of the three children occurs in an undated letter (probably of January, 1776) to Charlotte von Stein. It ends as follows: "I shall probably still come today, for I do not feel like your Fritz."[33] The interpretation of this passage is evident. The five-year-old boy may have run away from his mother, or have been unwilling to stay with her and Goethe was saying that, in contrast to the little boy's behavior, he would try his best to join her. This sounds like an innocent remark, but it is a far-reaching one if scrutinized for its possible unconscious implications. First of all there is Goethe's comparing himself with the little boy, as if he wanted to say: "Look at me, I love you more than your own little baby does." This suggests a competitive angle and an attempt at diverting the mother's attention from a beloved child to himself, which probably implies not only jealousy but also an initial demand to be loved by the beloved woman like her own progeny.

[33] [Ich komme wahrscheinlich heute noch, denn mir ist's nicht wie Ihrem Friz. (*Soph.* IV, 3:20; see also 244, *1*:20, n. 4)

The second remark to be found implies an indirect, mild reproach against her oldest son, an action of whose inadvertently increased Goethe's tension (letter of January 27, 1776). The third remark refers to Ernst, to whom he was sending a book (letter of February 12, 1776). In these three passages the patterns of his feelings for each individual child are indicated. Nevertheless, in the initial phase the children are mainly experienced by him as a nuisance, as is revealed in his nickname for them, namely *Grass-affen,* literally, "grass monkeys," that is to say, "young fools." In a letter of April 5, 1776, this is openly expressed: "How vexatious the seacats were to me yesterday, just at the moment when I had so much, so much to tell you."[34] Here the children are patently experienced as an annoying wedge between the lover and the beloved woman. This is all the more surprising since Goethe was extremely fond of children, and in his relationship to the earlier Lotte of the *Werther* time her siblings, of whom she took care as replacement for her deceased mother, played an integral role. Goethe quickly became their lasting idol and when he left Wetzlar they may have mourned his sudden departure more than his beloved Lotte. One gets the impression that in his relationship to Charlotte von Stein's children there was more conflict involved than with the siblings of that other Lotte. Charlotte Buff had been a virginal "mother." The oedipal aspect of the situation did not precipitate competition or contest. The little siblings of Werther's Lotte were creatures that—psychologically—had come from no-where, but the children of the Weimarian Lotte were constant reminders of her past and the indisputable testimonies that she had given something to a Freiherr von Stein that she would not grant to Goethe. The little children at Wetzlar brought out the potentialities Lotte possessed as a future mother, and this combination of supreme qualities as a future mother with the virginal attraction of a blooming girl made her so irresistible. The children of the Weimarian Lotte did not forecast any of Charlotte von Stein's future potentialities but were of interest rather as a sign of what Charlotte von Stein had been in the past. And so, her children were for quite a while "water monkeys" or "grass monkeys" or "the little ones," until they became permanently "children" and still later "those who are yours" [die Deinigen].

The tendency to assume the functions of a mother appears early in

---

[34] [Wie fatal waren mir die Meerkazzen gestern, iust im Augenblick da ich so viel so viel Ihnen zu sagen hatte.]

Meerkatze means literally "seacat," but is the name for a kind of long-tailed monkey and is used figuratively for an ugly person.

Goethe, but half-heartedly. On July 16, 1776, he wrote to Charlotte von Stein:

> Have fed Fritz. I am not meeting your sister. She is a sweet creature, such as I should like to have for myself and then nothing else [should be] loved. I am sick and tired of heart-sharing.[35]

Relying on the earlier-stated impression that in some of Goethe's letters sequences may be taken as free associations, I stress the significance of his mentioning his feeding the little boy and immediately thereafter expressing himself so strongly in favor of a girl whom he would not have to share with a competitor.

At the outset, general references to Charlotte von Stein's children as a unit prevailed, but gradually Fritz emerges as the principal figure, in relation to whom basic oedipal conflicts were acted out. The oldest, Karl, apparently reacted to Goethe in accordance with a positive Oedipus complex. Much later, when Goethe saw him again after a long separation, he wrote to Charlotte von Stein (August 19, 1784): "Karl is here, he has grown. . . . He will look like his father; it was a great pleasure for me to see him."[36] Whether the resemblance to his father had already been noticeable earlier and Goethe met him with greater coolness than his brothers, or whether Karl reacted with anger to the intruder in accordance with his age (eleven years) when Goethe first became interested in his mother, is undetermined. Be this as it may, he reported the following incident in his recollections of Goethe when he was an old man. After recalling the great pleasure he got from Goethe's valuable gifts he continued:

> My kind feelings towards this family friend suddenly turned, however, into a long-lasting hatred. The reason was the following. He was standing in the dining room holding forth in front of the fireplace and had raised both coattails in order not to burn them, or to warm himself better. Since he stood near me a little sideways the better to see the company near the fireplace, and I therefore [was] behind him to a certain extent, I silently caught hold of the bellows, stuck them unnoticed into the opening that usually is in the back underneath the buckles of the trousers, and greeted him with an unexpected blast of wind. His speech was interrupted by this. This made him very angry and he not only rebuked me harshly but also

---

[35] [Hab den Friz gefüttert. Deine Schwester seh ich nicht. Es ist ein liebes Geschöpf wie ich eins für mich haben mögte, und dann nichts weiter geliebt. ich bin des Herztheilens überdrüssig.]

[36] [Charles est ici, il a grandi. . . . Il resemblera a son pere, i'ai eu beaucoup de joie a le voir.]

threatened to slap me if it should happen again. I would have been too weak, as a boy of eleven, to defend myself against him, who was at least twenty-seven years old, but found myself dreadfully offended by this threat and looked upon it as a matter of honor which I had not met and settled satisfactorily. Unfortunately, I did not know a fitting answer and therefore thought the whole injustice to be on his side, considered him a bully, yet was afraid to tell him so.[37]

This recollection mirrors the mutual ambivalence in their relationship. Karl left home at the age of fifteen to study abroad.

Ernst, the second son, was always a frail boy; he died at the age of twenty after terrible sufferings. Goethe treated him with the greatest compassion. As will be seen later, I think that he played a significant role in Goethe's final breach with Charlotte von Stein.

If Karl was a son who reacted with aggression, and Ernst, perhaps because of his sickness, one who reacted with passivity, then Fritz was a kind of ideal youngster. He was vivacious, cute, interested in the world, and alert; he neither rebelled nor submitted, but was, apparently, bewitchingly charming in his boyish narcissism, which could adjust ingratiatingly to the kindness of adults without cramping his individuality. Aside from any bearing his love for the boy's mother had on his feelings for the youngster, Goethe's homoeroticism was greatly stimulated by the child. He pursued energetically his plan of having a statue made of Fritz in the nude, and protested when the sculptor thought Fritz's body too thin to serve as an attractive model (49, p. 172). In an early letter (March 19, 1776) he wrote: "Fritz was here. I kissed him a good deal."[38] This letter deserves particular attention, for in the wake of his kissing of Fritz he started to feel very bad. He "took flight" to Wieland, for he could not stand being

---

[37] [Mein Wohlwollen gegen diesen Hausfreund verkehrte sich aber plötzlich in einen lange anhaltenden Hass. Die Ursache war folgende. Er stand im Esssaal und perorierte vor dem Camin und hatte beide Rockschösse aufgenommen, um sie nicht zu verbrennen, oder um sich besser zu wärmen. Da er neben mir etwas seitwärts stand, um die Gesellschaft neben dem Camin besser anzusehen, und ich dadurch gewissermassen hinter ihn, so ergriff ich leise den Blasebalg, steckte ihn unvermerkt in die hinten gewöhnlich befindliche Öffnung unter der Hosenschnalle, und begrüsste ihn mit einem unverhofften Windstos. Seine Rede wurde dadurch unterbrochen. Diess machte ihn sehr böse, und er fuhr mich nicht nur gewaltig an, sondern drohte mir sogar mit Schlägen, wenn das wieder geschähe. Ich wär als Junge von etwa 11 Jahren zu schwach gewesen, mich gegen ihn, der wenigstens 27 Jahre alt war, zu wehren, fand mich aber durch diese Drohung entsetzlich beleidigt, und sah es für eine Ehrensache an, die ich nicht ordentlich ausgemacht und bestanden hätte. Unglückseeligerweise wusste ich keine passende Antwort und glaubte also alles Unrecht auf seiner Seite, hielt ihn für einen Grobian und fürchtete mich doch, es ihm zu sagen.] (543, pp. 7–8)

[38] [Friz war bey uns den hab ich viel geküsst.]

alone. The doctor was called and forbade him to go out, but the whole event sounds like an acute psychogenic episode at a time when his relationship to Charlotte von Stein was not yet settled.[39] The day before, he had written excitedly to Fahlmer concerning a settlement of family property. In such times of unstable object-relationships the danger of homosexual temptations may have become threateningly strong.

A relationship similar in its outward aspect to that which he had entertained with the children in Wetzlar also developed partly to Charlotte von Stein's children. He went on walks with them, sent toys, and tried to satisfy their little needs. It may be noteworthy how often when he sent food to Charlotte von Stein he wrote that it was for her and Fritz, as if he wanted to feed the youngster through his mother. Occasionally Fritz spent a night in his home. On New Year's Day of 1779, he wrote: "Fritz awakened me before four o'clock and so cackled in the New Year."[40] From about this time on a new theme appears: Goethe's gratitude to Charlotte von Stein for letting Fritz be with him. In the middle of January of the same year he wrote: "Thanks, dear angel, for Fritz."[41] "Association with children makes me joyful and young,"[42] he wrote around that time, and this probably remained true for most of his life (see 407). Being with a child yielded something positive and he obtained a narcissistic gain.[43] In the fall of 1780 there occurred the earlier reported masochistic identification with Fritz (see letter of November 2, 1780, above, p. 455). Whereas initially the identification with the child had led to a mild boasting about his own superiority, it now led to a sharing of a rejection, to a kind of consolation, as if he meant to say: "My love treats me no better than her favorite son. Why should I then feel unhappy and complain?", or, in other words, "Since Fritz is denied a full gratification of his desires why should I insist upon it?" This masochistic identification, which may have lasted longer than can be proved by documents

---

[39] The letter does not make it clear beyond doubt whether Goethe's illness began before or after Fritz's visit.

[40] [Friz hat mich vor vieren geweckt und das neue Jahr herbey gegäckelt.]

[41] [Dancke lieber Engel für Frizzen.]

[42] [der Umgang mit Kindern macht mich froh und jung] (Letter to Kraft of July 13, 1779)

[43] There are people in whose life the affinity to and interest in children plays a greater role than in others. Oddly enough, one rarely encounters a schizophrenic patient of whom this would not be true. I omit here a discussion of the deeper root of this predilection. It is connected with the fact that the lives of children pass closer to the primary process than those of adults. Sigmund Freud (178) points out the attraction which the infant's primary narcissism has for the adult. Goethe's interest was not so much in the infant phase, I think, but predominantly in the childhood period from the oedipal phase to early puberty.

at present available, may have been at work to facilitate his request to be allowed to use the familiar *Du*, a request that occurred a few months after the episode of November 2, 1780. This subterranean identification with the youngest possibly worked also as a secret barrier against temptations necessarily aroused by increased personal familiarity.

At this time also a new function of Fritz in Goethe's libidinal economy became evident: He served as a substitute for Charlotte von Stein. Before that time it had happened now and then that one of the children—but especially Fritz—served as messenger to carry one of those innumerable scraps of paper that were exchanged between them. Goethe wrote as a postscript on March 25, 1781: "I embraced you most affectionately in Fritz."[44] Since the letter had closed with an expression of greatest indebtedness to the love-object, the child was accepted in a situation of implied guilt as a substitute for his mother. Goethe was perhaps here retracing an old pathway—when by kissing his beloved Cornelia he gratified an oedipal impulse. This shift from the child as messenger to the child as substitute for the love-object is the shift from means to end. It is particularly impressive to watch this shift occurring within a single day. A few hours earlier he had written: "Send me Fritz soon; I will tell you more through him."[45] Here he asks for Fritz *expressis verbis* as a medium through which he can reach the love-object, but does not even hint at his functioning as a substitute.

When discussing that consequential month of March, 1781, I presented some of the reasons why, in my judgment, though a change had evidently occurred, the record did not permit the conclusion that a sexual relation had begun. I add here another reason, namely Goethe's using Fritz as a messenger. But first a qualification. It is extremely difficult to fathom what might have been considered indelicate or offensive in past times, even when those times are as relatively close to us as those of Goethe and Charlotte von Stein. Difficult as this is, it is even more difficult and almost impossible to pass judgment on such a matter with respect to particular personalities. Indeed, even among contemporaries one is struck in the course of psychoanalytic treatments by how vast the difference is from one person to another in matters of moral judgment. It is easier to inform oneself about what the law permitted or prohibited in past times, but even in a matter codified by law we may know all too little about the extent to which a particular law had any status in the sentiments and

---

[44] [Ich habe Sie in Frizzen aufs herzlichste umarmt.]

[45] [Schicken Sie mir Frizen bald durch den sag ich Ihnen mehr.]

I pointed out earlier (p. 519) that the dating of this letter is not quite certain.

actions of those who were supposed to have abided by it. The problem seems to become hopeless when it concerns questions of conduct that are not covered by law or statutes, but depend on individual tact, opinion and moral sentiment. Nevertheless, one hesitates to assume that Goethe would have used as a messenger to carry a billet-doux a boy who was his mistress's son, and that a few days after the inception of the physical relation, to boot. I admit the possibility thereof, I only strongly question the probability.

The change from messenger to substitute for the love-object, however, fits well into a close association that did not include physical consummation. It makes good sense that, in a situation in which the instinctual demand became increasingly strong and frustration therefore all the more difficult to bear, the child (a rival or an inferior as the case may have been) should have been made the object of love. Such a course is almost universal, and occurs when sibling rivalry changes under the impact of constant frustration to sibling love (see 193). The only external compensation he wanted was to be loved by the child as he loved him. Hence it is understandable that a few days earlier, when he was abroad and without present signs of Fritz's affection, the first direct reproach against Fritz should have occurred (March 13, 1781): "Not to forget Fritz. I dare say he could have written me once."[46] But such disappointments could not interfere with the broad emotional stream that flowed between the child and him, and when the boy accompanied him on a trip to Leipzig he was delighted. Here, of course, the afore-mentioned mechanisms could be extensively displayed, and upon his return he wrote as follows, to Charlotte von Stein (October 1, 1781):

> My dearest, I have always [throughout the trip] held discourse with you and [in the person of] your boy I conferred good and sweet things upon you. I have kept him warm and bedded him soft; I got delight from him and meditated upon his education.[47]

Here besides communicating with Charlotte von Stein through the child Goethe tried to appropriate the child to himself. Paternal and maternal functions were fused.

Quite in keeping with the narcissistic overevaluation of the child, he put Fritz in the position of an umpire. Thus six weeks later when he wrote to Lavater (November 14, 1781), who wanted to know how he liked

---

[46] [Frizzen nicht zu vergessen. Er hätte mir wohl einmal schreiben können.]

[47] [Meine Liebste ich habe mich immer mit dir unterhalten und dir in deinem Knaben gutes und liebes erzeigt. Ich hab ihn gewärmt und weich gelegt, mich an ihm ergötzt und seiner Bildung nachgedacht.]

the portrait of the Duke's brother painted by Tischbein,[48] he praised it highly in many respects, and then went on:

> Only, it made me wonder that a few unsophisticated people, and particularly a very well-balanced child extremely reliable in all his judgments about perceptible things, have not recognized it. I speculated about it especially since the boy guessed at a few kindred faces.[49]

It is of interest that Goethe accepts the child's judgment as a guide-rope in the evaluation of a work of art. Matters of art, such as analysis and art appreciation, were dear to his heart, and a faint implication of surrendering to the child's judgment can be read between the lines.

However, in a letter to Charlotte von Stein of about the end of May, 1782,[50] Goethe alludes to an event that must have had a profound effect on his feelings about the boy. Therefore I wish to record the letter in its entirety:

> I have already made a very nice beginning with Fritz today. He is with me the whole day and industrious, lively, and good. I hoped to be with you this evening and cannot renounce this hope. Towards five I will go through the yard and speak with a loud voice. If you want to see me, come to the window. Be calm, it will come right in the end. Only first get the child away from there and let him sleep over here when Ernst is [gone] away, for in any case it is no longer proper. Then we shall try to make a start at it and I want to be to him all that I can. Calm down. Farewell and do not fear. I am always yours and of those who are yours.[51]

It is difficult to reconstruct the events that prompted this letter. Fritz's own comments, written later when he annotated Goethe's letters, are not very helpful:

[48] Johann Heinrich Wilhelm Tischbein (1751–1829), painter of portraits, animals, and historical scenes, well-known in his time; Goethe's famous friend of his sojourn in Rome.

[49] [Nur hat es mich wundern müssen dass einige unbefangene Personen und besonders ein sehr wohl organisirtes, und in allen seinen Urtheilen über sinnliche Dinge höchst zuverlässiges Kind, es nicht erkannt haben. Ich machte dadrüber meine Betrachtungen, besonders da der Knabe auf einige verwandte Gesichter rieth. . . .]

[50] The letter is undated, but circumstances make it almost certain that it was written prior to May 25, 1782.

[51] [Ich hatte heute schon einen sehr schönen Anfang mit Fritzen gemacht. Er ist den ganzen Tag bey mir und fleisig munter und gut. Ich hoffte diesen Abend bey dir zu seyn und kann der Hoffnung nicht entsagen. Gegen fünfe will ich durch den Hof gehen und laut reden. Wenn du mich sehn magst so komm ans Fenster. Sey ruhig es wird sich geben. Thue nur vorerst das Kind drüben weg und lass ihn hüben schlafen wenn Ernst weg ist, denn es schickt sich auf alle Fälle nicht länger. Dann wollen wir es einzuleiten suchen, und ich will ihm alles seyn was ich kann. beruhige dich. Lebe wohl und fürchte nicht. Ich bin immer dein und der deinigen.]

After my teacher Kästner had become teacher of the [ducal] pages he continued to impart instruction to me and I slept in his lodgings. My second brother, Ernst, who was huntsman's boy to the Duke, went at this time to the country to a forester's in order to learn forestry. Therefore I was often alone among the pages; in order to change this, as became necessary, Goethe gave me a room in his house. The love and care with which he treated me was infinite and I owe him very much for this happy epoch of 1782–86, when he traveled to Italy.[52]

Düntzer accepted this explanation and said that Fritz had acquired "all kinds of unmannerly habits," and was without well-ordered activities among the pages. This was why his mother was to take him away from the ducal manor ("there") and let him sleep at home ("over here" in Goethe's letter) (107, *1*:176). Fritz's and Düntzer's explanations are unsatisfactory. Their reasoning would justify only a calm and deliberate decision, but by no means Charlotte von Stein's sudden and intense alarm; nor does it contribute to explain the conspiratorial undertone. Some details in Goethe's letters do not at all fill the bill either. Yet knowing or even proving that their explanation must be wrong and that Fritz's memory was deceived, does not tell us what really happened.[53] The facts as they seem assured by the evidence on hand do not carry us very far. In my judgment there cannot be great doubt about the following: The mother was evidently greatly upset about something in Fritz's behavior. Goethe suggested a measure to be instituted as soon as feasible; also a plan for the future was conceived, namely of Fritz's living in Goethe's house and being entrusted to his care, which should be gently introduced after the immediate measure had been taken. For the time being the boy would spend most of his daytime with Goethe.—This is not much, and speculation must set in when discussing what localities Goethe may have meant by "there" and "over here." Among several possible sequences of events I incline to the following, which I must admit does not follow rigorously from Goethe's letter. I suggest that the "there" of the letter may have referred to Charlotte von Stein's house, and the question may have been whether Fritz was to continue to sleep in his mother's bedroom. Charlotte

---

[52] [Nachdem mein Lehrer Kästner Pagenhofmeister geworden ertheilte er mir noch Unterricht, und ich schlief in seiner Wohnung. Mein zweiter Bruder Ernst, der Jagdpage des Herzogs war, ging zu dieser Zeit auf das Land zu einem Forstmanne, um das Forstwesen zu lernen. Hierdurch war ich öfter allein unter den Pagen, welches Goethe abzuändern, wie es nothwendig wurde, mir ein Zimmer in seinem Hause gab. Unendlich war die Sorge und Liebe, mit der er mich behandelte und ich verdanke ihm sehr viel in dieser glücklichen Epoche von 1782–86, wo er nach Italien reiste.] (243, *2*:550, 551, note to p. 51)

[53] It must also be considered that Fritz may not have told, and may never have known, the true reason for his being moved to Goethe's house.

von Stein was deeply attached to Fritz and it would not have been unlike her type to have treated the favorite son for an undue time like a little child. I wonder further whether Charlotte von Stein may not have surprised the boy when masturbating or whether Fritz showed a direct manifestation of an oedipal striving, such as exhibitionism or voyeurism, in accordance with his age of prepuberty. Perhaps Charlotte von Stein, always inclined towards feelings of guilt, had intimated to Goethe that she should have devoted more time to the boy. Thus Goethe may have felt indirectly responsible for the boy's difficulties. It is also noteworthy that the boy's father was not mentioned at all in the letter. Evidently plans and decisions were made without first hearing what his opinions were. To be sure, a year later, shortly before Fritz took up permanent residence in Goethe's house, Goethe urged Charlotte von Stein to make proper arrangements with her husband, but this request was no more than a gesture to confirm what she and Goethe had already decided upon a year before, regarding Fritz's education.[54]

The letter here under discussion, which, though undated, belongs to the end of May, 1782, was written around the time of the death of Goethe's father. It is important that just then, in his near environment, there lived a boy who, it is assumed, was involved in a conflict of early puberty, with possibly manifest oedipal implications. Such a situation must have had a stimulating effect upon his own past sexual conflicts. The attitude he took towards the boy was one of forgiveness and care; punishment was not at all the measure on which he relied in raising a child. It was the reflection of his own superego, which started to be more tolerant and benign to him. In serving the boy, he could eliminate feelings of guilt for sins he had himself committed.

The depth and direction that the father problem took appears in the ballad "The King of the Elves," which may have been written around that time.[55] This ballad is one of the most interesting psychological documents of that period. The father image is split into two: the father carrying the

[54] Was Goethe successful in his numerous endeavors to help younger people by educating them? Sarasin rightly speaks of the concealed hatred of the teacher towards the pupil (464, pp. 387–88), which appears faintly behind such endeavors in the inappropriate selection of the objects of his interest, and very distinctly in his way of raising his own son. Of Fritz, however, Wilhelm von Humboldt said (1809): "Stein is a very good man, yet his ability to work can be accepted only with reservation. What is more noteworthy, in these imperfections too he bears unmistakable traces of Goethe's education. I think it has harmed him that Goethe, as he easily does in general, emphasized too much the real and the practical and put too little stock in learning as such." (390, p. 362)

[55] Baumgart (14, 2:15) dates it 1781; Heinemann (258, *1*) dates it at the beginning of 1782.

child; and the King of the Elves, who wants the boy for himself. The one is the good father, the other the bad one; the former tries to rescue the child, the latter tempts him by blandishments and seduction and finally appropriates him for himself—he steals him from the good father. There is a direct sexual implication in the act of appropriation. The stanza says: " 'I love you, your beautiful form rouses me, and if you are not willing I will use force.' 'My father, my father, now he seizes me! Elf-King has done me harm.' "[56] The interesting feature in this ballad is that it is not father and mother that confront each other, but two fathers. The good father is pictured as a mother is usually represented: he holds the child in his arms, he keeps him warm, he gives him protection. Bode sees in the ballad a residue of Goethe's experiences with Fritz (49, p. 178).

It is necessary to refer here to a configuration that is rarely considered in psychoanalytic literature, namely the child's relationship to the father before the father becomes the rival and ideal of the oedipal phase. I wish to call this configuration *the preoedipal father*.[57] In some instances one finds a figure parallel to the preoedipal mother. As the latter is so often endowed by the boy with a penis, the former is endowed with breasts. From Bettina's reports it seems that Goethe's father assumed an important role in the earliest phase of the boy's life, carried him around, stood at his bedside and consoled him when he awoke in a panic. She reported:

> Once his father held him [Goethe] on his arm and let him look at the moon, when suddenly he fell back as if convulsed by something and became so beside himself that his father had to blow air into him so that he should not choke.[58]

About the child's preoedipal mother-relationship we know at least that it is biologically necessitated and, however its course may vary, depending on external conditions, every child has to pass through it. Yet is this also true of the preoedipal father-relationship? Or does that depend on fortuitous circumstances, such as the father's willingness and disposition to

[56] ["Ich liebe dich, mich reizt deine schöne Gestalt;/ Und bist du nicht willig, so brauch' ich Gewalt."/ "Mein Vater, mein Vater, jetzt fasst er mich an!/ Erlkönig hat mir ein Leids gethan!"] (*Soph.* I, 1:168)

[57] See Sigmund Freud (204, p. 250): "As regards the prehistory of the Oedipus complex in boys we are far from complete clarity. We know that that period includes an identification of an affectionate sort with the boy's father, an identification which is still free from any sense of rivalry in regard to his mother."

[58] [einmal hatte der Vater ihn auf dem Arm und liess ihn in den Mond sehen, da fiel er plötzlich wie von etwas erschüttert zurück und geriet so ausser sich, dass ihm der Vater Luft einblasen musste, damit er nicht ersticke.] (11, 2:160)

The episode is mentioned above, p. 183.

behave in a maternally affectionate manner towards the infant? Goethe —if Bettina's report can be trusted—obtained profuse impressions from which to evolve the imagery belonging to the preoedipal father. Melanie Klein and the so-called English School of psychoanalysis operate with the united parent image, meaning a configuration in which father and mother are not discrete entities. I doubt whether such imagery is really as common as is assumed. I rather think that it is difficult for the observer to discriminate between the images of the preoedipal father and the preoedipal mother. Since the infant does not hesitate to attribute the characteristics of both genders to each of them, they may appear identical to the observer, but are they also identical to the infant? From a literary product such as "The King of the Elves," I should conclude that they are not. In this ballad there is mirrored, I believe, the conflicting wishes in the male infant, on the one hand to be nursed, to be protected against forbidden impulses, and, on the other, to have these impulses libidinally satisfied by the father; in later years these wishes arouse formidable anxieties and guilt feelings, so that there is a tendency to project them into a representative who is divorced from the caring and nursing aspect of the preoedipal father.

Two factors may have precipitated preoccupation with that imagery in Goethe. First, his father's death (or the expectation of that event), and, secondly, the growing mutual attachment between himself and Fritz. The loss of the father as an old man, as he appeared to the adult, stimulated a longing for the tempting picture of the archaic father, of the days when the dichotomy of sexes had not yet complicated the life of the child. At the bottom of the imagery of the preoedipal father there is the fantasy that it was the father who gave life and food to the baby,[59] a fantasy that would be justified for Goethe if Bettina's report could be proved to have been according to fact. Simultaneously the reproach arises: "You have not protected me enough," which appears well justified when a father dies from senility. The anger at the vanishing father is denied and converted into the reproach of seduction that took advantage of childhood weakness. Homosexual gratifications are identified with death, in accordance with well-established unconscious imagery.

It is interesting to compare this ballad with the earlier ode "Ganymede" (discussed above, on p. 413), written between 1774 and 1781. In that poem, joyful, even blissful, surrender to the deity, a youthful boy's strivings upward to be united with the "all-loving father," are the central themes. In "The King of the Elves" the boy is completely passive and the

---

[59] The two horns of Moses are possibly a symbol of two breasts.

outcome depends on whether the bad father will outwit the good one or vice versa. The father-images in the two poems are from two different developmental levels, that of the Elf-King of early archaic origin. From the point of view of the constellation of reality circumstances, a reversal is noticeable, inasmuch as it is not a father-substitute that dies, but the infant. It sounds almost as if Goethe was trying to resist an impulse to follow his father, as if the death of the father had mobilized erotic longings to be united with the deceased. From this viewpoint the ballad contains a truth, namely the reproach: "By your death you have evoked my desire to die." We should be in a better position to evaluate this point if we had reliable data as to when Goethe wrote *The Fisherwoman*, which opens with "The King of the Elves." Goethe mentioned the arias of that play in his diary on August 5, 1781; the second rehearsal took place on June 21, 1782. The central theme of the play is a woman's pretending to have been drowned in order to frighten her father and her fiancé. She hopes this will make them more considerate of her wishes. When the truth is found out she is severely reprimanded and is reluctantly made to consent to an early marriage. The implications of this plot are clear if brought into connection with the death of Goethe's father. Yet the historical evidence does not favor its dating at a time after his father's demise, and unless we assume that recent news from Frankfurt had alarmed Goethe a coincidence has to be conceded.

His father's death and the strong relationship to a son-substitute reversed Goethe's whole standing in life. As long as a generation sees its elders still surviving there is a protective barrier against death: Father must die before death can seize the next generation. When his father died, the whole problem may have become aggravated for Goethe by the existence of a son-figure in his own life. Now he had to function as a protective barrier against death for a new oncoming generation. Thus "The King of the Elves" may also have served the purpose of reassurance: "After all, children may die before their fathers do."[60]

The whole conflictful problem having its center in progeny comes to the fore in the play *Elpenor*, which Goethe for obvious reasons could not finish. The history of its composition itself demonstrates the conflicts that underlie it. Twice when the Duchess was pregnant and Weimar was looking forward to celebrating the birth of an heir apparent, Goethe tried to write this tragedy. In 1781, a female was born dead, and therefore there was no occasion to finish the play for the churching of the Duchess. In 1783, when the Duchess was pregnant again, Goethe renewed his work on

[60] This of course had the factual basis, too, of the early deaths of Goethe's siblings.

it but failed to be ready with it on time; when all of Weimar was over-straining its poetic talents, Goethe's only contribution was a poem of four stanzas that no one would recognize as his if it were not for certain historical proof. In all respects, content as well as form, it was mediocre.

There is no doubt Goethe was inhibited in the composition of *Elpenor;* he wrote one and a half acts but never got beyond that, although in later years his interest in the dramatic subject was again aroused. The cause of the inhibition can be found if that fragment is studied. The bricks out of which Goethe built his plot are known: (1) an ancient Greco-Roman myth, and (2) a Chinese tale.

(1) Antiope, daughter of Nycteus, is made pregnant by Zeus; she leaves her father and takes refuge with Epopeus. Nycteus dies of grief and leaves the kingdom to his brother Lycus so that Antiope should be punished. Lycus kills Epopeus and takes Antiope home as a captive. She gives birth to twins. They are exposed, but found and raised by a shepherd, who calles them Zethus and Amphion. Dirce, wife to Lycus, mistreats Antiope, who flees again and joins her sons. Zethus, who does not recognize her, refuses her asylum. Dirce follows her and seeks to kill her. When the twins are informed by the shepherd that the fugitive is their mother they rescue her. They kill Dirce by tying her to a bull's horn. When the twins want to kill Lycus too, Hermes prohibits this but orders Lycus to surrender the kingdom to Amphion. (See 559, pp. 236–37)

This myth is a compound of several themes and it is not clear what its point is. It seems the subject matter is the badness of women. First Antiope causes the death of two men by her love-making with Zeus, and then Dirce causes trouble by her meanness to Antiope. The twins look like a resurrection of the two men who died, Nycteus and Epopeus, who must have loved Antiope and now reappear as her avengers. There is a hint of one twin's being the good and the other the bad. According to one version Amphion was the son of Zeus and Zethus the son of Epopeus. It is noteworthy that in Hyginius' version, which Goethe used, the tragic events lead to a peaceful solution inasmuch as a new murder is prevented.

(2) The Chinese play of *Tchao chi cou ell* or the "Little Orphan of the Family of Tchao,"[61] is far less vague in its plot construction. Tou ngan cou is the leader of the King Ling cong's army. He is jealous of Tchao tun, who is in charge of the civil administration. Tou ngan cou succeeds in slaughtering Tchao tun and his family except for the latter's son, Tchao

[61] This play aroused a great stir in eighteenth-century Europe and is also most delightful for the modern reader. For an English translation see 105, 3:197–237.

so, who is married to the King's daughter. By means of a falsified letter Tou ngan cou induces Tchao so to commit suicide. The Princess, however, is pregnant and gives birth to a boy, whom she entrusts to Tching yng, a physician, devoted to the house of Tchao. The Princess then hangs herself. Tou ngan cou cannot feel sure of his power as long as a member of the Tchao family is alive. Since the Princess's baby boy has been rescued and his whereabouts are not known, Tou ngan cou decides to have all children under six months killed. Tching yng, in order to save the infants of the country and to make it possible that the house of Tchao will be revenged, designates his own little son as the Tchao orphan and suffers his being put to death. Thus he succeeds in substituting the Tchao orphan for his own son. Tou ngan cou, out of gratitude for Tching yng's service, takes him into his palace and promises to adopt his son and make him his heir, for he himself has no children. Twenty years later the little Tchao, who is now called Ton tching, has finished his education under Tou ngan cou's supervision. He is greatly loved by his adoptive father and becomes an accomplished fighter. Tou ngan cou plans to dethrone the king, to put himself in his place and give his adopted son the office that he himself now holds. Tching yng informs the orphan Tchao of the true state of affairs. Incensed by the wickedness of his adoptive father, he kills him, and the house of Tchao is restored to its former honor.[62]

In this Chinese play we encounter themes that are in associative connection with several themes mentioned previously, particularly in connection with *Iphigenia,* but new themes appear too, for example the father who sacrifices his own child's life to save another person's child, and the child that loves a father-substitute but is forced to kill him. The hub of the play is the rescue of a baby that will later have the duty of avenging all the misdeeds committed against his family. The anguish of the man who dies without progeny is another theme that appears.

In Goethe's *Elpenor,* Antiope's husband, a king, has been treacherously slain on his way home from victory. After his death, Antiope goes with her little boy to visit her mother. However, she is ambushed and her son stolen. When she visits her husband's brother, Lycus, she and Lycus's son Elpenor are mutually attracted at first sight. By promising to make Elpenor the heir of her realm she induces Lycus to leave Elpenor to her care until he shall have grown up. The play opens on the morning when Lycus is to come to Antiope's court to take his son back home. On that day, Antiope informs Elpenor of what has happened in the

---

[62] For the content of the Chinese play see 36, pp. 94–123; 36A, 132–58. For other influences coming from French literature, see 489.

past and makes him swear that he will do everything in his power to avenge the past crime by finding and killing the perpetrator and his progeny. Elpenor swears and Antiope feels happy, for she has thus got rid of the burden of hatred. She makes Elpenor promise that if her son should return Elpenor will share the throne with him. Her son can be recognized by a birthmark that is located in the same place as one that Elpenor has. In the second act Polymetis, Lycus's servant, appears and heralds his master's early arrival. Polymetis is burdened by a dreadful secret regarding great crimes in which he became involved at the behest of Lycus. He is in a quandary whether or not to impart his knowledge to Elpenor, for it concerns him too. There the fragment stops.

From the plot construction it is clear that Elpenor is Antiope's son unbeknown to her and to him, and it is highly probable that it was Lycus who killed Antiope's husband. Many scholars have tried to work out how the play's further plot would run, but no one has succeeded in finding a satisfactory solution.[63]

A major part of the fragment is taken up by Evadne, servant of Antiope, a wise woman who helped Antiope in raising Elpenor and to whom the lad is deeply bound in gratitude and admiration. The connection between Elpenor and Fritz von Stein has been remarked by many.[64] The occasion for writing the play was the prospect of his friend and master's getting a male heir, but from its plot, fragmentary as it is, and from the themes in the sources Goethe used, one can see the formidable degree of ambivalence with which Goethe responded to the prospect of this event. In Fritz he had a substitute son and this adoption was probably meant to reduce the ambivalence by the boast: "I too have a son." But *Elpenor* shows that this quasi adoption, however valuable the other purposes it served, did not suffice to reduce Goethe's ambivalence and the deep frustration he felt at being childless.

The theme that is new for Goethe in the fragment, which he adopted from these two sources, is the parental and filial ignorance of their relationship, under certain circumstances. Children can be exchanged or re-

[63] Even the question of what the fragment actually reports is open to debate. Biedermann, who devoted much thought to this tragedy, summarizes the plot in a way that I cannot follow in some important details. See 36A, pp. 133–34.

[64] See in particular Alexander Wood, who, in an excellent paper (558) discusses the general biographical background of *Elpenor*. Wood puts special emphasis on the theme of the child that serves as a bridge between a man and a woman who without the child's help would not have found their way to each other. Wood speculates that this would have become the major theme of the missing part. Without attempting to evaluate how apt this observation may be for the continuation of the play, one may well note Fritz's increasing importance during those years for the relationship between Charlotte von Stein and Goethe.

placed and parents will not necessarily become aware of it, and, also, the child must be told *expressis verbis* who his parents are. Thus, by implication, the emotional relationship between child and parent is held superior to the biological one, which is declared a matter of accident. It even looks as if the author meant to show that circumstances may easily lead to the child's turning with hostility against his progenitor but feeling affection for those who raised him: Elpenor is even closer to Evadne than to Antiope. Also, the dreadful heritage that is left to children by their progenitors in the form of a mission or duty (a theme of no minor importance in *Iphigenia*) is sharply contrasted to the assistance given by those friendly persons who, bound by purely emotional, unbiological ties, help the younger generation to extricate themselves from these chains—if extrication is possible at all.

The connection of this view with Goethe's personal problems of this time is self-evident. Aside from that, Goethe, on the basis of his own conflicts, pointed out an undeniable truth, namely, that the inclination toward conflict (*Konfliktneigung*) is actually greater between those who are biologically related than between those whose emotional ties grew from accidental acquaintance or friendship. Did Goethe here betray a deep (and probably repressed) fear of having progeny? In cases of paranoid psychoses one can observe that the delusional persecutor regularly stands for a hostile, eminently aggressive, child, who will carry out the deed that his progenitor weighed against his own parents when he himself was a child; that is to say, the adult paranoiac fears that his own child will do to him that which he, when he was a child, desired to do to his own parents. The ambivalence of adults against the child arising from this deepest of all fears is adumbrated in the fragment. I must forgo demonstrating this in detail. Interestingly enough, Evadne seems to be the only one who is capable of unambivalent love for Elpenor. It seems that Goethe's own problem inadvertently became so clearly manifest in the play's content that he recoiled from leading the play to its end.

But this was only one of the roots of his inhibition. When he sent Schiller the manuscript of the fragment on June 24, 1798, Goethe wrote:

> I did not want to look at all into the other manuscript [*Elpenor*] which I enclose; it may be an example of an incredible mistake in choice of subject, and God knows for what else it may be a warning example.

To be sure, the subject was not commendable for the celebration of the birth of an heir apparent, but in 1798 Goethe was surely free to finish the play without consideration of the initial occasion. The subject was highly dramatic per se and contained the greatest potentiality. But for what else might it serve as a warning example? Goethe continued in his letter to Schiller:

> I am quite curious what you guess about the origin of this infelicitous product.[65]

Schiller, misunderstanding Goethe's question, returned the following most remarkable answer:

> [The drama] reminds one of a good school, although it is only a dilettantish product, and does not permit judgment as a work of art. It attests to an ethically refined soul, a beautiful and moderate sensibility, and a familiarity with good models. If it is not from a woman's hand, nevertheless it reminds one of a certain femininity of sentiment, in so far, that is, as a man can have it.[66]

It would be of interest to know what made Schiller sense a femininity in the author. From the content and the circumstances surrounding the writing of the play I should conclude that Goethe's inhibition in finishing it was connected with his femininity. The impulse to write it seems to have been directly connected with envy of childbearing. But this time that envy evidently could not be sublimated, and therefore the play could not be created. There is a hint in support of my hypothesis in a phrase used by young Tobler in a letter to Lavater about Goethe's writing *Elpenor:* "Goethe works on the new play in hope of a prince." [Goethe arbeitet in der Hoffnung eines Prinzen am neuen Stücke.] (250, *1*:110) The German idiom *guter Hoffnung sein,* or simply *in Hoffnung sein,* means "to be pregnant." Of course, it is quite clear what Tobler was referring to. If the Duchess gave birth to a baby girl, a tragedy that had a son as central

---

[65] [In das andere beyliegende Manuscript mochte ich gar nicht hineinsehen, es mag ein Beyspiel eines unglaublichen Vergreifens im Stoffe, und weiss Gott für was noch anders ein warnendes Beyspiel seyn. Ich bin recht neugierig was Sie diesem unglücklichen Producte für eine Nativität stellen.]

Die Nativität stellen should be translated "to cast a horoscope." But whether one takes it literally or figuratively, it is hard to see how Schiller could have misunderstood Goethe's letter. Gräf (261, part 2, *1*:286 n.) rightly says that Goethe assumed that Schiller knew Goethe had written it and wanted to find out in what period Schiller thought the fragment to have originated or what Schiller thought about its continuation. Yet Schiller misunderstood Goethe's phrasing and thought Goethe wanted him to guess who the author might have been.

[66] [Es (das Drama) erinnert an eine gute Schule, ob es gleich nur ein dilettantisches Produkt ist und kein Kunsturteil zulässt. Es zeugt von einer sittlich gebildeten Seele, einem schönen und gemässigten Sinn und von einer Vertrautheit mit guten Mustern. Wenn es nicht von weiblicher Hand ist, so erinnert es doch an eine gewisse Weiblichkeit der Empfindung, auch insofern ein Mann diese haben kann.] (256, *20*:589)

figure would be out of place. Goethe prognosticated male progeny and therefore worked hard on the play. But the way Tobler expressed that thought suggests that one person at least in Goethe's environment had unwittingly hit upon the unconscious process that was going on in Goethe. However, I do not want to base my impression on such a debatable reconstruction. In 1828 Goethe said to a visitor who spoke admiringly of the play:

> I too have a fondness for this fragment; I ought to have continued on *that* path if I wanted to bestow upon the Germans the gift of a theater. But how much, indeed, man starts, and accomplishes so little![67] [Italics mine]

This remark is indeed surprising. First of all, Goethe here expresses a fondness for this dramatic attempt despite his previous aversion to it; secondly, one cannot agree that this type of play would have constituted any particular contribution to the creation of a German theater. Goethe had written two plays of the same type as *Elpenor,* namely *Iphigenia* and *Tasso,* but they did not lead to a particular German theater. But it is exceedingly interesting that at the age of seventy-nine *Elpenor* is still associated in Goethe's mind with a gift, a wonderful gift to the whole nation. But alas, man cannot accomplish it. I think this statement must be understood as more than a historical reference; it contains the key to *Elpenor* if psychologically interpreted. There is a thing a man can try over and over to create and he will never accomplish it. *Elpenor* was born out of Goethe's despair at not having a child,[68] of having to accept another man's son as his own in order to assure himself of the love of a beloved woman, out of the despair that a biological barrier was set to his archaic wishes for magic omnipotence, which strove towards bearing a child himself. The conflict could not be sublimated because of the heightened ambivalence and its acuteness in the present. The whole situation was aggravated by the reality occasion requiring the play: the birth of a boy to his friend, the arousal of jealousy, the ensuing impulse to destroy the infant, and consequently the choice of a topic that, so far from glorifying the life of the young, cast the most gloomy shadow on their tragic existence. Barrenness or monstrosity were the unavoidable consequences.

[67] [Auch ich habe eine Vorliebe für dieses Fragment; auf *diesem* Wege hätte ich fortfahren sollen, wenn ich den Deutschen ein Theater hätte schenken wollen. Aber wie der Mensch denn so Vieles anfängt und so Weniges vollendet!] (250, 4:58)

[68] See also his letter to Kestner of March 15, 1783: "Do not begrudge me my trees; your sons are a good part better." [Misgönnt mir meine Bäume nicht, Eure Buben sind um ein gut Theil besser.]

Some of Goethe's utterances setting the act of mental creation in associative connection with childbearing have been quoted. In the months of the Duchess's pregnancy fell the remark quoted earlier (p. 81) from his letter to Knebel of November 21, 1782, about Werther's return into his mother's body. This remark was particularly crude. It suggested a strong reaction to a pregnancy occurring in his environment and referred to a process that was not creative at all, namely to the copying of an original. The plan to improve the original version did not require creativity of such a sort as to warrant so extreme a metaphor.[69] It also sounds like a disparaging remark about childbirth, as if he wanted to say: "Women are fussy about childbirth. It is the same as if I created a sensation about copying and revising *Werther*." The well-known sour-grapes mechanism may be assumed to have had its share in Goethe's simile.

In the same letter to Knebel (November 21, 1782) Goethe made a remark which is of far-reaching importance.

> And so I begin once more to live for myself and once more to recognize myself. As it never came to my mind in my father's home to connect the apparition of ghosts and the practice of law, so separate do I now keep the privy councilor and my other self, without which a P.C. can very well exist. Only in the innermost of my plans and intentions and enterprises I remain secretly loyal to myself and tie together again with a hidden knot my social, political, moral, and poetic life. *Sapienti sat.*[70]

This announcement of a new attempt at isolating functions synthesized only at a different level was preceded by an expression of disillusionment:

> The delusion that the beautiful seeds that ripen in my and my friends' existence must be sown in this soil, and that those heavenly jewels could be

[69] It is not clear what prompted Goethe to revise *Werther* at that time. Shortly after its publication he had promised Lotte's husband to do so, since he had made him appear in an unfavorable light. But psychologically Albert, Lotte's fiancé of the novel, was also a father-substitute. Now, after his father's death, the impulse to make a father-substitute appear in a favorable light and to convert all of Albert's contemptible qualities into unjustified exaggerations of Werther's hypersensitive mind might have grown strong enough to overcome previous inhibitions. What might earlier have had the flavor of defeat may have become the cherished exercise of filial duty after his father's demise. But Goethe did not get far and the revision of *Werther* still had to wait for a more opportune time.

[70] [Und so fange ich an mir selber wieder zu leben, und mich wieder zu erkennen. . . . Wie ich mir in meinem Väterlichen Hause nicht einfallen lies die Erscheinungen der Geister und die iuristische Praxis zu verbinden eben so getrennt lass ich ietzt den Geheimderath und mein andres selbst, ohne das ein Geh. R. sehr gut bestehen kann. Nur im innersten meiner Plane und Vorsäze, und Unternehmungen bleib ich mir geheimnissvoll selbst getreu und knüpfe so wieder mein gesellschafftliches, politisches, moralisches und poetisches Leben in einem verborgenen Knoten zusammen. Sapienti sat.]

mounted in the earthly crowns of these princes, has forsaken me, and I find my youthful happiness restored.[71]

Goethe was referring to the failure of his attempt to make Weimar a court of the Muses and to fulfill in the Duke (who developed more and more martial ambitions) the ideal of a prince.

The similes of this passage (the seed that must be sown, the heavenly jewels) are quite reminiscent of the problem just discussed. Goethe's acute homosexual disappointment was evidently based not only on the Duke's actual comportment but also on the expected arrival of an heir to the throne. The crushing load of administrative functions that he had voluntarily taken on apparently had served the purpose of preserving and increasing his princely friend's love. Now, in a state of deep disappointment, his activities could not be carried out with as much libido as before. "The Duke," he wrote to Knebel,

> finds his existence in the chase and the hunt. The jog trot of business continues orderly; he participates willingly to a passable degree and now and then he takes an interest in something good, plants and uproots [as the case may be]. The Duchess is quiet, lives the court life; I rarely see either of them.[72]

In this report written from one courtier to another Goethe could be quite open about the situation in Weimar of that time. Very interestingly he compared his activities in Weimar with law practice in his native city. The latter was indelibly associated with the picture of his father. In those years too there should have been an isolation of functions, but this isolation (if Goethe was capable of it at that time at all) was enforced by his father's pressure and the young Goethe had not yet found himself. He was for some hours lover and then again poet and very few hours an attorney, but all these activities either got mixed up with one another or kept his existence constantly excited and tense, or were separated by a gap.

The new accomplishment of isolating and synthesizing that Goethe described has a double aspect. Until then psychological isolation of functions apparently had not been necessary, although in Weimar nonpoetic

[71] [Der Wahn, die schönen Körner die in meinem und meiner Freunde daseyn reifen, müssten auf diesen Boden gesät, und iene himmlische Juwelen könnten in die irdischen Kronen dieser Fürsten gefasst werden, hat mich ganz verlassen und ich finde mein iugendliches Glück wiederhergestellt.]

[72] [Der Herzog hat seine Existenz im Hezen und Jagen. Der Schlendrian der Geschäffte geht ordentlich, er nimmt einen willigen und leidlichen Theil dran, und lässt sich hie und da ein Gutes angelegen seyn, pflanzt und reisst aus pp. Die Herzoginn ist stille lebt das Hofleben beyde seh ich selten.]

activities took up even more of his time and interests than in Frankfurt. But these were carried out not only in the service of a beloved woman and of a beloved Duke, to both of whom his artistic creations were also devoted, but also in the service of an ethical mission. Temporarily a unification of the male and female love-objects (mother and father) was established, that is to say, the two basic oedipal strivings were no longer disparate but harmonized. Partly because of reality factors, but partly also because of his father's death and the Duchess's pregnancy, old conflicts were stirred up and the ambivalence in the relationship to his father was transferred to his relationship with the Duke. Under the impact of such circumstances isolation was instituted in a constructive way.[73] Instead of leading to conflict or division of the ego it was integrated by a deeper synthesis within which the ego was one with itself. In this instance isolation made the ego's diversified activities possible, which otherwise would have hampered one another and led to neurotic psychopathology. The isolation of activities without conflict made possible by the underlying synthesis marked the growth and strengthening that Goethe had achieved in the preceding seven years.[74] In the same letter Goethe also wrote:

> All the letters to me since 1772, and many papers of those times, have been lying at my place, tied in orderly packages; I separate them and have them bound. What a sight! Sometimes I become flushed with it all. But I do not give up, I want to see these ten years lying before me as a long valley through which one has wandered is seen from a hill.[75]

Here another aspect of constructive isolation, directly related to Goethe's main purpose of these years, is described, namely the gaining of understanding of self. Whereas up to then the process of elaboration upon self occurring within the transference relationship required the closest emotional and mental proximity to the object of transference, now distance is feasible, and important steps of the self-recognitive process are potentially separable from the vicissitude of transference by introducing the study of objective documents.

[73] See 170, p. 77, for the effect of a lack of the capacity to isolate upon Leonardo da Vinci's creativity.

[74] It must be repeated here that the unambivalent homosexual love was now flowing towards Fritz, which brought Goethe closer to the love-object and initiated the integration of a full father-identification. Thus the isolation of functions was accompanied with a unification of the image of the main love-object.

[75] [Alle Briefe an mich seit 72, und viele Papiere iener Zeiten, lagen bey mir in Päcken ziemlich ordentlich gebunden, ich sondre sie ab und lasse sie heften. Welch ein Anblick! mir wirds doch manchmal heis dabey. Aber ich lasse nicht ab, ich will diese zehn Jahre vor mir liegen sehen wie ein langes durchwandertes Thal vom Hügel gesehn wird.]

Whereas in his letter of four days earlier to Jacobi he had stressed his suffering ("I have suffered unspeakably"), he now wrote to Knebel:

> For some time I have been living very happily. I almost never get out of my house, I do my work, and in good hours write the fairy tales that it has ever been my habit to tell myself. . . . I see almost nobody, except those who have business to talk with me about; I have separated my political and social life wholly from my moral and poetic (externally, of course) and this proves best for me. Every week I give a big tea from which no one is excluded and so acquit myself of my duty to society in the easiest way. . . . In the evenings I am with [Charlotte von] Stein and I hold nothing hidden from her.[76]

It is interesting how the inner process of isolating functions was concretized in real, social performances. Yet the outward appearance of his relationship to Charlotte von Stein apparently was not touched very much except for the fact that a certain portion of the day was regularly allocated to her company, whereas earlier the desire to be with her might have changed his plans at any hour of the day.

It is worth while to note that Goethe's dawning isolation from the court (essentially the first seed of his relinquishing his activities) occurred at a time when the Duke was apparently quite convinced that his standing with posterity would not depend on his deeds alone or those of his progeny but also and perhaps principally on Goethe. On February 17 (two weeks after the birth of his heir) the Duke wrote to Merck in answer to a congratulatory letter:

> You are right to be happy for me. For if ever there have been good dispositions in me they have not before now, because of circumstances, been able to find a secure point where they could be bound together. Now, however, a firm hook has been driven in on which I can hang my pictures. *With the help of Goethe* and of good luck I mean to paint them in such a way that, if possible, posterity will say: "he too was a painter."[77] [Italics mine]

---

[76] [Seit einiger Zeit lebe ich sehr glücklich. Ich komme fast nicht aus dem Hause, versehe meine Arbeiten und schreibe in guten Stunden die Mährgen auf die ich mir selbst zu erzählen von ieher gewohnt bin. . . . Ich sehe fast niemand, ausser wer mich in Geschäfften zu sprechen hat, ich habe mein politisches und gesellschafftliches Leben ganz von meinem moralischen und poetischen getrennt (äusserlich versteht sich) und so befinde ich mich am besten. Alle Woche gebe ich einen grosen Thee wovon niemand ausgeschlossen ist, und entledige mich dadurch meiner Pflichten gegen die Sozietät auf's wohlfeilste. . . . Abends bin ich bey der Stein und habe nichts verborgnes vor ihr.]

[77] [Sie haben Recht, wenn Sie sich mit mir freuen. Denn wenn je gute Anlagen in meinem Wesen waren, so konnte sich Verhältnisse halber bis jetzt kein sicherer Punkt finden, wo sie zu verbinden waren. Nun ist aber ein fester Haken eingeschlagen, an welchen ich meine Bilder aufhängen kann. *Mit Hülfe Goethens* und des guten Glücks will ich sie so ausmalen, dass womöglich die Nachkommenschaft sagen soll: "ed egli fu pittore."] (51, *1*:301)

It is interesting that the Duke here used similes that Goethe had used to describe his relationship to the Duke. From this letter one could try to reconstruct those processes in the Duke that paralleled Goethe's.

It is reasonable to ask whether the happiness that Goethe avows at the beginning of his letter to Knebel is in contradiction to the expression of pain found in his letter to Jacobi of four days before (see above, pp. 769–70, 793). Does this quick change of face with regard to his general feelings reduce the reliability of these documents, from which I constantly draw the most sweeping psychological conclusions? His letter to Knebel was in reply to one in which Knebel had let him know how unhappy he was, and it may seem as if Goethe had, by contrast, to describe himself as being quite contented. Equivalent secondary motives were mentioned when I discussed the letters to Jacobi and Plessing. Such secondary motives, of course, must be assumed to have had their bearing on nearly every letter. The particular relationship Goethe had to the recipient imparted to each letter a particular deviation from whatever psychological truth may have been present, just as a compass needle is deflected by proximate sources of attraction. The seemingly contradictory messages to two friends reminds me strongly of the situation I described in Part I, when Goethe within twenty-four hours gave opposite reports to Cornelia and Behrisch (cf. above, p. 64). I surmise that these opposites had the same meaning now as fifteen years before. Goethe was in a crisis. In one communication the pain of that crisis, in the other the happiness over mastering it or working his way out of it, was described.

A year later (November 19, 1783) Goethe asked Charlotte von Stein to return the ode that was published in the same month in the *Tiefurt Journal.* The poem referred to was *The Divine,* which starts: "May man be noble, charitable and good."[78] The exact time of its composition is not known. Some scholars assign it to 1780, yet Goethe wrote of it to Charlotte von Stein as if it were an item quite familiar to her, which would suggest a much later date. There is one particular factor that makes this poem remarkable from the psychological viewpoint. It is in essence a poem about an abstract superego. In earlier poems such as *Ganymede* and *Limitations of Mankind,* in which man's relationship to the Deity is also the topic (both written prior to 1781) this relationship was pictured in an erotic—and unmistakably homoerotic—way; *The Divine* is free of the eroticizing tendency. The superego is pictured as the Divine in man, which makes him different from all other beings. The observation of man, Goethe continues, makes us surmise that the Divine exists: man's

[78] [Edel sei der Mensch/ Hülfreich und gut!]

example may teach us to believe in the gods. Nature does not know ethical discrimination, no more does destiny; it may destroy the innocent or the guilty. "Only man can achieve the impossible. He discriminates, chooses, and judges. He can bestow duration upon the moment."[79]

Goethe's Divine coincides in its functions with what psychoanalysis calls the superego. The stanza before the last offers a conception of the gods that amounts to a projection of man's superego. The ode is an outgrowth of that stage of internal development that I believe Goethe reached around the time just now under discussion. Here again an act of isolation is recognizable. Within the diversity of subjective experiences a series is isolated and attributed to a particular organization, which is lifted out of the stream of instinctual experiences and their derivatives and is desexualized (see 197, pp. 28–39; 278).

Yet does the full acceptance of this isolated structure make man happy or unhappy? Perhaps both. The full visualization and conscious experience of the superego is burdensome, because it brings to full realization the scope of duties and moral commands. But it also provides satisfaction because it gives independence and results in self-reliance.[80] This twofold aspect of his emotional state, and the resulting relative unconcern about his own emotions, was verbalized in the afore-mentioned letter to Kestner of March 15, 1783:

> Never mind the way my last letter sounded. I should be the most ungrateful person if I did not own that my situation is far happier than I deserve. To be sure, the hotness and toil of life still do not spare me, and so it may well happen that one becomes tired and worn at times, even cross-tempered perhaps for once.[81]

One consequence of such strengthening of the superego was a decrease in the violence of those emotions that were fed mainly by the id. The ego can now take notice of them without reverberating in its totality. After a short pause it turns again towards comprehensive goals.

[79] [Nur allein der Mensch/ Vermag das Unmögliche:/ Er unterscheidet,/ Wählet und richtet;/ Er kann dem Augenblick/ Dauer verleihen.] (*Soph.* I, 2:84)
This last idea particularly shows an incredibly modern and far-reaching concept of the functioning of the human mind, to say nothing of the implications about the physical universe.

[80] The latter is particularly important since in the ode the superego is not glorified as something outside of the ego but as a structure with which the ego feels itself one. For the narcissistic gain provided by the superego see 178, pp. 94–95.

[81] [Lasst euch den Ton meines lezten Briefs nicht anfechten. Ich wäre der undanckbarste Mensch wenn ich nicht bekennte dass meine Lage weit glücklicher ist als ich es verdiene. Freylich schont mich auch wieder die Hitze und Mühe des Lebens nicht, und da kann's denn wohl geschehen dass man zu Zeiten müde und matt auch wohl einmal mismutig wird.]

In one of Charlotte von Stein's letters (July 7, 1783) to Goethe's friend Knebel, there is a remark that illustrates the change that had taken place: "Goethe is wise," she wrote,

> experience and health can still make him a master. I consider myself fortunate that it has fallen to my lot to listen to his golden sentences.[82]

On May 1, 1784, she wrote to Knebel:

> Goethe ponders now over these things [plants and animals] with fertile thoughts, and everything that passes through his imagination becomes in the highest degree interesting.[83]

Another episode may illustrate how the superego made itself noticeable in the relationship. Charlotte von Stein's brother, who held a court position, looked forward for a long time to an increase in salary, which did not come through. Charlotte von Stein asked Goethe about it

> but because a gulf is fixed between the minister and the straightforwardness of friendship, I received answers that I did not understand.[84]

Here Charlotte von Stein very astutely described the isolation process that was so strong in Goethe at that time. Goethe, who was particularly eager to assist Charlotte von Stein in matters of everyday concerns, must have wished to help, but carrying the call of his heart into an official function would have had a guilt-arousing effect, and isolation can be observed here in full bloom. He may have been overscrupulous just because his feelings were so strongly engaged. An attitude of punctiliousness of this kind is often found in compulsive personalities, but in Goethe, I believe, without wanting to minimize the compulsive elements in his character, this instance was characteristic rather of that particular phase than of his personality in general. It may be adduced as an additional sign of the recentness of the attitude. What has not yet become fully integrated is performed with great exactness and scrupulousness.[85] The tension about the subject apparently became so strong that Charlotte von Stein avoided discussing it. She wrote her sister-in-law: "By word of mouth one cannot

---

[82] [Goethe (ist) weise. Erfahrung und Gesundheit können ihn noch zum Meister machen. Ich halte mich glücklich, dass mir beschieden ist, seine goldnen Sprüche zu hören.] (51, *1*:306)

[83] [Goethe grübelt jetzt gar denkreich in diesen Dingen, und Jedes, was erst durch seine Vorstellung gegangen ist, wird äusserst interessant.] (51, *1*:315)

[84] [. . . aber weil zwischen dem Minister und der Aufrichtigkeit der Freundschaft ein Abgrund gesetzt ist, so bekam ich Antworten, die ich nicht verstand.] (49, *1*:244)

[85] It also must be considered that Goethe's position as Secretary of the Treasury was constantly endangered. One wrong step might have made him liable to violent attacks. Favoritism has always been a temptation for those who have had the key to the cashbox.

talk with him [Goethe] about it without both of us hurting each other."
Here the extent to which Charlotte von Stein was forced into a position of
retreat became manifest. A year later (October 7, 1784) she wrote to her
sister-in-law about Goethe: "You are familiar with his manner; he thinks
much without saying anything; one could put under his image: El
penseroso."[86] This passage reflects with particular forcefulness the degree
to which Goethe's psychophysiognomic appearance had changed. One
is reminded of the change of appearance when children leave the Oedipus
phase and settle down in latency. The charming motor restlessness, the
graciousness of movement, the charming seductiveness, have vanished.
Rigidity and timidity and obedience appear instead. If one ever has the
opportunity of seeing a series of pictures taken of a child during these
years one is frightened by what looks like the gradual development of a
depression. Similarly one might conclude from Charlotte von Stein's remarks that Goethe was depressed during this period. But I think the assumption would be as erroneous in the one instance as in the other. The
mere fact of an aggrandizement of the superego must not be confused
with a pathological inflation, although the visible signs may bear a
resemblance. Sometimes it can be decided only retrospectively whether
the ego's seeming or real aloofness was brought about by a superego upsurge that was well adapted to the demands of the culture community
and the strength of the ego and could therefore be integrated, or
whether it was a pathological flare-up without any constructive, but
rather with harmful, consequences to the individual and the community.

There was an episode that is suggestive of Goethe's having reached the
fringe of a depression, but it involved a short period. The discussion of
this episode requires a somewhat long detour but it is psychologically of
importance because it makes it possible to take up threads left hanging in
a previous chapter.

The week end of November 17, 1782, seems to have been emotionally
disturbing to Goethe. He wrote three communications[87] to Charlotte von
Stein on that Sunday and one letter to his friend Jacobi, which was quoted
earlier (p. 769). The day before, he had written to Charlotte von Stein
that his soul was leaning towards solitude. The next morning he made
a pilgrimage to her house and went on to his garden out of town.
There was a rock there that he had dedicated to her. "[The stone] is now

---

[86] 107, *1*:226. The Duke had made a remark concerning Goethe's reticence about a year
earlier (107, *1*:197).

[87] The editor of the *Sophienausgabe* arranged these three communications in a sequence
different from the one I follow here.

the only bright spot in my garden. The most beautiful tears of heaven dripped down from it."[88] He hoped that this would not be a bad omen. Then he roamed about his house, now deserted,

> like Melusine[89] about hers whereto she was not to return, and I thought of the past, of which I understand nothing, and of the future, of which I know nothing. How much did I lose when I had to leave this quiet domicile! That was the second thread that held me; now I hang quite alone from you, and, thank God, this is the strongest.

Then he spoke of reading over his correspondence of the preceding decade (cf. Goethe's letter to Knebel of November 21, 1782) and continued:

> I comprehend less and less what I am and what I ought.

> Stay for me, dear Lotte, you are my anchor between these cliffs.

> Whatever it may be, I feel an infinite need to be alone. Under the pretext that I do not feel well I mean to excuse myself from Court and Council,[90] to stay at home, to square old debts and set my house in order.[91]

Since the court physician himself was sick, he believed he could the more readily do so. "For that, however, I need your leave; do not deny it to me."[92]

After finishing the letter he received a short communication from Charlotte von Stein. He thanked her and asked for a few lines more when she should have returned from church. He continued:

> The sight of you, a line from you, is so attractive to me. The only thing that is still really attractive to me. I should like [to come] to you so you

[88] I assume Goethe meant drops of dew or rain.

[89] This strange comparison will be discussed presently.

[90] As a matter of record, Goethe did not miss a single gathering of the Privy Council around that time. Cf. 257 p. lxxv.

[91] The German idiom, like the English, suggests impending death.

[92] [Unter deinen Fenstern grüst ich dich und ging nach deinem Steine. Er ist ietzt der einzige lichte Punckt in meinem Garten. Die schönsten Trähnen des Himmels rollten an ihm herunter, es soll hoff ich nichts zu bedeuten haben.

Ich strich um mein verlassen Häusgen, wie Melusine um das ihrige wohin sie nicht zurückkehren sollte, und dachte an die Vergangenheit von der ich nichts verstehe, und an die Zukunft von der ich nichts weis. Wie viel hab ich verlohren da ich ienen stillen Aufenthalt verlassen muste! Es war der zweyte Faden der mich hielt, ietzt hänge ich ganz allein an dir, und Gott sey Danck ist dies der stärckste.

. . . begreife immer weniger was ich bin und was ich soll.

Bleibe mir 1. Lotte du bist mein Ancker zwischen diesen Klippen.

Was es auch sey, so fühl ich ein unendliches Bedürfniss einsam zu seyn. Unter einem Vorwande dass ich nicht wohl sey will ich mich vom Hof und Conseil entschuldigen, zu Hause bleiben, alte Schulden abthun und mein Haus bestellen. . . . Dazu muss ich aber auch deinen Urlaub haben, versage mir ihn nicht.]

could behold from me myself how I love you. Thanks for your compassion, your suffering with me, and pardon me and love me.

In a postscript he asked her to send Fritz after the meal.[93]
And then follows the last message of that day:

I send you herewith a letter to Jacobi that I shall dispatch tomorrow, and I am coming after. Solitude is sweet to me, [but] not to see you, unbearable. Impossible when I feel you so close. Your Fritz has done me very well. Farewell, beloved one. If you do not send me any message I shall take it as a sign that I may and can come. For the third time yours.[94]

Evidently Goethe was extremely restless and could not find peace. Something held him back from the beloved woman and at last his longing for her got the better of him and he joined her. The struggle can be traced through a variety of substitute gratifications he experimented with: First he looked at her house and the rock that symbolized her, then he read a letter written by her, and last he passed some time with her son. This progression follows a pattern observed in some obsessional neurotics, whose compulsions are selected in such a way as to bring them closer to the forbidden gratification;[95] each substitute brought him, too, closer to the reality of the beloved woman: her house, her letter, her son. Finally, he reached her herself.

But what might have caused Goethe's reluctance to see the beloved woman on that day? My belief is that she was menstruating just then and that this was the reason why he tried to keep away from her, or why he thought she did not want him to be there.

Since Charlotte von Stein very clearly was a woman of the type that feels discriminated against and frustrated by being a woman, it is almost certain that she responded to menstruation with complaints, malaise, and irritability. Of course, such a reaction must not be expected to occur with strict regularity, but it is reasonable to anticipate relative frequency. I

[93] [Dein Anblick, eine Zeile von dir ist mir so anziehend. Das einzige was mir noch recht anziehend ist. Ich mögte zu dir, dass du mir's recht ansehen könntest wie ich dich liebe. Danck für dein Mitleiden. dein mit mir Leiden und verzeih mir und liebe mich. Schicke mir doch Fritzen nach Tische.]

[94] [Hier schick ich einen Brief an Jakobi den ich morgen absende und komme nach. Die Einsamkeit ist mir süs, dich nicht zu sehen unerträglich. Unmöglich wenn ich dich so nah fühle. Dein Fritz hat mir sehr wohl gethan. Adieu Geliebte. Wenn du mir nichts sagen lässest nehm ich's als ein Zeichen dass ich kommen darf und kann. Zum drittenmal dein. . . .]

[95] For the gradual accomplishment of direct wish-fulfillment in the symptom see 205, p. 112; and for clinical examples, see 135, p. 129.

therefore will examine what can be found from the historical record about her condition on days four weeks apart preceding and following the date in question (November 17, 1782) in order to weigh the probability of my assumption. The Sunday four weeks earlier, October 20, he may not have seen her, although the letters do not make it entirely clear. However, on the following day he wrote: "Did your toothache stay away? How are you otherwise?"[96] This wording is suspicious. The German word *ausbleiben* (stay away), which Goethe used here, is customarily used in connection with menstruation in twentieth-century German. Whether this was also the case in Goethe's time, I do not know. The vernacular regarding menstruation is broad in modern languages and individual couples readily develop their own vocabulary. Whether Charlotte von Stein had fallen into the pattern of chronically accounting for her menstrual indispositions by pleading toothache, we cannot know, but it is not unlikely that Goethe's use of *"ausgeblieben"* is a reflection of an at least unconscious awareness that the "otherwise" had to do with a state of affairs that recurred every month. The question cannot be pursued further back: no letter of September 22 has been preserved. Goethe met Charlotte von Stein on that day after a separation of about two weeks and left her apparently the same day. Around August 25, Charlotte von Stein was away from Weimar on her estate.

The evidence becomes more promising if an investigation is made into the four-week cycles following November 17. On December 16, 1782, Goethe wrote: "Tell me before everything else how you are, whether it is better with you? I cannot tell you how worried I am about you, how much I suffer for your sake!"[97] Again four weeks later, on January 13, 1783, he wrote: "It was impossible for me to go away today since you do not feel well. I need movement and I mean to take a run about and then be with you. Tell me a word [as to] how you are."[98] Thus for several months before and after November 17 there was a demonstrable four-week cycle of Charlotte von Stein's feeling bad.

The question of whether or not Charlotte von Stein's menstrual cycle can be determined from Goethe's letters is a challenging problem. As psychoanalysts know, the little child often reacts sensitively to the maternal cycle and responds to it despite the most scrupulous attempts of so

[96] [Ist dein Zahnweh ausgeblieben? Wie steht es sonst mit dir?]

[97] [Sage mir vor allen Dingen wie du dich befindest, ob es besser mit dir ist? ich kann dir nicht sagen wie sehr ich um dich besorgt bin. Wie sehr ich um dich leide.]

[98] [Es war mir unmöglich heute wegzugehn, da du nicht wohl bist. Ich brauche Bewegung und will spazieren lauffen und dann bey dir seyn. Sage mir ein Wort wie du dich befindest.]

many mothers to conceal it. A person as sensitive as Goethe probably was influenced by the deep biological changes that occur in the menstruating woman. A periodicity can be noticed at times in Goethe's writing letters to friends; they tend to come in bunches. I do not mean to suggest that Goethe did not write friends between such clusters. But it seems that the desire to write to certain close friends came in spurts and followed a periodicity. It is quite conceivable that at times when the female became periodically incompatible—for him emotionally, rather than specifically sexually—he turned longingly towards the male. But extensive research would be necessary to make out of these suggestions a hypothesis.

The material that refers to the week end of November 17, however, contains two passages that make it possible to be more definite. The one concerns the heavenly tears on the stone symbolizing the love-object. The identity of names is of course particularly suggestive (the German word for "stone" being *Stein*). The image definitely refers to a fluid on the body of the beloved woman. The other concerns Goethe's unmistakable identification with Melusine as he walks about his beloved garden house. The *tertium comparationis* referred to Melusine's being banished from her home but wandering about her house from time to time to see or nurse her children. Goethe's comparing himself with Melusine goes, in my opinion, far beyond the confines of this literal meaning. Goethe had become acquainted with this lore as a child. That it had been firmly integrated into his imagination may be seen from the fact that he not only referred to it on various occasions but wrote a novelette, *The New Melusine*.[99]

The problem that underlies the lore of the beautiful Melusine is that of menstruation,[100] or, in more general terms, the lore contains in a disguised form fantasies about the affinity between womanhood and blood, and the dangers connected therewith that threaten man. The central theme is Melusine's requirement that her husband, Raimund, must not see her on one day of each week. Every Saturday he is to leave her alone, ask nothing of her, not even speak to her or see her or let anyone else see her, but leave her wholly untrammeled. Melusine will reciprocate by being faithful to Raimund at all times, and will particularly on that day stay in her woman's apartment "quietly, chastely, and seclusively." When Raimund transgresses this prohibition, he sees her sitting in a basin. Her face

---

[99] I have been unable to find out exactly in what form Goethe met the tale as a child and what form he read as an adult. I follow in my interpretation the version Gustav Schwab gives (485).

[100] For a different interpretation see 456.

and the upper half of her body are wonderfully beautiful, but the lower part is a long, misshapen, serpentlike tail. Melusine's week-end condition is also called her unnatural condition.

The change of periodicity from the biological monthly to a weekly rhythm, which occurs in the lore, is a permissible disguise but sufficiently betrays the nature of the problem. When Raimund promises without hesitation to obey Melusine's request this is called a lighthearted and bold action. The lightheartedness and boldness of the promise may well be regarded as the reflection of the narrator's view of how difficult it may be expected to be for Raimund to curb his curiosity and sexual passion during the days of female bleeding when both curiosity and passion are at their peak (see 189). If the central theme is faintly disguised, one detail at least expresses the unrepressed content, namely Melusine's sitting in the basin. The central theme also shows up almost undisguised in the way she punishes her father for having transgressed a prohibition her mother had imposed on him. Her mother had married on the condition that her husband would never visit her during her confinement and thus pry into her secrets. Yet he kept this promise as little as Raimund did his. In the father's instance the prohibition of intercourse at a time when a woman is bleeding is outspoken. Another detail may be mentioned. Melusine leaves her husband but returns sporadically at night to nurse her two youngest children. There is a popular belief, with some basis in fact, that a nursing woman does not menstruate. Thus the time when Melusine is permitted to return to her home is when she is not bleeding.

It is of interest that in two respects the tale, which must have originated with a man and not a woman, distorts the unconscious content by substituting its opposite. First, when Raimund gives in to his curiosity he beholds a tail instead of the female pelvis, that is to say, he does not see blood but the organ that male curiosity would like so much to behold, namely the female phallus.[101] The basin in turn is a reference to the repressed content. Second, Melusine must leave Raimund after her secret is discovered. Here man's anger at menstruation, his impulse to send the woman away because of his disappointment in her, is converted into his being deserted by her.

Goethe went a step beyond this when he wrote Charlotte von Stein a week later (November 23, 1782):

---

[101] The castration complex, of course, also throws its shadow in the shape of a compromise-formation on the content of what the spier beholds: in this case a misshapen serpent tail.

Let me divine the breath of your love from a leaflet. Today I found an old verse:

> So in love with her I've sunk
> As if of her very blood I'd drunk.[102]

In this short letter there are a score of contradictions. What is the verse supposed to be saying about Charlotte von Stein's love? Why is Goethe's drinking of her blood connected with the breath of her love? The contradiction is the result of a force akin to that which replaces male horror of menstruation by female desertion. In the couplet the crisis of a few days before is denied and replaced by its opposite. It says, as it were: "Your bleeding did not give me the impulse to desert you or to run away but rather it made me love you the more; I feel as if I had drunk of your blood." The most disgusting is converted by poesy into the most appealing.

The question must of course be raised why Goethe's conflict about menstruation affected him on just that week end. Fortunately one can make a guess as to the answer. He had finished the third book of *Wilhelm Meister* a few days before and therefore probably was occupied with the next book of his novel. Now that book is the one that starts with the poem: "Know you the land where the lemon trees bloom?" a poem which I earlier interpreted as growing out of male sympathy with the castrated woman. In my reconstruction the need to write a poem about the pitifulness of the castrated woman was the day-residue that made him react pathologically to the coincidental menstruation of the beloved woman.[103] Or is it that such beautiful poetry is created when a poet is latently preoccupied with an artistic task and his personal everyday life offers him assistance in the form of an event around which the latent content can crystallize?[104]

---

[102] [Lass mich den Athem deiner Liebe aus einem Blättgen ahnden. Heut fand ich einen alten Vers:

> Bin so in Lieb zu ihr versuncken
> Als hätt ich von ihrem Blut getruncken.]

As far as I know these verses have not been traced to a previous source and I strongly suspect that they were written by Goethe, who, feeling guilty about them, concealed authorship.

[103] Of course, the sequence may have been the reverse, namely that Charlotte von Stein's menstruation evoked such imagery as could well be fitted into the continuation of the novel. The disentanglement of the time sequence of various factors is probably impossible.

[104] There is no concrete biographical record that throws any direct light upon the date of Goethe's writing the poem in question. The remarkable coincidence of the way in which Book IV starts and Goethe's experiences and moods on that week end and, further, the fact that Goethe started to write Book IV around that time impressed me sufficiently to see in all these facts an inner connection.

The general plan of *Wilhelm Meister* may have required having the next book start with a poem expressing Mignon's unhappiness. Then Charlotte von Stein's menstruation probably created the very conflict Goethe needed to generate the impulse that led to the writing of the poem. If this instance is correctly understood here it also makes more understandable the blending of the most personal and the most general which is so striking a feature of Goethe's poetry.

Yet more can be said about the effect of the Melusine lore on Goethe. In later years (1807) he wrote a novelette: *The New Melusine,*[105] which he incorporated as a first-person narrative in *Wilhelm Meisters Wanderjahre*. A synopsis follows.

While traveling in rather straitened circumstances, the hero meets a young woman traveling alone. She seems quite wealthy and proposes to engage him to perform a task for her. He is to convey a box for her to a certain city, there take a room and await her rejoining him. He readily agrees, goes there at once and does her bidding. However, since he is prodigal with the money she gives him, and gambles, he finds himself suddenly without means. Just when his despair has reached its peak he hears something moving in the adjoining room, where he has stored the box. It is she. She forgives his delinquent behavior, gives him more money, once more charges him to care for the box. The same sequence is repeated, with the exception that this time the hero is seriously wounded in a duel. At night she comes into his room and heals his wounds. He reproaches her for her frequent desertions, which were bound to get him into trouble. This time she promises to stay with him and they continue their journey together. He now feels certain she will stay with him, for she has become pregnant, but nevertheless one day she disappears. He continues traveling with the box entrusted to his care. One night he discovers that there is light coming from a small crevice in the dried-out wood of which the box is fashioned. He peeps through the crevice and sees a richly furnished room, tenanted by the woman whom he knew, shrunk to diminutive proportions. This discovery turns his feelings against his sweetheart. When she meets him again in human proportions she notices what has happened and seeks to leave him, but he quickly recovers his former passion for her and she consents to stay with him, but not without warning:

> "Examine yourself thoroughly," she said, "whether this discovery has not
> injured your love, whether you can forget that I am in twofold form at

[105] The history and interpretation of this story have been dealt with at length by Theodor Reik (449).

your side, whether the diminution of my person will not also diminish your inclination.[106]

The hero then asks himself whether it is really something so terrible to have a wife who from time to time becomes a dwarf so that she has to be carried in a box. Would it not be worse if she became a giant and put her husband in a box? Thus they decide to stay together but the woman asks that he promise her that he will never think of her reproachfully for being a dwarf. He gladly promises, yet he notices that his love has, after all, weakened, and that he feels jealous when she finds admirers at the frequent parties that they attend. At one of them, after he has drunk quite a bit, he cannot control himself and curses her, calling her "dwarf" and "nixie." In his anger he upsets his wine-filled glass. "When I saw the red wine flow over the tablecloth I again came to my senses."[107] The rest of the story is of no interest in the present connection. The woman has to leave him; if, however, he wants to stay with her he must become a dwarf himself. She is the daughter of the king of the dwarfs and was sent among the human race. By becoming pregnant by a human being she is to have put an end to the dwindling stature of her people. He agrees on the spur of the moment. Yet after having been transformed into a dwarf he cannot get accustomed to his new condition and returns to his human state.

The traces of the menstruation theme are more visible in Goethe's story than Reik pointed out; he, of course, noticed the theme (see 449, p. 163) but was more interested in Goethe's fear of impotence which, no doubt, is also contained in the story. Goethe changed Melusine's secret from being a nixie to being a dwarf. The distorted emphasis on the lack of a phallus was less offensive apparently than the distorted emphasis on menstruation, as it is expressed in the lore. As a further direct reminder of the original theme, I mention that the person who tells the story has the nickname Redcoat.[108]

[106] [Prüfe dich genau, sagte sie: ob diese Entdeckung deiner Liebe nicht geschadet habe, ob du vergessen kannst, dass ich in zweierlei Gestalten mich neben dir befinde, ob die Verringerung meines Wesens nicht auch deine Neigung vermindern werde.] (*Soph.* I, 25:144–45)

[107] [Als ich den rothen Wein über das Tischtuch fliessen sah, kam ich wieder zu mir selbst.] (*Soph.* I, 25:149)

[108] The nickname Redcoat [Rotmantel] was not original with Goethe but taken from a fairy tale by Musäus (1735–87), well-known for his *Volksmärchen der Deutschen*. In Musäus's tale *Mute Love* [Stumme Liebe] a ghost in a scarlet red cloak (also a barber as in Goethe's story) finds final peace after the hero has shaved his beard and hair. As a reward for this good deed, the ghost helps the hero in finding a treasure with which he can marry the lady of his heart. Other inner connections could be pointed out. For Musäus's

More important is Melusine's asking the narrator whether he will be able to forget "that I am in twofold form at your side." This twofold appearance makes no sense if the central issue of the story is man's conflict about woman's having no phallus, since this is a constant quality, but it is a definite reference to what impresses man as the two forms of female existence, namely, bleeding and nonbleeding. It must also be considered that the new Melusine stays with the hero only for short times before they are united. Yet when they decide to remain together the new Melusine is pregnant, that is to say, she has stopped bleeding. Thus she was living uninterruptedly with the narrator of the story only when she was not bleeding. Furthermore, there is to be remembered the decisive incident that leads to the protagonist's reproach of Melusine for being a dwarf. It is when he sees the red wine on the (white?) tablecloth that he becomes aware of his mistake. "I recognized the great mistake I had committed and was indeed inwardly contrite."[109] Now there is no intrinsic reason why the sight of the spilled wine should have had this effect on him. The seemingly unnecessary stress on red wine must also be considered. It is a trivial, innocuous detail, barely noticed in the flow of the action, which here reaches a dramatic peak, but it signals the return of the repressed in an almost undisguised form and is, I believe, the key to the unconscious content of the story.[110]

Another problem may be raised. Reik has discussed extensively the question of when Goethe thought out this story. Goethe himself claimed in *Dichtung und Wahrheit* that he told the fairy tale to Friederike in Sesenheim, but his biographers insist that the story must have originated at a later date and that he cannot have told it to Friederike. It was actually written much later (1807) and published still later (1816). It found, at last, its final place, as a seemingly inorganic part, a kind of space-filler, in one of Goethe's latest works. Reik tries to prove that Goethe was not mis-

---

Stumme Liebe see 404, pp. 415–85. Musäus's novelette-like fairy tales are not in high esteem despite their high artistic quality. See Dorothea Berger, who wrote an excellent article on the subject (19) and also collected Goethe's disparaging remarks about Musäus, but did not consider that by taking a figure from Musäus's tales into one of his own stories Goethe paid one of the highest compliments an author can pay.

[109] [Ich erkannte den grossen Fehler, den ich begangen hatte, und war recht innerlich zerknirscht.]

[110] Later I found a detail that convinced me that my interpretation of Goethe's imagery surrounding the lore of Melusine is correct. In Christiane's letters to Goethe the term "Meerweibchen" or "Meerweiblichkeit" (mermaid or mermaidhood) is used for menstruation. The editor of their correspondence tried, of course in vain, to trace this euphemism in dictionaries. As can be seen from the foregoing, it must have been introduced into their relationship by Goethe. Cf. 533.

taken and that a story at least similar to the one known as *The New Melusine* was told to Friederike by Goethe in 1771. Reik, I think, has not considered Goethe's inhibition in reporting the full history of his life when he wrote *Dichtung und Wahrheit*. Goethe felt it necessary to avoid any account of the pre-Italian Weimar years.[111] Discretion, tact, and respect for many people or their progeny in Weimar made it difficult to cover the years from 1775 to 1786. But I do not believe that this was the decisive factor, for Goethe wrote autobiographical works about periods of his life subsequent to 1786. It was particularly Charlotte von Stein he had to consider. To be sure, she lived until 1827, and her sons never became so remote from him that he could disregard them in writing about her, but nevertheless there were more and purely personal reasons for the aversion he evidently felt to writing about their relationship and its contribution to the development of his personality. Neither did he mention her to Eckermann, who was to write a lasting monument of what Goethe thought of his contemporaries. But when he was writing *Dichtung und Wahrheit* many incidents of his later life, which would not enter the biography for extraneous reasons, came to his mind, and I can well imagine that some of them he did not want to let go by. The alternative was to publish them, not as they had actually occurred, but worked into earlier phases of which he felt free to speak.

My claim is that if the invention of the plot of *The New Melusine* considerably antedated the time when the story was written, then one must assume that its basic fabric was born around the time we are here discussing. There is an element in the story that is identical with one that appears in his correspondence with Charlotte von Stein. When traveling abroad with Fritz he wrote her, on September 9, 1783:

> Only this evening do I write to my Lotte with whom I have occupied myself in silence all this time. I wished you were around me invisibly all day long and stepped forth in the evening when I am alone as if out of the wall; you would feel, what I feel now with so much joy, that I am and can be solely yours. How do I hope for the moment of seeing you again; you have tied me to yourself with all bonds.[112]

[111] A hint at this problem may be found in Goethe's remark to Mendelssohn about the year 1775 (see 250, 4:279; and 256, part 2, 20:702, where the remark is differently recorded).

[112] [Erst heute Abend schreib ich meiner Lotte mit der ich mich diese ganze Zeit im Stillen beschäfftigt habe. Ich wünschte du wärest den ganzen Tag um mich unsichtbar, und trätest Abends wenn ich alleine bin wie aus die Mauer hervor, du würdest fühlen, was ich ietzt mit so vieler Freude fühle, dass ich nur alleine dein bin und dein seyn kann. Wie hoffe ich auf den Augenblick dich wiederzusehen, du hast mich mit allen Banden an dich gebunden.]

Here we have the theme that appears repetitively in *The New Melusine* of the woman who accompanies a traveler in a box and suddenly enters through the door of the adjoining room. The passage just quoted compels the conclusion that Goethe had at that time the fantasy of a setup that would grant him maximum control over the beloved woman. She should be always with him but materialize in accordance with his needs and desires. The tale of 1807 unfolds another theme that must have been like a seed (or an unconscious association) in the passage in the letter, namely: "Even if I could conjure up your presence each time I desired it and you remained invisible the rest of the time, I know there are days when I should wish you to remain invisible not because my longings for you were silent but because your condition would prohibit my seeing you."[113] The selfish component of the whole conflict here comes to the fore. Menstruation makes a woman temporarily unavailable. Man then must bear his unsatisfied cravings and must wait. In a different context this was Goethe's complaint when he was abroad: "You are away and I must wait until my return to see you." Yet strangely enough he wished she should be invisibly around him during the day. One would rather expect the wish to be that she should be with him constantly, that is to say, during the daytime too. In this wish the idea shows up again that it is better when a man does not see a woman at certain times. Or was it a consolation, as if it had come to his mind that even if he could carry her with him invisibly there would be days when nature would keep them apart? And then he may have developed the story of a man who unwittingly carried a woman with him on all his travels and only accidentally discovered her presence, but could not make use of his charming companion.

Goethe's dating this story back to the amorous days of Sesenheim may also have been the result of a thought that in those early days he perhaps for the first time became consciously aware of his horror of menstruating women. The great role Friederike's sicknesses played in Goethe's relationship to her is well known and may be another manifestation of his feelings about menstruation. Morris found what he thought was a connection between Christiane, Goethe's later wife, and the writing of *The New Melusine*.[114] This is quite possible, since in that relationship the problem of menstruation might have been most painfully activated.

---

[113] Scholars have evaluated Goethe's story varyingly. Some read in it the reasons that compelled Goethe to abandon Friederike; Karl Heinemann in his commentary to the novel (258, 2:459) links it up with a fairy tale that Goethe mentions—without giving its title—in a letter to Charlotte von Stein of September 17, 1782.

[114] 399, pp. 92 ff. Morris refers to Christiane's illegitimate pregnancy, etc.

This preoccupation with menstruation does not presuppose a sexual relationship with Charlotte von Stein. While the "selfish component" that I spoke of earlier also refers, of course, to man's resentment against the taboo that renders the menstruating woman inaccessible to him, it must be noted that the problem touched upon is one that begins to play a role early in the boy's life, quite before there is any question of literal sexual accessibility. One must assume, although it cannot be clinically proved in each instance, that the child notices at an early age the biological change in his mother. Olfactory sensations are no doubt the most usual and predominant indicators of the periodic event. But the mother's irritability or unavoidable increased preoccupation with herself causes the child to experience the maternal period as a separation, and a separation that is all the more painful and confusing since the child's eyes attest to his mother's bodily presence. I know of undoubted instances of a child's reacting to his mother's pregnancy before she herself was aware of having become pregnant—so sensitively can children detect changes in the mother's endocrinologic milieu. Since menstruation is often equated with rejection, the child not infrequently develops the idea that these strange changes are voluntary arrangements by the mother that express a cessation of love.

The factor of volition on the part of the woman is present in the lore as well as in Goethe's story. Also both Melusines show signs of superiority to their male partners. They are more intelligent, or of higher birth, of greater will power and kindness, than the men whom they marry. The recollection of the mother's emotions at the time of her menstrual cycles may be of considerable conflict-arousing power (which is in no contradiction to the associative connection of menstruation with the castration complex). Melusine's maternal quality of superiority, particularly as she is described in *The New Melusine* (daughter of a king, with special emphasis on the difference in status between her and the hero), is again reminiscent of Charlotte von Stein.

Still another theme that shows up in Goethe's writings, as well as in the lore, is that Melusine is dangerous to male progeny. I shall not go into details here, but only record that in Goethe's writings Melusine is a figure propitious to girls, as can be seen in one of the stories in *Unterhaltungen deutscher Ausgewanderter* (*Soph.* I, 18:157), whereas when Werther is fascinated by a pretty well-house on the edge of the town and feels like Melusine with her sisters (*Soph.* I, 19:9), this of course was meant to forebode the ensuing catastrophe. Melusine's propitious effect on girls and her inauspicious effect on boys is important at a moment when Goethe is about to take Fritz into his charge. Apparently, in his doing so there was at work not only the impulse to be of service to Charlotte von Stein, but also the fear that mothers might do harm even to sons whom they loved.

Yet on two occasions that we have seen, in the morning hours of November 17, 1782, and in the passage from *Werther* just referred to, Goethe put himself in the position of Melusine. Thus in *Werther* he puts the feminine identification right at the beginning of the novel, which is in conformity with the ill course Werther's fate will take.

On November 17, 1782, however, he was—according to my theory—in the process of writing a poem about Mignon's longing and complaints. A temporary identification with the castrated woman was probably a necessary prerequisite to the poet's being able to write a poem of such outstanding beauty. When, a week later, Goethe sent Charlotte von Stein the old couplet with the line "As if of her very blood I'd drunk," the temporary Melusine-identification seems to have been reduced to its physical core and to have come close to its end. The spell once broken, the narcissistic object-relationship changed to one of a different type. The relative ease of swinging from identification to other forms of object-relation is noteworthy. Such freedom may have been a prerequisite to the writing of a novel like *Wilhelm Meister,* with its large number of acting persons and its richness of incident. The episode of November 17, 1782, may also again show that Goethe was on the way towards being dominated rather by artistic necessities than by the vicissitudes of his feelings for Charlotte von Stein, although, if I have correctly reconstructed it, it shows how intimately interwoven they were. My personal feeling is, however, that he had reached the point where he had shaped the relationship to Charlotte von Stein in accordance with his artistic needs, or, in other words, fetched out of the relationship that which he needed for his literary creations, whereas previously the reverse had been the case.

Occasionally, however, the two were still in competition, as the following letter shows. On December 1, 1782, he wrote:

> If I thought as much about my *Wilhelm* as I do about you, the novel would soon be finished. But it is another novel that is closer to my heart.[115]

Occasionally he seems to have become aware that despite their emotional closeness self-control took all too great a role in their relationship. "Let us live," he wrote December 5, 1782, "to our mutual joy and not be-

---

[115] [Wenn ich soviel an meinen Wilhelm als an dich dächte so wäre der Roman bald fertig. Aber es ist ein andrer Roman der meinem Herzen näher ist.]

come too wise."[116] But this remark was not precipitated by something she had done, as was a similar complaint during the Swiss journey (see above, pp. 425–26). In this letter he first cheerfully reported how much he had worked that morning. Did he start worrying that the intensity of his absorption in his work might be detrimental to his affection for the woman? Three days later (December 8, 1782), when the Duke again wanted him as a companion on a journey, he wrote Charlotte von Stein: "I might almost wish to pass through foreign air, and yet I cannot imagine myself separated from you."[117] The trip was no fun. He became anxious at the hour when he was accustomed to meeting the beloved woman and he apologized for having left. It was the month in which he was habitually depressed. The restlessness and vacillation seem to have been the peripheral ramification of his December depression, which was resolved only when, shortly after, he took a trip to Leipzig. Even then it is evident that, at the outset, the Duke's presence was a source of irritation. After the first day spent in his company he wrote a miserable letter predicting that he would feel bad in Leipzig. On Christmas Eve (1782) he wrote that he "would go out into the wide world if I had not you."[118] He even made the mistake of putting Weimar as the place from which the letter was sent, instead of Leipzig. It was only after the Duke had left that Goethe started to breathe freely again. The beginning of the next letter, of December 25, sounds quite different, as if a load had suddenly been lifted:

> I have spent my time today most right cheerfully, interrupted only by the news that you do not feel well. How enjoyable was the sight of your letter for me, how sad its content.[119]

Then he went into an enraptured account of his former teacher, Oeser, with whom he spent the most delightful hours. And so it went on and he extended his sojourn in Leipzig in order to attend a concert. Few were the remarks that expressed sentiments about Charlotte von Stein, such as the one of December 29, 1782: "To be sure, occasionally a moment of boredom passes, and often, often, the desire for you tears at my heart." Yet he continued: "I wish I might stay here a quarter of a year." By a

---

[116] [Lass uns einander zur Freude leben und nicht zu weise werden.]

[117] [Fast mögt ich wünschen einmal durch fremde Lufft durchzugehen, und kann mich doch nicht von dir getrennt dencken.]

[118] [wenn ich dich nicht hätte ich ging in die weite Welt.]

[119] [Ich habe meine Zeit heute recht sehr vergnügt zugebracht nur unterbrochen durch die Nachricht dass du nicht wohl bist. Wie erfreulich war mir der Anblick deines Briefs, wie traurig der Inhalt.]

sleight of hand, however, he smuggled his entertainment into his love: "I owe you my happiness at home and my amusement abroad, for the calmness and the equanimity with which I receive and give, rest on the basis of your love."[120]

He was aware of his unbearable behavior prior to his trip to Leipzig—as he had written her the previous day—and his explanation of it is noteworthy: "If I do not constantly have new ideas to elaborate upon I become as if sick."[121] Thus his staying away longer is declared to be for her sake. Yet this explanation permits two conclusions. First, Charlotte von Stein did not provide him with the stimulation he needed during the weeks of internal lull or impending depression, and, secondly, when he struggled with the depression his own capacities were inadequate to maintain an undisturbed relationship to the world in general and the beloved woman in particular. Yet it is surprising how easily he could recover and how quickly he found solace in the company of old Oeser. From this father-substitute he stole a big painter's brush (letter to Oeser of January 30, 1783). Thus what had once been a cause of serious conflict and unrest now became a slip or prank or gay misbehavior on the symbolic level. This prank, however, is the first harbinger of a character trait that would be quite typical in the aging Goethe, whose friends knew with what ease and gusto he appropriated objects of interest to him never to return them to their owners.[122]

The old problem of childbirth, however, kept its serious aspect. In this case it derived special seriousness from an aspect that the reader of today who has grown up in a republic can only with difficulty, by imagination and empathy, grasp, namely, the significance of the expectation of an heir to a royal family. But there is overwhelming evidence that the individual reacted to the major events in the dynastic family in accordance with the structure of his own Oedipus complex, as can still be observed in present-day monarchies.

Likewise it is scarcely imaginable what it meant to the dynastic feelings of the reigning family of Saxe-Weimar whether a boy or a girl

---

[120] [Mit unter läufft freylich ein Augenblick langer Weile und offt offt reisst das Verlangen zu dir an meinem Herzen.

Ich wünschte mich ein viertel Jahr hier aufhalten zu können. . . . ich bin dir mein Glück zu Hause, und mein Vergnügen auswärts schuldig, denn die Stille, der Gleichmuth mit dem ich empfange und gebe ruht auf dem Grunde deiner Liebe.]

[121] [Wenn ich nicht immer neue Ideen zu bearbeiten habe werde ich wie kranck.]

[122] See 307, pp. 289, 426, 648; and also Goethe's remark, "I need possession in order to obtain the correct conception of objects." [Mir ist der Besitz nötig, um den richtigen Begriff der Objekte zu bekommen.] (246, p. 3)

was born. No glory, no territorial aggrandizement, could outweigh a crown prince, and many a sovereign would rather have let the population of his domain perish than die without male offspring. Thus court and populace were greatly concerned that after a married life of eight years the ducal couple had no son. The lack of harmony between the Duke and Duchess aggravated the situation. The fact that there was no crown prince was an abiding reproach against the Duchess. Thus infinitely much depended on the outcome of her pregnancy.

Goethe, of course, could not keep himself apart from that feverish fear that ran through Weimar. His ambivalence towards the whole matter was mentioned earlier. It is remarkable how he coped with the situation when tension reached its peak two days before the birth of a sturdy prince. "I did not go outdoors," he wrote on February 1, 1783, to Charlotte von Stein,

> but looked around in old documents and books and found a few human things in a heap of formality.[123] Farewell, at the critical moment in which joy or care awaits us. Good night dearest.[124]

Retreat into work, withdrawal from others, apparently had become the mainstay when reality became threatening. It is interesting how retreat into work could serve the same psychological purpose as retreat into bed. On March 7, 1783, he wrote to Charlotte von Stein: "I have again slept myself out as usual, and I sorrow only for you."[125] It is not known what had upset him at that time, but it is of interest that both techniques were accessible to him and that he could switch from one to the other. I surmise that withdrawal into work as a countermeasure against tension or anxiety was preferred when the unpleasant feeling was correlated to an impending event, whereas prolonged sleep was the method of choice when the sources of anxiety lay in the past. The past could not be undone in reality and a temporary regression might lay the groundwork for a new start. Events of the future, however, can be influenced. Virtuous behavior, work in the service of the superego, may be accompanied with magical beliefs of putting the gods into a propitious mood. But it is remarkable that all further reference to the Prince's birth vanished from his correspondence with Charlotte von Stein and if it were not for a brief remark in

---

[123] Was not the Duchess's pregnancy also something human in a heap of formality?

[124] [Ich bin nicht ausgegangen, sondern habe mich in alten Ackten und Büchern umgesehen und manches menschliche in einem Wuste von Formalität gefunden, lebe wohl in dem kritischen Augenblicke wo uns Freude oder Sorge bevorsteht. Gute Nacht liebste.]

[125] [ich habe mich wieder herausgeschlafen wie gewöhnlich, und trage nur Leid um dich.]

a letter of February 4, 1783, "it storms once again sharply upon me,"[126] one would not know that Goethe was going through a bitter conflict. The solution he found this time was apparently to heap his sympathy and solicitude upon Charlotte von Stein, as if she were the mother for whose welfare he had trembled a few nights before. Thus Charlotte von Stein's complaints, which may well have been psychogenic, facilitated the transfer of his worries from the Duchess to the beloved woman.[127] Charlotte von Stein, thus, was not only the person on whom his loving inclinations could focus, but the one on whom all other emotions, such as sympathy and pity, whatever their source may have been, could center.

The diffusion towards which his libidinal strivings tended was checked, and when a rival object arose that might have deflected his libidinal interests by its great reality value, he kept the principal channels open, thus leading him back again to the one woman to whom he had sworn enduring loyalty. Thus he wrote a few hours after the prince's birth, on February 3, 1783: "I do not want to live if you are not well,"[128] a reaction that makes sense, of course, only if one considers the little boy's trepidation during his mother's many pregnancies. It is less surprising that a repressed ancient impulse is transferred to the person who stands in the center of the present emotional interest when the repressed impulse or emotion finds an associative connection with, or is directly or indirectly aroused by, that person. Many instances of this sort have been mentioned earlier, but in this case, although the archaic impulse was awakened by an obtrusive event associated with a person other than the love-object, the thus-stimulated archaic emotion nevertheless turned again towards her.

Such remarkable results of the transference probably were no longer everyday occurrences but happened only in times of crisis. The result was a particular intensification of the relationship. The next letter, of February 7, 1783, demonstrates this even more conspicuously.

> Already in the early morning I must beg for and ask for your love. My resolution to stay at home will probably not be carried out, for already I am anxious to see you. If I could do so for only an instant I should go again with pleasure to my work.[129]

---

[126] [denn es stürmt wieder einmal scharf auf mich zu]

[127] In a letter of March 28, 1783, Charlotte von Stein writes Knebel that she had been suffering for some time from a *Flussfieber* (243, 2:567). However unmistakable the somatic component of Charlotte von Stein's sickness may have been, Goethe's unusually strong reaction must also be referred to the Duchess's childbirth.

[128] [ich mag nicht leben wenn du nicht wohl bist.]

[129] [Schon am frühen Morgen muss ich um deine Liebe bitten und fragen. Mein Vorsaz zu hause zu bleiben wird wohl nicht ausgeführt denn schon verlangt mich dich zu sehen. Wenn ich es nur einen Augenblick könnte wollte ich gerne wieder an meine Arbeit gehn.]

The following night he had a pleasurable dream of Charlotte von Stein: "If you knew," he wrote on February 8, 1783,

> how gracefully you glided by in my dream before my waking soul in your form of yesterday, you yourself would have felt pleasure at having dressed yourself in that gown.[130]

This sequence, I believe, must be understood as a repetition of early childhood events. First the little boy's fear was repeated that his mother might have been annihilated by the incomprehensible but most dangerous generative process; a glimpse of her would provide reassurance of her continued existence. By the same token, a compulsive urge to see the love-object, if only for a second, is observed in the adult. In the subsequent dream, the unmutilated graceful shape—the grossness of the pregnant maternal body exorcised—is most pleasurably experienced, brought vividly before us by the "gliding" movement and the endearing diminutive applied to the word "gown" (*Kleidgen*). Yet I believe that such a dream not only expressed the joy that the beloved mother had come unscathed through dangers, but also denied the fact of the past pregnancy.

With the ending of such a crisis, the relationship—if trust can be put in the letters that have been preserved—lost this unusual intensity. A certain impatience, perhaps even a reproach, can be felt behind some lines, such as those at the beginning of the letter of March 1, 1783: "If only your nature would be as salutary to yourself as it is to me."[131] In these days also there falls a barely noticeable little incident. In his letter of May 4, 1783, Goethe wrote, in the middle of the communication, somewhat abruptly:

> The way you told me last evening that you had a story to tell me, made me feel anxious for a moment. I feared lest it might be something with regard to our love, and, I do not know why, for some time I have been worried. How strange when man's whole weighty happiness hangs on one such single thread.[132]

Such pangs of anxiety belonged to past times and formerly had occurred quite frequently, even over long periods. Why did he think that Charlotte von Stein had something to tell him that would be unfavorable to

---

[130] [Wenn du wüsstest wie artig du in deiner Gestrigen Gestalt in Traume und vor meiner wachenden Seele vorbeygleitest, du hättest selbst ein Vergnügen das Kleidgen angezogen zu haben.]

[131] [Wenn dir nur dein Wesen selbst so wohlthätig wäre als es mir ist.]

[132] [Die Art womit du mir gestern Abend sagtest du habest mir eine Geschichte zu erzählen ängstigte mich einen Augenblick. Ich fürchtete es sey etwas bezüglich auf unsre Liebe, und ich weis nicht warum, seit einiger Zeit bin ich in Sorgen. Wie wundersam wenn des Menschen ganzes schweeres Glück an so einem einzigem Faden hängt.]

their relationship? In reality it had to do with something quite different, and Goethe's anxious expectation must have been a momentary upsurge from the depth of the unconscious, unrelated to reality. The beloved woman had become dependent on him, after all, and in reality he was giving her more than she could give him. In the same letter Goethe told Charlotte von Stein that he had received a letter from the pregnant mistress of Prince Konstantin, the Duke's brother, evidently asking for mercy, for she had to leave the country. More will be said later about her and the meaning she may have had for Goethe (see below, p. 819). But her appeal to him in the name "of everything that I hold most dear" brought her plight into a sudden associative connection with Charlotte von Stein (as will be seen more clearly later), and may easily have caused him to expect Charlotte's ire.

Another remark must be quoted in this context. On his excursion into the Harz (September, 1783) he again met the Marchioness Branconi. He wrote Charlotte von Stein (September 20, 1783) about her:

> I shall tell you much of the beautiful woman; she did not know where she stood with me. I should have liked to tell her: "I love, I am loved, and I do not have even friendship left over to give away." Perhaps I shall see her once more in Göttingen or Cassel.[133]

Such impulses to boast, such extreme arguments against a personal relationship with an overwhelmingly beautiful woman, must also indicate something about his feelings with regard to Charlotte von Stein. Why did he visit the Marchioness at all, one is inclined to ask, if his feelings were so satiated that there was not even room for friendship left?

The sudden pang of anxiety (May 4, 1783) and the overemphasis of complete attachment (September 20, 1783) both seem to me to indicate a further progress in the intensity of his unconscious ambivalence towards Charlotte von Stein. The anxiety probably was the expression of a suppressed wish to break away from her, and the boast of not having the slightest feeling free is the maximum defense that can be mobilized against a strong temptation. A conflict was evidently present in such situations, and probably one of no minor proportions, but a pang of anxiety or a boast (without leading to a crisis) was sufficient to restore the equilibrium.

Two remarks appear to me as typical of the prevailing conscious feeling he had during that time about Charlotte von Stein. When preparing

[133] [Ich werde dir viel von der schönen Frau erzählen, sie wusste nicht woran sie mit mir war, und gern hätte ich ihr gesagt: ich liebe, ich werde geliebt, und habe auch nicht einmal Freundschafft zu vergeben übrig. Vielleicht seh ich sie noch einmal in Göttingen oder Cassel.]

for a short excursion with the Duke and Fritz, he wrote (April 14, 1783): "I am becoming more and more your own and find my happiness and my destiny in you."[134] Further, when with Fritz in Jena he wrote (May 28, 1783): "Love me, since this is the ground upon which my whole destiny is embroidered."[135] These two remarks, though ostensibly written with affection in the spirit of his great love and in the vein of previous remarks, nevertheless indicate a change in his love per se, aside from any possible feelings of ambivalence. The love-object had become the ground upon which the pattern of Goethe's destiny shone. To be sure, an ornament needs background; the two are inseparably attached to each other and one loses its existence without the other. Yet had not Goethe earlier felt that his loftiest aspiration was to become the ground upon which his love-object's every wish, her whole destiny, might, as an ornament, be embroidered? The reversal from background to ornament is a sign of narcissistic recovery after the ego's libidinal depletion in the process of extreme surrender to a fantastically loved object (cf. 193, pp. 111–16).

That this reversal was by no means the veiled expression of a withdrawal from the object can be seen from the remark in the first-quoted letter, of April 14, 1783, which expressed an assimilation of differences and an increase of familiarity. However, when he was on a short journey, the old anxiety returned. I have the impression, although the historical record is not quite definite and clear upon this matter, that Goethe, as has previously been remarked, bore up poorly whenever he had to leave Charlotte von Stein at the request of or in company with the Duke. On such occasions outcries are heard reminiscent of past days of great despair. On June 14, 1783, while in Gotha with the Duke on the most embarrassing mission of going to meet Prince Konstantin, Karl August's brother, he wrote: "I am incapable of expressing what affection, what longing, draws me to you,"[136] and two days later (June 16, 1783):

> I cannot absent myself from you for a moment; your image is much more vivid for me than the objects that surround me; I am more squeezed in than ever. . . . Longingly I ask to be with you again, for I have nothing of my own any more. Sometimes I wish it might be different, sometimes I wish to give my thoughts a different direction. It is and remains impossible.[137]

---

[134] [Ich werde dir immer eigner und finde um dich mein Glück und meine Bestimmung.]

[135] [Liebe mich, denn das ist der Grund worauf mein ganzes Schicksaal gestickt ist.]

[136] [Ich kann dir nicht ausdrücken, welche Neigung, welches Verlangen mich zu dir zieht.]

[137] [Ich kann mich keinen Augenblick von dir entfernen, dein Bild ist mir viel lebhaffter als die Gegenstände die mich umgeben, ich bin eingeschränckter als iemals. . . . Mit

We shall find later a motive that may to some extent account for such a distraught mood. But first the compulsive nature of his thoughts devoted to the love-object must be stressed. Compulsive features of this sort have been mentioned earlier (see pp. 599–600), but never before, I believe, did Goethe express himself in a way that proved so definitely the defensive nature of his affection. This compulsive quality is the most clear-cut proof that in this instance thinking, much as it may appear justified in terms of reality, had for Goethe the function of warding off an unconscious emotion or some other thought content, maybe of an aggressive nature. As suggested before, a certain predisposition towards dejected moods was prevalent when he was off alone with the Duke or on an official trip such as this one to meet the Prince, who was now on his way back after having gotten two mistresses pregnant. It would be interesting to know what went on on those trips. I wonder whether the Duke used them as occasions for sexual escapades, or whether Goethe was otherwise exposed to sexual temptations on those occasions and therefore turned towards Charlotte von Stein in this helpless way. The passages quoted above sound as if they had been written by someone suffering from homesickness. But why, then, was not Goethe homesick when he was away from Charlotte von Stein on an unofficial journey? His letters during his second journey through the Harz shortly thereafter, when he was separated from the love-object for a month (September 6 to October 6, 1783), were written in an entirely different vein.

The two following remarks may possibly throw some light on this matter. Goethe was occupied in those months with revising and partially rewriting *Werther*. Furthermore, his attention was drawn towards Werther's Lotte by two other incidents. One was his friend Knebel's sending him an English engraving in illustration of Werther's Lotte. It was meant as a gift for Charlotte von Stein, and when Goethe sent it to her, he wrote (April 19, 1783):

> Here is the English Lotte. She goes by a name like some saint in a woodcut.[138] She really resembles Mme. Darsaintcourt, but only in respect to her beauty.[139]

Sehnsucht verlang ich wieder bey dir zu seyn, denn ich habe nichts eignes mehr. Manchmal wünsch ich es mögte anders seyn manchmal wünsch ich meinen Gedancken eine andre Richtung zu geben. Es ist und bleibt unmöglich.]

[138] The German *"Englische"* signifies both "English" and "angelic." It is noteworthy that Goethe used the masculine gender when mentioning the saint.

[139] [Hier ist die Englische Lotte. Sie führt den Nahmen wie mancher Holzschnitts Heilige. Eigentlich sieht sie der Mad. Darsainkourt ähnlich nur *en beau*.]

The second was his sending Charlotte von Stein the English translation of *Werther*, on which occasion he wrote, on June 24, 1783: "Here, dear Lotte, at last, the *Werther*, and the Lotte who served as a portent of you."[140] Here, at last, we have found an important direct association between Charlotte von Stein, the earlier Lotte of Wetzlar, and the Prince's pregnant mistress. This association may help greatly in unraveling his distraught mood and the compulsive thoughts I have mentioned.

I have referred from time to time to Prince Konstantin, the Duke's brother, and it is now appropriate to present the pertinent details. His love for Karoline von Ilten, a poor girl, was briefly mentioned. The court was adamantly opposed to a legitimation of their relationship and Goethe got involved in carrying out the decision. Karoline stayed for a long time with Charlotte von Stein and Goethe felt pity for the charming, unhappy girl. A mild flirtation, if not infatuation, was quickly broken off by decisive action of Charlotte von Stein, and Goethe abstained from further flirtations. The Prince was sent abroad to forget his grief. Everything seemed to go as well as could be wished as long as the Prince was in Italy. Once in Paris, however, he fell in love with Mme. Darsaintcourt, took her to London, made her pregnant, and, when he grew tired of her, sent her to Weimar. Again Goethe, the eternal troubleshooter, had to get her away from Weimar and bring her to the point of returning to Paris. The situation seemed to have become hopeless when news arrived that the Prince was on his way to Weimar accompanied by an English mistress, she too pregnant. Now, on his short trip in June, Goethe had the mission of meeting the Prince, a highly difficult task for a man who for years had lived in abstinence. An identification with the amorous Prince was already indicated when Goethe came so close to Karoline von Ilten in the role of rescuer. For the two unfortunate pregnant mistresses, Goethe, of course, could not function as a rescuer, but, strangely enough, he discovered in the picture of his first Lotte a resemblance to the French mistress, and the first Lotte was the portent of the Weimarian Lotte.[141]

Thus we have an associative series from Werther's Lotte through Mme. Darsaintcourt to Charlotte von Stein. The woman who was the link between the two Lottes demonstrated particularly the great unhappiness an illicit relationship may bring upon a woman. But simultaneously

---

[140] [Hier liebe Lotte endlich den Werther, und die Lotte die auf dich vorgespuckt hat.]

[141] It may be proper to report briefly the further vicissitudes of the Prince. Genuinely perhaps a capable person, he felt frustrated in his ambitions and was really the victim of a destiny somewhat typical of a younger son in a reigning dynasty. In 1784 he entered military service and died in the war of 1793 against France.

Goethe—as I think—was identified with the culprit for more than the afore-mentioned reason. Konstantin was a kind of poor relation, who had to force his way into the dynastic circle. Goethe, after all, had also to fight for his membership in that group. Despite his solid and unquestioned standing in Weimar, he was a bourgeois in origin, that is to say, still an outsider. Thus horror of the consequences of illicit love, and the temptation to behave like the Duke's younger brother, who embarrassed the court apparently out of revenge for not having been granted the fulfillment of his serious affection for his first love, caused enough conflict to make him feel safe only in Charlotte von Stein's close proximity. Thus on closer examination we encounter a net of identifications mutually exclusive, and laden with forbidden desires and their concomitant feelings of guilt: The identification with the victims of the Prince's irresponsibility, an identification with the perpetrator, and the desire to be free of inhibitions and to act in accordance with an untrammeled pleasure principle; and feelings of guilt at not being able to assist the humiliated paramours, for having to be stern with the culprit, for loving a married woman, whom, if he had not been restrained by Charlotte's firmness, he might have harmed as the Prince had the two women. The compulsive thinking about the ideal love-object may then be seen as the last resort to keep immensely stimulated passions under control.

Goethe's renewed preoccupation with the revising of *Werther* may have been involved too. That revision was the fulfillment of the promise to rehabilitate Lotte's husband Albert, in whom everyone saw Lotte's real husband, who had complained bitterly of the disfigurement his person had suffered in Goethe's novel. Goethe's remark about Werther's Lotte having been a portent of the Lotte of Weimar, shows a transfer from one upon the other. My question is: Did the Duke now concomitantly play the role of Albert? When Goethe left on his own he did not have the feeling of being imposed upon, but when it was the Duke that called him away, was this not a replica of Albert's preventing him from being with the first Lotte? Perhaps it was the replica of something worse, since he was dependent on the Duke, stood deeply in his debt, and had to accept him as his superior. Just when he was trying to embellish Werther's Albert,[142] which, I make sure, did not come easy to him, he may have been particularly sensitive to the Duke and therefore have experienced the trips with or for him in the sense of the oedipal situation, namely as a deprivation of a mother, for whom he then felt homesick.

---

[142] Again Goethe did not succeed in this task, which was once more postponed until shortly before his departure to Italy.

Before dealing in detail with an extensive journey he made without the Duke, I wish to mention briefly a letter that shows that his ambivalence towards his father was still an area in which conflicts were easily stimulated, a sensitivity that may also explain the ridicule he heaped on a degraded father-figure in *Wilhelm Meister* (see above, p. 753 f.). This letter arises from his relationship with J. F. Fritsch, whose initial opposition to Goethe's appointment was discussed before (p. 381). No subsequent criticism of Goethe by Fritsch is known and I surmise that Fritsch became convinced that he had made an error of judgment regarding Goethe's administrative capacities. In turn, Goethe's behavior towards Fritsch became one of deference, if not submissiveness.[143] But in one of the numerous meetings of the governmental Council Fritsch ridiculed a certain statement Goethe had made. Goethe replied the next day (May 6, 1783):

I cannot close without discovering to Your Excellency how sensitive and painful and also how inexplicable to me were the manner and the sort in which in yesterday's council Your Excellency sought to return an innocent word underscored. Your Excellency knows best how I am accustomed to absorb the reminders and hints, whether in jest or in earnest, of an experienced, understanding, and highly estimable man. You know that to stand in a good relationship with you, as I have the good fortune to do, is one of my greatest comforts, encouragements and rewards. . . .

Then Goethe goes into a lengthy explanation of the word that had aroused Fritsch's ridicule and continues:

Pardon me, Your Excellency, if I take this matter perhaps too anxiously and seriously, yet as long as you have the kindness to honor me with your confidence, as up to now, then I cannot keep anything in my heart that oppresses me.

Consider it as a proof of how significant everything is to me that comes from you and how much it lies in your power to encourage me by one good word in every duty that I take upon myself with pleasure in accordance with my capacities.[144]

---

[143] This probably was also favored by Fritsch's being Master of the Masonic Lodge of which Goethe became a member in 1780. See 95.

[144] [Ich kann nicht schliessen ohne Ew. Exc. zu entdecken wie empfindlich und schmerzlich, und auch wie unerklärlich mir die Art und Weise gewesen, mit welcher mir Ew. Exc. in dem gestrigen Voto ein unschuldiges Wort unterstrichen haben zurückgeben wollen. Ew. Exc. ist am besten bekannt, wie ich die Erinnerungen und Wincke eines erfahrenen, verständigen und hochachtungswerthen Mannes in Scherz und Ernst aufzunehmen gewohnt bin, Sie wissen dass ein gutes Verhältniss in dem ich mit Ihnen zu stehen das

Fritsch reassured Goethe the same day and Goethe thanked him.

This letter sounds strange if one considers Goethe's usual independence in that period. A harmless bit of ridicule from this fifty-two-year-old man had an astounding effect on him. An uneasiness quite out of proportion to the innocuousness of the incident took possession of him. Fritsch apparently was the last remnant in Goethe's surroundings of what represented direct paternal authority. But it was not a combative spirit that made him rebel against the father-substitute. In this last island of submission to a father he wanted to preserve approval and absence of conflict. To what extent he was able to bear up under the crushing load of responsibilities only because it won the love of a father-substitute, to what extent he would perhaps have thrown off all these distracting petty business matters had it not been for the competitive struggle with Fritsch (who had been so sure that Goethe would ruin the dukedom), to what extent he was compelled to prove to himself and others that he could do better than even Fritsch—all this is not known, but it probably was one of the motives for Goethe's affinity for governmental functions. The letter also shows how insecure Goethe still felt in that area and how easily his fear could become aroused. In all, it exhibits a remarkable change in tolerance of an authoritarian person if one considers Goethe's intolerance of the days preceding his journey to Switzerland (see above, pp. 382–84).

But now to Goethe's trip with Fritz from September 6 to October 6, 1783 (Second Harz Journey). He left his keys with Charlotte von Stein to give her access to all his belongings. He hoped there would be no reason for her to need the keys, but he assured her that everything belonged to her. Despite this initial preparation, which sounds like a presentiment of death, and despite the longing for her which they express, the letters he sent during the ensuing absence sound happy. "I have much to tell you," he wrote, September 9, 1783:

> it will do me good to breathe in foreign air and to view my situation [lit.: relation] from a distance. [The beings of] strangers are the best mirror in which we can recognize our own. . . .[145] Receive me again the way you

---

Glück habe, eine meiner grössten Beruhigungen, Ermunterungen und Belohnungen ist. . . .

Verzeihen Ew. Exc. wenn ich diese Sache vielleicht zu ängstlich und ernstlich nehme, allein so lange Sie die Güte haben mich mit Vertrauen wie bisher zu beehren; so kann ich nichts auf dem Herzen behalten was mich drückt.

Sehen Sie es als einen Beweis an wie bedeutend mir alles ist was von Ihnen kommt, und wie sehr es in Ihrer Gewalt steht mich in iedem Geschäffte, dessen ich mich nach Kräfften gern unterziehe, mit Einem guten Wort aufzumuntern.]

[145] In a later inquiry into the meaning self-observation attained for Goethe after his return from Italy, this viewpoint will take an important place.

bid me farewell. There are all sorts of enjoyable [things] to fetch in the wide world but little consolation, which I find solely near you.[146]

And on September 11, 1783: "Let us indeed never, not even temporarily, misjudge what we are to each other."[147]

On September 20:

You will enjoy the scores of ideas I bring with me about human nature and substance too, and, what concerns you in particular, you can always do without me still for some time since you will enjoy [in the future] doubly the days [of which you are] deprived [now].

With ease Goethe slipped into a rationalization that made his absence appear as serving Charlotte von Stein's happiness. But some qualm apparently remained because he continued:

How happy do you make me through the feeling of certainty that I am yours, and so I really am, dear Lotte; it is impossible to belong to anyone more. The first days at a place, where so much new flows towards one, things go their way, but when this movement decreases a very anxious longing for you, inexpressible in words, arises.[148]

This anxious longing had not yet arisen at that time, for Goethe quickly drops the subject and passes on to the unimportant. Although he could have returned quickly to the object of his love, he made a detour to Cassel, assertedly because his little companion, Fritz, requested it. "This journey," he wrote, September 28,

does me a lot of good; it was entered upon just at the right time. . . . I gladly settle myself down at your side in my thoughts and anticipate the enjoyment of future winter evenings.[149]

[146] [Ich habe dir viel zu erzählen, es wird mir gut thun fremde Luft einzuathmen und mein Verhältniss von weitem zu betrachten. Die Existenzen fremder Menschen sind die besten Spiegel worinn wir die unsrige erkennen können. . . . empfange mich wieder wie du mich verabschiedet hast. Es ist in der weiten Welt allerley vergnügliches und wenig trost zu holen, den ich allein in deiner Nähe finde.]

[147] [Lass uns ia nie, auch nur vorübergehend verkennen was wir einander sind.]

[148] [Du wirst dich freuen über eine Menge Ideen die ich mitbringe auch über menschlich Natur und Wesen, und was dich eigentlich angeht, du kannst mich immer noch einige Zeit missen, denn du wirst der entbehrten Tage doppelt geniessen. Wie glücklich machst du mich durch das sichre Gefühl dass ich dein sey, ich bin's auch 1. Lotte, es ist unmöglich iemanden mehr anzugehören. Die ersten Tage an einem Orte wo soviel neues auf einen zuströmt geht es seinen Gang, aber wenn diese Bewegung abnimmt entsteht eine recht ängstliche Sehnsucht nach dir, die keine Worte ausdrücken.]

[149] [Diese Reise thut mir sehr wohl, sie war eben zur rechten Zeit eingeschlagen. . . . Ich mag mich so gerne in Gedancken bey dir niederlassen, und künftige Winterabende vorausgeniessen.]

Here the certitude of future reunion sufficed as a substitute for absence in the present. Indeed, the present without the company of the beloved woman may have become so pleasurable that love appeared for a moment like obedience to command. "You are loved as you wish it,"[150] he wrote on October 2, 1783. It is in keeping with this mood that the first letter after his return (October 7) contained the message that he did not know whether he would be able to see her that morning. The frequency of letters decreased glaringly during the ensuing weeks.

Significant as the deep enjoyment and the feeling of self-assurance and certitude despite a separation from the love-object may have been, there is a report of an incident that possibly was of greater psychological import. From Cassel he wrote (October 2, 1783):

> So here we are and very cheerful; pardon only, dear Lotte, that we are staying away for such a long time. If I followed Fritz then I should have to go to Frankfurt; he pesters me and does everything to persuade me. When I tell him that his mother is alone, he assures me that mine would take great pleasure in seeing us, etc.[151]

Fritz here accidentally touched upon a problem that must have been an exceedingly sore one with Goethe at that time. If he was able to absent himself from work and duties for a whole month, he should, of course, have seen his mother. In that historical period it was even more than nowadays a requirement of custom to be with one's father or mother when one of them was dying, or, at least, to be with the surviving one at the earliest possible moment. Goethe's persistence in staying away from Frankfurt was a serious breach of custom and ethical demand. Why the little boy so insistently demanded that Goethe should see his own mother, is not known. Did he simply hope to travel some more (and traveling he obviously loved)? Yet children are often more intuitive than adults want to admit. Did he sense the longing Goethe may have felt to see his mother, or the horror that may have made it impossible for him to enter the house in which he was born and from which his father had vanished forever? It is strange that Goethe defended himself by referring to Charlotte von Stein's being without her son, whereas his own mother had been unduly deprived of her son over a much longer period. At that time Fritz was living with Goethe, to boot. Fritz impressed on Goethe that he

---

[150] [Du wirst geliebt wie du es wünschest.]

[151] [Wir sind nun hier und sehr vergnügt, verzeihe nur 1. Lotte dass wir so lange ausbleiben. Wenn es Fritzen nachginge, so müsste ich nach Franckfurt, er plagt mich und thut alles mich zu bereden. Wenn ich ihm sage seine Mutter sey allein; so versichert er mir die meinige würde ein groses Vergnügen haben uns zu sehn u.s.w.]

was negligent, and was this perhaps Fritz's revenge for occasional reprimands he had to listen to when Goethe was displeased with him?

It is impossible to guess the source of Fritz's request, but one is forced to conclude that the child here took over a function of Goethe's superego, a step of great consequence. In some tribes (see 12) the child is addressed with words customarily used for the parents or superior beings. The three Magi adoring the Christ child show the same element in Christian mythology. I have described before how Goethe consciously assigned substitutive functions to Fritz, but that substitution drew him closer to the love-object. The new substitution was based on an unconscious process and may have had an opposite effect by draining important quantities of narcissistic libido away from Charlotte von Stein. By caring for Fritz, he could exorcise feelings of guilt, still an important ingredient in his relationship to Charlotte von Stein. The purpose of telling her about his decision not to go to his native city and see his mother, may, in turn, have been to arouse feelings of guilt in her, for he pointedly stressed that Fritz's return to her impressed him as more important. Simultaneously he successfully rationalized his inhibition and fear of meeting his mother.

Into this period falls also Goethe's famous poem "Ilmenau," written for the Duke's twenty-seventh birthday (September 3, 1783). This poem is a good example through which to demonstrate and discuss the change that Goethe's poetry had undergone. I shall compare it with "To Driver Cronus" (*An Schwager Kronos*), written nine years earlier, also on the occasion of a well-circumscribed event, though of a different order.

Goethe had been on his way back to Frankfurt from Darmstadt, whither he had accompanied Klopstock, who was regarded as the greatest German poet at that time. On the trip back the coach was delayed by little mishaps and these mishaps were the precipitating stimuli for his writing "To Driver Cronus." Analysis of this poem would reveal that it was written under the impact of his meeting the famous poet, who, in accordance with his age[152] and fame, was a father-substitute and aroused in Goethe envious feelings of rivalry and rebellion. Be this as it may, the impressive fact is that the reader can enjoy the full beauty of this poem in total ignorance of any biographical material. The rapidity and success with which the trivial delays of the journey could be converted by Goethe into a symbolic and universally meaningful frame of reference is astounding. The poem "To Driver Cronus" conveys a formidable passion. The symbols used are filled with emotion and the poem goes on with relentless, overbrimming vigor.

[152] Klopstock was born in 1724.

In "Ilmenau" an entirely different situation is encountered. It opens with a particularly delicate and sweet description of a valley, but soon refers to events and people that, though they are described poetically, must leave the reader with a feeling of dissatisfaction unless he is well versed in the circumstances of Goethe's life at that time and knows to what specific details Goethe is referring. If he is made aware of these by a running commentary, he will discover infinite beauty in this poem too. But it is most significant that so much poetical art and mastery was expended upon a work whose language was no longer for all humanity. A sociological factor is here revealed. The indomitable vigor of the young man for whom the world was too small had, of course, mankind as its audience. Now that he had become a part of the Weimarian court, his audience had shrunk. For those for whom Goethe wrote "Ilmenau," but only for those, no commentary was necessary in order to understand the poem.

The well-ordered society of Weimar set up strict boundaries, and there was no mankind waiting for messages beyond them. However, Goethe's change of environment was correlated with a change in Goethe's personality. "To Driver Cronus" was written under the impact of primary processes, hence the quick translation of everyday occurrences into universally understandable symbols. In "Ilmenau" there is a preponderance of the secondary process.[153] It is classic in its form. Yet this classic form had not yet taken full possession of Goethe at that time, for when we look at the early version of *Wilhelm Meister* we notice that Goethe was still quite capable of writing what may be briefly called vigorous language. And *Wilhelm Meister* was also a work that had the whole of mankind as its audience.

In searching for the innermost psychological core of the poem "To Driver Cronus" one will find full ambivalence against an old man and the boastful pride in youth. But the poem per se does not show that ambivalence. The impetuous instinctual striving fills the form to the brim, so to speak, and the reader's mind becomes replete with the lust for life and with the rejection of anything that may stand in its way. In "Ilmenau" the whole movement is slowed down and the ambivalence is in the open, although the poem is often regarded as a glorification of Karl August. It refers first, in a kind of dream, to the days of Goethe's arrival at Weimar, and then proceeds to the present, which is characterized by the

[153] All artistic production of course is based on secondary processes. No art is possible without providing form for the as yet unformed primary process, and the process of giving form corresponds to the secondary processes in thinking. In the above comparison of the two poems, "Ilmenau" and "To Cronus," I have used an abbreviated form of communication for two kinds of poetry that are well known in literature.

vast improvements achieved since then. To be sure, the poem ends with a eulogy of Karl August, but in a form that leaves it unclear whether the poet means to describe what Karl August is actually doing or what he should do or will do. Moreover, Goethe makes himself the central figure of the whole piece. His worries about the Duke, his anxieties, his failures, are described, and Ilmenau, a district that was the center of Goethe's administrative interest and activity, is held up as a model to him. Goethe's attempt at camouflaging his ambivalence was successful, in so far as his contemporaries and posterity accepted the poem as a eulogy and as an enrichment of German literature. But a careful reading of the poem reveals unmistakably the ambivalent tendency, which I have already documented by many examples.

In comparing the constellation of ambivalence in the two poems, one feels inclined to assume that the ambivalence behind the earlier poem was much greater than in the later, but unconscious; in the later poem, the ambivalence is more noticeable, perhaps because the poet was aware of it. A conscious conflict of the present entered into the work of art.

It would be an error to regard the fact that "Ilmenau" does not achieve a synthesis of the ambivalence as evidence of a decline in Goethe's poetic powers. The simultaneous writing of *Wilhelm Meister* proves that the creative ability had been fully preserved during the years of ego reorganization. The slow pace of the classic form, however, at least permitted the ego to elaborate upon the ambivalence, which had been lifted to the level of consciousness. Poems like "To Driver Cronus" must have been written with lightning speed, which helped get over the ambivalence, just as even profound ambivalence may be put aside for a short while during intercourse and, despite his aversion against women, a man may reinstate the other sex in its full beauty and glory in the moment of orgasm.[154]

The matured ego had learned to tolerate duration, where the beauty of the moment had prevailed earlier. Such a rhapsodic poem as "To Driver Cronus" reached—in my view—its extraordinary emotional pitch because it had to serve as a defense against a breakthrough of strong conscious ambivalence. It had to be written in the shortest possible time because of the labile condition of the ego's state. It is a challenging psychological problem that the weaker ego may be better prepared to accomplish certain artistic tasks than the stronger one. Without the pressure of accumulated, intense, unconscious ambivalence, the ego apparently has sufficient time left to go about in a planned, organized way that may make the writing of certain forms of poetry impossible. In writing prose, as in *Wil-*

[154] See Freud (163, pp. 151–54) for the significance of sexual overvaluation.

helm Meister, the ego was still capable of working with impetuosity and, though not with the same intensity as in *Werther,* yet still intensely enough to remind the reader now and again of the *Sturm und Drang* period.

The ability to sustain tension, where immediate discharge had occurred previously, can be shown in other poems. During February and March of 1782 Goethe wrote a poem on the occasion of the death of Mieding, who was the scenery builder of the Weimarian theater. Ambivalence came to the fore here in a particular way. Goethe used this poem to write some beautiful verses about Corona Schröter, the actress who had once come close to being Charlotte von Stein's rival. He apparently felt guilty at having celebrated Corona so unreservedly: he wrote Charlotte von Stein (March 17, 1782) that he hoped she would be satisfied in every sense with those verses. This poem also was not written in one spurt, and again it reveals ambivalence on the surface by starting as a eulogy for the dead artist and ending with the glorification of a woman he once loved.

Yet the unconscious function of "Ilmenau" may have been still something other than the expression of ambivalence. After the birth of a crown prince the desire for personal independence and personal glory may have been awakened in the Duke. Fate played into Goethe's hands by offering the possibility of virtually adopting Fritz and thus being provided with a son-substitute, which may have given Goethe the feeling of squaring accounts for his friend's success. But such victories cannot have contributed much towards a consolidation of their friendship, which, as reported earlier, showed signs of weakening. Therefore it may have been timely to remind the Duke of what he owed to Goethe. Thus "Ilmenau" was less a glorification of the Duke than a reminder that without Goethe's incessant worry, advice, and self-sacrifice the Duke would not have been what he at that time was, to all external appearance at least. Furthermore, the poem sounds like a final reckoning: "I have accompanied you so far, and see what I have accomplished. If you want to be independent, very well, go ahead, but without my responsibility." It also returned to Goethe his freedom of action. Thus, one could almost call it a farewell song.

My attempt at analyzing that period in Goethe's life during which Book IV of *Wilhelm Meister* was written has led far afield into the presentation of an as yet unorganized multitude of discrete facts, behind which we must now look for a supraordinate aspect. Just such an aspect can, I believe, be found in this very Book, in the figure of Mignon and her gradual integration into Wilhelm's life.[155] We know that during this time, in Goethe's actual life, his arrogation of Fritz as a substitute child took place. From the point of view suggested by the significance of this event, other trends in the material presented can also be integrated under a comprehensive aspect.

These trends are: the change in the character of Goethe's love, which I have expressed in the simile of a change from background to ornament; the friendly farewell to the Duke, precipitated by jealousy over the birth of a male heir;[156] a sporadic sensitivity to menstruation in the beloved woman. If we recall Bettina's report of the little boy's possessiveness towards his sister Cornelia, his insistence upon being the one to feed her and his anger if anyone else wanted to do so, we have the infantile roots of important events during this period. By making himself Cornelia's guardian (adopting Fritz) he eliminated not only the mother, but also the father (the farewell to the Duke), he asserted his individuality threatened by his mother's pregnancies and by sibling rivalry (the change from background to ornament) and rejected his mother as an efficient and beneficent power (panic precipitated by menstruation).

Although this view may have its validity, it remains somewhat artificial and I do not think that it really covers the underbrush of discrete details I have presented. However, while this unsatisfactoriness may be the result of defective analysis and presentation of the material, I still consider the possibility that it may reflect precisely the relative desultoriness prevalent in Goethe's life at that time and the concomitant inner unsteadiness and doubt. In my opinion this aspect found succinct expression in the last chapter of Book IV of *Wilhelm Meister*. There we find the following passage describing Wilhelm's state of mind as he ponders what to do next, after the troupe has been invited to join the Count and Countess at their castle:

. . . he vacillated between doubt and necessity. He could see beforehand that he was going to have to go to the Count's castle [with the other actors] and he had a thousand reasons not to do so. When man finds himself in circumstances that bear no relation to the place his spirit should occupy, when he is hemmed in, tied down, ensnarled, and he has struggled against

---

[155] Sarasin (464, pp. 384–89) has presented this problem in a definitive form. However, in view of psychoanalytic theories evolved since then one feels inclined to raise the question to what extent behind Goethe's unquestionable father-identification signs of an identification with the preoedipal mother are noticeable.

[156] The Lavater episode also belongs to this trend.

it for a long time, then he at last accustoms himself to a dark, good-natured patience and follows unruffled the clouded pathways of his destiny. When then sometimes a flash from a higher sphere casts light around him, he looks about with joy; his soul is lifted up; he feels [like] himself again; yet soon, drawn down by the weight of his circumstances, he again gives up the again-divined happiness with mild muttering, and abandons himself, after puny opposition, to the force that carries away the stronger as well as the weak. And yet one can call such a man happy in comparison with others who find themselves in circumstances in which our friend was found.[157]

After an account of his blissful feeling during the performance of his play and his longing to repeat it, Wilhelm goes on to ponder about Mignon:

The devotion of the child, this mysterious creature, gave his being a certain firmness, more strength and weight, which always happens when two good souls unite or even only come closer to each other.[158]

Wilhelm considers as further positive factors in his present existence his fleeting liking for Philine and the sublime sentiments created in him by the harpist's songs. These experiences made Wilhelm think that "he enjoyed at moments more true and worthy felicity than he could recall from his whole life [before]."[159] "Against this," Goethe continued,

all the miserable mundane burdens lay on the other [side of the] scale: the company in which he found himself and which one dared almost call bad; their incapacity as actors and their self-conceit regarding their capacities;

[157] [er schwankte zwischen Zweifel und Nothwendigkeit. Er konnte voraussehen, dass er mit auf das Schloss des Grafen werde gehen müssen, und hatte tausend Ursachen, es nicht zu thun. Wenn sich der Mensch in Umständen befindet, die zu dem Raume, den sein Geist einnehmen sollte, in keinem Verhältnisse stehen, wenn er eingeengt, umwunden und verstrickt ist und er lange dagegen gearbeitet hat, gewöhnt er sich endlich zu einer dunkeln gutmüthigen Geduld und folgt gelassen den trüben Pfaden seines Schicksales. Wenn dann manchmal ein Blitz aus einer höheren Sphäre ihn umleuchtet, schaut er freudig auf, die Seele erhebt sich, er fühlt sich wieder, doch bald, von der Schwere seines Zustandes niedergezogen, gibt er das wieder geahndete Glück mit gelindem Murren wieder auf und überlässt sich nach geringem Widerstreben der Gewalt, die den Stärkern wie den Schwachen dahin reisst. Und doch kann man einen solchen Menschen glücklich nennen in Vergleich mit andern, die sich in Umständen befinden, in denen sich unser Freund befand.] (*Soph.* I, 52:92–93)

[158] [Die Anhänglichkeit des Kindes, dieser geheimnissvollen Creatur, gab seinem Wesen eine gewisse Consistenz, mehr Stärke und Gewicht, welches immer geschieht, wenn zwei gute Seelen sich mit einander vereinigen oder auch nur sich einander nähern.] (*Soph.* I, 52:94)

[159] [Er genoss in Augenblicken mehr würckliche und würdigere Glückseligkeit, als er sich von seinem ganzen Leben erinnerte.]

Philine's intolerable demands;[160] Melina's limited policy;[161] his wife's demands;[162] the necessity of sooner or later abandoning the precious child to her fate; the lack of money and of any decent way at all of remedying it. Thus the scale swung to and fro, or, rather, the fabric was woven of such contradictorily dyed threads as to throw towards the eye colors simultaneously agreeable and disagreeable from one fold like a bad cross-eyed taffeta,[163] and, if I am permitted to pile up analogies, this pleat was twisted as if of silk and crude hemp, intertwined and tangled, to boot, so that it was impossible to separate one from the other; thus there remained nothing for our hero to do but either to resign himself to these fetters or to cut through everything all together. Such are the circumstances in which a good and even determined man drags himself along for years and does not dare to stir hand or foot, remains in a situation of incessant suffering unless the greatest exigency forces him to choose and to act. But even then it avails him naught. It happens rarely that man is able and that destiny permits him, after a series of sufferings, after a succession of relationships, to make a clean sweep with regard to himself and others; one resolves as unwillingly to go into bankruptcy as into death, and seeks to hold his own as long as possible by borrowing and paying and putting off, with promises and patches. The mind occupies itself, works constantly, on how it can bring about a free, whole, and clean situation; and the moment compels the mind to act always half in straits, perhaps even awry, to exchange one evil for another, and, if there is good luck, to totter from the rain into the gutter; this is what, often repeated, becomes master over the best head, what translates vehement, passionate men into a kind of madness that, in the event, is bound to become out-and-out incurable.

How much did Wilhelm sense the hardship of this state, and how vainly did he work to remove himself from it! His old bourgeois existence was separated from him at this point as by an abyss, and he was admitted and consecrated into a new class while he still thought to linger as a stranger in its vestibule. His mind became weary from pondering back and forth.[164]

---

[160] She did not conceal her eagerness to start an affair with Wilhelm, who had sworn chastity after his experience with Mariane.

[161] Melina, appointed as the group's director, instituted a line of policy which was disapproved by Wilhelm.

[162] She wished to be supervised and instructed in her acting by Wilhelm.

[163] It is noteworthy that Goethe used at this point a complicated analogy taken from color optics although he was not yet occupied with such physical problems at that time. The full meaning of this analogy can be understood in terms of his later color theories.

[164] [Dagegen legten sich alle leidige irdische Lasten auf die andere Schale: die Gesellschaft, in der er sich befand und die man beinahe schlecht nennen durfte, ihre Unfähigkeit als Schauspieler und die Einbildung auf ihre Fähigkeiten, die unerträgliche Ansprüche Philinens, die enge Politik Melina's, die Forderungen seiner Frau, die Nothwendigkeit, das theure Kind früher oder später seinem Schicksale zu überlassen, der Mangel an Gelde und an

This psychological description of Wilhelm's state of hesitation and passivity is most vivid, though somewhat circumstantial. It seems as if Goethe was groping for words and analogies in order to make his hero's indecisiveness, as well as his innocence (which is attested to by his sufferings) certain beyond doubt.[165] If we look upon *Wilhelm Meister* as an autobiographical record leading us from the hero's childhood to his maturity we may easily see in the just-described phase of Wilhelm's wavering about whether to come into closer contact with the nobility the equivalent of those days when Goethe was struggling at Frankfurt over whether to go to Weimar. However, I believe that this part of the novel also—or, perhaps even, rather—depicts the mood Goethe was in at the time of writing. The Frankfurt days, though they also had their doubts, had not been characterized by this gnawing, internally consuming, indecisiveness that Wilhelm now carries in himself without opportunity to discuss the problem frankly with anyone. It will be recalled that while Goethe was writing Book IV he was occupied with the problem of passivity or, to put it more precisely, he experienced his existence as essentially passive, much as Wilhelm's was in this section.

irgend einem schicklichen Mittel ihm abzuhelfen. So schwankte die Schale herüber und hinüber, oder vielmehr, aus so widersprechend gefärbten Faden war das Gewebe gewebt, dass es wie ein übel schielender Taft zugleich angenehme und widrige Farben aus Einer Falte dem Auge entgegen warf, und wenn mir Gleichnisse zu häufen erlaubt ist, wie aus Seide und grobem Hanfe war diese Flechte gezwirnt, geflochten und verknotet darzu, dass es unmöglich war, eins von dem andern zu sondern, und unserm Helden nichts übrig blieb, als sich in diese Bande zu ergeben oder alles mit einander durchzuschneiden. Solche Umstände sind es, in denen sich ein guter, auch entschloss'ner Mensch jahrelang hinschleppt und weder Hand noch Fuss zu rühren wagt, in einem immer leidenden Zustande bleibt, wenn ihn die grösste Noth nicht zu wählen und zu handeln treibt. Aber auch alsdann ist ihm nicht geholfen. Selten, dass der Mensch fähig ist und dass es ihm das Schicksal zulässt, nach einer Reihe von Leiden, nach einer Folge von Verbindungen mit sich selbst und andern ganz reine Wirthschaft zu machen; man entschliesst sich so ungern zum Bankerotte wie zum Tode und sucht sich mit Borgen und Zahlen und Vertrösten, mit Pactiren und Flicken so lange hinzuhalten als möglich. Der Geist beschäftigt sich, arbeitet immer, wie er zu einem freien, ganzen, reinen Zustande gelangen könne, und der Augenblick nöthigt ihn immer in der Enge halb, vielleicht gar schief zu handeln, ein Übel für das andre zu ergreifen und, wenn das Glück gross ist, aus dem Regen in die Traufe zu schwanken; diess ist es, was oft wiederholt, Herr über den besten Kopf wird, was heftige leidenschaftliche Menschen in eine Art von Wahnsinn versetzt, der in der Folge ganz und gar unheilbar werden muss.

Wie sehr fühlte Wilhelm die Beschwerden dieses Zustandes, und wie vergebens arbeitete er, um sich daraus zu versetzen! Sein altes bürgerliches Verhältniss war schon wie durch eine Kluft von ihm getrennt und er in einen neuen Stand aufgenommen und eingeweiht, da er noch als Fremdling in dessen Vorhöfen zu verweilen glaubte. Sein Geist ward vom Hin- und Widersinnen müde.] (*Soph.* I, 52:94–96)

[165] The analogies Goethe used are not too felicitous at times and themselves provide material for interpretation.

There are other parallels (regarding the good as well as the bad in Wilhelm's existence) that confirm this view. The dark, good-natured patience, the bliss felt during the performance of one's own plays; the devotion to a child that gave firmness and strength; the occasional flirtations with an actress (which, however, almost vanished around that time in Goethe's life); sublime experiences of art. Goethe would also have agreed in 1784 that he experienced "at moments more true and worthy felicity than he could recall from his whole life before." Whether he would as readily have agreed that his circumstances, like Wilhelm's, were unfortunate, I do not know. It may easily have been something more to be kept secret than to be discussed in the light of day. But the analogy of "circumstances that bear no relation to the place his spirit should occupy"; the state of being hemmed in; the impossibility of changing the present condition without cutting through all ties; the prospect of having to continue in the same way, etc.—all this was true of Goethe's actual situation around that time, with one exception: Goethe fixedly remained a paragon of the fulfillment of duty, a position Wilhelm had not reached. Doubt manifested itself in Wilhelm's relative social inactivity; in Goethe, however, in all probability, doubt manifested itself only in sentiments but did not impose itself on action. Thus one may tentatively say that the Wilhelm in Book IV is the Goethe of 1784 minus the accretion of ego strength acquired during his eight years of love for Charlotte von Stein. Indeed, we search in vain for an equivalent to Charlotte von Stein in the novel. Indirectly it may have constituted a glorification of her, for it possibly pictures the fate the author thought he would have suffered if he had had to continue in Weimar without her beneficent influence. At the same time this glaring absence of her from the novel may be caused by the poet's preconscious preoccupation with the question of whether or not he could exist without her tutelage. Yet, if we read this chapter of Book IV as a day-to-day record of Goethe's secret moods, we may assume that he was struggling intensely with a problem that came close to overtaxing his resources. The state of relative calmness and harmony he maintained in his relationship with Charlotte von Stein was evidently not the sum total of his emotional world. There must have been a constantly irritating problem in actual reality that gnawed at the very marrow of his bones. What may this problem have been?

It is necessary to introduce here a matter which, in my opinion, is basic to the early *Wilhelm Meister,* and which will occupy us more later in a different form. This is the problem of "the integrity or pureness of emotion." In *Wilhelm Meister* a question is indirectly raised as to the harm the emotional sphere may suffer through the impact of society. A direct reference can be found in Book III when Goethe describes an officer who

> was one of the good souls destined by nature to take a sincere interest in what happens to others and what others achieve. His calling, which condemned him to a hard and unyielding occupation, while it wrapped him about with a rough shell had made him inwardly still softer. In a strict service—where for years everything occurred in the most regulated order, where everything was precise, and brazen necessity was the only goddess to whom one sacrificed, where justice became harshness and cruelty and the concept of man and mankind entirely disappeared—his good soul, which in a life of freedom and free will would have shown its beauty and would have found its [own] existence, was completely cramped, his feelings blunted and almost annihilated.[166]

The impositions of Goethe's new environment were not quite as harsh as the ones he described but severe enough to make him raise the question of whether his emotions too became "cramped, blunted, and almost annihilated." In the struggle to preserve the pure, uncontaminated feeling, Goethe had to try to keep the infusion from the social environment out of his system, and this he could accomplish by an objectivation of this sinister influence. The danger of the moment was of an internal surrender to, or an imprisonment from the outside by, the encircling nobility. As was pointed out before, the world of the theater stood partly for the nobility, but starting in Book IV and increasingly in Book V Goethe proceeded to subject the nobility, its institutions, its effect on man, to a scathing criticism. The problem had also a more personal aspect. Goethe no doubt had a secret hankering towards the nobility from his early years on, as manifested by his fantasy of having a nobleman as a near ancestor. On the other hand, he was full of pride in his membership in the wealthy independent bourgeois class of Frankfurt.[167] His own elevation to the nobility

[166] [Der Officier war eine von den guten Seelen, die an dem, was andern widerfährt, und was andere leisten, einen herzlichen Antheil zu nehmen von der Natur bestimmt sind. Sein Stand, der ihn zu einem harten trotzigen Geschäfte verdammte, hatte ihn, indem er ihn mit einer rauhen Schale umzog, in sich noch weicher gemacht. In einem strengen Dienste, wo alles seit Jahren in der bestimmtesten Ordnung ging, wo alles abgemessen, die eherne Nothwendigkeit allein die Göttin war, der man opferte, wo die Gerechtigkeit zur Härte und Grausamkeit ward und der Begriff von Mensch und Menschheit gänzlich verschwand, war seine gute Seele, die in einem freien und willkürlichen Leben ihre Schönheit würde gezeigt und ihre Existenz würde gefunden haben, gänzlich verdruckt, seine Gefühle abgestumpft und fast zu Grunde gerichtet worden.] (*Soph.* I, 51:256)

[167] See 64 for the whole question of Goethe's ennoblement. Von Bradisch makes the far-reaching remark (p. 26), following Witkowski, that Goethe, in his native city, was only a member of the highest class of the bourgeois patriciate but that he was excluded from the

changed the situation to all external appearance but may have created new conflicts of a more internal nature.

A letter from the period here under discussion bears testimony to how much alive the conflict was. When the title of *Geheimer Kirchenrat* was bestowed upon Herder, the recipient, who chronically felt dissatisfied and discriminated against, wanted to refuse it because another less deserving person was honored in an identical way. Goethe advised Caroline Herder (letter of May 11, 1784) that her husband should regard the title neither as an honor nor as a disgrace, "for what prince can attach honor or disgrace upon *his* name!" (Goethe's italics) Yet, Goethe continued, if he did not accept the title it would mean the end of his stay at Weimar.

> So much do I tell you as a friend. If you want, expect, or hope to get away from here, then let the matter rest, let whoever wants to have titles [have them], and wait until you are delivered. If, however, you want to, if you must, stay [in Weimar], then conquer the disagreeableness of the moment and Herder should accept the decree as I [did] my patent of nobility.[168]

In his letter to the Herders one senses the narcissistic root of Goethe's resentment at being elevated to the nobility. If the nobility had accepted him as an equal as he was, without having to make an essential change in his hierarchical standing, he would have felt he was being treated in accordance with his real value. This, at least, must have been his conscious thinking about the matter. The childhood involvement (the superiority in prestige of the aristocratic patriciate, the coronation festivities, the threat to his father by a French count) had prompted both envy, which might be resolved by ennoblement, and revenge, which might take the form of

---

aristocratic patriciate. It is possible that it is in the exclusion from the highest stratum of the Frankfurt elite that one must seek the earliest sociological root of the whole problem class stratification posed in Goethe's life. His move to Weimar may have been revenge for an unknown early humiliation by, or the result of envy of, the native aristocratic patriciate. Cf. the refusal of the literary society "Arkadische Gesellschaft zu Phylandria" to accept Goethe as a member when he was fifteen years old (251, 6:4–7). Oddly enough this society transformed itself into an aristocratic Freemason lodge at approximately the time when Goethe applied. Goethe told Eckermann (September 26, 1827) that when he held the patent of nobility in his hands he had no more than he had possessed before, since "We Frankfurt patricians always considered ourselves equal to the nobility" [Wir Frankfurter Patricier hielten uns immer dem Adel gleich] (119, p. 514). This statement may have been the result of deeply repressed early doubts, envy, and humiliation.

[168] [denn welcher Fürst kann *seinem* Namen Ehre oder Schande anhängen! . . .

So viel sag ich als Freund. Habt Ihr Lust, Aussicht, Hoffnung, von hier wegzukommen, nun so lasst es dabei bewenden, lasst Titel haben, wer will, und wartet, bis Ihr erlöst werdet. Wollt Ihr aber, müsst Ihr aber bleiben, so überwindet das Unangenehme des Momentes und Herder nehme das Decret, wie ich meinen Adelsbrief.]

matching the nobility's condescension by spurning their offer of noble rank from the vantage ground of his, the bourgeois's, superior accomplishment.

Furthermore, now approximately eight years after his arrival, much that had appeared enticing in the world of nobility at the beginning had become routine, and many of the frightening defects and abuses had come forcefully and painfully to Goethe's awareness. The tremendous *élan* with which he had thought he would reorganize the state, and all the idealistic utopias implied in that *élan,* had petered out, and doubts as to the God-willed nature of aristocracy—to which Goethe occasionally gave expression—may have gripped him severely at that time.

In Book IV of *Wilhelm Meister,* when Goethe for the first time brings the Count and Countess into the novel, he already exposes them as lacking in judgment. When the Count meets the actors for the first time he gives his favors to the worst actor, and the Countess to Philine, who knows how to flatter her. This initial depreciative evaluation of the Count and Countess was probably taken directly from reality. I can well imagine how incessantly he felt puzzled by the repeated errors of judgment on the part of sovereigns regarding their subordinates. "This gentleman," Goethe wrote about the Count,

> this experienced man of the world, a very knowledgeable man, turns his applause—probably through the capricious error of the moment—towards the most miserable and most absurd of the whole company; and a witty, judicious, distinguished woman gives her favors to a loose creature who seems to make an effort purposely to incur the contempt of every well-meaning soul.[169]

What Goethe here expresses seems to be a paradox, mildly tempered by a reference to a "capricious error of the moment." In his opinion the Count and his wife were people of whom one could say only the best; they possessed superior qualities—but they made one mistake after another. The error of the moment was only an excuse, because Goethe goes on to report that both believed their secretary to be highly qualified and a good writer, although in this case they had had the opportunities of long acquaintance to find out that they were, in fact, grossly mistaken. This discrepancy between having all the good qualities and committing noth-

---

[169] [Dieser vornehme Herr, dieser erfahrne Weltmann, ein grosser Kenner, wendet, wahrscheinlich durch einen launigen Irrthum des Augenblickes, seinen Beifall dem Elendesten und Abgeschmacktesten der ganzen Gesellschaft zu, und eine witzige, kluge, fürtreffliche Dame schenkt ihre Gunst einer liederlichen Creatur, die sich die Verachtung jeder wohldenkenden Seele recht mit Fleiss zuzuziehen bemüht scheint.] (*Soph.* I, 52:92)

ing but errors was to puzzle Goethe for a long time, I believe. Although his adherence to the theory of the superiority of the nobility, a theory which evidently was wrong, stemmed from Goethe's ambivalent feelings about nobility, it had a great psychological effect on him in so far as it compelled him to see the individual aside from his actions. Man is all too much inclined to regard each action of a person as a vessel into which his whole personality is poured, whereas the action may flow from a personality that in its core is just the opposite of what the action per se may suggest. Thus the person renowned for charity may be envious and miserly; the soldier bearing decorations for bravery may be a coward at heart. In short, Goethe's bent in favor of the nobility prompted a dichotomy most penetratingly expressed in the Christian thesis that the repentant sinner is more welcome to the Lord than one who has never departed from the true path.

The dichotomy that Goethe here expresses did not have the depth of that which became the leading theme in *Faust,* namely that man, despite all his errors, vices, and even crimes, nevertheless, somewhere and somehow, remains conscious of the just and the good. The thesis to which Goethe adheres in *Wilhelm Meister* sounds rather like a construction jury-built to serve an immediate purpose, that of bridging a rift that yawned between him and the nobility and threatened to widen into a chasm. Yet it must not be forgotten that this problem concerned not only the people immediately about him but also the whole structure of the society in which he was living. He had the opportunity of studying the nerve centers of the Weimarian dukedom and he was familiar with all governmental departments. His quest for knowledge had penetrated into all the secrets of political, administrative, and economic life. He had studied the strengths and weaknesses of those who held power and of those who were the emissaries of power and dealt directly with the subjects, and of those whose weal and woe depended on the former. In all probability Goethe started out with the belief that the well-being of society depended on the well-meaning of the holders of power and of office. If a gentle spirit blew goodness into the community then all its members were bound to benefit and flourish. He must have listened to a good many political discussions in his native town, particularly in his grandfather's house, and probably observed some of the disadvantages of the cumbersome democratic administrative machinery. One catches a distant repercussion of the whole problem, which must once have been very acute, in a letter to his wife, Christiane. When she was in Frankfurt to take care of the estate of Goethe's mother, who had died shortly before, Goethe

wanted to acquire for Christiane and their son citizenship in the munici-
pality of Frankfurt. Much red tape—and embarrassment, to boot, in view
of the son's illegitimate birth—had to be gone through in order to obtain the document. Thus Goethe wrote her on October 25, 1808:

> I thought since Frankfurt now has a sovereign[170] one could circumvent
> various formalities; at least with us everything would be settled by a stroke
> of the Duke's pen, but there the old formalities of the free Imperial City
> persist which inconvenience us this time.[171]

And the following day he elaborated upon the same subject in a letter to
I. F. H. Schlosser:

> To be frank, we are in our condition so accustomed, or spoiled,[172] that in
> instances where something neglected is to be made up for, some failure is
> to be corrected, the sovereign, setting aside customary forms, draws the
> cloak of mercy and dedicates the past to oblivion. I well believe that things
> of this kind are not as easy there [in Frankfurt] under the scarcely
> changed [city] institutions.[173]

And Goethe for the time being dropped his plan.

The stroke of the sovereign's pen versus the formalities of the free Imperial City probably were the symbols of Goethe's hopes and fears when
he arrived in Weimar. If the idealist's spirit, the momentum of the poet's
inspired words, gave the right direction to the pen of the young Duke
whose mind had not yet been encumbered by prejudice, intrigue, routine,
and hardly even by unhealthy traditions, then a model state would arise
to be admired and copied by the whole of Germany. But the days of such
beliefs were gone and the poet worked his way through boring files to save
the dukedom from bankruptcy. If the dukedom survived at all, Goethe would be fortunate. The whole caste of the nobility had lost its glamour in Goethe's eyes, and when he was accused later of servility to nobility
it was on the basis of an external form which he showed and which was
taken for the essence of his attitude.

[170] Frankfurt belonged at that time to the Confederation of the Rhine.

[171] [Ich dachte da Franckfurt jetzt einen Souverain hat; so könnte man über verschiedne
Umständlichkeiten hinauskommen, wenigstens bey uns wäre alles mit Einem Federstrich des
Herzogs abgethan, so aber setzt man dort die alten Reichstädtischen Förmlichkeiten fort,
die uns diesmal inkommodiren.]

[172] Goethe's way of expression is particularly elegant: *gewöhnt*—accustomed; *verwöhnt*
—spoiled.

[173] [Aufrichtig zu seyn, so sind wir in unsern Verhältnissen gewöhnt, oder verwöhnt,
dass in Fällen, wo etwas versäumtes nachzuholen, etwas verfehltes zu verbessern ist, der
Souverain, mit Beseitigung üblicher Formen, den Mantel der Gnade überzieht und das
Vergangne der Vergessenheit widmet. Ich glaube wohl dass dorten, bey kaum veränderter
Verfassung desgleichen nicht so ganz leicht sey.]

Chapter 6

Wilhelm Meister, Book V
(Until October 16, 1784)

Whereas the way Goethe solved the problem of his relationship to the nobility in later years is not our concern now, the crisis brought forth by this problem in 1784 deserves our attention. The content of the fifth book of his novel suggests the existence of strong sensitive criticism and a despair that this class should prove able to serve the purpose to which God seemed to have appointed it.

Book V of *Wilhelm Meister* was written between November 12, 1783, and October 16, 1784. In it Goethe narrates the adventures of the troupe at the Count's castle. A new character is introduced: Jarno, an unusual person in the Prince's entourage. Wilhelm is attracted to him. On his advice, Wilhelm starts to read Shakespeare, and is enraptured by this new world. He expresses his thanks to Jarno, who deeply offends him by a disparaging remark about Mignon and the harpist. When the Count's princely guest has to depart for war, the troupe is soon requested to leave the Count's service. On their way to the next city they are ambushed by robbers. Wilhelm is severely injured. He falls unconscious. When he comes to he is lying on the ground. Philine and Mignon attend him; everyone else has fled. The troupe has lost all its property except Philine's.

The incidents reported present the nobility as selfish, without taste, and unreliable. They promise lightly but do not live up to the expectations they arouse in those who trust them. They easily fall prey to intrigues, and though they think themselves masters they can easily be gulled. Their decisions are quick but unstable; they can be got to change their minds if flattering arguments are raised. They are incapable of sustained effort except what is devoted to pleasure and entertainment. Although they support art their artistic taste is unreliable and flighty. They will make others feel comfortable by pretense:

> The company was also sometimes bidden one and all [to appear] before the nobility after dinner. They thought this to be a great honor for them and did not notice the number of dogs that they had brought in at the same time by huntsmen and servants, and the horses that were trotted out in the courtyard.[1]

An indictment based on the irreconcilability of friendship, one of the highest values, with power, is contained in the following remarks of Wilhelm:

> What touching examples of faithful servants who sacrificed themselves for their masters! . . . I see faithfulness in this case as the striving of a noble soul to become equal to a greater one. Through abiding devotion and love a servant becomes equal to his master, who otherwise would be entitled to regard him only as a paid, contemptible slave. And thus the virtues are only for the low estate. The convenience of being able easily to buy oneself off is too great for a man not to succumb to it. Yes, in this sense I believe I am able to claim that a nobleman [lit.: a great man] may have friends, but he cannot be a friend.[2]

To a certain extent Goethe was here trying to defend the nobility. Their incapacity for giving friendship was the unavoidable result of necessary external circumstances. Faithful service to the noble, however, was made a deed of the highest virtue. Thus the nobility was disclosed as being incapable of possessing a value that Goethe and his time considered exquisite and unique, perhaps even valued as the highest form of love. A few paragraphs earlier Goethe had written:

> Of that happiness which we must recognize as the highest because it is derived from the inner riches of nature, they [noblemen] rarely have a strong sensation. Only to us poor ones, who possess little or nothing, is it granted

---

[1] [Auch wurde die Gesellschaft manchmal samt und sonders nach Tafel vor die hohen Herrschaften gefordert. Sie schätzten sich es zur grössten Ehre und bemerkten nicht, dass man zu ebenderselben Zeit durch Jäger und Bediente eine Anzahl Hunde herein bringen und Pferde im Schlosshofe vorführen liess.] (*Soph.* I, 52:144)

[2] [Welche rührende Beispiele treuer Diener, die sich für ihre Herren aufopferten! . . . Ich sehe die Treue in diesem Falle als ein Bestreben einer edlen Seele an, einem Grössern gleich zu werden. Durch fortdauernde Anhänglichkeit und Liebe wird der Diener seinem Herrn gleich, der ihn sonst nur für einen bezahlten verachteten Sklaven anzusehen berechtigt ist. Und so sind die Tugenden nur für den geringen Stand. Die Bequemlichkeit, sich leichte loskaufen zu können, ist zu gross, als dass der Mensch ihr nicht unterliegen sollte. Ja, in diesem Sinne glaube ich behaupten zu können, dass ein Grosser wohl Freunde haben, aber nicht Freund sein könne.] (*Soph.* I, 52:178)

to enjoy the happiness of friendship in rich measure. We can neither raise our beloved ones to higher rank by grace nor advance them through favors, nor make them happy through gifts; we have nothing but ourselves. This whole self we have to devote [lit.: give up] and, if it is to have any value, to assure this good to our friend for eternity. What a happiness! What a joy for the giver and the receiver! What a more than earthly bliss does loyalty give us! It confers, so to speak, a heavenly certainty upon the transitory condition of man.[3]

By holding up inner riches and inner nobility, which Goethe possessed a-plenty, against mundane wealth and rank and title, criticism and elimination of feelings of inferiority could be condensed into one idea. Simultaneously a seed was sown out of which a principle could grow that would permit conflict-free integration of serving the nobility.

This integration had, to be sure, not yet been achieved by Goethe at that time. The impression one receives from this fifth book, however, is that the problem found a realistic elaboration, or, at least, that Goethe, although not yet in possession of a solution, had started to extricate the problem from the emotions involved. Here it is perhaps necessary to report an episode that appears in the final *Wilhelm Meister* but found no place in the early version. A friend of the Countess, with the intention of playing a practical joke on her, persuades Wilhelm to dress in the Count's clothes. He is supposed to act like the Count for a few moments while the latter is absent on a hunting party. Wilhelm cooperates, but the Count returns suddenly, unannounced. Entering the room where Wilhelm is waiting for the Countess, he takes Wilhelm for an apparition of himself and believes that this presages his own impending death. Under the impact of this warning, he reforms his way of life and becomes self-meditative. Those who knew of the connection between the two events ridicule him in secret. If one adds that the Countess falls in love with Wilhelm and that a passionate love scene takes place between them, one finds the elements of the oedipal situation. It is noteworthy that that part of the novel which contained a strong social criticism of the nobility was eroticized in

---

[3] [von jenem Glücke, das wir für das höchste erkennen müssen, weil es aus den innern Reichthümern der Natur genommen wird, haben sie selten eine erhöhte Empfindung. Nur uns Armen, die wir wenig oder nichts besitzen, ist es gegönnt, das Glück der Freundschaft in reichem Masse zu geniessen. Wir können unsere Geliebten weder durch Gnade erheben, noch durch Gunst befördern, noch durch Geschenke beglücken; wir haben nichts als uns selbst. Dieses ganze Selbst müssen wir hingeben und, wenn es einigen Werth haben soll, dem Freunde dieses Gut auf ewig versichern. Welch ein Glück! welch ein Genuss, für den Geber und Empfänger! welche überirdische Glückseligkeit gewährt uns die Treue! Sie gibt dem vorübergehenden Zustande des Menschen gleichsam eine himmlische Gewissheit.] (*Soph.* I, 52:177)

the final draft. The particular theme of struggling against a father-substitute by frightening him with a feigned mirror-image deserves a thorough analysis. Here it is sufficient to note that this means of coming to grips with the oedipal deed was not yet at Goethe's disposal when he was working on the first version of the novel.

To what extent can this crisis in Goethe's feeling about the nobility be confirmed from his correspondence? There are remarks not unlike some of those quoted earlier from preceding periods. One, characterizing the situation in general terms, is reminiscent of Talleyrand's famous remark made after the return of the Bourbons to the throne: "They have learned nothing and forgotten nothing." When Knebel wanted to return to Weimar Goethe hoped his friend would enjoy his stay but doubted that this would be the case, and wrote on April 24, 1784: "For you find too much changed to resume your old life and too little to be able to start anew."[4] This remark implies that what had been achieved up to then had been only mediocre. It sounds as if Goethe would at that time have preferred it if the old tradition had continued untouched by any reforms. Then a clear-cut situation against which criticism could be directed would have existed; but as things stood, much effort had been expended and concessions had been made, but not enough to come close to a state worthy of pride. Yet mediocrity was baneful to a man like Goethe, to whom extremes were the breath of his nostrils.

In the late spring and early summer Goethe was absent from Weimar for several weeks because the provincial Diet was meeting at Eisenach. There, as a representative of the court, his conflict must have been particularly acute. He had to negotiate with the representatives of the estates, among them those of the bourgeoisie from whom he sprang, and try to extract from them financial support of the noble class. He came of course into particularly close contact with all the sufferings of those who toiled for those who were in power. His own distress is verbalized in a letter to the Herders on June 20, 1784:

> In our negotiations a sole point interests me, and that one is finished. Besides, there is no joy to be plucked here. The poor people must always carry the bag and it is pretty much the same thing whether it becomes too heavy on the right side or the left.[5]

[4] [Denn du findest zu viel verändert um dein altes Leben anzuknüpfen und zu wenig verändert um von vorne anfangen zu können.]

[5] [Bey unsern Geschäfften interessirt mich ein einziger Punckt und der ist abgethan. Übrigens ist da keine Freude zu pflücken. Das arme Volck muss immer den Sack tragen und es ist ziemlich einerley ob er ihm auf der rechten oder lincken Seite zu schweer wird.]

Such deep groans are rather rare in his letters. Not only consideration for those around him but also self-defense against a conflict that could easily have undermined his whole existence, may have made him suppress much that he had to say. To what extent he had become internally alienated from the group of which he had become objectively a part, and also from the Duke, can be seen from a sentence in a letter to Charlotte von Stein upon his arrival in Eisenach on June 7, 1784: "I have arrived with the greatest composure and shall wait for everything with just the same equanimity."[6] Goethe kept up this attitude and, despite the Duke's presence, lived in nearly complete isolation, to the surprise of all the others. He went on in his letter to Charlotte von Stein: "How different from the foolish dark striving and seeking of four years ago, although I miss some charming sensation of previous times."[7] This means he had plenty of strength to bear isolation even in view of the continuous offer of company and the vivid memory of the beauty of intense feelings that had formerly carried him away and that had become rather rare now. But again that longing for an earlier emotional intensity gripped him.

While in Eisenach, Goethe became acquainted with Voltaire's *La Vie privée du roi de Prusse*. These memoirs were an attack against Frederick the Great, full of indiscretion and rancor. Goethe's joy over this pamphlet was unmistakable. Whatever cause there was from childhood reminiscences to feel favorably disposed to the King, Goethe had a more recent occasion to feel ill-disposed to him in the publication of his opinions regarding German literature.[8] But despite these and possibly many more personal reasons one is nevertheless astounded to read the following statement in a letter to Charlotte von Stein of June 5, 1784:

He [Voltaire] writes of the King in Prussia as Suetonius of the scandals of the rulers of the world, and, if the eyes of the world could and should be

[6] [Ich bin mit der grössten Gelassenheit angelangt und werde alles eben so gleichmütig abwarten.]

Düntzer (113, p. 209) sees in this passage a sign of how much the fraternal relationship with the Duke had vanished.

[7] [Wie unterschieden von dem Törigen dunckeln Streben und Suchen vor vier Jahren, ob ich gleich manche anmuthige Empfindung voriger Zeiten vermisse.]

It is commonly assumed that Goethe made a slip here. Indeed, the last time he had been in Eisenach was seven years earlier. However, if the events of four years earlier (1780) are reviewed one gets the impression that Goethe's relationship with Karl August had reached a peak at that time. He had just returned with him from his Swiss journey, traveled with him to Leipzig, read to him his *Faust*, etc. The seeming slip may indicate that the passage refers to the lack of the feeling of friendship between him and the Duke when compared with four years before.

[8] It is questionable whether Goethe knew at that time how far the Duke had gone in his plans to organize an alliance with others in favor of Prussia against Austria.

opened as to kings and princes, these pages would be again a precious balm. However, one will read them, as one does a satire upon women, put them aside, and fall again at their feet.[9]

The remark equating Frederick and the women who are satirized is an important indication of Goethe's latent homosexuality. But, more important, here we notice Goethe siding forcefully with an impetuous attack against an absolute, though enlightened, sovereign. Certainly there was a vast difference between the Duke and Frederick, but Goethe took a rather strong stand against kings and princes generally, and such a statement necessarily included his friend Karl August as well. How closely the writing of *Wilhelm Meister* became intertwined at this point with Goethe's reality situation may be seen from the fact that a whole episode in the novel was taken from impressions he received in Eisenach when the Prussian heir apparent to the throne arrived (see 113, p. 210).

All these conflicts did not intrude into the manifest relationship with Charlotte von Stein, whose outlook was an arch-aristocratic one. However, when he had to accompany the Duke on a secret diplomatic journey to Brunswick in August, 1784, a seemingly trivial incident occurred, which, I believe, must have aroused serious and ominous feelings in him. When he arrived in Brunswick he found a letter from Charlotte von Stein written in French. It is believed that they had agreed to write each other in French because that was the language used at that court (see 254, 2:652). This assumption has its merits, but Goethe's first letter (August 18, 1784) does not confirm it:

> To see these barbarous [alphabetic] characters, strange to my heart, was an entirely new sensation for me; these *vous*[10] made me tremble and I quickly turned the page to see whether there was a word of the cherished language that had become more dear every day through the expressions of true feelings with which you enriched it. Oh my dear, it is nearly impossible for me to keep up this game; my pen obeys only with regret and it is only with pain that I translate, that I travesty, the original sentiments of my heart.[11]

[9] [er schreibt vom König in Preusen wie Sueton die Scandala der Weltherrscher, und wenn der Welt über Könige und Fürsten die Augen aufgehen könnten und sollten so wären diese Blätter wieder eine köstliche Salbe. Allein man wird sie lesen, wie eine Satyre auf die Weiber, sie bey Seite legen und ihnen wieder zu Füssen fallen.]

[10] The former *vous* instead of the intimate *tu;* see Goethe's previously described argument with Charlotte von Stein when she suddenly wrote *Sie* instead of *Du* (above, p. 538).

[11] [Voiant ces caracteres barbares etrangers a mon coeur ce fut un tout nouveau sentiment pour moi, ces *Vous* me faisoit trembler et ie tournai vite la feuille pour Voir s'il n'y avoit pas un mot de la langue cherie qui m'est devenue tous les jours plus chere par les expressions du veritable sentiment d'ont tu l'enrichis. O ma chere il m'est presque impossible

Whatever the previous understanding may have been—whether there was a seriously meant agreement or playful talk of possibly corresponding in French—Charlotte von Stein's writing to him in French and using the odious formal way of addressing him clearly had an unfortunate effect. She touched here the very nerve center of his present existence, his beloved language. To all the sacrifices she had demanded and Goethe had—gladly or reluctantly—made, she added now a new one which was not necessary and which carried into their relationship an element of artificiality and ceremoniousness just at a time when Goethe was becoming alienated from court life. The path to her was the only channel left by which Goethe could let his feelings go. In the same letter he agreed to do what was requested of him, but the quickness with which he was ready to surrender to this demand too should have warned her. It is questionable why this so eminently sagacious and intuitive woman committed such an error. Did she feel the growing distance between Goethe and the court and fear lest it might lead to an open breach? Did she therefore put him under increased pressure and thus try to put out the flame of silent insurrection? Be this as it may, this little incident may perhaps indicate that selfish considerations became an integral part of Charlotte von Stein's motivation and that her intuitive knowledge of what Goethe needed and of what was necessary for his welfare and development had reached its limit and was on the decline.

Goethe quickly became accustomed to the necessity of writing in French, and soon his assurances of love flowed richly from his new pen. The letters, however, sound a little stiff. What ideas and sentiments may have been evoked by the change in medium of expression is not known. Two factors may be mentioned. First, as a youngster he wrote letters to his sister in a foreign tongue for the sake of linguistic exercise.[12] Charlotte von Stein's proposal may have reminded him painfully of that time when he was in Leipzig. A regression occurred also in other respects. When he wrote his letters in French he started to write in excellent penmanship in order to give Fritz, who accompanied him, a good example. Possibly this was again a sign of identification with the boy at a time when he was angry with Charlotte von Stein, as was seen once earlier. Secondly, as I have had occasion to know from other instances, the necessity of changing a medium of communication such as one's native lan-

---

de poursuivre ce jeu, ma plume n'obeit qu'a regret, et ce n'est qu'avec peine que je traduis, que je travestis les sentiments originaux de mon coeur.]

[12] The reason for his discontinuing a foreign language in that correspondence was discussed in Part I (see above, p. 68).

guage entails a more analytic attitude, in so far as the new medium requires a more precise logical analysis of the content than the accustomed one, which permits almost automatic communication. This can easily be seen when one tries to translate from his native tongue into a foreign one. Charlotte von Stein, by introducing French into their correspondence, brought into use a tool that might easily have been turned against her, by necessitating objectivation where the surrender to emotions might have been more advantageous.

Goethe was hungry for emotions. Since his own emotions submitted more and more to mastery by his ego, emotions of others became of increasing importance. At one point, in a letter of June 14, 1784, he compared himself to Carlin (1741–83), a French comedian famous for playing the role of Harlequin to the greatest amusement of his audience at a time when he himself was affected by melancholy. This comparison came to his mind when he

> made the Prince laugh so loud in the antechamber that everyone was surprised. It was not so much a *bon mot,* but it became one, and it cannot be repeated. It pleased me heartily to see him laugh so.

To be sure, Goethe here indirectly contrasts laughter and depression but a few sentences later he writes: "How do I envy you that you can love me so much and so much more calmly and happily."[13] Thus, despite an implied (almost ironical) criticism, his envy of emotions extended even to Charlotte von Stein. The artificiality of court life (gone were the days of the early impetuosity), which necessarily impeded strong and warm emotions, was not the primary reason. It sounds like true relief when he starts his letter of September 28, 1784: "And now not one single word of French any more."[14]

It will be remembered that similar complaints about emotions, or the lack of them, were voiced around the time of Goethe's second Swiss journey, and that the analysis of these complaints led to a discussion of Goethe's temporary depersonalization. This time, Goethe's complaints, I think, run in an entirely different direction, as is indicated by the following letter. This was written May 6 or 7, 1784, after Charlotte von Stein had sent him some of her hair—in accordance with the custom of the time:

---

[13] [Ich habe den Prinzen in der Antichambre so laut lachen gemacht dass alles sich verwunderte. Es war nicht so wohl ein *bon mot,* als es ward ein's und es lässt sich nicht wieder erzählen. Mich freute es herzlich ihn so lachen zu sehn. . . .

Wie beneid ich dich dass du mich so sehr, und so viel ruhiger und glücklicher lieben kannst.]

[14] [Und nun auch kein Wort Französch mehr.]

Most solemnly, dear Lotte, I want to plead with you, do not increase my love for you daily through your sweet behavior. Ah, my best, why must I tell you this! You know well how full of gratitude to you my heart is.

Since the time of Deïanira hardly any more dangerous garment has been given to a lover; I shut it away in my wallet—it would have consumed me.[15]

Goethe, by referring here to the garment drenched in Nessus's blood by Deïanira that caused Hercules unspeakable torment,[16] was hinting to the beloved woman that she should restrain herself in order not to arouse his sexual passion, a problem that will become increasingly serious. It is understandable that in the course of his general improvement, the abatement of anxiety and other psychopathology, his desire for an adequate sexual outlet became more vigorous. Her sending an amulet in the form of a lock of hair brought him close to the breaking point, where self-control became uncertain. Of course, in trying to maintain strict abstemiousness—which was the basis of their relationship—he had to subdue emotional intensities, since any kind of intense emotion may increase the sexual urge, particularly during periods of abstinence. Despite (or perhaps because of) this, one notices an intensification, a kind of rejuvenation, of his feelings for Charlotte von Stein, as if much that had come close to becoming routine now acquired a new glamour.

In searching for further causes of this resurgence in Goethe's love for Charlotte von Stein, one may consider the following sequence in his letter to her of June 3, 1784, written before leaving for Eisenach, where he knew he would have to stay for several weeks:

Everything is packed and I have only still to say good-bye to you; how intensely do I feel that you are the anchor to which my little ship holds fast in this roadstead! You fondly beloved one! May you be well in your quietude [Charlotte von Stein was in Kochberg], where you have much time to think of [the one who is] yours [i.e., Goethe].

I am reluctant to leave Herder; he is so very good, dear, and affectionate.[17]

[15] [Recht feyerlich liebe Lotte mögt ich dich bitten vermehre nicht durch dein süses Betragen täglich meine Liebe zu dir. Ach meine Beste warum muss ich dir das sagen! Du weist wohl wie voll Dancks mein Herz für dich ist.

Seit Dejanirens Zeiten ist wohl kein gefährlicher Gewand einem Geliebten gegeben worden, ich habe es in meine Brieftasche geschlossen, es hätte mich aufgezehrt.]

[16] See above, p. 322, for Goethe's use of the Hercules myth in another context.

[17] [Alles ist eingepackt und ich habe nur noch von dir Abschied zu nehmen, wie sehr fühle ich dass du der Ancker bist an dem mein Schifflein an dieser Rhede festhält! Du innig Geliebte! Möge dir in deiner Ruhe recht wohl seyn, wo du recht zeit hast an den deinigen zu dencken.

Herdern verlass ich ungern, er ist gar gut lieb und herzlich.]

Since this is a farewell letter it is surprising that it is not entirely devoted to Charlotte von Stein but turns abruptly to Herder, from whom Goethe feels reluctant to part. The next paragraph brings forth this aspect of his mood even more clearly:

At the last minute the Stolbergs[18] have provided us with a cheerful, re-juvenated day; it is very fine that through recollection I was once more bathed in those lakes of youth[19] before my departure. Farewell. More from Eisenach. I live wholly for you.[20]

Thus in Goethe's farewell letter there are two references to men to whom Goethe had aim-inhibited but intense homosexual ties. The reference to the Stolbergs is an expression of a longing for those years of youth when, as now, he was preparing for a journey, but in the company of loved, attractive young men. Incidentally, it was on that trip to Switzerland that he met Duke Karl August for the first time. This time he would again join a male group, but he had become disillusioned and no enjoyable experiences were in prospect.

The relationship to Herder has been described previously. After a period of jealous withdrawal Herder had lately come closer to Goethe. From the written record it seems almost certain that Goethe was always ready to maintain a close friendship with him. Nevertheless when it is noticed that with the decline in Goethe's relationship to Karl August his friendship with Herder improved, one wonders to what extent the ups and downs of that friendship were steered by Goethe's unconscious needs. Yet the alternative—that Herder's jealousies were a reaction to the vicissitudes in Goethe's relationship to the Duke—is also a possibility. As is often true of seeming alternatives, both factors were probably involved (circular causality). I even believe that the renewed intensity of his feelings for Herder was one of the factors that stimulated his feelings for Charlotte von Stein. Also in this instance, as in a case previously described, the heterosexual attachment was to serve as a barrier against homosexual temptation. Friendship with a loved man was, so to speak, the catalyst of an affection that drew him closer towards the female love-

[18] The two Counts Stolberg, brothers, with whom Goethe became acquainted in Frankfurt in the early years of *Sturm und Drang*.

[19] This turn of speech, "bathed through recollection in lakes," echoes historical events, since the Stolbergs—as mentioned before—had been in their younger years passionate nudists; they had indulged in nude bathing in lakes in Switzerland during Goethe's first journey there.

[20] [Die Stolbergs haben uns noch einen fröhligen verjüngten Tag gemacht, es ist gar hübsch dass ich vor der Abreise noch einmal in ienen Seen der Jugend durch die Erinnerung gebadet worden. Lebe wohl. Von Eisenach mehr. Ich lebe dir ganz.]

object. It would be a mistake to dissolve one into the other or to see in one nothing more than a defense against the other, but it is remarkable how the growing love for this man poured new momentum into his relationship with Charlotte von Stein. At one point it seemed that his affection for Herder might outweigh his love for her.

On March 27, 1784, while in Jena, Goethe made a far-reaching discovery. He identified the intermaxillary bone in the human skull.[21] For a long time it was believed that this bone was to be found only in animals, and important conclusions regarding the truth of the Bible had been drawn from the asserted fact that this structure was absent in the human species. Goethe wrote two letters on the day of the discovery. The context suggests that he wrote first to Herder.

In accordance with the precept of the Evangel I must acquaint you most speedily with a stroke of luck that has befallen me. I have found—not gold nor silver, but what gives me an unspeakable joy—the *os intermaxillare* in man!

I compared human and animal skulls with Loder,[22] got on the track, and behold, here it is. Only I beg you let it not be remarked by you, for it must be treated in secret. It should also greatly delight you, for it is like the keystone to man; it is not missing, it also is present! But how! I have thought about it also in connection with your totality,[23] how nicely it fits there. Farewell! Sunday evening I shall be with you. Don't answer this, the messenger will no longer find me.

Saturday night.[24]

---

[21] The question of whether, from the point of view of the history of comparative anatomy, this event was really a discovery has been answered in the negative by Jacob H. F. Kohlbrugge (see 335). See also 145, p. 73. It is of no importance in this context what the correct answer is. Goethe felt, acted, and wrote in accordance with his conviction that the discovery was his.

[22] Justus Christian Loder (1753–1832) was professor of anatomy and medicine in Jena from 1778 to 1803.

[23] This is a reference to certain philosophical thesis Herder evolved.

[24] [Nach Anleitung des Evangelii muss ich dich auf das eiligste mit einem Glücke bekannt machen, das mir zugestossen ist. Ich habe gefunden—weder Gold noch Silber, aber was mir eine unsägliche Freude macht—

das *os intermaxillare* am Menschen!

Ich verglich mit Lodern Menschen-und Thierschädel, kam auf die Spur und siehe da ist es. Nur bitt' ich dich, lass dich nichts merken, denn es muss geheim behandelt werden. Es soll dich auch recht herzlich freuen, denn es ist wie der Schlussstein zum Menschen, fehlt nicht, ist auch da! Aber wie! Ich habe mirs auch in Verbindung mit deinem Ganzen gedacht, wie schön es da wird. Lebe wohl! Sonntag Abend bin ich bei dir. Antworte mir nicht hierauf, der Bote findet mich nicht mehr.

Sonnabend Nachts.]

The tremendous tension of the first few sentences is remarkable. How intense this feeling must have been can be seen from the introductory reference to the "evangel," derived from the Greek word *euangelos* meaning "bringing good news." I wonder whether any other document can be found in Goethe's whole life that expresses so directly an equally triumphant feeling over an achievement. To feel like proclaiming the good tidings of the Gospels is, indeed, to feel the greatest joy and triumph.

Now let us see what he had to say to Charlotte von Stein about all this.

> For good morning to my Lotte, a few lines, because unfortunately I will not even be able to tell her good evening.

> A precious pleasure has come to me; I have made an anatomical discovery that is important and beautiful. You also are to have your part in it. But don't say a word to anyone. A letter announces it to Herder too, under the seal of secrecy. I have such a joy that all my bowels are stirred.

> Farewell. How much do I love you! How much do I feel it in joyful and sad moments. Do not answer me, but let me find a word from you at my house. Farewell my Lotte. It fares so well for me only because you love me. Saturday.[25]

In this particular context Goethe may mean that his good luck is referable to Charlotte von Stein's love.

The difference between these two letters is very striking. In the communication to Charlotte von Stein the announcement seems to fall in the midst of other statements and the letter starts with a sentence of love (although the possibility that the first sentence was written earlier must be considered),[26] whereas in the letter to Herder the discovery of the bone is the very hub of the whole piece. To Charlotte von Stein, his announcement is couched in general terms; to Herder, Goethe is far more specific. Herder's work is included immediately in Goethe's thoughts, since Herder asserted kinship between man and the kingdom of animals, man

---

[25] [Zum guten Morgen meiner Lotte ein Paar Zeilen, da ich ihr leider nicht einmal werde guten Abend sagen können.

Es ist mir ein köstliches Vergnügen geworden, ich habe eine anatomische Entdeckung gemacht die wichtig und schön ist. Du sollst auch dein Theil dran haben. Sage aber niemand ein Wort. Herdern kündigets auch ein Brief unter dem Siegel der Verschwiegenheit an. Ich habe eine solche Freude, dass sich mir alle Eingeweide bewegen.

Lebe wohl. Wie sehr lieb ich dich! Wie sehr fühl ichs in fröhlichen und traurigen Augenblicken. Antworte mir nicht, Aber lass mich in meinem Hause ein Wort von dir finden. Lebe wohl meine Lotte. Es geht mir nur so wohl weil du mich liebst. Sonnabend.]

[26] I owe thanks to Dr. Vulpius of the Goethe-Schiller Archiv in Weimar for letting me know that an inspection of this letter does not reveal any sign that parts of it were written at different times.

being a higher form of creature. To Charlotte von Stein a promise is rather artificially made: "You also are to have your part in it." Indeed, to Herder he even goes so far as to intimate that the discovery is to be seen in its peculiar beauty only in the context of Herder's theories. It seems as if Goethe was trying to include Herder, to approach closer to him, and almost to create the impression that he had made the discovery for his friend's benefit.

In comparing the two letters one senses some of the traditional disdain so easily developed by men for women. Here was an area where his friend was closer to him than Charlotte von Stein, although he usually let her participate in his scientific work and she showed an excellent understanding of natural science, despite her inclination to superstitious beliefs (41; 49, pp. 208–12). But the two letters seem to imply that Goethe did not consider Charlotte von Stein primarily capable of grasping the full import of his discovery, which is quite in contrast to his unfailing belief in Herder. Charlotte von Stein was rather made the confidante of the psychological effect, of the sentiments that were generated in him in that moment.

It is also important to establish whether or not the letter to Herder preceded that to Charlotte von Stein, as is commonly assumed. The sentence "A letter announces it to Herder too," may suggest that the letter to Herder had already been written when he was writing to her; however, he may have anticipated so vividly what he was going to say to Herder that the letter may have seemed already to be lying on his desk. The first sentence in the letter to Charlotte von Stein seems to have been written in the morning hours; the letter to Herder definitely at night. Still, it is conceivable that the letter to Charlotte von Stein was not written all at once. One feature, however, makes me believe that the letter to Herder was written first—his declaration that he is informing his friend with the greatest speed. This stress on speed, in contrast with the more leisurely pace of the letter to Charlotte von Stein, perhaps suggests the priority of the letter to Herder and the ensuing relaxation when he was writing to her. One further point is perhaps worth risking. The formulation Goethe uses in this sentence ("A letter announces," etc.), while not precisely odd, was certainly not dictated by any well-established idiom, or even by some usage customary to him. He could—and might—so easily have written the German equivalent of "I shall write to Herder, too," or "I have written to Herder, too," that it must occasion speculation why he did not. My guess would be that he perhaps feared it would offend her to learn he had written to Herder first, but wanted to avoid the outright falsehood of "I shall write." The sentence he composed is a satisfactorily neat equivocation if this was his intent.

All this would very clearly indicate that in this moment Goethe was drawn more powerfully towards his male friend. Goethe had here finally reached an area where he had established relative independence apparently with scarcely a feeling of guilt and with no manifestation of hostility against Charlotte von Stein.

Some further comments are necessary regarding the more important question of the exact dating of these two letters. Both letters are undated, the letter to Herder being marked Saturday night, the other simply Saturday, and it is not quite certain on what date they were written. All editors of the letters assume March 27, 1784, to be the correct date. The letter to Charlotte von Stein is extant in the original; that to Herder is preserved only in a presumably exact transcript which was found in Chancellor Müller's literary estate. It bears the date March 27, 1790. That year is quite impossible for many reasons and undoubtedly is an error. There is unquestionable evidence that the discovery was made in 1784 (cf. *Soph.* II, 8:280, 317) and scholars have accepted as correct the rest of the date as found in the transcript. However, there is documentary evidence that Goethe spent the morning hours of that day in Weimar. A letter to Charlotte von Stein has been preserved dated by Goethe March 27, 1784, which starts as follows: "Reluctantly as always I leave you; how much do I wish you could share the carriage ride [with me]. . . ."[27] If the date of this letter is taken as correct—and there is no reason to doubt it—then Goethe was certainly in Weimar on the morning of March 27. I do not know how long it took him to cover the twenty-five or so miles to Jena, but he might easily have arrived early enough to spend a few hours with Loder and to make the first observations which convinced him that the intermaxillary bone was also present in the human skull. But it does not sound plausible that after having sent a message to Charlotte von Stein before his departure for Jena, he should have sent her a second *morning* greeting from Jena (cf. the first sentence of his letter to Charlotte von Stein announcing the discovery) without mentioning the ride to Jena but as if it were his first greeting that day.

Can we ascertain beyond doubt a date prior to which Goethe must have made the discovery? On April 23, 1784, he wrote a letter to his friend Merck. He did not mention his discovery in this letter, no doubt because he was afraid that someone else might publish his discovery before he

---

[27] [Ungern wie immer entfern ich mich von dir, wie sehr wünscht ich du könntest die Spazierfahrt mit machen. . . .]

did.[28] Merck, who lived at some distance and with whom he had had no personal contact for some time, was, after all, engaged in osteological research and was in contact with anatomists, and Goethe apparently was not sure that he could rely on his discretion. But in this letter Goethe did write: "I have also dabbled somewhat in the meantime *in anatomicis.*"[29] He wanted to know how the horn of the rhinoceros sits on the nasal bone. He asked for a drawing of the anterior palatal bone from below, so as to get a full picture of the sutures. Though all this could refer to preparatory studies prior to the discovery, his announcement that he would perhaps publish something in the field clinches the point. No doubt he was engaged in collecting the material necessary for a comparative study[30] of the *os intermaxillare* but wanted to obtain information from his friend without letting the cat out of the bag. This proves that the anatomical discovery must have occurred before April 23.

The scholars believe that the Saturday of March 27 fills the bill, but it is not quite clear why their choice fell on that date unless one accepts without further question the annotation regarding day and month on Chancellor Müller's transcript. If we make ourselves independent of that not too reliable annotation and seek for ourselves what other week end prior to April 23 Goethe could have spent in Jena, we can begin by excluding the week ends of April 3 and April 17, for which there are letters extant to show those dates could not be the ones we are in search of. But there is no evidence regarding the week end of April 10. Here there is a gap in the dated letters preserved from April 6 to April 12, and Goethe may thus have spent the week end of the tenth in Jena.[31]

I have scrutinized these possibilities so carefully because, if the present tradition of assigning the anatomical discovery to March 27 is correct, some possibly far-reaching conclusions regarding the psychology of scientific discoveries, as exhibited in Goethe, could be drawn. Because of the

[28] This probably was also one of the reasons why he stressed so strongly his request for secrecy in his letters to Charlotte von Stein and Herder.

[29] Since he wanted to conceal the discovery it is understandable that he used a pejorative expression ("dabbled"—*gepfuscht*) for his research, which in German is pretty strong: "Ich habe die Zeit über auch verschiedenes in anatomici . . . gepfuscht." In the same sentence he also made a mistake in grammar and used an awkward turn of speech, all of which may indicate that he had to struggle against a desire to boast to his friend of his great discovery.

[30] Goethe wrote a paper on the *os intermaxillare* in the year of the discovery. The publication, however, was delayed until 1820.

[31] To look in the other direction, one has to go back to Sunday, February 8, to find another week end one cannot account for from extant documents and which Goethe might have spent in Jena.

possibility that the date of the discovery may have been arbitrarily attributed, the following hypothetical reconstruction is presented with a reservation.

In the early morning of March 24, 1784, the five-year-old princess, oldest and first-born daughter of the ducal pair, died after a sickness lasting for six hours (see 243, 2:580). The sickness was called in German *Stickfluss,* which is an ancient term for a suffocating catarrh, and this was undoubtedly the name by which the illness that caused her death was reported to Goethe.[32] From Goethe's letters one does not learn to what extent he was involved in the tragedy, whether he was called to court and witnessed the child's tragic end. In a letter to Charlotte von Stein of that day he wrote:

> For a good morning I send you here Aurora, who is carrying away a child; it would be better if she were bringing one. Towards eleven I [shall] visit you and tell you how much I take joy in the day that has reappeared me to you [sic!]. Adieu. Receive me as always.[33]

Did Goethe know of the bereavement when he wrote these lines? The reference to Aurora's carrying away a child suggests it. One author believes that he sent with the letter a drawing depicting Aurora's carrying away a child. But how does the rest of the letter agree with the event of that morning, which must have shaken everyone, whether he witnessed it or not? There is no direct reference found in Goethe's letters of these days to the tragic event. On the following evening he read to the Duchess from an unpublished book by Herder to help her in her sadness. Wieland wrote of the Duke: "He was found in this situation in his demeanor as a human being like one of our sort, which may be said to his glory" (113, p. 204). Only on March 31, 1784, did Goethe mention the sad event, in a letter to Jacobi, who had lost his wife, and on April 24 he wrote Knebel a long letter in the middle of which he devoted one sentence to the tragedy: "The death of the little Princess has shattered many hopes and has increased worries."[34] Since I will presently draw theoretical conclusions from what I suppose to have been the effect the Princess's death had on Goethe, I must add an account of the historical circumstances, as far as I have been able to determine them. Charlotte von Stein wrote Knebel on March 26,

---

[32] It does not weigh against this that the eyewitness reports, quoted below, do not refer to this symptomatology.

[33] [Zum guten Morgen schicke ich dir hier Aurora die ein Kind wegträgt, besser wäre es sie brächte es.

Gegen elfe besuche ich dich und sage dir wie sehr ich mich des Tags freue der mir zu dir wieder erschienen ist. Adieu. Empfange mich wie immer.]

[34] [Der Tod des Prinzesschens hat viele Hoffnungen zerstört und Sorgen vermehrt.]

1784 (two days after the death): ". . . but she [Waldner][35] is very sad because Tuesday morning after three o'clock our little Princess, without having been sick before, suddenly died. Even the physician when he was summoned at midnight found nothing threatening about her. She was snuffed out at play, and softly, for shortly before, she requested the doctor to feel the pulse of her doll" (43, p. 172).

The other report, somewhat similar, but worth recording, stems from Charlotte von Stein's sister-in-law.[36] She wrote:

Friday, March 25, 1784, evening:[37] I am just returning from a sight that moved me profoundly yet gently. From the coffin of a child—our dear little Princess . . . lies now dead, in the cold veil of death. . . . Her face looks almost lovelier than when awake. . . . In her little hands she held a fresh, blooming rose, which she herself had grown, with Waldner [her governess].

Poor Waldner—for her my heart bleeds, a mother who loses her only child cannot suffer more, feel deeper pain.

Wednesday the twenty-fourth at 3 A.M. she died without any further sickness but a mild cold, so that there was thought to be no danger, not even a sickness. Because she was somewhat restless, Waldner got up; she breathed somewhat heavily, said, however, that she was not in pain—yet Waldner had the doctor come, and then she wanted him to feel the pulse of her doll, and played and let herself be pampered; this was half an hour before her death. Now young Hufeland[38] went away again quite calm—Engelhardt[39] comes along soon after, and says, as soon as he sees her: "The child is dying." The Duke was called, Waldner took her on her lap—and she passed away! She [Waldner] had to be carried away lifeless, and she is still sick—she will not get over it so quickly. God give her peace and all who suffer.

The poor mother—and the grandmother too—is inconsolable. The Duchess Louise is quieter yet deeply grieved.

What should one say?

[35] Luise Adelaide von Waldner-Freundstein (1746–1830), lady in waiting to the Duchess, was in charge of the little Princess; she was quite close to Goethe and Charlotte von Stein.

[36] Sophie von Schardt (1755–1819), née von Bernstorff. In 1778 she came to Weimar as the wife of Charlotte's oldest brother and quickly became a favored member of the group around Goethe.

[37] Here the writer makes a mistake. That Friday was March 26.

[38] Christoph Wilhelm Hufeland (1762–1836) was active in Weimar from 1783 to 1793; he was also Goethe's physician. He later became very famous.

[39] Johann Christian Daniel Engelhardt, surgeon in Weimar.

This night she will be laid in the earth next her little sister. May they rest softly![40]

Düntzer (113, p. 205) reports that the body of the Princess lay in state on March 26, that on the twenty-seventh, at 3 A.M., the funeral took place, and that Goethe had to arrange for most of the ceremonies and even to select, with Herder, the place in the church where she would be buried.[41]

If the letters to Charlotte von Stein and Herder about his momentous discovery are correctly dated then one encounters here an extraordinary psychological situation. It was shown previously that events referring to death which one could rightly expect to have had a deep bearing upon him, find scarcely any direct mention in Goethe's diaries or letters, although there is no doubt about their having had the deepest effect upon him. This was true regarding Cornelia's and his father's death. In the instance of the Princess's demise, so movingly reported by Sophie von Schardt, this silence—which on the face of it might easily strike the observer as callous—again makes itself painfully noticeable. However, a few hours after the burial of the child he achieved a mental accomplishment of impressive proportions. The maximum of intuition and observation was condensed into a short span of time, and the ego, frightened and

---

[40] [Freitag den 25. März 1784. Abends. Ich komme eben von einem Anblick zurück, der mich tief doch sanft gerührt hat. Von dem Sarge eines Kindes—unsere liebe kleine Prinzess . . . liegt izt todt, in der kalten Hülle des Todes. . . . Ihr Gesicht sieht fast lieblicher wie im Wachen. . . . In ihren Händchen hielt sie eine frische blühende Rose, die sie noch mit der Waldner gezogen hatte.

Die arme Waldner—für die blutet mein Herz, eine Mutter, die ihr einziges Kind verliert, kann nicht mehr leiden, nicht tieferen Schmerz fühlen.

Mittwoch den 24. früh um 3 Uhr starb Sie, ohne weitere Krankheit als etwas Schnupfen, wobey an gar keine Gefahr gedacht wurd, nicht einmal an Krankheit. Weil sie die Nacht etwas unruhig war, stand die Waldner auf, sie athmete etwas schwer, sagte aber es thue ihr nichts weh—doch liess die Waldner den Doktor kommen, und da wollte das Kind, dass er ihrer Puppe den Puls fühlen sollte, und spielte und liess sich verziehen, das war eine halbe Stunde vor ihrem Tode. Nun ging der junge Hufeland wieder fort, ganz ruhig— kömmt Engelhard bald drauf und spricht so bald er sie sieht: "Das Kind ist sterbend." Der Herzog wurde gerufen, die Waldner nahm es auf den Schooss—und es verschied! Sie musste man leblos forttragen; und noch ist sie krank—sie wird es sobald nicht verwinden. Gott gebe ihr Ruhe, und allen Leidenden.

Die arme Mutter—und die Grossmutter auch ist untröstlich. Die Herzogin Louise ist stiller, doch tief betrübt.

Was soll man sagen?

Heut Nacht wird sie bey der kleinen Schwester in die Erde gelegt. Ruhet sanft!] (226, pp.191–93)

[41] Yet it is not clear whether or not he was present at the funeral. Goethe's presence at a funeral is said to be historically proved only in the instance of his friend the painter Georg Melchior Kraus, who died in 1806 from the consequences of the sack by the French.

horrified, converted dismay and horror into a day of feasting and celebration.[42]

There is an uncanny connection between the child's death and the discovery. The organ whose pathology killed the child was, according to the official diagnosis, the throat, and the discovery pertains to a structure in closest proximity to the fatal area, namely the upper bone of the jaw. Goethe's attention and intuition must have been keyed with greatest intensity to that area and his genius cunningly succeeded in extracting from the destructive a feat of love and peace. As the first sentence in Goethe's letter to Herder shows, the scientific discovery was for Goethe a religious act. Whether or not man's skull had a special bone structure to bear the incisors was a question that, if viewed in isolation, was of no importance or concern to Goethe at all. But, in the context in which it was raised, the question spelled life or death to Goethe's fundamental concepts of nature and of the universe. If there was no such bone, then there was a gap in the unending series of life formations that nature had created. Then man stood in isolation from the rest of organic life and nature was exposed as irregular, arbitrary, and whimsical. If the bone existed—and its theretofore assumed absence was at that time a strong bastion of the argument against man's kinship with the kingdom of animals—then harmony between man and nature was reestablished and man became part of nature, as Goethe viewed him with the greatest joy. Therefore from his vantage point he was right in intimating that he was announcing a new gospel when he let Herder know of his fortunate find.

The little Princess was dear to his heart. When she was born, after four years of marital life without issue, the Duke was deeply disappointed that his first born was a girl. In a letter of March 8, 1779, Goethe advised the Duke how to overcome his disappointment (see above p. 340). In a letter of October 10, 1780, to Charlotte von Stein he called the child "most charming" [allerliebst]. In a letter of February 3, 1782, to Knebel, he wrote the untranslatable sentence: "Das Prinzessgen wächst in seiner Prinzessheit" which breathes the pride and admiration he felt for the infant, and when the Duke was abroad Goethe reported to him a little incident referring to the charm of the child's narcissism (June 16, 1782). And to his superior, Fritsch (August 5, 1782): "Our little Princess . . . becomes daily

[42] If further research should cast doubt upon March 27 as the day of discovery, then I think one must assume that it took place on April 10. Even then I should suppose that there was a connection between the death of the Princess and the discovery, although two weeks would have elapsed since the burial, and the course of events would lose in dramatic tension.

more graceful and shows a very vivacious mind."[43] I think this little child was the first one whose development Goethe as an adult was able to watch from birth on over a period of years. As could not have been otherwise, he had paternal feelings for her, and his words show that mixture of empathy, love, admiration, and curiosity that a charming little girl was bound to evoke in an adult who was well known for his great affection for children. And now this child had vanished overnight. Nature had torn a real gap. The impact upon Goethe must have been extremely heavy, as can be seen from the absence of a manifest reaction. In such situations an ego may easily be drawn into the stream of destruction and may suffer harm by masochistic identification with the victim of destruction.[44] To a certain extent all of us perhaps do this without harmful effect by mourning. Yet Goethe's full turn towards reality, as manifested by his great discovery, is the very opposite of such a reaction. Impetuously he wrested a part of reality from nature, appropriated it, and formed a theory of life out of it, thus making the world accessible to our understanding and also more beautiful. Simultaneously it was a process of substitution: the empty place of the departed child was filled by the emergence of a new insight. And it was a specific feature of this insight that it was also in part a denial of nature's cruelty by so much as it proved the existence of basic harmony in the laws of organic existence. Yet, as mourning is a narcissistic process, this momentous discovery also carried the earmark of narcissism.

To what extent this assumed connection between the death of a child and a great discovery by Goethe foreshadowed a pattern generally implicit in Goethe's scientific work cannot be discussed now. However, an event that does need to be discussed in this context is a peculiar disturbance from which he suffered while delivering an address on the occasion of the opening of a new mine at Ilmenau on February 24, 1784, that is to say, exactly four weeks before the little child died. By way of preface to an attempt to obtain at least a hypothetical understanding of that disturbance a few words are necessary regarding Goethe's role in this undertaking.

In his early Weimar days, even prior to a definite appointment, he had shown a great interest in the silver mine of Ilmenau, which had been out of commission since 1739, when it had become flooded.[45] With great political circumspection and perseverance Goethe succeeded in setting up an

---

[43] [Unser Prinzesschen . . . wird täglich artiger und zeigt einen sehr lebhafften Geist.]

[44] I must remind the reader again of Goethe's feelings of guilt towards his younger sister, his inclination to identify with the menstruating woman, and the urge to undo the harmful effect that love-objects have to bear.

[45] For Goethe's activities in Ilmenau and also for some data regarding the history of Ilmenau see 113, *passim;* 115; 532.

administration, collecting funds, and getting experts for trustworthy advice. The magnitude of the work that had to be done—in a period when capitalism was just dawning—can perhaps be appraised when it is considered that the executive committee of the new mining company was appointed in 1777 and the first turn of the spade to start the new pit only occurred seven years later. How intensely Goethe was occupied with this undertaking is evident from the official documents. The amount of work that had to be done, the extent of knowledge Goethe had to acquire, the mass of data to be collected, and the magnitude of the obstacles to be overcome can be studied in two extensive reports written by Goethe himself (237; 238).

In order to reconstruct the emotional background of Goethe's state of mind on the day when he delivered his address one must consider that Ilmenau was not only a place where he wanted to realize a deed of great social import by giving wealth and work to a community that had become destitute by a series of grave mishaps, but had also been the witness of early excesses into which Goethe had been drawn shortly after his arrival in Weimar, when the Duke was still indulging his adolescent impetuosity and irresponsibility (see 512). Ilmenau was thus a symbol of the twofold nature set forth in *Faust.*

Goethe's speech is of interest here because, as observed before, of an unusual disturbance that occurred. It is asserted that Goethe had to interrupt his speech for ten minutes because he lost the sequence of ideas he wished to express. This incident is recorded in Eckermann's conversation of April 14, 1831 (119, p. 602). This particular report was written originally by Soret and incorporated by Eckermann into his famous book. Soret reports that at a party "one of the older gentlemen present who still remembered a few things from the first years of Goethe's presence there" described the incident. Some scholars doubt the authenticity of the story and even regard it as an invention, basing themselves on a letter of G. R. Voigt, a close collaborator of Goethe's, who wrote: "It [the speech] is intentionally written in a popular vein, but was delivered by Goethe superbly."[46] Houben, who examined Soret's manuscript, writes that the passage originally spoke of a pause of twenty minutes and that Eckermann

---

[46] [Sie ist mit Fleiss sehr populär gehalten, wurde aber von Goethe ganz vortrefflich gehalten.] (105, p. 45)

However, Voigt's letter is quoted only in part. The sentences following the one quoted are deleted. Furthermore, Voigt's letter was written to a person whom he was trying to induce to buy more shares in the mine, and in view of his great admiration of and affection for Goethe he may easily have thought it indiscreet to report to an outsider a rather personal incident in Goethe's life of no general interest.

reduced "the improbable" to ten minutes. Houben adds that even this duration is questionable and continues: "Twenty seconds would have been better" (306, 2:734). It may be worth while to report the incident as Soret recorded it:

> At a party that was given in the name of the Prince for a few officials, Herr Ackermann, Sr., recounted that Goethe at the opening of a new mine in Ilmenau [1784] asked that the nobilities and those who participated in the enterprise be invited together in order that he might make a speech to them; he had learned it by heart, but suddenly, in the middle of a sentence, his memory failed. He had the manuscript in his pocket but nevertheless he wanted to find the thread of his speech by himself; thus for some good twenty minutes he looked at his listeners with fixed eyes, without falling into embarrassed stammering; his dignified, serious appearance held them in a spell; soundless silence ruled; then he found his way again, and finished the speech as if nothing at all had happened.[47]

Goethe's outstanding ability in speaking, his art of reciting, the quickness of his wit in improvising, are well known. He was truly a perfect master not only of the written word but also of the spoken. Yet here is an instance of a serious breakdown in delivering a well-planned and carefully considered speech. The question of the duration of the incident is immaterial. Twenty minutes of silence for a crowd gathered to hear a short speech is hardly imaginable and Houben is right to consider ten minutes far too long a period. On the other hand the claim of twenty minutes, as Houben points out, may well be a correct description of the informant's impression, that is to say, even a few seconds may have appeared to a sympathetic listener like an eternity. The report does not sound malicious and does not follow typical patterns of irresponsible gossip, but turns into a very complimentary remark about Goethe's greatness and the respect in which he was held by those about him.

It cannot, of course, be confirmed or denied whether the incident really happened, but one cannot assume on the basis of the report per se that it was an invention. Goethe was more than once the victim of sudden

---

[47] [In einer Gesellschaft, die einigen Beamten im Namen des Prinzen gegeben wurde, erzählte Herr Ackermann, der Vater, dass Goethe bei Eröffnung des neuen Stollens in Ilmenau [1784] die Honoratioren und die an dem Unternehmen Beteiligten zusammenbitten liess, um ihnen eine Rede zu halten; er hatte sie auswendig gelernt, aber plötzlich, mitten in einem Satz, versagte sein Gedächtnis. Das Manuskript hatte er in der Tasche, aber er wollte nun einmal den Faden seiner Rede von selbst wiederfinden; so sah er wohl etwa zwanzig Minuten lang seine Zuhörer mit unverwandten Augen an, ohne sich auf Verlegenheitsgestammel einzulassen; sein würdig-ernstes Wesen hielt sie in Bann, es herrschte lautloses Schweigen; dann fand er sich wieder zurecht und beendete seine Rede, als ob nicht das geringste vorgefallen sei.] (307, p. 531)

uncontrollable emotions. I wish to cite an example from later years, which, though it has to do with a different mood, shows Goethe from a little-known side.

D. G. Kieser (1779–1862), professor of medicine in Jena, wrote in a letter of December 12, 1813:

> At six o'clock I went to Goethe. I found him alone, marvelously excited.
> . . . I spent two hours with him and for the first time I did not quite understand him. With the closest confidential trust, he made me acquainted with great plans and bespoke my cooperation. I thought it was [because of] the time after dinner, but there was not the tiniest drop [of wine], and nevertheless he became constantly more vivacious. I was too tired to put myself into the same mood, so I finally tore myself decently away. I was almost afraid for him. . . . I never saw him so terribly vehement, forcible, and rumbling; his eye glowed, often words were missing, and then his face swelled and his eyes glowed and the whole gesticulation had to make up for the missing word. I understood his words and plans, but not himself. . . . He spoke of his life, his deeds, his value, with a frankness and positiveness that I did not comprehend.[48]

In this report properties and an appearance are ascribed to Goethe as by no one else before or after, and nevertheless the authenticity of the report cannot be questioned simply because its content is unique.

If it is assumed that Goethe really was seized by a kind of paralysis or inhibition at Ilmenau the question arises what kind of disturbance it might have been. If one is not satisfied to classify it as simply a parapraxia, one may think of a short-lasting hysterical fugue or an epileptoid incident. Whatever the correct diagnosis may be it is well known that such parapraxias are prone to occur when the will is striving with particular intensity towards a goal (cf. 156). The whole arrangement that Goethe meticulously prepared for the delivery of his speech was unusual. All people of family who lived in Ilmenau were gathered together and the speech was distributed among the miners who were waiting outside the hall.

---

[48] [Um 6 Uhr ging ich zu Goethe. Ich fand ihn allein, wunderbar aufgeregt. . . . Ich war zwei Stunden bei ihm, und ich habe ihn zum ersten Male nicht ganz verstanden. Mit dem engsten konfidentiellen Zutrauen teilte er mir grosse Plane mit und forderte mich zur Mitwirkung auf. Ich glaubte, es sei die Zeit nach Tische, aber es gab kein Tröpfchen, und dennoch wurde er immer lebendiger. Ich war zu müde, um mich in dieselbe Stimmung zu versetzen; so habe ich mich endlich ordentlich losgerissen. Ich fürchtete mich beinah' vor ihm. . . . Ich sah ihn nie so furchtbar heftig, gewaltig, grollend; sein Auge glühte, oft mangelten die Worte, und dann schwoll sein Gesicht und die Augen glühten, und die ganze Gestikulation musste dann das fehlende Wort ersetzen. Ich habe seine Worte und Plane, aber ihn selbst nicht verstanden. . . . Er sprach über sein Leben, seine Taten, seinen Wert, mit einer Offenheit und Bestimmtheit, die ich nicht begriff.] (250, 2:209–10)

How much importance Goethe set on the speech and its timing can be seen from a letter to Charlotte von Stein of February 21, 1784, in which he asks her to send an enclosed copy of it to Herder at 10 A.M. on Tuesday, and to tell him that it was delivered that very moment "but he should let no one see it until I return."[49]

If the parapraxia occurred at all what could its cause have been?

It is noteworthy that the speech is written in a style unusual for Goethe: the language is rough and unpolished. As Voigt wrote, it was intentionally written in a popular vein, but the result was a loss of beauty, although Goethe possessed in rich measure the gift of combining the simplest language with the highest artistic standards, or better, he reached the highest standards in the simplicity of language. One senses a struggle against some internal resistance in the composition of the speech. Right at the beginning there is a small sign of ambivalence. The moment had approached, he said, for which this town had waited nearly half a century, and to which he had looked forward with desire since the moment he became part of this country. Only after this introduction did he start to speak about the Duke and his merits with respect to the opening of the mine, which I take as a slur against his master. W. Neumann (409, 2:65) advocates the opposite view. He even says Goethe with the flattery of the courtier attributed all merits to the Duke and mentioned his own contribution only in passing. However, the sequence of thoughts cleverly expressed Goethe's true feelings about the matter. The opening of the new mine must have been considered by him as due solely to his own merit. He must, of course, have held the belief—which, by the way, was erroneous—that an undertaking was here being started that would survive the usual destruction wrought on all things human by time and would be indelibly associated with his name. Poets often have an erroneous notion of the transiency of their own works when compared with the asserted durability of the external trappings of power, Horace being a famous example. Was Goethe really sure at that time of the eternal value of *Faust* and *Werther,* and did he not think perhaps that the Ilmenau mine would still be spreading its wealth all over the duchy at a time when no one would know that a man named Goethe had ever written poetry? His published works of art had decreased in number, the circle of his readers had shrunk to personal acquaintances, yet here was a deed that neither those

[49] [Innliegendes Exemplar der Rede schicke Dienstags früh um 10 Uhr an Herdern und schreibe ihm dazu dass sie in diesem Augenblick sey gehalten worden, er soll sie aber niemanden sehn lassen bis ich wiederkomme.]

This is reminiscent of Goethe's sending a poem to Cornelia with instructions when to recite it; see above, p. 43.

who were present nor their descendants could ever forget. It looks as if Goethe wished to impress indelibly upon a group that this was his work and his work alone, whereas in general his official functions were carried out with a tendency towards inconspicuousness. Indeed, Goethe's striving towards the good and the social and the betterment of the community found here a touching concrete social manifestation not comparable to any previous event in his life. Could it be that this implicit itch for self-glory, even at the cost of artistic production, left a feeling of guilt in him which made him silent? It is not probable, for the moment was too sweet to be marred by such vainglory.

In reading the speech in search of themes that might possibly have provoked the parapraxia, one's attention fixes particularly on one that is conspicuous for its possible symbolic implications. In the middle of the speech he said:

> Let us look at the slight opening which we shall make today in the surface of the earth, not with indifferent eyes; let us not regard the first strokes of the pickax as an insignificant ceremony! No, we want rather to feel vividly the importance of the action, and heartily take joy that we were appointed to perform it and to testify to it.[50]

This passage contains a wealth of symbolic implications. The slight opening which is to be made with a pickax, the person who is permitted to be the first to do it, the emphasis on looking and being looked at, all these factors suggest that the unconscious meaning of the ceremony was a defloration,[51] possibly of an incestuous nature since it concerns the earth, which is associated with mother. The emphasis upon himself and the putting of the Duke into the second place would suggest a similar situation. Since it is my theory that Goethe did not have intercourse during these years, I assume that the ceremony became a substitute. The element of penetration is strongly represented in the whole affair of mining and richly represented in Goethe's imagery concerning it. It is possible that the ceremony was strongly libidinized in Goethe. The great publicity involved created an exhibitionistic occasion of major proportions.

But the psychological situation reminds one so strongly of a scene in

[50] [Lassen Sie uns also die geringe Öffnung, die wir heute in die Oberfläche der Erde machen werden, nicht mit gleichgültigen Augen ansehen: lassen Sie uns die ersten Hiebe der Keilhaue nicht als eine unbedeutende Ceremonie betrachten! Nein, wir wollen vielmehr die Wichtigkeit dieser Handlung lebhaft empfinden, uns herzlich freuen, dass wir bestimmt waren, sie zu begehen und Zeugen derselben zu sein.] (*Soph.* I, 36:369–70)

[51] Further parts of the speech confirm this view. Goethe spoke of the pit as the door to the deep-lying gifts of nature; he compared the whole institution with a child that needs help, etc.

Part II of *Faust* that one cannot, I feel, help thinking of a connection between the two. The scene involved occurs when the tragedy approaches
its end. Mephisto, in fulfillment of his side of the contract, has offered and
provided Faust with everything the human cosmos affords in order that
Faust should find a moment to which he could say: "Would that you
might abide! you are so beauteous!"[52] But none of Mephisto's arts has
created such a moment for Faust. Now the old man, powerful, victorious,
honored, burdened with guilt and also with the memories of sublime pleasures no human before him had ever enjoyed, stands alone in his palace.
The Emperor, whose power he has sustained against a dangerous enemy,
has given him the coast as a fief. Faust has wrested land from the envious
ocean; he is rich. He hears the clanking of spades—it is the lemures digging his grave, but he does not know the meaning of the noise; he is blind
—worry, the eternal companion of man, has taken his sight. He thinks
workers are carrying out his plan of converting swamps into cultivable
soil. Faust is overwhelmed by the vision of creating paradisaic land and
protecting it against the onrush of destructive waves.

> And so—surrounded by dangers—childhood, man, and old age spend here
> their vigorous time. Such a throng I should like to see, standing on free soil
> with free people. To this moment I should say: "Would that you might
> abide, you are so beauteous!" The trace of my earthly days cannot perish
> in eternity. In the presentiment of such high bliss I enjoy now the highest
> moment.[53]

And this brings to an end Mephisto's bargain, and he derides Faust "who
resisted me so vigorously" for clinging "to the last, bad, empty moment."[54]

Clearly, Faust's last moment is an almost exact replica of the moment
when Goethe stood among the people of Ilmenau and dedicated the mine.
I do not want to enumerate the thoughts contained in the speech that can
be viewed as parallels to Faust's last words, but rather to point out the
striking similarity between the general meaning and the mood of the
two situations.

Although the sequence of Goethe's writing of the several scenes of

[52] [Verweile doch! du bist so schön!]

[53] [Und so verbringt, umrungen von Gefahr,/ Hier Kindheit, Mann und Greis sein
tüchtig Jahr./ Solch ein Gewimmel möcht' ich sehn,/ Auf freiem Grund mit freiem Volke
stehn./ Zum Augenblicke dürft' ich sagen:/ Verweile doch, du bist so schön!/ Es
kann die Spur von meinen Erdetagen/ Nicht in Äonen untergehn./ Im Vorgefühl von
solchem hohen Glück/ Geniess' ich jetzt den höchsten Augenblick.] (Lines 11577–11586,
Soph. I, 15:316)

[54] [Den letzten, schlechten, leeren Augenblick/ Der Arme wünscht ihn fest zu halten./
Der mir so kräftig widerstand.] (Lines 11589–11591)

Faust is halfway known, no historical evidence is obtainable regarding the sequence of the several steps that led to the creation of the general plan of the play. The plot is most remarkable in its ending: Faust's absolution and entrance into Heaven. The key to this denouement is the victory of good over evil in Faust. Faust's finding bliss in the creation of the socially good, and not in the sensual pleasures that were offered him overabundantly by Mephisto, made the solution valid and logical. It was a real masterpiece to give the tragedy this turn and to unhinge it in a perfectly valid way from the historical tradition of its predecessors. When did Goethe conceive of this idea? Did it dawn on him while he was delivering the address in Ilmenau? Did he experience this part of the tragedy in himself in that moment? Did he have the feeling that this was the peak of pleasure and that no other subsequent joy would be able to rival this one, of being with the crowd surrounding him and projecting himself across many generations into a distant future when the lives of the happy descendants of those present would still crystallize around the mine and thus be distantly profiting from his good works? But if it was the peak of his life and his greatest bliss then the feeling of impending death may likewise have arisen in his mind and a long silence may have ensued. The parapraxia, thus, may have been the acted-out symbol of death.[55] The reported lack of confusion and embarrassment during the time that the inhibition lasted in Goethe would well support this hypothesis, for here the parapraxia stood for death, replaced death, and saved from death. The parapraxia brought time literally to a standstill, for, as the informant tells us, Goethe's audience was awestruck and remained in deep silence. Should we call it a parapraxia? It was a wish-fulfillment and the ego was not divided, as would have been the case with a parapraxia. I can well imagine that Goethe was not even aware of having interrupted the flow of his speech and that his audience responded as if they sensed that he was not in a state of confusion but overwhelmed by the beautiful greatness of the moment, worthy, indeed, of the wish that it "might abide."

If it was the problem of death that caused the parapraxia then this would take us back to the Princess's death, which may have painfully reminded him of what had happened four weeks earlier in Ilmenau. In this

[55] Later I found in Goethe's letters a direct reference to this possibility. On March 3, 1784, he wrote a letter of condolence to his friend Jacobi, who had lost his wife: "The thought of you and your condition has constantly accompanied me on a journey otherwise joyful, for I have reopened the old mine of Ilmenau." [Der Gedancke an dich und deinen Zustand hat mich auf einer sonst frohen Reise, da ich das alte Ilmenauer Bergwerck wieder eröffnet, immer begleitet.] It was on February 20 that he was apprised of the death of his friend's wife, and on the following day he journeyed to Ilmenau.

or the preceding year[56] Goethe made a statement of no minor import in this context. During an excursion into the rocky mountains he wanted to reach a certain place of mineralogical interest. His friend Trebra[57] warned him of the danger in climbing there, but Goethe replied: "We must become famous first before we break our neck, therefore there is no danger now,"[58] and he went on without mishap. Here, strangely enough, obscurity functions as a protection against death. He, Goethe, can die only after having acquired fame. This sounds like a secondary elaboration through reversal of the frequent fear that success and fame will arouse the ire of the gods and lead to the destruction of destiny's favorite. If this is so, then, the idea seems to go, the obscure person can rest assured that he need not fear death. But did Goethe feel as secure as that after the speech in Ilmenau, and did the horrible *memento mori* of March 24—which meant, after all, the obscure person, the child, too, can die—spur his most creative potentialities, with the result of the great scientific discovery of three days later? On the other hand, if Goethe's half-joking challenge to Trebra was the sudden manifestation of an unconscious fantasy, then the great discovery was, after all, precipitated by a masochistic identification with the dying princess. Creating, which on the social level must be equated with becoming famous, was possibly associated in Goethe's unconscious with dying. Then the death of the child would have stimulated masochistic fantasies, which in turn activated self-destructive tendencies, which in turn resulted in an intuitive accomplishment of outstanding magnitude.

It may be the privilege of the genius that in certain circumstances self-destructive tendencies lead to creative processes. The dejected mood of the genius when the creative process is hindered by an internal or external interference confirms this view.[59] Where the neurotic or psychotic person develops a symptom, in a genius a creative process takes place. Of course, the distinction is not so clear-cut. The genius also develops symptoms, but

---

[56] It is generally assumed that the episode to be presently reported occurred in 1783 on the occasion of the second *Harzreise,* but it may have taken place during the third, in 1784. The psychological context would rather suggest 1783.

[57] Friedrich Wilhelm von Trebra (1740–1819), Chief Inspector of Mines in the Electorate of Saxony, stayed for a while in Ilmenau. Goethe held him in high respect and studied his geological publications. They corresponded with each other and their relationship was most friendly.

[58] [Wir müssen erst noch berühmt werden, ehe wir den Hals brechen, darum hat es jetzt keine Gefahr] (246, p. 47)

According to Trebra's own version Goethe's utterance was slightly different: "We still have to come to great honors before we break our necks" [wir müssen noch zu grossen Ehren kommen, ehe wir die Hälse brechen!] See 250, *1:*119.

[59] But the damming up of libidinal energy also leads to dejection.

these symptoms converge towards a creative process. Neurotic and psychotic symptoms are also discharge phenomena, and despite the patient's complaining about them tremendous displeasure develops if the symptoms are suppressed. This, as is well known, becomes most clear in compulsive neuroses, where unbearable anxiety breaks out as soon as the patient tries to abstain from a ritual. The artist's severe despair when artistic production is hampered is an analogous phenomenon. Furthermore, it is known that psychic symptomatology is a process with at least two sides: discharge of aggression against external reality, and simultaneous aggression against oneself. Of course, this formulation covers only a small area of symptom formation, but to a varying degree it is contained in almost every symptom. This I mention only to show that internal aggression within a creative process would not be without parallel in other areas of psychic life.

Hardly more than five weeks prior to his speech in Ilmenau we find Goethe dictating his paper "On Granite" (Über den Granit," *Soph.* II, 9:171–77). This was the result of keen observation over a long period of time on his many journeys through Thuringia. This paper was, as far as I know, the first in which Goethe tried to synthesize a mass of detailed observation. It was written in beautiful language, quite different from the speech in Ilmenau; poetry and science freely fused into each other and the result was a work of art of inestimable value, whatever its scientific significance may be.[60] As nearly always in Goethe's writings there is also a piece of self-confession included. Since those parts which are the product of a scientific attitude are of no import in this context, I select and put together only the passages that permit a psychological interpretation of the unconscious ideation out of which, in my opinion, the essay grew.

Evidently, for Goethe granite was not something dead. The meanings granite had for him transcended the objective frame of reference. His essay has less the character of a scientific paper as it has been conceived in more recent times than of what later became so well known as *Naturphilosophie.* Thus, such a statement as the following is encountered:

> For one will gladly grant me that all natural things stand in an exact connection, that the inquiring mind does not gladly let itself be excluded from something within reach.[61]

[60] Although the piece impresses the reader of today rather as a literary than as a scientific product it was meant by Goethe as a contribution to natural science and therefore it is always justly published among his *Naturwissenschaftliche Schriften.*

[61] [Denn man wird mir gerne zugeben, dass alle natürlichen Dinge in einem genauen Zusammenhange stehen, dass der forschende Geist sich nicht gerne von etwas Erreichbarem ausschliessen lässt.] (*Soph.* II, 9:173)

Without falling into the pitfalls of a primitive animistic philosophy, Goethe quite rightly from his point of view, wrote: "The human mind animates everything."[62] Granite conveyed to Goethe impressions that, although rooted in the deepest layers of human feeling, involved something that was beyond the human world and for which he must have felt a deep longing. He speaks of the dignity of the mineral and calls it the oldest son of nature. When he writes of "the old experience that the highest and the deepest is granite,"[63] he perhaps not only means it in the sense of a geologic observation but also attaches meanings derived from the world of human feelings. Granite is the basis of our earth and upon it all the mountains were formed.

> In the innermost entrails of the earth it [the basis] rests unshaken; its high backs rise whose peaks were never reached by the all-surrounding water.[64]

He admires the great variety of colors and mixtures in which granite appears. Its origin is mysterious. One cannot derive it from fire or water. There is the ring of a defense against the anticipated reproach that he, the poet, is occupying his mind with matters unworthy of poetry, when he writes:

> Thus everyone who knows the attraction that natural secrets have for man will not be surprised that I have left the circle of observations which I formerly trod, and have busied myself with a quite passionate concentration upon this [mineral]. I do not fear the reproach that it must be the spirit of contradiction that has led me from the contemplation and description of the human heart, the youngest, the most varied, the most mobile, the most changeable, the most shakable part of creation, to the observation of the oldest, firmest, deepest, most unshakable son of nature.[65]

[62] [der Menschengeist alles belebt.] (*Soph.* II, 9:174)

[63] [die alte Erfahrung, dass das Höchste und das Tiefste Granit sei]

[64] [In den innersten Eingeweiden der Erde ruht sie unerschüttert, ihre hohe Rücken steigen empor, deren Gipfel nie das alles umgebende Wasser erreichte.] I follow here the text of the first volume of Goethe, *Die Schriften zur Naturwissenschaft* (255, p. 58) for the text as given in the *Sophienausgabe* (II, 9:172) (where it says *erreichten*) is plainly corrupt.

[65] [Und so wird jeder, der den Reiz kennt, den natürliche Geheimnisse für den Menschen haben, sich nicht wundern, dass ich den Kreis der Beobachtungen, den ich sonst betreten, verlassen und mich mit einer recht leidenschaftlichen Neigung in diesen gewandt habe. Ich fürchte den Vorwurf nicht, dass es ein Geist des Widerspruchs sein müsse, der mich von Betrachtung und Schilderung des menschlichen Herzens, des jüngsten, mannichfaltigsten, beweglichsten, veränderlichsten, erschütterlichsten Theiles der Schöpfung zu der Beobachtung des ältesten, festesten, tiefsten, unerschütterlichsten Sohnes der Natur geführt hat.]

Goethe admits that the inconstancy of the human world, which he has noticed in others as well as in himself, has made him suffer and thus implies the reason for his increased interest in the sciences.

Indeed, without grudge one may grant me—who has suffered and [still] suffers quite a bit through the changeablenesses of human minds, through their quick movements, in myself and in others—the exalted quietness which that solitary, mute closeness of great, softly speaking nature provides.[66]

And then he proceeds to describe what moves him when he rests on the barren peak of granite surveying a wide landscape.

Here you rest directly upon a ground that extends to the deepest places of the earth; no newer layer[s] . . . have interposed themselves between you and the firm soil of the primeval world; you do not walk, as in those fertile, beautiful valleys, across a continual grave; these peaks have not begotten anything living nor devoured anything living; they are before all life and beyond all life.[67]

One is reminded here by contrast of a heartbreaking passage in *Werther* written exactly ten years earlier, in which Werther turns with horror away from nature. It starts: "Does it then have to be so, that that which makes man's bliss becomes again the source of his misery?"[68] And then follows a grandiose description of a landscape, also seen from a peak, surprisingly like the view described in the paper "On Granite." Werther first breaks out in a hymn on what such a magnificent view had meant to him in the happy days of his past. But now, alas, it is different.

It has been drawn away from before my soul like a curtain and the arena of unending life transforms itself before me into the abyss of the eternally open grave. Can you say: *This* is! since everything passes away? . . . There is no moment that would not consume you and yours around you, no moment when you are not, do not have to be, a destroyer; the most innocent walk costs the life of thousands of poor wormlings. . . . My heart

---

[66] [Ja man gönne mir, der ich durch die Abwechselungen der menschlichen Gesinnungen, durch die schnellen Bewegungen derselben in mir selbst und in andern manches gelitten habe und leide, die erhabene Ruhe, die jene einsame stumme Nähe der grossen, leise sprechenden Natur gewährt.]

[67] [Hier ruhst du unmittelbar auf einem Grunde, der bis zu den tiefsten Orten der Erde hinreicht, keine neuere Schicht . . . haben sich zwischen dich und den festen Boden der Urwelt gelegt, du gehst nicht wie in jenen fruchtbaren schönen Thälern über ein anhaltendes Grab, diese Gipfel haben nichts Lebendiges erzeugt und nichts Lebendiges verschlungen, sie sind vor allem Leben und über alles Leben.]

[68] [Musste denn das so sein, dass das, was des Menschen Glückseligkeit macht, wieder die Quelle seines Elendes würde?] (*Soph.* I, *19:73*)

is undermined by the consuming force that lies hidden in the all of nature, which has formed nothing that would not destroy its neighbor, itself. . . . I see nothing but an eternally swallowing, eternally ruminating monster.[69] [Goethe's italics]

There is a significant and deep connection between these two passages, which lie ten years apart. In the passage of 1784 there is still an undertone of Werther's lugubrious pondering, namely when Goethe calls the fertile beautiful valleys "a continual grave." But what unmeasurable difference otherwise! A mineral has been found that is the foundation on which all organic life rests and that does not create life and does not destroy it, a fulcrum beyond life and death but not separate from the rest of nature since it is the basis on which the more tumultuous and depressing acts of nature take shape. With one wide sweep of thought Goethe embraces the disquieting problems of bygone days, nature's cruelty, and the inconstancy of the human heart and human affairs in general, and he finds peace in the discovery and contemplation of a material that is also a product of nature yet nevertheless represents a form of existence that is a higher and lower form of synthesis than anything else encountered in man's universe. The archaic, primeval origin of the material alone makes it the matrix out of which the opposing forces of life and death unfolded. Thus Goethe thought he had found in the scientific contemplation of nature a symbol (not imagined or arbitrarily set up by the human mind to serve its need but existing and observable by the senses, and therefore purified of all dispute inherent in symbolism of human origin) that transcended the area of permanent conflict present in all and everything touched by life and human emotions.

After having described the structure that is before and beyond all life, Goethe returns to human nature. In the moment when he is in direct touch with these forces of the earth, he cannot escape the effect of the contemplation upon himself and he creates an analogy

the sublimity of which I cannot resist. So lonely, I tell myself while I look down this whole naked peak and barely glimpse afar a puny moss at the

---

[69] [Es hat sich vor meiner Seele wie ein Vorhang weggezogen, und der Schauplatz des unendlichen Lebens verwandelt sich vor mir in den Abgrund des ewig offnen Grabs. Kannst du sagen: *D a s* ist! da alles vorüber geht? . . . Da ist kein Augenblick, der nicht dich verzehrte und die Deinigen um dich her, kein Augenblick, da du nicht ein Zerstörer bist, sein musst; der harmloseste Spaziergang kostet tausend armen Würmchen das Leben. . . . mir untergräbt das Herz die verzehrende Kraft, die in dem All der Natur verborgen liegt; die nichts gebildet hat, das nicht seinen Nachbar, nicht sich selbst zerstörte. . . . Ich sehe nichts, als ein ewig verschlingendes, ewig wiederkäuendes Ungeheuer.] (*Soph.* I, 19:75–76)

foot, so lonely I say, would a man feel who wished to open his soul to nothing but the oldest, first, and deepest senses of truth.[70]

Here on this oldest altar he wanted to sacrifice to the being of all beings. Then follows an account of a cosmic view including the development of the earth from the beginning to the present.

Before ending the essay, with a scientific warning to identify the mineral correctly and not to confuse it with others, Goethe brings up the plutonic theory of the formation of the earth's crust, but leaves it undecided whether or not he accepts this theory. Later, having become a convinced neptunist, Goethe for a long time combated the theory. Apparently he refused to believe in the planet's having taken shape in what must have meant to him a destructive act. By the reference in 1784 to the plutonic theory, Goethe gives one more hint that the problem of destruction was one of the leading unconscious ideas in this essay.

In its psychological aspect the outstanding feature of this piece is the remarkable change from Werther's concept of nature to that of the scientific Goethe of 1784. Destruction finds a new place. Its existence is acknowledged, but the basis of the organic universe (granite) is beyond love and destruction, something sublime, mysterious, eternal, and unchanging, which yields a great consolation and protection against the pessimism and despair that result from the observation of the tragedies that pervade all forms of life. Although this newly evolved comprehensive view of the universe, organic and inorganic, was presented as if derived from external reality, it must have had a psychological counterpart of which it was reflection and projection. I am aware that the comparison I am about to suggest may appear farfetched, but I wish to present it nevertheless for what it is worth. I believe that most of the features presented in this essay, which Goethe drew from his associations with granite, were later compounded into the mythological figures that he called The Mothers in the second part of *Faust* (verses 6216–6306, 6427–6438). In discussing their source most commentators on *Faust* refer to Plato and Plutarch, following Eckermann's conversation of January 10, 1830 (119, pp. 306–07) but there seems general agreement that The Mothers are mainly mythological figures of Goethe's own creation. I believe Goethe's mythological creativity appeared nowhere else as powerfully as here. Faust is told by Mephisto that

---

[70] [. . . ein Gleichnis . . . dessen Erhabenheit ich nicht widerstehen kann. So einsam sage ich zu mir selber, indem ich diesen ganz nackten Gipfel hinab sehe, und kaum in der Ferne am Fusse ein geringwachsendes Moos erblicke, so einsam sage ich, wird es dem Menschen zu Muthe, der nur den ältsten, ersten, tiefsten Gefühlen der Wahrheit seine Seele eröffnen will.] (*Soph.* II, 9:174)

he must descend to The Mothers in order to acquire the power to make Helena appear before the Emperor. The Mothers are outside of space and time. No path leads to them; no lock or bolt is to be loosened in order to reach them; bleakness and solitude reign there. They are surrounded by the images of all creatures; they do not see real things but only the models of things. Whatever has existed is stored there. The instrument that will lead Faust to The Mothers is a key ("it scents the right place").[71] The key is small, but grows and glows and lightens in Faust's hand.

It is difficult to describe the mystery and greatness that surrounds these mythological figures, but here it is not a matter of conveying poetical values. They symbolize the primeval beginnings of life, and everything living returns to them. They too, like granite, are beyond life and death; they are beyond conflicts; everything that exists finds its place in their vicinity. That they are not beyond the erotic sphere is indicated by the symbolism of the key that grows in Faust's hand and leads to them. I believe they are not only called The Mothers, but they *are* the mothers, the mothers of an early time that, in individual development, can also be called primeval. Freud has called that period the preoedipal one. Mother alone existed for the child at that time; father, if perceived separately at all, was nothing but an intruder. I believe that Goethe's conception of the granite and his creation of The Mothers both go back to experiences pertaining to the preoedipal phase, which is viewed in both instances as a conflict-free resting in mother.[72] It is in keeping with fantasies about this early phase, as well as with early modes of experience, that it is pictured as timeless and not subject to change.

The preoedipal phase is one of great importance in the development of both sexes. Fear of the preoedipal mother may lead to the severest forms of psychopathology. The harmony expressed in Goethe's essay on granite, whose "dignity" he helped to establish, is, I believe, the expression of an incredible pacification and elimination of conflicts that had taken place during the ten years since he wrote that passage in *Werther,* which in its place must be interpreted as the image of the devouring and destroying preoedipal mother. The image of The Mothers in *Faust* shows that the psychological gain had been preserved far into old age. These extraordinary mythological figures were not conceived until Goethe was seventy-two years old, and probably not before he was even older than that (see

[71] [Der Schlüssel wird die rechte Stelle wittern.]

[72] Marie Bonaparte has shown in Edgar Allan Poe's work instances of the identity of mother and landscape. See 59, p. 253.

425, p. 642). Thus we may say that The Mothers already stood in the shadow of death, which rendered them for Goethe less sublime than granite, and all the more uncanny, yet left them free of any taint of cruelty, so conspicuous in Werther's way of experiencing nature.

If the hypothesis is accepted that at that time granite was for Goethe a symbolic representation of the preoedipal mother, Goethe's Ilmenau speech will also appear in a different light. I have not been able, however, to decide among several alternatives. Did the fantasy regarding mining pertain to a striving towards greater closeness to the primeval mother by digging into the ground, or did it symbolize a direct attack against the primeval mother? Or was the fantasy related to a later mother (the oedipal mother equated with rock formations of a younger date), who was vulnerable in contrast to a preoedipal mother? On the basis of pure specu-lation one would think of the following series: the invulnerability and neu-trality of the preoedipal mother is assured, as expressed in the essay "On Granite"; then there follows the actual attack against the oedipal and vulnerable mother by symbolic piercing of the earth's surface; when the death of the infant Princess threatened to actuate the conflict, activity was spurred to its maximum and with one genius stroke Goethe wrenched a secret from nature and reestablished man's belonging to mother nature by proving the structural unity of organism and nonorganism.

In order to find what triggered this series of reactions it is necessary to go still a step back. In December of 1783 he had, as so often in December, a depressionlike condition, less severe this time than the year before. On December 6 he canceled an evening party and wrote to Charlotte von Stein: "For if I cannot be with you I want to be alone."[73] On the following day—it would have been Cornelia's thirty-third birthday—he wrote a long letter to his mother. It was a reply to one she had written to him (which is not preserved) expressing alarm precipitated by news conveyed to her by a mutual acquaintance. From a previous letter to Goethe (June 17, 1781, 340, *1*:96) it is evident that she felt guilty whenever news of him reached her that did not sound wholly favorable. Believing that Goethe had left Frankfurt because he was discontented in his paternal home, she apparently felt responsible for any harm that he might suffer in Weimar and offered him her home as a refuge. From Goethe's reply one can make a probable reconstruction of what kind of gossip reached his mother this time. "You have never known me with thick head and belly," he wrote,

[73] [Denn wenn ich nicht mit dir seyn kann will ich allein seyn.]

and it is natural that one should become serious over serious things, particularly if one is pensive by nature and wants the good and the right in the world.[74]

Then he reminded her of the bad winter of 1769 when she had given up hope of ever seeing her son recovered and went to the Bible for an oracle. Had she known then how it would be in 1783 she would have rejoiced.

> Let us therefore accept these years nicely as a gift, as we have to regard our whole life in general, and acknowledge gratefully each year that is added.[75]

He went on to enumerate all the favorable points of his existence in Weimar. In a rather peremptory way he proceeded to advise her:

> Do you, for your part, take joy now in my existence, and also if I should go out of the world before you. I have not lived as a disgrace to you; I leave behind good friends and a good name, and that can be the best consolation for you that I do not totally die.

> In the meantime live quietly; perhaps destiny will give us still a graceful old age together which we should then also want to live out with gratitude.[76]

These words sound strange after the preceding encomium of his life in Weimar. Although in the eighteenth century man did not feel as well protected against illness as at present, I doubt that these lines were written out of a realistic appraisal of statistical chances for survival. It would be of interest to know what Goethe thought the average life expectancy in his time was. Be this as it may, he must have been under the temporary impact of a presentiment of death, for at first he speaks hypothetically of his death, but later as if it were certain he would die before his mother. The reference to what he will leave behind implies the question of progeny. Therefore it is not surprising that he informed his mother on this occasion that Fritz was living with him.

---

[74] [Sie haben mich nie mit dickem Kopf und Bauche gekannt, und dass man von ernsthafften Sachen ernsthafft wird, ist auch natürlich, besonders wenn man von Natur nachdencklich ist, und das Gute und Rechte in der Welt will.]

[75] [Lassen Sie uns hübsch diese Jahre daher als Geschenck annehmen, wie wir überhaupt unser ganzes Leben anzusehen haben und iedes Jahr das zugelegt wird mit Danck erkennen.]

[76] [Sie an Ihrer Seite vergnügen Sie Sich an meinem Daseyn ietzt und wenn ich auch vor Ihnen aus der Welt gehen sollte. Ich habe Ihnen nicht zur Schande gelebt, hinterlasse gute Freunde und einen guten Nahmen, und so kann es Ihnen der beste Trost seyn dass ich nicht ganz sterbe.

Indessen leben Sie ruhig, vielleicht giebt uns das Schicksal noch ein anmutiges Alter zusammen das wir denn auch mit Danck ausleben wollen.]

I do not know whether you have already been written[77] that I have with me the son of the Ducal Equerry [in the feminine gender] von Stein, my most worthy [lady] friend. He is a thoroughly good and beautiful child of ten years who provides me with many good hours and cheers my quietness and seriousness.[78]

Goethe refers in this letter to an event of the winter of 1768-1769, but I am not certain that he was aware that the day on which he wrote about it to his mother was exactly the fifteenth anniversary of it. It happened on December 7, 1768, that Goethe's sickness following his return from Leipzig reached its climax in the form of a severe colic and his family thought he would die. His mother in her despair consulted the Bible and the result of her bibliomancy was the auspicious verse of Jeremiah 31:5: "Thou shalt yet plant vines upon the mountains of Samaria: the planters shall plant, and shall eat them as common things." This passage from Scripture not only restored the courage and confidence of the despairing mother but also gave her the certitude of a heavenly pronouncement that her son was chosen for great things in the future. However, not only was the mother who consulted the oracle deeply impressed but so also was the son who was the object of the prophecy. On December 9, 1777, during the journey that took him to Plessing, at a time when his sister's recent death was still acutely on his mind, he wrote Charlotte von Stein:

It is just around this time, nine years ago, a few days more or less, that I was sick to death; my mother opened her Bible in the greatest distress of heart and found, as she has told me since: "One will again plant vines upon the mountains of Samaria, one will plant and pipe thereto." She found solace for the moment and some joy, as time passed, in the saying.

You see what stuff comes jumbled up to my mind.[79]

In 1777 the event apparently was recalled by Goethe in greater detail, although at that time too he misquoted the scripture as he did in 1783 when writing to his mother. In 1777, as the whole tone of the letter shows, he

[77] Goethe means by others, particularly his servant Seidel, who kept up a correspondence with his master's mother.

[78] [Ich weis nicht ob Ihnen schon geschrieben ist dass ich den Sohn der Oberstallmeister von Stein, meiner werthesten Freundin, bey mir habe, ein gar gutes schönes Kind von 10 Jahren, der mir viel gute Stunden macht und meine Stille und Ernst erheitert.]

[79] [Es ist eben um die Zeit, wenig Tage auf ab, dass ich vor neun Jahren kranck zum Todte war, meine Mutter schlug damals in der äusersten Noth ihres Herzens ihre Bibel auf und fand, wie sie mir nachher erzählt hat: "Man wird wiederum Weinberge pflanzen an den Bergen Samariä, pflanzen wird man und dazu pfeifen." Sie fand für den Augenblick Trost, und in der Folge manche Freude an dem Spruche.

Sie sehn was für Zeug mir durcheinander einfällt.]

was engulfed by a deep emotional experience (cf. p. 296) which it was difficult for him to master, whereas now in 1783 he uses the recollection of the same event as a means by which to comfort his mother. In order to understand subsequent events, it is important to know what the nature of Goethe's disease of December 7, 1768, was. In reality he was not close to death at all. When his physician dispensed an arcanum, which probably was nothing but a laxative, he recovered. The sudden aggravation of his condition on his sister's birthday and the ready subsidence after a bowel movement make the interpretation of fantasies of pregnancy and birth inescapable.[80] At that time there was strongly activated and expressed in the variety of physical symptoms the trifold problem: death, birth, and jealousy. This time, in 1784, the symptoms did not go beyond the usual indispositions that made him stay at home but did not make work impossible. Those about him must have noticed his depression. Thus Wieland wrote to Merck (January 5, 1784) that Goethe adapted himself well to everything, but

> suffers all too visibly in soul and body under the pressing burden with which he has loaded himself in our best [behalf]. It sometimes makes my heart ache to see how he withal keeps his equanimity and lets the woe like a hidden worm gnaw at his insides. He spares his health as much as possible, which also is much in need of it.[81]

The presence of a depression in Goethe without his being fully aware of it, or without the full reaction to it to which the ego would be entitled, is important. From his letter to his mother one may conclude that there was the idea that, just as his father and Cornelia had had to, he also would die before his mother; he wrote his mother rather like a husband than like a son. In 1768 the identification was, at least somatically, with the pregnant mother, as manifested by the constipation. When the mother wrote in 1783 that she had heard he had a "thick belly" (whatever she may have meant by it) this probably set a series of associations into motion. But the result this time was the claim that plenty had accumulated to be forwarded to posterity and that he and his mother might happily spend

---

[80] In order to find the reasons for Goethe's particularly severe regression in December, 1768, the failure of his first great love in Leipzig and his reality situation at home after his return have to be considered.

[81] [(Goethe) leidet aber nur allzu sichtlich an Seel' und Leib unter der drückenden Last, die er sich zu unserm Besten aufgeladen hat. Mir tut's zuweilen in Herzen weh zu sehen, wie er bei Dem allen *contenance* hält und den Gram gleich einem verborgenen Wurm an seinem Inwendigen nagen lässt. Seine Gesundheit schont er so viel wie möglich; auch hat sie es sehr vonnöten.] (51, *1*:312)

their years of old age together. Goethe's letter to his mother can easily be put into a meaningful connection with the subsequent steps, which have already been discussed, namely, the paper on granite, the parapraxia in Ilmenau, and the discovery of the intermaxillary bone.

From January, 1784, on, a correspondence developed between Goethe's mother and Fritz. Fritz's first letter was presumably written at Goethe's suggestion. Goethe's mother used this opportunity wisely and asked the boy to keep a diary recording the most important events in Goethe's life. The boy responded faithfully and sent her a monthly diary. It seems that she understood the unconscious meaning of Goethe's gesture. The boy should really serve as a child whose parents were supposed to be Goethe's mother and Goethe. Since Goethe surprised his mother suddenly with a grown-up boy living in his house it looks as if Goethe's was supposed to have been the childbearing part in the liaison. Thus, at last, the infantile wish was fulfilled in terms of a human symbol and the mother intuitively complied with Goethe's unconscious ideation.

During the period with which we are concerned in this part, expressions of the highest love and complete surrender to Charlotte von Stein again occurred, expressions of being incapable of living without her. During June and part of July he had to get along without her since governmental duties took him away from Weimar. On June 24, 1784, he wrote to her:

> Before I go to bed, still only one word instead of a thousand. It becomes such an unconquerable need for me to see you that I fear once again for my head. I do not know what will become of me. Good night. How much do I feel the bliss of sleep.[82]

And the next day:

> Today I have quite seriously turned over in my mind whether I should not hurry to you for a moment. It cannot be and cannot be. I have to summon up [all] my patience.[83]

And on June 28, 1784:

> Now it will soon be time, dear Lotte, that I come again near to where you are, for my being no longer holds together; I feel quite distinctly that I

[82] [Nur noch eh ich zu Bette gehe ein Wort für tausend. Es wird mir so ein unüberwindlich Bedürfniss dich zu sehen dass mir wieder einmal für meinen Kopf bange wird. Ich weis nicht was aus mir werden soll. Gute Nacht. Wie sehr fühle ich die Glückseeligkeit des Schlafs.]

[83] [Heute hab ich recht im Ernste überlegt ob ich nicht auf einen Augenblick zu dir eilen soll. Es geht nicht und geht nicht, ich muss meine Geduld zusammen nehmen.]

cannot abide without you. . . . Yes, dear Lotte, only now does it become clear how you are and remain a half of myself. I am no single, no autonomous being. I have leaned [with] all my weaknesses upon you, have protected my soft flanks through you, have filled up my breaches through you. When once I am away from you my condition becomes most strange. On the one side I am armed and steeled, on the other like a raw egg because I have neglected to harness myself where you are shield and shelter. How glad I am to belong wholly to you and to see you again very soon.

Everything in you I love and everything makes me love you more.[84]

Then he praises the beloved woman for her zeal in administering her country estate, of which her husband kept him informed. It makes him perceive her "active soul." "Lotte, stay with me, and whatever else may interest you, love me above everything."[85]

Goethe here faced a dilemma. He recognized the need to be with Charlotte von Stein in order to function in certain areas, but felt simultaneously the weakness implicit in depending on her for the help she gave him. What is heralded as a source of strength is simultaneously lamented as a potential source of infirmity. The ego is recognized as divided into an invulnerable part and a part most liable to be harmed unless protected by her presence. This double effect of the love-object upon the development of his personality was not due to accidental circumstances, and Goethe felt the one effect was mutually dependent on the other. He found himself here in a situation comparable to that of many patients undergoing psychoanalytic treatment. They may have succeeded in conquering difficult areas of their dealings with reality and feel quite strong and firmly rooted in these reality pursuits, but they also feel, partly with pain, partly with enjoyment, as if a portion of their existence were completely bound up with the vicissitudes of the psychoanalytic process or, more specifically, with the analyst. Sometimes at the height of a most sensitive and intense relationship to the analyst, when, in the treatment situation, all the freshness and

---

[84] [Nun wird es balde Zeit liebe Lotte dass ich wieder in deine Nähe komme denn mein Wesen hält nicht mehr zusammen, ich fühle recht deutlich dass ich nicht ohne dich bestehen kann. . . . Ja liebe Lotte ietzt wird es mir erst deutlich wie du meine eigne Hälfte bist und bleibst. Ich bin kein einzelnes kein selbstständiges Wesen. Alle meine Schwächen habe ich an dich angelehnt, meine weichen Seiten durch dich beschützt, meine Lücken durch dich ausgefüllt. Wenn ich nun entfernt von dir bin so wird mein Zustand höchst seltsam. Auf einer Seite bin ich gewaffnet und gestählt, auf der andern wie ein rohes Ey, weil ich da versäumt habe mich zu Harnischen wo du mir Schild und Schirm bist. Wie freue ich mich dir ganz anzugehören. Und dich nächstens wieder zu sehen.

Alles lieb' ich an dir und alles macht mich dich mehr lieben.]

[85] [Lotte bleibe mir und was dich auch interessiren mag, liebe mich über alles.]

longing and trust of the child's early hunger for affection and object love, uninhibited as it was before later disappointments and frustrations, resurge, the patient is able to accomplish considerable achievements in the world of his social reality. Needless to say, the analysis of transference provides the solution to this dilemma. The analyst, being exclusively concerned with the patient's welfare and pursuing no other goal, yields, in the form of interpretations, the understanding the patient needs in order to free himself from the transference relationship. But Charlotte von Stein could not provide this understanding, not only because neither she nor anyone else possessed it at that time, but also because she, of course, took Goethe as an integral part of her own life and inevitably expected selfish gratifications from him. Many a patient would gladly forgo most of his achievements in reality in exchange for the gratifications he wishes to obtain in the treatment situation. It is most difficult to speculate whether this would have been true of Goethe in his equivalent situation, and how he would have reacted if marriage to Charlotte von Stein had become possible, or if sexual gratifications had become available in his relationship with the beloved woman.

Although the sexual demand apparently did disquiet Goethe increasingly, the emphasis in Goethe's request to the love-object was put on "make me strong." Much as such remarks seem to be repetitious from previous years, one feels a different spirit behind them. Previously, while it was recognized that, despite all changes, the ego remained vulnerable in the area that was directly related to the love-object, the hope existed that this weakness too would be turned into a strength as time went on; now the idea dawned that this process was not to be achieved by any impact that the love-object itself could have on the loving subject. This insight must necessarily have led to the idea that action born out of the subject without direct relationship to the love-object was required. Goethe needed an identification with another figure in this particular situation if he was ever to become capable of mobilizing the energy necessary to convert the vulnerable part of his personality also into one shielded like the rest. (In analytic terminology, he was now struggling to find a means of overcoming his transference.)

Actually one finds a passage that indicates that such identifications, no doubt formed in earlier years, did become activated. On June 24, 1784, the very day on which he had expressed great concern for his equilibrium, he wrote to his friend the composer Kayser,[86] who was in Italy:

[86] Phillip Christoph Kayser, musician and composer, born 1755 in Frankfurt, died 1823 in Zürich; a friend of Goethe's from his Frankfurt days.

Your letters and remarks give me much pleasure and I find cause to envy you in that you are setting foot upon and wandering through the country that I, like a sinful prophet, see before me only in darkling distance.[87]

This refers to Moses, who was permitted only to see the land of Canaan but not to set foot upon its soil. Now what did this sudden comparison of himself with Moses mean?[88] What was the sin that prevented him from setting foot upon the soil of Italy? Moses' supreme goal, indeed the mission of his life, was to reach Canaan with his flock. Did Goethe have, and had he so long entertained, just such a passionate, dedicated determination, on the personal plane, to come at last to Italy, as Moses had on the social plane to reach the land of Canaan? Then why, one asks, did it not appear more often in his letters to Charlotte von Stein? Up to then—if the letters convey a just impression of what were the main topics of discourse between them, and if she still remembered what was in them— Charlotte von Stein knew only that he had written her for a map of Italy (November 26, 1783).[89] A little later (on December 14, 1783), he made a playful remark: "This evening I am coming to you; we mean to go together into distant countries; and together to be happy everywhere."[90] This was meant as a pleasantry since at that time they were reading books of travel together (see 107, *1*:205). Had she known of psychoanalysis, she would perhaps have had her suspicions aroused by an exaggerated remark he made in his letter of November 7, 1782, namely, that on the map of the whole world there was no place designated where he would not think of her with love and faithfulness.

In view of subsequent occurrences the question may be raised as to when the idea of a journey to Italy first took on concrete form in Goethe. Did it dawn on him when he asked for the map of Italy, or was the pleasantry of December 14 perhaps the ambiguous expression of a fantasy of leaving Weimar with Charlotte von Stein and spending the rest of his life abroad with her and Fritz? Such ideas occasionally occurred earlier but rather in the form: "How nice it would be if . . . , but I know it is impossible." Around that time (December 8, 1783?) also he probably wrote the remark:

[87] [Ihre Briefe und Bemerckungen machen mir viel Vergnügen und ich finde Ursache Sie zu beneiden dass Sie das Land betreten und durchwandern das ich wie ein sündiger Prophete nur in dämmernder Ferne vor mir liegen sehe.]

[88] For the role of Moses in Goethe's life see 76. For a psychoanalytic explanation of that influence see 364.

[89] This letter is undated and I follow the editors of the *Sophienausgabe* in assigning this date to it.

[90] [Diesen Abend komme ich zu dir, wir wollen zusammen in ferne Länder gehn; und zusammen überall glücklich seyn.]

How good it is that man knows nothing in advance. Not to see you for two whole days would have been unbearable for me yesterday morning.[91]

This remark too makes one wonder in the light of later events.

Another feature related to a general psychology of love becomes noticeable in this period. Charlotte von Stein became for him no longer only a live presence, but also part of the past, that is to say, their relationship became historically structured. Thus he wrote to her on September 6, 1784, from a journey:

How close to me your love is I am not to say. I also wrote you from here seven years ago. Little by little I come again always to where I have thought of you and had converse with you before.[92]

In one such "historical" reminiscence there is an implied reproach. When Goethe was in Ilmenau he recalled a little scene that had occurred eight years before. He referred to it in his letter of February 23, 1784, and later incorporated it in his revised edition of *Werther* (see 44) in the following way. Lotte behaves in a seductive way by having a canary peck first at her lips and then at Werther's, whose reaction is as follows:

She ought not to do it! ought not to arouse my imagination with these images of divine innocence and bliss and ought not to wake my heart from the sleep in which it is sometimes rocked by the indifference of life!—And why not? She trusts me so! She knows how I love her![93]

The discord between Goethe and Charlotte von Stein over the passionateness of his behavior had apparently disappeared from their relationship for a long time, and Goethe had acquired control over his passion in the presence of the beloved woman. But when he sat in that parlor in Ilmenau he recalled how seductively she had behaved at that time. That Goethe selected from among the many alternatives eligible to be incorporated in *Werther* this little episode, suggests many implications, foremost a reproach. Since Charlotte von Stein was not, like the first Lotte, innocent, it amounted almost to saying: "Lotte destroyed Werther by inadvertence; but you should have been wiser and should not have risked that what had been fantasy might become reality by inciting me beyond

[91] [Was doch gut ist dass der Mensch nichts voraus weis. Dich zwey ganzer Tage nicht zu sehen, wäre mir gestern früh unerträglich gewesen.]

[92] [Wie deine Liebe mir nah ist mag ich nicht sagen. Vor sieben Jahren schrieb ich dir auch von hier. Nach und nach komm ich immer wieder dahin wo ich schon deiner gedacht mich mit dir unterhalten hatte.]

[93] [Sie sollte es nicht thun! sollte nicht meine Einbildungskraft mit diesen Bildern himmlischer Unschuld und Seligkeit reizen und mein Herz aus dem Schlafe, in den es manchmal die Gleichgültigkeit des Lebens wiegt, nicht wecken!—Und warum nicht?— Sie traut mir so! sie weiss, wie ich sie liebe!] (*Soph.* I, 19:121)

necessity." It may be recalled that Goethe complained shortly after (letter of May 6, 1784; cf. above, p. 847) about Charlotte von Stein's arousing him unnecessarily.

Thus his relationship to Charlotte von Stein came to assume a historical structure, which, as it implied a beginning and a development, thus also implied an end. The feeling of acute and supreme love transcends, I think, the usual bonds of time, through which the experience of events is constantly structured. In a state of extreme love the present is over and over again experienced as so overwhelmingly new and surprising and incapable of being compared to anything that happened in the past or that can be expected to be experienced in the future, that past and future are overshadowed by the present, and therefore become degraded to negligible appendages of the dimension of present. I think similar observations can be made in the case of the way time is experienced by the religious person when worshipping God. The absolute unchangeability of God, his being beyond the past and the future but always present, as conceived by the religious person, constitutes one of the factors that tie the faithful to the image of God. The fact that Goethe could look at his relationship with the love-object somewhat in a historical way may indicate that he had obtained increased distance from her, could extricate himself enough to be able to adopt the position of a quasi-outsider looking back and viewing that by which he had previously felt himself to be completely surrounded.

This was a further step in the development that had started with his apologizing for repeating himself in the expression of his love. We find an even stronger statement of the same kind in a letter of this period too. It dates from the time when he was in Eisenach, where, as mentioned before, he suffered with particular intensity from their separation. "I have not had a cheerful impression yet since I came here," he wrote on June 14, 1784,

> and I shall have one [lit. it will become one for me] again only at the sight of you, you sweet sum total of my destiny.
>
> Even when I intend not to regale you with my monotonous passion, nevertheless it flows against my will from the pen.[94]

Here his love is called monotonous as if it had become a compulsion and was lacking in those glowing ever-changing colors that make the "I love you" of yesterday stale, but the "I love you" of today the sweetest and most

[94] [Noch habe ich keine fröhliche Empfindung gehabt seit ich hier bin und sie wird mir auch erst bey deinem Anblick wieder werden du lieber Innbegriff meines Schicksals.

Wenn ich mir auch vornehme dich nicht mit meiner monotonen Leidenschafft zu unterhalten; so fliest es mir widerwillen aus der Feder.]

original word that could be said. It was on that day, by the way, that he was so delighted at making the Prince laugh heartily, as mentioned before (see p. 846). The letter closed with: "Fritz has written to my mother and he advises me very strongly to visit her; he cannot comprehend that I have so much to do."[95] But I guess it was not only the boy who could not understand it; there were many others, including Goethe himself. Was it not of his mother that he knew that no monotony could ever exist between them? Was Charlotte von Stein made the sum total of his destiny as a necessary barrier against the temptation to regress to a closeness with his mother that it was an absolute necessity for him to overcome? Was he letting Fritz enjoy a pleasure that he had to deny to himself, and was he indirectly pleading with Charlotte von Stein to put up with this exchange?

The poetic work of this period that is known to have grown out of Goethe's relationship with Charlotte von Stein was "The Secrets" (*Die Geheimnisse*), which was started at this time, and the major part of it written, but never finished. Goethe's lyric inspiration devoted to Charlotte von Stein had apparently dried up for quite a while. His main creative momentum was turned towards *Wilhelm Meister,* a novel. A few most touching poems did get written in conjunction with the novel, and, although they perhaps still referred indirectly to Charlotte von Stein, it is important to note that his feelings for her no longer led to those sublime spontaneous lyric outbursts of the greatest poetry. This is perhaps the strongest indication of the extent to which the whole relationship had been removed from the level of the primary process to that of the secondary. Consequently the unconscious no longer made inroads that the ego seized with wild and beautiful verses.

With regard to "The Secrets," a certain strain, a need to force himself, was already revealed in the earliest reference to the whole undertaking in a letter to Charlotte von Stein, which was found only recently (see 545). There we read (July 24, 1784):

> When [or if?] I start the poem it comes about only for your sake. Much as I am known to you, and nothing in my whole being is new to you, I nevertheless hope some passages should be unexpected for you.[96]

Understandably, producing an extended poem on the basis of such a motivation was bound to become drudgery.

---

[95] [Fritz hat an meine Mutter geschrieben, und er räth mir gar sehr an sie zu besuchen er kann nicht begreifen dass ich so viel zu thun habe.]

[96] [Wenn ich das Gedicht anfange so geschieht es nur um deinetwillen; so sehr ich dir bekannt bin und an meinem ganzen Wesen dir nichts neues ist; so hoffe ich doch, es sollen Stellen dir unerwartet seyn.] (545, p. 221)

In March, 1785, he had the intention of writing two stanzas daily in order to get ahead with the work, but he did not succeed in adhering to this plan for long (see 261, Part I, *1:55*, n. 1). The work in its present form consists of two parts, which originally were united into one: The first, called "Dedication" (*Zueignung*) consisted of fourteen stanzas, and from 1815 on served to introduce Goethe's complete works and thus has obtained a prominent place; the second, "The Secrets" proper, consists of twenty-five stanzas in its present unfinished form. Three stanzas originally written for "The Secrets" were later dropped.

Before presenting the background material upon which conclusions regarding the unconscious meaning of the epic poem may be based, I wish briefly to outline its content.

As the poet hurries up a mountain on a brilliant morning, suddenly mist rises out of which a godlike woman approaches him. He recognizes in her the one for whom he was already longing as a boy and who assuaged the injuries life inflicted upon him. She gave quietness when he was shaken by passions and it is she through whom alone he wants to have happiness. Many are they who think to possess her. But they err as he did when he had many friends. Now he really knows her, but he is alone and must enjoy his happiness in solitude. The woman reprimands him mildly. She was right not to reveal herself to him, for he believed himself to be a superman as soon as he had outgrown his childhood days. Why has he neglected his manly duties? How different does he think he is from others? He should know himself and live at peace with the world. The poet asks her forgiveness; from now on he will acknowledge the full value of her gifts and he will tread the path with his brethren. The divine woman forgives him and the poet feels new joys arise. The mists vanish and he can again see valley and sky. Now the woman gives him a veil, which has been destined for him for a long time. The fortunate person who takes this gift with quietness in his soul can want for nothing. It is the veil of poetry received from the hand of truth. With it he can banish life's anxious suspense, the grave becomes a bed of clouds and the crises of life are pacified. The poem ends with the poet's appeal to his brethren. They go united towards the next day when the burden of life becomes oppressive:

> So we live, so wander we in bliss.
> And then also shall when our descendants mourn us,
> To their pleasure still our love endure.[97]

[97] [So leben wir, so wandeln wir beglückt./ Und dann auch soll, wenn Enkel um uns trauern,/ Zu ihrer Lust noch unsre Liebe dauern.] (Lines 110–12)

The godlike woman whom the poet, as he says, does not want to call by her name, is evidently his Muse, that is to say, Charlotte von Stein. Again he projects her influence, this time as a kind of guardian angel, into the past. Into this simple plot he wove thoughts about his own development and compared the *Sturm und Drang* period with the present, when poetry was not only to serve the expression of internal processes but also to contain truth, that is to say, the correct representation of reality in the poetic form becomes an integral part of his art.

On the surface, the "Dedication" appears to be an unambivalent expression serving to glorify Charlotte von Stein. How could he give her more praise than by equating her with his Muse? Indirectly Goethe here came back to thoughts expressed earlier, namely, that he had known her already in his childhood and that she had accompanied him through his whole life. The idea is restated that everything he was and is he owes to her. The fact of his isolation, however, the overcoming of which he describes in the poem as a task imposed by his Muse, appears biographically in a different light. By having the Muse speak like this, does he not suggest to Charlotte von Stein that she should give him freedom, that isolation had become unbearable to him and that he expects her to ease his struggle to accomplish real independence? "You have neglected to fulfill the manly duties"[98] sounds particularly ambiguous in this context and he may have been unconsciously referring to his bachelorhood.

But consciously Goethe complained at that time about a different kind of isolation. He wrote on August 13, 1784, to Charlotte von Stein: "I can assure you that outside of you, Herder, and Knebel I have now no audience whatsoever." [99] On August 22, 1784, in the artificial medium of the French language, he wrote to her:

> You have isolated me in the world. I have absolutely nothing to say to anyone soever. I speak only in order not to be silent and that's all.[100]

Interestingly enough, he added this to an otherwise finished letter so as not to send it, as he explains, with a blank page, for this would not have been adequate to the richness of his love. I have earlier described the constructive aspect of isolation in this period; now Goethe puts the harmful effect into the foreground. The poem that seemingly glorifies the love-object expresses by implication a grave accusation. Goethe seems to have

[98] [Versäumst die Pflicht des Mannes zu erfüllen!]

[99] [Ich kann dir versichern dass ausser dir Herders und Knebeln ich ietzt gar kein Publikum habe.]

[100] [Tu m'as isolé dans le monde je n'ai absolument rien a dire a qui que ce soit, je parle pour ne pas me taire et c'est tout.]

felt that, as long as he was so close to the love-object, he could not break through the isolation.

Again in French he wrote on August 30, 1784:

No, my love for you is not any more a passion, it is a disease, a disease which is more precious to me than the most perfect health and from which I do not want to recover.[101]

And then he wrote of his great poem, which was of such help when he was away from her. He was right. This love for her was a disease. It was almost identical with the transference neurosis that develops within the relationship of a patient to his analyst. His symptoms had taken a turn for the better. The depressions were milder; the capacity to work was inexhaustible; he pursued his literary work, the writing of the novel, consistently over the years, and each year added a new book to the manuscript. This devotion to a literary task over many years was certainly a new accomplishment in Goethe's life. But just as a patient does not want to move out of the orbit of the transference relationship, so Goethe also did not want to put an end to his disease, which was identical with his love for Charlotte von Stein. The fear as to whether he would be capable of continuing his new style of life without the protection of the love-object was still too great. The horror of the pain involved in tearing himself away from the beloved woman still seemed unbearable, quite aside from the feelings of guilt and self-reproach at the idea of abandoning the one to whom he owed so much. The poem must therefore be understood as an indirect plea that his great and understanding friend might be wise enough to act like a true Muse, who has nothing but the poet's welfare, that is to say, his creative potential, in her heart and dismiss him from the isolation that had built itself around him.

The manifest content of the poem is truly the greatest praise a poet could give to his love. And Charlotte von Stein could truly be proud. Despite the moderation of its language—all wildness and tempestuous outbreaks were banished—the devotion to form that gives every line its beauty was not pursued in such a way as to neglect other poetical values; and except for one printing of his works in 1808 (out of a lingering resentment against her?), this poem introduced the various editions of Goethe's complete works. Thus he indirectly let it be known what he owed her forever.

If now behind this manifest content there is discovered the foreshad-

---

[101] [Non mon amour pour toi n'est plus une passion c'est une maladie, une maladie qui m'est plus chere que la santé la plus parfaite, et dont je ne veux pas guerir.]

owing of an attempt at dissolving this tie, ought this attempt to be called an expression of ambivalence? I doubt it, at least at this stage. Here the demand was raised in the service of the superego, the reason given being to preserve artistic integrity. Apparently the pleasure principle would have been well served at least in part by maintaining the status quo. At this stage the wish was to part in love and gratitude at the request of the beloved woman. She too should apply the same sublime renunciation that he had learned from her in tormenting struggle and that had become integrated by him so intensely that it would never leave him again. A trace of ambivalence may perhaps be found in the fact that he sent the beginning of the poem, apparently the "Dedication"[102]—or so much of it as he produced at the first start—to the Herders, asking them to forward it to Charlotte von Stein. However, the sending of the piece to the Herders may also be read as a kind of publication, an act that made it a *poem* primarily, rather than first a communication, then a poem. So understood, it is a vivid and definite, albeit tiny, assertion of the primacy of his creative life over his love-relationship. Since it was destined to glorify Charlotte von Stein it ought rightly to have been sent to her first. As probably happened with the letters announcing the discovery of the intermaxillary bone, the first letter of the two which announced that a new poem was in the making was again written to Herder. This time there is no doubt, since the letter to the Herders carries the mark of "Sunday, August 8, 1784, evening, half past nine o'clock" and the one to Charlotte von Stein "evening, ten o'clock." The first sentence to Charlotte von Stein also shows to what extent the homosexual competition has grown: "Instead of repeating to you so often that I love you I am sending you through the Herders something that I have toiled over for you today."[103]

In the same letter he wrote further on:

> In order to occupy myself and to turn my restless thoughts away from you I have begun the promised poem. I send it to the Herders; you will receive it from them.[104]

His beginning to write the poem was precipitated by his carriage's breaking down while he was on a trip. This use of the involuntary stop-

---

[102] It is not quite clear whether the "Dedication" or "The Secrets" was meant.

[103] [Anstatt dir so offt zu wiederhohlen dass ich dich liebe schicke ich dir durch Herders etwas das ich heute für euch gearbeitet habe.]

The "you" (*euch*) is plural, meaning Charlotte von Stein and the Herders.

[104] [Um mich zu beschäfftigen und meine unruhigen Gedancken von dir abzuwenden habe ich den Anfang des versprochnen Gedichtes gemacht, ich schicke es an Herders von denen erhältst du es.]

page as an occasion for writing poetry is comparable to the situation mentioned earlier when he was delayed on his return from the trip on which he had accompanied Klopstock. Then too the energy dammed up by the stopped locomotion was discharged in writing poetry. In the case of Klopstock what was involved was liberation from a father-figure. This parallel may favor my interpretation that the "Dedication" was also a request for freedom.

The main poem, "The Secrets," impresses me as not contradicting my interpretation of the "Dedication." In "The Secrets" (*Soph.* I, *16*:169–83) there are many symbolic passages that have not yet been sufficiently explained (see 13), but that need not concern us in this context.

The plot is as follows: Brother Markus, while wandering through difficult countryside, unexpectedly comes upon a magnificent building. He is received with hospitality and announces to his hosts that he has been sent "by the order of higher beings." Twelve knights dwell there under the leadership of a thirteenth, called Humanus, "the saint, the sage, the best man my eyes have seen."[105] There is a connection between Markus's arrival and the impending departure of the leader. Markus learns the goal of this community and the story of Humanus. The unfinished poem breaks off with an account of a nightly vision of three youths carrying torches. The underlying general idea[106] apparently was to discuss various religions or religious aspects as represented by the twelve knightly monks and to show that each of them represented an individual ideal that was valid in its own right. Each of the knights was also to report his own experiences with Humanus. The reason for Humanus's leaving is not indicated either in the fragment or in Goethe's commentary. It is only evident that the general plan of the poem called for Markus's taking over Humanus's place.

Returning now to the biographical context within which the poem was planned and written, I should emphasize the theme of one man arriving in a well-organized, tightly knit group and another man leaving it. I surmise that the two events, which, viewed under the aspect of Goethe's biography, were ten years apart, are drawn into one in the poem and assigned to two different personages. Markus and Humanus may both be viewed as idealized pictures of Goethe himself, the one as he was when he arrived in Weimar and the other as it was thought he would be at his

---

[105] [Humanus heisst der Heilige, der Weise,/ Der beste Mann, den ich mit Augen sah.] (Lines 245–46)

[106] See Goethe's own commentary, *Die Geheimnisse, Soph.* I, *41*:100–05; see also 530, 2:183–94; 13.

anticipated departure, sketching the enormous distance he had covered in his personality development during that span. Of course, he was not quite as innocent and naive at his arrival in Weimar as Markus, and not quite as ideally serene as Humanus as he visualized him at the time of his anticipated departure, but the two modes of Goethe's appearance may be approximately likened to Markus and Humanus.[107]

A few stanzas of the poem are devoted to Humanus's biography, and the type of life history assigned to him is worth noting. Some elements are taken from Christian, others from ancient, mythology: a spirit announced him to his mother; a star shone brighter at his christening; a vulture mingled peacefully with pigeons; as a child he choked to death an adder that threatened his sister's life when the nurse ran away in fright; a spring widening into a rivulet sprang from the dry rock at the command of his sword.[108] When man is favored by nature, he of course accomplishes much. But what makes Humanus an object of just praise is that he conquered himself, thus freeing himself from all those forces that narrow down man's freedom. He served his father's harsh commands as faithfully as an orphan might have done who was in need of a reward. He did menial services and obeyed the orders of all older people when he served in the army. He nursed the wounded and everyone loved him for his imperturbable cheerfulness "and only his father seemed not to esteem him."[109] Yet Humanus bore the burden of parental discipline with ease; obedience was the alpha and omega of his regimen. As other boys are motivated by pleasure, or youth by honor, so was he driven only by the will of others.[110] In vain did his father invent new tests; he always had to praise the lad. At last, however, the father too admitted the son's excellence and acknowledged his rights as an adult.

It is surprising that Goethe makes the father conflict, and Humanus's behavior within its scope, the hub of his life story, as if complete and uncompromising submission to a father's demands determined a particular disposition towards later saintliness. It is the more impressive because Goethe's personality was so different from this type and he submitted so rarely to his father's demands. In view of this difference we may assume

[107] I do not wish to claim that Goethe was consciously entertaining a wish to leave when he wrote the poem. However, his evident inhibition in proceeding with his writing may have stemmed from the secret that was growing somewhere in his mind.

[108] Cf. Goethe's earlier-mentioned identification with Moses.

[109] [Und nur der Vater schien nicht sein zu achten.] (Line 216)

[110] [Und wie den Knaben Lust, den Jüngling Ehre,/ So zog ihn nur der fremde Wille fort.] (Lines 221–22)

In view of the ensuing Hamlet Problem (see later) this passage acquires prominent importance.

that Goethe's recent submission to the most trying work on files, briefs, and accounts also served as a delayed obedience to his father, as if he were trying to make up for previous disobedience. This delayed obedience (cf. 167, p. 35) Goethe set forth in Humanus as a true-to-fact behavior pattern of the past. Or, in other words, Goethe presented a life story that he would have liked his own to have been. Thus, the many reasons for feelings of guilt under this head were removed; the bitterness and rebellious feelings that had prevailed in his relationship to his father were soothed into patient and loving submission. My conclusion is that the peacefulness[111] between father and son as presented in "The Secrets" shows the kinder feelings Goethe himself had acquired by the working through of his Oedipus complex. Because he himself actually felt less bitter, or tried to feel less bitter, about his father, he could present the ideal hero of his epos as an erstwhile submissive youth.

One wonders further whether the mythological elements Goethe provides for Humanus's infancy and early childhood are elements that, though derived on the face of it from various mythologies, can be regarded as embellished childhood fantasies of Goethe's about his own past. There is also a strange contrast between Markus, a character with no history, and Humanus, whose destiny is historically formed before he is even born. Markus is merely a tool in the hands of providence, and comes and goes in accordance with the revealed will of a supreme force; Humanus accomplishes destiny's will by integrating it and making it his own. Markus tumbles, so to speak, into his exalted position; Humanus has acquired his by his own effort and merit. Markus's saintliness is a negative one: he did not preserve his innocent naiveté in the face of worldly temptations; he was born naive and he will die naive. This cannot be said of Humanus.[112] These two opposite biographical types are, I think, two aspects that dawned upon Goethe with regard to his own life history. He apparently started to view himself on the one hand as the executor of higher decision, on the other as someone who has actively formed his own destiny in accordance with a superior moral force, whose will and intention he was fortunate enough to grasp.

Goethe at this point apparently was capable of stepping out of the context of his own life and of visualizing it under different aspects. Simultaneously the desire arose to create a mythos of his own self or to think

---

[111] However, Humanus's father still bears obnoxious features, as the last remnants of Goethe's ambivalence. Over and over again he tests his son as if he were trying to overstrain his endurance.

[112] I am here going beyond the actual content of the fragment and expressing impressions that one receives from so much of it as was written.

of himself as the subject of a mythos. This capacity is one of the strongest expressions of the change from the state of being driven to that of actively forming. Goethe's thoughts about what man does and does not know about himself and what the pitfalls of gratifying the biographical impulse are, go back to 1782. On October 4 of that year he wrote to Lavater in direct reference to the latter's confessions:

It is always very interesting to read something of that sort, although I have noticed again in this instance that, if I may say so, the reader has to make his own psychological reckoning in order to derive a correct sum from such data. I cannot now set forth my idea, only this much of it: That which man notices in himself and feels appears to me the smallest part of his being. What he lacks strikes him more than what he possesses; he notices more what makes him uneasy than what gladdens him and enlarges his soul; for in all agreeable and good conditions the soul loses the consciousness of itself, as the body too, and is reminded of itself again only through unpleasant sensations; and so in most instances he who writes about himself and his past condition will set down the narrow and the painful, whereby a person, if I may say so, shrinks. To this, that which we have seen of his actions, that which we have read of his writings, has first to be added again chemically and only then does a picture again arise of the person as he perhaps may have been or be. This, of many thousand cogitations, one.[113]

In "The Secrets," in so far as it is an autobiographical poem one can see that Goethe was not liable to be victimized by the shrinking process to which he alluded in his letter to Lavater. By suspending his own life between two opposite poles (Humanus and Markus), he staked out a huge area of the human world and overstepped the relative narrowness of Wilhelm Meister's, which, in the last analysis, remains within the confines

---

[113] [Es ist immer sehr interessant dergleichen zu lesen, ob ich gleich wieder dabey die Bemerkung gemacht habe, dass wenn ich so sagen darf, der Leser eine eigene psychologische Rechnungsoperation zu machen hat um aus solchen Datis ein wahres Facit heraus zu ziehen. Ich kann meine Idee iezo nicht auseinander legen, nur so viel davon: Das was der Mensch an sich bemerkt und fühlt, scheint mir der geringste Theil seines Daseyns. Es fällt ihm mehr auf was ihm fehlt, als das was er besizt, er bemerkt mehr was ihn ängstiget, als das was ihn ergözt und seine Seele erweitert; denn in allen angenehmen und guten Zuständen verliert die Seele das Bewusstseyn ihrer Selbst, wie der Körper auch, und wird nur durch unangenehme Empfindungen wieder an sich erinnert; und so wird meistentheils, der über sich selbst und seinen vergangenen Zustand schreibt, das enge und schmerzliche aufzeichnen, dadurch denn eine Person, wenn ich so sagen darf, zusammenschrumpft. Hierzu muss erst wieder das, was wir von seinen Handlungen gesehen, was wir von seinen Schriften gelesen haben chymisch hinzu gethan werden und alsdenn entsteht erst wieder ein Bild des Menschen, wie er etwa mag seyn oder gewesen seyn. Dies von vielen tausend Betrachtungen Eine.]

of middle-class narrowness, at least up to the point at which the original version left off. Goethe's faculty for experiencing himself now on the plane, and through the medium of, symbols must also be viewed—if my assumption as to the poem's biographical momentum is correct—as the beginning of a new phase in his ability to handle the activity-passivity problem. In Humanus and Markus Goethe apparently was able to view himself simultaneously as an active and a passive being. At least we may read the poem as the beginning of an attempt at finding a solution in the form of a reconciliation of two seemingly irreconcilable functions, both of which are indispensable in human life. However, the attribution of the two functions to two different personages indicates the distance that had still to be covered. This freedom was envisioned in the context of an impending departure, a departure for which no hint of motivation is supplied. Some interpreters have thought Humanus was acting upon a premonition of death. However, it is possible that Humanus's motive for leaving had not yet taken on a specific form in the poem because the author himself was still engaged in an unconscious struggle about the equivalent decision in his own life. The explicit declaration of Humanus's motives may have been inhibited by whatever force held Goethe's plan to go to Italy in abeyance, that is to say, away from consciousness.

Be this as it may, the possibility that Goethe started at that time to visualize his life under the aspect of general principles and not under that of single situations (as it was visualized in *Wilhelm Meister*), is a biographical datum of no minor import. I believe that the appearance of such new elements in a life history depends on what stage of the father-identification one is dealing with. The father is one of the first figures in the boy's life around which he forms a mythos. In the child's fantasy everything in the father's life is the offspring of will and no accidental occurrence can obstruct the pathway predetermined by his higher decision. It is, therefore, no accident that the central situation in "The Secrets" concerns a young man who, so to speak, has not yet found a destiny but steps into the place of a man whose whole life history has been given significant form. In comparing Humanus's life with Markus's one is reminded of a difference the little boy feels when he looks at his father's life. Particularly during the latency period, he may easily regard it with envy, since by comparison his own life seems empty, meaningless, and without structure as against his father's exciting stories about past and present achievements and even his father's account of his own childhood. This step towards acquiring a "father-biography" for himself—as symbolized by Markus's stepping into the role of Humanus—may well have coincided with Goethe's feeling that he had reached the peak of self-conquest demanded from him by Charlotte von Stein. Furthermore, Humanus, by humble service, had at last acquired his father's consent to adulthood, so perhaps Goethe felt that his time of humble service had ended.

As so often, a clue to a very personal problem can be discovered in a remark which Goethe made around that time about the relations of another person. Goethe was in correspondence with the Duke of Gotha regarding a stipend for the painter Tischbein. The Duke apparently was not satisfied with Tischbein's paintings, and Goethe was trying to persuade the benefactor to continue his support, although he had to agree in part with the Duke's criticism. He wrote (April 19, 1784):

> The painting with the two figures really has much that is good, although I freely admit that for me too it has little attraction. If I may whisper something in Your Highness's ear I find in these figures the innocence of our artist's habits. Had he enjoyed the charms of the female anatomy with body and soul, he would have been carried away towards this beautiful part of creation with irresistible urges; certainly his paintings would breathe more life and voluptuousness and he would not produce enigmatic androgynes.[114]

I am not aware of any other direct reference to sexuality in Goethe's correspondence of that time. This one says bluntly that an artist cannot be a great painter if he does not know sexual pleasure from his own experience. Innocence of heart is declared to be incompatible with great art. Sexual passion and sexual gratification appear more or less suddenly and unannounced as cornerstones of artistic creation. But was this true only of Tischbein and the artist who uses a visual medium or did this revelation contain a principle that held true for art, for creation, in general? Does an ethical absolutism harm artistic production? Is it not true that great art can grow only where the ethical demand also creates a conflict? If the ethical demand led to supreme mastery and thus eliminated the seed of conflict, from where then would artistic creation derive its momentum?

[114] [Das Bild mit den beiden Figuren hat wirklich viel Gutes, ob ich gleich gerne gestehe, dass es auch für mich wenig Reiz hat. Darf ich aber Ew. Durchl. etwas in's Ohr sagen, so finde ich in diesen Gestalten die Unschuld der Sitten unsres Künstlers. Hätte er die Reize des weiblichen Körpers mit Leib und Seele genossen, würde er nach diesem schönen Theile der Schöpfung mit unwiderstehlichen Trieben hingerissen, gewiss seine Gemälde würden mehr Leben und Wollust athmen, und er würde keinen räthselhaften Zwitter produciren.]

Cf. Freud: "An abstinent artist is hardly conceivable: but an abstinent young *savant* is certainly no rarity." (165, p. 197)

Perhaps this problem can take us back to Humanus. Did Humanus have to leave because he had reached at last a total integration of an ethical principle of the highest sort and thus was removed out of the realm of conflict and no longer appropriately equipped to be a leader of a community? Answers to these questions would be of a speculative nature. One can only register that at a point when Goethe appears to have achieved man's most difficult renunciation, namely the sacrifice of his masculine, biological role, to a degree where it possibly was no longer experienced by him as a sacrifice, that is to say, when the pain of frustration was reduced to a bare minimum and a kind of conflict-free area *seemingly* was established, he turned vigorously towards a demand for sexual gratification. The demand, to be sure, is as yet upon theoretical grounds: for the sake of artistic integrity. In a different context, such as the letter written in French from Weimar on September 20, 1784, to Charlotte von Stein, one also finds in Goethe's correspondence sentiments that seem indirectly related to this problem. Goethe was being visited by his friend Jacobi and he wanted most eagerly that Charlotte von Stein, who was at her country estate at that time, should join them. He wrote:

> We do our duty so well, my dear Lotte, that in the long run one could doubt our love. Business and friendship hold me, household duties keep you; it is impossible for me to go and see you; I find your reasons that prevent you from coming valid enough, and nevertheless I am dissatisfied with you and with me for being so reasonable.
>
> Jacobi's presence would be doubly dear to me if you were with us. It is impossible for me to talk of you to anyone soever; I know that I should always say too little and at the same time fear lest I say too much. I should wish everyone to know you in order to feel my happiness, which I do not dare to pronounce. Really it is a crime of lese amity that I should be with a man like Jacobi, with a friend so true and so affectionate, without letting him see [to] the bottom of my soul, without making him acquainted with the treasure on which I feed. I hope that [Frau] Herder will talk to him of you and will tell him what I do not dare to tell him.[115]

[115] [Nous faisons si bien notre devoir ma chere Lotte qu'a la fin on pourroit douter de notre amour. Les affaires et l'amitié me fixent, l'oeconomie te retient, il m'est impossible d'aller te voir, je trouve tes raisons assez valables qui t'empechent de venir, et cependant je suis mecontent de toi et de moi que nous sommes si raisonnables.

La presence de Jacobi me seroit doublement chere si tu etois avec nous. Il m'est impossible de parler de toi a qui que ce soit, je sais que je dirois toujours trop peu, et je crains en meme temps de trop dire. Je voudrois que tout le monde te connut pour sentir mon bonheur que je n'ose prononcer. Vraiment c'est un crime de lese amité que j'existe avec une homme comme Jacobi avec un ami si vrai si tendre sans lui faire voir le fond de mon ame, sans lui faire connoitre le tresor dont je me nourris. J'espere que la Herder lui parlera de toi et lui dira ce que je n'ose lui dire.]

To be too reasonable about love? This is a new theme. Goethe apparently felt the urge to boast of his love for Charlotte von Stein and her love for him. The reasons for their separation at that time were indeed valid from the point of view of reality, and nevertheless Goethe was right to be surprised that they were capable of so much reason. It is also of importance to note that this theme came up in a situation of homosexual stimulation. Jacobi's wife had died shortly before and he was traveling in the company of his sister, a situation that necessarily touched a very sensitive spot in Goethe's life. Probably he needed Charlotte von Stein as a protection against the homosexual activation, just as she fulfilled the same function in his relationship to Herder (see above, p. 847). But why did Goethe feel inhibited from talking to Jacobi about Charlotte von Stein? He had spoken to Merck about her, but was not rewarded for his candor, as will be remembered (see above, p. 633). Did he fear a similar reaction in Jacobi? That is not probable, for Jacobi was an entirely different type from Merck. But it may be recalled that I suggested earlier (p. 361) that Goethe may have felt he was the object of derision in a passage in Jacobi's novel *Woldemar*. Be this as it may, a noteworthy remark was made by Goethe in conversing with Jacobi at the time of their meeting in Weimar in September 1784. Jacobi reports:

> I recall that I . . . once heard the question raised: How the human species might have been propagated if the fall of man had not occurred. Goethe answered quickly: "Without doubt through a rational conversation."[116]

This remark of course was meant sarcastically.[117] Later (1797) Goethe published the following distich under the title "Futile Prattle": "All rational conversations are impotent to propagate the world; neither through them is a work of art brought forth."[118] Unexpectedly we find here something of a proof that Goethe's previously reported remark to the Duke of Gotha really referred to himself. If the sarcastic remark to Jacobi, the satirical distich, and the passage in the letter to Charlotte von Stein of September 20, 1784,[119] are taken together, we find a well-substantiated series: intercourse replaced by reasonableness → danger of artistic

---

[116] [Ich erinnere mich, dass ich . . . einmal die Frage aufwerfen hörte: wie das menschliche Geschlecht wohl möchte fortgepflanzt worden sein, wenn der Sündenfall nicht eingetreten wäre? Goethe antwortete schnell: Ohne Zweifel durch einen vernünftigen Diskurs.] (250, *1*:122–23)

[117] Although the editor of the *Gespräche* called this a lightning of the mind (*Blitzstrahl des Geistes*); see 250, *5*:23.

[118] [Fortzupflanzen die Welt sind alle vernünft'gen Discurse/ Unvermögend; durch sie kommt auch kein Kunstwerk hervor.] (*Soph.* I, *1*:353, lines 109–10)

[119] To my feeling this passage was a frank sarcastic remark, perhaps the first sign of a direct critical attitude.

sterility → reproach against Charlotte von Stein for no longer increasing his creativity but rather destroying the nerve center of his existence as an artist.

The remark to Jacobi was not only born of sarcasm against Charlotte von Stein but was also directed against himself, as if he was saying: "People who claim that conversation propagates the race behave just as I do, who behave as if intercourse played no role in my life." But if reliance can be put in Jacobi's account, then Goethe's forebodings went beyond the problem of sex, for Jacobi also reported Goethe as saying during this visit: "I know well that in order to salvage the outside one should destroy [one's] inside, but I cannot really acquiesce in it."[120]

Thus the question was quite alive in Goethe at that time as to the usefulness and beneficial effect of lofty moral standards. This readiness to doubt betrays a man who was no longer in danger of being overwhelmed by an outbreak of passion. Passion could be mastered by him. He faced alternatives, and no longer necessities. Whereas earlier the ethical principle was an inescapable must, for the fulfillment of which no sacrifice was too great, the moral obligation now became something relative, to which it was feasible to adhere but no longer an iron necessity. In the intended epic of "The Secrets" Goethe followed a religious relativism. Not only was the maximum good of each religion to be presented, which was perfect in its own kind although quite different from the others, but also each of the twelve monk-knights was to describe Humanus as he saw him. Since every one of them had accepted Humanus as his superior, there was also introduced the notion that ideal behavior was a relative concept, dependent on its social effects and on the beliefs of those who judged those effects. Moral relativism is often an excuse for licentiousness. There is no indication of this in Goethe at that time. It rather seems that the integration of values had converted compulsion into freedom of choice.

---

[120] [Ich weiss wohl, dass man, um die dehors zu salvieren, das dedans zu grunde richten soll; aber ich kann mich denn doch nicht wohl dazu verstehen.] (250, *1*:122)

Part III

Solutions and New Problems

Part III
A

The Italian Journey
(September 3, 1786–June 18, 1788)

Chapter 1

Preliminary Solutions

W E ARE NOW entering the final phase of that period of Goethe's life which is under investigation in this study. It brings us to the day of September 3, 1786, when, unknown to Charlotte von Stein and probably to any other person except his servant, Goethe set out from Carlsbad on his journey to Italy. It was the most important day of his life, if I may say so, and a psychological fact of supreme magnitude hides behind the event. It had taken Goethe over ten years to return, in this respect, to exactly the same point at which he was when the Duke's messenger reached him to take him to Weimar on November 3, 1775. Then too he had been on the point of going to Italy.

I should like to group the material significant for this phase according to topics. First I wish to consider what the novel *Wilhelm Meister* reports and proceed to an attempt at understanding the bearing of Shakespeare's *Hamlet* and of Spinoza's *Ethics* on the final development that took him away from Weimar and from his beloved Charlotte von Stein.

Wilhelm Meister, Book VI, and the Fetish

The sixth book of *Wilhelm Meister* was written between October 16, 1784, and November 11, 1785. It was the last one Goethe wrote before his departure. Despite his efforts he did not get far beyond it. A synopsis of the plot follows.

Wilhelm's fortunes take a temporary turn for the better. As he lies wounded on a battlefield a new group of travelers appears on the scene. They are wealthy people who do their best to help him. He is taken to the town where the rest of the theatrical troupe have found a meager refuge. Wilhelm's actor friends hold him responsible for their plight, and Wilhelm promises to undo the damage they have suffered although it was not due to his fault. He remains with Mignon and the harpist when the others depart for another city to seek employment with Serlo, a well-known theater director. After a while Wilhelm is informed by Melina that Serlo has rejected their proposal. Wilhelm follows them but does not succeed in changing Serlo's mind. He becomes acquainted with Aurelia, Serlo's sister, an actress whose life story is reported in detail. Wilhelm expounds his concept of *Hamlet,* and when Serlo hears that he has once acted on the stage he wants to hire him for his company, but Wilhelm feels a strong aversion to making acting his profession. News reaches him that his father has died and that his mother intends soon to remarry. When Serlo promises to hire his actor friends too if Wilhelm accepts his offer, Wilhelm gives in and joins Serlo's group as an actor.

The beginning of this Book contains the psychological key to an understanding of this period in Goethe's life and is worth going into in detail. As will be seen, he describes here the psychological history of the formation of a fetish.

Wilhelm is left alone on the battlefield with Mignon, who tries to stop the bleeding of his wounds with her hair, and Philine, who rests his head upon her lap. They hear noises and fear a new attack, but to their great joy rescuers arrive in the form of another party of travelers. A beautiful woman approaches them, riding on a white horse and surrounded by an older man and several cavaliers and servants. Wilhelm

> had fixed his eyes upon the gentle, quiet, sympathetic features of the arriving woman. He thought he had never seen anything more worthy to be loved. An ample man's cloak, which did not fit her, concealed her figure from him. She had, as it seemed, borrowed this garment from one of her companions against the influences of the cold evening air.[1]

A surgeon is called to examine and treat the injured. The woman seems quite upset about Wilhelm's misfortune and busies herself a great deal regarding his care. To his surprise he hears her say to one of her companions that "he suffered for our sake!"[2] (As transpires later, the ambush

[1] [Er hatte seine Augen auf die sanften, stillen theilnehmenden Gesichtszüge der Ankommenden geheftet, er glaubte nie etwas Liebenswürdigeres gesehen zu haben. Ein weiter Mannsüberrock, der ihr nicht passte, verbarg ihm ihre Gestalt. Sie hatte, wie es schien, gegen die Einflüsse der kühlen Abendluft, dieses Kleid von einem ihrer Gesellschafter geborgt.] (*Soph.* I, 52:198)

[2] [Und er leidet doch um unsertwillen!] (*Soph.* I, 52:199)

was aimed at this party and the actors were taken by mistake for the wealthy travelers.) The surgeon starts to undress Wilhelm in order to treat his wounds. The young lady cannot detach herself from the sight of the injured but fears to offend propriety by remaining. She turns towards an older man and says:

> "My dear uncle, may I be generous at your expense?" Simultaneously she drew off the cloak and one saw that it was with the intention of yielding it up to the injured and unclothed man. Wilhelm, whom the healing sight of her eyes had thus far held fast, was now first, as the cloak fell, overwhelmed by her beautiful figure. She stepped closer to him and gave him the cloak by laying it softly over him. In this moment, when he wished to open his mouth and utter some words of thanks, the vivid impression of her presence affected his already assailed senses so strangely that it suddenly seemed to him as if her head were surrounded by rays which bit by bit spread over her whole image.[3]

The surgeon's ministrations caused him pain.

> The saint faded away before the eyes of the swooning man, he lost the knowledge of himself and when he came to himself again horsemen and carriage, the fair [damsel] together with her escort, had vanished.[4]

The cloak became Wilhelm's treasured possession. In vain did he try to identify his charming benefactress; she disappeared from his life as suddenly as she had made her appearance, but the cloak continued to have magic effects:

> An electric warmth seemed to pass over from the fine wool into his body, yes even to translate him into the most delicious sensations. From his first youth on he did not remember as delightful an impression as that which the beautiful owner of the garment had made on him; he still saw the cloak fall from her shoulders and that most noble figure surrounded by rays

---

[3] [Mein lieber Oheim, darf ich auf Ihre Kosten freigebig sein? Sie zog sogleich den Überrock aus und man sah, dass es in der Absicht geschah, um ihn dem Verwundeten und Unbekleideten hinzugeben. Wilhelm, den der heilsame Anblick ihrer Augen bisher festgehalten hatte, war erst, als der Überrock fiel, von ihrer schönen Gestalt überrascht. Sie trat näher zu ihm und reichte ihm den Rock, indem sie ihn sanft über ihn hinlegte. In diesem Augenblicke, da er den Mund öffnen und einige Worte des Dankes hervorbringen wollte, würkte der lebhafte Eindruck ihrer Gegenwart so sonderbar auf seine schon angegriffenen Sinnen, dass es ihm auf einmal vorkam, als sei ihr Haupt mit Strahlen umgeben, die sich nach und nach über ihr ganzes Bild ausbreiteten.] (*Soph.* I, 52:200)

[4] [Die Heilige verschwand vor den Augen des Hinsinkenden, er verlor die Kenntniss sein selbst, und als er wieder zu sich kam, waren Reuter und Wagen, die Schöne sammt ihrer Begleitung verschwunden.]

standing in front of him, and his soul hastened after the vanished [woman] into every corner of the world.[5]

The recollection of the whole event became a compulsive thought in Wilhelm.

Incessantly he called back that occurrence, which had made an indelible impression upon his mind. He saw the beautiful Amazon come forth riding out of the bushes, approach him, dismount, exert herself [for his sake], walk up and down; he saw the enwrapping garment fall from her shoulders; her face, her figure, shine and fade away. A thousand times his imagination repeated the scene, a thousand times he called back the sound of her sweet voice; just as often he envied Philine for having kissed her hand and just as often would he have taken this story for a dream, a fairy tale, if the garment had not been left behind, which assured him of the certainty of the vision.

Tied up with the so great care that he had for this garment was the most lively longing to clothe himself in it. In the morning as soon as he got up he threw it over him and all day long he was in worry lest a spot or some other damage might befall it through its being used.[6]

This early version of *Wilhelm Meister* ends with a renewed vision of the beloved Amazon. Immediately after Wilhelm has promised his friends that he will join them and become a professional actor, the novel says:

His thoughts strayed hither and thither and suddenly the place in the woodland filled his imagination again. On a white horse the lovely Amazon

[5] [Eine elektrische Wärme schien aus der feinen Wolle in seinen Körper überzugehen, ja sogar ihn in die behaglichste Empfindung zu versetzen. Von seiner ersten Jugend an erinnerte er sich keines so angenehmen Eindrucks, als den die schöne Besitzerin des Kleids auf ihn gemacht hatte, er sah noch den Rock von ihren Schultern fallen, die edelste Gestalt mit Strahlen umgeben vor sich stehen, und seine Seele eilte der Verschwundenen in alle Weltgegenden nach]. (*Soph.* I, 52:201–02)

[6] [Unaufhörlich rief er sich jene Begebenheit zurück, welche einen unauslöschlichen Eindruck auf sein Gemüthe gemacht hatte. Er sah die schöne Amazone reitend aus den Büschen hervorkommen, sich ihm nähern, absteigen, sich bemühen, hin und wieder gehen, er sah das umhüllende Kleid von ihren Schultern fallen, ihr Gesicht, ihre Gestalt glänzen und verschwinden. Tausendmal wiederholte seine Einbildungskraft die Scene, tausendmal rief er sich den Klang ihrer süssen Stimme zurück, eben so oft beneidete er Philine, die ihre Hand geküsst hatte, und eben so oft würde er diese Geschichte für einen Traum, für ein Märchen gehalten haben, wenn nicht das Kleid zurückgeblieben wäre, welches ihm die Gewissheit der Erscheinung versicherte.

Mit der grössten Sorgfalt für dieses Gewand war das lebhafteste Verlangen verbunden, sich damit zu bekleiden. Des Morgens, sobald er aufstand, warf er es über und war den ganzen Tag in Sorgen, es möchte ein Flecken oder sonst ein Schade durch den Gebrauch daran kommen.] (*Soph.* I, 52:216)

came out of the bushes, approached him, dismounted, her humane prompt-
ings bade her go and come; she stood, the garment fell from her shoulders
and covered the wounded man; her face, her figure, shone up again and
faded away.[7]

I have purposely reproduced here this whole series of reports. The
original theme is repeated with hardly any change. The monotonous
repetition is characteristic of intense sexual daydreams. In this instance
it was a fetishistic daydream. As Goethe reports with clinical correctness,
thousands of times Wilhelm went through identical fantasies in which the
fetish played the same role over and over again. Goethe's account of the
formation of Wilhelm's fetish sounds like a psychoanalytic textbook example.[8]

Let us consider the elements singly. A beautiful woman gives a male
garment to a prostrate man. This scene can easily be deciphered in terms
of the psychoanalytic view that the fetishist sees in the fetish a female
penis, that is to say, the penis of the mother. The beautiful Amazon is
recognizable as a mother-substitute. Wilhelm is in a situation of utter
prostration when he is given the wonderful object from which he will
derive delightful sensations. He is depicted in an unmanly dependent
situation; in the language of psychoanalysis, he is castrated, and in the
situation of castration a charming, loving mother-substitute gives Wilhelm a penis and restores his manhood. Since the cloak was borrowed
from the woman's old uncle a hint is given as to the origin of the penis.
Mother takes away the penis from father and gives it to the castrated
(impotent) boy. This is one of the meanings of Wilhelm's daydream.

The male cloak is described as wide and Wilhelm does not become
aware of the loveliness of the Amazon's figure as long as she wears the
garment. This element refers to a pregnancy. It allows interpretation
in three different directions.

(1) Children sometimes rationalize a mother's pregnancy as a protu-
berance caused by a garment. This fantasy contains an important wish-
fulfillment. It says: "Mother is not pregnant; she still has her lovely

[7] [Seine Gedanken schweiften hin und wieder, und auf einmal er füllte der Waldplatz
wieder seine Einbildungskraft. Auf einem Schimmel kam die liebenswürdige Amazone aus
den Büschen, nahte sich ihm, stieg ab, ihr menschenfreundliches Bemühen hiess sie gehen
und kommen, sie stand, das Kleid fiel von ihren Schultern und deckte den Verwundeten,
ihr Gesicht, ihre Gestalt glänzte wieder auf und verschwand.] (*Soph.* I, 52:284)

[8] See 206; 215. For the symbolism of the mantle see Ernest Jones (320), who sets forth
several reasons why the mantle is a suitable symbol of the penis. He also quotes two verses
from Goethe's *Faust*, Part I, in which Goethe used the mantle as a symbol. See also 373; 447.
Freud emphasized at various times the use of the mantle as a symbol.

virginal figure." Thus the cloak functions as an element of denial. Yet at the same time it also symbolizes the pregnancy. Once it is discarded, mother appears again slender and attractive.[9]

(2) As a comment on the radiance surrounding the vision of the Amazon I wish to quote an observation made by Dr. Phyllis Greenacre (264). She writes: "In my clinical experience the two events of childhood which are most likely to produce visual overstimulation are, first, the sight of the genitalia of an adult of the opposite sex; second, any glimpse of the process of birth." Under the impact of a shocking experience the memory, or screen memory, according to Dr. Greenacre, is endowed with a particular luminous effect, such as Goethe described in this instance. The reference of this imagery to birth may become more convincing when one considers that shortly after the disappearance of the vision of the Amazon a birth is actually described in the novel. When Wilhelm is taken to town, he has to share an overcrowded room with the theatrical troupe. Melina's wife is in labor in an adjoining room and gives birth to a dead child. Wilhelm's erstwhile friends wish to eject him. They look upon him as an intruder and hold him responsible for their misfortunes. There is quite a bit of talk about intruders. One man threatens with powerful curses to eject everyone present unless they let Wilhelm, the alleged intruder, share their presence. Again traits of reversal are found: "It was not I that was angry at the intrusion of a younger sibling, and it was not I that father threatened with punishment unless I was kind to the baby, but others that wanted to push me out."[10]

(3) Since the cloak originates from a man, the equation of penis and newborn baby can also be discovered in this instance. One must assume that Goethe was here describing his own personal sexual fantasies, which stemmed from a childhood memory of the type I have adumbrated above. The sequence is a typical one: The woman, the falling garment, the revelation, the idealization of the woman in order to replace a shattering observation. Voyeuristic and fetishistic features in Goethe's writings have been mentioned from time to time earlier. The fetish in this instance, however, shows certain traits that are particularly important and far-reaching. Wilhelm is in the state of castration when the woman appears. The garment, when he wraps himself up in it and keeps it clean and spotless, provides Wilhelm with delightful pleasures and serves as a constant companion from then on; that is to say, it eliminates the damage

---

[9] The dream Goethe had about Charlotte von Stein after the birth of the Duchess's son will be recalled (see above, p. 815).

[10] In the final version of the novel Wilhelm's sister was left out entirely.

he has suffered by castration. It restores bodily integrity and makes the physical pleasure now obtainable even greater.[11] But simultaneously when the garment falls from the woman's shoulders she changes into a slender woman. The disfigurement by pregnancy and the threat to mother's physical integrity by childbirth are likewise eliminated in that very moment. The garment thus restores the bodily integrity of the boy and of his mother.

I wonder how far it was the double function of the fetish as described in *Wilhelm Meister* that made it so indispensable.[12] There are of course all kinds of double functions and double aspects involved in the formation of a fetish, as Freud showed. These double aspects are not always represented in the same degree and clinically a variety of combinations is encountered. What is striking in Goethe's account is the harmonious balance between and synthesis of two functions which involve the whole body of the person who receives the fetish and the whole body of the person who gives it. This is also strongly represented by the kind of garment chosen as fetish, namely a cloak that envelops the whole body. Also all aggressive traits are eliminated from the manifest content, which compels one to call Wilhelm's fetish a particularly happy solution of problems inherently characterized by strong ambivalence. The last shade of guilt is eliminated when it turns out that Wilhelm's castration has saved the lady and her party from the same fate. The ambush, as will be remembered, was really aimed at the person from whom Wilhelm receives the garment. Thus the unconscious idea was: "I let myself be castrated not because I deserve punishment, but because I want to rescue *you:* if I had not submitted to injury, dreadful mishaps would have befallen *you."* Thus the fetish becomes a just reward and the garment replaces what Wilhelm had voluntarily sacrificed for the benefit of the charming lady. The fact that the lady in turn had received the garment from her old uncle effects further relief from guilt and gratifies guiltlessly an aggressive impulse against the father. Thus the recipient does not need to feel guilty about having received (that is to say, taken) the fetish from the woman, for the woman in turn took it from a father-substitute. Thus the final castration of the father and the acquisition of his penis are achieved by the son without the slightest trace of self-reproach, and, further, without impairment of the beautified maternal image. The mother remains throughout the full course of events guiltless, innocent, and unselfish, and the image

[11] The material in *Wilhelm Meister* suggests the fantasy of receiving a new penis better than the one possessed before.

[12] I do not know whether this double function is generally to be found in fetishists.

of her body remains unscathed, for what she is giving away is not really part of her own body but that of another. Dr. Greenacre in her study of fetishism (265) postulates an early disturbance in the formation of the body image as a necessary step towards the development of a fetish. Although I wonder whether this is specific for the formation of a fetish or is applicable rather to perversions in general, it is striking to find in the novel a reference that may be interpreted as a reflection of just such an occurrence. As mentioned above, the episode with the lovely Amazon[13] ends with Wilhelm's losing consciousness. The exact wording in the first draft is peculiar: "He lost the knowledge of himself" [Er verlor die Kenntniss sein selbst]. In the final version Goethe wrote: "He lost all consciousness" [er verlor alles Bewusstsein] (*Soph.* I, 22:46), a linguistically more acceptable version, but possibly from the psychological point of view a greatly weakened one.[14] I would raise the question of how far the peculiarity of wording in the first draft is a remote reflection of the very process postulated by Dr. Greenacre. The formation of a body image that is discrepant from the real biological structure can well be equated with the loss of knowledge of self. This seems to me to be the nucleus of a psychosis that can be found in nearly all instances of well-integrated perversions. Furthermore there is in the first version of *Wilhelm Meister* an episode that may provide an important clue to illuminate how such a disturbance of the body image developed in Goethe. It will be remembered that when Mignon's hystero-epileptic seizure was described I surmised that this was the residue of the boy's experience of his little sister's orgasm, kinesthetically perceived. In such a moment, of course, partial or total identification may occur and may leave a permanent trace or permanent confusion in the organization of the male body image. Wilhelm's perversion of wrapping the cloak around himself again suggests total identification.

The episode leading to the formation of a benign, all-protective, pleasure-giving fetish that restores injury to health, prostration to courage and hope, is counterpoised by what may be called an anti-fetish, the discussion of which necessitates further reporting of the plot.

When Wilhelm comes to Serlo, the director of a famous theatrical company, he also becomes acquainted with Serlo's sister Aurelia, an actress. She is attracted by Wilhelm and this attraction seems to border

---

[13] Goethe in calling the beautiful woman an Amazon confirms indirectly some of the interpretations I have suggested.

[14] It is plain from many instances that the final version of *Wilhelm Meister* lost some of the psychological poignancy that typifies the first draft. Cf. above, p. 261.

upon love. She makes him her confidant and tells him the story of her life. Raised by an aunt, who abandoned herself to her impulses without restraint and consequently to promiscuity, she herself became a person full of conflicts and inclined towards wild behavior. Serlo and Aurelia are intensely bound to each other in an exceedingly ambivalent relationship. From the early version of the novel it is not clear whether Aurelia herself had gone through a phase of promiscuity. At Serlo's urging, she had married a man she did not love and who was quite without merit. He fell sick and during his sickness she became acquainted with Lothario, in the relationship with whom her life became meaningful. Her husband died. She was passionately drawn towards Lothario, but he abandoned her. When Wilhelm meets her, she is depressed. She unburdens her heart to him and he tries in vain to help her. During one of their talks Serlo enters and tries to take from her night table a dagger which she keeps there. Aurelia attacks him "with incredible passion." They struggle with each other in earnest until Aurelia is victorious. She comes out of the fight with the bare dagger, and Serlo, who is left with the empty scabbard,[15] throws it on the floor. He asks Wilhelm, who is greatly surprised by this strange scene, to judge between them.

"What business has she with the sharp steel? Let her show it to you. This dagger is not suitable for any actress. Pointed and sharp like a knife and needles, why this nonsense? Hot-tempered as she is she will one day do herself some harm by accident. I have a deep-seated hatred for such absurdities. A serious thought of this kind [meaning suicide] is mad and such a dangerous plaything is improper." "I have it once more!" Aurelia cried out as she held the bare blade on high. "I mean to guard my faithful friend better this time. Forgive me!' she cried out as she kissed the steel, "for neglecting you so!"

Serlo seemed to get really angry. "Take it as you wish, brother," she continued, "I find you unjust; do you know then whether perhaps under this shape a precious talisman is bestowed upon me; what help and counsel I shall find in it in bad times; must then everything that looks dangerous indeed be harmful?"[16]

---

[15] "Scabbard" is in German *Scheide,* which is also the word for vagina.

[16] [Was hat sie mit dem scharfen Stahle zu thun? Lassen Sie sich ihn zeigen. Dieser Dolch geziemt keiner Schauspielerin. Spitz und scharf wie Messer und Nadeln, zu was die Posse? Heftig wie sie ist, thut sie sich einmal von ohngefähr ein Leid. Ich habe einen innerlichen Hass gegen solche Sonderbarkeiten. Ein ernstlicher Gedanke dieser Art ist toll und ein so gefährliches Spielwerk ist abgeschmackt.—Ich hab' ihn wieder! rief Aurelie, indem sie die blanke Klinge in die Höhe hielt. Ich will meinen treuen Freund nun besser verwahren. Verzeihe mir! rief sie aus, indem sie den Stahl küsste, dass ich dich so vernachlässigt! Serlo schien im Ernste böse zu werden. Nimm es wie du willst, Bruder, fuhr sie fort; ich

This dagger comes to prominence again in the course of the novel when Wilhelm swears to Aurelia that he will never trifle with women and never profess love to a woman unless he can devote his whole life to her. When Wilhelm stretches out his hand to seal the vow Aurelia snatches the dagger and strikes with the cutting edge across his hand.

"One has to mark you men sharply if you are to remember," she cried, with a satisfaction that soon, however, turned to busy eagerness.[17]

In the final version of the novel it turns out that the Amazon is Lothario's sister and Wilhelm later marries her. This connection between the several brother-sister pairs makes comparisons particularly challenging. We have Lothario-Amazon versus Serlo-Aurelia. The garment corresponds to the dagger. The Amazon's inner harmony is contrasted with Aurelia's personality divided within itself. Aurelia also has a kind of fetish; it is dangerous; she does not part with it; its function is to destroy men who have destroyed her. The phallic reference of the fetish is strongly emphasized. The fetish has not developed into a protection of the whole body.

Yet the question I want to raise is whether the dagger should really be called a fetish. Aurelia calls it a talisman. I think of it as an anti-fetish. It has some of the potentialities of becoming a fetish, but to a certain extent it is the opposite of a fetish. It is a potential destroyer of its bearer, as indicated by Aurelia's hints at suicide, and it makes closeness to a beloved object impossible. Significantly, it remains in the possession of the woman, and, as is well known, fetishism occurs in women rather rarely (see 265). It would be interesting to know whether in clinical cases of a well-developed and well-integrated fetish of the kind Goethe describes in Wilhelm's relationship with the Amazon, one can also find the open or secret effects of an anti-fetish. It may be noteworthy that Charlotte von Stein, who of course had read the draft of the novel, seems to have understood, belatedly, the meaning of the Amazon's garment. In a letter to Herder of September 20, 1787, when her fears were strong that she had lost her friend forever, she reported the following dream:

Last night I dreamed you fetched me to church for the [Holy] Supper, and since I tarried and could not find my cloak, the sexton too came along

---

finde dich ungerecht; weisst du denn, ob nicht etwa unter dieser Form mir ein köstlicher Talisman beschert ist; was für Hülfe und Rath ich zur schlimmen Zeit bei ihm finde; muss denn eben alles schädlich sein, was gefährlich aussieht?] (*Soph.* I, 52:252)

[17] [Man muss euch Männer scharf zeichnen, wenn ihr merken sollt, rief sie mit einer Zufriedenheit aus, die aber bald in emsige Hastigkeit überging.] (*Soph.* I, 52:273)

after and assured both of us that the other communicants did not want to wait any longer, and out of anxiety that I could not find my cloak, I woke up.[18]

It is not difficult to interpret the dream. Charlotte von Stein was longing for Goethe, who in the dream was replaced by Herder.[19] Therefore the preconscious wish was that Goethe should come to take her to church. The Lord's Supper seems to stand for a wedding. People attend a wedding and get restless if the bride and bridegroom do not appear. But she cannot go to church and will not be wed to Goethe because she has no cloak. Here I think the cloak stands for penis. In the novel, Wilhelm loves the Amazon and later marries her because she gave him the garment, and Wilhelm tries to find her again and travels about looking for her. Goethe traveled too, but away from Charlotte von Stein in order not to see her, as she must have feared. She had no coat to give Goethe. How strong, underlying the dream, was the desire to be with Goethe, may be seen from the concluding sentence of her letter to Herder: "Make the dream come true and [continue your] visit [with] me until the sexton calls you again."[20] Here Charlotte von Stein responds to the dream as if it were the sexton that had been the reason for anxiety and not the missing garment.[21]

At the time when Goethe wrote the fetish episode in *Wilhelm Meister* he must already have had some idea regarding his journey to Italy. What concrete form this plan took is not known: was it still in the shape of a daydream or was it felt as a vague restlessness aiming at action not yet clearly defined? It is quite probable that Goethe felt the wish and the need to go to Italy but did not yet have a definite plan of how to proceed. Goethe's desire to travel is well documented, but nevertheless one feels a certain phobic apprehension when the journeys involved took him far away from his accustomed environment. I mentioned earlier the relatively numerous superstitions that occurred in conjunction with his

[18] [Die Nacht träumte ich Sie hohlten mich in die Kirche zum Abendmahl und da ich zögerte und meinen Mantel nicht finden konnte, kam der Kirchner auch noch hinter drein, und versicherte uns beyden die übrigen Comunicanten wolten gar nicht mehr warten, und in der Angst dass ich meinen Mantel nicht finden konnte wachte ich auf.] (See 518)

[19] The probability of this substitution is made even greater when one considers that barely a month had passed since Goethe made a slip and sent Herder a letter he had written to Charlotte von Stein (see above, p. 532, and later).

[20] [lassen Sie mir den Traum aus gehen und besuchen mich bis Sie der Kirchner wieder rufft.]

[21] See Freud's remark that in a woman's dream a cloak means a man, and his quotation of Reik (210, p. 38). At this point it may be worth while to point out that the phallic symbolism of the cloak may be fortified by the cloaklike character of the foreskin. (See 414.)

traveling. In later years too one senses their presence; for example, in 1816 when an accident occurred on his way and he canceled the whole trip, writing to Zelter (July 22, 1816): "What man proposes is otherwise disposed; be it indeed that the upper or nether demons intermeddle."[22] Thus Wilhelm's going through ambush, rescue, and acquisition of a pleasure-giving fetish acquires particular significance, for Wilhelm's journey too is a quest for solutions basic to his existence. The episode therefore may also serve the purpose of warding off fear in the fantasy. The anti-fetish then seems like a warning not to rely too heavily on an illusory solution.

However, if the cloak episode is connected at all with a possible fear in Goethe of a voyage into a distant country, we can attribute to it only secondary importance, comparable to the role of the day residues in dream formation. The episode, of course, is far more important as a sign that Goethe was elaborating upon the earliest and most archaic fantasies regarding the relationship of the sexes. The unconscious material is presented in a clear and lucid way. In comparison I should say that when an adult patient in the course of analysis presents fantasies whose meaning is as transparent as this, an interpretation can be given directly, unless the fantasies are completely isolated. One may conclude that the patient has reached the point at which the symptom is ready to disappear and the main resistances have been overcome. Here it is not only a question of what Goethe's actual insight into his archaic fantasies may have been, but also how his whole ego reacted. Objection may be raised against translating poetic fantasies into data regarding knowledge of self. However, the lucidity of fantasy was accompanied with changes of personality that indicate he had become capable of mastery of the corresponding instinctual impulses, and resulted, as I shall try to demonstrate later, in the final overcoming of a serious and almost devastating symptom.

The Amazon episode shows, in my estimation, that the archaic fear-arousing fantasies led to the formation of an egosyntonic, comprehensive configuration particularly competent to appease ambivalence. The fact that Goethe had his hero, at this point in his development, find this solution is significant. The reader may remember that I recorded earlier a well-attested episode in Goethe's life when he skated in public wrapped in his mother's fur coat. At that time the action was meant as a joke with the aim of deriding his mother. What was joke in 1774 became now ten years later a conflict-solving, appeasing solution, which reduced

---

[22] [Was der Mensch denkt, wird anders gelenkt, es sey nun dass sich die obern oder untern Dämonen darein mischen.]

internal distance from women and eliminated reproach, hostility, and guilt feeling. The change from appropriating a piece of female attire in reality to obtaining a male garment from a woman in fantasy, the change from derision to gratitude, may also indicate how far the poet's ego had traveled in losing its fears of women. Goethe's parapraxia when dipping the pen given him by Charlotte von Stein into the burning candle (see above, p. 493) may now be seen to contain the basic elements of the Amazon episode, arranged in a different pattern.

We may now also look back and recall the letter of the sixteen-year-old boy to his sister (see above, pp. 33–34), when—probably with a twinkle in his eye—he wrote her that he and his friends had lost their way and that they would have had to roam around the whole night if a beneficent fairy had not, in order to show them the right way, tied the tails of parrots to trees, and that the boys mistook them for wisps of straw. In this fantasy of adolescence, all the elements of the Amazon cloak-fetish episode can be found: the voyage, the woman who rescues, the penis symbols appearing as the result of benevolent female actions.[23] Thus we can say that not only is the neurotic symptom the result of a regression, but also the solution of a dire conflict can be accomplished by the ego's groping back into the infinite store of childhood experiences and picking out that which matches the requirements of the present. Or is this only the privilege of the undaunted genius? Be this as it may, we have found an aspect that permits subsuming under one and the same principle the whimsical fantasy of the pubescent boy, the prank of the youth, the parapraxia of the unsettled struggler during the years of trial and error, and the final conflict-solving work of art of the mature man.

Although general psychoanalytic viewpoints permit the assumption that the figure of the Amazon is a derivative of maternal imagery, some material can be adduced to establish more particularly a connection between the two. It may be characteristic that this maternal imagery is missing in the early version and that these associative connections between the Amazon and a maternal representative were established only during the post-Italian period. Since this further progress occurred after the

---

[23] I also want to remind the reader that in the letter written early in 1765 to his sister, the boy described, preceding the episode of the benevolent fairy, an experience with an ugly, large snake which he killed by throwing a stone. In the fantasy of the pubescent, the dangerous, fear-arousing, paternal *membrum* is compared with the rescuing, benevolent female phallus. One may surmise that in the episode on the battlefield the equivalent of the snake mentioned in the early letter is the ambush and the subsequent serious injury Wilhelm suffers. Here the attack by the father is successful, and the son, hypocritically, submits to superior power, in order to receive otherwise forbidden bliss from a maternal figure.

Italian period, we do not need to pursue the minutiae of that process but will record only the result.

On three occasions in *Wilhelm Meisters Lehrjahre* Goethe refers to Antiochus, prince of Syria. The history of this prince is remarkable for the friendly solution of the Oedipus complex that it affords.[24] Antiochus, son of King Seleucus, fell secretly in passionate love with Stratonice, his stepmother, "who had already made Seleucus the father of a son." Afraid of professing his love he pretended sickness and tried to extinguish his life by refusing nourishment. Erasistratus, the court physician, who apparently was the first psychosomatic experimentalist, checked the patient's pulse whenever a woman came to visit him. He soon found out the object of the Prince's secret love. He devised an ingenious scheme for engaging Seleucus's assistance in rescuing the Prince. He told the King that the Prince was suffering from love for his (Erasistratus's) wife. The King was surprised that Erasistratus would not surrender his wife to the Prince in order to save him. " 'You,' replied Erasistratus, 'who are his father, would not do so, if he were in love with Stratonice.' " The King protested and assured the physician that no sacrifice would be too great for him in order to save his son. Thereupon, when informed of the truth, the King summoned a general assembly and made Antiochus king of some provinces and Stratonice his queen, uniting them in marriage. He added that he thought he had enough power over his son "that he should find in him no repugnance to obey his commands," and he hoped all his friends would prevail upon Stratonice to carry out the King's decision.

This story actually shows a psychological tendency similar to that of the Amazon episode in the early *Wilhelm Meister* inasmuch as the son is protected against feelings of guilt and the necessity of being aggressive. The King's tactfulness is surprising. No one at court is apprised of the Prince's objectionable passion and the Prince's wishes are fulfilled in the form of a command for filial obedience. Yet the oedipal nature of the Prince's passion is definitely expressed in the historical anecdote, whereas it is barely hinted at in the Amazon episode. By bringing in the Stratonice theme at three points in the final version Goethe conveys the impression that, at least preconsciously, he knew after his return from Italy the true source of Wilhelm's love. The three occasions are:

(1) Wilhelm, returning from Mariane on the day when he wanted to elope with her and shortly before he is to discover her unfaithfulness, becomes engaged in conversation with a man whom he does not know but

[24] See, for the following, 424, pp. 1095–96.

who had known him as a child in his grandfather's house. It turns out that Wilhelm's favorite painting in his grandfather's collection was that of the king's sick son "who is consumed by love for his father's bride."[25] Wilhelm says that the painting left an "inextinguishable impression" [unauslöschlichen Eindruck] on him. Interestingly enough, Wilhelm does not mention the happy solution of the situation but only his pity for the youth who has to conceal his passion, as well as for Stratonice "who has to devote herself to another man when her heart has already found the worthy object of a true and pure desire."[26] In view of the place at which Goethe introduced this theme it is clear that he wanted to let the reader know something about the unconscious meaning of Wilhelm's love.

(2) When Wilhelm recovers from the wounds suffered in the battle and recalls the Amazon scene over and over again, Goethe adds that

> all his dreams of youth became connected with this image. . . . the King's sick son came again to his mind, to whose couch the beautiful sympathetic Princess steps up with quiet modesty.[27]

The oedipal character of the Amazon episode is here revealed by its being viewed as a continuation of the Stratonice story.

(3) Wilhelm happens, later in the novel, to meet the Amazon and he wishes to marry her but feels inhibited for various reasons. He is supposed to depart on an important journey, but his affection holds him back. In this embarrassing situation a physician friend helps him out and declares him to be sick, which makes his departure impossible. The Amazon's brother, however, sees through the ruse and teases Wilhelm by saying that he suffers from Antiochus's sickness (*Soph.* I, 23:303).

Yet, concomitantly with the introduction of the direct oedipal theme, the image of Wilhelm's mother changes in the final version of the novel. Whereas in the early version she is described in consistently accusing and disparaging terms, in the final version all this is deleted and she is given approximately that appearance that is also now the one officially assigned to Goethe's mother: the understanding woman who tried to mediate between father and son.

[25] [wie der kranke Königssohn sich über die Braut seines Vaters in Liebe verzehrt.] (*Soph.* I, 21:106)

[26] [die sich einem andern widmen soll, wenn ihr Herz schon den würdigen Gegenstand eines wahren und reinen Verlangens gefunden hat!] (*Soph.* I, 21:106–07)

[27] [Alle seine Jugendträume knüpften sich an dieses Bild. . . . ihm fiel der kranke Königssohn wieder ein, an dessen Lager die schöne theilnehmende Prinzessin mit stiller Bescheidenheit herantritt.] (*Soph.* I, 22:57–58)

From the letters written by Goethe to his mother—all too few of which have been preserved and most of which I have quoted—one can see that he had a rather cool, reserved attitude towards her. Respect was not lacking, but in encouraging her he took a superior attitude of telling her how to live. Genuine, affectionate cordiality is missing, if I am not mistaken, and I should surmise that in the hateful picture of Wilhelm's mother in the early version there is more of Goethe's feeling than one would expect in the light of other sources. His obstinate aloofness from Frankfurt would, at least, not contradict, if it does not confirm, this view. His actual attitude, at least as far as it comes to the fore in letters, could be characterized as a tempered distrust, as if he had tried but never quite succeeded in overcoming the hatred to which he gave free rein in the first version.

In the Amazon, however, Wilhelm succeeded in establishing a grandiose reconciliation with the female sex.[28] Interestingly enough, this reconciliation with the other sex is described in isolation from Wilhelm's relationship to his mother. The aversion against the mother continues in the novel parallel to the seemingly unambivalent relationship that Wilhelm establishes with the Amazon. From Wilhelm's experience with the Amazon one can perhaps learn what had made his mother an image of disgust. The Amazon episode says that the woman has a penis, but that voluntarily and with pleasure she surrenders it to the male. In this fantasy the absence of a penis in the woman is regarded as the consequence of an act of benevolence and this enables Wilhelm to overcome his disgust.[29]

Thus the cloak fetish is a secondary configuration successfully formed in the defense against an original disgust at the female genital. I wish to summarize what I have presented at various places by way of hypothesis about the origin of this disgust. From the Titania verses (see above, p. 301) it seemed apparent that an early observation, in the mother or a substitute for her, regarding the anatomic difference between the sexes must have shocked the boy and caused a permanent de-

---

[28] I have not stressed, in synopsizing earlier books of *Wilhelm Meister,* that Wilhelm showed misogynous traits after his disappointment over Mariane's infidelity. The Tancred-Clorinda theme, taken from Tasso's epic, which runs through the background of the novel, is omitted in this discussion.

[29] At the time when Goethe was composing the sixth book of *Wilhelm Meister* he wrote to Knebel (May 5, 1785) that he was patching up the beggar's cloak that was on the verge of falling from his shoulders. I shall discuss this statement later (see below, p. 981) but wish to refer to it here because it illustrates the castration complex by the symbolic use of the cloak.

valuation of the mother.[30] We shall now also remember that Wilhelm's early history as delineated in the first version suggested, through the imagery of the puppet show, that such an observation had taken place. I refer to the passage when Wilhelm lifted the curtain and looked between the legs of the table (cf. above, p. 260). Goethe compared the effect of what Wilhelm saw with the effect the dawning knowledge of the sexual difference has on children. Since Wilhelm's mother is cruel to his father, starts an affair with another man, is unkind to Wilhelm—she is jealous and therefore denies the boy the opportunity to witness a repetition of the puppet show—she is the representative of the castrating type of woman, who is pictured as being envious of man's prerogative and therefore appropriates his organ, whereas the Amazon surrenders it to him.

The lasting effect these childhood experiences had on Goethe may be noticed from remarks he made at an advanced age. Thus he reportedly said to Riemer, on November 20, 1805:

> The argument whether male beauty in its perfection, or female, in its kind, stands higher can only be settled from [the viewpoint of] the greater or lesser approximation of the male or female form to the idea, for that is where the real stops. Man's formation patently goes beyond that of the woman and is by no means the penultimate stage.[31]

Chancellor Müller reports about his meeting with Goethe on April 7, 1830:

> Now the conversation turned to Greek love. . . . He developed how this aberration derived essentially from the fact that man, according to purely aesthetic measure, is far more beautiful, excellent, perfect than woman. Such a feeling once arisen then turns easily into the animallike, crudely physical. The love of boys is as old as mankind, and one could therefore say it lies in nature, although it is against nature. What civilization has wrested from nature one should not let go again; at no price should one surrender it. Likewise also the concept of the sanctity of marriage is such

---

[30] The progress made by Goethe can be seen with particular poignancy in a comparison of the Titania verses and the fetish episode in *Wilhelm Meister*. Here I shall limit myself to pointing out one factor, which impresses me as being of particular psychological interest. From the Titania verses I concluded that Goethe referred to a childhood recollection experienced after awakening from sleep; in the *Wilhelm Meister* episode the hero loses consciousness—that is to say, he falls asleep—upon receiving the fetish.

[31] [Der Streit, ob die männliche Schönheit in ihrer Vollkommenheit, oder die weibliche in ihrer Art höher stehe, kann nur aus der grössern oder geringern Annäherung der männlichen oder weiblichen Form an die Idee geschlichtet werden, denn in ihr hört das Reale auf; des Mannes Bildung geht offenbar über die des Weibes hinaus und ist keineswegs die vorletzte Stufe.] (250, 1:457)

an achievement of Christian civilization and of inestimable value, although marriage is essentially unnatural. . . . Everywhere one has a certain, unconquerable reserve towards unregulated love relations outside of marriage, and that is quite in order.[32]

The aesthetic measure was here again used—as commonly by manifest homosexuals—to explain homosexuality. Goethe acknowledged homosexuality to be forbidden; he objected to the practice of it because it would be a regression inimical to civilization. Heterosexuality is in the service of civilization. It is noteworthy that Goethe did not appeal to the sanction of any moral or ethical concept. He almost said here that man's natural endowment and inclination would as a matter of course draw him towards a body of his own sex, but that it was his duty to attach himself sexually to a woman.

The whole aversion to the physical aspect of love came forth in a remark to Riemer of November 12, 1813:

Cohabitation destroys beauty, and nothing is more [?] beautiful than until this moment.[33]

In the art of antiquity alone is eternal youth captured and represented. And what else is eternal youth than to have known no man, no woman?

Here, then, would be innocence. A madonna, who is mother and virgin simultaneously, is nothing.[34]

[32] [Nun fiel das Gespräch auf griechische Liebe. . . . Er entwickelte, wie diese Verirrung eigentlich daher komme, dass nach rein ästhetischem Massstabe der Mann immerhin weit schöner, vorzüglicher, vollendeter wie die Frau sei. Ein solches einmal entstandenes Gefühl schwenke dann leicht ins Tierische, grob Materielle hinüber. Die Knabenliebe sei so alt wie die Menschheit, und man könne daher sagen, sie liege in der Natur, ob sie gleich gegen die Natur sei. Was die Kultur der Natur abgewonnen habe, dürfe man nicht wieder fahren lassen, es um keinen Preis aufgeben. So sei auch der Begriff der Heiligkeit der Ehe eine solche Kultur-Errungenschaft des Christentums und von unschätzbarem Wert, obgleich die Ehe eigentlich unnatürlich sei. . . . überall hat man vor ungeregelten, ehelosen Liebesverhältnissen eine gewisse unbezwingliche Scheu, und das ist recht gut.] (250, 4:261)

[33] This passage may appear enigmatic until it is discerned that it is a praise of forepleasure. An important aspect of the creative artist's libidinal economy is here revealed. It is only in the state corresponding to forepleasure that he can be creative. Fulfillment puts an end to his momentum towards creativity. Concomitant to this is his fixation to the experience of forepleasure. See 267.

[34] [Die Begattung zerstört die Schönheit, und nichts ist schöner [sic] als bis zu diesem Moment.

In der Antiken Kunst allein ist die ewige Jugend festgehalten und dargestellt. Und was heisst ewige Jugend anders als keinen Mann, keine Frau erkannt zu haben.

Hier wäre also die Unschuld. Eine Madonna, die Mutter und Jungfrau zugleich ist, ist nichts.] (452A, p. 347)

The full implication of these remarks cannot be gone into here. Their extent may be briefly outlined: The aversion to copulation; the destructibility of the beauty of women in intercourse; the sinfulness of propagation in all circumstances; the affinity between sexual pleasures and death. Was Goethe here belatedly referring to a basic contradiction in Charlotte von Stein, namely that she wanted to be regarded by him as a madonna although she was a mother?[35] Did he try to draw an ideal human being in Mignon, not as an androgynous creature, as one might believe, but as a being without any sex organs?

In his *Versuch über die Metamorphose der Pflanzen,* Goethe also reported many personal experiences and their effect upon him in so far as they were connected with the subject matter of botany. Thus he also came to write of his reaction when Schelver[36] informed him that he had for a long time doubted, and now was convinced of the indefensibility of, the "doctrine which ascribes two sexes to the plants and animals." "In my studies of nature," Goethe continued,

> I had faithfully accepted the dogma of sexuality and therefore was now perplexed to hear just the opposite of my opinion. . . . Now the doubts from time to time aroused against the sexual system entered immediately before my soul and what I had thought about this topic became again alive; some aspects of nature that confronted me *more cheerfully* and more consequentially favored the new way of thinking.[37] [Italics mine].

In the context of Goethe's reaction to a scientific theory that denies the universality of sexual division in nature we encounter an attitude that reconfirms the one observed in the above-quoted conversations. He seemed to feel "That is what I always thought," and "This makes the world a brighter place to live in"; his horror here becomes unmistakable at the idea of human beings being constituted as essentially and conspicuously different by nature and at this difference's not being a mani-

[35] See the letter of October 7, 1776, where Goethe compared Charlotte von Stein with a madonna.

[36] Friedrich Josef Schelver (1778–1832), physician and botanist, superintendent of the botanical garden in Jena, professor at Jena, 1803–06; he wrote *Kritik der Lehre von den Geschlechtern der Pflanze.*

[37] [. . . Lehre, welche den Pflanzen wie den Thieren zwei Geschlechter zuschreibt. . . . Ich hatte das Dogma der Sexualität bei meinen Naturstudien gläubig angenommen und war desshalb jetzt betroffen, gerade das meiner Ansicht Entgegengesetzte zu vernehmen. . . . Nun traten mir die gegen das Geschlechtssystem von Zeit zu Zeit erregten Zweifel sogleich vor die Seele und, was ich selbst über diese Angelegenheit gedacht hatte, ward wieder lebendig; manche Anschauung der Natur, die mir nun heiterer und folgereicher entgegen trat, begünstigte die neue Vorstellungsart.] (*Soph.* II, 6:186–87)

festation of nature's luxuriously abundant form-creating store of variations but an unyielding, unvarying difference.

Wilhelm Meister, Book VI, and Hamlet

We must now turn towards the other theme of biographical signifi-cance that runs through Book VI of the early *Wilhelm Meister*. This is Shakespeare's *Hamlet*. We shall have to investigate what Goethe's own opinions were about *Hamlet,* as expressed through the medium of *Wil-helm Meister*. But we shall also have to form our own opinion about the meaning of the tragedy if we are to understand why Goethe turned to-ward this topic with the deepest interest during the period preceding his departure for Italy.

Wilhelm is more or less constantly preoccupied with *Hamlet* during this last book of the novel and this preoccupation is indirectly connected with the lovely woman who has disappeared. As Goethe wrote, nothing was more prone to take Wilhelm's mind off his longings than the study of *Hamlet*. Wilhelm was puzzled by Hamlet's personality until he con-ceived the idea of reconstructing what kind of personality Hamlet's might have been before his father's death. By putting together the few relevant clues contained in the play Wilhelm reconstructs a character sugges-tive of an ideal prince.

> He was a prince, a born prince, and wanted to govern solely so that thereby the good might be unimpeded good.[38]

Wilhelm draws a picture of a man who has all the morally good quali-ties, but is lacking in the aggressiveness and capacity to be merciless, if necessary; qualities that are indispensable for the task of being a true ruler. Hence, when the Prince's father dies suddenly—Wilhelm reasons—the Prince feels impoverished to find no difference between himself and any other nobleman. "Ambition and desire to command are not the passions that excite him." [39] Here apparently Goethe indicated that the Prince was an ideal prince as long as he could occupy the place of crown prince. But one who is ideal as crown prince would not necessarily have the stuff prerequisite for an ideal sovereign. Therefore he was bound to

---

[38] [er war ein Fürst, ein geborner Fürst, und wünschte zu regieren, nur damit der Gute ungehindert gut sein möchte.] (*Soph.* I, 52:224)

[39] [Ehrgeiz und Sucht zu gebieten sind nicht die Leidenschaften, die ihn beleben.] (*Soph.* I, 52:231)

feel lonely and abandoned when, by his father's death, he was deprived of the background indispensable to his fulfilling his proper role.

One cannot quite agree with Goethe on this point. Hamlet's status and role as crown prince are not disturbed by his father's death. Claudius does not hesitate to accept him as heir to the throne. Yet it is important to keep in mind that Goethe at that time considered the mere fact of the death of Hamlet's father to be sufficient explanation of Hamlet's sadness, since the only role he was prepared to play was that of son. The Queen's objectionable marriage was only the second blow, according to Goethe, and only deepened the depressed feelings that were the inescapable sequelae to the loss he had suffered.

> The reliable image fades which a well-brought-up child likes to form of his parents. In the dead [father] there is no help and in the living [mother] no support.[40]

When now Hamlet is informed of how his father's death was brought about one cannot expect to find a young hero thirsty for revenge,

> a born prince who feels joyful to be doubly and triply challenged by the usurper of his crown.[41]

In the famous exclamation: "The time is out of joint," etc., Goethe saw the key to Hamlet's behavior: "A great deed laid upon a soul that is not equal to the deed."[42] Thus Goethe sees the hub of the tragedy in the discrepancy between the strength that Hamlet would have needed in order to live up to the demands of the situation and the actual strength at his disposal. In poetical and moving terms Goethe gave expression to this thought:

> Here an oak tree is planted in a precious vase that should have received only lovely flowers in its womb; the roots stretch out and the vase is destroyed.

> A beautiful, pure, noble, most moral being, without the sensible strength that makes a hero, perishes under the burden which it can neither carry nor throw off. Every duty is sacred to him, [but] this one too heavy. The impossible is demanded of him; not the humanly impossible, no, [only]

---

[40] [Das zuverlässige Bild, das sich ein wohlgerathnes Kind so gern von seinen Eltern macht, verschwindet. Bei dem Todten ist keine Hülfe und an der Lebendigen kein Halt.] (*Soph.* I, 52:232)

[41] [Einen gebornen Fürsten, der sich glücklich fühlt, gegen den Usurpator seiner Krone doppelt und dreifach aufgefordert zu werden?] (*Soph.* I, 52:233)

[42] [Eine grosse That auf eine Seele gelegt, die der That nicht gewachsen ist.] (*Soph.* I, 52:234)

the impossible for him! How he shifts and turns and anguishes, how he steps back and forth, is always reminded and always reminds himself, and, in the end, almost fails to keep his goal in mind, all this, however, without ever becoming happy again.[43]

Was this also Goethe's mood at that time? From Rome he will later report the truth about his feelings of these days: "To you," he wrote on February 21, 1787, to Charlotte von Stein,

I am attached with all the fibers of my being. It is terrible how recollections often tear me apart. Oh, dear Lotte, you do not know with what power I have forced myself and still do, and that the thought of not possessing you —take it and put it and turn it how I will—nevertheless at bottom destroys and consumes me. I may give my love for you what forms I wish, always, always— Forgive me that once again I tell you what for so long has been stagnant and silenced. If I could tell you my sentiments, my thoughts during the days, [during] the most lonely hours. Farewell. Today I am confused and almost weak.[44]

This letter in itself well-nigh proves that Goethe was in a Hamlet mood before leaving for Italy.

In the novel Goethe says of Wilhelm that he and Hamlet started to become one person, and there were, I am sure, many reasons why Goethe found in Hamlet part of himself, if not all of himself. One reason for that identity may also have been—and by the same token this may also have been the reason why he thought this to be the principal issue in *Hamlet*—that Goethe was facing a task "not humanly impossible, but impossible for him" to fulfill, namely the task of sexual abstinence im-

---

[43] [Hier wird ein Eichbaum in ein köstliches Gefässe gepflanzt, das nur liebliche Blumen in seinem Schoss hätte aufnehmen sollen; die Wurzeln dehnen sich aus und das Gefäss wird zernichtet.

Ein schönes, reines, edles, höchst moralisches Wesen, ohne die sinnliche Stärke, die den Helden macht, geht unter einer Last zu Grunde, die er weder tragen noch abwerfen kann. Jede Pflicht ist ihm heilig, diese zu schwer. Das Unmögliche wird von ihm gefordert, nicht das Menschen Unmögliche, nein, das ihm Unmögliche! Wie er sich windet, dreht, ängstigt, vor-und zurücktritt, immer erinnert wird, sich immer erinnert und zuletzt fast seinen Zweck aus dem Sinne verliert, ohne jedoch jemals wieder froh zu werden.] (*Soph.* I, *52*:234)

[44] [An dir häng ich mit allen Fasern meines Wesens. Es ist entsetzlich was mich oft Erinnerungen zerreisen. Ach liebe Lotte du weist nicht welche Gewalt ich mir angethan habe und anthue und dass der Gedancke dich nicht zu besitzen mich doch im Grunde, ich mags nehmen und stellen und legen wie ich will, aufreibt und aufzehrt. Ich mag meiner Liebe zu dir Formen geben welche ich will, immer immer—Verzeih mir dass ich dir wieder einmal sage was so lange stockt und verstummt. Wenn ich dir meine Gesinnungen, meine Gedancken der Tage, der einsamsten Stunden sagen könnte. Leb wohl. Ich bin heute konfus und fast schwach.]

posed upon him by Charlotte von Stein. But—who knows—perhaps both tasks are impossible for man: for a son to avenge his father's death with purity in his heart, and for a man to spend a lifetime in sexual abstinence.

How strongly Goethe wanted to emphasize the spiritual identity of Wilhelm (Goethe)[45] and Hamlet may be seen from the fact that in the same part of the novel Wilhelm is informed of his father's death and that his mother will probably not wait a year before marrying again, this time to "a long and much loved friend,"[46] the "silly person" of whom we heard right at the beginning of the novel. Yet before going into the reason for Goethe's identification with Hamlet, a discussion of the tragedy is necessary.

In my *Discourse on Hamlet*[47] I try to present certain facets of Hamlet's development in the course of the tragedy. In my opinion the salient point of this development is the gradual integration of a task. When he first receives his father's command Hamlet feels unable to carry out the task immediately for many reasons, one of them being the absence of full ego participation. His road to internal freedom, which is reached as soon as his ego can fully participate in the execution of the deed, is marked by certain signposts, which I try to locate and define in the *Discourse*. In *Hamlet,* also, the relationship of the hero's ego to emotions is a central theme, as it is in *Wilhelm Meister*. Further, Goethe too found himself at that point in a situation of procrastination and had to prepare himself secretly for a deed, namely the departure for Italy, and in him too this entailed a struggle to execute the deed with the full participation of his ego. It may at first sight seem ludicrous to put Hamlet's deed and Goethe's deed side by side, but closer scrutiny will reveal surprising parallels.

The meaning, the symbolic value, the intensity of the emotional charge, and the consequences of Goethe's journey to Italy cannot be overrated.[48] One must make a historical study of, and identify oneself with, the climate and flavor of times forever gone, and, further, engage in sympathetic, repeated reading of documents to be able to capture the limitless charm and excitement that Italy stood for if one is to understand how

---

[45] The historical record proves that during that time Goethe was intensely engaged in the study of *Hamlet* and that *Wilhelm Meister* was evidently the depository of ideas that Goethe evolved at that time.

[46] [einen lang und viel geliebten Freund] (*Soph.* I, 52:275).

[47] Originally written as an appendix to the present work, this *Discourse* will, because of its length, have to be published as a separate book.

[48] I shall limit myself to the psychological aspect of Goethe's Italian journey. The cultural implications can be found in any standard biography.

the bare fact of journey there could acquire an emotional importance commensurate with the gruesome events of *Hamlet.* To a century unendowed with charm and of more homogeneous sophistication it must appear ridiculous that a trip to Italy should be a shaking event to a thirty-seven-year-old, world-famous author, the highest court official of a principality. The mere fact that ten years of work, self-discipline, self-renunciation, and self-evaluation should have been necessary as a prerequisite to his taking this step must be met by contemptuous shrugging of the shoulders in our times, just as might the necessity the ancient Romans felt themselves under to consult the intestines of animals before making a decision momentous to the state.

The evidence showing the subjective importance of Goethe's journey will only later be presented in its entirety. A few facts need to be mentioned here. His own journey to Italy (1740–41) had been the culminating event in the life of Goethe's father, Johann Caspar Goethe (1710–82). He kept a diary of that journey and devoted his best years to the writing, in the Italian language, of his *Italian Journey* (236).[49] The works of art he brought home from Italy were cherished treasures in his house and the boy Goethe received early and important impressions from them. The father's journey to Italy was a central theme that ran through Goethe's youth, as can be learned from *Dichtung und Wahrheit.*

Three times in the past Goethe had come close to going to Italy and three times he had turned back. Something prevented him. During his first Swiss journey, in 1775, when he was groping about in an effort to clarify his relationship to Lili, he stood on the St. Gotthard and sketched the "Parting Glance toward Italy" [Scheideblick nach Italien]. When he came back his father was quite disappointed, for he had hoped to hear that his son had arrived in Milan. Goethe's description of Switzerland did not impress him, for "whoever has not seen Naples, has not lived."[50] Four years later he stood in the same place, but this time he thought he knew why he turned back: "I feel very strange," he wrote,

> up here, where, at a different season, I sojourned four years ago for a few days, with quite different worries, sentiments, plans, and hopes, and, moved by I know not what, turned my back on Italy, not divining my future destiny, and went unwitting forward towards my present destination.[51]

[49] I have not consulted this book. It is a most remarkable fact that it has not been translated and published in German.

[50] [wer Neapel nicht gesehen, habe nicht gelebt]. (*Soph.* I, 29:155)

[51] [Ich komme mir sehr wunderbar hier oben vor; wo ich mich vor vier Jahren mit ganz andern Sorgen, Gesinnungen, Planen und Hoffnungen, in einer andern Jahrszeit, einige Tage

Thus he wrote to Charlotte von Stein in 1779, meaning that in 1775 a good star had held him back from descending into the valley that would have taken him south, away from Weimar and his Charlotte. In 1779 apparently there was no danger that he would fall victim to the Italian lure. But there was another time in 1775 when he might easily have gone to Italy. I repeat this incident for the sake of some details not mentioned before. He had been invited by Karl August to come to Weimar. The Duke offered to send one of his courtiers to Frankfurt with a newly made landau, and Goethe agreed to proceed to Weimar on a certain day. He took leave of everyone in his native town and held himself ready to depart. But the ducal emissary did not show up. In order to escape embarrassment he kept to his house incognito. This seclusion was beneficial, since he escaped distraction from outside and could concentrate upon his play *Egmont,* a drama he had started to write earlier when the gap between him and Lili painfully burdened his soul. His father had taken an immediate fancy to the plan of this tragedy and now, when Goethe was spending days of seclusion at home, there was even more opportunity for communication between them about the play, which was progressing considerably. He recited the tragedy to his father and tried to distract his father's attention from the delay in being taken to Weimar, for the appointed day had long since passed.

The father, who was a convinced commoner and never approved of his son's predilection for the nobility, became sarcastic about Goethe's waiting in vain for the messenger and found in it confirmation of his conviction that his son was being made the victim of aristocratic practical joking. More than a week passed and not even a letter arrived to explain the mysterious delay. His father's hypothesis gained in credibility. Goethe became frightened and the shattering of his plans spelled doom to his capacity to write. *Egmont* came to a standstill. This plight was skillfully used by his father, who put pressure on him to let the situation stay as it was and to proceed immediately to Italy. He promised "money and credit" if Goethe made a decision on the spot. It was hard for him to hold out any further. He promised that if by a certain date no messenger nor explaining letter reached him, he would proceed to Italy.

Wondrous things must come about, indeed, when aimless youth, which easily leads itself astray, is, into the bargain, driven upon a false path through the passionate error of [old] age. Yet that is just why it is youth

---

aufhielt, und mein künftiges Schicksal unvorahnend durch ein ich weiss nicht was bewegt Italien den Rücken zukehrte und meiner jetzigen Bestimmung unwissend entgegen ging.] (*Soph.* I, 19:299–300)

and life, that we usually learn to understand the strategy only when the campaign is over.[52]

Goethe departed believing fate would take him to Italy. But the Duke's aide-de-camp arrived in Frankfurt shortly after and was thunderstruck to hear that his master's favorite had left. An express courier was sent after him with the urgent plea that he not humiliate the tardy courier. Again there was doubt in Goethe's mind. Should he go on towards Italy or turn back towards Weimar? The doubt did not last long and he decided in favor of Weimar.

> No further! As if whipped by invisible spirits Time's sun-horses run away with the light carriage of our fate and nothing is left to us but, courageously poised, to hold the reins tight and to steer the wheels now to the right, now to the left, away from a rock here and from downfall there. Whither it goes, who knows? He hardly even remembers whence he came.[53]

These were the words that he quoted from *Egmont* and that he cried out to a person who warned him and tried to make him choose Italy. These were also the words with which he ended his autobiographical novel *Dichtung und Wahrheit*. Were they really the words that crossed his mind when he made the fateful decision? Egmont, whose tragedy he finished in Italy many years later, was the hero who was executed by the Spanish; who thought he could deal with foreigners and people outside his own class; who was warned not to trust those who were not of his own kind, but who trusted them nevertheless, and fell. Much could be said of him; faintly one might see in him Hamlet's shadow. In *Egmont,* too, a girl commits suicide, out of love for the hero, but also out of despair over his impending execution.

But this is not the salient point. Goethe's father planned his son's career as a kind of complement of his own. He recognized early his son's magnificent endowment but worried that he might squander it. The son's education was roughly to follow his own, under even more favorable conditions, if possible. The initial steps his son made in the adult world

[52] [Wunderbare Dinge müssen frelich entstehen, wenn eine planlose Jugend, die sich selbst so leicht missleitet, noch durch einen leidenschaftlichen Irrthum des Alters auf einen falschen Weg getrieben wird. Doch darum ist es Jugend und Leben überhaupt, dass wir die Strategie gewöhnlich erst einsehen lernen, wenn der Feldzug vorbei ist.] (*Soph.* I, 29:185)

[53] [. . . nicht weiter! Wie von unsichtbaren Geistern gepeitscht, gehen die Sonnenpferde der Zeit mit unsers Schicksals leichtem Wagen durch, und uns bleibt nichts als, muthig gefasst, die Zügel festzuhalten, und bald rechts, bald links, vom Steine hier, vom Sturze da, die Räder wegzulenken. Wohin es geht, wer weiss es? Erinnert er sich doch kaum, woher er kam.] (*Soph.* I, 29:192)

seemed to justify his hopes, despite numerous disappointments. The climactic event in his own life had been his journey to Italy. This was not to be missing from his son's life. He probably would have re-experienced his own great elation and have become young again to know that his son was treading the same path he had in 1740. If one adds his profound aversion against his son's becoming a courtier, an attendant of a prince, one can easily imagine how great a pressure he passionately put on Goethe to make him decide to go to Italy. Goethe reports that his father had laid out a precise itinerary for him, and he left Frankfurt with a little library that his father had assembled for the purpose of guiding him on his journey. One almost feels inclined to say it would have been more the journey of Goethe's father than of Goethe himself, if Goethe had proceeded to Italy in 1775. Goethe did not feel disinclined towards the project. His father's glowing reports of Italy were cherished recollections of his childhood and he was eager to behold with his very eyes what he had seen only in engravings or in fantasy. In this respect too he found himself in a situation similar to Hamlet's. The wish coincided with the father's command. And in both instances the fulfillment of the wish—at the first opportunity offered by reality—would not have been genuine but the effect of compliance with paternal authority.

One cannot predict what Goethe's subsequent life would have been if the messenger had not reached him and the journey to Italy had taken place at that time. The ten years at Weimar prior to his finally visiting Italy are regretted by many.[54] I disagree. Those ten years were just as necessary as Hamlet's four acts of procrastination. Hamlet responding in a direct and immediate way to his father's demand would have remained an immature, insipid person. Whether Goethe's maturation would have been delayed or accelerated if this most important event had occurred at a time when his ego was not yet ready for it, is a matter of speculation. The fact remains that up to 1786 he rejected three opportunities, and I am inclined to agree in the wisdom of his so acting. His delay was not a neurotic symptom but arose from a deep understanding of self, just as his determination to go to Italy now was not a flight, as has been claimed by many and at times by Goethe himself, but a fulfillment and an accomplishment. He was ready now to do it out of his own individuality. His identification with his father was no longer a foreign body. Acting in accordance with his father's wishes was no longer a simple obedience; the introject had become integrated and was now a part of his ego.

[54] As has already been pointed out, Goethe himself later spoke disparagingly of that decade.

This inner acceptance and integration of an early father-identification, which took its inception at that time and was carried out during the years spent in Italy, must be kept in mind in order to understand Goethe's interest in the *Hamlet* problem. How intense this identification process was can be seen in the difference in Goethe's physical appearance before and after Italy. Charlotte von Stein, though not a quite reliable informant about Goethe after their break, reported to Fritz (February 25, 1796) what is fairly well confirmed from other sources as to Goethe's appearance some years after his return to Weimar.

> I had not seen him [Goethe] for a few months. He was terribly stout, with short arms, which he held quite straight [with his hands] in both pockets of his trousers. . . .
>
> I should only like to know whether I too appear to Goethe so physiognomically changed as he to me. He has really returned to the earth from which we sprang. Poor Goethe, who formerly was so fond of us![55]

Deep-going reorganizations of the personality leave their unmistakable traces in the biological sphere of the body.[56]

How deeply Goethe's interest in *Hamlet* was bound up with his own father problem may be seen from the final version of *Wilhelm Meister*. Wilhelm at last directs *Hamlet*—as Goethe did after his return from Italy—and the ghost of Hamlet's father is mysteriously played by what must strike the reader as the ghost of Wilhelm Meister's father. The kinship between Wilhelm Meister (Goethe) and Hamlet appears to be so close that one feels driven to claim that it was not that Wilhelm looked upon Hamlet as his mirror image or at himself as that of Hamlet, but that the two became so intimately interfused that the borders between them became indiscernible and, finally, anything Wilhelm might have said about Hamlet amounted to a confession about himself—that is, about Goethe. When, accordingly, Wilhelm gives us an account of the principal issue of *Hamlet* which is, as I believe, erroneous, it must be regarded as having been prompted by a need on Goethe's part to conceal something that was true of him.

> Purgatory sends its ghost and demands revenge, but in vain. All circumstances come together and urge revenge, in vain! Neither this world nor

[55] [Ich hatte ihn seit ein paar Monaten nicht gesehen. Er war entsetzlich dick, mit kurzen Armen, die er ganz gestreckt in beiden Hosentaschen hielt. . . .

Ich möchte nur wissen, ob ich dem Goethe auch so physiognomisch verändert vorkomme, als er mir. Er ist recht zur Erde geworden, von der wir genommen sind. Der arme Goethe, der uns sonst so lieb hatte!] (51, *1*:549)

[56] Cf. Freud's remark about the aged Goethe (216, p. 198).

the nether world succeeds in setting right that which fate alone has reserved to itself. The hour of judgment comes. The evildoer falls with the good! One generation is mowed down and another enters.[57]

If this conclusion were correct, then Hamlet's tragedy as conceived by Shakespeare would be a tragedy of fate, which it definitely is not. When Loening connects this opinion of Goethe's with the influence of his studies in classical antiquity (372, p. 18) he is right, but it still was also the result of a personal conflict. When he was twenty-one Goethe held a different view. Then (1771) he said of Shakespeare's plays:

> They all revolve around the secret point—which no philosopher has yet seen or determined—in which the singularity of our ego, the asserted freedom of our will, collides with the necessary course of the whole. . . . And I cry out: "Nature! Nature! nothing so [much] Nature as Shakespeare's human beings.". . .
>
> He vied with Prometheus, modeled his human beings trait for trait after him, only *on a gigantic scale.*[58] [Goethe's italics]

Here the full place of individuality, its full bearing, is recognized and accepted; it is likewise understood that individuality and environment must clash. But in 1771 a course predetermined by fate is by no means part of his interpretation of Shakespeare. The later interpretation (of 1785) leaves no loophole. Man may struggle, he may even give in to his anxiety and try to escape, but reality directed by fate must catch up and destiny wins out.

Aside from the influence of antiquity there was a very personal reason for leaving so much up to fate. Since Goethe was on the verge of proceeding in an exceedingly active way and of again taking over the reins of his "destiny," the feeling of guilt was greatly relieved by declaring fate to be the true master of our lives. Material was adduced earlier to show Goethe's tendency to experience himself as the passive clay out of which a superior force molded the form of his life. Yet now, Goethe was actively engaged in giving actual shape to an identification that was in

---

[57] [das Fegefeuer sendet seinen Geist und fordert Rache, aber vergebens. Alle Umstände kommen zusammen und treiben die Rache, vergebens! weder Irdischen noch Unterirdischen gelingt es, das auszurichten, was sich das Schicksal allein vorbehalten hat. Die Gerichtsstunde kommt. Der Böse fällt mit dem Guten! Ein Geschlecht wird weggemäht und das andre tritt ein.] (*Soph.* I, 52:249)

[58] [. . . seine Stücke drehen sich alle um den geheimen Punckt,|: den noch kein Philosoph gesehen und bestimmt hat:| in dem das Eigenthümliche unsres Ich's, die prätendirte Freyheit unsres Willens, mit dem nothwendigen Gang des Ganzen zusammenstösst. . . .

Und ich rufe Natur! Natur! nichts so Natur als Shakespeares Menschen. . . .

Er wetteiferte mit dem Prometheus, bildete ihm Zug vor Zug seine Menschen nach, nur in *Colossalischer Grösse*] (*Soph.* I, 37:133–34).

the process of becoming an integrated part of his personality and that there was no longer any necessity to keep repressed. The demon is not only the symbolization of a potent wish of the id, but at times also a symbolization of the ambitious cunning of the ego.

In the journey to Italy the two met: the longing for the beauty of the country his father had visited, the lure of the tales to which he had listened since early childhood; and also the demand of the ego in competition with his father, its indomitable quest to conquer the world in a way that should make him superior to his father. Tacitly, also, the feeling of guilt is soothed by the fact that his father always wanted him to go to Italy. But behind the seeming obedience, belated though it was—again a significant similarity with Hamlet—the ego could now evolve and rejoice in its newly gained superiority.[59]

Thus the preoccupation with *Hamlet* served as a necessary preparatory process in carrying out and bringing to a temporary end a conflict as to father identification, whereas the preoccupation with the fetish and the Amazon served the purpose of bringing into abeyance a conflict about the mother.[60] The two processes were still isolated from each other. It will be a long time until the two are fused and the coming to terms with mother and father can be compounded into one act.

Spinoza

The last of the three great subjects that were on Goethe's mind at that time was Spinoza's *Ethics*.

It is not always quite easy to determine what Goethe derived from reading the work of a great man. It is most surprising, for example, to read, in a letter to Zelter of November 7, 1816: "Lately I have been reading Linnaeus[61] and I was astounded by this extraordinary man. I have learned infinitely much from him, but not botany." We in turn must be astounded to hear that someone has learned "infinitely much" from Linnaeus that is not related to botany. Our curiosity grows even sharper when Goethe continues: "Besides Shakespeare and Spinoza I would not

---

[59] The return to the father may also be seen in Goethe's proceeding incognito under the name of a commoner, although this was well rationalized by many reasons pertaining to the convenience of traveling. He also remained faithful to his "dramatic likeness" and called himself Johann Philip Möller, merchant of Leipzig.

[60] The second part of this statement can readily be proved; the first, however, is tenable only if my interpretation of the *Hamlet* tragedy is valid.

[61] Carolus Linnaeus (Card von Linné; 1707–78), famous Swedish botanist, whose system of classification is the beginning of modern taxonomy.

know of any [of the] departed who has had such an effect upon me."[62]

What, then, was the effect of these men upon Goethe?

In a draft of his "History of my Botanical Studies," Goethe—after emphasizing again the tremendous effect of these three men—set forth the sense in which he wanted to be understood regarding Linnaeus. He wrote that Linnaeus's effect upon him was brought about

> through the opposition to which he incited me. For, as I sought to assimilate his sharp, ingenious distinctions, his pertinent, expedient, but often arbitrary, laws, a schism appeared inside me: that which he tried forcibly to keep separated, had, according to the innermost need of my being, to strive towards union.[63]

I think that here, notwithstanding the relevance and correctness of this view, Goethe revealed some basic ambivalence against one of his intellectual mentors. To a certain extent this can also be shown in Goethe's relationship to Shakespeare. After a period of extreme enthusiasm—and an unmistakable application of what he had learned, in the tragedy *Götz von Berlichingen*—there can be found, despite the readiness of his unstinting praise, an un-, if not to say, anti-Shakespearean tendency in Goethe's plays. This tendency culminated in Goethe's article *Shakespeare and No End!* (Shakespeare und kein Ende!; *Soph.* I, *41*:52–71), where Shakespeare's importance as a playwright is questioned. His admiration and praise of Shakespeare remained, but one wonders to what extent Shakespeare was secretly used, like Linnaeus, as a source from which to learn how *not* to proceed in practice.

Such traces of ambivalence cannot, I believe, be found in Goethe's relationship to Spinoza.[64] That relationship was also a more personal one.

---

[62] [Diese Tage hab ich wieder Linné gelesen und bin über diesen ausserordentlichen Mann erschrocken. Ich habe unendlich viel von ihm gelernt, nur nicht Botanik. . . . Ausser Shakespeare und Spinoza wüsst ich nicht, dass irgend ein Abgeschiedener eine solche Wirkung auf mich gethan.]

[63] [. . . durch den Widerstreit zu welchem er mich aufforderte. Denn indem ich sein scharfes, geistreiches Absondern, seine treffenden, zweckmässigen, oft aber willkührlichen Gesetze in mich aufzunehmen versuchte, ging in meinem Innern ein Zwiespalt vor: das was er mit Gewalt auseinander zu halten suchte, musste, nach dem innersten Bedürfniss meines Wesens, zur Vereinigung anstreben.] (*Soph.* II, *6*:390–91)

[64] This statement must be revised to a certain extent. In *Dichtung und Wahrheit* Goethe also mentions an inner antagonism that bound him to Spinoza. After setting forth the great impression Spinoza made upon him, he continues: "By the way, here also one should not be mistaken, that precisely the closest associations follow only out of the opposite. Spinoza's all-smoothing calm was in contrast to my all-agitating strivings." [Übrigens möge auch hier nicht verkannt werden, dass eigentlich die innigsten Verbindungen nur aus dem Entgegengesetzten folgen. Die alles ausgleichende Ruhe Spinoza's contrastirte mit meinem alles aufregenden Streben.] (*Soph.* I, *28*:289) But Goethe was not engaged in competition with

The man was not only admired for his achievements, but he was revered as a person of purity, as a saint, as Goethe once called him.

The influence of Spinoza as a philosopher upon Goethe has been analyzed by Dilthey and others (see 103; 517). In this context questions pertaining to the history of ideas so brilliantly discussed by Dilthey are less important. Dilthey tries to reduce the bearing Spinoza's writings had on Goethe in favor of Shaftesbury's. Yet Goethe repeatedly emphasized the enlightenment he obtained from the Dutch philosopher. If Dilthey is right—and his arguments are striking—it would indirectly confirm my feeling that Goethe's Spinoza enthusiasm was directed less towards Spinoza the metaphysician than towards Spinoza the psychologist. A passage in a letter to Jacobi (June 9, 1785) also suggests this:

> I cannot say that I have ever read the writings of this splendid man in one sequence, so that the whole edifice of his thoughts would once have stood wholly displayed before my mind. The mode of my thoughts and of my life do not permit it. But when I look into [his writings] I believe I understand him; that is to say: for me he is never in contradiction with himself and I can take out of [his writings] influences *very salutary for my kind of mind and action.*[65] [My italics]

This is the problem that will occupy us in this context. What were these "salutary influences," or by what reason did Spinoza's *Ethics* have a salutary influence upon him? The internal kinship between certain metaphysical claims of Spinoza and Goethe's basic concepts of art, nature, and the Deity have been stressed by the scholars who have tried to answer this question. But Dilthey has shown that these basic concepts had been present in Goethe's writings prior to his deeper familiarity with Spinoza. Thus it is wrong to say that it was Spinoza's metaphysics to which Goethe responded as if it were a revelation. In order to come to grips with this problem it may be best to consult Goethe's autobiographical novel and check in what contexts Spinoza makes his appearance there. For this, as for so many other purposes, *Dichtung und Wahrheit* cannot be used to ascertain exact time relations. In reality, and

---

Spinoza. Perhaps the greater ease with which he seems to have accepted Spinoza as a master arose from the fact that their fields of creativity did not, like Shakespeare's and Linnaeus's, overlap with his own.

[65] [Ich kann nicht sagen dass ich iemals die Schrifften dieses trefflichen Mannes in einer Folge gelesen habe, dass mir iemals das ganze Gebäude seiner Gedancken völlig überschaulich vor der Seele gestanden hätte. Meine Vorstellungs und Lebensart erlauben's nicht. Aber wenn ich hinein sehe glaub ich ihn zu verstehen, das heist: er ist mir nie mit sich selbst in Widerspruch und ich kann für meine Sinnes und Handelns Weise sehr heilsame Einflüsse daher nehmen.]

contrary to what Goethe there claimed, Spinoza unfolded his influence upon him during the last year and a half before his departure for Italy, as Suphan has demonstrated (517). Moreover, Spinoza and Charlotte von Stein were, for Goethe, closely associated. An article on Spinoza written in Charlotte von Stein's hand is preserved, but it was evidently dictated by Goethe, and she shared his reading of Spinoza with a like passion. But Charlotte von Stein does not appear in Goethe's autobiographical writings and therefore the whole Spinoza experience had to be antedated and was assigned to the years of his early friendship with Jacobi, who actually brought Spinoza close to Goethe only from 1783 on.

Goethe mentions Spinoza in two different books in the novel, the first time in Part III, Book XIV, and the second, in Part IV, Book XVI. The latter reference, which introduces the last part of the work, holds a logical place in so far as the predominant theme of that part concerns the role of the demoniac element in Goethe's life. But the earlier reference seems at first glance somewhat inorganically placed. In Book XIV Goethe describes in detail his connections with various friends during the *Sturm und Drang* period. His early writings had made him famous overnight and all kinds of people sought his acquaintance and friendship. There were the poets of that period: Lenz, Wagner,[66] Klinger; and the philosophers and prophets: Basedow,[67] Lavater, the brothers Jacobi. It was a period of passionate male friendships, of mutual self-revelations, of enraptured outbursts, of finding oneself in others, and finding in turn the partner in oneself. In short, it was a time of heightened homosexuality, sublimated, or at least aim-inhibited, as it was, nevertheless indulging in embraces. Goethe came particularly close to Friedrich Jacobi who was in the throes of conflicts similar to his. No religious differences or ideological disharmonies separated them at that time; they got along together in a blissful interchange of emotions and sentiments. Having arrived at this point in his story, Goethe expressed satisfaction that he had absorbed, though still incompletely, the way of thinking of an extraordinary man. He continued:

> This mind, that affected me so decisively and that was to have such great influence on my way of thinking, was Spinoza. After I had searched in vain through the whole world for a means by which to mold my peculiar na-

[66] Heinrich Leopold Wagner (1747–1779), author and lawyer in Frankfurt. Goethe became acquainted with him in Strassburg. When Wagner moved to Frankfurt they became closer and an intimate friendship developed.

[67] Johann Bernhard Basedow (1723–90), pedagogue and founder of the renowned Philanthropinum in Dessau.

ture, I finally arrived at the *Ethics* of this man. Whatever I may have read in that work, whatever I may have read into it, I would not know how to account for; suffice it, I found here the calming of my passion, a great and free vista seemed to be opened upon the sensual and moral world. What, however, particularly attached me to him, was his limitless unselfishness, which radiated from every sentence. That remarkable word: "He who loves God aright must not demand that God love him in return," with all the premises on which it rests, with all the consequences that spring therefrom, filled all my cogitations. To be unselfish in everything, and most unselfish in love and friendship, this was my highest joy, my tenet, my daily use, so that the later bold words: "If I love you, what concern is it of yours?", are spoken right out of my heart.[68]

Now this turn is most surprising since these last words are the very ones Goethe has Philine use to Wilhelm Meister when he complains about her attempt to seduce him. Whoever would have ventured to assert a profound connection between Philine's almost cynical devil-may-care attitude and Spinoza's saintly purity of thought, emotion, and conduct? Despite Philine's sweetness and charm, the spirit of Spinoza can hardly be discovered in her, although she is one of Goethe's most human creations. But apparently he felt that Philine had drunk of Spinoza's spirit. How is one to explain this? It is strange to hear Philine's voice in the middle of an autobiographical chapter on a period of intense quasi-homosexual relationships. Was Goethe in debt to Spinoza for the ability to create this exceedingly female character? Philine is a liberator from homosexuality and in the final draft of *Wilhelm Meister* she succeeds by cunning and deceit in getting even Wilhelm, this shiest of the shy, into bed for one night. When Goethe as an old man wrote about these early male friendships he may have felt belated misgivings about the somber potentialities of that epoch. He may have thought with gratitude of

[68] [Dieser Geist, der so entschieden auf mich wirkte, und der auf meine ganze Denkweise so grossen Einfluss haben sollte, war Spinoza. Nachdem ich mich nämlich in aller Welt um ein Bildungsmittel meines wunderlichen Wesens vergebens umgesehn hatte, gerieth ich endlich an die Ethik dieses Mannes. Was ich mir aus dem Werke mag herausgelesen, was ich in dasselbe mag hineingelesen haben, davon wüsste ich keine Rechenschaft zu geben, genug ich fand hier eine Beruhigung meiner Leidenschaften, es schien sich mir eine grosse und freie Aussicht über die sinnliche und sittliche Welt aufzuthun. Was mich aber besonders an ihn fesselte, war die gränzenlose Uneigennützigkeit, die aus jedem Satze hervorleuchtete. Jenes wunderliche Wort: Wer Gott recht liebt, muss nicht verlangen, dass Gott ihn wieder liebe, mit allen den Vordersätzen worauf es ruht, mit allen den Folgen die daraus entspringen, erfüllte mein ganzes Nachdenken. Uneigennützig zu sein in allem, am uneigennützigsten in Liebe und Freundschaft, war meine höchste Lust, meine Maxime, meine Ausübung, so dass jenes freche spätere Wort: Wenn ich dich liebe, was geht's dich an? mir recht aus dem Herzen gesprochen ist.] (*Soph.* I, 28:288)

charming Philine, who, quite without ethical principles, desired to be a woman who rejoiced in her womanhood and did not suffer by it or regret it.[69]

How did Spinoza come to be the bridge to the solution of the conflict? Spinoza, according to Goethe, taught the most completely unselfish love of God. Nothing ought to be expected as a reward for one's own love of God. Loving God is, per se, such joy and fulfillment in itself that the mere expectation of a reward calls into question the genuineness of that love. After all, are we rewarded for listening to music or for enjoying art? The indulgence in these functions is so enjoyable that it is its own reward. The question may be raised: Is there a connection between Spinoza's unselfish love of God and Philine's love? I think there is an extremely important one, from the psychoanalytic viewpoint. How many conflicts does not this viewpoint solve for the believer? All the injustices and torments to which, on the face of it, the good and obedient children of God are customarily exposed have a rather perturbing effect upon the believer, and the rarity with which goodness coincides with having reason to rejoice becomes a source of doubt and perturbation for the faithful. Spinoza's separating the two removed a basic uneasiness that was not alien to Goethe either. Yet this specific uneasiness can also be observed in the imagery that many men form about the physical aspect of the relationship of the sexes, more specifically a doubt as to whether the woman finds cohabitation disgusting. One answer the male may put forward in his search for an explanation of why the woman then submits to cohabitation is: she does it as a sacrifice to the man, in order to please him. But what is the reward she obtains? In accordance with childhood theories about this topic, and in accordance with childhood narcissism, the little boy wonders how the performance assigned by nature to the female partner could arouse anything but disgust. The various alternative solutions he may find are of no interest here; it is only important to point out that the solution that Spinoza offered as balm for the faithful believer's qualms, offers itself, *mutatis mutandis,* also as fitting to allay the just-described doubts of the man who feels insecure about his biological role. When Goethe encounters Spinoza's teaching that being good and loving God are beautiful per se and don't require rewards, this new knowledge can be immediately transferred to the physical situation, and the fantasy is now formed: the act of serving man, of loving him, is in itself a source of pleasure. In fact, Philine is a woman able to enjoy intercourse per se, independently of what else a man may give her. She does

[69] Happy women are perhaps the exception in Goethe's work.

935

not look upon intercourse as a sacrifice that puts the man in debt to her, in contrast to Aurelia, who constantly complains how mean men are to her and how much she has to suffer from them. It may not be superfluous to remark that Cornelia and Charlotte von Stein also belonged to this latter type of woman.

If this reconstruction is correct then an important step in Goethe's sexual maturation can be discerned in it, namely the projection of his own homosexuality upon the woman, leading to the conclusion: "The woman loves the male in the same way as I should like to surrender completely to God (a masculine ideal) without any reservation," or, in other terms: "As I derive pleasure from unquestioning passive submission to God, so does the woman in her sexual submission to the male." This, then, would explain, in outline, how Goethe's acquaintance with Spinoza had a personal psychological effect upon him in helping him to overcome a conflict the manifest content of which seemed, at first glance, far afield from the problems Spinoza elaborates upon, and this would also explain Goethe's reference to Spinoza in the context of his description of a period of intense male friendships.

The second time Spinoza is mentioned by Goethe in *Dichtung und Wahrheit* (Part IV, Book XVI), the counterpart of this problem is presented. In this instance it is more difficult than in the former to outline the general problem that was preoccupying Goethe, for he does not attack it in a straight line but proceeds by detours until he reaches the principal point he has in mind. At a certain time, which he does not specify, Goethe achieved inner peace by rereading Spinoza. "I devoted myself to this reading [of Spinoza] and thought, as I looked into myself, I had never seen the world so distinctly."[70] Then he goes on to say that, since Spinoza's philosophy has been attacked and censured by others, he will expound it.

> Our physical as well as our social life, customs, habits, worldly-wiseness, philosophy, religion, yes, even many an accidental event—everything calls out to us: that we should renounce. So much of what inwardly most belongs to us we are not to figure forth to the outside; what we need from the outside as a complement of what we are is withdrawn from us, whereas so much is imposed upon us that is as alien as it is annoying. We are despoiled of the laboriously acquired, of the amicably permitted, and before we can grasp the meaning of all this we find ourselves required to give up our individuality, first piecemeal and then completely. Moreover, one is

---

[70] [Ich ergab mich dieser Lecture und glaubte, indem ich in mich selbst schaute, die Welt niemals so deutlich erblickt zu haben.] (*Soph.* I, 29:9)

wont not to esteem the person who acts rebellious in this respect; on the contrary, the more bitter the cup is, the sweeter a face is to be made, so as not to offend the serene onlooker by any grimace.[71]

Nature gave man "abounding strength, activity and tenacity" [reichliche Kraft, Thätigkeit und . . . Zähigkeit] for the accomplishment of this task. Man is further assisted in achieving renunciation and the integration of the ego-alien by "the easiness of mind with which he is indestructibly endowed."[72] Man can renounce on the spur of the moment, when he can reach out for something new and thus retrieve his former position. "We put one passion in the place of the other,"[73] and in this way we go through all kinds of activities and cry out at last: "All is vanity" [alles eitel]. Goethe considers such a maxim blasphemous. There are, as he said, only a few who can perform once and for all a total resignation and thus avoid the long series of partial resignations.

Goethe referred here to one of the most puzzling problems of ego psychology, namely, the means and techniques by which an ego can overcome the pleasure principle or, in other words, give up a deep and intense wish. In his answer he sets forth a mechanism that is well-known to psychoanalysis, namely displacement. At the same time he recognized that displacement can never constitute a true giving up of a wish. Displacement leads to an attempt at fulfilling one wish under the guise of another. Since the substitute gratification does not give the full pleasure sought, there remains a deficit of pleasure, which in turn requires a new displacement. Wrongly does the person who performed the displace-

---

[71] [Unser physisches sowohl als geselliges Leben, Sitten, Gewohnheiten, Weltklugheit, Philosophie, Religion, ja so manches zufällige Ereigniss, alles ruft uns zu: dass wir entsagen sollen. So manches, was uns innerlich eigenst angehört, sollen wir nicht nach aussen hervorbilden; was wir von aussen zu Ergänzung unsres Wesens bedürfen, wird uns entzogen, dagegen aber so vieles aufgedrungen, das uns so fremd als lästig ist. Man beraubt uns des mühsam Erworbenen, des freundlich Gestatteten, und ehe wir hierüber recht in's Klare sind, finden wir uns genöthigt, unsere Persönlichkeit erst stückweis und dann völlig aufzugeben. Dabei ist es aber hergebracht, dass man denjenigen nicht achtet, der sich desshalb ungebärdig stellt; vielmehr soll man, je bittrer der Kelch ist, eine desto süssere Miene machen, damit ja der gelassene Zuschauer nicht durch irgend eine Grimasse beleidigt werde.] (*Soph.* I, 29:9–10)

Goethe here raised the far-reaching question that I referred to in connection with *Hamlet*, namely, the necessity of integrating culture and societal demands, of making the alien egosyntonic (a process that was particularly painful for Goethe in his relationship to Charlotte von Stein).

[72] [Leichtsinn . . . der ihm unzerstörlich verliehen ist.]

The German word *Leichtsinn* (easiness of mind) has now a pejorative meaning of superficiality, levity, and carelessness, that it did not imply in Goethe's use of it. See 146, p. 405.

[73] [Wir setzen eine Leidenschaft an die Stelle der andern]

ment believe he has really resigned himself to the loss of pleasure, and therefore when the necessity of the next displacement arises, he laments that an act of renewed renunciation is demanded of him. To such people life must appear as a chain of impositions and all their efforts impress them as vain. Goethe here described most succinctly his own way of dealing with the world in Weimar until he reached the point of breaking the pattern of repeated delaying of final solutions.

Goethe then goes on to describe the technique of those who are capable of a total, true resignation. They convince themselves of the eternally necessary and true laws. Their concepts cannot be swayed by the evanescent. There is something superhuman in their capacity to achieve this, and therefore such men are called godless and inhuman. Goethe did not consider himself a Spinozist, for he did not know whether he understood Spinoza's philosophy correctly. Since he had failed to give poetical expression to the effect Spinoza had on him despite the intention of doing so, he wanted now to make up for the past omission.[74]

Nature works according to laws, Goethe continues in his account of Spinoza, which are unalterable even by the deity, and if such an alteration should occur, man would be horror-struck. The same feeling grips man when he sees a person offend universally valid ethical laws or act unreasonably against his own advantage and that of others. We then try to rid ourselves of such a person.

Thereupon Goethe begins his account of his talent for involuntary poetical creation, which I have quoted verbatim on page 83, and which opens with the sentence: "I had come to look upon the poetical talent that lay in me as wholly derived from nature." If we now consider this paragraph in the light of the context in which it appears and take special notice of the introductory sentence, we are forced to conclude that at first Goethe was horror-struck by his own profuse genius and that it took him a long time before he could accept it as a part of nature and not to be dreaded. The reason for this initial dread is almost obvious. A sensitive and conscientious person must feel that something eerie is happening when in automatic and effortless fashion the most beautiful poetical creations come to his mind. He must feel as if the supernatural has entered within the boundaries of his self. Thus those unalterable laws of nature, of which Goethe had spoken shortly before, became altered within

---

[74] The fact that Goethe did not use these passages to expound Spinoza's doctrines but meant them as a psychological record of his own subjective experience, makes this part of *Dichtung und Wahrheit* an important source for the reconstruction of what went on in Goethe during the year and a half or so before his departure for Italy.

himself. Secondarily, this manifestation of a superior power led to alarming consequences, as one can conclude from the text, in which Goethe is not as direct and blunt as is my presentation here.

(1) The poet felt disinclined to gain monetary profits from these divine gifts, but, there being no copyright laws in his time, others pirated his publications, drew profits from his productions—and mutilated them to boot.[75] Thus Goethe found himself, in the midst of poetical treasures, unable to support himself.

(2) Since the poetical production occurred automatically, effort and will power were of no avail during intervals when his genius was silent. In view of these circumstances it seemed advisable (if not imperative) to devote that "which may be human, reasonable, and sensible in me . . . to the affairs of the world . . . and thus not to let any of my powers go to waste."[76]

Then Goethe switches to a different theme. He describes youth that is unconcerned and takes the world as a place to live out its impulses, be they good or wild. At any rate they lead to "an occasional acting without reflection."[77] He then describes two such incidents from his own life— one when a fire broke out in the Jewish quarter and he organized the people in their fight against the flames, drenching his most elegant garments and arousing laughter among the bystanders; the other, which I had occasion to discuss earlier, when he skated dressed in a rather conspicuous garment belonging to his mother (cf. above, pp. 104–5).

An individuality like Goethe's could not, of course, develop smoothly, but necessarily deviated from side to side until he found a kind of life style upon which he could rely and which would give him the much-needed stability.

There must have been no end of such stories as the two he told. Why did he select just these two in this particular context? Are we entitled to assume that the question of Spinoza's influence was still lingering in his mind? I feel inclined to answer in the affirmative.[78]

Scrutinizing the two examples, one easily finds a common factor.

[75] This aversion of Goethe's to earning money from poetical products was not present in later years. He was very hard on his publishers and received sums that were considered enormous in those days. See 342, 7:351–52.

[76] [. . . was menschlich, vernünftig und verständig an mir sei . . . den Weltgeschäften . . . und dergestalt nichts von meinen Kräften ungebraucht lassen.]

[77] [. . . ein gelegentlichs Handeln ohne Bedenken] (*Soph.* I, 29:19)

[78] My hypothesis, however, may appear weakened if Eckermann's report of March 15, 1831, is taken into account. There Eckermann claimed that the two episodes that I brought into connection with Spinoza stood originally not in close sequence to the discussion of Spinoza but further removed to the end of Book XVI. "The pleasant anecdotes," writes

Both involve clothes, that is to say, there is in both an allusion to an exhibitionistic factor. The second example is more open in this respect. It reveals the desire of a young man to adorn himself after the manner permitted to women, and takes us back to the problem of homosexuality, which also arouses the horror of deviating from eternally valid moral laws.

Fully to examine the significance of the story of the fire in the Jewish quarter would require a broad discussion of Goethe's attitude towards the Jews. That, however, would lead far afield. Suffice it to say that his remarks about contemporary Jews were not always friendly and that apparently he was not in favor of full emancipation for them. His deep feeling about the Biblical Jew, his desire to make the Wandering Jew the topic of epical poetry, his admiration for Spinoza, his infatuation with the boy Mendelssohn, show his profound tie to Judaic tradition and Judaic culture and his appreciation of Jewish talent; yet all this did not result in a liberal attitude towards the Jewish question of his times (see 522). His story about the fire may be interpreted as an indication of an identification with the Jews. In it, he behaves as if he were one of them and he incurs ridicule, which was also customarily directed against the Jews in Frankfurt. Goethe had already adumbrated this identification with the degraded (circumcised?) Jew when he complained about the pirating publishers. He tells us that the first one[79] to offend him in that way offered him some Berlin porcelain as a compensation. "On this occasion," Goethe continued,

> it was bound to occur to me that the Berlin Jews when they married, were compelled to buy a certain quantity of porcelain in order to assure the sales of the Royal works.[80]

Eckermann regarding the advice he gave Goethe, "of the fire . . . and skating . . . could very aptly be connected with the passage where the unconscious, quite unpremeditated poetical production is discussed." [Die artigen Anekdoten vom Feuer . . . und Schlittschuhlaufen . . . würden sehr schicklich dort zu verknüpfen sein, wo von dem bewusstlosen ganz unvorbedachten poetischen Producieren die Rede ist.] (119, p. 319) Goethe complied with this suggestion. I do not know to what extent this relative distance from the Spinoza discussion as Goethe originally planned it disproves my conclusions. In defense of my reconstruction I suggest that Eckermann—whose identification with Goethe is very evident—sensed a connection that Goethe tried to camouflage. Goethe's tendency to keep something obscure in Book XVI of *Dichtung und Wahrheit* is to my mind unquestionable.

[79] Christian Friedrich Himburg, a Berlin bookdealer and publisher, brought out Goethe's works first in three volumes (1775–76) and then in four (1779) without obtaining Goethe's permission.

[80] [Bei dieser Gelegenheit musste mir einfallen, dass die Berliner Juden, wenn sie sich verheiratheten, ein gewisse Partie Porzellan zu nehmen verpflichtet waren, damit die königliche Fabrik einen sichern Absatz hätte.] (*Soph.* I, 29:15–16)

Here Goethe quite openly records that he was made to feel like a Jew when he had to bow helplessly to exploitation.

Thus we have the following elements in associative connection with Spinoza: to be exposed to horror-arousing, supernatural impulses (the inner genius), to be exposed to uncontrolled aggression (the pirating publishers), to be exposed to ridicule because of association with a degraded minority (the fire in the Jewish quarter), to be exposed to the impulse of wearing female attire (the skating episode). In short, one finds in association with Spinoza a mélange of those situations that are in general unalterable, such as the sex to which we belong, or our group membership or the inner force of drives, passions and appetites. Apparently Goethe had learned from Spinoza to accept without rebellion that part of nature and society that is unalterable.

Of course, the question arises immediately as to how Spinoza's *Ethics* could have had this effect upon him. The psychological content of Spinoza's *Ethics* has been compared with Freud's psychoanalytic doctrines (see 4), and by some considered to be superior in psychological correctness to Freud's latest views.[81] In this context, it is of course, immaterial whether Spinoza's psychology coincides with Freud's or not, but it is of importance only that they are comparable and show an affinity (which has been most stressed among analysts by A. A. Brill [69, p. 97]). As a person in mental distress may obtain enlightenment and succor by the perusal of Freud's work, Goethe derived knowledge directly applicable to a most personal problem from the *Ethics*. Indeed, I believe that, for such help as is to be gotten from reading alone, Spinoza's *Ethics* served better than Freud's works would have. Since Freud applied a strictly scientific method, his findings are outspoken and liable to arouse resistance, whereas Spinoza's psychological statements, always drenched in explicit or implied ethical views, can strike most deeply into a person without arousing feelings of guilt or anxiety.

In the following, therefore, I do not want to say anything about Spinoza's work per se but to investigate whether parts of it—and we must not forget that Goethe did not study the *Ethics* in a systematic way but browsed sporadically in it—could have had a direct effect on the course that his conflicts took. We should once more consider what his psychological problem was before leaving for Italy.

(1) In the course of the pre-Italian decade Goethe had acquired full control over the sexual drive. He had spent years in a highly sublimated

---

[81] See 27. For a fair appraisal see 32.

relationship of love and affection for an idealized and intensely adored woman. The moment was approaching when control should lead to gratification.

(2) Emotional outbreaks had become scarcer and scarcer and the unruliness of his emotions had given way to a tremendous capacity for regular and often boring practical work devoid of any artistic values. In his attempt at gaining control over his emotions he had gone beyond the salutary limit. In his hard fight against the irrational, he developed a hostility against emotions in general. The task in this area was identical with that which I have mentioned with regard to the heterosexual drive. After the ego had acquired domination over intense feelings, it had to learn to tolerate their reintroduction without their getting out of hand.

Whether it is logically justifiable or not, a person browsing in Spinoza may well be moved to adopt a friendly disposition towards his emotions. The mere fact of Spinoza's stressing the causality of all psychological phenomena, including the irrational, makes an emotion an object to be viewed with interest rather than dismissed with disapproval. Thus we read in the Introduction to "On the Origin and Nature of the Emotions": "Nothing happens in Nature which can be attributed to any vice of Nature, for she is always the same and everywhere one. . . . The emotions, therefore, of hatred, anger, envy, considered in themselves, follow from the same necessity and virtue of Nature as other individual things; they have therefore certain causes through which they are to be understood, and certain properties which are just as worthy of being known as the properties of any other thing in the contemplation alone of which we delight." (272, pp. 127–28) "To delight in the contemplation of an emotion"—this is an attitude that obviates immediate suppression or repression of the emotion, but also forestalls its growing to unmanageable proportions. It suggests the moving of the ego's center into the position of self-observation, so that the emotions may pass before that agency in our personality that registers and contemplates the flow of the stream of consciousness. The preservation of the full emotion with simultaneous maintenance of secondary processes is here suggested. Since Nature cannot create anything vicious, the existence of certain rights in man by virtue of Nature becomes an inescapable consequence.

> It is by the highest right of Nature that each person exists and consequently it is by the highest right of Nature that each person does those things which follow from the necessity of his nature; and therefore it is by the highest right of Nature that each person judges what is good and what is evil, consults his own advantage as he thinks best. (272, p. 216, Part 4, Proposition 37, Note 2)

Thus the emotion is not a product of Nature which is to be borne because Nature imposes it, but something to the experience and enjoyment of which man has an inalienable right.

Spinoza's thesis that body and mind are manifestations of the same unitary essence, and the concomitant bringing of the "decrees of the mind" and the "appetites of the body" (272, p. 133, Part 3, Prop. 2, Note) into close proximity and declaring them to have equal rights, must have worked with particular force against the schism between mind and body, which was and is the mainstay of all puritanism and therefore was also a principal tenet of Charlotte von Stein's.

Since Nature can never be vicious, sin has no place within her realm. "In a natural state sin cannot be conceived, but only in a civil state where it is decided by universal consent what is good and what is evil. . . . 'Sin,' therefore, is nothing but disobedience, which is punished by the Law of the State alone." (272, p. 217, Part 4, Prop. 37, Note 2). But if sin is man-made and Nature is beyond and above sin, then the concept of sin need have no binding power as a deterrent. It is reduced to the status of a convenient instrument for avoiding behavior offensive to the group.[82] Such a view, in turn, again conflicted with a basic concept of Protestant puritanism. But within the realm of pure value, too, everything is relative. "The good which hinders us from enjoying a greater good is really an evil, for good and evil . . . are affirmed of things in so far as we compare them with one another" (272, p. 235, Part 4, Prop. 45, Demonstration). Consequently an evil may even become a good in certain contexts,[83] which denies any possibility of attributing an absolute moral value to any particular action. From Goethe's letters to Charlotte von Stein it becomes evident that such moral evaluation of him was currently being made, and Goethe had to listen to many a hard word at times for an action that was probably beyond his control and, if suppressed, might have led to "greater evil" and therefore was really good.

But Spinoza also went into the area of motivation and condemned fear as a totally inacceptable motive for action. "He who is led by fear and does what is good in order that he may avoid what is evil is not led by reason" (272, p. 234, Part 4, Prop. 63).

All the emotions . . . which are related to reason, are not other than emotions of joy and desire. . . . The superstitious, who know better how to

[82] Perhaps Goethe's reasoning was born out of the Spinozistic spirit when he justified the illegitimate relationship to Christiane with the argument that it did not cause any damage to anyone.

[83] Cf. "a less evil is really a good" in the same Demonstration (272, p. 235, Part 4, Prop. 45).

rail at vice than to teach virtue, and who study not to lead man by reason, but to hold him in through fear . . . aim at nothing more than that others should be as miserable as themselves, and . . . they . . . become annoying and hateful to men. (272, p. 234, Part 4, Prop. 63, Dem. and Note)

Fear (of venereal disease) as will be seen later played a noteworthy role in Goethe's sexual inhibition, but fear of reprimand from Charlotte von Stein was also a strong force in inuring him to the iron discipline to which he had now submitted for years. Thus the condemnation of certain emotions and the surprising association of certain other emotions with certain values must have led to Goethe's making a changed evaluation of patterns that had become habitual with him.

"By 'joy' . . . I shall understand the passive states through which the mind passes to a greater perfection; by 'sorrow' . . . through which it passes to a less perfection" (272, p. 137, Part 3, Prop. 11, Note). And even more radically: "Joy is man's passage from a less to a greater perfection" (272, p. 175, Part 3, Definition 2, in "Definitions of the Emotions").

When Spinoza further declares remorse to be "a sign of weakness of mind" (272, p. 223, Part 4, Prop. 47, Note), or repentance not to be a virtue ("that is to say, it does not spring from reason; on the contrary, the man who repents of what he has done is doubly wretched or impotent" [272, p. 227, Part 4, Prop. 54]), and further that humility never originates from man's understanding of himself, but is due "to the fact that his power of action is restrained" (272, p. 226, Part 4, Prop. 53, Demonstration), these ideas must have revolutionized Goethe's thinking about himself. Remorse, repentance, and sorrow, which had played such a great role in the process of reorganizing and remodeling his personality, were suddenly pushed to the side of evil. Joy, which Charlotte von Stein was so little capable of experiencing, was called a sign of perfection. Indeed, Goethe here encountered a psychological theory that was well equipped to evolve in him those emotions that corresponded to his turning increasingly away from Christianity and towards enlightened pagansim. Joy, which is so firmly associated with the picture modern Europe had formed of ancient Greece, was here made a measure of ethical perfection. Thus we read in the *Ethics:*

I make a great distinction between mockery . . . and laughter; for laughter and merriment are nothing but joy, and therefore . . . are in themselves good. Nothing but a gloomy and sad superstition forbids enjoyment. . . . No God and no human being except an envious one, is delighted by my impotence or my trouble, or esteems as any virtue in us tears, sighs, fears; . . . on the contrary the greater the joy with which we are affected . . . the more do we necessarily partake of the divine nature. To make use of things . . . and to delight in them as much as possible . . . is the part of a wise man. (272, p. 222, Part 4, Prop. 45, Note 2)

Here any remnant of the medieval spirit, any tendency such as the *Sturm und Drang* revived, to see in profound and tearing conflicts a moral value, has disappeared, and there is expressed in impressively logical terms a philosophy that turns vigorously and joyfully towards the world and nevertheless is also acceptable to one who was raised in the Christian community.

It is the part of a wise man . . . to refresh and invigorate himself with moderate and pleasant eating and drinking, with sweet scents and the beauty of green plants, with ornaments, with music, . . . and with all things of this kind which one man can enjoy without hurting another. (272, p. 222, Part 4, Prop. 45, Note 2)

Charlotte von Stein, of course, was capable of enjoying most of these things; yet her enjoyment was not of the freely flowing kind that breathes from this quotation. Moreover, the quotation goes on to assert a proposition that she could not accept as a valid part of nature's planning for mankind: "For the human body is composed of a great number of parts of diverse nature, which constantly need new and varied nourishment in order that the whole of the body may be equally fit for everything which can follow from its nature." If God and world coincide, then the highest celebration of the deity is the enjoyment of the world. Charlotte von Stein, who came from a puritanical environment, undoubtedly used the world as a medium for reaching God, and therefore for her the concept of duty could never be separated from life. How great was the benefit Goethe had obtained from having had to integrate this mode of living has been shown earlier and will later be further discussed, but now was the time for Goethe to outgrow the reorganization that had been accomplished. Was the treasure Goethe had received to continue to be available to him only in symbiotic relation with the donor, or was he going to be able to use it in full freedom and independence? This phase must be likened to the dissolution of the transference to the analyst once the patient's symptoms have been removed. The necessity of that process was unknown to both. Charlotte von Stein thought that her mission was being in the highest degree fulfilled as long as Goethe served the idealism that had become part of her existence.

On November 23, 1783, he wrote to Charlotte von Stein:

> My throat is not yet quite well, but the rest of me has been brought again into equilibrium through sleep. Only my love for you cannot come into an equilibrium; it always swings quite, quite alone to you.[84]

Yet sixteen months later, on March 15, 1785, he wrote:

> I have only two gods, you and sleep. You two cure everything in me that is to be cured and are the alternate measures against the evil spirits.[85]

In the difference between the two letters one senses the dawn of independence. By putting the love-object on the same plane as sleep the idea is remotely implied that sleep could also cure his love, which he had called a disease.

Yet in Spinoza's *Ethics* passages are found that have direct application to the structure of Goethe's transference relationship to the love-object. Thus we read: "The emotions of overestimation and contempt are always evil" (272, p. 224, Part 4, Prop. 48). Overestimation was defined as consisting "in thinking too highly of another person in consequence of our love for him" (272, p. 179, Definitions of the Emotions, No. 21). Had Goethe read these lines a few years earlier he would perhaps have criticized them, for at that time he might have felt that love was impossible without overestimation of the object. That overestimation is, after all, what makes the difference between admiration and love. Be this as it may, Goethe vastly overestimated Charlotte von Stein. She had become the alpha and omega of his existence and he showed at times all the earmarks of a person who is using himself up in behalf of an exalted object. Goethe was proud of this self-surrender. One gets the impression that at times he experienced it as a ceremonial act or a ritual. Of course he had surrendered to other women before, but then it had been in passion, on the spur of the moment, prompted by the momentary impression that the object was exquisite. In the relationship to Charlotte von Stein there was duration. He had at last accomplished an abiding object-relationship that did not fluctuate with the accidents of the object's behavior, which so easily arouse ambivalence when the tie to the object is weak. Yet all the sacrifices involved in self-renunciation were possible only through the over-

---

[84] [Mein Hals ist noch nicht ganz gut mein übriges Wesen aber durch den Schlaf wieder in's Gleichgewicht gebracht. Nur meine Liebe zu dir kann in kein Gleichgewicht kommen, sie hängt immer ganz ganz allein zu dir.]

[85] [Ich habe nur zwey Götter dich und den Schlaf. Ihr heilet alles an mir was zu heilen ist und seyd die wechselsweisen Mittel gegen die bösen Geister.]

estimation of that object. Now, when it became necessary to liquidate this overestimation, Goethe obtained support in undergoing this painful process through reading—in the works of a philosopher whom, in turn, he perhaps overestimated—that overestimation was an evil. Spinoza's stand against the overestimation of an object found its parallel in a doubt concerning altruism. "No one endeavors to preserve his own being for the sake of another object," he wrote (272, p. 206, Part 4, Prop. 25), and went on: "For if a man endeavored to preserve his being for the sake of any other object, this object would then become the primary foundation of virtue . . . which . . . is an absurdity" (272, p. 206, Part 4, Prop. 25, Dem.). But this was just what Goethe had claimed when he wrote Charlotte von Stein that when she was away his virtue had gone away with her.

This loss of virtue when Charlotte von Stein was absent collided head-on with Spinoza's definition of virtue. "We do not know . . . that anything is certainly good, except that which actually conduces to understanding and, on the other hand, we do not know that anything is evil except that which can hinder us from understanding" (272, p. 207, Part 4, Prop. 27, Dem.). In the light of such views, what Goethe had thought to be virtue became evil, for Charlotte von Stein's absence prevented understanding, or, in the poet's terms, even made it impossible.

Spinoza's *Ethics* is not limited to a contemplation of man's mind but also advises how man ought to live, how, for example, to put an end to an unpleasant emotion. "If we detach a perturbation of the mind or an emotion from the thought of an external cause and connect it with other thoughts, then the love or hatred toward the external cause and the fluctuations of the mind which arise from these emotions will be destroyed" (272, pp. 255–56, Part 5, Prop. 2). To a certain extent true object-love is denied in this proposition. There is ascribed to man the capacity to organize his object-relations in accordance with his conscious volition. Any attachment to or aversion from an object can be changed. The impact of the world as the arouser of our emotion is denied. The organization or manipulation of images is made the key to all object-relations.

From psychopathology it is well known that some people involuntarily manipulate their object-relations in this way. Particularly by means of depersonalization "the fluctuations of the mind" that arise from emotions can be flattened out with relative ease by those who are able to avail themselves of this mechanism. I wonder how far Goethe may here have received theoretical support for using a mechanism that, though it belongs essentially to psychopathology, nevertheless stands the perturbed in good stead in an emotional crisis. At least it can be said that anyone who tries to live up to Spinoza's second proposition may very well tend to develop a depersonalization.

Whether Goethe really had this mechanism at his disposal I do not know. Close study of his whole work might establish whether he did or did not. Depersonalization is a symptom that, in a mild degree, can occur occasionally in any person, and often does. Sometimes it is the principal symptom that prompts a patient to seek treatment. However, less is known about those who are often depersonalized and do not sense it as a symptom at all. Sometimes, although rarely, one even encounters a patient who feels a mild enjoyment from the state of depersonalization. Less rare are those for whom depersonalization provides compensation, by soothing the sting of mental pain.

Spinoza continues this line of thought when he writes: "In so far as the mind understands all things as necessary, so far has it greater power over the emotions, or suffers less from them" (272, p. 258, Part 5, Prop. 6). Spinoza tries to prove this proposition by two examples. Sorrow is diminished if the loss of a good is recognized as unavoidable, and no one pities an infant for its weakness and lack of consciousness, because all human beings are born infants. An appeal to reason should facilitate the ego's power of denial. Insight into the necessity of events may make the emotional reaction appear ludicrous. In psychoanalytical terminology one probably would see in this attitude an act of intellectualization, that great helper in the ego's struggle against unpleasure. But the mechanism has also another aspect. Insight into the nexus of things and emotions may make the emotions appear as necessary and unavoidable consequences and thereby create a more tolerant attitude towards them. If the emotions connected with the sexual passion are recognized as necessary consequences of Nature, then the ego may strive towards integrating them and become more inclined towards gratifying them than when bodily appetites are regarded as extraneous and incompatible with the dignity of man.

The tendency towards intellectualization becomes particularly evident in Spinoza's proposition that man is less injured by and suffers less from an emotion when he contemplates at the time of experiencing it many and different causes related to the emotion. There is an inverse proportion, according to Spinoza, between the number of the causes contemplated and the pain (272, p. 260, Part 5, Prop. 9, Dem.). Spinoza's demonstration of this proposition is particularly interesting. An emotion is injurious in so far as it hinders the mind from thinking. If an emotion determines the mind to contemplation of a large number of objects it is less injurious than if it does so of a small number. From this it follows necessarily that "we possess the power of arranging and connecting the modifications of the body according to the order of the intellect" when we are agitated by emotions that are not contrary to human nature (272, p. 260, Part 5, Prop. 10). Now the permanent state of sexual dissatisfaction, unless the sexual urge is well repressed, hinders the power to concentrate upon and pay attention to matters not associated with the urge. The painful feeling resulting from the relentless but never appeased demand, and the energy that has to be expended in the struggle against a drive, are necessarily a drain upon the intellectual power unless the sexual drive is sublimated *in toto*. This Goethe did not succeed in doing, since his feeling for Charlotte von Stein constantly renewed the sexual wish. His occasional complaints will be recalled about Charlotte von Stein's seductive behavior, which made abstinence all the more difficult for him. Be this as it may, when Spinoza says that "he who possesses a body fit for many things possesses a mind of which the greater part is eternal" (272, p. 277, Part 5, Prop. 39), this again may be interpreted in the afore-mentioned manner, particularly in view of the Demonstration, which asserts that such a man is "least of all agitated by those emotions which are evil," that is to say, by emotions that are contrary to our nature. In the same Demonstration Spinoza likens the opposite of this type to an infant: ". . . he who, like an infant or child, possesses a body fit for very few things, and almost altogether dependent on external causes, has a mind which, considered in itself alone, is almost entirely unconscious of itself, of God, and of objects" (272, p. 277, Part 5, Prop. 39, Note). But the infant is so much different from the adult also in point of its sexual immaturity, and Goethe was actually inactive in this one area. When Goethe read: "The more perfection a thing possesses, the more it acts and the less it suffers; and conversely the more it acts, the more perfect it is" (272, p. 278, Part 5, Prop. 40), it must have struck him like a thunderbolt. It was shown earlier that Goethe at times experienced his existence as a passive process of being molded, and the feelings of passivity in his relationship with Charlotte von Stein were conscious and at times fear-arousing.

In his earlier-quoted letter of August 30, 1784, Goethe called his love for Charlotte von Stein a sickness, which, however, he preferred to perfect health. Now he had to read that "love and desire may be excessive," and

we see men sometimes so affected by one object that, although it is not present, they believe it to be before them; and if this happens to a man who is not asleep, we may say he is delirious or mad. Nor are those believed to be less mad who are inflamed by love, dreaming about nothing but a mistress or harlot day and night, for they excite our laughter. (272, pp. 220–21, Part 4, Prop. 44 and Dem.)

Many a belief Goethe cherished at that time was stripped of its illusionary glamour, and, through Spinoza, there was introduced a down-to-earth, realistic element into Goethe's thinking about what man's emotional life ought to be.

Thus one may say that in Spinoza's *Ethics* Goethe found a document that seemed to spread itself before him like a map of the human personality, with special emphasis upon the delineation of the emotions. Of course, I do not mean to claim that my interpretations are necessarily correct readings of Spinoza's Propositions, Demonstrations, and Notes. I have meant solely to offer an explanation for the effect that Spinoza had at that time upon Goethe. We have knowledge of three factors: (1) The text that Goethe read around that time; (2) the conflicts from which he was suffering; and, (3) the few contexts in which he referred directly to Spinoza in *Dichtung und Wahrheit*. In correlating these three elements I conclude that Spinoza's *Ethics* forced upon Goethe the verbalization of certain matters that otherwise would have remained on the preconscious level. Concomitant with this process of verbalization, of course, went a process of conceptualization, and what otherwise would have remained vague and ambiguous was forced into chains of clear and precise thought that provided the ego with counsel with regard to future action. That one result of this was greater tolerance—at least in thought—towards emotions originating from the sexual urge becomes an unavoidable conclusion.

All this must have strengthened in him those tendencies that strove towards a detachment from Charlotte von Stein. How far this process of detachment was also a conscious one is debatable. The likelihood is that at this time Goethe had not yet reached the point where he could admit to himself the necessity of a permanent separation from Charlotte von Stein. However, Spinoza's bearing upon Goethe's personality development must not be given too primary a place. The same book would probably have been put aside two or three years earlier. It could have the great effect it now did because Goethe had advanced to a stage where he needed just this philosophy. Spinoza's *Ethics* functioned as a catalyst in helping to transform preconscious contents into conscious ones. In his relationship to Charlotte von Stein the main task had been accomplished and he had acquired a degree of maturity that can never be accomplished merely by the perusal of a philosopher's writings. However, the book probably was of considerable importance as a corrective to the damage Charlotte von Stein might have caused by clinging to a function in Goethe's life that was outside the boundaries of the quasi-therapeutic area in which destiny assigned her a salutary effect. She was not aware what objectively her mission was. Sublime as she was in the phase when the transference had to be established and certain structural changes had to be accomplished in Goethe, so unwilling was she to function as a proper tool in the process of detachment. She could, of course, fulfill her objective function only in a personalized way, and this subjective factor stood in the way of her accomplishing the last step of letting Goethe derive the maximum benefit from the treasure she had so generously given him. Yet, as I shall presently show, she even—unwittingly, I am certain—made that step which greatly facilitated Goethe's loosing the bonds of his affection for her and thus inadvertently decreased the pain that unavoidably accompanies the discontinuance of a relationship in which such enormous quantities of libido are invested.

Yet first I wish to summarize Goethe's main psychological accomplishments during this phase: (1) He found at last a formula that helped him to overcome his fear of women. This formula followed the structure of a fetishistic fantasy. In a simplified way one may say a temporary solution was found for the problem of freeing himself from his mother and for accepting his sexual genital urges, that is to say, this progress had to do with the relationship of the ego to the id. (2) He found in *Hamlet* a model for working through the Oedipus complex in so far as it related to the father. At last an integrated identification with his father became feasible. In a simplified way one may say that this progress had to do mainly with the relationship of the ego to the superego. (3) He acquired, through the perusal of Spinoza's *Ethics,* a helm and compass by which to steer safely between the Scylla of his own emotionality and the Charybdis of the impositions of his environment. In a simplified way one may say that the *Ethics* provided him with knowledge regarding the mechanics of the ego itself.

Chapter 2

Hic Rhodus, hic salta

I T WOULD BE of interest to know for certain whether Goethe's relationship to Charlotte von Stein was inherently bound to be discontinued—as I believe—or whether it was something specific to Charlotte von Stein or possibly something accidental in her behavior that made it possible for Goethe to detach himself. If the latter alternative is more probable, one would wish to know whether many factors had to conspire to make the detachment possible or whether one factor was decisive. Whichever alternative of the many may be correct the following incident must have had its bearing on Goethe's dawning estrangement.

Charlotte von Stein's Mistake

At about that time Charlotte von Stein made a fateful mistake. Whether one can regard it objectively as a mistake is questionable—clearly it was the manifestation of a deep disturbance in her personality; however, in terms of its effect on her chances of preserving Goethe's attachment, it was a mistake. From the point of view of Goethe's interest—the poet's total development—one has to consider it salutary. The event in question concerned Charlotte von Stein's role as mother. She was deeply attached to her youngest son, Fritz, but had a remarkably ambivalent relationship to the two older children, Karl and Ernst. At Christmas, 1785, the latter returned from abroad a sick boy. His feet and legs were affected. Tuberculous caries developed. He was marked for death.

How did his mother react? She wrote (May 10, 1786) to her and Goethe's friend, Knebel:

> Today Ernst is measured for crutches. Trouble has landed on his neck good and early! *This* advantage he has, that he need not return from the delusion of youth since nature, as it seems, casts him forth at an early hour.[1]

And in another letter, to Lotte Lengfeld, who later became Schiller's wife: "Death would be the most tolerable for him, but I fear he will still for a long time have to fight with pain."[2]

When I described how Goethe's mother comported herself when death approached for Susanna von Klettenberg (see above, p. 472), I called attention to how very different the eighteenth century's outlook towards death was from ours. Yet even allowing for this difference in the spirit of the times, there still remains enough to be surprised about. The grim remark, seemingly devoid of any pity, about how early her son had become acquainted with the tragic aspect of life, may have been a defense against grief. But it is hard to see it as only that—to suppose that there was no compassion behind it. The same problem confronts us in the second letter, where a surprising measure of reasonableness of adjustment comes to the fore, and one misses the cry of despair that nature wrings when a mother suffers the worst fate of all, to know that her own child is doomed. Unfortunately, we can only speculate about how her demeanor struck her contemporaries—whether as coldness, or as concealing heart-rending pity. Our chief witness is Goethe, and he seems clearly to have been repelled by the whole episode. Goethe was not so well "adjusted," and he undertook a fight against death. He consulted renowned physicians; he made plans with Herder to keep the patient occupied, and he strongly advised Charlotte von Stein to take her son with her on her trip to Carlsbad in order to make the medical facilities of that place available to him. She refused, but went on herself, leaving the boy under the care of others. Although Goethe later doubted, probably correctly, whether his advice had been good, her apparent lack of motherly feeling chilled him. He wrote to her at Carlsbad on July 9, 1786:

---

[1] [Heute werden dem Ernst Krücken angemessen. Dem sind die Übel hübsch bei Zeiten auf den Hals gerückt! *Den* Vorteil hat er, dass er nicht braucht vom Wahn der Jugend zurückzukommen, da ihn die Natur frühzeitig, wie es scheint, hinausweist.] (Italics by Charlotte von Stein) (49, p. 259)

[2] [Der Tod wäre das Erträglichste für ihn, aber ich fürchte, er wird noch lange mit Schmerzen zu kämpfen haben.] (49, p. 259)

... and since my wish to know him in Carlsbad is not to be fulfilled, there is nothing more for me to wish for the poor boy. His capacity for suffering goes beyond all imagination.[3]

His profound dissatisfaction is unmistakable in these words. Goethe avoided any openly critical expression concerning Charlotte von Stein at that time. His anger and disgust must have been intense for him to have allowed even this brief remark to enter. That resentment at her absence was implied is made clear by the situation that obtained. The other leg showed signs of disease and the surgeons thought it advisable to open it, yet they hesitated for fear of reproach. "I do not understand the matter at all,"[4] he wrote and then added the above-quoted sharp remark. Evidently it would have been the mother's duty to be present in order to authorize the procedure and to attend her son. A tendency to identify with the suffering boy was present in Goethe. His letter was written when the whole court was impatiently awaiting the outcome of the Duchess's pregnancy. The baby had already been expected for quite a while and Goethe could not leave on his vacation before the event took place. Thus he started his letter of July 9:

I am just about as overripe as the princely fruit, and in like wise abide my deliverance. My affairs are concluded and I have to go away if I am not to start over again from the beginning.[5]

This may serve as an indication of the direction of Goethe's identification. The letter was written shortly before he left for Carlsbad, whence he went on secretly to Italy.

The impression of a rebirth is inescapable (see 298, p. 59). Here a dying son deserted by his mother, there an infant that persists in clinging to the womb; Goethe fighting desperately to save the one who was doomed, and waiting impatiently for the appearance of the other. He himself was bringing to an end one period of his life and waiting eagerly to enter a new one. He was both of them, the dying and the about-to-be-born, in one. But (to be sure, only in his imagination) the one mother was causing the death of her child by her frigid unmotherliness and the other was tardy in giving up her baby as if she wanted to keep it forever. In comparison with the former he must have felt superior in motherly feelings. Although

[3] [. . . und da mein Wunsch ihn im Carlsbad zu wissen nicht erfüllt worden; so habe ich für den armen Jungen keinen mehr zu thun. Seine Leidenskrafft geht über alle Begriffe.]

[4] [Ich verstehe nichts davon]

[5] [Ich bin nun fast so überreif wie die fürstliche Frucht, und harre eben so meiner Erlösung; meine Geschäffte sind geschlossen und wenn ich nicht wieder von vorne anfangen will muss ich gehen.]

Fritz was closer to his heart than the other two children he nevertheless did not hesitate to turn towards poor Ernst with pity, kindness, and care.

At such a moment Goethe's ambivalence against his mother, so impressively expressed in the first version of *Wilhelm Meister,* must have been set ablaze, and he could not resist setting himself up as being a better mother than Charlotte von Stein was. And in that moment one of the most important links between him and the love-object must have been broken. Charlotte von Stein had denied herself to him as the provider of sexual release. To be sure, by enforcing a constant demand for maximum sublimation and compelling Goethe to endure maximum tension she served him best. But the imposition of such a great sacrifice necessarily led to her being constantly put in a more and more exalted position. If he was to act and feel like a saint then she too had to live the life of a saint. In "The Four Seasons" (Vier Jahreszeiten)[6] there is the following distich:

"That is the true love which remains always and always the same [as itself], whether one grants it everything, whether one denies it everything."[7]

Whether such a love would still be human is questionable. As an ideal, it is undoubtedly valid; indeed, an ideal could scarcely be otherwise. Goethe had perhaps come close to this ideal type of love at the pinnacle of his attachment to Charlotte von Stein, but at the time when he decided to depart for Italy it had a different character. The fact alone that he was able to prepare for the journey and set out without telling her of his intention shows to what extent he had detached himself from her. She seems to have been not unaware that something had changed. In the aforementioned letter to Knebel (May 10, 1786) she wrote:

Goethe lives in his contemplations, but he does not communicate them; this [communicating] is a virtue that only you possess! But I pity poor Goethe: He who feels well, speaks! I, unfortunately, sometimes cannot speak for two reasons, because I know nothing and because I suffer.[8]

However, here this astute woman erred. Goethe's silence did not warrant pity. It was not the silence of withdrawal, or paralyzing conflict, but the

[6] The part of this collection of distichs (1796) entitled "Summer" is usually referred to Goethe's relationship with Christiane Vulpius.

[7] [Das ist die wahre Liebe, die immer und immer sich gleich bleibt,/ Wenn man ihr alles gewährt, wenn man ihr alles versagt.] (*Soph.* I, 1:349)

[8] [Goethe lebt in seinen Betrachtungen, aber er teilt sie nicht mit, Dies [Mitteilen] ist eine Tugend, die Sie nur besitzen! Aber ich bedaure den armen Goethe: Wem wohl ist, Der spricht! Mir versagt leider manchmal die Sprache aus doppelten Ursachen, weil ich Nichts weiss und weil ich leide.] (43, p. 186)

silence of the man who is rallying his energies for consequential action and wants to act in full independence.

Goethe's letters of this period present some particularly provocative problems. Foremost is the challenging question whether from his letters Charlotte von Stein could have discerned that his departure, catastrophic for her, was impending. At this point one feels with particular annoyance our ignorance as to whether the correspondence we have is complete. Should we assume that all or almost all of Goethe's letters to Charlotte von Stein have been preserved?[9] The scholar, so often cheated by accidents of the past, has to bow to reality and accept gratefully that which has reached him from the distant shores of a bygone generation. I am forced to proceed as if what we have is a complete or almost complete file of letters.

From the point of view of this assumption, I must admit that, if the fact of Goethe's journey to Italy had not been known to me, it would not have struck me that the writer of these letters was during that period secretly preparing for a journey into distant countries. One would gladly assume that Goethe acted upon a sudden inspiration and perhaps did not know until the last moment what he was going to do. We often let our demon, the projection of our unconscious wishes, take care on the spur of the moment of the most important decisions and actions. Yet there is unquestionable evidence that while he was writing his most amorous letters Goethe knew he would soon be absent from Weimar for a long time. In his autobiographical scheme one finds in the entry for 1785: "Journey to Italy proposed."[10] To be sure, this was written many years later and Goethe's tendency to antedate has been mentioned earlier. I have quoted previously (cf. above, p. 880) Goethe's undated letter to Charlotte von Stein which has been assigned by scholars to November 27, 1783, and have suggested that his request there for maps of Italy may adumbrate the intention to visit that country. If the dating of this communication and my suggestion are correct, this would mean a surprisingly early inception of the project. One stands on firm and indisputable grounds in citing a

[9] That some letters have been lost is known. In the first place, there is objective evidence of the chance destruction of certain ones. Also, some others, which Goethe borrowed back from Charlotte von Stein in the course of preparing his *Italian Journey,* he then destroyed, and we do not know how much of their original content has been kept in that book, and how much is gone forever. The real question, of course, is whether what is missing is missing essentially by hazard or as the result of some conscious or unconscious process of selection, that is, whether our view of the relationship between Goethe and Charlotte von Stein would be materially altered if the missing part could be recovered.

[10] [Reise nach Italien Vorgesetzt] (*Soph.* I, 26:359)

much later letter, of July 12, 1786, to Jacobi, who was in England at that time:

> When you return I shall have pushed on to another side of the world; do not write me until you have a letter from me again that informs you of my place of residence.[11]

This passage dispels beyond doubt any possibility of an improvised journey undertaken on the spur of the moment, arising suddenly out of an acute crisis. Likewise the exact instructions he left with his faithful servant prove how deliberate and well-organized the planning of the journey was. Yet throughout this period, when he was writing Book VI of *Wilhelm Meister,* and when he journeyed to Carlsbad, where he joined Charlotte von Stein before leaving for Italy, he wrote some of his most charming love letters.

I shall now give an account of some of the events in Goethe's personal life before his departure. During December, 1784, he was again seized by a serious depression. Unfortunately, the Duke invited him to join him in Frankfurt. Goethe felt unable to accept. He mentioned the matter to Charlotte von Stein in his letter of December 5, 1784, and spoke of "bad recollections" [bösen Erinnerungen] of 1779, when he had had to visit the various courts in company with the Duke on their way back from Switzerland.[12] But this time all that the Duke asked was that Goethe meet him in his native city and travel with him from there to Weimar, so the reference to those court visits was patently a rationalization. To what bad recollection was he referring, then? That journey of 1779 was the last time Goethe had seen his father, whose mental deterioration was then already noticeable. As I tried to show earlier, Goethe was in the process of integrating a father-identification. Just as Hamlet shunned the Polonius identification, so for Goethe any vivid recollection of the deteriorated father (enhanced by the mother's vivid descriptions) might have endangered that process. Moreover, the time of his sister's birthday was at hand when the Duke's invitation arrived. Accordingly, on December 6 (a day before her birthday) he wrote the Duke of his reluctant decision not to accept the invitation.

> So many inner as well as external reasons hold me back that I cannot follow your call. . . . I . . . am afraid of new ideas that lie outside my ap-

[11] [wenn du wiederkommst werde ich nach einer andern Weltseite geruckt seyn, schreibe mir nicht eher bis du wieder einen Brief von mir hast der dir den Ort meines Aufenthaltes anzeigt.]

[12] Cf. Goethe's letter to Merck of April 7, 1780, p. 410 above.

pointed circle. I have enough of them anyhow and too much; the household is narrow and the soul insatiable.

I have so often noticed that when one returns home the soul, instead of narrowing itself to the condition that one finds, rather spreads to the breadth of that from which he comes, and if that doesn't work then one tries to bring and cram in as many new ideas as possible, without paying attention right away to whether or not they really go in and are suitable. Even in recent times, when I have even only felt at home when abroad, I have not been able to protect myself entirely from this evil, or, if you wish, from this natural consequence.[13]

Goethe is guilty here of some circumlocution. He evidently did not want to speak of the personal reason that made it impossible for him to see his mother and the abode of his youth. His reference to the confusion new "ideas" would create must be understood as a fear of an emotional upheaval. Frankfurt was associated with early humiliations, defeat, a senescent father, and a dead sister, but also with the acquisition of world fame; Weimar with honor, work, responsibility, as well as loyal, kind and loving service to an idealized woman, but also with a contraction of his audience to two or three minds. Both existences were stretched out between dichotomies.

Only at the end of the letter does he hint at the true difficulty:

It costs me more than appears to hold myself together, and only the conviction of its necessity and unfailing benefit could bring me to the passive diet I now hang on to so tight.[14]

The external adjustment did not show the inner conflict involved. The "passive diet" did not meet the inner demand but was accepted only by force of necessity. Indeed if Goethe had accepted his present existence as satisfactory it would have amounted to a defeat; it was acceptable only as

[13] [Soviele innre sowie äussere Ursachen halten mich ab, dass ich Ihrem Rufe nicht folgen kann. . . . ich . . . fürchte mich vor neuen Ideen die ausser dem Kreise meiner Bestimmung liegen. Ich habe deren so genug und zu viel, der Haushalt ist eng und die Seele unersättlich.

Ich habe so oft bemerckt dass wenn man wieder nach Hause kommt die Seele statt sich nach dem Zustand den man findet einzuengen, lieber den Zustand zu der Weite aus der man kömmt ausdehnen möchte, und wenn das nicht geht so sucht man doch so viel als möglich von neuen Ideen hereinzubringen und zu pfropfen, ohne gleich zu bemercken ob sie auch hereingehen und passen oder nicht. Selbst in den letzten Zeiten, da ich doch jetzt selbst in der Fremde nur zu Hause bin, hab ich mich vor diesem Übel, oder wenn Sie wollen vor dieser natürlichen Folge nicht ganz sichern können.]

[14] [Es kostet mich mehr mich zusammen zu halten als es scheint, und nur die Überzeugung der Nothwendigkeit und des unfehlbaren Nutzens hat mich zu der passiven Diät bringen können an der ich jetzto so fest hange.]

a transitory phase of schooling himself for future tasks. Between the lines Goethe was here really warning the Duke to expect a profound reorganization of his life.

Moreover, Goethe's condition was then aggravated by the depression that almost regularly occurred around the time of Cornelia's birthday. On December 12, 1784, he wrote to Charlotte von Stein:

> Dear Lotte, it nevertheless seems as if the month were to have its way; I want only to be good and quiet and await the Holy Christ. The worst of it is that in such hours the feeling of your love also is darkened.[15]

At the bottom of the depression loving and being loved could not be felt any more. I believe that this is the first time that Goethe directly and in simple language admitted the encumbrance of the depression upon his love. Yet there is the faint possibility that in previous years the depression did not dash his affection as it did now when the early signs of detachment were becoming apparent.

Be this as it may, three days later, on December 15, 1784, he wrote to Knebel: "December has tormented me less this time than usual." [Mich hat der Dezember diesmal weniger als sonst geplagt.] Was this falsification, carelessness, or actually the truth? Ulterior motives scarcely were at work. The last-mentioned letter to Charlotte von Stein had a postscript.

> Thus much had I written when your very best, dearest little note arrived. How do I thank you, sweet Lotte, for your love and for its certainty.[16]

Thus, apparently, the feeling of abandonment could be dispersed upon the sight of the beloved handwriting. Both statements, consequently, may after all have been true—that he was tormented by depressive feelings of momentary intensity and that that December he was "tormented less than usual." The ego apparently was resilient enough to be plunged into a deep depression for a while and to return quickly to daylight again.

For his artistic production this state was, of course, detrimental. Thus he wrote Knebel in the same letter of December 15, 1784: "Nevertheless I got nothing but official matters out of the way. An operetta in between times—that is all."[17] After the ending of Book VI of *Wilhelm*

---

[15] [Liebe Lotte es scheint doch als wenn der Monat sein Recht behaupten wollte ich will nur hübsch still seyn und des heiligen Christs harren. Dass schlimmste dabey ist dass mir auch in solchen Stunden das Gefühl deiner Liebe verdunckelt wird.]

[16] [Soviel hatte ich geschrieben als dein allerbestes liebstes Zettelgen kommt. Wie danck ich dir süse Lotte für deine Liebe und für ihre Gewissheit.]

[17] [Doch hab ich nichts als Geschäffte bey Seite gebracht. Eine Operette in Zwischenstunden das ist alles.]

Meister a stagnation had set in. There are only a few references, such as, to Charlotte von Stein, on May 21, 1786: "I have written at *Wilhelm* and with each page I hope for the joy of reading it to you. Yet I have some worry about this book."[18] And two days later (May 23, 1786):

> I have written at *Wilhelm* and now think that it shall soon go well with this book also; if only it were not such a peculiar matter with all these things; one cannot ponder and devise much concerning them. What comes spontaneously is best.[19]

The intuitive, creative stream had come to a standstill and poetic production was labor and toil. The "passive diet" extended into the field of artistic creativity.

Progress in the Detachment from the Love-Object

The narrowing-in process that was enforced by the prevalence of a process of detachment was occasionally projected upon the environment and Goethe wrote as if the problem had been the small number of persons with whom he could maintain satisfactory contact. Thus he wrote in the afore-mentioned letter of December 15, 1784, to Knebel: "[Charlotte von] Stein and Herder are of the greatest value to me and are almost my only present capital from which I draw interest." Goethe had an ambivalent attitude in this matter. In the same letter he wrote: "I . . . wish at times I could share your seclusion, although I live almost as lonely except for official affairs."[20] Thus he vacillated between the desire for complete seclusion and for more company, which was apparently the direct offshoot of being attached to a woman from whom he had, spiritually at least, to detach himself, if he wanted to reacquire his full artistic genius.

The process of detachment did not—as I remarked before—exclude his giving assurances of the greatest love. The December depression of 1784 was of only brief duration,[21] and in the following months letters were sent, at times even daily, with the most charming expressions of love.

---

[18] [An Wilhelm hab ich geschrieben und bey ieder Seite hoffe ich auf die Freude sie dir vorzulesen. Einige Sorge hab ich doch für dieses Buch.]

[19] [Ich habe an Wilhelm geschrieben und dencke nun bald auch dieses Buch soll glücken, wenn es nur nicht mit allen diesen Dingen so eine gar wunderliche Sache wäre, es lässt sich daran nicht viel sinnen und dichten, was freywillig kommt ist das beste.]

[20] [Die Stein und Herder sind mir vom grösten Werth und sind beynahe meine einzigen hiesigen Capitale von denen ich Zinsen ziehe. . . . Ich . . . wünschte zu Zeiten deine Abgeschiedenheit theilen zu können, ob ich gleich ausser Geschäfften fast eben so einsam lebe.]

[21] Even to Charlotte von Stein, who had witnessed his depression, Goethe claimed in a letter of December 19, 1784, that he had not felt that well in a December for a long time.

This period was introduced with a particular gesture of denial that he had any thought of leaving, which in the light of what he must already more than unconsciously have known, smacks of hypocrisy. We read in his letter of January 11, 1785, referring to a play in which freedom was glorified:

> I am so much spoiled that I cannot comprehend at all . . . what *freedom* means. . . . Everyone seeks his heaven abroad; how happy I am that I have mine so close.[22] [Goethe's italics]

Denial worked and on February 19, 1785, he wrote a letter that sounds very happy:

> I am so industrious and therewithal so cheerful, things go so well with me, that I think I am in heaven, compared with the usual. In this paradise nothing is lacking to me but that my little chamber does not harbor you and my little stove does not warm you.[23]

Shortly thereafter he went to Jena to spend some time with Knebel, a pattern that became habitual later during the years he lived with Christiane, when friendship with Schiller also took him to Jena. This time it seems that it was the birth of a prince who died after a few hours that drove him away from Weimar. Did Charlotte von Stein notice that this trip, which was prompted by a conflict, was not necessitated by any considerations of duty? As soon as he arrived in Jena, he of course assured her of how much he missed her. Thus he wrote on March 7, 1785: "You alone are missing, otherwise a forecourt of heaven would be here." The next day there followed an enthusiastic report of how nice it was to be in Jena with Knebel. Towards the end of the letter he wrote: "If I had hopes of seeing you here everything would be fine and good. Also my serenity is interrupted by the thought that you are suffering."[24] Here the emotions about Charlotte von Stein, if they were consequential at all, are tacked on at the end, like an afterthought. Yet the following day (March 9, 1785) sounded quite different:

> As far as my work goes I could stay here still for a long time; as to my feelings I should have to be soon again with you. Scarcely a few days are

[22] [Ich bin so weit verdorben dass ich gar nicht begreifen kann was . . . *Freyheit* heist. . . . Jeder sucht seinen Himmel ausserwärts, wie glücklich bin ich dass ich meinen so nah habe.]

[23] [Ich bin so fleisig und dabey so vergnügt, es geht mir so gut von statten dass ich meine ich sey gegen sonst im Himmel. In diesem Paradiese fehlt mir nichts als dass mein kleines Cabinet dich nicht beherbergt, und mein Windöfgen dich nicht wärmt.]

[24] [Du fehlst allein sonst wäre ein Vorhof des Himmels hier. . . . Wenn ich Hoffnung hätte dich hier zu sehen wäre alles trefflich und gut. Auch unterbricht meine Ruhe der Gedancke dass du leidest.]

gone and already I miss you very markedly. . . . Farewell, most beloved, indispensable one. I take joy in nothing but what I can share with you.[25]

And on the following day, March 10, his whole letter ran:

I can assure you d[ear] L[otte] that things won't go right with me here; I should have done more at home. Solitude, I see well, is not the most quieting [thing]. Since I am away from you, I feel a lack that I cannot conquer with anything. Farewell, I shall come soon.[26]

This looks like a typical sequence: at the outset enjoying being at a distance from the love-object, thinking of her a little, starting to worry, being unable to stand being absent from her, and, in the end, having to rush back to her.

On the occasion of earlier separations the sequence to be observed was, I believe, different, in that the pain of separation was greatest immediately after departure, then gave way to an enjoyment of the new environment, until the longing for the love-object set in again. If I am correct as to this change of rhythm, I should draw the conclusion that Goethe was now trying to convince himself that Charlotte von Stein was indispensable to him.

How should these signs of ambivalence be evaluated? Whether Goethe had ever reached a relationship to Charlotte von Stein that was entirely free of ambivalence is debatable. Relationships truly free of ambivalence are patently so rare that one may assume that Goethe's affection for Charlotte von Stein too was never quite free of it. Suffice it to say that it

---

[25] [Meiner Arbeit nach könnte ich noch lange hier bleiben, meinem Gefühl nach müsste ich balde wieder zu dir. Kaum sind einige Tage herum; so fehlst du mir schon sehr mercklich. . . . Lebe wohl. Geliebteste, unentbehrliche. Mich freut nichts als was ich mit dir theilen kann.]

[26] [Ich kann dich versichern 1. L. dass es mit mir hier nicht recht fort will, ich hätte zu Hause mehr gethan. Die Einsamkeit mercke ich wohl ist nicht das ruhigste. Da ich von dir entfernt bin, fühle ich einen Mangel, den ich mit nichts überwinden kann. Lebe wohl, ich komme bald.]

We shall see further on that Goethe succeeded only later, in his relationship with Christiane Vulpius, in enduring solitude over long periods of time, and in using such periods most productively. Specific features in the relationship with Christiane made it possible that absence from the beloved object should create longing but not anxiety. Charlotte von Stein probably never became a "pure" object; her picture always contained—even if at times only to a small degree—narcissistic structural elements of Goethe's own personality projected upon her; as Goethe expressed it indirectly in a poem that has been quoted, she was at times his superego. The fact that object and personality structure did not become sufficiently separated—which for many reasons was the case in Goethe's relationship with Charlotte—made Goethe somewhat more dependent on the object than is compatible with mental health.

was far less ambivalent than it had ever been to any other woman. Yet its narcissistic admixture must not be overlooked. In addition, the absence of sexual gratification has to be considered. Sexual gratification temporarily releases the ego from its tie to the object. It may, of course, also make the object more valuable, but it nevertheless decreases the object-hunger for a moment to zero. The denial of sexual gratification may make an object useless in certain circumstances, but a strong sexual desire kept in suspense, combined with a strong attachment to the object, may result in an object-relationship seemingly free of ambivalence. Goethe, apparently, had given up hope of a sexual relationship with Charlotte von Stein. I imagine that if she had granted it at that time the relationship would either have collapsed or become indissoluble—alternatives both of which would, in my view, have been injurious to Goethe. As we know from the one letter from Italy, he had to struggle against sexual temptations, but this does not prove at all that he realistically expected sexual gratification from her at that time, or that that gratification would really have solved the principal problems of the pre-Italian decade. It seems that primarily he wanted to avoid any acute temptation of that sort. On November 22, 1784, he wrote to Charlotte von Stein: "Farewell, and, if a request counts with you, then do not awaken Amor when the unquiet boy has found a cushion and slumbers."[27]

It is probable that a woman of Charlotte von Stein's type, despite her aversion to the sexual drive, tested from time to time whether Goethe still harbored passionate feelings for her. She was after all not a stick. To suppose that her strictness in sexual conduct was the result of a lack of passion would be to deny what is known to be true of the hysterical personality type to which she certainly belonged. I assume she wanted chastity combined with the periodic assurance that her feminine charms still kept the fire burning. Goethe, however, once abstinence became an integral part of their relationship, wanted any sexual implication radically avoided.

The ambivalence in conjunction with Goethe's short trip to Jena, however, concerned a different problem. Though he had to part from her for internal reasons, it seems that when he was separated from her and took note of his relative well-being, a countermove started with the aim of establishing it as certain that a separation was out of the question. Here I must quote a pertinent argument of one of Goethe's biographers, Wilhelm Bode (48, pp. 100–01). Bode's contention is that there may be

---

[27] [Lebe wohl und wenn Eine Bitte bey dir statt findet so wecke den Amor nicht wenn der unruhige Knabe ein Küssen gefunden hat und schlummert.]

more sincerity in the single and never-repeated assurance of love by a man who considers repetition unnecessary than in such endless vows of love as Goethe's, which might have been prompted by an insight into what women want to hear. According to this view, most of Goethe's love letters to Charlotte von Stein would have to be considered as predominantly the result of Goethe's skill in female psychology or as a testimony to his sensitivity to what women like to hear from their admirers. This evaluation of Goethe's letters is realistic and rests on empirically arrived at generalizations free of any idealization of the man. I, however, believe that a personality like Goethe's could not have persisted in pretended kindness and goodness in one and the same relationship to a woman over a period of ten years. That goodness was characteristic of Goethe I do not doubt, but so was cruelty. In discussing his character, one group of biographers has enumerated instances of the former and the hostile ones instances of the latter. But both traits belonged to him and are equally typical of him. The type of genius to which Goethe belonged necessarily shows both because both are indispensable for his kind of creativity. Surely goodness would have required an occasional visit to Frankfurt, and there was never a woman who would have enjoyed being with Goethe more than his mother; nevertheless he adamantly persisted in staying away for years and years, although in the long run it required more effort not to go to Frankfurt than to go. To believe that Goethe could for a decade have sacrificed so much, given so much to, and taken so much from, a woman out of the goodness of his heart would require a change in basic concepts regarding the psychology of the creative genius. For these and other reasons I feel inclined to agree with Georg Simmel, who—contrary to Bode's reasoning—states:

> That Goethe was, in his dealings with women whom he came face to face with in reality, an expert in the sense of practical psychology, is by no means certain. (497, pp. 192–93)

Yet Bode called attention to an element that, I am sure, one senses between the lines of Goethe's letters to Charlotte von Stein. They occasionally sound insincere. I explain this insincerity as a reflection of the difference between what Goethe actually felt about Charlotte von Stein and what he wanted to feel, or thought he ought to feel, about the love-object. In earlier relationships Goethe had been overwhelmed by his ambivalence and had freely given in to it. In his relationship to Charlotte von Stein he followed an ideal model. His human frailty could not live up to this ideal as completely as he would so much have liked. When his actual affection lagged behind, he went through the motions of an unambivalent relationship. Of course, the desire not to hurt the love-object is part and parcel of such a relationship, so that Bode's belief that Goethe on this occasion was "a thoroughly goodhearted man" (48, p. 100) is in that sense vindicated. But the momentum of his "goodheartedness" in moments of insincerity derived from his selfish desire to live up to the ideal of what a relationship ought to be. When this factor fell by the wayside he was sufficiently cruel to abolish this relationship too.

When Bode claims that Goethe played with most women and that he considered most of them "dolls and toys" (48, p. 67), I am convinced that this does not apply to anything that can be found in any of the letters he wrote to Charlotte von Stein.[28] Repetition merely for the sake of politeness, or as a mere psychological maneuver motivated by secondary intentions in order to manipulate the situation, cannot be assumed to have been the driving force, although such secondary motivations were also present. He had actively to intervene in order to retain Charlotte von Stein's love, but secondary motives grew only out of comprehensive primary motives deeply embedded in the unconscious. What sounds like repetition to our deaf ears was more than repetition. It arose out of the constantly repeated attempt at solving conflicts. Our ignorance is not yet able to decipher the meaning of each single instance; our tools of psychology are not sensitive enough to respond in a sufficiently differentiated way, but it is evident that the flash of Goethe's love when he was separated from Charlotte von Stein in 1785 was different in meaning from that in previous years.

What did it mean when upon his return from Jena Goethe wrote (March 15, 1785) to Charlotte von Stein, as quoted before: "I have only two gods, you and sleep"?[29] Is this praise or blame? Did he experience with Charlotte von Stein that which he found in sleep? Sleep is usually considered to be a physiological phenomenon and to be enforced by physiological necessities, but it is also an exquisite psychological phenomenon

[28] Yet even those who share this conviction may raise the argument that I have imputed too much to these letters to Charlotte von Stein and that I have often overinterpreted their meanings. I believe, however, that these letters cannot be interpreted too much. The scholar, although constantly in danger of putting the wrong things into them, cannot put *too much* into them. Interpretations of the kind I suggest in this study are liable to error because of limitations in which the science of psychology finds itself at present. Nevertheless, although a more refined technique may in the future demonstrate a number of my interpretations to be erroneous, it is not to be expected that future psychology will reduce the depth of this historical record. On the contrary, it can be expected that much deeper meanings will later be extracted from this correspondence. Therefore, while conceding the possibility of error in the interpretation of details I reject the argument of overinterpretation.

[29] [Ich habe nur zwey Götter dich und den Schlaf.]

and no two individuals sleep the same way, psychologically speaking; in the differentiated personalities the psychological processes during sleep are individually different. By this statement I do not mean simply that the content of psychic processes varies from individual to individual, as documented by the relative preservation of individuality in dreams, but rather that, as I believe, the metapsychological cathexes in sleep are individually different. There are people who reach the maximum of their object-relationship in sleep. Sleep for them is not a turning away from the world and a crawling into themselves but the maximum coalescence with an object. This is not the place to pursue the difficult problem of the psychology and psychopathology of sleep, but Goethe's statement about Charlotte von Stein and sleep—not indeed complimentary to her—may throw an important sidelight on the stage this relationship had reached. If, that is to say, sleep had become for Goethe a process of coalescence with an object, then it had become a substitute for the physical coalescence that is biologically and psychologically enforced by nature in intercourse. However, the fact that sleep could be compared with Charlotte von Stein at all shows the degree of regression and the prevalence of sporadic passivity, which became characteristic of one aspect of the relationship and which may also indicate how far Goethe had outgrown previous forms of this great love.

The end of April again took him to Jena to see Knebel. This time what seems to have been uppermost was his utter despair over the Duke's increasing bellicosity and military aspirations. Upon his return he thanked Knebel (April 30, 1785):

> How good it is to talk back and forth intimately with friends about one's condition! I went away from you with much freer spirits and have again tackled my work as if it were to be for eternity. I thank you for having made me feel that I am so closely interwoven in your existence; far be it from me intentionally to sever such ties.[30]

This letter should be compared with the one he wrote to Charlotte von Stein ten days earlier (April 20, 1785):

> I am feeling well, dear guardian spirit, and am happy at your well-being. We are to stay always together, my love. Be without worry as to that. To-

---

[30] [Wie gut es ist vertraulich über seinen Zustand mit Freunden hin und wiederreden! ich ging mit viel freyerem Muthe von dir weg und habe meine Arbeiten wieder angegriffen als wenn es für ewig seyn sollte.

Ich dancke dir dass du mich hast fühlen lassen dass ich so nah in dein Daseyn verwebt bin, fern sey es von mir solche Bande vorsetzlich zu trennen.]

wards evening I am coming to see you and we shall chat as much as we want.[31]

The letter to Knebel does indeed sound much more sincere and cordial and one wonders whether Charlotte von Stein still had the power to elicit in him such bursts of energetic work as Knebel evidently could. I stress this factor because it may also indicate a lessening of her influence as a representative of the superego. When he was in need of advice now he went to a man, and felt at home in his company. Concomitantly his admiration for Herder grew. Charlotte von Stein, I believe, had become an everyday part of his life and was taken for granted. From the last-quoted letter to her it seems that she was worried about being abandoned by him.

As his relationship with Charlotte von Stein was essentially different from those that preceded and followed it, the process of detachment also was different. In previous love-relationships acute crises prevailed, as well as sudden dramatic decisions. He was driven, and there was hardly any deliberation in his behavior. The process of detaching himself from Charlotte von Stein was a slow pitiable affair with many ups and downs. I am even certain that Goethe was not aware that he was on the verge of breaking with her. Whereas there had been some powerful force that drove him away from previous sweethearts, such as sickness, fear, ambivalence, jealousy, or cessation of desire, nothing of these is noticeable in his dealings with Charlotte von Stein during this time.

When he was on his way to Carlsbad to join her he was delayed for a few days by a toothache. He was in despair over losing time he had expected to spend with her. His letter of June 27, 1785, ends:

> Farewell, you dear alpha and omega, you sum total of my joys and pains; since I do not have you, what can I possess; since you are mine, what can be lacking to me?[32]

However, this did not prevent him from going hiking in the mountains in the company of Knebel, or from making mineralogical studies, before going on to Carlsbad.

When Charlotte von Stein left Carlsbad Goethe stayed on, but immediately started to complain. When he in turn left Carlsbad he wrote six hours later in anticipation of seeing her again (August 18, 1785):

[31] [Ich befinde mich wohl mein lieber Schutzgeist und freue mich deines Wohlseyns. Wir wollen immer zusammen bleiben meine Liebe. Darüber sey ohne Sorge. Gegen Abend komm ich zu dir und wir schwäzen uns recht aus.]

[32] [Lebe wohl du liebes a und o du Inbegriff meiner Freuden und Schmerzen, da ich dich nicht habe was kann ich besitzen, da du mein bist was kann mir fehlen.]

At last here six hours from Carlsbad, again on the way to you, my beloved, my friend, only security of my life. What is everything else, what every other human being? The more I come to know of them the more I see that nothing more remains for me to seek in the world, that I have found everything in you.[33]

And when she was absent at her estate in Kochberg, he wrote on September 8, 1785, in the early morning hours:

Love me, you best of all female beings that I have ever come to know; keep me very, very solely loved and believe that I am yours and want and have to remain yours. The thought of being with you for the winter can make all bleak days bright.[34]

And on September 17, 1785:

If only you could come back soon! Since Fritz is missing to me too[35] I could become sick with longing. I cannot describe to you in what frame of mind I am. What I do fades away from me, and what I write seems to me nothing. Oh, come back so that I may feel again my existence. Good night my best. When shall I be able to say it to you again by word of mouth?[36]

On September 11, 1785, he wrote her:

Your absence is a real touchstone of myself. I see how little I subsist by myself [alone] and how necessary your existence remains for me so that mine should become a whole [existence].[37]

This is reminiscent of earlier expressions of affection, but the sentence with which this letter opens has to be read if the correct interpretation is to be found:

[33] [Endlich hier sechs Stunden von Carlsbad, wieder auf dem Weege zu dir meine Geliebte, meine Freundinn, einzige Sicherheit meines Lebens. Was ist alles andre, was iedes andre menschliche Geschöpf. Je mehr ich ihrer kennen lerne, ie mehr seh ich dass mir in der Welt nichts mehr zu suchen übrig bleibt, dass ich in dir alles gefunden habe.]

[34] [Liebe mich du bestes aller weiblichen Wesen das ich ie kennen gelernt behalte mich recht, recht einzig lieb und glaube dass ich dein bin und dein bleiben will und muss. Der Gedancke den Winter mit dir zu seyn kann alle trübe Tage heiter machen.]

[35] Fritz was on a trip to Frankfurt to meet Goethe's mother.

[36] [Wenn du doch balde wieder kommen könntest! da mir auch Fritz fehlt möcht ich kranck werden für Sehnsucht. Ich kann dir nicht beschreiben wie mir zu Muthe ist.

Was ich thue verschwindet mir und was ich schreibe scheint mir nichts. O komme wieder damit ich wieder mein Daseyn fühle. Gute Nacht beste. Wann werd ich dir es wieder mündlich sagen können.]

[37] [Deine Entfernung ist mir ein rechter Probstein meiner Selbst. Ich sehe wie wenig ich für mich bestehe und wie nothwendig mir dein Daseyn bleibt dass aus dem meinigen ein Ganzes werde.]

If you knew, dearest soul, how deeply I miss you [lit.: you are missing to me], you would have little peace in your solitude, you would wish every hour to fly over here to me and to share with me a life that without you becomes wholly tasteless and unbearable.[38]

This opening sentence clearly contains a reproach. It is no longer a request for love or pity and is no longer meant to convince the beloved woman of the intensity of his affection but reproves her for not knowing how he feels and for preferring enjoyable solitude to fulfilling a function for which he evidently held her responsible. His reprehension of her preference for solitude is a measure of his own horror at it.

This, taken together with his reference, in the portion of this letter quoted earlier, to the "touchstone" (*Probstein*), is suggestive of a defense against masturbatory temptations, which, particularly in view of Fritz's absence, may have become unendurable. However, as will be seen later, Goethe had reached the point where he was able to enter into heterosexual relations, and this changed the meaning of a masturbatory temptation. Initially, masturbation probably meant a defeat of the ego. But now that he had reached a new phase of maturity, masturbation would have constituted a reproach against Charlotte von Stein. If it occurred now, it would mean that she had put him into an unbearable situation, for she was responsible for protecting him against this kind of temptation, not necessarily by providing him with physical gratification, but by giving him that kind of emotional satisfaction that made the ego strong enough to bear abstinence. The plea for the love-object's presence as a complement to his existence—a plea so often raised in his letters—may be understood either as an expression of weakness or as a justified demand by an adult who needs complementation for the sake of a full existence. I believe that a change from the former to the latter can be discerned, although fear of the new, uncertainty as to what would happen if he had to enter a new relationship, was probably also a powerful force which compelled him to convince himself over and over again of Charlotte von Stein's indispensability. In the past, too, the time immediately after a break, when there was no direct contact with the beloved woman left behind, was the most painful one.

Remarks seemingly casual yet harboring reproaches and criticism, and even threats, occurred. His letter of October 1, 1785, is a good example of how many contradictory impulses and tendencies were simultaneously at

---

[38] [Wüsstest du liebste Seele wie sehr du mir fehlst du würdest wenig Ruhe in deiner Einsamkeit haben, du würdest iede Stunde wünschen zu mir herüber zu fliegen und ein Leben mit mir zu theilen das mir ohne dich ganz und gar abgeschmackt und unerträglich wird.]

work, and what gyrations he had to go through in order to synthesize them. Towards four in the morning he wrote her that a fire alarm had wakened him. He gave the location of the conflagration and described the measures taken. There was no breeze and the fire was speedily extinguished. Goethe was proud that his system of firefighting, which he was able to observe in action on this occasion, proved its value. He took it as an act of destiny that he was present at Weimar that night, for it was very much against his will that he was there. Only now he started to talk of "a kind of despair" [Einer Art Verzweiflung] in which he had arrived from Jena the evening before. There he had spent some time with the Princess Gallitzin.[39] Goethe wanted to continue his trip to Kochberg, but he could not find a horse, and when he was about to set forth on foot it started to rain, the wind blew and he had to give over. The letter closes:

Sleep quietly and dream of me. May but the feeling of how necessary you are for me become thoroughly lively in you and lead you to me soon.[40]

Why did Goethe feel this despair when he left Jena? I think the reason must be sought in his meeting the Princess Gallitzin. She was, indeed, an extraordinarily remarkable person. Although she was a member of the upper nobility, she withdrew from court life and devoted herself exclusively to her studies and to the raising of her children. Even this slight information may suggest that she possessed in a great measure qualities that Goethe may have sought in Charlotte von Stein, but which she possessed to a smaller degree than the Princess. In Jena Goethe also met the famous philosopher Hemsterhuis,[41] who was close to the Princess and accompanied her on her journeys. Possibly this philosopher had a relationship to the Princess similar to that which Goethe had or wished to have with Charlotte von Stein. Oddly enough, the Princess claimed in later years that Goethe had written her once that she alone had found the key to his heart that had been for so long closed (254, 2:672, note to letter 1456). Some scholars doubt the correctness of this claim and it may indeed have been exaggerated, but still Goethe's "kind of despair" when returning from Jena, the slackening of his effort to reach Kochberg, may indicate

[39] Adelheid Amalia, Fürstin von Gallitzin (1748–1806). Born in Berlin, she married a Russian prince but withdrew from court. She spent her later life in solitude. She was in close contact with a select group of outstanding philosophers.

[40] [Schlafe ruhig und träume von mir. Mögte doch das Gefühl wie nötig du mir bist recht lebendig in dir werden und dich bald zu mir führen.]

[41] Frans Hemsterhuis (1721–90), a Dutch philosopher of renown. His philosophy was based on Plato and Socrates, but was also greatly influenced by Locke, Shaftesbury, and Leibniz.

that the Princess's later report was not without foundation. After all, there had been times when neither rain nor storm would have prevented him from making his way to Charlotte von Stein.

Tentatively I suggest that Goethe found in the Princess a woman who was superior to Charlotte as an ideal, and that it was his awareness of this circumstance, which, after all, implied criticism of the beloved woman, that resulted in psychic malaise. Indeed, Goethe's letter proceeds in a most strained way. He starts out with the conflagration and uses it as a rationalization for not having gone to Kochberg. The meeting with the Princess, whom he called in a letter to Jacobi (October 21, 1785) "this splendid soul" [Diese herrliche Seele], among other laudatory epithets, is handled in a rather cursory manner. How bad his conscience was can be seen from his calling in fate to justify his absence from Kochberg.

Fritz too was now used for new purposes. When his return from Frankfurt was impending and Charlotte von Stein was absent in Kochberg, postponing her return to Weimar, Goethe threatened he would not let Fritz go to Kochberg since this would encourage her to stay away. The lad seemed to have made a very satisfactory development. After having sent him to Frankfurt to see his mother—probably as a substitute for himself—Goethe now played his own mother against Charlotte von Stein. "He [Fritz]," he wrote her on October 6, 1785,

> has in Frankfurt come really to know freedom for the first time and my mother has taught him still all the more thoroughly the philosophy of the gay life.[42]

The philosophy of the gay life was no part of Charlotte von Stein's inventory. It was just the absence of such a philosophy that had made her an invaluable ideal to Goethe. His attachment to her, who was so stable, served as a counterpoise against remnants of identification with the mercurial, quick-tempered, gay mother. But now, after he had attained a considerable degree of internal security, the philosophy of the gay life was no longer a danger and there was, probably, a longing for the fleshpots of Egypt. We know that he kept almost defiantly away from them, but his stress on the great benefit Fritz had derived from this philosophy must be taken as a hint of resentment at Charlotte von Stein's stern, puritanic outlook. I wish to remind the reader of the two passages I quoted from her letters earlier when describing her character (cf. above, pp. 143–44). There she admitted her inability to love instinctively and that love needed justi-

---

[42] [Er hat in Franckfurt erst recht Freyheit kennen lernen, und meine Mutter hat ihn die Philosophie des lustigen Lebens erst noch recht ausführlich kennen gelehrt.]

fication by the mutual moral improvement which it spreads to those who love each other. Yet at this point it must be stressed again that one of the prerequisites of Goethe's forming an idealizing relationship of "transference" to Charlotte von Stein was just the fact that she was the antitype of his mother. However, what had been auspicious as an initiating factor—and not least in facilitating the transference was her similarity to Cornelia with regard to frigidity and sex repression—finally became an encumbrance.

Goethe's mother was just the opposite. Her primary demand was for pleasure. The combination of enjoyment or love with a superego demand was alien to her personality structure. By contrasting Goethe's mother and Charlotte von Stein so sharply we can now qualify the process described earlier as a reorganization of Goethe's superego. It had been a feature of his superego—deriving ultimately from an identification, favored by constitutional-biological forces, with a mother who herself was not strikingly able to control her pleasure-seeking impulses—that it was characterized by a relative unreliability. The aim here was to replace this with a kind of superego that would function more reliably as an inhibitory agency and thus afford better protection against the terrible onrush of drives, passions, and affects to which Goethe had been almost constantly exposed in earlier years.[43] This protection had by and large been achieved, and therefore Goethe could indulge without danger his longing for the emotionally permissive maternal climate, that is, he could permit himself the longing for it, but he could not yet expose himself to its direct impact.

Yet from Charlotte von Stein's two statements we learn that her inhibiting and inhibited behavior was not only the effect of an unconscious, neurotic conflict, but was also based on a conscious, deliberate, well-organized system, steeped, to be sure, in all the intense emotions with which a strong ethical system is rooted in a personality.

Yet it will be remembered that Fritz showed a behavior or symptoms that alarmed Charlotte von Stein and prompted Goethe's taking over the place of the father. Charlotte von Stein probably thought thereby to attach Goethe more closely to herself, and probably succeeded. His paternal desires, his jealousy of those who brought forth progeny, were partly satisfied, but simultaneously Charlotte von Stein was revealed as wanting

---

[43] Goethe, as I shall have to point out from time to time, continued all his life long to be exposed to the danger of being overwhelmed by interior forces. Yet in his relationship to Charlotte von Stein this danger was greatly reduced and occurred only in unusual circumstances, whereas before it had been constant.

in the qualities of a mother. When Fritz was handed over to Goethe, Goethe took it as a sign of Charlotte's love, as a renewed assurance that she would not leave him, but it also gave him a superior position and made her dependent on him. The tables were now turned and Goethe was giving more than he received. His toleration of abstinence, which had been a necessary sacrifice in the healing process he underwent during the Weimarian decade, became gradually a favor he granted to the woman to whom he owed so much. But gratitude and favors are not good foundations for a love that is to endure. The longing for the pleasure-giving mother arose and was now accepted because it was no longer as dangerous as it might have been years before. When he stressed to Charlotte von Stein (October 3, 1785) that the trip to Frankfurt was of "unspeakable value" [unsäglichem Werthe] to Fritz, and on the same day stressed to his mother that all she was doing for the boy gave him (Goethe) "joy as something that happens expressly to please me,"[44] may we take this as a sign of a fantasy that Fritz was now reborn through his own mother? One passage betrays a direct aggression against Charlotte von Stein. In the letter of October 6, 1785, he encloses a letter from Fritz to one of Charlotte's guests and adds: "[Fritz] apologizes that he does not also write to you." This sounds like tacitly condoning the son's negligence. The tone becomes even more threatening when he goes on: "Be sure to come soon and in good health; my heart bit by bit is getting used to being alone."[45]

When, in November, he made an apparently unnecessary detour before returning to Weimar from an official trip, Charlotte von Stein seems to have protested the delay. At least this is suggested by a sentence in his letter of November 13, 1785:

Don't go regretting my few days' longer absence; I am coming and hurry back to you if possible with a fuller soul.

How happy will I be to be able to express to you how much I feel your value and how you alone of all beings in the world can make me happy.

The vicissitudes of my journey will when I tell you them convince you more thereof than the warmest assurances could hardly do. I am yours and must be yours. Everything leads, drives, urges me again to you. I don't want to say more. Tuesday evening I shall be with you again if nothing

[44] [Freude als etwas das ganz eigens mir zu Liebe geschieht]

[45] [. . . entschuldigt sich dass er nicht auch dir schreibt. . . . Komme ja bald und gesund zurück mein Gemüthe gewöhnt sich nach und nach an's alleine seyn.]

unexpected happens. I am already with you, my heart consumes itself for you.[46]

In this letter the ambivalence is not camouflaged. The whole assurance of love is supposed to compensate for his bad conscience over having extended his absence from Weimar.

Are we entitled to see in such a letter a tactical move, such as Bode assumed (cf. above, pp. 963–64) to be at work in most of his letters to Charlotte von Stein? This particular letter sounds as if written by design, as if he meant deliberately to pile one assurance of love upon another in order to appease Charlotte von Stein's anticipated anger and also his present bad conscience. This possibility cannot be denied, but an alternative is that the wish to be absent from Charlotte von Stein had reached the preconscious stage and that the strong assurance of love was needed as a defense against a growing impulse that was vigorously rejected by a conscious striving. To a certain extent one may see from this defense how much Goethe truly loved her. This sounds paradoxical, but the fact can be well proved that, while he was approaching the time when forces in him would demand a final break, yet the conscious part of his personality maintained the erstwhile beloved woman as the only and exclusive love-object and went on, except for occasional barely noticeable stirrings on the surface, to serve and bow in loyalty and devotion to that one person who had become for him the symbol of everything that could be loved in this world.

And what of the woman whom he had loved so uncompromisingly, with such unutterable intensity that he did not want to admit to himself that the time of love was approaching its end, she who had reproached him so often and had caused him so many bitter hours? She seems to have fully recognized him in his uniqueness and in his greatness. Most simple, but most touching, words are to be found in her letter to Knebel of April 20, 1785:

> It is strange that just now when I received your letter I was thinking quiet-sadly about the same topic of which you write to me. But unfortunately there is nothing to change on the one side where our friend [Goethe] has

---

[46] [Lass dich die paar Tage längerer Abwesenheit nicht reuen, ich komme und eile wo möglich mit vollerer Seele zu dir zurück.

Wie glücklich werde ich seyn dir ausdrucken zu können wie sehr ich deinen Werth fühle und wie allein du vor allen Wesen der Welt mich glücklich machen kannst.

Die Schicksale meiner Wanderschafft werden dich, wenn ich sie dir erzähle, mehr davon überzeugen als die wärmsten Versicherungen kaum thun können. Ich bin dein und muss dein seyn. Alless leitet, treibt, drängt mich wieder zu dir. Ich mag nichts weiter sagen. Dienstag Abend bin ich wieder bey dir wenn nichts sonderliches vorkommt. Ich bin schon bey dir, mein Herz verzehrt sich für dich.]

given up hope, because there is no hope, and morally false rhythms and sounds prevail in our system.[47] But, sage that he is, he will, I trust, get it into order as time goes on.

Aside from this our friend goes the way appropriate to him. You other philosophers know well that certain necessary laws in the moral self as well as in the physical are tied to those things. Therefore an understanding, noble, generous, charitable, unselfish [man] cannot have a pleasurable part in this world, or, if he does want to enjoy it, then he must forsake his heaven.

These people remain once and for all those whom one reveres in spirit and in truth like the one God. No earthly altars are built for them.

Only it is necessary that when these heavenly souls are once tied, through the offices [they hold], to the children of this world, they make this point very plain to themselves and repeat always in their hearts: "Father, forgive them; for they know not what they do."

In this way must we bestead our friend.

You may well laugh at my resigning myself so dryly. One who feels in himself much effective vitality may have a different view.[48]

The creativity of the artistic genius has always, I believe, been regarded as a manifestation of divine powers, and at last Charlotte von Stein, who had seen her friend in his greatest weakness and frailty, in his most ungodlike distresses and tribulations, accepted him as he was and pleaded with the world to honor in him the godlike spirit, but also

[47] Charlotte von Stein refers here to political questions that troubled Goethe and about which nothing could be done. See below, pp. 977–78.

[48] [Es ist sonderbar, dass eben, da ich Ihren Brief erhalte, ich still-traurig über denselben Gegenstand nachdachte, davon Sie mir schreiben. Aber leider ist's da auf der einen Seite, wo unser Freund die Hoffnung aufgegeben, Nichts zu ändern, weil Nichts zu hoffen ist und moralisch-unrichtiger Takt und Töne in unserm System herrschen. Aber als ein weiser Mann wird er sich's wohl mit der Zeit zurechtlegen.

Überdies geht unser Freund seinen ihm gehörigen Weg. Sie andere Philosophen wissen ja, dass gewisse notwendige Gesetze in der moralischen Natur so gut als in der physischen mit denen Dingen verknüpft sind. So kann ein Verständiger, Edler, Grossmütiger, Wohltätiger, Uneigennütziger keinen vergnüglichen Teil mit dieser Welt haben; oder wenn er ihn geniessen will, so muss er seinen Himmel verlassen.

Diese Menschen bleiben nun einmal Die, welche man wie den einigen Gott im Geist und in der Wahrheit verehrt. Keine irdischen Altäre werden ihnen nicht gebaut.

Nur ist es notwendig, dass, wenn einmal diese himmlischen Seelen durch Ämter mit den Menschenkindern gebunden sind, sie sich Dieses recht deutlich machen und immer in ihrem Herzen wiederholen: Vater, vergib ihnen, denn sie wissen nicht, was sie tun!

Auf diesem Weg müssen wir unserm Freund beistehen.—

Sie werden mich wohl über die trockene Ergebung auslachen. Wer in sich viel Lebenskraft-Wirksamkeit fühlt, Dem mag's vielleicht anders vorkommen.] (43, pp. 181–82)

pleaded with him to exercise mercy upon mankind, which traditionally honors the evil and despicable but tramples ruthlessly upon the few who one day will bear testimony that man was born a better being than the record of history suggests. In these few lines, which may rightly be called naive, Charlotte von Stein shows the best side of herself, and though in subsequent years she was often victimized by her jealousies and moral narrowness, these words in their simplicity prove how great she was and how deeply she was immersed in Goethe's greatness, a greatness that had made her too a greater person than she had been before. Gone were the days when she had written on the back of a letter of Goethe's of October 7, 1776:

> If what I feel is wrong, and if I [shall] have to atone for a sin so dear to me, my conscience does not want to tell me: destroy it, thou Heaven! when it could accuse me.[49]

In 1776 we find a coquettish flirting with guilt feelings, that peculiar mixture of Protestant renunciation with rococo sensuality; in the letter of 1785, however, there is no intimation of feelings of guilt and no easy sensuality, but a touching seriousness about the inescapable tragedy of the great man and an unfaltering willingness to sacrifice for him.

It is not known, however, whether this woman, who had superstitious beliefs about dreams, could read the handwriting on the wall when Goethe happened to make a slip. On December 26, 1785, he wrote her:

> I well knew on the Holy Evening that I still had something to bestow on you, yet could not call it to my mind. Here I send it after.[50]

Again the warding off set in, yet betrayed the impulse that had to be warded off. He wrote the following day:

> I want always to send you something and say something to you so that you should remain certain of my remembrance.[51]

Thus Goethe struggled against the full recognition of what the meaning of this period of his relationship to the love-object was.

[49] [Obs unrecht ist was ich empfinde—und ob ich büssen muss die mir so liebe Sünde will mein Gewissen mir nicht sagen; vernicht' es Himmel du! wenn michs je könt anklagen.] (254, *1*:568)

The verses were written on a letter (cf. above, p. 210) in which Goethe reproachingly called Charlotte von Stein a Madonna.

[50] [Ich wusste wohl am heiligen Abend dass ich dir noch etwas zu bescheeren hatte, konnt mich's aber nicht besinnen. Hier schick ich's nach.]

[51] [Ich mögte dir immer etwas schicken und etwas sagen damit du meines Andenckens gewiss bliebest.]

Male Friendships and the Court

In Goethe's dealings with men there were quite different trends. He came to a full insight into the gulf that separated him from the Duke. In a letter to Knebel of April 2, 1785, his dilemma is more succinctly than ever described:

> The passion for war that has got like a kind of itch under the skin of our princes wearies me like a bad dream in which one wants to get away and should and his feet fail him. They appear to me like such dreamers and I feel as if I were dreaming with them. Let them [keep] the happy self-deception.[52]

In an outburst of despair he declared he had reached the end of his patience and hope and pleaded with his friend to throw in his lot with him. What caused Goethe to feel so annoyed was the Duke's obstinately and successfully pursuing his goal of strengthening Prussia by the formation of an alliance of the smaller princely states. Goethe apparently foresaw that this would upset the balance of power and lead to war. His state of mind was described in a letter from Knebel to Herder of May 7, 1785:

> Goethe has here again plucked up some spirit. . . . His heart has a deep sound of friendship. His maturing feeling for that which is human in life, deprives him . . . of all joy in his political state. This is not hopeful, either for his friends or for the wretched country.[53]

Goethe here faced a reality situation that was heart-rending. He was sincerely attached to the Duke. Much of the self-discipline he imposed upon himself was also meant as an example to the prince. Now he was working to get the finances of the exhausted country straightened out and it seemed he would be able to avert a debacle. The Duke accepted Goethe as a leader and actually had undergone quite a few changes to his advantage. He was receptive to Goethe's enthusiasm and even became interested in science. But apparently the realm of high politics he considered his private domain, and despite long discussions he insisted upon

---

[52] [Die Kriegslust die wie eine Art von Krätze unsern Prinzen unter der Haut sizt, fatigirt mich wie ein böser Traum, in dem man fort will und soll und einen die Füse versagen. Sie kommen mir wie solche Träumende vor und mir ists als wenn ich mit ihnen träumte. Lass ihnen den glücklichen Selbstbetrug.]

[53] [Goethe hat sich hier wieder etwas Mut geholt. . . . sein Herz hat einen tiefen Ton der Freundschaft. Sein reifendes Gefühl für Das, was menschlich im Leben ist, nimmt ihm . . . alle Freude seines politischen Zustandes. Dies ist nicht trostvoll, weder für seine Freunde, noch für das armselige Land.] (51, *1*:330)

his determination to realize his ambitions in that field. The Duke's relative lack of interest in the government of the state proper, as against his concentration upon a dangerous foreign policy, meant to Goethe that this part of his mission had come to naught. However, this did not result in a turning away from or rejection of the master who frustrated him so extremely. The letter of December 26, 1784, is an important document in this respect. Goethe here came to grips with the question of the Duke's maintaining a herd of wild boars and sows for his hunting pleasure. The beasts caused immense damage and aroused the anger of the populace. Goethe thought it his duty to persuade the Duke to give up this source of pleasure. The letter is a veritable masterpiece of diplomacy and tact, sprinkled with humorous innuendo and radiating a flow of warm affection (see Appendix M).

The whole affair appears ridiculous today, although not so long ago, and more still than many are aware, the welfare of the poor has been readily sacrificed to the pleasure of the wealthy. One can easily imagine with what feelings Goethe worked upon such a document. He knew that it would be a bitter pill for the Duke to swallow to part with those trappings of fancied virility. When the letter is read the degree of empathy by identification with a type alien to him and in a matter so odious, becomes strikingly clear. The capacity to identify and to understand and nevertheless to object and to condemn is not given to many. Here we see Goethe in full mastery of his aim-inhibited homosexual feelings. Neither love nor hatred succeeded in interfering with the gentle care he had determined to give his once so much beloved friend.

Before leaving on one of those diplomatic trips that Goethe hated and condemned, the Duke increased Goethe's salary and gave him a bonus for his vacation. Goethe on this occasion called the Duke "a great friend of conscience-cleansing" [ein groser Freund von Gewissensreiningungen], in a letter to Charlotte von Stein of May 24, 1785. Nevertheless, the following day he wrote a submissive letter to Fritsch thanking the Duke and the Privy Council for this useful honor. The letter to Fritsch was in keeping with the sacred rules of a princely court and was impersonal in tone, and at no point, of course, would the reader suppose that the writer had his own theory as to princely magnanimity, a theory which—whether correct or incorrect—shows how little the bearer of the ducal favor could be bribed in his judgment. Thus Goethe had acquired a remarkable detachment of outlook and judgment without damage to his feelings, that is to say, without undergoing a new wave of repression. The new paths of his sublimated homosexual feelings will be discussed in greater detail in Appendices N and R.

I quote below a letter that shows the harmonious equilibrium Goethe had acquired in his friendships with men, and that brings forward again his just-cited ability to identify and understand and nevertheless to criticize. This time it had to do with his friend Jacobi, who was engaged in a literary conflict with the philosopher Mendelssohn about Spinozism. Jacobi had embarrassed Goethe by unauthorizedly publishing, and revealing the authorship of, a poem by Goethe. Yet Goethe had made himself guilty by a tactlessness committed towards Jacobi, as reported earlier (see above, pp. 358 ff), and perhaps therefore did not respond very strongly to Jacobi's transgression, as a letter of September 11, 1785, shows. Here, however, Goethe's current tendency to forgive a friend is of less interest than his tact in handling precarious situations. Thus he wrote Jacobi after having received the latter's polemic against Mendelssohn (311) (May 5, 1786):

> I have read your booklet with sympathy, not with joy. It is and remains a polemic, a philosophical one, and I have such a disinclination against all literary squabbles. . . . You had to write these pages, that I see, and I expected them, only I should have wished that the *species facti* had been more simply reported; all that is passionate therein I cannot approve. . . . The more concise the better. You will say that this is my way; everyone has his own. Well, I must let it go. . . . When self-assurance vents itself in scorn of others, even of the lowliest, it must strike one adversely. A reckless person may make sport of others, humiliate, debase [them], because [in so doing] he exposes himself. Whoever cares about self-respect would seem to have renounced the right to belittle others. And what are we all then that we dare exalt ourselves much?[54]

He then tells Jacobi for how much he envies him: children, friends, wealth, house, estate, etc.

> Yet in return God has also punished you with metaphysics . . . whereas he blessed me with physics so that I may delight in the contemplation of his works, few only of which he has wished to give me as my own.

> As for the rest, you are a good person, so that one can be your friend without being of your opinion, for how far apart we are I have seen all the more from your booklet itself. . . . Forgive that I have written it down just as

[54] This high degree of tolerance and this aversion against discord seems to be particularly characteristic of this period of Goethe's life, since he later did not adhere to such principles but during one period attacked his adversaries vitriolically. The letter is characteristic of Goethe's efforts to master aggression at that time.

it was in my heart; I am so alone here and would write much more still if I were not loath to take a new sheet.[55]

Again, particularly in a paragraph I have omitted because of its involved metaphors, Goethe did not spare his critical vein and defended elevated pursuits as he had done with the Duke. With Jacobi, of course, he could be more candid, and, in order to avoid grieving his friend he added words of praise. Of interest also is the passage about the many works of God he had not received as his own, meaning in particular, I believe, children. Although behind this admission there may have been the tactical purpose of appeasing by humbleness his friend's possible reaction to forthright criticism, it nevertheless sounds like a genuine complaint about essentials missing in his life. This is all the more remarkable since it must be doubted that this idea was ever expressed to Charlotte von Stein. There he claimed that being with her gave him everything his heart could desire. Of course, the verbalization of this feeling would have implied a reproach against her and therefore was not suitable for discussion between them. Yet I believe that there is a still deeper reason why this feeling was perhaps expressed only to a man: It may have involved a wish originating from unsatiated homosexual libido; this would account for its being brought up in a letter to a friend who was far away.

These letters to Jacobi and the Duke must not be misinterpreted as resulting from a glibly moralizing attitude. He had by no means lost the capacity for being hard upon someone he did not hold in esteem. His aversion against Lavater made him want to express it by leaving Weimar when Lavater came to visit. Yet he had to wait until the Duchess was delivered of her baby, and thus an encounter became necessary. He wrote Charlotte von Stein about it on July 21, 1786:

> The gods know better than we know what is good for us, therefore they have compelled me to see him [Lavater]. . . . He has stayed in my house.

[55] [Dein Büchlein habe ich mit Antheil gelesen, nicht mit Freude. Es ist und bleibt eine Streitschrifft, eine Philosophische und ich habe eine solche Abneigung von allen litterarischen Händeln. . . . Du musstest diese Bogen schreiben, das seh ich und erwartete sie, nur hätte ich gewünscht die Species fackti wäre simpler vorgetragen, alles Leidenschafftliche dabey kann ich nicht billigen. . . . Je knapper ie besser. Du wirst sagen es ist meine Manier, ieder hat die seine! Gut ich muss es geschehen lassen. . . . Wenn Selbstgefühl sich in Verachtung andrer, auch der geringsten auslässt, muss es widrig auffallen. Ein leichtsinniger Mensch darf andre zum besten haben, erniedrigen, wegwerfen, weil er sich selbst einmal Preis giebt. Wer auf sich etwas hält scheint dem Rechte entsagt zu haben andre gering zu schätzen. Und was sind wir denn alle dass wir uns viel erheben dürfen. . . . Dagegen hat dich aber auch Gott mit der Metaphisick gestraft . . . mich dagegen mit der Phisick gesegnet, damit mir es im Anschauen seiner Wercke wohl werde, deren er mir nur wenige zu eigen geben wollen. Übrigens bist du ein guter Mensch, dass man dein Freund seyn kann ohne deiner

Not one heartfelt, intimate word has been exchanged between us and I am rid of hatred and love for eternity. He has thus shown himself to me with his perfections and peculiarities in these few hours, and my soul was like a glass of pure water. . . . I have also drawn a heavy line under *his* existence and now know what, on balance, remains for me of him.[56] [Goethe's italics]

The first question that comes to one's mind is, under what *other* existence he had "drawn a heavy line." I have found no commentary on this question in the literature. He did not change his attitude towards anyone around that time as far as I know, yet since he was, at least preconsciously, in the process of "drawing a heavy line" under his relationship with Charlotte von Stein, I wonder how far he unconsciously betrayed that which he himself did not want to have true. Oddly enough, if this was an unintended confession it occurred in conjunction with the description of an unpleasant relationship to a man.

On May 5, 1785, Goethe ends a short letter to Knebel as follows: "I am patching up the beggar's cloak that wants to fall from my shoulders."[57] The sentence intrudes abruptly into a context that does not elucidate its meaning. It is a statement of despair. Consciously, it referred, in all probability, to the difficulties Goethe had to cope with as a person acting on the political stage. Although no catastrophe was in the offing, he must have felt as if he were going into bankruptcy politically. The reorganization, the re-formation, of the state was not succeeding. All he could do was patchwork. Introducing here and there reforms such as denying the crowd of courtiers the privilege of taking their daily meals at court[58] in order to save money—that much his efforts could accomplish, but the transformation of this feudal principality into a prosperous state, that was

---

Meynung zu seyn, denn wie wir von einander abstehn hab ich erst recht wieder aus dem Büchlein selbst gesehn. . . .

Vergieb dass ich so hingeschrieben habe wie mirs eben um's Herz war, ich bin hier so allein und schriebe wohl noch viel mehr wenn ich mich nicht scheute ein neu Blat zu nehmen.]

[56] [Die Götter wissen besser was uns gut ist, als wir es wissen, drum haben sie mich gezwungen ihn zu sehen. . . . Er hat bey mir gewohnt. Kein herzlich, vertraulich Wort ist unter uns gewechselt worden und ich bin Hass und Liebe auf ewig los. Er hat sich in den wenigen Stunden mit seinen Vollkommenheiten und Eigenheiten so vor mir gezeigt, und meine Seele war wie ein Glas rein Wasser. Ich habe auch unter *seine* Existenz einen grosen Strich gemacht und weis nun was mir *per Saldo* von ihm übrig bleibt.]

[57] [Ich flicke an dem Bettlermantel der mir von den Schultern fallen will.]

[58] This reform had also the effect of forcing Charlotte von Stein's husband to spend more time at home than previously and thus curtailed the time Goethe could spend with the beloved woman undisturbed. Was this reform introduced out of ambivalence against Charlotte von Stein?

beyond either Goethe's financial genius or the potentialities of the existing reality.[59] The social group, however, that was obstinate and did not want to give up its parasitic battening on the meager fat of the land was precisely the one that Charlotte von Stein represented impeccably and to perfection. He had kept his side of the bargain and had become a perfect servant of that aristocratic society which, according to Charlotte von Stein, he had at the outset threatened by his impetuous *Sturm und Drang* behavior. He bent his best efforts to rescuing that society, which was in danger of falling apart and now was patched up enough so it could crawl at its lethargic pace towards an ignominious end. But in the course of this work Goethe had become acquainted with the personal and social weaknesses of the nobility and it may have dawned upon him that an adequate reform would have had to go so far as to touch upon basic principles that were sacred to him, such as the privileged position itself of the nobility.

As an example of what problems bore upon his mind I shall record Goethe's reaction to the Diamond Necklace Affair, in which Queen Marie Antoinette appeared heavily compromised. He wrote later:

> Already in the year 1785 the Necklace Affair had made an indescribable impression upon me. In the immoral abyss of city, court, and state, which here opened up, the most horrible consequences appeared, ghostlike, before me, the apparition of which I could not for quite a while get rid of, whereby I behaved in such a strange way that my friends . . . confessed to me, much later, that at that time I seemed to them as if insane.[60]

Goethe's hyperreaction was characteristic. He rightly foresaw that the exposure to contempt of a person who holds a place of high authority must undermine the political basis of the whole state. However, I can hardly suppose that behind Goethe's unusually strong reaction to the historical event there was no personal factor hiding. After all, what he was reacting to was a woman's compromising herself, a queen to boot, who

[59] I may have apportioned too little merit to Goethe as Secretary of the Treasury. In the reorganization of the tax structure of Ilmenau (see 532, pp. 108–34) he succeeded in making essential changes. Yet whatever the objective value of Goethe's work was it did not measure up to what he knew needed to be done.

[60] [Schon im Jahr 1785 hatte die Halsbandgeschichte einen unaussprechlichen Eindruck auf mich gemacht. In dem unsittlichen Stadt-, Hof- und Staats-Abgrunde, der sich hier eröffnete, erschienen mir die greulichsten Folgen gespensterhaft, deren Erscheinung ich geraume Zeit nicht los werden konnte; wobei ich mich so seltsam benahm, dass Freunde . . . mir nur spät . . . gestanden, dass ich ihnen damals wie wahnsinnig vorgekommen sei.] (*Soph.* I, 35:11)

The event continued to haunt Goethe, and in Sicily he inquired into the history of Cagliostro, who had also played a role, though a minor one, in the Affair. Goethe got rid of the subject only after having written a play about it.

might serve so well as a mother-substitute. Yet the fact that the alleged evildoing of a queen struck such a resounding note in him that he was considered temporarily out of his mind proves that there was a problem in connection with which a spark could set off explosive reactions. Historical events that elicit deep feelings in us—particularly if the events do not directly affect our everyday lives—derive their power from our projections. This can be observed over and over again in the course of a psychoanalytic investigation, and it is not much of an exaggeration to say that a person who has become well acquainted with his unconscious conflicts will regard with self-possession and objectivity even grave historical events.[61]

It is not probable that, despite its saliency as a political news item, the Necklace Affair and its effect upon his unconscious remained isolated from the imagery centering in Charlotte von Stein, and had no associative connection with fantasies regarding the evilness of women. Here an experience must be mentioned that breathes all the warmth and secular religiosity (as I wish to call it) that so touchingly characterized Goethe before he integrated aristocratic patterns of living. On November 11, 1785, while in Ilmenau, he added to a finished letter to Charlotte von Stein the following account:

> I had yet another precious scene that I wished I could reproduce for you. I had a bookbinder called in to bind the *Wilhelm Meister* book in my presence; he recalled an appeal he had filed with the tax commission, and as he worked he told me his history and spoke about his life. Each word he said was as heavy as gold and I refer you to a dozen of Lavater's pleonasms in order to express the reverence that I felt for this man.[62]

Goethe evidently was deeply moved by the simplicity and concreteness of the craftsman's account and many of Goethe's poetical works could be associated with this episode, which is reminiscent of medieval nearness to earth. Charlotte von Stein, I believe, persisted in her admiration for Lavater, and Goethe may well have used the naive, unsophisticated but unspeakably human religiosity of this simple man as a weapon against

---

[61] Of course, there is a definite limit to this capacity even under optimal conditions. Instances in which seeming objectivity serves as a defense against the outbreak of strong emotions must be considered too.

[62] [Ich habe noch eine köstliche Scene gehabt die ich wünschte dir wiederzugeben zu können. Ich lies einen Buchbinder rufen um mir das Buch Wilhelms in meiner Gegenwart zu heften, er erinnerte eine Bitte die er bey der Steuerkommission angebracht und unter der Arbeit erzählte er mir seine Geschichte und sprach über sein Leben. Jedes Wort das er sagte war so schwer wie Gold und ich verweise dich auf ein Dutzend Lavaterische Pleonasmen um dir die Ehrfurcht auszudrücken die ich für den Menschen empfand.]

the irritation of his obnoxious erstwhile friend's unending sanctimonious effusions. But was it not also a weapon—and an all the heavier one for that matter—against Charlotte von Stein and the society for which she stood, against her dogmatic, cold puritanism, which weighed like lead and not like gold? Here in this small town of Ilmenau, on a November day, away from all the brilliance of a sophisticated society, he became deeply steeped in the message spoken by a voice that he had not heard for a long time, and I can easily imagine that he felt as if he were listening to one of the mythical figures from the Old Testament who always had such a great meaning for him.

I imagine that there was one particular factor that appealed to him. I have earlier characterized the change that had taken place in him during the Weimarian decade by contrasting the primary and the secondary process. Here now was a man who freely spoke of all his sufferings—and I am sure they were plenty—but he did not get upset and spoke in a simple religious way about life. Here Goethe encountered mastery too, mastery over far greater adversity even than most members of the elite had to bear, and nevertheless he could hear the full swing of a deep emotionality behind every word; mastery despite the unchecked fullness of emotion; without a substitute in the form of a theory, philosophy, cynicism, or witticism. Here he encountered, apparently, the man whose ideal Spinoza outlined, the man who loved God and thought his love to be reward enough and therefore went on loving despite all adversity. A member of the elite cannot love God in that way—even if he does disregard adversity—because he is provided with narcissistic gratifications that obviate true humbleness. Can one imagine the first Minister of the principality, the novelist and dramatist, accepting the love of God as reward for his love of God? Here he was suddenly overwhelmed by a world that was filled with that spirituality he had always sought and that he had wished to integrate under Charlotte von Stein's guidance. Yet here in this world of the humble craftsman it was taken for granted; it was not cultivated; it grew in Nature's soil; it was not tinged by the idea of sacrifice and renunciation and martyrdom. It probably was the most touching synthesis of the highest Christian principles and the spirit of classic antiquity (as Goethe saw it, following Winckelmann) : noble simplicity and quiet greatness.

Hypomanic Interlude and the Dethronement of Psychology

Such an experience, although it was a source of strength for Goethe, may have increased his antagonism against Weimar and the many there to whom he was still deeply attached. In that struggle—and how great the struggle must have been I shall discuss later—shortly before leaving Weimar, he was seized by a spell, perhaps comparable to a hypomania, seemingly in a supreme attempt at eliminating the conflict involved in his decision to leave. On July 9, 1786, he wrote to Charlotte von Stein:

> This time I sit at the fireplace and defy the cold and the wet. I am driven, delighted, and tortured by a thousand ideas. The vegetable kingdom raves once again in my soul; I cannot get rid of it for a moment, yet I make nice progress. Now that I am going through my old writing,[63] many old evils also are roused. It is a wonderful epoch for me, in which just you are lacking. A week from today I hope to be not far from you. . . .

> I most enjoy now the plant world, which persecutes me: and this is right when a subject is to be appropriated. Everything forces itself upon me; I do not meditate any longer upon it, everything comes to meet me and the enormous realm simplifies itself in my soul so much that I shall soon be able to solve [lit.: do at sight] instantly the most difficult task.

> If I only could communicate the vision [lit.: sight] and the joy; yet it is impossible. And it is no dream, no fantasy; it is a becoming aware of the essential form with which nature, as it were, only plays, and playing brings forth the manifold life. Had I time in the brief span of life I would make bold to extend it to all realms of nature—to the whole realm.[64]

In this letter Goethe again praised nature for its infinite consistency; the entirety of nature is beheld in visionlike fashion as the infinite number of variations of one primordial pattern. Goethe gave heightened and enraptured expression to a thought which was in his essay "On Granite" (see above, p. 867) and in his letter to Knebel of April 2, 1785, when he wrote: "The consistency of nature is a beautiful consolation for man's in-

---

[63] Goethe was working on a new edition of his collected works.

[64] [Diesmal sitz ich am Kamine und trotze der Kälte und Nässe. Ich bin von tausend Vorstellungen getrieben, beglückt und gepeinigt. Das Pflanzenreich rasst einmal wieder in meinem Gemüthe, ich kann es nicht einen Augenblick loswerden, mache aber auch schöne Fortschritte. Da ich meine alte Schrifften durchgehe, werden auch viel alte Übel rege. Es ist eine wunderbare Epoche für mich, in der du mir eben fehlst. Heut über acht Tage hoff ich nicht weit von dir zu seyn. . . .

Am meisten freut mich ietzo das Pflanzenwesen, das mich verfolgt; und das ists recht wie einem eine Sache zu eigen wird. Es zwingt sich mir alles auf, ich sinne nicht mehr drüber, es kommt mir alles entgegen und das ungeheure Reich simplificirt sich mir in der Seele, dass ich bald die schwerste Aufgabe gleich weglesen kann.

Wenn ich nur jemanden den Blick und die Freude mittheilen könnte, es ist aber nicht möglich. Und es ist kein Traum keine Phantasie; es ist ein Gewahrwerden der wesentlichen Form, mit der die Natur gleichsam nur immer spielt und spielend das manigfaltige Leben hervorbringt. Hätt ich Zeit in dem kurzem Lebensraum; so getraut ich mich es auf alle Reiche der Natur—auf ihr ganzes Reich—auszudehnen.]

consistency."[65] Did this vision of consistency pervading the whole realm of nature grow out of an acute awareness of gross inconsistency in the human world or in himself? As we shall see later the decision to go to Italy was the result of an iron consistency, based upon a merciless insistence that the laws of his own existence be carried out to the dot, whatever the price in pain to himself might be. Yet man's conscious mind is only rarely in harmony with the deepest layer of his personality. Often when he is fulfilling the primordial essence of his being he feels torn and divided, since the aim of this primordial essence is in conflict with what reason and the present moment demand. Thus one part of man would like to follow the seduction and behest of the moment but is compelled to bow to other stronger forces that originate in an archaic, demonic world.

The concept of nature that Goethe evolved in his letter to Charlotte von Stein became the leitmotif of his philosophy. In nature the basic pattern is varied over and over again; the confusing and infinite series of forms are only variations of an identical pattern. This is the consistency of nature that he could not find in man. Man is inconsistent, and such laws of harmony cannot be discovered in his world. Goethe's despair over the inconsistency of man was the reflection of his own inconsistency. In the essay "On Granite" he admitted taking flight to nature from what he had discovered in his own heart and in the conduct of man.

It was not until almost a century and a half later that the basic harmony of man was discovered by Freud, in the repetitious compulsion. All the infiniteness of patterns, of actions seemingly contradictory, can be viewed as variations, as repetitions, of a primordial constellation deeply imbedded in man's unconscious. What seems gross inconsistency in human life, science can unravel as the reflection of an identical core. Thus modern science would, if anything, rather say "the consistency of human life is a beautiful consolation for nature's inconsistency."[66]

The intensity of conflict in Goethe seems to have been unusually high on that ninth of July; the ego weakened by conflict was tossed around in the struggle. There were two aspects involved. Goethe was on the verge of acceding to the repetitious compulsion, for his journey to Italy reinstituted that which was most archaic in him. Yet against this accession to the repetitious compulsion part of his personality rebelled, longing for a

---

[65] [Die Consequenz der Natur tröstet schön über die Inconsequenz der Menschen.]

[66] Following some ideas of Paul Schilder's, I assume that Goethe's vision regarding the consistency of nature was—at least at that time—paralleled by a basic pattern of his own personality. See 471.

continuation of the present and dreading the demand of the unconscious. Against this torn condition Goethe mobilized an imagery about nature that he wanted to have been true about himself. The harmonious panorama of nature that he beheld coincided with what he wished to behold when he turned his eye upon his inner universe. His rhapsodic view of nature was a projection of a wished-for, but direly lacking, state of his own mind. Thus we understand how his vision consoled and comforted him and why he felt incapable of conveying his joy to others.

A person temporarily in doubt as to where to go or in what direction to proceed may suffer a weakening of his sense of identity. Goethe's hypomanic spell, which made reality an open and well-ordered book, had its recoil and resulted in a heightened feeling of self that found succor in the perception of the harmony of nature. Thus he had written to Charlotte von Stein at the beginning of this phase (June 15, 1786):

> How legible the book of nature becomes for me I cannot express to you; my prolonged spelling-out has helped me; now suddenly everything moves and my quiet joy is unspeakable. As much new as I find, I still find nothing unexpected; everything fits and joins up, because I have no system and want nothing but the truth for its own sake.
>
> How all this will now increase, of this I think with joy.[67]

The ego claimed it was well protected against surprise, that the new coincided with the expected—a constellation which, if actualized, would testify to maximum strength. Yet we know his ego was at that time in a phase of maximum tension and insecurity. It is worth while to go back and see what happened ten years earlier when Goethe was in a comparable reality situation before leaving Frankfurt for Weimar.

A few months before that decisive step there were signs of depression and meekness. To Jacobi he wrote on March 21, 1775:

> My heart and mind are now turned elsewhere so entirely that I feel almost indifferent about my own flesh and blood. I cannot say anything to you— for what could be said? Nor do I want to think of tomorrow and the next day; therefore farewell! . . . I feel as if I were skating for the first time

---

[67] [Wie lesbar mir das Buch der Natur wird kann ich dir nicht ausdrücken, mein langes Buchstabiren hat mir geholfen, ietzt ruckts auf einmal, und meine stille Freude ist unaussprechlich. So viel neues ich finde, find ich doch nichts unerwartetes es passt alles und schliest sich an, weil ich kein System habe und nichts will als die Wahrheit um ihrer selbst willen.

Wie sich das nun vermehren wird daran denck ich mit Freuden.]

unassisted and wheeling about on the path of life and were supposed already to enter the race, and this is where my whole soul strives.[68]

Here is an expression of a feeling of weakness where there should have been strength and firmness. But then gradually a state developed that is also reminiscent of hypomania though its clinical manifestations were quite different from those of the summer of 1786. I refer to such a torn mood as was reflected in his letters (quoted earlier, pp. 120–21) to the Countess Stolberg, with their rapid changes, the scarcely finished sentences, and pages covering many days, with little paragraphs added after a long time. Then too he had been groping for a point of stability. A good example is the letter written at night on October 26, 1775, to the Countess's brother, Friedrich Leopold:

> I feel an urge, brother, to write you, in this moment when I am so far, so far distant from you . . . ; floating in the wonderful infinite sacred ocean of our *father,* the inapprehensible yet tangible. Oh brother! Namable yet infinite feelings harrow me—and how I love you, you feel since I am thinking of you at this moment under old linden trees.

> The wretched lying-in-the-dust Fritz! and the wriggling of worms, I swear to you by my heart! If this is not children's babbling and the rattling of the Werthers and all that rabble! Against the inner testimony of my soul![69] [Goethe's italics]

Thus abruptly he broke off the letter.[70] In this communication one finds the flash of an attempt at dissolving in the image of a father whom one can touch but not apprehend. Yet this attempt at identification was of questionable effect and, by and large, Goethe remained on the level he had described to Bürger a week earlier (October 18, 1775) in the following words:

[68] [. . . mein Herz und Sinn ist ietzt so ganz wo anders hingewandt, dass mein eigen Fleisch und Blut mir fast gleichgültig ist. Sagen kann ich dir nichts—denn was lässt sich sagen. Will auch nicht an morgen und übermorgen dencken drum Ade! . . . mir ist als wenn ich auf Schlittschuen zum erstenmal allein liefe und dummelte auf dem Pfade des Lebens und sollte schon um die Wette laufen und das wohin all meine Seele strebt.]

[69] [Ich fühl einen Drang Bruder dir zu schreiben in diesem Augenblick, dass ich so weit so weit von dir . . . entfernt binn; schwebend im herrlich unendlich heiligen Ocean unsers *Vaters* des ungreifflichen aber des berührlichen. O Bruder! Nennbaare aber unendliche Gefühle durchwühlen mich—und wie ich dich liebe fühlst du da ich unter alten Linden in dem Augenblick dein Gedencke.

Das Erbärmliche liegen am Staube Friz! und das winden der Würmer ich schwöre dir bey meinem Herzen! Wenn das nicht Kindergelall und Gerassel ist der Werther und all das Gezeug! Gegen das innre Zeugniss meiner Seele!—]

[70] The fact that this communication is preserved only in the form of a rough draft has no bearing on my conclusions.

Whatever human nature can collect by way of contradiction, the Fairy—
Fond or Fiend, how should I call her?—has presented to me as a New
Year's gift for [17]75; however, this excellent disposition was given me al-
ready with the christening-gift.[71]

These two specimens may suffice to illustrate the vast difference between 1775 and 1786. In two identical external situations identical mood
swings set in that can be classified as approximately hypomanic. Yet in one
instance the rent in personality becomes quite apparent and attempts are
made in vain to find at least temporary equilibrium in a vague dissolution in the father; in the other instance the hypomanic mood comes to the
fore only in an occasional paragraph of a letter as a manifestation of accelerated mental activity. The letter is now used far less as a channel for
direct discharge of the heightened tension, as had happened in 1775; it
rather bears witness to the hypomanic mood indirectly by the rapidity and
crowding of thoughts. Also, the synthesizing power of the ego was strong
enough, as against the centrifugal forces, to condense a consistent visionary image of nature, that is to say, the main channel was an intensified way
of experiencing nature without being overwhelmed by the inner emotional turmoil. Particularly by the integration of science, reality had become a structure of such intense interest that even at a point of crisis Goethe could attach himself so solidly to it as to submerge the crisis in it.
Indeed, one may go further and say that a crisis became a signal for an increase in interest in reality. The hypomanic mood did not lead to a series
of gross wish-fulfillments but rather to a flow of images that depicted
reality in a seemingly consistent logical frame. The fact that wish-fulfillments can be discerned behind the logical context does not signify a de-
thronement of the reality principle in favor of the pleasure principle, but
rather proves in this instance a harmonious participation of the whole personality in the formation of a visionary theory. It is of interest that in both
episodes a turn towards reality is noticeable, but in the earlier one this did
not lead to more than a vague, fantastic feeling of dissolution in a father-
imago.

I have referred earlier to the decline in Goethe's striving towards con-
secutive, rational self-recognition during the post-Italian era (cf. above,
p. 571), when interest in natural science bloomed, but no indication of an
interest in a scientific psychology can be discovered. Just now, before his
departure for Carlsbad, we can observe the intensity of his interest in

[71] [Was die menschliche Natur nur von Widersprüchen sammeln kann, hat mir die Fee
Hold oder Unhold, wie soll ich sie nennen? zum Neujahrsgeschenck von 75 gereicht, zwar
war die treffliche Anlage schon mit dem Pathengeschenck gemacht.]

science, which had developed during the preceding few years; concomitantly, the decline in his interest in psychology can already be observed around this time. On September 5, 1785, Goethe wrote to Charlotte von Stein:

> Last evening I accomplished quite a clever feat of psychology. [Frau] Herder was still most hypochondriacally tense about everything unpleasant that she had had to encounter in Carlsbad, particularly from her roommate. I had her tell and confess everything to me, the rude behavior of others and her own mistakes, with the minutest circumstances and consequences, and at the end I *absolved* her and I made her understand jokingly under this formula that these things are now done with and thrown into the depths of the sea. She herself became cheerful about it and is really cured.[72] [Goethe's italics]

Freud called this incident "an example of psychotherapeutic influence" (207, p. 210). Indeed, it is amazing to see Goethe here using on the spur of the moment a device that comes close to—if it is not quite identical with—Freud's cathartic method. The basic principle, at least, was identical in both, in (1) the confession in the greatest detail of everything, including the seemingly trivial, and (2) the intention of freeing the mind from what is troubling it by confession and detailed description.

It is surprising that Goethe should have held in his hands the essentials necessary to develop psychoanalysis and have passed them by and looked upon them as if they were a pleasantry or a joke, although he was aware of the effect they had upon a person. Historically one is reminded of the situation, so splendidly presented by Sachs (461), when the ancient Romans devised extraordinary machines for theaters and circuses but were incapable of applying the same ingenuity to serious pursuits, where they might have made possible the survival of their civilization. It may be a general principle in the history of the great discoveries that man first creates for mere sleight-of-hand that which implicitly contains the most serious and consequential. The creative unconscious can first show itself, perhaps, when the searching and imagining mind is not engaged in a serious pursuit. Perhaps all truth is first verbalized in a joke.

But aside from any historical meaning, what does this little episode

[72] [Gestern Abend habe ich ein recht Psychologisches Kunststück gemacht. Die Herder war immer noch auf das hypochondrischte gespannt über alles was ihr in Carlsbad unangenemes begegnet war. Besonders von ihrer Hausgenossin. Ich lies mir alles erzählen und beichten, fremde Unarten und eigne Fehler, mit den kleinsten Umständen und Folgen, und zuletzt *absolvirte* ich sie und machte ihr scherzhafft unter dieser Formel begreifflich, dass diese Dinge nun abgethan und in die Tiefe des Meeres geworfen seyen. Sie ward selbst lustig drüber und ist würcklich kurirt.]

mean in terms of Goethe's life? This episode, which he described in a letter to Charlotte von Stein and which shows that he knew of a method whereby to free a person from unpleasant preoccupations, occurs at a time when the desire to see into his own motivations has weakened and no longer shows that passionate interest observed during the earlier part of his stay at Weimar. After all, he had become strong enough not to feel that his existence was threatened by the erratic outbreak of irrational forces, and he was therefore beginning to come under the influence of a resistance. But the degree to which psychological understanding had grown in him can be seen from the ease with which he evolved this technique—playfully, like an act of legerdemain. Yet the playfulness, the lack of wonderment about the observation, and also the reluctance to draw any conclusions, show how far he had withdrawn from psychology.

Nevertheless, after the knowledge of man and the knowledge of self had become an integral part of his mental life, Goethe remained, of course, the great observer of man to his latest years, and man was the center of his contemplation for his whole life. How astute an observer he remained can be seen—to cite an example at random—from a remark he made to Eckermann about children, on March 17, 1830, when he said that "they can serve us as the finest barometers by which to observe the degree of favor or disfavor in which their people hold us."[73] Although it is doubtful whether Goethe meant to allude to the unconscious interaction between parents and children in the sense of modern depth psychology, nevertheless the remark per se shows how closely Goethe observed human behavior realistically and in detail. However, he never made use of psychological observation for the purpose of developing a science of psychology in the sense in which his observation of nature was for the purpose of evolving systematized, rational insight, that is to say, a theory of nature. Possibly there was an automatic reluctance, lest a scientific psychology might interfere with artistic creation, but whether such a factor was operative or not I should rather assume that his increasing moving away from psychology must have been prompted by motives that lay buried more deeply in the structure of his personality. It is to be noted that his experiment with Herder's wife was born out of ambivalence. He was really making game of her. She was a troublesome person, with whom Goethe had serious difficulties in later years. The way he wrote about her to Charlotte von Stein suggests that he did not take her problems seriously. Goethe here followed a trend—still present to a certain extent in our

---

[73] [. . . so können sie uns als die trefflichsten Barometer dienen, um an ihnen den Grad unserer Gunst oder Ungunst bei den Ihrigen wahrzunehmen.] (119, p. 591).

times—towards regarding neurotic troubles as undignified trivialities. Therefore he did not marvel over the effect of his experiment, although the first sentence of his report sounds as if for a moment the idea flashed through his mind that something serious was involved. Yet it is important to keep in mind that the experiment was born out of ambivalence against a person and was motivated by the intention of exorcising a trivial, unpleasant manifestation of the mind.

The idea that the innermost laws of the mind can be determined by the study of psychopathology was not ripe in Goethe's time. Imbued with the classical ideal of beauty, he was likewise imbued with the horror of sickness, defect, and above all, disturbances of the mind. Insanity, as presented in the tragedy *Iphigenia,* was accepted as a stage in the process of purification, a steppingstone towards health,[74] or, in the final version of *Wilhelm Meister,* as the result of apostasy conjoined with incest and therefore deserving lethal punishment. Goethe was here under the domination of the castration complex, which prevented the acceptance of the defective as something lovable. Yet the path to the development of a valid psychology begins with the study of psychopathology.[75]

It may appear contradictory that Goethe studied anatomy so ardently and did not recoil from dissections. Yet if Goethe's basic principle of nature's consistency and man's inconsistency is kept in mind the contradiction will be eliminated. The study of anatomy led to the understanding of the harmony of the body. "Therefore," he wrote, in *Dichtung und Wahrheit,*

anatomy was also of double value to me because it taught me to endure the most repulsive sight while gratifying my thirst for knowledge.[76]

---

[74] Cf. Freud (207, p. 210): "a striking instance of expiation, of the freeing of a suffering mind from the burden of guilt."

[75] Notwithstanding the absence of a scientific psychology in Goethe's work it is noteworthy that a little-known paper by him contains the germ of a theory of parapraxia that in important respects comes quite close to Freud's. See "Mistakes of Hearing, Writing and Printing" [Hör-, Schreib- und Druckfehler] (*Soph.* I, *41* [Part 1]: 182–88). This is set forth with particular clarity when Goethe claims that the scribe to whom one dictates "substitutes his inherent inclination, passion, and need for the heard word, inserts the name of a beloved person or of a desired good morsel" [seine inwohnende Neigung, Leidenschaft und Bedürfniss an die Stelle des gehörten Wortes setzt, den Namen einer geliebten Person oder eines gewünschten guten Bissens einfügt] (*Soph.* I, *41* [Part 1]: 185) A passage on p. 188 indicates that Goethe recognized that a theory of attention is incompetent to explain parapraxias.

[76] [Die Anatomie war mir auch desshalb doppelt werth, weil sie mich den widerwärtigsten Anblick ertragen lehrte, indem sie meine Wissbegierde befriedigte.] (*Soph.* I, 27:257)

Dissection revealed the secret of nature's beauty and consistency, just as subjecting Orestes to a psychotic seizure was a step in leading him to the reestablishment of equilibrium. Since man appeared inconsistent and contradictory, the scientific study of man necessarily had first to lay bare man's contradictoriness. Thus psychological experiment and the provocation of an ambivalent reaction were closely knit together in Goethe, as his playful dealings with Caroline Herder demonstrate. The consistency of man was a state that could only be attained in a work of art. Faust is in a permanent state of conflict—which, measured by the classical ideal, is inconsistent—but achieves consistency in the moment of death, that is to say, in Heaven. Multaretuli, in a fictitious conversation between Goethe and Eckermann (300), has Goethe take a positive attitude towards psychoanalysis (cf. also 207, p. 208); this I believe, can be justified only upon the supposition that Goethe would have discovered in psychoanalysis a science that demonstrated the consistency and logic of conflict, thus transforming the seeming inconsistency into consistency. Then man would have obtained his fitting place in nature, whose consistency was the object of Goethe's unending admiration.

The scientific investigation of nature brought Goethe closer to nature. The more he studied it the more it became a unit, a totality. How he achieved this need not concern us here. But it may help us explain that in the period immediately preceding his Italian journey he was deeply steeped in the study of infusoria. He preserved specimens in solution, observed them through the microscope, exposed them to sunshine, poured urine into the solutions, and faithfully made sketches of his observations. All this at a time when he was going through the throes of a severe struggle of ambivalence, that is to say, a phase of inconsistency according to his own view. Here in nature's slime there was no ambivalence; little cells moved faster or slower, propagated or disappeared, and man could only gaze and marvel, and wait for inspiration to recognize God's *or* Nature's consistency within the manifoldness of forms and processes that are so confusing at first sight.

Chapter 3

Italy

Last Days in Carlsbad

I WISH NOW to return to Goethe's sojourn in Carlsbad, which he reached belatedly because of the delayed birth of the Princess. He probably did not arrive before July 27, spent two weeks with the beloved woman, and accompanied her towards home as far as Schneeberg, where he visited the mines. Then he went back to Carlsbad for two more weeks and from there left on September 3 for Italy.

The remarkable feature in his letters after his separation from Charlotte von Stein in Schneeberg was his repeated talking of their living together. Thus he wrote on August 16, 1786:

> Now farewell and love me; before I leave Carlsbad I shall write you; I am immensely close to you. You ought to be always with me; we should live well.[1]

And on August 23, 1786:

> In any case, I have still to stay a week; then, however, everything will end so gently and the fruit will fall off ripe.

> And then I shall live with *you* in the free world and, in felicitous solitude, without name and station, come closer to the earth from which we spring.[2]
> [Goethe's italics]

[1] [Nun lebe wohl und liebe mich, eh ich von Carlsbad gehe schreib ich dir, ich bin dir herzlich nah. Du solltest immer mit mir seyn wir wollten gut leben.]

[2] [Auf alle Fälle muss ich noch eine Woche bleiben, dann wird aber auch alles so sanfte endigen und die Früchte reif abfallen. Und dann werde ich in der freyen Welt mit *dir* leben, und in glücklicher Einsamkeit, ohne Nahmen und Stand, der Erde näher kommen aus der wir genommen sind.]

Goethe here outlines a fantasy, a daydream, that contains a wish-fulfill-ment, namely, to live alone with the beloved woman, without anyone's knowing who or what they were. It seems puzzling that at a time when he was in the process of doing this very thing for himself alone, the wish to live alone with the beloved woman should have become so strong. Why should he have given a quasi promise to live with her in a world of their own when he knew that he was separating himself from her for a long time?

One conclusion that may be drawn is that he was afraid of what he was in the process of doing, and also that he harbored wishes to give up all he had accomplished in the preceding ten years and turn away from fame, from artistic production, in order to spend the rest of his life in exclusive devotion to the beloved woman, in her service and adoration.[3] But, then, why did he nevertheless go to Italy, and why was he afraid of that journey?

In a moment of despondency, Goethe wrote Charlotte von Stein nine weeks before he left for Italy, on June 25, 1786:

> I am correcting *Werther* and always find that the author did ill not to have shot himself after having finished the writing.[4]

This statement may be regarded as the offshoot of a momentary constella-tion. First, in rereading *Werther* in order to make the changes necessary before the impending publication of his collected works, he was, I be-lieve, bound to be drawn again into a *Wertherstimmung,* if only because the feeling inevitably arose that never again would he be able to pour forth such a beautiful work. Secondly, Charlotte von Stein seems to have been annoyed with him. At least Goethe wrote, in the passage before that just quoted:

> Only continue to hold me dear, and let us at least preserve a good that we shall never find again, even if there are moments when we cannot enjoy it.[5]

---

[3] Here again is an instance in which one must consider the question that Bode raises of whether Goethe deliberately pretended or lied for the sake of playing up to what he assumed Charlotte von Stein would like to hear. Close scrutiny will show, however, that Goethe did not behave like a man who was knowledgeable in the ways of a woman's heart. By such strong statements as that quoted above, he made it, if anything, more difficult for Charlotte von Stein to accept the burden of the ensuing separation. Such statements have to be under-stood as the result of conflicts in Goethe, or his defenses against them, or his attempts at finding at least temporary solutions.

[4] [Ich korrigire am Werther und finde immer dass der Verfasser übel gethan hat sich nicht nach geendigter Schrifft zu erschiesen.]

[5] [Behalte mich nur lieb und lass uns ein Gut, das wir nie wiederfinden werden, wenigstens bewahren, wenn auch Augenblicke sind wo wir dessen nicht geniessen können.]

Yet the regret he felt at that moment over not having followed in the footsteps of his brain child, was more than an expression of merely momentary discouragement. He had again reached an end, as he had when the departure from Frankfurt became a necessity in 1775. On July 9, 1786, while waiting impatiently for the birth of the princely baby, the delay in which kept him from joining Charlotte von Stein in Carlsbad, he wrote her the above-quoted sentence (cf. p. 954), "My affairs are concluded and I have to go away if I am not to start over again from the beginning."[6] Ostensibly this was meant to characterize the momentary situation in Weimar, when external circumstances forced him to delay his departure, but he knew at that time that he would not come back to Weimar for a long time and I believe one may read into this terse statement a broader reference to his general situation in Weimar. Weimar had nothing new to offer but only relative comfort and repetition. "Nothing extraordinary can be accomplished in this workaday world,"[7] he wrote to Charlotte von Stein in the same letter. Though the event alluded to was quite distant from Goethe's orbit, it nevertheless belonged to the world in which he lived. It was, indeed, one of the most hilarious and bizarre occurrences ever to happen at the court of Weimar, at which there was no dearth of extravagant people. The Countess von Werthern (not the Duke's former sweetheart) arranged to have herself pronounced dead and to have a dummy interred in her stead, while she eloped with her sweetheart to Africa. After a year or so the couple returned and her brother promised to acknowledge her as his rightful sister if she "duly" got a divorce and "duly" married her lover. The prospect of such a commonplace ending to an affair that had started so promisingly was what prompted Goethe's remark about the workaday world. But Goethe's adventurous "elopement" to Weimar was also on the verge of ending in retirement from Parnassus, and the turn that the romantic passions of the attractive Countess took may have been—had he been in need of it—an additional warning to him.

What would he really have done if he had returned from his vacation in Carlsbad in 1786 and resumed his customary ways? He had exhausted all the potentialities that had been latent in the Weimarian situation at his arrival in 1775. He had integrated a philosophy of hard work and steeped himself in the most monotonous drudgery, that is to say, he had integrated the reality principle to an extent no observer would have held

[6] [. . . meine Geschäffte sind geschlossen und wenn ich nicht wieder von vorne anfangen will muss ich gehen.]

[7] [Es lässt sich in dieser Werckeltags Welt nichts auserordentliches zu Stande bringen]

him capable of; further he had maintained a loyal, devoted relationship to a single person over a period of a decade; he had learned to master the sudden impulses imposed by ambivalence and acquired the power of making sacrifices for a beloved object without reservation and without obtaining a pleasure premium as a reward. He had maintained his equilibrium despite two profound losses—sister and father. He had trained himself to integrate the aspect of science, and to a certain extent had deviated from the artist's path—as far as an artist ever can—without, however, losing his creative urge. Although he discovered himself as a scientist, he also discovered that it was his destiny to be an author and that the art of literature was his mission in life. His material existence had become secure. He earned a large salary, was the favorite of a powerful duke, and had become deeply rooted in a well-delineated group. He was, moreover, the center of a small group of friends who were stable, well-adjusted, and of superior caliber, quite different from the type who were attracted to Weimar by him in the period after his first appearance there. In the terminology of general psychology one can say that Goethe showed all the earmarks of maturity and good adjustment. He was a settled man. When he left Carlsbad at the age of thirty-seven plus one week, in order to go to Italy instead of returning to Weimar, where all who knew him expected him, with the exception of his servant Seidel, he had reached a developmental phase in which for most people adventure and new beginning have stopped and the justified desire arises to reap the profit of toil and planning, a phase when, in other words, the curve of the *élan vital* flattens without showing any further peaks. Reason and comfort dictated going back and continuing the work he had organized and led so promisingly for ten years. But had he acted in accordance with reason and comfort—that is to say, had he continued to live in accordance with the "good adjustment" that is so much vaunted in our times—life would have become a repetition, since, as has been said, the potentialities of the initial Weimarian situation had been fully realized.

Yet repetition on this level was incompatible with the dynamics of an eternally creative existence.

If man were not condemned by nature to his talent, one would have to scold oneself as foolish for loading oneself through a long life with always new torment and repeated toil.[8]

---

[8] [Wenn der Mensch nicht von Natur zu seinem Talent verdammt wäre, so müsste man sich als thörig schelten, dass man sich in einem langen Leben immer neue Pein und wiederholtes Mühsal auflastet.]

So he wrote to his friend Zelter on April 22, 1828, that is to say, some four years prior to his death. Here Goethe repudiated responsibility for the lifelong creative urge that forced him to act contrary to reason, comfort, and the much-vaunted common sense of the average man. "Condemned by nature to talent"—that is, to genius—the ego experiences itself as a powerless appendage to the creative urge, which relentlessly drives on the genius, who partakes of one sector more of life than the ordinary man. There is an idea impressively expounded by Georg Simmel (496, p. 37) concerning the relationship between individuality and social function that can also be applied to the genius. Just as certain public personages, such as kings and ministers, must, in certain instances, forgo large areas of their individuality if they are to attain ideal fulfillment of their socially assigned functions, so the genius has one responsibility more than the ordinary person, namely, to carry out the demand of his artistic destiny. During some periods artistic destiny and individualistic strivings may go parallel and stay in harmony, but at times they part and then the individual's first reaction may be one of anguish, such as Goethe expressed in his regret at not having committed suicide. These remarks regarding artistic destiny may seem metaphysical, but I think they ought to be considered as referring to a psychological dimension that must be accounted for in the case of the genius. This dimension, although deeply permeating all life sectors of the individual, may in a state of conflict be experienced subjectively as an isolated agency independent from and outside of the personality, not connected with any other strivings.

Another equally powerful—probably preconscious—factor was driving Goethe away from Weimar: the dammed-up, ungratified sexual desire, which he had not until then succeeded in satisfying. In view of later events, it appears highly probable that there were fantasies present regarding sexual adventures in the country of Latin and Greek civilization, and that it may also have been the fear-provoking aspect of these fantasies that prompted Goethe's desolate remark about *Werther*.

It is important to consider how many factors might have made it appear attractive to him to continue a routine that had become so firmly established in him, and how many important narcissistic and erotic pleasures were waiting for him in Weimar if he returned. Thus the pleasurable illusory prospect of living with Charlotte von Stein in a world of their own served the purpose of denying the realistic possibility of losing her.

The interpretation of Goethe's journey to Italy as a flight—specifically, as a flight from Charlotte von Stein—is encountered in many of the biographies of Goethe, but it is an erroneous interpretation, notwithstanding some remarks along these lines by Goethe himself in later years.[9] The motives for these remarks will be discussed later; they are the same as those that later prompted him to cover with silence his whole relationship to Charlotte von Stein.

Thus far, in trying to get a picture of what may have induced Goethe to go to Italy, we have found a multiplicity of motives and reasons, such as the Duke's military ambitions, dissatisfaction with administrative overwork, ambivalence towards Charlotte von Stein, a childhood longing to see the country of which his father had told him so much, sexual desires, the inner necessity of acting out an identification with his father, the exhaustion of potential inner growth under existing conditions. It behooves us to bring some order into this variety.

Once more I want to show that it was not predominantly the unpleasantness of Weimar that drove him away, as Lukács very radically proposes by emphasizing Goethe's disgust with the social conditions in Weimar (375, p. 14). There was no more painful thorn in his flesh than the Duke's bellicosity, and nevertheless Goethe wrote to him on his way away from Weimar, on July 24, 1786, as follows:

> The hope of still spending this day with you has not only deceived me but has also deprived me of a farewell. . . . I thank you that you still wish to give me leave with a friendly word.
>
> Hold me dear, give my regards to your lady wife, whom I left in a state of great joy and good health,[10] and live yourself well and happy.
>
> I go in order to correct all kinds of defects and to replenish all kinds of gaps; may the healthy spirit of the world assist me![11]

And on September 2, the day before he left from Carlsbad for Italy:

> Forgive me that at our farewell I spoke only vaguely about my journeyings and staying away; even now I do not yet know what will become of me.
>
> You are happy, you are going towards a desired and chosen destination, your domestic affairs are in good order, on a good path, and I know you

---

[9] Gräf is one of the few who defend the view that a flight from Charlotte von Stein was not among Goethe's motives for temporarily leaving Weimar. See 252, *1*:xvii.

[10] The Duchess had given birth to a healthy baby princess.

[11] [Die Hoffnung den heutigen Tag noch mit Ihnen zuzubringen hat mich nicht allein getäuscht, sondern auch um ein Lebe wohl gebracht. . . . Ich dancke Ihnen dass Sie mich noch mit einem freundlichen Worte beurlauben wollen.

Behalten Sie mich lieb, empfehlen Sie mich Ihrer Frau Gemahlinn, die ich mit herzlichen Freuden wohl verlassen habe, und leben selbst gesund und froh.

Ich gehe allerley Mängel zu verbessern und allerley Lücken auszufüllen, stehe mir der gesunde Geist der Welt bey!]

permit that I, too, should now think of myself—yes, you yourself have often exhorted me to do so. In general, I am surely at this moment dispensable, and, as for the particular assignments that I have been charged with, these I have arranged in such a way that they can go on smoothly without me for a while; indeed, I could die and it would not cause a ripple. I pass over many concordances with this constellation and only ask you for an indefinite leave. . . . My health has greatly gained and I also hope for the best for my elasticity of spirit, that when left to itself for a while it can enjoy the free world.

. . . Fare you well, this I wish sincerely; hold me dear, and believe that when I desire to make my existence more complete, I, in doing so, only hope to enjoy it more than up to now with you and in your [domain]. May you have joy in everything you undertake and enjoy a good outcome. If I let my pen run on it would yet say much; only one more farewell and a request to remember me earnestly to your lady wife.[12]

In evaluating this letter one must have in mind that the Duke was Goethe's chief and that Goethe was not quite sure how the prospect of his long absence would be received. But whatever its utilitarian motives may have been the letter breathes genuine affection. Despite serious disagreements and some estrangement, a strong tie of affection remained, and one gets the impression that it was not easy for Goethe to part from his friend, and that he tried to add one more farewell after another in order to delay the moment of the final good-bye.

Important as this letter is by way of proof that positive feelings prevailed even in the relationship to the Duke, it is even more important for the clue it contains in the passage in which he claims that even his death

[12] [Verzeihen Sie dass ich beym Abschiede von meinem Reisen und Aussenbleiben nur unbestimmt sprach, selbst ietzt weiss ich noch nicht was aus mir werden soll.

Sie sind glücklich, Sie gehen einer gewünschten und gewählten Bestimmung entgegen, Ihre häusliche Angelegenheiten sind in guter Ordnung, auf gutem Weege, und ich weis Sie erlauben mir auch dass ich nun an mich dencke, ja Sie haben mich selbst oft dazu aufgefodert. Im Allgemeinen bin ich in diesem Augenblicke gewiss entbehrlich, und was die besondern Geschäffte betrifft die mir aufgetragen sind, diese hab ich so gestellt, dass sie eine Zeitlang bequem ohne mich fortgehen können; ja ich dürfte sterben und es würde keinen Ruck thun. Noch viele Zusammenstimmungen dieser Constellation übergehe ich, und bitte Sie nur um einen unbestimmten Urlaub. . . . hat meine Gesundheit viel gewonnen und ich hoffe auch für die Elasticität meines Geistes das Beste, wenn er eine Zeitlang, sich selbst gelassen, der freyen Welt geniessen kann.

. . . Leben Sie wohl das wünsch ich herzlich, behalten Sie mich lieb und glauben Sie: dass, wenn ich wünsche meine Existenz ganzer zu machen, ich dabey nur hoffe sie mit Ihnen und in dem Ihrigen, besser als bisher, zu geniessen.

Mögten Sie in allem was Sie unternehmen Glück haben und Sich eines guten Ausganges erfreuen. Wenn ich meiner Feder den Lauf liesse mögte sie wohl noch viel sagen, nur noch ein Lebe wohl und eine Bitte mich Ihrer Frau Gemahlinn angelegentlich zu empfehlen.]

would not cause a great change. The patent meaning is that his administrative affairs were in good order and that his leaving would not be any dereliction of duty, but the passage also suggests that his departure may have had the meaning of his own death.[13] In such terms, his stay in Italy and return to Weimar would have had the meaning of a rebirth.[14]

How did Goethe manipulate the situation in order to act out this fantasy? He insisted on complete incognito for the largest part of the journey and for a long period no one except his servant was permitted to know his whereabouts. Many passages could be quoted to show the zeal and circumspection invested in keeping his closest friends, even Charlotte von Stein, ignorant of his whereabouts. As far as they knew, he might just as well have been dead, so little did they learn of him. For a long time he left out the place from which he wrote when writing to them, and only after he had arrived in Rome in November, 1786, did he reveal to his Weimarian friends where he was. He was aware how unusual this procedure was. In his last letter to the Duke, quoted from earlier, he wrote (September 2, 1786):

> Circumstances . . . compel me to lose myself in regions of the world where I am totally unknown. I am going quite alone under an alias and I hope for the best from this somewhat peculiar-seeming undertaking.[15]

To lose oneself in regions where one is unknown signifies, I believe, a state of deep regression in which personal identity and the feeling thereof are temporarily abolished. With skill he made others go through a period of tense expectancy, such as he had just gone through before the Princess was born, by making his subordinates expect his return from one week to the next. This procedure extended to almost everyone in Weimar, including Charlotte von Stein. He wrote to the Duke in the same communication: "It is good that . . . I shall even in absence be effective, like someone who is constantly expected."[16]

---

[13] See 551 for the symbolic meaning of taking trips; see also 158, p. 385.

[14] See 298. Yet this hypothesis loses much of its explanatory value when we learn that Goethe quite consciously experienced this journey as a rebirth. He wrote to Herder on December 2, 1786: "I count a second birthday, a true rebirth, from the day when I entered Rome." [Ich zähle einen zweyten Geburtstag, eine wahre Wiedergeburt von dem Tage da ich Rom betrat.] However, the identification of "the day of entering Rome" with a second day of birth may be an important clue to our unraveling one of the many unconscious motivations of Goethe's journey.

[15] [Umstände . . . zwingen mich in Gegenden der Welt mich zu verlieren, wo ich ganz unbekannt bin, ich gehe ganz allein unter einem fremden Nahmen und hoffe von dieser etwas sonderbar scheinenden Unternehmung das beste.]

[16] [. . . es ist gut dass . . . ich auch abwesend, als ein immer erwarteter, würcke.]

Goethe, as he wrote in the diary that he began on the first day of his journey, had wanted to set out on his birthday but was prevented by the editorial work on his collected works. Yet it is evident that the delay of a week—insignificant for any practical purposes—disturbed a fantasy he had formed and to which he tried hard to adhere. On September 11, 1786, while in Botzen, he wrote in his diary that he felt as if he had been born and raised there and were returning from a northern country. Later in the day he jotted down: "I feel like a child that has first to re-learn how to live."[17] The desire to isolate the past, to interpolate a long period between the pre-Italian and post-Italian residence in Weimar, was evident. Yet apparently Goethe desired that into this interpolated period no artistic problem of the past should intrude. For practical reasons this was not possible. Too many unfinished and sketchily written works dotted the path of the preceding ten years, and he had to set out on his journey with a good many manuscripts. Among the work he accomplished was the putting into verse of some important tragedies; thus there literally took place a process of artistic rebirth.[18]

How far he went in his strivings to isolate himself may be seen in his pleading with his servant-secretary Seidel not to mail him any letters to Rome before he should have arrived there. The way this idea developed can be well observed in his letters to Seidel. From Carlsbad he wrote, August 13, 1786:

> Nothing has yet happened that could prevent me from carrying out my plan. I shall start the journey towards the end of the month. By the mail that leaves Weimar on the eighteenth send me the last letters . . . from then on do not send [anything] prior to hearing from me.[19]

And shortly before his departure on September 2:

> When I consider everything, I cannot give you any earlier address than that in Rome, and that is [follows alias and address], but you are not to write to me there until you have again a letter from me, unless there is an emergency.[20]

[17] [Mir ists wie einem Kinde, das erst wieder leben lernen muss.] (*Soph.* III, *1*:180)

[18] How strongly he objected initially to this work can be seen from a diary entry of September 5, in which he calls the work on *Iphigenia* "a foul task" [eine böse arbeit].

[19] [Noch hat sich nichts zugetragen, das mich an Ausführung meines Plans hindern könnte. Gegen Ende des Monats werde ich die Reise antreten. Mit der Post welche Freytag den 18. von Weimar abgeht schicke mir das letzte von Briefen . . . alsdann sammle und schicke nicht eher bis du von mir hörst.]

[20] [Wenn ich alles überlege, so kann ich dir keine frühere Adresse als nach Rom geben und zwar: . . . . du schreibst mir aber nicht dorthin als bis du wieder einen Brief von mir hast, es müsste denn ein Nothfall sein.]

On his journey he wrote Seidel from Verona on September 18, 1786:

You are not to send anything after me, unless it should be absolutely necessary, for I want to enter *Rome* without the expectation of northern news. From Rome I shall write immediately and then there will be time [enough].[21] [Goethe's italics]

Rome, Sicily and the Father-Identification

On the sixth day after his arrival in Rome, that is, on November 4, 1786, Goethe wrote Seidel: "I have arrived here happily; send me now everything that you have gathered up."[22] The goal of isolation had succeeded; he had at last arrived in his beloved Rome without the past marring this culminating moment of his life. The details of the way he organized this trip to Rome were part of its symbolic meaning. To the Duke (letter from Rome of November 3) he called it: "the, as it were, subterranean journey hither."[23]

There is a metaphoric way in German of expressing the idea of being born, namely, "to see the light of the world" [Das Licht der Welt erblicken]. That was Goethe's mood as he entered Rome. His letter to Seidel ended thus: "The law and the prophets are now fulfilled, and I have peace from the Roman ghosts for my lifetime."[24] The fulfillment of the law and the prophets—this must refer to the birth and crucifixion of Christ, and it expressed the inexorable impulse that forced Goethe to reach Rome. Imagery of birth and rebirth had its share in this impulse. But this imagery was at least preconscious, if not quite conscious, and there must have been another, deeply unconscious factor at work in order to prompt such impetuous haste.

It is not clear what obsessed him, as he hurried through Italy, with the fear that something might interfere at the last minute and detain him from reaching the citadel of Western culture. On November 3, 1786, he wrote Karl August:

Scarcely did I dare to tell myself where I was going; even on my way I was still afraid, and only under the Porta del Popolo was I sure I should have Rome [Rome should be mine].[25]

[21] [Du schickst mir nichts nach, es wäre denn höchst nötig, denn ich will *Rom* ohne Erwartung nordischer Nachrichten betreten. Von Rom schreib ich gleich und dann ist es Zeit.]

[22] [Ich bin hier glücklich angelangt, schicke mir nun alles, was du gesammelt hast.]

[23] [die gleichsam unterirdische Reise hierher.]

[24] [Das Gesetz und die Propheten sind nun erfüllt, und ich habe Ruhe von den Römischen Gespenstern auf Zeitlebens.]

[25] [Kaum wagte ich mir selbst zu sagen wohin ich ging, selbst unterwegs fürchtete ich noch und nur unter der *Porta del Popolo* war ich mir gewiss Rom zu haben.]

In this letter also he described the obsessive nature of this desire to "have" Rome.

> Yes, these last years it became a kind of disease of which only the sight and the presence [of Rome] could cure me. Now I may confess, towards the end I could no longer look at a Latin book, at a drawing of an Italian region. The craving to see this country was overripe.[26]

In his first letter from Rome to his friends in Weimar, when he at last revealed his whereabouts, he wrote on November 1, 1786:

> The craving to come to Rome was so great, grew so much with each moment, that there was no staying any more and I stopped in Florence only for three hours.

> Now I am here and quiet and, as it seems, quieted for my whole life.

> For, one may really say, a new life starts when one sees with his eyes the whole that he knows partly in and out [by heart]. All the dreams of my youth I now see alive; the first engravings that I remember (my father had his views of Rome hung in an antechamber) I see now in reality and everything that I have known already for a long time in paintings and drawings, engravings and woodcuts, in plaster and cork, now stands together before me. Wherever I go I find [old] acquaintance in a new world; everything is as I imagined it and everything [is] new.

> I can say the same thing about my observations, about my ideas. I have not had a wholly new thought [and have] found nothing wholly strange, but the old [thoughts] have become so definite, so alive, so coherent, that they could pass for new.

> When Pygmalion's Elise, whom he had formed completely in accordance with his desires and to whom he had given as much of truth and of existence as an artist can, at last came towards him and said: *"It is I!"*, how otherwise was she alive than the sculptured stone.[27] [Goethe's italics]

[26] [Ja die letzten Jahren wurd es eine Art von Kranckheit, von der mich nur der Anblick und die Gegenwart heilen konnte. Jetzt darf ich es gestehen Zuletzt durft ich kein Lateinisch Buch mehr ansehn, keine Zeichnung einer italiänischen Gegend. Die Begierde dieses Land zu sehn war überreif.]

[27] [Die Begierde nach Rom zu kommen war so gross, wuchs so sehr mit jedem Augenblicke, dass kein Bleibens mehr war, und ich mich nur drey Stunden in Florenz aufhielt.

Nun bin ich hier und ruhig und wie es scheint auf mein ganzes Leben beruhigt.

Denn es geht, man darf wohl sagen, ein neues Leben an, wenn man das Ganze mit Augen sieht, das man Theilweise in und auswendig kennt. Alle Träume meiner Jugend seh ich nun lebendig, die ersten Kupferbilder deren ich mich erinnre (mein Vater hatte die Prospeckte von Rom auf einem Vorsaale aufgehängt) seh ich nun in Wahrheit, und alles was ich in Gemählden und Zeichnungen, Kupfern und Holzschnitten in Gyps und Korck schon

Goethe here describes a significant kind of subjective experience, namely, the experience of the almost thoroughly familiar as new. His first days in Rome were evidently replete with impressions, observations, perceptions, all of which bore sharply the mark of newness. Yet, at the same time, all of them were deeply connected with earliest childhood memories. The tension and discrepancy between the new and the familiar, each not only imbedded within the other, but even well-nigh intimately fused with the other, resulted in an incomparable and unique effect, which kept Goethe in constant pleasurable excitement. It was a twofold return to childhood. Childhood is a time in which the experience of the new is the average experience, since the child experiences almost everything as new. Thus the influx of so many new impressions in Rome must have called again into being a quality that is typical of childhood experience. But since this newness was closely associated with images most familiar from childhood, the new per se also stimulated the resurgence of childhood memories.

Goethe went through a subtle change in ego state as a result of this interaction of emotional qualities such as the new/the known, and the present/the past, and thus one is reminded of the ego-change Freud felt at his first view of the Acropolis (212). However, there was one great difference. The feeling of guilt as a result of accomplishing what his father had not succeeded in doing, which led in Freud to depersonalization, was absent in Goethe,[28] since his father had been in Rome and had told his children of the wonders of the city in enraptured terms. Thus when Goethe arrived in Rome he did not outdo his father but appropriated, as it were, what his father had once upon a time possessed. However, his father had had the privilege of visiting Rome at an earlier age than Goethe by seven years. There are two passages in which one senses a mild irrita-

---

lange gekannt steht nun beysammen vor mir, wohin ich gehe find ich eine Bekanntschaft in einer neuen Welt, es ist alles wie ich mir's dachte und alles neu.

Eben so kann ich von meinen Beobachtungen von meinen Ideen sagen. Ich habe keinen ganz neuen Gedancken gehabt, nichts ganz fremd gefunden, aber die alten sind so bestimmt, so lebendig, so zusammenhängend geworden, dass sie für neu gelten können.

Da Pygmalions Elise, die er sich ganz nach seinen Wünschen geformt, und ihr so viel Wahrheit und Daseyn gegeben hatte, als der Künstler vermag, endlich auf ihn zukam und sagte: *ich bins!* wie anders war die Lebendige, als der gebildete Stein.]

In this comparison of the "alive" [die Lebendige] with "sculptured stone" [gebildete Stein] the deepest root of Goethe's conflict is perhaps buried. The name of the sweetheart he was in the process of abandoning was, after all, von Stein.

[28] Whether Goethe also had, after all, an experience of depersonalization in the form of *déjà vu* experiences is, though probable, nevertheless a matter of speculation. See 159, pp. 265–68.

tion about this and a quick compensatory move. In the beginning of the above-quoted letter to his friends of November 1, 1786, he wrote:

At last I have arrived in this capital of the old world! If I had seen it fifteen years ago, in good company, led by a well-informed man, I should have held myself fortunate. If, however, I am to see it alone with my own eyes and visit [it], then it is well that this joy fell to me so late.[29]

It is an important clue to keep in mind for subsequent conclusions that this time factor was the subject of the very first remark Goethe made to his friends in this, his first message to them after a long silence. Why start out in such a defensive way and claim that it was, after all, better for him to reach Rome at such an age and not earlier? The connection with his father is more outspoken in his first letter to his mother from Rome (November 4, 1786). After announcing his arrival and giving his itinerary, he writes how wonderful it is

that I see now in reality the objects . . . of which I so often heard my father tell. . . .

To be sure, I see all these things a little late, yet thereby with all the more profit and much in a short time.[30]

The hidden rivalry with the father is here almost manifest, as if he wanted to say: "Though you saw Rome at an earlier age than I (though you were mature earlier than I?) I still take more joy from it than you and am superior to you." A hidden reference to competition with a father-substitute can already be found in his travel diary entry for September 8, 1786, in which he writes of the mountain *Martinswand,* well-known in the folk story, which tells that the Emperor Maximilian, when he was stranded in its wilderness, was rescued by an angel. Goethe's remark is that he would dare to go to the point where the Emperor went and return without the help of an angel.[31]

I shall try to bring these statements about Rome under one psychologi-

[29] [Endlich bin ich in dieser Hauptstadt der alten Welt angelangt! Wenn ich sie in guter Begleitung, angeführt von einem recht verständigen Manne, vor funfzehn Jahren gesehen hätte, wollte ich mich glücklich preisen. Sollte ich sie aber allein, mit eignen Augen sehen und besuchen; so ist es gut dass mir diese Freude so spät zu Theil ward.]

[30] [dass ich nun die Gegenstände in der Natur sehe . . . von denen ich den Vater so oft erzählen hörte. . . .

Alle diese Dinge seh ich freylich ein wenig späte, doch mit desto mehr Nutzen und viel in kurzer Zeit.]

[31] As if he had to restrain himself, Goethe added that actually to do so and climb to the spot where the Emperor had been would be "a sacrilegious enterprise" [ein frevelhafftes Unternehmen]. (*Soph.* III, *1*:159)

cal aspect. Rome meant a place where his father had been, of which his father spoke boastfully, the beauty of which he praised, a place that Goethe felt an obsession to go to; once he had got there Rome meant a place that gave him the feeling that he would be quieted for the rest of his life, something that was very familiar from childhood but appeared as new to the adult, something one knew from pictures and drawings and that nevertheless looked quite different in nature, like Pygmalion's statue come to life, and something that one can *have*—an extremely unusual expression to apply to a city. All this forces me to believe that Rome had for Goethe the symbolic meaning of the female genital, or, speaking more generally, of the female body, or, speaking more specifically, of the mother. The haste and urgency to rush to Rome were fed by the energy released from his unconscious by the fact that entering into Rome meant for him taking possession of his mother. The repeated hesitation in the past about entering Italy and going to Rome was caused by the unconscious identity of Rome and the mother. Earlier he had not been strong enough to perform the deed in its symbolic guise. But the ten years in Weimar and the transformation he had undergone within his relationship with Charlotte von Stein had at last brought about the maturity necessary for this thrust, and without fear he accepted female genitality indelibly associated with the image of the mother in man's unconscious.

From this point of view one can understand why there should have risen to dangerous, almost pathological, proportions Goethe's fears lest he not succeed in reaching Rome. This fear can be felt in his diary entry of October 27, 1786, that is, two days before he got there:

> Rome! Rome!—I no longer take off my clothes so as to be ready first thing in the morning. Still two nights! And if the angel of the Lord does not smite us on the way, we are there![32]

A psychological inquiry leads inescapably to the assertion that Goethe was not on a flight when he entered Rome but that the preceding decade had been the indispensable prerequisite of that triumphal entry. And indeed no Roman imperator ever entered Rome in such elation and exuberance as Goethe. And in however low esteem Goethe later held the pre-Italian decade, he owed to it such indescribably beautiful feelings as probably no other human being experienced. However, it is understandable that Goethe was not aware of this connection, but isolated the present

---

[32] [Rom! Rom!—Ich ziehe mich gar nicht mehr aus um früh gleich bey der Hand zu seyn. Noch zwey Nächte! und wenn uns der Engel des Herrn nicht auf dem Wege schlägt; sind wir da.]

from the past. Subjectively it had to seem to him that he was succumbing to Italy's beauty, and to have been aware that he was now reaping the harvest of a decade of toil and resignation would have marred the exuberance of the moment. Thus he wrote in his diary on September 11, 1786, that now was the moment to see "whether the creases that have beaten and pressed themselves into my mind can again be effaced."[33] He was thinking at this point of all the traces that the sufferings and dreariness of the last few years had left in him, but actually he was in the process of straightening out conflicts that dated back to early childhood and had gradually become accessible to the integrative powers of the ego. I mentioned earlier Freud's subjective experience when he faced the Acropolis. When Goethe's various reports of his journey are read over, an amazing parallel is found between one part of his journey and Freud's journey to Athens. Freud has vividly described his reactions when it was suggested to him that he go to Athens. He objected, hesitated, doubted, and fell into a bad humor. This was a puzzling, seemingly paradoxical, reaction, since he unquestionably had a desire to visit that very place. When he analyzed this reaction many years after having actually been there, he discovered its root. It issued from a conflict about fulfilling a wish the fulfillment of which made him superior to his father.[34] The fact that impressed me so much in Goethe's behavior after I had read Freud's clinical autobiographical essay, was the absolute certainty of aim with which Goethe rushed to Rome and Naples, in contrast to the grave doubts and procrastination which beset his journey to Sicily. His father's journey had not taken him further south than Naples, and as soon as Goethe felt the impulse to visit regions where he knew his father had never set foot he showed a reaction almost identical with that Freud reports over the prospect of going to Greece. Goethe's first reference to Sicily is in the letter of December 29, 1786, to Charlotte von Stein: "I am not going to Sicily. I am not sufficiently prepared, have neither money nor time enough."[35] On

[33] [ob die Falten, die sich in mein Gemüth geschlagen und gedruckt haben, wieder auszutilgen sind.] (*Soph.* III, *1*:175)

[34] See 212, pp. 311–12. This conflict can be encountered in almost all male persons. Clinically two extreme types are encountered: one which must in all circumstances achieve superiority over the father in all respects, and the other, which is compelled to maintain a place of inferiority. In most instances a mixture of both can be observed: some superiority is acceded to as the price for suffering an inferiority in some other sector.

[35] [Nach Sicilien geh ich nicht; ich bin nicht vorbereitet genug, habe weder Geld noch Zeit genug.]

Cf. Freud (212, p. 303): "We [my brother and I] discussed the plan [of going to Athens] . . . agreed that it was quite impracticable and saw nothing but difficulties in the way of carrying it out. . . ."

January 6, 1787, in a letter to his friends in Weimar, he stated his plans again quite definitely as leading him to Naples and back to Rome, but then he added:

> But now, Sicily still lies down there. A journey thither would have to be made only in the fall and when better prepared; also not just a mere trip across and around, which is soon made but from which one brings back only the *I-have-seen-it!* for his pains and money. One would have first to settle down in Palermo and later in Catania in order to make secure and useful excursions. . . .[36] [Goethe's italics]

In the same letter Goethe declared that he was too much alone to make a decision and that his friends ought to get together "to decide about my fate."[37] They should, however, assume, as he could assure them, that he felt more inclined to come home than to stay in Italy. This was, no doubt, a hypocritical statement, probably not with the intent of deceiving others but resulting from self-deception. In his letter of January 17, 1787, to Charlotte von Stein he expressed his eagerness to hear what she thought about his various plans, but did not mention Sicily. On February 2, 1787, to Charlotte von Stein, he went a step further and said he had to leave Rome and make a pause, was looking forward to Naples and to Sicily, "if you want to do without me for a longer time."[38] On the following day he was more definite in getting his friends to advise him to go to Sicily. Thus he wrote the Herders (February 3, 1787) he would organize his journey however they told him, and "as the spirit drives. I could go to Sicily immediately after Easter, since the country can be traveled still in April and May, although hot enough, and I should have to see it anyhow."[39] Here at last the cat was out of the bag and it becomes clear that Goethe's mind had been made up from the beginning that he would go to Sicily. The "I could go" becomes, within that very sentence "I should have to go."[40] On February 19, 1787, he wrote to Knebel: "As to Sicily, I let destiny dis-

[36] [Nun aber liegt Sicilien noch daunten. Dahin wäre eine Reise nur mehr vorbereitet und im Herbste zu thun, auch nicht eine blose Durch und Umreise, die bald gemacht ist, wo von man aber nur das: *ich habs gesehen!* für seine Mühe und Geld mitbringt. Man müsste in Palermo nachher in Catanea sich erst festsetzen um sichre und nützliche Exkursionen zu machen.]

[37] [über mein Schicksal zu entscheiden]

[38] [wenn ihr mich länger entbehren wollt]

[39] [wie der Geist treibt. Ich könnte nach Ostern gleich nach Sizilien gehn, denn das Land ist im April und May noch bereisbar, obschon heis genug, und sehn müsst ich's denn doch.]

[40] Cf. Freud (212, p. 304): "Later on we [my brother and I] recognized that we had accepted the suggestion that we should go to Athens . . . instantly and most readily."

pose. I am prepared; if luck lures me, I shall go."[41] As so often, destiny had to decide in conformity with his own wishes and fears. On April 18, 1787, more than two weeks after he had landed in Sicily, he wrote to Charlotte von Stein:

> I can only repeat to you that I am well and cheerful and that now my journey is taking shape. In Naples it would have ended too blunt.[42]

I believe this passage is renewed proof of how important it was for Goethe to excel over his father by accomplishing this last leg of the journey, which took him furthest from the beloved woman and coincided, as he claimed thirty-one years later, with a significant turn in his "adventure."[43] The journey would have ended "too blunt" and the crowning touch would have been missing had he not added this part of the journey. The day before, that is, after having been sixteen days in Sicily, he wrote to Fritz:

> I feel fine and have perhaps not been in all my life in such high spirits and so delighted for sixteen days in a row.[44]

One can easily imagine what this meant when it is considered that it was Goethe who wrote:

> Everything in the world can be borne
> Except a succession of beautiful days.[45]

What may have accounted for its being so difficult for him to bear happiness will not be investigated here. Suffice it to know that Goethe did not possess that kind of temperament that is capable of easily experiencing pleasure. Thus he was aware of the unusualness of his feeling happy over such a long stretch of time. Since he had been in Rome much longer but had not been able there to find that particular pleasure over a span of time comparable to that which he now mentioned to Fritz, the conclusion is inescapable that there must have been some particular psychological

---

[41] [Wegen Sicilien lass ich das Schicksal walten. Vorbereitet bin ich, wenn das Glück mich lockt, geh ich.]

[42] [Ich kann dir nur wiederhohlen dass ich wohl und vergnügt bin und dass nun meine Reise eine Gestalt nimmt. In Neapel hätte sie zu stumpf aufgehört.]
This letter is the only one preserved of those he wrote to Charlotte von Stein from Sicily.

[43] Meaning the relationship with Charlotte von Stein; see later, p. 1082.

[44] [Ich befinde mich wohl und bin vielleicht in meinem Leben nicht 16 Tage hinter einander so heiter und vergnügt gewesen als hier.]

[45] [Alles in der Welt lässt sich ertragen,/ Nur nicht eine Reihe von schönen Tagen.] (*Soph.* I, 2:230)

difference between the two experiences. It would be wrong to attribute this long duration of joy exclusively to reality factors, such as the infinite beauty of Sicily. That, to be sure, Goethe never ceased to praise, but the rest of Italy was surely beautiful enough to provide sixteen happy days if all other psychological factors had been identical. But after the symbolic appropriation of his mother by his entry into Rome, Goethe was able now to be where his father had never been and he could indulge in seeing and enjoying landscapes whose beauty his father did not even imagine. His father had boasted of Naples' beauty (see above, p. 924); now the son could boast of something the father had not known. In a manner acceptable to the ego, the defeat of the father could be celebrated, with, nevertheless, no ensuing feeling of guilt, no hesitation, but, rather, uninterrupted happiness.

The point has now been reached where the crucial psychological process that took place during the Italian journey can be set forth. One aspect of that process can be described as a full father-identification, which went so far as to result in a characteristically changed physical appearance—as I pointed out on page 928. However, there was more involved than an identification. In his moving to Weimar, besides its obvious meaning of rebellion against his father, there had also been involved an attempt at identifying with his father. The Italian journey seems, however—as can, I believe, be proved by the evidence, presently to be adduced, that a very important neurotic symptom subsided in Italy—to have led to a significant decrease of anxiety concerning his father. I should therefore suggest that an already existing father-identification became integrated. The preexisting identification, important as it may have been as a stimulus to action, had not been accepted by the ego and therefore led to neurotic anxiety or its substitutes. In technical terms, one may say that the identification had taken place in the superego, whereas in the course of the journey this part of the superego was taken over by the ego. The ego no longer required that its superego be patterned in accordance with the father, but was now able to feel secure in the conviction of being as strong, as potent, and as invincible as father had been. The elimination of the high tension between ego and superego must have led to a feeling of triumph that easily resulted in a feeling of superiority to the father. Indeed, when the father-image has been totally integrated the resulting conclusion must be: "I am no longer afraid of father," which, in turn, must give the ego the feeling of being stronger than the father.

Before presenting further clinical material for the support of my metapsychological conclusion I wish to call attention to a curious manifestation of a group attitude. Among the many Germans who offer themselves as representatives of the nation there has not been one who could rival Goethe. No other German's life has been so carefully scrutinized and investigated, and the Goethe literature is so large that even if he devoted his entire life to it no one could rightly claim he had read everything that has been printed about Goethe. For all practical purposes, not the smallest incident has been left untouched by the scientific probing of the scholars, and I doubt whether there is any other person—with the possible exception of Napoleon—whose life is so richly documented as Goethe's. All the more astounding is it, then, that two publications that must be appraised as being eminently important for an understanding of Goethe's life have not been translated into German, but are available only in the language in which they were originally written, namely Italian. The one is the account by Johann Kaspar Goethe, the poet's father, of his Italian journey,[46] and the other is a little book by Carletta (84), which proves—as I believe beyond doubt—that the sexual adventure described by Goethe in his *Roman Elegies* must have been in accordance with truth, and not, as so many have claimed, a poetic transposition of experiences with his sweetheart and later wife Christiane Vulpius, with whom he started a relationship shortly after his return from Italy. Apparently the nation did not want to take cognizance of the full impact the poet's father had on his son, and must, further, have felt hurt and disillusioned by the relationship that Goethe maintained with a young Italian widow. The very offensive, but undeniable, fact of a common-law relationship with Christiane lasting over eighteen years was somehow made palatable to the nation by its belated legitimation, but a predominantly sexual love for Faustina, free of conflict and characterized by freely flowing sensuousness and enjoyment, apparently was incompatible with the image that the nation had formed of its greatest son.

However, let us return now to the father's account of *his* Italian journey which, as I said, has never been published in German and has been largely neglected by most biographers. From the little that has been published, one gets the impression that this travel report was written with unusual warmth, interest and circumspection. Here a man who considered a journey through Italy the consummation of the best the world

---

[46] *Viaggio in Italia* (236). Cf. above, p. 924. I wish to stress the late date of publication (1932–33). Reinsch (451), who had an opportunity to study the original document, claims that Farinelli published the diary "with many deviations from the original." The German reader has access to this diary only in selections. For those parts which have been published in German, see 56; 232; 451.

could offer tried hard to report everything an enthusiastic traveler might experience and observe. The great variety of topics that aroused his interest, the realism of his approach to everything new that came to his attention, and the very personal viewpoints that he adopted are among the factors that surprise the reader. I wish to illustrate this by some examples. In Ferrara, he followed the trail of the poet Torquato Tasso, since he admired particularly his *Jerusalem Delivered*. He compared the once flourishing condition of this principality with its contemporary poverty and wrote:

> This city is one of the most important in the Papal States, well built, with broad streets and large palaces, but not populated enough. The inhabitants are for the most part poor, for the powerful ones, and particularly the Holy Father, seldom leave them the necessary. Therefore it astounded me to see the environs and particularly the vineyards in a better condition than one might expect in view of the miserable condition of the winegrowers and other people.

> Being under this sad impression, I should not want the people to pray for my soul even if I had died there as a prince. Surely people would take vengeance and wish me the opposite of a heavenly bliss. For it is the custom here that when one of the great ones' time has come, it is ordered that all the inhabitants unite their prayers for his salvation. I witnessed this for a recently deceased bishop during my sojourn. Everyone ran into the churches, which were as much frequented as on the great holidays. This had for me the advantage that all the temples stood open and I could make my rounds through them without impediment. (232, pp. 63–64)

At the seashore, wandering barefoot, he gathered starfish and sea horses for his collection of natural curiosities and wrote:

> As far as the starfish are concerned I have always held them to be plants of changing appearance. One recognizes only with great attention the animal life. They also have their corresponding organs, but they do not live long, I believe, outside of water. In this example the truth reveals itself, as the modern natural philosophers [*Physiker*] have pointed out with much acumen, of the close connection of the three states of nature, namely the animal, vegetable, and mineral kingdoms. This brings to my memory that the coral, which without doubt must be classed among the plants, transforms itself back into stone.

> Indeed one notices in the creation of all things, from the archangel to the smallest particle of dust, a conspicuous kinship from step to step up to the highest creator, and in such manner that even the sublimest spirits do not

recognize where the one kind starts and the other leaves off. I recall having read that there is supposed to be a tree in the kingdom of Borneo the leaves of which finally come to life and then move around upon the stalk like a foot until they fall off. Likewise there are supposed to be grains in Sicily that are able to transform themselves into animals. But when one gives credence to these tales, it appears to me that many sensible reasons can be found for both observations without charging nature with a miracle on the occasion of the transition from the plant to the animal condition. Nature is like a chain, of which created things are the links. (232, pp. 69–70)

This last quotation particularly gives a glimpse into how close the connection was between Goethe's world of ideas and his father's. Evidence of this could be multiplied by many other examples even from the excerpts available in German publications. It cannot be foretold what further significant connections may be discovered when the original is adequately studied by scholars prepared to recognize such significances.

Furthermore, the parallels between the journeys of father and son are sometimes uncanny. When Goethe left Italy in 1788 he was still, so to speak, inferior to his father in so far as the latter had visited Venice twice —the second time on his return trip to Central Europe—but Goethe only once, although he had kept fairly accurately to his father's route. Promptly —one feels tempted to say—fate played into Goethe's hands, and in 1790 he was asked to go to Venice to meet the Dowager Duchess on her return trip from Italy. Thus he also saw Venice twice and caught up with his father, and again had experiences quite reminiscent in detail of his father's stay in Venice. When I used the term uncanny before, I had in mind a detail that cannot have been due to Goethe's involuntary selection, nor is there any reason to suppose him to have been fabricating experiences in order to provide parallels. The analogous incidents I refer to are the following: When Goethe's father traveled through the Austrian province of Styria on his way to Venice, he was apprised of the death of Christian Wolff, one of the foremost German philosophers of his time. He later learned, however, that this news was erroneous, that it was a relative of the philosopher bearing the same name who had died (232, pp. 38–40). When Goethe came to Innsbruck, the capital of Tyrolia, also an Austrian province, on his return from Venice during his second Italian journey, he was met with the news that his friend Herder had died. The same night it was discovered that this was wrong and that Herder's name had been confused with that of Heinicke.[47] The two incidents are so similar down

---

[47] Samuel Heinicke (1729–1790), teacher of the deaf and dumb in Leipzig.

to their smallest details that one hesitates to think of a coincidence, particularly in view of the many other parallels. I do not wish to speculate as to whether Goethe made up the story or became the victim of a fantasy. The incident is mentioned in his letter to Herder of June 9, 1790, and so far as I know is not documented by others. Goethe wrote that a stranger greeted them with the news, etc. It is perhaps odd that this stranger was not identified and one wonders whether Goethe himself contributed to this slip. Of course, if Goethe was in any part the fabricator of this episode, while it would diminish the uncanniness it would confirm the identification to an almost unbearably obvious degree.

Be this as it may, one has to conclude that Goethe became intimately familiar with all the details of his father's travel diary. He probably also felt the intense passion, longing, and pride with which his father's writings were imbued. One can easily imagine the boy's envy of his father's writing this journal and the father's zeal in using it in his teaching of the boy.[48] Yet Goethe's father also suffered from feelings of inferiority. He stressed in his introduction that he was not setting down his impressions in order to appear before the public (see 56, p. 7). Thus Goethe also felt his father's inhibition. His own later writing of the *Italian Journey,* a real gem of literary beauty, may not only have gratified the childhood wish also to write a book about Italy, like his father, but have fulfilled in addition the childhood wish to write a better account and, unlike his father, not to be afraid to submit it to the world of readers.

Indeed, one is led to some interesting conclusions if he pursues the question of why, in the light of the evident merits of the father's diary, Johann Kaspar was for so long—and to some extent still is—held in low esteem, as a rather mediocre, limited mind. One of the occasions taken for ridiculing him—by Goethe's friend Merck, among others—was a letter he wrote to the secretary of Count von Seckendorf, Johann Philipp Strecker, when he reached Venice for the second time, on his way back to Frankfurt. Johann Kaspar complained bitterly about the iniquities travelers are exposed to in Italy. Thus he wrote for example:

> And I am surprised, since all travelers have fared the same as I and still do, that people do not leave the Italians their old walls on which they pride themselves so much, and instead visit only France, England, Holland and

[48] Here may also be one of the roots of Goethe's frequent regret over not being better acquainted with Italian. Yet one is reminded, too, of Freud's remark regarding the mechanism of "retiring in favour of someone else" (192, p. 159 n). Probably Goethe needed small islands where he left his father's superiority untouched. A similar situation will be encountered later in the discussion of Goethe's musical development.

Lower-Saxony. . . . Truly is it said that in all Europe one cannot for his money travel with greater discomfort and annoyance than in the said Italy. One brings home nothing but a head full of oddities for all of which if he should carry them to the market of his native city one would not get two pennies cash.[49]

Oddly enough, when Goethe went to Italy for the second time he passed some critical judgments on Italy that sounded quite different from his earlier enraptured praise and came close to his father's letter. He wrote to Karl August on April 3, 1790, from Venice: "Moreover, I must confess confidentially that my love for Italy is struck a fatal blow by this journey."[50] And to Herder on the same day: "A little more intolerant towards the swinish life of this nation than the last time."[51] As little as these remarks correctly reflect Goethe's attitude toward Italy, so little does Johann Kaspar's letter do justice to him or to his understanding of Italy, which finds true expression in his book. He apparently was giving vent in the letter to some acutely aroused feeling of annoyance, a feeling that did not prevent him from preserving the greatest admiration for Italy.

I am puzzled about how this letter of Johann Kaspar's ever got into Merck's possession, and raise the question—quite hypothetically—whether Goethe himself may have let it fall into Merck's hands.[52] The letter somehow conforms to the impression that Goethe left regarding his father in *Dichtung und Wahrheit*. We encounter here a particularly challenging problem of the psychology of biographical writing. When one reads *Dichtung und Wahrheit* quite closely and in detail one finds a good many positive statements about Goethe's father. To be sure, there are also quite a few of a negative nature. In any case, there is nothing from which the reader could guess that Goethe's father spent on his son almost half of his annual income during his years of university studies (see 482, p. viii). Thus a certain degree of ambivalence towards his father, even when the poet was getting on in years, can be detected. But the picture of Goethe's

[49] [Und ich wundere mich, da es doch allen Reisenden gleich wie mir ergangen und noch ergehet, dass man denen Italienern ihre alten Mauern, worauf sie sich so viel einbilden, nicht lässet, und davor Frankreich, England, Holland und Niedersachsen alleine besuchet. . . . Genau gesagt ist es, dass man in ganz Europa vor sein Geldt nicht unbequemer und verdriesslicher reiset, als in besagtem Italien. Man bringt nichts mehr mit nach Hause als einen Kopf voller Curiosideten, vor welche man insgesammt, wenn man sie in seiner Vatterstadt auf den Markt tragen sollte, nicht zwey baare Heller bekäme.] (482, pp. 5–7)

[50] [Übrigens muss ich im Vertrauen gestehen, dass meiner Liebe für Italien durch diese Reise ein tödtlicher Stos versetzt wird.]

[51] [Ein wenig intoleranter gegen das Sauleben dieser Nation als vorigemal.]

[52] This suggestion must now be dropped in view of a recent publication by Ernst Beutler (30, p. 50) in which he reports that Strecker was Merck's cousin.

father that has usually been derived by those who read the poet's auto-biography has been worse than would conform with the literal signifi-cance of its wording. Nevertheless, I believe that Goethe himself must be held responsible for this impression. Those who read the autobiography ap-parently do not respond so much to the literal meaning as to what is be-tween the lines. Goethe, so to speak, laid the foundation for his own leg-end. This man who rightly assumed prerogatives denied to other mortals also arrogated the privilege of forcing upon posterity beliefs about him-self in conformity with his own wishes. And this was not achieved by the blunt and customary means of lie or falsification[53] but rather by highly artistic and formal means that draw the reader's imagination in certain directions without his noticing that he is being made the victim of the poet's luring voice.

A problem opens up here that is of general psychological interest. This concerns the effect that an identification leaves upon the ego. Identifica-tions may manifest themselves in a great variety of ways. Moreover, al-most any given psychological phenomenon may be the manifestation of an identification, from such trivial actions as the choice of a necktie to such deeply rooted personal traits as gait or pitch of voice. Conversely, an identification may not lead to any manifestation observable from the out-side but exhaust itself in fantasies and daydreams (cf. 153 *passim*). Be-side the variations in manifestation there is the variation in content. There are some subjects who habitually identify only with surface prop-erties of the object, such as a gesture, and others whose identifications center in the core of the object's personality structure (see 444; 445). Fur-thermore, the range of the identification's effect on an ego must be con-sidered. It may extend to almost the whole ego, or only to the way it deals with outer reality, or its relationship with ego-ideal and superego. The whole problem, of course, becomes still more complex when a sub-ject who has actually made a structural identification, combats it and only permits himself manifestations in the form of superficial traits. Thus we may consider three variables, manifestation, content, and structural ef-fect, when studying identification in a particular individual.

Insufficient as is this abbreviated commentary on so broad a subject as identification, it may facilitate insight into the character of Goethe's

---

[53] There have been authors who deliberately modified crucial data about their lives, such as Tolstoy, who gives the reader erroneous information about the date of his mother's death. I do not think that Goethe ever resorted to such a technique but rather used the innuendo, the hint, the creation of impressions by indirection. Evidently he relied on unconscious tech-niques in misleading the reader.

identification with his father. It seems reasonable to ask why Goethe actually had to go to Italy in order to carry out his identification with his father. It is the privilege of the poet that he may enjoy the gratifications of most extensive identifications without undergoing the trouble and labor they so often entail. By creating characters and letting them act in conformity with wishes that stem from identifications, many poets, if not all, have found an effective medium for acting out their identifications.[54] Goethe, of course, had this medium at his disposal, and in writing his tragedy *Tasso* probably also gave way specifically to early identifications that may have stemmed from his father's accounts about Italy. Therefore it is reasonable to ask why Goethe had actually to go to Italy, instead of dealing with the problem by a purely internal change or by artistic creation, as the case may be. To be sure, there were many other motives behind the journey, as I have already shown, but the role of the identification must have been the most potent force and therefore one has to tackle the question of why this identification had to manifest itself in the form of real actions.

[54] Probably one should not speak here of acting out, since by writing works of literature the poet touches upon reality only in an indirect way. See 191, pp. 17, 18–19; 462; 166.

Chapter 4

Goethe's Sexual Life

First Cohabitation

I MIGHT REFER here to the fact that it was a general characteristic of Goethe's that he was not disposed to content himself with a modest role in worldly affairs, such as fate and society so often assign to the poet, but that he had to be painter, stage manager, scientist, minister, architect—in short, had to play in social actuality all the roles that the poet usually plays only on the imaginary level. Fortunately I can in this instance go beyond a general statement and be more specific. Goethe had this time to go through the motions of the father-identification, and had to live it out by means of real actions, because it had become closely connected with a turn in his relationship to the other sex. He had to concretize the identification because this was the only way of achieving sexual intercourse. Since the unconscious goal of the Italian journey was also that of entering the situation of genital heterosexual gratification, he had to act out the identification, for this goal, though it also entailed an internal change, went beyond it and necessarily had to involve the volitional kinesthetic system.

It seems—as I observed previously—that Goethe had sexual intercourse for the first time in his life during his second sojourn in Rome, after his return from Sicily. That he had intercourse in Rome can be proved; that it was for the first time is, of course beyond proof, but nevertheless an assumption of such high probability that I tend to consider it a certainty. I turn now to the first part of the statement.

In the *Roman Elegies* Goethe describes in classical hexameters an erotic adventure of unquestionable sexual character, marked by a physical, sensu-

1019

ous enjoyment that Goethe compared to the unchristian, antique, suddenly arising and often short-lasting, passions of the Greek gods. According to the *Elegies,* he fell in love with one Faustina, a young widow, who worked as a waitress in a Roman *osteria* owned by her family. There are some references to an uncle, a mother, and her own child. These are, in the main, the only realistic details that are mentioned, and that might be susceptible of documentary proof. In 1899 Carletta published his little book *Goethe a Roma,* in which he brought forward documentary evidence that a person conforming in all respects to the particulars mentioned in the *Roman Elegies* actually lived in a neighborhood in which Goethe was said to have spent some of his residence in Rome. This was Faustina, born 1764, the third daughter of the innkeeper Agostino di Giovanni, married and widowed in 1784, mother of a little boy, the issue of her short-lasting marriage. This evidence was all the more astounding since the name Faustina was, according to Carletta, an extremely rare one among poor people, and therefore it is highly probable that even the name of the sweetheart was not one chosen for purely poetical reasons but was also in accordance with historical truth. Despite this impressive historical finding most German scholars have continued to insist that the Faustina praised beyond measure by Goethe was in reality his German sweetheart Christiane.[1] Additional evidence of Faustina's historicity may be found in one of the many Goethe reminiscences that were published after his death. In 1880 there appeared the recollections of J. K. W. Zahn[2] regarding his stay in Weimar when he visited Goethe in 1827. He had just returned from Italy and Goethe showed immediate interest in him, particularly because he was the possessor of copies of some Pompeian frescoes. Goethe's tendency to become absorbed by artistic impressions that appealed to him is well known, and he delighted in looking at the pictures. Zahn's account of the various incidents, his characterizations of the people he met with Goethe, and his references to certain habits and mannerisms of the poet all sound credible and seem to be authentic, since many other

[1] See, e.g., Ludwig Geiger, in the introduction to the *Italian Journey* (248, 26:xliv–xlv. Geiger seems to feel indignant at the idea that Goethe could have been the lover of a Roman waitress. Since the fact that Goethe had sexual adventures in Rome is evidenced by his correspondence (see later), Geiger does not deny the possibility that Goethe may "not have resisted the charms" of a Roman waitress, but the idea that such a person might have been depicted as Faustina in the beautiful *Elegies* is rejected. Among the many reasons that may have been operative in disposing scholars to feel bad about accepting Carletta's Faustina identification one has to consider nationalistic and class prejudices.

[2] Johann Karl Wilhelm Zahn (1800–71), architect and painter.

observers report the same.[3] Goethe became quite enthusiastic and Italian recollections were stimulated. At one point in his recollections Zahn reported the following conversation:

> "Are you also acquainted with the Osteria alla Campana?", he [Goethe] further inquired. "The tavern at the Bell? Of course. We German artists celebrated your birthday there just last year." "Is the Falernian [wine] still so good?" "Superb!" "And what did the kitchen afford?" "Oh, you get *stuffato,* a kind of stew, macaroni, and a pastry, which they call *fritti."* "Everything is still as it was in my time!" Goethe said and smiled with satisfaction. Then he continued: "That *osteria* was my usual resort. There I met a Roman [woman] who inspired me to [write] the *Elegies.* She used to come there in the company of her uncle, and under the eyes of that good man we would arrange our assignations by dipping our finger in the spilled wine and writing the hour on the table."[4]

Furthermore, in Goethe's literary estate an annotation was found written by his secretary:

> A tradition among German artists has preserved the name of the *osteria* in which Goethe experienced the graceful adventure which he has described in the fifteenth Roman Elegy.[5]

Furthermore, there are passages in Goethe's correspondence with Duke Karl August that furnish additional evidence that Goethe indulged in sexual relations at that time, though no reference was made to a particular woman. We shall quote these passages later in a different context.

The reader must excuse the circumstantiality and detailedness with

[3] Zahn's visit and one detail of his report are verified in Chancellor Müller's conversation with Goethe of September 11, 1827 (246, p. 157). Also, there are letters preserved written by Goethe to Zahn, and Goethe referred to him in some of his publications.

[4] [Kennen Sie auch die Osteria alla Campana? fragte er weiter.—Die Weinschenke zur Glocke? Gewiss. Wir deutschen Künstler haben noch im vorigen Jahre Ihren Geburtstag dortselbst gefeiert.—Ist der Falerner noch immer gut?—Vortrefflich!—Und was liefert die Küche?—Ah, man erhält Stuffato, eine Art Schmorbraten, Maccaroni und ein Gebackenes, das sie Fritti nennen.—Es ist noch alles, wie zu meiner Zeit! sagte Goethe und schmunzelte behaglich. Dann fuhr er fort: In dieser Osteria hatte ich meinen gewöhnlichen Verkehr. Hier traf ich die Römerin, die mich zu den Elegien begeisterte. In Begleitung ihres Oheims kam sie hierher, und unter den Augen des guten Mannes verabredeten wir unsere Zusammenkünfte, indem wir den Finger in den verschütteten Wein tauchten und die Stunde auf den Tisch schrieben.] (250, 3:445)

The details that Goethe referred to here appear in the *Elegies.*

[5] [Eine Tradition unter den deutschen Malern hat den Namen der Osterie aufbewahrt, in welcher Goethe das anmuthige Abentheuer erlebte, das er in der funfzehnten römischen Elegie beschrieben hat . . .] (*Soph.* I, 42 [part 2]: 358)

which I have gone about to prove that Goethe must have had sexual intercourse in Rome. I have thought it necessary in order to show that Goethe's correspondence and literary works do contain direct and unmistakable proof thereof at least in this instance, and I surmise that intercourse was to Goethe an event of such importance, magnitude, and unusualness that he was bound to leave evidence thereof to posterity. The same is true of his relationship to Christiane. Even if no children had issued from this relationship, and even if he had not married her, and even if he had broken it off after a few years, posterity would have learned of it from his letters and literary works, and—in this instance—also from the letters of his contemporaries. No relationship of Goethe's to any other woman carries such earmarks. Even his most intimate letters to Behrisch dating from his student years in Leipzig do not contain evidence of sexual intercourse. They were written in the greatest sexual excitement; they show ample evidence of conflict and struggle; but not only do they not contain one open word about intercourse, but also they are devoid of the bliss and temporary contentment characteristic of the adolescent or young man who has found transitory relief in a biologically adequate union with a person of the other sex.

The other part of my statement, that Goethe had intercourse in Rome for the first time, is much more difficult to prove. The evidence therefor can only be indirect. Yet if no direct evidence is available for Goethe's abstinence from intercourse for the first four decades of his life, his correspondence with the Duke during his second Roman sojourn contains passages which, if any reliance is to be reposed in documentary evidence, it must be concluded were written by a man for whom intercourse was a novelty. I wish to quote these passages, but first remind the reader of the profound change that had taken place in Goethe's relationship to the Duke during his stay in Italy, as forecast already by his warm letters of farewell from Carlsbad.

On September 28, 1787, Goethe wrote Karl August:

> I am at the peaceful side of the world, you at the martial end, and taking everything into account one could not have a more antipodean existence.[6]

This passage expresses a readiness on Goethe's part to acknowledge how diametrically different their existences were without feeling the urge to interfere. He looked upon their two existences as on a par. This step of

---

[6] [Ich bin an der friedlichen Seite der Welt, Sie am kriegrischen Ende und alles berechnet man könnte keine antipodischere Existenz haben.]

Karl August had joined the Duke of Brunswick in his military expedition against Holland. Cf. 113, p. 279.

accepting Karl August as the representative of a different type, by definitely dropping any implication of being the Duke's mentor made it possible for him to approach the Duke for advice on an intimate matter, as will presently be seen.[7] The first such approach is in a letter of December 29, 1787.

Karl August had at last succeeded in participating in military action and was with the Prussian army in the Netherlands when Goethe sent him this letter. In accordance with the afore-mentioned change, Goethe did not berate or criticize him for his martial aspirations, but—in my estimation rather facetiously—remarked that the Duke's great luck with women had probably not deserted him in Holland. Then he continued:

> The sweet little god has relegated me to a bad corner of the world. The public girls of pleasure are unsafe as everywhere. The *zitelle* (unmarried girls) are more virtuous than anywhere else; they do not let themselves be touched and ask immediately when one plays up to them: "E che concluderemo?" [and what will be the understanding?] For either one must marry them or get them married, and once they have a husband then the mass is sung.[8] Yes, one can almost say that all married women are at the disposal of the person who is willing to provide for the family. Thus these are bad conditions and to nibble[9] is only possible with those who are as unsafe as public creatures. As far as the *heart* is concerned, it does not find a place in the terminology of the Ministry of Love hereabouts.[10] [Goethe's italics]

And then he mentions "the love of men for each other, a strange phenomenon . . . which I have seen nowhere else so marked,"[11] and which he regarded as the direct consequence of the attitudes of Italian women. It seldom reached the highest degree of sensuousness and usually remained in moderate forms, he reported.

---

[7] For the vicissitudes of Goethe's relationship to the Duke see Appendix R.

[8] I understand this passage in the sense that as soon as they have the respectable façade of marriage, they are ready to live with any man who is willing to support them.

[9] The literal meaning of the term Goethe uses here amounts approximately to "to trifle with tidbits" (as distinct from settling down to a meal).

[10] [Mich hat der süsse kleine Gott in einen bösen Weltwinckel relegirt. Die öffentlichen Mädchen der Lust sind unsicher wie überall. Die Zitellen (unverheurathete Mädchen) sind keuscher als irgendwo, sie lassen sich nicht anrühren und fragen gleich, wenn man artig mit ihnen thut: e che concluderemo? Denn entweder man soll sie heurathen oder sie verheurathen, und wenn sie einen Mann haben, dann ist die Messe gesungen. Ja man kann fast sagen, dass alle verheurathete Weiber dem zu Gebote stehn, der die Familie erhalten will. Das sind denn alles böse Bedingungen und zu naschen ist nur bey denen, die so unsicher sind als öffentliche Creaturen. Was das *Herz* betrifft; so gehört es gar nicht in die Terminologie der hiesigen Liebeskanzley.]

[11] [Ein sonderbar Phenomen . . . das ich nirgends so starck als hier gesehen habe, es ist die Liebe der Männer untereinander]

Here Goethe attacked the sexual problem in a direct and realistic way. His introductory remark about the Duke's habitual success with women now appears in a new light. It sounds like a pretext for writing about such matters at all, by implying that the Duke, as a well-known expert in amorous matters, might be interested in what was going on in Italy in that sphere. But Goethe shows up in the account that follows as a tyro. His reasoning leads to the conclusion that one cannot have intercourse in Italy unless he is ready to marry, or to risk a venereal disease, or to support an entire family. Goethe's fear of venereal diseases was excessive.[12] Widespread as venereal diseases were at that time (all historical accounts agree that contemporary European cities were hotbeds of venereal diseases), nevertheless Goethe's horror went beyond what can be called reality anxiety and makes sense only if regarded as based on the neurotic ground of intolerable castration anxiety. Bode rightly says that Goethe was no more exposed to this danger than other men and must therefore have been "more fearful and cautious" than his contemporaries (54, p. 38).[13]

We shall now understand better Goethe's letter of December 29, 1787, and guess what really was concealed behind the facetious appearance he tried to give his communication by calling it a "contribution to the statistical knowledge of the country."[14] The idea about homosexuality implies that most men must become homosexuals if women behave as they do in Italy. It sounds as if he were putting the following question to the Duke: "What should I do? These are the conditions here; I cannot find a girl; how do you go about succeeding with women whereever you go?" Further, he intimated to the Duke that, if heterosexual gratifications were not available, the necessity of homosexual relations would arise. The beautiful examples of male friendship encountered in Italy reminded Goethe of the ancient classical tradition. Now, Goethe and Karl August were united by a friendship that was itself reminiscent of classical examples. They had acted on the stage as Orestes and Pylades, to cite only one external manifestation. Therefore, aside from asking for advice, Goethe apparently was

[12] Goethe's *Elegies* give eloquent expression to the haunting fears he had of venereal diseases; particularly one which he did not publish, where he used metaphors about the disease like: "The uncanny birth of poisonous slime" [Ungeheure Geburt giftigen Schlammes]; "the worm that pounces upon the enjoying man" [der Wurm, packt den geniessenden an]; "It pollutes the springs, slavers, transforms Amor's animating dew into poison" [besudelt die Quellen, geifert, wandelt in Gift Amors belebenden Thau]. For quotations, see *Soph.* I, 1:419.

[13] I do not agree with Bode's conclusion that this cautiousness betrays a weakness of the drive. An intense fear of castration regularly has strong sexual urges behind it.

[14] [Beytrag zur statistischen Kenntniss des Landes.]

worried as to whether a sexual affair might harm their friendship. In other words, he might have wanted to know whether his princely friend would be jealous of or resent his indulging in sexual love and gratification. Of course, Goethe also implied that he was in danger of losing himself in homosexuality unless he should find a way of gratifying his urges in a heterosexual relationship. Thus he implicitly warned the Duke of possible unfaithfulness to him (whether by a manifest relationship or by an intense friendship was left open) unless the Duke helped him to make heterosexual love possible.

As will presently be seen, it seems that the Duke—probably unconsciously—understood what was going on in Goethe's mind.

Goethe had been preoccupied with potential sexual adventures since his arrival in Italy. Already in Vicenza he wrote in the diary that he kept for Charlotte von Stein, on September 25, 1786:

> I have looked at all of them [women in Vicenza] quite sharply and have not in this week seen more than one of whom I should wish to say with certainty that her charms were for sale.[15]

This entry suggests a kind of compulsive looking over of women in order to ascertain the possibility, or the impossibility, as the case might be, of obtaining sexual gratification. And on October 1, 1786, in Venice, he again wrote in the diary:

> Today for the first time a vendible sweetheart accosted me in full daylight in a small street by the Rialto.[16]

With his arrival in Rome Goethe apparently made a new step ahead in his approach towards women. Thus he wrote the Duke on February 3, 1787:

> Here as everywhere else one cannot occupy oneself with the fair sex without wasting time.

> The girls, or rather the young women, who present themselves as models at the painters' are sometimes the most darling and ready to let themselves be inspected and enjoyed. It would be in this way a very convenient pleasure, if the French influences [meaning venereal diseases] did not make this

---

[15] [Ich habe sie alle recht scharf angesehn und in denen acht Tagen nicht mehr als Eine gesehen, von der ich gewiss sagen mögte dass ihre Reitze feil sind.] (*Soph.* III, *1*:230)

[16] [Heut hat mich zum erstenmal ein feiler Schatz bey hellem Tage in einem Gässgen beym Rialto angeredet.] (*Soph.* III, *1*:253)

Goethe's mentioning prostitutes in the diary intended for Charlotte von Stein provides almost certain evidence that he did not become involved with them—at least prior to his arrival in Rome.

paradise uncertain also. I bring the portrait of one such creature with me; one cannot see anything more gracious.[17]

One can gauge from this passage how intensely Goethe's sexual excitement must have been aroused by the sight of nude women in closest proximity. Even in this situation the fear of infection made him recoil from the gratification so easily accessible.

Yet now, in December of 1787, during his second stay in Rome, he seemed to be determined to be more active, and his letter to the Duke betrays a more realistic approach. Goethe's next letter to him, on January 25, 1788, does not refer directly to the sexual question. He begins by thanking Karl August profusely for his letter. He would have considered the day on which he received Karl August's communication "the most cheerful" [den fröhlichsten] he spent in Rome if the Duke had not reported ill health. Was the communication referred to one written as a reply to Goethe's last letter, of December 29?[18] I believe so, for in December Goethe wrote the Duke he could without worry write about "more serious" [etwas bedeutenderes] subjects—meaning politics—since none of his letters showed signs of having been opened,[19] and Karl August gave an outline of the political situation in the letter to which Goethe was responding in January. Was Goethe's great delight over Karl August's letter also because of some remarks concerning the sexual problem? Goethe's next remark sounds like a sexual innuendo:

Immediately upon receipt of the letter I took to the open, for as Tristram believes the horizontal position to be that in which one enjoys joy and bears pain the best, so, with me, it is the wandering in the open air.[20]

Goethe's reference is to the passage in *Tristram Shandy* when Tristram before retiring to his room to surrender to his grief says: "I am persuaded

---

[17] [Mit dem schönen Geschlechte kann man sich hier, wie überall, nicht ohne Zeitverlust einlassen.

Die Mädgen oder vielmehr die jungen Frauen, die als Modelle sich bey den Mahlern einfinden, sind allerliebst mit unter und gefällig sich beschauen und geniessen zu lassen. Es wäre auf diese Weise eine sehr bequeme Lust, wenn die französchen Einflüsse nicht auch dieses Paradies unsicher machten. Ich bringe das Portrait von so einem Geschöpfe mit, man kann nichts zierlichers sehn.]

[18] Since Karl August's letters to Goethe of this period are not extant one has to resort to reconstructions.

[19] Actually Goethe was kept under surveillance in Rome for a while at the order of the Austrian government. Neither did Goethe know that the first letter his mother sent him to Rome was intercepted and sent to Vienna. See 541, 1:389.

[20] [Ich lief gleich nach erhaltnem Brief ins Weite, denn wie Tristram die horizontale Lage für diejenige hält, in welcher man Freude und Schmerz am besten geniesst und trägt; so ist es bey mir das Wandeln in freyer Luft]

of it, Madam, as much as can be, that both man and woman bear pain or sorrow (and, for ought I know, pleasure too) best in a horizontal position." Did Goethe here insinuate that he had not yet found a solution to his problem since he still adhered to the vertical?

In his training as an artist he made practical progress as he faithfully informed his master.

> Towards the end of October I returned to the city[21] and then a new epoch began. The human figure now attracted my glance and just as previously I turned my eye away from it as from the brightness of the sun, so I could now look at it with delight and dwell upon it. I betook myself to school, learned to sketch the head with its parts. . . . To this I devoted November and December. . . . With the first of January, I descended from the face to the clavicle, spread myself out over the breast and so on . . . then looked at the forms of antiquity, compared them with nature, and imprinted its characteristics well [in mind].[22]

Goethe here described, after he had overcome it, a visual inhibition. He had not been able to look at the nude body, which blinded him like the sun.[23] From his letter to Seidel of December 29, 1787, one can determine fairly accurately the time when this inhibition ceased:

> I am now occupied with the form of the human body, of which one can have outside of Rome only an imperfect grasp.[24]

What he had "whispered" into the ears of the Duke of Gotha about the painter Tischbein, with whom he spent much time in Italy, will come back to mind (see above, p. 893). Goethe's visual inhibition bears witness to his excessive rejection of sexuality, to wit, of voyeuristic desires and the feelings of guilt attached thereto. That he could now freely gaze at the female body shows that one neurotic symptom, at least, had disappeared.

We are now prepared for Goethe's decisive letter of February 16, 1788, which started in a vein of levity at the Duke's expense:

[21] Most of October Goethe spent in the country in the vicinity of Rome.

[22] [Gegen Ende Oktobers kam ich wieder in die Stadt und da ging eine neue Epoche an. Die Menschengestalt zog nunmehr meine Blicke auf sich und wie ich vorher, gleichsam wie von dem Glanz der Sonne, meine Augen von ihr weggewendet, so konnte ich nun mit Entzücken sie betrachten und auf ihr verweilen. Ich begab mich in die Schule, lernte den Kopf mit seinen Theilen zeichnen. . . . Damit brachte ich November und December hin. . . . Mit dem ersten Januar stieg ich vom Angesicht aufs Schlüsselbein, verbreitete mich auf die Brust und so weiter, . . . dann die Antiken Formen, mit der Natur verglichen und das karackteristische sich wohl eingeprägt.]

[23] In German, unlike most other languages, the word for sun is feminine in gender.

[24] [Ich bin jetzt mit der Form des menschlichen Körpers beschäftigt, davon man ausser Rom nur einen unvollkommnen Begriff haben kann.]

I was kindhearted enough while reading your letter . . . to think of hemorrhoids, but now indeed I see that the neighborhood has suffered.[25] If only through this vexatious inoculation everything bad has been driven out of the body! I shall not fail to defy all the evil spirits with the mysterious sigil [follow the signs for Mercury, Libra, Aries, Leo, and Scorpio].[26] You write so persuasively that one would have to be a *cervello tosto* [scatterbrain] not to be lured into the sweet flower garden. It seems that your kind thoughts of January 22 had a direct effect in Rome, for I can already report some lovely strolls. This much is certain, and you as a *doctor longe experientissimus* [scholar of long and great experience] are perfectly right, that a moderate movement of that kind refreshes the spirits and brings the body to a delicious equilibrium. As I have more than once experienced such [movement] in my life, contrariwise have also felt the discomfort when I wanted to get myself from the broad way to the narrow path of abstinence and safety.[27]

Here, at last, there is documentary evidence that Goethe had sexual intercourse and we must be grateful that he added a description of the effect that it had upon him, as will presently be seen. The Duke apparently reacted to Goethe's letters as Goethe had wished. But—at least if one takes the reply at face value—Goethe had already had sexual experiences before the Duke's encouraging letter reached him. Goethe added words of agreement with the Duke concerning the effect of intercourse: it refreshes the spirits and restores equilibrium to the body—a strange description indeed, bespeaking more the elimination of displeasure than the actual feeling of pleasure that ought to be felt in orgasm. Goethe here wrote like a man for whom sexual intercourse is a novelty. Otherwise, why would he have had to make a general remark about how an orgasm feels or what effect it has? This is a crucial point, presently to be discussed. First of all, in view

[25] The Duke had written to Goethe from Mainz, where he was under treatment for a gonorrheal infection that he had contracted in the Netherlands.

[26] The emphasis here is on Mercury as curer of syphilis.

[27] [Ich war gutmüthig genug, bey Lesung Ihres Briefs . . . an Hämorroiden zu dencken und sehe nun freylich dass die Nachbarschaft gelitten hat. Wenn nur durch diese verdrüssliche Inoculation alles Böse aufeinmal aus dem Körper getrieben worden ist. Ich werde nicht verfehlen mit dem geheimnissvollen Sigillo . . . den bösen Geistern zu trutzen. Sie schreiben so überzeugend, dass man ein *cervello tosto* sein müsste, um nicht in den süssen Blumen Garten gelockt zu werden. Es scheint dass Ihre gute Gedancken unterm 22. Jan. unmittelbar nach Rom gewürckt haben, denn ich könnte schon von einigen anmutigen Spazirgängen erzählen. So viel ist gewiss und haben Sie, als ein *Doctor longe experientissimus,* vollkommen recht, dass eine dergleichen mässige Bewegung, das Gemüth erfrischt und den Körper in ein köstliches Gleichgewicht bringt. Wie ich solches in meinem Leben mehr als einmal erfahren, dagegen auch die Unbequemlichkeit gespürt habe, wenn ich mich von dem breiten Wege, auf dem engen Pfad der Enthaltsamkeit und Sicherheit einleiten wollte.]

of the general scarcity of direct references to genital sexuality in his correspondence (not only with the Duke but also with all others, even his most intimate friends), and this during the uninhibited, wild years of the *Sturm und Drang* as well, this passage must be called most unusual for Goethe. Since he was not given to repeating information already conveyed in his communications but all his longer letters have the sparkle of "newness," one can hardly suppose that he was repeating something he had told the Duke at an earlier time. Because Goethe refers here to the barest facts of sexual life, namely that he had had intercourse previously, the conclusion becomes inescapable that he had never heretofore avowed to the Duke that he had had any intercourse before.[28] But why did Goethe find it necessary to tell the Duke that he had enjoyed sexual gratification "more than once"? This was something one would take for granted in a man close to forty, but he nevertheless considered it unobvious enough to make a special point of it.

To be sure, this passage seems also to disprove my earlier contention that he had intercourse in Rome for the first time, since he here writes of having felt the effect of "the moderate movement" "more than once" in his life.[29] The intended implication was in all probability that sexual gratifications had occurred several times in the past. Yet before we take this casual remark of Goethe's at its face value two questions have to be considered. First, would he have been ready to admit to the Duke at that time that he had never had intercourse before? Would he not have felt humiliated that the great author, the favorite of women, the powerful minister of state, had not yet gained carnal knowledge of the other sex at the age of thirty-nine? The fact that he stuck in this little remark—the content of which everyone would have taken for granted—suggests, I believe, rather the opposite of what it ostensibly conveyed.[30] Particularly in

---

[28] This is also a definite proof, in my mind, that no sexual transgressions ever occurred during the wild time at Stützerbach, as has repeatedly been claimed, for why would Goethe mention a fact that would have been well known to the Duke from experiences they shared?

[29] One might possibly reason that the "more than once" refers to incidents in Rome that occurred after the first intercourse there, but such an interpretation is strained and barely compatible with Goethe's wording: "more than once *in my life*."

[30] Bode seems to be of the same opinion. He writes about this passage: "It is most peculiar that he [Goethe] should declare it at all to a friend so intimate and so openhearted as Karl August that woman was not unknown to him." See 54, pp. 30–31. The analyst is here, indeed, in an unaccustomed situation. More frequently than not he assumes that processes of a sexual nature are at work where others feel unable to perceive them. In this instance the analyst denies the occurrence of sexual events where common sense and general opinion take them for granted. In inquiring among colleagues I have found that most of them scouted my hypothesis. One of them suggested that the main evidence (Goethe's letter to the Duke of February 16) cannot be used for my purpose, since Goethe's words may have

view of the Duke's phenomenal success with women—and his probable bragging about it—Goethe must have felt quite embarrassed about his total lack of experience, and it is understandable that he should have slipped in the awkward reference to "more than once."

While this may suffice to explain what prompted Goethe to lay claim to having had sexual experience, it must be acknowledged that, even under the prompting of such strong motives, it would not have been like him to have resorted to an outright lie—the less so since it was gratuitous: he did not have to raise the matter at all. The problem can, I believe, be resolved, if one raises the second question, namely: What exactly is the meaning of the words Goethe used, and why did he express himself in just this way? It is rather striking that Goethe uses a metaphorical—one might almost say a euphemistic—turn of phrase: "moderate movement of that kind." He was certainly not in general inclined to prissiness in his use of words, and the Duke was certainly not someone whom he might have had to be afraid of shocking by forthrightness. To be sure, in the first context to which it refers, when it is said that "moderate movement refreshes the spirits," the phrase unequivocally signifies intercourse. But in its second reference, which is where it is in context with the significant "more than once," it is picked up only indirectly, with the indefinite word "such" [*welches*]. For one so sensitive to words and their arrangement as Goethe, this could hardly have been accidental. I am led inescapably to the conclusion that Goethe chose these words, and this arrangement, because, while they could seem to say to the Duke: "I have had sexual intercourse 'more than once' before," they would at the same time spare Goethe the culpability for an outright lie, because, strictly interpreted, it could be contended that they meant only: "I have had the experience of *such movements* [i.e., movements *like* but not *identical with* these] before."

My thesis is not that Goethe never had emissions before, but only that he had refrained from intercourse.[31] To be sure, I feel strongly that after

been facetious. To be sure, some passages of the letter are written in a facetious vein and Goethe perhaps would not have minded if most of the letter had been read by the Duke in that spirit, but I think that Goethe was quite sparing of self-irony and the seeming facetiousness was aimed at covering up a deep embarrassment.

[31] The claim that there was such a long period of abstinence from intercourse may be difficult to credit. However, I have had the opportunity to observe strict adherence to the principle of marital fidelity and rejection also of premarital intercourse in a certain type of man, that can be characterized by membership in a Protestant sect, origin in a small to middle-sized urban community, and professional excellence. These men had spent the years of greatest sexual urgency without benefit of intercourse. If Packe is right, John Stuart Mill's life too included a period of twenty years of great intimacy with a woman (who later became his wife) but without intercourse. (See 417, pp. 317–20.)

his arrival in Weimar a long period of complete sexual abstinence started under the influence of Charlotte von Stein. Thus one may tentatively summarize Goethe's sexual development so far as its physical aspect is concerned, by assuming the following five phases: (1) In childhood the well-known sexual contacts with the younger sister (in Goethe's instance undetermined with regard to their specific nature) and masturbation (sporadic or consistent?); (2) masturbation in puberty—possibly separated from (1) by the frequent dip in sexual activity during the latency period—and petting with a passionately loved girl (Leipzig); (3) masturbation probably continued into manhood years, until (4) a period of complete abstinence sets in after the arrival in Weimar; (5) first intercourse at the age of thirty-nine and intercourse sporadically repeated to an unknown date, prior to his wife's death in 1816. (For Goethe's relationship to Christiane see Appendix Q.)

How far the evidence on record may be considered sufficient proof that Goethe did not have intercourse prior to his second residence in Rome, I do not know. Bode, who weighed in great detail all the historical documents, including Goethe's autobiographical statements, did not find evidence to the contrary.[32] And if Charlotte von Stein may be called in as an indirect witness one must refer to a statement she assertedly made after she discovered Goethe's relationship with Christiane:

> Since he [Goethe] is such a preeminent human being and also is already forty years old, he should not do anything through which he brings himself down to the level of others.[33]

This remark, if correctly recorded, definitely suggests that Charlotte von Stein did not know anything about any previous sexual relationship of Goethe's, which would, in view of her intimate knowledge of his past, confirm anew the hypothesis I have adopted here. This hypothesis, which, as far as I know, was, among modern scholars, propounded for the first time by Bode[34] is so surprising not only for its inherent improbability but

---

[32] See Bode (54, pp. 4–28, 57–68). Particular attention is called to Bode's discussion (pp. 6–7) of a passage in *Dichtung und Wahrheit* which has been interpreted by many as a reference of Goethe's to contact with prostitutes during his early student years. Bode very ably sets the record right.

[33] [Da er ein so vorzüglicher Mensch ist, auch schon vierzig Jahr alt ist, so sollte er nichts tun, wodurch er sich zu den Andern so herabwürdigt.] (51, *1*:419)

See also Bode's remark in 54, p. 34.

[34] Eduard Hitschmann's opinion regarding this question is not quite definite. He assumes that Goethe experienced in Rome "uninhibited enjoyment" [ungehemmten Genuss] for the first time (see 298, p. 57).

also because Goethe is described by many biographers as a man whose life was studded with love adventures and who was, if anything, rather loose and uninhibited in his dealings with the fair sex.

Yet if one studies Goethe's correspondence one gets the impression of a curtain's being lifted and of being able to look behind the scenes that Goethe so impressively built for the events of *Dichtung und Wahrheit,* which, after all, was the main source of Goethe's Don Juan reputation. No one would surmise after reading *Dichtung und Wahrheit* that its author at the age of thirty-nine wrote to his friend about intercourse as Goethe did in his February letter to the Duke. There we behold a man who, with sarcasm, pretense of casualness, and concealed embarrassment, under the sway of an urge to confess informs his friend that he too has at last accomplished cohabitation. If in later years he intentionally or inadvertently cultivated the myth of having had extensive genital experience, he must have been deeply ashamed of something regarding his sexual life. Was it a feeling of shame that he was so late in manifesting adulthood? I doubt it, for he could have presented himself to the reader as a man of superior will power, who went through life with the determination to avoid sin. Yet at no point did he exhibit the slightest inclination to create such an image of himself.

The Delay in Goethe's Sexual Maturation

As said before, there exists a relatively large literature in which it is asserted that Goethe had many friendships of a sexual nature. Thus there have been many who have contended that Goethe had intercourse with Friederike Brion and that he abandoned her because of a pregnancy, or that he was Charlotte von Stein's lover, even Fritz's father. Undoubtedly some of these assertions were made in a disparaging and belittling spirit, with the intention of dethroning Goethe from the elevated position that he held, but, as so often happens, enemies are ambivalent, and to a certain extent their attacks may be considered as acts of friendship despite their hostile motivations. It seems very probable that Goethe had the—perhaps unconscious—intention of creating the impression that his life had been beset by many love adventures. Bode (54, pp. 57–59) makes the very astute remark that most of the accusations leveled against Goethe's morality in his conduct towards women were based—except in the case of his common-law wife—on his own biographical writings. Had he died before returning from Italy we would not know—so Bode argues—anything about his erotic life. Bode also contends that even a close acquaintance of Goethe's would not, when he was twenty-five or thirty, have had anything sensational, or even very much at all, to report about Goethe's love-life. I agree with Bode that it was Goethe's doing that made him liable to be suspected of all kinds of sexual irregularities as a young man, but his relationship with Charlotte von Stein was an exception. It was only after his letters to her were published in 1848, that is to say, long after his death, that it was asserted that he had maintained an illegitimate relationship with her, and the indignation that arose was because she was married. Goethe himself observed silence in his writings and conversations about this particular relationship, in contrast with so many others about which he let the world know perhaps even more than could with accuracy be reported.

Before entering a full discussion of Goethe's sexual inhibition I want to make two biographical remarks. The physical, emotional, and spiritual climate of Italy, of course, had an eroticizing effect upon Goethe. His diary shows that he was surprised by the southern freedom in all physical matters. He cannot find words to praise the climate and its influence upon his well-being. The publicness of Italian private life, the open windows, the open doors, the ensuing stimulation of voyeurism and exhibitionism, the Italian freedom in expressing emotionality, the remoteness of his Weimarian friends and of Charlotte von Stein, new friendships with artists—all these factors must have conspired to give rise to a veritable upsurge of sexual wishes and impulses, and a corresponding reduction of fears and inhibition.

These factors, which can be taken for granted, are of secondary importance. A truly remarkable conclusion, however, is forced upon us when the exact date of the beginning of the Faustina episode is determined. This is not so easy to settle as it at first appears. His correspondence with the Duke seems to leave no doubt that it fell in the month of January or February, 1788. However, it is desirable to deal with a previous event that for a while made me believe that the episode began a few months earlier. Suphan (518, pp. 495–504) published a letter from Charlotte von Stein to Herder of August 31, 1787, which reveals that Goethe had made a suspicious slip around that time. By mistake, he had addressed to Herder a letter written to Charlotte von Stein and had thus suddenly let Herder know of the suspicious *Du* that obtained between them and that had been kept secret from the world. Charlotte von Stein was evidently embarrassed. The meaning of Goethe's slip can only be guessed at. He may have been unconsciously trying to expose Charlotte von Stein and thus force her into a separation. She seems to have understood the slip in this way because, in the letter referred to, she wrote to Herder of her fear that she would never see Goethe again, a fear "that renews itself for me terribly today."[35] This would suggest that he wanted to let the beloved woman know that a change had occurred in Italy, which in turn would suggest the beginning of the Faustina episode. However, Goethe's letters to Karl August make this assumption impossible, and therefore Goethe's slip, if it has this meaning of infidelity, has to be interpreted as an involuntary revelation of an intention rather than of an accomplished fact.

Another detail that suggests January as the beginning of the Faustina episode is to be found in the second volume of Goethe's *Italian Journey*. In the report devoted to the month of January, 1788, there is the charming poem: "Cupid, loose, self-willed boy" (Cupido, loser, eigensinniger Knabe)[36] in which Goethe complains about the mischief Cupid causes in his room, how he meant to stay only for a few hours but now has been there for days and nights. Although Goethe as an old man claimed that one should not think of Cupid as a "daemon"[37] in this poem but rather as "an assemblage of active spirits"[38] that have a distracting effect on a man who is seriously striving for knowledge, one may nevertheless surmise that this erotic poem signalized the beginning of Goethe's amorous adventure with Faustina.

I have spent so much effort upon the precisest possible dating of the Faustina episode because it permits the revelation of a deep, quasi-biological factor that extends to the bottommost layers of Goethe's personality, a factor that may help to explain why the first intercourse had to take place at that very time. Goethe, surprisingly enough, had at that time reached the age at which his father had married. Johann Kaspar Goethe was baptized on July 27, 1710, and was married August 20, 1748. He was at that time thirty-eight years and twenty-four days old.[39] Goethe reached the same age on September 21, 1787. The time of Goethe's first intercourse, with Faustina, deviates by about three months, a difference which I will discuss later. Of course, I do not suppose that Goethe was aware of this coincidence in time. I believe rather that we are dealing here with puzzling connections—established by deep archaic identifications—between generations, of which we may occasionally become dimly aware, but

---

[35] [. . . die sich mir heute schrecklich erneuert]

[36] *Soph.* I, *32*:213. Some authors declare that the poem was already written in November or December, 1787. Goethe called it his *Leibliedchen.*

[37] Goethe apparently as an old man tried to deprive this charming poem of its unquestionably erotic, sensuous quality by asking that Cupid should not be taken as a god symbolizing the instinctual, passionate aspect of life.

[38] [eine Versammlung thätiger Geister] (*Soph.* I, *32*:213)

[39] I neglect the probably very few days between birth and christening.

which we are not yet capable of understanding. One is reminded of Freud's theory of the repetitious compulsion, which perhaps not only dominates the lives of individuals but also attaches one generation to another, in a fashion comparable to that in which, according to the belief of antiquity, the effect of an event may extend through many generations, exemplified in the fate of the Tantalides, or in the promised punishment of the Decalogue. It would, of course, be of no minor interest to know whether Goethe's father had premarital intercourse or not. Aside from a courtship with a lady in Milan during his Italian journey, nothing is known about J. K. Goethe's dealings with women prior to his marriage, unless one can draw conclusions from his remarks about women in his Italian diary. I think it is quite impossible from the material on hand to speculate upon the stages of his sexual development. For Goethe's imagery about his father, however, the time of his father's marriage may have functioned as the time of first intercourse.

The approximate coincidence of Goethe's age at this first intercourse with his father's age at the time of marriage touches upon difficult problems of psychology. It is hardly possible that a conscious motive was involved, and even if a conscious motive were conceivable we should have to see in it the reflection of a vastly deeper force, beyond the scope of conscious volition. It is not yet known what contents are really conveyed from one person to another either by intuition or observation, or, for all we know, by the bare fact of identification itself. Indeed, man's knowledge (and here the term is used in its widest possible meaning) of his fellow men is vastly greater than it may appear to be if conscious knowledge alone is considered. This can easily be proved by the surprising reactivity of the infant and little child to even minor changes in parental mood and attitude and also by the fruitless attempts of parents to guard secrets from their children. We also do not know what personality data are attached to the biological image a person presents to his environment. Here we move into the realm of speculation. If Goethe's father was a personality type disposed to delaying the consummation of his sexual proclivities until marriage it is conceivable that the son took over a similar or even identical rhythm of sexual development, particularly in view of their constitutional similarity.[40]

[40] Only lately did I come across a passage that permits the hope that some important, concrete evidence may one day be unearthed regarding Johann Kaspar's sexual life. Von der Schulenburg mentions a passage in the diary of Christian Senckenberg, who was his physician. He claimed that "Johann Kaspar owed it only to him that he could marry." [. . . Johann Kaspar nur ihm, Senckenberg zu verdanken hatte, dass er heiraten konnte] (483, p. 78). Von der Schulenburg insinuates that Johann Kaspar may have contracted

A problem arises here to which Kinsey has given much thought (329, pp. 394–447). Do sexual patterns change in the course of generations, or do children behave sexually the way their parents did? If I understand Kinsey correctly, his statistical data permit the conclusion that sons who continue their fathers' group-membership (in terms of employment and educational level) repeat as adults their fathers' sexual patterns. Many of those, however, who will later shift membership to a different level do acquire at an early age the sex habits of the group in which they will land as adults. This finding is, in my estimation, quite surprising, and offers much food for thought and further research.

It is difficult to apply the finding to Goethe's life. He actually obtained membership in a group superior in social status and prestige to his father's group. However, social ascent did not in that historical period necessarily manifest itself in a rise to higher education or the accumulation of greater wealth. As far as I know, the prevailing sexual patterns within the reigning nobility were quite different from those of the bourgeois class. There were not, I believe, those sliding differences Kinsey describes as going through our society from the lowest social level to the highest. The sexual patterns that prevailed, for example, in the family of Karl August are incommensurable with a bourgeois pattern. The Duke had a number of mistresses and he could have married them off, made them part of the nobility, etc. It was an honor, after all, to be the mistress of a noble, and this, of course, had no parallel in bourgeois society.

---

syphilis when he was in Venice. I do not wish to discuss here all the reasons that speak against an assumption of syphilis in Johann Kaspar; I only want to say that the disorder that may be assumed with greatest probability in view of Senckenberg's remark, is a phimosis. The correction, by surgical intervention, of this defect, which makes intercourse impossible, may easily make the surgeon feel entitled to such a remark. A phimosis cured in later life, would also, in my estimation, fit very well with what we know of Johann Kaspar's life and character. He was, after all, a man who had the best chances in life, but made the poorest use of them for himself. It also would tend to confirm the probability that Johann Kaspar actually had not had intercourse before he married. I wish to stress that I only hypothetically suggest that Goethe's father may have been circumcised. If this was actually the case, it would contribute a great deal to the understanding of some aspects in Goethe's psychology, such as the surprising ease with which he converted castration fear into feelings of victory (see, for example, Appendix D). It also would greatly help in explaining Goethe's antisemitism, which at times was quite strong, and also such details as his undue reaction to hearing of Marie Antoinette's Necklace Affair (autumn, 1785; cf. above, p. 982). Louis XVI, her husband, suffered from a phimosis. His potency was restored by surgery only after marriage and this fact may have been known at the court of Weimar.

About the psychology of circumcision see 414. More specifically, it may be appropriate at this point to suggest that Goethe's repeated references to imagery of skins, cast snakeskins, being caught in a skin, etc., should be read in the light of the possibility that he was aware of such an experience in his father's life.

It is of interest that for several generations Goethe's paternal family had been moving uninterruptedly into higher social strata. The picture may be briefly outlined as follows. Hans Goethe the younger (died 1686), Goethe's great-great-grandfather, was a distiller in his last occupation, changed domiciles at least three times. Hans Christian Goethe (1633–94), the great-grandfather, was master in the guild of the farriers, and a deputy. His oldest son, Friedrich Georg Goethe (1657–1730), Goethe's grandfather, settled down in Frankfurt after traveling for twelve years. He became a tailor and by 1704 had accumulated a fortune of 15,000 gulden. By a second marriage he acquired an inn, and he left an estate of over 90,000 gulden. Johann Kaspar, Goethe's father, attended one of the best secondary schools in Germany, acquired a doctor's degree in law, and later the rank of "Imperial Councilor."[41] Goethe himself, then, could continue the family ascent only by entering the superior class of the nobility, since his father had in a sense almost reached the top of the bourgeois class.[42] It is important to keep in mind that for five generations or longer this family had been moving with great momentum towards the top of the social structure.

Kinsey's data comprise, unfortunately, only two generations at the most. If we knew more about the variation of sexual patterns in successive generations that ascend, descend, or remain stable in terms of position in the social hierarchy, we could perhaps speculate successfully about a sociobiological factor that might possibly have a great bearing upon such phenomena as the delay of Goethe's heterosexual relations.[43]

The earliest identifications with the image of the father, which form the core of the ego but also extend deeply into the realm of the instinctual drives (the id), are the focus at which the person's biological endowment and the history of preceding generations cross. In these moments of early

[41] For the data used see 63, pp. 11–17.

[42] Interestingly enough, Lili (Anna Elisabeth Schönemann), to whom Goethe was engaged for a short while, came from a family that actually belonged to the highest stratum of Frankfurt's bourgeois society, superior to that of Goethe's family.

[43] I should like to make a remark, again speculative, concerning Kinsey's findings. The variations of sexual patterns Kinsey found going vertically through the structure of our society may be correlated to degrees of actual or attempted sublimation, that is to say, inhibition. Are the members of higher classes of contemporary society exposed to the necessity of greater sublimation or inhibition than those of lower ones, and is this why one finds sexual patterns of higher classes among those who belong to lower classes but will move upward in the social hierarchy? The structure of Goethe's society perhaps did not show the correlation between group-membership and necessity of sublimation, which possibly is valid only for a bourgeois society. There was perhaps a kind of break between bourgeois and feudal class without parallel in contemporary society.

identification the further destiny of the individual is perhaps decided. I think it is quite wrong to believe that Goethe's mother was assigned a maximum share in the poet's destiny; rather, one senses dimly a victory of Goethe's father in the unfolding of the son's life, a victory that took on manifest form also in his son's final literary creation, as will presently be seen.

During his Italian journey Johann Kaspar came through Rovigo, a small and poor town in the vicinity of Padua. There, in the church of Madonna del Socorro, he found the following inscription dedicated to the image of the Madonna:

> Oh pilgrim, you who raise your brows because as you gaze you are struck with amazement before Mary's majesty, which you gather from her image as in Scripture, hear: No brush can paint with justice the miracles that radiate from her countenance; in highest art, throughout space and time, nothing gleams but Mary's bliss.[44]

Johann Kaspar Goethe was deeply moved by these verses and Goethe as a boy must have heard them more than once from him. The striking coincidence is that these verses express the spirit and the emotional climate of the closing scene of the second part of *Faust,* and particularly of the seven verses of the Chorus Mysticus with which the play ends and which contains Goethe's final message to the world:

> All that is mortal
> Is but an Image;
> The Imperfect
> Here becomes event.
> The Indescribable
> Here has been done;
> The eternal female [element]
> Draws us upwards.[45]

From its face value no one would guess that in this closing scene, in which Goethe gives ecstatic homage—unsurpassed by any other verses ever written—to the Mother of the Lord, there hides a full and final iden-

---

[44] [Der Du nach oben wölbst, o Pilger, Deine Brauen,/ Weil im Erschauen/ Dich Staunen vor Mariens Herrlichkeiten trifft,/ Die von dem Bild Du liest, wie in des Buches Schrift,/ Vernimm: Kein Pinsel mag gerecht zu malen/ Die Wunder, die von ihrem Antlitz strahlen./ In höchster Kunst, begrenzt von Raum und Zeit,/ Erschimmert nur Mariens Seligkeit.] (232, p. 62)

[45] [Alles Vergängliche/ Ist nur ein Gleichniss;/ Das Unzulängliche/ Hier wird's Ereigniss;/ Das Unbeschreibliche/ Hier ist's gethan;/ Das Ewig-Weibliche/ Zieht uns hinan.]

tification with his father, inasmuch as in these lines the spirit of his father's favorite poem rises up. In the final phase of his beautiful life he apparently succeeded in establishing a synthesis which, close as he may earlier have gotten to it at times, had been essentially beyond his reach. At this moment, loving and adoring mother coincided with accepting father as an ideal. The father is not mentioned because the ego and the ideal have become an ideally harmonious unit. In other words, the oedipal conflict has been dissolved without being denied, and the split between ego and superego eliminated. The peace and harmony of the infantile ego[46] is restored on the highest level accessible to man's development in full acceptance of reality.

But here I have glanced ahead to the final period of Goethe's life, which is outside of the scope of this investigation and from which Goethe was still far away in 1788.

I pointed out before that in September, 1787, Goethe reached the age his father had when he married. I believe that the importance of this coincidence cannot be overrated. It helps explain why Goethe was indomitably drawn towards Italy, why there was nothing that could have stopped him;[47] it helps explain the intense passion he felt before and during the journey. But perhaps I do overrate the coincidence of ages in its bearing on the first intercourse. The identity of ages was reached, after all, in September, 1787, and the adventure with Faustina apparently started some three and a half months later. It would not be surprising—or in view of present knowledge of the id and the unconscious it might even have to be expected—if the unconscious did not proceed reliably and exactly in respect to time relations.

It may, nevertheless, be worth while to investigate some of the events of September, 1787. A very important event—from the literary point of view—was the belated finishing of the play *Egmont,* which I mentioned several times before (see above, pp. 578, 925). Goethe had worked on this play off and on for about fifteen years and had tried repeatedly to finish it but had not succeeded, prior to his second Roman sojourn.[48] Goethe himself marveled over this. Under the date of July 6, 1787, in the second Roman sojourn of the *Italian Journey,* he wrote: "It is quite peculiar that I have been so often held back from concluding the play and that it should

[46] Cf. in the closing scene of *Faust* the choir of the blissful boys who died in infancy.

[47] In this context it is also important to point to the German phonetic identity of *"gen Italien"* [toward Italy] and *"Genitalien"* [genitals] (see 158, p. 232) which might have held a focal point in Goethe's unconscious and preconscious ideation.

[48] For the documentary evidence of Goethe's struggle in writing *Egmont,* see 261, part 2, *1*:198–213.

now get finished in Rome."[49] Under September 1, 1787, one finds the entry: "Today I can say *Egmont* has been finished"[50]; and on September 5: "I have to write on a morning that becomes a festive morning for me, for today *Egmont* has become, in the true meaning of the word, quite completely finished."[51] And on September 15, 1787, the manuscript was dispatched to Herder.[52]

We are coming quite close here to the earlier-mentioned date of September 21, 1787. This becomes important and meaningful if three aspects are considered:

(1) To see *Egmont* finished was the greatest desire of his father

. . . who got a quite particular fancy for this play, and wished nothing more than to see it finished and printed.[53]

The particular affinity between *Egmont* and these memories of his father may easily have been the reason for Goethe's procrastination in finishing the play and also for his finishing it on this particular day.[54]

(2) A biographical connection between *Egmont* and Goethe's father comes almost overtly to the fore in the way Goethe characterized the principal figure. Egmont is the most narcissistic type Goethe created among the main heroes of his works: gay, unconcerned about the future, vain, reveling in his power, in his prestige and success, highly endowed to experience pleasure,[55] and absolutely lovable.[56] Apparently Goethe here drew a picture of a father-imago which was characteristic of a certain developmental phase of his relationship to his father. It is unnecessary to demonstrate that Egmont was the character in the play with whom Goethe identified.[57] Of course the bad father who takes vengeance appears

---

[49] [Es ist recht sonderbar, dass ich so oft bin abgehalten worden das Stück zu endigen, und dass es nun in Rom fertig werden soll.] (*Soph.* I, 32:29)

[50] [Heute kann ich sagen ist Egmont fertig geworden] (*Soph.* I, 32:73)

[51] [Ich muss an einem Morgen schreiben, der ein festlicher Morgen für mich wird. Denn heute ist Egmont eigentlich recht völlig fertig geworden.] (*Soph.* I, 32:75)

[52] According to some sources this happened on September 6.

[53] [. . . der eine ganz eigne Neigung zu diesem Stück gewann, und nichts mehr wünschte, als es fertig und gedruckt zu sehen.] (*Soph.* I, 29:182)

[54] The element of belated atonement for disobedience may easily have had its bearing.

[55] How far Goethe was ahead of his time in the concept of modern man can be seen when Schiller's critical review of Goethe's *Egmont* is considered. See the reprint of that review (133, pp. 1–8).

[56] Here I should like to refer to what I have said in my *Discourse on Hamlet* about Hamlet's relationship to Yorick. I surmise that the dynamic constellation that led Hamlet toward the Yorick imagery is comparable to that which induced Goethe to create Egmont.

[57] In 1796 Goethe read the role of Egmont during a rehearsal. See 261, part 2, *1*:227.

here too. It is Alba who brings Egmont to ruin and causes his death, but Egmont has features of a paternal figure; after all, he is the leader of a nation.

(3) Furthermore, an aspect of the content of *Egmont* is to be considered. In this play Goethe, for the first time, presents a sensuous, at times even frivolous, lighthearted sexual relationship—that between the great Count Egmont and Klärchen, the low-born girl who loves him and commits suicide prior to his fall and tragic end. Goethe here strangely anticipated the kind of relationship he would later have with his sweetheart Christiane, without the tragic implications. I infer from critical remarks that Charlotte von Stein made about the Klärchen scenes after Goethe's return from Italy that they were written there. She was familiar with the play as far as it had grown prior to Goethe's departure for Italy, and no criticism by her of *Egmont* is known up to then. Of course, Egmont's free turning towards Klärchen without a trace of guilt and his enjoyment of the girl's sincere and devoted love shocked Charlotte von Stein, as it was bound to, as a sign of the direction his yearnings were taking. Since this criticism—as said before—occurred later, the conclusion is justified that the erotic interplay within the political action originated in Italy.

The creation of the Klärchen episode proves that Goethe had become internally ready to experience such a relationship himself. The erotically uninhibited Philine had been rejected by Wilhelm, though he had had to use all his will power to escape her seduction. Between Klärchen and Egmont sincere mutual love extends across the societal gap that separates them. The writing of the love scenes between Egmont and Klärchen was, so to speak, an internal rehearsal of an anticipated heterosexual relationship, and simultaneously expressed its acceptance. Thus it might have been more to the point if I had said earlier that by the time Goethe reached the age at which his father married, the last inhibition to his entering a heterosexual relationship had fallen.

If my reasoning is accepted it might be taken to mean that once he had finished *Egmont,* on the day bearing the decisive unconscious meaning, Goethe's unconscious released him, so to speak, from his inhibition, and he now made full use of the first opportunity that offered itself. Such a view of the events would be static and mechanical. The unconscious would, of course, have been competent to supply motives—and means— adequate to prompt the ego so to manipulate the reality situation by previous arrangements that the decisive date would coincide with the physical fulfillment. Already on September 28, 1787, he wrote to the Duke:

I still hold myself in seclusion and even—I do not know whether it is praise- or blameworthy—women have no part in me.[58]

The "still" indicates Goethe's awareness that he was ready to give way to another style of living. Thus the love scenes in *Egmont* would be the result of internal rehearsing and anticipation and the *Roman Elegies* the result of that which was experienced in reality.

About the delay of three and a half months that separates Goethe's age at first intercourse and his father's age at marriage I have a theory that I set down only with hesitation, because it will inevitably sound fantastic, whatever its merits.

We have seen that Goethe's relationship to Rome was marked by its dichronous organization. He first took possession of the city but then had to leave only to return again. This first visit, I believe, must be understood as literally an act of penetration. He had, in my opinion, rehearsed this act shortly before he left Weimar. On August 16, 1786, while visiting the mines at Schneeberg, he wrote to Charlotte von Stein:

This morning as I was descending into the shaft I left your ring off my finger. I kept missing something; that is how I feel also over missing your company and I always have something to tell you.[59]

Thus we see Goethe leaving off his finger the symbol that tied him to the beloved woman. When he penetrated into Mother Earth, he separated himself from the woman, who had become a transitory object. Now, in anticipation of the penetration of Rome, he wanted to perform the equivalent act unattached to any other woman.[60] I see in Goethe's symptomatic act an almost voluntary, deliberate, symbolic ritual of a final farewell to the beloved woman. After the penetration into Rome he had to go to Sicily. I have explained this part of his journey as a step to make himself superior to his father. After his return to Rome (the second penetration) we observe Goethe—if my reconstruction is correct—again arrange a dichronous sequence: (1) the completion of *Egmont* and the celebration thereof; and (2) the beginning of the Faustina episode, three and a half months later.

[58] [Noch halte ich mich immer in der Stille und sogar (ich weiss nicht, ob es lobens oder scheltenswerth ist) die Frauen haben keinen Theil an mir.]

[59] [Heute früh lies ich beym Einfahren in die Grube deinen Ring vom Finger, es fehlte mir immer etwas, so ist mir's auch da mir deine Gesellschafft fehlt und ich dir immer etwas zu sagen habe.]

This happened the first day after he left Charlotte von Stein. Winterstein (551, p. 496) rightly considered this occurrence an important symptomatic act. Hitschmann (298, p. 54) misinterpreted it as a losing of the ring, which it is evident is not what Goethe meant.

[60] Cf. what was said before about Goethe's speech in Ilmenau, p. 858.

The dichronous arrangement makes me raise the question of how far Goethe's intercourse with Faustina was a reenactment of his own conception. Since Goethe was born on August 28, 1749, the date of his mother's last menstruation would be around November 21, 1748, that is to say, about three months after his parents' marriage, on August 20, 1748. If we consider this possibility and repeat now the same figuring about the presumptive date of his having been conceived as we did earlier about his date of birth we actually come quite close to the time when in all probability he started his relationship with Faustina.

Thus, possibly, Goethe unconsciously achieved by skilled acting out the most grandiose narcissistic wish-fulfillment man can achieve, namely, that of becoming his own progenitor (cf. 171, p. 173).

If this idea could be proved it would indicate that Goethe was after all not acting out a father-identification but was, rather, raising himself in that moment far above his progenitor and even eliminating him symbolically by acting out a fantasy of self-conception.

Having put this theory forward for whatever it may be worth, I return to my first thesis, that the delay of three months may be a negligible factor, and that the Faustina episode grew out of a deep father-identification.

According to Freud, the unconscious is heedless of time relations, and the analysis of dreams reveals the arbitrariness of the unconscious with respect to the firmly organized time relation that is a cornerstone of conscious mentation. Yet, despite the unquestionable amorality of the unconscious in regard to time—and the child shares this amorality even in its conscious life until a superego is established—one wonders whether perhaps this is true only with respect to a certain type or kind of time. The id, the repressed, the archaic, does not know and has no regard for time in so far as it is a principle of order, particularly in the sense of Newtonian time. Time as an aggregate of time points, one of which represents the ever-shifting *now* and the other time points to come and time points past —this kind of time is accessible to the ego only after an inhibitory barrier has been erected between the ego and the id.[61]

But Newtonian time is a refined conception, and there are many other modes of time experience. There are clinical observations that are, I believe, competent to show that in certain circumstances the id is also bound to the time category.[62] It is a frequent observation that patients develop

[61] For a splendid discussion of the time problem from the point of view of psychoanalysis, see 58.

[62] I cannot abstain from citing an instance from Freud's work which, despite objections presently to be discussed, may contribute to the problem in question. In 1919 Freud added to

psychopathology, such as a depression, at annual intervals, around the birthday of a younger sibling (as Goethe did) or any other day of biographical importance. The ego is quite unaware of this connection, and the observer is compelled to assume that the time relation between the anniversary and the original event is deeply repressed. Even after the patient's insight has reached the point where he does not regard the timing of the depression as a mere coincidence with the date of the past event but perceives the causal relationship between the two, he will often still develop the depression again around the time of the respective anniversary. Indeed, sometimes the association between a certain time period and a traumatic event is so tight and was established in such an early developmental period that even prolonged and intensive psychoanalytic treatment cannot disjoin them and the patient infallibly develops a depression at the predestined period. Here, I believe, is a proof that certain processes in the id carry a distinct time mark indelibly attached to certain images. Further, the rhythm to which instinctual processes are obedient presupposes the rule of time in this province of the personality too. But this is an entirely different time from that which the ego uses in its dealings with

---

his *Interpretation of Dreams* a footnote in which he reported a dream of his own. The concluding remark is as follows: "Before I could call out again I woke up, feeling no anxiety but with my heart beating rapidly. My bedside clock showed that it was two-thirty" (158, pp. 558–59). If we consider that it was not Freud's habit—at least not in his publications—to record the time of awakening when his sleep was interrupted by a dream (cf. 158, p. 456), and further that this part is printed in italics in the German edition together with the rest of the dream-text, then we may deduce that psychologically this time reference belongs to the dream and we shall not be surprised to hear that the infantile trauma to which this dream refers occurred "when I was between two and three years old." The German text is perhaps even more suggestive. It says: *"als ich über zwei und noch nicht drei Jahre alt war"* (when I was more than two and not yet three years old). However, later Freud wrote that the trauma occurred when he was "a child of little more than two years old" (195, p. 198). Thus we may tentatively conclude that the age at which the infantile trauma was suffered was represented by the hour of awakening (2½).

Dr. Otto Isakower kindly called to my attention that the age at which the trauma was suffered cannot have been an item of particular concealment. In favor of this objection one may say that Freud does not write about the dream as if the age of the trauma had been unknown to him at the time of the dream. However, the trauma was tentatively dated in 1889 to the age of "under two years" (157, p. 56). One could perhaps assume an inner unwillingness to ascertain the correct age for reasons which lead too far afield to discuss at length here. The awakening at 2:30 would then be a vigorous assertion of a truth the self would like to deny. Dr. Isakower further asserts that Freud, as is known from Jones's biography (321, 2:180; 3:381–82, 389–90), was occupied at that time with problems of the relation between dreams and telepathy and therefore was compelled to hold fast the exact time of the dream since that dealt with the possible death of his oldest son, who at that time was at the front in World War I. This argument seems to deprive the example of its usefulness for the purpose for which I brought it up.

external reality. Archaic time disregards this reality completely, and it may insist that the yesterday is today, or the today is past, or the past is future, but it still is coping with time and not going beyond it. Its archaic nature reveals itself in just those depressions I mentioned before. If there is jealousy of a younger sibling, or a feeling of guilt because of death wishes, why should the conflict be activated and become acute around the time of an anniversary? In adult reality the guilt is a constant one if it has any reality at all. It should be possible to correlate the intensity of the conflict with changes in the relationship with the sibling, but the anniversary per se is essentially a superficial factor, an accidental circumstance. Nevertheless, the id acts as if the conflict were attached to a certain and limited time period. By clinging in such a way to a time mark it shows its profoundly conservative nature.

This discussion of archaic time is, of course, incomplete. I only wanted to make the point here that despite the powerlessness of logical time relations over the id, the id itself is still governed by time relations, though of a different kind. Therefore, it is not necessarily in contradiction to the present theory of the id to claim, as I have done, that age-identity was one of the most potent factors in Goethe's sexual development. Among the many objections that may be raised against my contention there will be doubt as to whether the id is so precise. My thesis would require the assumption that some compartment in Goethe's personality *knew* of the twenty-first of September as being the crucial day. The dispatching of *Egmont* on September 15, and Goethe's expression of doubt (September 28) as to whether it was a good thing for him to stay away from women, show, in my estimation, that around the day that I have calculated by reference to his father's biography, something crucial was set into motion.

The occasional clinical glimpses I have been able to get into the working of unconscious time relations tend to confirm such a preciseness. The unconscious is in this respect also quite contradictory. One sometimes observes that the repressed image that the unconscious has preserved of a person is astoundingly correct and reality-adequate, and far more precise than the opinion based upon conscious judgment; at other times the unconscious is stupid, so to speak, and the images it has preserved of a past reality are faulty, inadequate, and poor. I think one of the factors that decides which pattern is to develop is the degree and kind of ambivalence towards the image in question. One would surmise that the little boy initially had a strong, intense, almost unambivalent love for his father, stimulated by the father's affection for the infant. If Bettina's reports are correct, one may be certain of strongly tender, even maternal, feelings in the father towards his oldest son. (Cf. above, pp. 183, 781 f.) In view of his father's age of over thirty-nine at the time of Goethe's birth, and his exclusive devotion, undistracted by a professional life, this is highly probable. But before we say more about the basic unambivalent relationship there is more to be said about the ambivalent one.

Of course—and this preserved Goethe from retreat into passive homosexuality—one encounters later the image of the defeated, weak father, as happened in reality in the episode with the French Count Thoranc (an important childhood experience in view of Goethe's later ties to the nobility and his great admiration for Napoleon). The psychological effect of this episode can still be noticed in a quarrel Goethe instigated with his father after his return from Leipzig and shortly before leaving for Strassburg on April 1, 1770. Well knowing what pride his father took in his house, which had been remodeled in accordance with his specifications, Goethe started to criticize some of its furnishings. This, apparently, his father let go by without angry reply. But shortly thereafter the son tried to convince him that he should shift the staircase to one side of the building in order to achieve greater privacy for the several stories. As an argument in favor of his suggestion he said that "the anxious scene" [*die ängstliche Scene*] that had taken place with Count Thoranc—then eleven years earlier—would not have occurred if the staircase had been built after the manner of staircases in Leipzig. The father flew off the handle and "got into an incredible rage,"[63] a scene that hastened Goethe's departure. Here Goethe was really telling his father that if he had been as smart as the inhabitants of Leipzig—that is to say, as smart as his son, who had become in Leipzig like the inhabitants of that city—he would have saved himself much trouble. It is of interest that even at the age of twenty-one Goethe would still bring up his father's past defeat and mock him with it.[64]

The appearance of Count Thoranc in the house of the Goethes had shaken the paternal authority, and there are indications that concomitantly the boy entered a phase of mild delinquency. He was less supervised by

[63] [in einen unglaublichen Zorn gerieth] (*Soph.* I, 27:228–29)

[64] Yet no one can escape the repetitious compulsion. When Goethe made alterations in his final abode on the Frauenplan in Weimar he spent much thought and effort on the alteration of the staircase. I do not know for sure, but from the description I surmise he did not follow the ingenious plan of the inhabitants of Leipzig. Anyhow, the staircase did not prevent the French from endangering his life after the battle of Jena, when grenadiers penetrated into his house. This episode throws an interesting sidelight upon the Thoranc episode —not further to be discussed here—for Goethe soon thereafter married his common-law wife.

the father, attended French plays, and came into contact with actors and actresses.[65]

The many subsequent arguments with and acts of rebellion against his father have been so often stressed by biographers that I forgo enumerating them. Yet, despite the unfavorable description of his father that Goethe presented in *Dichtung und Wahrheit,* one feels between the lines a surprising degree of affection. It is necessary to mention here an episode that Goethe recounted in the second part of his *Italian Journey,* which was devoted to the second sojourn in Rome. This has been treated by literary scholars under the name of "The Beautiful Milanese."[66] Goethe met her during an excursion to Castel Gandolfo in October, 1787. It is the only love episode Goethe recounts in his *Italian Journey.* It is written with a particular simplicity and exquisiteness. All in all, Goethe mentions her five times. This concentration on her, sporadic though it is, leaves the impression that she was the only woman on whom his attention focused during this seven-month period. It is difficult to describe in what the charm of this relatively short and very simple story lies. He first mentions her in passing and casually in a letter of October 8, 1787, reporting only that he felt interested in a Milanese who distinguished herself favorably from the Roman women. A few pages later, in a report concerning the same month, he comes back to her and describes her most favorably in detail. He was seated between her and a Roman girl, and was reproached by the latter's mother for showing so much interest in the former. He tried to excuse himself, but realized that his heart had been conquered by her. "One really has no regard in such a moment for the danger that threatens us under these flattering features."[67] The next morning he met her again. She spoke casually of the lack of education from which women suffer and deplored her ignorance of the English language. Goethe immediately gave her a lesson, employing for the purpose an English newspaper article in which the falling of a woman into the water and her fortunate rescue were related. She proved an excellent pupil and expressed joy over the rapid progress she had made in this one hour. Goethe became quite excited by the attraction he felt for this woman, and his feelings did not remain quite unnoticed by others. In the evening, while admiring a beautiful

[65] Sarasin (464, pp. 371–73) has shown the meaning of this period in Goethe's life.

[66] Here again, as in the case of Faustina, Carletta (84) was able to prove that the beautiful Milanese was a historical person. Her true name was Maddalena Riggi (1765–1825).

[67] [Übersieht man doch in solchem Augenblicke die Gefahr nicht, die uns unter diesen schmeichelhaften Zügen bedroht.] (*Soph.* I, *32*:123)

sunset, he casually listened to a conversation, which revolved around a dowry. At the end he asked who the bride was and learned to his consternation that it was the beautiful Milanese. Goethe found it strange that a mutual inclination should be so abruptly destroyed just as it was starting to germinate.

> I was surely old and experienced enough to pull myself together, though painfully, on the spot. "It would be strange enough," I exclaimed, "if a Werther-like fate had sought you out in Rome to spoil for you such auspicious and, till now, well-maintained, conditions."[68]

Goethe stayed away from the beautiful woman, and everyone was satisfied with his conduct except for one incident, which brought in the inevitable interlocking of love and orality. From one of his excursions he brought back mushrooms, which he gave to his host's cook to be prepared for the meal. When the host was told that this rare dish was contributed by a guest he became angry.

> This culinary adventure gave me the occasion to consider—with silent amusement—that I myself, infected with a quite peculiar poison, had come under suspicion of poisoning a whole party through the same imprudence.[69]

Goethe quickly found his equilibrium by looking upon the woman as a bride and future wife.

The beautiful Milanese is brought to the reader's attention for the third time by the sad news that her fiancé had withdrawn from the engagement and that the young woman had become seriously ill over the shock. Goethe was most eager to be kept informed of the course of her illness, from which she soon recovered. The fourth reference (report for February, 1788) concerned an accidental meeting with the Milanese, who thanked Goethe and assured him that her friends' sympathy, and particularly his own, had caused her to recover. When Goethe relates his farewell visits in Rome we hear of the Milanese for the last time. There was a good chance that another young man, undaunted by her poverty, would soon marry her. The concluding conversation of the two who had for a moment been drawn close by mutual love, I shall not repeat. Suffice it to

---

[68] [Ich hatte Jahre und Erfahrungen hinreichend, um mich, obwohl schmerzhaft, doch auf der Stelle zusammen zu nehmen. Es wäre wunderbar genug, rief ich aus, wenn ein wertherähnliches Schicksal dich in Rom aufgesucht hätte, um dir so bedeutende, bisher wohlbewahrte Zustände zu verderben.] (*Soph.* I, 32:128)

[69] [Dieses culinarische Abenteuer gab mir Anlass, in stillem Humor zu bedenken, dass ich selbst, von einem ganz eignen Gifte angesteckt, in Verdacht gekommen sei, durch gleiche Unvorsichtigkeit eine ganze Gesellschaft zu vergiften.] (*Soph.* I, 32:130)

say that the reappearance of the beautiful Milanese two pages before the ending of the *Italian Journey* lends her particular emphasis.

What is the psychological meaning of the whole report? The objective content is trivial. A man falls in love with a girl for one day, learns she is engaged, withdraws; becomes alarmed when he hears she is suffering from illness brought on by the desertion of her fiancé, informs himself every day of her condition, is gently thanked by her, and says farewell to her before his departure. So far as the concrete facts go it is not easy to make out why Goethe included this episode in his Roman report. But one cannot leave it at that. The style in which it is written is most poetical and some parts unforgettably convey the impression of strong emotions behind the surface calm of the presentation.

Several features are notable. Goethe's role is here the reverse of that he acted in the Friederike adventure. It is a girl that is jilted by a man and falls seriously ill, and this time Goethe is not the spoiler but the rescuer. It will be remembered that Goethe did penance to Friederike by having Weislingen poisoned in the play *Götz von Berlichingen*. In this aspect also we encounter a reversal, inasmuch as in the mushroom episode he provides his company with a delicious—though ambiguous (*zweideutig,* as Goethe calls it)—dish, but is suspected of endangering others with poison. The theme of rescue appears already in the newspaper article which he uses in teaching the beautiful girl.[70] Goethe's eagerness to teach the young lady is reminiscent of his ambitions for Cornelia's education. Goethe corresponded with her from Leipzig upon this very topic of female education. He witnessed his father's linguistic lessons to Cornelia and in Rome proved himself—I am sure—a better teacher than his father, against whose didactic peculiarities Cornelia had rebelled. But most significant is the reference to Werther, when Goethe says how strange it would be if a fate like Werther's befell him in Rome. Once more there was a woman engaged to another man and loved by Goethe. But this time he is master of the situation and no longer is overwhelmed by it. He can withdraw, and promptly it is the woman who is exposed to Werther's sufferings. However, though she is deserted by her lover, she does not commit suicide. She falls seriously ill and is rescued by Goethe. Here Goethe very emphatically stressed that he was still capable of feeling Werther's sentiments but was definitely immune to the temptation of suicide. There could have been no better way to demonstrate the profound change that had taken place between his arrival in Weimar and this moment.

[70] Hárnik has pointed out the psychoanalytic meaning of this detail (see 275, p. 121).

However, the charming episode of Goethe's love for the beautiful Milanese acquires supreme psychological importance when it is considered that Goethe's father maintained a romantic and most honorable relationship with a young woman in Milan at the conclusion of his Italian journey. That Goethe's relationship to the beautiful Milanese and his father's relationship to the young woman in Milan are more than a coincidence is, in my estimation, proved by the fact that both episodes cover a period of exactly seven months. It is scarcely credible that all these parallels are due to chance, particularly if we observe that both father and son end their books on their Italian journey with a reference to their Milanese sweethearts.

Johann Kaspar's love spent itself in letters. He was most desirous to meet the Italian woman, whom he had observed from his window. Their correspondence at first took place from window to window, each party gazing through a telescope at what the other had written. As soon as the lady had given her permission, an exchange of letters began, each writing eight, from July, 1740, to February 6, 1741.[71] In these letters Johann Kaspar tried to persuade the woman to join him in a tryst, which she refused to do despite her love for him. I could enumerate some similarities between these letters and Goethe's report of his acquaintance with the beautiful Milanese. But more important than this is Goethe's unconscious taking over the exact time relation (seven months in both instances)[72] from his father's almost novellike travel report, and showing again this puzzling element of time organization in the repressed. It also shows again the depth of identification with the father. Since Goethe had intercourse in Rome, in addition to his courtship of the Milanese, he acted out in one time period two events that were separated by eight years—his father's romance with the young woman in Milan and his father's marriage—thus also illustrating how careless the unconscious can be with respect to the time organization, however much it may be regardful of what might be called "time status."

In the light of this episode, we may now also uncover another aspect in *Werther*. Since the chapter with the Milanese and Goethe's behavior in conjunction with her was consciously experienced as in contrast to the fate of Werther, and since in the Roman adventure Goethe wanted to experience also what his father had experienced in Milan, we may deduce

---

[71] I owe thanks to Dr. F. H. Reinsch, who owns a microfilm of Johann Kaspar Goethe's manuscripts, for his kindness in checking the dates of the love letters confirming that the pertinent data have been correctly recorded in Glaser's book.

[72] In Goethe's instance, from October 8, 1787, to April 23, 1788, when he left Rome.

that the Werther episode already had the meaning of establishing a contrast with the father. Werther, by not daring to take the beloved woman away from her fiancé but rather committing suicide, manifests the passive aspect of the Oedipus complex. He apparently attains the highest level of submissiveness by destroying himself rather than carry out the positive oedipal impulses towards his mother. Now, however, we hear that his father had fallen in love as a young man and sworn eternal love but without great to-do had peacefully married someone else eight years later. Did Werther not teach his father a lesson of how a young man ought to love and die, and do we not find at the bottom of the novel a satire on his father's pedestrian, bourgeois, unromantic way of loving?[73] Yet, then, on the other hand, the Faustina episode also means: father did return from Italy a virgin and waited eight years for intercourse; I, however, fared better. A certain insatiability in the relationship to his father, the absolute need always and in everything to get more than his father got, is unmistakable. But Werther's rebellion cost him his life, whereas the later signs in Goethe's life of competition with his father contained infinitely less self-destruction but led to profit, pleasure, and renewed glory.

Thus Goethe, like all other male inhabitants of this planet, could not escape a profound ambivalence towards his father. This point, which on principle could be taken for granted, is discussed again in this context because the unfolding of events during the second sojourn in Rome seems to prove that this ambivalence was not the only or even the most decisive relationship to his father. Somehow it strikes me as a manifestation of a touching loyalty when a man sacrifices his masculinity for the exact period of time he believes his father had been deprived of the sexual joy. The anxieties and the pathology involved in such a delay are evident, but here I want to stress—since this attitude cannot possibly have been maintained by conscious motivation—the very factor of unconscious (and probably therefore unshakable) loyalty to and love for his father which must have been present despite and above anxiety. I assume that the early intense relationship to his father, in which active and passive attitudes as well as object-love and identification were not yet strictly separated, was stronger and much more decisive than the subsequent strongly ambivalent relationship. I further surmise that this early positive and all-embracing

[73] An external parallel between *Werther* and Johann Kaspar's novellike love correspondence can also be seen in *Werther's* being written as a series of letters. Epistolary fiction was, of course, the preferred literary form of the century. Yet it is noteworthy that there was not only the historical link of Goethe's novel with its predecessors but also a very personal one that in turn contains a double aspect, namely, the use of this form by his father and possibly the impression it had made on the boy in his early youth.

father-relationship protected him against the devastating effects that the conflict brought about by ambivalence towards the father has caused in the lives of so many in their exercise of the great gifts they obtained from nature.

We have pursued the poet's ways of dealing with a problem on the symbolic level (entrance into Rome, entrance into mines), and on the reality level (Faustina episode). We have examined records to observe his reactions to both. No doubt the reaction on the symbolic level carried more weight. His ego was far more agitated on the way to Rome than on the way to Faustina, I should judge, not only from his letter to the Duke, but also from the *Roman Elegies*. Despite the occasional warmth, despite the imagery, at times quite sensuous and erotic, there is spread over that whole work what I should call a sublime coldness, created, if by nothing else, by its poetical structure in imitation of ancient poetry. That the adventure with Faustina freed Goethe from tension, that it provided a feeling of security and certainty, I should not doubt; but that Goethe achieved what may be called a normal orgasm with full reverberation of the entire psychobiological organism, with a deep regression of the ego, is highly questionable. He felt deeply grateful for what he had received, for there was probably doubt in him as to whether he would ever achieve it. In immediate consequence thereof one notices that rivalry with men temporarily disappeared almost completely, as can be seen from his letters to the Duke and to Herder.

The original title of the *Italian Journey* was "From my life . . . I also in Arcadia" [Aus meinem Leben . . . Auch ich in Arkadien]. Panofsky (418, p. 319) has presented in an admirable and definitive essay the literary and artistic history of this apothegm. Having been created as a saddening *memento mori* to remind man that death reigns even in Arcadia, the land of beauty, music and art, it lost its elegiac meaning and came to stand in Goethe's instance for: "I, too, was in the land of joy and beauty." Goethe was sixty-seven when he published the *Italian Journey,* and although the aging poet reported there the most beautiful experiences of the time of his life's peak, I believe the Janus-meaning of the saying can still be felt. In the brief motto *Et in Arcadia ego,* I see the exhibitionistic phallic attitude as well as the idea of coincidence of orgasm and death. On the one hand it implies pride and bragging ("I also had intercourse, accomplished what father accomplished, and the world ought to admire me for it"); on the other, it refers to the feeling of a deathlike prostration starting with the onset of the postcoital period, the *post-coitum-omne-animal-triste,* which is unbearable to the phallic type of personality.[74]

Goethe's Sexual Impediment and His Attitude Towards Emotions

There cannot be further delayed the discussion of the difficult question of what exactly Goethe's sexual impediment was prior to 1788. The historical record suggests early sexual contact of one kind or another with his younger sister; intense, at times extremely passionate, relationships of varying length with women during adolescence and early manhood; a platonic relationship with a married woman seven years his senior covering a decade; and first intercourse at the age of thirty-nine with a twenty-three-year-old woman.

Evidently the delay in intercourse was not due to lack of desire or interest in the other sex, or to a phlegmatic temperament, or to lack of opportunity. The strength of the drives cannot be disputed after reading the letters written from Leipzig, or *Werther,* or certain of his poems. When Bode (54, p. 39) reasons that Goethe's sexual desires must have been weak since he left his common-law wife sometimes for more than half a year, he draws a conclusion that is not supported by psychoanalytic findings. (I discuss this question extensively in Appendix T.) The sexual desires of a person may, of course, be inordinately strong without necessarily showing up in a corresponding frequency of sexual intercourse, even when no external obstacle to this gratification is present. Thus the mere paucity of sexual contacts does not gainsay what other evidence shows: that Goethe possessed strong and rather unruly drives. As is prone to happen in an intensely creative personality, these drives were diverted into the unending stream of highest productivity. Yet we have often seen Goethe in a state of the greatest unrest, actively struggling with his aroused instincts. Besides the pouring of instinctual energies into the creative process there was a personal, voluntary, factor that acted as a barrier between him and sexual intercourse. Reik (449, pp. 170–71 and *passim*) has tried to explain this barrier as a disturbance comparable to an obsessive neurosis, based on castration fear, unconscious aggression, fear of retaliation, and identification with an overly strict father. Bode (54, pp. 39–40) accepts the theory of a doctor friend, Wilhelm Meyer in Weimar, that Goethe suffered from psychic impotence.

---

[74] Here it must also be repeated that the gay Egmont is, after all, decapitated, and that at no other place did Goethe express his horror of venereal disease as strongly as in the *Roman Elegies*. For other signs of ambivalence in the *Elegies* see 298, pp. 57–58.

Before discussing these two theories a few general remarks have to be made about neurosis and emotions in Goethe. There is no doubt that Goethe—according to his own testimony—exhibited a score of phenomena belonging to the realm of psychopathology. If these phenomena are taken out of context and considered as entities in themselves they have to be called neurotic symptoms. They include fear of heights, fear of darkness, horror at the sight of a meat market, suicidal impulses, hallucinations, hypochondriasis, compulsions—to enumerate a few. If the accounts of all these phenomena were collected from Goethe's works, biographical records, and the testimony of others, a huge collection of direct psychopathological data would be obtained, that is to say, one would have a collection of almost all the symptoms listed in textbooks of psychopathology with the sole exception of manifest perversions.

Despite the fact that Goethe's life was undoubtedly replete with a great variety of neurotic symptoms, it is quite questionable what conclusions should be drawn from such a list. One conclusion is clear: without these phenomena he would never have become the great artist and man that he was. They were intimately connected with his total personality. They were not obstacles to the unfolding of his creativeness, but if anything prerequisites and stimuli. It is most questionable whether they ought to be called neurotic symptoms at all, since the dynamic position they held seems to be essentially different from that in the neurotic or psychotic (cf. Appendix T). This conclusion, I believe, becomes rigorous unless one divides the personality of such a genius into a neurotic part and a creative part, a tendency unacceptable from the point of view of more recent concepts of the personality and one that is refutable by clinical evidence, as I shall presently try to demonstrate.[75] One may raise the objection that this proposition is also valid for the clinically neurotic patient. Phobic soldiers, it was found, for example, may perform deeds of heroism. Without the phobia they would perhaps have behaved the way the average soldier behaves, that is to say, they would not necessarily have acted beyond the call of duty. This is quite true and should not be questioned. There is no doubt that neurotic symptoms may, by compensation or denial, lead to socially valuable, constructive actions (see 138). But there is no valid psychological point of view from which it can be claimed that phobias are the indispensable prerequisite of heroism. The same soldier who became a hero in order to compensate for the phobia

[75] I do not doubt, however, that the line can be drawn between the neurotic and non-neurotic part of a particular personality.

might have performed in a still more heroic way if he had made and integrated an early identification with a strong father-image.

It is different with Goethe's creativity. It is unthinkable that his *Werther* would ever have been written unless he himself had been plagued for a while by suicidal impulses and had gone through the throes of a depression. Essentially the same is true of the other psychopathological phenomena. As nearly everything that concerns the psychology of the genius is a riddle, so also is this difference between a bona-fide neurotic symptom and the so-called neurotic symptomatology of the genius puzzling and mysterious. Furthermore, one can observe that, in Goethe's case, at least, most of the neurotic symptoms did not interfere with the ego's freedom of choice. One even senses that whenever the ego was threatened with curtailment of its freedom by neurotic anxiety or inhibition this became a challenge to be compensated for by particularly intense effort. I wish to cite one of the most remarkable instances, namely Goethe's attempt at fighting the anxiety that, as is well known, every soldier suffers when exposed to the hail of bullets for the first time. When Goethe followed the Duke on his military expedition against the French revolutionary armies (1792) he had an opportunity to watch this phenomenon, about which he reported the following in his *Campagne in Frankreich 1792:*

> I had heard so much about bullet-fever and wished to know how this matter really stood. Boredom and a spirit that is roused by any danger to audacity, even temerity, tempted me to ride quite collectedly up to the forework of La Lune. This was again occupied by our [troops], yet it offered a wild sight: roofs shot to pieces, trusses of wheat strewn about; upon them here and there the fatally wounded stretched out; and meanwhile sometimes a cannon ball straying over here rattled on the remnants of the brick roofs.

> Quite alone, left to myself, I rode to the left upon the heights and could plainly oversee the fortunate position of the French. . . . I encountered good company, officers I knew of the general staff and of the regiment, who were greatly astonished to find me here. They wanted to take me back again with them; I told them, however, of certain plans, and, without further ado, they left me to my well-known peculiar stubbornness.

> Now I had got quite into the region where the bullets were playing over; the sound is strange enough, as if compounded of the humming of a spinning top, the bubbling of water, and the whistling of a bird. They were less dangerous because of the wet ground: wherever one of them hit, it re-

mained stuck, and thus my foolish experimental ride was at least safe from the danger of ricochets.

In these circumstances, though, I was soon able to remark that something unusual was going on within myself. I observed it painstakingly, and yet the sensation could only be communicated by analogy. It seems as if one were in a very hot locality and at the same time completely permeated by the same heat, so that one feels oneself perfectly the same as the element in which one finds oneself. The eyes lose none of their strength or of their clearness, yet it is as if the world had a certain brown-red shade,[76] which makes the state [of mind] even more fear-arousing. I was not able to note anything concerning the movement of the blood, rather everything seemed to me to be swallowed up in that blaze. This, then, elucidates in what sense one might call this state a fever. However, it remains notable that that horrid, fearsome [element] is brought to us only through the ears, for the cannon thunder, the howling, whistling, and crashing of the bullets through the air, is yet the essential cause of these sensations.

After I had ridden back and was in perfect safety, I thought it remarkable that all that blaze was immediately extinguished and not the least of any feverish commotion had remained. This state, by the way, belongs among those least to be desired; accordingly, I have scarcely found one among my dear and noble comrades in arms who would have a really passionate impulse towards it.[77]

[76] It is noteworthy that Goethe referred to a similar phenomenon in an earlier reported context. On that fateful evening when he was apprised of the engagement of the beautiful Milanese, nature also appeared changed in a peculiar way. Goethe wrote: "A hue was drawn over the landscape which was not ascribable either to the sunset or the evening air alone." [Es hatte sich ein Ton über die Gegend gezogen, der weder dem Untergang der Sonne noch den Lüften des Abends allein zuzuschreiben war.] (*Soph.* I, 32:126) It is my impression that Goethe was in both passages hinting at a fantasy of the end of the world. Cf. 178, pp. 74–76; 173, pp. 68–71, particularly p. 69, where Freud distinguishes two types of this fantasy.

[77] [Ich hatte so viel vom Kanonenfieber gehört und wünschte zu wissen wie es eigentlich damit beschaffen sei. Lange Weile und ein Geist den jede Gefahr zur Kühnheit, ja zur Verwegenheit aufruft, verleitete mich ganz gelassen nach dem Vorwerk La Lune hinaufzureiten. Dieses war wieder von den Unsrigen besetzt, gewährte jedoch einen gar wilden Anblick. Die zerschossenen Dächer, die herumgestreuten Weizenbündel, die darauf hie und da ausgestreckten tödtlich Verwundeten und dazwischen noch manchmal eine Kanonenkugel, die sich herüberverirrend in den Überresten der Ziegeldächer klapperte.

Ganz allein, mir selbst gelassen, ritt ich links auf den Höhen weg und konnte deutlich die glückliche Stellung der Franzosen überschauen. . . .

Mir begegnete gute Gesellschaft, es waren bekannte Officiere vom Generalstabe und vom Regimente, höchst verwundert mich hier zu finden. Sie wollten mich wieder mit sich zurücknehmen, ich sprach ihnen aber von besondern Absichten und sie überliessen mich ohne weiteres meinem bekannten wunderlichen Eigensinn.

Ich war nun vollkommen in die Region gelangt wo die Kugeln herüber spielten; der Ton

It is not the point here to discuss the techniques the ego uses for the purpose of gaining or preserving relative freedom of action, as in the just-quoted example.[78] Goethe's biography itself shows that whatever his quasi-neurotic symptoms may have been they led neither to limitations of the ego's main purpose of productivity and creativity nor to an inhibition of functions the ego needed for other accomplishments.[79]

In this adventure we have an instance of Goethe's being attracted to doing the very thing he was afraid of. In the light of this—which was, indeed, typical—one is puzzled at such an attempt as Reik's to account for Goethe's abstinence from sexual intercourse as arising from a fear of it. Reik's extensive study of all the reasons for this fear leaves untouched the question of why this man, who almost never recoiled from an action out of fear—even fear for his life—should have shrunk from sexual intercourse out of fear. What one would have expected from him, indeed, is that he would have felt the more compelled to engage in an activity the more he feared it. At least it would be reasonable to assume he would have sought sexual pleasure, if for no other reason than curiosity. And his

---

ist wundersam genug, als wär' er zusammengesetzt aus dem Brummen des Kreisels, dem Butteln des Wassers und dem Pfeifen eines Vogels. Sie waren weniger gefährlich wegen des feuchten Erdbodens; wo eine hinschlug blieb sie stecken, und so ward mein thörichter Versuchsritt wenigstens vor der Gefahr des Ricochetirens gesichert.

Unter diesen Umständen konnt' ich jedoch bald bemerken dass etwas Ungewöhnliches in mir vorgehe; ich achtete genau darauf und doch würde sich die Empfindung nur gleichnissweise mittheilen lassen. Es schien als wäre man an einem sehr heissen Orte, und zugleich von derselben Hitze völlig durchdrungen, so dass man sich mit demselben Element, in welchem man sich befindet, vollkommen gleich fühlt. Die Augen verlieren nichts an ihrer Stärke, noch Deutlichkeit: aber es ist doch als wenn die Welt einen gewissen braunröthlichen Ton hätte, der den Zustand so wie die Gegenstände noch apprehensiver macht. Von Bewegung des Blutes habe ich nichts bemerken können, sondern mir schien vielmehr alles in jener Gluth verschlungen zu sein. Hieraus erhellet nun in welchem Sinne man diesen Zustand ein Fieber nennen könne. Bemerkenswerth bleibt es indessen, dass jenes grässlich Bängliche nur durch die Ohren zu uns gebracht wird; denn der Kanonendonner, das Heulen, Pfeifen, Schmettern der Kugeln durch die Luft ist doch eigentlich Ursache an diesen Empfindungen. Als ich zurückgeritten und völlig in Sicherheit war, fand ich bemerkenswerth, dass alle jene Gluth sogleich erloschen und nicht das Mindeste von einer fieberhaften Bewegung übrig geblieben sei. Es gehört übrigens dieser Zustand unter die am wenigsten wünschenswerthen; wie ich denn auch unter meinen lieben und edlen Kriegskameraden kaum einen gefunden habe der einen eigentlich leidenschaftlichen Trieb hiernach geäussert hätte.] (*Soph.* I, *33:* 72–74)

[78] I do not wish to raise here the question of character traits in Goethe that came more strongly to the fore with the progress of age, such as a difficulty in making decisions, a formality, even ceremoniousness. I wish to center in this context only on manifest psychopathology, which, in appearance, is identical with the clinically encountered psychopathology of neurotics.

[79] This factor can scarcely be emphasized sufficiently. Goethe's life history abounds in examples of this sort; a very remarkable one is presented in Appendix H.

curiosity was boundless. He felt compelled to know and investigate, to see and watch. Furthermore, one may rightly say that Goethe's counterphobic mechanisms were adequate to carry him through all fears; why should they have failed to protect him in intercourse? To be sure, it is a frequent clinical observation that mechanisms effective in complicated and fear-arousing life situations come to naught in the direct sexual situation. But the type of man is also known that even compulsively indulges in frequent intercourse in order to convince himself and those about him that he is not afraid of women. Of course, neither alternative can be proven: that Goethe's counterphobic attitudes would have been strong enough to carry him through intercourse without anxiety on the one hand, or the possibility that in intercourse the limit of his defenses would have been exceeded. In view of the total picture, I should rather conclude that if Goethe had been capable of intercourse he would have behaved like most young men and would have indulged in intercourse despite his fears. This, after all, did happen in Rome. As the *Roman Elegies* prove, anxiety concerning venereal diseases was still strongly on his mind, but he nevertheless had intercourse with Faustina, whom he declared—arbitrarily—to be free of disease. A good many Faustinas had previously crossed his way, but in Rome Goethe was ready to take his chance despite his fear.

According to my theory, Goethe suffered from a sexual impediment that made intercourse impossible. I believe one can guess fairly accurately at the nature of the difficulty if one studies the biographical record—from which, of course, Goethe left out any description of that of which he was ashamed.

Goethe apparently suffered from premature ejaculation precipitated by sexual foreplay, particularly by kissing, or perhaps even exclusively by kissing. It would fit into the general picture of his hyperemotionality, against which he later often protected himself by ceremoniousness and which, despite all precautions, was even then frequently interrupted by periods of intensely flowing emotions. Instances of his being overwhelmed by an emotion can be seen in his reports of weeping when he thought of the vicissitudes of his characters. His great art of acting, with its perfect presentation of emotions, must not be interpreted as a sign of control over emotions, but as an instantaneous unfolding at the appearance of the proper signal. His incredible poetic creativity, the quick coming to his mind of perfectly formed poems and songs, the more or less constant preoccupation with plots, fantasies, and poetic elaboration upon what he heard and observed—all this shows that he was continuously possessed by the tendency towards immediate discharge, if not by action and physical gratification, then at least by artistic creations or by fantasy.

If there should be any doubt left as to what danger Goethe was actually in of being overwhelmed by a sudden emotion I want to add one more example, from a period in his life when such incidents had become rare. An informant reported with respect to an observation of 1807:

I had been told how he had lost [several children] through death during those years, and how his paternal grief over this overpowered him to such an extent that he threw himself to the ground in unrestrained expressions of grief. . . . Once, on a fine summer's day, the great poet was sitting outdoors there in Carlsbad, at a table with wooden benches, together with some Weimarian acquaintances. . . . Thereupon, absorbed in conversation, one saw Goethe's son coming down a hill. The young man was at that time studying in Heidelberg and, engaged in a hiking trip, he had directed it towards Carlsbad in order to surprise his father there by a visit. Thus, approaching the party at the table in such a manner that his father had his back turned to him and could not see his approach, he motioned eagerly to those sitting opposite to keep quiet and not to draw his father's attention to his arrival. Thus, finally, he sneaked up behind his father's back and, following a customary Weimarian jest, he suddenly put his hands over his father's eyes. As Goethe now disentangles himself and turns around and thus most unexpectedly sees his son, the joyful paternal feeling gets hold of him in a way that deeply moved those who were present. The boundless expressions of being overwhelmed by emotions which the august man exhibited were of such force that the witnesses of this scene were really frightened, and, out of concern for his mental state, wished his calming down.[80]

[80] [Es ist mir erzählt worden, wie er in jenen Jahren Kinder durch den Tod verloren hat, und wie ihn der Vaterschmerz dabei so überwältigte, dass er sich in ungemässigten Äusserungen desselben an die Erde warf. . . .

. . . Einst, an einem schönen Sommertage, sass der grosse Dichter dort in Karlsbad im Freien mit weimarischen Bekannten an einem Tisch mit Holzbänken an beiden Seiten. . . . Da sah man, in das Gespräch vertieft, Goethes Sohn von einer Anhöhe herabkommen. Der junge Mann studierte zu dieser Zeit in Heidelberg und hatte eine unternommene Fussreise auch nach Karlsbad geleitet, um den Vater dort mit seinem Besuche zu überraschen. Als er sich nun der Gesellschaft an jenem Tisch so näherte, dass ihn der Vater im Rücken hatte und seine Annäherung nicht bemerken konnte, winkte er den Gegenübersitzenden eifrig zu, sich still zu verhalten und den Vater nicht auf seine Ankunft aufmerksam zu machen. So schlich er endlich leise bis an den Rücken des Vaters heran und hielt ihm plötzlich nach dem gebräuchlichen weimarischen Scherze die Hände vor die Augen. Wie nun Goethe sich loswindet und umkehrt und so höchst unerwartet den Sohn erblickt, da ergreift ihn das freudige väterliche Gefühl auf eine Weise, die in den anderen gegenwärtigen Personen eine tiefe Erschütterung hervorbrachte. Die masslosen Äusserungen der Gefühlsüberwältigung, mit welcher der erhabene Mann hier erschien, waren von solcher Stärke, dass die Zeugen dieser

Despite the unquestionable presence in Goethe of signs that are characteristic of the obsessional-compulsive personality, I nevertheless believe that in him the basic structure—that is to say, the basic ego-emotion relationship—was that of a hysterical personality, and many physical conversion symptoms can be cited in support of this opinion.

In view of all these factors it is not improbable that the psychological basis of his personality tended towards a full emotional discharge on minimal provocation. This must not be thought of as a weakness of the sexual impulse or desire, but rather as a tendency of the instinct itself—formed in accordance with the way his emotions unfolded—to present itself immediately with its full force. From his letters as a young man one can see how the emotion, once stimulated, rushed with surprising rapidity to an almost unbearable peak. This of course often resulted in contradictory behavior. Also it gave him at times the appearance of unpredictability, since his emotions were prone to develop to a maximum over incidents that looked inconsequential to the beholder.

I wish now to justify my hypothesis that it was kissing that aroused Goethe to such an extent that it was accompanied with full discharge. Reik (449), in his effort to explain Goethe's flight from his sweetheart Friederike Brion in Sesenheim in 1771, discussed at length an episode that played a great role in Goethe's relationship with her. Before he met Friederike—so Goethe reports in *Dichtung und Wahrheit*—he had had a strange experience with a girl, Lucinda, in Strassburg. She had fallen in love with him, but believed her sister Emilie had won him over for herself. In order to prevent Emilie from enjoying her victory, the defeated Lucinda put a curse on Goethe, predicting misfortune for the girl who should next kiss his lips. The episode is worth reporting at length:

> She [Lucinda] stood before me and seemed to be meditating upon something. Thereupon she said: "I know that I have lost you; I make no further claims upon you. But you, sister, shall not have him either!" With these words, she took proper hold of me by the head, thrusting with both hands through my locks, pressed my face to hers, and kissed me repeatedly upon the mouth. "Now," she exclaimed, "fear my curse. Unhappiness upon unhappiness for ever and ever upon her who first after me will kiss these

Szene wirklich dabei erschraken und in Besorgnis für seinen Geist die Beruhigung herbeiwünschten.] (250, *1*:508–09)

However, in evaluating the basic relationship of Goethe's ego to emotions one must distinguish several phases: the pre-Weimarian *Sturm und Drang* period; the acquisition of self-mastery, and the maintenance of it, during the middle years; the weakening of the ego through the process of aging and the concomitant reappearance of the ego's weakness *vis-à-vis* strong emotions. I have not discussed the aging-process phase in this section.

lips! Now dare to carry on again with him; I know Heaven will listen to me this time. And you, sir, hurry now, hurry away as fast as you can!"[81]

Thereafter, Goethe felt inhibited from kissing Friederike, fearing that Lucinda's curse would be fulfilled upon his new sweetheart. Reik is right in saying (449, pp. 97–98) that at the basis of this fear lay the fear that a disaster would befall him (Goethe). But, if the above-quoted passage, the account of Lucinda's curse, is read carefully, one may conclude that the disaster had already befallen Goethe when he was kissed by Lucinda. From this report I should reconstruct the following scene to have happened in reality. A girl, while passionately kissing Goethe, noticed that, by a premature ejaculation, he had cheated her of the pleasure of which she was urgently desirous. As women so often do, she experienced this as an aggression against her, as a token that Goethe did not want to have intercourse with her. Accordingly, she put a curse on the next—or all following—girls, so that they should suffer the same fate. Of course, the curse was directed at Goethe. Her wish was that he should suffer the same mishap for the rest of his life, but, since she presumably experienced Goethe's premature ejaculation as an aggression against herself, she identified herself with the women with whom she anticipated Goethe would seek to have intercourse, and wished them to have the same effect as she had upon her lover.

I agree with Reik that it is immaterial whether the Lucinda episode, or any like it, really took place at all, or in any such way as the aging Goethe reported it. But I think that in the Lucinda episode Goethe came his closest to intimating what the sexual difficulty of his adult years was. When he wrote this episode he was looking back upon years of successful intercourse with Christiane, and the sense of shame had abated so much that he could hint at the truth in the story of Lucinda's curse. The figment —if it was a figment—he used is not so different from the explanation men had been proffering for centuries to explain instances of impotence. In earlier times, witches had been burned to death for having, allegedly, deprived men of their generative faculties (see 502, pp. 54–61, 117–22).

---

[81] [Sie stand vor mir und schien auf etwas zu sinnen. Drauf sagte sie: Ich weiss, dass ich Sie verloren habe; ich mache keine weitern Ansprüche auf Sie. Aber du sollst ihn auch nicht haben, Schwester! Sie fasste mich mit diesen Worten ganz eigentlich bei'm Kopf, indem sie mir mit beiden Händen in die Locken fuhr, mein Gesicht an das ihre drückte und mich zu wiederholten Malen auf den Mund küsste. Nun, rief sie aus, fürchte meine Verwünschung. Unglück über Unglück für immer und immer auf diejenige, die zum ersten Male nach mir diese Lippen küsst! Wage es nun wieder mit ihm anzubinden; ich weiss, der Himmel erhört mich diessmal. Und Sie, mein Herr, eilen Sie nun, eilen Sie was Sie können!] (*Dichtung und Wahrheit,* Book IX, *Soph.* I, 27:291–92)

Goethe's story sounds as if, remembering his sexual weakness, he thought belatedly to explain it by the theory that a woman must have cast a spell over him.

But an equivalent reality event may likewise have taken place. For a while Goethe may have been quite ready to accept his defect as a means of obtaining temporary relief from sexual tension, and also as a means of protecting the girl from the evil effects intercourse was bound, in his estimation, to have. Yet how much distress must he then have felt when he discovered that women did not share his belief in his protectiveness and suddenly made him aware that they regarded his sexual peculiarity as an aggression against them. Or, having solved the sexual problem to his satisfaction for a long time by means of his defect, Goethe may have wanted to resort to more mature pursuits only to find suddenly that what he had thought a blessing now to be dispensed with was a reaction he could not control.

It would help us in testing these assumptions if we could reconstruct who the person was in contact with whom changes of this sort occurred. I do not think that Reik has really explained adequately why Goethe had to leave Friederike. His explanation would fit a person who was suffering from a true clinical obsessive neurosis and who therefore had to protect himself by acts of avoidance. Reik's assumptions as to the contents of Goethe's unconscious may be correct, but if Goethe had had only these issues (castration fears, death wishes, fears of retaliation) to cope with I believe that, despite their fear-arousing effect, his ego would have been strong enough to go ahead and overrule them by action. In other words, my reasoning does not dispute the assumption that such contents were part and parcel of Goethe's unconscious—they are found far too often in male imagery about the sexual act for us to doubt their existence in Goethe's—but I must turn against the conclusion that Reik drew as to the effect such imagery had on the poet's ego structure.

It is far more probable that the unconscious fears, combined with the ego's tendency towards maximal emotional upsurge, once excited, led to a premature ejaculation, provoked through kissing. Here Goethe's ego was caught in a trap. No effort, no training, no determination, no counterphobic attitude, could help out. The more the ego exposed itself to danger, the less it could succeed, for what was involved was automatic, reflex actions which it was powerless directly to come to grips with. There was only one method of preventing the dreaded event and this was, not to kiss. But how could a girl be passionately loved if one did not kiss her?

I do not know of an instance from Goethe's life that might show conclusively a compulsion or obsession to interfere with an essential or important pursuit he was determined to follow. He was superstitious, like all people who maintain a lively communication with their unconscious. But he directed his superstitions well, so that they carried him along on the path to accomplishments. When, with regard to kissing, he had to resort to avoidance we should not interpret this as constituting a phobia but as the only valid means available for getting rid of a symptom that could not possibly be overcome by will power or counterphobic techniques. When bullets whizzed around him, Goethe could move on despite trepidation, but a reflex of the vegetative nervous system was beyond the scope of effort. Checking Goethe's own reports on the way he behaved so as to avoid kisses I do not find much against my assumption. He wrote:

Since the time that passionate girl cursed and hallowed my lips (for each consecration includes both), I guarded myself, superstitiously enough, against ever kissing a girl, because I feared to hurt her in an unspeakable *mental* way. I therefore conquered each voluptuous impulse through which youth feels urged to win this favor—meaning little or much—from an attractive girl. However, even in most prudish company an annoying test waited for me. Those little more or less ingenious games through which a gay youthful circle gathers and unites, are mainly based on forfeits. In claiming them kisses have a considerable redemption value. I had resolved once for all not to kiss and as a lack or impediment incites us to activities towards which we would not have been inclined otherwise I summoned all my talents and sense of humor to get through [such situations] and in so doing rather to win than to lose, for and before the company [engaged in the game].[82] [Italics mine]

Goethe explicitly says he had to fight against his voluptuousness. The compulsive-obsessional or the phobic patient does not report fighting

[82] [Seitdem jenes leidenschaftliche Mädchen meine Lippen verwünscht und geheiligt (denn jede Weihe enthält ja beides), hatte ich mich, abergläubisch genug, in Acht genommen, irgend ein Mädchen zu küssen, weil ich solches auf eine unerhörte geistige Weise zu beschädigen fürchtete. Ich überwand daher jede Lüsternheit, durch die sich der Jüngling gedrungen fühlt, diese viel oder wenig sagende Gunst einem reizenden Mädchen abzugewinnen, Aber selbst in der sittigsten Gesellschaft erwartete mich eine lästige Prüfung. Eben jene, mehr oder minder geistreichen, sogenannten kleinen Spiele, durch welche ein munterer jugendlicher Kreis gesammelt und vereinigt wird, sind grossentheils auf Pfänder gegründet, bei deren Einforderung die Küsse keinen unbedeutenden Lösewerth haben. Ich hatte mir nun ein-für allemal vorgenommen, nicht zu küssen, und wie uns irgend ein Mangel oder Hinderniss zu Thätigkeiten aufregt, zu denen man sich sonst nicht hingeneigt hätte, so bot ich alles auf, was an mir von Talent und Humor war, mich durchzuwinden und dabei vor der Gesellschaft und für die Gesellschaft eher zu gewinnen als zu verlieren.] (*Dichtung und Wahrheit* Book XI, *Soph.* I, 28:13)

against voluptuousness. It takes a long analysis before he discovers that his symptoms are a defense against drives. Goethe let us know that he was struggling against a gratification that he could easily have achieved by simply kissing a girl. The fear of the "mental damage" he might bring upon the girl by his kissing her was only too much rooted in reality. In accordance with Lucinda's curse ("unhappiness upon unhappiness") one would rather have expected in Goethe fear of a damage more conspicuous than we associate with a mental damage. However, in view of the reaction he may on one occasion have noticed in a girl following his sexual peculiarity, he may easily have begun to fear lest his sexual weakness poison the girl's mind. From the great effect that the Friederike episode had upon Goethe and from the fact of his taking flight from her, I should surmise that it was in the relationship with her that Goethe was forced to take cognizance that his premature ejaculations were symptoms, and that he was suffering here from a real defect. Friederike, in her loveliest innocence—it can well be imagined—succumbed to his charms. Whereas Goethe for a while reached gratification while dancing and kissing, the situation finally came about when the girl wanted to surrender herself to him, and Goethe himself, being twenty-two years old, felt driven to perform the act, but discovered to his horror and humiliation that he was prevented by a premature ejaculation. Thereupon he turned in flight.

Years earlier, in Leipzig, when he was seized by his infatuation for Käthchen Schönkopf, the situation had been essentially different. There we see him in the middle of the impetuous storms of adolescence. The way he is described by friends of that time also impresses one with the juvenile element, the pretense and the effort to pose as a man. To a certain extent one may compare it with an experimental phase. He still needed a tutor, who appeared in the form of Behrisch. Wild and passionate desires are found side by side with overmoralistic tendencies. The sexual defect did not frighten him at that time for it provided relief without involving him in danger. I find what I regard as an account of the defect, as well as of the ego's reaction to it, in a letter of the seventeen-year-old boy to Behrisch on October 12, 1766. I have quoted this poem earlier (cf. pp. 52–53) but want to repeat it because of its great importance in this context. The poem was written in English upon his return from a tryst at which he was able to be with his girl alone for four hours, an opportunity rarely offered. In the opening lines,

> What pleasure, God! of like a flame to born
> A virteous fire, that ne'er to vice kan turn,

Goethe gives what I regard as an unmistakable reference to the reliable protection against sin provided by his defect. Then follows the description of the sexual foreplay:

> What volupty! when trembling in my arms,
> The bosom of my maid my bosom warmeth!
> Perpetual kisses of her lips o'erflow,
> In holy embrace mighty virtue show.

After the assurance of virtue—that is to say, in accordance with the requirement during the Leipzig period of avoiding intercourse—Goethe proceeded to describe the orgasm:

> When I then, rapt, in never felt extase,
> My maid! I say, and she, my dearest! says.
> When then, my heart, of love and virtue hot,
> Cries: come ye angels! Come! See and envy me not.

"Come ye angels! Come! See and envy me not" is a typical response of the adolescent to orgasm, namely, the expression of a feeling of being the only one who experiences such delights and that even the most blissful beings, angels, have reason to envy him. The integration of the defect is described with particular clearness. Orgasm is capable of being combined with virtue and the ego revels in triumph at having gained the greatest pleasure without any negative consequences. One also gets the impression that Käthchen was immature enough not to mind the juvenile nature of her lover's love life. The fact that Käthchen married soon after Goethe's departure also reflects the general emotional climate of that relationship.

The almost psychotic character of Goethe's reaction to frustrations, which I described earlier, should not make one assume a necessarily deep object-relationship. The two hemorrhages that forced him to return to his native city—whether they were tuberculous or psychogenic is still debatable—might be compared to a genitalization of the whole body. The hemorrhages would then stand for ejaculation and the choice of the mouth as the leading pathological zone would confirm the nature of the basic sexual disturbance.

During the time that he was courting Friederike, Goethe described a physical symptom that was unquestionably psychogenic. After a meal he felt "as if his throat were throttled,"[83] a symptom that had been absent in Sesenheim and that he was able to combat in Strassburg by not drinking a certain red wine that was served at the boardinghouse and that he liked

---

[83] [die Kehle wie zugeschnürt] (*Soph.* I, 28:8)

very much. I should explain the symptom as a displacement from below to above and an attempt to impede the ejaculation by a constriction.[84]

When Goethe arrived in Strassburg he had reached a more mature level than that of Leipzig. What might have been satisfactory at the earlier stage did not suffice any more. The progress is also revealed in his love poetry, which became charmingly masculine. When he was now impeded by his defect, particularly if it happened that the girl turned towards him without reservation and expected genital gratification, then it was bound to have a disturbing effect upon him. What had been welcome relief in Leipzig became a curse in Sesenheim. The feeling of shame must have been very intense. I believe that by shifting the accent in *Dichtung und Wahrheit* from shame to guilt the aging Goethe achieved a restoration of his self-esteem. Since behind the premature ejaculation there lurked aggression, a feeling of guilt was probably already present at the time of the flight from Sesenheim. Yet the immediate reaction probably was mostly shame, which one senses behind some details recorded in *Dichtung und Wahrheit*. There one notices a shifting of the shame to details (which he probably had to invent in order to attach humiliation to them) and a considerable readiness to accuse himself of guilt in order to hide his shame.[85] It was easier for him to present himself as a guilt-laden Don Juan than as a young man with a physical impediment.

I shall give some examples of shameful or embarrassing events Goethe described in *Dichtung und Wahrheit* in conjunction with the Sesenheim episode. Such features appear as early as his account of the way in which he first established contact with the Sesenheim family. There are two instances of disguise to which Reik (449, pp. 57–69) has devoted much thought. On his way to Sesenheim Goethe tried by means of behavior, clothes, and style of hairdress to give himself the appearance of a poor student of theology. This was assertedly his appearance when he met Friederike for the first time. The next morning he felt so ashamed about the wretchedness of his attire that he wanted to return quickly to Strassburg, change his clothes and come back. Not far from the Brion family manor he met the son of an innkeeper who looked somewhat like himself. He borrowed the lad's clothes and returned to Sesenheim, thus fooling all members of the family, who at first sight thought him to be the innkeeper's son, George.

There is no need to go into the details of this masquerade. It sounds

---

[84] The avoidance of red wine may also point to menstruation fears; cf. my discussion of *The New Melusine,* above p. 803.

[85] For a study that aims at the differentiation of shame and guilt see 420.

somewhat forced or strained, and many authors have claimed—on good grounds, as I believe—that these two episodes of disguise did not occur at all.[86] Be this as it may—and in this context historical truth is far less important than meaning—these two opening episodes involved intense embarrassment and shame, and, according to his report, Goethe had to apologize to a score of people and do a lot of explaining. According to Reik's interpretation (449, p. 65) the two disguises were expressions of ambivalence and of a feeling of superiority, the first one expressing: "If I were a student of theology you would be glad to welcome me," and the second: "The innkeeper's son is the proper fellow for you, I am not suited for you," but also: "I wish I were George so I could marry you." I can follow Reik when he points to the ambivalence, but my main interpretation goes in another direction. Goethe said that in the first disguise he was imitating a person who is called a "Latin horseman" [ein lateinischer Reiter]. To my surprise, I have found this expression explained in a way that seems to fit exactly into the explanation that I derived earlier from the psychoanalytic implication. Karl Heinemann, the editor of the Bibliographical Institute edition of Goethe's works, supposes that the expression was formed after a common enough Italian idiom, "fare il latino a cavallo," which ordinarily means: "to achieve success in something despite difficulties."[87]

This I think is the key to the first disguise. It is the expression of an attempt or wish to identify with a man who will succeed in performing sexually in all circumstances. In the second disguise, Goethe, I believe, expressed the wish to get away from the sophistication of his own social group. As a boy he got about enough to move among a good cross-section of the urban population and he certainly noted the difference between the sex customs of the lower classes and those of his own. George was beneath the social status of Friederike, whose place was between George's and Goethe's. I do not believe that in the attempt at identification with George, the innkeeper's son, Goethe was motivated by any desire for marriage but solely by the wish to be able to carry out intercourse, as if he meant to say: "If I had the masculinity of an innkeeper's son I should sleep with my sweetheart even if my social status were below hers." The two episodes of disguise, in all probability freely invented by the poet, gave occasion to describe the feeling of embarrassment indelibly attached to his recollection of Sesenheim, and thus it is to be expected that these products

[86] For a comparison between Goethe's account and historical truth, see 525, pp. 159–283.

[87] 258, *12*:271, n. 2; Richard M. Meyer (248, *23*:333, n. to p. 260, 1. 25) explains the metaphor as meaning "a poor, helpless pedant on horseback."

of the poet's imagination also reflect the incident that was the historically true source of the embarrassment he could well remember.

In Goethe's account of how he felt after he had given Friederike the forbidden kiss I find also a confirmation of his sexual weakness. He wrote:

> Yet I do not want to conceal the still more painful that lay in the background for me. A certain arrogance sustained that superstition [regarding the curse] in me; my lips—hallowed or cursed—impressed me as more important than usual, and I was conscious, with no little self-complacency, of my abstemious comportment in depriving myself of quite a few innocent pleasures, partly in order to preserve that magic privilege, partly in order not to hurt an innocent being if I gave it up.

> Now, however [after having kissed Friederike], everything was lost and irretrievably; I was returned to a common condition. I thought I had injured the dearest person, had harmed her irretrievably; and thus that curse, instead of my getting rid of it, recoiled from my lips into my very heart.[88]

This passage describes the hypercathexis of the oral zone, which is indispensable for the kind of sexual disturbance I have assumed Goethe to have suffered from prior to his journey to Italy. It also describes the futility of voluntary effort in combating the symptom.

It is remarkable that Goethe's choice of sweethearts subsequent to Friederike fell rather on women with whom sexual intercourse was made extremely difficult if not impossible by external circumstances themselves. Lotte in Wetzlar was engaged, at least secretly; Lili was a member of a superior class and his engagement to her also tended towards postponing the sexual act. Precisely from Lili herself stems a report that indirectly confirms some assumptions I have made about Friederike. Many years after her engagement to Goethe, Lili, who had married von Türckheim, called Goethe "the creator of her moral existence" [Schöpfer ihrer moralischen Existenz]. She also confessed that her passion for Goethe was stronger than her sense of duty and virtue, and

---

[88] [Was aber noch Schmerzlicheres für mich im Hintergrunde lag, will ich nicht verhehlen. Ein gewisser Dünkel unterhielt bei mir jenen Aberglauben; meine Lippen—geweiht oder verwünscht—kamen mir bedeutender vor als sonst, und mit nicht geringer Selbstgefälligkeit war ich mir meines enthaltsamen Betragens bewusst, indem ich mir manche unschuldige Freude versagte, theils um jenen magischen Vorzug zu bewahren, theils um ein harmloses Wesen nicht zu verletzen, wenn ich ihn aufgäbe.

Nunmehr aber war alles verloren und unwiederbringlich; ich war in einen gemeinen Zustand zurückgekehrt, ich glaubte das liebste Wesen verletzt, ihr unwiederbringlich geschadet zu haben; und so war jene Verwünschung, anstatt dass ich sie hätte los werden sollen, von meinen Lippen in mein eigenes Herz zurückgeschlagen.] (*Dichtung und Wahrheit, Soph.* I, 28:23)

if his magnanimity had not steadfastly rejected the sacrifice that she wanted to make for him, she would later have looked back upon her past deprived of her self-respect and of public esteem.[89]

These words are not known directly from Lili herself but are contained in the report of Henriette von Beaulieu-Marconnay, who met her and later published the conversation. From this report it seems evident that Lili felt in favor of a sexual relationship during her engagement. Others have denied this and claimed that these words meant a willingness to elope (see 453, p. 29). Since Goethe and Lili were engaged, I do not see that an elopement would have been looked upon as boding such disastrous consequences for the bride's future. If Lili really expressed herself in such words as reported by Mme. Beaulieu-Marconnay I think one must conclude that Goethe, despite his longing and passion, did not request genital gratification but that it was rather the sweetheart who was ready to give in to her drives and Goethe who rejected the idea.

I have discussed this episode in detail because it may appear improbable that Friederike, the daughter of a vicar, should have been at all ready to go so far in deviating from the prescribed standards of conduct. Goethe described Friederike, however, as a naive, sincere person, absolutely devoted to him. From the point of view of the young man, it is rather a sign of virtue when a virtuous and inexperienced girl is ready to surrender to him in full trust in his honesty and sincerity. After having seen Friederike for the first time, Goethe asked his companion, who had taken him to Sesenheim, whether the girl had ever been in love, was then in love, or engaged. When the answer was no, Goethe could not believe it. He would have understood her gayness [*Heiterkeit*] better if "she had loved and lost and recovered, or if she were affianced."[90] I am inclined to interpret this remark—independent of what its meaning is in the literal context of the story—as an expression of regret in the aging Goethe that the unsuccessful Sesenheim adventure took place with a girl who was in love for the first time. In these circumstances his sexual deficiency must have embarrassed him with particular intensity and must also have resulted in a greater feeling of guilt than would have been the case with a hussy. As a matter of fact, Friederike remained unmarried, as if she had been severely traumatized by her acquaintance with Goethe.[91]

---

[89] [. . . wenn seine Grossmut die Opfer, welche sie ihm bringen wollte, nicht standhaft zurückgewiesen hätte, so würde sie späterhin ihrer Selbstachtung und der bürgerlichen Ehre beraubt auf die Vergangenheit zurückgeschaut haben.] (250, *1*:62–63)

[90] [Hätte sie geliebt und verloren und sich wieder gefasst, oder wäre sie Braut.] (*Soph.* I, 27:357)

[91] For Friederike's life after Goethe left her, see 52.

In his relationship with Lili, a girl of great sophistication, Goethe behaved differently and apparently refused a sexual adventure. However, it must also be taken into account that during the period of ardent love for Lili Goethe's visits with the girl in Offenbach occurred. The identity of that girl is quite enigmatic, but nearly all young friends and acquaintances who belonged to the *Sturm und Drang* circle visited her and spent nights in her home (see 388). In Weimar he allied himself with a woman with whom the probability of having intercourse was minimal. But, as I tried to prove earlier, intercourse was not accessible to him as a way of achieving sexual relief.

The question arises here whether Goethe tried with Charlotte von Stein to continue his habitual technique of obtaining gratification. And here, I think, there is again a point of biographical evidence that supports my hypothesis. Charlotte von Stein evidently complained about Goethe's behavior. But what kind of behavior did she mean? Is it conceivable that this type of woman would, after having objected to Goethe's trying to have a sexual relationship with her, then reconcile herself with him? Is it not much more probable that he tried to embrace her in the passionate way in which he customarily elicited an ejaculation and that she, feeling, of course, that this embrace would lead to or was aimed at a genital discharge, forbade him ever to try such a maneuver with her? Whether he ever dared again to go that far can, of course, no more be known than whether he did so at all, but it is important to keep in mind that the restraints she imposed on him in all probability excluded passionate kissing. As frequent passages in Goethe's letters show, kisses were exchanged between him and Charlotte von Stein. If my guess is correct that she did prohibit passionate kissing then thereby she contributed yet another factor to Goethe's recovery. He, so to speak, learned the art of unpassionate, merely affectionate, kissing by knowing that to overstep a certain threshold would be followed by the immediate loss of the love-object.

We possess a short note by Goethe which throws an important light upon his sexual life during the early years in Weimar. It will be recalled that he spent many hours off and on in wild dancing with the girls of rural neighborhoods: "The wheel of the petticoats," he jotted down.

> The red stockings. When the wind of the whirling petticoats passes under one's nose. The pursing up and puckering of the little mouths of the girls and the casting down of their eyes [when] they feel the prick. Trouser-button. To ride on wool-sacks. To stamp so that the boards thunder. . . .[92]

[92] [Das Rad der Unterröcke. Die rothen Strümpfe Wenn einem der Wind der schwingenden Unterröcke unter die Nase geht. Das mäulgen ziehen, rümpfen (?) Augen niederschlagen

The editors of the Sophienausgabe believe that these notes were written in 1777 and refer to observations Goethe made on the occasion of a country dance. I see in them a reflection of his own experiences. Here we see how the sexual urge is channelized into the motor system, how the passionate dancing leads to excitement without discharge. It is important that even in such intimate sketches no mention is made of intercourse, although these years of steady companionship with the Duke, who allegedly indulged freely in sexual escapades, gave ample opportunity for intercourse with girls of a socially lower stratum.

We shall now understand in its full extent Goethe's entry in his diary of August 7, 1779: "May the idea of the pure, which extends right to the morsel I take into my mouth, become ever more shining in me."[93] The mouth was the organ of sin, for it was the stimulation of it that led to an ejaculation. Under the influence of Charlotte von Stein, Goethe was determined to eradicate the symptom. The best way to reach such a goal was to enlarge its scope. If all pleasure that can be derived from the mouth is forbidden, then one can be sure that direct sexual implication has been excluded. It must also be considered that when such a perversion is suppressed, the libidinal cathexis of eating may grow stronger by displacement. Thus Goethe's including the morsel of food he eats in the concept of purity was consistent with the principal aim of that time. Goethe's entry about the purity of the morsel can be proffered as circumstantial evidence of the correctness of my reconstruction. With the disappearance of the symptom in Italy Goethe also became freer in his eating habits, as was noticed by others.

It is of interest to watch the consistent rise in social status of Goethe's sweethearts, starting with Gretchen and culminating in Charlotte von Stein, the cultivated noblewoman. When he finally began genital relationships Goethe returned to where he had set out and chose a mistress who belonged to low social status. It may be recalled that when Goethe as a boy first saw and fell in love with Gretchen she was doing the work of a waitress. Christiane had a social status somewhat higher than Faustina, the waitress, but Goethe did not go beyond that, and remained with her. Thus he did not repeat in his genital life the sociological sequences he had passed through during that part of his love life that had been impeded by the sexual defect. The problem of this arrest in his psychosexual develop-

---

der Mägdlein die den Schwanz spüren. Hosenknopf. Auf Wollsack reiten Stampfen dass die Dielen donnern.] (*Soph.* I, 53:424)

[93] [Möge die Idee des reinen die sich bis auf den Bissen erstreckt den ich in den Mund nehme, immer lichter in mir werden.]

ment is of no minor importance. Evidently he never succeeded in establishing a genital relationship with a partner who was his equal in refinement and sophistication. It is possible that because of the delay in starting intercourse no time was left to add that development, which others usually go through at a much earlier age. It is likewise possible that the artist, when he achieves a synthesis of sexual gratification and adequate object-relationship, when he blends the physical and the spiritual—without feeling of guilt—into a happy, blissful experience, loses the momentum and impetus for further artistic productivity (see Appendix T). In *Faust,* Part II, Goethe makes the moment of death and the moment of highest bliss coincide. Such a sexual peculiarity as I have tried to reconstruct must, despite the concomitant feelings of embarrassment, humiliation, and inferiority, have harbored some supreme advantages that were of paramount necessity to Goethe's development as an artist. The disorder was so structured that it did not make genital discharges impossible. If Goethe had suffered from an obsessional neurosis of such severity as to block genital gratification completely, I do not know whether his psychic apparatus would have been able to withstand the terrific strain of the pre-Weimarian years or whether he would not have become a victim of suicide or psychosis.

Furthermore, the defect did not isolate Goethe. It required the searching and finding of a partner. Masturbation would have involved a feeling of guilt greater than probably occurred with this perversion. It would also have thrown a shadow on his strivings toward the object world. By the technique of gratification that I have posited Goethe was compelled over and over again to turn towards objects without ever finding full gratification. I believe that this is a particularly important point. If the perversion had provided him with a deep-going and really satisfactory discharge, artistic creation probably would not have continued to be the main channel through which his libido flowed towards the world. One has only to compare the *Roman Elegies* with the poetry written for Marianne Willemer, a woman Goethe never possessed sexually. The *Elegies* are beautiful, but this kind of poetry would never have made Goethe the poet that he was. The constant striving for the object, the almost reaching it, but the never fully possessing it, the joy of recognizing the beauty of the beloved object, the joy of obtaining the foretaste of supreme bliss but never coming to a full rest—all these factors and many more conspired to render Goethe's poetry one of the most beautiful creations. The psychological prerequisites of such creations cannot be based on a repeated total gratification of the sexual urge. Only if the very core of the personality still harbors needs that are beyond gratification and that have to be diverted into the creative process, can supreme works of art be produced. It was perhaps just this factor that made the perversion an indispensable part of the ego's capacity for work. The pleasure it provided gave a foretaste of the bliss that might be achieved but that never came within reach, each time escaping elusively. This perversion was bound to have an extremely stimulating effect upon the ego's longing to capture in words that which the body persistently refused to provide, but only made divinable in vain promises.

Equally important was it that the perversion simultaneously protected the ego against a damaging overburdening of ungratified libido. The psychological structure of Goethe's sexual defect makes the Moses identification particularly understandable. Goethe too was condemned to seeing the promised land from afar without being permitted for many years to set foot upon it. Such an essentially wholesome identification as this with Moses might easily have been replaced by an equation with Tantalus, who is punished by eternal thirst in the midst of water which recedes as soon as he stoops to drink it. Tantalus is the prototype of the masochistic personality, quite different from Moses, who, though denied the final gratification, is the arch-image of the grandiose nation-founding father.

At this point a few remarks must be added regarding Goethe's orality. The oral zone—always under the supposition that my hypothesis is correct—was the leading zone, which set the mechanism of ejaculation into motion, and therefore it is reasonable to expect signs in Goethe of intense orality in other respects. I do not wish to dwell on his strong predilection for alcohol, or the great role that food played in his life, or the importance that conversation, talking, or reciting had for him, but I do wish briefly to call attention to the fact that Goethe's language was very oral and that his choice of metaphors was so frequently given an oral frame of reference. I wish to quote one example to serve for many. On January 6, 1787, he wrote from Italy to his friends in Weimar of his intention to return home after Easter, and then continued:

> I shall by then have lapped up [94] still a few vessels out of the great ocean and my most urgent need will have been satisfied. I am cured of a gigantic passion and disease, again restored to the enjoyment of life, to the enjoyment of history, of poetry, of Antiquity.[95]

[94] The German word *schlürfen* combines the meanings of to sip and to lap.

[95] [Ich werde bis dahin noch einige Schaalen aus dem grosen Ocean geschlürft haben und mein dringendstes Bedürfniss wird befriedigt seyn. Ich bin von einer ungeheuren Leidenschafft und Kranckheit geheilt, wieder zum Lebensgenuss, zum Genuss der Geschichte, der Dichtkunst der Alterthümer genessen.]

Here we encounter oral imagery symbolizing all the good things life can give him before he returns home. The oral imagery is general and moving from it to the specific he indicated what the good things were in particular. The relationship between orality, food, and the prospects of love comes to the fore in the following passage from Goethe's letter to Jacobi of September 11, 1785, in which he is writing about Fritz:

> Do you know what! I mean to train him up for your girl; she surely never would get a more attractive and better man, since, after all, I cannot become your son-in-law. But do not give her punch to drink and other such trash; keep her unspoiled as I do the boy, who is accustomed to the purest diet.[96]

Here the belief in the moral and ethical effect of the right kind of food is very succinctly (though possibly facetiously) expressed. In a letter to Charlotte von Stein of January 3, 1780, in which he told her of a new idea for a play, he asked her to keep this information confidential or else someone else could "snatch the roast from before my mouth."[97] Here the whole not yet fully formed artistic idea is compared (if not equated) with a luring dish, which is perceived but only enjoyed in anticipation.

Of course, anal references can also be found but they are much fewer, I believe. The strong oral undertone of Goethe's language cannot be missed. Yet ascertaining the oral flavor of many communications and thus illustrating the importance of the oral zone by examples does not carry us very far. I suggested earlier that the oral zone was the trigger that set the genital process into motion. We find such pathology in oral-dependent patients, but we also find it in persons in whom genital strivings are strongly developed but in whom these genital strivings do not lead to corresponding manifestations, that is to say, the same oral perversion may be built on quite different fixation points of libidinal development and may be related to quite different ego structures. In one patient the oral aim is made the main ego goal; they want to suck and they do suck, and are parasitic; in the other the oral aim is only the façade of strong phallic tendencies that are not revealed as such because of castration anxiety. During the initial phase of Goethe's relationship to Charlotte von Stein, when his letters contained such frequent references to food, we already saw him very vigorously engaged in oral activities. It was his delight to provide

---

[96] [Weist du was! ich will ihn deinem Mädgen erziehen, einen hübschern und bessern Mann kriegt sie doch nicht, da ich doch einmal dein Schwiegersohn nicht werden kann. Aber gieb ihr nicht Punsch zu trincken und des andern Quarcks, halte sie unverdorben wie ich den Buben, der an die reinste Diät gewöhnt ist.]

[97] [den Braten vorm Maul wegnehmen]

the beloved woman and her children with delicacies, and he also threw himself with great activity into the affairs of the principality—giving food, so to speak, to all the inhabitants of Weimar. The phallic tendency finds expression only in such passages as the following, written towards the end of a letter from Eisenach of September 6, 1777:

> Dearest! You indeed all alone I hold dear; this I sense from my dealings with the rest of women.

> You are not jealous of me, otherwise I would tell you a remedy [against it]. The sheath of the souvenir I do not have, but your scarf I have about me.[98]

The sequence of thoughts is rather clear from the psychoanalytic viewpoint. It is (1) I love you—this is clear because I cannot fall in love with another woman; (2) how nice it would be if you were jealous—then I could make a suggestion as to what you should do so as to make it unnecessary; (3) I do not have the sheath of the souvenir. This "free" association reveals, if there had been any doubt, the nature of the remedy he intimated against jealousy, that is to say, intercourse. It is of interest that, despite his great intimacy with Charlotte von Stein Goethe wrote in such a circumlocutory way about intercourse. He slipped in an intimation and revealed the truth by means of a symbol, abruptly following the intimation. I conclude from this that the direct genital demand was also veiled when he was with her. Thus food became the substitute for the physical gratification that Charlotte von Stein denied, as can be seen from the beginning of his letter of February 8, 1781, reporting about the nosebleed incurred assertedly by a dietary indiscretion.[99]

All this material may strengthen the probability of my hypothesis as to the specific character of Goethe's sexual disturbance. But I must emphasize again—particularly in view of the readiness with which true oral dependency is assumed in a patient, as can be seen from a perusal of contemporary psychoanalytic literature—that this great role which the oral erogenic zone played must not lead to the conclusion that the clinical picture presented constituted an oral character. The mouth functioned as a trigger to activate the genital mechanism, and also, in the situation of unrelieved frustration, as an organ substitute for the genital. In such a fusion,

[98] [Liebste! Ich habe Sie doch ganz allein lieb, das spür ich an der Wirthschafft mit den übrigen Frauen.

Eifersüchtig auf mich sind Sie nicht, sonst wollt ich Ihnen ein Mittel sagen. das Futteral zum Souvenir hab ich nicht, aber Ihr Halstuch hab ich um.]

[99] See above, p. 490; see also the letter of December 12, 1780, about the preference for bean soup, above, p. 486.

mouth–genital, the crucial point is the extent to which the genital becomes the executor of the mouth or to which it preserves its independence and only secondarily uses the mouth for its own purposes.

Be this as it may, in Rome we find Goethe in full possession of his genital function. The evidence does not permit the conclusion that the full orgastic psychic experience was restored—and perhaps it never was restored—but the physiological functioning of the genital mechanism was no longer impaired, that is to say, sexual excitement could be borne without immediate discharge; forepleasure did not activate the ejaculation, and the fear of castration abated so much that Goethe was capable of exposing himself to the risks unavoidably involved in intercourse, particularly outside of marriage.

Recovery

It would, of course, be of the greatest interest to know what factors brought about the successful cure of Goethe's sexual defect. On the basis of the evidence that has been presented bearing on a father-identification, one may be tempted to regard the recovery as spontaneous: now that he had reached the age at which his father married, he no longer felt "unworthy," and feelings of guilt, envy, castration fears, that formerly prevented him from engaging in intercourse, subsided. Spontaneous recoveries from sexual defects do, of course, occur, but rarely at so late an age. Particularly in view of the extent to which every event in Goethe's life seems to fall into a pattern of psychological meaningfulness, it would be a grave mistake to assume that some combination of accidental (non-meaningful) factors—which after all is covered by the loose term "spontaneous"—was at work when an event of such great importance as this took place in Goethe's life. At thirty-nine or forty a man's sexual habits are usually set and the spontaneous disappearance of a symptom of the kind I have supposed to have been present in Goethe would be most unusual. To be sure, it might be argued that Goethe could not be called really impotent even if my hypothesis of ejaculation while kissing is correct. It is possible that Goethe used this device for sexual relief because he did not desire to indulge in intercourse, whatever the reasons for his disinclination may have been. But—so the argument might continue—if he had tried intercourse his sexual organs might have functioned adequately. Thus the discussion would shift exclusively to the reasons for Goethe's abstaining from intercourse, and half the problem would be removed at one stroke. The Friederike episode, however, strongly suggests a humiliating experience, and it is not probable that a young man of Goethe's temper, curiosity, and inquisitiveness seriously intended never to have sexual intercourse. Furthermore, if a man up to the age of thirty-nine never has intercourse with a woman although he has ample opportunity to do so, and although he is not prevented by adherence to a rigorous religious or moral system, he may be considered clinically impotent.

What then were the factors responsible for Goethe's recovery? Aside from the biological factor of age, which decreased the sexual impetuosity of early manhood and favored mastery over immediate discharge,[100] I believe that his relationship to Charlotte von Stein had had a therapeutic effect upon him, as I have intimated before. His ego had acquired the capacity to bear excitement without dissipating it in immediate discharge, and—as I believe—this had been effected by certain features of his experience with her. Of course, the factors that are primarily referable to Charlotte von Stein cannot be neatly separated from Goethe's own genius and propensity towards recovery. The artificial nature of the following analysis is readily conceded, yet this artificiality does not disprove its possible correctness. Goethe's encounter with Charlotte von Stein was an event out of which a new Goethe arose. The totality of that experience is undeniable, and the factors to be sifted may have been essential or unessential, but they were at work.

In inquiring into what tools Charlotte von Stein had at her disposal one may think first of interpretations, which play such a paramount and almost exclusive role in psychoanalytic therapy. Interpretation in that sense she could not supply, but a passage in one of the many letters shows that in at least one instance she made a statement that can be likened to a psychoanalytic interpretation. On March 19, 1776, that is to say, pretty early in the relationship, Goethe wrote a letter to her (from which I quoted earlier, p. 774), apparently late at night and in one of those wild moods which, though not quite as intense as during the years of puberty, were somewhat reminiscent of them:

> I have to tell you still a word, dear lady. I became sick tonight and that in a rabid way; pulled myself together again. Still have to stay here, however. Took flight to Wieland because I should have been quite alone at home. Wanted to [go to see] you today. Hufeland [the court physician] forbids me to go out. Good-bye. Only one line from your hand.[101]

---

[100] An additional auxiliary element in the technique by which Goethe may have been able to maintain potency will be discussed in Appendix O.

[101] [Ich muss Ihnen noch ein Wort sagen liebe Frau. ich bin heute Nacht kranck worden und zwar toll, habe mich wieder zusammen genommen. Muss aber noch hier bleiben. bin zu Wielanden geflüchtet weil ich ganz allein zu Hause wär. Wollte heut zu Ihnen. Hufeland verbietet mir auszugehn. Ade. Nur eine Zeile von Ihrer Hand.]

The beginning of next day's letter was as follows:

> You were mistaken, angel. Of all things on earth that could be harmful and lethal to me, pique is the last. Of course, material for it is never wanting, only I do not work it up. How are you, best lady? Today I would already be far from you except for this accident, and this is also pleasing to me at this moment because I am still close to you—. Never mind; since for once I have to have the weakness for women I would rather have it for you than for another. Adieu, angel.[102]

The background of these letters is the following. Goethe was to have traveled to Leipzig, and had to postpone the trip for a few days because of his sickness. Charlotte von Stein evidently expressed, in answering the first letter, the opinion that his sickness was caused by pique. Goethe rejected this "interpretation" and tried to disprove it by claiming that he did not work up pique even when occasion offered. The rest of the letter might seem to prove his point since it suggests that he wanted to postpone his departure in order still to be near the beloved woman. However, he had the day before written an urgent letter to Johanna Fahlmer regarding his financial situation, which had become most pressing. He pleaded with her not to tell anybody of his impending trip to Leipzig. Perhaps he feared the anger of his father, who might have interpreted this trip as a new waste of money and effort. Thus the impending trip was charged with a feeling of guilt. Also it was the first time that he would be returning to the city where he had received such consequential impressions during his student years and he may have been afraid of the depth of emotions to which he would be exposed.[103]

Tentatively we may say that Charlotte von Stein's interpretation, namely, her connecting his sickness with pique, was probably correct, particularly in view of Goethe's prompt denial.[104] Since her letter is not preserved we do not know whether her interpretation fulfilled the require-

---

[102] [Sie irrten sich Engel. Unter allem was mir auf Erden schädlich und tödlich seyn könnte ist Ärgerniss das lezte. An Stoff dazu fehlts freylich niemals, nur verarbeit ich ihn nicht. Wie befinden Sie Sich beste Frau, heute wär ich schon weit von Ihnen ohne den Zufall, und der ist mir auch lieb in dem Augenblick weil ich Ihnen noch nah bin—Lassen Sie's gut seyn, weil ich doch nun einmal die Schwachheit für die Weiber haben muss, will ich sie lieber für Sie haben als für eine andre. Adieu Engel.]

[103] The letter of March 25, 1776 (quoted above on p. 506 f.) to Charlotte von Stein written on his way to Leipzig is actually one of the most moving he ever wrote and betrays that he was exposed to a feeling that came from the very depth of his heart.

[104] The difference between "clarification" and "interpretation" has been clearly and precisely set forth by Edward Bibring (31, pp. 754–59). Did Charlotte von Stein's "interpretations" ever transcend the level of clarifications? I do not know, but am inclined to assume that at times they did, without, however, ever reaching the depth and precision that are required of correct, psychoanalytic interpretations.

ments of a psychoanalytic interpretation. Probably it did not. But nevertheless it is historically important to have evidence that instances comparable to psychoanalytic interpretations occurred at all, even if these interpretations were superficial ones, such as are currently given by so-called dynamic psychiatrists. It is one of the most surprising facts about man's mental functioning that even a mediocre observer must know more about a subject than the subject can know about himself, even if we assume the subject to be an astute observer of self. Mannerisms, speech habits, gestures, gait, facial expressions, must remain to a large degree unnoticed by the subject but come quickly to the attention of the subject's fellow men. This of course does not mean to say that these fellow men would be able to verbalize all their preconscious or unconscious observations. The impressions we receive from one another usually remain below the conscious level. It can be safely said that we know far more about one another than we know that we do. If we really relied only on our conscious knowledge of others we probably could not be very active socially. Unwittingly we use a wealth of impressions and unconscious experiences to steer our way through the complicated maze of social contexts.

Merely by her superior position as an observer Charlotte von Stein would have been in a position to convey to Goethe a wealth of data about himself that was unknown to him. In her case we may suppose that the knowledge she accumulated about Goethe did not rest primarily in the preconscious or unconscious, since she was geared to observation and consciously wanted to grasp as much as possible of the enigmatic personality. Thus, even if she conveyed no more to him than that which one's fellow man can commonly observe in his neighbor, but which is not known to the person himself, this would have made her an indispensable source of self-enlightenment to Goethe. This is attested to by a letter he wrote her from Naples on May 25, 1787, after her initial anger and vituperation over his having left her in ignorance about his journey to Italy had calmed down, but at a time when her communications still expressed sadness over his disloyalty and lack of consideration:

> Everything that gives me testimony of your love is infinitely valuable to me, and so are now, since you are composed again, your sad little notes. May I bring you only happiness in the future. You have said golden things to me about myself and about my most intimate circumstances; I listen all silent to the whisper of my guardian spirit.[105]

[105] [Alles was mir ein Zeugniss deiner Liebe giebt, ist mir unendlich werth, auch sind es mir jetzt, da du wieder gefasst bist, deine traurigen Zettelchen. Möge ich dir künftig nur Freude bringen. Du hast mir goldne Sachen über mich selbst und über meine nächsten Verhältnisse gesagt, ich horche ganz still auf das Lispeln meines Schutzgeistes.]

Her letters to him Charlotte von Stein destroyed, and of course there is no record of their years of conversation, so we have no idea what these golden things may have been, and can only guess how many, if any, would have to be considered equivalents of—or outright—psychoanalytic interpretations. The one example I have quoted indicates that her remarks probably went beyond the low level of common-sense judgments. Be this as it may, she got Goethe to the point of listening. Usually we object to our fellow men's telling us that which has remained unobserved by ourselves, but Charlotte von Stein held Goethe in a "transference" that prevented him from breaking off the relationship when she had to call his attention to something that was embarrassing or that hurt the vanity and pride of a man as excessively sensitive as he was.

Whatever the role of interpretations may have been in this relationship, I should not surmise that it was the most important factor in promoting his recovery from the sexual disturbance I have posited. I should think that the repeated exposure to sexual excitement without providing a discharge made the ego acquire the capacity to bear tension. Unfortunately, there is not the slightest indication regarding Goethe's history as to masturbation, aside from the one reference in the *Triumph der Empfindsamkeit*, where he took a facetious but rather tolerant attitude. But I should surmise that during most of these years of his association with Charlotte von Stein he kept himself completely free of voluntary sexual gratification and that it was this particular circumstance that made him feel so very grateful for what she had done for him. For he must have felt himself incapable of bearing the extreme deprivation of complete abstinence without Charlotte von Stein's help and influence.[106] His assurances of gratitude and expressions of felicity about his state are very numerous and it is therefore most astounding to read in his letter to her of June 8, 1787, from Rome:

> I am given back again to myself and only all the more yours. Rather than the life of the last years I should have wished death for myself, and even at [this] distance I am more to you than I was to you formerly.[107]

[106] But how far did Goethe's abstinence go? Did it also preclude nocturnal emissions and spermatorrhea? About the former I shall have something to say in Appendix P; about the latter no fruitful speculation suggests itself.

[107] [Ich bin mir selbst wiedergegeben und nur umsomehr dein. Wie das Leben der letzten Jahre wollt ich mir eher den Todt gewünscht haben und selbst in der Entfernung bin ich dir mehr als ich dir damals war.]

This was written upon his return from Sicily and we know the second Roman sojourn was the time destined for the consummation of the sexual act.

Evidently Goethe had changed his outlook upon the last decade completely. In the same letter he claimed to have discovered a new viewpoint:

> I have come to know happy people, who are so only because they are *whole;* the least also, when he is whole, can be happy and perfect in his own way; this too I will and must achieve now, and I can—at least I know where it lies and how it stands; I have come inexpressibly to know myself on this journey.[108] [Goethe's italics]

That which was new was the emphasis on the state of being whole (*ganz*). This was the new yardstick of perfection, and it did not depend on mastery, work, or devotion, for the humblest or least of men could achieve it. Could it be, perhaps, that only the humble or low achieve it? Yes, he was attacking the whole climate and ideology of the last decade when he wrote, also in the same letter—to be sure, in a different context, namely in reference to Catholic Church ceremonies—the following:

> Also a harmful truth is useful, because it can be detrimental only for a moment and then leads to other truths that are always useful and must become very useful, and conversely a useful error is harmful because it can be so [useful] only momentarily and induces other errors that become always more harmful.[109]

Such a statement, though perhaps applicable to pompous church rituals, may have been aimed also at Charlotte von Stein's puritanic teachings, which asserted social usefulness as a person's uppermost duty.

Goethe had already introduced into his correspondence the new viewpoint of the undivided existence during his first stay in Rome, but at that time he was not yet quite sure that he would come out of the new venture unscathed. When he received letters from Charlotte von Stein that were, apparently, reproachful, he answered on January 20, 1787:

> Your letter of January 1 has come to me and has brought me joy and pain. I cannot say anything further about it than: I have only *one* existence; this I have this time staked *wholly,* and am still staking it. If I do get out of it physically and mentally, if my nature, my mind, my good luck, conquer

---

[108] [Übrigens habe ich glückliche Menschen kennen lernen, die es nur sind weil sie *ganz* sind, auch der Geringste wenn er ganz ist kann glücklich und in seiner Art vollkommen seyn, das will und muss ich nun auch erlangen, und ich kanns, wenigstens weiss ich wo es liegt und wie es steht, ich habe mich auf dieser Reise unsäglich kennen lernen.]

[109] [. . . auch eine schädliche Wahrheit ist nützlich, weil sie nur Augenblicke schädlich seyn kann und alsdann zu andern Wahrheiten führt, die immer nützlich und sehr nützlich werden müssen und umgekehrt ist ein nützlicher Irrthum schädlich, weil er es nur augenblicklich seyn kann und in andre Irrthümer verleitet die immer schädlicher werden.]

the crisis, I shall make up to you a thousandfold what is to be made up. If I perish, then I perish; I was no use any more anyhow.[110] [Goethe's italics]

What was it that made him write about his great happiness of a few months before as if of death? Had he not been undivided before? And if he was divided, why had it not disturbed him before? Had Goethe been lying during those earlier years when he spoke of his existence in exalted terms? The answer is that that which had provided bliss in the pre-Italian years had been the feeling of living up to his highest ethical demand through sexual abstinence. Rightly he had felt that his achieving this state of abstinence had been made possible by his relationship to Charlotte von Stein, that she was the first woman whose influence had had this effect upon him, and therefore he loved her and thought himself incomparably happy with her. Yet in the June of 1787, a few months before taking up sex relations and at a time when he felt potent, the retrospective glance cast at the years of abstinence saw only the pain of frustration. Abstinence now had become an unnecessary ballast, feared and hated by Goethe, whereas it had been in previous years the mainstay of his existence, a state which he could not have borne unsupported and unprotected by his feelings for an idealized love-object. Goethe later destroyed most of the letters he wrote to Charlotte von Stein from Naples and Sicily. He preserved one intentionally and afterwards sent it to his most beloved friend Zelter, who had put so many of his poems to music, with the following words (February 16, 1818):

Since I receive so much loveliness from your own hand and as against that return so little, therefore I am sending you an ancient page, which I was unable to burn when I consigned to the fire all papers referring to Naples and Sicily. It is such a nice word upon the turning point of the whole adventure and casts a glimmer of light backwards and forwards. I wish it to be yours! Preserve it piously. How nice one really is when we are young! And so on and eternally.[111]

[110] [Dein Brief vom 1. Jan. ist mir gekommen und hat mir Freude und Schmertzen gebracht. Dazu kann ich nichts weiter sagen als: ich habe nur *Eine* Existenz, diese hab ich diesmal *ganz* gespielt und spiele sie noch. Komm ich leiblich und geistlich davon, überwältigt meine Natur, mein Geist, mein Glück, diese Krise, so ersetz ich dir tausendfältig was zu ersetzen ist.— Komm ich um, so komm ich um, ich war ohne dies zu nichts mehr nütze.]

[111] [Da ich so manches Liebe von deiner eignen Hand empfange und dagegen wenig erwidere, so sende ich dir ein uralt Blättchen, das ich nicht verbrennen konnte, als ich alle Papiere, auf Neapel und Sicilien bezüglich, dem Feuer widmete. Es ist ein so hübsches Wort auf dem Wendepunct des ganzen Abentheuers, und giebt einen Dämmerschein rückwärts und forwärts. Ich gönne es dir! Bewahre es fromm. Was man doch artig ist wenn wir jung sind! und sofort und ewig.]

This was Goethe's reaction at the age of sixty-nine to the letter he had written thirty-one years previously (April 18, 1787):

My dear, still a word of farewell from Palermo. I can only repeat to you that I am well and cheerful and that now my journey is taking shape. In Naples it would have ended too blunt. From my pages you see only a few things in detail; about the whole, about what is innermost in me and the happy consequences that I feel, I cannot and do not want to say anything. This is an indescribably beautiful country, although I am acquainted with only a small part of the coast. How much joy do I obtain every day from my little knowledge of natural things, and how much more would I have to know for my joy to become perfect. I am succeeding happily in what I am preparing for [all of?] you! I have wept tears of joy already that I shall give [all of?] you joy.[112] Farewell, most beloved, my heart is with you, and now that the great distance, the absence, has, so to speak, cleansed away that which during this last time had been stagnant between us, so the beautiful flame of love, of fidelity, of remembrance, burns and shines forth again joyfully in my heart. Regards to the Herders and everybody. And think of me.[113]

I must admit that if Goethe had not written to Zelter that this letter was a commentary upon "the turning point of the whole adventure" its psychological importance would have escaped me. The real turning point was, of course, Goethe's departure to Italy, but at that time Goethe apparently was not cognizant at all of its consequences, improbable as this may sound. On the one hand we must assume that Goethe had preserved sufficient naiveté to believe that Charlotte von Stein would be as

[112] It is difficult to decide which alternative is correct of the two possible meanings the German word *Euch* may have here. Does it refer to Charlotte von Stein plus her son and other friends, as I have indicated by translating it as "all of you," or is it a more formal mode of address to her alone? If the latter is the case it has far-reaching psychological implications.

[113] [Meine Liebe noch ein Wort des Abschieds aus Palermo. Ich kann dir nur wiederhohlen dass ich wohl und vergnügt bin und dass nun meine Reise eine Gestalt nimmt. In Neapel hätte sie zu stumpf aufgehört. Aus meinen Blättern siehst du nur einiges im Detail, vom Ganzen, von meinem Innersten und den glücklichen Folgen die ich fühle kann und mag ich nichts sagen. Dies ist ein unsäglich schönes Land, ob ich gleich nur ein Stückchen Küste davon kenne. Wie viel Freude macht mir mit jedem Tage mein bischen Wissen der natürlichen Dinge und wie viel mehr müsste ich wissen wenn meine Freude vollkommen seyn sollte. Was ich Euch bereite, geräth mir glücklich, ich habe schon Freudenthränen vergossen dass ich Euch Freude machen werde. Leb wohl Geliebteste mein Herz ist bey dir und jetzt da die Weite Ferne, die Abwesenheit alles gleichsam weggeläutert hat was die letzte Zeit über zwischen uns stockte so brennt und leuchtet die schöne Flamme der Liebe der Treue, des Andenckens wieder fröhlich in meinem Herzen. Grüse Herders und alle. und gedencke mein.]

happy about his journey as he was. He had elevated her to such a superior position that he had completely lost the feeling for her as a frail human being, or he disregarded it in order to be able to go ahead without having to fear the unavoidable consequences. But now when he wrote this letter he knew that something was going to change, for the turning point had come, and still he anticipated that the beloved woman would also accept this new turn. In Sicily, it seems, it dawned on him what the true cause of his unhappiness was and what had militated against full happiness in the presence of the beloved woman. This would also agree well with his addressing her twice with *Euch* instead of with *Dir*. It was here, apparently, that he made the decision to separate the physical aspect of love from her, and this may even have appeared to him as a sacrifice. Now he would be able to be always pleasant and cheerful in her presence and to serve her without inner resentment. Thus we understand how the old Goethe shook his head and thought that he was awfully cute when young (however, he was not quite so young in Sicily as the old man wanted it to seem). Thus, he must around that time have come to a new resolution. This was apparently the decision to divide his love life between a pure, unsexual love for Charlotte von Stein and a sexual, instinctual relationship to another woman. His reference to the beautiful flame of love, fidelity, and remembrance suggests this. Up to then he had wanted to find both in Charlotte von Stein and this had held him in conflict. The envisioned division of his love-life was to establish conflict-free harmony.

We find, then, the following phases in Goethe's relationship to Charlotte von Stein. At the beginning he approached her as he would have dealt at that time with any other woman whom he liked, in his wild and slightly fresh way. She responded quite negatively to his comparative lack of manners and even expressed pity.[114] After a brief attempt at breaking away he again turned towards her, although she kept him at a distance and over and over again imposed prohibitions upon him. Then came the period when she permitted the *Du* and left no doubt in his mind that he was the most important person in her life, even surrendered her favorite child to him, but still never relented in her ethical and moral demands. More and more she became the exclusive object of his affection, admiration, and also of his sexual desires. Then, in Sicily, he determined to withdraw the sexual part of his love from her and thought he could continue forever with what remained, that is to say, a sublimated, tender,

---

[114] See *Rino,* a skit written by Charlotte von Stein in 1776 (244, *1:*471–74) in which Gertrude (Charlotte) says of Goethe: "He is not at all master over himself; the poor man, I pity him."

affectionate relationship based on respect, admiration and friendship, a platonic relationship that would remain undisturbed by sexual wishes, for these would be gratified in the relationship to some other woman. Since he did not want to recognize that Charlotte von Stein was not really the person he thought her to be—and in order to endure abstinence he had had to make himself believe that she was a woman above and beyond sexual wishes—he could also be firmly convinced in Sicily that she would be above jealousy. The unconscious revenge he was in the process of taking I do not mean to deny, but apparently this was a highly repressed process if it was present at all. He still apparently adhered to the conscious conviction that a life without closeness to Charlotte von Stein was impossible.[115]

After this digression we must return to our main question, namely, what factors in Goethe's relationship to Charlotte von Stein were responsible for his recovery from his sexual defect. Only two have been mentioned: interpretation, and the repeated exposure to tension, particularly sexual tension, without concomitant discharge. Regarding the variety of clinical situations in which sexual arousal without subsequent discharge are encountered I wish to mention only two. There are women who derive sadistic pleasure from exciting a man sexually and denying him gratification, and there are patients who try to arouse themselves for the purpose of denying themselves gratification, a process they masochistically enjoy. This takes on at times the following shape: a patient may masturbate, suddenly stop short of ejaculation and repeat the whole procedure an indefinite number of times. This self-teasing is always a sign of pregenital fixations. Probably a pregenital component such as masochism was at work in Goethe's relationship to Charlotte von Stein. Instances of masochism were discussed earlier. But here I am not thinking of those conspicuously masochistic episodes but rather of the probability that the incessant sexual

---

[115] As a matter of fact the division of his love-life that he envisioned in Sicily persisted for Goethe. After his return he had his "bed sweetheart" (*Bettschatz*), Christiane, and also fell in love sporadically with other women. If Goethe really had had a sexual relationship with Charlotte von Stein, his relationship with Christiane would have been a regression. Charlotte von Stein would have been his peer as a human being, an adequate partner in terms of personality traits, a cultivated, intelligent woman with impeccable manners, far above those of Christiane. His quick infatuation with the latter after his return from Italy would suggest—still supposing that a sexual relationship with Charlotte von Stein existed—that a higher development that had been attained before his Italian journey had been undone by his stay in the South and replaced with an inferior object-choice. There is no reason to assume that Goethe should have suffered a regression at a time when he was undergoing such a vast thrust forward in all other respects. The letter to Charlotte from Sicily would make no sense at all if a sexual relationship between the two were assumed.

frustration that was imposed upon Goethe must presuppose at least a minimum of masochistic gratification. It is important to note that Goethe did not use the frustration imposed upon him by the love-object for purposes of self-pity or accusations against the frustrating person, as is commonly the case clinically with patients suffering from masochism. Goethe reached under this regimen a high degree of self-discipline and only accused Charlotte von Stein vehemently later, when frustration by her had been replaced with gratification by Christiane. Was Charlotte von Stein being sadistic when she denied Goethe sexual gratification? To answer this question we must come back to her personality again. She undoubtedly showed frequent signs of conversion hysteria. She was sexually frigid, probably on a hysterical basis (see above, pp. 143–44, for her inability to love instinctively). Her attitude towards her emotions can be seen from the following statement she made in later years after her break with Goethe: "When I am able to make myself quite [like] a statue then I feel best; I must not permit myself either joy or pain."[116] Here the compulsive-schizoid factor comes to the fore. One does indeed encounter in such women strong sadistic impulses, which are expressed in their hysterical as well as compulsive symptomatology. Her great idealism and the idealistic demand she put upon those about her were partly the result of the inherent sadism. The seductiveness of which Goethe occasionally complained was the expression of a strong instinctual urge that was warded off by the frigidity. When Goethe thought that an idealistic relationship with her would be compatible with a simultaneously entertained sensual-sexual one with another woman, he did not want to recognize that Charlotte von Stein's idealism was built upon frigidity and sexual aversion, which always betray absence of true mastery over the sexual impulse. Her occasional seductiveness—apparently interpreted by Goethe as signs of an innocent naiveté—aimed at the reassurance that he was still sexually in love with her. The unconscious aim of her overt insistence upon purity and asexuality was protection against a direct sexual involvement which she unconsciously desired; the unconscious aim of her seductiveness was the assurance that her femininity had a thrilling effect upon the beloved partner. It was probably this inherent contradiction that kept their relationship going for such a long time. Unconsciously Goethe must have felt the live sexual desires present in her. Yet at the same time he was certain that she would never give way to the impetuousness of his passions. It is my impression that at the slightest indication that she would do so, Goethe's

[116] [Wenn ich mich recht zur Statue machen kann, ist mir am wohlsten; ich darf mir weder Freude noch Leid erlauben.] (534, p. 145)

conflict would have broken out forcibly and he would have exposed his sexual deficiency. The history of his sexual life shows pretty impressively that even after his recovery, as sigualized in his experience with Faustina, it was only a woman inferior to him in social status, education, and manners that he ever loved with overt sexuality. However much sexual passion may have been present in his relations to other women, it never led to the genital union. If Charlotte von Stein's ethical ideology had been fully integrated by her, and the sexual desire for Goethe had been not just rendered unconscious but truly abolished, Goethe's relationship with her would probably have taken a turn similar to that which he had with Susanna von Klettenberg, whose influence, though strong during a short period, left no such permanent traces upon him as did Charlotte von Stein's.

However, Charlotte von Stein defies simple classification. She has been written about in all kinds of ways. Incidents that permit describing her as a sadistic character are plentiful. Her lack of motherliness towards Ernst has been mentioned. Her husband was seriously handicapped in later years and dependent on her nursing care, which she dutifully gave him. But once when she heard a thumping noise on the staircase behind her, well knowing her husband had fallen, she did not even turn around but pointed backwards and told the butler: "Just pick him up" [Heb er mal auf] (49, p. 368).

Of which Charlotte von Stein should we then think? Of the woman with the impeccable behavior; the sophisticated woman who even in old age studied books of science and immersed herself undaunted in the knowledge of her times? Or the stern, domineering one? Here the only point in question is to determine what in her was relevant for the relationship to Goethe and why it became relevant, and what effect it had on him. Therefore, when I speak of the sadistic root of some of Charlotte von Stein's attitudes towards Goethe, this needs some qualification. The sadism was in the service of an idealistic ideology, and the desire for erotic-sexual gratification belonged wholly to the unconscious. Exhausted by seven pregnancies, disgusted with her role as a woman, Charlotte von Stein entertained no hope or desire for a love adventure when Goethe appeared at the court in Weimar. But she grasped immediately that there was a task for her to do, a role that she could fulfill in the poet's life. That the impetus to carry out this task was supplied by a strong unconscious desire or impulse for a sexual union, though it made her very unhappy later, was fortunate for Goethe. It increased her effort and interest and made her averse to compromise. It also kept Goethe, probably pretty continuously, in tension, and thus enforced a change in his ego which at last made him able to bear sexual tension. Although these processes have a remote similarity to teasing and self-teasing—processes that drain and weaken the ego and wear down the ego's capacity to bear tension—they were essentially different from these since they were carried out in the service of the superego. In the course of incessant repetition, they provided the ego with that stamina which is indispensable in male human sexuality.

Furthermore—as Goethe recognized early in the relationship—the image of Charlotte von Stein absorbed all the various images that had up to then contributed to his conception of "woman," that is to say, mainly the images of his mother and sister. This unification of objects cannot be assessed too highly. Although Goethe fought against a full transference and probably was afraid of giving up all objects in favor of the one, he could not resist or ward off this process, which took place in his unconscious. He became incapable of writing to his sister and limited the relationship to his mother to the bare minimum.[117] He repeatedly felt tempted to see her again but stayed away and sent Fritz, whom he wanted to adopt, instead. It is difficult to determine when Goethe made a sister transference and when a mother transference. Others have noticed the similarity between Charlotte von Stein and Cornelia, but clinical experience shows that at the core of the sibling relationship there is often an important attitude towards one of the parents. How strongly and how long the sister transference persisted can be seen from a letter from Rome, after Charlotte von Stein had reproached him for having left her ignorant for so long about his whereabouts (January 17, 1787): "Since the death of my sister nothing has grieved me so much as the pain I have caused you by my departure and silence."[118] This is one of his few direct references to his sister's death and it is significant that it is made in a situation in which he had hurt Charlotte von Stein, as if he meant to say: "I will destroy you as I did my sister and you will desert me out of revenge as my sister did."

Charlotte von Stein and Goethe's mother were to a certain extent antipodes, but Charlotte's function as ethical and moral authority provided the implication of the forbidding and guiding mother—and also of the father, as I have tried repeatedly to demonstrate. Yet it should be recalled that Cornelia had a greater bearing on the poet's early creations than his mother. Goethe's first great play was written for Cornelia's sake. Cornelia,

[117] Goethe's inhibitions in his relationship to his mother and sister were not exclusively based on the transference factor that I am stressing in this context.

[118] [Seit dem Todte meiner Schwester hat mich nichts so betrübt, als die Schmerzen die ich dir durch mein Scheiden und Schweigen verursacht.]

however, seems not to have had her influence by means of authority but rather by pleading and affectionate urging. Goethe labored under the conscious belief that only between sisters could a pure relationship exist; witness a conversation with Eckermann of March 28, 1827. They were discussing Sophocles' belief that only a sister could love a brother in a pure way without sexual involvement. Goethe replied: "I should think that the love of a sister for a sister would be still purer and more sexless."[119] Whether Goethe would have thought this valid also for brothers I do not know. I think the underlying idea was partly that women cannot among themselves get very far in their sexual gratifications anyway, since they do not have a penis at their disposal—an idea frequently present in the male phallic phase. Yet I can well imagine that the task of sublimation was easier for Goethe in a homosexual transference than in a heterosexual one. For this reason too and not only because of Charlotte von Stein's relative severity, it is probable that she also at times meant a homosexual object to Goethe.

Thus we observe that all object-related forces in Goethe inclined toward the one love-object and became absorbed into the relationship to her. The unification of a series of similar and diverse objects into one impresses me as a process exceedingly important for Goethe's recovery. The dispersal of libido as a means of avoiding a high level of tension was thus successfully counteracted. This tendency towards dispersal was strikingly seen—as I wish to remind the reader—when Goethe quickly conjured up an imaginary letter relationship to the Countess von Stolberg when he fell in love with Lili (see above, p. 119). When dispersal was not possible in a relationship, flight became necessary. In other words, in the relationship with Charlotte von Stein an organizational process (see 277, p. 386) probably took place within the representations of the object world, and the ego learned to accept the object in its totality and integrity.

In genital disturbances of the kind I have assumed were present in Goethe, one frequently finds a pathological representation of the object in the unconscious, inasmuch as it is pictured as suffering from an essential defect; the absence of a penis has the meaning of a mutilation and consequently the female is viewed as vulnerable, frail, and liable to be injured. Furthermore, this imagery of the woman justifiably complaining about her injury finds its counterpart simultaneously in an imagery of the woman's cruelly seeking revenge for the grave injustice she has suffered. Thus the unconscious object-representation contains per se features that

---

[119] [Ich dächte, dass die Liebe von Schwester zur Schwester noch reiner und geschlechtsloser wäre!] (119, p. 479)

arouse fears in the male in two respects. He unconsciously dreads lest he cause still greater injury to the female, and he fears lest he suffer harm from her. The apparent contradictoriness of these two groups of images does not preclude their simultaneous existence in the unconscious and their double effect as sources of anxiety. The close association of these two sources in Goethe can be demonstrated in an example to which I have referred previously. The defectiveness of the object was emphasized in the Friederike episode. In conjunction with the same object its cruelty also came to the fore. In the creation of Weislingen, the weak-willed villain in *Götz von Berlichingen,* who jilts Maria, an innocent girl, and is later poisoned by his wife, Adelheid, Goethe wanted to do penance for his selfishness towards Friederike. Yet in the play Weislingen is the victim of Adelheid, a ruthless, ambitious, and vicious woman. In this association between Maria (Friederike), Weislingen, and Adelheid, the triad of defective object, castration, and cruel object is impressively illustrated. For a person like Goethe the impairment of the object was so intolerable that it probably led to a fear of even the sight of the castrated woman.[120]

What were now the specific ways in which the particular anxieties were overcome by Goethe before he left for Italy? He had gradually substituted in his relationship to Charlotte von Stein benevolent action for anxiety. It was favorable for Goethe's recovery that she was of that type that suffers from its femininity. The reader may recall my previous report regarding Charlote von Stein's complaints about the injustice of having to bear children and her strong feeling that women were discriminated against by nature (see p. 144). Goethe's intimacy had, thus, to be with a woman who suffered precisely from that which aroused his fears of women. But he learned to undo the harm. Under his very eyes the almost destroyed woman found a new purpose in her existence and the zest for life reappeared. Unending were the services he devoted to her: her new quarters, food, the care of her children, her health, etc. Here too he could rid himself of feelings of guilt regarding his mother, sister, and father. The castrated woman was brought to life again and he experienced actively that childbirth was not the final downfall of the fair sex. Consequently, one layer of his relationship to Charlotte von Stein consisted of a consistent and continuous chain of beneficent actions which probably had its effect on the unconscious object-representation. The reality experience of having made a despairing woman turn again in friendship towards the world corrected a deficient imagery by depriving it, at least to some extent, of its

---

[120] See 449, p. 100 and *passim*. For the way this conflict was overcome in his relationship to Christiane see Appendix Q.

fear-arousing quality. Clinically one can observe that patients suffering from sensitivity as high-pitched as Goethe's experience unavoidable frustrations, even of minor degree, as a serious threat, such as castration. The intensity of such experiences can be noted in Goethe's use of the following conceit in his letter to Charlotte von Stein of September 13, 1778, when he complains about vexations:

> Often I shake my head and harden myself again and finally I feel like that piglet from which the Frenchman had devoured the crisp roasted skin and sent it again into the kitchen in order to have a second skin roasted on.[121]

Here Goethe clearly states how he experienced reality's impositions. I see in a certain type of event repeatedly recurring in their relationship a specific antidote against this type of anxiety. As we have seen, Charlotte von Stein often withdrew from Goethe, left for Kochberg or made herself otherwise inaccessible. This loss of the object—temporary in reality but experienced as forever by the unconscious—with all the pangs and fears in its wake, was regularly followed by the object's reappearance. The ego thus experienced repeatedly that no harm to itself was connected with the desertion by the object; further, that the disappearance of the object was not an act of aggression, and—most important—that the object returned unimpaired. Thus in a situation of supreme deprivation the ego received maximum reassurance regarding its own integrity and that of a beloved object. We may say that Goethe went innumerable times through a process reminiscent or symbolic of castration and emerged unharmed, and that this repetition apparently reduced his castration fears immensely.

Charlotte von Stein, by the fact that she represented all the past love-objects (including those of the infantile period) acquired a unique and exclusive position comparable to that of the analyst. This, however, she could not use as the analyst does. The patient, because of the transference tie, is capable of bearing the displeasure aroused by the analyst's interpretations, and thus the analyst can gradually bore his way to the earliest conflicts. This use of the transference was not accessible to Charlotte von Stein. But all in all one can say that Charlotte von Stein provided those situational factors that were correlated to Goethe's defect in a specific way, so that his being frequently exposed to them sealed off infantile sources of anxiety and strengthened his ego, lifting it to a higher level of object-relation. The specificity of correlation varied. In one instance there

---

[121] [Offt schüttl ich den Kopf und härte mich wieder, und endlich kom ich mir vor, wie ienes Ferckel dem der Franzos die knupperig gebratne Haut abgefressen hatte, und es wieder in die Küche schickte, um ihm die zweite anbraten zu lassen.]

was the repetition of the danger situation until the ego got accustomed to it and no longer regarded it as dangerous. In another, it was the influence brought upon the unconscious to prevent the dissipation of cathexis but to achieve its concentration upon one unified image. In still another it was the forcing of the ego to let tension increase to a maximum without letting it be reduced by habitual—possibly low-level—discharges.

And how did Goethe experience his relationship to Charlotte von Stein consciously? At one point (November 9, 1784) he called her his "dear leader of the soul" [liebe Seelenführerin[n]], an expression that would fit exactly the assumptions I have been making regarding their relationship.[122] Yet "leader of the soul" was only one aspect, and might have led to mere intellectualizations. The "leader role" was complemented by an equally strong emotional background. It was the synthesis of the two that made the relationship what it was. How well he understood the whole process was revealed in an undated letter, evidently written during the initial phase of their acquaintance, in which he projects the writing of a history of his life for Charlotte von Stein alone: "For it is more than *confession* when one also avows that for which one does not need *absolution*."[123] (Goethe's italics) Goethe was right. In confession, only material correlated to feelings of guilt is verbalized. In analysis, all limitations of communication are broken down and the stream of information must extend to the totality of life. Goethe wanted to embrace that totality in his communication with Charlotte von Stein. It was also to include the seemingly trivial. According to Goethe's own words, one cannot think of his relationship to Charlotte von Stein as simply a confessional revelation of the younger man to the older and more experienced woman. The confessional part was present, but it held a subordinate place. Only its extension to his whole existence made his communication what it was. On June 14, 1780, he wrote her: "You see I always tell of the *I*"[124] (Goethe's italics). And again he was right. Everything that happened in this relationship served primarily—if not always exclusively—an ego purpose, and this in a different sense from that which usually obtains in love relationships. There is always some selfishness at the bottom of love—to the despair of some moralists and all theologians—or else it would be self-destructive and no love. But in Goethe's love for Charlotte von Stein—if it ever was

---

[122] However, he added that he had learned this epithet from Hemsterhuis (cf. above, p. 970), who was close to Princess Gallitzin, and I compared their relationship with Goethe's to Charlotte von Stein. About the historical background of this type of relationship see 147.

[123] [Denn es ist mehr als *Beichte* wenn man auch das bekennt worüber man nicht *Absolution* bedarf.] (*Soph.* IV, 3:26)

[124] [Sie sehen ich erzähle immer vom *ich*.]

real love—there was an additional element of selfishness, namely, the purpose of recovery from a disease. To a certain extent one may claim that it was Goethe who used Charlotte von Stein for the selfish purpose of recovering from his psychopathology, as something that threatened his future. Freud has described processes arranged by the ego and endowed with the function of inducing a recovery. Freud thought that the anxiety that regularly or sporadically overwhelms the patient after a trauma in the course of a traumatic neurosis serves the purpose of reducing or even eliminating the effect of the trauma, although the patient complains about this anxiety as the foremost symptom. It is conceivable that the ego might go to much greater trouble in order to induce recovery from a chronic symptom. Yes, to a certain extent one may say that Charlotte von Stein was a puppet in the whole play, unconscious of the role Goethe's hypnotizing personality had forced upon her.

That Charlotte von Stein of course experienced this relationship in completely different terms does not require any additional comment.

Despite the respects in which this relationship was similar to or comparable with psychoanalysis—which I may have unduly stressed—it showed simultaneously a great dissimilarity. The psychoanalytic situation, as it has developed during the one hundred and fifty odd years since Charlotte von Stein suffered the heartbreaking desertion by Goethe, makes it possible for one individual to put himself entirely at the service of another, without the slightest demand for gratitude or personal obligation. There is perhaps no other situation in life in which an individual loses his freedom so completely as in the psychoanalytic, and surely in no other is he given back his freedom again so completely. One of Freud's greatest ethical achievements, perhaps, was that he gave the world an instrument wherewith to put an end to the despair over the situation which Lord Acton described so justly: "Power tends to corrupt; absolute power corrupts absolutely." Charlotte von Stein acted out of self-interest during the last phase of their relationship, and she was not able to move within the frame of reference that makes it easy for the analyst to escape the temptations set up by the patient's transference. There is no other institution but the psychoanalytic situation in which it is out of the question for the recipient of benefits to balance what he has received by any gift of his.

Yet there were very essential differences between psychoanalysis and Goethe's relationship to Charlotte von Stein quite beyond the sphere of the difference between her attitude and that of the psychoanalyst. What Charlotte von Stein did for Goethe, when compared with a modern psychoanalytic treatment, appears like an ox-drawn cart compared with a modern airplane. Her effect upon him did not, of course, lead to a cure, as this term is understood nowadays, but only to the clinical removal of Goethe's sexual defect, which could probably be achieved today by means of therapy lasting a few months. When Goethe left Charlotte von Stein he was fixated to the phallic level and still suffering from considerable psychopathology. To be sure, some of his childhood fears had disappeared. In his letter of January 4, 1787, to Fritz, however, he described the disgusting scenes connected with the public slaughter of pigs. I have mentioned before his phobic flight from the butcher stalls in his native city. Whether he lost that fear during his association with Charlotte von Stein is not known. After all, the spontaneous disappearance of childhood phobias is a general occurrence. Therefore it is not clear whether his conversations with Charlotte von Stein really penetrated to the childhood neurosis. However, in the early chapters of *Wilhelm Meister* crucial childhood events were outlined and it is conceivable that in his dealings with Charlotte von Stein some childhood amnesia was lifted. Whatever interpretations she may have given him, they cannot have had the preciseness and encompassing nature that analytic interpretations have. Moreover, a bona-fide analysis does not limit itself to the unearthing of childhood memories—as some "neo-Freudian" psychoanalysts seem to think—but requires a reconstruction of the unconscious processes underlying these childhood memories; that is to say, childhood memories must not only become conscious but must also be understood. It is not probable that Goethe penetrated to such depth under the effect of his relationship to Charlotte von Stein. Yet the fact that childhood memories which quite probably had vanished from consciousness were recovered is an outstanding fact. The synthesizing of these memories into a work of art, which was so necessary for him, may have had an effect equivalent to that of the workingthrough process in psychoanalytic treatment.

Chapter 5

General Remarks

Historical Deliberations

THE DANGER of suffering permanent harm in the course of the delicate surgery Goethe underwent was eminently great to Goethe the artist. It must not be forgotten that it was not only a matter of his recovery, but recovery without decrease of artistic potential, an unspeakably difficult undertaking in view of the intimate connection between psychopathology and artistic creativity in Goethe (and probably in all geniuses).[1] Here we are to take cognizance that as compared with what goes on in a modern psychoanalytic treatment, there was in Goethe's therapeutic relationship to Charlotte von Stein a lack of verbalization of certain contents and processes. If the reorganizational process that took place in Goethe during the pre-Italian Weimarian years did not have an untoward effect on his capacity for artistic creation, then we perhaps may suggest that this limitation of verbalization, which would seem to be a deficiency from the modern point of view, may have been an advantage from the point of view of Goethe's artistic potential. The psychoanalytic treatment of the genius is still an area of ignorance.

[1] Robert H. Jokl (318) claims that a correctly performed psychoanalysis can never endanger or impair individual artistic creativeness. However, a distinction must be made between talent and genius. Jokl refers in the clinical part of his paper only to talent. I have never had any sort of practical experience with any kind of genius and therefore can only utter an opinion derived from impressions based on the study of Goethe's life. This opinion is contradictory to Dr. Jokl's. I think sublimations are vulnerable, and in view of present-day ignorance regarding the psychology of genius we should be cautious and rather assume that too great familiarity with the repressed part of the personality might possibly impede the automatic process of artistic creation in the genius. If an analyst should venture upon the analysis of a genius I think he should be aware of this possibility.

After the lull in his creativity at Weimar, Goethe left for Italy with his creative potential geared to function at its maximum for the rest of his existence, during which he would create still more than he had before he met the woman. To be sure, I should say his artistic potential was inclining towards zero when he came to Weimar. He had produced the utmost values that could spring from the *Sturm und Drang*. If he had died at about that time we should consider him the greatest German poet, and add that his early passing away did not, however, cause very great harm to German literature since he had given his best and could not have produced new forms of art comparable to what he had given the world in *Werther* and his poetry.[2] No one could have divined, let alone known, that in this poet there still lay at that time the seed of two more entirely new styles that would rise to new heights and that Goethe's genius capacity encompassed more than just the scope of the *Sturm und Drang*. The increase of Goethe's artistic potential to the height that it reached at the time of his departure for Italy was caused by the many changes he underwent during his attachment to Charlotte von Stein. Briefly and in a simplified form these can be described as the change from relying predominantly on the primary processes in artistic production to invoking increasingly secondary ones. Since mastery was the keynote of the time in which Charlotte von Stein's influence was so overwhelming it is understandable that the secondary processes acquired a new power over Goethe's artistry. Whether such changes can be brought about in a genius by verbalization and insight, or whether they must be left to the accident and arbitrariness of unregulated life, is a moot question.

The other great service that Goethe owed Charlotte von Stein because of her having helped him attain his potency was the protection against a psychosis. I have the impression that the sexual relief he obtained from Christiane—little as he may have availed himself of it—sufficed to unburden his ego to the extent that it should not become overstrained. However, as we shall see later, in one corner of his gigantic work there lies the indisputable evidence of a benign partial psychosis, well-integrated and overlaid with broad embellishments of secondary elaborations which preserved him from a serious break with the world. This psychosis concerned only an area of his scientific work and did not militate against his artistic productions.

[2] One may easily react in this way to Mozart's early death, and Goethe's life is a glaring example of how easily one may be deceived in such a question. It may be different in the case of the genius of action: What was left for Alexander the Great to conquer when he died at the age of thirty-three?

The danger of an outbreak of a psychosis in a genius, particularly an artistic genius, should not be underrated. I believe that every genius is a potential psychotic, because the production of great art is due to the deflection of a psychosis. A block or impairment of this diversion towards the creative therefore necessarily leads to a manifest psychosis. Art and psychosis are closely related. When Goethe wept over the fate that befell the heroes of his imagination, that is to say, when the products of his imagination temporarily acquired greater power over him than actual reality, he behaved to a certain extent like a psychotic.[3] As Freud said, the dream is a short-lasting psychosis (217, p. 61). The connection between dream and art I mention only in passing, and in order to provide occasion to hint at the grounds on which I postulate that the creation of great art may involve the transformation of psychotic-like structures by means of mechanisms that resemble sublimation. If Goethe had not surmounted his sexual defect it is questionable whether his ego would have been able to bear up under the internal strain. This, I believe, is not in contradiction to my earlier hypothesis that he was consistently abstinent sexually for some years before the Italian journey. The transference to an exalted, beloved, idealized object, of course, made it possible to bear this protracted period of frustration without harm. A continuation of the relationship would not have been favorable for Goethe's further artistic development, and the question was whether Goethe would be able to bear up after the discontinuance of the transference relation. Since Charlotte von Stein was not ready to set him free—the equivalent to dissolving the transference, which in psychoanalysis takes place by analysis of the transference—Goethe had to break away by force, which was one of the many meanings of the Italian journey. The capacity to perform intercourse facilitated the process of dispensing with the attachment to the exalted ideal object. From then on the doomlike surrender to a woman beloved beyond everything else lost its dangerous quality and Goethe thereafter went sporadically through such episodes, not only with impunity but rather to the greatest benefit of his artistic inspiration.

The study of Goethe's relationship to Charlotte von Stein provides an insight that may have surprising implications. We know exactly, or fairly exactly, how mankind managed to cope with problems of external reality before the help of modern technology. Applied science has become integrated so quickly that we have difficulty in imagining how a community can survive without antibiotics or the radio. Psychiatry and psychoanaly-

[3] See Walter Muschg (405, p. 108): the poet's kinship with the criminal, the insane, is unmistakable.

sis are in the process of being integrated in a similar way, at least in this country. An American army, for example, without the assistance of psychiatrists is as unthinkable as one without sulfa drugs or penicillin. When we consider problems of mental hygiene in times prior to the advent of modern psychotherapeutic methods our attention is usually directed towards the efficacy of institutions. The usual example is the institution by the Catholic Church of confession. Mythology, the catharsis of the Greek drama, religion, the Church etc., are other institutions that are studied under this aspect. The relationship between Goethe and Charlotte von Stein, however, teaches us that non-institutional, purely interpersonal, configurations had, in special circumstances, a function that amounted to a rude equivalent of psychotherapy based on scientific insight, as the ox-drawn cart was the equivalent of a modern railroad in a society that was based on a primitive technology. It would be an important branch of the history of mental science to find and study other forms of interpersonal relations that may have served the same function. It is probable that the structure of the pattern changed together with changing history. After all, the Goethe–Charlotte von Stein episode, despite its individual uniqueness, fitted only into the eighteenth century (see 354). The way it started, the course it took, and its ending, the way it worked and the manner in which it achieved the purpose for which it was destined, all this is drenched in the spirit of that era, and one may expect essential changes in typical interpersonal relationships from century to century. But there have at all times been young men with sexual defects, and the percentage of those who overcame them must have been significant. In other words, the question must be asked: How did people overcome their neuroses in earlier years? When Eckermann suffered an episode of severe hypochondriasis his physician thought his "skin systems were corrupted." He told him that if he had come two weeks later he would have been lost, and prescribed warm baths and flannel underwear to be worn directly next the skin. The effect was excellent and the patient quickly recovered (see 306, *1*:26). We know today that the physician was wrong in his diagnosis, but his advice was evidently excellent if what we are concerned with is the speediest possible recovery. The treatment he prescribed probably served as a substitute for a wish-fulfillment of a return to the womb, and may thus have been based on an intuitive, unconscious, understanding by the physician. Of course, Eckermann was not cured of his hypochondriasis and subsequently suffered many bouts of the disease.

Be this as it may, I think one ought to look beyond the narrow horizon of how the professional man—and this includes the priest, the sorcerer, the medicine man—coped with psychopathology. The historical example that I have studied concerns the intimate processes between two people, both of whom were only vaguely aware of the objective functions they mutually played in their relationship. Goethe—as I have tried to prove by means of quotations—knew that this relationship was more than love. At least he hinted at this when he called Charlotte von Stein the "leader of his soul." Charlotte von Stein, I am sure, was not aware that it was her function to cure Goethe from a sexual defect. Apparently she thought the opposite, namely, that he would be for the rest of his life different from other men and not indulge in sexual activity, which was so odious to her (see above, p. 1031). This shows that she had misunderstood the great service she had rendered Goethe. But there are innumerable analogous situations in man's attempts at coping with reality. Discoveries are made by error, and a man may be oblivious of the significance of what he has found. Thus Goethe's recovery and the circumstances leading to it must historically be considered a harbinger of things to come. What Freud scientifically and systematically evolved a hundred years later can be found here as a seed. In other words, the antecedents of the historical climate that favored, a century later, the discovery of psychoanalysis can be observed in this episode. But there must have been innumerable other antecedents, in terms of the relationship between two people, that served the same purpose. It would be a challenging task to pursue the type of modifications which interpersonal relations underwent under the impact of this function.[4]

The Joseph Identification

We have reached the end of this investigation and there could be no better conclusion than to point to an aspect of Goethe's life history that is connected with a comprehensive and far-reaching cultural configuration that has played a role in Western intellectual life and history that is perhaps still not fully understood. I mean the importance of Goethe's identification with the Old Testament figure of Joseph.[5]

A few general remarks must be made about this identification. A

[4] In my enthusiasm over having discovered in Goethe's relationship to Charlotte von Stein basic similarities—faint though they may have been—to a psychoanalytic treatment I have certainly underemphasized the differences. Therefore I wish to cite at least one: the freedom to express hostility and aggression against the object of transference was excluded from their relationship. Aggression could be expressed only through innuendo or parapraxia or under other guises. But in the form of feelings of guilt at least one aspect entered their relationship. The relief of feelings of guilt by constructive action had its therapeutic bearing also on the effect of aggression on the personality make-up.

[5] Kris termed such identifications *gelebte Vita,* which he translated as "enacted biography." See also, for the following, 347, p. 83.

person's ego-development is supported by his identification not only with persons who are important in his environment but also with traditional characters whose destiny has its repository in the annals of history, in mythology, religion, and art. The choice of a historical person with whom the growing ego will identify depends on various factors. In the forefront are certain subjective factors, such as the needs of the identifying person, his fears, and particularly the history of his own oedipal conflict. But one can also observe that the appeal of traditional figures for identification varies with the historical period. The aspect that prompts identification with a traditional figure changes. A detail that may be quite meaningful for one generation may go unnoticed by another; thus, the interpretation of a myth, of the life of a saint, will change (see 271). But an element of chance cannot be denied in determining what traditional character may become decisive in a personality's development. The circumstances in which a person becomes acquainted with the object to be identified with, the person (often a teacher) under whose guidance the subject familiarizes himself with the traditional figure, and, last but not least, the age of the identifying person at the time of acquaintance—all these play a great role. The one great traditional figure unsurpassed as an object of identification in Western society is Christ, and every member of that society is exposed at one time or another in his development to the appeal for identification with Christ. The majority of members are even taught the obligation of identifying with certain aspects of the Saviour's personality as represented by tradition. The Christ identification, valuable though it may be for the community—and it or something like it may have been indispensable for the development of Western civilization—is dangerous for the individual, in view of the magnitude of the personal sacrifices involved and the excessive amount of destructive energy that must be directed against the person's own self in order to carry it out.

But in the Old Testament there looms the figure of Joseph, undoubtedly an antecedent of Christ but less dangerous to the person who identifies with him. Joseph, indeed, might have a greater appeal to an ambitious adolescent than Christ, with his certain doom though belated glory. The myth of Joseph is too well known to require recital, yet some of its salient features may be enumerated. He is the oldest son of his father's second wife. He is the son of the wife who was most loved by his father. His life goes through cycles. Defeat is followed by victory. Victory and defeat stand in causal relationship. His hardship brings him into a situation that contains the seed of a fabulous success: If his brothers had not tried to get rid of him he would not have come into the house of Potiphar; if

Potiphar's wife had not falsely preferred charges against him, he would not have been sent to jail; if he had not been sent to jail Pharaoh would never have heard of his oneirocritical art.

He brings good luck to father-substitutes: Potiphar's wealth multiplies under Joseph's stewardship; Joseph brings almost the whole land of the country into Pharaoh's possession.

He is the preferred son, in whom the father or his substitute reposes unreserved confidence. Potiphar and Pharaoh transfer to him the administration of their entire estates, without any system of checking.

He is unaggressive and never in rebellion against his father or a father-substitute, but nevertheless he acquires the greatest power. This power, however, is not arrogated power, but power peacefully delegated to him by a father-substitute. Although he is in command of the whole situation and the father-substitute does not interfere with his use of power, it is still shared power, working to the benefit of the supraordinated authority, which he never fully replaces.

He resists the temptation to carry out the oedipal crime. The Joseph myth is perhaps one of the oldest attempts at creating the picture of a man who seemingly has reached a level beyond the Oedipus complex. He calls his first son Manasseh, that is to say, forgetfulness, because, as he says, God has made him forget all about his hardships and his father's home.[6] Thus he indicates that his oedipal wishes and resentments have been completely repressed. He follows the exogamous type of marriage and is given by Pharaoh the daughter of the priest of On as a wife. Yet this priest has the name of Potiphera, a name suspiciously reminiscent of Potiphar, to whom he has so exquisitely fulfilled his filial duty. Ignoring the derivations of philologists, I tentatively suggest that here, despite all defenses, the basic oedipal constellation possibly comes to the fore. From the analytic point of view the remnants of the oedipal situation are also indicated by the necessity of marrying in accordance with exogamy. Of course, many other features of this beautiful myth could be pointed out, but suffice it to stress once more its secular nature versus the spirituality of the Christ-myth, and the perfection of the solution it brings to the oedipal conflict. The gruesomeness of physical martyrdom is replaced by joy and serenity. Prudence and sagacity, though they do not obviate tragic complications, lead to success, the rescue of the whole country and the reunion of the family. Without bloodshed, merely by the power of his superior intellect, the favored son climbs to the highest rung of fame. A whole country—

---

[6] Cited after J. M. Powis' University of Chicago translation of the Bible.

that is to say, the whole known world—gathers around his seat, listens to his advice and bows in reverence.

The external course of Goethe's life reflects the story of Joseph to a certain extent: his arrival in a foreign country, his fabulous rise to power, the inherent trust of Weimar's Pharaoh, the gathering of the whole known world around his seat to listen to his words. If we consider the implication of Joseph's mother having been young and his father aging, we find another parallel between their histories, aside from their having both been very arrogant youths. In both life histories we also find the exogamous type of marriage, in Goethe's life less by ethnic than by social discrepancy. In his relationship with Charlotte von Stein—if the interpretation advanced in this study is correct—we may see a distorted replica of the episode of Potiphar's wife.

Strangely enough, there seems to be ample historical evidence that external factors also favored—and probably accomplished—Goethe's identification with Joseph.[7] While Count Thoranc was residing in the house of the Goethes, he ordered several artists to paint for him. The young boy wrote a composition in which he described a cycle of twelve pictures representing Joseph's history; a few of these were carried out, as he wrote in *Dichtung und Wahrheit,* and it is possible that he posed as a model for some of these Joseph paintings. Goethe's first major poetical effort was also devoted to a Joseph epos.

Before discussing Goethe's own words about Joseph and the Joseph epos I wish to cite a biographical detail of Goethe's youth that must have had the gravest consequences in the formation of his character, but about which one can only speculate, since Goethe himself treated it cursorily.

Goethe's father was the guardian of Balthasar Johann David Clauer (1732–1796; see above, p. 101). This apparently gifted man had lost his father in 1735 and his mother in 1750. Johann Kaspar Goethe had promised the boy's mother that he would not forsake her son. Clauer succeeded in graduating as a doctor of law in 1753, but in 1755 he appeared with his servant in Goethe's house and continued to live there, with a few interruptions, until 1783. The young man apparently suffered from a gradually progressing schizophrenic psychosis, possibly of the hebephrenic type. Thus Goethe as a boy lived for many years side by side with a kind of older brother. At least it does not seem far-fetched that a child would regard a ward of his father's who lived in the same house and was for all practical purposes a part of the family, as a sibling. Were there perhaps

[7] For the presentation of the historical material see 475; 421.

also fantasies in the boy that his father had been married before and that Clauer was the issue of that previous marriage? If so, it would bring Goethe's family constellation much closer to that of the Biblical Joseph. Be this as it may, the presence of a schizophrenic adult in the house must have had a bearing on the growing child.[8]

Goethe was the preferred son, just like Joseph, and he was mentally superior to the deteriorating Clauer and made full use of his superiority, again behaving as Joseph did with his brothers. Strangely enough, Goethe mentions this sick housemate just in connection with his Joseph epos.

What made this labor much easier for me was a circumstance that threatened to make my work and my authorship in general very voluminous. A young man of many capabilities, who however had become demented through strain and conceit, dwelt as a ward in my father's house; he lived at peace with the family and was very quiet and wrapped up in himself, and, if one let him proceed in his accustomed way, contented and obliging. This one had written his academic notes with great pains and had acquired a fluent and legible hand. He liked best to be occupied with writing and was glad to be given something to copy; still more, however, he liked to be dictated to, because then he felt translated back to his happy academic years. Nothing could have been more welcome to my father, whose handwriting was not fluent . . . and therefore he was in the habit . . . of dictating to this young man for a few hours a day. I found it no less convenient in between times to see that which was going fleetingly through my head fixed on paper by a strange hand and my gift of invention and of imitation grew with the ease with which it was seized and preserved.[9]

[8] Speculating about possible misadventures when two little children grow up in the company of a hebephrenic subject, one may think of exhibitionistic incidents and sexual games between him and Cornelia. Here may be an important root of Cornelia's disgust with sex and Goethe's long-lasting aversion against direct sexual contacts.

[9] [Was mir diese Arbeit sehr erleichterte, war ein Umstand, der dieses Werk und überhaupt meine Autorschaft höchst voluminos zu machen drohte. Ein junger Mann von vielen Fähigkeiten, der aber durch Anstrengung und Dünkel blödsinnig geworden war, wohnte als Mündel in meines Vaters Hause, lebte ruhig mit der Familie und war sehr still und in sich gekehrt, und wenn man ihn auf seine gewohnte Weise verfahren liess, zufrieden und gefällig. Dieser hatte seine akademischen Hefte mit grosser Sorgfalt geschrieben, und sich eine flüchtige leserliche Hand erworben. Er beschäftigte sich am liebsten mit Schreiben, und sah es gern, wenn man ihm etwas zu copiren gab; noch lieber aber, wenn man ihm dictirte, weil er sich alsdann in seine glücklichen akademischen Jahre versetzt fühlte. Meinem Vater, der keine expedite Hand schrieb . . . konnte nichts erwünschter sein, und er pflegte daher . . . diesem jungen Manne gewöhnlich einige Stunden des Tags zu dictiren. Ich fand es nicht minder bequem, in der Zwischenzeit alles was mir flüchtig durch den Kopf ging, von einer fremden Hand auf dem Papier fixirt zu sehen, und meine Erfindungs-und Nachahmungsgabe wuchs mit der Leichtigkeit des Auffassens und Aufbewahrens.] (*Soph.* I, 26:223–24)

Here the older brother, so to speak, is made secretary of the young boy, who in turn imitates the father.[10] I mentioned earlier the narcissistic pleasure the little boy must have experienced when his mother carried forward her fairy tales exactly as he had told his grandmother that he thought they ought to go. Now we encounter a comparable experience in the latency period and adolescence, one that provided unusual narcissistic gratification and stimulation.[11] The virtually automatic conversion into visible and permanent form of fleeting thoughts must have led to an overcathexis of thoughts, fantasies, and daydreams.

But in order to get the full meaning of Goethe's brief account of Clauer's stay in his house one has to compare it with the vivid interest in the Joseph myth that Goethe expressed in the preceding paragraphs.[12]

From the viewpoint of the Joseph identification, we can then speculate that Goethe's Italian journey provided a break with the image of the virtuous Joseph who fled from Potiphar's wife. In Italy Goethe became less virtuous, and probably outgrew the Joseph identification. I discussed earlier Goethe's identification with his father in Italy; this would take us to Jacob, Joseph's father, who courted two sisters. Goethe came quite close to Charlotte's younger sister, and when he took Christiane into his house, she came with her sister. Nevertheless, it cannot be stated clearly how far the Joseph identification changed to a Jacob identification. It does not seem to have played a major role; one may perceive it shadowlike in the background.[13]

Thus we can dimly see the decade 1776–1786 of Goethe's life against a background still more comprehensive than individual vicissitudes can

[10] From Leipzig he writes his sister (March 14, 1766) in French: "I will forgive you if you do not always write in your own hand. What keeps you from having your thoughts written down by the scribe, who writes so nicely and quickly?" [Je te pardonnerai, si tu n'ecris pas toujours de ta propre main. Qui est ce qui t'empèche de faire ecrire tes pensees par l'ecrivain qui ecrit si joliment et si vitement.]

[11] In the supplementary notes to his autobiography Goethe devoted one paragraph to the period of 1749–1764. The last sentence reads: "voluminous scribbling in several languages favored by early dictating" [Vielschreiberei in mehreren Sprachen, durch frühzeitiges Dictiren begünstigt]. (*Soph.* I, 35:3). The importance of Clauer was suggested by Sarasin (464, p. 399).

[12] Joseph then reappeared decades later, under his Persian name Jussuph, in the *Westöstlicher Diwan*.

[13] The question of the role of the Joseph identification in the life of Napoleon was raised by Freud (see 213). To the parallels between Goethe's and Freud's lives which I have occasionally cited I want to add one more. In Freud's life too the Joseph identification played a great role. Not only was he a dream interpreter like Joseph (cf. 158, p. 484 n.) but he too was the older son of his father's second wife. This identity regarding the family position is, in my opinion, most remarkable.

form; but even if individual life loses in stature and relevance when viewed under the aspect of the long history of man's civilization, we are still deeply moved when we observe the daily struggle, sacrifice, and joy of these two minds, whose encounter will remain as enigmatic and challenging an intertwining as two human souls have ever experienced.

Part III
B

Goethe and Science

Chapter 1

The History of a Partial Psychosis

A PROBLEM NOW confronts us that has come up from time to time in the course of this book but that I have put off discussing until it could be dealt with, if not in isolation from other factors, at least without still further impeding consideration of matters that then more urgently needed to be considered. I mean Goethe's relationship to science.

At one point we found Goethe writing a semiscientific essay *On Granite,* at another his discovery of the *os intermaxillare* burst more or less suddenly upon us, but it was not clear why a scientific discovery should have appeared at that juncture, and not a poem or a new chapter in his novel. As a matter of fact, Goethe's immediate elation over his anatomical discovery was greater than that which he evinced over any other of the many things he had cause to be proud of during that pre-Italian decade. Whether the direction of Goethe's creativity at any given moment was determined by specific circumstances has been to some extent discussed, but the fullest attention must still be given to the fact that, for periods that became longer as time passed, his mind was preoccupied, even prepossessed, by problems that are distinctly different from art, and that definitely belong to science. This is so surprising and unusual that an attempt must be made to get closer to the problem it poses, even if it entails some risk that speculation will occasionally predominate over well-founded interpretation.

In Goethe's biographies the fact is always mentioned and even stressed that his interest in the natural sciences was awakened early and that he attended courses in medicine and other scientific branches during his university years. However, one may surmise that Goethe's scientific strivings in Weimar had a different psychological meaning from those of his early years, although the two cannot, of course, have been completely unrelated. Goethe's attendance at science courses, although at that time of the early dawn of science not as unremarkable as it would be considered today, may easily have been the outcrop of his general interest. A firebird like Goethe had also, of course, to orient himself as to the progress mankind was making in the realm of science. Still, there is, so far as I know, no record in those early years to indicate that he ever thought of making science his career or that his interest went beyond that with which he habitually met new intellectual realms. His tremendous thirst for knowledge is not our subject matter but is simply something accepted as a fact in this context.

During the years in Weimar, however, one notices that science and scientific strivings become an integral part of his life, something without which he would probably have been just as badly off as he would have been without writing poems or tragedies. Indeed, there was if anything perhaps more constancy in his scientific interests, perhaps even more loyalty and devotion to them in his later years than to artistic pursuits.

The strangeness of this phenomenon, namely, that an artistic genius of such formidable proportions should devote so much time, energy, and thought to science, has, of course, aroused the interest of many, and the literature on this subject is quite extensive (see 473). A good way to start investigating the phenomenon may be to give an example of how Goethe approached science, or better, how he behaved in an actual situation of scientific inquiry. On July 2, 1792, he wrote to Sömmering:[1]

> I must inform you on this occasion of an experiment that seems to me very important and that points to quite a few things. I cast upon the wall in the usual way the colored so-called *spectrum solis* and brought a luminous stone prepared in Bologna [2] into the yellow and yellow-red part of the spectrum and found to my surprise that it did not thereupon emit the slightest light in darkness. Thereupon I put it in the green and blue part; then too it emitted no light in the darkness; at last, after I put it in the violet part, it at that moment attracted light and shone brightly in the darkness. I have repeated this experiment very often in the presence of several friends and it always succeeded. It can be most prettily observed when the sun stands high, because then one can cast the colored image upon the floor of the dark room. One puts two pieces of the luminous stone, the one in the yellow-red, the other in the blue-red color, and closes for a moment the opening in the shutters. There will then appear only one luminous stone shining, to wit, as I said before, the one placed on the blue-red side.

[1] Samuel Thomas von Sömmering (1755–1830), professor of anatomy, 1797–1805, physician in Frankfurt am Main, outstanding anatomist and physiologist.

[2] Apparently what is called "Bologna stone," that is, phosphorescent barium sulphate.

I have already varied this experiment very much and will repeat it as early as possible and probe it further. I do not dare to conclude anything from it but what it itself directly declares, namely, that the two counterposed color borders manifest a quite different, indeed an opposite, effect, and since both are considered only appearances, show such a real and pretty long-lasting influence upon a body.[3]

Scheumann (469, p. 136) is certain that Goethe was the first to observe this phenomenon, namely that, as we should put it today, fluorescence of a substance depends on the wave length of the light to which the substance has been exposed. This little episode, about which Goethe wrote in a perhaps casual way, gives cause for several conclusions. It shows that Goethe was a keen observer. In keeping with the fact that the times were gone when man relied on Aristotle or church authority, perception and observation held a paramount place in his scientific outlook. For Goethe, knowledge was not based primarily on tradition, but there was, instead, an insatiable desire to make first-hand observations. It is very important that this fact be established. Despite his passions, despite his artistic genius, he behaved in this respect like a modern scientist. Indeed, his passion for direct observation was even greater than is nowadays typical. Modern science relies more and more on machines or technical devices—and surrenders to them the task of observation, reserving for the human mind the function of choosing what use to make of what the technical instrument has observed. A comparison of a modern physician with one of fifty or seventy-five years ago will demonstrate this change in the status of direct observation. In the textbooks of the earlier period

---

[3] [Ich muss Ihnen bei dieser Gelegenheit einen Versuch mittheilen, der mir sehr wichtig scheint and der auf manches hindeutet. Ich warf auf die gewöhnliche Weise das farbige sogenannte *Spectrum solis* an die Wand und brachte einen in Bologna zubereiteten Leuchtstein in den gelben und gelbrothen Theil des Farbenbildes, und fand zu meiner Verwunderung, dass er darauf im Dunkeln nicht das mindeste Licht von sich gab. Darauf brachte ich ihn in den grünen und blauen Theil, auch alsdann gab er im Dunkeln kein Licht von sich, endlich nachdem ich ihn in den violetten Theil legte, zog er in dem Augenblicke Licht an und leuchtete sehr lebhaft im Finstern. Ich habe diesen Versuch sehr oft in Gegenwart mehrerer Freunde wiederholt, und er ist immer gelungen. Am schönsten macht er sich, wenn die Sonne hoch steht, da man denn das farbige Bild auf den Fussboden der dunkeln Kammer werfen kann. Man legt zwei Stücke Leuchtstein, das eine in die gelbrothe, das andere in die blaurothe Farbe, und schliesst im Augenblick die Öffnung im Fensterladen. Es wird alsdann nur ein Leuchtstein glühend erscheinen, und zwar, wie oben gesagt, derjenige, der auf der blaurothen Seite gelegen.

Ich habe diesen Versuch schon sehr vermannichfaltigt und werde ihn sobald als möglich wiederholen und ihn weiter durcharbeiten. Ich wage nichts daraus weiter zu folgern, als was er gleichsam selbst ausspricht: dass nämlich die beiden einander gegenüberstehenden Farbenränder eine ganz verschiedene Wirkung, ja eine entgegengesetzte äussern, und da sie beide nur für Erscheinung gehalten werden, einen solchen reellen und ziemlich lange dauernden Einfluss auf einen Körper zeigen.]

one will find descriptions of hundreds of little signs that might be taken to indicate whether a patient was suffering from this or that disorder. Whether a dullness on percussion was heard slightly more to the right or the left was a highly consequential observation. Modern medicine, however, has replaced the unreliable sense organ by precise and reliable instruments of registration. The work of the highly trained sense organ is now done by the laboratory and X rays.[4] The old physician had a passion for examining the patient over and over again; he could scarcely satiate his mind with the gathering of observational data. A similar urge to observe phenomena in a natural setting played a paramount role in Goethe's life. His perceptive system was constantly geared to grasp phenomena which, common or uncommon, were not usually subjected to scrutiny. I think that the whole question of Goethe as a scientist revolves around the question of perception and observation. Yet the above-quoted letter to Sömmering contains more than an expression of Goethe's readiness to register an unusual phenomenon, of his clarity and precision in describing the phenomenon and the circumstances in which it can be observed. In the second part he turns towards the meaning of his observations, that is to say, the conclusions that one can draw from them. Here he displays a lack of courage quite unlike his boldness when he believed he had discovered the *os intermaxillare* (see above, pp. 849 ff). It is questionable whether the conclusion that he adds has the value of a conclusion at all, or is not merely a repetitive statement about the content of the observation side by side with the a priori statement that the two color borders are "considered *only* appearances," which has nothing to do with the observation per se. One may be surprised at this soberness, almost bordering on lack of imagination. The observation as such sounds most thrilling, and the fantasy of even a mediocre mind would be greatly stimulated by such a strange phenomenon—the more so since Goethe had every reason to believe what was probably the case, that it had never been noticed before.

The great role that perception and observation played in Goethe's life must be contrasted with the place experiment (and mathematics?) held for him. To these he responded with a yes, pronounced in a soft voice, followed by a very loud no. His attitude towards experiment can perhaps be formulated, though oversimply, in the following way: An experiment is constructive if it repeats in a leisurely way that which has been observed in nature. But the mere experiment, divorced from the broad flow of liv-

---

[4] This great progress with regard to the precision of diagnostic apparatus has been followed by less desirable consequences which can be briefly summarized in the phrase "the dehumanization of medicine."

ing and creative nature, is destructive and must mislead the observer. Therefore Goethe never grasped the meaning of Newton's classical experiments in the field of color and persistently tried to explain them in terms of his own—amazingly accurate—observations made in natural settings.

There was undoubtedly a horror at the prospect of isolating factors, elements, situations. This horror was even one of the reasons that for a long time kept him from Schiller.[5] Already in an early paper (1793) on this topic, "The Experiment as the Mediator between Object and Subject" (*Der Versuch als Vermittler von Object und Subject, Soph.* II, *11:* 21–37), Goethe's principal attitude comes to the fore. It seems from this paper rather clear that what was involved was not so much an intellectual difficulty as a psychological one. At the beginning of the paper Goethe brilliantly and profoundly expounds the aim of science and the difficulties encountered in accomplishing this aim. The necessity of eliminating the subjective factor is clearly recognized. The great importance that the experiment has in scientific procedures is also recognized. Yet, after six printed pages that would, I believe, find approval, by and large, even today, Goethe raises his objections against experiments. He does not reject them outright—how could he have?—but one feels the desire to do so.[6]

First he warns against conclusions drawn from a single experiment. Yet if two experiments are combined there is danger that their proximity may give rise to exaggerated notions of the significance of their relationship. They may appear to follow one from the other, yet a long series of them might have to be interpolated in order to establish "a natural connection." Even a series of experiments does not prove anything.

> Nothing is more dangerous than to wish to confirm any proposition directly through experiments, and the greatest errors came into existence just because the danger and inadequacy of this method are not understood.[7]

I do not wish to retrace all of Goethe's steps but only to record his alarm at the discrepancy of observational data inherent in an actual experimental situation, and the tendency sometimes to arrive at far-reaching conclusions, in terms of hypotheses and theories, on the basis of one experiment.

[5] See *Glückliches Ereignis, Soph.* II, *11:*13–20, particularly pp. 16 and 17.
[6] See Martin Gebhardt (228, p. 35): "He [Goethe] hated experiments even when he performed them by necessity."
[7] [. . . dass nichts gefährlicher sei als irgend einen Satz unmittelbar durch Versuche bestätigen zu wollen, und dass die grössten Irrthümer eben dadurch entstanden sind, dass man die Gefahr und die Unzulänglichkeit dieser Methode nicht eingesehen.] (*Soph.* II, *11:*28)

In living nature nothing happens in isolation. Practical experiences appear to us in isolated form and if we consider experiments isolated facts, we do not prove that they are facts.[8] Goethe's antidote against such dangers was the empirical formation of experiences of a higher order. He cited his own contributions to optics as an example of how to obtain such experiences of a higher type. The experiments he recorded in that area formed, as he thought, a series each of which touched the subsequent one, so that all of them together in reality constituted only one experiment. In an aphorism Goethe became particularly categorical about his aversion against experiments.

> Man himself, inasmuch as he makes use of his healthy senses, is the greatest and most exact physical apparatus there can be; and that is just the greatest evil of modern physics—that one has, as it were, detached the experiment from man and wishes to gain knowledge of nature merely through that which artificial instruments show, nay, to limit and prove that which nature can achieve.[9]

Here it is clearly outspoken that the isolating effect of experiments, their driving a wedge between nature and man, aroused Goethe's displeasure. It is noteworthy that Freud thought Leonardo's paucity in artistic production was due to his inability to isolate phenomena (170, p. 77), and very surprisingly a similar inability is encountered here in Goethe's scientific work, although, as I have tried to show, the mechanism of isolation played such a constructive and perhaps lifesaving role at certain times during his Weimarian years before he went to Italy.[10]

What, then, may have caused this disturbance in Goethe? I think one of the reasons was that isolation, to him, meant destruction. And Goethe was right as to this qualitative property of the experience. Isolation is always a mechanism that is kept in motion by destructive energy, or energy

---

[8] In his *Chromatology* (*Soph.* II, 2:17) Goethe says quite openly that nothing can be proved by experiments beyond the purely perceptive.

[9] [Der Mensch an sich selbst, insofern er sich seiner gesunden Sinne bedient, ist der grösste und genauste physikalische Apparat, den es geben kann; und das ist eben das grösste Unheil der neuern Physik, dass man die Experimente gleichsam vom Menschen abgesondert hat, und bloss in dem, was künstliche Instrumente zeigen, die Natur erkennen, ja was sie leisten kann dadurch beschränken und beweisen will.] (*Soph.* II, *11*:118)

Goethe's apparent horror that a machine should replace life is reminiscent of certain anxieties that Hanns Sachs has explained (461).

[10] Cf. above, p. 1228. And yet, this process of isolation, beneficial as it was, was nevertheless the first step Goethe took towards divorcing himself from those activities that took up most of his time before he went to Italy.

that genetically stems from the destructive. "Nature is reduced to silence," wrote Goethe, "when put to the rack; its faithful answer to an honest question is: Yes! Yes! No! No! Anything else is of evil."[11] Nature on the rack, however, is precisely nature caught in isolating experiments,[12] which do not speak the language of the gospel in simple yea and nay but necessitate hypotheses and theories. Such statements indicate that, at least in this situation, isolation became for Goethe a truly destructive function, which therefore could not be used in a flexible way. This pathology surrounding the mechanism of isolation had its worst effect on Goethe in making Newton's theory unacceptable to him per se, quite aside from any experimental arrangement:

> All people, however educated they were, had been indoctrinated with the split-up light and unfortunately sought to trace back the living [light] which they enjoyed to that dead hypothesis.[13]

But quite aside from the implication of destruction one gets the impression that the place that perception, particularly visual perception, held in Goethe's personality must be considered here. Perception and observation fulfilled in Goethe far more than that for which they are destined, so to speak, namely, to supply data in terms of which the ego can orient itself about what is going on in the outer world. By perception and observation the world is to be re-created—or perhaps even be created, as Goethe thought. When he exclaims: "In our eye lies the law,"[14] and thus tries to combat Newton, he is partly right, since without perceptive organs there would be no colors, but Goethe goes much further. In the papers found after his death the following appears: "The senses do not deceive; judgment deceives,"[15] and in 1815 he wrote the verses: "Allah need create no more, we create his world,"[16] and one of the *Xenien* (also published

---

[11] [Die Natur verstummt auf der Folter; ihre treue Antwort auf redliche Frage ist: Ja! Ja! Nein! Nein! Alles Übrige ist vom Übel.] (*Soph.* II, *11*:152)

[12] See Goethe's *Chromatology* (*Soph.* II, 2:69), when he carries on the controversy against Newton's experiments: "This is the so-called *Experimentum crucis,* with which the investigator puts nature to the rack. . . ." [Es ist dieses das sogenannte Experimentum crucis, wobei der Forscher die Natur auf die Folter spannte. . . .]

[13] [. . . alle Personen, so gebildet sie auch waren, hatten das gespaltene Licht eingelernt und wollten leider das lebendige, woran sie sich erfreuten, auf jene todte Hypothese zurückgeführt wissen.] (*Campagne in Frankreich 1792, Soph.* I, *33*:197.)

[14] [in unserm Auge liegt das Gesetz] (*Soph.* II, 5:195.)

I have torn this quotation out of context. In its actual context Goethe's words convey a different meaning.

[15] [Die Sinne triegen nicht, das Urtheil triegt.] (*Soph.* I, 42 [part 2]:259)

[16] [Allah braucht nicht mehr zu schaffen,/ Wir erschaffen seine Welt.] (*Wiederfinden, Soph.* I, 3:76)

after his death) says: "What is the most difficult of all? What you think to be the easiest: to see with your eyes what lies before your eyes."[17]

We have here three steps. Man's only reliable tool for linking himself with the world is his sense organs; the world is over and over again re-created by man; the most difficult creative act is to perceive that which is perceptible. A synthesis of these three steps lies in Goethe's idea of the *aperçu* which I think was his basic tool of scientific research. He gives a practical example of how he thought an *aperçu* works. Galileo, he wrote,

> by evolving from swinging church lamps the principle of the pendulum and of falling bodies, led natural science back again to man and already in his early youth demonstrated that for the genius one instance has the value of thousands. Everything depends in science on that which is called an *aperçu*, [that is to say] on the perceiving of what lies essentially at the bottom of the appearances. And such a perceiving is infinitely fruitful.[18]

And at another place he compares the firm *aperçu* with "an inoculated disease: one will not get rid of it until it is fought through."[19] Goethe called his discovery of the intermaxillary bone an *aperçu*.[20] And in discussing the nature of productivity with Eckermann on March 11, 1828, he said:

> Every productivity of the *highest sort*, every outstanding *aperçu*, every discovery, every great thought that bears fruit and has consequences, stands outside of personal control and is above all earthly power.[21] [Houben's italics]

I think what Goethe meant was the moments when perceptions and thought-contents coincide, are fused or synthesized into a unit the parts of which the self cannot discriminate, so that consequently the thought-content has the clarity, definiteness, and relevance that one expects to en-

---

[17] [Was ist das Schwerste von allem? Was dir das Leichteste dünkt,/ Mit den Augen zu sehn, was vor den Augen dir liegt.] (*Xenien. Aus dem Nachlass.* No. 45. *Soph.* I, 5 [part 1]:275)

[18] [. . . führte die Naturlehre wieder in den Menschen zurück und zeigte schon in früher Jugend, dass dem Genie Ein Fall für tausend gelte, indem er sich aus schwingenden Kirchenlampen die Lehre des Pendels und des Falles der Körper entwickelte. Alles kommt in der Wissenschaft auf das an, was man ein Aperçu nennt, auf ein Gewahrwerden dessen, was eigentlich den Erscheinungen zum Grunde liegt. Und ein solches Gewahrwerden ist bis in's Unendliche fruchtbar.] (*Soph.* II, 3:246–47)

[19] [Ein entschiedenes Aperçu ist wie eine inoculirte Krankheit anzusehen: man wird sie nicht los bis sie durchgekämpft ist.] (*Soph.* II, 4:302)

[20] To Eckermann, August 2, 1830; see 119, p. 597.

[21] [Jede Produktivität *höchster Art*, jedes bedeutende Aperçü, jede Erfindung, jeder grosse Gedanke der Früchte bringt und Folge hat, steht in niemandes Gewalt und ist über aller irdischen Macht erhaben.] (119, p. 539)

counter only in a perception. The content of perceptions, after all, does not admit doubt. Any person feels a joy whenever a desired conclusion, a narcissistically cathected opinion, reaches that degree of incontestability that is inherent in perceptions. In short, an *aperçu* is a thought that has become perception. What is involved is an experience close to religious revelation, in which belief becomes accessible to the sense organs. When Goethe called his discovery of the intermaxillary bone an *aperçu* he was right. When he perceived the *sutura incisiva* originating from the *foramen incisivum* on the lower plane of the palate (see 273, p. 12), he was not only perceiving a new bone but he was simultaneously perceiving the position of man as part of nature. In such situations the observer is not aware of how many assumptions, theories, and conclusions are being registered by him as perceptions and does not realize that what he believes to be the content of his perceptions is actually far beyond all sense data.[22] Goethe had difficulties with Newton's experiments because they did not provide him with such a perceptive situation. Only after a logical analysis of all factors could he have drawn the conclusion that Newton drew. Goethe's tendency, however, was to accept only that which he could experience as sense data.[23] In pathological instances this very situation leads to fixed ideas and delusions. The perceptive systems of the schizophrenic are more active than those of the nonschizophrenic. His perceptive system has not undergone that degree of "taming" to which the nondelusional has subjected his.

Yet the artist keeps up this perceptive dimension. Every person once had it, probably, and it may be slumbering in all of us, but usually it is mastered, suppressed, or inhibited and only let loose in the dream process. The artist, however, has the privilege of keeping it intact without becoming the prey of psychosis.

If we wish to evaluate Goethe's standing as a scientist a general idea must first be considered.

Muschg (406) investigates the various dimensions of literary art. He rightly includes in his study almost all documents involving words except scientific work. He then distinguishes four types: the magician, the prophet, the priest, the minstrel. In a simplified form I should translate

[22] See 531, pp. 12–18. This becomes very clear when one follows the discussion between Goethe and Schiller about what experience and what ideas are. For a summary of Goethe's and Schiller's relationship, see 60, Introduction.

[23] See Gebhardt (228, p. 150): "Goethe . . . perhaps did not devote himself to . . . experiments within the electrical field because man is lacking in a sense organ for electrical stimuli and therefore apparatuses alone can be intermediaries for the respective laws. We know, however, that Goethe was very skeptical about this."

this into four sociological functions: (1) The artist creates a new world in the present; (2) he announces the coming of a new society and participates in its creation; (3) he preserves the existing society, and (4) he is the source of pleasure. There is much to be said about each function, but here I wish to restrict myself to only a few words about Goethe's relationship to these four functions. His artistic life extended to the fullest in all four dimensions. The near-miracle of his life was that all four dimensions took on manifest form in reality as well as in the purely artistic medium.

In the function of minstrel, that is to say, providing entertainment, he is theater-director and actor, organizer of masquerades, planner of skating parties, arranger of feasts; in the function of priest, that is to say, conserving contemporary society, he is the loyal servant of his duke, treasurer of state finances, introducer of reforms, builder of roads, adviser upon appointments, policy-maker, negotiater with the Imperial Diet, fighter against the revolution; as a prophet, that is to say, as a builder of the future society, he creates learned institutions, preaches humanism and tolerance, fights church religion, propagates the cult of nature as a manifestation of a deity, opens new fields of science, and sets forth in his literary work a new philosophy.

The magic function is, of course, an all-embracing one. The word, knowledge, action, imagery—all psychic functions—can be utilized for this purpose. He was poet, painter, architect, and scientist. He built mines, organized meteorological stations, and predicted the weather.

An artist can achieve any or all of this, but he usually can do so only within the scope of his particular medium. Shakespeare was King and Queen and Saint and Sinner, Hamlet and King Lear, but how much of this was he able to act out in reality? Michelangelo was Moses and a slave and Lorenzo de' Medici, but the same question has to be asked concerning him. Goethe, however, had the privilege of creating a world through his artistic medium and also of acting out a diversity of lives in reality. It is no coincidence that *Wilhelm Meister* has as a principal character a man who has the intense desire to become an actor. The actor, after all, is the artist who may, at least for a limited span of time, be in reality that which the author may taste in fantasy only. If Goethe's life is viewed thus broadly, the question of whether his scientific theories were correct or not becomes most insignificant. Then only his activity as a scientist merits interest and is surprising only as a psychological datum. When Gebhardt writes: "Goethe always remained unconsciously poet when he wanted consciously to be a physicist" (228, p. 151), he may be correct. But he is correct only in so far as Goethe, the man, is equated and identified with Goethe,

the poet; the question remains whether Goethe, the artist, really represents the essence of that man. It is true, if we knew of Goethe only as a painter or as a physicist, or as a statesman, or as a stage-director, or as everything he was other than literary artist, we should not consider him the genius that we do.

Yet just what our judgment of Goethe would be in such a case is an idle question at bottom, for his literary achievements are unthinkable without those other nonliterary activities and achievements. Perhaps the greater part of his literary works was a series of *aperçus,* and it may have been because such a vast part of the world had gone through his perceptions that he was able to re-create the whole world in his literary productions.

A psychological analysis, in so far as it strives to be scientific, cannot rest with ascertaining that Goethe was unconsciously a poet when he aimed at being a physicist, even though such a statement may be undeniably correct. Goethe himself would have protested very vigorously against his being "reduced" to a poet. Repeatedly he said to Eckermann:

> I do not pride myself at all on anything that I have achieved as a poet. Notable poets have lived in my time, still more notable ones before me, and there will be some after me. Yet I take real pride that in my century I am the only one who knows the truth in the difficult science of chromatology and for that reason I have a consciousness of superiority over many.[24]

This sentence is of extraordinary importance. The genius's evaluation of himself is often—perhaps even regularly—faulty.[25] But an error in self-evaluation is an important clue. We must conclude that for Goethe chromatology was of all his works the closest to him. I should like to compare it with the following. The highest feelings of superiority, of real achievement, one sometimes experiences in a dream. One wakes up with the feeling of having made a tremendous discovery or of having delivered an outstanding speech. Yet when one remembers the words actually spoken in the dream he discovers to his surprise that they were nonsense words. How can the ego derive this feeling of superiority from mere nonsense words? One factor in the explanation is this: the words in the

[24] [Auf Alles was ich als Poet geleistet habe, bilde ich mir gar nichts ein. Es haben treffliche Dichter mit mir gelebt, es lebten noch Trefflichere vor mir, und es werden ihrer nach mir seyn. Dass ich aber in meinem Jahrhundert in der schwierigen Wissenschaft der Farbenlehre der Einzige bin, der das Rechte weiss, darauf thue ich mir etwas zu gute, und ich habe daher ein Bewusstsein der Superiorität über Viele.] (119, p. 261)

[25] The one that has always impressed me as the most astounding example besides the one quoted is that by Jean-Jacques Rousseau, who thought that his greatest accomplishment was an opera he composed.

dream are cathected with a large quantity of narcissistic energy.[26] This is what makes them so extremely valuable to the dreamer. He cannot escape the feeling of having achieved something tremendous because he is confronting his own unbounded ego. We encounter a similar situation when we study the attitude of delusional patients towards their own delusional productions. They can as little detach themselves from those delusions as the normal person could deny his own identity. Part of the patient's identity is invested in his delusion, and therefore he must overrate it. That is why it is so important to study Goethe's misjudgment upon his *Chromatology,* because his final judgment indicates the probability that he there set down thoughts of particularly great closeness and importance to him.

What were the antecedents of this final comprehensive statement by Goethe about himself? We have some information about this subject since in his *Chromatology,* which consists of over a thousand pages, Goethe devoted twenty-eight pages to the "Confession of the Author" [Confession des Verfassers] *(Soph.* II, 4:283–311). This confession contains many remarkable features, only a few of which will be discussed here. To begin with, I propose to take Goethe's interest in color for granted and to consider only the circumstances in which he conceived the idea that Newton was in error in his demonstration that white light contained the colors of the spectrum. Goethe had heard of Newton's theory as a student and had accepted it.

> Like all the world I was convinced that the whole collection of colors is contained in light; nothing different was ever told me and never did I find the slightest reason to doubt it because I was not interested further in the matter.[27]

When, after the Italian journey, Goethe started to grapple with the problem of color, he wished to repeat Newton's original experiments. The opportunity to do so presented itself when Hofrat Büttner[28] moved to Jena, for this scientist possessed the necessary refracting prisms. Goethe borrowed the chest containing the optical instruments but put off performing the experiment. First he did not have proper quarters for arrang-

---

[26] I disregard here the latent dream-thoughts which may lead to such a dream.

[27] [Wie alle Welt war ich überzeugt, dass die sämmtlichen Farben im Licht enthalten seien; nie war es mir anders gesagt worden, und niemals hatte ich die geringste Ursache gefunden, daran zu zweifeln, weil ich bei der Sache nicht weiter interessirt war.] *(Soph.* II, 4:292)

[28] Christian Wilhelm Büttner (1716–1801), natural philosopher and linguist, professor at Göttingen, sold his library and laboratory to Karl August and retired to Jena.

ing to have a small ray of sunlight enter an otherwise darkened room. Then, when he had moved to a house where conditions were appropriate, he was again detained by other matters. Hofrat Büttner became restless and with increasing urgency requested the return of his prisms. Goethe excused himself, promised, but still put off the experiment. At last Büttner seems to have become seriously worried and sent a messenger to carry the chest away. Goethe could not delay any further, but, rather than let the prisms go without having used them at all, he took one out of the chest and looked through it, expecting to see all-white light dissolved into many-colored light, as he had understood should happen according to Newton. But to his amazement he observed that the white wall still appeared white, and that only where white bordered upon dark did colors make their appearance.

> It did not need long reflection before I recognized that a boundary was necessary in order to bring forth colors, and immediately, as if by an instinct, I said aloud to myself that the Newtonian principle was wrong.[29]

From this moment on, no argument, no experiment, no persuasion, no objection to his own theories,[30] could make Goethe change the conviction that had appeared with meteorlike suddenness on his horizon, never to loosen its grip on his mind. Years of hard work, hundreds of pages, poems, articles, almost every medium at his disposal, he devoted to prove, to convince, to persuade, that white light was pure and did not contain colors. A word against his theories could threaten even a well-founded and sincere friendship; acceptance of his theories was repaid with affection. The only discordant note I know of that ever arose between Goethe and Eckermann, his most loyal admirer, occurred when the latter showed that one of Goethe's theories could not be correct but needed revision. Such an extreme sensitivity was plainly unusual for Goethe and made a reasonable discussion of the problem impossible. The time-honored vanity and pride of authors cannot explain this deviation

---

[29] [Es bedurfte keiner langen Überlegung, so erkannte ich, dass eine Gränze nothwendig sei, um Farben hervorzubringen, und ich sprach wie durch einen Instinct sogleich vor mich laut aus, dass die Newtonische Lehre falsch sei.] (*Soph.* II, 4:296)

[30] The reader may be interested to know what Goethe's own chromatological theories were. Despite my study of Goethe's relevant publications on the subject I have never gained a clear understanding and therefore quote the shortest and most precise summary I have found in the literature: ". . . that colors are not a quality of different rays, but phenomena due to the meeting of light and darkness, of white and black. The predominance of light produces yellow, the predominance of darkness produces blue. Both together produce green. Red is between blue and yellow, of which it is but a modification." (486, p. 99) For a concise statement see 531, pp. 39–47.

from his usual standards. Even Eckermann noticed that Goethe responded in this area quite differently from the way he did in any other. Thus he wrote:

> Goethe could ill abide contradiction of his *Chromatology,* whereas he always showed himself accessible in regard to his poetical works and gratefully received every well-founded objection.[31]

Eckermann tried to explain this difference by the contrast between the success of Goethe's literary works and the vituperation and disapproval that his *Chromatology* encountered for half a century. This scarcely seems like a satisfactory explanation.

Goethe's irritability about anything concerning Newton developed gradually. An early reference to the new idea does not sound very aggressive, although the reference to a "revolution" may indicate a smoldering attack against a father-figure. Thus he wrote in a letter to J. F. Reichardt, of May 30, 1791:

> Among the works in which I am now most interested is a new theory of light, of shadow, and of colors. . . . If I do not deceive myself it must produce some sort of revolution in natural science as well as in art.[32]

Johann Friedrich Reichardt (1752–1814), conductor and composer, was at that time greatly admired by Goethe. Reichardt set many of Goethe's poems to music. Serious discord later developed between them.

Newton, I believe, makes his first appearance in Goethe's letters in one to Knebel of October 8, 1791:

> I take very great pleasure and consolation from a Jesuit Grimaldi,[33] who concerned himself with light and colors at approximately the same time as Newton. His book *De Lumine Coloribus et Iride* was printed five years before Newton gave his optical lectures and much earlier than he published his *Optics*. Grimaldi is a far keener observer than Newton and quite, methinks, on the right path, from which this Father of the Church [Newton] turned us away.[34]

---

[31] [. . . Goethe in seiner Farbenlehre nicht gut Widersprüche vertragen konnte, während er bey seinen poetischen Werken sich immer durchaus lässlich erwies und jede gegründete Einwendung mit Dank aufnahm.] (119, p. 260)

[32] [Unter den Arbeiten die mich jetzt am meisten interessiren, ist eine neue Theorie des Lichts, des Schattens und der Farben. . . . Wenn ich mich nicht betrüge, so muss sie mancherlei Revolutionen sowohl in der Naturlehre als in der Kunst hervorbringen.]

[33] Francesco Maria Grimaldi (1618–63), professor of mathematics at Bologna.

[34] [An einem Jesuiten Grimaldi welcher ohngefähr zu eben der Zeit mit Neuton sich um das Licht und die Farben bekümmerte, habe ich sehr grosse Freude und Trost. Sein Buch *de Lumine Coloribus et Iride* ist fünf Jahre früher gedruckt als Neuton seine Optische

Goethe tries here to belittle Newton by raising the question of priority, despite the fact that he evidently regards Grimaldi's work as not only earlier, but different. What there was about this difference that prompted Goethe to a friendly attitude will be cited later.

How seriously Goethe's likening of Newton to a church Father was meant can be seen from his letter to Zelter of March 13, 1822:

> My opponents do not confound me; who would not have to become accustomed to this in the world—but particularly in Germany! The noble physical antagonists [meaning his opponents among the physicists] impress me like Catholic clerics who should want to refute a Protestant by means of the Council of Trent.[35]

It is of interest to quote here from Goethe's conversation with Eckermann of February 19, 1829, on the occasion of a disagreement between them about the theory of colors: "'I fare with my chromatology,' he continued a little more serenely and mildly, 'just as the Christian religion has. One believes for a while he has faithful disciples, and, in the twinkling of an eye, they deviate and form a sect. You are a heretic like the others too, for you are not the first who has deviated from me.'"[36] When this quotation is compared with the letter to Zelter one discovers a typical example of projection.

His irritability on this subject assumed regrettable forms in publication and outright invectives were hurled against Newton and his work, such as:

> Nasty lawyer's trick; sophistical misrepresentation of nature; our man of honor; the author behaves despicably; whether indeed one might find in the history of science anything so foolish and ridiculous in the way of explanation; sheer nonsense.[37]

Vorlesungen hielt und viel früher als er seine Optik herausgab. Grimaldi ist ein weit schärferer Beobachter als Neuton und ganz dünckt mich auf dem rechten Wege von dem uns dieser Kirchenvater abgebracht hat.]

[35] [Meine Gegner irren mich nicht, wer müsste diess nicht in der Welt, besonders aber in Deutschland gewohnt werden! Die edlen physischen Widersacher besonders kommen mir vor wie katholische Pfaffen, die einen Protestanten aus dem tridentinischen Concilium widerlegen wollten.]

[36] [Es geht mir mit meiner Farbenlehre, fuhr er darauf etwas heiterer und milder fort, gerade wie mit der christlichen Religion. Man glaubt eine Weile treue Schüler zu haben, und ehe man es sich versieht, weichen sie ab und bilden eine Sekte. Sie sind ein Ketzer, wie die anderen auch, denn Sie sind der erste nicht, der von mir abgewichen ist.] (119, p. 260)

[37] [Schlimmer Advokatenstreiche; Sophistische Entstellung der Natur; Unser Ehrenmann; Der Autor benimmt sich schändlich; Ob wohl in der Geschichte der Wissenschaften etwas ähnlich Närrisches und Lächerliches von Erklärungsart zu finden sein möchte?; Barer Unsinn.] (248, *40*:xlii)

This attitude went so far as a direct accusation of intentional dishonesty when Goethe quoted the following verse from his own work: "Yet I well see, lying becomes necessary and [this] beyond all measure."[38] The dishonesty, maliciousness, and stupidity imputed to Newton had its counterpart in Goethe's conviction that it was because of a conspiracy on the part of his contemporaries, motivated by vanity, that he was denied the recognition due him. He was very certain that his revelation about Newton would have a sensational effect and that he was virtually destined to give the deathblow to an error that had kept mankind in thrall. When recognition was not forthcoming, he evolved the theory that he was the victim of the clannishness of a guild towards him, an outsider and layman.[39] In later years a different note was to be struck. When a book was published by J. B. Wilbrand,[40] whom, in general, Goethe appreciated as a scientist but who expressed himself in agreement with Newton's theory of the spectrum, Goethe wrote him on August 5, 1820:

> I regretted that a man who had renounced so many prejudices . . . could still not have freed himself from the most unconscionable of all juggleries, the Newtonian spectrum. . . . I have not found [in your book] . . . the slightest notice even . . . of my chromatology, at which I fell into [such] an astonishment that it came close to despair.[41]

At the beginning there were visible remnants of the Christ identification, which I have mentioned from time to time. Thus he wrote in a draft, after having compared the Newtonian school with the Roman Church: "And so it is well known to me what awaits me when now I step forth to demonstrate. . . ."[42] But later he wrote, concerning the year

[38] [Aber ich sehe wohl, Lügen bedarf's, und über die Massen!] (*Soph.* II, 2:281)

[39] Goethe at first considered the possibility that he might fail in convincing his contemporaries. In a draft he wrote: "Since I prepare the whole matter for revision and, if I should not excite the attention of my contemporaries, who are occupied otherwise, I commend my work to the following century." [Da ich nun die ganze Angelegenheit zur Revision vorbereite, und wenn ich die anders beschäftigte Aufmerksamkeit meiner Zeitgenossen nicht erregen sollte, meine Arbeit dem folgenden Jahrhundert empfehle.] (*Soph.* II, 5 [part 1]: 177)

[40] Johann Bernhard Wilbrand (1779–1846), professor of anatomy and physiology at Giessen.

[41] [. . . bedauerte ich, dass ein Mann, der sich schon von so vielen Vorurtheilen losgesagt . . . hatte, sich noch nicht von der schmählichsten aller Taschenspielereyen, dem Newtonischen Spectrum, habe retten können. . . . Nun find ich . . . aber von meiner Farbenlehre selbst . . . auch nicht die mindeste Notiz, worüber ich in ein Erstaunen gerieth, das der Verzweiflung nah war;]

[42] [Und so ist mir recht wohl bekannt, was mich erwartet, indem ich gegenwärtig auftrete, um zu zeigen . . .] (*Soph.* II, 5 [part 1]:165)

See also Goethe's comparison of the "Newtonian crowd" with "mob, Pharisees, or

1810, in which the *Chromatology* was finished and published in its entirety: "About its effect I was little concerned. . . . Yet I did not expect such a perfect lack of interest and rejecting unfriendliness."[43] There are several passages in his conversations with Eckermann that show the imagery he formed around scholars in the field: they are vain, ambitious, petty, and reject everyone who is an outsider.

Another example, perhaps even more impressive than those already cited, can be found in Soret's notes (December 30, 1823). Goethe complained of a young man who published a work on optics that contained views quite similar to Goethe's but who avoided referring to Goethe by name in order not to endanger his prestige, in view of the disrepute in which Goethe was held as a physicist.[44] Later the author visited Goethe and apologized. Soret thought that Goethe's struggle was not only against Newton, but that a profound change was necessary in the generally accepted view, "and if you were right a thousand times, nevertheless you have to be wrong for quite a while."[45] Thereupon Goethe replied:

"I shall be the worse off, because, proud of my discovery, I persuaded myself with complete arrogance: This Newton, whom all the world admires, these unrelenting mathematicians, these algebraic geniuses, these keen observers, they are all mistaken; I alone as against them am right, I alone hold the philosophers' stone in my hand, which they, after all, could find so easily, which would come to light as clear as the sun for them if they would only open their eyes and see correctly. In this conviction I knocked on the head—and smartly—all traditional opinions; I have been fought against, or, even more, my ideas have been ridiculed, but I have not lost faith in my work, be it only to have had the pleasure the better to see through mankind's weaknesses."

While his words bubbled forth inexhaustibly with a force of expression that I am not capable of reproducing, his eyes glowed with an extraordi-

---

scribes" [Volk Pharisäern oder Schriftgelehrten] (*Soph.* I, 42:526). The martyr attitude is clearly expressed in *Xenien* No. 169 and 171 (*Soph.* I, 5:229) and particularly in epigram No. 79 (*Soph.* I, 1:325)

[43] [Um die Wirkung war ich wenig bekümmert, . . . Einer so vollkommenen Untheilnahme und abweisenden Unfreundlichkeit war ich aber doch nicht gewärtig;] (*Soph.* I, 36:55)

[44] The author was the physiologist Johannes Evangelister Purkinje (1787–1869) who visited Goethe in December, 1822. He later became famous for his discovery of the effect that was named after him. Since Purkinje was less interested in the physical aspect of chromatology than in the subjective, he naturally found much to agree with in Goethe's theories.

[45] This quotation should serve as an example of the extent to which Goethe was supported in his views by his circle.

nary fire, the joy of triumph shone from them, while an ironical smile played about his lips; his fine head was more imposing than ever.[46]

Soret was a reliable reporter with regard to the content of the conversation and in view of his awe and admiration for Goethe his interpretation of Goethe's physiognomic expression is quite understandable, but in a psychoanalytic inquiry a reservation will be made as to this interpretation. It is reasonable to connect the affect and the facial expression noticed by Soret because they were evidently unusual for Goethe, with the psychopathology I have postulated as being at the bottom of Goethe's disturbance.

The remarkable feature surrounding this whole episode in Goethe's life, which can be labeled *chromatology* for short, is that it has the character of a paranoid psychosis. Now we know for certain that Goethe was not suffering from a psychosis in the sense in which that word is usually used when referring to a personality whose ego is in the grip of a psychosis. Goethe's psychosis must have been a partial psychosis.[47]

The episode begins with an experience that fulfills typical clinical conditions of a grave disorder. It is characteristic of the starting point at which a schizophrenic disorder will manifest itself for the first time. Yet the question of whether or not Goethe suffered from a schizophrenic disorder I will not take up now but limit myself to the study of the structure and history of the disorder.

When Goethe was looking into the prism while Büttner's messenger waited, a sudden mental flash occurred that had a permanent effect within

[46] ["... und hätten Sie tausendmal recht, so müssen Sie zunächst geraume Zeit unrecht haben."

"Und mir wird es um so schlimmer ergehen, weil ich, stolz auf meine Entdeckung, mir voller Hochmut einredete: dieser Newton, den die ganze Welt bewundert, diese unerbittlichen Mathematiker, diese Rechengenies, diese scharfsinnigen Beobachter, sie alle sind im Irrtum, ich allein bin gegen sie im Recht, ich allein habe den Stein der Weisen in der Hand, den sie doch so leicht finden könnten, der sonnenklar für sie am Tage läge, wenn sie nur die Augen öffnen und ordentlich sehen wollten. Mit dieser Überzeugung habe ich alle überkommenen Meinungen, und tüchtig, vor den Kopf gestossen; man hat mich bekämpft, oder noch mehr: man hat meine Ideen lächerlich gemacht, aber ich bin an meinem Werk nicht irre geworden, sei es auch nur, um das Vergnügen gehabt zu haben, die Schwäche der Menschheit besser zu durchschauen."

Während seine Worte unerschöpflich hervorsprudelten mit einer Kraft des Ausdrucks, die ich nicht wiedergeben vermag, funkelten seine Augen in ungewöhnlichem Feuer, Siegesfreude leuchtete aus ihnen, während um seine Lippen ein ironisches Lächeln spielte; sein schöner Kopf war imposanter denn je.] (307, p. 91)

[47] By "partial psychosis" I mean a circumscribed area in the personality that has the structure of a psychosis, is well encapsulated, and tends to distort sporadically certain ego functions when they are called into play in its service.

a rather well-circumscribed area of his personality. It elicited thoughts and feelings regarding a genius whose personality and doctrine suddenly appeared to him in a different light from before.

We are familiar from clinical experience with the meaning of such sudden flashes. They are characteristic of the "primal experience."[48] They are experienced sometimes as an inner illumination. The world appears suddenly changed, dead or distant or unnaturally close, or the patient suddenly recognizes a comprehensive truth that had not dawned on him before. It is not necessary to go through the whole phenomenology of this most interesting symptom. Goethe reported similar experiences on other occasions. The discovery of the *os intermaxillare* and his thoughts while contemplating a sheep skull in the Jewish graveyard at Venice seem to have been accompanied with similar feelings. But in these two instances what was involved was a process in which something that was latently present for a time took on a concrete form, or, in other words, a perceptual configuration was suddenly discovered to which a previously existing thought could be harmoniously attached, or into which it could be synthesized.

The flash regarding Newton was differently structured. It involved a thought, so Goethe claimed, for which he was in no way prepared, and the accent was on a negative content—"Newton is wrong"—whereas the other two experiences stressed that certain relationships existed.

In studying the history of Goethe's relationship to Newton, one discovers that he felt adoration for him in his younger years. When he was collaborating with Lavater in the latter's famous physiognomic studies, Goethe wrote for Lavater a few character analyses ostensibly based on scrutiny of the subjects' countenances. One of them was devoted to Newton. Goethe's analysis was written in typical *Sturm und Drang* language, which makes translation most difficult. He wrote as follows:

1

. . . The *eyes* full of inner strength to seize the object; to grasp it, not merely *to illuminate* it, not *to store* it in the memory, but to devour it and make it *immanent* in the great All that is in the head.—Eyes full of the power of creation—and eyebrows full of the most luminous, most solid fertility.

[48] By "primal experience" I render the German term *Primäres Wahnerlebnis* (see 383). Because the approach toward schizophrenia is in this country different from that which prevailed in Germany, the concept of primal delusional experiences seems not to have found its way into American usage.

. . . It [the brow] seems to express rather elevated, formidable thinking than abstract. Powerful urge, urge of confidence and of certainty hovers over it.

Remarkable is the purity, the calm, of the whole in the presence of visible inner exertion. . . .

2

. . . A republican he is who, without commanding, reigns, [who] has ever to withstand, [who] has organized, established, built up, many affairs. How firmly he seizes sensory impressions—makes trial designs, not without trust in himself and in his overpowering strength. . . .

4

. . . The brow, how crowded in the recollection of effects! Presentiment of future soul's anguish within present strength!

. . . The lips [a] buttress—[of] inner strength. . . .[49] [Goethe's italics]

The analysis of Newton was, as can be seen, written with particular passion and in the strongest, most positive terms, in such a vein as that in which a modern physiognomist would write about Albert Einstein, who, like Newton in the eighteenth century, stimulating public imagination, filled a place of fame. It is of particular interest to note the great emphasis Goethe put on Newton's eyes (quite different from his other analyses), which may be put into a meaningful connection with the later conflict. It is also surprising how many subjects Goethe chose for physiognomic analy-

1

[49] [. . . Voll innerer Kraft die *Augen,* den Gegenstand zu fassen; ihn zu ergreifen, nicht bloss *zu beleuchten;* nicht ihn ins Gedächtniss *aufzuhäufen;* sondern ihn zu verschlingen, und in das grosse All, das im Haupte ist, *immanieren* zu lassen.—Augen voll Schöpfungskraft —und Augenbrauen voll der lichtvollsten, solidesten Fruchtbarkeit.

. . . Mehr hohes, gewaltiges Denken, als abstraktes scheint sie [die Stirn] auszudrücken. Mächtiger Drang, Drang der Zuversicht und der Gewissheit schwebt drauf.

. . . Auffallend ist die Reinheit, die Ruhe des Ganzen, bey der sichtbaren innern Anstrengung. . . .

2

. . . Ein Republikaner ist's, der, ohne zu befehlen, herrscht, immer widerstehen muss, viele Geschäffte geordnet, eingerichtet, gebaut hat. Wie fest ergreift er sinnlichen Eindruck, —macht prüfenden Entwurf, nicht ohne Zutrauen zu sich und seiner übermannenden Kraft. . . .

4

. . . Die *Stirn,* wie gedrängt in Erinnerung von Würkungen! Ahndung künftiger Seelennoth in gegenwärtiger Kraft!

. . . Die Lippe Widerhalt—innerer Kraft. . . .] (*Soph.* I, 37:359)

See also the work of Eduard von der Hellen (286) who by splendid analysis established those few parts of the work published under Lavater's name that were written by Goethe.

sis who were in one way or another idealized father-substitutes, or who represented himself in an idealized shape (ego-ideal) : Klopstock, Homer, Rameau, Scipio, Titus, Brutus. Thus in the primal experiences the image of an illustrious beloved father changed to one of a malicious, vicious, hated one. However, for completeness' sake, it must be stated that Goethe's psychogram of Newton contains characteristics that sound feminine. Qualities such as purity, calm, inner exertion, fertility, power of creation, may indicate that already in this early encounter Goethe projected upon Newton the imagery of a primeval mother, or we may be dealing here with a father-image of an archaic period as described earlier (see above, p. 781).

The primal experience was the starting point of the disturbance, but what was its further course? One can reconstruct some of the underlying processes if one assumes that Goethe's paranoid statements about Newton's personality were the result of his own projections. Since he wrote extensively about what he thought the psychological prerequisites were from which Newton's alleged error grew, this writing may become an important source of information.

But is one justified in assuming that this material is the residue of projections? I think that evidence can be adduced that necessitates such an assumption. In the closing paragraph of his discussion of Newton's *Optics,* we read this opinion by Goethe of Newton:

And do we not notice in life, in some other instances [as well] that when we seize with animation a wrong *aperçu,* our own or somebody else's, then it may gradually become a fixed idea and at last degenerate into a complete partial insanity, which manifests itself principally in that one not only passionately sticks to everything that is favorable to such a type of thought, eliminating without hesitation everything that slightly contradicts [it], but also interprets in his favor that which is conspicuously contrary.[50]

Today we know that this is applicable word for word to Goethe himself, and therefore I conclude that the psychic processes assumed in his adversary were projections of processes that actually went on in him.

And strangely enough, the account Goethe here gives of the failing

---

[50] [Und bemerken wir nicht im Leben, in manchen andern Fällen: wenn wir ein falsches Aperçu, ein eigenes oder fremdes, mit Lebhaftigkeit ergreifen, so kann es nach und nach zur fixen Idee werden, und zuletzt in einen völligen partiellen Wahnsinn ausarten, der sich hauptsächlich dadurch manifestirt, dass man nicht allein alles einer solchen Vorstellungsart Günstige mit Leidenschaft festhält, alles zart Widersprechende ohne weiteres beseitigt, sondern auch das auffallend Entgegengesetzte zu seinen Gunsten auslegt.] (*Soph.* II, 4:41)

with which he taxes his illustrious opponent, but which was actually his own, is an astoundingly accurate one. But the quoted passage also confirms us in the assertion that Goethe actually was seized by a partial psychosis. After all, even if he had been right in all his theories and conclusions regarding the nature of light, he had no valid reason to suppose that Newton had been seized by partial insanity. Therefore the attribution of partial insanity to his opponent appears rather like the consequence of some unconscious awareness of the presence of major psychopathology in himself.

I wish to cite two further passages which seem to bring forth even more strongly the projective nature of Goethe's elaborations upon Newton's personality. At one point Goethe surmised "that Newton perhaps found so much delight in his theory because it offered new difficulties with each empirical step."[51] This would really be an unusual source from which to gain pleasure, but it was Goethe who wrote in an outline of his biography:

My life a single adventure.

No adventure [obtainable] through striving for development of that which nature has endowed me with.

Striving to appropriate that which she [i.e., nature] has not endowed me with.

As much true tendency as false.

Therefore eternal torture without proper enjoyment.[52]

(But an earlier quotation [see above, p. 664] may be remembered that showed the great attraction such a situation had for Goethe.) In the book in which he attacked Newton so severely he wrote, under the heading "Confession of the Author," about his endeavors as a painter—which, after all, are what brought him to chromatology:

Yes, I felt for this [painting], for which I truly had no aptitude, a far greater drive than for that which was easy and comfortable for me by nature. Indeed, it is certain that false tendencies influence man more often with greater passion than the genuine ones and that he aspires with greater zeal after that in which he is bound to fail than after that in which he could succeed.[53]

---

[51] [. . . dass vielleicht Newton an seiner Theorie soviel Gefallen gefunden, weil sie ihm, bei jedem Erfahrungsschritte, neue Schwierigkeiten darbot.] (*Soph.* II, 4:104)

[52] [Mein Leben ein einzig Abentheuer./ Keine Abentheuer durch Streben nach Ausbildung dessen was die Natur in mich gelegt hatte./ Streben nach Erwerb dessen was sie nicht in mich gelegt hat./ Eben soviel wahre also falsche Tendenz./ Desshalb ewige Mar [ter] ohne eigentl. Genuss.] (*Soph.* I, 26:364)

[53] [. . . ja ich fühlte hiezu, wozu ich eigentlich keine Anlage hatte, einen weit grössern Trieb als zu demjenigen was mir von Natur leicht und bequem war. So gewiss ist es,

In another part of his *Chromatology,* in attacking the validity of Newton's experiment Goethe makes the following strange statement:

The truth about Newton's gift of observation and the exactness of his experiments everyone who has eyes and senses will perceive with surprise; indeed, one may boldly state: who could, by means of such a hocus-pocus, have cheated a man of such extraordinary gifts as Newton was if he had not cheated himself? *Only someone who knows the power of self-deception* and knows that it borders quite closely on dishonesty, *he alone will be able to explain Newton's method* and that of his school.[54] [Italics mine]

But Goethe claimed that he had that power of explanation, and thus indirectly admitted that he knew "the power of self-deception . . . that borders quite closely on dishonesty." Here we find what may be Goethe's unwitting self-betrayal of the projective origin of the portrait he drew of Newton.

As one reads Goethe's angry attacks against Newton, his repetitious arguments, and his expressions of regret at Newton's stubbornness, one gets the impression that Goethe is speaking as if of a living person,[55] who in the face of however many convincing arguments Goethe thought to pile up, still spitefully refused to give ground. Goethe also held Newton responsible for the equally stubborn insistence of nearly all subsequent physicists on agreeing in principle with his theory of light. This fuzziness regarding objects of his anger, this unawareness that he was treating a person who had been dead for a long time as if he were a contemporary who could still be convinced of an error, makes the diagnosis still more probable, quite aside from the tendency towards concretization of thinking of which Goethe made himself guilty in his theory of color (see 288, p. 350 and *passim*).

Goethe's keenness in describing his own psychopathology by imputing it to Newton offers an invaluable source of psychological data

---

dass die falschen Tendenzen den Menschen öfters mit grösserer Leidenschaft entzünden, als die wahrhaften, und dass er demjenigen weit eifriger nachstrebt was ihm misslingen muss, als was im gelingen könnte.] (*Soph.* II, 4:286)

[54] [Wie es dagegen um die Newtonische Beobachtungsgabe und um die Genauigkeit seiner Experimente stehe, wird jeder, der Augen und Sinn hat, mit Verwunderung gewahr werden; ja man darf dreist sagen, wer hätte einen Mann von so ausserordentlichen Gaben, wie Newton war, durch ein solches Hocuspocus betrügen können, wenn er sich nicht selbst betrogen hätte? Nur derjenige, der die Gewalt des Selbstbetruges kennt, und weiss, dass er ganz nahe an die Unredlichkeit gränzt, wird allein das Verfahren Newtons und seiner Schule sich erklären können.] (*Soph.* II, 2:27)

[55] Dr. Otto Isakower suggests in a personal communication that Goethe would have become a paranoiac if Newton had still been alive during Goethe's adult years.

regarding Goethe's own conflicts. In discussing Newton's character Goethe gave the following psychological analysis:

> Every being that feels itself as a oneness wants to preserve itself in its own condition undivided and undisturbed. This is an eternal, necessary given of nature, and thus one can say every single [being] has character. . . . In this sense we may ascribe character to the weak, yes, even to the coward, for he gives up what other people esteem above all but does not belong to his nature: honor, glory, only for the sake of preserving his personality. . . . A character is called strong when it powerfully opposes all external hindrances and tries to enforce its individuality even at the risk of losing its personality. A character is called great when its strength is simultaneously combined with great, boundless, infinite properties and capacities, and through it quite original, unexpected intentions, plans, and deeds come to light.[56]

Goethe then goes on to show that this is quite independent of any ethical evaluation of an action. Ethics are based on the strivings for the good. Strength of character is beyond good or evil, and Newton showed a strong character by adhering to an error with great tenacity despite all warnings he assertedly received from without and from within.

> And here enters a principal enigma of ethics, which, however, does not remain insoluble to a person who dares to look into the abysses of human nature.[57]

He then expounds the psychology of error:

> Man is subject to error, and as he errs, in one instance or constantly, so he instantly becomes false towards himself and others. . . . If one devotes to a person more love, more respect, than he deserves, then immediately one must become false to oneself and others. . . .

> Reason and conscience, however, do not let their rights be taken away. One can lie to them, but cannot deceive them. Indeed, we do not go too far

---

[56] [Jedes Wesen das sich als eine Einheit fühlt, will sich in seinem eigenen Zustand ungetrennt und unverrückt erhalten. Diess ist eine ewige nothwendige Gabe der Natur, und so kann man sagen, jedes Einzelne habe Charakter. . . . In diesem Sinne dürfen wir dem Schwachen, ja dem Feigen selbst Charakter zuschreiben: denn er gibt auf, was andere Menschen über alles schätzen, was aber nicht zu seiner Natur gehört: die Ehre, den Ruhm, nur damit er seine Persönlichkeit erhalte. . . . Einen starken Charakter nennt man, wenn er sich allen äusserlichen Hindernissen mächtig entgegensetzt und seine Eigenthümlichkeit, selbst mit Gefahr seine Persönlichkeit zu verlieren, durchzusetzen sucht. Einen grossen Charakter nennt man, wenn die Stärke desselben zugleich mit grossen, unübersehlichen, unendlichen Eigenschaften, Fähigkeiten, verbunden ist und durch ihn ganz originelle unerwartete Absichten, Plane und Thaten zum Vorschein kommen.] (*Soph.* II, 4:99–103)

[57] [Und hier tritt nun ein ethisches Haupträthsel ein, das aber demjenigen, der in die Abgründe der menschlichen Natur zu blicken wagte, nicht unauflösbar bleibt.]

when we say: the more moral, the more reasonable, man is, the more mendacious he becomes as soon as he errs, the more monstrous the error must become as soon as he perseveres in it.[58]

It is fearsome, Goethe continues, when a strong character, in order to remain faithful to himself, becomes disloyal to the world.

> Yet this does not yet solve the whole enigma; a more mysterious one still lies behind it: that is to say, there can be found in man a higher consciousness, by which he obtains a certain survey over the inescapable nature inherent in him, which, despite all freedom, he is nowise able to change. To get wholly clear about this is well-nigh impossible; to blame oneself for a moment at a time is well enough, but it is given to no one to blame himself perpetually.[59]

I regret to stop quoting here. Who else has ever written so clearly and succinctly about the dynamics of a psychosis? Goethe starts out with the subject's strivings for identity and ends with the burden of feeling of guilt. If he had also given due weight to the impact of forbidden id-wishes, the picture would have been complete. A psychosis does indeed make it possible for an individual to struggle, usually at the cost of some pain, against the more painful disturbance of the feeling of identity and to escape a crushing feeling of guilt. Did he really learn all this from the study of Newton's life? It is not reasonable to assume so, but rather to suggest that Goethe was here referring in general terms to the emotional conflicts that made Newton's theory of light unacceptable to him and forced him to set up his own. And when he suggests that Newton's theory of color has to be viewed as a "congealed *aperçu*" [ein erstarrtes Aperçu] he is describing the damaged structure of a part of his own psychic apparatus, which in that area had lost its elasticity. Here Goethe could not go forwards or backwards but had to persevere rigidly in the

[58] [Der Mensch ist dem Irren unterworfen, und wie er in einer Folge, wie er anhaltend irrt, so wird er sogleich falsch gegen sich und gegen andere. . . . Man widme einer Person mehr Liebe, mehr Achtung als sie verdient, sogleich muss man falsch gegen sich und andre werden. . . .

Dagegen lassen Vernunft und Gewissen sich ihre Rechte nicht nehmen. Man kann sie belügen aber nicht täuschen. Ja wir thun nicht zu viel, wenn wir sagen: je moralischer, je vernünftiger der Mensch ist, desto lügenhafter wird er, sobald er irrt, desto ungeheurer muss der Irrthum werden, sobald er darin verharrt.]

[59] [Allein hiermit ist noch nicht das ganze Räthsel aufgelöst; noch ein Geheimnissvolleres liegt dahinter. Es kann sich nämlich im Menschen ein höheres Bewusstsein finden, so dass er über die nothwendige ihm einwohnende Natur, an der er durch alle Freiheit nicht zu verändern vermag, eine gewisse Übersicht erhält. Hierüber völlig in's Klare zu kommen ist beinahe unmöglich; sich in einzelnen Augenblicken zu schelten, geht wohl an, aber niemanden ist gegeben, sich fortwährend zu tadeln.]

position that had forced itself upon him, and I do not doubt that he was right when he said that by his inquiry into optics he contracted "a disease of development that was to have the greatest influence upon [his] life and actions."[60]

A full elucidation of a primal experience usually clarifies almost the entire psychopathology. Although there is no possibility of elucidating fully Goethe's primal experience, namely the revelation he had when looking through the prisms, it may nevertheless be worth while to investigate that experience as far as one can.

The first question concerns the exact date of its occurrence. Regrettably, this cannot be established upon the basis of published documents, so far as I am familiar with them. However, two dates can be established that mark the limits of the interval during which it must have occurred. The earlier date is determined by Goethe's remark in the "Confession of the Author" that he gained an opportunity to arrange for repeating Newton's experiments when he moved to a new house in which the necessary conditions were fulfilled. Since this house must have been the one in which he lived from November, 1789, to June, 1792, the experience cannot have occurred prior to November, 1789. The latest possible date of the primal experience is given through the earliest reference in his letters to chromatological studies. In a letter to the Duke of May 17, 1791, he refers to his chromatological work in terms that indicate that the letter was written after he had undergone the primal experience: "The theory of the blue color," he wrote, "I have also written down during these days." And the following day:

> I can also announce with vivid joy that since yesterday I have reduced the phenomena of colors as shown by the prism, the rainbow, the magnifying glasses, etc., to the simplest principle. First and foremost I have been prompted to it by a contradiction of Herder's which struck this spark in me.[61]

This is, I think, the earliest known record referring to Goethe's work upon colors. Documentary evidence thereafter becomes more frequent. Thus I think one has to conclude that the primal experience occurred

---

[60] [. . . eine Entwickelungskrankheit eingeimpft, die auf Leben und Thätigkeit den grössten Einfluss haben sollte.] (*Soph.* I, 35:14)

[61] [Die Theorie der blauen Farbe habe ich auch in diesen Tagen geschrieben. . . . Noch kann ich mit lebhafter Freude melden, dass ich seit gestern die Phänomene der Farben wie sie das Prisma, der Regenbogen, die Vergrösserungsgläser pp zeigen auf das einfachste Principium reducirt habe. Vorzüglich bin ich durch einen Widerspruch Herders dazu animirt worden der diesen Funcken herausschlug.]

somewhere between November, 1789, and May 17, 1791.[62] Goethe himself claimed that the experience occurred in 1790. In the Tag-und Jahres-Heften he wrote for the year 1790: ". . . to my great amazement I discovered *the Newtonian hypothesis to be wrong and untenable.*"[63] (Goethe's italics) Further, among annotations in preparation of *Dichtung und Wahrheit,* there is also a short summary of events of 1790. Toward the end of the summary he wrote: "Change of apartment. *Aperçu* of the prismatic appearance of colors."[64] Yet Goethe's testimony is not quite reliable, for both of these remarks were written many years later and in the second there is an evident mistake, since Goethe's move to the new dwelling was in 1789.

If one knew whether Goethe reacted immediately to the primal experience or whether it brewed in him for some time before he set actively to work, it would also help to fix the date earlier or later in the possible period. This, too, however, is open to speculation.

More concrete evidence can be adduced regarding the next question: What, to Goethe, was the unconscious meaning of light? Light, to him, meant something pure, and it had a female quality. In discussing Newton's sixth experiment, the crucial one, in which a ray of light is broken into its components by means of a prism, Goethe accuses Newton of putting Nature to the rack to force an admission of something that Newton had stipulated beforehand. He then continued:

> Nature, however, is like a steadfast and noble-minded person, who, even under all tortures, perseveres in the truth. If it stands otherwise in the register, then the inquisitor has listened wrong or the clerk written it down wrong. If such a spurious deposition should pass muster for a little time, nevertheless someone will still be found thereafter who may take the part of the injured innocence, as we have now armed ourselves to venture this service of chivalry for our friend [*feminine in German*]. We now want to hear first how Newton goes to work.[65]

[62] Rupprecht Matthaei (379) has spent much thought on the exact dating of the first glance through the prism and reached the conclusion that it must have occurred in January or February, 1790. This date agrees well with the theory I shall presently suggest.

[63] [. . . entdeckte ich zu meinem grossen Erstaunen: *die Newtonische Hypothese sei falsch und nicht zu halten*] (*Soph.* I, *35*:13–14)

[64] [Veränderung der Wohnung. Aperçu der prismatischen Farbenerscheinung.] (*Soph.* I, *53*:386)

[65] [Allein die Natur gleicht einer standhaften und edelmüthigen Person, welche selbst unter allen Qualen bei der Wahrheit verharrt. Steht es anders im Protocoll, so hat der Inquisitor falsch gehört, der Schreiber falsch niedergeschrieben. Sollte darauf eine solche untergeschobene Aussage für eine kleine Zeit gelten, so findet sich doch wohl in der Folge noch jemand, welcher sich der gekränkten Unschuld annehmen mag; wie wir uns denn

The predominantly feminine meaning of light to Goethe's unconscious is evident from this passage. The imagery is of Newton's committing a dastardly attack upon female purity. Goethe must defend female innocence against such attack, so that the woman may once more shine in her true and innocent light. Goethe seems actually to have had feelings of physical disgust in conjunction with Newton's concept of light. At one point at least he calls Newton's white "nauseating."[66] Another even stronger statement is the following:

> *The most repugnant,* however, that has ever come before my eyes, was Biot's [67] chapter on entoptic colors, there called polarization of light. In accordance with a false analogy with a magnet, light also was there twisted into two poles, and thus it was sought, no less than before, to explain colors by means of a differentiation of the most immutable and most untouchable.[68] [Italics mine]

The most immutable and the most untouchable becomes the most repugnant as soon as someone tries to change it and touch it—this seems to dictate the assumption that the whole complex of light had become associated with unconscious imagery of the virginal mother.

From this point of view it is also understandable why Goethe wrote in such approbatory terms about the physicist Grimaldi (see above, p. 895). Although Grimaldi anticipated in part Newton's theory of light, yet Goethe could praise the "prudence and subtlety"[69] with which he investigated the subject, and one senses a certain joy in Goethe when he reports that for Grimaldi light was "a fluid, which, however, he tried to the utmost to refine."[70] There is, likewise, a laudatory tone in Goethe's report that Grimaldi strove to convince the reader "of the subtlety of such a tenuous material being, which appears only like a spiritual exhalation."[71]

---

gegenwärtig gerüstet haben, für unsere Freundin diesen Ritterdienst zu wagen. Wir wollen nun zuerst vernehmen, wie Newton zu Werke geht.] (*Soph.* II, 2:69)

[66] [das ekelhafte Newtonische Weiss] ("Confession of the Author," *Soph.* II, 4:302)

[67] Jean Baptiste Biot (1774–1862), French physicist, who made researches in almost all branches of physics, was most famous for his work relating to the polarization of light.

[68] [Das Widerwärtigste aber, was mir jemals vor Augen gekommen, war *Biot's* Capitel über die entoptischen Farben, dort Polarisation des Lichts genannt. So hatte man denn, nach falscher Analogie eines Magnetstabs, das Licht auch in zwei Pole verzerrt und also, nicht weniger wie vorher, die Farben aus einer Differenzirung des Unveränderlichsten und Unantastbarsten erklären wollen.] (*Soph.* I, 36:121)

[69] [Vorsicht und Zartheit] (*Soph.* II, 3:310)

[70] [eine Flüssigkeit, die er jedoch auf's äusserste zu verfeinern sucht.] (*Soph.* II, 3:310)

[71] [von der Zartheit eines so subtilen materiellen Wesens, das gleichsam nur wie ein geistiger Aushauch wirkt.] (*Soph.* II, 3:311)

The collation of the analogies Goethe used when reporting Newton's theory with those used for Grimaldi shows that Goethe responded to their respective theories not in accordance with their soundness or unsoundness but in accordance with the feelings they aroused in him, as if he were reading subjective expressions of opinion regarding a living person close to his heart.

We have now gleaned two important components of the unconscious complex with which Goethe was wrestling in his chromatological studies. A father-figure (Newton) was trying to do violence to an untouchable, pure, immutable, virginal mother (light). He might succeed transitorily in defaming her, and his authority might be great enough to make the world believe his damnable accusations. Goethe, however, would restore the innocence of the debased mother. One point remains vague. Had the father actually soiled the mother or had he only lyingly alleged that the mother was impure, and would Goethe (the son) prove that despite the father's evil doings the mother's purity had never been impaired, or was it his task to undo a violence that the father had actually perpetrated upon her? The actual physical disgust Goethe felt when he came across a reference to the composite nature of light may indicate which version predominated.

When we now return to the primal experience we may be in a position to see the importance of an element to which we have not yet paid attention, namely, the significance of Goethe's delay in availing himself of Hofrat Büttner's prisms. As was reported earlier, Goethe left them unused for many months. Notwithstanding his manifold obligations and activities, it is surprising that, if only out of curiosity, he did not cast one glance through the instrument. This procrastination strikes me as being most unusual in Goethe and I evaluate it as a prodromal symptom of the disease. The contents manifested cannot have been formed on the spur of the moment but must have lain dormant, probably from childhood on. Therefore it would be of importance to know what was in Goethe's mind the moment before he was seized by the primal experience. And of that moment, in the presence of Büttner's waiting messenger, he tells us that he wanted to take a quick glance through the instrument,

> which I had not done since my earliest youth. I recalled indeed that everything had appeared many-colored; in what way, however, was no longer present to my mind.[72]

[72] [was ich seit meiner frühsten Jugend nicht gethan hatte. Ich erinnerte mich wohl, dass alles bunt erschien, auf welche Weise jedoch, war mir nicht mehr gegenwärtig.] (*Soph.* II, 4:295)

1137

Thus we have the following sequence. Goethe in his earliest youth looked through a prism. He had a vague recollection of what he had seen through it. We know that this recollection was wrong because not all white light appears many-colored in a prism. As an adult, Goethe had wanted for a long time to look again through a prism. Even after moving to a new house where the necessary conditions could easily have been set up, he again postponed doing so. In a moment of haste, when he was bent on returning the prism to its owner, he recalled the vague impression from his earliest youth. He thereupon looked through the prism. The ensuing perception did not confirm the content of the childhood memory. In this moment the primal experience seized him.

From this sequence I conclude that Goethe's postponement of looking through the prisms was the result of an inner inhibition. He was afraid of what he might see. In view of his superior memory it is all the more remarkable that he had the wrong recollection of what one sees when looking through a prism. To his amazement he did not perceive anything disgusting, as he had thought he would, in accordance with the assertion of a father-figure (Newton). In this moment he was struck by the idea that the father-figure was utterly wrong and malicious, and further there came to him in a flash the basis of a new theory, which would disprove the existence of the disgusting feature asserted by the father-figure.

The whole puzzle may find a quick solution when one considers that Goethe's first child, a son, was born on December 25, 1789, probably in the very house in which Goethe was subjected to the primal experience. A few conclusions may follow. The object of Goethe's voyeuristic impulse as a child probably was his mother's pregnancy. Was there a desire not to notice it, to deny the existence of the protruding belly? Goethe spoke of Newton's wanting to split [zerspalten] light. Was he afraid as a child that his mother would fall apart? Be this as it may, he was probably puzzled by the problem of whether his mother could have become pregnant without impurity. The father seemed to claim or deny that he did something to mother, or perhaps others claimed that the father caused it. But was it true? Cannot a baby be born without the mother's becoming soiled? Now Goethe's son was born, on the twenty-fifth of December like the Christ child, and not quite two months before the child's birth Goethe had moved away from his house on the Frauenplan to a more remote house on the edge of town on *Mary* Street (Marienstrasse) (see 260, p. 53). The child issued from Christiane, who was of low social status and whom Goethe could not yet bring himself to marry. In all probability the conditions in his home on the Frauenplan made it appear more convenient to move away from the center of town, where he lived in great proximity to Charlotte von Stein, to the outskirts, where he felt less observed. Like the Holy Family this family too took flight into Egypt.

My feeling is that the primal experience took place after the child's birth. Goethe's emotional state during these months can be reconstructed. Christiane's easygoing ways, the simple warmth of her youthful affection unencumbered by conflicts, problems, or reproaches, made his home a place of delightful pleasure never before experienced. Nevertheless, some of his deepest fears had come true. A crime had been committed. An innocent girl who was always loving to him was publicly exposed to humiliation. Bode reports the following about the legal aspect of Goethe's situation:

> Secular or church punishment in cases of illegitimate births had shortly before been abolished in the Weimarian area; but there were heavy punishments for the concealment of such pregnancies. The progenitor of such children still had to pay some fines: one and a half talers to the verger, as much to the leader of the choir of the native township, and five talers to the lying-in hospital in Jena. These statutes were in force for Goethe and Christiane. Whether they were carried out or waived through the sovereign's clemency has not been transmitted to posterity.[73]

The appearance of the son on the day Christ was born must have made the situation even uncannier for Goethe.[74] Christiane's imperturbable devotion to him and her utter lack of recrimination must have further fanned Goethe's feelings of guilt to barely endurable proportions. The general view is that Goethe could not marry his sweetheart at that time because it would have been impossible to introduce her at court. But Goethe's position was firmly enough established so that, if the marriage had not been publicly announced, this too would have been forgiven him. The whole community gossiped about his living with Christiane and no one was ignorant of her lack of manners and education. If Goethe did not marry her at that time it was because of an internal inhibition. This, of course, aggravated the feeling of guilt all the more.

In such circumstances, truly most dangerous to his equilibrium, he generated at the first occasion that offered itself a primal experience whose unconscious meaning was: It is not true that women become pregnant by impregnation; virgin birth is possible; father did evil things to mother; it

[73] (50, p. 3.) One must still add the memory of the execution of the two women guilty of infanticide in Goethe's native town; cf. above, p. 726.

[74] Charlotte von Stein's birthday was also on December 25.

is my mission in life to restore mother's honor and wipe out the malicious calumnies heaped upon her.

It is not necessary to separate in this interpretation the factors related to the actual precipitating situation of the present and those related to the infantile situation of the past, but it is worth while to remind the reader once more of some of the analogies used by Goethe in this context: the inquisition, the torture of an innocent woman, the falsification of her statements in order to make condemnation possible. Had Christiane's illegitimate pregnancy occurred in earlier times she might have been exposed to treatment quite like this. As a matter of fact, Goethe's own behavior resulted in an equivalent exposure of Christiane, inasmuch as he knew of the calumnies she would have to endure. Thus the primal experience also meant the denial of a misdeed in the present and its projection upon the father. But the unconscious core of the delusion, probably, was the much-needed conviction that he was not guilty of having begotten the child.[75]

The relationship to Christiane continued undisturbed; he worked assiduously and acted like the sanest of the sane. When Morris claims that the recognition of his error regarding chromatology "would have shaken this powerful nature irreparably in its foundations"[76] he reveals the deepest teleological meaning of Goethe's *Chromatology*. Apparently Goethe could maintain his equilibrium and stability only on the supposition that light was pure and uniform, untouchable, and undisturbed. A delusion helps the ego to bridge a rent in its structure (see 412).

Goethe's authority and fame on the one hand, and the relative social insignificance of the delusional system and its limitations to a well-defined area on the other, made it possible for Goethe to live out and maintain undisturbed to his last day that delusional system. To the many privileges he was destined to enjoy one must add also that of integrating a psychosis without suffering the punishment most mortals must bear for such a daring and hazardous step. For the unpleasantness of being held in disrepute by scholars for his wrong physical theories must, indeed, be considered a slight punishment only. Favored by destiny as he was, his *Chromatology* is still cited with praise by physiologists and psychologists,

---

[75] Oddly enough, in Goethe's own theory of the nature of color a remote implication of the doctrine of the Trinity may be found. According to Goethe, colors are the result of light, darkness, and opaqueness (*Trübe*).

[76] [. . . hätte diese mächtige Natur in ihren Grundlagen unheilbar erschüttert] (248, 40:xlix)

since the subjective part of his work is still as valid as it was when it was written, and he was the first correctly and accurately to observe and describe after-images, contrast, and allied phenomena in a systematic way (cf. 285). It is remarkable how free of interference by any psycho-pathology his capacity for observation of subjective color phenomena was and how productive he was in observing nature for unusual color phenomena. Ever ready to gather the unknown, he kept an astute eye on the subtle and faithfully recorded the noteworthy. But as soon as his mind turned towards the logical analysis of Newton's experimental situation he was tripped by his unconscious, and the ego's valiant struggle to maintain the denial of horrible guilt deprived reason of its sublime functions.

The question of how he succeeded in limiting this pathological way of combating an unconscious conflict to this one well-defined situation is puzzling. From a purely psychological or, better, clinical, point of view one can only state that the great importance natural science had for Goethe lay in the possibility it offered of a framework into which he could insert a psychosis without further damage to the functioning of his personality in the community. May one perhaps assume that in science there were objectively given properties that favored Goethe's attaching the psychosis to them? In other words, was there a specific relationship between the two, or was it due to accidental circumstances that his psychosis evolved in the field of science? Could it just as well have evolved in the field of art? It may sound like a useless question to ask why Goethe did not choose Shakespeare, rather than Newton, as the target for his paranoid reaction. However, speculation upon such a question may, after all, clarify some points. First of all, when Goethe's great admiration or even longing for Shakespeare began, his craving for an exalted father-substitute was still quite strong; he had not yet found his own full identity; his personality was still in flux and needed an ideal after which to pattern itself; the feeling of guilt had not reached that intensity which was present when he had ensnared himself in irremediable guilt. Secondly, in Shakespeare he faced a father-image with which he might have felt capable of competing successfully. Shakespeare's greatness was, at the time of the primal experience, well-synthesized; the substitute father against whom the aggression was directed had to be one whose image was accessible to alteration.

Yet here I wish to introduce a more general factor, going beyond the accidental vicissitudes of man's life. I believe that Goethe had reached at the time of the onset of his psychosis, when he was forty or forty-one years old, his absolute peak of life.[77] As was remarked before, as Goethe grew older his identification with the pedantic father became increasingly apparent (cf. 216, p. 198). The psychobiological roots of these identifications go back to an early age. The actual manifestations of the identification, however, are held in abeyance, particularly in individualistic and rebellious personalities. But aging peels off the integuments that conceal such old and repressed identifications, and my suggestion is that the starting point, barely noticeable to the onlooker, of the reactivation of such old identifications—or the time when the counterforces that hold down the identifications weaken—coincides with man's reaching the peak of his psychobiological existence.

One may see in Goethe's partial psychosis an attempt at fighting against the resurrection of an ancient identification, which had distasteful features for him. All such processes have a multitude of meanings and functions, but I wish to point out only that possibly there was in this psychosis an attempt at externalizing the arena of struggle. Since, despite its great repugnance, these psychobiological processes cannot be kept in check by the ego and it has to suffer them, it may easily select as a scapegoat someone against whom it can proceed actively and without restraint, so as to suffer with less pain within its own borders that which it cannot slow down in its relentless course. In other words, one of the functions of Goethe's psychosis, if my hypothesis is correct, was a struggle against aging, carried out by a process of externalizing an internal danger. His own child was of course a permanent reminder to Goethe that he was getting older. His permitting the child, at least for that time, to remain illegitimate—an act so openly hostile that its significance is evident— amounted also to a denial that he had a son.[78] It is further clear that if a psychopathological process of such magnitude and gravity had extended

---

[77] I cannot offer anything like proof in favor of my suggestion that Goethe's peak of life occurred around this time. The suggestion as such is not essential to my theory but adds a psychobiological factor which may or may not have had its bearing. I was struck when I found in Jones's biography of Freud the sentence "Eighteen ninety-seven was the acme of Freud's life" (321, 1:267). Freud was then forty-one years old and in view of the similarities between him and Goethe I thought my guess might thus find indirect confirmation. In this context it is of interest to note that Goethe and Freud reached almost identical ages. There is a difference of only thirty-eight days.

For more concrete evidence see H. C. Lehman (361, p. 162): "It has been found that literary masterpieces of the first rank have been produced most frequently by authors who were from ages 40 to 44 inclusive." See also 362, p. 73, which favors my above assumption. Although I did not find any direct confirmation of my assumption in Charlotte Bühler's book on *Lebensläufe* (74), neither did I find anything that would either disprove or contradict it.

[78] About Goethe and his son see Appendix Q.

into the field of his artistic creativity it would have caused a far greater upheaval in Goethe than it did when it touched the field of chromatology exclusively. But it is striking that this process took hold of just the one creative activity that was typified—among all the many in which Goethe indulged—by its constant reference to a frame of true or false. In this connection it comes to my mind that the few people I have known with extraordinary mathematical gifts have shown particularly bizarre personality traits. Mathematics is the most exact branch of science and it always puzzled me how personalities so profoundly under the sway of irrational forces could maintain the discipline and control so intensely required in the area of mathematical thinking.

Returning to Goethe, it must be considered that his creations in the field of art did not flow in a constant stream, but were produced in spurts.[79] In order to create something extraordinary he had to be under high emotional tension. This usually centered in a woman with whom he fell passionately and almost compulsively in love without sexual discharge. As Möbius convincingly showed, whether this happened did not depend —despite appearances—on external circumstance: when the emotional crisis occurred he found the woman who seemed to inspire him (395, 1:205–27).

Our present way of thinking leads us to believe that these spurts are correlated to biological factors. The artistic creations were then the beautiful vases into which the sporadic outbreaks of passion and emotions were poured. Common sense would suggest that just such spells of extraordinary emotional tension are particularly likely to give rise to psychopathology, that is to say, to the partial psychosis. However, one can observe that more frequently than not science—and therefore also chromatology—occupied his mind during just those intervals when his mind was not required to withstand the onslaught of heavy emotional spurts. Possibly this seeming contradiction is attributable to our relative ignorance of the laws of emotional processes. What now appears to be correlated to biological rhythms may later be recognized as the effect of early traumata. Periods that now appear to be characterized by relative emotional calm may later be recognized as periods that contained great emotional tension but in which that tension was successfully combated by the ego's defenses. What now appears like a peak of emotional tension may actually be a period of weakened defense. It is further possible that the ego is sometimes less careful in applying the reality principle where it believes itself

[79] Möbius studied the rhythm of Goethe's creativity and the psychopathology involved with great astuteness and in detail (see 395).

1143

well protected by the completeness of its control over its reality-testing functions. Something similar can be observed when a slip or parapraxia occurs. Just when the ego is paying particular attention to what it is performing, or feels certain of itself for other reasons, its vigilance may be misdirected and the parapraxia will take place. Artistic creation also may give direct vent and discharge to the unconscious conflict, whereas the necessity of sticking to the hard-and-fast rules of scientific research may, precisely for a personality like Goethe's, constitute an unbearable burden, driving the fettered ego, by way of compensation, to give free range to that which is most deeply repressed.[80] This content then finds expression in a context and under conditions in which the ego is fully convinced that it is perfectly secure against being made the victim of irrational forces.

In the case of the afore-mentioned mathematicians the process must have been reversed. They were constantly threatened by a break with reality, and mathematics was the only island where the ego could safely stride within the secure walls of unsubvertible rules.

Thus science offered an area for Goethe's creativity at times when, for whatever reason, artistic creativity was at a low ebb. Yet was Goethe truly creative in science? The question has been debated back and forth and I wish to emphasize only one aspect which has impressed me by its seriousness.

A large proportion of those who have elaborated upon Goethe's contribution to science have not been well acquainted with the scientific literature of Goethe's time and that preceding him. In an extremely thoughtful and well-documented study (335), Kohlbrugge, on the basis of wide acquaintance with the scientific literature of the eighteenth and nineteenth centuries, cited many examples of the following kind.

In a letter to Merck of October 27, 1782, Goethe made a prediction that petrifaction would soon be correlated with the epochs of the world. Bielschowsky, one of the most popular of Goethe's biographers, does not hesitate to claim, upon the evidence of this letter, that Goethe was the first to recognize the importance "of those stony documents" for geology (see 335, p. 147). Kohlbrugge, however, easily proves that this idea had come to Goethe from his reading of Buffon[81] and other contemporaries. Kohlbrugge examines most of the findings and theories for which Goethe

---

[80] Freud's discussion of the relationship between attention and parapraxia, the absence of parapraxia in automatic behavior vs. the probability of its occurrence when a particular effort is being made, contains the basic formulations of this problem; cf. 187, p. 29.

[81] Georges Louis Leclerc, Comte de Buffon (1707–88), French naturalist, famous for his *Epoques de la nature* (1779).

has been given credit and is forced to the conclusion that in nearly all instances Goethe was either in error or was following what others had said before him.[82] Kohlbrugge also recognizes that this does not detract at all from Goethe's greatness and we find the following statement:

How much would we be deprived of if Goethe had really been a modern, exact, I almost feel inclined to say "boring," natural scientist. We should be glad that this he was not, that among the few things in which he was found wanting, there was this gift.[83]

Goethe's struggle and aversion against mathematics are well known.[84] Many psychological factors could be unearthed that would have a bearing on this aversion. Wolfram von den Steinen, in his excellent book *Das Zeitalter Goethes* (506), stresses those sectors of the cultural life surrounding Goethe whose importance he did not grasp. Of those cited, the most important seems to me the rise of the machine age, which took place during Goethe's lifetime and which remained unremarked by him.[85] I wonder to what extent Goethe rejected exactly that which in the course of history actually destroyed his society and culture and that which, in the last analysis, poses those problems that we are facing today and that seem beyond our ingenuity to master. It would be interesting to know how far our technology would have developed without the rise of mathematics that has taken place since Leibniz, that is to say, if mathematics had not developed beyond the calculus. If I may express an opinion, although I am quite unburdened by any knowledge upon the subject, I should venture the amiable illusion that technical knowledge might not have developed beyond the limit past which it injures mankind. Goethe stands just at that border. He had premonitions of what was to come but expressed it somewhat fantastically. He said to Eckermann (October 23, 1828) that the time would come when God would lose his enjoyment of mankind and everything would have to be destroyed for "a rejuvenated creation."[86] Goethe

---

[82] Kohlbrugge's conclusions do not seem to be the result of a hidden opposition or hostility to Goethe, which no doubt characterizes part of the literature about him. It seems rather that Kohlbrugge feels regretfully compelled to adopt conclusions that conspicuously contradict those of many other authors.

[83] 335, p. 150. See also 514. It is of interest to notice through what mental gyrations one must go when one neglects this point of view. See 322. For a happy synthesis arrived at by analyzing Goethe's attitudes as a natural philosopher see 38, cf. 531.

[84] For a discussion of this broad topic see 126; 86; 374.

[85] Max Geitel, *Entlegene Spuren Goethes* (230), reports all the manifold incidents in Goethe's life in connection with technique, trade, machines. But as the title itself indicates this did not involve central problems. The point of view I have taken here is too extreme and has been corrected in Appendix V.

[86] [zu einer verjüngten Schöpfung] (119, p. 554)

thought this would happen after thousands of years. But this strange prediction must have grown out of a deep doubt and the vague feeling of some uncanny process in which Western man had become entangled. Goethe wrote to Zelter on February 28, 1811:

> The mathematicians are silly fellows and they are so far away from divining what the essential points are that one has to condone their conceit. . . . I wonder what sort [of person] the first one will be who will understand this situation and deal honestly with it; for not all of them are blockheads and not all of them are malicious. Furthermore, at this point, I see all the more clearly what I have known already for quite a time without saying anything about it, that the culture mathematics gives to the mind is most one-sided and limited.[87]

Yet in attacking so violently "the culture mathematics gives to the mind" does not Goethe attack that aspect of our civilization that would give him the greatest discomfort were he alive today, namely, that it is based primarily on the usufruct of the technical sciences to the denigration of art and religion, with which it largely dispenses? And as, I believe, I have noticed in all paranoid psychoses in which cultural issues of our time are given prominence, Goethe's psychosis, too, had an essentially conservative content. It covered the area where the individual felt threatened and with all the power at his command he tried to stem the tide. But in vain! Did Goethe know that he was fighting a losing battle? A passage in another letter to Zelter, of March 18, 1811, seems to betray this. In turning against the physicist Weiss,[88] Goethe wrote about him: "an impotent hatred is the most terrible sensation; for, to be exact, one should not hate anyone except when he could annihilate him."[89] Here again we encounter projection in full bloom, for Goethe's hatred was an impotent one. Not only was it

---

[87] [Die Mathematiker sind närrische Kerls, und sind so weit entfernt auch nur zu ahnden, worauf es ankommt, dass man ihnen ihren Dünkel nachsehen muss. Ich bin sehr neugierig auf den ersten, der die Sache einsieht und sich redlich dabey benimmt: denn sie haben doch nicht alle ein Brett vor dem Kopfe, und nicht alle haben bösen Willen. Übrigens wird mir denn doch bey dieser Gelegenheit immer deutlicher, was ich schon lange im Stillen weiss, dass diejenige Cultur, welche die Mathematik dem Geiste giebt, äusserst einseitig und beschränkt ist.]

This quotation gives only a one-sided view of Goethe's relationship to mathematics. It says more about the way he felt about mathematicians. For a comprehensive and definitive presentation of the subject, see 116; 117.

[88] Christian Samuel Weiss (1780–1851), professor at the University of Leipzig, from 1810 professor at the University of Berlin; he lectured against Goethe's chromatology in 1811.

[89] [ein ohnmächtiger Hass ist die schrecklichste Empfindung; denn eigentlich sollte man Niemand hassen, als den man vernichten könnte.]

directed against the *manes* of his father and, as a paranoid hatred, directed in its root against an object of the past, almost never capable of satiation, but it was also aimed at the inroads of a new culture, which, however incompatible it was with what was dear to Goethe, he was powerless to prevent. These two factors made Goethe's hatred a self-perpetuating one, which the self could not eliminate. Such hatred is possible only when the ego knows at least unconsciously that its cause will never be carried to victory.

Goethe has been called the first modern European. His encyclopedic stature is reminiscent of Aristotle. Yet that he included much that stemmed from the medieval age cannot be overlooked. The medieval age is not meant here in the sense of the Dark Ages but of the period that believed in alchemy and that could see the works of God as clearly as modern man sees the world of objects. Just as Goethe possessed an incredible breadth of identifications with everything human, so also a manifoldness of civilizations and cultures left a residue in him. He can be called a great compounder of the past. But those features in modern science that were destined in the end to cause and necessitate a break with the idea of God, he could not integrate, and they remained alien to him. I think it was Goethe's religiosity that made him repudiate a system purified of the last vestiges of anthropomorphism, and one must not forget that Goethe still stood under the last wave of the medieval tradition.[90]

Yet that science played such a great role in his life, that he devoted so much time and effort and thought to scientific problems, shows that he had grasped the spirit of the age in which he was living. I have meant only to suggest here a historical factor that may have had a great bearing on why certain aspects of science never could become relevant to him. This factor is not in opposition to the psychological one. We saw that around modern physics he evolved a system of paranoid ideas correlated to archaic problems of childhood. Thus the archaic and infantile in his personality succeeded in undermining that which had been least integrated by his personality, and that was modern science; but it could not endanger that which had become a well-organized part of his personality, namely, his artistic creativity. Thus he fought a battle against a reality whose outline he dimly perceived on the horizon but which it would have been too painful for his ego to integrate.

[90] I should have written this chapter quite differently and should have saved myself much doubt if I could have read R. D. Gray's excellently documented and convincing study (263) before writing this essay.

At this point I wish to take up once more the diagnostic question. It can be properly discussed only if Goethe's partial psychosis is not regarded in isolation but is brought into genetic connection with the psychotic episode or episodes that he suffered in his student years in Leipzig. The several episodes may then appear as phases of the same disease. I adduce as external evidence that the Leipzig episode was precipitated by a gesture of his sweetheart to her eye (letter to Behrisch, beginning of October, 1767). Although the specificity of this precipitating element establishes only a superficial similarity to the later phase, in which the eye had also a leading function, the seeming coincidence still may be the clue to a deeper connection. The voyeuristic and homosexual elements were certainly pronounced in both phases. It would be a challenging task to analyze both phases side by side. They are comparable to the course tuberculosis may take: an acute phase in adolescence with spontaneous recovery followed by a phase in the middle years with the formation of a cavity that causes a minimum of clinical symptoms. Thus we may assume that Goethe's psychic disease, which had been acute for a short time during his adolescence, became subterranean, to manifest itself again in that unfortunate moment when Goethe looked through the prism, not to leave him again. Viewed in this way the diagnosis of schizophrenia, improbable and surprising as it may be, becomes conceivable. It is unnecessary to say how much one hesitates to draw such a conclusion in view of the superb efficiency of a vast array of ego-functions, of an unusual degree of flexibility and strong object-relations. *Non nostrum tantas componere lites.*

Chapter 2

Finale to an Experiment in Love

LEAVING THE DIFFICULT diagnostic problem, I have now to append Goethe's farewell to Charlotte von Stein, for his separation from her bore a consequence relevant to the subject matter. I wish to discuss first Goethe's letter of June 8, 1789. I call this his last letter to her, for although, after an interval of seven years, their correspondence started anew, the 130 letters—the majority of them short—that followed, up to her death in 1826, have nothing to do with that Charlotte von Stein whom he had so excessively loved. Seemingly she had become removed to the periphery of his life.

It was the twelfth anniversary of Cornelia's death when he wrote this "last" letter. There is no indication that he was aware of the meaning of that day, but one can scarcely imagine that not even his unconscious had taken notice. It was also probably the day when he took the last and definite step in discontinuing his relationship with the woman erstwhile beloved beyond measure. It had become evident that their relationship was untenable. On June 1, 1789, he wrote her a long letter of justification, piling one argument upon another to prove that he had not changed since his return from Italy, that he was still a man who cared for his friends and assisted them; justifying his love for Christiane[1] by the well-known statement:

---

[1] For Goethe's relationship to Christiane see Appendix Q.

And what sort of relationship is it? Who is deprived by it? Who lays claim to the feelings that I grant this poor creature? Who to the hours I spend with her?[2]

He calls her son Fritz as a witness of his unchanged concern.

And it would have had to be by a miracle if I should have lost solely to you the best and fondest relationship.[3]

He reproaches her for her unbearable behavior towards him in constantly finding fault "before there could have been any question of a relationship that seems to hurt you so much."[4] He attacks her by expressing regret that she had again taken up the drinking of coffee, and reminded her that she had given up this habit for his love's sake. Thus by implication he let her know that he was not the only one that was guilty of giving in to instincts, but that by regressing to forbidden oral gratifications she, too, had betrayed their mutual contract of high morality. But what an incredible mental short-circuit, what a childish argument to raise, in view of the deep anguish and humiliation the woman saw herself as being exposed to by his behavior! It is noteworthy that this slip should have been made by Goethe and it probably was expressive of a secret admission of having hurt her that he used such an inadequate argument.

The final letter of June 8 shows this even more clearly. He starts out by assuring her how hard it had been for him to write the previous letter and by surmising that it was equally unpleasant for her to read it. Yet at least "the lips are opened"[5] and he wishes they may never be closed again for them. His confidence in her was his greatest bliss and if it should be broken off he must become a changed person. He did not want to complain about his situation at Weimar, but it was a painful one, and he enumerated all the unfavorable features: the cold, humid summer, the severe winter; the Duke, the many inconsistencies, the futility of work, the general dissatisfaction of everyone at court. If besides all this there also arose discord with a close friend, the situation might become unbearable. Thus in a veiled way he threatened to leave Weimar. He quickly added that all this was said for her benefit as well as his and expressed his deepest

[2] [Und welch ein Verhältniss ist es? Wer wird dadurch verkürzt? wer macht Anspruch an die Empfindungen die ich dem armen Geschöpf gönne? Wer an die Stunden die ich mit ihr zubringe?]

[3] [Und es müsste durch ein Wunder geschehen, wenn ich allein zu dir, das beste, innigste Verhältniss verlohren haben sollte.]

[4] [. . . eh von einem Verhältniss die Rede seyn konnte das dich so sehr zu kräncken scheint.]

[5] [. . . ist doch wenigstens die Lippe eröfnet]

regret that he should be the cause of sadness to her in all these circumstances.

And then the letter takes an unexpected turn:

I do not wish to say anything by way of excuse. I only want to ask you fondly: Help me yourself, so that the relationship that is repugnant to you may not degenerate but remain the way it is.

Restore your confidence in me again, look at the matter from a natural viewpoint, permit me to say a sensible, true word about it to you, and I can hope that everything between us shall be reestablished in purity and goodness.[6]

And then he proceeds to chat about everyday matters.

What the answer to this letter was—if there was one—is not known, but a silence of seven years ensued, broken only by two short communications that have been lost (see 254, 2:717).

The first letter written after this interval, on September 7, 1796, concerned some assistance Charlotte von Stein needed for Fritz. It begins: "You receive, dear friend, a page that may be shown to the Duchess [also] if necessary." And it ends:

Permit also further that my poor boy [his son August] may enjoy your presence and may form himself through seeing you. I cannot think about it without being moved that you wish him well so much.[7]

This referred to Charlotte von Stein's having, from time to time, taken little August as a visitor to her home.

The desperate and sudden cry for help in the letter of June 8, 1789, and the deep emotion when he thought about how kind Charlotte von Stein was to his "poor boy," may belong together. The question is: did Goethe know, when he wrote to Charlotte von Stein on June 8, that Christiane was pregnant? She was then in her third month of pregnancy and it is not probable that she tried to conceal the fact from her lover. Of what was Goethe thinking when he expressed the fear in his letter to

---

[6] [Zu meiner Entschuldigung will ich nichts sagen. Nur mag ich dich gern bitten: Hilf mir selbst, dass das Verhältniss das dir zuwider ist, nicht ausarte, sondern stehen bleibe wie es steht.

Schenke mir dein Vertrauen wieder, sieh die Sache aus einem natürlichen Gesichtspunckte an, erlaube mir dir ein gelassnes wahres Wort darüber zu sagen und ich kann hoffen es soll sich alles zwischen uns rein und gut herstellen.]

[7] [Sie erhalten, liebe Freundinn, ein ostensibles Blatt um es allenfalls der Herzoginn zu zeigen. . . . Erlauben Sie auch ferner meinem armen Jungen, dass er sich Ihrer Gegenwart erfreuen und sich an Ihrem Anblick bilden dürfe. Ich kann nicht ohne Rührung daran dencken dass Sie ihm so wohl wollen.]

Charlotte von Stein that his relationship to Christiane might degenerate?[8]
Was he thinking of marriage or desertion? Did he need Charlotte von
Stein's moral support to do either one or the other—since apparently he
despaired of continuing as things were?

I should surmise that his first reaction was despair and anxiety and a
desire to be again with the woman who had succeeded in keeping him
free from feelings of guilt for so many years. The desire for confession and
absolution was probably quite strong, and Charlotte von Stein could
probably have had him back at that moment, at least for a while.[9] Yet he
set up one condition, namely, that his relationship to Christiane continue.
But this was just the point where Charlotte von Stein could not compromise, since here was the border beyond which she could not make herself
the instrument of his salvation. If she had been able to live quite in the
service of this great man, she would cheerfully have taken the hand he
stretched out towards her. For Goethe it probably was better that she
acted selfishly. Here the Cornelia situation was revived. Cornelia too had
been jealous and had not wanted to share the admired brother with a
rival. But Cornelia had gone away twice—once when she married and
once when she died—and he had survived. And survive he would also
this time. Here may be the secret reason for his having written the letter
on the anniversary of his sister's death. It was written in a way that indirectly forced Charlotte von Stein to break with him. The request for
reconciliation—aimed at clearing his conscience—coupled with the request
to acquiesce in his living with Christiane, can also be considered a letter

[8] Was Goethe referring in that sentence to his relationship to Charlotte von Stein? By
taking it as a reference to Christiane I follow in my interpretation that which is current.

[9] Bode presents a historical example of a woman who was in a situation comparable to
Charlotte von Stein's and who acted in the opposite way. This is the story of the afore-
mentioned Zimmermann—who played a role before and shortly after Goethe and Charlotte
von Stein met (see above, p. 148)—and the wife of Hofrat von Döring. This woman had
become the sole mainstay of his wretched existence after his daughter had died and his son
had fallen into incurable derangement. When her husband was appointed to another city and
Zimmermann felt he could not go on without her, she chose a young girl as a wife for him.
The marriage worked out beautifully. (See 49, pp. 309–310.) Bode's unfavorable comparison of Charlotte von Stein's behavior with this instance is not quite fair. Goethe's relationship with her had from the start taken its character from the fact that when he arrived in Weimar he had been specifically in need of a woman who was totally interested in
him without sexual involvement. If Charlotte von Stein had been a woman who could have
acted like the wife of Hofrat Döring, she would never have been able to give Goethe what
he got from her during that pre-Italian decade. It was just that total possession without
reservation (except the sexual one) that made it possible for him to recover. Since knowledge
of the psychology of such constellations did not exist at that time, it had to be a woman
whose emotional make-up fitted the bill. Yet that emotional make-up rendered impossible a
smooth ending to this exquisite experiment in love.

of dismissal, as a kind of ultimatum that Goethe may have been convinced beforehand would prove inacceptable.

And now we may be able to understand the contradiction, several times mentioned, between Goethe's emotions—as expressed in his letters shortly before and during his Italian Journey—and his actions. Evidently the image of the beloved woman was so deeply ingrained in his existence that a conscious thought or a conscious intent of separation was unacceptable to him. Consciously he evidently clung to the very last moment to the illusion that his "alliance of souls" [Seelenbund] would be permanent. I can well imagine that if a doubt that threatened this certitude had entered his consciousness he might not have been able to go to Italy. Therefore the repeated reassurances and expressions of love from Italy were quite logical; the pain of the impending separation might otherwise have paralyzed the vigor of his action. His actions, indeed, were in conformity with the iron necessity of further development and growth, yet the emotions were still clustered about the pleasures of a past developmental phase, a constellation rarely encountered in clinical psychopathology.

Yet whatever criticisms Goethe may have voiced against Charlotte von Stein, the glaring absence of later references to her in Goethe's written record proves that he must later too have been aware of the incomparable, unique role this woman had played in his life. Certain experiences are surrounded by the halo of sacredness and therefore remain locked away in memory. Yet a glimpse of that uniqueness can be caught in the lines Goethe added to a poem, written for his friends on the occasion of his seventy-seventh birthday, when he sent a copy of it to Charlotte von Stein (August 29, 1826):

> The enclosed poem, my dearest, should really close: "To see inclination, however, and love of those living in direct neighborly affiliation, sustained through so long times, is the supreme [value] that can be granted human beings."

> And so [may it be] for ever and ever! [10]

These were the last words of Goethe's to reach Charlotte von Stein, who died four months later.

And what Goethe meant to Charlotte von Stein up to the last minute of her life, despite the violent attacks she had for a time hurled against him

---

[10] [Beyliegendes Gedicht, meine Theuerste, sollte eigentlich schliessen: Neigung aber und Liebe unmittelbar nachbarlich-angeschlossen lebender, durch so viele Zeiten sich erhalten zu sehen, ist das allerhöchste was dem Menschen gewährt seyn kann.

Und so für und für!]

and his sweetheart, can be seen from her last will, in which she ordered that her funeral procession was not to pass in front of Goethe's house because she wanted to spare him a sight that she knew would distress him. But the Master of Ceremonies insisted that the funeral of so noble a woman must be led throughout the city, and thus this wish, too, like so many others of hers while she was alive, came to naught.

Chapter 3

The End of Self-Cognition

W<small>HATEVER THEIR FEELINGS</small> about each other may have been during the thirty-seven years following Goethe's fateful letter of June 8, 1789, the fact is indubitable that during the fourteen years of Goethe's association with Charlotte von Stein he was passionately striving for self-knowledge. Over and over again feelings, impulses, and wishes were confessed and in hard discipline subjected to mastery. On that day when he dismissed Charlotte von Stein he dismissed also the self-analytic attitude. I wish to quote some passages which may show Goethe's thoughts about self-knowledge in later years (cf. 293). Chancellor Müller reported Goethe as saying, in a conversation of March 8, 1824:

> I assert man can never learn to know himself, can never look upon himself purely as an object. Others know me better than I myself. Only my relations to external reality can I learn to know and to appraise aright; one should limit oneself to this. With all the striving for self-knowledge that the priests and morality preach to us we do not get ahead in life, do not arrive either at results or at true inner improvement.

Apparently as an afterthought, Goethe added:

> Yet I do not wish to give out this opinion as a gospel.[1]

[1] [Ich behaupte, der Mensch kann sich nie selbst kennenlernen, sich nie rein als Objekt betrachten. Andere kennen mich besser als ich mich selbst. Nur meine Bezüge zur Aussenwelt kann ich kennen und richtig würdigen lernen, darauf sollte man sich beschränken. Mit allem Streben nach Selbstkenntnis, das die Priester, das die Moral uns predigen, kommen wir nicht weiter im Leben, gelangen weder zu Resultaten noch zu wahrer innerer Besserung. Doch will ich diese Ansicht nicht eben für ein Evangelium ausgeben.] (246, p. 101)

Eckermann records a conversation of April 10, 1829, expressing similar views. Goethe said:

At all times it has been said and repeated that one should strive to know oneself. This is a strange demand, which no one has yet satisfied, and which, really, no one ought to satisfy. For all his thinking and striving man is dependent on external reality, on the world around him, and he has [enough] to do to know it and to make it serviceable to the extent that he needs it for his purposes. About himself he only knows when he enjoys or suffers, and thus, also, solely through sufferings and joys is he taught about himself that which he is to seek for or to avoid. Moreover, man is, however, a dark creature; he does not know either from where he comes or whither he goes; he knows little about the world and least about himself. I do not know myself either and God protect me too therefrom.[2]

These strong words against self-knowledge can be confirmed also by Goethe's written word. In a short paper about the scientific approach towards nature, the following passage appears:

I confess that from way back the great and so meaningful-sounding task: *know thyself* has always appeared to me in a suspicious light as a trick of secretly banded-together priests, who wished to confuse man by means of unattainable demands and who wished to lead him away from activity in connection with external reality towards a false inner contemplativeness. Man knows himself only in so far as he knows the world, which he can perceive only in himself, himself only in it. Every new object thoroughly looked at opens up in us a new faculty. I therefore paid great attention in more mature years to how far others might perhaps know me, so that in them and by means of them, as in so many mirrors, I might acquire more precise knowledge about myself and my inwardness.[3]

---

[2] [Man hat zu allen Zeiten gesagt und wiederholt, man solle trachten sich selber zu kennen. Diess ist eine seltsame Forderung, der bis jetzt niemand genüget hat und der eigentlich niemand genügen soll. Der Mensch ist mit allem seinem Sinnen und Trachten aufs Äussere angewiesen, auf die Welt um ihn her, und er hat zu thun, diese insoweit zu kennen und sich insoweit dienstbar zu machen, als er es zu seinen Zwecken bedarf. Von sich selber weiss er bloss wenn er geniesst oder leidet, und so wird er auch bloss durch Leiden und Freuden über sich belehrt, was er zu suchen oder zu meiden hat. Übrigens aber ist der Mensch ein dunkeles Wesen, er weiss nicht woher er kommt, noch wohin er geht, er weiss wenig von der Welt und am wenigsten von sich selber. Ich kenne mich auch nicht und Gott soll mich auch davor behüten.] (119, p. 285)

[3] [Hiebei bekenn' ich, dass mir von jeher die grosse und so bedeutend klingende Aufgabe: *erkenne dich selbst,* immer verdächtig vorkam, als eine List geheim verbündeter Priester, die den Menschen durch unerreichbare Forderungen verwirren und von der Thätigkeit gegen die Aussenwelt zu einer innern falschen Beschaulichkeit verleiten wollten. Der Mensch kennt nur sich selbst, in sofern er die Welt kennt, die er nur in sich und sich nur in ihr gewahr wird. Jeder neue Gegenstand, wohl beschaut, schliesst ein neues Organ in uns auf. . . . Ich habe daher in reiferen Jahren grosse Aufmerksamkeit gehegt, in wiefern

Here, in a theoretical context, self-observation is asserted to be futile and is replaced by observation of those who know the subject. By studying one's reflection in others one gains knowledge about oneself. Self-observation is here indirectly limited to one's social effect, and the unconscious, of which Goethe was so well aware during earlier years when he was in contact with Charlotte von Stein, is, in the last analysis, denied. In a significant passage Goethe has Antonio, Tasso's antagonist, express similar views:

It is, indeed, pleasurable to occupy oneself with oneself, if only it were as useful. Inwardly no man learns to know what is innermost in him, for he measures himself after his own measure, sometimes too small and unfortunately often too great. Man knows himself only in man; only life teaches everyone what he is.[4]

Here too Goethe does not supply a counterargument but has Tasso agree with Antonio's reasoning although it is directed against him.

In another context, Goethe differentiates between two kinds of self-knowledge:

If we then look at the important word: *know thyself,* we must not interpret it in an ascetic sense. In any case there is not meant by this the autognosis [knowledge of self] of our modern hypochondriacs, humoralists and Heautontimorumenos [self-tormentors], but it means quite simply: Pay attention somewhat to yourself, take notice of yourself so as to become aware of how things stand in your relationship to your equals and the world. For this purpose no psychological tortures are needed: every capable person knows and experiences what this means; it is good advice, which amounts to the greatest practical advantage for everyone.[5]

andere mich wohl erkennen möchten, damit ich in und an ihnen, wie an so viel Spiegeln, über mich selbst und über mein Inneres deutlicher werden könnte.] ("Bedeutende Förderniss durch ein einziges geistreiches Wort," published in 1823; *Soph.* II, *11*:58–64)

This passage adds new insight into the mechanism of projection, which played such a great role in Goethe's partial psychosis.

[4] [Es ist wohl angenehm, sich mit sich selbst/ Beschäft'gen, wenn es nur so nützlich wäre./ Inwendig lernt kein Mensch sein Innerstes/ Erkennen; denn er misst nach eignem Mass/ Sich bald zu klein und leider oft zu gross./ Der Mensch erkennt sich nur im Menschen, nur/ Das Leben lehret jedem was er sei.] (*Tasso, Soph.,* I, *10*:154)

[5] [Nehmen wir sodann das bedeutende Wort vor: *Erkenne dich selbst,* so müssen wir es nicht im ascetischen Sinne auslegen. Es ist keineswegs die Heautognosie unserer modernen Hypochondristen, Humoristen und Heautontimorumenen damit gemeint; sondern es heisst ganz einfach: Gib einigermassen Acht auf dich selbst, nimm Notiz von dir selbst, damit du gewahr werdest, wie du zu deines Gleichen und der Welt zu stehen kommst. Hiezu bedarf es keiner psychologischen Quälereien; jeder tüchtige Mensch weiss und erfährt, was es heissen soll; es ist ein guter Rath, der einem jeden praktisch zum grössten Vortheil gedeiht.] (240, no. 657)

On the basis of such statements, Richard M. Meyer[6] claimed that Goethe rejected "the renowned 'know yourself' . . . only in so far as it drives us into paralyzing rumination about the basis of our individuality; a practical self-knowledge appeared indispensable to him." I think this interpretation is wrong. It is true that Goethe distinguished between healthy and unhealthy self-knowledge. But what he called practical self-knowledge is not what is really meant by self-knowledge, and I am sure not what the inscription on the Delphic temple really meant. Goethe's concept was limited to what is nowadays called "interpersonal relationship." "Be aware of what is really going on between you and your fellow men; do not deceive yourself about your footing in the world." This is essentially different from an introspective process, with knowledge gained exclusively by the use of the self-observatory function. It admits the self only in so far as it is a socially effective self and inasmuch as it can be observed in its functional relation with the group.

In one of the *Xenien* Goethe gave an explanation of this attitude:

No one will know himself; no one will separate himself from his self-ego; yet he should attempt every day what is outwardly finite and clear, what he is and what he was, what he can and what he might.[7]

Here the possibility of self-knowledge is denied because it means the separation from a part of oneself. Again the advice to keep an eye on the surface configuration is repeated. Interestingly, to know oneself is regarded as a loss, as involving a separation from a part of one's ego. The reasoning seems to be that no one would bear the pain of losing a part of his most valuable possession. To acquire self-knowledge is indeed painful, and always constitutes a loss as well as an increase of knowledge. It means a retrenchment of the daemonic, which Goethe revered as the driving force of his existence. Nevertheless, he was aware of the dangers that surround the genius's not knowing himself. Thus he wrote, thinking of Byron:

Great talents are rare and it is rarely that they know themselves, but vigorous unconscious acting and meditating have most unhappy as well as pleasant consequences, and in such conflict an outstanding life fades away.[8]

---

[6] See Introduction to *Dichtung und Wahrheit* (248, 22:vii).

[7] [Niemand wird sich selber kennen,/ Sich von seinem Selbst-Ich trennen;/ Doch probir' er jeden Tag,/ Was nach aussen endlich, klar,/ Was er ist und was er war,/ Was er kann und was er mag.] (Aus dem Nachlass, *Zahme Xenien*, VII, 19–24, Soph. I, 5:84)

[8] [Grosse Talente sind selten, und selten ist es, dass sie sich selbst erkennen; nun aber hat kräftiges unbewusstes Handeln und Sinnen so höchst erfreuliche als unerfreuliche Folgen, und in solchem Conflict schwindet ein bedeutendes Leben vorüber.] (240, No. 260)

Goethe felt close to Byron and he must have sensed that Byron's fate could easily have become his own. Yet what he indicated in the above passage is the very thought that self-knowledge would have protected Byron from his ill fate. Was it that Goethe had an unconscious awareness that he had manipulated his own daemon well and that self-knowledge had forced his daemon into a path that led away from the threatening downfall?

Goethe, who suffered from a latent hypochondriasis, feared what he might discover if he looked into himself: "When man meditates on his physical or moral condition he usually finds himself sick."[9] Here he followed somewhat Hamlet's "conscience does make cowards of us all," but on another occasion he showed surprising insight regarding motives that may prompt a turning away from self-observation:

> One tolerates upbraiding for his defects; he lets himself be punished; he patiently suffers quite a bit for the sake of his defects; but he becomes impatient when he has to put them by.[10]

Self-observation always prompts an impulse towards self-change. This impulse may become completely suppressed or may be warded off in various ways. A subject under my observation once took the attitude that he did not need to change because he knew so much about himself. The mere knowledge of defects was heralded as a moral value entitling him to praise from others. This, however, belongs to the psychopathology of self-observation. The function of self-observation and the function of self-criticism are separate, but that one should activate the other can hardly be avoided unless the ego institutes countermeasures. In Goethe's case, where perception and action were extremely closely allied, it may be assumed that the defenses against the impulse to change the self were rather weak and self-observation may have been a potential source of constant irritation. In view of his strong narcissism the necessity of changing was, as in most instances, experienced as painful. Action directed toward the external world, however, is intrinsically more pleasurable:

> How can one learn to know oneself? Never through contemplation, but rather through action. Try to do your duty and you will know right away what you are made of.[11]

[9] [Wenn der Mensch über sein Physisches oder Moralisches nachdenkt, findet er sich gewöhnlich krank.] (1821; 240, No. 98)

[10] [Man lässt sich seine Mängel vorhalten, man lässt sich strafen, man leidet manches um ihrer willen mit Geduld; aber ungeduldig wird man, wenn man sie ablegen soll.] (240, No. 17)

[11] [Wie kann man sich selbst kennen lernen? Durch Betrachten niemals, wohl aber durch Handeln. Versuche, deine Pflicht zu thun, und du weisst gleich, was an dir ist.] (1829; 240, No. 442)

Self-observation replaced by fulfillment of duty towards the world! Here again Goethe anticipated Freud's theory that self-observation is a function of man's superego. But fulfillment of duties, of course, cannot provide man with that knowledge which he obtains by introspection.

At times it sounds as if Goethe would have liked to reach the bottom of self-knowledge but felt frustrated.

> Many know much, [yet] they are a long way from wisdom. Other people are for you a play; no one has learned all about himself.[12]

In the same publication Goethe also indicates the reason why he felt exasperated about self-knowledge.

> Know thyself—What is that supposed to mean? It means: Just be! and also do not be! It is a saying of the dear sages which contradicts itself in [its] brevity.[13]

Here, in resorting to a rationalization in his persistent fight against self-knowledge, Goethe at the same time recorded a deep truth. A person who observes himself changes, by so doing, the object of his inquiry. The problem encountered in this context is similar to that which modern physics has to contend with in the investigation of the structure of matter. Inquiry per se changes essentially that which is to be explored, and in human beings the observer himself ceases to be the same self in the act of assuming the attitude of observer. To a certain extent one can say that self-observation is impossible since in what is called self-observation there can only be observed a system as it is in the condition of self-observation, that is to say, the only self-observation possible is that of a self-observing person.

Self-observation, the faculty for which is the most outstanding difference between man and animal, leaves a gap in the ego. Therefore this acquisition by the species is bound to result in quite a few antinomies, some of which were synthesized by Goethe into general statements.

When Goethe went on: "Know thyself!—What would the reward be? If I know myself, at once I have to run away,"[14] he was referring to something that can no longer be called typical, at least in the sense that it would

---

[12] [Ihrer viele wissen viel,/ Von der Weisheit sind sie weit entfernt./ Andre Leute sind euch ein Spiel;/ Sich selbst hat niemand ausgelernt.] (*Proverbial* [*Sprichwörtlich*] 500–04, *Soph.* I, 2:245)

Cf. Henry IV of France: *Multi multa sciunt, se autem nemo.*

[13] [Erkenne dich!—Was soll das heissen?/ Es heisst: sei nur! und sei auch nicht!/ Es ist eben ein Spruch der lieben Weisen,/ Der sich in der Kürze widerspricht.] (*Soph.* I, 2:248)

[14] [Erkenne dich!—Was hab' ich da für Lohn?/ Erkenn' ich mich, so muss ich gleich davon.] (*Soph.* I, 2:248)

be inherent in the self-observatory function.[15] Actually man should have the stamina to hold a firm position even in the face of an ego divided in itself. Goethe here described the urge immediately to undo the gap inevitably produced by the activation of the self-observatory function as soon as it comes to the subject's awareness.

This sensitivity of Goethe's to the division of the ego is, in my opinion, connected with the problem of freedom. As Goethe apparently was earlier particularly sensitive to the reduction, or even temporary annihilation, of the ego through orgasm, this sensitivity seems to have been revived in the situation of self-observation. In saying: "A person has only to declare himself to be free and on the instant he feels himself contingent. If he dares declare himself contingent, then he feels himself free,"[16] Goethe described a basic antinomy regarding man's feeling of independence (freedom) and dependence (contingency) with respect to his standing in the universe. This antinomy grows out of man's capacity to observe himself. The declaration of freedom provokes the announcement of inner forces that limit the ego's freedom; the acknowledgment of these inner forces establishes a situation in which the ego can raise itself again above the limitation. Goethe expounded this problem in a letter to Rochlitz of November 23, 1829:

> *Act prudently* is the practical side of: *know thyself*. Both must be regarded neither as law nor as demand. . . . People would be more sensible and happier if they knew how to find the difference between the infinite goal and the contingent purpose and reconnoitered to find out bit by bit how far precisely their means do reach.[17]

Yet it seems as if Goethe himself never quite succeeded in establishing harmony between the infinite goal (know thyself) and the contingent purpose (prudent action).

It was, however, in his autobiography (Part 3, Book XIII) that Goethe made a definitive statement about his thoughts regarding self-cognition. Since this exposition was combined with a deep insight into the uncon-

---

[15] Although from psychoanalytic experience it is known that, depending on the depth of self-knowledge, every subject reaches the point where he turns away from the content gained by self-observation.

[16] [Es darf sich einer nur für frei erklären, so fühlt er sich den Augenblick als bedingt. Wagt er es, sich für bedingt zu erklären, so fühlt er sich frei.] (240, No. 44)

[17] [*Handle besonnen,* ist die praktische Seite von: *Erkenne dich selbst.* Beides darf weder als Gesetz noch als Forderung betrachtet werden. . . . Die Menschen würden verständiger und glücklicher seyn wenn sie zwischen dem unendlichen Ziel und dem bedingten Zweck den Unterschied zu finden wüssten und sich nach und nach ablauerten, wie weit ihre Mittel denn eigentlich reichten.]

scious I will quote the passage extensively; it also shows that Goethe's aversion left untouched his understanding of man.

> What, however, makes a sensitive youth most apprehensive, is the irresistible return of our errors; for how late do we learn to understand that while developing our virtues, we at the same time cultivate our errors. The former are founded on the latter as on their root and these branch out in secret as vigorously and in like variety as those in obvious [open, palpable, visible] light. Since we usually exercise our virtues with volition and consciousness yet our errors take us unconsciously by surprise, we rarely derive pleasure from the former, but always tribulation and anguish from the latter. Here is the gravest point of self-cognition that renders it almost impossible.[18]

It is impressive to watch the genius set side by side the claim of the impossibility of self-cognition and a decisive result of this very function. Evidently he exercised this function (how could he not?) profusely, but let it do its indispensable work subterraneously, thus avoiding unpleasant interference with the area of consciousness.

Be this as it may, the passages quoted here tend to prove that there was a latent conflict in Goethe regarding the function of self-observation and self-discernment. In other words, he was constantly on the verge of being—or an indeterminate number of times actually was—thrown into acute conflicts by the manifest activation of self-discernment. His main defense, in my opinion, was a grandiose shift from self-observation to observation of nature. The "subtle empiricism"[19] he once suggested in the study of nature—advising that one make oneself identical with the object —is one that ought essentially to be applied to self-observation, in which the observer must identify temporarily with all the contents he can perceive. Chiefly because of his aversion against this process he had to shift it to his inquiry into the universe, and conceived the idea that a physical content should be treated like a subjective one. When Goethe wrote: "We confess rather our moral errors, defects, and infirmities than our scientific ones,"[20] he surely was not describing a phenomenon generally valid. True,

---

[18] [Was aber den fühlenden Jüngling am meisten ängstigt, ist die unaufhaltsame Wiederkehr unserer Fehler: denn wie spät lernen wir einsehen, dass wir, indem wir unsere Tugenden ausbilden, unsere Fehler zugleich mit anbauen. Jene ruhen auf diesen wie auf ihrer Wurzel, und diese verzweigen sich insgeheim eben so stark und so mannichfaltig als jene im offenbaren Lichte. Weil wir nun unsere Tugenden meist mit Willen und Bewusstsein ausüben, von unseren Fehlern aber unbewusst überrascht werden, so machen uns jene selten einige Freude, diese hingegen beständig Noth und Qual. Hier liegt der schwerste Punct der Selbsterkenntniss, der sie beinah unmöglich macht.] (*Soph.* I, 28:211–12)

[19] [Zarte Empirie] (1829; 240, No. 565)

[20] [Wir gestehen lieber unsre moralischen Irrthümer, Fehler und Gebrechen als unsre wissenschaftlichen]. (*Aus dem Nachlass,* 240, No. 1264)

the scientist charges his inquiries, theories, discoveries, with great narcissism, but in general his moral values are closer to his ego than his work. Goethe meant the aphorism as one of his many attacks against the professional scientist. Even if he had been right, we must take it as primarily a self-admission of what his scientific work meant to him, namely, a substitute for the constant active working on his own personality. Thus it may be claimed that the root of his scientific work was a resistance against self-discernment, or in other words against a continuation of the process that had primarily absorbed him during his years with Charlotte von Stein. His systematic interest in natural science began shortly after his acquaintance with her; it led to his triumphal discovery of the *os intermaxillare,* which he announced first to Herder and then to her; and it took greater and greater hold of him the more his relationship with her cooled off, finally giving him the opportunity to rationalize a partial psychosis.

The "know thyself," which was the center and hub of his relationship with Charlotte von Stein, became a dreaded memento of a period concerning which his feelings may have been partly of humiliation. It may have hurt his narcissism deeply that during these ten years Charlotte von Stein had held a position of superiority over him such as no other person ever did in his adult life and that he was mainly the receiving party. The following epigram may have been written as a revolt against this unmanly dependency:

> I always thought to learn in good humor something from others. I was forty years old when this error left me. I was always foolish enough to believe I was teaching others. You, fate, [may you] teach everyone as he needs it.[21]

Goethe was forty years old in 1789 when he definitely broke with Charlotte von Stein and became a father. His relationship to her had been one of continuously learning, but at the age of forty, according to the epigram, he substituted fate as his teacher for someone else who remained unnamed. The known circumstances of Goethe's life at that time suggest Charlotte von Stein.[22]

---

[21] [Immer glaubt ich gut (müthig?) von anderen etwas zu lernen,/ Vierzig Jahr war ich alt, da mich der Irrthum verliess./ Thöricht war ich immer dass andre zu lehren ich glaubte/ Lehre jeden du selbst, Schicksal, wie er es bedarf.] (*Venetianische Epigramme,* No. 45; *Soph.* I, 5, [part 2]:376)

[22] Goethe's distrust of and fight against psychological introspection, coming after a protracted period of the most intensive introspection, can be compared with a historical process that is taking place under our very eyes. We are witnessing what is evidently a piecemeal destruction of Freud's psychological achievement, which was based on introspection and interpretation. By insidiously changing methods, falsifying concepts, and simplifying issues, the corrupters of psychoanalysis are transmogrifying it into what they call more exact science

I have quoted extensively the formidable words which Goethe used against self-recognition, strange indeed for a man who found ultimate accomplishment and fulfillment in ancient Greece, which considered self-knowledge as the consummation of all values. Strangely enough, the pleasure principle, which Goethe so successfully combated in the pre-Italian years, was embraced in disfavor of the pain the Delphic oracle commended, and the hopelessness of all psychology was declared man's irrevocable fate. Yet one cannot forget his frequent remarks in his letters to Charlotte von Stein about "the skins he shed," symbols of his progress in self-awareness through insight, and of a jubilant triumph in being able to live up to the demands of reason. Unquestionably the peak of this relationship with its great strides in self-recognition coincided with an alarming deficit in artistic production. It may have been the recollection that at a time when the process of self-cognition had its full momentum he was not productive artistically, that induced him decades later to warn in such harsh terms against strivings for knowledge of self.

Yet Goethe's genius saved him from really escaping psychology. His consciously setting aside introspection did not alter his grasp of man. When he wrote his friend Knebel (April 8, 1812) that in the last analysis we are capable of doing the good only "inasmuch as we are acquainted with ourselves"[23] and further, when he wrote in 1813 about Shakespeare that "the cognition of himself" enabled him to recognize others[24] he admitted that he knew all the time from whence his artistic genius drew the lifeblood of its creations. To be sure, his characters never again vibrated with that hotness of life that was so typical of the pre-Weimarian years. The earlier *Wilhelm Meister* was the last creation that can be put to any extent into that category.

Yet we know from a statement Goethe once made (see above, p. 261) that in his post-Italian years the vividness of his childhood memories faded away. That is to say, he went through a phase of second repression after the revival of the repressed during the pre-Italian decade. This second wave of repression found actual as well as symbolic representation in his striking out most of Wilhelm Meister's childhood history in the final draft of his novel. I believe that this second wave of repression was necessary in order to realize the full artistic potential.

---

and a therapeutically more effective treatment method. Yet all these changes, allegedly undertaken for the sake of improvement, make out of psychology a behavioristic science forever divorced from man's living soul. It is the reaction against a burden that is too heavy to carry and which therefore is cut to fit the shoulders of the epigones.

[23] [wir handeln eigentlich nur gut, insofern wir mit uns selbst bekannt sind]

[24] Das Erkennen seiner selbst, welches ihm die Einleitung gibt, auch fremde Gemüthsarten innig zu erkennen.] (*Shakespeare und kein Ende! Soph.* I, 41:52–53)

The creation of great art requires the interplay of the ego and the repressed, the former at times giving in to the latter, at times warding it off, at times alluding to it, at times denying it. I surmise that in order to restore the interplay of the almost infinite gamut of mechanisms by means of which the ego is able to deal with the repressed (and here I include also those mechanisms that are beyond the range of the defenses), and which are indispensable for the maximum artistic output, this secondary repression was necessary. That we find in its wake the traces of a psychosis ought not to disturb us, for it left Goethe's genius without a blemish.

Part IV
Appendices

Appendix A

Remarks Upon the Problem of the Relationship Between
Psychosis and Artistic Creativity

1

Tʜᴇ ꜰᴏʀʙɪᴅᴅɪɴɢ ᴄᴏᴍᴘʟᴇxɪᴛʏ of this problem militates against setting down anything more than a few tentative suggestions. A little is known regarding the negative aspect of the relationship between mental disorders and artistic creativity. The question has been raised in two ways: What are the creative products of patients who suffer from such disorders, and what are the effects of mental disorders upon the creative genius? Well-known examples of the latter are Hölderlin, Van Gogh, Nietzsche, Maupassant. That a mental disorder can impair any function and consequently also the artistically creative one is more or less self-evident. On the other hand, that there is a relationship between mental imbalance and artistic creativity has been presumed or conjectured since early times. The eeriness surrounding the genius led in the Middle Ages to the belief that he had concluded a pact with the devil. Such superstitions and equivalent theories may sometimes have grown out of the feeling that the genius's creations stem from a realm which the ordinary man does not dare to tread.

Goethe's Leipzig episode, which is what calls forth these remarks, is significant for the fact that here a psychotic episode and the blossoming of a new mastery of the literary resources of language stand side by side.

Three groups of questions suggest themselves: (1) What was the nature of what Goethe brought forth? Was it really original with him? (2) What was the nature of the acute psychopathology he suffered from? (3) What are the connections, if any, between the two?

Many have claimed that a new German literature was brought forth by Goethe in Leipzig, and perhaps no one has advanced this claim better than Friedrich Gundolf. I wish to quote a few pertinent remarks from his commentary on six poems,[1] which, of those Goethe wrote in Leipzig, impress him most as showing elements essentially new in German lyric poetry:

> With the Leipzig Book of Songs . . . the series of love songs starts which for the first time in modern High German do not only talk *about* love, but themselves are love-become-music [Klang gewordene Liebe]. . . . Here not only concepts, motives, and images stemming from the realm of love are presented or reference taken to love, and it is not only said: "I love"— but the spell lies in the *sound,* in the rhythm, in *magic,* and not in the conceptual aspect of the language. Here the ego does not put forth its state of excitation, but the excitation of the ego presents itself in the language as melodic rhythmic language structure. (Gundolf's italics) (270, p. 59; my translation)

Such a claim as Gundolf here makes is not difficult to assert but it is difficult, if possible at all, to prove. I shall try presently to exemplify the new quality that Goethe assertedly introduced into German literature but I wish first to fix more precisely what it is that needs to be shown if the claim is to be validated. To begin with, I think we can swiftly agree that the quality under discussion had not shown itself in Goethe's poetry before. Anyone who reads Goethe's poems in chronological sequence will be struck by the qualitative difference between certain lines of his Leipzig poems and everything he had written earlier. It is not so simple with the question of whether these elements were original with Goethe and truly new in German literature. I propose, first, that the discussion be limited to poetry written in High German. Surely the boundaries of a language must also be the boundaries of a literature, and whether or not the new elements existed, for example, in the poetry of Walther von der Vogelweide (c. 1170–c. 1230, greatest of the minnesingers) is a question that would require the comparison of incommensurables to resolve. For the same reason, the lyric poetry of the Middle Ages will be omitted.

In High German literature only two poets before Goethe came close to the specific, seemingly new, elements of which we get a glimmering in some of Goethe's Leipzig lyric lines. These two are Johann Christian Günther[2] and

---

[1] The six poems are: "The Night" [Die Nacht], *Soph.* I, *1*:44; "The Butterfly" [Der Schmetterling], *Soph.* I, *1*:51; "Wedding Song" [Hochzeitlied], *Soph.* I, *1*:50; "Inconstancy" [Unbeständigkeit], *Soph.* I, *1*:64; "The Bliss of Love" [Das Glück der Liebe], *Soph.* I, *1*:48; "To the Moon" [An den Mond] *Soph.* I, *1*:49. About Goethe's language at that time and words coined and reshaped by him and integrated into the German language see 76.

[2] Johann Christian Günther (1695–1723), born in Lower Silesia, died in Jena, lived a restless and dissipated life of a kind that is characteristic of a certain type of genius. Goethe acknowledged Günther's great contribution to German literature and called him "a poet in the full sense of the word" [ein Poet im vollen Sinne des Worts] (*Soph.* I, 27:81), and summed up his life in the one sentence: "He did not know how to tame himself, and thus his life melted away from him as did his [writing] poetry." [Er wusste sich nicht zu zähmen, und so zerran ihm sein Leben wie sein Dichten.]

Klopstock. Close though these two—and particularly Klopstock—may have been, neither of them, however, as far as I can see, ever achieved that synthesis with the artistic medium that appears in Goethe's lines. In Klopstock, too, there is discernible a modicum of rational deliberation, a modicum of detachment from, rather than immersion in, the content of the poetry. I do not by this comment refer to the poet's subjective detachment but only to the effect his poetry has on the reader.

I select six lines of a poem by Goethe in which I find the new element most unmistakably expressed. The "literal" translation I place after the German, since translation at this point can only convey the ostensible topics of the poem and cannot possibly render those elements that are here considered essentially new to German literature.

> Und durchstreich mit leisem Tritte,
> Diesen ausgestorbnen Wald.
> Luna bricht die Nacht der Eichen,
> Zephirs melden ihren Lauf,
> Und die Bircken streun mit Neigen
> Ihr den süssten Weyrauch auf.

(And I roam with soft step through this died-out forest. Luna breaks the night of the oak trees; zephyrs announce her course, and the birches as they bow strew about the sweetest incense for her.)

This is probably the original version of the poem.[3] It was sent to Behrisch with other poems in May, 1768, and was called "Die Nacht" (The Night). It was published in 1770 in the collection *New Songs* [Neue Lieder]. In the first two lines of the poem Goethe sets forth how he leaves the cottage of his sweetheart. Then follow the six quoted verses. The second stanza ends in typical rococo style. The poet enjoys the coolness of the summer night and, although he can barely grasp its delights, he would gladly forgo a thousand such nights if his girl would grant him one.

I should perhaps stress right at this point that not one of the six poems is written entirely in the new spirit. In each instance, at least in my judgment, only parts show the imprint of the new lyricism. I must further stress that a psychological evaluation of the poem with respect to the points in question depends almost entirely on its language, yet not on language alone, for its

---

[3] I take this text from Morris (251, *1*:244. The next version can be found in the same volume on p. 352. There the first line reads "[I] am walking with veiled step" [Wandle mit verhülltem Tritte]. For different versions of the poem see *Soph.* I, *1*:376. It would be a challenging task to subject all these variations to a psychological analysis. It is my impression that the later versions, although they may be improvements in some poetic respects, are more removed from the primary process and thus weakened in the immediate impact of their imagery.

imagery too is essential. Yet the same imagery—though it too was, I think, new in German literature—could have been presented in language that would by no means have created the specific inner experience that the poem in its present form affords. This inner experience can only be described in approximation. The description must inevitably be lacking in that specificity which would be necessary for a demonstration of what the nature of these new elements really is.

Let us consider first the imagery. If I say that it is characterized by richness, flexibility, originality, and beauty, I am once more saying something that can be said of a large number of poems. Evidently the specialness lies in a subtler aspect. One point to be observed is that tension is created at times by the synthesis of innately contrasting images, such as "died-out forest" (that is, as it were, a non-forest), or "soft step" (that is, a soundless sound, the German word *Tritt* denoting action implying some sound). In another version tension is generated by slightly different means: "soft step" becomes "veiled step," in which data are brought together from different sense areas that cannot be combined in actuality (steps cannot be veiled but by stepping softly, a reference to the auditory sphere, whereas the act of veiling refers to visual impression). The image of "breaking the night" belongs to a similar mode: the use of a verb that is basically applicable only to concrete objects, concretizes the concept of night so that it gains in actuality and reality.

A surprising and eminently artistic turn lies in the poet's speaking of "the night of the oak trees," as if nature had not in general the appearance of night but only in so far as the oak trees were involved. By this turn Goethe actually compels the reader to put himself into the oak trees and then to look out to see himself surrounded by the oak trees' darkness. This imagery is, moreover, imposed upon the reader at the moment when the whole phenomenon is on the verge of dissolution, or has already faded, because Luna has broken that very night. Of course nature is—as almost always in poetry—anthropomorphized in this poem. The breezes, which bring movements into the "died-out forest," are the messengers of the moon, and thus, since they are themselves the very symbols of easy and rapid motion, they endow the moon, too, with motion, which otherwise, because of the subjective imperceptibility of her change in position, we experience as a static source of light. Still further tension is created by the poet's leaving it to our imagination whether Luna's speed is founded upon the speed of her messengers or vice versa. The final image of bowing birches strewing incense for Luna is a particularly charming one, since the natural form of these trees and the usual slight movement of their leaves, even in absence of a perceptible breeze, suggest this very allegory. But this pleasingly easy imagery, having the quality of resolving tension, is still enriched by the "sweetest incense," which introduces a new sensual area, one that participates most intensely in the experience of a beautiful summer night. And this odor, by being presented as prepared by the trees in celebration of Luna, absorbs the variety of preceding elements into itself. What has been unfolded is thus at the end compounded again into a single unit.[4]

To turn now to the way poetic meter is used here, I wish to quote a relevant remark of Gundolf's about the difference between meter and rhythm: "Meter bears a relationship to rhythm like that of a seismograph to an earthquake, the thermometer to temperature . . . in short, like that of the conceptual means for the ascertainment of a state of a movement to that state or that movement itself" (270, p. 61). Meter is a quantitative factor and rhythm a dynamic one. If a poet tries to fulfill the requirements of meter he fills a form with words; form and content do not fuse into a unit. Rhythm, which is an organic principle, shatters meter even when it fulfills all its rules, as happens in Goethe's six lines. As one listens to them one does not hear them as verses whose form has been dictated by a metric principle; they seem rather, just as much as prose, to have had their rhythmic stamp given to them by the very shape of the thought and feeling being expressed. To be sure, Klopstock came close to the same achievement, but significantly enough the metric system to be followed was placed in front of many of his odes,[5] which would be most incongruous with Goethe's poetry. These six lines are remarkable in that Goethe had not at that time attained the freedom he acquired later in the use of a free meter, but, while being obedient to strict rules, he is still able to make the meter seem to disappear, so that the words flow with complete freedom, following their own inherent laws and those of the imagery attached to them. The same idea can be expressed in more general terms. The poetic medium has lost, so far as we can discern, a property which is among those most essentially its own. I should like to compare that medium to the air that is between the beholder's eyes and the object he beholds. It is imperceptible to the beholder and therefore devoid of any interfering quality. To make the medium's qualities imperceptible is, of course, the art of the true master. As long as we perceive in the sound of a violin that it is produced by the rubbing of a string with a bow the greatest artistry has not been achieved. Yet in these six lines Goethe succeeded in doing just this. The words flow with such ease, the meter is so completely converted into rhythm, that the character peculiar to the medium becomes imperceptible.

In inquiring into the psychological effect of these verses one may call attention to still another peculiarity: Words and images, so it appears to me, flow in such a way that, though the germs of visual imagery are, up to a certain point, evoked, they are not permitted to blossom forth to full concretization. This result is achieved not only by the rapidity and richness of the sequences but also

---

[4] Again I can only refer the reader to the best of Klopstock's poems, such as *Die Frühlingsfeier,* to see for himself how genuinely new even in the use of imagery these six verses by Goethe are.

[5] This is the case, at least, in the edition of his complete works of 1823 (333). I do not know whether this agreed with Klopstock's intention.

because some of the imagery itself defies full visualization. Right at the outset the "softness" of the step cannot be fully visualized; another difficulty is raised by the forest devoid of life. Is it a soundless forest, or literally a dead forest, or a living forest depleted of moss and flowers and animals? The "breaking of the night," in turn, requires, if the metaphor is to be translated into a visual image, some further step than such an expression as "clearing up" would have necessitated. The announcement of Luna by the breezes is again a metaphor with great appeal to visualization but by no means one that leads directly to a pure visual image.

Only the final imagery about the birches permits at last easy and rapid visualization. Thus it may be that one of the factors that create the specific effect in the reader is that the flow of stimuli is structured in such a way as simultaneously to inhibit the blossoming forth of the full potential reaction until all the dammed-up tension can be concentrated in, and thus fortify, the final image.

Of course, whether this actually takes place depends on the individual's subjective artistic experience itself. No amount of analysis can persuade that these characteristics are there; indeed, for many, the further such analysis goes, the more it will destroy the possibility of the specific uniqueness' being grasped. Moreover, it is unfortunately true that the same terms I have applied to these lines may be applied with at least seeming propriety to certain characteristics in the poetry of others without its being true that that poetry is capable of evoking a comparable reaction in the reader. I even venture to say that if the effect of these lines were accessible to satisfactory analysis that very fact would perhaps disprove the point I am driving at, which is that in these six lines Goethe produces the impression that that particular night cannot be presented poetically in any other way if it is to be presented adequately, that the poem actually conveys more than the reader would have been able to experience had he himself experienced the night in question, that, indeed, it conveys the utmost that there is to be conveyed about such a summer night, and, in short, that the key to this achievement is his having found the way to create a poem that shall seem to the reader to be identical with the subject.

The existence of this reaction in the reader has not, to be sure, been checked experimentally. I am also aware that no properties of the literary work have been described with that precision necessary as a basis for the investigator's correlating them with this unique effect in the reader. Yet because it cannot be demonstrated as one demonstrates a hallucination that the creation of identity between the poem and its referent has taken place, should the inquiry into the prerequisites of such an act therefore be dismissed? I believe we ought to proceed as if the phenomenon itself had been well established, and seek to explain what the prerequisites were of Goethe's thus—more or less suddenly—emerging as the first German poet to write this kind of poetry.

The study of that emergence makes us the witness of the very moment when a new cultural element was being introduced into the category of language. This new element had in its own way historical antecedents, and it is reasonable to assume that Goethe might not have been able to evolve it if he had had to start German poetry from scratch. But whatever and however numerous these antecedents may have been, they are not the same as this particular element which appeared in Goethe's lyrics. This element is original with and singular to Goethe. To what extent it can also be found in other German poets subsequently, or to what extent it is also encountered in other literatures, are not subjects of this inquiry.

Since the origin or introduction of any new cultural element is a matter for the widest discussion in history and anthropology, the importance of Goethe's Leipzig period goes beyond the area of psychology or of the history of literature.

In a further attempt at putting into more general terms the characteristics of the phenomenon in question I wish to state that the linguistic aspect is characterized by its integration of two opposites. It fulfills the most primitive function of language and, simultaneously, the most sublime one. The most archaic function of language, observable even in animals, is its eliciting of certain emotions or reactions in the recipient of the message. This function does not presuppose the formation of words, but is, under certain conditions, already attached to the utterance of mere sounds. A scream of pain or terror or any reflex sound caused by a strong affect will evoke in the recipient a similar emotion, sometimes even of the strength of the emotion that supposedly brought forth the stimulus. Here is the most archaic situation, growing from the instinctual sphere, in which the auditory stimulus replaces the object itself, that is to say, the auditory stimulus evokes in the recipient feelings of such strength as equal or surpass that of the feelings evoked by the object's presence. The most sublime aspect of language has to do with purely formal qualities, belonging to the realm of aesthetics (whatever this concept may cover). The formal aspect requires compliance with certain implicit standards, the origin and meaning of which has never been satisfactorily elucidated and which change not only from period to period but to a certain extent at the hands of each poet. The new element in Goethe's lyric consists of the integration of the instinctual and the formal (sublimated) into a perfect linguistic unit, in which the two layers of existence, innately contradictory and seemingly mutually exclusive, are so intricately blended that the listener resonates to both of them simultaneously and without opportunity of differentiating them. This formulation in turn, though valid in itself, remains still too general to cover the specific instance.

This new synthesis of instinct and language was preceded by and overlapped with Goethe's Anacreontic poetry, born out of the contemporary rococo. In Goethe's Anacreontic poetry, instinctual content played an all-important role. As Gundolf put it, in this phase of Goethe's lyric he sang about love and sex, whereas in the new poetry it is the special combination of what is being written about and the way it is being written that becomes the direct expression of emotions. This profound change requires inevitably the supposition that there had arisen in Goethe a new relationship to the main objects of poetry. One must conclude from the literary evidence that Goethe was able to identify, or, more precisely, to identify more closely, with nature or other people or whatever became the topic of poetry than he had been able to during his rococo period. Whereas until then Goethe had written poems about what he perceived in nature and about the feeling these perceptions elicited in him, it seems that now the frontiers of separation or isolation between object, emotional response, and artistic medium were so much obliterated that all these formed one unit. One can express the same idea by repeating that Goethe's verses were no longer a medium through which the poet conveyed contents that were outside of them, or a medium through which the listener became acquainted with such contents; the verses lost their medial character and were so formed that those contents were to be found in the structure of the verses itself.

Such profound changes in the literary product require further the assumption that the interplay between mechanisms that are indispensable for artistic creation must likewise have changed. In view of the central interest that is being devoted to ego psychology at present, one is particularly eager to know more about just this aspect of the problem. Unfortunately, clinical observation must surrender at this point to mere speculation. Did the change within the array of ego-mechanisms pertain to projection, or identification (cf. 331, pp. 300–01), or their harmonious interplay? It seems in some poems as if a feminine identification had been successfully acted out, but identification with a butterfly or a tree can likewise be encountered. We shall return to this question presently.[6]

2

The diagnosis of Goethe's psychopathology in Leipzig is no easy matter. There occurred two short-lasting attacks, which, though separated by an interval of twenty-eight days, I do not keep apart when I speak of Goethe's psychotic episode.[7] It started with his attributing to a gesture of his sweetheart a delusional meaning, followed by a nightmare to which for a short while he reacted as if its content had occurred in reality. Temporary confusion, panic, rage, acute attacks of jealousy, a host of somatic sensations, and insomnia were the other more outstanding symptoms. I believe that most psychiatrists will agree that all this permits the diagnosis of a short-lasting psychosis. Agreement, however, will be harder to achieve as to the type of psychosis. Some experts to

[6] For an abundance of source material and a detailed discussion of the relationship between adolescence and literary creativity, see 24.

[7] I have not reported Goethe's accidental fall from a horse which occurred between the two attacks.

whom I read the pertinent letters had no doubt that the psychopathology they revealed amounted to no more than that so often encountered in a certain type of adolescence rich in conflicts and protracted. They were certain that it did not constitute a malignancy such as schizophrenia. They considered the degree of his insight into and detachment from his internal processes, though often reduced, sufficient evidence to preclude such a diagnosis.

Protracted adolescence of the type Goethe showed is indeed always replete with the strangest and most bizarre forms of psychopathology, which can be sufficiently explained by the heavy impact and demands puberty puts on the psychic apparatus. To take such adolescent complications as warranting the diagnosis of schizophrenia may easily result from the present vogue for diluting (and thus making utterly meaningless) the concept of schizophrenia to such an extent that every kind of psychopathology—if only it is intense, unusual, or bizarre enough—finds its place in that classification. Indeed, if no more were known about Goethe's psychopathology than what is contained in the Leipzig documents, I should perhaps drop my suggestion of the diagnosis of schizophrenia, were it not for two circumstances. The eerie mood that runs throughout the letter to Behrisch at the beginning of October, 1767, as well as the intensity of the suffering and despair that one senses, perhaps goes beyond what we mean by the vague term "normal adolescent psychopathology."

In this context it is also proper to call attention to a feature of some of Goethe's Leipzig letters that showed up also in his behavior and was noticed with pain by his friends:[8] a tendency towards affectation, mannerism and pretension. Gundolf quite rightly says that much stronger urges and sensations seem to underlie the poetry of such of Goethe's predecessors as Günther and Klopstock than Goethe's Leipzig poems, and that the sensations (emotions) underlying the Leipzig poems were "light and shallow" [*leicht und flach*]. These circumstances, too, may favor the view of a young man going through a schizophrenic episode, though they do not, of course, prove it beyond a doubt.

Be this as it may, as I shall set forth in detail in Section 3 of this Appendix, Goethe at the age of forty-one, that is to say twenty-three years after Leipzig, evolved a delusional system which, apparently, persisted to the end of his life. It became partitioned off and did not branch out. Since its content pertained to a peripheral matter and Goethe was protected by his enormous prestige, it was not followed by social consequences. It came to the attention of some of his intimates who respected his idiosyncrasy and did not draw the grave conclusions that it deserved.

However, in view of this later psychopathology the earlier episode may appear in a different light, for the two are not disconnected in content. Thus we observe an acute psychotic episode, with paranoid ideas, at the age of eighteen, which becomes subterraneous and reappears twenty-three years later in the

[8] See the letter of Goethe's friend Thorn (51, *1*:5–6).

form of a chronic paranoid system, a clinical situation that perhaps permits the diagnosis of schizophrenia.

Nevertheless, it will appear most improbable to associate a diagnosis of a disorder that so frequently leads to disintegration with a personality of such unique eminence as Goethe's, in whom precisely the highest ego-functions operated unimpaired by any disease. Two arguments, for whatever they may be worth, I wish to adduce here.

The first is the analogy with somatic pathology. Untreated tuberculosis, for example, as is well known, will in most instances lead to an utter destruction of the organism. But in earlier years, when there were many such cases, instances were by no means rare in which a florid tuberculosis during adolescence subsided by spontaneous recovery. In later years, perhaps between fifty and sixty, the subject might develop a small cavity, which, leading only temporarily to minor clinical symptoms, then became encapsulated, to be found only accidentally at autopsy. Yet both courses, the malignant as well as the benign, still belong to the same internal disease: tuberculosis.

Secondly, the fact that the highest mental functions were not affected in Goethe's instance does not militate per se against the diagnosis, as I shall demonstrate briefly in the following. I had the opportunity of observing over a period of years a young schizophrenic whose pathology was extensive and had impaired all aspects of his interpersonal relationships. He was unable to form positive object-relations, tormented those about him with reproaches ranging from petty to serious and bizarre, developed a paranoid system about a certain physical function, and possibly hallucinated at times. Yet it was most impressive to observe throughout the years of his psychosis that his capacity for producing certain kinds of intellectual work persevered unimpaired. He was a person of extraordinary gifts for abstract thinking and during the time of psychosis he published one paper after another in his particular field. His highly specialized and difficult work was his only tie to the world, and one might say that all other functions were sacrificed to the one great talent that he possessed.

On the basis of our present knowledge the features his case exhibited cannot, I think, yet be explained. What he reported was at times most puzzling. Thus sometimes when he looked up from his work for a few seconds he responded to his perceptions with delusions, but in the next moment, when he resumed his work, he pursued the most abstract thinking process with precision and correctness.[9]

In the case of this patient the ravages of a malignant disorder filled the clinical picture most conspicuously, whereas in Goethe's life the effect of the disorder can be discovered only with difficulty. But the constellation, if my hy-

---

[9] I feel strongly that such clinical findings disprove the current opinion that those processes denoted at present by terms such as "sublimation" or "neutralization" depend on qualitative changes of (libidinal or aggressive) energy; they prove rather that those processes are correlated to structure independently of the kind of energy that structure is activated by.

pothesis is correct, would still be the same in both instances: a malignant psychosis despite excellent operation of higher ego-functions. Reducing the problem to a purely clinical aspect, the difference can be considered a quantitative one, a far larger area of the ego being affected in one case than in the other.

3

If Goethe suffered from a schizophrenic disorder it is also remarkable that only its later phase damaged his productivity by temporarily draining away considerable energy from the artistic realm, whereas the initial phase, in my view of the clinical situation, made an indispensable contribution to the awakening of his genius. About this possible connection I wish to make a few tentative remarks.

In schizophrenia, ego-structure is dissolved. Upon how extensive the process is and what area it affects will the course and outcome of the disease depend. In describing Goethe's artistic achievement in poetry (which almost certainly started after the episode) I have mentioned the synthesis of instinct and linguistic form. The prerequisite of such a synthesis was a greater closeness of the ego to the instinct. The instinct had to be permitted to make an inroad upon the ego and to become amalgamated with ego-structure. We are dealing here with seemingly regressive processes of which Goethe evidently was incapable prior to the episode, judging from his previous Anacreontic poetry.

In my estimation the clinical record indicates that during the psychotic episode actual ego-structure was dissolved. The consequent freeing of instinctual energy, however, did not lead to physical discharges, but the energy was intercepted by uninjured ego-functions and used for the creation of poetry.

In reality, of course, such processes are infinitely more complicated and I have tried to devise only a simplified hypothetical model of what may have underlain the clinical observation.

The complication stems from various quarters. The dissolution of ego-structure is not per se a pathological process, for—as I believe—healthy growth is only possible if there is an appropriate balance between the formation and dissolution of ego-structure. This is a point of view that has never, to my knowledge, been discussed,[10] and the details of which I cannot present here. Yet if the dissolution of ego-structure during a schizophrenic attack is made the focal point, one would like to qualify this statement by adding the difference between it and equivalent healthy processes. Perhaps the time of dissolution ought to have ended with the onset of puberty, and subsequent dissolving processes are pathological. I do not know and cannot add any pertinent remark.

Furthermore, as mentioned before, what specific ego-mechanisms were involved in the new poetry still remains obscure. It seems as if, after the episode, Goethe was drawn into the objects, whereas before he partook of nature by

[10] See, however, 202, in which the problem is implicitly contained.

taking in the objects with which he identified. The usual mechanism of identification, after all, consists of the incorporation of a part of the world. The reverse mechanism, that of letting the ego flow into objects, is an exquisite schizophrenic mechanism, which causes—I think always—great pain to the ego, which thus feels deprived of its identity and responds with anxiety to a state of extreme impoverishment. The outstanding feature in Goethe's case was, if my theory is correct, that the self abandoned itself freely to being sucked in by external objects and did not, in the process, become truly impoverished but, like Jonah in the monster's belly, retained its identity along with sufficient composure to be able to write down all its experiences on its dangerous journey. An ego that is sucked in by objects that arouse its interest is one that has been weakened by dissolution of structure, but an ego that, under such adverse conditions, maintains its fortitude and synthesizes defeat into the victory of creation, proves that a basic fount of resourcefulness has been preserved. The difference in outcome between Goethe's and the usual schizophrenic psychosis may also have depended on the level of the libidinal development he had attained. As I shall suggest later, one of the most significant features in the make-up of the genius may be that he had reached the genital level, which we know the schizophrenic patient does not commonly succeed in doing.

By referring at this point to Goethe's libidinal development, I indirectly make the relation of libido and aggression the decisive factor, which brings me again in accord with well-established theories.

One feels tempted to ask whether schizophrenia has not a bearing upon the creation of the new and original far more often than is generally known.[11] In studying schizophrenic patients one is very frequently astounded by the originality of their approach to the world. They are freer of tradition than other patients. Despite the intermingling of archaism, one can learn from almost every schizophrenic a new aspect of the world. For many reasons, of which one is the extension of the involvement to higher ego-functions, his disease rarely leads to a constructive result. I am inclined tentatively to suggest the following. We commonly feel bedazzled by the multitude of past geniuses whose works we have had an opportunity to love and admire—for the life-span of one individual permits thorough acquaintance with the works of only a small number. Yet if the huge number of human beings that have populated this planet in the course of generations is considered, it is clear that it is more appropriate to speak of a paucity than of a multitude, especially if we bear in mind that there must certainly have existed more persons of the highest endowment than ever ripened into geniuses. Could the paucity of genius be partly explained by the small probability that the disease in question will befall a highly endowed person and will dissolve only so small an area of ego-structure as to effect liberation without casting a malignant spell upon higher ego-functions?

[11] Cf. Jaspers' study (314, p. 169) in which the implication of a schizophrenic process in the work of genius is discussed.

The possibly productive role this disorder has played in history will not be further discussed here. It is a comprehensive topic, which I have mentioned here only in order to add some weight to my initial diagnostic suggestion. It may now sound not quite so improbable as it did at first glimpse. Also we may now understand better why so many human beings are evidently inhibited in their creativity. I mentioned earlier (on p. 70 f.) the feeling of guilt aroused by the rebellion which, if not regularly contained in creation, is very frequently present. In view of the great role which instinctual unsublimated energy plays in the process of creation, we may, following Anna Freud, who speaks of the anxiety that is aroused by the strength of the drives (153, pp. 63–64), also speak of the anxiety that is aroused by the impulse to create per se. When Wälder says: "The ego experiences each excessive *crescendo* of the instinctual forces as danger for itself and independently of any consequences menacing from the outside a danger to be destroyed and its organization overwhelmed" (538, pp. 47–48), this viewpoint can be transferred *mutatis mutandis* to the deepest fears by which the ego is kept from using its highest creative potential. In the process of creating, the ego feels exposed to dangers. It is not difficult to reconstruct what these dangers are. Under the creative spell, the ego does not feel in control of its vicissitudes, and old castration anxieties may be aroused. I have an hypothesis to propose in terms of which this fear may be seen as not quite irrational. But, further, it is probable that the fear is linked to more primitive fears. The ego becomes absorbed in one purpose to the temporary detriment of other functions, and thus a deep anxiety may arise of being devoured by the creative process, or the created work, as the case may be. Concomitant with the creation of a masterwork part of the ego or the personality becomes temporarily split off from the rest of the organization and deposited in the work of art (see 462, p. 49; 350). Will it ever regain possession of that which it relinquishes in that process? The genius, with his immeasurable fund of resources, does not persevere long—if at all—in a deflated state, but the person of talent may look upon the process of creation as an immense inflation of the ego (leading almost to bursting), followed by a phase of paralysis and prostration, reflecting the old saying: *Post coitum omne animal triste.* Thus in the process of creation a mixture of two groups of traits can be found; one consisting of derivatives of male genital sexuality (about which I will have more to say in Appendix T), the other of female genitality with particular emphasis on pregnancy and birth. I think that the prospect of becoming entangled simultaneously in the activation of two heterogeneous functions is particularly liable to arouse the deepest fears in a mind that faces the prospect of losing itself in creative processes.

In consideration of these fears it becomes understandable that the ordinary person, in contrast to the genius, recoils from the advice that Freud indirectly gave when he wrote (178, p. 85):

A strong egoism is a protection against falling ill, but in the last resort we must begin to love in order not to fall ill, and we are bound to fall ill if, in consequence of frustration, we are unable to love. This follows somewhat on the lines of Heine's picture of the psychogenesis of the Creation:

> Krankheit ist wohl der letzte Grund
> Des ganzen Schöpferdrangs gewesen;
> Erschaffend konnte ich genesen
> Erschaffend wurde ich gesund.

> (Sickness, methinks, has been the final cause
> Of the whole urge to create;
> By creating was I able to recover
> By creating I became well.)

Perhaps in many cases neurosis and psychosis cause less pain than the creation of unique beauty.

Appendix B

Bibliographical Remarks Concerning Goethe's Correspondence with Charlotte von Stein

Since goethe's letters to Charlotte von Stein form the principal document on which this inquiry rests it may be fitting to add a few bibliographical remarks. According to a friendly communication of Dr. Vulpius of the Goethe-Schiller Archiv in Weimar, all known letters written by Goethe to Charlotte von Stein have been published and no communication is held unpublished in the archives. When these letters were published for the first time in 1848 (242) they were received with great surprise, for, unlike other women who had a lasting influence upon Goethe, Charlotte von Stein had not been known as one of Goethe's idols. Of course, as soon as this material became known, a large number of publications devoted to her appeared. Yet, of all the relationships Goethe entertained, the one to Charlotte von Stein must still be called the most enigmatic.

The reader may be interested in the frequency distribution of Goethe's letters to Charlotte von Stein. As might well be expected, a certain number of letters resist all attempts at being fitted into chronological sequence and some have been dated differently by various editors. In the accompanying chart I again follow the dating of the *Sophienausgabe*. If a letter covers a longer period of time I have counted each instance of Goethe's evidently adding a new part to his letter. If a letter of the same day contains parts marked as written at different times I have also counted such parts singly. I have not tried to fit into this chart letters not preserved in their original form which were among those that Goethe requested as aids in the writing of a book (such as his reports on a trip to Switzerland or Italy), but have included only those that are contained in the IV. Abteilung of the *Sophienausgabe*. (Since Goethe sent Charlotte von Stein the diary he wrote for her in Italy in lieu of letters, and since many letters written from Italy found their way into Goethe's *Italian Journey* and were not returned to the recipient, the chart is particularly misleading for the time Goethe spent in Italy, September, 1786–June, 1788.) The numerical frequency changes do not necessarily reflect changes in the intensity of the relationship, for— aside from the loss of some letters—their monthly number depended on numerous extraneous factors such as his or her absence from Weimar, although the reader should be aware that he also wrote many letters to her while they were at the same place. The chart, therefore, does not intend more than to give a bird's-eye view of the physical distribution in time of Goethe's letters as they are preserved, and no further conclusion can be drawn from it.

In order to evaluate the historical evidence on hand and to judge the numerical aspect of these letters (which number 1944, in my way of counting), the reader should be acquainted with the extent of Goethe's correspondence. In the fifty volumes of the *Sophienausgabe* (IV. Abteilung, *Briefe,* published 1887–1912), 13,683 letters (including drafts and parts of letters quoted in the letters of other people) are published. Since that publication more letters have been published and, of course, an unknown, but unfortunately very substantial, number of letters has not reached posterity. For a comparison it is also important to know that there are fewer than four hundred letters preserved written by Goethe to his wife, who stands next to Charlotte von Stein in the number of preserved letters she received. Yet even if we forget about the number of letters preserved and think of the possible number of letters Goethe wrote to this or that person, the known number written to Charlotte von Stein must be considered large in absolute as well as relative terms.

Goethe's letters to her were given by Charlotte von Stein to her son Fritz (1772–1844) during her lifetime. He wrote a commentary which does not go beyond the year 1789. It was apparently not meant for publication and is said to be replete with mistakes. It has, regrettably, never been published in its entirety. Fritz's nephew Karl von Stein and his wife, Luise, pasted the letters into seven folio volumes, not without trimming them to fit in some instances (see 254, *1:* 551, and, for the following, p. 552). Fritz von Stein probably had based his arrangement on a tradition derived from his mother. Since he kept them loosely in envelopes they may easily have become mixed up by his relatives when they pasted them in the folios. The sequence of the letters in the seven folio volumes now in the Archives at Weimar is regarded as quite unreliable and is therefore not followed by modern editors.

The seven folios contain the majority of Goethe's letters to Charlotte von Stein. Some of the Italian letters, except for one which Goethe presented to a friend in 1818, were found in Goethe's literary estate. One letter, written on July 23, 24, and 25, 1784, was found in 1942 (see 545).

It goes almost without saying that the large number of Goethe's communications to Charlotte von Stein contains some of great length covering several printed pages and some that consist of only a few lines. Except for two letters, all are unmarred and they are quite legible. After their break, Charlotte von

Stein asked Goethe to return her letters, and she destroyed them. Eighty-seven letters written by Charlotte von Stein to Goethe between 1794 and 1826 have been published by Petersen (254, 3:601–33). As far as I know there is no English translation of Goethe's correspondence with Charlotte von Stein.

FREQUENCY OF GOETHE'S LETTERS TO CHARLOTTE VON STEIN

YEAR	MONTHS												TOTAL
	Jan.	*Feb.*	*Mar.*	*Apr.*	*May*	*June*	*July*	*Aug.*	*Sept.*	*Oct.*	*Nov.*	*Dec.*	
1776	13	3	15	7	17	16	11	11	11	1	5	7	117
1777	5	8	20	6	13	7	9	7	7	5	8	14	109
1778	10	7	5	5	13	14	5	8	8	4	4	9	92
1779	6	5	11	6	7	4	3	5	13	17	12	3	92
1780	5	5	10	13	20	12	4	13	23	10	19	20	154
1781	18	30	34	29	18	13	14	13	11	9	16	24	229
1782	20	19	23	19	21	21	30	34	18	21	29	22	277
1783	15	7	9	19	9	12	12	13	10	10	14	19	149
1784	17	13	18	10	11	25	12	21	9	12	15	11	174
1785	6	8	18	19	7	10	1	5	14	12	18	23	141
1786	22	13	14	10	8	9	9	6	4	1	5	11	112
1787	10	10	0	1	1	3	1	2	0	0	0	1	29
1788	2	0	0	0	0	0	2	3	0	0	0	0	7
1789	0	3	0	0	0	2	0	0	0	0	0	0	5
1796	0	0	0	0	0	0	0	0	1	1	0	0	2
1800	0	0	0	1	0	0	0	0	0	0	0	0	1
1801	0	0	0	0	1	0	0	0	0	0	0	0	1
1802	0	1	0	0	0	0	0	0	0	0	0	0	1
1804	1	0	1	4	1	2	1	2	0	0	1	1	14
1805	3	1	0	0	0	1	0	1	0	0	0	0	6
1806	0	1	2	0	0	0	1	0	0	0	0	0	4
1807	0	0	1	2	1	2	0	2	0	1	2	3	14
1808	2	4	4	3	1	1	1	1	0	0	0	0	17
1809	2	0	0	1	2	1	0	0	1	1	2	2	12
1810	0	0	1	0	1	0	0	0	0	0	1	0	3
1811	0	0	0	1	0	0	0	1	1	2	0	0	5
1812	0	0	2	0	0	0	1	1	0	1	0	1	6
1813	1	0	1	0	0	0	0	0	0	0	2	1	5
1814	2	0	2	0	0	0	0	0	0	0	0	0	4
1815	0	0	0	0	0	0	0	0	0	0	0	1	1
1816	0	1	0	0	0	0	0	0	0	0	1	0	2
1817	0	0	1	0	0	0	0	0	0	0	0	0	1
1819	0	0	0	0	0	2	0	0	0	0	0	0	2
1821	0	0	0	0	0	0	1	0	0	0	0	0	1
1825	0	0	0	0	0	0	0	0	1	0	0	0	1
1826	0	0	0	0	0	1	0	1	0	0	0	0	2
									Dated letters				1944
									Undated letters				151

Appendix C

Further Remarks Concerning Goethe's Attitude Towards Work

IN AN INQUIRY into Goethe's psychology of work one has to take note that Goethe's artistic output rested on two different techniques of production: on the one hand the automatic, principally intuitive and seemingly effortless one (which can barely be associated with work), and on the other a laborious, painstaking, meticulous way of producing (which bears all the earmarks we commonly associate with work). Though for obvious reasons the two techniques are always blended in the series of actual, creative acts, the ego feels quite differently according as the one or the other technique prevails, and this difference in subjective experience alone justifies their separate discussion. The history of these two techniques, their meanings, the way they complemented each other, the specific problems involved in each—these, no doubt, would be the main headings in a study devoted to this subject. But little that is definite can yet be said about these various points.

I wish first to contrast the two techniques by quoting some pertinent remarks of Goethe's.

On April 6, 1829, he said to Eckermann of one of his poems that he would not be able to produce such a poem a second time and that he was unable to say how he came to do it "as happens to us very often."[1] In his conversation of January 2, 1824, he even claimed that the great can thrive only by means of undisturbed somnambulistic production. On March 11, 1828, he went further and assumed that no creativity of supreme kind, no distinguished *aperçu*, no consequential great thought, is within any person's power and is beyond all human control.

> Things like these man must regard as unforeseen gifts from above, as God's pure children which he has to accept and revere with joyful thanks.[2]

[1] [wie uns denn dieses sehr oft geschieht] (119, p. 272)

[2] [Dergleichen hat der Mensch als unverhofte Geschenke von oben, als reine Kinder Gottes zu betrachten, die er mit freudigem Dank zu empfangen und zu verehren hat.] (119, p. 539)

On February 24, 1824, he made a remark about the inefficiency of the thinking process.

All the thinking for the sake of thinking does not help; one must be right by nature so that the good flashes [of thought] always stand before us like God's free children and call out to us: here we are![3]

The following passage, from December 16, 1828, informs us about the other kind of productivity:

I carried this ballad[4] about in me for a long time before writing it down; years of pondering are involved in it, and I tried [to write] it from three to four times before it would come out for me as it now is.[5]

Here is an example of Goethe's capacity for working hard in order to get a piece to suit him. Thus only part of his literary work was the product of intuitive, unwilled creation.

It is highly probable that the first-mentioned literary technique—of automatic, intuitive creation—was the derivative of an unconscious urge to bear children, as can not the least be seen from the comparison of *Einfälle* with children, but what could have been the unconscious root of the second technique? Eckermann's report of his interview with Goethe on March 14, 1830, may point us in the right direction. Goethe, in speaking about his ballads, said the following:

I owe them chiefly to Schiller, who spurred me on [to write them] because he always needed something new for his *Horae*.[6] I had had them in my head already for many years; they occupied my mind as charming images, as beautiful dreams that came and went, and with which fantasy playfully rejoiced me. Reluctantly, I resolved to say farewell to these splendid appari-

---

The contribution of the unconscious to creative thinking will not be disputed by the analyst. Nevertheless, one wonders whether Goethe overemphasized this factor for a personal reason related to his attitude towards work, which is something that always requires conscious effort.

[3] [. . . dass alles Denken zum Denken nichts hilft; man muss von Natur richtig seyn, so dass die guten Einfälle immer wie freye Kinder Gottes vor uns dastehen und uns zurufen: da sind wir!] (119, p. 70)

[4] Goethe refers here to a poem published in 1820 under the title "Ballad" [Ballade] (*Soph.* I, 3:3–6). It was written in 1813. Its story is as follows: The sons of a knight call in a beggar to tell them a fairy tale. He recites the ballad of the king who is defeated and travels as a beggar with his little daughter. A knight asks for her and marries her. At this point in the story, the knight returns and is irate at his son's associating with a beggar and orders him to be thrown into the dungeon. The beggar, however, is the returning king, who had been deprived of his castle by the knight.

[5] [Ich habe die Ballade lange mit mir herumgetragen ehe ich sie niederschrieb; es stecken Jahre von Nachdenken darin, und ich habe sie drey bis vier Mal versucht, ehe sie mir so gelingen wollte wie sie jetzt ist.] (119, pp. 240–41)

[6] A literary magazine of which only three volumes (1795–97) were published under the editorship of Schiller.

tions that had befriended me so long, at the same time that I endowed them with a body by means of inadequate, meager words. When they were put on paper I beheld them with an admixture of woefulness; it was as if I had to part forever from a beloved friend.

On other occasions it went quite differently for me with my poems. I had thereof not the slightest impressions or forewarning beforehand, but they suddenly overwhelmed me and wanted to be made on the instant, so that I felt driven to write them down there and then instinctively and after the fashion of a dream.[7]

Here the two modes of production are contrasted with clarity and precision, and more is said this time about the mode that involved work and effort. The result of this mode was always poorer than the investment in it warranted, whereas the result of intuitive creation was comparable to a windfall. With no investment at all, the greatest wealth was then harvested. The setting down of work accomplished by means of effort, however, Goethe compares to separation from a friend.

This latter remark suggests strongly the comparison of the two techniques of production with two phases of female biological production: on the one hand conception and on the other gestation and parturition, the latter of which is frequently experienced as separation and loss. However, I feel more inclined to see in the two modes of production the reflection of two general aspects of femininity. The one puts emphasis on female passivity, stressing woman's submission to male activity. In this aspect women are nothing but the vessels into which man pours his creative powers, out of which grows new life. This aspect, of course, generalizes the phase of conception. The ego similarly feels passive like a mere tool when it is fertilized by creative ideas that seem to come from an unknown, or at least apparently ego-alien, territory. The other aspect stresses female activity, as if it were the mother who solely by her own powers creates the fetus and makes it grow by planned and purposeful activity, thus actively enriching the world by the addition of new life. This aspect of femininity (see 99, 1:282–83) would then be the equivalent of Goethe's second technique of production.

[7] [Ich verdanke sie grössenteils Schillern, der mich dazu trieb, weil er immer etwas Neues für seine Horen brauchte. Ich hatte sie alle schon seit vielen Jahren im Kopf, sie beschäftigten meinen Geist als anmuthige Bilder, als schöne Träume die kamen und gingen und womit die Phantasie mich spielend beglückte. Ich entschloss mich ungern dazu, diesen mir seit so lange befreundeten glänzenden Erscheinungen ein Lebewohl zu sagen, indem ich ihnen durch das ungenügende dürftige Wort einen Körper verlieh. Als sie auf dem Papiere standen betrachtete ich sie mit einem Gemisch von Wehmut; es war mir als sollte ich mich für immer von einem geliebten Freunde trennen.

Zu anderen Zeiten ging es mir mit meinen Gedichten gänzlich anders. Ich hatte davon vorher durchaus keine Eindrücke und keine Ahnung, sondern sie kamen plötzlich über mich und wollten augenblicklich gemacht seyn, so dass ich sie auf der Stelle instinktmässig und traumartig nieder zu schreiben mich getrieben fühlte.] (119, pp. 576–77)

How exquisitely female this mode was despite the feeling of activity can be discovered from the fact that such productions were usually for the sake of some other person. His first major production, *Götz von Berlichingen,* was accomplished at Cornelia's instance, that is to say, to please her. For a long while Charlotte von Stein held this place, and later—as in the case of the ballads referred to above—Schiller. The need to have such a counterplayer in order to be able to endure the displeasure of drudgery and separation (gestation and parturition), besides betraying the feminine component also indicates the intensity of conflict attached to work.

Intuitive creation did not involve this conflict. God's children leaped forth from Goethe's head like Pallas Athena springing from the head of Zeus. This kind of creation apparently left the ego enriched and strengthened. It was at times a sublime joy despite the passivity of the ego inherent in it. The process of effortless production, in turn, contained its specific conflicts, which I do not discuss in this context (cf. above, p. 105). Work by effort impoverished the ego and drained its stamina; it could be performed only when a beloved person requested it. It may even be doubtful whether the second part of *Faust* would have been finished if Eckermann had not continued the function of his illustrious predecessors. The necessity of working for the sake of somebody else if work was to be performed at all, shows that work never acquired in Goethe that degree of autonomy that is commonly expected in the adult. The child's work depends almost entirely upon his good relations to a teacher or a mentor of some sort. His work performance is intimately correlated with the existence of unimpaired ties of affection, and we grant the child this privilege in accordance with the weakness which the reality principle necessarily has in tender years.

Yet the pain that evidently occurred when a work of art, the plan for which had remained inchoate in the poet for a long time, gradually took concrete form and thus took its departure from him, does not seem to have been the strongest deterrent to the performance of such work. A deeper problem hides behind the struggle through which Goethe had to go in order to work. A hint as to what that problem was that underlay Goethe's seemingly neurotic work disturbance is provided in Eckermann's report of a conversation of February 4, 1829. Goethe then said:

> The conviction of our future existence originates for me in the conception of activity; for if I act unceasingly until my end then nature is obligated to assign another form of existence to me when the present form is incapable of sustaining my spirit any longer.[8]

[8] [Die Überzeugung unserer Fortdauer entspringt mir aus dem Begriff der Thätigkeit; denn wenn ich bis an mein Ende rastlos wirke, so ist die Natur verpflichtet, mir eine andere Form des Daseyns anzuweisen, wenn die jetzige meinem Geist nicht ferner auszuhalten vermag.] (119, pp. 244–45)

Here activity, death, and immortality are brought into a meaningful connection. One can scarcely say anything definitive about the relations among these three concepts in Goethe's unconscious. Goethe's statement seems to express only a belief in a proportion between one's activity and one's claim to immortality, but it is man's plight that in order to become immortal, he has first to die. However, according to those who believe in it, immortality is a quality of every human soul and not the privilege of the active man only. I wonder, therefore, whether there was in Goethe—despite the prima facie implication of the opposite—the unconscious idea that every man must in accordance with his constitution fulfill a certain measure of activity before he is prepared for death. Thus every psychological process involving the quality of activity would have meant to Goethe coming one step closer to death. In this light it may become better understandable why Goethe felt inhibited in making active work a constant part of his life and why he needed a compensatory gratification in the form of love when he had the active, voluntary impulse to produce by effort.

Two more instances may be cited to show that this hypothesis may have merit. When Faust at the end of the tragedy accepts work for the sake of society as an integral part of life, as well-nigh the only source of valid pleasure from which he does not want to part, at that moment death wins power over him and he succumbs. Furthermore, when, seven months before his own demise, Goethe had finished the play, he was in a mood that is best characterized by the following statement he made to Eckermann:

My further life from now on I can consider as a pure gift, and now basically it does not matter at all whether I do anything more, or what.[9]

Both instances may serve to show how easily acceptance and integration of the idea of work or accomplishment of work led to the idea of death.

The relation between the fear of activity and the fear of death must have been based on a deep-seated disturbance of the ego. Such psychopathology extends to layers of the personality that usually become accessible to investigation only in the course of a psychoanalytic procedure. If a guess may nevertheless be ventured on the basis of clinical experience I should surmise that the horror of work may have been connected with a disturbance of time experience. I wish to cite the following clinical instance: A patient tried to avoid a situation in which he would look forward with great joy to a future event. His justification was that if he looked forward to the coming of an event with joyful expectation time would pass faster than if he remained in a state of composure, and that this rapid passing of time he experienced as a proportionately faster approach towards death. This conclusion was based on the belief that a person's life-span is fixed, and the flow of subjective time is something concrete, and the two are rigidly bound up with each other. Moreover, the decisive factor of

[9] [Mein ferneres Leben kann ich nunmehr als ein reines Geschenk ansehen, und es ist jetzt im Grunde ganz einerley, ob und was ich noch etwa thue.] (119, p. 401)

objective time was measured exclusively in terms of the subjective experience of time. This deep aversion against a strong pleasurable emotion showed up clinically in an aversion against sexual experiences in any form. Significantly enough, this patient tried to extend his life-span by betting. The hours preceding the event that would determine whether he had won or lost stretched out for him to excruciating eternities.[10]

In this patient's life a pleasurable emotion was the accelerant of time-consumption; in Goethe's life, I surmise, it was the feeling of activity. However, in this connection one may recall Goethe's strange statement: "Everything in the world can be borne except a succession of beautiful days" (cf. above, p. 1010).

I wish now to suggest another source of Goethe's work inhibition by quoting a remark which seemingly takes us far afield from the subject matter. On February 26, 1824, while looking with Eckermann at some etchings by Roos[11] that depicted sheep in a very realistic way, Goethe remarked:

> I always feel apprehensive when I look at these animals. The narrowness, the stupor, the dreaminess, the yawning, of their condition draw me into fellow-feeling therewith; one dreads becoming an animal and could well believe that the artist himself was one.[12]

In this brief remark an important feeling is expressed as to the relation between the creator of a work of art and his creation. The underlying fantasy is of an identity between the two. There is also a hint as to the origin of that fantasy: It is based on an archaic fear of changing into what one is looking at when it elicits strong visual impressions. Goethe apparently felt a primitive dread of becoming, under the impact of the painting's attractiveness, that which was depicted in the painting, and assumed that the converse relationship must have existed between the painter and the painting; thus the painting was seen as deriving its character from having acquired part of its creator's nature, and perhaps there was also the feeling that the created work may have had a reciprocal effect upon its creator.

Fears as to such a reciprocal effect, or recoil, can also be discovered in a statement Goethe made about his own drawing. There he tried to keep reality at a distance. Once he said to Eckermann (April 10, 1829):

> I had a certain fear of making [drawing] the objects as pressing in upon me; rather was the fainter, the more moderate, to my mind. When I made a landscape and came closer from the faint distances through the middle

---

[10] Ought one to recall here occasional behavior patterns that suggest there was a gambler hidden in Goethe?

[11] Johann Heinrich Roos (1631–85), well-known painter of animals, active in Frankfurt.

[12] [Mir wird immer bange, wenn ich diese Thiere ansehe. Das Beschränkte, Dumpfe, Träumende, Gähnende ihres Zustandes zieht mich in das Mitgefühl desselben hinein; man fürchtet zum Thier zu werden, und möchte fast glauben, der Künstler sei selber eins gewesen.] (119, p. 75)

ground, then I was always afraid to give the foreground the appropriate strength.[13]

Goethe's aversion against rereading most of his works is well-known. On January 2, 1824, he said to Eckermann about *Werther:*

> That, too, is a creature that, like the pelican, I have nourished with my own heart's blood. . . . Besides I have reread the book . . . only once since its publication and I have been wary of doing it another time. It is pure bombshells!—It makes me feel uncanny and I fear to reexperience the pathological condition from which it originated.[14]

How intense such fears were and how great their effect can be learned from a letter to Schiller of December 9, 1797, in which he wrote:

> I know myself, albeit not well enough to know whether I could write a true tragedy, but I am appalled at the very undertaking and am almost convinced that I could destroy myself by the very attempt.[15]

There seems even to be an element of warding off in his raising the question of whether perhaps the pathos of Greek tragedy was to the ancients "only aesthetic play," in contrast to the situation of the modern writer for whom "the truthfulness to nature has to assist in order to bring forth such a work."[16] Thus comprehensively he expresses his fears of the destructive effects the creation of such works may have on the creator.

Goethe himself noticed that he often became estranged from the works he had produced. One gets the impression that he had, as it were, to get away as speedily as possible from what he just had created.[17] Twice in his conversations with Eckermann he reported instances in which he did not recognize his own writings. He even claimed that it did not take a long time before he looked

---

[13] [. . . ich hatte eine gewisse Furcht die Gegenstände auf mich eindringend zu machen, vielmehr war das Schwächere, das Mässige nach meinem Sinn. Machte ich eine Landschaft und kam ich aus den schwachen Fernen durch die Mittelgründe heran, so fürchtete ich immer dem Vordergrund die gehörige Kraft zu geben.] (119, p. 286)

[14] [Das ist auch so ein Geschöpf, das ich gleich dem Pelikan mit dem Blut meines eigenen Herzens gefüttert habe. . . . Übrigens habe ich das Buch . . . seit seinem Erscheinen nur ein einziges Mal wieder gelesen, und mich gehüthet es abermals zu thun. Es sind lauter Brandraketen!—Es wird mir unheimlich dabei und ich fürchte, den pathologischen Zustand wieder durch zu empfinden aus dem es hervorging.] (119, pp. 430–31)

[15] [Ich kenne mich zwar nicht selbst genug um zu wissen, ob ich eine wahre Tragödie schreiben könnte, ich erschrecke aber blos vor dem Unternehmen und bin beynahe überzeugt dass ich mich durch den blossen Versuch zerstören könnte.]

[16] [nur ästhetisches Spiel . . . die Naturwahrheit mitwirken muss um ein solches Werk hervorzubringen.]

[17] There are, of course, well-known exceptions to this attitude and the question of which creations were quickly abandoned after their creation and which retained affection for a while would be a worthwhile subject for inquiry.

upon a production as something thoroughly strange, and he once compared one of his works to a cast snakeskin (January 12, 1827).

It would be wrong to suppose that all these inhibitions and apprehensions about his own writings may have been based on self-consciousness, humility, or embarrassment. How sure he was of his genius can be seen from a remark he made to Eckermann on January 2, 1824:

> My idea of the excellent was in each phase of my life's development never much beyond that which I also was capable *of producing* in each phase.[18] [Eckermann's italics]

Creation (the cast serpent skin) was an attempt to get rid of something. Looking at it, reexperiencing it, meant the revival of a dangerous past, an invitation or stimulation to regress.[19]

Yet planned, voluntary, conscious work also involves repeated looking, actual or mental, at the product of one's work. Unconscious, intuitive creation spares this very phase and thus serves as a successful defense against this inroad of anxiety. Somnambulistic creation evades the feeling of guilt that would be caused by the audacious making of children; conscious work requires an extensive "conflict-free sphere" (276) because of the unavoidably close contact with an object, the presence and effect of which cannot be denied by the working ego. Thus the somnambulistic way of creating contains the seed of denial that the work of art has been produced by its creator at all, and also protects him against being devoured by it.[20]

A clinical symptom such as an inability to work must also be interpreted in terms of the community to which the patient exhibiting the symptom belongs. An inability to work did not, for example, necessarily indicate a bad prognosis in a Central European patient, at least during the period between the two World Wars, whereas the same symptom in an American nearly regularly is indicative of a serious disturbance. Work evidently plays a different role in American civilization than it does in the Central European. Work seems to be the last activity a patient suffering from a neurosis gives up in this country whereas it might easily be the first pursuit to fall victim in his Continental counterpart. In the light of this cultural factor one may have to evaluate Goethe's attitude toward work in terms different from those one would feel inclined to use in relation to the present.

In the final version of the semiautobiographical *Wilhelm Meister,* there is a passage which, I am confident, expressed the conviction not only of Wilhelm,

---

[18] [meine Idee vom Vortrefflichen war auf jeder meiner Lebens-und Entwicklungsstufen nie viel grösser als was ich auch auf jeder Stufe *zu machen* im Stande war.] (119, p. 429)

[19] This part of Goethe's fears challenges being linked up with his hostile feelings against progeny, which I discuss in Appendix Q.

[20] For the fear of being devoured see 370, pp. 104–12. See also, for various aspects of intuitive work, 349.

but, at least in part, of the author. This is a letter in which Wilhelm, writing to his brother-in-law, justifies his total rejection of a bourgeois way of life, of which the brother-in-law is the exponent.

What help is it to me to produce good iron when my inner self is full of slag? And what, to put a country estate in order when I am at odds with myself?

To say it to you in one word: to develop myself, just as I stand here, that was dimly from my youth on my desire and my intention. I still hold these very ideas, only the means that shall make it possible for me are somewhat clearer. . . .

Were I a nobleman, our quarrel would soon be disposed of; since, however, I am only a commoner, I have to take a path of my own, and I wish that you may understand me. I do not know how it is in foreign countries, but in Germany only for the nobleman is a certain general—if I may say so, personal—education possible. A commoner can acquire worth and, at the very most, develop his mind; his individuality, however, will be lost, whatever stand he may take. . . . He [the nobleman] is a public figure, and the more refined his movements, the more sonorous his voice, the more restrained and measured his whole being is, the more perfect he is. If towards high and low, towards friends and relatives, he remains always the very same, there is nothing in him to find fault with, one may not wish him different. . . . If he knows how to control himself outwardly in every moment of his life, no one has any further demand to make upon him, and all the rest that he has in and around himself—capability, talent, wealth—all seems to be only surplus.

Now, imagine any commoner who might think merely to lay some claim to these privileges; he is bound to fail utterly, and he is bound to become the more unhappy the more his temperament has given him capacity and drive to be of that sort.

If the nobleman in ordinary life knows no limitations at all, if one can create out of him kings and kinglike figures, then he may everywhere step forth before his peers with quiet self-assurance; he may press forward everywhere, whereas nothing is more becoming to the commoner than the pure unspoken sense of the boundary line that has been drawn for him. He must not ask: What are you? but only: What do you have? What understanding, what knowledge, what ability, how much property? As the nobleman gives everything by the presentation of his person, so the commoner by his personality gives nothing and is supposed to give nothing. The former may and should make an [impressive] seeming; the latter should only be, and whatever he wants to seem is ridiculous or in bad taste. The former should do and effect, the latter should render and provide; he should cultivate single abilities so as to become useful, and it is already presupposed that there is no harmony in his being nor ought be, because, in order to make himself useful in one way, he must neglect everything else.

This difference is by no means the fault of the arrogance of the noblemen and the submissiveness of the commoners, but of the constitution of society itself; whether anything of this will one day change and what will change, concerns me little. . . .

As a matter of fact, I have an irresistible propensity for just that harmonious development of my nature which my birth denies me. . . . Now, I don't deny to you that my drive becomes daily more unconquerable to be a public figure and to be pleasing and influential in a larger circle. In addition there is my inclination towards poetry and towards everything that is tied up with it, and the need to cultivate my mind and my taste so that I may gradually, in that enjoyment too, which I cannot do without, take the good really for good and the beautiful for beautiful.[21]

---

[21] [Was hilft es mir, gutes Eisen zu fabriciren, wenn mein eigenes Inneres voller Schlacken ist? und was, ein Landgut in Ordnung zu bringen, wenn ich mit mir selber uneins bin?

Dass ich dir's mit Einem Worte sage, mich selbst, ganz wie ich da bin, auszubilden, das war dunkel von Jugend auf mein Wunsch und meine Absicht. Noch hege ich eben diese Gesinnungen, nur dass mir die Mittel, die mir es möglich machen werden, etwas deutlicher sind. . . .

Wäre ich ein Edelmann, so wäre unser Streit bald abgethan; da ich aber nur ein Bürger bin, so muss ich einen eigenen Weg nehmen, und ich wünsche, dass du mich verstehen mögest. Ich weiss nicht wie es in fremden Ländern ist, aber in Deutschland ist nur dem Edelmann eine gewisse allgemeine, wenn ich sagen darf personelle, Ausbildung möglich. Ein Bürger kann sich Verdienst erwerben und zur höchsten Noth seinen Geist ausbilden; seine Persönlichkeit geht aber verloren, er mag sich stellen wie er will. . . . Er ist eine öffentliche Person, und je ausgebildeter seine Bewegungen, je sonorer seine Stimme, je gehaltner und gemessener sein ganzes Wesen ist, desto vollkommner ist er. Wenn er gegen Hohe und Niedre, gegen Freunde und Verwandte immer eben derselbe bleibt, so ist nichts an ihm auszusetzen, man darf ihn nicht anders wünschen. . . . Wenn er sich äusserlich in jedem Momente seines Lebens zu beherrschen weiss, so hat niemand eine weitere Forderung an ihn zu machen, und alles Übrige, was er an und um sich hat, Fähigkeit, Talent, Reichthum, alles scheinen nur Zugaben zu sein.

Nun denke dir irgend einen Bürger, der an jene Vorzüge nur einigen Anspruch zu machen gedächte; durchaus muss es ihm misslingen, und er müsste desto unglücklicher werden, je mehr sein Naturell ihm zu jener Art zu sein Fähigkeit und Trieb gegeben hätte.

Wenn der Edelmann im gemeinen Leben gar keine Gränzen kennt, wenn man aus ihm Könige oder königähnliche Figuren erschaffen kann; so darf er überall mit einem stillen Bewusstsein vor Seinesgleichen treten; er darf überall vorwärts dringen, anstatt dass dem Bürger nichts besser ansteht, als das reine stille Gefühl der Gränzlinie, die ihm gezogen ist. Er darf nicht fragen: was bist du? sondern nur: was hast du? welche Einsicht, welche Kenntniss, welche Fähigkeit, wie viel Vermögen? Wenn der Edelmann durch die Darstellung seiner Person alles gibt, so gibt der Bürger durch seine Persönlichkeit nichts und soll nichts geben. Jener darf und soll scheinen; dieser soll nur sein, und was er scheinen will, ist lächerlich und

Here the sociological background of Goethe's attitude toward work is presented. Work was degradation to the nobleman, sole purpose to the bourgeois. Out of this realistic, historical, sociological fact Goethe made a spiritual antinomy. Work limits the development of the personality; it pours energy into a function that in the last analysis always leads to the production of something material.

By working, man blunts a facet of his personality. Whereas the nobleman has one purpose in life, namely, to evolve more and more individualized personality structure, the bourgeois has to forgo this aspect of human existence, for individuality militates against submission to the narrow domain of the reality principle concerned with man's dealings with his physical environment. The development and exercise of the tools with which to grapple with the immediate physical reality absorb the whole momentum of bourgeois existence. Goethe turned forcefully against such a limitation and accepted production only on condition that it did not interfere with the evolvement of personality structure. What he had in mind was the aristocracy of the mind, a spiritual aristocracy, whose royal prince he was, and which was indeed incompatible with the ethics and ideology of the bourgeoisie of his times. Of course, the imitation of the way of life of the hereditary aristocracy was absolutely alien to him and, as Thomas Mann (377) so rightly points out, Goethe is the greatest representative of the bourgeois class, but he used an actually existing class difference to erect his own ideal form of existence by transforming a physical property into a spiritual one. This sociological factor does not, I believe, contradict my previous psychological deductions, such as his repugnance for certain forms of femininity and his anxiety about being devoured. The bourgeois whose life is exhausted in utilitarian activity is bound to a physical existence as is the childbearing female and he is devoured by the pursuit of goals that did not grow out of the free interplay of personality forces but were imposed upon him by a narrow, aspiritual reality, such as that which—as it may have seemed to the boy—prompted the mother to lose herself in the infant.

Taking all this together, I do not consider Goethe's attitude towards work as

---

abgeschmackt. Jener soll thun und wirken, dieser soll leisten und schaffen; er soll einzelne Fähigkeiten ausbilden, um brauchbar zu werden, und es wird schon vorausgesetzt, dass in seinem Wesen keine Harmonie sei, nicht sein dürfe, weil er, um sich auf eine Weise brauchbar zu machen, alles Übrige vernachlässigen muss.

An diesem Unterschiede ist nicht etwa die Anmassung der Edelleute und die Nachgiebigkeit der Bürger, sondern die Verfassung der Gesellschaft selbst Schuld; ob sich daran einmal etwas ändern wird und was sich ändern wird, bekümmert mich wenig . . .

Ich habe nun einmal gerade zu jener harmonischen Ausbildung meiner Natur, die mir meine Geburt versagt, eine unwiderstehliche Neigung. . . . Nun läugne ich dir nicht, dass mein Trieb täglich unüberwindlicher wird, eine öffentliche Person zu sein, und in einem weitern Kreise zu gefallen und zu wirken. Dazu kömmt meine Neigung zur Dichtkunst und zu allem, was mit ihr in Verbindung steht, und das Bedürfniss, meinen Geist und Geschmack auszubilden, damit ich nach und nach auch bei dem Genuss, den ich nicht entbehren kann, nur das Gute wirklich für gut und das Schöne für schön halte.] (*Soph.* I, 22:148–52)

the sign of a neurosis. Had he integrated the mode of living that we subsume under the concept of work, he would have lost the highest quality of his immense productivity. Paradoxically enough, a relatively unrestrained personality like Goethe's can achieve more in terms of actual output than one that has to work in order to achieve and to produce. We are dealing here indirectly with the flexibility and the rapidity of the primary process, which, when harnessed to the secondary processes, are greater than those of the secondary processes alone.

Also the hard pre-Italian decade, in which Goethe's personality evolved new structure and in which he acquired the gifts of self-control and self-sacrifice and which was so replete with work, did not lessen his closeness to his own unconscious, which as a result of his alliance with Charlotte von Stein he learned to use more wisely than he could otherwise have done.

At this point I wish to discuss briefly how modern psychotherapy would approach a problem such as Goethe's attitude towards work.

(1) According to one school, which is to a certain extent quite fashionable, it would be dangerous to discuss with such a patient his childhood conflicts or those of his youth; one is advised rather to make the patient face the full brunt of his present conflicts and to give him maximum encouragement to tackle the tasks that reality imposes. In such a technique there is much of what Alfred Adler thought to be the most efficacious method of dealing with a neurotic. All the possibilities of successful work that the patient's environment offered would be discussed. His present and past attempts at escaping responsibility would constitute an important part of these interviews. In accordance with the adage "Nothing succeeds like success,"[22] maximum pressure would be put on him to start working. His strong tendencies to be dependent would be stressed. The therapist would strictly avoid the patient's becoming dependent on him and he would probably, in such a case as Goethe's, prove that the patient desired to be fed by the Duke just as he had been fed by his father, without having to earn his livelihood by unpleasant work.

A principle of this technique is to confront the patient with a behavior to which he was unaccustomed in his parents. Since Goethe's mother was always kind and indulgent, and rather inclined to pamper and admire her son, it would be logical for a woman therapist adhering to this school to impose demands on the patient and to spur his ambitions.

Charlotte von Stein's trust in this point of common-sense methods was crowned with success, so that Goethe quickly shed his dependency on the Duke and became a hard-working man, but we must remain aware that in the process Goethe became in turn entirely dependent on Charlotte von Stein.

(2) Another approach would be to keep unequivocal neutrality on all ques-

---

[22] See 7, p. 40: "Like the adage 'Nothing succeeds like success,' there is no more powerful therapeutic factor than the performance of activities which were formerly neurotically impaired or inhibited." It goes without saying that such a blind belief in work and success is the result of a contemporary prejudice, an unpsychological, purely utilitarian viewpoint, which has no place in a psychological, scientific treatise.

tions of work and not to give any advice or encouragement to the patient, but consistently to show him what the genetic and dynamic background of his inability to work really was.

With such a technique it is quite probable that gradually some of his identifications would become visible: first, of course, the more recent ones, such as Goethe's with his brother-in-law Schlosser, and later that with the father, thus leading the patient as well as the analyst deep into the patient's childhood. Only after a considerable period of intensive therapy would the series of other conflicts about death and transmogrification of the ego come to the patient's awareness. Of course, in view of the patient's pent-up avidity to find an adequate field of action, and because of the great variety of his capabilities, he would start working quite before the deepest roots of his work disturbance had been uncovered. Awareness of the conflict about the sister, brother-in-law, and father might be sufficient to free him from anxiety so much as to make it possible for him to accept work as an integral part of life.

The patient would not meet the uncovering of identifications without rebellion against the therapist, a rebellion comparable to Goethe's violent protest against Charlotte von Stein at the beginning of their acquaintance when she berated his pleasure-seeking conduct. Whereas the analyst uses the patient's resistance caused by an interpretation for the purposes of the therapy, Charlotte von Stein could only wait and hope that Goethe would find his way back to her when he had left her in an angry mood.

Here is one point where the difference between a scientific method of therapy and an approach based on common sense and intuition becomes evident. The analysis of resistance is one of the fulcrums of the psychoanalytic therapy. Charlotte von Stein, with all her intuition and sagacity, could not cope with this problem when Goethe turned against her for pointing out his unreasonableness.

(3) A third technical possibility may be the following. Since it is a difficult task to analyze a patient in a social vacuum, and an adult man in Western society lives in a social vacuum when he is without work, a tentative agreement may be made between the analyst and the patient either before the treatment begins or during its initial phase that the patient will, by an exercise of will power, engage in some work that is relatively to his liking, even if he feels a strong revulsion against doing so. The rationale of such an agreement would be that it gives the patient an opportunity to test his objections against work. The agreement must be understood to be of a temporary nature and the work chosen by the patient on a quasi-experimental basis must not be considered by him as being related to a final choice. This technique would follow Freud's advice concerning the treatment of phobias (169).

The probability is great that the patient will in such circumstances choose an area of activity that will permit him to discharge in action what the psychoanalytic process would prefer to encounter as the content of his thoughts. Inadvertently he will use his tentative choice for what Freud called "acting out."

Indeed, one aspect of Goethe's professional life during his first Weimar decade was that of a grandiose and dramatic acting out. On the stage of the court of Weimar he tried to demonstrate to himself and the world that he could be not only a better educator of princes than his brother-in-law but also a better administrator than that one and his own father together. Had he been in a so-called orthodox analysis, he would in time have found out that here he was trying to solve a childhood conflict by inefficient means, namely, by playing a role designed to prove the cherished conviction that he was superior to his father. Of course, nothing in Goethe's life was merely waste and the hard discipline he imposed on himself bore fruit, but it took ten valuable years before he discovered that to be a high state functionary in a principality could not possibly be his life's mission.

Charlotte von Stein's temporary victory over Goethe in the domestication of his unruliness and the taming of his poetic frenzies was partly prompted by her selfishness, which is encountered at times in the subsequent history of their relationship. The course an analysis takes depends not only on the scientific knowledge at the therapist's disposal but also on the extent to which he has overcome his own conflicts and neurosis. In this respect Charlotte von Stein was severely handicapped. She often acted upon motives that may have impressed her and others as unselfish, but that were quite probably of ambitious origin. How far she may have thought by her influence on Goethe to be able indirectly to dominate the court of Weimar, and thus have been led to disregard Goethe's real needs, must remain undetermined.

Earlier it was said that in an efficient analysis Goethe would have reproduced certain thoughts, images, and feelings from which he could have learned about his identifications with men who played an ambivalent role in his early and late life, such as his father and his brother-in-law. Instead he assumed their roles, albeit in a distorted way, and performed them on the historical stage of the country of his choice. It was further stated that this acting out was an inefficient means of solving a problem. The question involved, difficult to solve, is which identifications in a patient need to be eliminated or changed and which should be preserved. The fabric of man's ego consists to a great extent of identifications, and identification is per se a mechanism indispensable for the ego's development and thus for social behavior (see 193; 304). Some of these identifications prove beneficial and helpful, others are burdensome and the ego could operate far more effectively without them than with them.

The psychopathology of identification is a vast subject and only one aspect may be briefly considered. The effect of an identification on the general economy of the ego may depend on the quantity of guilt-feeling it arouses. Goethe's work in the service of the state involved pain and sacrifice, and encompassed an area far wider than it was really necessary for him to embrace. As Germany's foremost poet he could have rested content with an assignment somehow connected with his literary interests. The immoderateness and self-destructiveness inherent in his work as a civil servant imply a profound hankering for self-punishment. Yet only with the refined technique of psychoanalysis can the role of a particular identification in the ego's total economy be measured. A psychotherapy based on the principle of success will measure the value of an identification in terms of its social utility, a standard inacceptable to a sound psychology. Charlotte von Stein, to the extent that she identified the patient with his and her community, was not able to become aware of the poisonous side-effects of the current manifestations of an old identification, but was limited to excessive preoccupation with the beneficial effect the identification had on the community and on the prestige of her favorite.

But the fact that she persistently held up the reality principle and made Goethe face up to social reality and distinguish it from the product of his sensitivity or irascibility meant that she did in part fulfill a function that psychoanalysis consistently tries to accomplish. This consistent upholding of the reality principle and the making of herself a representative of it is one of the unique and unusual features in the relationship between Goethe and her. In Western imagery the woman is very often pictured as the one great force that operates to distract man from the reality principle and onto the path of the pleasure principle, but in this initial phase of their relationship, when one would have expected Charlotte von Stein to have attempted to capture the great hero by flattery and fawning, she unerringly compelled him to take cognizance of the reality factor, risking by so doing the loss of his love for her and even forcing reality on him when it amounted to a hindrance to his freedom of artistic production.

In the discussion of that aspect of the reality principle that had evidently led to a conflict in Goethe's life, we must not forget a point of view that seems quite crucial but is neglected by most of those analysts who have tried—in vain—to improve upon Freud's principal theories and technique. There is agreement that after a successful analysis the ego should be capable of operating in accordance with the reality principle. The acceptance of the reality principle does not, of course, mean submission to the demands of the social environment or a giving in to social pressures but rather that the ego operates in accordance with the maximum benefit to the personality as well as to the community. The metapsychology of the integration of the reality principle is a difficult chapter and will not be pursued here, but I wish to stress that the test of a sound integration of the reality principle is not simply whether there is reality-adequate *behavior*. The overt actions of a person, however well-adapted to reality they may be, are in themselves not reliable indices of maturity, and many a person tries to cover with ostensibly reality-adequate behavior a dire lack of personal maturity. The fact that a patient speedily fits himself into a social context is regarded nowadays by many therapists as entitling them to chalk up a therapeutic success. A different attitude is found in Freud's report on the analysis of a patient suffering from the sequelae to a severe infantile neurosis (188). From this report it is very probable, if still less than perfectly certain, that the patient's work problem was one of the last to be solved in the course of the treatment, and that during that whole period the patient did no work whatsoever. By imposing upon a patient the necessity of working, a therapist may inadvertently block important avenues through which the patient might achieve indispensable knowledge of self. Particularly in matters of work and social behavior the danger is great that a patient may fall into a pattern of behavior that is not integrated at all but merely satisfies his pride and ambition—and those of his therapist. It seems, then, that it is more appropriate to postpone "success," and to wait until such time as the ego is strong enough to participate in its fullness in the accomplishment of the hard tasks that are part of reality.

This consideration is not applicable to Goethe's life, for though, during the pre-Italian decade, he integrated the capacity to work, he thereafter found himself privileged, as befits a genius, to limit or even forgo work, according as he wished, as soon as it had achieved the purpose for which it was destined in his life.

These additional remarks should not be concluded without renewed citation of the work record of Goethe's father. Johann Caspar was prevented from practicing law in Frankfurt through his appointment as *Kaiserlicher Rat*. A political career in his native city was blocked by his temperament, his views, and, perhaps, his obstinacy.[23] He was a man who kept himself constantly busy but who had no occupation, trade, or profession. The idea of work, the ethos of work, so to speak, was strongly represented in him, as can be seen from Goethe's remarks in *Dichtung und Wahrheit,* but work per se, in the sense of a regulated daily occupation that he would have regarded it as his duty to pursue, held no place in his life. Valid as the circumstances might have been that prevented him from engaging in such work, it is hardly possible to rest at considering this lack as a matter of the chance effect of external circumstances. It must also have been the manifestation of internal factors of his own personality. In studying the historical record, one gets the impression of a gifted, compulsive personality, socially minded but righteous, ambitious but naive, with many-sided interests, who may have been spoiled in his childhood and youth and probably suffered from the parvenu stigma that to some extent was attached to his status.[24] Many conflicts can be adduced to explain this absence of a work record in Johann Caspar's life, but here only his effect upon Goethe is of interest. I have stressed the importance of the fact that his father was not distracted by a profession from a comprehensive devotion to the rearing and education of his children. I

[23] Schulenburg's study (483) contains the historical reasons that prevented his participation in the administration of the city.

[24] From the point of view of the highest bourgeois circles in Frankfurt, J. C. Goethe was inferior both in point of wealth and in the length of time his family had enjoyed such wealth as it had. Schulenburg's recent biography (483) shows how great the gap was between the status of the bourgeois patriciate and that of Goethe.

wish to add now the importance of his personality inasmuch as the idea of work was so strong in him although it did not lead to actual work. Goethe's, too, was a personality that kept itself constantly busy, with an almost incredible intensity, but he always reserved the freedom to organize his busyness beyond the restricting pale of work. I feel inclined to assume that had the boy identified with a father to whom a daily gainful occupation was of importance he would not have been capable of organizing his multifarious activities so magnificently that he never became dominated by them, as must happen with work. Had his father been a loafer or a lazy person to whom work had no value per se at all, the danger of Goethe's accepting a parasitic existence would have been great under the impact of temptations that were by no means slight at the court of Weimar.

Appendix D

Remarks Concerning a Cover Memory of the Aging Goethe Ridiculing Castration Fear

THE FOLLOWING CHARMING childhood episode, which Goethe reports at the end of the second book of *Dichtung und Wahrheit,* requires a brief introduction. *Rat* J. K. Goethe, intensely interested in the education of his children, had the foremost literary works of the German tongue in his library and actively encouraged their zealous perusal by his children. However, so strongly did he hold rhyme to be an indispensable feature of poetry that he would not put Klopstock's[1] *Messias,* written in unrhymed hexameters, on his shelves. He came close to breaking off an affectionate tie to an old friend of the family who extolled the beauty of Klopstock's poem, until the friend desisted from further favorable comments.

Yet "to make proselytes is the natural wish of every human being,"[2] Goethe remarked, and the friend smuggled the forbidden volume into the family circle, where it was rapturously acclaimed by the rest of the family. Goethe went on to report:

My mother kept it concealed and we of the family took possession of it whenever we could in order to learn by heart, in our leisure time, hidden in some corner, the most outstanding passages, and particularly to fix in our memory as quickly as possible the tenderest and most vehement ones.

---

[1] Gottlieb Friedrich Klopstock (1724–1803), renowned German poet, famous for his epic, *The Messiah,* and his odes. He introduced a new era in German literature. The first three cantos of the epic were published in 1748, the next seven in 1755, cantos eleven to fifteen in 1764 and the last five in 1773.

[2] [Proselyten zu machen, ist der natürlicheste Wunsch eines jeden Menschen] (*Soph.* I, 26:124)

[3] Portia, a Roman patrician, has a dream (Canto VII, lines 403–48) in which Socrates appears to her and denies the truth of ancient mythology and affirms the truth of Christian eschatology.

We vied with each other in reciting Portia's dream[3] and we divided between us the wild, despairing colloquy between Satan and Adramelech,[4] who had been tossed into the dead sea. The first role, as the most violent one, fell to my lot; the other, a little more plaintive, my sister took on. The mutual maledictions, horrid, to be sure, yet euphonious, just flowed from our lips and we seized on every opportunity to greet each other in this hellish idiom.

It was on a Saturday evening in winter—our father always had himself shaved by [artificial] light in order to be able to dress conveniently for church on Sunday morning—we were sitting on a footstool behind the stove, and, while the barber lathered, murmured rather softly our customary curses. Now, however, Adramelech had to take hold of Satan with iron hands: my sister grabbed me powerfully and recited, though quietly enough, yet with ever-growing passion:

> Help me! I implore you; if you demand it I'll worship
> You, Monster, you outcast, you black evil-doer.
> Help me! I suffer the pain of avenging eternal death! . . .
> Erewhile, I could hate you with hot, with furious hatred!
> Now I no longer can! This, too, is piercing grief![5]

Up to this point, everything had gone along passably, but now with awful voice she cried aloud the following words:

> Oh, how I am crushed!

The good surgeon [i.e., the barber] was startled and spilled the soap basin over Father's chest. There rose a great turmoil and a stern inquisition was held, particularly in view of the misfortune that might have occurred if the process of shaving had already been under way. In order to exculpate ourselves of any suspicion of wantonness, we owned up to our devilish roles, and the misfortune brought on by the hexameters was too patent for them not to be denounced and banned anew.

Thus are children and common folk wont to transform the great and the sublime into a game, even into a farce, and how else should they be able to endure and to tolerate it![6]

---

[4] Adramelech, Satan's vassal and erstwhile competitor, is thrown with his master into hell, where both of them suffer the greatest torments.

[5] Goethe did not quote these verses correctly.

[6] [Die Mutter hielt es heimlich, und wir Geschwister bemächtigten uns desselben wann wir konnten, um in Freistunden, in irgend einem Winkel verborgen, die auffallendsten Stellen auswendig zu lernen, und besonders die zartesten und heftigsten so geschwind als möglich in's Gedächtniss zu fassen.

Portia's Traum recitirten wir um die Wette, und in das wilde verzweifelnde Gespräch zwischen Satan und Adramelech, welche in's todte Meer gestürzt worden, hatten wir uns

This childhood memory—whether or not it is a bona fide account—has to be interpreted as a cover memory. It refers, under the cloak of Klopstock's beautiful verses, to an intimate aspect of the sibling relationship. If the interpretation is based on this record solely, one is tempted to assume that—as so often happens in cover memories—essential matters were converted into their opposites and it was not the little girl who grabbed the older brother but rather the other way around. Then the historical truth contained in the story told by the aging poet would be of a violent attack by the sexually aroused boy against his weaker sister, who turned towards him with a plea for mercy. Did she succeed in arousing his pity? The cover memory does not tell. It only intimates that the sister screamed and that by so doing she brought the father to the scene of the intended crime. Of what happened to the boy, again we are not informed.

Although clinical observation derived from other instances strongly suggests the interpretation of the literary evidence as I have presented it here, it has been seen in my discussion of an episode in Wilhelm Meister's relationship to Mignon (see above, pp. 759–60) that the boy's attitude toward his sister may actually have been a more passive one. However, it is quite possible that active phases alternated with passive ones or were intermittently replaced by them or became intermingled with them. A reconstruction detailed enough to establish the

getheilt. Die erste Rolle, als die gewaltsamste, war auf mein Theil gekommen, die andere, um ein wenig kläglicher, übernahm meine Schwester. Die wechselseitigen, zwar grässlichen aber doch wohlklingenden Verwünschungen flossen nur so vom Munde, und wir ergriffen jede Gelegenheit, uns mit diesen höllischen Redensarten zu begrüssen.

Es war ein Samstagsabend im Winter—der Vater liess sich immer bei Licht rasiren, um Sonntags früh sich zur Kirche bequemlich anziehen zu können—wir sassen auf einem Schemel hinter dem Ofen und murmelten, während der Barbier einseifte, unsere herkömmlichen Flüche ziemlich leise. Nun hatte aber Adramelech den Satan mit eisernen Händen zu fassen; meine Schwester packte mich gewaltig an, und recitirte, zwar leise genug aber doch mit steigender Leidenschaft:

Hilf mir! ich flehe dich an, ich bete, wenn du es forderst,/ Ungeheuer, dich an! Verworfner, schwarzer Verbrecher,/ Hilf mir! ich leide die Pein des rächenden ewigen Todes! . . . / Vormals konnt' ich mit heissem, mit grimmigem Hasse dich hassen!/ Jetzt vermag ich's nicht mehr! Auch diess ist stechender Jammer!

Bisher war alles leidlich gegangen; aber laut, mit fürchterlicher Stimme rief sie die folgenden Worte:

O wie bin ich zermalmt! . . .

Der gute Chirurgus erschrak und goss dem Vater das Seifenbecken in die Brust. Da gab es einen grossen Aufstand, und eine strenge Untersuchung ward gehalten, besonders in Betracht des Unglücks das hätte entstehen können, wenn man schon im Rasiren begriffen gewesen wäre. Um allen Verdacht des Muthwillens von uns abzulehnen, bekannten wir uns zu unsern teuflischen Rollen, und das Unglück, das die Hexameter angerichtet hatten, war zu offenbar, als dass man sie nicht auf's neue hätte verrufen und verbannen sollen.

So pflegen Kinder und Volk das Grosse, das Erhabene in ein Spiel, ja in eine Posse zu verwandeln; und wie sollten sie auch sonst im Stande sein es auszuhalten und zu ertragen!]
(*Soph.* I, 26:124–26)

exact sequence of sexual activity and passivity does not seem possible from the literary record.

Whatever the right answer to this difficult problem may be, the mechanism of denial can certainly be observed in operation at full force and very efficiently in Goethe's narration. Castration as the possible consequence to masculine transgression of the incest tabu is refuted in the strongest possible way, for the poet wants to make us believe that the brother's sexual desire for his sister endangers the father's safety by bringing him to the brink of injury by a knife. "Thus are children and common folk wont to transform the great . . . into a farce, and how else should they. . . ." How perfectly was Goethe able to change a trauma that threatened himself into one that might have endangered the very person from whom he feared to suffer it! How charmingly does the poet confess the defensive character of the cover memory, admitting that without it life would become unbearable. The posing of game and farce over against the great and the sublime can only be an expression of the unconscious insight that he, the great Goethe, was making mirth and banter out of tragic childhood events.

How different does all this sound from the aging Goethe's aversion against using the word death (see 500, pp. 308–10). Thus the loss of the ego had not ceased to hold its eternal terror for him either.[7]

[7] Another interpretation of this passage from *Dichtung und Wahrheit* must be considered in the light of the possibility, discussed more fully elsewhere, that *Rat* Goethe had been circumcised for the correction of a phimosis. The aging Goethe may, in this episode, have been hinting, probably unconsciously, at this state of affairs. In that case, the story would have to be interpreted, not as signifying Goethe's denial of his own anxiety and transformation of it into its opposite (*Rat* Goethe's danger of being cut by the barber's knife), but as an expression of Goethe's ridicule of a father whom he regarded as maimed in reality.

Appendix E

Further Psychoanalytic Remarks about *A Midsummer Night's Dream*

SHAKESPEARE's *A Midsummer Night's Dream* can be broken down into underlying psychological factors from various points of view. That some of them seem mutually contradictory does not prove they cannot coexist within the synthesis that brought them into an artistic whole. There is a definite contrast between the Theseus-Hippolyta and Oberon-Titania pairs on the one hand and the Lysander-Hermia and Demetrius-Helena pairs on the other. The difficulties that arise between Theseus and Hippolyta and between Oberon and Titania are of a nature that is typical of men who know the secrets of love and sex and treat their spouses accordingly. Lysander-Hermia and Demetrius-Helena behave like young inexperienced people, like juveniles, one feels inclined to say. They love impetuously and go about the pursuit of love in a direct, concrete, unpsychological way; they are not burdened by fears and doubts, in their unawareness of the mystery which lies in the fact that human beings are sexual beings. Pyramus and Thisbe also belong to this group, but they are overwhelmed by the traumatic effect of the crude facts of sexuality. Thus one may set up a series: Pyramus, who cannot bear the sight of menstruation and kills himself; Theseus, who can control himself and wait until the new moon shall avert the unpleasant event; Oberon, who tries to force the woman (who in turn tries to deny the fact of menstruation) into intercourse.

Yet a deeper analysis permits further interpretation. Theseus, after all, is the hero who defeated the Amazons and thus put himself in possession of the beloved Hippolyta. He says:

> Hippolyta, I wooed thee with my sword,
> And won thy love doing thee injuries:
> But will I wed thee in another key,
> With pomp, with triumph, and with revelling.

The relationship of the sexes is here still thought of as a predominantly aggressive one, and the woman is still regarded as a castrated being. Yet once she is tamed, Theseus wants to spare her any further humiliation. The nuptial hour is not to be until the new moon, that is to say, Hippolyta is not to bleed. The underlying unconscious imagery is that menstruation is brought about by the first intercourse. The image of the nonmenstruating virgin would be apt in reference to an Amazon, who must be ever ready for participation in battle. Thus Theseus wants to deflower the Amazon without making her bleed and (probably) make her a woman who will not have to menstruate.

Oberon's relationship to Titania is far more complicated.[1] Titania is spiteful, she behaves like a man, denies her dependency or weakness—which means, in this context, her menstruation. She acts as if only the possession of a penis makes a human being valuable—witness her insistence on keeping the boy. The dream episode in which she falls in love with Bottom may then stand for Oberon's attempt at teaching her the consequences of her refusal to accept femaleness. The exclusive love of the penis, the overestimation of the male organ, is tantamount to the love of an ass, the huge penis in a brainless person. Actually, one finds clinically in women in whom the masculine complex plays a major role an attitude of scorn for men. These women are in danger of falling into a relationship of sexual bondage (*sexuelle Hörigkeit*) to inferior men, exactly as happened to Titania. Oberon's causing Titania to become infatuated with an ass would then not be the result of an intention to punish or humiliate, but rather to edify her and to warn her by demonstrating to her the dangerous consequences of looking upon femaleness as a state of castration. Oberon, according to this interpretation, is the man who turns towards the woman as a being in her own right and does not look at her as a castrated being. He represents true masculinity, which has overcome the castration complex.

One senses yet another area of imagery, namely, that of the phallic woman. Titania's insistence on keeping the boy would mean her unwillingness to give up a phallus. The image in Goethe's verses of Bottom in Titania's arms would be a ridiculing reference to the worthlessness of the female phallus. The red mouse jumping out of the witch's mouth, an imagery used by Goethe in the *Walpurgis Night* (see above, p. 306) would be a clever condensation of menstruation and a small female phallus. The symbol would stand for the idea, actually frequently found in men, that the woman loses a penis when menstruating. Imagery referring to the female phallus can be found in many places in Goethe's writings. Of the many possible interpretations for aspects of *A Midsummer Night's Dream,* I believe those about menstruation and the female phallus are the ones that became importantly relevant in Goethe's unconscious.

---

[1] I owe thanks to Dr. Edith Jacobson for having called my attention to the following interpretation.

Appendix F

Further Examples of the Blood Myth in *Iphigenia*

ANOTHER EXAMPLE OF the blood myth is the solution of the tragic knot suggested by Orestes to his sister. He pleads with her that she should take flight with Pylades from these inhospitable shores and start a new life in beautiful Greece:

> Let my body, unsouled upon the altar of the goddess, be hurled from the rock into the sea, [let] my blood reeking thereover bring a curse upon the shore of the barbarians.[1]

The solution offered by Orestes moves on the level of early oedipal imagery. Only blood can avenge blood. Blood sacrificed before a goddess (a mother-substitute) will reconcile mother and simultaneously wreak vengeance upon Thoas, a father-substitute. Thus Orestes' blood will recoil indirectly upon Agamemnon, whose fault brought the predicament upon Orestes. Revenge, wish-fulfillment, and punishment become synthesized into one act—thus following the structure of the neurotic symptom—and magic restores an equilibrium that had been disturbed by the misdeeds of an ancestor.

A strangely phrased reference to blood sacrifice is found in Thoas's soliloquy when he becomes suspicious of Iphigenia (last act, second scene). He deliberates upon how Iphigenia would have fared if she had come to these shores when his ancestor still insisted upon the savage customs from which he, under her influence, has desisted. He concludes that she would have been happy to survive and she "would quite gladly have annually washed herself up again to life with strange blood."[2] The equivalent passage in the final version reads:

[1] [Lass meinen vor dem Altar der Göttin entseelten Körper vom Fels in's Meer gestürzt, mein drüber rauchend Blut Fluch auf das Ufer der Barbaren bringen.] (*Soph.* I, 39: 362–63)

[2] [. . . hätte sich gar gern mit fremdem Blut zum Leben jährlich wieder aufgewaschen.] (*Soph.* I, 39:388)

She would have . . . shed strange blood before the altar.[3]

The original sentence of 1779 is certainly oddly phrased.[4] The reference to periodicity ("annually") is in this context particularly interesting. The implication seems to be that by immolating men in obedience to her masters she would regain each time a new lease on life. Against the cruder background of the unconscious, the thought may express the fantasy that the priestess in performing the sacrifice draws blood from young men, which she needs for her own rejuvenation, that is to say, the female menstrual blood is so extracted from men, who must die for the woman's welfare.

This typically male imagery finds its counterpart to a certain extent shortly thereafter in a dialogue between Iphigenia and Thoas. When suspected by Thoas of dishonesty, Iphigenia decides to tell the truth. But before doing so she tries to justify a step that might be called foolish and that might lead to the destruction of all three of them. She asks whether man alone has the right to perform unheard-of deeds, which, besides, are regularly deeds of aggression:

Does there remain nothing for us [women], and has a woman, like your Amazons, to deny her sex and rob you of the right of the sword and avenge in your blood the oppression [which we suffer at the hands of men]?[5]

With particular finesse the wording "your Amazons" shifts the responsibility for the unfemale type to man's overbearingness. The whole problem of bleeding is here made one that is imposed upon women by man's aggression. In other words, the woman who denies her sex (rejects menstruation) is forced to do to men that which she denies in herself.

[3] [Sie . . . hätte . . . fremdes Blut vor dem Altar vergossen] (lines 1794–95)

[4] Fischer (146, p. 61) interprets the passage as meaning "to attain new life through the washing of the hands in blood."

[5] [Ist uns nichts übrig, und muss ein Weib wie eure Amazonen ihr Geschlecht verläugnen, das Recht des Schwerts euch rauben und in eurem Blut die Unterdrückung rächen?] (*Soph.* I, 39:393)

Appendix G

Anna Amalia's Letter to Fritsch of May 13, 1776

ALTHOUGH THIS LETTER has no direct bearing upon any particular psychological problem connected with Goethe, I give a translation of it in full because it conveys more impressively than any general account could the atmosphere that prevailed at Weimar in Goethe's early years there. The particular moment at which the Duchess's intervention solved a seeming impasse was most dramatic. After his accession to the throne, the Duke had failed to induce Fritsch, president of the Privy Council since 1772, to accept Goethe as a member of the Council. He had written him letters, flattering, persuasive, and replete with good reasoning. Goethe apparently functioned as an adviser in this correspondence, which guaranteed that no avenue of approach would be missed. Yet all these endeavors were of no avail. Fritsch did not budge in his determination and the Duke appeared to face the alternatives of running his government either without Goethe or without Fritsch. The two alternatives were equally unpalatable to him, and, indeed, the consequences of either would have been incalculable for Goethe: It meant either living a poetical existence in accordance with the customary notion of how a poet ought to live, aloof from a societal reality he craved, or assuming a responsibility that he would never have been able to carry and that, if assumed, would surely have ended in his downfall. I surmise that it was Goethe's influence that made the Duke appeal for help to his mother, the Dowager Duchess Anna Amalia. The following letter which she wrote to Fritsch, who had been her prime minister, made him reconsider his decision and the day was won for Goethe.

You know the feelings that I entertain towards you, and it is just these feelings that press the pen into my hand to entreat you to listen to a friend who only wants the best [outcome]. My son, the Duke, has demonstrated his trust in me by showing me the correspondence that has passed between him and you regarding the new institutions that have to be set up. In connection therewith I note with pain that you have the intention of forsaking my son, and this at a moment when he needs you the most. The reasons you offer have distressed me deeply; they are not worthy of a man of spirit like you who knows the world; you are prejudiced against Goethe, whom you perhaps know only through untrue reports or whom you judge from a wrong point of view. You know how close my son's glory is to my heart and how much I have worked and am still daily working so that he should be surrounded by men of honor. If I were convinced that Goethe belonged to those servile creatures to whom no other interest is sacred but their own and who act only out of ambition, then I should be the first to step forth against him. I do not wish to speak of his talents, of his genius, I talk only of his morality; his religion is that of a true and good Christian, which teaches him to love his neighbor and to try to make him happy; this, after all, is the first and cardinal wish of our Creator. Yet, let us now leave Goethe and talk of you.

Bethink yourself, my friend; you who are so religious, so conscientious, could you forsake a young sovereign, who shows trust in your talents and in your goodness of heart, moreover, at a moment when you are so much needed by him and that (permit me to say this to you) only because of a wrong idea that you yourself have put in your head? You say that my son will be everywhere blamed for seating Goethe in the Council; yet will you not be blamed, too, you who forsake my son's service over such a trivial reason? Make Goethe's acquaintance, try to get to know him; you know that I assay my people thoroughly first before I judge them, that experience has taught me a great deal through such acquaintance, and that I therefore judge without prejudice; believe a friend, who truly cares for you for reasons of gratitude as well as of attachment. Even if the Duke, my son, has taken an overhasty step, have you not done your duty sufficiently by drawing his attention to it—and if he insists on it, is it then your fault? Methinks, the world would take it amiss of you, if you forsook a prince who was in need of your insight, your uprightness; judge for yourself whether this is compatible with the religion you profess. Once more, bethink yourself; I know you as grateful; I ask you, out of your love for me, do not forsake my son in these circumstances; I advise you so and ask it of you equally out of love for my son and out of love for you yourself.

I am with all possible friendship,

Sir,

Your very well-inclined friend,

Amelie.[1]

---

[1] [Sie kennen die Gesinnungen, die ich für Sie hege, und eben diese sind es, die mir die Feder in die Hand drücken, um Sie zu beschwören, einer Freundin Gehör zu schenken, die nur das Beste will. Mein Sohn, der Herzog, hat mir das Vertrauen bewiesen, mir die Korrespondenz zu zeigen, die zwischen ihm und Ihnen stattgefunden hat in betreff der neuen

Einrichtungen, die gemacht werden müssen; ich ersehe daraus mit Schmerz, dass Sie die Absicht haben, meinen Sohn zu verlassen und dies in einem Augenblicke, wo er ihrer am notwendigsten bedarf; die Gründe, welche Sie anführen, haben mich tief bekümmert, sie sind eines geistreichen Mannes wie Sie, der die Welt kennt, nicht würdig; Sie sind eingenommen gegen Goethe, den Sie vielleicht nur aus unwahren Berichten kennen oder den Sie von einem falschen Gesichtspunkte aus beurteilen. Sie wissen, wie sehr mir der Ruhm meines Sohnes am Herzen liegt, und wie sehr ich darauf hingearbeitet habe und noch täglich arbeite, dass er von Ehrenmännern umgeben sei; wäre ich überzeugt, dass Goethe zu diesen kriechenden Geschöpfen gehörte, denen kein anderes Interesse heilig ist, als ihr eigenes und die nur aus Ehrgeiz thätig sind, so würde ich die Erste sein, gegen ihn aufzutreten. Ich will Ihnen nicht von seinen Talenten, von seinem Genie sprechen; ich rede nur von seiner Moral, seine Religion ist die eines wahren und guten Christen, die ihn lehrt, seinen Nächsten zu lieben und zu versuchen ihn glücklich zu machen; das ist doch der erste, hauptsächlichste Wille unseres Schöpfers. Aber lassen wir jetzt Goethe und reden wir von Ihnen.

Gehen Sie in sich mein Freund, Sie, der Sie so religiös, so gewissenhaft sind, können Sie einen jungen Regenten verlassen, der Vertrauen zeigt in Ihre Talente und in Ihre Herzensgüte, noch dazu in einem Augenblicke, wo Sie ihm so notwendig sind und das (erlauben Sie dass ich es Ihnen sage) nur einer unrichtigen Idee wegen, die Sie sich in den Kopf gesetzt haben. Sie sagen, man würde meinen Sohn überall tadeln, wenn er Goethe in das Conseil setze; aber wird man Sie nicht auch tadeln, Sie, der Sie den Dienst meines Sohnes einer so geringfügigen Ursache wegen verlassen? Machen Sie Goethes Bekanntschaft, suchen Sie ihn kennen zu lernen; Sie wissen, dass ich meine Leute erst gehörig prüfe bevor ich über sie urteile, dass die Erfahrung mich in solcher Bekanntschaft vielfach belehrt hat und dass ich dann ohne Vorurteil richte; glauben Sie einer Freundin, die Ihnen wahrhaft zugethan ist sowohl aus Dankbarkeit wie aus Anhänglichkeit. Selbst wenn der Herzog, mein Sohn, einen übereilten Schritt gethan hätte, haben Sie dann nicht hinglänglich Ihre Pflicht gethan, wenn Sie darauf aufmerksam machten,—und wenn er darauf besteht, ist das dann Ihr Fehler? Mich dünkt, die Welt würde es Ihnen verargen, wenn Sie einen Fürsten verlassen, der Ihrer Einsicht, Ihrer Rechtschaffenheit bedarf; urteilen Sie selbst, ob sich das mit der Religion, die Sie bekennen, verträgt. Noch einmal, gehen Sie in sich; ich kenne Sie als dankbar; ich bitte Sie aus Liebe für mich, verlassen Sie unter diesen Umständen meinen Sohn nicht; ich rate es Ihnen und bitte Sie eben so sehr aus Liebe zu meinem Sohne und aus Liebe für Sie selbst.

Ich bin mit aller möglichen Freundschaft

mein Herr

Ihre sehr wohlgeneigte Freundin

Amelie.] (61, pp. 115–17)

Appendix H

Supplementary Notes Concerning Goethe's Second Swiss Journey
An Unconscious Factor in Goethe's Desire to Travel

In order to come closer to an understanding of Goethe's attack of anxiety on November 11, 1779, one also has to consider an effect that nature had on him particularly in conjunction with traveling. In the letter of November 11, 1779, in which he told Charlotte von Stein of the deep impression the story of St. Alexis made on him (cf. above, p. 588), he mapped out his plan for the next leg of his journey. This involved a difficult and dangerous sector against which many local people had warned. Here an attitude is encountered in Goethe that had been apparent two years earlier, when he insisted upon ascending the Brocken in a season when it was said to be impossible (cf. above, p. 447).[1] A high mountain became to him a challenge. The more he was told that it was impossible to climb it the more he felt driven to do so, and he was ready to gamble at a high risk. Thus he wrote about the intended expedition:

> The outcome will decide which was right, our courage and confidence that it must succeed, or the prudence of some persons who wanted to dissuade us forcibly from this path. This much is certain, that both prudence and courage must acknowledge luck [to be] superior to them.[2]

[1] The situation in Switzerland actually reminded Goethe of the Brocken. On November 2, 1779, the day before the Duke and his party set out on the journey into Savoy, against the advice of many, he wrote to Charlotte von Stein: "If it is possible to get on [the top of] the Brocken in December, then these portals of horrors [the Savoy mountains] must also let us pass at the beginning of November." [. . . Wenn es möglich ist im Dezember auf den Brocken zu kommen, so müssen auch Anfangs November uns diese Pforten der Schröcknisse auch noch durchlassen.]

[2] [Der Ausgang wird entscheiden, ob unser Muth und Zutrauen, dass es gehen müsse, oder die Klugheit einiger Personen, die uns diesen Weg mit Gewalt widerrathen wollen, Recht behalten wird. So viel ist gewiss, dass beide, Klugheit und Muth, das Glück über sich erkennen müssen.] (*Soph.* I, *19*:286–87)

Here the attitude of the gambler comes to the fore. Some twenty years later, on his third journey to Switzerland, Goethe made the remark that the urge to gamble spreads in uncertain times, when the future may harbor great luck or great misfortune, and he wrote to Schiller at that time (October 14, 1797):

> Traveling resembles gambling; gain and loss are always involved and in most cases from the unexpected side; one receives more or less than one hopes. . . . For natures like mine that are fond of settling down and holding fast to things, a journey is of inestimable value; it enlivens, sets right, enlightens, and educates.[3]

Some psychoanalytic findings have, although quite contrary to common sense, made their way into the public awareness, such as the finding that many gamblers suffer from intense masochism. The secret urge to lose is an astounding thing to discover in a gambler, but it is found in those who are addicted to gambling or who do it compulsively. This view has apparently become so popular that a newspaper columnist (W. C. Heinz) began an article on horse betting in the New York *World-Telegram & Sun* with a psychiatrist's statement "that people don't bet on horse races to win, but to lose," and ended with a reference to the heroism of being able to accept defeat: "For the price of a bet the horse player buys a pedestal for himself." The masochistic element can also be discovered in Goethe's way of gambling with nature, but in addition it provided him with a feeling of triumph, such as he experienced profoundly when he conquered the Brocken.

The masochism of the gambler may have been emphasized so strongly by psychiatrists because, for obvious reasons, they are commonly dealing with unsuccessful gamblers. Most gambling in present society is institutionalized, and as a social reality is structured in such a way that the individual gambler cannot win. Heinz may have been correct in viewing gambling as having become the meeting-ground of masochists. In Goethe's case gambling evidently tended to provide him with an opportunity to conquer masochism. As Goethe occasionally remarked, he felt averse to formalized gambling, such as playing cards. It may have been the factor of institutionalization that made it unpalatable for him. His wrestling with the challenges nature offered permitted more freedom and activity than institutionalized gambling provides. In Goethe's urge to travel one can discover what Fenichel has so impressively described as a counterphobic attitude (see 138). Yet when a serious omen frightened him he abstained from the journey. Thus when, on July 20, 1816, he left Weimar with his friend Johann Heinrich Meyer to drive to Baden-Baden and the carriage was overturned, he returned to Weimar and canceled the whole journey. Of course,

---

[3] [Die Reise gleicht einem Spiel, es ist immer Gewinn und Verlust dabey, und meist von der unerwarteten Seite, man empfängt mehr oder weniger als man hofft. . . . Für Naturen wie die meine, die sich gerne festsetzen und die Dinge festhalten, ist eine Reise unschätzbar, sie belebt, berichtigt, belehrt und bildet.]

there were reality reasons for this change of mind,[4] but one feels a superstitious attitude behind such decisions. In a letter to Zelter of July 22, 1816, he writes of the interference by "the upper or nether demons"[5] in connection with the incident. (See above, p. 912)

The preconscious motive of outwitting fate, of proving superiority and fortitude against all odds, was not always strong enough to keep in abeyance the masochistic temptation, which it usually succeeded in warding off. The attack of anxiety on November 11, 1789, illustrates such an incident.

Goethe's Acrophobia

Goethe's phobic attack in the Savoy Alps was classified by me as a claustrophobia. I do not need to repeat the interpretation I derived from his writings. Here I wish to add Goethe's account of another type of phobia he suffered from[6] and of how he cured himself of it in Strassburg, 1770–71.

In *Dichtung und Wahrheit,* Goethe writes:

Particularly, however, a vertigo frightened me that came over me whenever I looked down from a height. All these defects I tried to remedy and that, because I did not want to lose any time, in a somewhat violent way. . . . I climbed, all by myself, up to the highest point of the minster steeple and sat in the so-called neck underneath the knob or crown, as it is called, for perhaps a quarter of an hour, until I dared to step out again into the free air where one stands on a platform that would scarcely measure an ell square, without being able to hold on to anything in particular, and sees before him the unending land, while the immediate surroundings and [architectural] ornaments hide the church and everything upon which and above which he stands. It is perfectly as if one saw oneself lifted up into the air in a Montgolfière. This kind of agony and torment I repeated so many times, until the impression became quite indifferent to me; later I profited greatly from these preparatory exercises on mountain trips and geological surveys, on large constructions, where I competed with the carpenters in running over free-lying [i.e., unfastened] beams and projections of the building, in Rome, moreover, where one has to practice such daring feats, in order to see important works of art more closely.[7]

---

[4] Wolfgang Vulpius (536, p. 140) rightly suggests that Goethe's disinclination to meet Marianne von Willemer, his beloved Suleika, out of fear that his passionate attachment to her might be rekindled, was the decisive motive in his dropping any further plans for continuing the trip.

[5] [die obern oder untern Dämonen]

[6] The problem of whether or not we are dealing here with bona fide neuroses will be taken up later. This much may be said here: these formations, which in Goethe resemble neurotic psychopathology to a T, nevertheless probably do not belong to this type of psychopathology at all.

[7] [Besonders aber ängstigte mich ein Schwindel, der mich jedesmal befiel, wenn ich von einer Höhe herunter blickte. Allen diesen Mängeln suchte ich abzuhelfen, und zwar, weil

Unfortunately, Goethe did not report why he crammed himself first into the narrow space underneath the knob before exposing himself on the platform to the sight that aroused vertigo. Did the anxiety already set in when he secluded himself in the narrow space or did anxiety set in on the platform only after a preceding seclusion in a narrow space? His way of overcoming the phobia strikes me as a ritualistic repetition of birth. First, he confined himself in a narrow space, possibly feeling well-protected and free of anxiety, as is indicated by his saying: "until I dared to step out again"; then the state of security is disturbed and he exposes himself to an experience which is the very opposite of the one he has just left. Being completely surrounded by walls is replaced by almost floating in free space. I cannot imagine a better symbolization of the contrast between the prenatal and postnatal states.[8]

Jery and Bätely

A short play that Goethe wrote on his second Swiss journey must be briefly mentioned. This is a one-act musical comedy, which he wanted to have set to music by his friend Philipp Christoph Kayser (1775–1823), about whom more will be said later.[9]

What Goethe really felt about this play is difficult to say. It may be significant that when no alto voice could be found for the performance by the amateur group in Weimar he changed the role of Bätely's mother into that of her father, without any other change in the text than that of pronouns and their corresponding nouns.[10]

---

ich keine Zeit verlieren wollte, auf eine etwas heftige Weise. . . . Ich erstieg ganz allein den höchsten Gipfel des Münsterthurms und sass in dem sogenannten Hals, unter dem Knopf oder der Krone, wie man's nennt, wohl eine Viertelstunde lang, bis ich es wagte wieder heraus in die freie Luft zu treten, wo man auf einer Platte, die kaum eine Elle in's Gevierte haben wird, ohne sich sonderlich anhalten zu können, stehend das unendliche Land vor sich sieht, indessen die nächsten Umgebungen und Zierrathen die Kirche und alles, worauf und worüber man steht, verbergen. Es ist völlig als ob man sich auf einer Montgolfiere in die Luft erhoben sähe. Dergleichen Angst und Qual wiederholte ich so oft, bis der Eindruck mir ganz gleichgültig ward, und ich habe nachher bei Bergreisen und geologischen Studien, bei grossen Bauten, wo ich mit den Zimmerleuten um die Wette über die freiliegenden Balken und über die Gesimse des Gebäudes herlief, ja in Rom, wo man eben dergleichen Wagstücke ausüben muss, um bedeutende Kunstwerke näher zu sehen, von jenen Vorübungen grossen Vortheil gezogen.] (*Soph.* I, 27:256–57)

[8] Many other examples could be cited of Goethe's overcoming by deliberate effort what seem like neurotic symptoms. I shall take up the problem more fully later but wish to stress this observation here, for it throws doubt on whether the psychopathology Goethe reports in these instances is to be regarded as neurotic. It is an indispensable sign of a phobia that it cannot be mastered by will power.

[9] Kayser did not supply the music in time for the performance in Weimar. Seckendorff, as usual, helped out. Later the play was set to music by the well-known composer Johann Friedrich Reichardt (1752–1814).

[10] Cf. above, on p. 341, the similar ease with which Goethe rewrote *Lila*. There too the changes involved the replacement of a character with one of the opposite sex.

The play takes place in Switzerland, against a rustic setting. All four characters in the cast belong to the rural population, but Goethe did not intend to give a characterization of Swiss life. The characters were "out of my own factory" [aus meiner Fabrick], as he wrote Charlotte von Stein on January 3, 1780, thus suggesting the personal background of the plot. Jery is in love with Bätely, who, however, rejects all her suitors. Yet Jery does not give up hope despite Bätely's consistent rejection of him. Jery meets Thomas, a former friend of his, who quickly finds out why Jery is so sad. Thomas offers himself as a go-between to win Bätely's heart for Jery. However, he does not get very far with her. When he tries to get into her good graces she gets quite angry at him and retires into her house. Thomas feels incensed and decides to teach her a lesson. He drives his cattle onto Bätely's grounds and causes great damage to her property and her father's. Bätely feels quite helpless. Her father tries to engage the help of their neighbors. They refuse because Bätely has caused the unhappiness of so many young men. When Jery hears of Thomas's offensive behavior, he refuses to listen to his explanations and attacks him. They wrestle, but Thomas is stronger than Jery; he injures and defeats him. Bätely feels pity and gratitude for Jery. She bandages his wounds and tries to console him for his defeat. She is ready to marry him. Jery forgives Thomas.

The play is simple and innocuous and aside from some lovely songs it has no great literary merit. But from the biographical point of view it throws an interesting sidelight on some problems previously discussed. Pniower (248, 8:332) is, in my opinion, right, when he connects the wrestling match between Jery and Thomas with an entry (October 13, 1779) in the diary that Goethe's servant, Seidel, kept, under his master's supervision, on the trip. There we read: "Two fellows had to wrestle with each other in the Swiss manner on the grass before the inn."[11]

Despite their vast difference in artistic value, one feels inclined to compare this play with *Iphigenia* in regard to the content of their plots. In *Iphigenia* emphasis is put on the great friendship between two men who try to combat female aggression. In the little musical comedy one man tries to win a reluctant girl for his friend and the two men become enemies over this attempt. That the theme of a woman's endangering male friendship was in the air may be seen in Goethe's diary entries about himself, the Duke, and Corona Schröter. In *Iphigenia* one of the main themes was the woman's wish to make the male bleed; in the comedy, the woman soothes her suitor's wounds, which were indirectly caused by her, though the proximate cause was a male rival.[12] The theme

---

[11] [Vor dem Wirthshaus musten zwei Bursche nach Schweizermanier in dem Gras mit einander ringen.] (*Soph.* IV, 4:82)

Apparently the two were engaged to demonstrate to the foreign travelers the Swiss style of wrestling. I have mentioned this scene as one of the factors precipitating Goethe's ensuing phobic attack.

[12] There is an implication that Thomas falls in love with Bätely himself and that he might change from a go-between to a suitor.

of castration is still alive. Bätely falls in love as soon as Jery feels defeated. The courting male is looked upon by her as an aggressor. When Jery wants to withdraw because he has failed in his efforts to protect Bätely—that is to say, as soon as he admits weakness—the way is open and Bätely can love him.

On the other hand, the play emphasizes the weakness of women. Originally it was Bätely and her mother who were incapable of taking care of their property and depended on Jery's assistance. In the final version, too, there are numerous references to the necessity of Bätely's marrying because of her father's old age and her own inability to manage once her father shall have died. One feels inclined to assume that the problem that occupied Goethe in this play had to do with the question of whether a man's love for a woman must necessarily lead to discord among men. The ironical attitude towards women is pretty plain. But the play also ridicules the bragging, crude behavior of men who believe that every woman must cater to their wishes. Thus it makes fun of the aggressive behavior in both men and women, and takes sides in favor of Jery's silent suffering, as if Goethe were trying to provide himself with the consoling assurance that passivity rather than aggressive insistence leads ultimately to the fulfillment of wishes. Yet if one tries to translate the manifest content of the comedy into the terms of the unconscious, I wonder whether one does not have to assume that the underlying unconscious idea was rather a doubt as to the adequacy of Jery's goodness and sweetness.

A Telepathic Experience Claimed by the Aged Goethe

For completeness' sake I wish to mention briefly an experience that Goethe reported in *Dichtung und Wahrheit*, Book XI. After his farewell from Friederike, he rode away, his heart full of pain, toward Drusenheim:

> Then one of the most peculiar presentiments came over me; I saw myself, to wit—not with the eyes of the body, but of the mind—coming again towards myself on the same path on horseback and that in a garment [such] as I have never worn; it was light gray with some gold.[13]

When, eight years later, Goethe rode on horseback to visit Friederike on the occasion of his second journey to Switzerland, as I reported in the main text, he wore exactly such a garment, "not out of choice, but by accident."[14]

This report is a challenge to the psychologist. Reik devotes much acumen to explaining it (449, pp. 188–205); Rank discusses it in connection with the problem of the double, and reports Freud's opinion that the apparition served as a "justifying excuse" [rechtfertigende Entschuldigung] for his turning away

---

[13] [. . . da überfiel mich eine der sonderbarsten Ahnungen. Ich sah nämlich, nicht mit den Augen des Leibes, sondern des Geistes, mich mir selbst, denselben Weg, zu Pferde wieder entgegen kommen, und zwar in einem Kleide, wie ich es nie getragen: es war hechtgrau mit etwas Gold.] (*Soph.* I, 28:83)

[14] [nicht aus Wahl, sondern aus Zufall.]

unfaithfully towards new goals (437, p. 56). Doubts as to the veracity of Goethe's report have arisen. As a matter of fact, not the slightest hint of a reference to it can be discovered in his correspondence of that time with Charlotte von Stein. It is difficult to imagine that he could have omitted an event of such extraordinary peculiarity from his letters to her, although it is conceivable that its eeriness detained him from doing so. Be this as it may, it is my guess that this report has to be explained by reference to factors in the aging Goethe. It is highly probable that the whole account owes its origin, if not outright to poetic invention, yet to the particular problems that were on Goethe's mind at the time when he was writing this chapter of *Dichtung und Wahrheit*. In that case the event does not belong to the subject matter of this study. Nevertheless, I wish to point out that in *Wilhelm Meisters Lehrjahre* Goethe reported a certain widespread superstition that a person who sees his own apparition will soon die. This superstition plays a prime role in the novel at a characteristic juncture to which I refer on p. 841. I surmise that when Goethe was relating his Sesenheim experiences he may have been troubled by the idea that as a punishment for his irresponsible behavior towards his sweetheart, he should have died; that he felt very guilty towards the girl is well attested. The mistaken recollection of the apparition, meaning: "I was marked for death," would then be the result of a joy that a benign fate spared him premature, if well-deserved, death.

Thus the preconscious or unconscious reasoning of the aging poet may have been: "I was destined to die as a young man, for I saw my own apparition, but I survived and therefore I do not have to fear death now."

Appendix I

Commentary on the Psychology of Goethe's Drawing

ANY PROBLEM CONNECTED with Goethe as a pictorial artist seems to be beset with particular difficulty. Hermann's proposed general theory concerning Goethe's drawing (294), despite its attractiveness, is not quite satisfactory. Basing himself on Goethe's report that he started to draw when separated from his first sweetheart, Gretchen, he concludes that the youngster's taking up drawing occurred because of a regression to hand eroticism enforced by the loss of a love-object. In the same paper he links Goethe's poetic propensities with oral eroticism.

Was Goethe's drawing really a regressive function? As an adult he certainly also drew when his relationship to a love-object was at its peak. To be sure, drawing apparently occurred very frequently when he was not in the company of the love-object, but this is likewise true of his writing poetry. In the case of the three pigsty sketches—accompanied in at least two instances with poems of considerable beauty—one feels inclined to correlate the drawing with aggressive, and the poetical faculty with libidinal, tendencies. The possibility that the poems in turn imply ambivalence would not necessarily militate against this assumption, since the sketches openly show contents attributable to ambivalence, whereas in his poetic strivings Goethe succeeded in synthesizing the negative into beautiful forms which, as such, appear free of ambivalence.

If this instance is typical then one would feel inclined to assert generally that the creation of literary works has in Goethe's case to be correlated mainly with libidinal processes, whereas the energy invested in pictorial functions was derived mainly from the aggressive-destructive drives. The explanatory value of this theory is self-evident. If it is sound it would also make it understandable why Goethe was beset by doubts as to the field in which his best talents lay, and why it took him so long to settle upon the literary arts as his proper domain. According to this theory, the great value of the pictorial arts as a medium for the release of negative, aggressive, feelings would have rendered them indispensable and that is why it would have been so difficult for Goethe to wrest himself away from drawing, an area in which, objectively, he was never able to achieve anything above the average.

However, it can be shown that the theory in this form is far too simple to be competent to explain the clinical data. Even if the pigsty sketches were used for aggressive purposes this would not prove in the least that the energy used in the process of drawing was correspondingly of aggressive origin. The interplay between libidinal and destructive energies is far too intricate for it to be possible to allocate them to neatly separated functions.

Literary products also, as is shown in the text, frequently served aggressive purposes, and an example is presented (p. 468 above) of drawing that definitely served libidinal, friendly, unaggressive, tendencies.

Words, of course, in Goethe's case also served a magical function, and thus frequently released hostile feelings. In an early childhood episode, which he recorded in Book III of *Dichtung und Wahrheit,* this can be seen with particular clarity. In a dispute with the mother of a boy artist, he inadvertently used when speaking of the boy the well-known German adage expressing the inherent frailty of human affairs: "Today red, tomorrow dead." When the boy fell seriously ill and had probably died, he remembered having spoken these words. Yet instead of expressing a feeling of guilt, as one would expect, he went on:

> Such portents by means of an untimely, even unbecomingly, uttered word, were already held in respect by the ancients and it remains most noteworthy that the forms of belief and superstition have always been the same among all peoples and at all times.[1]

From Goethe's account it is evident that he had been jealous of this boy and felt a homosexual liking for him.

A comparable episode—only this time it was Goethe who was the victim of the magic of words—occurred years later when a girl put a curse on him, with the result that he suffered from a rather long-lasting compulsive inhibition against kissing.

Both instances illustrate that for Goethe, as for everyone else, words were endowed with direct, archaic magical power, which was also fed by strong aggressive strivings. It is striking to compare the long-lasting effect that the magic of words of the curse-casting girl had upon him with the ease with which he dismissed the disastrous effect that he believed his own words had upon the ambivalently loved male rival. It is also proper to remind the reader in this context of the Leipzig nightmare, which was broken off partly by the dreamer's

---

[1] [Dergleichen Vordeutungen durch ein unzeitig, ja unschicklich ausgesprochenes Wort standen bei den Alten schon im Ansehen, und es bleibt höchst merkwürdig, dass die Formen des Glaubens und Aberglaubens bei allen Völkern und zu allen Zeiten immer dieselben geblieben sind.] (*Soph.* I, 26:151)

quoting Shakespearean rhymes (see above, p. 61). These examples may suffice to demonstrate on the one hand the relative lack of guilt-feelings attached to the verbal medium, and on the other the exquisite synthetic and defensive value that this medium possessed for Goethe. The pictorial arts, I surmise, never acquired these functions, at least not as intensely as the literary arts. The reason, possibly, lies in the displacement of guilt-feelings from the verbal to the pictorial art. The sublime heights to which he could carry the art of words may partly have been made possible by his possessing in the pictorial art a channel through which he could drain off negative impulses. We must recall that Goethe himself once compared his drawing with the sucking of the infant.[2] If we accept Goethe's remark as valid we may use it as an argument against Hermann. Again we ought to be distrustful of simplified theories. It may accord with psychoanalytic common sense to correlate the various creations of art with libidinal processes in the respective executive organs, and such common-sense conclusions may occasionally be confirmed by clinical observations, but in general it must be expected that common sense will prove as little dependable in psychoanalysis as it has in other fields of science.

A certain organ may become the carrier of libidinal charges that stem from other organs. Thus Goethe may have been quite right when he observed that—as it would be expressed in psychoanalytic terminology—drawing was for him an oral activity. Yet that which strikes one in browsing through a collection of Goethe's drawings is the lack of any features that would indicate frenzy or ecstasy. The passions out of which his first great literary works grew are totally absent from his drawings. Do the pictorial arts lend themselves as well to somnambulistic creativity as the literary ones? I do not know. For Goethe, drawing, I believe, remained drudgery, and he could not integrate this function into a passionately driving creative process. This inability possibly speaks in favor of the assumption that the drawing function was per se cathected with all too much destructive energy, which in turn impeded such automatic creative processes as played an enormous role in Goethe's literary productivity as well as creativity.

A comparison of Goethe's imagery of Prometheus, the progenitor of mankind, with the childbearing function will reveal other reasons for Goethe's relative failure as a pictorial artist. I refer more extensively (p. 477 above) to Goethe's dramatic fragment *Prometheus* (1773), which reveals some basic conflicts in a very open fashion. Here I wish only to mention that in this fragment Prometheus forms human shapes from clay against the will of Jupiter. However, he cannot pour life into the forms and therefore he wonders for a moment whether he ought not make peace with Jupiter in order to gain life for his lifeless statues. Then Minerva, his sister, out of love for him, takes him "to the spring of life" [zum Quell des Lebens] (*Soph.* I, 39:203) and—also transgressing Jupiter's commandment—animates the clay figures.

[2] See letter to Charlotte von Stein of September 14, 1777, pp. 439–40 above.

I believe the *Prometheus* fragment to be one of Goethe's most personal works. It is written in a dithyrambic style and as one reads it one senses the rapidity with which it was written. For these and other reasons I make so bold as to draw direct conclusions from it concerning the structure of a certain unconscious conflict in Goethe. The two elements I have selected from the plot are (1) the forming of clay figures as an act of rebellion against the father; (2) male incapacity to bring forth life, which is a privilege nature gave the female. These two elements can be transposed to the drawing function. When drawing, the artist is partly in the situation Prometheus was in when he wanted to create live human beings. Did drawing have for Goethe the unconscious meaning of rebellion against his father? Further, when we read—what is discussed later in greater detail—the surprising fact that Goethe felt inhibited in drawing the human figure (an inhibition he learned to overcome only in Italy when he was in his late thirties), we are bound to ask: Did the male inability to bring forth biological life throw its shadow on the products of his pictorial ambitions?

One gets the impression that in pictorial art Goethe did not transcend the stage of wanting to reproduce nature. He himself was aware of his limitation at at least one point in his autobiography, when he reports his ambition to capture pictorially the details of nature, but, "as little as nature has destined me to be a descriptive poet,"[3] so little did he succeed in accomplishing this other goal.

But why should Goethe in the pictorial arts have been primarily fixated to the details of nature and not have been able to wrest himself away from the detail and turn towards the object in its totality? We face here the difference between reproduction and creation, or re-creation. In drawing, Goethe apparently tried to suck in the world (infantile orality) and to reproduce it (spit it out) in the form in which it had been appropriated.[4] In the literary productions the stimulation by the world served only as a rousing agent to set into motion the creative processes which led to the bringing forth of an original product, which, though it still showed traces of the reality from which it stemmed, was nevertheless thoroughly drenched in the individuality of its creator.

A lack in the pictorial art of the freedom which he possessed fully in the literary arts may have been one of the reasons why Goethe was bound to fail as an artist. This lack of freedom can perhaps be brought into meaningful con-

---

[3] [so wenig mich die Natur zu einem descriptiven Dichter bestimmt hatte] (*Soph.* I, 27:16)

[4] The connection between orality and drawing in Goethe would require speculation following the example which Freud has given in his analysis of judgment (203). It would be necessary to study how far Goethe's drawing was related to the pleasure—or reality—ego, and how far he tried to *discover* or *rediscover* objects, respectively, by drawing them. I am not aware of material in Goethe's writings that might help here and I am lacking in clinical observations that I could tentatively substitute.

nection with problems of bisexuality. Reproducing nature pictorially may have become for Goethe identical with the childbearing function and, because of that literal identity, have evoked anxiety, feelings of guilt, and also a feeling of inferiority. In the world of words Goethe found a world of meanings, whereas the world of pictures remained for him a world of similarities. No barrier arose for the poet when he sought to pour life into something in the world of meaningful words, whereas this process was evidently inhibited in the creation of concrete visual pictures.

I remind the reader of Hoffer's studies in the genetic importance of the mouth-hand relationship (301; 302) and raise the question whether there was an early disturbance in the formation of that relationship in Goethe which hampered his development as a pictorial artist. The pouring of life into words—unimpeded by the detour over the hand which drawing necessitates—reminds me of the age-old image of a divine power breathing life into the human body.[5]

Words, though they are written down by the adult, are, particularly to the child, the unvisual products of breath, and breath became the exquisite medium through which Goethe fertilized the world without being hampered by feelings of guilt or anxiety.

Thus I have proposed several avenues through which Goethe's relative failure as a pictorial artist can be approached. Yet these avenues are isolated from one another. It is not evident what they have in common and we do not know where to turn in order to find the basic factor, the common denominator, in this issue.

Here I am aware of my shortcomings with particular vividness and I can only apologize by referring to the fact that all subjects related to talent and individual endowment are still dark spots on the psychoanalytic chart of the human personality. Nevertheless, I still prefer this inadequate attempt to such a statement as that nature had given Goethe the genius of poetry while he just had not the stuff to be a great painter.

[5] Ernest Jones (319) has discussed the meaning of breath as a fertilizing agent.

Appendix J

Distribution of "Du" and "Sie" in Goethe's Letters to Charlotte von Stein in the Spring of 1781

Goethe addressed Charlotte von Stein with *Du* on two occasions when writing her from Neuenheiligen. The last letter written from there (see above, p. 517) resumed the customary *Sie*, which was retained after his return to Weimar. On March 22 he suddenly wrote a letter in which the *Du* was used throughout (above, p. 780) and this was repeated on the following day. On the same day another communication followed in which the *Sie*

March	April		May
25 ±	1 +	17 +	1 ±
26 ±	2 +	18 −	3 +
26 ±	3 +	18 −	6 −
27 +	5 −	19 −	7 +
28 ±	6 +	20 +	9 −
28 +	7 −	22 +	10 +
30 +	8 +	23 +	12 ±
31 ±	9 +	24 +	14 +
	10 +	25 +	21 +
	11 +	27 ±	23 +
	12 +	27 +	25 +
	13 −	28 +	27 ±
	14 −		28 +
	15 −		30 +
	16*		31 +

+ = *Du*
− = *Sie*
± = *Both*

* In this letter Goethe uses the third person.

was used but which closed with the enigmatic "my new one" (above, p. 519).

I add a table containing all the dates on which Goethe wrote to Charlotte von Stein from March 23 to the end of May, 1781. Each date is followed by an index indicating whether the *Du* (+) or *Sie* (−) was used throughout the letter. The letters in which both occurred are marked by ±. I have listed only those letters the dates of which are beyond any doubt.

From this point on the *Du* was used regularly with the following few exceptions. On June 5 two letters were sent. In the second sentence of the second communication the *Sie* occurs once. It strikes me as an oversight. On June 20 there was a short letter in which Goethe addressed Charlotte von Stein with *Sie*. In the case of this letter I suspect it may have been conveyed by a person who was not quite reliable and therefore the *Sie* was enforced by external necessity. Yet as late as September 22, 1781, a solitary *Sie* can still be found. Interestingly enough, this occurred when Goethe had a feeling of uncanniness.

From the table it can be seen that there was an interval in which Goethe was wavering in the form of address. It took about nine weeks before the *Du* became an integrated and permanent part of his relationship with Charlotte von Stein. Yet within this period of wavering the types of address are not evenly distributed but occur periodically. Thus, following the letter ending with "my new one" (March 23) no letter occurred in which *Sie* was used throughout until April 5, when the first letter of that type was written. The *Sie* letters become more frequent from April 12 on, until on April 20 a new period of *Du* starts, etc.

The questionable letter recorded in the main text on pp. 782–83, which uses *Sie* consistently and which the editors of the *Sophienausgabe* assign to March 25, would be a foreign body and its assignment to that date is highly improbable for statistical reasons alone. (Since the dating of this letter is questionable it does not appear in the chart.)

The uncertainty in the use of *Du* and *Sie* during this interval indicates the great emotional meaning that this matter of usage had for Goethe.

Whereas in his initial stay at Weimar, when *Du* and *Sie* were not used consistently, one receives the impression that the type of address depended on intensities and qualities of emotions, the key to the variation of address in 1781 is not known to me. Emotions, to be sure, had their effect, but I surmise that other factors (probably correlated with some unknown structural component) had a predominant bearing. The choice of address in 1781, therefore, has to be assigned to processes of a more meaningful order than had been the case in 1776.

Appendix K

Further Remarks Concerning the Gretchen Episode

GOETHE'S REPORT OF the Gretchen episode in Books V and VI of *Dichtung und Wahrheit* is a document of eminent psychological importance since it contains an account of the pubescent boy's first amorous experience. To be sure, that account is, for a variety of reasons, not accessible to an adequate or reliable interpretation. Yet it would be hard to find another episode in Goethe's voluminous writings—all of which, after all, must be regarded as autobiographical—concerning which the psychologist would want to know with like curiosity whether or not Goethe's report contains a kernel of historical truth.

Usually the biographer takes a report as a road sign pointing in a certain direction and the question of historical truth sinks to secondary importance. But in this instance the reality meaning of the account would be of the greatest assistance to an understanding of the gradual unfolding of the subject's love-life. Was Goethe's account based on historical truth at all or was it entirely poetic invention? Düntzer (112) tries, on not quite convincing grounds, to prove the historical authenticity of the Gretchen episode. Goethe's mother referred to a Gretchen, according to Bettina von Arnim,[1] but her reports are not always trustworthy. According to tradition, Goethe in 1828 told Stieler[2] that Gretchen was pure poetic invention (112, p. 32), but this report is second-

---

[1] See 11, 2:168. Bettina reported that her informant spoke of "the pretty Gretchen; he was very fond of her; she was the first I knew of that he cared for" [das schöne Gretchen, er hatte sie sehr gern: das war die erste, von der ich weiss, dass er sie lieb hatte.] But Goethe's mother claimed that Gretchen lived in Offenbach, which would be different from his report. And in Bettina's recital there is no indication of any misdemeanor connected with the infatuation. But plenty of reasons can be thought of for the informant's not mentioning anything of that sort or Bettina's discreetly by-passing it in her communication.

[2] Karl Stieler (1781–1858) of Mainz, favorite portrait painter of the Bavarian kings, who painted Goethe's portrait.

hand and again is open to doubt. Further historical research might unearth material that would shed light on this episode. Since, as Goethe claimed, his love-affair came under the scrutiny of an extensive investigation involving a large group of people engaged in all kinds of dishonest practices, one would expect to find a wealth of documentary evidence. Kriegk reports finding files referring to a trial of two court employees which took place five and a half weeks after the time when, if Goethe's report is correct, the Gretchen affair blew up.[3] But this evidence is rather scanty by comparison with the extent of the evildoing Goethe reports of the group in which he says he was moving at that time. The Gretchen episode will be reported in greater detail in the following.

One of Goethe's early friends, whom he calls "Pylades," boasted to an acquaintance about Goethe's poetic abilities. This acquaintance expressed disbelief, and when Pylades, in the company of the boy-poet, met the skeptic by chance, Goethe on the spot performed the feat with which the man challenged him to prove his talent.

The test was whether Goethe could compose a letter in verse in which a young bashful girl reveals to a young man her love for him. Only later did Goethe learn that this verse-letter was used for a practical joke on another man. This person, in turn, wanted to answer in verse, and Goethe was invited by the whole group to help them out by again composing a letter. At this gathering he met Gretchen for the first time, a meeting of which he later wrote: "It was the first permanent impression which a female being made on me."[4]

Goethe furnished the answer as requested and after a short while he was asked in turn to compose the letter with which the fictitious girl would answer. It was from the reading of this letter that Gretchen realized that he was in love with her. As soon as they were alone she implored him to stop writing fictitious letters since she was certain only evil could result from doing such things. Goethe promised that he would not pass on the letter to the man who had commissioned him, but in the course of his conversation he brought the girl to the point of signing the letter he had composed, thus creating the impression that she had written the love-letter for him.

I was beside myself with delight, leaped to my feet, and wanted to embrace her.—"No kissing!" she said, "that is something so vulgar; but love, if it is possible."[5]

---

[3] 343, quoted after the annotations to Goethe's *Werke* (248, *12*:500–01). This book was not accessible to me. My efforts to get a transcript or extracts of the important diaries of Johann Christian von Senckenberg (1707–72), famous physician, scientist, and community-spirited citizen of Frankfurt, were in vain.

[4] [Es war der erste bleibende Eindruck, den ein weibliches Wesen auf mich gemacht hatte.] (*Dichtung und Wahrheit,* Book V, *Soph.* I, 26:267)

[5] [Ich kannte mich nicht vor Entzücken, sprang auf und wollte sie umarmen.— "Nicht küssen! sagte sie: das ist so was Gemeines; aber lieben, wenn's möglich ist."] (*Soph.* I, 26:271)

In Goethe's narrative he assures her that she has saved him by her warnings and then goes on:

> The first love inclinations of an unspoiled youth take throughout a spiritual turn. Nature seems to want that one sex become aware through its senses of the good and the beautiful in the other. And so arose in me too through the sight of this girl and through my inclination towards her a new world of the beautiful and the excellent.[6]

Extensive and intensive occupation with a particular topic unavoidably conduces to bias. Accordingly, I am not sure whether I am being objective when I observe that important parts of Goethe's account, up to this point at least, seem almost to parallel important events in and aspects of his relationship to Charlotte von Stein. But I cannot help feeling that Goethe's asking Gretchen to sign the letter and his subsequent elation as if she had written the letter herself is quite reminiscent of his "correcting" Charlotte von Stein's letter and then calming down as if she had never hurt his feelings (cf. above, pp. 538–40). Furthermore, the way he describes Gretchen—her aversion against any kind of physical contact, her rejection of kissing, and her emphasis on love "if it is possible," as if love were a task to be fulfilled—makes her nearly identical with Charlotte von Stein in her outlook on this subject. Charlotte von Stein's function as a mediator in perceiving the world of the beautiful and excellent has been shown by so many examples that no further demonstration is necessary of the parallel in this respect.

The Gretchen episode ended in catastrophe. One day it was discovered that the group to which Gretchen belonged was engaged in a variety of criminal activities. Suspicion also fell on the boy and he was sharply interrogated. His innocence was established, but he was abruptly separated from his sweetheart. He was told that she was not incriminated, but that she had preferred to leave town. He never saw her again. This sudden turn of events—the separation from the girl, the interrogation, the fear that he might have injured the girl and his friends by his confession and defense—all this together caused what would nowadays be called a nervous breakdown. He refused food, cried, became depressed, raved, and finally fell into physical sickness. It took a long time for him to recover. His parents hired a young man to serve as his daily companion. There was the fear that he might do violence to himself. According to Goethe, his illness stopped abruptly when his new companion told him that Gretchen had stated in her interrogation that she had always looked upon him as a child and that her inclination towards him had always been of a sisterly nature.

---

[6] [Die ersten Liebesneigungen einer unverdorbenen Jugend nehmen durchaus eine geistige Wendung. Die Natur scheint zu wollen, dass ein Geschlecht in dem andern das Gute und Schöne sinnlich gewahr werde. Und so war auch mir durch den Anblick dieses Mädchens, durch meine Neigung zu ihr, eine neue Welt des Schönen und Vortrefflichen aufgegangen.] (*Soph.* I, 26:272)

I hastily assured my friend that now all was over! Also I no longer spoke of her and no longer mentioned her name; yet I could not give up the evil habit of thinking about her, of calling up her appearance, her character, and her conduct, which now appeared to me in an entirely different light. I found it unbearable that a girl at most a few years older than I should consider me a child, when I thought I could pass as a quite intelligent and capable young fellow. Now her cold, aloof nature, which formerly had stirred me so much, struck me as quite disagreeable; the familiarities she permitted herself towards me, but forbade me to return, were utterly hateful to me.[7]

Strangely enough, elements of this résumé about Gretchen are again to be found in Goethe's relationship to Charlotte von Stein at one time or another. The following example seems to me characteristic for several reasons. Once, as he was rushing to her after having finished his day's work, he saw lights in the windows of the casino where Weimar's nobility foregathered weekly. He hoped he would nevertheless find her still at home, and hurried, but she had left already. He grumbled and tried to console himself, yet ended his letter to her thus:

If you had known how much I needed a glance from you, you would have stayed at home. I do not want to be a child. Adieu.[8]

The last statement comes abruptly. It cannot be considered a childish desire to have wanted her to spend the evening with him. The statement may refer to reproaches she had delivered on some previous occasion when he felt disappointed at her absence.

An interesting further point of parallelism is that Gretchen, in her way, also belonged to a group in which he was a stranger by status and social background. The just-mentioned letter was written on a Tuesday when Weimar's aristocracy gathered in the casino, where Goethe could not join them, since he had not yet been made a member of the nobility at that time. Thus he was literally as well as symbolically separated from Charlotte von Stein as he had been from Gretchen. To be excluded from a group by an insurmountable bar-

---

[7] [. . . ich versicherte hastig meinen Freund, dass nun alles abgethan sei! Auch sprach ich nicht mehr von ihr, nannte ihren Namen nicht mehr; doch konnte ich die böse Gewohnheit nicht lassen, an sie zu denken, mir ihre Gestalt, ihr Wesen, ihr Betragen zu vergegenwärtigen, das mir denn nun freilich jetzt in einem ganz anderen Lichte erschien. Ich fand es unerträglich, dass ein Mädchen höchstens ein paar Jahre älter als ich, mich für ein Kind halten sollte, der ich doch für einen ganz gescheidten und geschickten Jungen zu gelten glaubte. Nun kam mir ihr kaltes, abstossendes Wesen, das mich sonst so angereizt hatte, ganz widerlich vor; die Familiaritäten, die sie sich gegen mich erlaubte, mir aber zu erwidern nicht gestattete, waren mir ganz verhasst.] (*Soph.* I, 27:8–9)

[8] [Wenn du gewusst hättest wie ich eines Blickes von dir bedarf, du wärst zu Hause geblieben. Ich will kein Kind seyn. Adieu.] (January 29, 1782)

rier causes a particularly severe distress. It is one of the great unhappinesses from which some children, if not all, suffer at times.

Goethe's reproach against Gretchen for having taken liberties that were not permitted to him also has its counterpart in his relationship to Charlotte von Stein. To make the parallel complete it must be added that in Goethe's account the whole Gretchen episode is intertwined with a political event that took place in Frankfurt in 1763 and that deeply impressed the young boy's fantasy, namely, the coronation of Emperor Joseph. As has been abundantly shown, Goethe's love for Charlotte von Stein and his political work can likewise scarcely be kept apart.

As Goethe described it in *Dichtung und Wahrheit* his interest in the historical event was based mainly on the desire to explain to Gretchen all the confusing details of such an elaborate ceremony. He wrote:

> On the whole and generally speaking this infinitely varied world surrounding me made only a very simple impression on me. . . . I had no inclination but towards Gretchen and no other intention but to see and grasp everything really correctly in order to be able to go over it again with her and to explain it to her.[9]

The same aspect played a great role in his relationship to Charlotte von Stein, as will be remembered. At times his letters to her even sound as if his whole interest in administrative and political activity was only to provide a background for his love for her. On October 29, 1781, he wrote:

> My soul is firmly tied to you; your love is the beautiful light of all my days; your approbation is my best glory and if I much prize a good name abroad, then it is for your sake, in order not to bring discredit on you.[10]

[9] [Überhaupt und im ganzen genommen machte diese unendlich mannichfaltige Welt, die mich umgab, auf mich nur sehr einfachen Eindruck. . . . Ich hatte keine Neigung als zu Gretchen, und keine andere Absicht, als nur alles recht gut zu sehen und zu fassen, um es mit ihr wiederholen und ihr erklären zu können.] (*Soph.* I, 26:313–14)

[10] [Meine Seele ist an dich fest gebunden, deine Liebe ist das schöne Licht aller meiner Tage, dein Beyfall ist mein bester Ruhm, und wenn ich einen guten Nahmen von aussen recht schäze, so ists um deinetwillen, dass ich dir keine Schande mache.]

There is still another detail recorded in the Gretchen episode which is reminiscent of the Weimarian days. The friend whom the boy entertained with his stories and who made him acquainted with Gretchen and the ill-fated group of men, Goethe in *Dichtung und Wahrheit* calls Pylades. Now, this name also occurs in *Iphigenia,* and, as may be recalled, this role was acted by the Duke. When the boyhood Pylades is described as having been successful with women, the parallel becomes even more striking, in view of the Duke's numerous love-affairs. As he held power over Pylades by the stories he told him (*Dichtung und Wahrheit,* Book II) and gained Gretchen's passing interest by his poems, so he won his great position of power in Weimar by his standing as the greatest German poet and so, too, did he gain Charlotte von Stein's unfailing interest by the beautiful poems dedicated to her. If we could only be sure of the historical veracity of the Gretchen episode, how nicely could the triumphs of the adult be described as almost literal repetitions of childhood events.

Thus in both instances—in the administration of the duchy as well as in the coronation of 1763—important aspects of social reality assertedly became meaningful to him only in so far as they served his love for a woman. In these instances it seemed as if certain reality functions of an innately unerotic nature could be activated only if they were embedded in an erotic relationship. As a matter of fact, Goethe's almost exclusive devotion to administrative duties decreased as soon as he became psychologically prepared to break away from Charlotte von Stein, as is demonstrated in the text.

The hidden similarities between the Gretchen episode and some biographically verified facts concerning his relationship with Charlotte von Stein cause great embarrassment to the biographer who would like so much to separate fact from fiction. Undoubtedly there is the possibility that the Gretchen episode was entirely fictional, as some biographers have supposed. It is not a matter here of deciding about this or that detail. Assuming the Gretchen episode to have been built around a real event, it can be taken for granted that Goethe rearranged facts or added and deleted details in order to synthesize the event into a dramatic story. It is not probable (albeit not impossible) that the misdeeds of the gang were discovered just at the time when the coronation festivities had reached their peak—a detail that lends dramatic momentum to Goethe's narration but may easily strain the truth, as far as the real events are concerned. Yet it would help if one could know for certain that at that age Goethe was deeply in love with a girl older than he, and that that early romance ended in a catastrophe that threatened his social position in his native community. On the other hand, in view of the great significance Charlotte von Stein had for the course his life took, he may—as mentioned previously—at times have felt the urge to give her a proper place in his autobiography, and yet have been as little able to do so as he was to write freely about the Duke and his spouse. It would not have been unlike Goethe to have recorded some aspects of the history of that relationship in a place where he could be certain it would not be discovered. Likewise it is possible that, in the fashion of a cover memory, some of the essential features of his love for Charlotte von Stein were projected into the past, quite probably without his even being aware that the embellishment of a perhaps trivial incident stemmed from the dramatic events of a much later date.

The third possibility, of course, is that his adult relationship to the beloved woman bore, by repetition, the earmarks of an adventure of early puberty.

Which of these alternatives is the correct one? The analyst would feel inclined to assume that the Gretchen episode—real or invented—was genetically connected with childhood experiences, and that the repetitive elements in his relationship with Charlotte von Stein were enforced by the repetitious compulsion, which plays such a great role in the life of individuals, neurotic or otherwise, as well as of groups.

Another frequently stated detail comes again to one's mind. Goethe's mother claimed she loved only one man, an emperor whose coronation she witnessed as a child. Doubtful as it may be that this claim was true, the possibility cannot be denied that the boy heard her talking of that fantasy, or that he reacted to a feeling or behavior pattern that was linked up in her with coronations. Then the Gretchen episode would mean an acting out of an accusation against mother and/or revenge for her unfaithfulness. The mother's infatuation was directed toward an emperor who played an unhappy and tragic role in history and did not possess the splendor imagination usually attributes to emperors. Our young lover, too, did not play for long a splendid role, as if he might have thought that only the unhappy and unsuccessful aroused his mother's abiding affection.

Before leaving off this psychological evaluation of the Gretchen episode one more detail must be brought up. Originally Goethe intended to conclude his account of his first love affair with a résumé of Prévost's famous novel, *Manon Lescaut.* He dropped the idea and closed the chapter with the following lines in which he explains how, after the break with Gretchen, he

> . . . had time enough to figure forth to myself self-torturingly the strangest novel of sad events and of an inevitable tragic catastrophe.[11]

In the originally intended ending of this chapter, Goethe tells us that, so long as his relationship with Gretchen lasted, the novel served to enhance its delightfulness, but once they had broken off, it made him the more wretched (see *Soph.* I, 26:381). This formulation seems to open a longer period in which Goethe could have read *Manon Lescaut* than that referred to in the final form, where, for all that is explicitly said, the book was not read until all was over between them. Nevertheless, the difference is not really very great, for it is plainly a matter of indifference to Goethe—and to us—just when he read it, since his preoccupation with it has the character of his dallying with fantasies of his own, rather than the Abbé Prévost's. This thought is insinuated in the concluding passage of the final draft when he writes: "I had time enough to figure forth. . . ." How deeply the effect of this novel went one may see from a remark at the end of the original, unpublished, draft. The aging Goethe praised the great art of the author of *Manon Lescaut* and admitted that as a youth he had been unaware of this aspect but had been moved only by its content. As a youngster he had fancied himself capable of such love and faithfulness as Des Grieux's and he believed Gretchen to be infinitely better than Manon. After telling of the novel's effect upon him during and after his love-affair, he makes the puzzling remark: *"In order that there should be fulfilled for me what stands written"*[12] (Goethe's italics). The interpretation admits only a Christ identification, to which I have referred throughout the text. The

---

[11] [. . . hatte Zeit genug mir den seltsamsten Roman von traurigen Ereignissen und einer unvermeidlich tragischen Katastrophe selbstquälerisch auszumahlen.] (*Soph.* I, 26:342)

[12] [Damit an mir erfüllt würde, was geschrieben steht.] (*Soph.* I, 26:381)

readiness with which Goethe in his old age attributes the Christ identification to his young self may suggest an early inception for that identification. In any case, its erotic-sexual genesis is demonstrated with particular clarity.

It can be concluded that *Manon Lescaut* was the artistically expressed content of his own daydreams, which makes it necessary to pay some attention to it.

In this novel Western literature was enriched by the creation of a new type of woman. If all that had been involved had been the beautiful, sensuous, seductive, pleasure-seeking type of woman, *Manon Lescaut* would not, I think, have become as famous as it is. But with great psychological finesse Prévost added to a well-known literary type a feature that made Manon vastly more interesting than her predecessors, and simultaneously greatly stimulated men's fantasy. Manon is not just a selfish girl who turns wherever she can the better obtain the means of gratifying her sensuality, her cravings for luxury and abundance. She is capable of love and she really loves. This composite of selfishness and love is what makes her what she is, for her love is not the ever-changing desire for a variety of men; in reality she is quite constant in her love, and when she assures Des Grieux that he and only he is the man she loves, she is not lying —at least not consciously—but is expressing a truth more far-reaching than perhaps she knows. But she is a victim of circumstances. On the spur of the moment she cannot resist the tempting appeal of the prospect of pleasure. Her defense, when her infidelity has been proved, consists of repentance and the assurance that it had been committed for her lover's sake.

By creating this figure Prévost anticipated a type of psychopathic personality that can be found described in our psychiatric textbooks. Indeed, I think his description is the more just, for in the textbooks the so-called psychopathic personality is usually presented as shallow, which in general it is not. Manon is not shallow. She has passion, psychological vigor and depth.

From clinical observation one can gather that it is Manon's passion that can bind a man to her eternally, as happens with Des Grieux. Clinically one finds relatively often that compulsive, narcissistic men, culturally endowed and capable of sublimation, become associated with this type of woman, or are preoccupied in their fantasies with such as she. It is always men who are greatly inhibited in the free flow of emotions, affects, and the gratification of their drives, that one finds so involved. Their ambitions take them far afield from adequate instinctual releases. The unbounded capacity of the Manon type for surrendering to the primary process has a fascinating effect on some of those who are seriously inhibited in surrendering to it themselves. Des Grieux belongs to this type of man. Whenever he can disentangle himself from Manon he behaves in a manner perfectly adjusted to reality and shows all the traits of the gifted man who is fully capable of sublimation; but Manon's presence shatters his sublimations: he must surrender to her and commit self-destructive acts. The fact that these women, aside from their abundant capacity for providing pleasure, arrogate the place of man's ego-ideal gives them inescapable power over men.[13]

In reading Prévost's novel one is reminded of the sexual daydreams and novellike narrations that are often heard in psychoanalyses. The masochistic element is indisputable. Des Grieux knows that Manon's plans must ruin him, but nevertheless he must give in to her demands. In the novel a rhythm becomes noticeable that is reminiscent of the ups and downs of the manic-depressive personality. At one point, De Grieux says: "Throughout my life I have noticed that heaven when it wanted to hit me with its hardest punishments, always selected that time when my good luck seemed to me to be most firmly established."

This sounds like masochistic reveries about orgasm, and, in Prévost's novel, male masochistic reverie is carried to a peak. There is apparently a deeper masochistic gratification in being ruined by a woman by whom one is loved than by a rejecting woman. This fantasy also—or perhaps primarily—serves as a better protection against aggression.

What is found in the two drafts of *Dichtung und Wahrheit* about *Manon Lescaut* can, thus, be used to prove the extent to which Goethe must during his adolescence have been preoccupied with disguised masochistic fantasies, and it is probably quite significant that in his imagery the angel Gretchen changed at the end into something like a psychopathic personality—a sequence that will be found later at a decisive point in his life in actuality.[14] It may or may not have been without meaning that when Goethe was writing his autobiography he asked Charlotte von Stein for a copy of *Manon Lescaut* (August 30, 1811) in exchange for his sending her the poetical work by Caroline von Günderode[15] for which she had asked. The woman who ruins men and the woman who is ruined by a man were put in the same context inadvertently, as it seemed, and without meaningful connection, solely because of external coincidences. Yet Goethe had written the résumé of *Manon Lescaut* which he needed for his autobiography on May 16, 1811 (see *Soph.* III, 4:206), and we do not know why he later asked for another copy from the woman he had so ardently loved in former years.[16]

The little detail of Goethe's bringing in Prévost's novel sounds like a true-to-life memory. From the artistic viewpoint it would have been in bad taste to give a résumé of *Manon Lescaut,* and, as said before, Goethe dropped the idea. However, he reread the novel, because, apparently, he did not remember its con-

---

[13] Cf. 416 for a detailed analysis of this problem.

[14] I am referring here to Goethe's association with Christiane Vulpius subsequent to his sublime experiences with Charlotte von Stein.

[15] Caroline von Günderode (1780–1806), a hypersensitive German poetess who committed suicide for unrequited love. Goethe came to be well informed about her in 1810 when he met Bettina von Arnim, who had been a close friend of hers.

[16] It seems Charlotte von Stein had a copy of the French original. Cf. Goethe's entry of September 1, 1811, *Soph.* III, 4:230.

tent very well. He may have remembered that the novel played a role in his fantasies of that time.

In the synopsis from which I quoted earlier, one finds the following entry for the year 1763:

Peace of Hubertsburg February 15. Coronation. Dreadful things. Back to poetic a[rt].[17]

What those dreadful things were that perturbed the young boy we do not know. Was it really the Gretchen episode? It must have been something sexual. Perhaps it involved the inception of masturbation, some humiliating experience of being discovered, which, in a highly disguised fashion, found a representation in the published autobiography.

Some details of the Gretchen episode actually point in this direction: the interrogation; a confession after much pressure; the subsequent isolation; the supervision by a tutor hired for that particular purpose. Since in the Gretchen episode vicious young men prevail, by whom the innocent boy is unwittingly abused for malicious purposes, one may think of a homosexual abuse or mutual masturbation.

The Gretchen episode as recorded in *Dichtung und Wahrheit* then would be the poetic end product of two trains of thought, principally:

(1) The poet may have been trying to bring consolation to his wounded pride by saying: If I had suppressed forbidden sexual impulses I should have gotten into far more serious troubles, namely, have been exploited by an irresponsible gang and publicly humiliated.

(2) The poet may further have been offering an excuse by saying that even if he had resisted masturbatory—homosexual—impulses and turned towards a girl in his quest for sexual release, good luck would not have been on his side, for boys of the age of fourteen are treated by older girls like children and are not given the privileges of adults.

The possibility that sexual transgressions were the historical core of the Gretchen episode may account for the absence of legal documents, which is unaccountable if the "dreadful things" of 1763 were really of the nature Goethe led posterity to believe.

[17] [Hubertsburger Friede 15 Febr. Krönung Ungeheures Zurück in die Dichtk.] (*Soph.* I, 26:355)

Appendix L

Remarks on Engel's Novel *Herr Lorenz Stark*

Goethe's contemptuous remark about J. J. Engel's novel *Herr Lorenz Stark* (125) (see above, p. 715) which was a kind of best seller in its time, suggests some hypothetical remarks. The novel, though well written, was certainly mediocre. The main character is Lorenz Stark, the father, a self-made, wily, well-meaning man who has the bad habit of frequent sarcasms, with which he gets on the nerves of those around him. The author characterizes him as follows:

> The failings of which this excellent man had not a few and which often were extremely annoying to those who had to live with him were so intimately interwoven with the best of his qualities that these, as it seemed, could hardly exist without those. Since he was in fact smarter than almost all those with whom he had to deal, he was very self-willed and dogmatic.

The main conflict around which the novel revolves is that between the father on the one side and on the other his son, who is assisted by his sister and brother-in-law, a prominent physician. The whole constellation is reminiscent of Goethe's circumstances in Frankfurt. One is inclined to say that, if Cornelia had stayed in her native city with Schlosser and if Goethe had been a mediocre person, his life might easily have taken such a course as is depicted in Engel's novel. The son, who works in his father's business, is almost despised by his father for his love of nice clothes, his addiction to parties, to gambling. He seems to have a weak character and is averse to marriage.

Unbeknown to the father, the son has actually stopped his easy way of living but spends most of his free time with a young widow, who, mother of two children, has been left in straitened circumstances by a frivolous husband. The son loves this woman but is not strong enough to marry her and is in constant discord with his father. Thus he decides to move away from his parental home to a foreign city. His mother, sister, and brother-in-law easily dissuade him from this step, for the hardship that he anticipates abroad is itself enough to frighten him. The denouement can be easily guessed. The father is gradually apprised of his son's good deeds and is reconciled to the son's wish to marry the widow. All ends well through the persistent cunning and assistance of the sister and brother-in-law, for whom the father has affection and respect.

As a matter of fact, one feels inclined to surmise that somewhere such a spineless, self-indulgent, dependent creature lay hidden in Goethe, or that he was at times afraid that he might succumb to such inclinations. He was indeed right to turn against the type of father represented by Lorenz Stark because of his emasculating effect. Goethe was protected against this effect by the sharpness of his oedipal conflict, which acted as a fulcrum for his activity. His father's unpleasant qualities were just sufficiently pronounced to prevent a passive submission and his inclination to be domineering was not intense enough to suppress the son's gifted dispositions. So much for a few external factors in Goethe's oedipal situation that can be brought into connection with Engel's work.

Regarding the intrinsic factors of the father conflict, Engel's novel is utterly lacking in the daemonic element that is so pronounced in Goethe's life, and which can be discovered in every life history once its unconscious elements are uncovered. If Engel's portrait of the father-son relationship were really typical, this relationship would be innately conflict-free, and any conflicts that did arise would be due to the son's weakness or deficiencies. Obedience and good will would be quite sufficient to insure a harmonious living-together.

If the relations between generations were really structured in this way the Oedipus complex would be nothing but a construction of the psychoanalyst, as so many critics claim. Goethe's remark against *Lorenz Stark* sprang not only from his artistic disapproval but out of his intense feeling about the tragedy inherent in the father-son relationship, a tragic aspect that was minimized and represented frivolously in Engel's novel.

Appendix M

Goethe's Letter of December 26, 1784, to Karl August

THE FOLLOWING LETTER may serve as evidence of the mastery Goethe had acquired in handling human situations of even a precarious nature. Since he held on the social plane the position of a courtier the danger of loss of dignity was at times great, yet the following document will demonstrate that his character was solid and proud enough, and his understanding of human foibles and vanities sufficient, to blend sociopolitical necessities with friendship and duty, without humiliation to himself, or either flattery or defiance towards the Duke. Thus he wrote:

Your kind letter relieved my worries and I am very glad that you have not taken amiss my refusal [to meet the Duke in Frankfurt; cf. above, p. 957], for, in my considered opinion, I could not for more than one reason leave [this] place. I wish that whatever you do on this journey and whatever you may encounter may be of use and benefit to you.

Also the joy of hunting I grant you with all my heart and nourish the hope that you, in turn, after your return will free your people from worry over a threatening evil. I mean the rooting inhabitants of Ettersburg. I dislike mentioning these animals, since I have protested right from the beginning against their being quartered and it might well look like dogmatic obstinacy that I now again take the field against them. Only the general demand can move me to break an almost sworn silence and I the rather write, since it will be one of the first matters that will be brought before you on your return. Of the damage itself and the relation of such a herd to our region I say nothing, I speak only of the impression it makes on the people. Never before have I seen anything so generally disapproved; there is only one voice concerning it. Estate owners, tenants, [your] subjects, servants, even the hunting set, all join in the desire to see these guests extirpated.

From the government in Erfurt[1] a memorandum about it has been sent to ours.

What has struck me in this connection and what I should like to tell you is the attitude of the people towards you that reveals itself therein. Most of them are simply astounded, as if the animals had fallen like hail from the skies: the generality does not ascribe the evil to you; others do, as it were with reluctance, and all of them unite upon this, that the blame belongs on those who, instead of raising objections against it, prevented you by their ingratiating pretenses from realizing the damage that is incurred by it. Nobody is capable of supposing that you could be led by some passion into such an error for the purpose of settling and deciding something that flatly contradicts your usual way of thinking and acting, your known intentions and wishes. The Land Commissioner[2] actually told me to my face that it was impossible, and I believe that he would utterly have denied [to me] that those creatures existed if they had not, the very next night, at Lützendorf [a ducal estate at the Ettersburg], rooted up and felled a row of newly planted trees together with their poles.

If my wishes were to be fulfilled, these archenemies of culture would quietly and little by little be sacrificed to the table without any bustle of hunting, so that, with the returning spring sun, the dwellers about the Ettersberg might be able once again to look upon their fields with happy heart.

One describes the situation of the farmer as lamentable, and certainly it is; with what ills does he have to battle!—I do not wish to add anything that you know for yourself. I have seen you renounce so many things and hope that you will with this passion make a New Year's present to your [people] and hold out for myself [as a reward] for the agitation of my mind, which the colony since its inception has caused me, only the skull of the common mother of this loathsome tribe, that I may place it in my cabinet with twofold pleasure.

May the page that I am just finishing come to hand at a good hour.

Four weeks ago I would not have written it; it is just the result of a state of mind I have got myself into by an initially amusing idea.

I pondered over the nine-year period that I have spent here and the various epochs of my mental attitudes; I tried to make the past quite plain to myself so as to obtain a clear grasp of the present, and, after all sorts of contemplations, I proposed to myself to fancy that I had just now arrived at

---

[1] Carl von Dalberg, who was a friend of the Duke's as well as of Goethe's, and whose fields adjoined the Ettersburg.

[2] George Batty, an agronomist whose judgment was highly esteemed in Weimar and whose able advice had contributed to Goethe's success as an administrator.

this place, just now entered a service where the people and affairs are quite familiar, the capacity, however, and the desire to be effective still new. I looked at everything now from this point of view; the idea gladdened me, entertained me, and was not without profit, and I was the more able to do so since I do not at all suffer from any adverse relationship and am really stepping into a clean future.[3]

[3] [Ihr gütiger Brief hat mich ausser Sorgen gesetzt und ich freue mich sehr dass Sie meine Weigerung nicht übel aufgenommen haben, denn ich konnte nach meiner Überzeugung aus mehr als einer Ursache den Ort nicht verlassen. Ich wünsche dass alles was Sie auf der Reise thun und was Ihnen begegnet zu Nutzen und Frommen gereichen möge.

Auch die Jagdlust gönn ich Ihnen von Herzen und nähre die Hoffnung dass Sie dagegen nach Ihrer Rückkunft die Ihrigen von der Sorge eines drohenden Übels befreyen werden. Ich meine die wühlenden Bewohner des Ettersbergs. Ungern erwähn ich dieser Thiere weil ich gleich Anfangs gegen deren Einquartirung protestirt und es einer Rechthaberey ähnlich sehn könnte dass ich nun wieder gegen sie zu Felde ziehe. Nur die allgemeine Aufforderung kann mich bewegen ein fast gelobtes Stillschweigen zu brechen und ich schreibe lieber, denn es wird eine der ersten Sachen seyn die Ihnen bey Ihrer Rückkunft vorgebracht werden. Von dem Schaden selbst und dem Verhältniss einer solchen Heerde zu unsrer Gegend sag ich nichts, ich rede nur von dem Eindrucke den es auf die Menschen macht. Noch habe ich nichts so allgemein missbilligen sehn, es ist darüber nur Eine Stimme. Gutsbesitzer, Pächter, Unterthanen, Dienerschafft, die Jägerey selbst alles vereinigt sich in dem Wunsche diese Gäste vertilgt zu sehn. Von der Regierung zu Erfurt ist ein Communicat deswegen an die unsrige ergangen.

Was mir dabey aufgefallen ist und was ich Ihnen gern sage, sind die Gesinnungen der Menschen gegen Sie die sich dabey offenbaren. Die meisten sind nur wie erstaunt als wenn die Thiere wie Hagel vom Himmel fielen, die Menge schreibt Ihnen nicht das Übel zu, andre gleichsam nur ungern und Alle vereinigen sich darinne dass die Schuld an denen liege die statt Vorstellungen dagegen zu machen, Sie durch gefälliges Vorspiegeln verhinderten das Unheil das dadurch angerichtet werde einzusehn. Niemand kann sich dencken dass Sie durch eine Leidenschafft in einen solchen Irrthum geführt werden könnten um etwas zu beschliesen und vorzunehmen was Ihrer übrigen Denckens und Handlens Art, Ihren bekannten Absichten und Wünschen geradezu widerspricht.

Der Landkommissair hat mir gerade in's Gesicht gesagt dass es unmöglich sey, und ich glaube er hätte mir die Existenz dieser Creaturen völlig geläugnet wenn sie ihm nicht bey Lützendorf eine Reihe frisch gesetzter Bäume gleich die Nacht drauf zusammt den Pfälen ausgehoben und umgelegt hätten.

Könnten meine Wünsche erfüllt werden; so würden diese Erbfeinde der Cultur, ohne Jagdgeräusch, in der Stille nach und nach der Tafel aufgeopfert, dass mit der zurückkehrenden Frühlingssonne die Umwohner des Ettersbergs wieder mit frohem Gemüth ihre Felder ansehen könnten.

Man beschreibt den Zustand des Landmanns kläglich und er ist's gewiss, mit welchen Übeln hat er zu kämpfen—Ich mag nichts hinzusetzen was Sie selbst wissen. Ich habe Sie so manchem entsagen sehn und hoffe Sie werden mit dieser Leidenschafft den Ihrigen ein Neujahrsgeschenk machen, und halte mir für die Beunruhigung des Gemüths, die mir die Colonie seit ihrer Entstehung verursacht, nur den Schädel der gemeinsamen Mutter des verhassten Geschlechtes aus, um ihn in meinem Cabinete mit doppelter Freude aufzustellen. Möge das Blat was ich eben endige Ihnen zur guten Stunde in die Hand kommen.

Vor vier Wochen hätte ich es nicht geschrieben, es ist nur die Folge einer Gemüthslage in die ich mich durch einen im Anfange scherzhafften Einfall versetzt habe.

Ich überdachte die neun Jahre Zeit die ich hier zugebracht habe und die mancherley

Epochen meiner Gedenckensart, ich suchte mir das Vergangne recht deutlich zu machen, um einen klaren Begriff vom gegenwärtigen zu fassen und nach allerley Betrachtungen nahm ich mir vor mir einzubilden als wenn ich erst ietzt an diesen Ort käme, erst ietzt in einen Dienst träte wo mir Personen und Sachen zwar bekannt, die Krafft aber und der Wunsch zu würcken noch neu seyen. Ich betrachtete nun alles aus diesem Gesichtspuncte, die Idee heiterte mich auf, unterhielt mich und war nicht ohne Nutzen, und ich konnte es um so eher da ich von keinem widrigen Verhältniss etwas leide, und würcklich in eine reine Zukunft trete.]

Appendix N

Notes on an Aspect of Goethe's Relationship to Music

From 1784 on, that is to say towards the end of his pre-Italian stay in Weimar, a phenomenon that deserves careful study became increasingly conspicuous in Goethe's life, although it is quite improbable that its meaning can be deciphered to our satisfaction with the psychological tools at the disposal of the present-day psychologist. This phenomenon was embedded within the more comprehensive one of Goethe's relationship to music. The psychology of music is an elusive topic and I bow reluctantly to the necessity of dealing with it even in this less elusive form, namely, Goethe's at times incredibly intense desire to write libretti and to see them put to music.

Offhand, this desire strikes one as very strange. If a man has won world fame by a novel and has been pouring out one poem after another, most of which, even without being put to music, sound like music—why should such a master spend time and effort upon writing texts for music, particularly when most of his time has to be spent on reorganizing the financial condition of a principality, when he is already engaged in mineralogical research and the investigation of the life of amoebas, and when he can hardly find the time to finish a novel in which he seeks to give artistic structure to the deepest problems that have been agitating his being?

Goethe's poems were put to music by many of his contemporaries but he associated with three composers for the express purpose of having them take a lasting interest in that task. These were: Philipp Christoph Kayser (1755–1823), Johann Friedrich Reichardt (1752–1814), and Karl Friedrich Zelter (1758–1832). In this context only Goethe's relationship to the first will be discussed in detail, for the other two appeared in his life only after his return from Italy. His relationship to the second was quite ambivalent and much argument and discord occurred in it. Zelter became a cherished and loved friend of the aging poet.

Goethe already took a great interest in Kayser in Frankfurt. Kayser[1] was the son of the organist at St. Catherine Church in Frankfurt. At the age of seven his piano playing was remarkable and later he was also admired as a poet and thinker, being a member of the youthful group in which Goethe moved before he left for Weimar. In this circle he was looked upon as a musical genius. He was a kind of Werther embroiled in hopeless love; he lived in great unhappiness with his family, and Goethe apparently tried to help him from 1771 on when he returned from Strassburg. Since Kayser was so unhappy in Frankfurt Goethe advised him to go to Zurich where he had in Lavater a loving and admiring friend. Accordingly Kayser left Frankfurt in 1775, shortly before Goethe's departure.

Kayser was successful in Zurich and at the beginning he seemed happy, probably for the first time in his life. When Goethe later wrote *Jery und Bätely*, he harbored the express intention of having it set to music by his friend. Yet Kayser was too slow and it was given musical form by a Weimar courtier. In 1781 Goethe made a new attempt at helping the composer by inviting him to Weimar. Goethe wanted to introduce him into the court of Weimar, probably with the hope of having him settle close to him. Yet Kayser's accomplishments were not such that this could be seriously considered. Goethe was determined to see his friend instructed by the foremost musical genius of that time, Gluck. He arranged for a trip to Vienna for him and also wanted to finance it, but the composer was too unadaptable to fall in readily with the plans of his benefactor. Later, in 1784, Kayser went to Italy, with the plan of unearthing the music of the ancients, and Goethe again assisted in the financing of the trip. Goethe's correspondence with the composer, for whom he predicted a great future, was lively, and around 1784 Goethe conceived a plot for a comic opera wholly in verse, *Jest, Cunning, and Vengeance* [*Scherz, List und Rache*] (*Soph.* I, *12*:117–80), having Kayser in mind all the time as the prospective composer. The manuscript was duly forwarded to him and Kayser sent the music act by act to the impatiently waiting author. The text was purposely written so as to make music possible throughout the play, in contrast to Goethe's earlier libretti in which sung parts alternated with spoken ones.

There were only three persons in Goethe's cast: the Doctor, Scapin, and Scapine. Its plot is as follows:

Scapin and Scapine wish to take revenge upon the Doctor, who alienated their aunt from them and has now become her heir. Scapin manages to become a servant in the Doctor's household. Scapine intrudes as a patient, feigns sickness, and seeks help from the Doctor. The Doctor mixes a medicine. Scapin lures him out of the room by pretending that a fire has broken out. Scapine quickly pours the medicine out the window and puts a jar of arsenic on the table instead of the innocuous drug the Doctor had used. Upon the Doctor's

---

[1] For Kayser's biography see 46, *1*:49; 443.

return she feigns death and the Doctor believes he has killed her by mistakenly dispensing arsenic. Scapin forces him to pay a large sum of money in return for disposing of Scapine's body. At night Scapine awakens the Doctor by screaming in the cellar and blackmails him anew. When they have obtained all the money they wanted, Scapin and Scapine make fun of the Doctor, who only too late recognizes that he has been gulled by two scoundrels.

Although Kayser met Goethe's expectations this time and sent his compositions as requested it turned out when the musical score was finished that no opera had been created that could be performed. More will be said about the libretto later. Goethe was not disheartened by this failure. Before Kayser had finished his composition Goethe started to work on a new libretto. When he was in Italy he had Kayser follow him and spent some happy months with him. Kayser became his guide for music as Tischbein was for painting and drawing. They became very close and Goethe traveled back to Weimar in Kayser's company. Apparently there was the plan that Kayser should settle in Weimar permanently. A few weeks later Kayser had to join the Dowager Duchess on her trip to Italy. Yet it seems that he could not long stand the ceremoniousness of court life and soon insisted upon leaving the Duchess's entourage. This breach of etiquette made his employment at the court impossible. He returned to Zurich and there lived a quiet, withdrawn life, greatly respected by the few who knew him intimately but thought of as a bizarre, melancholic, misanthropic person by those who knew him superficially.

Goethe lost all interest in him. The precipitating cause of Goethe's withdrawal from this man for whom he felt intense affection for a few years is not known with certainty. When Kayser later requested a recommendation for employment in Frankfurt his letter remained unanswered, and when Goethe came to Zurich during his third Swiss journey he shunned not only Lavater's company but also Kayser's. However, in his *Italian Journey* Goethe wrote with warmth and justice about his friend.

To return to the libretto, I should like to add a few remarks.

In my estimation it is excellently written as long as it pursues a lighter vein. But Goethe tried to include dramatic elements which do not fit at all into a comic opera. Thus, for example, before feigning death Scapine goes through the motions of a seemingly hallucinated encounter with Greek mythological figures. In the last act when she is luring the Doctor into the cellar she acts dramatically like a ghost and the text is not written in a comic way, but takes on dramatic turns. This I think—aside from its literary weakness—poses impossible tasks for the composer. Kayser was a mediocre musician, to be sure, and did not possess the talent to write an opera of any consequence, but even a real musical talent would not have been able to make a good opera out of Goethe's libretto. As a matter of fact, none of Goethe's many libretti was ever set to music by any composer of renown.

Yet there are exquisite libretti in which the tragic and the comical interchange, da Ponte's libretto for *Don Giovanni* being the best example.[2] A comparison of this with Goethe's will, I believe, prove my point. Da Ponte's libretto strikes me as a masterpiece. The comic and the tragic are consistently interwoven and distributed in accordance with character type. When Leporello is making fun under the guise of seriousness this is consistently brought to the listener's attention, whereas in Goethe's libretto there are long passages that the reader could never recognize as serving a comical purpose if he were not familiar with earlier situations. It may be remembered that something similar happened to Goethe when he wrote *Der Triumph der Empfindsamkeit* and combined it with the *Proserpina* play. He blamed himself severely in later years for having linked comedy with tragedy, but the mishandling can be considered as typical.

It is curious that this greatest poet of his times lacked the capacity to write a libretto that could measure up to da Ponte's. I do not wish to enter into speculation about what makes da Ponte's libretto so great, but this much may be said: da Ponte's technique was not one that would have been alien to Goethe nor one that Goethe did not himself apply at times in his masterly fashion. Thus Goethe's failure as a writer of libretti was not due to lack of ability but to an inhibition in applying his talent to this particular task. In other words, one may assume that when Goethe wrote a play with the purpose of providing a composer with a text his Muse deserted him. Therefore one may conclude that a deep ambivalence towards music here came to the fore. In his conversation with Eckermann of December 9, 1824, Goethe said:

> I want to warn you of something right away. Composers will come and will want to have an opera [libretto]; but be unyielding in this matter and refuse since this is also an affair that leads to nothing and with which one wastes one's time.[3]

This warning sounds strange since it was Goethe who looked for composers and at times produced so rapidly texts to be set to music that one could not keep pace with his productions. The belated complaint about the importunate composers sounds rather like sour grapes, a motive that—though secondary—must be considered. No doubt, ambition played a great role in Goethe's life. He had to be a jack of all trades, branching out into almost all fields of art and engaging in almost all human pursuits. Yet music probably was a field in which, despite

[2] Lorenzo da Ponte (1749–1838), a contemporary of Goethe, holds a minor place in the history of Italian literature. Nevertheless, his libretto of *Don Giovanni* is vastly superior to any libretto of Goethe's and is considered by some the best libretto ever written. In later life he became professor of Italian literature at Columbia University in New York.

[3] [Nun will ich Sie gleich noch vor etwas warnen. Es werden die Componisten kommen und eine Oper haben wollen, aber da seyn Sie gleichfalls nur standhaft und lehnen Sie ab, denn das ist auch eine Sache, die zu nichts führt und womit man seine Zeit verdirbt.] (119, p. 102)

his many pertinent remarks on the subject (see 296), he remained a layman. By "layman" I mean here a person who cannot jot down a tune. The extent of Goethe's musicality may be seen from a letter to Herder (middle of July, 1772) in which he perhaps half jestingly wrote: "I can write, but I cannot cut a pen . . . ; I can play the violoncello, but I cannot tune it."[4] It is known how important it was for Goethe to *do* things, not only to understand them. This was also one of the reasons why he had to draw and paint despite the relative mediocrity of his talent. I speak elsewhere of his reaction to his lack in mathematical talents. Any awareness of a limitation amounted to a deep narcissistic injury. In analytic terminology, one would say that imperfection was equated with castration. At least, the ego responded with remarkable defense reactions to the fact that certain areas of mental life were not actively accessible to him. A great variety of contents and qualities can acquire a hostile meaning, depending on individuality and culture. Frequently the foreign or alien is equated with the hostile. In Goethe, I believe, that which could not be mastered by production or activity acquired this quality. He apparently could integrate only by active production. Thus, music—that vast realm of the most human orbit, more human still than all the arts that cluster around the verbal functions, penetrating more directly into man's emotions, being a mystery and a miracle to a searching mind that can only listen to music but not create music—must have been a challenge to Goethe in so far as he depended in this area upon others, saw others create, and remained forever an outsider.

In view of the influence that environmental factors had upon Goethe in the formation of his interests and talents a short discussion of these factors in their relationship to music is in place. Here we notice right at the beginning of his musical education a trauma that he suffered under peculiar circumstances. In *Dichtung und Wahrheit,* Goethe narrates that at the time when his parents were looking for an able piano teacher to whom the little boy and his sister should be entrusted, Goethe witnessed a piano lesson of one of his friends. He was quite enraptured by the hilarious way in which his friend's teacher taught the skill of piano playing. Each finger, each key, and each note had the funniest name, and the boy felt most amusingly entertained throughout the hour. He insisted that this teacher be hired, but was rudely disappointed when his lessons took a drab and boring course and nothing of this hilarity and mirth was to be noticed. His sister accused him severely of having deceived her and was convinced that he had told her a fib. Yet the boy found a sudden solution to this puzzle when one of his friends came for a visit at the time of a piano lesson. The teacher immediately applied his engaging way of teaching and Goethe's friend left as eager as Goethe had been to take lessons with such an entertaining teacher. Then the boy realized that the amusing technique was only a bait to catch pupils.

---

[4] [Ich kann schreiben, aber keine Federn schneiden . . . das Violincell spielen, aber nicht stimmen.]

Although historical evidence speaks in favor of Goethe's starting his piano lessons at the age of fourteen,[5] I have the impression that the reported episode may have occurred at an earlier age. I surmise that a fourteen-year-old boy would not respond so intensely to the pranks of a teacher. Be this as it may, we here see Goethe betrayed and duped by an older male whom he had approached with admiration and affection. And music, which should have served as a bridge to the realization of joyous expectations that centered in the teacher, became the culprit when the same male later behaved in a way that humiliated the lad in his sister's eyes and showed him up as a fool.

Approximately a year later Goethe suffered similar disappointment, again in conjunction with music. He greatly admired a certain Johann André,[6] a man eight years his senior, who was the composer of an operetta. This operetta was performed in a quasi-esoteric literary society to which Goethe applied for membership at the age of fifteen. André was a member and Goethe introduced himself to him in connection with this application. He praised the musical piece to its author apparently in an arrogant manner, and thereby evoked an unfavorable impression, which André did not conceal. Goethe was not accepted as a member.[7] André in a letter called him more a chatterbox than a person of soundness.[8] Yet a few years later André composed the tunes for Goethe's first *Singspiel,* an opera with set pieces and spoken lines, *Erwin und Elmire,* which was performed in Berlin twenty-one times between 1775 and 1782 and thus achieved the largest number of performances of all Goethe's *Singspiele* (see 46, *1:*49).

I cite Goethe's relationship to André because it demonstrates a function of Goethe's *Singspiele.* They are intended, in my opinion, to win male friendship. In the André episode we see an admired man, by whom Goethe had earlier been rejected, now engaged in lending his talents to the adornment of one of Goethe's creations.

But in order to reach a more fundamental aspect of the meaning that music may have had for Goethe we must go further back in his history. Music was an important part of Goethe's home life as he described it in *Dichtung und Wahrheit,* Book I. Goethe's first mention of music in that autobiographical novel is important. In reference to his father's Italian teacher, Domenico Giovinazzi,[9] who helped his father in writing his account of his Italian journey in Italian and who later became the teacher of the little boy and his sister, Goethe reported:

---

[5] For the biography of Goethe's piano teacher, Johann Andreas Bismann, see 389, particularly p. 248.

[6] Johann André (1741–1799), composer, conductor, and music publisher, lived in the vicinity of Frankfurt. Originally a merchant, he became proficient in the musical field though he never received a musical education.

[7] See for Goethe's relationship to the Arcadian Society of Philandria (Arkadische Gesellschaft zu Phylandria), 251, *1:*94–95; 6:4–7, 15.

[8] [er hat mehr ein gutes Plappermaul, als Gründlichkeit.]

[9] For Giovinazzi's biography see 389, pp. 56–73.

The old man did not sing badly and my mother had to put up with accompanying him and herself daily on the piano.[10]

This was perhaps one of Goethe's earliest childhood memories of music.

The passage deserves particular attention. It appears in a context devoted to his father. Thirty printed lines earlier there occurs Goethe's first reference to his father in the autobiography, in which there is reported how he frightened his children back into their bedrooms by masquerading as a ghost. As will be recalled, Goethe took a critical view of his father for such unwise behavior. A few lines later he mentions the etchings of Rome that adorned the foyer and that made an indelible impression on him as a boy. On this occasion he remembers his father in a friendly, though possibly mildly ironic, vein. He writes:

The otherwise very laconic father was indeed occasionally so obliging as to grant us a description of the subject [of the etchings].[11]

The etchings provided an occasion to mention his father's predilection for Italy and Italian, the natural history collection his father brought from Italy, and the book on his Italian journey to which he devoted so much of his time. Then follows the introduction of Giovinazzi and the musical episode I have cited above.

Thus we have the father described in the following sequence leading to the description of the musical life: (1) the *frightening* father (disguised as a ghost); (2) the *kind* father who teaches the son; (3) the *admired* father who accumulates knowledge and writes a book.[12] My contention is that the Giovinazzi report is a screen memory for the fourth link in the sequence, namely for the *accused* and *hated* father who does evil to the mother. A clue to the possibility that the train of thought underlying the Giovinazzi episode was quite different from what it appeared to be on the surface is to be found in the fact that one word in the account of that episode was evidently not historically accurate—Goethe's assertion that his mother had to accompany Giovinazzi *daily*.

We are accurately informed about the expenditures of *Rat* Goethe (see 458). From 1753 to 1755 Giovinazzi received an annual salary of ten gulden (see 389, p. 57), which makes his daily appearance in the house of Goethe's father highly improbable. According to my hypothesis Giovinazzi, the old man,[13] would stand for the father, who daily forces mother to do something

[10] [Auch sang der Alte nicht übel, und meine Mutter musste sich bequemen, ihn und sich selbst mit dem Claviere täglich zu accompagniren.] (*Soph.* I, 26:18)

[11] [. . . der sonst sehr lakonische Vater hatte wohl manchmal die Gefälligkeit, eine Beschreibung des Gegenstandes vernehmen zu lassen.] (*Soph.* I, 26:17)

[12] The various signs of implied criticism, interspersed in this sequence and attesting ambivalence, should not distract from the general development of the imagery attached to the father.

[13] Giovinazzi was born around 1690; see 387.

she does not like to do ("mother had to put up with"), that is to say, who forces the mother to submit to intercourse. Music would be a kind of symbol for the aggressive male aspect of the relationship between the sexes. Goethe's mother loved to play the piano, at least in later years (see 283, pp. 292–93), but when she married her education was rather poor and *Rat* Goethe spent much zeal upon teaching her. Since he encouraged her also to improve her piano playing the little boy may have been right in feeling that his mother was reluctant to conform to the demands of her pedantic husband, who, much older than she, held the place of a father in her life.[14]

Music was one of the many pursuits with which Goethe as a boy came into contact in his father's house. In earlier years he tried to accomplish at least the mastery of an instrument. He played the piano and cello for a while but it does not seem to have got him far. The father played the flute and the lute, and here may have been one of his father's skills that the son never succeeded in matching. In Book I Goethe says of his father: "He esteemed my inborn talents all the more as he was lacking in them, for he had acquired everything only through indescribable industry, perseverance, and repetition."[15] That he was probably right can easily be imagined. But this statement may be turned around and one may conclude that Goethe was profoundly impressed by any and all of his father's talents. As can be shown over and over again he had to achieve more than his father had in all respects. It may sound ridiculous to compare the two at all and to view Goethe's output in terms of what he produced beyond his father's obvious limitations. However, it would be quite inappropriate to measure the two in objective terms. In this instance one can only compare, on the one hand, that which is represented in the mind of the adult as a faint childhood recollection charged with enormous emotional quantities, with, on the other, the feeling that the adult self evolves regarding its own accomplishments. Thus it may easily happen that an objectively minor factor becomes overcharged with infantile emotions and the adult ego is then forced to spend its greatest effort in a direction that is dictated by a seemingly trivial childhood event. Thus the musical accomplishments of Goethe's father, moderate though they were, may have had a greater effect upon Goethe than one might assume from the gross facts of his life history. One gets a glimpse of what seems like still-suppressed anger over his father's occupation with music when the aging

[14] Goethe says about his father in *Dichtung und Wahrheit:* "In the first years of their marriage he pressed my mother to write assiduously as well as to play the piano and sing, in connection with which she also saw herself compelled to acquire some little knowledge and scanty skill in the Italian language." [So hatte er meine Mutter in den ersten Jahren ihrer Verheirathung zum fleissigen Schreiben angehalten, wie zum Clavierspielen und Singen; wobei sie sich genöthigt sah, auch in der italiänischen Sprache einige Kenntniss und nothdürftige Fertigkeit zur erwerben.] (*Soph.* I, 26:18)

[15] [Er schätzte meine angebornen Gaben um so mehr als sie ihm mangelten; denn er hatte alles nur durch unsäglichen Fleiss, Anhaltsamkeit, und Wiederholung erworben.] (*Soph.* I, 26:45)

poet does not let an opportunity pass of twitting his progenitor. In talking of the way his father spent his days during a certain period he wrote: "My father . . . spent more time on tuning his lute than playing it."[16] The dry humor in this report of a perhaps valid observation betrays the suppressed spite that such recollections apparently evoked in Goethe.

I wish to add a further detail that seems to me of importance. Goethe when telling us of Giovinazzi and his mother mentions the aria "Solitario bosco ambroso"[17] which he had learned by heart merely from hearing it, before he understood its meaning. The following is a literal translation of the aria.

> Solitary shaded wood
>> To thee comes the afflicted heart
>> To find some rest
>> From this horror, amid thy silences.
> Every object that delights some other
>> For me no longer is joyous;
>> I have lost my peace
>> I myself am in hatred with me.
> My Phyllis, my lovely flame,
>> Tell me, O trees, is she perhaps here?
>> Alas, I seek her in every place
>> And still I know that she is gone.
> How many times, O agreeable leaves,
>> Has your shadow provided cover.
>> Such a blessed procession of hours,
>> How rapidly did it run away!
> Tell me at least, you friends the leaves,
>> If my love I shall see again.
>> Ah, it is echo that answers me,
>> And it seems to me it answers "No."

[16] [Mein Vater . . . stimmte seine Laute länger als er darauf spielte.] (*Soph.* I, 27:198)

[17] The full text of this aria became the subject of my curiosity. In the current Goethe literature, Pietro Metastasio (1698–1782), famous for many libretti, is given as (or presumed to be) the author, and Domenico Corri (1746–1825), an Italian who spent most of his life in Britain, as the composer. I could not find the aria in Metastasio's complete works, and, despite intensive inquiry among the experts I found no one who was able to locate it until Professor Siegmund Levarie (who called attention to what should have been clear from the beginning—the impossibility of Corri's being the composer because of his age) found the full text in *The Oxford Book of Italian Verse* (Oxford, 1952), pp. 279–80. The author is Paolo Rolli (1676–1765), who was famous in his time as the author of *Canzonette*. The composer was, in all probability, Willem de Fesch (1667–1757); born in Antwerp, his pleasant melodies became popular among amateur musicians because they were easy to perform. I owe great thanks to Professor Levarie, who has published in the meantime the result of his research (366).

For the literal translation of this aria I am indebted to Mr. Seymour A. Copstein, to whom I wish to express my gratitude on this occasion.

I hear a sweet murmuring;
   It might perhaps be a sigh,
   A sigh from my object of worship,
   That says to me, "I shall return!"
Ah, it is the sound of the river that shatters
   Among these stones its cool liquid,
   And does not murmur, but weeps,
   Out of pity for my sorrow.
But if she returns, in vain and belated
   Will the return be, O gods!
   How piteously her sweet regard
   Will weep over my ashes.

This aria takes on special interest when one considers that it may have been the first literary piece in which Goethe became familiar with the *Werther* theme, and one feels compelled to assume an almost direct connection between it and the following passage in a letter from Werther to Lotte that she receives after his death:

> When you climb up the hill on a fine summer evening, then remember me as I so often came up the valley, and then throw a glance over there to the churchyard to my grave, how the wind rocks the high grass now this way, now that, in the glow of the sinking sun.[18]

This passage has always impressed me intensely. One may regard it almost as the pinnacle of the novel. It is here that the reader is for the first time apprised of Werther's decision to commit suicide. Rarely will a sentence be found in which so many images are compounded without the use of general symbols. The images are concise, articulate, and penetratingly clear. A maximum effect is obtained by the organization of the time dimensions: Werther writing in the present of what Lotte will be thinking when, years after his death, she remembers him as he had been in the past. The spatial relations are similarly organized: Lotte ascending the hill, looking back into the valley where Werther had walked, the grave beyond the valley in the light of the setting sun, with the addition of the image of the swaying grass, which captures a spatial dimension of infinite extension by the description of a strictly local event, since in our imagination wind does not start at a particular point nor stop there. In this brief passage five space relations and four time relations are compounded. All this is achieved without leaving room for the most minute doubt in the reader. Just the opposite: with a minimum of words, an incredible breadth of images is forced upon the reader's imagination without a resting point's being supplied,

[18] [Wenn du hinauf steigst auf den Berg, an einem schönen Sommerabende, dann erinnere dich meiner, wie ich so oft das Thal herauf kam, und dann blicke nach dem Kirchhofe hinüber nach meinem Grabe, wie der Wind das hohe Gras im Scheine der sinkenden Sonne hin-und herwiegt.] (*Soph.* I, *19*:160)

and within seconds he has to change the direction of the time flow as well as of the spatial direction several times.

In view of such intensely pregnant imagery it is of interest to consider the possibility that the passage was in genetic connection with early imagery that was introduced to the child's mind by music. Goethe claims he did not understand the meaning of the words of the aria, as he later in the novel also claims that as a boy of ten or eleven he did not understand the plays when he went daily to French performances during the occupation of Frankfurt. I doubt the correctness of both claims. A boy endowed with such a flourishing fantasy life, with such sensitivity and intuition, as Goethe had, must have caught on rapidly. Goethe—it seems to me—pretended ignorance where there was no ignorance, as the child feigns naiveté in order to conceal his sexual knowledge, suspicions, and anxieties. To be sure, his fantasy may often have gone astray from the true meaning of the words, but the general trend of works in the literary arts cannot long have escaped him. His disclaiming understanding appears to me rather to be the expression of a denial of forbidden fantasies which must have been all too frequent at that age. Here, however, we are involved in a seeming contradiction. I interpreted the Giovinazzi–mother recollection as a cover memory of parental intercourse, in which the father played a sadistic role. Now the content of the aria leads us onto the path of Werther, whose lot was an unmanly one, in which he was the victim of brutal and superior forces. Indeed, the mother accompanying the Italian teacher is a figure in a triangle situation if we add the father, who, though he stands in the background, was still the driving force that compelled her to do her assertedly daily musical exercises.

Giovinazzi himself was a colorful person. He was a Dominican monk who rebelled against the Church, left the monastery, and fled Italy. He became a Protestant in Zurich and had to struggle hard before he was legally permitted to earn a living in Frankfurt. In 1735 his first wife died and shortly thereafter he married a woman of over thirty, who was so physically afflicted and infirm that she could not be married in church and needed a special dispensation for a private wedding (see 389, p. 65).

In a letter to his sister of September 27, 1767, when he was in Leipzig, Goethe complains of his shortcomings in Italian and there are implied complaints about the instruction he had received. However, he also lets us know that he had written "l' Opera Comique La Sposa Rapita, et bien d'autres choses"—"the comic opera, *The Abducted Wife,* and a good many other things"—which he burnt because his father made fun of his faulty language. Here, in the relatively early Leipzig days, we already encounter the ambition to write a libretto, this time in Italian, with a suspicious title to boot, and associated with anger at his father. We are again in the middle of the oedipal situation.

Reconsidering the triangle situation father–mother–Giovinazzi indelibly attached to early musical impressions, I suggest that music was very closely associated in Goethe's development with masturbatory activities.[19] In making such a suggestion I am indulging in pure speculation, for so elusive a point can hardly be expected to be confirmed by the record. Yet the problem is so challenging, for Goethe was driven to embrace all manifestations of man's artistic propensities and the study of what facilitated success in one area and obstructed it in another might help solve some of the problems that have from time to time arisen here. Up to this point one can only draw the conclusion that the closeness of music to a repressed, highly charged, forbidden instinctual process may have hampered Goethe's relationship to music.

Returning to Goethe's adult years I wish to quote a passage from a letter to Kayser that may throw further light on the question of Goethe's zeal to produce a libretto. "The author of a musical play," he wrote on May 5, 1786,

> as he surrenders it to the composer, must look upon it as upon a son or pupil that he is devoting to the service of a new master. There is no question any more of what the father or teacher wants to make out of the boy, but of what his master wants to shape him into; [it is] fortunate when he understands the craft better than the first tutors.[20]

The finished product, the opera, would thus become a work in which the efforts of two persons become inseparably blended with each other. The contribution of each would become unidentifiable, the end product being the testimony to the profoundest intermingling of two minds, a process that it was, I think, one of the principal functions of libretti to serve.

Yet Goethe's analogy is ambiguous. It sets in contrast the father, or first tutor, with the master, who will decide the final fate of the pupil. Characteristically, the mother is omitted from this analogy. Partly Goethe is here shifting responsibility so that it shall be as if the final outcome did not depend on the father's or first tutor's ability but solely on the will and ability of the last master. The passage was written at a time when Goethe still entertained some hopes of a successful outcome of Kayser's endeavors, but a doubt had perhaps already set in. Before starting work on the libretto for Kayser, Goethe wrote him (June 28, 1784) about the Italian *opera buffa:*

> I am particularly delighted by the delicacy and grace with which the composer hovers like a heavenly being over the poet's earthy nature.[21]

[19] The beginning of the aria with its stress on solitude may be adduced as a peripheral confirmatory sign.

[20] [Der Dichter eines musikalischen Stückes, wie er es dem Componisten hingiebt, muss es ansehn, wie einen Sohn oder Zögling den er eines neuen Herren Diensten wiedmet. Es fragt sich nicht mehr was Vater oder Lehrer aus dem Knaben machen wollen sondern wozu ihn sein Gebieter bilden will, glücklich wenn er das Handwerck besser versteht als die ersten Erzieher.]

[21] [Besonders erfreut mich die Delikatesse und Grazie womit der Componist gleichsam als ein himmlisches Wesen über der irdischen Natur des Dichters schwebt.]

The imagery derives from the Old Testament and again refers to male creativity. The poet, so to speak, shapes the earthly form, into which the composer then pours life.

Goethe felt challenged at that time by the Italian *opera buffa* and was striving towards the creation of the same genre in German. Notwithstanding the implication of national competition, we again encounter a specific image of the cooperation of two males in the creation of a masterpiece (new life). Yet this cooperation was not without a competitive element. Sternfeld makes the parody the central issue of his excellent treatise on *Goethe and Music* (511). He uses the term "parody" in its broader and constructive meaning as applying to a productive technique "by which actual melodies gave birth to many of Goethe's poems" (511, p. 7). It can be historically proved that an amazingly large number of poems were written by Goethe to existing tunes. Thus Goethe by replacing the text of existing songs with his own lines may have given vent to unconscious competitive strivings. The song is a unit in which words are held together like mounted jewelry. The new text pushes the old one out of its traditional and rightful shrine, and I wonder whether the suggestion is justified of an analogy with a child putting himself into the place of the fetus in the pregnant mother. Yet this competitive angle should not distract from the awareness of how sensitive Goethe was to music, which comes so strongly to the fore when one reads Sternfeld's introduction to his book.

Be this as it may, we encounter here two different situations with regard to Goethe's relationship to music. In one he faced music and wrote words into it; in the other he wrote words and wooed music. The psychological background of the two situations is different though they may have grown from the same unconscious matrix, which included such factors as homosexuality, competitiveness, infantile sexual theories.

As I said at the outset, I do not wish to enter into a discussion of music, but nevertheless this much may be said, that music is closer to the primary process than the literary arts. This is probably not true for some musical experts, for whom music may be something tantamount to a science or even an actual science, but for the majority of listeners, and certainly for Goethe, this is the sort of meaning it has. The closeness of music to the primary process is manifested by its direct rooting in the emotional sphere. The average person can say as little about music as he can about primary emotional or instinctual experiences. When he listens to music that moves him, he comes face to face with strong emotions whose origin he cannot trace to any particular source accessible to verbalization. Music is shrouded in mystery more than other forms of art, and secondary processes are almost excluded from the experience of it.

It is not clear to me how far my view resembles or differs from that expressed by authors like Kohut and Levarie (336; 337) when they claim that the main function of the secondary processes in the average listener is to avert anxiety and to facilitate the ego's surrender to the enjoyment of the archaic, which is for the most part beyond understanding. The task that faces the ego in this surrender appears to me essentially different from that involved in accomplishing the surrender required in the other arts.

How was it with Goethe's ability to surrender to music? On June 19, 1805, he wrote to Zelter:

I know music rather through reflection than through enjoyment and therefore only in general.[22]

This statement should be compared with his letter to Zelter of August 24, 1823.

But now to what is really the most surprising! The enormous power of music over me these days! The voice of Milder,[23] the sonority of Szymanowska,[24] yes even the public exhibitions of the local rifle regiment, unclench me as one in friendship lets a balled fist go limp. To explain this somewhat I tell myself: You have not heard any music at all for two years and longer . . . and so this organ, in so far as it is in you, has locked itself up and set itself apart; now suddenly the heavenly pounces upon you through the medium of great talents and exerts its whole power over you. . . . I am fully convinced that at the first beat of your singing academy I should have to leave the hall. . . .

. . . you would through gradual guidance and examination cure me of morbid irritability which is to be regarded as the real cause of that phenomenon, and little by little make me capable of absorbing the entire fullness of the most beautiful revelation of God.[25]

---

[22] [Ich kenne Musik mehr durch Nachdenken als durch Genuss und also nur im Allgemeinen.]

I do not intend by quoting this letter, or by any other statement in this Appendix, to question the value of Goethe's contribution to the theory of music, which is considered by some to have been considerable. See 367.

[23] Pauline Anna Milder-Hauptmann (1785–1838), operatic singer.

[24] Marie Szymanowska (1790–1831), famous pianist at the Russian court, met Goethe in Marienbad in 1823 and went in the same year to Weimar where she again played for Goethe.

[25] [Nun aber doch das eigentlich Wunderbarste! Die ungeheure Gewalt der Musik auf mich in diesen Tagen! Die Stimme der Milder, das Klangreiche der Szymanowska, ja sogar die öffentlichen musikalischen Exhibitionen des hiesigen Jägercorps, falten mich aus einander, wie man eine geballte Faust freundlich flach lässt. Zu einiger Erklärung sag' ich mir: du hast seit zwey Jahren und länger gar keine Musik gehört . . . und so hat sich dieses Organ, insofern es in dir ist, zugeschlossen und abgesondert; nun fällt die Himmlische auf einmal über dich her, durch Vermittlung grosser Talente, und übt ihre ganze Gewalt über dich aus. . . . Ich bin völlig überzeugt, dass ich im ersten Tacte deiner Singakademie den Saal verlassen müsste.

. . . Du würdest mich durch allmähliche Leitung und Prüfung von einer krankhaften Reizbarkeit heilen, die denn doch eigentlich als die Ursache jenes Phänomens anzusehen ist, und mich nach und nach fähig machen, die ganze Fülle der schönsten Offenbarung Gottes in mich aufzunehmen.]

A comparison of these two passages (1805 and 1823) is so instructive because in the first Goethe reveals an attitude towards music in which one can see his inhibition against surrendering to its impact, whereas in the second he describes the danger of such a surrender. In 1823 he again went through the throes of one of his puberty crises, fell in love with a nineteen-year-old girl, whom, for a while, he seriously intended to marry. Everything was ready in him for a total surrender, but he was well aware that he would not be capable of surrendering to music without bringing harm upon himself.

Here a careful analysis of his relationship to Marie Szymanowska should follow, but this would take us too far afield. Suffice it to say that he tried to find consolation by substituting music for the girl he could not marry, but it is questionable which was the greater strain upon his psychic apparatus: his hopeless love or the impact of music.

Quite rightly he knew that he could let music take hold of him only by piecemeal influx under the guidance of a friend who, if necessary, would substitute, so to speak, for him. Music was to Goethe probably a potentially anxiety-arousing medium, as happens, according to Kohut and Levarie, when the secondary processes do not fulfill their function. Yet this would at least not contradict, if it does not indeed confirm, my earlier suggestion that the effect of music was for Goethe identical with that of a forbidden instinctual process, such as masturbation.

Yet just because of its closeness to the primary process music was also endowed with the capacity of initiating or stimulating the artistic process in Goethe. This double aspect of stimulant and of threat makes an inquiry into Goethe's relationship to music rather difficult. However, that aspect, of psychic economy, is outside the scope of this essay and I mention it here only because in some periods Goethe needed the help of an outside force to compensate for the weakening of inner defenses.

Goethe's craving for the music to his libretto during the two years prior to his departure for Italy was perhaps an attempt at making up for the absence of creative lyric outbursts. The pre-Italian Weimarian decade can, as was pointed out earlier, be roughly characterized as marked by a gradual change from the prevalence of primary processes in artistic creation to the prevalence of secondary processes, or, in literary terms, from the *Sturm und Drang* production to the classical.[26] Charlotte von Stein's great contribution to this change has been consistently described, but it seems that towards the end the secondary processes had grown rank and fettered the ego's ability to use the primary process. Already when he was writing his *Iphigenia,* Goethe wrote Charlotte

[26] The primary process, I must repeat, is always involved in artistic creation, unless that creation proceeds as an imitative technique, and the above classification is not intended to indicate more than the contrast between a phase in which the ego tries to accept the primary process to the largest extent possible and a phase in which the ego tries to elaborate upon it to the largest extent possible.

von Stein (February 14, 1799) that he asked some musicians to play for him in the adjoining room. "I have had music brought to me, to soothe the soul and to unloose the spirits."[27] (Cf. above, p. 488) Evidently Goethe was in need of a kind of catalyst. Such a need had been unthinkable when he was at work on the early masterpieces, like *Werther*. When he was writing *Iphigenia* music served this purpose, but it was only a subordinate means in a process that started from the preconsciously formed artistic intent and led to the last form-giving step. In the case of the libretto the situation was different; there, since music was to provide the final beauty for the whole artistic creation, the product became dependent on the genius of another person and Goethe temporarily relinquished his artistic independence.

It now becomes necessary to make a few suggestions regarding the psychological meaning of Goethe's *Singspiele*. These are usually divided into two groups: those that followed French models and those for which the prototype is the Italian *opera buffa*. For my purposes this differentiation is not necessary. I wish to raise two points especially. The first comes quickly to attention, and that is the preponderance of women as chief characters in the *Singspiele*, in contrast to the serious plays, in which male heroes predominate. Such titles as *Erwin und Elmire, Claudine von Villa Bella, Jery und Bätely, Die Fischerin, Lila,* demonstrate the point sufficiently.

The second point is less clearly demonstrable. I shall attempt to show it principally in the instance of Goethe's first *Singspiel, Erwin und Elmire*. I follow here the first version of the play, begun at the end of 1773 and finished, at the latest, by the beginning of 1775.

The principal character is Elmire, who torments herself with violent self-reproaches for the way she has treated Erwin. Erwin, who had been in love with her, has left her because of her arrogant treatment of him. Elmire believes she will die of grief, since her rejection of him was uncalled for; indeed, she herself was enamored of him. Her confidant, Bernardo, tries in vain to soothe her. Finally he persuades her to confide in a saintly man whom he has met by chance in the quietness of his secluded habitation. Erwin has in the meantime retired into solitude. He thinks constantly of Elmire and reproaches himself for having taken flight. Bernardo visits him and tries in vain to induce him to return. Erwin is determined to renounce the world since it is impossible to obtain Elmire's love. He is angry at Bernardo for disrupting his meditations. Bernardo assures him that Elmire loves him and declares that he will prove it to him. He gives him the clothes of a hermit. Elmire arrives and meets Erwin disguised as an old hermit. She confesses her sins to him and reproaches herself again for her unjustified cruelty towards Erwin, who is thus convinced of Elmire's love. Then Erwin and Elmire become united.

In reading the play one is reminded (more than this outline may reveal)

---

[27] [Musick hab ich mir kommen lassen die Seele zu lindern und die Geister zu entbinden.] (See also a letter of February 22, 1779.)

of *Werther*. The relations between the two works are not simple. Elmire is presented as in part an unworthy character who unnecessarily brings suffering upon Erwin, but at the same time she is herself unhappy, suffers, and expects death; the depth of her disappointment and inconsolability is reminiscent of Werther's own. Werther's death finds a mitigated counterpart in Erwin's voluntary retirement and all conflicts are resolved in a happy ending.

I see in this *Singspiel* (1) the presentation of Werther's conflict in a woman; (2) an open accusation against a woman, a factor that was concealed in *Werther* and there remained only implicit; (3) the undoing of the tragic; (4) the repetition of the *Wertherstimmung* on a lower, almost burlesque, level. *Erwin und Elmire* was written at about the same time as *Werther*: the actual writing of it down started a few months before; it was interrupted and finished after the novel had been completed. Apparently Goethe needed a lower medium in which he could express something that had no place in the tragic and serious presentation of a deep conflict. One is reminded of the construction of many of Shakespeare's plays. There the main action is diversified in side actions. In these Shakespeare presents other possible solutions than that contained in the principal plot, or developments other than the main one, such as might occur under different conditions. In other instances these variations show up in the parts of the fools and clowns. Rarely is the action in a play by Shakespeare one-dimensional and one is inclined to see in it the full declension, as it were, a kind of paradigm of all possible variations on one and the same conflict. This richness of action, which makes Shakespeare's theater the all-comprehensive stage of the human world, is missing from Goethe's work—as perhaps it is from that of all other dramatists. Thus no one single work of Goethe's can convey the greatness of his mind, whereas Shakespeare wrote some plays that even singly reveal the whole greatness of their author.

Seen as part of the whole of Goethe's work, or even of a large section of it, the *Singspiele* too can be seen in their ultimate exquisiteness, while they must be rated as productions of minor quality. I do not know if what I have shown with regard to *Erwin und Elmire* is valid for all his *Singspiele,* but I have the strong impression that they were for him a depository for all the dross, the bizarre, the awkward, that found no niche in his works of beauty and sublimity. They were the crippled children, which were to be made into angels by the strokes of the composer, for music can transform everything into beauty.

By the creation of sublime works Goethe gave his gifts to mankind, but then he wanted also to be loved and that that love should come to him by having a friend cast a cloak of beauty over the dross. Having a work set to music may have given Goethe the unconscious consolation and reassurance that he also was loved by the world.

Freud in his book on jokes and their relationship to the unconscious (161) showed that the desire to throw off the yoke of necessities that are imposed upon us, persists in the adult. Even the necessity of adhering to the ordinary reasonableness is occasionally thrown off, as can be seen in the pleasure derived from nonsense jokes.

In the *Singspiele* Goethe apparently applied a similar mechanism. They are caricatures of his own works in which he throws off the yoke of aesthetic necessities. In the fragment *Die ungleichen Hausgenossen* [The Unequal Housefellows], which he started to write as soon as he had finished *Scherz, List und Rache,* and which was also written to be set to music by Kayser, this can be demonstrated even more clearly than in *Erwin und Elmire.* As far as can be concluded from the fragment, the central issue of this play was the disagreements between a sentimental poet and an old servant who were both employed at the same court. We have here a farcical presentation of the serious problem that is in the center of Goethe's tragedy *Tasso.*[28]

It is more difficult to uncover this principle—if it is one—in the play *Scherz, List und Rache.* I suggest the not quite satisfactory hypothesis that it is the farcical counterpart of *Wilhelm Meister.* One of the play's features is its small number of characters—only three. In *Wilhelm Meister* there is a large and sometimes confusing number of people who come and go and often leave the reader uncertain about their vicissitudes. The majority of the personages are of a dubious character. Most of them are not outright bad, but almost every one of them is sufficiently objectionable to be denied the quality of being unquestionably sympathetic. In the play all three characters are outright scoundrels. They abandon themselves freely to their vices and are thus free from conflict. Thus the play was perhaps in a very concealed form a simplified version and a caricature of *Wilhelm Meister.*

Goethe's *Singspiele* also offer an opportunity to discuss again the question of what the dynamic constellation has to be in order that the artistically creative person may bring forth a work of art. I do not intend to discuss the various theories here but only to point out that an examination of these instances shows that the establishment of a rule is quite impossible: If we compare the psychological background of *Werther* with that of the *Singspiele* we encounter opposed constellations.

Werther was written in a state of deprivation. Whatever the trauma may have been, in a state of isolation the author created a work of the greatest beauty, a process whose function was to restore the balance of its creator. When he wrote *Scherz, List und Rache,* the author was engaged in the strongest object-relationship of his adult years, but turned towards a person of the same sex and created for the benefit of the homosexual object a work that is of secondary quality despite the author's zeal, ambition, and care. The proximate motive for this work was Goethe's desire to make Kayser famous. How intense his feelings for Kayser were may be seen from two letters. When Kayser was wrongly in-

---

[28] A similar relationship can be found between Goethe's Carnival plays [Fastnachtsspiele] and serious works. Morris (398) has given an example of this.

formed that Goethe was going to Italy and expressed his worry Goethe answered (August 15, 1776): "We are not going to Italy. This for your calming. I bear you always in [my] heart."[29] And in the closing passage of his last letter to him before his departure for Italy Goethe wrote, on May 5, 1786: "Farewell, you sole survivor to me from my youth, grown up to this point in incredible silence. Farewell."[30] Also in later years despite a complete separation Goethe spoke of Kayser with evident affection (see also 46, 2:212–13; 118, 7:276) and in a letter to Zelter of January 5, 1822, he called him "the pious one." Kayser must have stood for part of Goethe himself in the sense that Kayser's life history might have become Goethe's own (the withdrawal into a small group, the refusal to adapt to societal exigencies). Goethe may already in 1775 have recognized in Kayser that type of person whose good luck and success are curtailed by their overscrupulousness and by the suffocation of free growth by the weight of their superego. That is to say, they are tripped up by what from the point of view of society must be called their goodness.

In the letter to Kayser of June 24, 1784, quoted from in the text (see above, p. 880), written when Kayser was in Italy, Goethe compared himself with Moses forbidden to enter the promised land. This, however, implies that Goethe believed that Kayser did have the privilege of reaching Canaan because he was purer and free from sin. Goethe probably established a connection between Kayser's innocence and naiveté and his failure as a creative artist. This must have burdened him with particular intensity since Kayser consistently withstood the lure of court life, whereas Goethe's success was based partly on his willingness to make a compromise on that score. Thus in the instance of this *Singspiel* at least, the created work seems to have had the function of revealing the author's own deficiency in the hope that the loving care of a friend would embellish moral ugliness. Yet the surrender of the defective as a gift to the friend was to serve as a steppingstone on that friend's path to glory.

We encounter here an exquisite situation of aim-inhibited homosexuality. It is also understandable that this great interest in Kayser occurred during a time of a weakening in Goethe's tie to Karl August. In the relationship to him, too, Goethe wished to raise a loved male to a superior level. Karl August, how-

---

[29] [Wir gehen nicht nach Italien. Diess zu deiner Beruhigung. Ich trag dich immer im Herzen.]

[30] [Leben Sie wohl, Sie einziger mir aus meiner Jugend überbliebner, in unglaublicher Stille herangewachsner. Leben Sie wohl.]

If speculation were permitted one might find many unconscious reasons for Goethe's fondness for Kayser. There is the name, which means "emperor" in German. Bettina's account of Goethe's mother's unfulfilled love for a tragic *Kaiser* was recorded earlier. This Kayser too was usually wrapped in melancholy. Goethe's jealousy of Kayser in early years must have been intense: a boy, younger than he, considered a genius at a time when his own future career was most dubious, must sharply have stimulated his sense of rivalry, in view of his great ambitiousness. Thus threads lead to Kayser from father, mother, and siblings, and the emotional charges of Kayser's image in the unconscious must have been unusually great.

ever, started to go his own way, which differed from Goethe's ideal, and now Kayser, probably, was to serve as a substitute.

One may easily object that Goethe's aims were primarily directed at the creation of a German opera and that the homosexual implications were of a secondary order, the unavoidable concomitant, so to speak, when a poet co-operates with a composer. An historical accident provides the disproof of this suggestion. In December of 1785 Goethe heard Mozart's *Abduction from the Seraglio*. In his letters to Kayser one sees that he had to overcome a considerable resistance in order to acknowledge the beauty of Mozart's music.[31] He must have felt that here a true German opera was in the making and Bode rightly raises the question why Goethe did not turn to Mozart in order to have his libretti set to music (46, *1*:1061). The reason may easily have been that the libidinal tie to Kayser was too great at that time to permit him to deal flexibly with his libretti in terms of purely artistic requirements.

Yet Goethe's turn towards Kayser and music must be viewed within a more comprehensive crisis, which may have been going on for quite a long period but was fully verbalized at around that time. Goethe began to have doubts about the German language, the elemental medium through which he existed as an artist.

When Goethe was in Gotha he wrote to Charlotte von Stein on January 26, 1786, after having read Reichardt's German theatrical annual:[32]

My poor operetta [*The Unequal House-fellows*] [which I have just] be-gun, I pity as one could pity a child that is to be born to a Negro woman in slavery. Under this brazen sky! Which I do not reprehend otherwise, for operettas do not indeed have to exist. If I had only known twenty years earlier what I know [now]. I should at least have acquired the Italian [language] enough to have been able to work for the lyric theater, and I should have conquered it. I only pity good Kayser that he wastes his music on this barbarous language. . . . With the excrements of the Weimarian poverty Reichardt seasons the wretchedness of his—or rather the German —theater. Farewell. I have no one but you to whom I can lament my great vexation. . . . I read out my pieces here and I feel ashamed from my heart that they are admired. . . . You just have to take the place of everything else for me, I hold myself to you![33]

---

[31] In later years Goethe paid Mozart the highest tribute that a poet-author can pay a composer. Cf. his reply of December 30, 1797, to Schiller's letter of December 29, 1797.

[32] Heinrich August Reichardt (1751–1828), theatrical manager of the court theater in Gotha, and librarian; he published from 1775 to 1800 the annual *Deutsche Theaterkalender*.

[33] [Meine arme angefangne Operette dauert mich, wie man ein Kind bedauern kann, das von einem Negersweib in der Sclaverey gebohren werden soll. Unter diesem ehrnen Him-mel! den ich sonst nicht schelte, denn es muss ia keine Operetten geben. Hätte ich nur vor zwanzig Jahren gewusst was ich weis. Ich hätte mir wenigstens das Italiänische so zugeeignet, dass ich fürs Lyrische Theater hätte arbeiten können, und ich hätte es gezwungen. Der gute

Apparently Goethe was in a generally low mood: the sky, the German theater, the operetta, his operetta in particular, and then, most important, the German language, depressed him. To be sure, the German language is hard, rasping, and lacking in the melodious beauty of Italian, of which Goethe was so envious.

> Had I the Italian language in my power as [I have] the unhappy German, I should invite you immediately for a voyage beyond the Alps and we should certainly make [our] happiness.[34]

So he wrote to Kayser on May 5, 1786, four months before he actually went to Italy. But the poor instrument of the German language had grown under his hands into something eminently beautiful. One even has the impression that the hardness of the German language challenged him and that it was just this hardness that stimulated his poetic genius. Moreover, to Eckermann he freely admitted that the poorness of German literature gave him the opportunity to rise. Had he been born later it would have been his despair, so he claimed.[35] Indeed, would he have been able to create a rich literature in a language that had been used by Dante and Tasso? Therefore he had reason in reality to be grateful to the difficulty of the German language which had withstood full mastery prior to his appearance. To be sure, the German language is lacking in the virility of the French, the sagacity of the English, and the beauty of the Italian, if such subjective impressions may cursorily be set down, but nevertheless this had not hindered Goethe at all in his literary efforts and it is evident that he here projected an inner void into an external—though really existing— difficulty. This despair over the German language—including also a despair over what he had created—he hurled at Charlotte von Stein, and it probably was connected with the person to whom he confessed this feeling. It will be remembered how unfavorably he responded when Charlotte von Stein introduced French into their correspondence and now he proposed that she should make up to him for his having to deal with an allegedly unmanageable language. The request could not be fulfilled. How could it? What is a poet without language? And how could the poet be repaid by a human being for the loss of this tool?

The longing for Italian leads us back to his early years when his mother was singing Italian arias and his father was perfecting his Italian in order to write his devoted account of his Journey. When Goethe lamented the crudity of

---

Kayser dauert mich nur, dass er seine Musick an diese barbarische Sprache verschwendet. . . . Mit den Exkrementen der Weimarischen Armuth würzt Herr Reichardt seine oder vielmehr die deutsche Theater Miserie. Lebe wohl. Ich habe niemanden als dich dem ich meinen grosen Verdruss klagen kann. Ich lese nun meine Sachen hier vor und schäme mich von Herzen indem man sie bewundert. . . . du musst mir eben alles ersezen, ich halte mich an dich.]

[34] [Hätt ich die Italiänische Sprache in meiner Gewalt wie die unglückliche Teutsche, ich lüde Sie gleich zu einer Reise ienseits der Alpen ein und wir wollten gewiss Glück machen.]

[35] Goethe to Eckermann, January 2, 1824, 119, p. 429.

German and rejected it as an unacceptable medium he was acting under the full sway of his castration complex, which probably also was an important source of his longing to find a composer for his libretti, as if he wanted to say: "I do not possess that which it takes to produce something perfect." But I think that this complaint about the German language, in his letter to Charlotte von Stein, is a veiled reproach against her for having deprived him temporarily of his poetic genius, for it was around that time also that his work on *Wilhelm Meister* had come to a standstill.

Thus the crisis in which Goethe was with regard to the German language was an expression of the crisis which existed in his relationship with Charlotte von Stein. Elsewhere, I try to demonstrate (cf. Appendix T) that Goethe's relationship to the artistic medium, that is, language, was the model for his object-relations. Here this process can be seen in reverse. At the peak of the crisis in the object-relation Goethe also feels alienated from his language. All the more reason for turning to music, from which he evidently hoped to obtain that beauty which he had lost in poetry.

Appendix O

Additional Remarks Concerning Goethe's *Roman Elegies*[1]

I HAVE DRAWN the conclusion in the text that Goethe's sexual impediment was prompted by overstimulation during sexual foreplay. Various scattered bits of information gave me the idea that kissing was the trigger stimulus. In Rome, according to all evidence, the sexual difficulty was overcome. I have further tried to outline the great variety of factors that effectuated the recovery. There were two main groups: those of the past, chiefly related to Charlotte von Stein, and those of the present (situational factors). With regard to the latter one has to consider a technical point, namely, whether, in order to bypass the danger point, Goethe avoided kissing Faustina. The only source, it seems, of material that might possibly throw some light on such a subtle point, is what, if anything, Goethe says about kissing in the 490 lines of the *Roman Elegies,* his only poetical testimony to his love adventure. The first fact that strikes one—surprising in itself in view of the great role kissing plays in Goethe's love lyrics—is that kissing appears in but three psychologically meaningful contexts.[2]

(1) In Elegy V (line 105, *Soph.* I, *1:239*) the first reference to kissing is encountered. In this Elegy Goethe expresses his joy at being on classical soil where the present and the past speak to him more loudly, more charmingly. He peruses

---

[1] I am indebted to Mr. Seymour A. Copstein for having suggested the investigation the results of which are reported in this appendix.

[2] Kissing is mentioned a fourth time (Elegy XIII, line 269), in a context that is not psychologically relevant since it figures as a mere description or enumeration of the things that commonly occur when two people fall in love with each other.

> Glance and squeeze of hands, and kisses, affectionate words,
> Syllables of delightful meaning a loving couple exchange.
> [Blick und Händedruck, und Küsse, gemüthliche Worte,
> Sylben köstlichen Sinns, wechselt ein liebendes Paar.] (*Soph.* I,
> *1:250*)

the work of the ancients during the daytime; at night, however, Amor keeps him busy in a different way. He is doubly happy even if his education is halved by the time he spends on love. But doesn't he gain knowledge too when he espies the form of his mistress's bosom? Then he understands better the statues of marble.

> I think and compare;
> See with a feeling eye and feel with a seeing hand.[3]

Even if the sweetheart steals a few hours of the day she gives nightly hours as a compensation.

Not all the time, though, are there kisses; there is sensible conversation.[4]

Thus the first reference to kissing is a negative one. This is surprising, indeed. Also the context in which the restricting sentence appears is significant. In this Elegy the passionate aspect of love, its instinctual side, steps into the background and the poet emphasizes its educative value, its contribution to the understanding of ancient sculptures. Rational discourse is made possible by the absence of kissing. It is in this Elegy that Goethe reports having composed poetry in his mistress's arms and having safely counted out on her back the feet of hexameters with his fingers.

(2) In Elegy XIII another relevant remark is encountered. In this Elegy Goethe reproaches Amor for having induced him to enter a love-affair by the promise that his poetry would thus acquire sparkle and colorfulness. True, Amor kept his promise and there are subjects a-plenty for cantos. But, alas, love-talk does not need the prosodical measure. Aurora, too, the friend of the Muses, has been bribed into alliance with Amor and awakens the poet on the altar of the god when he finds the abundance of his sweetheart's locks on his bosom. His mistress is still asleep. She moves. He believes he will again see her eyes open. Oh, no, they should stay closed. He wants to keep his eyes resting on her sublime and noble body and limbs and enjoy the silent delight of pure beholding.

> Did Ariadne sleep so beautifully, Theseus? were you able to take flight?
> One sole kiss for these lips! Oh, Theseus, now leave!
> Look into her eye! She awakens!—Eternally now she holds you fast.[5]

Goethe refers to an episode in Theseus's life that has many times found poetic elaboration, notably in the *Epithalamium* of Catullus. When Theseus landed on Crete to slay the Minotaur he fell in love with Ariadne, the King's daughter. After Theseus had slain the monster with Ariadne's help, he carried

---

[3] [. . . ich denk' und vergleiche,/ Sehe mit fühlendem Aug', fühle mit sehender Hand.

[4] [Wird doch nicht immer geküsst, es wird vernünftig gesprochen.]

[5] [Schlief Ariadne so schön; Theseus, du konntest entfliehn?/ Diesen Lippen ein einziger Kuss! O Theseus, nun scheide!/ Blick' ihr in's Auge! Sie wacht!—Ewig nun hält sie dich fest.] (*Soph.* I, 1:251)

her off, but abandoned her on the island of Naxos while she slept. When she awakens she is married to Dionysus.

There is a certain similarity between this passage and the one first cited. Again a complaint is lodged against the mistress for her distracting effect, a complaint, however, that is overruled as soon as it is raised, in favor of the beauty and pleasure of the whole love experience. In both instances the love of the woman is justified by, or brought into connection with, the beauty of the art of sculpture. Also, in both the visual component of eroticism is stressed.

In the latter, the kiss appears as the last gesture of farewell. By bringing in the myth of Theseus and Ariadne the erotic meaning of the kiss is replaced with a destructive imagery of separation, almost reminiscent of the kiss of death. To be sure, Goethe lets us know that he did not act like Theseus, and, somewhat hypocritically, he asks how Theseus could desert his Ariadne. Yet Faustina fared with Goethe somewhat like her mythological predecessor. Also Goethe was, like Theseus, in a foreign country and Faustina was a very fleeting love-object in whom Goethe was interested almost solely for sexual reasons, as it seems.

In this Elegy again a negative aspect in regard to kissing seems to prevail, although it is not as outspoken as in the first sample, for Goethe only insinuates that he might have tried to act like Theseus but did not. Yet the very reference to this particular point of the Theseus myth has to be considered as a significant element.

(3) Goethe's reference to kisses in Elegy XVIII is perhaps the most interesting and illuminating one. Here Goethe speaks of feeling peevish when he spends a night alone, but he feels horror at the idea that serpent and poison have to be dreaded "under the roses of pleasure" [unter den Rosen der Lust] (line 374). This is the famous Elegy in which he inveighs wrathfully against venereal disease. But with his sweetheart the poet is free of this anxiety.

> Thus Faustina makes my happiness: gladly she shares
> Her couch with me and keeps faith exactly with the faithful.[6]

Goethe then refers to another source of anxiety, the act of defloration, by putting himself in contrast to rash youth that desires "a charming obstacle" [reizendes Hindernis], whereas he prefers long and easy enjoyment under secure conditions.

> What a bliss it is! We exchange safe kisses,
> Breath and life we confidently suck in and infuse.
> In this way we enjoy the long nights, and listen,
> Bosom to bosom pressed, to storms and rain and shower.[7]

[6] [Darum macht Faustine mein Glück; sie theilet das Lager/ Gerne mit mir, und bewahrt Treue dem Treuen genau.] (*Soph.* I, *1*:257, lines 377–78)

[7] [Welche Seligkeit ist's! Wir wechseln sichere Küsse,/ Athem und Leben getrost saugen und flössen wir ein./ So erfreuen wir uns der langen Nächte, wir lauschen,/ Busen an Busen gedrängt, Stürmen und Regen und Guss.] (*Soph.* I, *1*:257, lines 381–85)

This imagery is quite surprisingly reminiscent of the twice-quoted (cf. above pp. 679, 189) Leipzig letter-poem of October 12, 1766, in English. Particularly the lines:

> What volupty! When trembling in my arms,
> The bosom of my maid my bosom warmeth!
> Perpetual kisses of her lips o'erflow,

seem to be worthy of renewed quotation. The whole Elegy stands under the sign of anxiety. Feelings about the dangers of venereal diseases, of defloration, intrude (fears which we can be certain inhibited him from intercourse in Leipzig), and in that moment kisses are heralded as "safe" and reminiscences of early love play (bosom to bosom) reappear. In Leipzig kisses were "safe" because they evoked ejaculations and therefore protected against the necessity of intercourse; in Rome the meaning of "safe" changes and refers to freedom from venereal diseases. "Safe" might have had here still another meaning that does not become evident from the context. If Goethe has overcome his deficiency, then he does not need to worry any more about the detrimental effects kissing might have. Kissing would then have really become a *safe* part of foreplay.

Yet there is testimony that Goethe did not feel so safe as he pretended. In the second Elegy of the four that Goethe held back from publication, he elaborates extensively on the danger of venereal diseases. In antiquity man fared better. When Propertius was surprised by Cynthia he was found unfaithful but in good health. Goethe goes on:

> Nowadays, who is not wary of breaking boring faithfulness!
> Whom love does not hold back, apprehensiveness does.
> And even there, who knows! Any kind of pleasure is a risk,
> Nowhere does one lay one's head safely in a woman's lap.
> Safe is no longer the marriage bed, nor adultery;
> Husband, wife, and friend, one is injured in the other.[8]

Thus also in Rome with Faustina Goethe could not rid himself of the specter of disease. Nevertheless, he was sufficiently free of anxiety to risk intercourse. Whether he protected himself against impotence (and infection?) by not kissing Faustina or by kissing her only when it could not be avoided cannot be answered with certainty, but the three quotations I have discussed make it seem very probable—or, to formulate it with greater caution, what we find Goethe saying about kissing and kisses in the *Roman Elegies* does not contradict or disprove the assumption—that in Rome he overcame psychosexual impotence

---

[8] [Jetzt wer hütet sich nicht langweilige Treue zu brechen!/ Wen die Liebe nicht hält, hält die Besorglichkeit auf./ Und auch da, wer weis! gewagt ist jegliche Freude,/ Nirgend legt man das Haupt ruhig dem Weib in den Schoos./ Sicher ist nicht das Ehbett mehr, nicht sicher der Ehbruch;/ Gatte, Gattin und Freund eins ist im andern verletzt.] (*Soph.* I, 53:5)

from which he had suffered until then in the form of premature ejaculations prompted by the overstimulation of kissing.

Now we shall also understand better a poem that Goethe wrote for Charlotte von Stein (letter of November 2, 1776) when he was suffering from a sore lip. He dedicated it "To the Spirit of Janus Secundus" [An den Geist des Johannes Sekundus],[9] who was famous for his series of poems *Basia* (The Kisses) in which he glorified the art of kissing.

Goethe's poem starts:

> Dear, saintly, great kisser,
> You who have almost outdone me
> In languishing breathing blissfulness![10]

Whom else should he tell his complaints to if not him whose songs have restored his benumbed heart? His lip bleeds and aches:

> My lip that is so much accustomed
> To swell from love's sweetest happiness
> And, like a golden portal of heaven,
> To splutter lulling bliss in and out.[11]

The lip is not sore from the bite of the sweetheart, who

> Would like to have more from me, and would like
> To kiss me up whole, and devour and [do] what [ever] she could![12]

His lips are sore from the cold winds and no medicine will cure them because in it there is "no drop of all-healing poisonous balm of love."[13]

The imagery in regard to kissing and lips is self-explanatory. But I wish to remind the reader that according to my reconstruction Charlotte von Stein forbade Goethe to kiss her at all, or, at least, to kiss her passionately. The poem, thus, would be a consolation. It claims that the mistress wants to kiss and kiss but that a physical ailment prevents him from indulging in the delight both of them crave. From the fall of 1777 on Goethe suffered considerably from ailments connected with the mouth (see 415, p. 34). Psychosomaticists may find a connection between Charlotte von Stein's prohibition, assumed by me, and the type of disorder that became noticeable from that time on. Be this as it may, the

---

[9] (*Soph.* I, 2:316–17). Johannes (Janus) Secundus (1511–36) was a Dutch poet, painter and sculptor.

[10] [Lieber, heiliger, groser Küsser,/ Der du mir's in lechzend athmender/ Glückseeligkeit fast vorgethan hast!]

[11] [Meine Lippe, die so viel gewohnt ist/ Von der Liebe süsstem Glück zu schwellen/ Und, wie eine goldne Himmelspforte,/ Lallende Seeligkeit, aus und einzustammeln.]

[12] [Mehr mögt' haben von mir, und mögte mich Ganzen/ Ganz erküssen, und fressen, und was sie könnte!]

[13] [der Liebe alles heilendem Gift Balsam]

poem dedicated to Goethe's predecessor reflects a conflict about kissing that was raging at that time.

The Insel-Edition of Goethe's lyric work, following a chronological sequence, puts the final version of the just-quoted poem—considerably different from the original—as the first one of the period 1788/93,[14] which, after all, stands under Christiane's sign. Christiane, to be sure, was not averse to kissing, but may Goethe now have needed a physical protective barrier against over-stimulation? It is, of course, speculation when I suggest that this may have been the reason why Goethe turned again towards this poem at that time (assuming the dating of this poem in the Insel-Edition to be correct). I thought for a while I had discerned some concrete evidence of the reason for Goethe's attachment to the "Spirit of Johannes Secundus" when I found in a German translation of the *Basia* the following epilogue:

> Not naked,
> No, not naked it is
> That you are most beautiful;
> Entirely draped in the adornment of your garments,
> This way, yes so
> You overcome me
> Entirely.
> Your kisses, yes,
> Your kisses—
> And nothing else.[15]

This epilogue, so precisely expressing the kind of psychopathology I have thought existed in Goethe, was welcomed by me as renewed confirmation of my reconstruction and I did not hesitate to assume that Goethe had found in the *Basia* a frank, poetical representation of what he was secretly suffering from. When, however, I tried to establish the original Latin text I did not find an "epilogue" and all editions that I consulted, Latin as well as translations, end with the eighteenth or nineteenth poem by Secundus. Did Blei, the German translator, insert as an epilogue another of Secundus's poems, or did he use poetical license and is the epilogue contraband of the translator's vintage? I do not know, but feel inclined to assume the latter.[16] Nevertheless, I wanted to bring this strange coincidence to the reader's attention. It is worth recording that Blei's translation of the *Basia* is preceded by Goethe's original poem dedicated

---

[14] See 253, p. 277. No other editor as far as I know dates the final version in this way.

[15] [Nicht nackt,/ Nein, nicht nackt ist's,/ Dass du am schönsten bist,/ Ganz bekleidet in deiner Gewänder Schmuck/ So, ja so/ Bezwingst du mich/ Ganz./ Deine Küsse, ja,/ Deine Küsse—/ Und nichts sonst.] (488, p. 35)

[16] Blei himself is no longer alive. An inquiry addressed to the University of Leyden has brought a valued response from the Chief Librarian, Dr. A. Kessen, that confirms that the "Epilogue" is missing from all recorded editions of the Latin, and also from the numerous other translations.

to the poet Secundus. It looks as if Blei was under the impression of Goethe's poem when he composed the—by the way very free—translation. Is it possible that in the epilogue he was expressing in a poetical fashion something he had intuitively grasped from between the lines of Goethe's poem, or Secundus's poems, or both?

Appendix P

Goethe's Pheasant Dream

Even a superficial inquiry into the psychological background of Goethe's Italian journey would remain incomplete without an attempt to interpret a certain dream that Goethe had towards the end of the year 1785, at a time when he must evidently have already been quite preoccupied with his forthcoming journey.

Regrettably, the date of the dream cannot be determined exactly. In that part of his *Italian Journey* devoted to his trip from Ferrara to Rome, he wrote from Bologna under the date of "October 19, evening" [1786] that he had had the following dream "something like a year ago":[1]

I dreamed [lit.: it dreamed me] namely: I landed with a rather large boat[2] on a fertile island, richly covered with vegetation, of which I knew that right there the finest pheasants were to be had. Moreover, I immediately bargained with the natives for such fowl, which they also immediately, [having] killed, brought forward in plenty. They were pheasants right enough, but, as dreams are wont to recast everything, so one glimpsed long tails colorfully bedecked with eyes, like those of peacocks or rare birds of paradise. These were brought to me in the boat in threescore [bunches], laid with their heads towards the inside, heaped up so gracefully that the long varicolored feather-tails, hanging towards the outside, formed in the sunshine the most magnificent sheaf that one could imagine, and actually in such plenty that there was only a little space left over fore and aft for the steersman and the oarsmen. Thus we cut through the calm tide, and meanwhile I already named to myself the friends to whom I wished to impart these varicolored treasures. Landing at last in a large harbor, I got lost

---

[1] [es wird eben ein Jahr sein]

[2] The German word *Kahn* means a particular kind of boat, something like a wherry.

among ships with enormous masts, where I climbed from deck to deck to look for a safe landing place for my small boat.

We delight in such delusional images, which, since they spring from ourselves, most likely must have some analogy to the rest of our life and vicissitudes.[3]

The first question to be answered is, of course, whether Goethe actually had such a dream or invented this beautiful account for poetical reasons. In the diary he kept for Charlotte von Stein during this part of the journey one finds, again from Bologna under the date October 19, 1786, evening:

The pheasant dream starts to be fulfilled. For, verily, what I am loading up [with] I can liken to the delicious fowl, and the development I also divine.[4]

A letter to the Herders of December 13, 1786, closes with the following postscript: "Remember the pheasant dream, which is now being fulfilled, if only the end turn out more consoling."[5] And December 29, 1786, to Charlotte von Stein: "Loaded with pheasants, I am thinking only of my return and of bringing and dedicating the best to all of you."[6] And the last reference: on February 17, 1787, he wrote to Herder, after expressing his understanding of Herder's difficult situation and of his wife's worries over her children: "In [all] my bliss I would become sad about you if I did not see that I am enjoying for your sake too and prepare magnificent feasts of pheasants for you."[7]

[3] [Es träumte mir nämlich: ich landete mit einem ziemlich grossen Kahn an einer fruchtbaren, reich bewachsenen Insel, von der mir bewusst war, dass daselbst die schönsten Fasanen zu haben seien. Auch handelte ich sogleich mit den Einwohnern um solches Gefieder, welches sie auch sogleich häufig, getödtet, herbeibrachten. Es waren wohl Fasanen, wie aber der Traum alles umzubilden pflegt, so erblickte man lange, farbig beaugte Schweife, wie von Pfauen oder seltenen Paradiesvögeln. Diese brachte man mir schockweise in's Schiff, legte sie mit den Köpfen nach innen, so zierlich gehäuft, dass die langen bunten Federschweife, nach aussen hängend, im Sonnenglanz den herrlichsten Schober bildeten, den man sich denken kann, und zwar so reich, dass für den Steuernden und die Rudernden kaum hinten und vorn geringe Räume verblieben. So durchschnitten wir die ruhige Fluth und ich nannte mir indessen schon die Freunde, denen ich von diesen bunten Schätzen mittheilen wollte. Zuletzt in einem grossen Hafen landend, verlor ich mich zwischen ungeheuer bemasteten Schiffen, wo ich von Verdeck auf Verdeck stieg, um meinem kleinen Kahn einen sichern Landungsplatz zu suchen.

An solchen Wahnbildern ergötzen wir uns, die, weil sie aus uns selbst entspringen, wohl Analogie mit unserm übrigen Leben und Schicksalen haben müssen.] (*Soph.* I, *30*:168–69)

[4] [Der Phasanen Traum fängt an in Erfüllung zu gehn. Denn warrlich was ich auflade kann ich wohl mit dem köstlichen Geflügel vergleichen, und die Entwicklung ahnd ich auch.] (*Soph.* III, *1*:306)

[5] [Gedenckt des Phasanen Traums der nun in Erfüllung geht, wenn nur das Ende tröstlicher wird!]

[6] [Beladen mit Phasanen denck ich nur an die Rückkehr und Euch das Beste zu bringen und zu widmen.]

[7] [Ich würde in meinem Glücke traurig über Euch werden, wenn ich nicht sähe, dass ich auch für Euch geniesse und Euch herrliche Gastmäler von Phasanen zubereite.]

This may suffice as a historical proof that, prior to his departure for Italy, Goethe really had a dream in which pheasants played a prominent role. He had evidently told others about the dream, which must have left an unusually deep impression upon him, and therefore could refer to it in his letters as something generally known to his intimate friends.

Yet did Goethe record the dream as it was actually dreamed when he included it in his *Italian Journey* some twenty-eight years later? As is well known, the psychoanalyst does not in general mind very much whether the dream he is called on to interpret is correctly reported or altered, for the alteration also contains the same trend as those preconscious and unconscious forces that led to the original dream. However, if the alterations are made on purpose, involve purposive omissions, or consist of fancied adornments, the basic trend of the repressed material may get lost. Furthermore, the usefulness of an altered dream record depends also on what problem one is seeking to solve by means of examination of the dream record. I believe that the inquiry into certain problems of dream psychology does not suffer if carried out with even purposively altered dream records, but that for the elucidation of other problems an accurate dream record is indispensable. I make this point because I wish to admit from the beginning that my interpretation of Goethe's pheasant dream is in part open to objection because of our ignorance as to the reliability of Goethe's report. We know for certain only that Goethe had a pleasing dream about pheasants, but whether its content was quite of the kind he let us know cannot be determined. After all, Goethe did not write his *Italian Journey* primarily as a person interested in the factualness of his report but primarily as an artist, and the result was a work of exceptional beauty. His pheasant dream sounds like a short story and may give the impression that alterations were made for the sake of artistic beauty, but in view of the peculiarity of Goethe's dream-life one could just as well imagine that the goal of literary beauty also left its imprint on the manifest content of his dreams and it is conceivable that in his report we confront the bona fide description of a real dream as he recalled it at the time he put it in writing.

There are in this dream only a few elements that are so clear that their interpretation will scarcely meet any objection. Since Goethe was at the time of the dream preoccupied with his Italian journey one may safely assume that the "fertile island, richly covered with vegetation" meant Italy, which is as a matter of fact a peninsula. Thus in the dream Goethe anticipated his arrival in Italy and the dream must refer to a wish that Goethe hoped would be fulfilled in Italy. The pheasants and the tails like peacocks' are compelling symbols of the erected penis. The large number, that is to say, the accumulation of the same symbol, may indicate by contrast the singular instance, in which the dreamer is interested, namely the state of his own oversized genital.[8] Since he buys the

---

[8] Cf. Freud: ". . . the notion of something irreplaceable, when it is active in the unconscious, frequently appears as broken up . . ." (171, p. 169).

pheasants from the inhabitants of the island, we may translate the dream up to that point as saying: "I will arrive in Italy, I will become sexually excited and have powerful erections elicited by impressions received there." The erection is evidently visualized as enormous, for the pheasants threaten to crowd out all other men and almost no space is left either "fore" or "aft." Then follows a period of tranquillity occupied with thoughts of his friends at home with whom he wishes to share his treasures.[9]

The dream ends with the return from Italy to an unspecified harbor. It is not Weimar or any other familiar neighborhood. The boat, by comparison with others, has become small, that is to say the erection has ceased; he sees enormous masts, another symbol of the erected penis, referring this time not to his own organ, but to those of others. The search for "a safe landing place for my small boat" may suggest—if further symbolic interpretations are admissible—the desire to find also upon his return from Italy a safe sexual partner, the word "safe" referring here to the absence of venereal disease as well as forgiveness for possible impotence, that is to say, a healthy girl who will not humiliate him because of his "small boat" even in view of the enormous masts of other ships.

Among the many points that require discussion the prevalence of castration symbols—the beautiful fowl are killed—may be raised first. The dream was evidently experienced by Goethe as a happy and propitious one. When his affairs in Italy were particularly pleasing he recalled it almost with the feeling of recognizing the benevolent hand of Providence. This is, of course, surprising in view of the rich representation of castration and the seemingly unsatisfactory ending of the dream. In the dream Goethe is by no means assured of finding a safe landing place for his small boat, and the dream breaks off while he is still searching for one. Goethe was aware of this factor, as can be seen from his aforementioned letter to Herder of December 13, 1786, in which he expressed the hope that the end of his journey would be more consoling than his dream's ending was.

It is almost always risky to try to get at the very bottom of a dream by the interpretation of symbols alone. When the symbols are of multifarious significa-

---

[9] The German word *mitteilen,* "share," is ambiguous as Goethe uses it here. The usual meaning of the word is to share *information.* Yet *teilen* means to divide and there is no doubt in my mind that Goethe was thinking of treasures that he would share with his friends. I actually remembered this part of the dream in this way and only in translating it noticed that the literal meaning of the word was "to give information." Paul Fischer, the reliable guide through Goethe's vocabulary, says under *teilen* that Goethe used the phrase "einem etwas teilen" in the meaning of "es ihm mitteilen" (to inform him of something) or "mit ihm teilen" (to share with him) (see 146, p. 621). The word "impart," which I use in the translation, has both meanings, that of sharing and that of communicating, and does justice to the imagery of the dream. As will be recalled, Goethe in reality *informed* the Duke of his sexual adventure and he *shared* his exciting Italian experiences with his friends by means of a large number of letters, and brought home small specimens of the wonderful things he had the pleasure of beholding in Italy.

tion, only the context can help decide what psychological content ought to be put in the place of the respective symbol. Schools other than that of depth psychology are in a more favorable position. Buder (73), who interpreted Goethe's dream in a threefold fashion (as she thought Adler, Freud, and Jung would have done), seems to consider the interpretation reached by the application of Jung's analytic psychology as carrying one furthest. She does not hesitate to equate the boat carrying the magnificent sheaf with the image of Dionysus that is brought to a harbor. The sight of this image has a healing effect. The dreamer senses that this god lives in him and he is forced to acknowledge as valid nature's necessity. She even sees the image as being brought to Athens and adds an elaborate mythological scene. That nothing of this evolves in the dream is explained by the fact that the scene shifts, in her opinion, to the Nordic world, symbolized by the ships with huge masts. Again she adds a mythological fantasy, taken this time from Nordic history. Such a technique cannot run into any difficulties and by its nature knows no barrier. To be sure, her interpretation does not convey anything to us that could not be learned from the study of Goethe's published writings, and it does not become clear why Goethe, if at that time such thoughts were in his mind at all, should have banished them into a dream.

In the effort to unearth a factor that may have a specific relationship to this dream I turn to the context in which the dream was remembered and reported at length. This context is not a reliable substitute for the dreamer's free associations, which are missing to us, but we may reach out tentatively towards it and see how far it can help out in the interpretative endeavor. For this purpose I shall use the final version of Goethe's report, the *Italian Journey,* and also the diary that he kept during the journey, which differ in some respects.

In the following I have picked those items in the *Italian Journey* under October 19 that may have been connected with Goethe's recalling the pheasant dream on that day and may therefore have been in associative connection with the dream itself.

Goethe spent the day in Bologna in becoming further acquainted with Italian art. Yet he fared with art as he did with life: "The more one gets into it, the broader it becomes."[10] He discovered new stars in the sky of Italian painting, but he felt perplexed. It was the so-called Second School of Bologna, of the end of the sixteenth and the beginning of the seventeenth century, that made him feel that he was still lacking in knowledge and judgment. It was mostly the subject matter of those paintings, which impressed him as foolish, that prevented Goethe from admiring and loving them. He turned vigorously against the customary subjects of Christian iconography and he deplored that such beautiful painting should be marred by the horridness of the subjects represented. In the afternoon he was in a milder mood and admired a madonna

[10] [je weiter man hineinkommt, je breiter wird sie (die Kunst).] (*Soph.* I, *30*:163)

nursing the Christ child. Even a painting that showed a circumcision elicited a positive comment: "I pardoned the insufferable subject."[11] Goethe compared himself to "Bileam, the confused prophet, who blessed when he intended to curse."[12] Yet any objection he might have had came to naught in the face of Raphael, whom he could hardly find sufficient words to praise. A St. Agatha of the school of Raphael made him think of his Iphigenia, which in turn reminded him that he had not gone on with the rewriting of that tragedy as he had planned but had instead evolved a plot for *Iphigenia in Delphi,* which went as follows:

Electra, convinced that Orestes will bring Diana's image from Tauris to Apollo's temple, dedicates as an expiatory sacrifice the ax with which so many crimes had been committed in her family's history. However, she is wrongly informed, by a Greek who had accompanied Orestes, that her brother has been killed in Tauris. Passionate Electra breaks out into incredible rage. When Iphigenia arrives with her brother in Delphi the Greek points her out to Electra as the one who murdered Orestes. Electra wants to kill Iphigenia, whom she does not recognize as her sister, with the very ax she had dedicated, but a happy turn averts the tragic deed.

Goethe felt he would not have the opportunity to shape this plot into a play: "But where should one get hands and time [for this], even if the spirit were willing!"[13] And then Goethe proceeded to the dream report. An account of his visit to the Scientific Institute[14] follows, and concludes his report of October 19. In this account we find a sentence pertinent in this context:

An earlier observation here came again into my thoughts, that man, in the course of all-altering time, so difficultly rids himself of what a thing at first was, even if its function has subsequently altered.[15]

Here Goethe discovered—in a historical setting—the mechanism of fixation, which plays such a great role in the life of the neurotic.

If we compare these reports from the final version with Goethe's diaries we see that he did not follow the original outline exactly. From the diary we know that Goethe was quite excited on October 19. There we read:

[11] [Ich verzieh den unleidlichen Gegenstand.] (*Soph.* I, *30:*16)

[12] [Bileam, dem confusen Propheten, welcher segnete, da er zu fluchen gedachte.]

[13] [Wo soll man aber Hände und Zeit hernehmen, wenn auch der Geist willig wäre!] (*Soph.* I, *30:*168)

[14] This was an organization, independent of the University of Bologna at that time, located in an Italian palazzo.

[15] [Mir fiel eine frühere Bemerkung hier wieder in die Gedanken, dass sich der Mensch, im Gange der alles verändernden Zeit, so schwer los macht von dem, was eine Sache zuerst gewesen, wenn ihre Bestimmung in der Folge sich auch verändert.] (*Soph.* I, *30:*170)

Goethe proved this proposition by pointing to the basilica form of the churches, the disproportionate size of Italian courtrooms, and the monastic character of scientific workrooms.

The world runs away from under my feet and an inexpressible passion drives me on.[16]

The sight of a painting by Raphael and a walk into the mountains quieted him down a little. Addressing himself to Charlotte von Stein he wrote:

I tell you everything [about] how it is [with] me and I am not ashamed of any weakness before you.[17]

Then he went on to praise Raphael.

The next theme towards which he turned was Albrecht Dürer, whom he pitied for not having been in Italy. In the *Italian Journey* Goethe wrote in a similar vein about Dürer, under the heading of October 18. There, however, he noted that Dürer had been in Venice, and his regret was that he had not got deeper into Italy. When he was writing the diary, had Goethe forgotten that Dürer had also been in Italy, or was he ignorant of the fact at that time? If he had forgotten, then we may conclude that he was trying to repress recollections regarding his father's Italian journey, since Dürer was undoubtedly a father-substitute for Goethe. As he wrote in the book and in the diary, he thought that Dürer's fate was also his, "only that I know a little bit better how to help myself."[18] It is after his remark about Dürer that Goethe mentions the pheasant dream in his diary, as quoted earlier. There then follows the comment on Raphael's Agatha and his discourse on the horridness of Christian iconography, with which we are familiar from his book. He describes a view from a tower in Bologna, which in the *Italian Journey* is recorded under October 18. He got quite incensed about a tower that was built on a slant and spoke of a "suspended tower" [der hängende Turm].

At this point I leave off the citation of details. We get an approximate idea of the range of themes with which Goethe was preoccupied around this time. Actually, material referrable to the castration complex is prevalent: his intense condemnation of Christian iconography, that is to say, circumcision, martyrdom, physical suffering; the strong reaction to the inclined tower. We also find the competitive attitude towards men in the question of whether he or Albrecht Dürer was better able to cope with the world. We further discover the whole series of problems contained in the sibling relationship, which shows up in the plot for a new tragedy, *Iphigenia in Delphi*. Thus we are able—though indirectly—to adduce historical evidence that the positive Oedipus complex, castration complex, and the sister conflict were condensed into the dream.

Yet these are abiding themes, which, in various forms, pervade Goethe's

[16] [Mir läuft die Welt unter den Füssen fort und eine unsägliche Leidenschafft treibt mich weiter.] (*Soph.* III, *1:*305)

[17] [Ich sage dir alles wie mir ist und ich schäme mich vor dir keiner Schwachheit.] (*Soph.* III, *1:*305)

[18] [nur dass ich mir ein klein wenig besser zu helfen weiss.] (*Soph.* I, *30:*161; *Soph.* III, *1:*306)

entire life; indeed, these are the eternal themes about which, modified by individual fate, all of us dream whenever we do dream, though often in such disguised form that they do not become apparent in each instance.[19]

It is to be observed that a study of id contents which probably were worked into the dream does not carry us beyond what has been derived with greater precision and benefit to our knowledge from other biographical sources.

Perhaps we will be more fortunate if we consider the specific mood Goethe was in on the nineteenth, namely, the feeling that the world was running away from under his feet. This mood can be reencountered to a certain extent in the remark with which Goethe introduced his report of the pheasant dream in the *Italian Journey*. There he wrote, after complaining that he did not find time to write the new tragedy about Iphigenia:

> While I feel apprehensive under the pressure of such a superabundance of the good and desirable, I must remind my friends of a dream that seemed to me significant enough, something like a year ago.[20]

Furthermore, in a sudden upsurge of what must have been an indomitable urge to go to Rome, he wrote in his diary for Charlotte von Stein on October 19:

> I want to contain myself and bide my time; [if] I have been patient these thirty years then I will still endure two weeks yet.[21]

The three remarks I have quoted have one factor in common: they refer to situations in which there is an imbalance between the quantity of stimuli impinging upon the psychic apparatus and the energy of the psychic apparatus that is free to be devoted to the binding of incoming stimuli. There are essentially two different constellations of such imbalance: Either the incoming stimuli exceed the capacity of the psychic apparatus, or the psychic apparatus has larger quantities of energy at its disposal than are satiated by the influx of external stimuli. The first two remarks—"the world runs away from under my feet" and "the pressure of superabundance makes me feel apprehensive"—refer to the former constellation. The last remark—"I will still wait two weeks more"—refers to the latter.

Now, these two constellations take on clinical prominence in a case of a certain dysfunction of the genital apparatus, namely, *ejaculatio praecox*. The person experiencing a premature ejaculation has the feeling that the world is, so to speak, running away under his feet, that all too strong a stimulation is exciting

[19] Buder claims that the analyst who adheres to Freud would interpret the dreamer's desire to land the small boat in the harbor as an expression of the longing to return into the mother, and, in further consequence, as the fear of the *vagina dentata*. I think that Buder is mistaken here.

[20] [Indem ich mich nun in dem Drang einer solchen Überfüllung des Guten und Wünschenswerthen geängstigt fühle, so muss ich meine Freunde an einen Traum erinnern, der mir, es wird eben ein Jahr sein, bedeutend genug schien.] (*Soph.* I, *30*:168)

[21] [Ich will mich auch fassen und abwarten, hab ich mich diese 30 Jahre geduldet, werd ich doch noch 14 Tage überstehn.] (*Soph.* III, *1*:310)

him, and therefore he has to reduce it before the peak has been reached; yet simultaneously he has the feeling of frustration and he feels pained that an expectation that has been raised cannot now be fulfilled. The first and the last fear particularly (the world is running away, and I fear I will not be able to bear further waiting) are almost literally like the reports one hears from patients suffering from *ejaculatio praecox*. Further, Goethe's complaint about not having enough time to carry out his dramatic plans (a complaint that impresses me as quite unusual for him) points in the same direction. The patient suffering from premature ejaculation is acting as if he were in a hurry and had not enough time for intercourse. Therefore I conclude that the pheasant dream was connected with Goethe's sexual dysfunction, which I have described as a premature ejaculation under the impact of exciting kisses.

Returning now to the dream to see whether this can be confirmed, I wish to point out first a stylistic peculiarity. In the second sentence the word "immediately" [sogleich] appears twice. This may indicate that a problem of *immediacy* played a great role in the latent dream thoughts, since nothing in the ostensible narrative requires that immediacy be stressed. I further suggest that the conspicuous symbolism of the erected penis (as expressed by the beautiful birds' tails) reflected an erection that the sleeper was having at the time of the dream. This dream element would, if my assumption is correct, partly belong to Silberer's "autosymbolic phenomena" (see 491; 493).

As a second assumption I introduce the idea that the sexual excitement expressed by the erection would have led to an ejaculation had it not been for the specific content of that dream. In other words, the function of this dream was—paradoxically—the prevention of an ejaculation, and the wish-fulfillment lay in the fact that no ejaculation occurred.

Usually sexual excitement that occurs during sleep and leads to an erection produces imagery that corresponds to the prevalent instinctual aim. The final imagery of the orgastic dream is correlated to the concomitant sexual sensations. In the instance of Goethe's dream, however, it was not the corresponding erotic imagery but the symbolization of the erection itself that became the manifest dream content. This part of the dream means: "I do not have the erection now, but I will have an erection when I am in Italy," or in other words: "Now that I am in Italy" (as feigned in the dream) "I have an erection." This makes good sense, for we were able to conclude from various sources that Goethe consciously or unconsciously planned to have intercourse in Italy.

Simultaneously the choice of symbol served the purpose of preventing an ejaculation. The erected penis was symbolized by something dead, which has to be interpreted along two different lines: (1) The symbol's quality of deadness represents the threat of punishment (a superego element); (2) by making the penis dead its manifestation of life, namely the ejaculation, is prevented.

I think in this second interpretation we encounter a particularly important function. As will be recalled, it became clear from Goethe's letter to the Duke that intercourse in Rome did not have a very profound effect upon him, inasmuch as the actual pleasure gained in cohabitation was not overwhelming. I suggest that in the endeavor to prevent a premature ejaculation the male organ became depersonalized. The unconscious or even preconscious fantasy of the erected penis being a dead organ may have helped Goethe in maintaining his potency while simultaneously reducing greatly the pleasure potential.

Invalid as the idea is, one not infrequently hears from male patients that quickness of ejaculation is a sign not only of particularly great passion, but even of potency and masculinity. It is possible that a similar idea evolved in Goethe regarding his premature ejaculations. He may have imagined that his dysfunction was caused by a superabundance of passion and, therefore, of life, and consequently the imagery of a dead penis deprived of the ejaculatory function may have loomed as a welcome fantasy.

In mythology, folklore, and art it is the erected penis that is taken as the symbol of creativity. The ejaculation, less suitable for representation, plays a minor role.[22] In unconscious imagery erection and ejaculation frequently evoke quite different imagery and seem to have quite different meanings. The strongest responses of guilt, shame, and despair I have noticed, I believe, in instances of inhibited ejaculation. Erective inability or premature ejaculations seem to become far more easily eroticized than ejaculatory inhibition. I mention such details in passing in order to make the reader aware that the dynamics and phenomenology of psychopathology are quite different with respect to each single function of male potency and that the differentiation of symbolic representation regarding erection and ejaculation is not as improbable as it may seem at first hearing. For a man who ejaculates prior to intromission an inability to ejaculate will appear as a most desirable goal, and therefore the imagery of an erected but dead penis—though it may appear contradictory—is quite conceivable in the male who is trying to ward off the quick ejaculatory response to stimulation. It is to be remembered that one of the functions of the pre-Italian decade for Goethe was learning to bear stimulation without immediate discharge. His fight against genital releases must also have included a fight against genital discharge during sleep or dreams. The closer he came to the moment of departing for Italy the more pressing the question became whether or not he would be able to bear sexual tension without immediate release even in a situation of maximum stimulation, like foreplay leading to cohabitation and cohabitation itself. Thus an ego that had integrated the idea of control and postponement of gratification to such an extent that even in sleep a strong genital impulse could be mastered despite a strong erection, that is to say, an ego that even when sleeping, at a time of its great weakness, could fulfill one of its most difficult tasks, an ego so prepared could optimistically look forward to facing the same task when awake. It should further be considered that in view of Goethe's intention to have intercourse in Italy the idea must have arisen of

---

[22] I do not consider here fertility rites in which emphasis is often put on ejaculation.

saving the precious seminal fluid for that time and not dissipating it in a nocturnal emission prior to that moment of greatest import. Thus there were many reasons why the ego had to fight against a nocturnal ejaculation around the time the pheasant dream was dreamed.[23]

In the further course of the dream we encounter another element that seems to confirm my hypothesis. After having elaborately presented in symbolic terms the erection and the pleasure derived therefrom, Goethe reports how "we cut through the calm tide." The word "tide" [Flut], referring to a phenomenon of nature characterized by contraction and expansion, is again well suited to symbolize the constellation I have in mind. At any rate the concept or image of tide is associated with movement and the calmly cutting through the tide would express the dreamer's serene joy at maintaining an erection for a long period of time without perturbation.

From numerous clinical examples it is known how the patient who suffers from premature ejaculation tries to avoid the occurrence of the symptom. He usually diverts his mind to trivialities during intercourse: he then compulsively counts or focuses on other emotionally neutral contents. I find what I believe is a similar element in this part of Goethe's dream. While crossing the calm tide he names the friends with whom he will share the treasure, or whom he will inform of the treasure. The naming of friends is reminiscent of a compulsive trait. By thinking of friends he diverts his mind to contents that it is most forbidden to connect with an ejaculation and that therefore serve as a potent deterrent against a sexual discharge. Concomitantly this preoccupation with males may have granted forbidden gratification under the guise of a defense against an orgasm.

Towards the end of the dream the boat has become small, that is to say, the erection has ceased, without having led to an ejaculation. The dream ends with a question: "Will I find a safe landing place?" The worry, according to this question, no longer was lest there be ejaculation before intromission but was about external factors, such as the availability of healthy women. The wish-fulfillment is found, paradoxically, in the not having an ejaculation during sleep.

Usually the main contribution of the ego to the dream is the wish to sleep (158, pp. 570–73). Here the ego's striving goes beyond this goal. To the wish to sleep is added the wish to avoid orgasm. This wish of the ego is made acceptable to the id (is made id-syntonic, so to speak) by the promise that a far greater wish than mere ejaculation will later be fulfilled in Italy. By this means the id can be lured into cooperation. The exhibitionistic element is plain in the dream

---

[23] Cf. Freud's observation that there are people who "seem to possess the faculty of consciously directing their dreams." Such a person may think while dreaming: "I won't go on with this dream any further and exhaust myself with an emission; I'll hold it back for a real situation instead." (158, pp. 571–72) However, in the instance of Goethe's pheasant dream I am not thinking of such a conscious direction of dreams.

and is a further premium with which to assuage the id, which insists on immediate gratification. It is as if the following thought had been activated in the ego: "Is not there more to be proud of if I can boast of an enormous erection sustained over a long period of time than if I gain immediate pleasure?" Such associative bridges, valid as they are, are in my estimation of secondary importance. They are auxiliary measures. The dream per se I take as a token that demonstrates the extent to which the ability to tolerate excitation and to forbear had become integrated by Goethe's personality.

Although the narcissistic element is present in this dream, I may have over-stressed its importance. The dream stands in the service of an unfulfilled longing for an object. It is quite significant that, as can be seen from the letters I have quoted, the pheasant dream usually came to his mind in connection with an unselfish impulse, such as the sharing with a friend or a return to Weimar. Also the three other times Goethe referred to the dream in the *Italian Journey* it was in combination with expressions of friendly object-relations. Thus at least we do not find any disproof of my thesis that this dream meant to Goethe a declaration: "See, I can master selfish, pleasure-seeking strivings for the sake of the love of an object."

However, one may dimly perceive in the background a wish-fulfillment of a less propitious nature. The dream, after all, may also mean: "I will be in Italy; I will be sexually excited; I will have powerful erections; I will not grant myself sexual gratifications but rather bear frustration in order to boast to my friends upon my return that I can withstand temptations in all circumstances." This interpretation would mean that Goethe still had powerful fears of intercourse at the time of the dream and that he could envisage a happy journey to Italy only if reassured of the safeguard of abstinence, to which he had grown accustomed in Weimar. However this may be, the triumphant admonition: "Remember the pheasant dream" which accompanied him throughout his *Italian Journey* implies more of wish-fulfillment and mastery than avoidance of anxiety usually can yield.

And here it is also appropriate to recall the paragraph that Goethe put after his report of the pheasant dream and in which he described so succinctly the concept of fixation. By referring to the difficulty man encounters in wresting himself away from the way he initially used a thing and in adapting his tools to purposes that vary with the course of time, Goethe had preconsciously in mind, I think—though he used churches, courtrooms, and ateliers as illustrations—the new use to which he put his genital apparatus.

In one more dimension the pheasant dream may serve us as a clue. We have come from time to time upon the problem of activity and passivity, and we have noted the singular bearing that this antinomy had upon Goethe's life, the difficulty he encountered in combining or synthesizing the two. In this dream we may learn that the mere fact of waiting for gratifications—even when they were assured for the proximate future—was experienced by Goethe as a castration threat, that is to say, as a hated relegation to passivity and femininity. Even—or perhaps especially—the psychobiological structure of male genitality, which entails delay between erection and ejaculation, in short the factor of forepleasure, was experienced by him as castration and passivity, and for this reason, too, the enduring of excitation could be visualized in the dream only by a symbol of castration. Here we can descry a biological root of the difficulty that Goethe encountered in integrating passivity, and thus also the reality principle. Yet in sleep man *is* passive, and the dream is imprinted upon a passive ego, which yearns for sleep. Had Goethe's ego not felt that deep aversion to exposure to passivity would his manifest dreams ever have turned out, as they often did, as nothing more or less than perfect poems?[24]

[24] The pheasant dream gives ample opportunity to discuss aspects of dream interpretation, particularly since we possess an interpretation of the dream according to the analytical psychology of Jung, as mentioned before (see 73). Therefore I do not wish to leave my discussion of Goethe's dream without mentioning at least the following. Buder is in error in supposing that Freud's interpretation of dreams aimed exclusively at ascertaining fixations or the infantile or the morbid. The opposite attitude, according to her, is that of the analytic psychologist of Jung's school: "Not that which still is, but that which is not yet but wishes to become, is put in the center of attention." [Nicht das, was noch ist, sondern das was noch nicht ist, aber werden will, wird in den Blickpunkt gerückt.] (73, p. 509) And further: "In the dream images those things speak that wish to become in a person." [In den Traumbildern sprechen die Dinge, die in einem Menschen werden wollen.] (73, p. 512) This statement is in agreement with the theory that in dreams the fulfillments of wishes are hidden. But when Buder states that the healthy person surrenders to the effect of these images, which gradually become "forces in his life," and that these forces, which formed the dream imagery, give shape to man's reality, whereas the inhibited, sick person cannot put "dream impulses" into reality, this idea must be rejected. The neurotic person often harbors wishes that cannot be fulfilled and part of his neurosis consists in his refusal to accept frustration of these very wishes. Clinical observation, then, shows only all too often that he permits "dream impulses" to impose themselves upon his life in reality, whereas he would fare better if he kept the wishes for the impossible or the forbidden away from his life's pursuit. Goethe wished in this dream for the capacity to sustain an erection, a wish the fulfillment of which did not belong to the impossible or the forbidden—at least from the viewpoint of reality. He acquired this capacity during the ten hard pre-Italian years of self-discipline and fulfillment of duties. The coincidence that in this particular dream the dream wish was one that was ego-acceptable and also adequate to the ego's capacities was misused by Buder to give the impression that psychoanalysis had overlooked a general dream function. Insufficient knowledge of the processes that occupied the pre-Italian decade and ignorance of the most powerful unconscious forces that are revealed in Goethe's biography may make the pheasant dream appear either as if it were a telepathic one (its main content was fulfilled in Italy—the Faustina episode) or as if the dream had carried into Goethe's life new elements, that had not existed before, and that stimulated him to actions otherwise omitted. In reality, what happened in Italy was the fulfillment of an old childhood wish, and the whole episode with Charlotte von Stein was an attempt at recovery from a symptom. Buder, however, follows the tradition of one school of thought and sees in Goethe's relationship with Charlotte von Stein nothing but regressive features. If a dream is taken out of context and one fails to make an exact analysis of all elements associated with it, then it may of course serve as confirmatory evidence of any kind of arbitrary interpretation.

Appendix Q

Notes on Goethe's Relationship with Christiane Vulpius and the General Problem of Morality in the Life of the Genius

LITTLE HAS BEEN known about the earlier life of Christiane Vulpius,[1] who became Goethe's mistress and later his wife. Only recently has some new information been forthcoming. Christiane was born June 1, 1765, in Weimar, and baptized on June 3. She lost her mother during her early years. Her brother, three years older than she, studied law and history and tried to make a living as a free-lance writer. Christiane seems to have had scarcely any schooling. She worked in an artificial-flower factory, where she earned a little money. This establishment was not an enterprise primarily for profit but was intended to provide useful occupation for middle-class girls.

Christiane came of a Protestant family that had settled in Weimar in the sixteenth century. We find ministers and lawyers among her ancestors. Her grandfather was "Juris Practicus" and court lawyer of the Duke of Saxony. Her father, Johann Friedrich Vulpius, failed to maintain his ancestor's high status. He was only an "official copying clerk" [Amtskopist],[2] that is to say, a subordinate official. He was married twice. From the first marriage issued six children, from the second there were four. Only Christian August (1762–1827), who later became a popular author of robber and horror novels; [Johanna] Christiane [Sophia] (1765–1816), his third child, later Goethe's wife; and

[1] For Christiane's biography see 134; 535; 536. (I obtained this last only recently.)

[2] See 66. In Wolfgang Vulpius's biography of Christiane (536) more about him can be found. He was a student of law in Jena, but apparently never finished his studies. After submitting a large number of applications over a period of nine years he at last obtained an inferior position in 1759. After seven years he received his only promotion—to "Amtsarchivar." Around 1778 he appropriated some money due the government. The seriousness of the misdemeanor cannot be established because of the loss of the pertinent documents during the war. He lost his employment and his family had to live under very precarious conditions. But it is of interest to note that Christiane's ancestors on the paternal side belonged to a group of more cultivated social background than Goethe's paternal ancestors.

1286

Sophie Ernestine Louise (1775–1806), Christiane's stepsister, survived. When he died in 1786 he left his family destitute. According to unconfirmed gossip he was a chronic alcoholic.

This seems to be all that is known about Christiane's origins. There is an unverified tradition that Goethe met Christiane for the first time in the flower factory when he was showing a visiting officer around. Allegedly the visitor was fresh to Christiane, and she effectively cut him short.[3]

At the request of her older brother, who had lost his employment, Christiane petitioned the all-powerful Minister Goethe in his behalf.[4] She submitted her petition as Goethe was passing through the park. This incident led—immediately as it is assumed—to an amorous adventure.

Goethe looked upon July 12, 1788, as the beginning of their relationship (see 252, *1*:486). In a letter to Schiller of July 13, 1796, he remarked that his marriage was eight years old and the French Revolution seven around that day,[5] a remark of broad significance—though made as a pleasantry—as to the great effect that his encounter with Christiane had upon his life.

Christiane soon moved into Goethe's house.[6] Her stepsister, ten years younger than she, and her aunt Juliane, an unmarried sister of her father's, soon joined her. Christiane took over the management of Goethe's complicated household. She participated in parties only after their relationship was legalized. The dates of Goethe's children are as follows: August—December 25, 1789, to October 27, 1830; a male stillbirth on October 14, 1791; Caroline—November 21 to December 3, 1793; Karl—October 30 to November 16, 1795; Kathinka —December 16 to 19, 1802.[7]

---

[3] It is often assumed that Goethe's poem "Der neue Pausias und sein Blumenmädchen," refers to this incident. In that poem it is related how a man attempts a sexual attack against a flower girl, whom Pausias successfully defends. He then falls in love with the girl, who secludes herself out of shame over the incident. The necessity for work forces her to leave her abode and thus she meets Pausias again and they become united. Goethe introduced this poem in an unusual way—with a quotation from Pliny's letters explaining who Pausias was. It is asserted this was done to avoid the impression that he was referring to Christiane in the poem.

[4] Wolfgang Vulpius's recent biography makes it certain that Goethe had previous knowledge of Christiane and the misfortunes of her family. Goethe was present in the Privy Council when her father's misdemeanor was discussed; he also had to deal with official documents referring to the Duke's granting her father a pardon and making him overseer of road construction. He also was present at the Privy Council when Christiane's petitions for assistance to her mother and siblings came up.

[5] The remark was made in a letter in response to one from Schiller inviting him to the christening of his second son, Ernst Friedrich Wilhelm (1796–1841). Goethe replied he would have come even uninvited, "if these ceremonies did not put me so out of humor." [Wenn mich diese Zeremonien nicht gar zu sehr verstimmten.]

[6] The exact date of this move is not known. It seems that from October, 1788, on she was well established in Goethe's house.

[7] The stillbirth as well as the infantile mortality and several miscarriages are explained by Kleine as suggestive of erythroblastosis foetalis. See 332.

It is of interest to record here Goethe's tendency to absent himself from Weimar around the time of his children's birth. In this, his behavior was quite different from that towards the Duchess when she approached the time of delivery; he then acted like her guardian spirit.

That Goethe tried to be absent when the birth of a child impended, and that his departures on those occasions had the character of a flight, can best be seen in a letter written by Christiane during October, 1793, in which she asked what name she should give the *Krabskrälligkeit;*[8] "for after all it has to have a given name" (252, *1*:40). Since she added that she thought "it" would wait until an answer had arrived it is plain that Goethe had left at a time when the birth was expected. The other term which they used for the unborn child, namely "das Pfuiteufelchen," "the-little-it's-a-damned-shame," is also a pejorative term. Goethe's frequent absences in Jena during his years of matrimony will be discussed later. Most of their vacations were spent apart.

On October 19, 1806, they were officially married, but the odium of an illegitimate relationship could not be wiped out. On January 9, 1815, Christiane suffered a stroke from which she recovered quickly. In the middle of May, 1816, another similar episode took place. But at the end of May her condition worsened and on June 6 she died, after days of almost continuous convulsions.

Much has been written—in terms mostly vituperative—about Goethe's choice of Christiane as a love-object and his long association with her. However, at times public and scholarly opinion has changed and Christiane has been extolled as "the only fitting companion for Goethe" (252, *1*:xv). Gräf, who studied their relationship most intimately, regarded this opinion as peculiar. In his sympathetic and understanding introduction to his exemplary edition of their correspondence, he reaches the conclusion that, despite the many good points that can be cited in favor of Christiane, their association was "a dangerous, only half-successful, experiment" (252, *1*:liii). I myself am strongly of the opinion, which I shall try to establish, that Christiane was the only type of woman Goethe could successfully have made his mate.

I believe it is a mistake to speak of "Goethe's relationship to Christiane" as if it was a single unchanging entity, for in this relationship distinct phases are quite noticeable and the meaning Christiane had for Goethe varied in essential respects from phase to phase. For the present inquiry only the first phase is of importance and these notes will be predominantly devoted to it.

The first question, of course, concerns Goethe's choice of object. Why did he select Christiane at all? It seems that at the outset Goethe did not regard his choice of Christiane as one that would lead to a permanent relationship, let alone one that would result at last in marriage. Initially it was probably a mere infatuation, arising on the spur of the moment and excited by purely

---

[8] An untranslatable personal term she and Goethe apparently used for a child, or perhaps an expected child, literally: "crab-clawed-hood"; "crab" being a common term of contempt for "child," roughly equivalent to English "brat."

sexual motives. Nevertheless, I believe that certain outward features of their first meeting had an appeal to Goethe's unconscious. As mentioned, Christiane submitted to Goethe a petition in behalf of her brother, who had failed as an author and poet. The imagery of a sister who tries actively to rescue a brother, whereas he relies passively on her willingness to sacrifice, fits well into fantasies we may assume Goethe entertained, in view of his own relationship to Cornelia. Vulpius's ill fate possibly struck him as an outcome that might easily have become his own had he not been protected by his daemon.[9] Thus by appropriating Christiane he deprived a brother of a devoted sister, who was functioning as his guardian angel. At the same time, by taking care of the brother—which Goethe actually did—he could accomplish in real life a female identification. I believe that there may be support for my suggestion that a kind of sister imagery surrounded Christiane's person in Goethe's fantasy in a detail whose peculiar circumstances have not yet been clarified. Christiane's birthday was June 1. Goethe, however, persistently celebrated it on August 6. To be sure, it is not certain whether this was arranged by him or whether Christiane was uncertain of the date. Gräf suggests that Christiane confounded her own birthday with that of a sister Sophie, who was born August 6, 1781 (252, *1*:482). This, however, does not strike me as very probable, since Christiane was sixteen when Sophie was born.[10]

It is more probable that Goethe had his share in the shift of the birthday. Christiane was willing to an unusual degree to comply with Goethe's wishes, and it would fit well into the picture one gets of her that she submitted readily without protest to Goethe's desire to exchange her sister's birthday for her own. If it was Goethe's doing to shift Christiane's birthday away from June we may be reasonably sure that it was because the June date established for him an explicit association between her and Cornelia, whose death occurred on June 8, 1777.[11] As fate proceeds sometimes like a sentimental playwright, so it fell out that Christiane died on June 6, 1816, which brought the day of her death almost exactly to the anniversary of Cornelia's death, so that when Goethe wrote those verses that were ostensibly devoted to Christiane's death—

> In vain, oh sun, you seek to shine
> Through the bleak clouds!
> The whole profit of my life
> Is to lament her loss.[12]

[9] See above, p. 31 for my assumption that in Goethe's relationship to Lenz the same mechanism was operative.

[10] Her brother Christian thought that Christiane was born on June 6.

[11] If my reconstruction is correct, we see here an instance of the return of the warded-off content. For the new birthday chosen for Christiane was again that of a sister, albeit Christiane's sister.

[12] [Du versuchst, o Sonne, vergebens/ Durch die düstren Wolken zu scheinen!/ Der ganze Gewinn meines Lebens/ Ist ihren Verlust zu beweinen.] (*Soph.* I, 4:61)

—fate had made it possible for him to express something he had felt over the years about Cornelia. How great the trauma of his losing Cornelia was he had intimated only once, in his letter to Charlotte von Stein of January 17, 1787, from Rome. Then for a lightninglike moment he drew aside the curtain from before that which had been too painful to put into words, and wrote, "Since the death of my sister nothing has grieved me so much. . . ."[13]

Whatever the unconscious meaning of Christiane may have been, external factors, of course, also had their bearing on his choice. Christiane was pretty, rather than beautiful. I have recorded earlier that Goethe was usually attracted rather by pretty women than by beautiful ones. She was seventeen years younger than he. The desire to be rejuvenated by the physical love of a young, healthy, sturdy, attractive girl can, on good grounds, be assumed. The whole Italian episode was one of rejuvenation, and the forbidding northern country that Goethe was once more compelled to live in threatened to undo the gain he had obtained in the south. Christiane's relatively low social status permitted the continuation of what had been started with Faustina in Rome. Goethe very definitely did not want to tie himself down to a woman, and Christiane apparently offered all that the moment needed without boding any dangers for the future. The first intimate meeting may have been like an experiment to test whether the Roman voluptuous love could be repeated in Weimar. Again we encounter secret, short-lasting meetings, with pains not to be observed by the neighbors.

According to Karl von Stein's account, Goethe's infatuation became known accidentally. His brother Fritz, apparently still in possession of the keys to Goethe's garden house, dropped in and met a young lady who also behaved as if she were at home there. It seems that it was in this way that Goethe's relationship with Christiane became known. There was an unbelievably malicious reaction to Goethe's illicit affair. The history of this shameful gossip and intrigue has often been reported and does not need any commentary here.

Apparently the girl showed so many qualities and pervaded the atmosphere around her with such an affectionate climate that what had been intended as a passing entertainment became a serious and necessary part of his existence.[14] Once intercourse had been introduced into his life in Rome, Goethe probably could not do without it, and whatever the frequency of his indulgence in it may have been, it seems to have been necessary for him that it be available. Goethe was unbelievably lucky in his choice of Christiane, since—this is my impression —only a woman of her type could have given him what he urgently needed without doing him any harm. It is most remarkable how this unsophisticated woman, who was capable of comprehending her lover's objective greatness al-

---

[13] [Seit dem Todte meiner Schwester hat mich nichts so betrübt. . . .]

[14] Cf. Goethe's epigram, *Soph.* I, 1:465; cf. also Appendix S.

most alone by her awareness of his prestige in her environment, subordinated herself to Goethe's needs without surrendering her individuality or creating feelings of guilt in him by silence or reticence. She apparently gave herself to him as she was, and one feature of the way she was was her gratitude for what he did for her, a longing to be with him as much as possible and to fill her place and perform her functions in a way that would please and satisfy him. Although Goethe exposed her to humiliation by not marrying her and by letting her go through five illegitimate pregnancies, not once in her letters did she hint at a desire to become his legitimate wife. There were, of course, plenty of opportunities for insinuating such a request in what she wrote, but, to my mind, there is a question whether she even proposed such an expectation to herself inwardly. She apparently had an unshakable trust that he knew best what ought to be done and accepted his decisions as final. At the same time she also felt that nothing ought to interfere with his work and subordinated her own wishes and needs without hesitation to the necessities of his creativity. Her letter to him of November 24, 1798, when he was in Jena, may serve as one example, from among the many that could be cited, of this attitude.

I thank you for the nice roast venison. Now the winter entertainments start with us and I do not want to let them be spoiled for me by anything. I love you and only you alone; I take care of my little boy and keep my household in order, and make fun [of them]. But they cannot leave a person alone. The day before yesterday Meissel[15] comes [up] in the theater and asks me without ceremony whether it is true that you are going to be married —you are already providing yourself with carriage and horses.[16] I became so angry at that moment that I gave him a particularly malicious answer and I am convinced that I will not be asked again. Yet because I always think of it I dreamed of it this night. That was a bad dream, which I must tell you when you come. In the course of it I cried so and screamed so loud that Ernestine woke me up and there was my whole pillow wet. I am very glad that it was only a dream. And your dear letter made me joyful again and happy. The ice is quite good and I want to go skating again. . . . We look forward with great pleasure to the masked ball. If you were here, it would, of course, be an even greater joy to us; yet since I hear that it goes well with your work, that is better than all masked-ball pleasures, for I know that when it goes well with you with your work, then you return in

[15] Gottlieb Meissel, secretary employed at the ducal Chancery. Goethe mentioned him in a letter to C. S. Voight of June 5, 1800.

[16] Goethe planned at that time to keep his own horses and carriage, and actually did so later. The rumor in Weimar was that Goethe would marry Amalie von Imhoff (1776–1831), Charlotte von Stein's beautiful and very talented niece. Apparently there were some who tried to arrange a match between the two "so that male and female genius would combine." See 49, p. 479.

really good spirits. And then we want to be very cheerful together. Yet, by all signs, we shall have a heavy winter for the snow is already a yard deep here. Farewell and keep on loving me.[17]

This sample is in certain respects typical of their correspondence up to the year 1804 or 1805. Unfortunately only letters from 1792 on have been preserved, but I surmise that this close affection, cordiality, and mutual reliance, which can be observed in these twelve years (1792–1804), and which is documented by about 380 letters, started fairly soon after their first acquaintance. Christiane's letters have been held in disrepute because of their execrable spelling. Yet Goethe's spelling was at times quite bad, and his mother's, though not as bad as Christiane's, would nowadays be considered a sign of complete lack of education. Christiane's spelling was purely phonetic and there is no indication that it disturbed the recipient in any way. Gräf did not publish her letters in their original spelling but substituted correct orthography. Thus he gave a text which is very readable but reveals, surprisingly, that the two correspondents communicated on the same level during those years. It is perhaps one of the most touching signs of Goethe's humaneness that in the letters of that period not one sentence can be found that betrays strain, condescension, or an effort to lower his level to hers. The letters flow with perfect ease, affection, and warmth without a line that one could suppose might have caused Christiane any difficulty in understanding or grasping its full meaning. This is an incredible feat if the difference between their educational levels is considered. Is today's reader deceived by Goethe? Did he really "talk down" to her, and were those letters really written with conscious effort and intent? I do not believe so. The suppressed tendency would have been bound to show up somewhere—in corrections, slips, or some awkwardness. But the fact is they are just

[17] [Ich danke Dir vor das Rehebrätchen. Itzo gehen bei uns die Winterfreuden an, und ich will mir sie durch nichts lassen verbittern. Die Weimarer thäten es gerne, aber ich achte auf nichts. Ich habe Dich lieb und ganz allein lieb, sorge für mein Bübchen und halte mein Hauswesen in Ordnung, und mache mich lustig. Aber sie können einen gar nicht in Ruhe lassen. Vorgestern in [der] Komödie kommt Meissel und fragt mich ohne Umstände, ob es wahr wär, dass Du heurathst, Du schafftest Dir ja schon Kutsche und Pferde an. Ich wurde den Augenblick so böse, dass ich ihm eine recht malicieuse Antwort gab, und ich bin überzeugt, der fragt mich nicht wieder. Weil [ich] aber immer daran denke, so habe ich heute Nacht davon geträumt. Das war ein schlimmer Traum, den muss ich Dir, wenn Du kommst, erzählen. Ich habe dabei so geweint und laut geschrien, dass mich Ernestine aufgeweckt hat, und da war mein ganzes Kopfkissen nass. Ich bin sehr froh, dass es nur ein Traum war. Und Dein lieber Brief macht mich wieder froh und zufrieden. Es gibt recht gutes Eis, und ich will wieder Schlittschuh fahren. . . . Auf die Redoute freuen mir uns sehr. Wenn Du hier wärst, wäre uns freilich noch lieber; aber da ich höre, dass es Dir mit Deinen Arbeiten gut gehet, das ist besser als Redouten-Freude, weil ich weiss, wenn es Dir mit Deiner Arbeit gut geht, Du auch recht vergnügt wiederkömmst. Und dann wollen mir sehr vergnügt zusammen sein. Aber allem Anschein nach kriegen mir einen starken Winter, denn hier liegt der Schnee schon eine Elle hoch. Leb wohl und behalte mich lieb.] (252, 1:226–27)

as much Goethe's as the rest of his letters and are nevertheless perfectly focused upon and aimed at this lovely, uneducated girl, who was only interested in dancing, parties, her household duties, and, above all, Goethe's and their son's physical well-being and good spirits.

I wish to present just one specimen from the many to show in what vein Goethe's letters were written. He wrote Christiane on March 26, 1797, as follows:

> I am sending you herewith, my dear child, some money so that you may be taken care of this week. How gladly would I come to you right away to-day, for I actually have nothing more to do here. Only I should like to wait until Schiller has finished a piece of his work that he wants to read to me.[18] Everything else I could do as well over there in the neighborhood of my dear children. I yearn greatly to see you again and [will] return happy, since everything has succeeded according to my wish.[19] Fare very well and keep on loving me.[20]

One gets the impression that Goethe poured into his letters to Christiane a side of his personality that he could express only in this relationship: an avoidance of abstractions and a predilection for concreteness. That immediate contact with reality in which the physical prevails: food, wine, the home, money, the house, health, and the child, were the favored topics of his letters. There are innumerable references to wine, the choice and preparation of food, what was eaten or was to be eaten—interests that do not sound at all feigned but were live and direct in him. Also his concern for her dress was genuine. This is particularly evident in one letter (May 17, 1793) when he wrote her during his stay in Frankfurt that his mother had given him a skirt and some material for her. Two postscripts show that he was preoccupied with how she should use the material and for what occasions, and in his letter of August 15, 1797, he asked, "Do write me how the black silk dress turned out, and when you wore it for the first time."[21] His correspondence up to 1804 shows distinctly the features of a genuine object-relationship uncomplicated by manifest conflicts, providing him with happiness and satisfaction without sacrifice, and exhibits him as primarily interested in the love-object's welfare and benefit. There is no precedent for this relationship in Goethe's life and he never again estab-

---

[18] Probably parts of his tragedy *Die Piccolomini;* see 252, 1:491.

[19] Goethe probably refers to his writing *Hermann und Dorothea.*

[20] [Hier schicke ich dir, mein liebes Kind, etwas Geld damit du diese Woche versorgt seyst. Wie gern käme ich gleich heute zu dir, denn ich habe eigentlich hier nichts mehr zu thun. Nur möchte ich abwarten biss Schiller mit einem Stück seiner Arbeit fertig ist, das er mir vorlesen will. Alles andre könnt ich recht wohl drüben, in der Nachbarschaft meiner lieben Kinder thun. Ich sehne mich recht euch wieder zu sehen und komme vergnügt zurück, da mir alles nach Wunsch gelungen ist. Lebe recht wohl, und behalte mich lieb.]

[21] [Schreibe mir ja, wie das schwarzseidne Kleid gerathen ist, und wann Du es zum ersten Mal angehabt hast.]

lished one comparable to it. It was the meridian of his life and whatever conflicts may have agitated him during these twelve years, they did not daunt the sunny happiness which one captures in reading these letters. Following Heinz Hartmann's concept of the ego's conflict-free sphere, I feel inclined to speak here of a conflict-free area in interpersonal relations, whatever conflicts may have seethed beneath the conflict-free surface. This mind, endowed with an incredibly wide span, was also able to live honestly, fully, and sincerely on a plane that looks at first glimpse as un-Goethe-like as any that one could think of.

Thus the question of his not marrying her for eighteen years, and of his frequent absences in Jena, acquires particular prominence. Most authors explain the former by the impossibility of his introducing Christiane at court in view of her lack of education and manners. This argument, I believe, is not valid, since Goethe's position was such that he would not have had to introduce her at court even if they had got married then. My explanation, which follows, is hypothetical.

Goethe evidently felt unable to commit himself and to establish an official relationship, which it would hardly have been possible to abrogate.[22] Yet even without marriage this relationship became for all practical purposes indissoluble; the latent possibility of such separation, however, which is always implied in an illegitimate relationship, probably had its bearing. I think that by keeping the relationship an illegitimate one, Goethe was trying to keep it on a level of high emotional tension. He may also have been trying to keep it isolated from the rest of his multifarious existence. Christiane really did not belong at court and in the company of highly sophisticated people. As soon as she became a person who also had to play an official role she would also have become a person no longer able to fulfill her functions to perfection. Marriage would have burdened Christiane with duties that she was actually not equal to. The Christiane of the period up to 1805 is actually a far more charming and sympathetic person than the *Frau Geheime Räthin* of from 1806 on. By temperament modest, tenderhearted, and extremely ready to help others, she may have suffered some diminution in these virtues by her elevation to the status of Goethe's wife, and, as was bound to happen, elements that did not fit her at all were carried into her existence by the act of legitimation. The slandered, sometimes even ostracized, Christiane Vulpius may have been happier than Christiane von Goethe.

Yet another aspect must be considered in the discussion of Goethe's opposing or putting off marriage. Christiane felt guilty about the illegitimate relationship and she was overjoyed when Goethe's mother, upon being apprised of their living together, showed no signs of moral indignation or disapproval.[23]

---

[22] However, divorces were not unusual or impossible. For example, the parents of the girl who was later Goethe's daughter-in-law were divorced.

[23] Goethe told his mother of his common-law marriage and of his son only while he was in Frankfurt, in August, 1792.

When Goethe was again in Frankfurt the next year and Christiane was sent gifts and greetings from his mother as well as from him, she was overjoyed and wrote her without Goethe's previous permission. She apprised Goethe of this step (June 7, 1793) with some foreboding, expressed her joy about the gifts and added: "What I am most happy over is that your dear mother is not angry with me; this makes me very glad since it had a few times distressed me" (252, 1:21). Male prerogatives perhaps were viewed at that time as covering a broader area than nowadays, but even today a girl may worry over how her lover's mother will respond to her conduct, although the lover carries the brunt of responsibility for the relationship, as was evidently true in the case of Christiane and Goethe. This factor—of Christiane's accepting the whole responsibility, of her never accusing Goethe but regarding herself as to blame and taking the attitude that he was being granted only what was his due—all this must have been a source of the greatest relief for Goethe, who thus obtained absolution even before he asked for it. Moreover, the whole question of guilt—which, in my opinion, was inseparably attached for Goethe to direct sexual pursuits—was thus shifted to an extraneous social factor, which must have facilitated the physical relationship. The problem was no longer, at least on the preconscious level: "What damage am I doing to the female body?" but "What damage am I doing to a girl's reputation?" This was a scruple it was infinitely easier to cope with than the repressed content of the destructive effect of cohabitation. Circumstances here played into Goethe's hands to find a workable rationalization for one of his most threatening conflicts, which might otherwise easily have aroused acute fears. Thus, paradoxically, the very illegitimacy of the relationship may have reduced Goethe's feelings of guilt.

Goethe's frequent and long absences in Jena are actually an aspect of the consummate adequacy of his new living conditions. He openly told Christiane that he could not work at Weimar. She accepted this without resentment as ungrudgingly as if there had been a plain and simple reason for it. Goethe's absences were rarely enforced by external circumstances, though he did occasionally have official business to transact in Jena. Evidently Christiane's and his son's presence made work impossible. Thus his life was divided between the latently homosexual circle in Jena, where he maintained his close friendship with Schiller and was completely devoted to production, and Weimar, where he had his "cheerful days" [vergnügte Tage], as they so frequently called them in their letters. Goethe did not hold it against Christiane that he was not able to work at Weimar—he was quite aware that it was his peculiarity—and Christiane, as mentioned before, did not see in this a reproach against herself. The need for isolation during periods of productivity cannot be viewed as a sign of ambivalence on Goethe's part. If it happened that he felt a longing for her and would have preferred to return to Weimar or to have her come to Jena, he strictly abstained from either alternative if there was the slightest danger it would impair his capacity to proceed with the creative work upon which he was engaged. Strangely enough Christiane understood this, and, despite her incessant expressions of how pleasureless life was for her without Goethe, she never suggested that he ought to give preference to her wishes but limited herself—at least in her letters—to the wish that he might soon succeed in finishing his work. It is only with extreme rarity that such suggestions occur as the following of September 25, 1799: "Perhaps your work would go better here than usual" (252, *1:261*).

Goethe himself was perfectly clear as to his own special need. When once he had to stay at Weimar at a time critical for his production, he sent his family to Jena and asked Schiller to keep an eye on his son. He wrote him, August 7, 1799:

> Since I could not get away to Jena my [loved] ones had to give way, for this remains once for all: that I cannot bring forth the least bit without solitude.[24]

It becomes clear from other evidence that a friend who evoked too strong a feeling in him might also have the same effect. Thus, he wrote from Weimar to Schiller about his friend Meyer, who lived for many years in his house and who had become an integral part of his ménage (December 9, 1797):

> I believe I will not bring Meyer with me to Jena, for I have again renewed the experience that I can work only in absolute solitude, and that not perhaps only some conversation, but even the very presence in the house of loved and treasured persons totally drains off my poetic sources. I would be now in a kind of despair—because indeed any trace of a productive interest has disappeared—if I were not sure of recovering it in the first week in Jena.[25]

A spell of creativity was accompanied with a latent apprehension that an external stimulus might put an end to the process just at the moment when the subjective configuration was about to take on material form. "I therefore ask you," he wrote Christiane on November 20, 1798, "not to come over unexpectedly. I must again hold to my wonted way and work here in one stretch so long as I want and am able to."[26] In the following letter, which he wrote her on

---

[24] [. . . da ich nicht nach Jena entweichen konnte, so mussten die Meinigen weichen, denn dabey bleibt es nun einmal: dass ich ohne absolute Einsamkeit nicht das mindeste hervorbringen kann.]

[25] [Meyern werde ich wohl nicht mitbringen, denn ich habe die Erfahrung wieder erneuert: dass ich nur in einer absoluten Einsamkeit arbeiten kann, und dass nicht etwa nur ein Gespräch, sondern sogar schon die häusliche Gegenwart geliebter und geschätzter Personen meine poetische Quellen gänzlich ableitet. Ich würde jetzt in einer Art von Verzweiflung seyn, weil auch jede Spur eines productiven Interesse bey mir verschwunden ist, wenn ich nicht gewiss wäre es in den ersten 8 Tagen in Jena wiederzufinden.]

[26] [Ich bitte dich daher nicht unvermuthet herüber zu kommen, ich muss es wieder auf meine gewöhnliche Art halten und hier solange in Einem Stücke arbeiten als ich mag und kann.]

May 30, 1809, one senses the anxiety of the genius lest the trivial conquer the sublime:

> During this next week turn away from me everything that you can, for I am just now so involved in work[27] as I have not been able for a year to seize it. If I should be disturbed now, everything would be lost that I see quite near before me and that can be accomplished in a short time.[28]

The psychological conditions that are necessary for the creative act are not within the ego's free decision. Whatever the creative genius may wish he is still dependent on the interplay of self-acting forces which the conscious part of the personality must let operate in their own way without any attempt at interference. Yet this necessity for isolation was probably for Goethe an occasion for a feeling of guilt—perhaps quite rightly, for it was a manifestation of a tendency to keep Christiane out of important areas of his existence. Nevertheless, she was regularly informed about the mechanics of his production—whether work was progressing satisfactorily, whether he was working upon some poems or a novel, whether he was generating new ideas which he could use in future productions. The realm of meanings and values and contents, however, does not find reflection in their letters. Yet the resultant was that each of them felt he was obtaining more from the other than he gave, and each expressed the desire to give the other as much as he was receiving.

Thus this was one of the few really happy marriages involving an artistic genius that we know of. Both partners thrived and both felt they were getting what most they wanted by being to each other what they were. Only one instance occurs (in Riemer's[29] diary)—and this from the period after they had become married—in which it appears that Christiane was made unhappy by Goethe. She thought on that occasion that he had given her just reason for jealousy. In Riemer's diary of May 14, 1810, the following is found: "To Knebel's, where Goethe and his wife. Jealous weeping by the latter. Therefore soon home. Afterwards together, but she without participation."[30] And on May 15: "At noon the *Geheime Räthin* for dinner. Ill humor out of jealousy. Thereafter appeased."[31] I have not succeeded in finding out who was the object of

---

[27] Goethe was at that time involved in work upon his novel *The Elective Affinities*.

[28] [Wende alles was du kannst die nächsten acht Tage von mir ab: denn ich bin gerade jetzt in der Arbeit so begriffen wie ich sie seit einem Jahre nicht habe anfassen können. Würde ich jetzo gestört, so wäre alles für mich verloren was ich ganz nahe vor mir sehe und was in kurzer Zeit zu erreichen ist.]

[29] Friedrich Wilhelm Riemer (1774–1845) started in Goethe's house as tutor of his son, August, from 1803 to 1812. During that period and also subsequently until Goethe died, he collaborated closely with him.

[30] [Zu Knebel, wo Goethe und seine Frau. Eifersüchtiges Weinen derselben. Desshalb bald nach Hause. Nachher zusammen, doch Sie ohne Antheil.]

[31] [Mittags die Geh. Räthin zu Tische. Verdriesslichkeiten aus Eifersucht. Apaisiert hernach.] (252, 2:418)

Christiane's jealousy. Whoever it may have been, Goethe wrote Christiane two years later in a postscript to his letter of November 6, 1812:

Last evening I also saw Minchen[32] again. I left it to accident how I should meet her. Accident also proved to be most kind and it went just right. She is now a few years older. Her looks and comportment, etc., however, are still so pretty and so charming that I do not reproach myself at all for having once loved her more than was fitting.[33]

Christiane was accused in various quarters of unbecoming conduct (even of alcoholism), but there is scarcely anything to suggest that Goethe was not satisfied with her comportment. The only reference of this sort I have been able to find in his letters occurs in his letter of July 20, 1803, on a summer vacation. Goethe wrote:

Do me the favor, however, during the time that remains, of not carrying the dancing to excess, and conclude your stay with a moderate enjoyment.[34]

Except for this one admonition, he encouraged her to find enjoyment, to go to dances, to have as much fun as possible, and in turn he was happy when she reported incidents of amusement. Christiane was what may be called a kinesthetic personality type. Movement, and particularly rhythmic movement, was almost an addiction with her and she could not dance enough. She was aware that she was unable to sit still for any length of time (letter to Goethe of November 30, 1803) and I wonder whether this predilection for the kinesthetic system was also one of the factors that made her so lovable for Goethe.[35]

I have the impression that around 1805 an internal break occurred in their relationship. I believe that two factors especially contributed to the gradual disappearance of that warmth and affection and closeness that flow so strongly in Goethe's letters of the first phase. In discussing Goethe's relationship to Char-

---

[32] Christiane Friederike Wilhelmine Herzlieb, whom Goethe usually called Minchen, was born May 22, 1789. She lost her parents early and came as a foster-child to Frommann in Jena, who was the publisher of some of Goethe's works. Goethe knew her as a child and fell in love with her around 1807 when he wrote his sonnets, most of which were devoted to her. She probably also had a bearing on Goethe's *The Elective Affinities*. The intensity of Goethe's feelings for her and the extent of her influence on Goethe's work have often been debated.

[33] [Gestern Abend habe ich auch Minchen wieder gesehen. Ich überliess es dem Zufall wie ich mit ihr zusammen kommen sollte. Der hat sich auch recht artig erwiesen, und es war eben recht. Sie ist nun eben um ein paar Jahre älter. An Gestalt und Betragen u.s.w. aber immer noch so hübsch und so artig, dass ich mir gar nicht übel nehme sie einmal mehr als billig geliebt zu haben.]

[34] [Thue mir aber nun die Liebe und übertreib es diese letzte Zeit nicht mit Tanzen und schliesse deinen Aufenthalt mit einem mässigen Genuss.]

[35] See above, p. 1180, for the role of the kinesthetic system in Wilhelm Meister's relationship to Mignon.

lotte von Stein we noticed that Goethe frequently needed a counterpoise to his attachment to a woman in the form of male friendships. First the Duke served this function and later Herder. After Goethe's return from Italy his friendship with the Duke took on a new momentum. On three occasions he joined him in military enterprises which took him from Christiane for long periods of time. From 1794 he maintained a very intense relationship with Schiller. In that year the long stays in Jena took their beginning. In 1805, however, Schiller died, and I think that the loss of this most important homosexual tie had a profound bearing on his acute feelings for Christiane. Moreover, I surmise that Goethe discontinued his sexual relationship with Christiane around that time or limited it at least to an exceptional occurrence. Nor, as far as is known, did he depart thereafter, any more than he had before, from his pattern of abstaining from sexual relations with anyone else. The warmth and directness of affection faded away and assurance of love and gratitude became quite rare. Their mutual interest in each other became a matter of routine. Goethe never ceased his absorbing interest in her welfare, except in one instance shortly before their relationship was ended by Christiane's death, an incident which would take us too far afield.

After almost eighteen years of unmarried living together he abruptly decided to make her his wife. She had rescued him from the violence of marauding French invaders and he apparently considered it a matter of gratitude to make her his legitimate wife. Many factors were at work to make him prefer legitimation. I do not wish to discuss any of these save one: I think he was no longer in love with her and that marriage could no longer endanger their relationship. Her place in his life had become solid in so far as it had become routinized. As time progressed Goethe's letters to her no longer even sounded as if they were written for her. From 1806 Christiane had an attractive companion, Caroline Ulrich,[36] and in his letters Goethe almost regularly included greetings to her of a tender sort, calling her Caroline or Uli, or referring to her as "your attractive secretary." She wrote Christiane's letters and I assume that she also read Goethe's letters to her. In his letter of June 6, 1813, he wrote Christiane:

> If you cannot read my letter Uli will help out; I am almost in the habit of [writing in the style of] her handwriting, it almost looks as if I were in love with her.[37]

Indeed, one quite often gets the impression (which cannot be verified) that Goethe's letters to Christiane were meant more for her "attractive secretary" than for their ostensible recipient. I do not suppose that this was done intentionally, but I believe that the knowledge that Caroline would read his letters

[36] Caroline Wilhelmina Johanne Ulrich (1790–1855), married, in 1814, Friedrich Wilhelm Riemer (1774–1845), Goethe's secretary and collaborator.

[37] [Wenn du meinen Brief nicht lesen kannst, so wird Uli aushelfen, ich gewöhne mir fast ihre Hand an, es sieht fast aus als wenn ich in sie verliebt wäre.]

became for Goethe a source of greater zest and interest in writing to his wife than would otherwise have been the case. Besides, there were letters addressed to Christiane that were evidently meant for Riemer, his own collaborator, or for Professor Meyer, who was his expert friend in matters of the visual arts, as well as long letters that apparently were meant to be diary entries—notes for eventual later publications. In all these communications one does not get the impression of a personal contact on Goethe's part with Christiane.

The third phase set in with Christiane's first stroke, from which she quickly recovered only to succumb a year later. This third phase is replete with grave problems not to be discussed here. But it must be emphasized that, whatever Goethe's feelings and conflicts may have been in later years, Christiane felt protected and loved by him to the last moment.

Christiane's premarital years with Goethe were saddened by the malicious gossip that was rampant in Weimar, the relative isolation in which she lived, and her worry about Goethe's health. The idea that she might have to face the Weimarian clique alone stood like a specter behind her. This is proved by her letters to the only friend she had, the physician Nicolaus Meyer (see 392), as well as by her great care that Goethe should never in any circumstances be annoyed by this worry. Occasionally she could not master her grief and there are a few letters in which she complained bitterly about the hostility and tactlessness of those about her. But such outbreaks of despair and anger were isolated and commonly she quickly found her way back to that unfailing trust in her great friend who never spared encouragement to make her disregard the hypocrisy and arrogance from which he himself perhaps had to suffer even more than his mistress.

One cannot leave off even a superficial discussion of this intriguing relationship without spending at least a few words on the image Goethe formed of Christiane. I omit any attempt at a reconstruction based on his poetry but refer here only to direct evidence. He once said to O. L. B. Wolff:[38]

> Ought one really believe that this person [Christiane] has lived with me already twenty years? But that is just what attracts me to her, that she does not give up anything of her nature and remains as she was.[39]

Here Goethe refers to the image of Christiane's indestructibility symbolized by a relative immunity to external influences. The hold the world may take on a person is implicitly viewed as a threat. Christiane, undisturbed by what the world said and wanted—but also unaffected by the ways of her giant friend—pursued the lines dictated by her temperament and constitution, and this im-

---

[38] Oskar Ludwig Bernhard Wolff (1799–1851) studied medicine, history and philosophy; he was a teacher in Hamburg, and was well-known as a mimetic improvisator.

[39] [Sollte man wohl glauben, dass diese Person schon zwanzig Jahre mit mir gelebt hat? Aber das gefällt mir eben an ihr, dass sie nichts von ihrem Wesen aufgibt und bleibt, wie sie war.] (250, *1*:554)

pressed him as strong and reliable, thereby relieving him of the neurotic fear that as a male he might easily injure the female. Further, Goethe is said to have told Christine Reinhard:[40]

> First I must tell you that of all my works my wife has not read a line. The intellectual realm has no existence for her; she was created for the management of a household. Here she unburdens me of all worries; here she hustles and bustles; it is her empire.[41]

Goethe's assertion that Christiane had not read a line of his works appears unfounded at first sight, for from two letters and various diary entries one can prove that she read certain of his works[42] and that he himself read parts of *Dichtung und Wahrheit* to her. But actually these letters and diary entries date from after 1807, when Countess Reinhard reports Goethe's having made this remark, so that at that time Christiane was perhaps not actually acquainted with a single line of her husband's works. Be this as it may, Goethe's remark strikes me as one of approval. I surmise that he wanted to think of Christiane as a person who was untainted and unaffected by culture, a being superior by its closeness to nature, a "force of nature" (Naturwesen), as he called her; this imagery too, which refers again to indestructibility, perhaps facilitated cohabitation.

It is remarkable that in Goethe's letters to Christiane even before Caroline Ulrich's secretaryship no sexual allusions can be found, although Christiane was at times relatively free in her letters, reporting on matters of menstruation and probably referring to the male genital under the euphemism of "Mr. Nicefoot" [Herr Schönfuss]. One is entitled to conclude that even in his relationship to Christiane Goethe did not entirely discard his sexual inhibitions. The fear of destroying the woman by the sexual act, though weakened, had not vanished.

But did the same thing happen with respect to his fear of being harmed by passionate love (castration fear)? In the elegy "Amyntas" (*Soph.* I, *1*:288–89) there is to be found, I think, the mechanism by means of which Goethe had, at least in part, conquered this fear. Before discussing its content the biographical background will be considered. It was written on September 19, 1797, when

---

[40] Countess Christine Reinhard (d. 1815), wife of Count Karl Friedrich Reinhard (1761–1837), who became acquainted with Goethe in 1807. An important correspondence developed from their friendship. The quoted passage is from a letter from the Countess to her mother shortly after she made Goethe's acquaintance.

[41] [Zuerst muss ich Ihnen sagen, dass von allen meinen Werken meine Frau keine Zeile gelesen hat. Das Reich des Geistes hat kein Dasein für sie, für die Haushaltung ist sie geschaffen. Hier überhebt sie mich aller Sorgen, hier lebt und webt sie; es ist ihr Königreich.] (250, *1*:498)

[42] See Goethe's letters of September 22, 1809, Christiane's letter of July 11, 1810, Goethe's diary of February to April, 1811. Christiane was also familiar with Goethe's dramatic works, for she was a passionate theatergoer and, therefore, never missed any performance of a Goethe play.

Goethe was on his third journey to Switzerland,[43] which took him away from Christiane for several months. Originally the plan had been to go to Italy. Christiane had vigorously opposed his going so far away. This was, I believe, the only situation that she absolutely refused to tolerate. Evidently the idea of his traveling that far was too closely associated in her mind with a permanent loss. Goethe himself may have felt similarly. In his letter to Christiane from Zurich on October 25, 1797, he wrote: "It is indeed a bad thing: once one has left, it is almost as if he were dead."[44] Moreover it is evident from Goethe's letters to Christiane of that time that he felt a strong longing to be back home with her, which may at times have interfered with his full enjoyment of the journey.

Goethe's elegy "Amyntas" is historically connected with the eleventh elegy or bucolic idyl of Theocritus, the famous poet of the Hellenistic period (third century B.C.). This elegy was directed towards the physician Nicias, who had recommended as the only cure or remedy for love renunciation and occupation with the Muses.[45] It begins: "It seems there's no medicine for love, Nicias . . . but only the Pierian Maids," and ends, after setting forth Polyphemus' love song, with: "Thus did Polyphemus tend his love-sickness with music, and got more comfort thereout than he could have had for any gold" (120, pp. 141, 147). Goethe starts as follows:

> Nicias, excellent man, you physician of body and soul!
> Sick, that I am indeed; but your cure is hard.[46]

Amyntas recognizes that Nicias's advice has its merits, but he has lost the will power to live up to it. Amyntas cannot refute Nicias and tells himself all the harsh words which he learned from him. Yet in vain! Does not the storm rage and the sun set? And thus nature tells him:

> You, too, Amyntas, are
> Bowed down by the strict law of inflexible powers.[47]

And then Amyntas proceeds to tell what he had learned from an apple tree which bore only little fruit since ivy had profusely taken root in it. (The plan for the elegy sprang into being when Goethe on his trip saw a tree embraced by ivy; see *Soph.* III, 2:153.) He tried to cut away the ivy in order to restore the tree's full productivity, but the tree besought him not to proceed:

[43] Cf. above, p. 550, for the homosexual meaning Switzerland had, in my opinion, in Goethe's imagery.

[44] [Freylich ists eine böse Sache, wenn man einmal weggeht, so ists beynahe, als wenn man tod wäre.]

[45] However, it is possible that this idyl was meant as a letter from Theocritus to Nicias, with whom he had studied medicine in his youth, reporting the consolation Theocritus himself had found in the Muses. See 120, pp. xii, 139.

[46] [Nikias, trefflicher Mann, du Arzt des Leibs und der Seele!/ Krank, ich bin es fürwahr; aber dein Mittel ist hart.]

[47] [. . . auch du bist, Amyntas,/ Unter das strenge Gesetz ehrner Gewalten gebeugt.]

Together with this network,
Which you destroy amain, you cruelly tear the life out of me.[48]

Then the tree refers to the ivy as something which he himself has fed and nourished. And should he not love the plant that needs him alone?

Nourishment she takes from me; what I would need, she enjoys,
And so she sucks out the marrow, sucks out the soul from me.[49]

The dangerous guest seizes half of the succor which the strong roots send upward, and nothing reaches the top.

Yes, it is the traitress! She wheedles me out of life and goods,
She wheedles me out of strength to strive, wheedles me out of hope.[50]

But the tree feels only her and enjoys the choking embrace. Likewise Amyntas prays Nicias to hold back his knife and to spare the poor one who, willingly coerced, pines away in loving pleasures.

Sweet is every lavishness; oh, let me enjoy the pleasantest!
Who surrenders to love, is he sparing with life?[51]

Although some authors believe that this poem is not referrable to Goethe's relationship to Christiane, and others, like Gräf, interpret it as an expression of the grief he occasionally felt in his relationship with her,[52] and Hitschmann cites it as a testimony of Goethe's castration fear (298, p. 61), nevertheless I think that it exhibits a mechanism by means of which Goethe overcame his castration fear, and that it also expresses—though indirectly—the highest praise of Christiane.

In order to do justice to this poem other details of the situation in which it originated have to be considered. It was written when Goethe was moving in a direction away from Christiane, at a time when he felt guilty over leaving her alone in order to satisfy his own strivings for pleasure by seeking out the company of his friend Meyer, to whom he had strong homosexual ties. In the poem Goethe accepts and acknowledges the sexual drive as an inflexible law which no one can escape. Sexual desire is no longer viewed as extraneous or alien but as a part of nature. True, the fulfillment of that urge is pictured as reducing

[48] [. . . du reissest mit diesem Geflechte,/ Das du gewaltig zerstörst, grausam das Leben mir aus.]

[49] [Nahrung nimmt sie von mir; was ich bedürfte, geniesst sie,/ Und so saugt sie das Mark, sauget die Seele mir aus.]

[50] [Ja, die Verrätherin ist's! sie schmeichelt mir Leben und Güter,/ Schmeichelt die strebende Kraft, schmeichelt die Hoffnung mir ab.]

[51] [Süss ist jede Verschwendung; o, lass mich der schönsten geniessen!/ Wer sich der Liebe vertraut, hält er sein Leben zu Rath?]

[52] 252, *1*:liii. "We divine something of the deep sadness of the feeling of isolation which must sometimes have seized the great man."

man's virility and creativity, but this loss has acquired a definitely maternal coloring. It is visualized as a life-giving and life-preserving force or sacrifice, not in the sense of leading to new life in the form of a child but in the meaning of giving life to the woman who loves man and is loved by man. It is noteworthy that here the artist's maternal creative power is secondarily turned towards the female companion and the sexual object is visualized as a product of the creative (maternal) man. I say secondarily because we have to assume that the creativity of the artistic genius is a derivative of a maternally creative force which is now diverted away from the formation of works of art towards giving life to a woman by means of the sexual act. Furthermore, Amyntas (Goethe) pictures obedience to Nicias's advice of sexual abstinence as an act of castration—with the removal of the ivy the life of the tree is simultaneously destroyed. The idea that renunciation of genital activity amounts to a form of castration is, of course, a potent antidote against the castration fears that lead to abstention from cohabitation. It is also remarkable that the initial imagery of castration (cutting the ivy in order to liberate the tree) is directed against the symbol of the female, that is to say, intercourse is no longer visualized as an act of destruction of the female body but the act of withholding intercourse has acquired the meaning of an aggression against the female body.

We notice here a further progress in the understanding of female needs; intercourse is accepted as a process by which woman's life is enriched. The threat to man is outweighed by the enormous pleasure premium provided by the feeling of giving life to a human being and by the physical repercussion of pleasure derived from the sexual act. What Goethe really intimates in the poem is that castration is unavoidable whether man renounces intercourse or indulges in it. So why should he abstain, since abstention deprives man of pleasure and makes the woman wither away? The situation set forth by means of these symbols represents a general aspect of the relationship of the sexes. We find an intimation of what I have previously described in the lives of compulsive personalities as the surrender of their instinctualness and passionateness to a woman, who is clinically more often than not a psychopathic personality. The sexual functions are unevenly distributed in the symbolic frame. The man gives everything and the woman enjoys everything. The woman is all sex and the man all kindness. Sexual passion is enjoyed through beholding the sexual release in the partner. The man's own excitement is denied and his pleasure is declared to be gained mainly by empathy. The incapacity of the ego to surrender to instinctiveness is overcome by enjoying the sexual surrender in the female partner. The circle is closed by the fantasy that the partner's passionate discharges are accomplished through male activity. To a certain extent the castration complex is presented here in unusually strong terms, for it is claimed that a human being without a penis cannot live at all unless it is given life by masculine powers. Yet, strangely enough, this inflated castration complex also harbors its solution, namely the requirement that it is the male duty to provide the female with life. Thus Goethe did not truly overcome his castration fears in his love of Christiane but he found countermeasures (a) by a full identification with the image of the phallic mother, (b) by oral regression, (c) by integration of phallic needs as a part of nature, (d) by substituting for the imagery of castration that occurs in the course of cohabitation, the imagery of castration caused by exposure to ungratified genital needs.

It is further remarkable that in this solution there was also contained a soothing of Goethe's envy and jealousy of female creativity. Since the relationship of the tree to the ivy is a maternal one, the simile amounts to saying, "Women may boast of their childbearing capacity; their existence is made possible only by men's being *their* mothers." Thus the child becomes indirectly a product of the male. In the symbolism used in the elegy there is no place for the child at all, for the female is completely absorbed in her relationship to the male and thus acquires all the earmarks of a child.

I believe this process was greatly facilitated by Christiane's childlike nature, which manifests itself abundantly in her letters. She put herself on a plane with her little son, August. Thus in her letter of April 6, 1799, she wrote Goethe how she and August, as they lay in bed, argued about who would greet Goethe first upon his return to Weimar (252, *1*:245) and shortly after (November 23, 1799) she complained that August daily showed more reasoning power "so that I am often frightened by him" (252, *1*:275–76). This attitude comes to the fore very clearly when Christiane calls herself and August "your children," which Goethe also did when writing about both of them. Thus Christiane was for Goethe a kind of Mignon, though not a mysterious romantic Mignon but a kind of astute, uncorrupted child with a live, appealing intelligence. It was probably this kind of intelligence that was meant in the following account by Knebel's wife:

> Goethe often told us that when he was preoccupied with something in his mind and the ideas pressed too hard upon him, he then sometimes got too far off and could not find his way back by his own effort; how he then went to her [Christiane] and simply laid the matter before her and often could not help being astounded at how she, with her simple, natural astuteness, always knew at once the right way out, and he already owed her a good deal in this respect.[53]

Yet although the child-father (mother) relationship was quite pronounced in their relationship this did not show up directly in their letters, except for epithets

___

[53] [Goethe hat uns oft gesagt, dass, wenn er mit einer Sache in seinem Geiste beschäftigt wäre, sich die Ideen zu stark bei ihm drängten, er dann manchmal zu weit käme und sich selbst nicht mehr zurechtfinden könne, wie er dann zu ihr ginge, ihr einfach die Sache vorlege und oft erstaunen müsste, wie sie mit ihrem einfachen, natürlichen Scharfblicke immer gleich dass Richtige herauszufinden wisse und er ihr in dieser Beziehung schon manches verdanke.] (62, p. 269)

such as "my children." As I said before, the letters sound like communications between two equal partners, and if we did not know about Goethe and Christiane from other sources the child relation could easily be overlooked. This I believe is an additional sign that Goethe had here achieved a conflict-free relationship by projecting into his spouse the image of child, a projection greatly facilitated by Christiane's personality.

What was Christiane's personality type? Her contemporaries and later interpreters have tried repeatedly to give a picture of her that would agree with the diagnosis of psychopathic personality. Her many illegitimate children, her long common-law marriage, her excessive drinking,[54] her insatiable dancing, sometimes until the early morning hours and with men much younger than she, and other factors might be cited in justification of such a diagnosis. If we examine the fact of Christiane's drinking, for example, we must concede that its clinical evaluation does not lead to this diagnosis. She drank much, without doubt, but I do not think that she drank more than Goethe himself and rather believe that it was far less. Furthermore, we must consider that in Christiane's time—as can be seen from some of her letters—a belief in the salubrious effect of alcohol was far more widespread than today. No incident is recorded of pathological inebriation—in contrast to August von Goethe—and intake of alcohol does not seem to have led to any social dysfunctions. The diagnosis of her terminal illness is quite questionable and there is no strict reason for bringing it into connection with her drinking habits.

Still, even though an examination singly of each trait in Christiane's personality make-up presumably would not confirm the diagnosis of psychopathic personality, one feels nevertheless that her life was pervaded by some factor of instability. Furthermore, in some instances latent pathology of a parent becomes manifest in the children (not necessarily by inheritance). The fact that August von Goethe very definitely showed traits of psychopathy would not of itself make me feel that we are dealing with a latent form of his disorder in Christiane but it certainly must command attention.

As is well known, adults in their choice of love-objects tend toward types of personalities that were of importance in their childhood. Thus it is highly probable that Goethe's selection of Charlotte von Stein followed the sister type. What is remarkable, however, is that these choices frequently show a personality relief more distinctly than was the case in the original. Thus from the pathology in the son-in-law one may often draw conclusions as to what the latent conflicts had been in a woman's father. It is my impression that August von Goethe followed the maternal type in making Ottilie von Pogwisch his wife. And she later showed the classical features of the psychopathic personality (see 305). Thus I believe that, oddly enough, we may from the study of Ottilie's personality draw the conclusion that Christiane actually harbored a psychopathic personality. Ac-

---

[54] I agree with Etta Federn (134, *passim*) who tries to prove that the commonly encountered description of Christiane as suffering from chronic alcoholism is not correct.

tually Christiane was much sicker than one can prove from the record of her manifest behavior. The greatness and affection of the man whom she loved protected her, I believe, against severe manifestations of her disorder; I speculate that if she had had to live under psychologically less propitious conditions her clinical record would have been quite different. Thus it can be said that she was essentially an impulse-ridden personality, that strivings for gratification prevailed in her over control, sacrifice, or renunciation. Fortunately for her and for Goethe the gratifications she sought fitted halfway into the requirements of society, although occasionally she came close to transgressing the tolerable. One may be sure it would have been better if after the age of forty she had dropped the practice of dancing. A woman of forty, I have the impression, was expected at that time to comport herself as a somewhat staid matron and her appearance at public balls unescorted by her husband was considered undignified. Yet by indulging in that craving she was not really behaving in a dissocial way and certainly she was not doing anybody any harm.

If we take the example of her passion for dancing as representative of a good many other features we may conclude that she was the antitype of Charlotte von Stein. This, I believe, is the salient point. As Goethe needed Charlotte von Stein in his pre-Italian period, just so urgently did he after his return from Italy need the opposite type of woman, whom he found in Christiane.[55] In almost all respects—as could easily be demonstrated point for point—Christiane was the counterimage of Charlotte von Stein. This makes good sense. Goethe had acquired mastery over himself during the pre-Italian decade. Despite occasional emotional break-throughs he integrated this mastery and he now needed a companion in whom he could enjoy exactly what he had renounced. Christiane's passionate temperament was for Goethe a necessary complement which facilitated his own maintaining a state of mastery. The basic equation between the ego and its emotions was now changed in Goethe inasmuch as secondary processes prevailed. In Christiane he could enjoy a mode of existence in which this basic equation was the opposite and quite reminiscent of his own bygone days.

To deplore the fact that Christiane did not partake in Goethe's mental greatness or to blame her for it is totally to misunderstand the whole situation. Goethe had a wide circle at his disposal from which to get stimulation. A sophisticated and highly differentiated wife who participated in his productions would never have conceded him the creative isolation he needed or the fervid relationships to women who inspired in him new outbreaks of poetic creativity. Women in whom reality, fantasy, and projection were fused into just that configuration which he needed for his sporadic spells of inspiration would have been com-

---

[55] If Goethe's selection of Charlotte von Stein followed the sister type we may see in Goethe's mother the *imago* of Christiane. There certainly is a similarity in character structure between the two. The switch from the sister *imago* to that of the mother, probably repeating the developmental sequence in reverse order, gives occasion for far-reaching speculations.

pletely out of the question as companions of his everyday life. Thus I conclude that Christiane was the ideally fitted companion for Goethe; she gave him the maximum of pleasure and joy a genius is permitted to taste during his earthly days and never encumbered his genius creativity. Goethe in his choice of Christiane followed the ideal type of experience that is almost regularly encountered in his life.

Yet the fact remains that Goethe lived for seventeen years in a relationship that was against the laws of his country, the prescriptions of his own superego, and the moral and ethical precepts of his group. It was not a rebellious step directed against the group, a kind of protest in order to introduce a betterment by arousing public attention. It was a step that his own conscience did not approve of and thus we have to deal with the question of the morality—or immorality—of the genius. In what follows I do not introduce the moral and ethical standard as an absolute one but as a code of behavior that society expects its members to live up to, and which the individual citizen accepts as potentially, if not actually, binding.

The question of Goethe's infringement upon such a standard comes even more strikingly to the fore in Goethe's relationship to his son. While Christiane, in the last analysis, did not suffer any serious harm through Goethe's breach of morals this cannot be said of his son, August. When he had to live among the children of Weimar's elite but was frowned upon because of his illegitimate birth—legally corrected only when he was eleven—we can easily imagine the many injuries he had to suffer in his early years. Moreover, Goethe does not seem to have interfered with Christiane's indulging the boy in wine, which she let him partake of in great quantities. From Bode's biography (50) one gets the impression that August, though of course in no way approaching the genius of his father, was a man of above average intelligence and with ample resources to have been able to live a satisfactory and constructive life. His career at the court of Weimar was halfway successful, but as a human being he was utterly ruined by a maximum dependency, mental as well as emotional, on his father. Even when he was a married man and father of two children he reported every morning to his father and was unable to keep a secret from him. Goethe used him as a welcome agent to take care of all the unpleasant chores that would have distracted him from his main pursuits. Thus August kept order in his father's voluminous collections, regulated the household, and appeared as his father's representative at official occasions, reciting the poem his father had composed for the occasion. His development was quite promising until an event, enforced by his father, threw a shadow upon him (this at least is the impression obtained from Bode's biography). When Germany's youth volunteered in the war of liberation August too joined the ranks, but Goethe arranged that his son should not participate in actual warfare but stay in Weimar in a soft job free from any danger. August was jeered at and humiliated by the returning warriors and a duel over the matter would very probably have taken place if Goethe had not again interfered. From then on August's psychopathology seems to have taken on serious forms.

The possibility of psychopathy in the case of his mother was discussed earlier, but there is no doubt about the diagnosis in the case of August's wife, Ottilie. She was gifted, ambitious, impulse-ridden and without restraints. August behaved towards her in a way reminiscent of his father's dealings with Christiane: always forgiving, protecting, reconciling. But Ottilie was not the woman to appreciate August's kindness. Constantly dissatisfied, always longing for other men, eternally feeling frustrated, she undermined the little support August might have derived from marriage. Three children issued from the marriage. The two boys were captivated by their grandfather's charm and wooing and August was again the one to hold the place for his father. His children really were Goethe's children. The extent of his tragic unhappiness, his restlessness, his sensitivity, his incapacity to bear life at all towards the end of his existence, are well documented. Chronic alcoholism became August's way of escape. After an accident at the age of forty, he died in Rome two years prior to his illustrious father's demise, and was buried close to the pyramid of Cestius where Goethe while in Rome once expressed the wish to be buried. Thus his was a sham life, for he was devoured by his father, who appropriated life wherever it was available to draw it into the incessantly grinding jaws of his infinite productivity.[56]

We confront here a very serious problem. No man who is endowed with intelligence and originality ever went through life without doing some harm in addition to the many good deeds he may have done. Many acts of destruction must certainly have dotted Goethe's path. But even detailed scrutiny of the record of his life does not show any manifestation of serious destructiveness. Of course he did many things—aside from his common-law marriage—which did not meet with the approbation of his contemporaries or posterity.[57] To cite only

[56] One grasps fully the tragedy to which the son of a genius is subjected only when one stands before August von Goethe's grave at the Cestius pyramid and reads the inscription *"Goethe filius Patri antevertens obiit anno XL"* (Goethe's son preceding his father died in his fortieth year). Here he is deprived of his very name and his death is viewed as significant only for the moment it fills in his father's life. This inscription epitomizes the attitude society takes towards the son, and at the same time embraces an aspect of the hidden attitude of the father. For the forfeited independence, individuality, and personal identity—forced upon him by the way the world undermines his morale and, more basically, by the fact that his father's crushing greatness inevitably strips him of an appropriate figure with which to identify—the son receives meager compensation in the impoverished niche the annals of history reserve for him through the mere fact of his having been associated with the genius. Here there should be mentioned in passing the different effect the genius often has on his female progeny.

[57] I do not consider here, of course, those contemporary accusations which were at times quite grave, but which are now known to have been unsubstantiated, such as Klopstock's reproach of debauchery, which allegedly occurred during the early years of Goethe's stay in Weimar; also, a further accusation that Goethe perjured himself when he denied author-

one, when he prepared the last edition of his works he tried to secure for his progeny a stable income and therefore petitioned the government of the German League to prohibit the pirating of his works and to grant him a copyright. Börne castigated Goethe very severely for not having demanded this prerogative for all German authors, who were threatened with financial ruin by the absence of legal protection (see 522, p. 107). To be sure, if Goethe had made this matter of his own advantage an occasion for taking a step towards the general protection of all German writers he would have been functioning as a kind of liberal reformer or even revolutionary. No doubt to demand a just right for a whole group is morally superior to demanding that right for oneself alone. But Goethe was not in these latter years a revolutionary or a vigorous social reformer. His relative selfishness in this instance did not, however, actively harm anyone. Moreover, the old man had no hope of any great personal advantage from a favorable decision upon his petition, for he himself was well provided and knew that he would not live much longer. His motive was an unselfish one in the service of his progeny, although the unselfishness was limited to a small circle with which direct "selfish" identification was possible. I cite this example as one of many that could be used to show that in Goethe's life—as in any other—there were many actions that can be criticized if a particular and particularly strict yardstick is applied.

The two instances above, his illegitimate relationship with Christiane and the indirect ruination of his son, fall into a different category. They cannot be justified, particularly the latter, whatever moral yardstick is applied, although in the relationship to his son no purposeful conscious act of destruction occurred. Nevertheless, a closer study of his relationship to August reveals that despite Goethe's undoubted affection, worry, and care, his unconscious aggression could not be deflected and actually reached its goal in the early, tragic downfall of the young man.

The study of the relationship between the genius and progeny has received new impetus from the Sterbas' book *Beethoven and His Nephew* (508). The authors go to great lengths to prove that Beethoven had a psychosis and that the basis of all of his recriminations against his nephew was delusional. In my opinion the psychological problem would be exactly the same if Beethoven's nephew had been a scoundrel and a good-for-nothing. Thus, Goethe did not accuse his son of any misdemeanor and there are no psychotic symptoms observable in his direct dealings with his son, yet nevertheless we discover in this area of his existence a constellation that—though different in the form of its manifestation—is essentially the same as that described by the Sterbas in Beethoven's life. Goethe's psychosis started shortly after his son's birth and was attached to scientific content. Thus the father–son relationship was

---

ship of a farce which ridiculed Wieland. The play was actually written by Goethe's friend Heinrich Leopold Wagner, but it is almost certain that Goethe would not have been called to Weimar if the widespread allegation of his authorship had been given credence there.

kept free of the signs of a manifest psychosis. Nevertheless, August von Goethe suffered his martyrdom and died in the most tragic circumstances, and he was probably far more profoundly hurt and damaged by Goethe than Beethoven's nephew was by his uncle. Why did an equivalent process show up in such unmitigated fashion in Beethoven's life and why was it so well covered up in Goethe's? If Goethe had not been able to work his way out of the *Sturm und Drang* period, and the process of personality reorganization that took place during the pre-Italian years had not occurred, his relationship to August might easily have taken a turn similar to that observed in Beethoven's case. Yet, it may be added, he probably would never have had intercourse, as Beethoven probably never had, and would not have begotten a child. Beethoven preserved up to his death a structural relationship to emotion such as we studied in Goethe in the period before he came to Weimar: the unopposed spread of emotion, engulfing the whole ego, which had to bow powerlessly before it. What appeared as dissociality, rudeness, brutality, in Beethoven's everyday life was the cornerstone of his creativity. A mastered emotion would never have led to those musical compositions which we admire.

The problem we confront here has the following origin. The response of society to a genius is almost invariably divided. Some of his contemporaries admire him; others feel provoked, and reject or even persecute him, and attempt to justify their negative response by referring, among other things, to unethical or immoral actions, which—also most invariably—can be discovered in the life of the genius. After his death a process of idealization gradually transforms the image of the genius into one that conforms to the wishes of those who delight in the beauty of his creations. The psychology of society's response to genius is of no concern here for its own sake; I only wish to sketch an outline of this reaction as a reminder that there is no doubt that a marked discrepancy exists between what society would like to believe about a genius—particularly of bygone days—and what the scholar actually finds out in the course of his research. The relative immorality of the genius is a topic that ought perhaps be discussed only by experts. Man, disillusioned in his most tender expectations by the emergence of science, deprived of the consolation of religion, has really little left to believe in. The only radiant illusions that still remain are the over-whelmingly beautiful creations of the few geniuses that have so far walked the earth. Quite understandably, it is reasoned that the beautiful can originate only from the beautiful. And who would like whenever he sees a healthy beautiful baby to recall St. Augustine's depressing statement: *"Intra feces et urinas nascimur"*? Yet it is true too of the products of male creativity—at least of such men as Goethe and Beethoven—that they are born *intra feces et urinas*. Much as I wish that the illusion of the higher morality of the genius should for social reasons be preserved, I also believe—for reasons presently to be stated— that the structure of the personality of the genius has to be investigated what-ever immorality may be uncovered in the course of the inquiry.

It is reasonable to raise the question of whether a society wants angels or artistic geniuses. It is perhaps a disquieting thought that Goethe, who lived in an illegitimate relationship with a woman and had her pregnant five times without an attempt at hushing it up, would never have been permitted in a modern, industrialized republic, such as this country is, to hold a position of public power and authority such as he held in Weimar.[58] Yet the station he held in Weimar was as indispensable to his creativity as we should readily acknowledge food and a domicile are for a creative artist. From this point of view it becomes important for society to take notice that the artistic genius must necessarily be immoral in certain areas if he is to be creative. Whatever legendary elements there may be in the traditional tale that Phidias was twice guilty of stealing money, it contains a deep psychological truth. Whether this is true of all artistic geniuses I do not know. It is possible that in periods when the genius did not experience himself as a separate individualized unit, quite different laws governed the creative process. What the psychology was of those incredible Romanesque and early Gothic sculptors whose names we do not know but whose artistic genius still adorns the cathedrals cannot be fathomed. Perhaps there have been times when the creative genius, unburdened by the desire to pour *his* feelings, *his* conflicts, *his* personality, into his creations, was agitated by motives that did not impose on him the necessity of discharging destruction to the extent that we observe in other historical periods. This is a moot question. But the geniuses whose lives are sufficiently documented do show it surprisingly often. Even Mozart, whose life falls into an entirely different category from that of Goethe or Beethoven, is suggestive of the same problem when the famous letters to Bäsle are recalled (401).

The findings of the Sterbas can be summarized in one statement: Beethoven wanted to devour his nephew. Whether we should regard this impulse as destructive or loving in its psychological meaning is questionable. In studying this impulse one almost feels inclined to think of Karl Abraham's "preambivalent phase" (2). Whatever its psychological meaning, its social effect was destructive, and ethical evaluations of actions are predominantly, though not exclusively, determined by their social effects. In Beethoven's case, the object he tried to devour fell into his hands by the accident of his brother's early death. But I am convinced he would have found an equivalent object if fate had not provided this one. The grave dilemma in which the artistic genius stands with regard to his object-relations is dealt with at a different place. Suffice it to say here that the genius must not indulge in the full pleasure of such a relationship but

[58] The detrimental effect of certain forms of democracy on artistic genius has been noticed by many. Cf. the following entry in Tolstoy's notebook for a possible explanation of what appears to be a paradox: "A man living under a despotic government, such as Turkey and Russia, may be more or less free, though he will be exposed to the violence of a rule in which he has no say, but a subject in a constitutional government, while always recognizing the lawfulness of the rule under which he finds himself, is always a slave" (499, p. 647).

has to destroy the object in order to preserve the full momentum of the creative process.[59] As a matter of fact we have seen that Goethe's artistic output decreased when his relationship to Charlotte von Stein became too intense, and the Sterbas point out the years of relative unproductiveness in Beethoven's life because of his dealings with his nephew. In the life of the genius the love-object is always sacrificed in favor of the artistic object which the genius intends to create. Amidst the terrible destruction Beethoven heaped upon his nephew there arise the *Missa Solemnis* and the Ninth Symphony and the later quartets. And only this counts in the eye of eternity. All the crimes a genius may commit pale and are forgotten and do not count if they served the aliveness of creation. The genius therefore cannot be immoral. Only the man of talent who metes out destruction by imitating the genius and whose creations are dispensable, can be immoral. In reading the Sterbas' book one feels their astonishment over Beethoven's crassness, but they do not emphasize that this was evidently a necessary part of the personality that was to be able to create his music. In Goethe the whole problem is veiled by his manners, erudition, and sophistication, but, strangely enough, August von Goethe had to die whereas Beethoven's nephew, despite an attempt at suicide, survived his uncle. At one point the Sterbas perhaps do Beethoven an actual injustice. They marvel at the nephew's good adjustment in later life and attribute it either to constitutional factors or to "the good foundation of emotional stability" (508, p. 300) which he received from his mother, whom Beethoven so brutally maligned. Yet the third alternative they do not mention: that, despite all of Beethoven's destructive actions, his nephew felt throughout the years that he was infinitely loved by him, a love which made him suffer and which for evident reasons he could not endure, but yet a love which despite all temporary tragedies resulted in the education of an able citizen who later filled his mediocre place to perfection. Goethe's subterranean aggression against his son, which was masked by gentleness, love, and affection, had far more serious effects than Beethoven's apparent hostility; August—except for one incident[60]—found no situation in which he was able to turn against his father and free himself of a domination that necessarily had to end in his downfall. If we rise above the transitory, how shall we decide? Do we seriously propose that Beethoven's nephew should have lived a happy childhood and adolescence but we ought to be without the *Missa* and the quartets? Should August von Goethe have lived to be seventy or eighty and have been spared his torments but we should be without *Dichtung und Wahrheit* and *Faust II?*

If we insist that the concept of morality so wholesomely applied to the life of the ordinary man must also be applied to the genius then we must strive

---

[59] This conflict, as is also discussed elsewhere (see Appendix U), necessarily breaks out with particular intensity when there is progeny or its equivalent.

[60] When Goethe wanted to remarry at the age of seventy-four some unpleasant scenes occurred between father and son.

actively for the suppression of talent in the young. The early appearance of talent announces the potential appearance of a genius, which in turn makes the prospect of destructive acts highly probable. The chance that this destruction will strike just one or a few of those objects that are closest to him is eminently great. Therefore I am convinced that society, which owes so much to the genius, has the duty to compensate particularly the genius's offspring for the deep injuries which he is bound to suffer.

A destructive process equivalent to that observed in the object-relations of the genius is encountered on a higher plane. Shakespeare's creativity made it impossible that great tragedy should ever again be written in the English language, and with Goethe German literature was brought to a close for all practical purposes. The genius realizes all the potentialities that are inherent in a certain artistic medium and therefore despite all the stimulating effects which he leaves to succeeding generations he more frequently than not stifles, at least in those that follow soon after him, a development into giants of like stature. This is why artistic geniuses appear serially and are not distributed uniformly throughout history (see 353). Goethe's destructive effect was particularly great in this respect because, in all branches of literature except comedy, he went to the very limit of what can be created in the German language.

The direct manifestations of destruction in his personal life are much less. One has to penetrate far below the surface to find that which was quite open to inspection in Beethoven's life. Goethe owed this relative good luck partly to Charlotte von Stein's influence and the reorganization of his personality that she brought about, and partly to Christiane, who was so constituted and behaved in such a way as permitted him to keep the center of his creativity outside of their relationship. Thus the unavoidable destructive side effects attached to acts of creativeness were diverted from the center in which the realistic life of the citizen and husband, Goethe, his bourgeois existence so to speak, took place. Yet the relationship to offspring is an area of such delicacy, a focus of formidable conflict-arousing forces of such magnitude, that even this infinitely wise man could not make his way across it without leaving the trace of unrequited wrong.

Appendix R

Supplementary Notes on the Relationship of Goethe and Karl August

A COMPREHENSIVE INQUIRY into the relationship between the genius and his Duke, the like of which will hardly be found in the annals of history, would fill a book. In this supplement I wish to summarize aspects previously mentioned and also to discuss briefly a new period in their friendship which I shall follow up only as far as 1790.

The beginning of their friendship stood under the sign of the *Sturm und Drang*. Both were enchanted by each other from their first encounter on. They fitted each other like hand and glove. It was not only a matter of personalities but likewise of circumstances: the young prince on the verge of taking over the government of his principality, and the famous poet, seven years his senior, ready to put his genius in the service of the prince's welfare and future. They were mutually in need of each other and if ever the biological principle of symbiosis can be applied to the relationships of adults this was an ideal example.

The clear-cut delineation of this initial phase, which requires no interpretation, is somewhat darkened by the obscureness of Goethe's relationship to the Duchess. As will be recalled, I drew the conclusion that Goethe was in love with her. The record does not demonstrate this beyond doubt. Devotion, interest, loyalty, affection, and concern on Goethe's side are evident. If love was present it had to be kept a secret and it is not surprising that the scholar is limited to circumstantial evidence. The few items of such evidence I have cited, to my ear speak strongly the voice of a conscious and intense love. The psychological origin of that love is, of course, still more difficult to unravel. Did it stand as a defense against the strong homosexual implication of the friendship that drew the two men to each other? Was it the result of extreme jealousy of her as a competitor for his friend's affections? Was Goethe's love for the Duke also a defense against the temptation that the Duchess spelled for him? All this remains unclear. Whatever the truth, Goethe preserved for the rest of his days a strong feeling for the Duchess, and in *Tasso,* I believe we may be sure, he expressed a very personal problem which takes us directly back to her.

In the first phase of his friendship with Karl August, Goethe seems to have been of greater psychological importance to the Duke than was his Duchess. Notwithstanding the incompatibility of the Duke and the Duchess I am not sure that that marriage would not have worked out better if Goethe had been absent from the court of Weimar during these early years. To be sure, he exerted great effort to bring those two as close together as possible and to remove the obstacles that seemed to keep them apart, but I wonder whether he was aware to what extent even his mere presence was bound to divert the prince from his spouse. From time to time we have noticed rough spots in Goethe's personality that often made enduring friendships difficult, but we can be certain that he consistently showed his best side when he was with the Duke. Aside from his personal liking for him, the awe and respect of the commoner for his sovereign automatically held any manifestations of ambivalence to the unavoidable minimum. If one tries to imagine Goethe actively striving to be engaging, charming, bewitching, almost seductive, one may get an inkling of the fascination that must have emanated from this man, who was by nature a constant firework, bristling with wit, fantasy, ingenuity, *esprit,* and zest of life. What woman could have competed successfully with his constant presence? Perhaps it could have been accomplished by a woman who knew how to attract the fiery young prince over and over again by strong sensuous gratifications in the sexual sphere. But Louise was inhibited, seclusive, a woman who herself had to be awakened by understanding guidance and gentleness in order to find herself and to evolve the extremely fine qualities that were dormant in her. Goethe quickly recognized them and she probably was able much more easily to reveal them to him than to her impatient and impetuous husband. I surmise that she had a strong feeling for Goethe and was afraid of it and therefore tended more towards Herder, in whose company she felt more secure than in that of the man to whom she probably felt more attracted.

Be this as it may, the Duke was completely enraptured by Goethe. We see them together most of the time. When the Duke is sick or injured Goethe nurses him; when the Duke goes hunting Goethe is his companion; he reads to him and he administers his dukedom for him. The Duke's whole existence is channelized through Goethe's life. Yet Goethe's function as an agent of the Duke's pleasure is probably of less importance than his function as an ego-ideal. Goethe felt responsible, as the Duke's mentor, for the prince's development, for his present and future stature as a monarch. The unconscious background of this feeling of responsibility has been discussed. He suffered because of the Duke's many weaknesses, but there is no indication that he ever lowered his standards to that of the ingratiating courtier who values security and advantage over honesty. Whatever formal appearance their relationship may have taken the broad stream of mutual feelings for each other as human beings remains undisputed. From Goethe's letter to Charlotte von Stein we know the course his growing ambivalence towards the Duke took. This ambivalence was never, I am sure, expressed in its true form to the Duke. I assume that he was sensitive enough to feel that things had changed between him and Goethe. However, he need not have experienced this as a consequence of Goethe's way of feeling about him but may have felt it as a welcome change befitting his growing maturity and strivings for independence. I have tried to show that Goethe, Charlotte von Stein, and the Duke formed a triangular relationship. I have further tried to show in what way Goethe's feelings about the Duke—aside from reality factors—were correlated to the vicissitudes of his relationship to Charlotte von Stein. The double aspect inherent in the Duke's position as pupil and master (the reality factor suggesting simultaneously the younger brother and the father) carried a certain uncertainty into Goethe's relationship, which enforced the simultaneous activation of contrary attitudes, not to speak of the unconscious factors involved. The fact that the Duke could serve as an object of Goethe's active as well as passive unconscious homosexuality made him an important part of that triangle. Charlotte von Stein became a unified object inasmuch as she gradually absorbed the images of all other love-objects. The Duke, because of his double significance to Goethe, was perhaps destined to play an equivalent role with regard to homosexual libido. However, Charlotte von Stein, because of her great importance as a superego representative, also absorbed much of the homosexual libido.

Yet, though the Duke could not by his direct personal contact contribute as much as Charlotte von Stein to the reorganization of Goethe's personality, one must attribute to him an indirectly indispensable role. First, he was Charlotte von Stein's sovereign and I have repeatedly stressed that Goethe's sacrifices for the Duke and the principality stood in a strong associative connection with the beloved woman. This, in turn, facilitated the healing of an old conflict brought about by mutually contradictory attitudes towards his father and mother. Concomitant with Goethe's mounting discontent with the Duke we noticed that Goethe occasionally used Charlotte von Stein as an agent to carry out aggressive impulses directed against him. The example I cited concerned Goethe's asking her to inform the Duke that he could not reckon on his friend's company any more on his many trips (cf. above, p. 970). Here Goethe repeated incidents which must have occurred with some frequency in his parental home.[1]

---

[1] I have not set forth in the text an incident that occurred when Goethe was visiting his parental home in the Duke's company in 1779–80 on the occasion of his second Swiss journey. The mental state of Goethe's father was evidently deteriorating at that time and a scene most humiliating to Goethe took place. In the midst of that visit Goethe's father—without provocation as far as is known—gave vent to an outbreak of savage anger against the Duke and declared he would never pay the expenses incurred by the visit of the Duke

Yet we noticed that at that time he shifted his positive feelings to Herder and towards the end of his pre-Italian period a new triangle was formed, with Herder replacing the Duke and at times threatening Charlotte von Stein's predominance more than the Duke did. Secondly, the Duke served to some extent as an outlet for those positive as well as negative impulses that might have injured Goethe's relationship to Charlotte von Stein. No doubt, some ambivalence which really was directed at Charlotte von Stein was occasionally displaced upon him and thus Goethe was able to maintain a smoother, more conflict-free relationship to Charlotte von Stein than would otherwise have been possible. I do not think that this is necessarily a contradiction of the function I have attributed to Charlotte von Stein of becoming a unified object, for I believe that those impulses that might have disturbed this process were wholesomely directed against the Duke. He served temporarily as an outlet for charges that could not find a constructive place within the relationship with the beloved woman. In turn we observed one situation in which Goethe's love for Charlotte von Stein received new impetus from the impact that the Duke's relationship with the Countess von Werthern had upon the poet. I refer to the episode that led to Goethe's asking Charlotte von Stein for the privilege of addressing her with the intimate *Du*. In that episode he apparently responded to an identification with the Duke and tried to put into reality something that he had observed in his princely friend. The oedipal structure of the triangle situation here becomes particularly conspicuous.

We know the reality factor that caused Goethe's disappointment in the Duke. The latter was determined to pursue his own way in high politics and to play a prominent role in the European balance of power. This implied the prospect of military adventures and was a blow to Goethe's ambition to get the Duke to concentrate upon the peaceful improvement of his dukedom. Here was an area in which the Duke was determined to satisfy his own ambition independently of Goethe's wishes and Goethe gradually recognized the limitation of his influence. A permanent alienation seemed unavoidable. Yet with Goethe's farewell to the Duke prior to his departure for Italy a new element becomes noticeable in his letters. It looks as if Goethe, on the verge of separating from the beloved woman, discovered anew the deep feeling of friendship and affection that tied him to this man, a feeling that blossomed richly during subsequent years. The fact that this wave of friendship started with the prospect of a separation may indicate that the homosexual danger was the principal factor that had previously created the ebb in their friendship. However, it is difficult here to keep reality factors and purely psychological factors apart.

---

and his entourage. This was all the more embarrassing since apparently this happened in the presence of the Duke's subordinates. The motivation for this outbreak is clear: the Duke had deprived the aging man of his son, his only solace. (Unbeknown to Goethe the Duke sent Goethe's mother a large sum of money after his return to Weimar.) The incident forcefully brings out reality factors that contributed to the way Goethe felt about his father.

The Duke was, after all, Goethe's sovereign, master, and employer. Goethe's journey to Italy had the function not only of breaking up his relationship with Charlotte von Stein but also of putting an end to his crushing administrative load. Could he have been sure beforehand that the Duke would not take it amiss when he absented himself from Weimar for a long period of time without prior discussion and permission? He had truly become the center of the whole governmental machinery and suddenly he behaved as if he expected it to run without him. To be sure, Goethe took his precautions and delegated his functions to others, and, indeed, no harm resulted to the principality from his absence, but he was justifiably in doubt as to whether the Duke would accept his secret arrangements favorably or turn in anger against his wayward friend. When, because of accidental circumstances, Goethe during his stay in Rome did not receive any communication from his master for a long time he seems to have become greatly worried and he appealed to his friends to intercede with the Duke on his behalf. However, Goethe's doubt as to his friend's understanding was not warranted and, although the Duke's letters from this period are not preserved, one recognizes from Goethe's answers that he had no reason to complain of feelings of resentment in his princely friend. Goethe's gratitude and relief were great. All this may suggest that he was forced to submit to the Duke by the need for employment, support, and economic survival. Though these and other reality factors are, to be sure, relevant, I am certain that personal feelings of affection were the primary motives.

During his stay in Italy Goethe made further progress in the modification of his homosexuality. The step forward in heterosexual adjustment, the genital gratification by intercourse, also had its effect on his homosexuality and he was able to accept latent, passive homosexuality without rebellion. He at last conceded to the Duke his right to a martial career and reconciled himself to the Duke's deviating from the ideal he had formed for his erstwhile pupil. Whether or not Goethe was right in having objected so long to the Duke's ambitions I do not know, but we may be sure that it was not only considerations having to do with the reality situation that were responsible for his objections. Apparently Goethe could not well bear his friend's aggressive, sadistic, destructive behavior (indelible accompaniments of the image of war or the military in general), that is to say, he could not tolerate in his friend that with which he could not identify. It must not be forgotten that the principal character in Goethe's first major play was a martial hero, Götz von Berlichingen. Possibly in those ambitions that were for such a long time objectionable to Goethe, the Duke expressed strivings that Goethe himself held in repression. Aggressiveness in a man may have had a frightening effect upon Goethe. From his Italian letters however, we see Goethe accept, even favor, the Duke's aggressiveness. It appears that he had become capable of loving a man on a less narcissistic level than before. Prior to this change the basic formula of his friendship was: "I love you for your outstanding qualities, which I too possess, perhaps even in a higher degree, or which I should like to possess," and he could, by and large, love a man only as far as he could identify with him. Part of this was observed in his difficulties with Lavater. Now, however, he could grant a male love-object its independent existence without feeling that it infringed his own feelings of affection.

Yet Goethe's personal conflicts, that is, the meaning that the Duke had for his unconscious, ought not make us overlook the Duke's personality. The Duke apparently really understood his friend, and therefore Goethe was spared all those tragic conflicts that so often separate the creative genius and his patron. The Duke intuitively grasped what Goethe needed and when Goethe submitted alternatives as to his own future in Weimar the Duke was ready at hand to select that which proved most constructive for Goethe. It speaks greatly in favor of the superior quality of the Duke that he never felt competitive in this relationship, never tried to exploit Goethe and never was exploited by him, but that each partner gave the other the best he could in terms of his endowment and social position.

During his stay in Italy Goethe made the Duke his adviser in sexual matters, as I explain in the text. One almost feels inclined to think that Goethe made an inner bargain of the following sort: "You will permit me to have sexual intercourse and I will permit you to indulge in bellicose pursuits." The time sequence does not favor this assumption inasmuch as Goethe seems to have reconciled himself with the Duke's peculiarities before he had his adventure with Faustina; but if we consider that Goethe consciously or preconsciously planned to have a sexual adventure during his journey it makes good sense that he first straightened out his relationship with the Duke. Another factor that may have to be considered as having a more than accidental connection with Goethe's delayed heterosexual adjustment is the fact that two of his best friends married late: Heinrich Meyer in 1803 at the age of forty-three, after having lived for almost ten years in Goethe's house; and Knebel, in 1798 at the age of fifty-three.

Goethe—probably without consciously intending to—endangered his friends' marriages. About the Duke and the Duchess I have already written. But it is striking that when Goethe took care of Herder's family during the latter's absence in Italy, Herder's wife wrote so much and so enthusiastically about Goethe that Herder became quite worried.[2] Herder's wife was a person who irritated Goethe and a conscious intention to court her is out of the question; nevertheless, this temporary complication in Herder's marriage, though quickly straightened out, reflects what was probably an important complex in Goethe. Woman was considered a factor that interfered with male friendship, and if it was a woman that was loved by a friend of Goethe's she aroused aggression in the form of conscious or unconscious strivings to estrange her from her spouse. Such a mechanism can be seen, almost openly, in Goethe's closest friend,

[2] See 51, *1*:421, for Caroline Herder's letter reassuring her husband of her faithfulness.

Knebel, who was an inveterate bachelor, but married the Duke's mistress when she returned to Weimar after having given birth to an illegitimate son (376, pp. 171–73). We may assume that fear of retaliation by the jealous male and defense against the aggression directed against male competitors that is implicit in choosing a spouse were also among the unconscious factors that held Goethe back in heterosexual pursuits. Certain passages in his correspondence with the Duke from Italy quoted earlier seem to confirm this aspect.

As observed before, Goethe's asserting himself sexually facilitated a conflict-free, smooth relationship with the Duke. The danger of homosexuality was reduced and his inner sense of self-sufficiency was fortified, so that he was later able to accept his friend as his master without internal rebellion. As soon as his forebodings as to the Duke's possible resentment were removed, letter after letter followed expressing gratitude, loyalty, and full devotion for the future. In his letter of May 27–29, 1787, from Naples, this culminated in the following response to the Duke's granting him all the privileges he wanted after his return to Weimar:

And therefore take my best thanks for your intentions in wishing so generously to relieve me. As our matters now stand you can do so without disadvantage to affairs, indeed I will become more to you than I often have been up to now if you let me do only what no one but me can do and assign the rest to others. My relationship to [official] affairs arose from my personal [relationship] to you; now, after so many years, let a new relationship to you arise out of the hitherto-existing official relationship. I am ready for each and all, where[ever] and how[ever] you will want to use me. Ask me about the symphony you intend to play; I will be glad at any time to state my opinion, thus also my personal relationship to Schmidt[3] will put me in a position to cooperate in all matters in accordance with your wishes. Already I see how this journey has benefited me, how it has enlightened me and gladdened my existence. As you have sustained me up to now, care for me further and do me more good than I can myself, than I dare wish or ask. Give me to myself, to my fatherland, give me again to you yourself that I may start a new life, and a new life with you! I lay my whole destiny trustingly in your hands. I have seen such a great and beautiful piece [of the] world and the upshot is that I want to live only with you and in your country. If I can do so less loaded with details, which I was not born for, then I can live to your happiness and that of many people.[4]

[3] Johann Cristoph Schmidt (1728–1807) succeeded Goethe in the Privy Council.

[4] [Und darum nehmen Sie den besten Danck für Ihre Gesinnungen, dass Sie mich so gütig erleichtern wollen. Wie jetzt unsre Sachen stehn, können Sie es ohne Nachteil der Geschäfte, ja ich werde Ihnen mehr werden als ich oft bisher war, wenn Sie mich nur das thun lassen was niemand als ich thun kann und das übrige andern auftragen. Mein Verhältniss zu den Geschäften ist aus meinem persönlichen zu Ihnen entstanden, lassen Sie nun

It is evident that in the course of gaining a new attitude towards the female sex he also changed to new superego representatives. Thus he continued a process that had already started in Weimar, and Charlotte von Stein lost this function while he was still in Italy, despite the many diary notes he wrote for her. From the last-quoted letter on, he gave the Duke a regular account of his activity as an artist and of his plans for the future and let him know details he did not communicate to anyone else (541, *1*:388). On December 7, 1787, he wrote: "The aim of my efforts and peregrinations is and remains the wish to adorn your life. May it be granted me."[5] Such a statement brings most clearly to the fore how Goethe was inclined at that time to elevate the Duke to the status of his superego and to reduce his own existence to nothing but an ornament of his princely friend's life. This almost masochistic attitude became at times dangerously strong, as the following passage in his letter of March 17, 1788, may show:

I may well say: I have in this year and a half found myself again; but as what?—As an artist. What I am still besides, you will judge and make use of. As each of your letters makes me see distinctly, you have—by dint of your abidingly effective life—more and more extended and sharpened that sovereign's knowledge of the use to which people can be put. I gladly submit myself to that judgment. Receive me as your guest; let me fulfill the whole measure of my existence and enjoy life at your side; thus my strength will, like a dammed-up, purified spring now opened from a height, be easy to be led here or there according to your will. . . . I can say but: "Lord, here I am; make of thy servant what thou wishest." Any place, any little place that you reserve for me, shall be agreeable to me; gladly will I come and go, sit down and stand up.[6]

---

ein neu Verhältniss zu Ihnen nach so manchen Jahren, aus dem bisherigen Geschäfts-Verhältniss entstehn. Ich bin zu allen und jeden bereit, wo und wie Sie mich brauchen wollen. Fragen Sie mich über die Symphonie die Sie zu spielen gedencken; ich will gern jederzeit meine Meynung sagen, so wird auch mein persönlich Verhältniss zu Schmidten mich in den Stand setzen, nach Ihrem Verlangen, in allen Sachen mitzuwürken. Schon sehe ich, was mir die Reise genützt, wie sie mich aufgeklärt und meine Existenz erheitert hat. Wie sie mich bisher getragen haben, sorgen Sie ferner für mich und thun Sie mir mehr wohl, als ich selbst kann, als ich wünschen und verlangen darf. Geben Sie mich mir selbst, meinem Vaterlande, geben Sie mich Sich selbst wieder, dass ich ein neues Leben und ein neues Leben mit Ihnen anfange! Ich lege mein ganzes Schicksal zutraulich in Ihre Hände. Ich habe so ein grosses und schönes Stück Welt gesehn, und das Resultat ist: dass ich nur mit Ihnen und in dem Ihrigen leben mag. Kann ich es, weniger von Detail überhäuft, zu dem ich nicht gebohren bin; so kann ich zu Ihrer und zu vieler Menschen Freude leben. . . .]

[5] [Das Ende meiner Bemühungen und Wandrungen, ist und bleibt der Wunsch Ihr Leben zu zieren. Möge er mir gewährt werden.]

[6] [Ich darf wohl sagen: ich habe mich in dieser anderthalbjährigen Einsamkeit selbst wiedergefunden; aber als was?—Als Künstler! Was ich sonst noch bin, werden Sie beurtheilen und nutzen. Sie haben durch Ihr fortdauerndes würckendes Leben, jene fürstliche Kenntniss: wozu die Menschen zu brauchen sind, immer mehr erweitert und geschärft, wie

Here we learn why Goethe so easily permitted someone else to dispose his existence as he thought fit. He had discovered—what he had learned earlier in his contact with Charlotte von Stein, and now definitely integrated—that the purpose and mission of his existence were in the world of art. In this circle he carried full responsibility; about the rest he apparently cared less, and therefore was ready to give its due to the community—represented by the Duke—which supported him so generously. To a certain extent he now continued without the feeling of sacrifice a process that he had maintained for the preceding few years with great effort. What he had been doing during that period—gladly, as he pretended, but actually, as we know, with the greatest internal pressure—was now to be continued on a reduced scale. Goethe rightly anticipated that on this reduced scale he would be able to balance harmoniously the societal demands and his artistic mission. The fact that he could now surrender the major parts of his responsibilities, that he no longer had to be the first one in all affairs of the dukedom, that he put the Duke into the place that, as the prince of the state, was his by law and tradition, that he granted him the final voice in disposing his own services to the state—all this shows that aggression had been tamed and that he had become humble. This very radical change was the manifestation of a new phase in the solution of a homosexual conflict. What had heretofore had to be acted out in reality would now be done within the artistic medium. A token of this is to be seen, I believe, in certain occasional remarks Goethe made about *Wilhelm Meister,* which he left unfinished when he went to Italy. Apparently he had in mind at that time at least to make this novel a kind of educational tool by means of which to exert some influence upon the Duke. I surmise that once he had relinquished his former role as an educator of the prince and decided to subordinate himself to the Duke's wishes he decided to seek to accomplish by means of a work of art what direct action had been unable to render acceptable. In one instance, in the form of a joke, he alluded to the magical role he attributed to poetry. The Duke was again suffering from the sequelae of a venereal infection and Goethe wrote him (April 6, 1789): "I will shortly deal with it with the greatest abuse in hexameters and pentameters" (thus referring to the elegy that had as its topic the curse of venereal diseases, *Soph.* I, *1:*219–20) and added: "This however, is of no help toward a cure."[7] This little additional remark, however, sounds to me like an inverted admission of his belief in the magical power of

mir jeder Ihrer Briefe deutlich sehen lässt; dieser Beurtheilung unterwerfe ich mich gern. Nehmen Sie mich als Gast auf, lassen Sie mich an Ihrer Seite das ganze Maas meiner Existenz ausfüllen und des Lebens geniessen; so wird meine Kraft, wie eine nun geöffnete, gesammelte, gereinigte Quelle von einer Höhe, nach Ihrem Willen leicht dahin oder dorthin zu leiten seyn. . . . Ich kann nur sagen: Herr hie bin ich, mache aus deinem Knecht was du willst. Jeder Platz, jedes Plätzchen die Sie mir aufheben, sollen mir lieb seyn, ich will gerne gehen und kommen, niedersitzen und aufstehn.]

7 [Ich werde ihm ehstens in Hexametern und Pentametern aufs schmählichste begegnen, das hilft aber nicht zur Cur.]

poetry (see 203). In view of his great attachment to the Duke and the fact that he was himself free of the disease despite his own sinful indulgence, the impetus to the elegy may have derived in part from the impulse to compass the Duke's recovery. There may well have been an unconscious feeling of guilt about the Duke's disease. How far identification and feelings of guilt went can be seen from a letter of the middle of February, 1790. The second page is missing except for the following paragraph (which was suppressed in the *Sophienausgabe*):

> If only another evil did not hold you fast in Berlin! About this I much less console myself. Particularly since I feel myself so secure in this respect. Unfortunately the caution and frugality of your Domestic Councilor and poet, who rarely sleeps alone and there keeps *penem purissimum* [his penis most clean] would not well be suitable to the mode of life of a military political prince.[8]

This remark is of great biographical value although its conscious intent is not known, since it is preserved out of context. Whatever Goethe may have intended by it, it betrays an unconscious relation between the two men characteristic of the period. It sounds almost like an apology on Goethe's side for being a coward in sexual matters while letting his friend and master expose himself to the dangers of a martial existence, which also included a dangerous love-life.

About this time he also continued what he had started in Italy, and kept the Duke abreast of his own progress in sexual matters. Thus he informed the Duke when he resumed sexual intercourse after his son's birth. In communications of that sort he avoided direct language but used Latin or symbolic terms, as in the last-quoted letter and one of February 6, 1790, in which he wrote: "With the permission of the goddess Lucina one has also begun again to enjoy love."[9] By "Lucina" Goethe referred to childbirth and menstruation; the impersonal pronoun weakens the sentence even more. Also the German idiom *der Liebe pflegen* is less committal than "to enjoy love," which is about as close to the German as one can get in English.

Evidently Goethe had the need to make confessions to the Duke in sexual matters. Goethe's sexual problems make it understandable that he should have needed a father confessor. In an earlier letter to the Duke he made a remark that casts the problem in a different light. When the Duke was absent in Ilmenau Goethe wrote (July 5, 1789):

---

[8] [Wenn nur nicht ein ander Übel Sie in Berlin festhielte! Darüber tröst ich mich weniger. Besonders da ich mich von dieser Seite so sicher fühle; Leider will sich die Vorsicht und Genügsamkeit Ihres Häusslichen Rathes und Dichters, der selten alleine schläft und dort *penem purissimum* erhält, nicht für die Lebensweise eines militarischen politischen Prinzen schicken.] (541, *1*:405)

[9] [Mit Vergünstigung der Göttin *Lucina* hat man auch der Liebe wieder zu pflegen angefangen.]

Probably you had snow in the woods; since the day before yesterday the sun shines again for us; yet one becomes so accustomed to the variation [of the weather] that he no longer either enjoys it or feels afflicted. I think more and more about my home life, which indeed it is quite meet I should.[10]

Here again Goethe referred to a respect in which his situation was more favorable than the Duke's. He enjoyed sunshine but the Duke was exposed to snow. Then follows the denial that any pleasure accrued to him from this, or, even, from nature in general. Now, there is no doubt that nature in all its infinite variations and effects was extremely meaningful to Goethe. The remark that the unending changes in nature do not provoke any particular emotions in him sounds most un-Goetheish.[11] However, we may recall that Christiane was pregnant at the time of this letter. The last sentence quoted refers to the cause of his relative insensitivity to nature: he was increasingly preoccupied with his "home life."

Was Goethe afraid lest this preoccupation put an end to his poetry? As a matter of fact it seemed during 1788–93 as if Goethe's lyrical flow had stopped. His main poetical productions were the *Roman Elegies* and the *Venetian Epigrams,* neither of which can be called lyrical. Yet lyrical poetry, the automatic transformation of any kind of impression into lyrical verse, was Goethe's mainstay. The ebb in lyrical production might easily have aroused a feeling of guilt in Goethe toward the Duke, who had most generously granted all his requests for relief from responsibilities, in return for Goethe's promise of full devotion to the career of an artist, who would thus adorn his master's life. Yet instead, his first action after his return to Weimar was to make his mistress pregnant, and although he finished the play *Tasso* (actually a year later than he had

---

[10] [Wahrscheinlich haben Sie auf dem Walde Schnee gehabt, seit vorgestern scheint uns wieder die Sonne, man wird aber der Abwechslung so gewohnt dass man sich nicht mehr freut noch betrübt. Ich dencke immer mehr auf die Haus Existenz, das sich denn auch ganz gut für mich ziemt.]

[11] However, there is an epigram—in almost direct reference to the quoted passage in the letter to Karl August—that expresses the idea that Goethe temporarily lost his lyrical interest in nature under the impact of his love for Christiane.

Oh how much attention I paid formerly to all times of the year;

Greeted the coming spring, longed after the fall!

But now there is neither summer nor winter, since me, most fortunate one,

The wings of Amor cover, eternal spring hovers round me.

[O, wie achtet' ich sonst auf alle Zeiten des Jahres,/ Grüsste den kommenden Lenz, sehnte dem Herbste mich nach!/ Aber nun ist nicht Sommer noch Winter, seit mich beglückten/ Amors Fittich bedeckt, ewiger Frühling umschwebt.] (*Soph.* I, *1*:328, Epigram 91)

It is most impressive with what superb objectivity Goethe examined the effects of the new way of living that evolved in his relationship with Christiane. This epigram sounds almost like a warning against the loss that the artist may incur by coming too close to an object.

planned) around the time when the above-quoted letter was written, he may have looked with apprehension upon his poetical future. A year later he wrote Knebel on July 9, 1790:

> My state of mind drives me more than ever to natural science and I am only surprised that in prosaic Germany a cloudlet of poetry[12] still remains hovering over my head.[13]

Yet this interest in science, which took up more and more of his time, was not the only quarter from which his Muse was threatened. After he had at last finished *Tasso* he wrote Herder pointedly (August 10, 1789): "Now we are free of any passion to undertake such an extended composition. The fragmental fashion of erotic jesting pleases me more."[14] Goethe was referring here to the *Roman Elegies* and the *Venetian Epigrams,* works which (particularly the latter) had an agglomerate structure ("fragmental fashion") and were characterized by a strongly erotic flavor.[15] This freedom from any passion for extended poetical works that Goethe confessed and was glad of did not promise a rich literary harvest for his immediate future and he may thus rightly have felt he stood in debt to his princely friend. This may be one of the reasons why he now produced an epigram to extol the Duke. Although in this piece Goethe freely admits how small is his master's power and domain he nevertheless holds him up to the nation as a model: every German should in like fashion turn his strength both outwards and inwards as he does.

> . . . then it would be a feast to be a German with Germans.

But, Goethe continues, why praise him whose deeds themselves have won his renown? Besides, such praise will perhaps seem to have been bought by bribery.

> For he has given me what the great rarely grant,
> Inclination, leisure, confidence, fields and garden and house.[16]

Only him has the poet to thank, and indeed he was in need of much, since, as a poet, he knew nothing about earning a livelihood. Europe praised him, but did not give him anything. Germany imitated him, France read him, and England received in friendship "the distracted guest" [den zerrütteten Gast]. But of what avail is it to him, the poet, if even the Chinese paint Lotte and Wer-

---

[12] By "cloudlet of poetry" Goethe meant his *Venetian Epigrams.*

[13] [Mein Gemüth treibt mich mehr als jemals zur Naturwissenschaft, und mich wundert nur dass in dem prosaischen Deutschland noch ein Wölckchen Poesie über meinem Scheitel schweben bleibt.]

[14] [Nun sind wir frey von aller Leidenschaft solch eine konsequente Composition zu unternehmen. Die Fragmenten Art erotischer Spässe behagt mir besser.]

[15] Goethe's writing two essays on erotic topics at this time (probably for Karl August) is discussed in Appendix S.

[16] [. . . da wär's ein Fest, Deutscher mit Deutschen zu sein./ Denn mir hat er gegeben, was Grosse selten gewähren,/ Neigung, Musse, Vertraun, Felder und Garten und Haus.]

ther? Never has an emperor or a king asked and been concerned about him, "and he was to me Augustus and Maecenas."[17]

As in the Ilmenau poem (cf. above, p. 1287) Goethe himself does not come off badly in praising the Duke.[18] But the self-praise is set forth in a way that redounds to the Duke's aggrandizement, and in the end he introduces a lofty compliment by equating the Duke with the Roman emperor.

Yet did Goethe really look upon the decrease of literary productions (which proved temporary) as a source of potential disappointment to the Duke? The great discoveries he thought he was in the process of making in the fields of color physics and botany he may easily have deemed a satisfactory equivalent.

How did the Duke respond to Goethe's choice of sweetheart? When did he meet her for the first time? What was his opinion regarding her? How did he judge his friend's erotic taste? One searches in vain for Christiane's name in the correspondence between the two. In his letter to the Duke before his marriage Goethe referred to her three times and this by implication only. A fair insight into Christiane's bearing upon Goethe's relationship to the Duke can be gleaned from Goethe's letters to him after he legitimized his common-law marriage in 1806. This took place five days after the battle of Jena (October 14), when Germany and the Duke were disastrously defeated by Napoleon, Weimar was sacked, and Goethe's life was saved by Christiane's brave and energetic interference with French marauders who had intruded into Goethe's bedroom. His marriage itself was announced to the Duke only on December 25, 1806, that is, nine weeks after it had taken place. According to the arrangement and dating of his correspondence in the *Sophienausgabe,* the letter in which the announcement was made was his third to the Duke after the ceremony had taken place.[19] In this letter Goethe first informed the Duke that Karoline Jagemann[20] had that day borne the Duke an illegitimate son. Since bad days are so often recalled, the good ones ought also to be remembered, he added. It

---

[17] [und Er war mir August und Mäcen] (*Soph.* I, 1:315–16)

[18] Goethe's real ambivalence is evident in his following this epigram with one in which the man of action and the man of art are put on a par. It ends: "My friend, only go on living and writing poetry!" [Mein Freund, lebe nur, dichte nur fort!]

[19] The *Sophienausgabe* records, between October 19, when he married, and December 25, 1806, when he informed Karl August of his change of status, three letters of Goethe to the Duke: (1) between October 19 and 26; (2) middle of December; (3) December 25, 1806. In the more recent edition of the correspondence between Goethe and Karl August (541, 1:473) it is claimed that these three letters were published separately in error, and that they are parts of one letter. Be this as it may, the whole structure of the letters betrays Goethe's procrastination in writing to the Duke. I have not been successful in determining what the actual possibilities of communication were between Weimar and the Duke from the disastrous battle of Jena until the end of December. In Goethe's diary there is no expression of alarm about the Duke's whereabouts.

[20] Karoline Jagemann (1777–1848), famous actress and singer, active in Weimar from 1797, from 1802 the Duke's mistress, gave birth on December 25 to Carl Wolfgang (1806–95).

struck him that seventeen years before that day his own son, August, was born. He was sure he would have the Duke's permission to give his son a father and mother through a nuptial bond "as he [August] had long deserved."[21] Why did Goethe wait with the news of his marriage until the Duke's illegitimate son was born? If we follow the sequence of letters as published in the *Sophienausgabe* we notice the following development until Goethe summoned up courage to let the secret out of the bag.

In the first letter, apparently written between October 19 and 26, 1806, he wrote:

> To go to Jena I could not make up my mind, just as I have already torn up many a letter to you like this one: the upheaval of things is still too near; whatever one says is inadequate or inadmissible and so one keeps silent or holds oneself back rather than talk.[22]

The internal difficulty of communicating with the Duke comes rather clearly to the fore in Goethe's having destroyed several attempted letters to him. Such wavering, I am confident, was most unusual for Goethe. Furthermore, Goethe insinuates that he was preoccupied with something that he did not want to put into words. The reader who speculates about the content of Goethe's preoccupation will think not so much of a very personal incident but rather of the general effect that the catastrophic political situation and the upheaval in Weimar had on him and that may have led to depressed spirits, so that the moment of personal communication seemed not yet to have arrived.

In the letter apparently written in the middle of December, after having told the Duke that he had not "suffered" any attack of his disease, Goethe added:

> But I have suffered something from October 14 on, something also physical, which still stands too close to me for me to be able to express it. May heaven give us all years in order to get this object into the [right] focus.[23]

Although Goethe alludes to October 14 (the date of the invasion of Weimar) as the day since which he "suffered something physical," this passage has nevertheless to be referred to his marriage, which actually took place on the nineteenth, for Goethe looked on the day on which he was rescued as spiritually the day of their wedding. In this letter Goethe comes a small step closer to the confession—indeed, he felt like one who confesses—that burdened him and

[21] [wie er es lange verdient hatte]

[22] [Nach Jena zu gehen konnt ich mich nicht entschliesen, so wie ich manche Briefe an Sie wie diesen schon zerrissen habe. Die Umwendung der Dinge steht einem noch zu nahe, alles was man sagt ist unzulänglich oder unzulässig und so schweigt man lieber oder nimmt sich zurücke als dass man spräche.]

[23] [Aber erlitten habe ich etwas vom 14. Octbr an, auch etwas physisches das mir noch zu nahe steht um es ausdrücken zu können. Geb uns allen der Himmel Jahre um diesen Gegenstand in den Sehewinckel zu bringen.]

seemed to brook no further delay. Yet only in the letter of December 25 does he at last find the necessary courage and determination.

Why did he remind the Duke that this was also the birthday of his own son? And why did he justify his marriage by declaring it to be a duty to his off-spring? Fate, by a trick worthy of a soap opera, played into Goethe's hands. I believe that Goethe had calculatedly waited until the Duke's son was born, but he could hardly have foreseen that the awkward problem of communication would be made so easy by the coincidence of birthdays.[24] I must conclude that Goethe tried to put the Duke into a sentimental mood, in which he would look graciously upon his friend's decision. Whether the technique he used was a gracious one I do not know. It strikes me as possibly tactless that he stressed the effect of his marriage on his son at a moment when the Duke was being apprised of the birth of a son whose legitimate father he could never become.[25]

Be this as it may, Goethe's procrastination and circumstantiality sound as if Karl August had not been friendlily disposed towards Christiane. This is partly confirmed by an entry in the diary of Chancellor Müller, a sober and reliable informant, intimately acquainted with conditions at the court of Weimar. In a long conversation the Duke conveyed to him a variety of indiscretions. As-sertedly he said that "[Christiane] Vulpius has spoiled everything; she has alienated him [Goethe] from society."[26] Was it really Goethe's alienation from society that troubled the Duke? Or was he jealous of his friend? I think we can be reasonably certain it was the latter. Goethe in turn evidently resented the Duke's mistress, and his only serious dissension with the Duke in 1817 occurred because of her. The Duke's resentment might have expressed itself in a different way if Goethe had chosen as a spouse a woman of a different sort from Christiane, but I think he would have resented any woman Goethe seriously loved. His characterization of Charlotte von Stein as "no great light" [kein grosses Licht] (250, 4:478) was certainly out of place. Goethe must have known of the Duke's jealousy, and, it seems, he felt guilty over his attachment to Christiane. His conscience, I surmise, sided with the Duke and he re-proached himself for being unfaithful to his friend, who represented brother, father, and grandfather. When, at last, he confessed his marriage to the Duke he claimed it was only for the sake of his son, thus out of love not for a woman, but for a male, and thus he indirectly appealed to what we may be sure was the Duke's desire to marry his mistress in order to obtain his newborn son as a legitimate offspring.

This situation may likewise suggest another aspect of Goethe's homosexual-ity. As I have set forth before, it was Christiane's energetic and lifesaving pres-

---

[24] Notice should also be taken that Goethe's son was given the Duke's middle name and the Duke's son his father's first and Goethe's middle name.

[25] The Duke, unlike Goethe, did not tarry long but solved his mistress's problem by nobilification in 1809. Carl Wolfgang was made hereditary owner of a baronial estate.

[26] [Die Vulpius habe alles verdorben, ihn der Gesellschaft entfremdet.] (250, 4:478)

ence of mind that made him decide to marry her. Despite her ignorance of French she cowed the aggressive intruders so thoroughly that they preferred to abstain from any further violence. One can easily imagine how dramatic this scene must have been and how deeply Goethe must have been moved when this woman without hesitation was ready to sacrifice her life rather than let her spouse suffer harm. But Karl August had not been capable of protecting Weimar and the battle of Jena was lost despite his service in the Prussian army.[27] In general, women seemed at that moment to be the only ones who could stave off Napoleon's aggressive designs. The Duchess met Napoleon with so much fortitude and indignation that the dictator, irate about the Duke's support of the enemy, relented in his design to deprive him of his dukedom and conceded far more lenient terms than he had originally intended. Thus the Duke owed the preservation of his dukedom to his wife's stalwart character and Goethe his life to his mistress's natural, motherly instincts. Now, the Duke was also a person who nourished, fed, and supported Goethe. Dimly one discerns the competition between two mother-images in Goethe's conflict about his attachment and gratitude to the Duke and to Christiane.[28] That, in marrying, Goethe was probably turning from one mother to another, may have been one of the unconscious roots of his feeling of guilt towards the Duke. It contained the reproach, "You lost the battle of Jena, which would almost have destroyed my life, if Christiane had not won the battle on the Frauenplan."[29]

[27] If Karl August had pursued a policy of neutrality, in accordance with Goethe's advice prior to 1786, Weimar would have suffered much less by the French victory. Also it should not be forgotten that Goethe was an ardent admirer of Napoleon.

[28] I omit the childhood experience of the Königsleutenant and its consequence upon Goethe's quick decision to marry.

[29] I take up a more archaic conflict between homosexuality and heterosexuality in Appendix S.

Appendix S

Remarks Concerning Goethe's Erotic Poetry and a Translation by Professor Moses Hadas of Two Latin Essays by Goethe

Iₙ 1790 GOETHE composed in Latin two essays which were published posthumously under the titles: "Annotations to the Anthology 'Priapeia'" [Bemerkungen zur Sammlung "Priapeia"] and "Annotations to Augustine's 'De Civitate Dei'" [Bemerkungen zu Augustinus "De civitate dei"] (*Soph*. I, *53*:197–207).

The first he almost certainly wrote in 1790, that is, shortly after his son's birth. In it he set forth what purports to be some textual criticism of the 1664 edition of the *Priapeia*, prepared by Schoppe to which were added the commentary of the famous Renaissance philologist, Scaliger.[1]

The *Priapeia* is a collection of about eighty-nine short Latin poems in the form of jesting epigrams applied to statues of the god Priapus. The identity of the editor, who also wrote the introductory epigram, is not known. The epigrams have been attributed to a variety of poets of the Augustan period. It is believed that some were written by Ovid, Catullus, and Tibullus. Some items are believed to be later inclusions. The collection stems from a time when

---

[1] "Priapei, sive diversorum poetarum in Priapum lusus; illustrati commentariis Gasperis Schoppii, Franci. . . . Huic editioni accedunt Iosephi Scaligeri in Priapei Commentarii, ac Friderici Linden-Bruch in eadem notae. Patavii, apud Gerhardum Nicolaum V. Sub signo Angeli Aurati, 1664." Quoted after *Soph*. I, *53*:491. This edition was not accessible to me. A copy bound with "Titi Petronii Arbitri, Equitis Romani, Satyricon . . . Lipsiae, 1731," is in Goethe's library.

The English translation of 1890 (431) also provides ample footnotes and commentaries regarding the origin of the compilation, its various editions, and the background of Roman sexual customs.

Caspar Schoppe (1576–1649), called Scioppius, was a German scholar and a convert to Roman Catholicism who became famous for his virulent writings against the Protestants and against Joseph Justus Scaliger, formerly his intimate friend. Scaliger (1540–1609), a renowned Renaissance savant, was the founder of modern literary criticism of ancient literature.

the worship of Priapus was no longer the primitive worship of generative energy, but had degenerated into a sensuous cult of pleasure and licentiousness. The representations of Priapus in sculpture are varied, but always show him with a huge erected penis. Besides being installed in temples consecrated to him, statues of him were set up at crossroads and in orchards, where they served as scarecrows and to protect the gardens against thievery.

A substantial number of the epigrams are devoted to this guarding function. Intruders are warned of the punishment that awaits them: if it is a boy he will be sodomized, if a girl she will be fornicated, if an adult man, he will have to perform irrumation. The majority of sexual remarks refer to sodomy; the act with boys is praised, as in Epigram 4, where Priapus gives free all that is in his garden if the boy will give him what his garden possesses. The collection contains a large variety of sexual insinuations and references, but the general trend can be characterized in the following way. It is a narcissistic glorification of the erected phallus accompanied with a measureless contempt for women. The most desirable sexual gratification seems to be sodomy with a boy; contempt for the male who submits after maturation is undisguised. The peak of contemptuousness is expressed toward fellatio, regardless of whether it is performed by male or female. The female element seems appreciated only when young and then mainly in the situation of coitus per anum, clearly as a substitute for boys. Intercourse implies an aggressive action and women are repeatedly presented as old, physically repulsive, with huge vagina infested with worms, rather like corpses.

Thus the *Priapeia* is a literary illustration of the phallic phase as Freud has described it (see 198). A translation by Professor Moses Hadas of Goethe's essay on the *Priapeia* follows:

To Prince Augustus:[2]

It is not vouchsafed to man, as it is to the sparrows,[3] to enjoy Venus, continually, and many persons join with Scioppius in deploring this circumstance. But I have always been of a mind, most excellent prince, not anxiously to yearn for what chance has denied, and hence I have always endeavored to fill out the intervals by which nature has separated my pleasures with some useful or agreeable occupation.

[2] Some doubt has been raised as to the identity of the "Princeps Augustus" to whom these two essays were dedicated. Besides Karl August, the Duke of Weimar, August (1747–1806), the brother of the Duke of Gotha, has been suggested. He is said to have been an adept in ancient literature. But in my mind there can be no doubt that these essays were meant for Karl August. As I have noted in Appendix R, Goethe was at that time inclined to compare Karl August with the Roman Emperor Augustus (and with Maecenas). Since in both essays Goethe is partly facetious, partly serious, it would make good sense if he attributed to the Duke the role of Augustus.

[3] Cf. *Priapeia* (431), Epigram xxv, 1.5: "Vernis passeribus salaciores" [(neighboring women) more lecherous than sparrows in the spring]

Upon this system too I have amused the long nights of the winter which is presently retiring by passing them alternately with Venus and with the more indulgent Muses.

Herewith, excellent prince, I present you with a few pages which testify to my gayer lucubrations.

Carmen 26

In the fifth line, *ut semper "placeant" spectantibus* [that *they* should always give pleasure to the spectators] I prefer to read the singular *"placeat"* [that *she* should give pleasure]. The courtesan, the people's darling, is depositing her cymbals, along with her rattles and tambourines, before Priapus, not that these *instruments* should give pleasure [placeant], but that by means of the gift *she* might win the god's favor for herself and by his aid always afford pleasure [placeat] and that the desired erection should always be ready for those who lust for her and make ready to enter her.[4]

Carmen 45

Scaliger's opinion seems to approach the true meaning of this poem more closely than does Scioppius's. Priapus, rebuking a certain catamite who is curling the hair of his head to look like a girl, scolds him in the rustic manner, saying: "You don't suppose you'll make yourself the more a girl if you take pains to curl the hairs around your penis with an iron and crisp them with a curling iron?"[5]

Carmen 54

> E D si scribas, temonemque insuper addas
> Qui medium D vult scindere, pictus erit.

This poem teaches us to draw a monogram, which we present to your view here:

[4] The Latin text accompanying the English edition of the *Priapeia* (431, p. 27) reads *placeat* as Goethe suggested.

[5] The corresponding Latin verses

> Num tandem prior est puellae, quaeso,
> Quam sunt, mentula quos habet, capilli?

are translated in the English edition as follows: "But is a girl, prithee, of more value than are the hairs which deck thy mentule?" The editor adds as an explanation: "Is it worth while disturbing a hair even on thy mentule, much less thy head, to take the semblance of a girl?" (431, p. 43). Thus, where the Latin author ridicules the girl-imitating behavior of a boy on the ground that to be a boy is to be a sexually more attractive object (to a man), Goethe sees the meaning as a scolding of the boy for supposing that he could make himself as sexually attractive (to a man) as a girl is.

It is to be understood as follows. If you write E D and add a bar [*temonem*], that is, a thick line so oriented that it would bisect the D, you will have the figure of a "phallus." It is the kind of drawing which children and uneducated people are wont to use. In the same way as we here see the neck of the phallus represented by a bar, so children are wont to draw the arms and legs of people.[6]

Carmen 68

The sense of this poem is plainly as follows. Priapus, set up in the garden of a certain Greekling, hears his master reciting Greek, and though he is an uneducated rustic, he thinks that he has learned a number of Greek words. It is, to be sure, easy, for Romans employ Greek words with only the terminations slightly altered. What the Greeks call *psolon* [penis], the Romans call *psolum* [penis], and what the Romans call *culus* [buttocks] the Greeks call *coleon*. Hence I believe that the fifth line should be emended as follows:

Psoleon ille vocat quod psolum subinde vocamus.[7]

Thus it will fit well with the verse that follows:

Id quod nos culum, coleon ille vocat [What we call "culus," he calls "coleon"].

In the final distich, having succeeded so well in the comparison of the Greek language with the Latin, Priapus girds himself to explain the word *smerdaleos* [terrible] also, and rejoices in the discovery of a relationship with a Latin word. He thinks it is to be derived from *merda* [excrement], and he asserts that the penis of the pederasts, which he had heard spoken of as *smerdaleam,* that is "terrible" to the pathic, is quite properly called *merdaceam,* that is, "befouled with excrement," forasmuch as it is wont

hesterno occurrere luto
[to encounter yesterday's filth].

So Lindenbrog notes, from an ancient epigram,

---

[6] In this epigram Goethe quite failed to grasp the underlying (homosexual) significance.

The translation in the English edition (431, p. 53) is as follows: "If thou writest E, D, and then addest a joining line, that which wishes to cleave through the middle of D (thee) will be represented." The editor rightly points to the ambiguity of the D in the second line, which stands for the Latin word *te* (you). Thus the D is meant to picture the anus to be cloven by the mentule.

[7] That is, "He calls 'psoleon' [penis] what we call 'psolum' [penis]." The line read, in Goethe's edition:

Psoleon ille vocat, quod nos Psoloenta vocamus,

which might be translated:

"He calls prick what we call pricking."

Et non laudatur mentula, merdacea est—
[The penis is not praised; it is befouled with excrement].

Carmen 75

According to the opinion of Scaliger, this poem should be divided into two parts; the last two verses should be separated from the four preceding, and then the interpretation, it seems to me, is quite easy. First the poem introduces Priapus grieving that his weapons have fallen from his loins, *forsan injuria temporis,* [perchance by the injury of time]. Girls look at the mutilated figure with sidelong glance and despise it for being unequipped. Hence, in order somehow to recall to their minds that he is a god, he admonishes them to sacrifice at the altar which was regularly set up near a statue of Priapus, and then he intimates that the penis which is now lifeless like a piece of kindling wood would be of service to them.

mentula nunc exanimis [The penis which is now lifeless], the penis which is now separated from my body and lies apart. I agree with Scioppius that we should read *arae si dederitis,* [if you will have offered to the altar].[8]

Carmen 77

"Do not fix a *fibula* [safety-pin] on Priapus." We know well enough that a fibula was fixed on the *membrum virile* of singers and other young men whose lechery they wished to restrain, and in such a way that it seemed attached to the prepuce. I am indeed astonished that this fact should have escaped Scioppius, who is most devoted to the archaeology of the phallus, so that he should make the frigid suggestion that this was a proverbial expression for Priapus.[9]

---

[8] Here Goethe seems to prefer Scioppius's reading *"arae"* on the ground that it permits the interpretation: "If the penis is unerect and lifeless—mere kindling wood—then it is good at least for a sacrifice *on the altar of* Priapus, if nothing else"; whereas Goethe apparently believes that the reading "aram" would require the interpretation: "The penis now useless can be revived if the courtesans *dedicate an altar* to Priapus," i.e., devote themselves, as it were, professionally, to sexual intercourse.

[9] In this epigram, of which Goethe quotes only the last line, Priapus complains that, although he is growing old, he is still not without power to perform sodomy, even if only on other old ones, such as Nestor or Priam, and that therefore he is not served, but hindered, by those well-meaning ones who build high the fences around his orchard domain, for, in doing so, while they lighten his guardian task, they deprive him of his sexual prey—in short, they put a fibula on his penis. Goethe is surprised that Scioppius does not explain that "to put a fibula on" means, in such a context, "to pin up the prepuce so as to prevent erection," a widespread practice among public performers in the ancient world. Actually, since it is hard to see how Scioppius could have known that the expression was "proverbial" without knowing also that the practice was common, we are led to conclude that Goethe felt deeply the extent of the deprivation involved in the practice, so that here, too, he is to be seen reacting to a limitation upon genital activity.

Carmen 80

I suspect that lines 4 and 5 should be emended as follows:

> Non habet haec aliud mentula majus *ea*
> Num vilior Tydeus? qui, siquid credis Homero.

And I explain the poem in this fashion. The speaker is Priapus, who has been newly made and just set up in a garden; by some chance the artisan has carved his penis less than a foot long. The girls approach him and object that the penis is not long and thick enough and that it does not stand up well, and they also manipulate it with their hands as if they wished it to be more erect. Priapus complains at the girls' disappointment with the size and at their dissatisfaction: though his penis is not of a size worthy of Priapus, it does surpass all human penises. Then to exculpate the smallness of his own organ he cites the example of Tydeus, who, though small in body, was said to be most pugnacious in character.[10] Soon he suspects that his newness and shyness have affected him adversely, so that his organ should not achieve its proper erection. He thinks he ought to get rid of his shyness, for he was made on purpose to stand under the open sky with scrotum exposed.[11]

Carmen 84

Ex quo natus es, et potes renasci, [Whence you are born and can be reborn]. Scioppius wrongly deduces from the words *potes renasci,* [you can be reborn], that the figure of Priapus had been fashioned out of a trunk which had not been uprooted. To me this verse seems to say nothing else than the following: Your effigy has been made from wood of this forest, and another trunk which is growing there will bestow upon us a god like yourself; hence if we do not, by your care, escape a shortage of wood, we shall not hesitate to burn you up. We would rather be without a god than go cold.

Carmen 86

I emend the next to last verse as follows;

---

[10] Cf. "Tydeus was short of stature, but a man of war; yea even when I [Athene] would not have him fight. . . ." (*Iliad,* V, 801 f.)

[11] Goethe's emendation changes *eo* of his edition to the *ea* quoted above. The editor of the English edition acknowledges that he does not understand this epigram (which he gives as No. 81), and reports that Scioppius could not either. Interestingly enough, he translates it substantially as Goethe paraphrases it—i.e., as if it read *"ea."*

Goethe's explanation focuses on the parallel between the inadequate penis and Tydeus, who is not daunted by his smallness of stature, but willingly joins combat (*Ingenio pugnax, corpore parvus erat*). So, if the penis got over its shyness it would sustain an erection and prove equal to its opportunities. Thus here again Goethe seems to seize upon an occasion for exhorting to heterosexual activity.

Vicinus prope dives est negligensque Priapum—[12]

[There is a rich man near by, one who is neglectful of Priapus.] Thus I think that the beauty which the poem has hitherto lacked can be restored to it. In the whole poem Priapus praises the devoutness to himself of the humble squatters of a marshy farmhouse, and in return for their dutifulness he must secure that the master's little garden and vineyard be protected. And so he asks that the boys refrain from raiding them and rather attack the garden of the rich neighbor who is neglectful of Priapus. He assures them that they will find it unguarded. The piety of the poor man and the negligence of the rich man thus juxtaposed are made clear; he is not presented as complaining of the neglect of his own divinity and thus castigating himself, contrary to the logic of myth and of poetry alike.

In the second essay Goethe elaborates on some passages in Augustine's *De Civitate Dei*. He cites from Book VI, Chapter 9, and Book VII, Chapters 2 and 3, in which Augustine presents an extensive *reductio ad absurdum* of the mythology of Roman erotic gods and goddesses as far as he was acquainted with the subject, his chief source having been Varro.[13] Goethe quite candidly embraces the pagan gods Augustine ridiculed.

The translation by Professor Hadas follows:

Notes on St. Augustine, *De Civitate Dei*

Some days ago, excellent prince, I was informed, to my very great pleasure, that you found delight in occupying yourself day and night with the lucubrations of my great grandfather Casper Schoppius on the subject of the male organ of Priapus. I am moved by this information to dedicate to you, as a patron of erotic trifles, a little dissertation which I worked out, to indulge my nature, in the winter season when I was shut up in my study.

The nights were long and virtually of iron, and the days were like the nights. Having just returned from a most happy journey to Italy they troubled me so sore and so afflicted me as almost to extinguish all desire of life.

You know the lot of that mediterranean Thuringia, of ours, most perceptive prince: we bestow effort on the arts, but we take no pleasure in the arts; poor in science, we trade in science; we cultivate the commonwealth, but we do not consider the interests of the commonwealth. Reflecting upon these matters, I determined to institute a different plan of life.

You yourself are aware, excellent prince, that from my earliest years I have diligently pursued the study of subjects human and divine, and you

---

[12] Goethe's text gave "Priapus," i.e., the nominative.

[13] Marcus Terentius Varro (116–27 B.C.), Roman polyhistor and writer, one of the most fertile minds of ancient times. Augustine quoted profusely from the religious sections of his *Antiquitatum rerum humanarum et divinarum libri XLI* (Antiquities of Things Human and Divine), a work now lost.

cannot be ignorant that my theory has somewhat been tempered and p
. . .[14] by my practice. I thought it would be disgraceful for me not to
illustrate that chapter, plainly divine and human, concerning generation
and creation.

Opportunity was not wanting, and I seized upon it and sweated through
many nights in the fashioning of man. I do not blush to confess this, with
Schoppian integrity, although I have seen others, and especially country
folk, perform that divine work offhand, more like a god.

By the learned, beloved prince, all things are dealt with learnedly, as by
the pure purely; I could thus do no other than investigate and scrutinize
with the greatest diligence the opinion of the ancients on this act.

First of all I was struck by the religious ingenuity of the ancients, which
assigned the whole business of generation to numerous gods and goddesses
and with most accurate distinctions attributed separate functions to separate deities.

Pray receive the exposition in this little dissertation, from Varro according to St. Augustine.

All are agreed that Love, whom the Latins call Cupid and the Greeks
Eros, is the original source and moving force of propagation and of life.
Some declare that Love has entered into a three-fold matrimony with air
and earth and water, because it is not possible to inhabit any of these three
elements with impunity; it is not possible to stir a foot out of the house, nor
to take the air of a public promenade, nor to sail nor to fish nor to hunt nor
to play music or lead a dance without acknowledging Love's sway, and
suddenly with some girl . . .

Love,

then, we hold, must be given first place, and ungrudgingly. When spirits
are joined there follows a desire to meet in some safe retreat, to converse
securely, and to unfold the feelings of the mind with mutual communion.
Over this process presides the god

Domiducus.

When you have taken the girl to your home she is suffused with a certain shyness, with a certain dread. And so, in order that she should not
flee away, the goddess

Manturna

must be invoked; she will assist your blandishments, will multiply the
pleasure of kisses, will fix the girl firmly upon your knees, and will con-
strain her as you lead her to the couch. Then suddenly will appear the
goddess

Virginensis,

who will assist you as you loosen her girdle, will quiet the girl's efforts at
resistance with whispers, will skillfully arrange the disposition of her limbs

[14] A lacuna in the text, beginning with the letter "p."

upon the couch, will remove inconvenient garments, will guide you in your eagerness, and will part her thighs for you as you recline over them. At this juncture you will not be failed by the god

Subigus,

who, as you are fumbling about the approach and applying tender belly to belly, which the Greeks call *depsein* or *pepainein*.[15] . . . And when you have done this prettily and not like a boor, then that she may find the burden convenient the goddess

Prema

will assist the girl that she should willingly and with pleasure bear your weight pressing upon her and resting upon her with all your body. Then let the goddess

Pertunda

attend; though St. Augustine (*De Civitate Dei,* Book VII)[16] is of opinion that her assistance is superfluous after that of the god Subigus and the goddess Prema, and though she need but rarely be invoked in our times, we nevertheless believe that she ought not be neglected, for however rare a thing may be it may still happen. With her help, then, the knocked-on door will be opened by the god

Janus.

Let the little door of the thrice and four times adorable little shrine be opened and the appropriate duties of the amiable religion be performed. Nor will the god

Saturnus

fail, who will bring the seed. The god

Liber

will release you, and the goddess

Libera

will come up and propel the girl's seed to meet yours. Then if everything proceeds orderly, the god

Vitumnus

will [bestow] life [for the birth, and] the god

Sentinus

[will bestow] perception.[17]

What now is the psychological meaning of these two essays or, in other words, what function is to be attributed to them?

[15] The Greek word *depsein* means to work, or knead (something), e.g., wax, until it is soft; *pepainein* is to grow soft and warm; a typical use is in Theocritus 2.140: *chròs epì chrōtì pepaíneto*, "flesh upon flesh grows soft and warm."

[16] *Sic;* the passage is actually in Book *VI*, Chapter 9.

[17] Goethe broke off his text before setting down the Latin words whose meanings are conveyed by those in square brackets in this last sentence. They are supplied from St. Augustine's text.

1339

A large number of shorter or longer essays by Goethe on a variety of topics have been preserved. Some of them fall into the area of philology, such as, for example: "Idioms that an author avoids, but leaves the reader to insert at his pleasure" [Redensarten, welche der Schriftsteller vermeidet, sie jedoch dem Leser beliebig einzuschalten überlässt] (*Soph.* I, 41 (part 1):118–20), or "Phaeton, tragedy by Euripides. Attempt at reconstruction from fragments" [Phaeton, Tragödie des Euripides. Versuch einer Wiederherstellung aus Bruchstücken] (*Soph.* I, 41 (part 2):32–47).

The two essays dedicated to Prince Augustus, however, though belonging to philology, are quite different from others, not only in being in Latin (the only instances in Goethe's work, I believe, besides his law thesis and his treatise on the *os intermaxillare*) but also in content, structure, and intent. Goethe tries here to act like his humanist forefathers; he addresses his master officially, and he intends to delight him by his philological research. This research, dry and unimaginative in itself, explores topics of intense emotional value. Under the guise of philology the forbidden and the obscene are brought to light and made the subject of communication. This combination of dry objectivity with the indecent makes the charm of these seemingly casual compositions.

Psychologically, however, they are not as casual as their author wishes to make it appear. First of all, Goethe's introducing himself as a great-grandson of the humanist who edited the work on Priapus is quite striking. According to the *Sophienausgabe* Goethe mentions this ancestor only in these two essays, in the one on the *Priapeia* under the Latinized form of "Scioppius" and in the other as "Schoppius" (Schoppe in German).

Whether such kinship actually existed or not,[18] it probably was not incidental that an ancestor is here stressed, for the essays were written during the winter of 1790, that is to say, shortly before or after the birth of his illegitimate son, on December 25, 1789. Thus Goethe stresses a direct kinship with an ancestor who was also known for intense preoccupation with forbidden sexual matters. But Goethe also slips in a reference to the uprightness and sound moral principles of his ancestor, thus indirectly vindicating himself, who, like Scioppius, complains that the pleasures of Venus are not always available to man. Goethe here refers (without openly saying so) to the fact that his own sexual pleasures were interrupted by Christiane's pregnancy and puerperium. In a letter to Karl August of February 6, 1790 (quoted in Appendix R), he announces that he has resumed intercourse. It is noteworthy that parts of the essay on the *Priapeia* are written on an official document dated February 5, 1790, and that in the just-mentioned letter to the Duke he wrote: "Yesterday the first

---

[18] I owe thanks to Professor J. A. Von Bradisch whose courtesy made it possible for me to go through the most detailed family tree of Goethe available, which traces Goethe's ancestors back in part to the thirty-second generation, in the eighth century. The name of "Schoppe" does not appear in it. See 434.

eroticon was put on paper in this year."[19] It is usually assumed that the essay on the *Priapeia* was written before that on St. Augustine. However, I believe that a careful perusal shows that it probably was the other way around. The answer to this question is important, for, if my impression is correct, then the writing of the essays was connected with a time of protracted abstinence and its termination.

Be this as it may, the two essays grew out of Goethe's intense sexual interests of that time. They are indirect witnesses in favor of the assumption that intercourse was for Goethe really something new. He was fascinated by the subject like someone who has started to fathom its full meaning and now cannot wrest his mind from his interest in it. Goethe is here reminiscent of the preadolescent youth that boasts of its sexual knowledge and lets others know: "I too know now what *it* is." He presents himself as a man sophisticated in sexual matters and manners for whom perversions and secrets of love are so familiar that he can treat them with the coolness appropriate to a literary study. The heightened interest in the male organ, the emphasis on its erectile power, makes it probable that Goethe—at least at that time—had not reached the genital phase but was fixated to the phallic phase.[20]

And still an inhibitory trend is also noticeable. Goethe's age was not puritanically minded; lasciviousness was not alien to a late rococo court, and Goethe's use of the Latin language must be looked upon as defensive. I wonder whether he would have been able at that time to put the content of these essays into German words, symbols close to his ego and replete with feelings that were absent for him from the Latin language, which was relatively neutral. This point is particularly important since the essays were a communication to a friend and thus were sources of greater preconscious shame and embarrassment than if they had been written for his own enjoyment alone. Yet this remark is not to be taken as a denial of the victorious accomplishment, characteristic of that period, of a more tolerant attitude towards sexual subjects. I also wonder whether we do not catch a faint glimpse of that inner trend towards continued opposition to genitality in Goethe's remark about the country folk, whom he has seen "perform that divine work offhand, more like a god." Is this remark a biographical one? Was it made in the sense of an excuse, to indicate that he did not surrender lightheartedly to the animalistic urge like common people, but went through the business of "the fashioning of man" rather as a duty or a task that a man who pursues "the study of subjects human and divine" has to fulfill?

It is perhaps easier to guess the meaning which these essays had in terms of Goethe's relationship to the Duke. In the discussion of Goethe's sexual develop-

---

[19] [Gestern ist das erste Erotikon in diesem Jahre zu Papier gekommen.]

For the records that permit such a precise dating of the first essay see *Soph.* I, *53:*492.

[20] See 198. Dr. Anna Freud has reported behavior similar to Goethe's in patients who embark on heterosexual intercourse after having been successfully treated for homosexuality.

ment, there was reported the somewhat humiliating position he had to take when he confessed to the Duke his helplessness and inexperience in sexual matters and at one point even insinuated that he had never before had intercourse. The erudition he now displayed in matters of erotic literature, the cynicism of his remarks about women (such as the rarity with which in our times the assistance of the goddess Pertunda will be invoked), and, further, the free discussion of perversions, the phallic boasting, may have been born of a desire to compensate for past humiliations and to demonstrate that he had successfully caught up with deprivations of the past. To a certain extent he thereby fitted himself into the general sensuous atmosphere, alien to his works up to then, of a late rococo court. Yet this gesture of erotic acclimatization may also have aimed at compensating for Karl August's critical attitude towards Goethe's sweetheart (cf. Appendix R), as if Goethe tried to prove that even if he did not possess a refined sophisticated mistress, he nevertheless possessed refinement and sophistication in his erotic tastes.

A point relating to Goethe's own feeling about intercourse must be set forth here. There is ample evidence that Goethe was at that time quite preoccupied with the genital aspect of sexuality. If one adds the possibility that he was in a state of temporary frustration because of Christiane's pregnancy and puerperium the question may rightly be raised why this state led only to his writing the after all cut-and-dried philological essays and not some deeper poetical creations. It may be contended that the genital function is not suitable to direct poetical presentation and the necessary circumlocution and recourse to symbols would not be to the taste of a man primarily interested in the direct gratification of the sexual urge. Notwithstanding the validity of this argument I wish to cite an example of Goethe's early rococo poetry in which he succeeded in dealing with an incident of a genital nature without resorting to circumlocution.

This piece is from the book of poems, *Annette* (Leipzig, 1767; *Soph.* I, 37: 11–48). It is the second of two narratives in verse, both called "Triumph of Virtue." The poet once came unawares upon his girl when she was alone and naked. Thus he had an opportunity to behold what she never permitted him to see. He was beside himself with unexpected joy, but yet the girl angrily thrust him back with one hand and covered herself with the other. She insisted that he leave immediately. Yet this was out of the question. One does not easily encounter again such an opportunity. Then Goethe describes his sensation when his hand touched her bosom, and when it rose and fell as the girl breathed deeply. She grew silent and the attacker's cruelty softened. If a young man is ever to reach his goal by cunning mischief then girls must not keep silent when they are alone with him. His narrative goes on:

> My arm embraced with sinews strained
> The soft hip. Almost—almost—yet the course of victory

Was quickly stopped by a fervent flow of tears
Irresistibly.[21]

Then follow the girl's implorations that he should spare her, her regret over not following her mother's teaching, and a prayer to God to intervene. The poet adds some moralistic warnings directed to all seducers. He takes flight and reports the rewarding words his sweetheart spoke to him the following day when he met her with her mother.

It is noteworthy how far Goethe had come here, at the age of seventeen, in the evolvement of erotic poetry. To be sure, he was greatly influenced by the spirit of the time, and quite immature, suggestive without depth and moralistic in puerile fashion. But he was not bashful about presenting erotic details and went as far as one can without being outright offensive.

We know that at that time Goethe was in an acute conflict regarding a solution of the sexual problem, and his pent-up sexual craving induced him to put this conflict into verse: the desire for intercourse, how close he got to fulfillment, the defenses against it. Quite a few of the situational details are such as he may have experienced in reality and he was not blocked from using them in a work of art.

Such a constellation was missing when the two essays were written: a philological inquiry dressed up in Latin prose instead of passionate, lyrical verses. Yet in Leipzig intercourse, though desired, was feared, and rejected as morally objectionable (cf. 154). The art of writing poems did not bring the poet closer to intercourse. Just the opposite: it was a potent tool in his struggle against it.[22] In 1790 intercourse was a fact and cherished by the poet in its pleasure-giving reality. Poetry about intercourse now might threaten its actual integration. As Goethe pleaded with the Muses not to make a fairy tale out of his sweetheart (cf. Appendix T) so also he had to keep this new-found land out of his poetry.

At one point, however, Goethe presented erection directly. In one of the posthumously published *Roman Elegies* he writes about the god Priapus whose statue stands in a yard forgotten and desecrated by the droppings of the birds, but who is restored by the poet's labor. Goethe has the god Priapus speak as follows:

---

[21] [Mein Arm umschlang mit angestrengten Sehnen/ Die weiche Hüfte. Fast—fast—doch des Sieges Lauf/ Hielt schnell ein glüh'nder Strom von Thränen/ Unwiderstehlich auf.] (*Soph.* I, 37:30)

[22] Among the many scraps and bits of papers that were found in Goethe's literary estate there is one on which Goethe contrasts himself with a person who complained about the foolishness of his writings: "The difference between you and me is that your intoxication is slept off, mine stands on the paper." [der Unterschied von mir zu ihnen ist der ihr Rausch ist ausgeschlafen, meiner steht aufm Papier]. (*Soph.* I, 38:482)

The girl is not shocked by me and not the matron,
Hideous I am no longer, am only monstrous strong.
Therefore your splendid brush should also a half-foot long
Swell up from your middle when your darling so bids.
The limb shall not tire before you have the dozen figures
Thoroughly enjoyed, as Philaenis[23] artfully devised them.[24]

It should be observed that the word "brush" in line 3 (German *Ruthe*), though etymologically the same as English "rod," has the meaning in this context of a fox's brush. Here the spell-casting effect of poetry in the sense of guaranteeing maximal physical strength is clearly set forth.

The preoccupation with genital pleasures had its stimulating effect upon his desire for literary creation. The outcome is a compromise that least threatens the genital impulse. This, I think, is how the two essays originated. The writing of certain parts of them may have had a directly stimulating effect upon the author. The enumeration of the various gods and goddesses and of what they do to assist man, although it is carried to the ostensible goal of procreation, actually is so much devoted to the intercourse itself and its foreplay that it sounds like a putting into words of elements of sexual daydreams. The ego, apparently, was primarily interested in acquiring physical pleasure.

Still, another, almost diametrically different, interpretation cannot be ruled out. The choice of St. Augustine's pejorative remarks about ancient gods as a literary subject is not surprising. Here Goethe had an opportunity to remonstrate against Christian contempt for paganism and with emphasized opposition to the Father of the Church he could set forth the appealing charm and humanity of ancient gods. This is a favorite theme of Goethe's.

His preoccupation with the *Priapeia* is of a sort that was less wont to appear in his writings. Therefore it may be worth while to speculate about the topics of the nine epigrams that he chose for literary comment among the eighty-nine or so. They may be cursorily described as follows: the wish of a dancer that she may successfully entice men; the vituperation of a catamite (misunderstood by Goethe as an exhortation not to imitate girls because they are preferable to men); the presentation of the penis by drawing (with the omission of the homosexual implication of the drawing); a philologic pun on the Roman and Greek languages with an implied denigration of homosexuality (its anal, fecal, aspect); three epigrams in which Priapus complains about the weakness of

---

[23] An ancient Greek woman reputed to have written a treatise on the sexual positions. She is referred to in Carmen LXIII of the *Priapeia* (431, pp. 60, 121).

[24] [Nicht das Mädchen entsetzt sich vor mir, und nicht die Matrone,/ Hässlich bin ich nicht mehr, bin ungeheuer nur starck./ Dafür soll dir denn auch halbfuslang die prächtige Ruthe/ Strozzen vom Mittel herauf, wenn es die Liebste gebeut./ Soll das Glied nicht ermüden, als bis ihr die Duzzend Figuren/ Durchgenossen wie sie künstlich Philänis erfand.] (*Soph.* I, 53:7)

erection; the replaceability of Priapus; the poor man who reveres Priapus is better protected than the rich man who neglects him.

It can be noticed that out of the abundance of phallic boasting in the *Priapeia* Goethe chose just such epigrams as are not very representative of that meaning or interpreted them so as to weaken that aspect of them. Yet his perusal of the compilation and his literary preoccupation with it must be looked upon as an expression of his being in the midst of an intense phallic phase. Thus, I conclude that Goethe used the literary essay to fight against an impulse that may have grown stronger the longer he lived with Christiane. I have mentioned before the unmitigated hostility against women that is characteristic of the *Priapeia*. May it not be that this hostility of the literary piece coincided with a secret tendency in Goethe himself? I have also reported Goethe's plea that poetry should not, as it had done regularly in the past, again transfigure (and thus deprive him of) his sweetheart. The Muses were benign and they granted his request, Goethe setting out for a career as a scientist. Yet did Goethe not harbor a longing for his beloved art, and was it not necessary for him to devaluate the woman and sexual pleasure with her in order to regain that level and kind of conflict that were indispensable to him for the creation of art? Thus we may be face to face, in the psychological background of these cut-and-dried Latin essays, with a very complicated psychic structure, an unconscious wish to debase and reject women and, simultaneously, a strong defense against this wish. The interesting point in this situation is that poetry (the Muse) usually served the function of severing the object-relationship, whereas in order to find his way back to art, Goethe apparently had, in this instance, to weaken the object-relationship by a different set of mechanisms. One may say that this time he had to carry out himself, as it were, what his Muse had done for him in previous instances.

However, in order to give a more complete survey of Goethe's erotic poetry we have briefly to discuss a middle phase between the early rococo period and 1790. This middle phase is best represented by *Merry-Andrew's Wedding, or the Way of the World, a microcosmic drama* [Hanswursts Hochzeit oder der Lauf der Welt ein mikrokosmisches Drama] (*Soph.* I, 38:45–52, 435–449). This farcical play of bitter irony is directed against the hypocrisy of the world. Here we find a free indulgence in extremely obscene words, mostly of anal quality, somewhat reminiscent of certain of Mozart's letters, cited earlier, to his cousin Bäsle (401).

The indulgence in the vulgar and obscene, seemingly for its own sake, is characteristic of that period, in which Goethe out of the abundance of his strength and lust for life, did not wish to acknowledge any limit imposed by external societal forces. Such pronounced displays of contempt for society were all the more necessary since outbreaks of the kind were not correlated to phases of freedom from inner inhibition. It is also noteworthy that although there is some obscenity referring to genital sexuality, anal obscenity greatly prevailed in that period, a circumstance that may reflect the genital inhibition. This view may appear all the more acceptable when it is considered that the farce probably was written in 1775 and had as its secret target the social circle of Goethe's fiancée, Lili, and its conventions, which Goethe, of course, was expected to bow to.[25]

Morris, very cleverly, suggests an inner kinship between the farce of *Merry-Andrew's Wedding* and the *Prometheus* fragment of 1773 (see 398). In *Prometheus* we find a dramatic reference to intercourse (cf. above, p. 712) that cannot be classified as belonging to erotic literature in the sense in which the word is used in this context, but it is noteworthy that Goethe here approached the problem with eminent tragic seriousness, equating orgasm and death.[26]

The obscenities of the farcical plays, however, had the function of discharge of crude, barely formed, pent-up instinctual forces. The erotic productions of 1790 are quite different. They are not crude by any means. The *Roman Elegies,* with which this period started, are of outstanding literary value despite their relative coldness. They were probably all written in Weimar at a time when the Roman adventure was a matter of the past and poetry could no longer interfere with the cherished pursuit of reality.

The next step was the two Latin essays. These in turn were followed by the *Venetian Epigrams.* Most of these were written in 1790 when he was in Venice (March 31 to May 2) and in Silesia, yet some, and precisely most of those that refer to Christiane, were already written in Weimar. I imagine that the epigrammatic form reduced the danger of the alienating effect that poetry cast upon his personal relationships. Epigrams do not divert the poet's imagination for a long time. Moreover they are at least as much a matter of the intellect as of the heart. For Goethe it was the ideal form in which to appease his creative urge and still be able to indulge in sensuous pleasure and maintain a strong attachment to Christiane and his son.

When he was sent to Venice to accompany the Dowager Duchess back to Weimar, he had to wait for quite a while. Italy did not mean what it had meant to him not so long before. The memory of Faustina reappeared—

> Beautiful is the country; yet, alas, Faustina I do not find again.
> This is no longer Italy that I left with pangs.[27]

—although he was filled with longing for home, sweetheart, and the newborn baby. He wrote to Herder (May 28, 1790):

[25] See *Soph.* I, *38*:435. See also 562.

[26] A complete discussion of Goethe's erotic poetry would have to include the poem "The Diary" [Das Tagebuch] (*Soph.* I, *5*:345–50), which reveals an aspect of sexuality of the aging Goethe. This is outside the scope of this appendix.

[27] [Schön ist das Land; doch ach! Faustinen find' ich nicht wieder./ Das ist Italien nicht mehr, das ich mit Schmerzen verliess.] (*Soph.* I, *1*:308)

They [Christiane and the baby] are very close to me and I gladly admit that I love the girl passionately. How much I am tied to her, I have felt only on this journey.[28]

In this state of conflict—of sexual longing and excitement on the one hand, and on the other his love for Christiane that militated against any serious love-affair —we find as a compromise a heightened interest in prostitutes.

Generally, Goethe's sexual interests in Venice betray regressive features and therefore some of the posthumously published epigrams are an important source for the study of Goethe's sexual psychopathology. Concomitantly, aggressive features become more pronounced and we find among them some of his most radical expressions of contempt for Christian values, such as the following:

> Much can I endure. Most of the onerous tasks
> I bear with quiet courage as a god bade me.
> A few, however, are averse to me like poison and serpent;
> Four: tobacco smoke, bedbugs, and garlic and Christ.[29]

The sensuality in the Catholic church ceremonies of Venice offended his Protestant simplicity; his hostility to Newton, of course, Lavater and other subjects such as the French Revolution found their way into the epigrams. Many more such aggressive epigrams could be quoted, but Goethe's aggression is not our concern here.

The pieces dealing with sexual topics do, however, concern us. Goethe describes how he sat with two prostitutes in a tavern, how they tried to seduce him and he resisted. From his firm refusal they recognized him immediately as a stranger. Goethe concludes:

> Oh now you know why the Venetian creeps along pale.[30]

Thus we see that the syphiliphobia was still on his mind. Yet no longer were there, as in the *Roman Elegies,* those acrimonious outbreaks against disease as the spoiler of all erotic-sexual pleasures.

Remarkable, however, is Goethe's solution of the homosexual problem. As I have suggested, his relationship to Cornelia had the character of that to a mirror-image and afforded him the opportunity to project the image of his own body onto that of a female body. Thus we read in the *Venetian Epigrams:*

[28] [. . . sie liegen mir sehr nahe und ich gestehe gern, dass ich das Mädchen leidenschaftlich liebe. Wie sehr ich an sie geknüpft bin, habe ich erst auf dieser Reise gefühlt.]

[29] [Vieles kann ich ertragen. Die meisten beschwerlichen Dinge/ Duld' ich mit ruhigem Muth, wie es ein Gott mir gebeut./ Wenige sind mir jedoch wie Gift und Schlange zuwider;/ Viere: Rauch des Tabaks, Wanzen und Knoblauch und +] (*Soph.* I, *1*:323, Epigram 66)

In most editions the last word is omitted. Goethe is said to have told his son the missing word was one meaning borborygmus, but in the manuscript it says Christ. Cf. 258, *1*:218.

[30] [O so wisst ihr warum blass der Venetier schleicht.] (*Soph.* I, *53*:15, Epigram 37 of those posthumously published)

Boys I loved, too, to be sure, yet I am fonder of the girls;
If I have my fill of her as a girl, she still serves me as a boy.[31]

Or the following expressing the same thought in terms of mythological symbols:

Do not turn, sweet child, your little legs up towards the sky;
Jupiter sees you, the rogue, and Ganymede worries.[32]

The girl meant here is not Christiane but one of a troupe of jugglers consisting of a father and his four children, whom he watched in Venice. The girl makes her appearance on and off in the epigrams under the name of Bettina. The homosexual solution with regard to the anatomical differences between the sexes apparently did not always function adequately, and as he beheld this girl with her confusing contortions of limbs an old conflict of his broke out.

As if carved by the most artistic hand, the sweet little figure,
Soft and without bone, as only the mollusk swims!
Everything is limb, and everything joint, and everything pleasing,
Everything built according to measure, everything moved according to free will.
Human beings have I known, and animals, as well birds as fish,
Many a particular worm, miracles of great Nature;
And yet I marvel at you, Bettina, sweet miracle,
You who are everything at the same time, and an angel in addition.[33]

As he watches Bettina, Goethe is reminded of Breughel's paintings with their grotesque figures, of Dürer's apocalyptical images, of sphinxes, sirens, centaurs:

Thus Bettina perplexes us, confusing her lovely limbs,
Yet she gives us joy immediately when she treads [on] her soles.[34]

The falling apart of the body image is also expressed in the following unfinished epigram:

[31] [Knaben liebt ich wohl auch, doch lieber sind mir die Mädchen,/ Hab ich als Mädchen sie satt, dient sie als Knabe mir noch.] (*Soph.* I, 53:16, Epigram 40 of those posthumously published; written in Silesia in 1790)

This idea was already expressed in antiquity and reappears also in modern literature.

[32] [Kehre nicht, liebliches Kind, die Beinchen hinauf zu dem Himmel; Jupiter sieht dich, der Schalk, und Ganymed ist besorgt.] (*Soph.* I, 1:317; Epigram 38)

[33] [Wie, von der künstlichsten Hand geschnitzt, das liebe Figürchen,/ Weich und ohne Gebein, wie die Molluska nur schwimmt!/ Alles ist Glied, und alles Gelenk, und alles gefällig,/ Alles nach Massen gebaut, alles nach Willkür bewegt./ Menschen hab' ich gekannt, und Thiere, so Vögel als Fische,/ Manches besondre Gewürm, Wunder der grossen Natur;/ Und doch staun' ich dich an, Bettine, liebliches Wunder,/ Die du alles zugleich bist, und ein Engel dazu.] (*Soph.* I, 1:317, Epigram 37)

[34] [So verwirrt uns Bettine, die holden Glieder verwechselnd;/ Doch erfreut sie uns gleich, wenn sie die Sohlen betritt.] (*Soph.* I, 1:318, Epigram 41)

What about you is above, what below what before what behind?
Each movement full of danger seems [a] worry;
And so gracefully you do it, one desires the danger renewed.[35]

The anxiety that is on the verge of breaking out in view of the confusing body image is counteracted by emphasis on female self-sufficiency.

What I am most apprehensive about: Bettina becomes always more dexterous,
Ever more movable becomes every little limb of hers;
Finally she brings her little tongue, in addition, into the graceful c . . .
Plays with the pretty self, does not pay much heed to men.[36]

Yet perhaps reality provided imagery that confirmed the fantasy of the female phallus as may be guessed from the following epigram, part of which is illegible.

To spread out the graceful thighs the father commands,
Childlike the sweet part . . . [illegible] down upon the carpet,
Alas, he who will some day love you first, will find the blossom
Already vanished; your profession took it early away.[37]

Since the illegible part apparently refers to something falling out of the genital onto the carpet, I wonder whether the little girl had been taught to make coins disappear and reappear in the genital. If this supposition is correct then we may conclude that childhood fantasies of a penis hidden somewhere in the female body may easily have been activated.

We meet here on the occasion of his second Italian journey a Goethe quite different from that of the first. At that time he reported with gladness that he had learned to overcome his inhibition against looking at the naked human body. In Venice, now, there are no inhibitions of that sort to overcome but he is found in the midst of free indulgence in pregenital pleasures. What his actual sexual releases were during this stay in Italy is difficult to reconstruct. It is conceivable that he became involved in genital releases elicited by perversions, but one may just as well suppose that the gratification stopped at the mere pleasure of looking. Ordinary intercourse does not seem probable; his longing for Chris-

---

[35] [Was ist oben was unten an dir was vorne was hinten?/ Voller Gefahr scheint jede Bewegung Sorge/ Und so zierlich du's machst wünscht die Gefahr man erneut.] (*Soph.* I, 5:377)

[36] [Was ich am meisten besorge: Bettina wird immer geschickter,/ Immer beweglicher wird jegliches Gliedchen an ihr;/ Endlich bringt sie das Züngelchen noch ins zierliche F . . ./ Spielt mit dem artigen Selbst, achtet die Männer nicht viel.] (*Soph.* I, 53:14, Epigram 34 of those posthumously published)

[37] [Auszuspannen befiehlt der Vater die zierlichen Schenkel,/ Kindisch der liebliche Teil . . . [unleserlich] den Teppich herab./ Ach wer einst zuerst dich liebet, er findet die Blüte/ Schon verschwunden, sie nahm frühe das Handwerk hinweg.] (*Soph.* I, 53:14–15, Epigram 35 of those posthumously published)

tiane, his expectation that she would be faithful and the consequent equivalent obligation on his part; further, his timidity about venereal diseases probably sufficed to keep his passion under control. A warning seems to sound in his malicious epigram (Number 39 of those posthumously published) against the younger Camper, who lectured in Rome on his famous father's anatomical theories when Goethe was there, and who apparently contracted syphilis. Here an important difference can be demonstrated. His outbreaks against venereal disease in the *Roman Elegies* appear to have been based on an anxiety that, though well rationalized, bears neurotic earmarks. The passionateness of his aggressive and anxious feelings on the topic appears now in Venice to have changed to sarcastic irony; neurotic anxiety seems to have been replaced almost entirely with reality anxiety. Something of this kind seems characteristic of Goethe's erotic feelings in general, so far as he expressed them in his *Venetian Epigrams*. Sex is deprived of its spiritual meaning. It is observed and taken apart with the skill of the anatomist's scalpel. The resultant is an unpoetical, almost cynical, attitude even in matters of the greatest intimacy. Thus he wrote, evidently in reference to Christiane:

For a long time I sought me a woman, I sought, yet I found only wenches.
At last I caught you, little wench, for myself, yet I found a woman.[38]

This sober looking straight at facts and not permitting oneself to cover them with the veil of poetry was applied not only to others but also to himself.

Why does the crowd so bustle and scream? It wants to feed itself,
Beget children and feed them, as best it can.
Mark this, traveler, and do the same at home!
More man cannot attain, however he sets about it.[39]

This objective, cold, cynical attitude makes him set forth an unconscious reason for his aversion against the German language, an aversion from which he suffered at times quite intensely during these years.

Give me instead of "the tail"[40] another word, O Priapus,
For I, German, I am as a poet badly plagued.
In Greek I call you phallus, that would sound fine to the ears,
And in Latin also *Mentula* is a bearable word.

[38] [Lange sucht ich ein Weib mir, ich suchte, da fand ich nur Dirnen,/ Endlich erhascht ich dich mir Dirnchen, da fand ich ein Weib.] (*Soph.* I, 53:17, Epigram 46 of those posthumously published)

[39] [Warum treibt sich das Volk so, und schreit? Es will sich ernähren,/ Kinder zeugen, und die nähren, so gut es vermag./ Merke dir, Reisender, das, und thue zu Hause desgleichen!/ Weiter bringt es kein Mensch, stell' er sich, wie er auch will.] (*Soph.* I, 1:310, Epigram 10)

[40] The German word *Schwanz* here translated "tail" is also a vulgar word for "penis."

Mentula would come from Mens [Mind], the tail is something from behind,
And from behind never was for me a joyful pleasure.[41]

With the gradual withdrawal of genital libido from creative activity and its
investment in genital activities, the libido free to be disposed in artistic pursuits
perhaps took on an anal quality, and Goethe attributed this to the German
language, nourishing the illusion that it was the artistic medium and not the
author that was at fault. As a matter of fact Goethe's literary products of that
time, despite their stress on genitality, have an anal quality in terms of formal
features; one has also to think of the *dirty* subjects they deal with.

If we look now at the main literary creations of that period, the *Roman
Elegies,* the two essays, and the *Venetian Epigrams,* we are able to observe
here with great precision the detrimental effect that extensive physical gratification of the passions and its integration has on artistic creativity.

Goethe must have noticed the difference in the emotional background that
made him take up his pen this time. In Epigram 27 he says that the nine Muses
often had nodded at him yet he did not pay attention to them when he had his
girl in his lap. Now he has left his sweetheart, but the Muses have also left him.

> Olympus is still filled with gods; you came to rescue me,
> Boredom! You are saluted as mother of the Muses.[42]

The genius can be inspired even by boredom, but then his artistic product cannot be of that quality that thrives when passionate conflict moves his heart. And
as everything—with very few exceptions—that Goethe wrote is beautiful and
interesting, to say the least of the average of his productions, the *Venetian
Epigrams* too are beautiful and interesting, but no more, and had Goethe
never transcended this level, while he would still be considered an eminent
German poet he would have been of significance only to a small group that
shared his language and it would not be clear whether or not he should be called
a genius.

Yet at the same time we can derive an important general psychological conclusion. It is not the mere fact of frustration that is prerequisite to genius creations, for Goethe probably was frustrated in Venice and possibly, since physical
genital gratifications per se were acceptable to him at that time, he may even
have felt particularly frustrated in view of the alluring sensuous temptations
that abounded in Venice. And still the poetic outcome was not illustrious. Yet

---

[41] [Gieb mir statt "Der Sch . . ." ein ander Wort o Priapus/ Denn ich Deutscher ich bin
übel als Dichter geplagt./ Griechisch nennt ich dich phallos, das klänge doch prächtig den
Ohren,/ Und lateinisch ist auch *Mentula* leidlich ein Wort./ *Mentula* käme von **Mens,** der
Sch . . . ist etwas von hinten,/ Und nach hinten war mir niemals ein froher Genuss.]
(*Soph.* I, 53:15–16, Epigram 38 of those posthumously published)

[42] [Doch von Göttern ist voll der Olymp; du kamst mich zu retten,/ Langeweile! du
bist Mutter der Musen gegrüsst.] (*Soph.* I, 1:313)

we notice that physical gratification was not only sought by him at that time but cherished, welcomed, and heartily accepted as a prospect. Thus the effect upon creativity depends on the personality's attitude towards frustration and it is not the intensity of frustration per se that counts. Probably the condition that will squeeze the last ounce of creativity out of the genius's infinite endowment comes into existence when the greatest *inner* longing for gratification combines with the most total *inner* rejection of it to produce the most supreme frustration.

To conclude, I wish to return to the biographical detail. Goethe's loyalties were divided between Christiane and the Duke at that time. This division was no longer a direct expression of the original sexual conflict of the pre-Italian period but it shows some similarity with it. What is new is the form of solution that Goethe found. In 1790 the conflict was easily solved by writing the two essays and the erotic-sexual poetry and thus making the Duke share his erotic pleasures. As I have pointed out, the successful performance of sexual intercourse permitted a freer expression of homosexuality, reduced its intensity and relieved feelings of guilt.[43] The poetry of that time also had the function of exposing the sexually appropriated female to the sight of the beloved friend. It created a situation *à trois*, which Freud has described with regard to obscene ribaldry. "A person who laughs at smut that he hears is laughing as though he were the spectator of an act of sexual aggression" (161, p. 97). The sexual pleasures enjoyed in the physical relationship with women are used to excite the friend and to compensate him for the loss he has suffered by the poet's heterosexual amorousness.[44]

By this reservation in his relationship to Christiane he avoided a full surrender to the female and kept a route open to disentangle himself emotionally if the need should arise. But the intensity of these complications was, during that period, kept at a level at which one can no longer speak of "dangerous conflict."

[43] The reader may not consider my previous statement about the *Priapeia* as incompatible with this conclusion. The "Notes on the *Priapeia*" are both an expression of and a defense against homosexuality. The homosexuality that was expressed was not primarily in rivalry with the heterosexual trend; but the homosexuality against which the defensive function was directed spelled a profoundly aggressive rejection of the female.

[44] I omit discussion of the opposite trend, namely, that of exciting the friend's jealousy and arousing his interest.

Appendix T

Tentative Notes on the Psychology of Genius[1]

From time to time in the course of this inquiry observations have been made and conclusions drawn that might have some bearing on the psychology of genius. This material has, however, been presented haphazard and piecemeal, in accordance with the needs of the moment. I shall now try to pull these scattered remarks together into a more systematic form.

First there is a problem of definition. There are a few historical personalities concerning whom there is agreement—among the public at large, and, with negligible exceptions, among the experts—that they are geniuses. Such, for example, are Dante, Shakespeare, Leonardo, Michelangelo, Rembrandt, Mozart, Goethe, Beethoven. But though there might be agreement that all these names belong in the category "genius," I believe that the concept "genius" cannot be satisfactorily defined. This is indeed a curious situation—that we should be prepared to agree upon whether a certain person belongs in a category and still not be able to agree on a valid criterion for determining who shall belong to it. Accordingly, the following is not meant as a definition of "genius" but simply as a brief statement of the reasons why I have included the above names in my arbitrarily selected list: They were persons who were capable of re-creating the human cosmos, or part of it, in a way that was significant and not comparable to any previous re-creation.[2]

[1] I have been so bold as to give this appendix a general title although this section refers to tentative conclusions I have drawn only from the study of Goethe. Since Goethe may for various reasons be looked upon as an ideal type of creativity, the generality of the title may not be entirely misplaced. However, it is to be expected that only a few of the propositions I express, if any, will be valid for a general theory of genius. It goes without saying that only in a typology of geniushood could an outline of the whole area be given. The reader is advised to peruse "The Childhood of the Artist" by Dr. Phyllis Greenacre (266) which has been published since this section was written.

[2] I am aware that the vagueness of the terms "significant" and "not comparable" renders this statement useless as a definition. But even if satisfactory definition is impossible such a statement may have a certain limited utility in the context in which it is offered.

The human cosmos finds representation in an individual way in every human being; no two persons ever experience it in exactly the same way. The genius is, in this respect, not different qualitatively from the rest of mankind. Yet already in the act of receiving individually significant impressions of the outer world, of appropriating it by sense organs, feelings, or thoughts, the genius is, nevertheless, significantly different from the nongenius. Whereas the ordinary person in taking the world into his own personality system utilizes the modes of doing so that prevail in his particular society and his particular historical moment, the genius, though inescapably limited also by historical juncture, will still show more independence. There is even to be encountered in the genius the paradox that his way of experiencing the world bears more deeply engraved the earmarks of his historical times than that of his contemporaries and, nevertheless, is formed in a more individual and original way than theirs. Precisely in Goethe's work can it be very definitely shown that the act of perception itself already contains the very essence of genius and partakes of the nature of a re-creation.

However, the other aspect of genius—the presentation of the human world in a significant, incomparable, and understandable way—must also be present before a person can be said to belong to this category. There are, after all, people who have the capacity of a genius in regard to the re-creation of the world in the perceptive area but who are unable to pour these experiences into relevant, significant, and understandable forms. For example, the psychotic patient, too, as we know, perceives the world in an absolutely original way and re-creates it, often very profusely, in works of art, but his re-creation is in forms that are not understandable to mankind. Here an important aspect of genius can be shown. The artistic productions of the psychotic become understandable as soon as we have penetrated into the structure of his personality (see 346A). The understanding of his personality often coincides with the understanding of his creations. The creations of genius, too, can at times be understood better when his personality structure is understood, but the genius's creation, however much it may contain of his own personality, also contains an aspect of reality in which the rest of mankind can participate without any knowledge of his personality structure. This feature is missing in the psychotic's creations. However, the problem of the psychotic genius will have to be left untouched in this context.

Furthermore, we must distinguish in the genius between his faculties and his personality, that is to say, between the raw material at his disposal and the form his personality gives to this raw material (cf. 276). There is no doubt that there are people who possess all the raw material necessary for genius but who squander it, or are inhibited, or commit early suicide—by violence or by default. Otto Weininger has always impressed me as a person who had all the possibilities of becoming a genius as far as the possession of raw material went but was lacking in that additional requirement which I vaguely call personality here. He ended his life at the age of twenty-one. Clinically we also encounter the type of person who has the personality of a genius but lacks the raw material.

Thus in the genius two or more entities are blended, each of which has a different history, structure, and meaning. What I have called the "raw material" can more sophisticatedly be called the biological, constitutional factor. In every genius, I suppose, there will be found at one point or another a faculty probably of a biological nature that makes him superior and unique. In Mozart this can be demonstrated objectively. At the age of fourteen Mozart succeeded in writing out from memory after a single hearing the famous *Miserere* of Gregorio Allegri (1582–1652), which had been kept secret by the papacy upon threat of excommunication (see 526, p. 99). This extraordinary feat is, as far as I know, without equal before or since. This faculty, however, which Mozart demonstrated in this instance, does not demonstrate his genius. It is conceivable that a person might some day perform an equivalent feat without showing any signs of talent for composing music. Yet it demonstrates that Mozart also possessed a primary, mainly biological, capacity, such as has perhaps never since been encountered in any other person.[3] Thus we may suppose that Mozart's very biological substructure already contained an objective faculty that was unique.

In Goethe we also observe such a factor. For example, his dream function, which we may classify as biological, may at times have been different from what is usually encountered in the study of dreams. It is true that instances are known of dreams containing an objectively valid answer to a problem with which the waking ego has struggled in vain (see 158, 5:555, 579). Yet, that Goethe should ever have had dreams the manifest content of which consisted of nothing more nor less than perfectly formed poems betrays a dream function endowed with constructive capabilities that must be extremely rare. I have reported in the text the uncanny feelings Goethe had about his genius capacities. Their biological rooting in the dream function may have been not the least source of Goethe's apprehension. It should be remembered here, as in the main text, that it is immaterial for present purposes whether in this instance the dream was lifting into consciousness a content that the waking ego was inhibited in grasping, or whether what here emerged from the dream was something that had originally been formed in the conscious mind only subsequently to be repressed: in either case the unconscious was playing a role not only extremely rare, if not indeed without precedent, but also one that must have had its roots in the very biological structure itself. We know, too, from Goethe's account that his unattended-to free associations also appeared on the conscious level during the daytime as fully formed poems and songs. There were in all probability still other unique biological factors at Goethe's disposal whose existence escaped documentation.

Of course, the fate of the biological factor is not independent of external circumstances. Mozart's father was a musician and Mozart grew up in an environment in which music was the center of everyday life. About Goethe we hear from Bettina von Arnim

[3] There are other indications that Mozart's auditory sense was incomparably developed.

how he had already at the age of nine weeks anxiety dreams, how grand-mother and grandfather, mother and father and the wet nurse, stood around his cradle and listened, what violent movements were revealed in his features, how, when he woke up, he broke out into very distressed crying; often also he screamed so vehemently that he lost his breath and his parents feared for his life; they arranged for a bell; when they noticed that he became restless in his sleep, they rang and rattled it vigorously so as to make him forget the dream immediately upon awakening.[4]

It is generally accepted that particular stimuli shape the *anlage,* and early stimulation such as Bettina describes conceivably helped to form out of Goethe's "dream *anlage*" the constructive function from which he derived such great profit.

This of course is mere speculation, but with this speculation we have reached the topic of the genius's environment, that is, the special genesis of genius. As I have several times pointed out, Goethe was raised by parents both of whom found the consummation of their lives in this child. Of course, this fact was characteristic not only of them but also of him. A less intelligent, charming, inquisitive, talented, eager child would not have stimulated his parents to the extent to which the child Goethe did.[5] But the bare reality factors independent of the child's constitution are of no minor importance. If Goethe's father had been a practitioner of a profession, if his mother had been older and had felt closer to her husband, not so much of parental strivings, interests, and wishes would have extended to their oldest son. One may raise the question whether Goethe's disposition towards genius was so penetratingly strong that it would have led to equally profuse and supreme manifestations even if the details of his environment had been different. I doubt it. If Mozart had been kidnapped at the age of one and grown up among gypsies, or had lived as a prince at court, he would not have become the great composer he did. Likewise a Goethe living with a father who devoted himself to his little son for only an hour or two in the evening and whose interests were divided between family and a thriving law practice, would have found the opportunity for the evolvement of the "raw material" slumbering in him seriously impaired.

There also arises the question of the conscious and unconscious parental atti-

---

[4] [wie er schon mit neun Wochen ängstliche Träume gehabt, wie Grossmutter und Grossvater, Mutter und Vater und die Amme um seine Wiege gestanden und lauschten, welche heftige Bewegungen sich in seinen Mienen zeigten, und wenn er erwachte, in ein sehr betrübtes Weinen verfallen, oft auch sehr heftig geschrieen hat, so dass ihm der Atem entging und die Eltern für sein Leben besorgt waren; sie schafften eine Klingel an; wenn sie merkten, dass er im Schlaf unruhig ward, klingelten und rasselten sie heftig, damit er beim Aufwachen gleich den Traum vergessen möge.] (11, part 2:160).

[5] Anna Freud has repeatedly stressed the easily overlooked fact that parental behavior is not solely the product of parental conflicts but also contains their reactions to the child's personality. See 90.

tudes towards the child. From clinical experience we learn repeatedly that despite the best conscious intentions and wishes and efforts of the parents it is the unconscious part of the parental motives and attitudes that tips the scales.

As to the unconscious motives of Goethe's parents we know nothing, but we are compelled to assume that in their unconscious too the unambivalent prevailed over the ambivalent. It is even reasonable to speculate whether perhaps in this instance the child found himself with parents who in their unconscious had a relationship free of ambivalence to the child. But even if this was the case the reality factor of the father's circumstances allowing full devotion to the boy's upbringing must not be underrated. Also the more feminine behavior of the father during the preoedipal phase, that is to say, a rarely occurring adjustment of the father to the particular needs of the growing child, must not be overlooked.

In the relationship between the child Goethe and his mother that which has always struck me as the most remarkable feature—aside from her immediate infatuation with the baby, her willingness to serve the child, her making him the fulfillment of all her wishes—is the fairy-tale telling situation reported by Bettina. Especially if, as Bettina tells us, it occurred repeatedly, I feel that this may have been a center in which the child's genius endowment was kindled.

Furthermore, the presence of J. C. Goethe's psychotic secretary can scarcely be overrated. Here the appearance of the primary process in a very peculiar form is most striking. This young man devoted himself to bringing the child's fantasies instantly into a material form, that is to say, if a simplified description is permitted, the primary process of another person was for the child's sake brought into the service of a reality function, which in turn facilitated the materialization of the child's own primary process, or at least of its derivatives in the form of daydreams and free associations. This combination of circumstances is hardly less unusual and fantastic than that which we encounter in the fairy-tale situation.

The influence of the many pregnancies of Goethe's mother and of the early death of these children in establishing Goethe's confidence and optimism has been described by Freud (see 185). To this we must add that he returned to blooming life from serious childhood disorders. The child surrounded by childbirths and child deaths himself went through death only to regain life anew, a chain of processes that resulted in the evolvement of that indomitable narcissism which could never be totally defeated by even the greatest exertions and demands upon the psychic apparatus.

Yet oddly enough just such a series of events (pregnancies and child deaths and numerous serious diseases) brings so much ill fate into the lives of those who are later defeated by their psychopathology. Perhaps his parent's unshakable affection for the child Goethe converted the curse that early traumata usually constitute into a strengthening of the ego. Did this mother perhaps not withdraw emotionally from her oldest son when she went through her many pregnancies and did the boy perhaps not have to fear the loss of maternal affection at occasions when other children feel deserted? Here again speculation must fill the gaps of our ignorance.

Although it has not always been explicitly stated, Goethe's relationship to his sister has been made the center of this inquiry, and there is little to be added here. If he had been an only child or one among many, either situation would have had a less favorable effect. The early intimate contact with the other sex, though it may have increased latent homosexuality, resulted in protection against its manifest form, which personalities of Goethe's type are always in danger of developing.[6] The twinlike character of the relationship between these two I have several times stressed. That Cornelia was also a mirror-image of himself caused him to seek a woman when he was prompted to narcissistic regressions, whereas on such occasions different childhood conditions might later have easily made him become a victim of manifest homosexuality, which in his instance would not have been conducive to creativity.

The closeness in age of the next sibling, so often a stumbling block in the life of the neurotic, worked advantageously in Goethe's instance. Identification with the sister could take place without precipitating damaging regressions. At the same time there was, we noticed, an identification with the mother and acting out of the fantasy of having given life to the baby. Yet here a few additional remarks are warranted. Always supposing that Bettina's secondhand account conveys an essentially correct record of Goethe's childhood situation, the triangle relationship of the boy, Cornelia, and their mother, allows further comment. Consider, for example, the earmarks here of a particularly early-developed altruism. The little boy—he must have been around three at that time—instead, apparently, of intensifying his own oral needs under the impression of his younger sister's gratifications, made himself actively instrumental in bringing gratification to her. He reportedly became quite angry when anyone else sought to do so, which would signify an intense arrogation of maternal functions by identification, and likewise an intense insistence upon carrying them out. At the same time it shows an identification or empathy with the infant's oral needs, that is to say, childhood jealousy and envy were early converted into acceptance of supplying the sister's oral needs as a valid task to be solved by him.[7] Here we encounter a particularly happy synthesis of two identifications into a positive object-relationship. We may see in this early situation the prototype or preformation of his adult creativity, when the needs of others would incessantly be gratified by his

---

[6] Cf. *Dichtung und Wahrheit*, Book XVIII: "The habit of dealing becomingly and courteously with young ladies without the immediate consequence of a definitive constraint and possession, I owed only to her [Cornelia]." [Die Gewohnheit mit jungen Frauenzimmern anständig und verbindlich umzugehen, ohne dass sogleich eine entscheidende Beschränkung und Aneignung erfolgt wäre, hatte ich nur ihr zu danken.] (*Soph.* I, 29:100)

[7] Of course, the recorded data do not permit a conclusion as to whether this accomplishment was achieved by a surrender to the sister of demands of his own which he wished to have gratified.

pouring forth one work of art after another. The narcissistic needs of the creative personality would likewise be gratified in the same act. What enabled the little boy to achieve this early synthesis is not known; yet the boy's capacity to synthesize his own oral needs as well as the jealousy of his mother into a constructive act of altruism was an early harbinger of the later genius.

In noting this early development of altruism one is reminded of a passage in Freud's writings. In discussing the predisposition to obsessional neurosis, Freud wrote:

> I cannot tell if it may seem too rash if on the basis of such indications as we possess, I suggest the possibility that a chronological outstripping of libidinal development by ego development should be included in the disposition to obsessional neurosis. A precocity of this kind would necessitate the choice of an object under the influence of ego-instincts, at a time at which the sexual instincts had not yet assumed their final shape, and a fixation at the stage of the pregenital sexual organization would thus be left. (176, p. 325)

A satisfactorily precise understanding of this hypothesis eludes me, for there is a doubt in my mind whether Freud meant a premature evolvement of ego-functions proper, or rather of what is now called the superego. Goethe's early development of altruism in a crucial phase of infantile development has to be accounted an important step in ego-development. I observed a similar development in a patient who later suffered from a schizophrenic disorder. At the age of one and a half—as her mother reliably reported—she was more concerned with the gratifications of her fifteen-months-older brother than with her own. She developed similar attitudes later towards her three-year-younger sister, but subsequent analysis showed that this step had overstrained her resources; it seems that in this instance conformity and feelings of guilt prevailed over true affection for the sister, although these were present, too.

A factor that particularly impresses me in Goethe's early altruism, and that I wish to stress, is the passion that apparently was contained in it, as can be seen in the anger that broke out when he was prevented from expressing it. This makes me believe that the child's altruism was fused with strong passional elements and that the pleasure gain from his altruistic activity was considerable. I speculate that in my patient the pleasure gain derived from the equivalent activity was much less. It is conceivable that in the child Goethe the early evolvement of ego-functions was in the service of strong pleasurable object-relations, and that it was this that prevented unfortunate consequences such as are so often observed in patients who come to clinical attention. In them, the progress in ego-development is made at the cost of a deep injury to the child's potential capacity for love and affection. Goethe's early altruism seems to have favored particularly strong ties to objects.

Thus Goethe spent his childhood with a partner of almost the same age, who stimulated his activity, kept his erotic feelings alive, made the attachment to the other sex an indelible part of his life, and left enough feelings of guilt to stimulate the incessant urge to undo part of his ambivalence by the creation of new and perfect life.

Crucial and decisive as Goethe's relationship to his sister was, behind it looms, of course, the fountainhead of human destiny, his relationship to his mother and father. In this relationship, as is true of all kinds of psychopathology, the relevant features of the genius's development will once be found, but nothing relevant can be added by me now except perhaps for two remarks. In *Dichtung und Wahrheit,* Book VI, Goethe characterizes the triangle of the mother and her two surviving children in the following terms:

> A mother almost still a child, who grew up to consciousness only with and in her two oldest children; these three, as they became aware of the world with healthy glance, fit to live and demanding immediate enjoyment.[8]

Although Goethe is attempting, in this statement, to indicate a contrast with his relationship to his father, it can be considered in its own right. Here, without denying the mother-relationship, he speaks of it as if it had been almost a sibling-relationship; yet this is not set forth in terms of the pleasure and enjoyment that accrued to him from this constellation, but in terms of his mother's finding her identity in that process. At least that is how I understand the word *Bewusstsein* (literally "consciousness"), which Goethe uses in this context. Fischer in his dictionary notes that at times the word *Bewusstsein* has in Goethe's writings the meaning of *Selbstbewusstsein,* "consciousness of self" (146). This, I believe, suggests that Goethe was under the impression that his mother acquired her individuality through her contact with the two children, that she, so to speak, woke up, became adult, found herself, in short, acquired a sense of identity.[9] As a matter of fact, I have observed in some immature mothers that important phases of structurization of the personality were activated and accomplished through pregnancy and child-rearing. It is a process equivalent to that described

---

[8] [eine Mutter fast noch ein Kind, welche erst mit und in ihren beiden Ältesten zum Bewusstsein heranwuchs; diese drei, wie sie die Welt mit gesundem Blicke gewahr wurden, lebensfähig und nach gegenwärtigem Genuss verlangend.] (*Soph.* I, 27:21)

[9] In view of a clinical observation I have made since I described this root of Goethe's geniushood I would put more stress on this source than I did originally. I had occasion to observe a young man who, no doubt artistically endowed, obtained great proficiency in one of the arts. To my surprise, the unconscious reservoir of his ambition, devotion to and love of his art was the fantasy, coinciding partly with reality, that he was the only one in the family who provided his mother with the artistic stimulation of which she was fond and in need. By providing her with this he thus not only established a particular closeness but obtained superiority over her at an early age by the active attitude of giving. It was not an attitude of receptivity, of profiting from her interest in art, but without doubt the conviction that his mother received from him what no other member of the family was able or inclined to give her; he here acted out a positive oedipal impulse without having to pay the price of a feeling of guilt.

by Freud in women of a certain type in whose characters one finds vestiges of relations to men with whom they had been in love (197, p. 37). However, acquisitions of structure that are related to the context with the infant are, it seems, often deeper-going, longer-lasting, and more basic, as compared with those that derive from the object-relationship to men. Since Goethe's mother was young and, in some respects, unstable all her life, I can well imagine that she may have belonged to the afore-mentioned type of immature mother. Although it is questionable whether each of her children had such an effect upon her, some evidence can be drawn from her correspondence regarding her relationship to her first born. I wish to take this effect, however, as assured and discuss the consequences that the child's effect upon his mother may have had upon Goethe's development.[10] From this point of view it would appear that the fairy-tale situation was only the concretization of a general feature of the background against which Goethe's childhood development took place, namely, that any step forward in his own development provided his mother with a stimulus for further growth. I perceive in Goethe's remark a high degree of emotional closeness and intimacy between the child and the mother, but these degrees bear the opposite signs from those that are customarily found in that relationship. The child did not experience himself primarily as the recipient, but rather denied the status of childhood dependency. During the process of growing up, when, biologically, outside stuff was taken in and transformed into the substance the organism was in need of, the child apparently had the feeling of giving something out to his mother. Whether he experienced this in an active form remains undetermined. It may well have been a feeling that inner activity automatically had equivalent effects in his mother.[11] In her lecture on "Emotional Factors in Education" (given at Cleveland, Ohio, on September 20, 1956), Dr. Anna Freud assigned to the mother who raises her child the function of lending the child her own ego, its strength, patience, knowledge, and so forth, until the child has sufficiently matured. In Goethe's instance, strangely enough, it seems to have been the other way around, and it was the child who lent his rapidly growing ego to his mother for her maturation. The reader may recall (see Appendix Q) that a comparable situation obtained between Goethe's son, August, and Christiane, but that Christiane became frightened. Such constellations can be beneficial only when they are integrated by both mother and child. Thus in Goethe's brief remark one solution to the problem of his creativity may be found. In an early situation —and one of the most important in the child's development—he entertains a relationship in which fundamental features of automorphism are found adumbrated, inasmuch as the mere process of growth was experienced as being coin-

---

[10] This point would not be essentially weakened if it should some day turn out that Goethe was here less under the influence of a reality factor than of a fantasy. My own feeling is that Goethe recorded as an old man an impression that was true to reality.

[11] Possibly this was the psychobiological origin of the keystone feeling of which Goethe twice wrote.

cident with a constructive action he performed upon and for the beloved mother. The unconscious equivalent of the egosyntonic idea that the mother found her identity through contact with the child was probably the idea that the child had begotten or given birth to her. An idea expressed in a poem in *Westöstlicher-Diwan* may be a late derivative of this early notion:

> Allah does not need to be active any more,
> We create his world.[12]

It is difficult to decide—but quite consequential—to what developmental phase this mechanism is to be attributed. Did the child form it already in the preoedipal phase, or was it a solution that was found on a compensatory basis in the oedipal phase? The context in which Goethe made the autobiographical remark strongly suggests an oedipal constellation, since it follows an ambivalent description of his father. And yet one feels doubtful. In this remark Goethe indicates a very tight bond between mother, sister and himself and draws a line of demarcation between this group and the father. The remark suggests a sharp border of the ego where it adjoins the image of the father, in contradiction, possibly, to a partial fusion of his self with mother–sister imagery, as if the identity of self had been only partially established, namely, at those places only where there was an opportunity of setting himself into contrast with his father. I therefore conclude that a preoedipal formation was successfully taken over into the oedipal phase and constructively used for a working through of the oedipal conflict. This would mean that the decisive process had already taken place in an early phase of infancy, but as far as I am familiar with the record I believe that it cannot be specified in a more detailed fashion.

Regarding the father-relationship, I can only repeat what I have said earlier. Goethe's ambivalence shows up very sharply; but it is a singular ambivalence, for one finds at its bottom an almost unambivalent loyalty, devotion and respect, perhaps even love. In turn this unambivalent core of the relationship to the father is singular in so far as it seems simultaneously to have been identical with an incredible self-elevation above the father, the two diametrically opposed attitudes, mutually exclusive, not leading to conflict because they were synthesized into one. I derive this strange conclusion from the clinical findings concerning Goethe's first intercourse. The reader may recall that the record strongly suggests its having taken place when Goethe was the same age his father had reached when he married (cf. p. 1654). However, I added as an additional hypothesis—incredible though it sounded—that it occurred at the age when his father begot his oldest son, which would mean that Goethe reenacted in his first intercourse a self-conception or self-procreation. At such archaic levels conception and procreation become identical. Now I may add that the difference be-

---

[12] [Allah braucht nicht mehr zu schaffen,/ Wir erschaffen seine Welt.] (*Soph.* I, 6:189)

Schaffen and *erschaffen* are here put into contrast. There may be a doubt about the connotation of the former. It is sometimes used in the sense of "to create," but also "to be active," or "to be active creatively." Cf. 146, p. 520.

tween the two interpretations is perhaps not quite as great as I thought, for in the act of self-procreation a man essentially repeats what his father did. To be sure, he repeats it in a more narcissistic way than happens when he identifies with the father who takes possession of the mother for the first time. However, a man who postpones his first intercourse as long as Goethe did and then identifies with the father who begets the identifying person synthesizes the two attitudes that I have outlined above: he endures the enormous deprivation which he believes his father had to endure and thus expresses his loyalty, but simultaneously he deprives his father of the procreative role to which he owes his life and thus expresses his rivalry and incapacity to bear the father's superiority. Furthermore, if Goethe's father was circumcised—as the enigmatic note of his physician may mean (see p. 1035 n)—there may have been an important reality factor that favored precisely the attitude that I have just described. The little boy then would have grown up in admiration of the largeness of his father's genital and would simultaneously have had the feeling that, after all, his small penis was superior to his father's.

Another general factor can be unraveled from Goethe's history, a factor which is not easy to describe. In general terms one can posit four modes of psychopathological manifestation: neurotic, delinquent, psychotic, and perverted. In the text it is shown that all four modes were manifested in Goethe's life and that all four were at his disposal. He had to struggle with inordinate neurotic fears, he indulged in aggression and destruction, and he was powerlessly overwhelmed at times by patent inroads of the unconscious.[13] A fixation to any one mode of manifestation would have seriously limited the wealth of his contacts with reality, the extreme variety of his resources for taking in the world and re-creating it. This latitude in forms of psychopathology was made possible by fortunate external circumstances. One such circumstance came about when, after a very carefully supervised childhood, the rebuilding of his father's house when the boy was five years and eight months old forced his father temporarily to relax his supervision and the child was exposed to what we may call the seamy side of life. This is described by Goethe in the first book of *Dichtung und Wahrheit*. Then, when he was nine and a half, the French occupied Frankfurt, and Count Thoranc, the famous *Königsleutnant,* was billeted in his father's house, and a few months later paternal authority was shattered in a violent scene between the father and the Count. Here again external influences assisted the boy in freeing himself from authority that might have reduced his freedom by an all too early solidification of his personality. The reduction of paternal authority brought him outside of the area of direct supervision by his father and was followed by a phase that may be evaluated clinically as one of mild delinquency. Thus he was protected against too great an effect of the latency period, during which time the superego develops. Had he remained continuously under his father's governance,

[13] Appendix S, in discussing Goethe's erotic poetry, sets forth some of his fantasies concerning perverted inclinations.

identification with him would have manifested itself much earlier and probably would have led to inhibition. The Gretchen episode in his fifteenth year in turn brought him back again under closer supervision and thus the danger of the development of real delinquency was averted. By chance, fate provided him with sequences that an enlightened educator might try to establish for a child by a planned adaptation of his environment, namely, after a step in ego-development has been accomplished, to grant relative freedom before new pressure is brought upon the child. If constantly increasing pressure is exerted upon a child the danger is great of a development characterized by compulsiveness and unfreedom. In psychoanalysis an interpretation is followed by a period of working through; when raising a child, an equivalent process must be granted, that is to say, after an ego-adaptation has been enforced by external pressure, time must be granted to the child to integrate the new adaptation so that it shall become egosyntonic. This propitious sequence of phases in Goethe's upbringing was one of the concomitant factors, I believe, that caused in the adult a balance between anxiety and aggression, or, in clinical language, between neurotic and delinquent psychopathology. Various symptoms have been described that bear the sign manual of neurotic psychopathology; Goethe's overt neglect, however, of father and mother, manifested by the long periods during which he stayed away from Frankfurt at times when his presence there was indicated, his illegitimate liaison, his tardiness in adopting his son, and many other incidents are manifestations of aggression or, as I prefer to call it, of delinquency.

Yet as soon as one studies the function of these various forms of psychopathology one notices that they do not follow the usual laws found in the psychoanalysis of clinical cases. In the instance of the seemingly neurotic psychopathology this becomes particularly clear. Goethe apparently always maintained at least that minimum of distance from symptoms which betokens that his seemingly neurotic psychopathology belongs in a different category, outside the area of neuroses. The bona fide neurotic symptom reduces the ego's reactibility, whether this reduction pertains to action, perception, thought, or internal freedom: in one or another area the neurotic symptom impinges on function. In Goethe, however, one can observe that, with one exception, the neurotic symptoms never penetrated so deeply into the structure of the ego as to cause an impairment of function. I have recorded some of the instances, dating to a time prior to his arrival at Weimar, which prove that, as soon as the necessity arose, his ego found ways and means of sealing off the respective symptom by a sort of partitioning sequestration. This ingenuity and resourcefulness of the ego is absolutely unneurotic, and therefore we are not entitled to look upon Goethe's many anxieties as neurotic anxieties, although they have much in common with them in their history and content. As soon as the two sets of phenomena are viewed in their functional aspect the difference between them becomes amply clear. The bona fide neurotic symptom puts forceful constraint upon the ego; the equivalent symptom in the genius, however, does not show this effect at all;

we find so-called symptoms with particular frequency during phases in which a new creation is being prepared and we must look at them as an internal rehearsal of the work of art which is to be created. Freud attributed to thought processes the function of "an experimental kind of acting" (172, p. 221). An equivalent function can be detected in the seemingly neurotic psychopathology of the genius. If the genius did not have at his disposal this internal arena upon which to carry out his conflict (without moving in a straight line towards the final, reality-adequate, purposeful action leading to gratification or to a solution) many works of art could not be created. Art often, if not always, evolves out of the tension that results from the damming up of energy diverted from original goals by the practical (and inner) impossibility of directly gratifying wishes. What appears then as neurotic manifestation of inner conflicts is in reality the back and forth movement of as yet unbound energy which is in the process of being formed into the prestages of creative actions. This phase may vary greatly in length and in clinical conspicuousness, ranging all the way from such a phase as that prior to Goethe's retreat in 1774 when he wrote *Werther* to the zero of those instances when he woke up with a finished poem in his mind. The greater and the more formidable the resulting work of art, the longer, probably, and the stronger will be the preceding phase of internal rehearsal. The mentation upon *Faust* covered Goethe's whole adult life and even went back to his childhood. When I reconstructed the inner processes that went on in Goethe while he was presenting his speech on the occasion of the opening of the Ilmenau mine (see above, p. 858) I tried to capture one little episode of "neurotic" internal rehearsing—in this case one which I believe led ultimately to the solution of the *Faust* problem.

The extent to which the creative artist needs the "neurotic" conflict can be seen from the way he acts and feels when his environment takes on a shape that eliminates the seed of conflict. When Schiller was helped out by a friend at a time of tragic destitution, he could not bear up under relatively favorable conditions longer than a year; he went away and wrote his benefactor:

> My heart is contracted and the lights of my imagination are extinguished. I am in need of a crisis. Nature brings about a destruction in order to bring forth anew. It may well be that you do not understand me, but I understand myself all right.[14]

Instructive as this sample is and much as it supports my thesis, it is not applicable to Goethe's life. His existence was far too broad, his sensitivity far too delicate, his ability to extract what he needed for works of art from whatever situations arose far too formidable, for it to have been necessary for him to take

---

[14] [Mein Herz ist zusammengezogen, und die Lichter meiner Phantasie sind ausgelöscht. Ich bedarf einer Krisis. Die Natur bereitet eine Zerstörung, um neu zu gebären. Kann wohl sein, dass Du mich nicht verstehst, aber ich verstehe mich schon.] (Quoted after 406, pp. 286–87)

purposeful steps towards the preparation of conflicts. Goethe would have been able to enact neurotic rehearsing even in a vacuum, so to speak.

A different, though comparable, aspect is also valid for Goethe's delinquent syndrome. Again—with rare exceptions—we do not encounter the ego bound to aggressive actions. There is again distance between ego and aggression, in the form of reflection and deliberation. Aggression in Goethe's life took a position equivalent to an act of self-preservation. Yet in his case the aggression did not primarily serve so much the purpose of preserving life and existence or of pleasure gain as the purpose of safeguarding the creative process and keeping it free from interference. As aggression is healthy and necessary in the fight for the preservation of self and love-objects, it acquires an equivalent meaning when the genius faces the alternatives of either acting in accordance with the mores and thus endangering the creative process, or infringing upon standards of conduct but thus guaranteeing optimal creative output. Goethe's feelings of guilt were not mute when he deliberately caused pain to people towards whom he felt affection and for whom he assumed responsibility. It is, however, remarkable that in his letters and diaries he rather avoided an elaboration upon his feelings of guilt. Nevertheless, that they existed cannot be doubted, as occasional remarks made years later when the acuteness of the situation had faded away may prove, or as a study of some of his works will also demonstrate. I have quoted documents that may sound as if Goethe was cold, at times even brutal. The reader may recall some surprising letters written immediately upon his sister's death, and yet we know from one sentence in a letter written some ten years later (January 17, 1787, to Charlotte von Stein) when he felt guilt-ridden and saddened, how overwhelmingly he had been seized by despair at that time. It looks as if he prevented himself from dissipating his feelings of guilt, which evidently provided momentum towards creation.

We shall return later to another aspect of the role of aggression in the genius. Here I wish to point out that the thesis I have thus far advanced—that the psychopathology of Goethe (and of any other genius for that matter) is not to be classified or viewed in the same way as the psychopathology commonly encountered clinically—is not valid without exception. If my reconstruction of Goethe's sexual dysfunction and my clinical evaluation of the history of his writing the *Chromatology* are correct—as I shall assume in the following discussion—we face in these two instances patent exceptions to the above-stated rule. A premature ejaculation precipitated by kissing or any other form of foreplay is definitely beyond the scope of neurotic rehearsal. It is a dysfunction, and results in a limitation of the ego. In this instance the ego was forcibly constrained and had to bow to the pathology imposed upon it. Similarly, the attitudes of Goethe towards color theory and the way his *Chromatology* originated do not show mental distance permitting reflection upon alternatives. In this area Goethe behaved in a way identical with the unbending determination of the delusional psychotic.

In order to view these two instances in proper proportion we must consider the structure of the object-relations of the genius. Man, who is born in a state of extreme self-centeredness, without regard for other human beings and without a subjective desire for human contact, develops into the state of adulthood, which is characterized by intense longings for mental, emotional, and physical contacts with one or more members of the species. Further, within man's object-relations the most intense and the most sublime experiences of joy, pleasure, and delight occur, comprising the physical as well as the emotional and spiritual spheres. The development from the infant into the adult state is difficult, complicated, fraught with potential mishaps, deviations, and tragedies, and the final outcome is only exceptionally completely satisfactory. Nevertheless, any lag in the full evolvement of object-relations must in general be regarded as belonging to the realm of psychopathology and must be considered a deficit phenomenon.

As far as I can see there is only one exception to this rule, namely the artistic genius. As soon as he achieves a satisfactory mode of object-relationship—and for the genius only an ideal mode is likely to be satisfactory—he simultaneously loses the capacity for creating great art. My way of presenting this problem here may unintentionally give the impression that these alternatives (object-relationship versus genius creativity) are matters of choice, or of willed strivings. In the genius there are safety devices that come automatically into play and protect him against ever losing himself in the pleasures of a true object-relationship. The presence of these safeguards, of course, does not obviate the deepest and most heart-rending conflicts and sufferings in the genius, for all the forces that tend in others towards the pleasures of object-relations are at work in him too but are blocked or diverted before they have reached their goal. As a matter of fact, there is a remark in one of Goethe's letters that shows some awareness of this constellation at a surprisingly early age. Thus he wrote to Behrisch from Leipzig on November 7, 1767, about his sweetheart Annette:

> I often say to myself: If she were now yours, and no one but death could challenge you for her, shut you out from her embraces? [I] tell you what I feel about it, all the thoughts that I revolve—and when I am finished, then I beg God not to give her to me. If ever a prayer has been heard, it will be this one, and the fulfillment would need—fie, this is an ugly, blasphemous thought, a thought that is intended to displace the prayer.[15]

Notwithstanding the fears, doubts and scruples that lie behind such a remark, one nevertheless feels that here the dawning genius vaguely senses what he owes to his destiny and very seriously shies away from the temptation of a full object-

---

[15] [Ich sage mir oft: wenn sie nun deine wäre, und niemand als der Tod dir sie streitig machen, dir ihre Umarmung verwehren könnte? Sage dir was ich da fühle, was ich alles herumdencke—und wenn ich am Ende bin; so bitte ich Gott, sie mir nicht zu geben. Ist je ein Gebet erhört worden, so wirds dieses, und die Erfüllung brauchte—pfuy das ist ein hässlicher gotteslästerlicher Gedancke, ein Gedancke, der das Gebet zu verdrängen gerichtet ist.]

relationship despite the unique bliss it holds forth. This remark was made at a time when the relationship between the lovers temporarily took a pleasurable and promising turn, between the two spells that impressed me as paranoid episodes.[16]

Why has it to be thus in the genius? When great art is created the result is something that carries all the earmarks of life, yet is still more beautiful, even more pleasing, than life itself, for it comes closer to our ideals than reality, with its many flaws, can. Reality is never ideal, but art is, or, at least, comes closer to being so. The idea is trite and has often been expressed, but nevertheless I shall cite just one example in proof thereof. Even if there existed a landscape as beautiful, harmonious, mysterious and full of meaning as a particular landscape painting by Rembrandt it would not retain this ideal character, for it would require a certain season or a certain illumination and the addition of one edifice constructed by man might destroy it; that is to say, its ideal appearance is transitory. Rembrandt's landscape is not subject to these limitations.[17]

The pouring of life into perfect forms of art requires a specific inner condition in the creative artist, a condition that presupposes a total immersion in or total devotion to the task of creation. In general it may be said that objects are of importance to the genius only in so far as the experiences with them will serve the comprehensive goal of creating life in the form of art, that is to say, only those objects that are potential stimuli of future works of art can become relevant in the genius's life. As soon as the longing for the objects themselves successfully competes with the urge to create, creativeness must lose in momentum. When the relation to the object provides real happiness and causes gratifications that reduce tension to a normal level, again no momentum towards creation remains, and either no work of art will issue or only one of second quality. If, however, the longing for and the love of the object is experienced at maximum but the possession of the object is frustrated, then the full momentum towards the re-creation of the object in the form of a work of art will be preserved. Thus maximum tension combined with maximum frustration is one of the constellations that may enable a genius to produce works in keeping with his innate talents. Where relevant documents have reached us, we can observe in Goethe that true object-relations did not subsist between him and those women who inspired his most beautiful poetry; for him they were pure catalysts of creativeness, vehicles by means of which he could be transported to the sphere in which art is

---

[16] Wilhelm Dilthey (104, p. 225) quotes this passage but erroneously dates it after the second paranoid spell. He explains it by Goethe's knowledge that no one single relationship would suffice him, and by his striving for experiences in their total fullness and in freedom. I do not dispute that the pleasure principle too was at work in Goethe's remark to Behrisch, but I am convinced that only consideration of the reality principle, which is different for the genius from what it is for the ordinary person, does full justice to this passage.

[17] The possibility of the painting's being destroyed or of its visibility depending on illumination falls into a different category of limitations and does not militate against its ideal character.

generated. As soon as the object has served such a purpose it is dropped and hence so many geniuses are decried as selfish, cruel, or egotistic. No doubt, the genius's actual behavior bespeaks aggression. To a great extent, psychological aggression is also involved in such relationships, because the object is psychologically destroyed during the creation of the work of art. The genius must never permit himself to be lured into full and satisfactory object-relationships. Here is the point in which the profound suffering of the truly great ones centers. They are permitted to sense the delights of object-relations, they present them to the world in all their beauties, complications, and involvements, but as real persons they must endure the dire deprivation of just these gratifications. I must repeat here the passage quoted earlier (p. 997) from Goethe's letter of April 22, 1828, to Zelter.

> If man were not condemned by nature to his talent one would have to scold oneself as foolish for loading oneself through a long life with always new torment and repeated toil.[18]

And to Eckermann on January 27, 1824:

> I have always been esteemed one of fortune's particular favorites, nor do I wish to complain or to berate the course of my life. Yet at bottom it has been nothing but toil and work, and I dare say that in all my seventy-five years I have not had one month of real ease. It was the eternal rolling of a stone that wanted ever to be lifted anew. . . . My real [good] fortune was my poetical meditation and creation.[19]

Such passages sound genuine. The old man knew well that to the beholder his life must appear as one constantly favored by fortune, but looking back he discovered little of happiness. Who would not like to exchange his existence for such a stupendous life as Goethe's was, but who would be willing to give up as a price the pleasures Goethe never enjoyed in the real love of real human beings?

There are other factors in the genius most unpropitious to true object-relations. The relationship that is most distinctive for the genius, in my opinion, is that which he has to his artistic medium, the medium in which he forms his works of art. It is ever accessible to and completely mastered by the genius. It is the soil in which he flourishes. The genius may labor and toil and struggle with his particular medium or a masterpiece may arise with ease, but he always wins

---

[18] [Wenn der Mensch nicht von Natur zu seinem Talent verdammt wäre, so müsste man sich als thörig schelten, dass man sich in einem langen Leben immer neue Pein und wiederholtes Mühsal auflastet.]

[19] [Man hat mich immer als einen vom Glück besonders Begünstigten gepriesen; auch will ich mich nicht beklagen, und den Gang meines Lebens nicht schelten. Allein im Grunde ist es nichts als Mühe und Arbeit gewesen, und ich kann wohl sagen, dass ich in meinen fünf und siebzig Jahren keine vier Wochen eigentliches Behagen gehabt. Es war das ewige Wälzen eines Steines, der immer von neuem gehoben seyn wollte. . . . Mein eigentliches Glück war mein poetisches Sinnen und Schaffen.] (119, pp. 65–66)

the victory, and this factor, I believe, holds an extreme importance also in the genius's pseudo object-relations. He wants to mold out of real persons his ideal works of art and responds with aggression and hostility and despair when the human medium proves to be less pliable than the artistic medium. This basic process of tearing a part of reality away and transforming it into a work of art, when performed in human relations, must lead to catastrophes. First of all, human beings are not prone to surrender their individuality; and, secondly, if by happy coincidence a genius does find an object that is willing to surrender, this willingness, in turn, mars the ideal image of the object; and, thirdly, even if this consequence could be excluded, the ideally pliable object would compete with the artistic object that is in the process of being born and would thus become the enemy of the genius. From all these factors it becomes evident that true intense and abiding object-relations resulting in mutual happiness are incompatible with the productivity and creativity of the genius. Goethe's relationship with Christiane was an exception in so far as he here succeeded in isolating his artistic existence from his physical existence, and it was a particularly happy solution that this isolation could be carried out without generating a conflict. A woman who was his peer in human values would not have tolerated this situation. She would either have remonstrated against being removed from the central sphere of her partner's existence or she would have surrendered by making a sacrifice. Both responses would have dampened Goethe's artistic potential. Goethe, at one point at least, was aware of the mutual exclusiveness of true object-relations and the creation of great art. In 1790 he wrote the following epigram:

Your fate, O Midas, was a sad one: in your trembling hands
You, hungry, hoary one, felt the heavy, transformed fare.
My fate, similar to yours, is more cheerful: for what I touch
Becomes under my hands immediately an adroit poem.
Fond Muses, I do not remonstrate; I only wish that you do not
Transform my sweetheart into a fairy tale when I press her firmly to my
   bosom.[20]

This was written while Goethe was in Venice longing to return to Christiane and their infant son. Here Goethe himself testified that the genius poet is constantly on the verge of destroying the object-relationship by transforming it into a work of art. This had happened to Goethe repeatedly, but he did not want it to happen yet again in his relationship with Christiane. Since such processes are not accessible to volition we may well understand his appeal to the Muses.[21]

[20] [Traurig, Midas, war dein Geschick: in bebenden Händen/ Fühltest du, hungriger Greis, schwere verwandelte Kost./ Mir, im ähnlichen Fall, gehts lust'ger; denn was ich berühre,/ Wird mir unter der Hand gleich ein behendes Gedicht./ Holde Musen, ich sträube mich nicht, nur dass ihr mein Liebchen,/ Drück' ich es fest an die Brust, nicht mir zum Mährchen verkehrt.] (*Soph.* I, 1:330)

[21] In his last play, *When We Dead Awake,* Ibsen presents the very plight of the artist by using a symbolism hidden in realistic events. A sculptor, inspired by the beauty of his model,

Actually his relationship with Christiane was kept free from the Midas curse. It is also interesting to note from the artistic medium how this was accomplished. I cite elsewhere Goethe's quasi-linguistic essays upon the *Priapeia* and *De Civitate Dei* (see Appendix S). By expressing under the cloak of linguistic essays thoughts that would otherwise have led to poetry, he protected the live, amorous relationship. Goethe had at that time incorporated cohabitation into his way of living. As with all other significant matters, so also this newly gained sexual activity was bound to be drawn into the scope of poetic elaboration. The two philological essays permitted literary occupation with the subject of eros and sex without ensnaring Goethe in the pitfalls of poetry, where he would gradually have witnessed the atrophy of the object-relationship to Christiane. In the *Roman Elegies* and the *Venetian Epigrams,* which reflect his erotic-sexual preoccupation, he took a step closer to the dangerous poetry. However, in the *Roman Elegies* he turned in hexameters and pentameters towards Faustina, with whom his relationship was expendable, indeed, he no doubt regarded it as transitory from the start; in the *Venetian Epigrams* he wrote poetry which he himself called a "fragmentary kind" [Fragmenten Art] (to Herder, August 10, 1789). It is the peculiarity of this poetical form that it has the structure of an aggregate. Any number of additional thoughts, ideas, pictures, or fancies may be annexed without thereby creating a peak, or capping the edifice. The epigram really ends almost as soon as it has started and I believe it is a poetical form that is the least likely to be injurious to an object-relationship, because it cannot serve as an outlet for a complex and comprehensive emotion. The *Venetian Epigrams* are precisely such an aggregate of manifold "snapshots," momentary thoughts, etc. Even a short lyrical poem will typically have a greater potential as a medium of discharge than Goethe's 103 epigrams.

Yet even the two lyrical poems of that period that certainly refer to Christiane exhibit a feature that seems to confirm the view presented here. In one, "Morning Complaints" (*Morgen Klagen*), Goethe describes a night in which he waited in vain for his mistress's visit and ends with a complaint about her absence when he searches for her in the garden after the sun has risen; in the other, "The Visit" (*Der Besuch*), he enters his mistress's room, finds her asleep, and does not wake her up because she looks so sweet when sleeping. What de Buisonjé said about the first of these two poems is true of both, namely, that unresolved tension is preserved to the end of the poem (93, p. 110). Thus his

---

created a masterpiece which made him world famous. The model as a human being, however, meant to him nothing but an "episode." On meeting her years later, he falls passionately in love with her. When they are about to consummate their passion, both are crushed by an avalanche. I think Ibsen's play must be understood in terms of the conclusions that are to be drawn from Goethe's life history. True and consummated object love kills the artist's creative potential; in Ibsen's play the object that subverted the artist's mission is likewise drawn into the destructive process. Whether this comes to pass because of tragic guilt or the artist's revenge remains a moot question.

only two lyrical poems of that period that certainly refer to Christiane express unresolved frustration, although this was a period replete with gratifying experiences of physical release. I consider this seeming contradiction renewed proof that the poet protected himself against an effect that poetry regularly had upon his object-relationships. Goethe's choice of Christiane and the structure of his relationship to her were surprisingly free from manifest psychopathology so long as one has regard only to the behavioristic aspect, but concomitantly it had the least effect upon his creativity.

From the foregoing it will also become evident why the question of progeny is bound to become a center of conflict in the genius's life. In connection with Mephisto's remark: "However, we depend ultimately on creatures which we have produced,"[22] Goethe made the afore-mentioned statement of December 16, 1829, to Eckermann: "A father who has six sons is lost, let him take whatever stand he wants."[23] Here Goethe expressed some paranoid fears regarding progeny. My observations suggest that the major part of paranoid symptomatology in adult psychotics is referable to this conflict. The patient reacts according to the following equation: "My children will do to me that which I wanted to do to my parents when I was a child," and this, the reader may believe, was nothing kind or friendly. That a similar equation also played a role in Goethe's life is very probable, though not decisive. Progeny must necessarily become an issue of conflict for the genius. Here he is most deeply challenged and affronted, since one of his unconscious motors, ever and again stimulating him to new creations, is the deep wish to create a child.[24] The existence of his own progeny must precipitate new jealousy in the genius and also the depressing insight that all the works he has created do not measure up to the sublimeness of a living creature.[25] Yet instantly the expectation, described earlier, arises that his progeny—which he tries to arrogate ultimately as his own creation—will be a material out of which he will mold something ideal. Here the genius follows an imagery that is almost universally encountered, according to which most parents hope and expect that their children will be better and prettier and more successful than they themselves have been. But the genius wants to achieve all this by his own effort, and he expects, indeed, that the child will be pliable like an artistic medium. We know that Goethe actually achieved August's complete surrender. Yet children thus treated can never develop into ideal forms and therefore the genius's relationship to his progeny is bound to end in manifest or latent tragedy, unless ini-

---

[22] [Am Ende hängen wir doch ab von Creaturen die wir machten.] (*Faust* II, verses 7003–04)

[23] [Ein Vater, der sechs Söhne hat, ist verloren, er mag sich stellen wie er will.] (119, p. 299)

[24] In the book by the Sterbas, *Beethoven and His Nephew* (508), this comes superbly to the fore. This is also to be seen in Goethe's life though there it is not as outspoken as in Beethoven and did not lead to equally strong repercussions.

[25] The opposite misgiving, namely, a despair that the child does not live up to the ideal of the created work, is, of course, also visible.

tial ambivalence early causes him to abandon them, as J. J. Rousseau did with his progeny.

If we return now to Goethe's particular sexual dysfunction, we notice that it reflected exactly the structure of his object-relations. Passionate love drove him towards objects, but the sexual apparatus denied full union with the object. The danger of fixation to an object thus became greatly reduced, and the physical impairment forced him over and over again to turn anew towards the same object or others and to pour his feelings, left ungratified by the absence of adequate final consummation, into the unending stream of his lyrics. I have previously described how the physical limitation favored poetical production and prevented the full enjoyment of object-relations. After his recovery, as can be proved from documents, he limited the frequency of cohabitation and preferred long periods of abstinence.

Productive as the effect of Goethe's dysfunction was, its neurotic nature, I believe, is unquestionable. After all, *mens sana in corpore sano* will never produce great art. If we consider the goals we have inherited from our ancestors since the dawn of civilization and call them "nature," we have to conclude that the creation of great art is against nature. However, it is not the presence or absence of a neurosis that decides for or against the genius's capacities, but rather the *kind* of symptoms from which he suffers, and the *part* of the personality that is affected by them. The actual neurotic symptom (in contrast to "neurotic" rehearsing) in the genius impresses me as an adaptation of the psychobiological organism, which, in this instance, has to carry out a task opposed to basic drives deeply impressed upon the biological matrix.[26] Therefore, the "natural" condition of the psychobiological organism has to be subjected to a transformatory process which brings the organism and the task to be accomplished into a proper correlation.

In Goethe's partial psychosis revealed in the history of his *Chromatology* we are dealing with phenomena of a quite different order. I cannot discover any constructive value for the creative process in this form of psychopathology and am inclined to regard it as a deficit phenomenon, which drained potential artistic productivity. It had, of course, its inestimable value in maintaining the adequacy of the rest of Goethe's personality and quite possibly a manifest catastrophe would have occurred if his psychic apparatus had not been safeguarded by this avenue of discharge. It is admirable how well this partial psychosis was integrated into the rest of his personality, and that its manner of appearance did not create a real dissension between the artist and the community, that the content of the psychosis was so superbly apt as to lead to conclusions that appeared almost correct (and actually contained a large body of correct assertions).

All this shows the tremendous power in Goethe of synthesizing and organizing, but it does not contribute anything to the understanding of the psychosis per se. It will be remembered that it took its inception at a time when Goethe

[26] To a certain extent this was anticipated by Ferenczi. Cf. 140.

must have felt desperately guilty because his sweetheart was pregnant (or had given birth to a boy). Evidently this conflict was beyond the realm of "neurotic" rehearsal. At least, in checking various sources one does not find any report that indicates conspicuous changes in his mood or behavior. On November 10, 1789, Sophie von Schardt, Charlotte von Stein's sister-in-law, wrote:

> Goethe has almost buried himself [lit.: is almost buried] in order to finish the sixth and seventh volumes of his works. He tells me that he will become more sociable again immediately [afterwards].[27]

And on December 5 of the same year Karoline von Beulwitz wrote Schiller:

> Goethe was pleasant. He grieves me so: his sweetheart has been in labor for five days and will probably die. He looked milder than usual and [was] absent-minded.[28]

Whether the remark about Christiane rested purely on rumor or had some basis in reality I have not been able to ascertain.[29] The former quotation shows that Goethe had the tendency to absent himself from company at that time and I doubt that this was enforced primarily by his preparing his works for publication. If we did not know of Goethe's letter to Charlotte von Stein of June 8, 1789, with its urgent appeal for help, we should have to rely on assumptions regarding his state of mind during these months. In studying the preserved record one feels inclined to believe that Goethe's psychological constellation was at that time similar to what it was after Cornelia's death as well as in the period before and after his father's death, that is to say, there was an extreme internal upheaval combined with extreme external impassiveness, at least in relation to these events. Yet in these two situations he was relatively protected by his live transference to an exalted object, whereas now he was confronted by dangers that originated in the object of his love and had been caused by his own doing. Also during the months following the birth of the child no sign of "neurotic" rehearsal can be found, that is to say, in all probability the upsetting experiences during Christiane's pregnancy did not lead to the activation of automorphic mechanisms. It seems to me that here the impact of reality was too great, the problem too forbidding, the issue too (literally) unspeakably sad for it to lead to the creation of art. But perhaps I overestimate the quantitative factor. This situation, after all, was different also in quality from the numerous others that had led to creative outbursts. It was no longer a question of using a neurotic feeling of guilt for artistic purposes; now the ego was hopelessly entangled in a situation in which no rationalization could serve conscience as an agent of absolution.

[27] [Goethe ist beinahe begraben, um den 6. und 7. Band seiner Werke fertig zu machen. Er sagt mir, dass er sogleich wieder geselliger werden würde.] (51, *1*:435)

[28] [Goethe war artig. Er dauert mich so: sein Liebchen ist in Kindesnöten seit fünf Tagen und wird vermutlich sterben. Er sah milder aus als gewöhnlich und zerstreut.] (51, *1*:436)

[29] August was not born until December 25. This excludes the possibility that she could have been suffering labor.

Perhaps the genius's conscience is subtle enough to recoil from converting real guilt into a source of narcissistic pleasure.[30] In conjunction with Christiane's puerperium a permanent, incurable structural injury to the psychic apparatus in the form of a delusion was observed instead of an artistic creation. I conclude from this one example, which illustrates the substitution of a psychotic symptom for a work of art, that great works of art are derivations of psychotic symptoms. At this point I leave it open whether works of art are to be regarded as the result of a defense against, or of sublimation[31] of psychotic symptoms. In any case, one of the prerequisites for the creation of great art is a tendency—even a strong tendency—towards psychosis (probably of the schizophrenic variety), which is mastered or diverted by (automorphic) countermechanisms that transform this tendency towards psychosis into the molding of an artistic product. Or, in other words, we may say that if the genius were prevented by external forces from creating art he would become psychotic.

I wish to interpolate here a few remarks on sleep, dream, and awakening. Under the impact of nocturnal conflicts a sleeper forms dreams, at the bottom of which lie wish-fulfillments. In aggravated conditions (from the dreamer's viewpoint to be called extraordinarily grave), the capacity to form a dream embodying a wish-fulfillment breaks down, and instead a nightmare evolves. In like manner, we may imagine, in the genius inner conflict usually leads to artistic productions; however, when confronted with inner conflicts of extraordinary gravity, that are beyond the scope of being shaped into a comprehensive work of art, he too succumbs to psychosis. Freud called the dream a short-lasting psychosis (217, p. 61), as it obviously is: during the dream the ego accepts a hallucination as valid reality. The dream spares the sleeper from awakening; without the capacity for dreaming, whenever his conflicts reached a certain level his sleep would be interrupted and he would return to the perception of external reality. From a certain viewpoint one may turn Freud's evaluation of the dream into its opposite and say that the interruption of sleep (awakening and returning to external reality) because of an internal conflict is the equivalent of a psychosis. This reversal may at first sight seem bizarre, but closer examination may justify its validity. Objectively the dreamer replaces an internal conflict by another internal process, namely the dream, and thus maintains an adequate function of the psychic apparatus, namely sleep. Full awakening in such a situation is a disturbance injurious to a life-necessary biological function. Since the return to full reality is biologically justified only when either the need for sleep has been gratified or a changed external situation necessitates the sleeper's participation,

---

[30] Did Goethe face reality guilt also after Cornelia's and his father's death? After all, he had abstained from writing to his sister and from giving her the minimal consolation she was justified in expecting, and he had absented himself for twenty-nine months from his native city before the death of his father, whom he had deserted in 1775.

[31] I use the term "sublimation" here for any technique that modifies instincts and, by the use of instinctual energy thus saved, leads to the creation of art.

a sleeper who instead of dreaming wakes up (a symptom I have occasionally found in schizophrenic patients) is behaving in a situation of internal conflict as if external stimulation were interfering with the gratification of a biological function. Hartmann (276) has shown that the pleasure and reality principles have a relative scope. Thus we may say that a person who wakes from sleep for internal reasons is reacting contrary to the reality principle despite his turning towards reality. Adjustment to reality requires the periodic withdrawal from reality. A sleeping person who wakes up rather than dreams is infringing upon the reality principle.

Yet even if a turn towards reality, instead of dreaming, is accepted as a disturbance falling within the scope of the reality principle, the likening of this disturbance to a psychotic symptom may be argued against on good grounds. However, we are accustomed to associating with the term "psychosis" all those states in which the inner reality supersedes external reality. This is exemplified most clearly by hallucinations, when the true image of reality does not reach the perceptual end of the psychic apparatus but is replaced by an image born from fantasy, wishfulness, or anxiety. Yet the limitation of the concept to this aspect still betrays a rationalistic viewpoint. Man's inner reality has the same claim to relevancy as man's outer reality, and certain constellations in which stimuli that originate in inner reality cannot reach the perceptual end of the psychic apparatus but are replaced by images of outer reality have to be included in the concept of psychosis. The fact that both realities (external as well as internal) have their rightful claims means that the ideal functioning of the psychic apparatus is a process that continuously harmonizes these two realities. It is incorrect to believe that the psychotic disturbance consists exclusively in the imposition of inner reality upon the representation of external reality, as exemplified by hallucinations. In most schizophrenic patients we as commonly find symptoms of the reverse order, namely, the inability of the patient to let the inner reality flow towards the perceptive organs stimulated by external reality (as I shall presently exemplify by a remark on depersonalization). It is an error dating back at least to Descartes (see 513) to believe that man's adequate perception of the world rests exclusively upon the stimulation of perceptive systems by external stimuli. Only a disturbed perception of reality can result from such a one-sided process. The psychic apparatus has its own contribution to make even in the simplest act of perception, if only in the form of the implied feeling that it is *my* perception, that it is a *live* perception, etc.—in short, all that which makes the difference between a depersonalized perception and a normal one.

Thus we see that in almost every psychological act the two realities have to be blended and that the functioning of the psychic apparatus in favor of the one or the other leads to serious disturbances. The dream in its phenomenological aspect is a short-lasting psychosis, yet it serves the purpose of the reality principle in the broader sense of Hartmann's definition; nevertheless awakening instead of dreaming can rightly be likened to a psychotic reaction when the functional

context is considered. Then we see that the perceptual system functions in regard to inner reality in a way that is comparable to the formation of hallucinations, in which the psychic apparatus refuses the perception of external reality by replacing it with an image born from inner reality.

Returning now to Goethe's *Chromatology,* we may say that up to that point in his career almost all inner conflicts, with a few exceptions presently to be discussed, were appeased by the creation of works in a variety of artistic media. This may be likened to the sleeper's situation when the inner conflict leads to a dream. In Leipzig, however, the artistic form of solution was still in the process of development. The future genius had not yet integrated creativeness to such an extent as to be able to use it as an efficient mediator in a formidable conflict.[32] At that time there were, as we noticed, manifestations of a psychosis; furthermore the active cooperation and assistance of an older friend was necessary to preserve Goethe's personality from permanent damage.

To be sure, the death of his sister and his father had a different effect, in so far as they led neither to productions nor to psychotic manifestations, although they aroused conflicts in him. I have attempted to explain this as the result of the fact that at that time Goethe's reactions were absorbed by the transference relationship to Charlotte von Stein. Be this as it may, the conflict centering in Christiane's illegitimate pregnancy was outside the scope of what could be solved by artistic productions, and instead we notice a process—equivalent to the dreamer's awakening—of intensive turning towards reality, in the form of Goethe's primal experience, with its misconception of a sector of reality.

I have earlier spoken of the genius's creations as a sublimation of a psychosis. Without wanting to go into a discussion of the concept of sublimation or neutralization, at this point I must still justify the application of these concepts to such a structure as a psychosis. The term "psychosis" is used by definition for a

---

[32] Goethe was apparently aware of the one great step forward he owed to his Leipzig period. When writing about that period in Book VII of *Dichtung und Wahrheit* he summarized its effect in the following famous passage:

And thus that trend began from which throughout my whole life I could not deviate, namely, to transform whatever delighted or vexed or otherwise preoccupied me, into an image, a poem, and to come to terms with myself about it, in order to correct my concepts of external things as well as to put myself at rest inwardly concerning them. No one was more in need of this gift than I, whose nature constantly threw him from one extreme to the other. Everything of mine that has thus become known is only fragments of a grand confession, which this little book is a venturesome attempt to make complete. [Und so begann diejenige Richtung, von der ich mein ganzes Leben über nicht abweichen konnte, nämlich dasjenige was mich erfreute oder quälte, oder sonst beschäftigte, in ein Bild, ein Gedicht zu verwandeln und darüber mit mir selbst abzuschliessen, um sowohl meine Begriffe von den äussern Dingen zu berichtigen, als mich im Innern desshalb zu beruhigen. Die Gabe hierzu war wohl niemand nöthiger als mir, den seine Natur immerfort aus einem Extreme in das andere warf. Alles was daher von mir bekannt geworden, sind nur Bruchstücke einer grossen Confession, welche vollständig zu machen dieses Büchlein ein gewagter Versuch ist.] (*Soph.* I, 27:109–110)

particular vicissitude of drives. There is no doubt that the psychic apparatus learns to use drives to achieve things far outside their original goals, that is to say, to redirect the energy of instinctual demands away from the physical gratifications originally sought. I believe that this view must be extended to configurations which are more complicated than drives. I believe that neurotic or psychotic symptoms per se may undergo such processes. In a psychoanalytic treatment the symptom is dissolved, the instinctual energy enchained in the symptom is thus made free, and concomitantly the possibility is created of direct physical gratification of the drive or of its use for other adequate egosyntonic purposes. I believe that a similar process may occur—without previous dissolution of the symptom—by sublimation of configurations more complex than drives, such as symptoms that are the result of the interaction between drives and ego mechanisms. One may learn from a patient's life history that an infantile compulsive neurosis developed into compulsive character traits. There is no strict clinical proof that in such instances the compulsive symptoms were first dissolved before the instinctual energy was freed to develop into a character trait. It is far more probable that under the impact of external or internal factors the compulsive symptom per se underwent a developmental transformation into a character trait.[33] On closer reflection this view regarding the direct transformation of symptoms gains in probability, particularly with regard to psychosis. As Hartmann has suggested (279, p. 189), the energy of the schizophrenic defense mechanism also has not been sufficiently sublimated or neutralized. Thus according to this theory the neutralizing process operates upon the instinctual charges which are invested in the derivatives of instincts as well as in the ego-mechanisms. It is only one step further in the same direction when I suggest that such a process engulfs simultaneously drive and defense mechanism, that is to say, a symptom. This viewpoint can easily be applied also to the ego's capacity to create works of art and thus provides an approximate theoretical picture of what is meant by the statement that works of art may be the result of sublimation of psychotic symptoms.[34]

The psychotic symptom is the result of a conflict between ego and reality (see 201). That struggle becomes so much more intense and dramatic in the schizophrenic than in the nonpsychotic because the former faces in external reality a projection of his own drives. Reality is the background upon which the schizophrenic projects his drives and by acting out his conflict within the scope of reality he gratifies or defends himself against drives. The schizophrenic becomes as violently agitated, shaken, and affected by reality as the psychobiological organism is agitated and shaken by the struggle with ungratified drives.

Yet this is a feature that the psychotic, particularly the schizophrenic, shares

[33] For the sublimation of instinctual energy into a character trait see 164.

[34] A clinical illustration of this claim can be found in a letter Haydn wrote to his publisher. See 446, pp. 180–81. With even greater clarity the episode is set forth by Heinrich Eduard Jacob (310, p. 354).

with the genius. The genius's personality is so deeply moved and agitated by reality because reality is for him also the carrier of unsublimated, direct instinctual forces. The momentum of Werther's violent emotional turmoils in his relationship with nature is identical with the passionate momentum of the child's experiences with the preoedipal mother. Even the artistic end product still shares an important aspect of the psychotic symptom. It replaces external reality by the genius's own product—like a hallucination—though no longer in the psychotic's autoplastic form but in the artist's automorphic form. Despite its extraordinary social value, despite its perfect fitting into man-made culture, the work of art still contains this important aspect which is also contained in the psychotic symptom. Of course, it would be a grave mistake to equate art and psychosis—clinically and socially they are quite unlike; only a structural analysis reveals their partial identity, in history and in one aspect of structure. Yet this partial identity makes it understandable why we may occasionally encounter in the genius a psychotic symptom instead of a work of art. I believe that this is not as true of the person of artistic talent. He may switch from artistic production to other relatively adequate activities without harm. In the genius creativity is far more deeply rooted. Creativity is the only mode at his disposal of solving conflicts, even if only temporarily, and when this mode is blocked the psychic apparatus can no longer synthesize reality but must show a rent in the form of a psychotic symptom. The talent *can* create, the genius *has to* create.[35]

Yet as soon as I have drawn this conclusion I must admit that I have myself presented evidence to the contrary in my account of Goethe's relationship with Charlotte von Stein. There I presented clinical evidence that a deep structural change occurred in Goethe's personality, not in connection with the process of artistic production, but within the framework of live and intense contact with another human being. Perhaps it is an outstanding feature of Goethe's life that it also contains the exception to the afore-mentioned rule of the relative equivalence of psychotic symptom and work of art. Goethe synthesized into his existence several artistic lives, as Korff has demonstrated so impressively in his grandiose panorama of the development of German mental, artistic, and spiritual life between 1770 and 1830 (338). He was the foremost representative and spokesman not only of the *Sturm und Drang,* but likewise of the classic, romantic, and high-romantic periods. In this study, however, only the development of the *Sturm und Drang* Goethe to the classical Goethe has been paid attention to. When he arrived at Weimar he had achieved, in the form of *Götz von Berlichingen* and *Werther,* the utmost of which he was capable through the *Sturm und Drang.* Indeed, the whole movement was played out. One by one those who had formed its inner circle drifted away. Heinrich Leopold Wagner became a lawyer and died at the age of thirty-two; Lenz became psychotic; Friedrich Maximilian Klinger (1752–1831) entered the Austrian military serv-

---

[35] The problems of the talent as presented by Edmund Bergler (20) do not seem to be relevant for the genius.

ice in 1778 and later had a brilliant career in the Russian army. Not one of Goethe's generation was able to carry on the momentum of the *Sturm und Drang*. Goethe, however, had the genius to surmount such a fate. The maximum of certain artistic patterns had been accomplished and the artistic potential in the direction of the novel and the tragic play had dwindled to zero.[36] In order to increase the general artistic potential a structural change in Goethe's personality became a necessity. A special and a general problem must be considered here. The special one concerns Goethe's career. It is in keeping with the infiniteness of his genius that his literary range also embraced areas that usually are covered by two or more generations. His change from *Sturm und Drang* to classical art and later to the romantic movement is exceptional and he would have validated his claim to the status of genius through his accomplishments during any one of these three periods alone.

The general problem, however, is of greater interest here. This has to do with the difference between the solution of a conflict and a structural change. A dream, for example, may make an important contribution to the solution of a conflict, or, at least, to its reduction. This, to be sure, is not a necessary effect, for very often the dream may increase or even precipitate conflicts, but some dreams, probably because their wish-fulfillments are experienced as a reality, release the sleeper with a decreased tension in a particular conflict area.[37] This effect is regularly to be observed in the creations of the genius: the creation of a work of art or of a series of works of art results in a temporary reduction of conflict tension. However, it does not result in a structural change. The proud words with which Freud characterized the effect of psychoanalytic therapy, "Where id was, there shall ego be" (210, p. 112), are not applicable to the effect of artistic production upon the genius's personality. Since the genius needs the impact of the unconscious and his conscious ego must eternally be involved with the unconscious parts of the various provinces of his personality, an actual structural change would reduce his creative potential. The immensity, the inexhaustibility, of the genius's creativity (limited only by the biological factor) is based on the fact that, in him, the conflict, though temporarily reduced or removed, rearises with full force after only a short pause, sometimes even instantaneously. Whether the same group of conflicts pervade his whole output or the conflicts change in the course of his career is irrelevant in this context; the inexhaustible "spontaneous tendency to conflict" (214, p. 347), which in some patients makes successful psychoanalytic treatment almost impossible, compels the genius to hurry from one creative act to

---

[36] However, I do not have it in mind to characterize in this way Goethe's artistic potential as a lyrical poet. This form of artistic expression was so closely ingrained in his life that it was never, I believe, in danger of becoming exhausted. The constellation was different with regard to major literature (novels and plays).

[37] See Freud's discussion (158, p. 579) of A. Maeder's theory that this is a function of the dream.

another. This, however, presupposes that the created work, however great its momentary solacing power, does not have structural effects of import, for then the "spontaneous tendency to conflict" would die down and the momentum as well as the intensity of the creative urge would gradually dwindle to zero.

The purely artistic task—aside from all personal implications—that confronted Goethe when he arrived in Weimar, necessitated a strong object-relationship. This had to be of a kind different from that which I described earlier as typical of the genius, for in this phase creation had become impossible by the exhaustion of a certain form of art, and he did not need a conflict to kindle creativity but a relationship that would increase his artistic potential by assisting him in a reorganization of his personality. I think that this sets into just proportion what I said earlier about the genius's creativeness, object-relationship, conflict, and artistic potential.

I wish now to turn towards the distinct role that masochism plays in the life of the artistic genius. The concept of masochism has undergone a broad extension through Freud's work (199). Originally a designation for a well-circumscribed perversion, the term has acquired the meaning of a biological force which is indispensable for life, and of a certain type of character formation (moral masochism). The question of whether or not masochistic perversions play a larger role statistically in the lives of artistic geniuses than in other groups will not be raised here. The question that concerns us is the place of pain in the life of the artistic genius. In most instances his life is beset with unending sufferings and complaints. Walter Muschg has given a most impressive account in the "Tragic History of Literature" (406) of the incredible sufferings creative man has to undergo. They are reminiscent of the stations of the cross, or of an inferno. Nothing man ever suffered is missing: hunger, persecution, diseases, abject poverty, depressions, self-reproaches, self-accusations, eternal feelings of torment. Disloyalty, unfaithfulness, drunkenness, drug addiction, sexual deviation, are not exceptional. All kinds of eccentricity and queerness, distorted character formation and quarrelsomeness may be attributed to the majority. Everything that man wants to be free from besets the lives of the creative with very few exceptions, and even in these one is tempted to surmise that if a fuller and more accurate record were available we should have to revise drastically our notion that they were indeed exceptional. It is one of those human mysteries that the most beautiful productions, which provide tortured mankind with consolation, inspiration, and refuge from the intolerable, grew out of pain and so often out of evil. As one scrutinizes the life history of an individual genius one cannot help feeling the deepest pity for a man who left behind so many admirable creations but himself did not enjoy many moments of happiness. And then one may easily raise the question of how much more this artist might have created if he had been spared all his misfortunes, if his contemporaries had recognized his genius and had given him freedom to live the kind of life he craved. Yet one also notices that some were offered such opportunities but, under one pretext or another, did not accept them, or else soon quit the favorable opportunity or brought it to nothing. I have demonstrated this earlier in an example drawn from Schiller's life. Therefore, if one considers how many life histories of creative writers are known and how regularly they contain reports of great suffering, one must conclude that suffering, so far from being an obstacle or impediment to creativity, is one of its prerequisites.[38] To be sure, the creative writer has his moments of exhilaration, triumph, and joy, but they are rare and short-lasting, whereas the periods of pain are long-lasting. But even the joyful moments have often an undertone of unease, as if the psychic apparatus of the sensitive, creative personality reacted with pain to strong emotions even when they were pleasurable.

Here one must recall again Goethe's statement about how difficult it is to endure a succession of happy days.[39] I should like to compare this situation with that in the child, in whom, as Freud pointed out (163, p. 203), any kind of strong emotional excitement may lead to sexual excitement. One gets the impression that in the creative genius strong emotions do not lead so much to sexual stimulation but rather to pain. Quite possibly this pain is one of the many psychological forces that compel him to form the emotional experience into a work of literature. Muschg expressed this idea in the following beautiful analogy: "There are animate beings in nature which, in reacting to a defect, that is to say, a painful interference with their organism, produce pearls. The witchery of these creations lies not only in their form and their substance,

[38] In studying the lives of some geniuses, such as Dostoevski, one gets the impression that man does his best creating when he is caught in the pincers of grave dangers that threaten from within as well as without, whether the outward ones are real or only assumed. It seems at times as if the self had to conquer formidable internal resistance against creating and as if this resistance could be overcome only when the ego felt itself surrounded by threats. A situation seems then to arise in which the creative act becomes compellingly necessary as the only route left open for survival. However, in view of the complexity of the human mind one hesitates to assert that no genius creations can be produced without great suffering and feels inclined to speak here only of statistical frequency.

[39] The problem we encounter when observing the productive effect of masochism in the artist has its bearing also upon the creativity of the scientist. Cf. Freud's letter of April 16, 1896: "I have come back with a lordly feeling of independence and feel too well; since returning I have been very lazy, because the *moderate misery necessary for intensive work* refuses to appear" (321, *1*:305; italics by Jones). I see a symbolic representation of the creative genius's masochism in the Prometheus myth. Freud interprets Prometheus's punishment, with regard to its libidinal meaning, with the observation that the "daily consumption and renewal [of the liver] is an apt description of the behavior of the appetite of love, which, though gratified daily, is daily renewed" (211, p. 291). I think this interpretation may be complemented by observing that, if Prometheus's gratification of love is conjoined with suffering, there may be seen in this suffering the masochism that strives actively to create a new world. If my view is correct the myth reverses the time sequence. The creative mind does not suffer as punishment for the fulfillment of forbidden wishes, but creates because it suffers. For other reversals in the Prometheus myth see 211.

but also in man's unconscious horror as to their source and the history of their origin. This is the beauty that man values most highly, against reason, and collects with greatest pleasure—at bottom there is no beauty that is not constituted so. In man's world similar mysterious creatures live who respond to a deeply afflicted disturbance of their existence with the creation of beauty: a value genetically connected with disease and threat to life. Only the hidden connection in origin can explain why this product of suffering and nearness to death encounters such great praise." (405, p. 111) Here the essential connection between suffering and artistic creation is most clearly outspoken. Do we know of any other human activity to which suffering is an indispensable prerequisite? The psychological conclusion is that the artistic genius must not, like other mortals, avoid pain as much as possible or try to reduce it to the unavoidable minimum, but that he must turn towards suffering, not necessarily seeking it, but at least lending it a willing ear, and must let it enter freely into the confines of his personality. A real flight from pain would end in an inhibition of the creative impulse.

Does this bending towards pain, this openness to the influx of pain, belong in the category of masochistic manifestations? In order to answer this question I wish to return to Freud's theory. What originally had looked like a threat to life, a power counteracting all and every purpose of life, the masochist's craving for suffering came to be recognized as the exaggeration or distortion of something that is apparently to be found in everybody and that, when it occurs in right proportions, is actually life-preserving and beneficial. According to Freud's theory, masochism is the end product of destructive forces that are active in man and that would be potentially able to lead him quickly to death, if they did not become eroticized, that is to say, mitigated, changed in their effects, and transformed into life-supporting forces. I should like to go a step further here and raise again the question whether men's ability to bear displeasure and pain at all rests on his masochism. Ferenczi answered this question in the affirmative.[40] According to Freud's early theory displeasure is due to an increase of stimulation in the pyschic apparatus. This theory was later changed, but is still true in its basic aspect. On the early level the human being tries to avoid displeasure and his biological structure is such as to provide him with manifold apparatuses that work against an accumulation of tension and displeasure. But in the course of development man acquires a remarkable capacity to tolerate pain and tension. To what extent is man's masochism one of the prerequisites for the evolvement of such a capacity? Of course, masochism alone would never endow man with that capacity. In perverted masochists one observes a craving for a special kind of pain to be provided in special circumstances. Deviations from this special pattern arouse anxiety. The masochistic pervert is usually sensitive to pain; indeed, his general tolerance of pain outside of the unique setup that is so precious to him is lower than that of the nonmasochist. It

[40] See 142. For a criticism of this hypothesis see 276, p. 142.

looks as if the masochist has invested all of his masochism in the perverse situation and has not much energy left to tolerate pain arising from other sources.

In some types of moral masochism the situation is different. The realm of pain tolerance is broadened in them, and among those who have accomplished great achievements for mankind there are many who were moral masochists. But the heightened sensitivity to criticism or opposition betrays the pathological background in these instances, too.

What I have in mind is a hypothetical question: What would be the effect of painful stimuli on man if he were without masochism? Is it possible that under such conditions deleterious stimuli would not cause pain at all but would wreak direct damage on the psychic apparatus?

Freud designed a metapsychological model illustrating the processes that occur within the psychic apparatus when it is stimulated by pain. He suggested that narcissistic energy flows to the points of invasion and thus binds the inflow of stimuli (178, pp. 82–83). Is it possible that this energy stems from masochism? These questions cannot be answered yet, but the little that is known of the artistic genius suggests that such hypotheses may be tenable. According to this view, the ordinary person would have just enough masochism to bind the unavoidable influx of painful stimuli that could not otherwise be dealt with. In the creative genius, the heightened masochism would lead to a decrease of the defenses against pain. By not using opportunities of avoidance of or defense against pain, the genius reveals the presence of more masochism than the ordinary person, but by his valiant defense against pain once it has shaken the very bottom of his self, in the form of the created work of art, the genius reveals his difference from the clinical moral masochist, in whom pain has become so strongly libidinized that he surrenders to the influx of pain and exhausts himself in the act of suffering. Thus we can discern an important dichotomy: masochism in the ordinary person for the sake of survival; masochism in the genius for the sake of creation. If art is taken as a unique manifestation of life, one may consequently surmise that the artist is here showing in a visible way traits that exist less conspicuously in the rest of mankind. And further, if artistic production is an intensified manifestation of life then perhaps what becomes conspicuous in the artist is one of the prerequisites of life in general, as described by Freud.[41]

Yet my hypothetical comparison of masochism in a variety of instances shows how easily masochism may work against the creation of great art. A bit

[41] I have described Goethe's masochistic tendencies at large but these never constituted masochism in the narrower sense of a perversion. I have found only one instance in Goethe's life that may be classified as such. In Book II of *Dichtung und Wahrheit* (*Soph.* I, 26:102–03) an episode is reported that apparently occurred during the latency period, when the boy exposed himself more or less voluntarily to a prolonged beating by three boys who he knew disliked him. The self-imposed passivity and suffering of avoidable pain was followed by a terrible outbreak of aggression against the three.

too much or too little may upset the balance necessary for the unique setup required for great creations. Masochism may thus be likened to a powerful drug, which, dispensed in the right quantities, is highly beneficial, but, given in too large doses, kills. The tolerable range, moreover, is very narrow and it is therefore easily understandable that so many instances come to clinical observation in which masochism is encountered as the force that undermined and shattered a personality. Furthermore, that quantity of masochism that may be highly beneficial to a genius will, when it occurs in a person not endowed for creation, lead to disease. We may also surmise that works of art remain uncreated because a person endowed with a great artistic potential has an insufficient fund of masochism or overformidable defenses against it and therefore is not equipped to submit to the often excruciating pain inherent in the creative process.

Here we must recall what was said earlier about the genius's object-relations: his great craving for objects versus the impossibility of his gratifying these cravings through a true contact with real objects. This principle is probably true of the genius's relationship not only with love-objects but with any kind of object. The creative artist needs the outer world. He constantly receives stimulation and inspiration from it. But at the same time that world, which is so important, is a source of a great danger. If he really fell in love, if he really made a complete turn towards objects, what then would impel him still to depict reality in his creations? If all his impulses flowed towards an object how would he still have energy left for the supreme effort to give artistic form to his experiences in and with the world? Therefore any object that arouses his interest becomes a danger to his artistic production, although his interest in objects is the mainstay and one of the most important prerequisites of his creativity.

Here another important root of the artist's masochism is encountered. Precisely in the sector in which he feels the strongest impulse towards seeking fulfillment and gratification of intense desires and cravings, he must make a supreme sacrifice and abstain, if he wishes to continue as an artist on the highest level of which he is capable. Of course, these terms must be taken in their broadest meaning. Abstention need not necessarily mean physical separation or absence of physical gratification (although it seems to have meant this in a number of instances), but it does mean that the artist must not obtain from objects those pleasures that others enjoy in their relationship with the world. There always must remain a significant residuum of unfulfilled craving, of which the average person remains free by gratifying his cravings through his contact with objects. That is to say, the genius is potentially capable of the strongest object-relations but in the outcome they are diverted and channelized into the creative process.

This of course must give the genius a feeling of despair—as, indeed, it does too to those about him who wish him well—since no matter what he obtains by way of realistic wish-fulfillment, he is always compelled to remain dissatisfied. An oversupply of wish-fulfillments might become a temptation and if the genius accepted all the sources of gratification that the world sometimes offers him he would be stripped of his artistic potentialities. But here we have the clinical picture of the masochist. Only a masochist can constantly seek the pain of renunciation in the face of the offer of gratification.

Yet it must not be forgotten that masochism is only a prerequisite of artistic creativity and that the decisive factor is the use to which a person puts it. Only if the artistic creation becomes more important for the artist than the real love-object, so that the original drive follows the pathway that the structured part of the personality has mapped out regardless of the depth of pleasure to be obtained, only then is a work created that has life and blood and that gives the impression that it cannot be surpassed as life cannot be surpassed. Thus, whatever of instinctual energies flows into the creative process, that kind of satisfaction that is reached in the physical sphere cannot be attained. This is one of the reasons why artistic creation can offer only short-lasting, temporary decreases of tension, and why a genius like Goethe was almost continually under the compelling spell to create. Often (and sometimes for long periods of time) that inner call to create does not lead to creative action, but potentially the genius is constantly on the verge of creating, and only when that potentiality is incessantly in him, only then is he a genius.

The turning of instinctual energies towards creation is, of course, a perilous process, since the drives never cease utterly to impel towards their original goals but ever tempt to resort to archaic gratifications. The ego, speaking in anthropomorphic language, must lure the drives towards these new goals that are so far distant from their innate bent. The ego has to provide a steep gradient for their discharge in the form of tension between the provinces of the personality among themselves on the one hand, and towards reality on the other. When this gradient flattens out, it signalizes a reduction of structure. Then a tendency has won out that is directed against the accumulation of such intensity as is necessary for great achievement. Concomitantly, regressions to pregenital levels set in and the goal to which the artist ought to aspire can no longer be attained; the instincts then no longer work in the service of the ego, or the ego has given up its aspiration for maximum achievement and a kind of short circuit occurs.

There are branches of literature, such as pornography, that appeal directly to instinctual life. In this instance the sole function of literature is reduced to the sexual arousal of the reader, and when that has been accomplished the artistic value vanishes.[42] I do not wish to enter into a detailed discussion of such literature. Still, it is remarkable how far great artists can go in their directness in presenting or referring to sexual topics without becoming pornographic. This,

---

[42] The mutual exclusiveness of art and sexual gratification is a problem that involves an important aspect of the psychology of art.

of course, is not what was meant by my assertion that great art depends on the instincts. The great achievement of the literary genius is his ability to make us feel the affects and passions of others (or of himself) without generating in us identical affects and passions. We feel them only by small specimens or in a different quality but in a way that makes us able to anticipate what their full reality must feel like. To experience inwardly all the events, affects, tragedies, vicissitudes, that the poets present, without the expenditure of cathexis, which would be necessary if all this were experienced in full reality, sets an enormous amount of energy free in the person enjoying literary art. What happens to the psychic energy thus liberated need not occupy us here, except for one factor, namely, that it is bound partly by the formal quality of the work of art. The pleasure of artistic enjoyment is due to this liberated psychic energy. In pornographic literature, in which that artistic quality is lacking, the reader becomes sexually excited approximately in the way he would in a reality situation of forepleasure, and no artistic experience can take shape.[43]

I may be reproached for confusing an element of content with a dynamic-economic one when I claim that instinctual energy enters the creative process at its fullest wherever great art results, and it may be said that, of course, just as contents drawn from external reality enter the work of art so also contents from all layers of the human personality may enter it, even must enter it, and that this necessity does not prove the existence of correlated energic processes in the artist. Indeed, virtually all literary creations have man's inner life as their content at least to a certain degree, and if that were all there was to it my hypothesis would not be required. I am cognizant of the validity of this objection, but tentatively uphold a hypothesis that is parallel to Freud's clinical observation that certain psychotic manifestations are "a concrete representation and external projection of libidinal cathexis" (173, p. 78). The great works of art are similarly such concrete representations and only if instincts find concretization in a work of art is man moved by it. I have left aside the question of the forms in which the instinctual energies find concretization and add only the meager remark that the perfect form is that which creates maximum tension in the subject while precipitating the minimum danger of prompting regression either to the original aims of instincts or to truly archaic ego states.

A factor bearing on this problem can be demonstrated in the development of the artist's fantasy life. In the ordinary person, a comparison of his fantasy life as a child and as an adult shows a marked difference between the two, that is to say, a break has occurred in the course of its development. The matter cannot be gone into in detail here (see 166) but this much may be said, that an exact clinical follow-up shows a gradual reduction of the flourish-

---

[43] For the laws of psychic economy in a range of cultural configurations see Freud's book on jokes and their relation to the unconscious and Kris's repeatedly cited collection of essays on a variety of topics, *Psychoanalytic Explorations in Art* (346).

ing childhood fantasy life. In some instances one can establish fairly exactly the point at which the switch from the one to the other took place. In one case the patient recounted to a friend some of the fantasies he had formed about classmates. With this process of verbalization the fantasies became buried and the imagery he produced took on adult forms, but I had the impression that this change would have taken place in any circumstances even without the preceding incident of verbalization.

In general, it seems that a break in fantasy life occurs in the early latency period and another in early or middle puberty. It is important to characterize at least roughly what the differences between these two types of the imaginative function are.

The adult's fantasy life has become greatly reduced by the growth of secondary processes, which do not necessarily exclude intense daydreaming but in general restrict it and make it less vivid. This becomes evident when the child's fantasy life is observed. Only a few stimuli are necessary for the child to form extensive and intense fantasies. They are often so intense that the child attributes to them the same reality value that he should attribute to actual reality, or even more. The poet preserves this faculty of believing in his fantasies and he frequently lives more in them than in reality itself.

At the bottom of the matter there is found a characteristic difference between two ways of experiencing emotions. The adult, in his everyday orientation, usually bases full conviction only upon sense data, or insight derived from the content of sense data. Emotions are in essence not perceptible in the sense that actions or concrete objects are. The child, however, being swayed by emotions not subject to the secondary processes, believes he perceives the emotions and they evidently acquire for him a degree of concreteness that in the adult is reserved for concrete objects of actions. The poet experiences his own emotions and those of others with that vivacity that is encountered in children. His own emotions and his perception of emotions in others do not fade. In him the reduction to which the emotional sphere is subjected in the latency period and following the upsurge of puberty, has not taken place. Certain inhibitory effects concomitant with the growth of the superego are absent from his development,[44] and this concreteness of the emotional sphere is a fulcrum upon which the creative process over and over again turns. The experience of emotions as of primary evidential value, as having the quality that ought be reserved for sense data, can also be observed in his experience of nature. I have given examples of this in Goethe and have tried to show how the most intimate emotional conflicts found displacement onto objects of nature. It is only in dreams that the ordinary adult can perceive the world again in childhood fashion, only there that the bare perceptual skeleton becomes again the bearer of connotations that under normal conditions can never be attached to perceptions

[44] I do not consider here the possibility that these inhibitions also develop in the genius but melt in the course of a pubertal psychosis.

per se. An impressive specimen of such a process is to be found in Goethe's psychograms based on silhouettes. Whether these psychological analyses were correct or not is not decisive. The faculty of responding to a simple configuration with a wealth of associations and the disposition to take these associations as valid indices of the personality to be evaluated can here be observed in full operation.

To a genius like Goethe, for whom the afore-mentioned indices of childhood imaginative life were characteristic, an artificial medium like silhouettes may, however, become an impediment. Thus he wrote to Lavater on September 20, 1780: "Now that I make no more physiognomical pretensions, my sense becomes very sharp and agreeable; I know almost in the first minute what to make of people."[45] Yet four days later, after having joined a new group of people, he wrote Charlotte von Stein: "Since my coming here my writing makes a pause. One cannot at once, as of rocks and woods, say what to make of people, and [it is] better not to repeat to oneself every impression, but let it continue for a while."[46] In this passage—besides the reference to the meaning of landscapes or nature in the poet's life—Goethe expresses the restraint that he had to put upon the rush of associations that instantly arose upon his meeting people and that might easily have encumbered reality-adequate contact. This passage is particularly instructive because it refers to a change in Goethe's approach to people from reliance on immediate impressions to careful observation. Apparently Goethe had until then taken his own emotional responses to people for granted and had to learn in the course of the reorganization of the reality principle (cf. above pp. 914–41) that there are certain things in man that cannot be known by immediate impressions but that require prolonged observation. We behold Goethe here becoming aware of the change from an infantile mode of response to an adult one that is dominated by secondary processes.

In the child and the poet the imaginative life is, apparently, closer to the primary process than in the ordinary adult. The ordinary adult subjects his psychic life so strongly to the secondary process that his imaginative life becomes well-ordered but pale. Great resistances must often be removed by the psychoanalytic technique in order to get the adult to form conscious fantasies. Anxiety and remorse prevent him from taking up again that function which is found so charmingly in children. Yet even after the removal of obstacles and when the patient becomes more courageous in putting fantasies into the limelight of full consciousness, the fantasy life that is forthcoming is stunted by comparison with that of children.

To return to our starting point, it must be emphasized, however, that the

---

[45] [Seitdem ich keine Phisiognomische Prätension mehr mache wird mein Sinn sehr scharf und lieblich, ich weis fast in der ersten Minute wie ich mit den Leuten dran bin.]

[46] [Seit dem ich hier bin macht mein Schreiben eine Pause. Es lässt sich nicht so wie von Felsen und Wäldern sogleich sagen, wie man mit Menschen dran ist, und besser man wiederholt sich nicht ieden Eindruck, sondern lässts eine Weile fortgehen.]

fantasy life of children is a highly erotic one; it is not fed by sublimated energy. Of course, compared with the impulsive actions in which the infant and the child indulge before the level of well-formed and coherent fantasies has been reached, it appears as an enormous step forward. If the poet went beyond it he would lose one of the most important functions by which to build his artistic creations.

Furthermore it seems necessary that the artist preserve the reactibility of nearly all archaic layers, not only the childhood imaginative life, but also the pregenital sources of libido. It has frequently been reported of geniuses—and noticed with the greatest surprise—that their pregenitality is exceedingly strong. This can be observed abundantly in Goethe's life and I wish once more to remind the reader of Mozart's letters to his cousin. The Sterbas made the same observation about Beethoven and explain it by a regression (508, p. 121). Psychoanalytic case reports on artists are, of course, replete with observations of this kind. The abundance of pregenitality in the genius requires explanation of two different orders: (1) Horace's *Nil humanum a me alienum puto* was not only valid for this poet but maintains its validity for all artistically creative minds of magnitude. Whatever the genius's conscious value judgment may be about the disgusting and the evil—and pregenitality comprises a large part of it—he has to resonate to this extensive sector of the human world too; if his defenses were so strong that his pregenitality paled, this would deprive him of much of that on which his artistry thrives. I venture to compare this with man's genital life. If it is devoid of any pregenital admixture it is sure to become stale and inhibited. The point is only that no pregenital element should crowd out all others. As a matter of fact, according to my observations pregenital interests are in the genius pretty evenly spread among the variety of possible manifestations. Yet still more important is (2), a factor that can easily be derived from my remarks about the rivalry in the genius between investing drives in object-relationships leading to gratification as against investing them in the creative process that leads to a work of art. The pregenital drives harbor far less of such a rivalry than the genital drive. In most pregenital gratifications the object is used up. It disappears in the course of satisfaction and does not become a competitor with the genius's principal goal. In view of the absence of complete gratification within the framework of a full object-relationship the pregenital gratifications acquire a heightened importance in the life of a genius. Here he can indulge in satisfactions with greater freedom than otherwise and in a compensatory fashion he may make up for the loss of pleasure he suffers in other areas of life. The strongly narcissistic quality that is attached to all pregenital activities functions to protect him against becoming lost in an object. Therefore I especially doubt the regressive character of the pregenitality one observes in the genius, although pregenitality does not pervade all phases evenly and occurs in varying degree at different times. I rather look upon pregenitality as a prerequisite of the kind of life a genius has to lead. How, specifically, it happens that the genius is able to preserve such strong investments in pregenital functions, I do not know. It is part of the process that makes him preserve so many constructive patterns of his childhood.

We find something similar in some forms of so-called psychopathy. On the one hand, many so-called psychopaths grope for an artistic medium as an outlet; on the other, many artists have been compared to psychopathic personalities. The comparison appears justified, because the great artist has preserved a vast array of childhood functions, interests, and ways of living. But occasionally psychopathic personality and genius have been equated, and this, in my estimation, is a grave error, as even a superficial comparison would lead us to discover. In the former's life destructiveness prevails (self-destruction as well as behavior destructive to others), whereas in the latter we encounter the sublimest examples of constructiveness.

An approach to a psychology of artistic creation, however, must not stop at demonstrating how much of the infantile and of the preadult is still alive in the artist. It behooves psychology to investigate how the artist can and does use the infantile in the creative process. The equipment of the artistic genius contains many factors that in ordinary circumstances ought not to evolve at all or should be absorbed in the course of development under ordinary conditions, but are indispensable for the creative process.[47] Although it may be unnecessary, I wish to repeat that the genius too is liable to evolve his own psychopathology, as I have also tried to show in Goethe. In the nongenius certain manifestations can be taken as bona fide signs of psychopathology, whereas in the genius when such signs appear a preliminary inquiry is necessary in order to find out whether or not the seeming symptom is a prerequisite of the creative process. One such symptom is the female identification, which is so dangerous to normal development of the male but without which male creativity cannot evolve to its maximum potentiality. Here again the outcome will depend on quantitative factors. If the female identification goes too far, that is to say, if the artist performs an almost total identification with the mother, this may encroach severely on the creative potential.[48] Yet if the heterosexual relationship is of a kind that excludes female identification, then the urge to create will suffer greatly. One thing is certain: that the normal outcome of the passing of the Oedipus complex (see 202), that is to say, the total absorption of the Oedipus complex in adult functions, will counteract the development of artistic creativity. If the Oedipus complex has come to a complete rest, the urge to

---

[47] With due apology for using the banal term "mental health," I wish to state that that which appears like the psychopathy of the genius is in reality a sign of his mental health.

[48] Manifest homosexuality in our day is at times combined with the greatest achievements; at other times it damages the creative function severely. Evidently the manifestation of homosexuality is not the decisive factor. Manifest homosexuality as such does not exclude unconscious strong heterosexual object-relationships. The effect of homosexuality on creativity, I surmise, depends mainly on concomitant inner factors. The clinical manifestation per se seems to be neutral as far as the creative function is concerned.

project either an inner conflict or its solution into a self-created configuration can no longer be very strong. The liveliness and the acuteness of the positive feeling for the mother or a mother-substitute and the feelings that are attached to the predominantly unconscious recollections of the mother are an important prerequisite for the poet's creativity during his years of manhood.

The necessity the poet is under to preserve so much of the infantile and childhood period, which the ordinary man may discard but the loss of which would deprive the artist of the impulsion to strive for new differentiations, can be paralleled with Bolk's theory of the origin of men (see 57). Bolk found it a prerequisite for the evolutionary process leading to the creation of the human species that parturition take place when the fetus was still at a developmental level earlier than that at which other closely related species bring forth their young. It was the "infantilisms" of the human neonatus that made a higher differentiation of the human species possible. The artist apparently must not achieve full adulthood if he is to be able to undergo a further differentiation that would become impossible if the secondary processes took full hold of him. One respect in which he must not grow up completely is his relationship to his parents, particularly to his mother. This incompleteness of maturing occurs, of course, in many others without their becoming artists, not to speak of geniuses. The majority of those who do not achieve the passing of the Oedipus complex become neurotics or worse, and cannot in general use the developmental deficit for constructive purposes.

It may be possible to state more specifically in what the developmental deficit of the genius consists. It seems to me to lie in the structure of his superego. The formation of the superego does not take place in one act, as one may learn the alphabet, but is the result of a relatively long-lasting process. Its antecedents are to be found far back in early infantile times in the form of archaic anxieties. The main phase of its formation occurs in connection with the oedipal complex, the modification and transformation of which is the hardest task the child's ego has to accomplish. The superego is not a uniform, static structure but must be thought of as many-layered (cf. 470). These multifarious layers do not all reach the same degree of development, some being very highly developed and endowed with a strong effect upon the personality, others being stunted in their growth and fixed at an early phase of their origin. It may even happen that a layer that ought to have developed for the sake of adequate functioning of the personality, did not germinate at all. We then speak of lacunae (see 317). The effect of such lacunae will, of course, depend greatly on their site, that is, whether they affect early archaic layers still quite close to the instincts and scarcely to be called superego yet at all, or later layers far removed from the id and destined to regulate functions of a higher order.

Generally, some of these last must regularly be even overdeveloped in the artist. The postulates of the aesthetic laws, the obligations that the true artist has to discharge in the service of his art, all such demands must be intensely represented in the superego. All the more must this be the case in the genius. It is the superego that represents necessities of form, aesthetic rule, and structure. We regard the superego as a conservative force and therefore I must stress that when I speak here of the representation of aesthetic demands in the artist's superego, I do not have in mind any necessity of upholding traditional laws. Goethe's *Sturm und Drang* period is significant for its rebellion against rules that were traditional, at least in the German linguistic area, and Goethe's predilection for Shakespeare as a superego representative contained a strongly rebellious aspect. Yet despite the rebellious aspect of Goethe's *Sturm und Drang* creations, they still followed an artistic ideal that was incorporated in his superego. To be sure, it was a self-willed and self-chosen superego, so to speak, introduced into his life by Herder, whom he accepted as an admired, though ambivalently loved, authority. Nevertheless, however rebellious the work of art, and however possibly immoral or amoral its content, to say that it is a work of art must mean that it lives up to aesthetic postulates, and these must be embodied in the superego of its author. This part of the many-layered superego must be firmly established in the genius. However, if his whole superego achieved a like degree of structuralization there would be no momentum towards a creative act. I am referring here to the tension that has, I believe, to be present within one and the same structure (superego) if that urge to create which is encountered in the genius is to prevail. I surmise that the lacunae of the artistic genius's superego lie in the middle areas. The early archaic layers and some of the late, highly developed ones are well established, but the middle layers, which can be attributed to the latency period, seem to be much more weakly developed or even partly missing. Thus the genius is equipped with an archaic, crudely demanding, sadistic superego and at the same time one that is highly developed and refined but no less demanding. I suspect that the created work of art has also the function of an attempt at filling, in a concrete form, those vast lacunae of the genius's own superego.

It is because of these lacunae in the superego that so many investigators of the psychology of genius have found a kinship with psychotics and criminals. As is to be expected, in these two forms of psychopathology superego lacunae can easily be demonstrated. The capacity of the genius for solving the tension ensuing from his particular structuralization of the superego by the creation of a masterwork that is considered by the culture group as a correct, social, and highly valued act, shields the underlying superego pathology from direct scrutiny. Of course, one would like to know what the genius's secret is, why he does not become a victim of psychosis and criminality, but converts psychopathology into creations. Is it that his superego psychopathology is different in structure and genesis from that encountered in these two groups, or is it that he is endowed with extraordinary gifts and this enables him to compensate in a way unique to himself? I surmise that his path of development is, from early phases on, different from that so often encountered in the two afore-mentioned groups.

Although I am unable to demonstrate subtle points in the development of genius I wish to point to a gross factor. Lacunae in the superego, such as those just cited, aside from their topography, may derive from three different clinical constellations:[49] (1) The subject may have identified with inadequate objects, which themselves were instances of defective superegos. (2) For mainly internal reasons the subject's superego development may have been disturbed so that the end result was a defective one. (3) The superego may have developed by and large adequately, but parts of it were dissolved by later disease. The lacunae in such an instance are the secondary result of a disease in a personality that has up to this point made an adequate adjustment. I think that these three etiological constellations result in different clinical manifestations. The little we have been able to reconstruct about Goethe's developmental history makes it appear that he belonged to type 3. If my impression that in Leipzig he went through a short-lasting psychosis (possibly of the schizophrenic type) is correct, he would have suffered during that period a loss of parts of ego (superego) structure. By creating works of art the genius would then be attempting to concretize in external reality a structure that had once upon a time been part of his own self. According to this theory, the genius would, by creating, not so much be reestablishing a lost object or reproducing an ideal object of the past, subsequently proved imperfect—although this mechanism is nevertheless also involved—but rather would be re-creating a part of his self that he had once possessed but irretrievably lost. The work of art according to this theory would be the active concretization of a projected internal void,[50] yet a void that had once been fully occupied by structure. It would make good sense that this former—more satisfactory while more complete and therefore more harmonious—ego state is still represented in unconscious memory systems and that the longing for this state contributes to the pressure by which the genius is driven towards making his existence complete by creating. To seek the happiness of childhood is an important force in the lives of many people, yet in the ordinary instance this seeking is based partly on an illusion; partly it pertains to a state to which the ego has lost its rightful claim; and partly it is directed towards certain stimuli with which the ego was supplied by external reality. The genius's craving for the reexperience of a past state is for obvious reasons far better justified.

If single episodes of the life of a poet like Goethe are taken out of context they are quite reminiscent of, perhaps even identical with, events we frequently encounter in the history of disorders. But if the total picture in any cross-section of the lives of geniuses is considered—even from a time period when

---

[49] For defective superego development, see 3.

[50] That this can be only a subordinate function in the creative process—though possibly one of the most archaic ones—is clear.

they have not yet achieved artistic mastery—one gets the impression that the artists already as children were different in significant aspects from their psychopathological counterparts. This, at least, is the impression gained from biographies of such as Mozart and Goethe.[51]

The fact of symptomatic similarity between two groups does not prove like similarity between the dynamic and genetic factors leading to the particular symptomatology. Plato's theory regarding madness may have a proper place in a rational clinical deliberation on the artist's psychopathology. Two passages in the *Phaedrus* are of consequence for this problem. Plato distinguishes between madness as the outgrowth of disease and madness as "a divine release of the soul from the yoke of custom and convention" (422, *1*:268). A radical and uncompromising thesis is expressed in the following words: "But he who, having no touch of the Muses' madness in his soul, comes to the door and thinks that he will get into the temple by the help of art—he, I say, and his poetry are not admitted, the sane man disappears and is nowhere when he enters into rivalry with the madman." (See 422, *1*:249–50; 406, pp. 259–92.) The impression one receives from many a biography could not be put in a more precise symbolic form. Here madness is postulated as an indispensable prerequisite of great literary art. Since our rational age cannot accept a particular heavenly influence as the cause of the poet's psychopathology, Plato's theory can help us only as a formulation of the problem but does not contribute anything to the answer we are seeking. But the imagery Plato devised to distinguish the great poet from the lesser may offer some clue. There is the poet who tries to achieve his goal by art without madness, and who must therefore fail.

If we compare the psychopathology of the adult neurotic with that of the poet we find a difference that seems significant for us, namely, a different attitude towards passivity. The neurotic in general puts up a hard struggle against his wishes for passive gratification and responds to them with intense anxiety. As Freud suggested, the mastery of this problem is really the greatest difficulty in the analysis of male patients (214, p. 356). The poet, of course, also has conflicts about passivity, but strangely enough in some situations—and possibly in those that are most important for the creative process—he puts himself uncompromisingly at the service of a power that is experienced by him as external. Throughout the history of occidental culture (and, I think, of many other cultures) one over and over again finds great artists claiming that an external inspiration overcame them. That inspiration is really the equivalent of Plato's divine madness.

---

[51] Nevertheless, it is conceivable that future research will demonstrate that it is either the content of the genius's identification, that is to say, the kind of people with whom he had an opportunity to identify, or the inherited endowment pushing him towards certain channels of discharge, or both, that decide his fate and safeguard him against a psychotic or criminal outcome.

The inspiration is attributed to a variety of forces, depending on personal and historical factors. It is sometimes a female deity, more often, I think, a masculine god, but it is impressive to what a degree the artist subjectively feels quite passive at a time when he objectively reaches a peak of activity. His way of feeling has its counterpart in the way the woman feels about bearing children or about the moment of conception. The psychology of artistic creation really includes two problems: the one of inspiration (see 349; 98) (conception) and the other of forming the work of art (giving birth). It is difficult to keep these two aspects apart because in the actual process of creating they often become intermingled or even coincide, as frequently in the case of lyric poetry. An outstanding example would be Goethe's report of writing his poems in a state of semisleep. In such an instance the earliest awareness of inspiration coincides with the bringing forth of the finished product. Usually the artist is not that fortunate and inspiration leads only to an idea, to a fragment or scrap, and the process of forming out of it the perfect work requires hard and painful labor, which may, however, be interrupted by renewed flashes of inspiration. Goethe's *Werther* seems to have been written in a period of constant and prolonged inspiration covering several weeks. Here one should rather speak of a frenzy, ecstasy, or delirium.

Among the artists there seem to be at least two essentially different types of ways of experiencing the act of creation. Anton Chekhov wrote: "Medicine is my legal spouse, while literature is my mistress. When I get tired of one, I go and sleep with the other. . . ." (87, p. 17) This should be compared with what Goethe wrote when he was going through the tedious labor of getting his *Elective Affinities* ready for publication: "I am here for longer than seven weeks and I have an impression of myself like that pregnant woman who has no other desire than that the child be born, whatever it may be or become."[52] It is my feeling that the latter type is more typical of the genius. The possibility of switching horses is subtly expressed in Chekhov's remark, the inescapability in Goethe's. I also think that the narcissistic component, so important in the mother-infant relationship, creates a stronger tie and affinity to the germinating work of art than a pure object-relationship. Although the genius gratifies his "object hunger" by creating a work of art, the strong narcissistic component must not be overlooked. It is in the mother-infant relationship that object-relationship and narcissistic gratification coincide and both mutually support each other.

It is more difficult, however, to gain knowledge about the conception of a work of art. There is often a distinct reluctance in the artist to say very much about the moment when a work of art was conceived. I have the impression that the artist can more easily identify with the pregnant mother than with the

---

[52] [Ich befinde mich seit länger als sieben Wochen hier und komme mir vor wie jene Schwangere, die weiter nichts wünscht, als dass das Kind zur Welt komme, es sey übrigens und entstehe was will.] (To C. F. von Reinhard, October 1, 1809)

woman who is conceiving. This is different from religious imagery with its emphasis on the spiritual conception of the Lord. Furthermore, the moment when the work of art is conceived is probably vague and not easy to describe. But I wonder whether the poet is really interested in knowing about this phase of the creative process. It is beset with its own peculiar dangers. The poet cannot foresee all that his unconscious may pour forth. If he submits to the flash of divine inspiration he may expose himself to a grave danger in so far as deeply repressed contents may break through far beyond the tolerance of the self. The process of forming and elaborating and achieving the final form of the work of art, painful as this phase may be and desperate as some artists may feel about it, nevertheless harbors less danger to the psychic apparatus than the moment of artistic inspiration. The elaborating process is somewhat closer to volition, that is to say, to consciousness. For the neurotic, most of the derivatives of the unconscious are dangers; for the poet they are God-sent harbingers of great works. Yet the contents of his inspiration are experienced as coming from the outside and passively he submits himself to that external force in whatever way he may symbolize it. The knowledge that the passive surrender will lead to the birth of an artistic work may give the poet the courage to surrender with a minimum of anxiety. In his dark Leipzig period Goethe seemed to react like a neurotic, if not like a psychotic. The situation of being passively devoured became the content of a nightmare and Shakespeare's verses were the saving magic wand (see above, p. 61). Here the power of escaping danger is still borrowed from a father-substitute; later he will surrender passively and find the magic power in himself. I think one of the secrets of the great poet is that he can keep passivity and activity in proper balance and does not react to either of them with an unmanageable feeling of guilt. He can accept the birth of a work of art as an act of restitution after having bowed passively to inspiration. The moment of inspiration, of course, is not necessarily only a moment of passive masochistic surrender, but the incorporation of divine inspiration by passive surrender may then mean an act of taking something away from a father or mother-substitute that, in turn, is given back in the shape of the work of art.

The difference between the neurotic and the artist may possibly require the postulation of a fourth psychological principle. Freud in laborious and painstaking work established the existence of three principles dominating the variety of processes within the psychic apparatus. The principle of constancy aims at keeping the tension and quantity of psychic energy in the psychic apparatus at the lowest possible (and therefore optimal) level. It works against any and all deviations from that level. The pleasure principle, which also aims at reducing the tension of the psychic apparatus to that optimum, achieves this by detouring around any powerful increases or decreases in tension, generating maximum pleasure. The reality principle, which interposes long delays in the reduction of tension in adjustment to the necessities of reality, enforces control, that is to say, the faculty of bearing tensions and excitation over long periods of time. The promise of pleasure in the future makes possible the endurance of displeasure over these periods of time. My question concerns whether at a later stage of development there does not emerge a fourth principle, one that is not necessarily as indispensable to life as are the constancy, pleasure, and reality principles, but that may still acquire a considerable power over the sequence and course of psychic processes and the distribution of energy in the psychic apparatus. I wonder whether a psychic apparatus is able under exceptional conditions to regulate the distribution of energy independently of the laws of pleasure. Of the three classically asserted principles, the reality principle goes farthest in removing energic processes from domination by pleasure, and it is impressive how much pain and displeasure the apparatus can bear in the service of that principle. But it does not divorce itself essentially from the pleasure principle—indeed, it is perhaps its most forceful guardian and protector. Can a psychic apparatus be structured in such a way as to operate over considerable periods of time while engaging in processes that do not result in pleasure and, moreover, do not even hold forth the promise of resulting in pleasure? One gets the impression that perhaps such an improbable event does take place in the life of a genius. When he is filled with the irresistible necessity to create he may sacrifice his self for the great goal of bringing forth the work that he potentially senses in himself. He will live up to that necessity regardless of whether there is a chance that fame or compensation awaits in the future (cf. 406, p. 443; 289).

It may sound like a blatant contradiction now to attempt to hypothesize a fourth principle entirely "beyond the pleasure principle" after I have so strongly stressed that the drives are involved in the creative process and declared them to be the indispensable source of those energies that are discharged in that process. The clinical situation is indeed contradictory and inconclusive. There is no doubt that the path of the genius is studded with pleasures of a beauty and sublimity such as the average person does not experience. I am not referring here to the pleasures of success or the pleasure of seeing one's own creation alive and becoming a living part of the existence of others. It is said that Mozart, lying on his deathbed in his home, followed in his mind with incredible joy all the details of the performance of *The Magic Flute* as it was being performed in the theater where he had attended it only once. I am thinking rather of moments such as the one I described when I outlined the events that led to Goethe's writing "Über allen Gipfeln ist Ruh" ("The Song of Repose"; cf. above, pp. 694–724). The creative process leads the genius into a depth of experience that is scarcely reached by others and this depth of experience itself provides incomparable pleasure and joy. I have to interpolate a general statement here. Human existence is structured in such a way that pleasure cannot be excluded over a long period of time. It is quite impressive to observe the operation of this basic law in situations where one would expect that all sources of pleasure gain had been closed, such as in prisons or during long-lasting, painful diseases. Even here one notices that after a while pleasure, concealed or sometimes even almost openly expressed, is experienced. Thus I do not mean by suggesting a fourth principle operative in the lives of geniuses that they lead a kind of existence actually devoid of pleasure. What I want to say is that the genius would create even if he were deprived of pleasure gain, that he would continue his work even without that minimum pleasure that is automatically given by the mere fact of living. Thus the creative process seems so fundamental to his existence that it would continue even if it resulted in a life without pleasure. This supraordinated, all-comprehensive necessity to create gives the genius at times a feeling of being only an appendage to creation, as if he had been cheated out of all pleasure. To be sure, there are moments or even periods when the genius actually renounces all pleasures, exposes himself to pure displeasure and makes a sacrifice of which no other personality type is capable.[53]

The source from which the genius derives this unique capacity is, I think, still a puzzle. This particular capacity is usually forgotten in the discussion of the psychology of genius and greater attention is paid to the equally puzzling question of the origin of the genius's unique artistic capacities. These capacities, of course, constitute one of the prerequisites and probably are deeply rooted in the biological inheritance, as units that defy further psychological analysis. But their flowering, their being used for the creative maximum, the genius's subordinating his own opportunities for pleasure to their operation, these and many other factors are of a psychological nature and will some day be understood in psychological terms.[54] What I speak of here goes beyond what is commonly observed in the lives of human beings who put their existence in the service of the superego. Great as the sacrifices may be that are occasioned in the lives of such people, the operation of an obscured pleasure principle is still observable. The genius seems to transcend even that degree of renunciation, and, although he is almost constantly coping with uninhibited, instinctual energies, he channels them towards goals that seem to be beyond the antinomies of pleasure and displeasure. It seems it is just in this particular constellation that the genius's unusual capacity for sacrifice is to be observed. His dealing with the accumulation of large amounts of instinctual energies over and over

[53] The martyr comes to one's mind at this point and many a genius has experienced his life as one of martyrdom. Notwithstanding a certain similarity between some types of genius and the martyr, there is one great difference. In the hour of supreme suffering the martyr has, typically, lost the opportunity of choice. Although the true martyr will not regret his past decisions and will voluntarily bear suffering, he is, if a religious martyr, certain of reward once earthly pain has ceased. The unrecognized genius may or may not be certain of compensation in the form of later fame; it plays a lesser role in his make-up than the martyr's certainty of victory. Horace's prediction that the walls of Rome would be standing at a time when his work would have been forgotten is an example of that difference.

[54] In our own historical period such an instance of supreme sacrifice in the service of creation is well documented. I have in mind Freud's self-analysis, in which, temporarily, the genius achieved an almost complete renunciation of the pleasure principle.

again confronts him with the temptation of letting them flow towards their original goals, and possibly in each creative step there lies also an act of renunciation in so far as the potentially available physical gratification is rejected in favor of the concretization of instinctual energy in the form of a masterwork. One gets the impression that after long and painful detours the genius reaches a stage where actually the pleasures inherent in creativity gradually weaken and he becomes possessed by art. Whatever pleasure there may be left in life, it has become a secondary and dispensable adjunct of living in art. Creating is no longer experienced as a mission or a duty, but has become a matter of course. The narcissistic gain has been reduced and the genius feels himself no longer a living entity, but, so to speak, an embodied principle. Whether man has ever actually achieved such a form of existence is difficult to prove; that man may harbor that potentiality and that some who are chosen approximate it, one may assume. The neurotic, who is fixated to the sway of the pleasure principle, cannot extricate himself from the open or tacit expectation of pleasurable recompense. The genius, however, may grow away from the sensual and pleasurable in steady approximation to an existence in which the ego accepts and integrates the call to create without wasting energy on pursuits that do not directly serve the realization of superego values. In this situation I think one can no longer speak of "pleasure" in the sense in which this term is used when one speaks of "the pleasure principle." Pleasure presupposes at least a minimal discharge of energy. In this stage the discharge that takes place in the creative process may become negligible and creating be tantamount to an identification with a value.

It may be worth while to consider the possibility that such a principle is potentially at work in everyone who develops a superego. This would be the most recent acquisition of the species in its phylogenetic development, and the least anchored in the biological layer of the personality, and therefore the one most difficult to discern in the manifoldness of psychic processes.

Be this as it may, in the midst of the many as yet unresolved uncertainties in the psychology of the artistic genius there is one fact that is fairly securely established, namely, the superiority of men over women in the creation of the highest cultural values. Without falling prey to Victorian views and other exaggerations the fact remains that the peak accomplishments of cultural creations have been achieved by men. Women's endowment for cultural production is eminent and a large number of women have created values that match almost the best of what men have created, but not the very best. In terms of the highest standards of artistic creation one does not find one single woman among the geniuses. This fact is extremely surprising. If one considers one after another those functions that one must regard as essential for the act of artistic creation one must admit that many of them are usually found to be even more highly developed in women than in men, such as intuitiveness, playfulness, emotionality, and many more. An attempt is often made to explain this considerable difference in creative abilities on the basis of sociological factors. The inferior societal position, the lack of, or at least circumscription of, educational opportunities, the early discouragement of the growing girl by her awareness of the high regard in which the male element is held by those about her—these and other factors of the same sort are, we are asked to believe, responsible for the absence of females from the galaxy of the world's geniuses. This explanation sounds very convincing and many historical facts can be cited in its favor. But it does not explain why these allegedly detrimental historical conditions have not prevented the evolvement of superior talents in women. As soon as we abstract the genius quality we find a huge number of women who have all the skills and talents and abilities and endowment that we find in their talented male counterparts. The difference evidently resides exclusively in the area of the genius quality. It would be strange indeed if a societal factor permitted the evolvement of skill, ability, and talents, but selectively suppressed just that which makes a genius.

On the other hand we encounter—and not so rarely—the stamp of genius in a man who grew up under the worst "societal" conditions. I do not consider it a disproof of this thesis when anthropologists prove that at certain stages of societal development woman's contribution to civilization was greater than men's. Man's cultural potentiality is not as firmly anchored in the biological layer as breathing or seeing. In every man the cultural potentiality may become suppressed or even destroyed and societies are thinkable in which the social milieu makes the generation of male cultural endowment impossible. But in such societies, I surmise, female achievement will not reach that maximum that can be observed under conditions favorable to the sprouting of male capabilities.

In speculating about the reason why this rare capacity of genius occurs only in men, the first idea that comes to one's mind is that woman's creative ability exhausts itself in her larger contribution to the propagative process. As various authors have pointed out, the development of women is more complicated than that of men. Women have to grapple with tasks with which male development is not concerned. The change from clitoris to vagina as leading genital zone, the change of sex of the principal, infantile love-objects (from the preoedipal mother to the oedipal father), are such special tasks. Furthermore, the periodic intrusion of the physical factor in the form of menstruation works against sublimation. Here one has to consider also the internal cyclic endocrine changes, which have no parallel in male life, where endocrine changes span long periods of time. The internal change of the endocrine milieu within short periods of time when compared with the relative constant of the male endocrine milieu, shows with particular clarity the additional burden, of no minor proportion, that the female psychic apparatus has to bear. Last, but not least, from early years on the girl's development is hampered by penis envy, the compensation for which, by the growth of breasts and the maturation of the childbearing capacity, arrives too late to heal the injuries suffered at a tender age.

Notwithstanding the relevance of such factors one still wonders why their presence should militate so strongly against the evolvement of the genius quality, particularly in view of the eminent endowment found in such a large number of females. Envy sometimes functions as a positive spur to achievement and the boy's envy of the maternal capacity to bear children plays, more frequently than not, a role like that of penis envy in female development. Without belittling the effect of the factors so far enumerated, I still feel that it is another aspect of the male–female biological structure difference that accounts for the potentiality of genius in the man and forestalls this potentiality in the woman. I have in mind the fact that generative material is potentially present in the male in unlimited amount—that is to say, the male gonads have the capacity to produce their contribution to the generative material in enormous quantity, whereas in the female the generative material is there from the outset and cannot be increased in quantity in the course of postnatal development. The number of ovula in the ovaries is fixed at birth. The fact that the supply of ova is huge and far exceeds the number that could actually be used by the individual for the generative possibilities of a lifetime, should not mislead us as to the possible psychological consequences of its being biologically fixed and predetermined. To be sure, although there is no doubt that biological processes have their bearing upon psychic processes and the structure of the psychic apparatus, we have no reliable code to decipher their relationship and are incapable of reliable correlations between these two groups of factors. Therefore the following does not amount to anything but a hypothesis. In the male the potential generative material is practically unlimited. With each ejaculation several millions of sperms leave the body and spermatogenesis is probably a continuous process as soon as maturation has started. The biological data suggest that the biological creativity of females is limited when compared with the male. The unlimited biological generative capacity of the male is, according to this hypothesis, the biological equivalent of man's superior creativity. The divertibility of the female biological potential towards other areas is limited when compared with the equivalent potentiality in the male. The creative function in women is, so to speak, bound up in the generative material and is therefore less accessible to the diversion of which the male creative function seems extremely capable.

Indeed, if two marked differences are found in two groups of people there may be a certain probability that they are not merely coincidental but closely correlated. Thus—expressed in negative terms—man's incapacity to bear children would be one of the prerequisites of his cultural endowment. It has been stated by others that men's envy of women for their privilege of childbearing is one of the roots of men's cultural superiority. I do not agree with this view.

Envy possesses, no doubt, an importance that can hardly be overrated in man's life. But, though envy may increase the momentum of a function, it cannot really create something new that would not exist without it. Envy, I have no doubt, plays a great role in the artist's life and the craving to create something equally as wonderful as the infant that mother bore must have been an important factor in the lives of many a genius, and it certainly was in Goethe. Envy, however, is a potent motive in the lives of women, too, and applies not only to the penis but to man's cultural achievements as well; nevertheless, this envy does not provide women with that momentum that would enable them to become men's equal in the creation of cultural values.

It may also be the structure of bisexuality that is significant. Men's feminine components, being less bound to an anatomical structure in the male organism than masculinity in women, may be more readily accessible to sublimation than masculinity in woman. Here may be another biological root for the capacity of some men to create, under propitious circumstances, works almost comparable in perfection to the biological creations of women. Biological functions, however, are more reliable and more precise than mental ones. The vast majority of women can conceive and bear children. Still, the transformation of female creative functions in the male into an unbiological medium depends on innumerable imponderables, and only in exceptional circumstances does this transformation result in the appearance of a genius. Still, this fact—that men, and only men, can, in exceptional circumstances, reach this high level of cultural achievements—apparently also depends on male physiology inasmuch as that obviates the exhaustion of male creativity in the act of propagation. Hence, it would not be quite correct to construe contrasts or opposites between male and female creativity. As was remarked before, female contribution to civilization is enormous and the peak achievements of women tower far above the average of all men, most of whom stay aloof from the cultural process. Thus women, of course, are exquisitely capable of sublimation and of developing single, highly specialized talents. Goethe wrote Lavater (July 24, 1780):

> You use the word "talent" as if it were the opposite of genius. . . . Yet we ought to consider that that very talent cannot be anything but the language of genius.[55]

I think Goethe was right. The genius and the talent have in common that both have talents, but the genius has the additional gift of creating out of his talents something that is not accessible to the talent. This additional synthesis, this language of the genius, it is that is lacking in women. Hence there is no essential contrast between female and male creativity. Women, too, develop single, highly specialized functions that probably are not more highly developed

[55] [. . . brauchst du das Wort *Talent* als wenn es der Gegensaz von Genie wäre. . . . Wir sollten aber bedenken dass das eigentliche Talent nichts sein kann als die Sprache des Genies.]

in the genius, who, however, can add to his work a distinctive mark. As a good mother centers her innermost interest on the child, a genius has only one interest at heart, that is to say, his creation. This unflinching interest, this complete surrender, which is noticeable in the artistic genius, can only be matched by the mother's relationship to the child.

One more word about the male sublimation. It has been stated that sublimations depend on pregenital energies and that sublimatory processes do not take hold of genital libido (97). This may be a valid viewpoint for the clinical instances that come to our attention. Yet the genius may possibly acquire his unique capacities by the diversion of genital libido towards creation.[56] He renounces, so to speak, his phallicity for the sake of incomparable originality. This may be one more reason for the great rarity of genius. The probability that a psychobiological organism can ever give up striving for the greatest possible pleasure with which nature has endowed the psychobiological organism, is indeed very small.[57]

This additional hypothesis could easily be misunderstood. It does not mean to suggest that the genius quality requires lack of genital activity. Frequency of genital activity is no indicator at all of the degree of genital sublimation; what counts is only such factors as actual pleasures gained or exhaustion of the biological pleasure potential, and the meaning of the genital function in the conscious and unconscious systems. (I enlarge on this subject in Appendix U.) Likewise complete absence of genital activity always signifies supreme inhibitions—the archenemy of sublimation. As I have tried to demonstrate, genital activities are documented in Goethe's life, but it seems that they did not play that central role which man's biological structure suggests they should. I wish to repeat here Dr. Paul Kramer's suggestion that the fullest possible orgastic experience would be shattering to the sensitive and delicate fabric of the genius's psychic apparatus. Consequently the sublimation of genital energy would also serve the biological survival of the individual genius, who protects himself automatically against a tension level beyond his capacity of endurance. We discover here a biological root of defense, which perhaps is at the bottom of all

---

[56] See 359. Also Helene Deutsch assumes that "the best sublimations" derive from genital libido (98, p. 417).

[57] I add belatedly here a report it would have been very profitable to cite at several points earlier. An informant as reliable and sober as Chancellor von Müller writes that Karl August told him on May 27, 1828, the following:

Goethe, he claimed, has always ascribed too much to women; has loved his own ideas in them; has never really felt great passion. [Goethe habe stets zu viel in die Weiber gelegt, seine eigenen Ideen in ihnen geliebt, eigentliche grosse Leidenschaft nicht empfunden.] (250, 4:478)

The conversation was a very frank one and many indiscretions were communicated by the Duke. It is of the greatest importance that the Duke, who had spent in intimate closeness with Goethe the early years of his stay in Weimar when Goethe was believed to have indulged in excesses, considered him as not feeling passionately about women.

sublimation. Yet the fact that the genital function seems to have played a secondary role in the life of Goethe (who went to extremes in all other dimensions of life) makes it probable that we are dealing here not with an inhibition but with the rare instance of a true phallic sublimation. As all other males wish to infuse the unique and most individual stuff the organism can produce within another human being, the genius is primarily driven to spread unique and most individual symbols throughout the human world, and to find in that activity the consummation of his existence. Thus it looks as if the unique feature in the genius's bisexuality is the synthesis of his biological maleness and femaleness into one act of creation. Creation per se is indelibly steeped in the female part of the biological substructure; the sublimation of the male biological factor, the infinite richness, the eternal creative flow, the transposition of the biologically unique into the mentally unique form, is the result of phallic creativeness.

In trying to bring psychology of genius into the most general biological context one feels tempted to compare it to a certain biological form of adjustment described by Parr (419; see also 276, pp. 24–27). This author stressed the element of activity in adaptation, which, according to his theory, is based on an act of choice by means of which organisms select the best-suited environment. In a fashion comparable to this form of adaptation the artistic genius creates his own environment, which suits him better than the reality he actually encounters. For the true genius there is no place in this world and no combination of living conditions that can offer him a secure frame of existence. Therefore, he is forced to select a frame that has not yet been realized but is stored in him as a potentiality. He spends his life, apparently, in constantly giving visible shape and real structure to that kind of world which is the only one suitable for him to live in, and thus his "maladjustment" to the world as it is is also one of the many prerequisites to genius.

Appendix U

Remarks on the Problem of the Transformation of Instinctual Energy

AN INVESTIGATION OF the kind I have set forth in these notes may rightly arouse the expectation of new findings and thus an accretion to the theories of psychoanalysis. This expectation has not been confirmed, for whatever reason. However, one point has become clear. To set this point forth fully, so that it could take whatever place it deserves in contributing to a change in present psychoanalytic theory, would require a long disquisition including consideration of basic concepts of psychoanalysis and particularly of hypothesis as to the origin of the ego. Since this is not possible here, I shall be as brief as I can.

After having studied the record of those years of Goethe's life that are the subject matter of this inquiry, I feel quite certain that the energic processes we are wont to denote under the term "sublimation" do not constitute a transformation of energy of instinctual quality into indifferent energy. Furthermore, the existence of such a thing as indifferent energy must be doubted quite generally.

This proposition requires a few words about the concept of sublimation. It was introduced in 1905 when Freud gave a general outline of his theory of libido. He meant by it a process by means of which libido, the energy of the sexual drives, is diverted towards goals that are noninstinctual. Freud was here referring to the extraordinary contribution of drives to cultural achievements of the highest order. Sublimation was thus defined in a precise manner. Its clinical index was the cultural achievement, which is easily recognizable and therefore reliable as a defining feature (however, see 22; 25). Though Freud in his early definition did not explicitly say so, the term per se perhaps implied, aside from the elevation of the aim of the instincts, a process that may be likened to rarefication, or purification, which libido has to undergo before it can be used for the work of cultural value.

In 1923 Freud introduced, in his book *The Ego and the Id,* the concept of an indifferent, desexualized energy, and sublimation was now described as a change in the quality of libidinal energy.[1] According to this view, libidinal energy, before it can be used for noninstinctual goals, has to be transformed into an energy that is free of any specific quality. With this redefinition of sublimation the concept was greatly extended and covered many psychological phenomena that were no longer connected with cultural achievements. Subsequently equivalent ideas were suggested regarding the energy of the aggressive-destructive instincts,[2] and the concept of neutralization was introduced.[3]

It is always difficult to contend that an event observers assert they have witnessed did not take place at all; I therefore hesitate to dispute the existence of sublimation in terms of energy transformation or neutralization (as defined at present) and limit myself to the contention that, if it does exist, it is of minor importance in the total economy of the personality.

It may be that automatisms, well-integrated behavior patterns, subordinated and routinely activated parts of comprehensive action sequences, run on indifferent energy—I don't know. Future physiological and pathophysiological inquiries will decide the question. At present, it seems to me, the theoretical assumption is sufficient that small quantities of instinctual energy are the fuel used up by automatisms and the like.

Of more far-reaching importance is the question of the source of the energy that is used in thinking, which, after all, takes the central role in man's coming to terms with his surroundings. According to Freud's later formulations "the energy for the work of thought itself must be supplied from sublimated erotic sources."[4]

Earlier, however, Freud (1911) thought that the energic processes in think-

---

[1] A passage in Freud's paper on Schreber's Memoirs may be understood as containing a reference to a qualitative change of libido by means of sublimation in patients who are fixated to the stage of narcissism. Freud says that "some unusually intense wave of libido, finding no other outlet, may . . . undo the sublimation" (173, p. 62).

[2] It was Robert Waelder who, as far as I know, first extended the concept of sublimation to aggression. This occurred in a discussion of Freud's "Analysis Terminable and Interminable" (October 6, 1937), in the *Wiener Psychoanalytische Vereinigung,* in connection with his setting forth the consequences of Freud's introducing a "spontaneous tendency to conflict" (cf. 214, p. 347) as a neurosogenic factor. For an early indirect reference to the sublimation of aggression see 170, p. 74: "During the work of investigation love and hate threw off their positive and negative signs and were both alike transformed into intellectual interest." See also Freud's letter No. 33 (321, 3:464).

[3] For the best and most complete theoretical discourse on the subject of sublimation see 280. Kris (350, pp. 27–28; 352, pp. 30–31) suggests using the term *neutralization* to designate energy transformations and *sublimation* for the displacement of goals.

[4] 197, p. 64. In this context Freud was certainly thinking of desexualized energy.

ing consist of the displacement of minimal quantities of energy combined with minimum discharge. This required the damming up of libido and the raising of the level of the whole cathectic process (172, p. 221). Freud did not there say *expressis verbis* that by "energy" he meant libido, but the context requires this assumption. A passage in a less known paper by Freud supports this. "Strictly speaking," he writes, "all mental states, including those that we usually regard as 'processes of thought' are to some degree 'affective,' and not one of them is without its physical manifestations or is incapable of modifying somatic process" (162, p. 288).

I feel inclined to adhere to Freud's earlier assumption that thinking uses the shift of small quantities of energy, and energy which Freud evidently regarded as libidinal.

Thinking, which, under optimal conditions, is, of all ego functions, the one most removed from the instincts, may well serve as a sample in which to test whether or not, in terms of psychoanalytic theory, it is rigorously necessary to assume the operation of an indifferent energy. The probability that the energy used in thinking is instinctual becomes even greater in the light of the following statement by Freud. He says of the desexualized libido that "it would still retain the main purpose of Eros—that of uniting and binding—in so far as it helped towards establishing that unity, or tendency to unity, which is particularly characteristic of the ego" (197, p. 64). Indeed, to speak broadly, the thought processes also lead either to the synthesis of contents that are disparate or to the disjoining of the commensurate, and thus the general goals of the two principal groups of drives (Eros and Thanatos) are also demonstrable in thinking.

It seems to contradict the concept of an indifferent energy that the energy here spoken of is regularly discharged in a way that still bears the earmarks of characteristics essential to those drives from which it allegedly derives. Physiological research will have the last word in this matter too. The historical argument I have used in citing Freud's early theories proves little of itself. But I am certain that present clinical observations and psychoanalytic knowledge in general do not compel the assumption of an indifferent energy underlying thought processes. The matter at present is moot in this respect. The assumption that, in thinking, small instinctual energies are displaced or shifted is justifiable, and cannot be rejected on an empirical basis. The crucial question here is structure. Whatever the quality of the underlying energy may be, special structures must be evolved for logical or reality-adequate thinking to take place (see 439). What in quantitative terms of psychic economy Freud in 1911 called the "raise of level" [Niveauerhöhung] would nowadays be regarded as a matter of structure.

To turn now to the biographical record, hardly any indifferent energy can be clinically demonstrated during Goethe's creative spells. He is in a semi-somnambulistic state, or excited, overwhelmed by passions, irritable, driven, weeping, etc. When his libido is halfway gratified and the asserted indifferent energy would thus be ready to be disposed of, undisturbed by the instincts, the quality of his output is lowered, as was observed particularly during the time following his Italian journey. Yet his creations on the occasions of the adolescent crises that occurred throughout his life, when his whole state of mind was flooded with instinctual energy, reached the very pinnacle of accomplishment.[5]

I presume the reasoning against this clinical argument may run as follows: The overflow of libido during creative spells does not argue against the theory of neutralization. True, there may be a serious libidinal upheaval underlying a creative spell, but the upheaval can lead to creation only if and when sufficient indifferent energy is mobilized to keep the productive functions going. The ego may need conflicts and libidinal damming-up in order to use its store of indifferent energy to the best purpose. Without the fire of conflict, it may be reasoned, the ego loses its maximum momentum towards creation. The consequence thus would be that the ego, under the impact of the threat that originates in the id, resorts to maximum achievement by optimal use of its store of indifferent energy.

This construction sounds reasonable, but whence comes that relative calm after the creative spell? By neutralization of instinctual energy only relatively little instinctual energy can be discharged or used up. Moreover, it is not probable that at a period when such intense libidinal outbreaks occur the ego can keep any of its structures free of the instinctual flood that bursts into its confines. It is not probable that just those functions in which the self takes the most passionate interest during a creative spell are charged with indifferent energy, while all the surrounding structures are greatly cathected with instinctual energy. Would one not be right in assuming that at times of maximal libidinization of the whole personality an impairment is observed in the operation of those functions of which it is claimed that their optimal use requires cathexis by indifferent energy? Is it not more probable that the secret of genius lies in the total integration of new goals, which are now pursued by the instincts with that intensity and cunning with which otherwise physical gratification is pursued? Is not the genius's secret the total diversion towards the process of creation of the drive that has physical discharge as its aim?[6]

This ability to divert such enormous quantities of instinctual energy as are involved in the creative process towards nonphysical aims is a matter of structure, of structure endowed with particular capacities for synthesis and organi-

---

[5] It is of interest to note here that the only adolescent crisis for which this was not true was his very first, which occurred when he was still chronologically an adolescent. Then, it seems, the creative spell set in towards the end of the critical period or after it was over.

[6] Hartmann warns against a confusion of self, goal, and ego-function when discussing energic problems (280, p. 21). But it seems to me the clinical record clearly establishes that in Goethe these functions that served the concretization of passionately desired aims were also cathected with instinctual energy.

zation. I assume that it is this additional structurization that uses up great quantities of instinctual energy. If I try to prove from the clinical record that the artistic genius uses libido (or aggression) in the creation of his masterworks, that creating is an instinctual process in a particularly highly structured personality, I am not really saying anything new, for in his inquiry into Leonardo's life Freud found the same picture. He was struck by Leonardo's "overpowerful instinct for research and the atrophy of his sexual life" (170, p. 80). About this drive Freud wrote: "We consider it probable that an instinct like this of excessive strength was already active in the subject's earliest childhood. . . . We make the further assumption that it found reinforcement from what were originally sexual instinctual forces, so that later it could take the place of a part of the subject's sexual life. Thus a person of this sort would, for example, pursue research with the same passionate devotion that another would give to his love, and he would be able to investigate instead of loving." (170, p. 77) Here the original drive to investigate is taken out of the context of the sexual drives and its passionateness is attributed to its having assimilated the total or part of the libidinal drive-force. In an earlier paragraph Freud had written, as quoted earlier, that love and hate had been transformed into intellectual interest (170, p. 74). Here Freud unhesitatingly attributes Leonardo's genius achievement to libido in its instinctual form.[7]

Freud sets forth in theoretical terms a process equivalent to that which has been presented in these notes as underlying Goethe's passionate drive to create. His drive to inquire, also strong beyond measure, rarely acquired the exclusiveness that is observed in Leonardo.[8]

Yet if, in two instances of genius, we find the most creative—and well-nigh the most characteristic—ego-functions so powerfully endowed with instinctual cathexis, that is to say, if we find instinctual cathexis just in that area where the ego achieves that which is most characteristic of its structure, what then is the probability that indifferent energy is relevant in those other instances, in which the nongenius, the ordinary ego, learns, draws, judges, thinks, recalls, memorizes, initiates?

Let us turn now to everyday psychoanalytic clinical experience to see what it can tell us of this matter. In the vast majority of patients we do not find the instinctual factor that I have described in the pursuits of the genius. Most patients do show a lack of passion in those areas of ego-structure that have not been affected by neuroses and that adequately serve the reality principle. Such pursuits do not serve physical gratifications but aim at the realization of ego aims, inasmuch as they lie in external reality, are carried out with flexibility,

---

[7] The reference to other drives was in accordance with the classification of instincts Freud was employing at that time as sexual instincts and ego instincts, a classification he later dropped.

[8] The instance of exclusiveness in connection with his *Chromatology* was based on an impairment of the investigatory function.

awareness, calmness, deliberation, and devotion, often even under trying conditions. All these indices, mainly derived from patients' reports regarding the conscious mode of their experiences and partly from the observation of actual behavior, are lacking in those characteristics that we customarily attribute to instinctual processes. What is the significance of this glaring discrepancy between the abundance of passion in the pursuits of the genius and the lack of it in the nongenius? In the pursuits of the two we are dealing, after all, with equivalent processes. From other comparable discrepancies we know that the seeming lack of the instinctual factor is due to repression or inhibition. In the instances referred to here, when the activation of ego-functions results in the attainment of its goal repression is not probable, but the comparison speaks strongly in favor of an inhibition. Indeed, we know that all those egos that set out on their pursuits in the way I have described, actually realized only a small part of their potentialities. The genius, however, contrives the realization of the maximum achievements that lie as a germ in the confines of his self.

The vast majority of persons leave the oedipal phase with an ego that bears the marks of deep injury. The tribulations endured in the struggle to find a way out of the dangers and disappointments suffered in the first passionate relationships of infancy put a hobble on almost all reality-related ego-functions. This general dampening effect upon the ego cannot be called neurotic or psychopathological so long as the minimum demands of reality can still be fulfilled. The borderline between normalcy and disease is here particularly ill-defined. The process that seems characteristic of the genius can by no means be called a prerequisite of health, even though it shows the maximum realization of what a self may be capable of achieving in propitious circumstances. Under ordinary conditions the manifestly instinctual factor is more or less restricted to the physical area, and the ego, feeling defeated in its early attempts at instinctual gratification, tries to isolate passionate pursuits from reality pursuits. Under the influence of a warning and forbidding superego, narcissistic pursuits that serve the tacit goal of ego aggrandizement are engaged in with relative timidity and inhibition, and the ordinary person thinks, acts, creates, and works with a minimum of—or even without any—originality, that is, without full passionate participation of self.

According to this view, that which is called "indifferent energy" is inhibited instinctual energy—it would be more precise to say "the energy of inhibited ego-functions." The ego-structure of the ordinary person is not of a kind that is capable of maintaining its working capacity under the impact of optimal sexualization or instinctualization. We discover here what impresses me as an important point of theory. The study of the instinctualization of those ego-functions that serve reality purposes leads to contradictory observations. In many instances we observe an impairment of function under the impact of sexualization, but this is by no means a rule. Notwithstanding the clinical material cited as regards the genius one also occasionally observes in the ordinary person a sudden sprouting of an ego-function when the removal of a feeling of guilt permits the ego to cathect one of its functions with freely flowing erotic energy (cf. 280, p. 23).

I conclude that there is no general law regarding the efficiency of ego-functions in terms of inhibition[9] of, or degrees of, sexualization. The relationship between the quality of function and the degree of sexualization is a relative, not an absolute, one. Depending on the structure of the ego, increasing sexualization of ego-functions may improve efficiency or hamper it. There are patients who are sensitive to such sexualization and others who are even incapable of maintaining adequate functioning over long periods of time unless they can derive sexual pleasure from such activities. A very typical situation can be observed during the onset of a schizophrenic psychosis, when ego-structure weakens or even dissolves. An ego thus injured is incapable of maintaining the proper operation of all its ego-functions and one can observe how sometimes one ego-function after another is drawn into an injurious process of instinctualization. However, to be exact, it is not the instinctualization per se that leads to dysfunction but the injury that is done to ego-structure.

It should not be forgotten that Freud, very rightly, called sexuality an ego-function too (205, p. 87), and what has been said about ego-functions up to this point refers to those that do not serve the aim of physical gratification. I bring this up because precisely in Goethe one can observe that the ego-functions that serve sexual gratification were stunted and those that serve creative and reality pursuits operated so superbly with instinctual energies. When a shift in organization occurred and ego-functions that serve sexual pursuits were adequately activated, the quality of the creative function was, though not disturbed, yet certainly somewhat reduced in efficiency. Apparently the *locus minoris resistentiae* in Goethe's ego-structure lay in the capacity to tolerate maximum genital pleasure, and even after the genital function was restored, I surmise, orgasm did not reach its full peak. Yet in the creative area the drive was permitted to flow freely and there the ego was structured in such a way that it could withstand the demand put upon it by the drives that found release through creativity.

Hartmann sees the proof of neutralization principally in the stability of ego-functions, their resistivity against regression and sexualization, which he calls degrees of secondary autonomy of the ego (280, p. 11). Yet I think one can regard the stability of ego-functions as firmly established only when they also operate adequately so long as they are charged with great quantities of instinctual energy. The highest degree of secondary autonomy is then achieved. The creative function in Goethe—notwithstanding the varying quality and quantity of its output—shows this maximum of secondary autonomy. I think this is generally true of the artistic genius. If anything, he can never invest too

[9] When I speak here of inhibition I do not mean absence of libidinal cathexis, but, rather, low-grade cathexis.

much of instinctual energy in the creative process and, so long as adequate ego-structure is concomitantly present, the quality of function must improve with increasing investment. Only in such a case can we rightly speak of a genius personality.

A general remark about the instincts is necessary here. According to Freud's account, libido exhibits two seemingly contradictory properties. In many contexts libido is described as flexible and easily displaceable. The primary process, for example, is described as a shifting of libidinal cathexis from one idea or image to another, in disregard of the requirements of logic or external reality; similarly it is said that when instinctual gratifications are blocked in one way libido seeks discharge in collateral ways. On the other hand, Freud described the tenacity of libido, which shows up clinically in some forms of resistance, its property of insisting on a certain form of gratification, its tendency to regress to earlier forms of gratification and to achieve gratification at all costs.[10] Does it depend exclusively on the nature of the ego-structure whether instinctual energies are to appear flexible or tenacious? A good deal could be said in favor of this view, and still one feels inclined to say that much also depends on the properties of the instinctual energies. This is of importance in a discussion of ego-functions and their endowment with secondary autonomy; they too should be simultaneously flexible and tenacious, depending on the requirements of the ego itself and of external reality. When Goethe let reality pursuits, such as administration and government, engross a broad area of his life to the detriment of creative pursuits, and performed his duties in that area with such tenacity, even stubbornness, he was not, as I have tried to demonstrate, acting unwisely. At a later point of his development it was important to reorganize this mode of existing and his ego was flexible enough to evolve a new form of reality pursuits. But this change from tenacity to flexibility is not necessarily alien to the way the instincts work.

Another property of the drives must be mentioned here. Drives per se are not necessarily as irrational as they so often appear. If they have a strong admixture of masochism then they work quite strongly against the ego's purposes and true advantage. But the admixture of masochism is only incidental, though very frequent in subjects that come to the analyst's attention. If we look at Goethe, and in this instance we are concerned not only with the genius but with a property that can frequently be observed in life, we notice that many of his decisions were made at the prompting of his drives and passions, and not on the

---

[10] In Freud's Leonardo study (170) two essentially contradictory statements are found that illustrate the two aspects under which the problem may be viewed. On page 74 Freud says in a laudatory sense that the "persistence, constancy and penetration" that Leonardo showed in his investigating are "derived from passion"; on page 133, however, he says of Leonardo's research that it "seems to have contained some of the features which distinguish the activity of unconscious instincts—insatiability, unyielding rigidity and the lack of an ability to adapt to real circumstances."

basis of rational insight. After all, the reasons his father raised against his moving to Weimar were rational and well taken. All arguments spoke in favor of his rooting his professional life in his native city, and his urge to join the Duke was an impulsive one. We encounter an equivalent situation when he temporarily removes himself from Weimar and stays so long in Italy. Again the reality principle and rational deliberation would have warned strongly against this step, which again was certainly an impulsive one growing out of the bottommost depth of the repetition compulsion. And still, in both instances we know impulse and instinct made the right choice against rational and cool deliberation. Goethe would have called it his daemon, on whom he could rely. The daemon, however, is a personification of the instincts that do their work unbeknown to the ego.

I am trying here to demonstrate a factor that plays its great role in a certain type of healthy person and can be called "drive dependability" (*Triebsicherheit*), a factor that can sometimes already be observed in infants and children. Of course, the type that, contrariwise, is always led astray by his instinctual impulses vastly predominates in the psychoanalyst's clinical material. Such "drive dependability" as one finds in Goethe, combined with eminent ego-structure, was responsible for a life story of such magnificence as even the highest degree of neutralization could never achieve.

We can now perhaps say more about the person whose ego-functions are threatened by sexualization. What is the difference between a patient suffering from hysterical abasia and the farmer who plows the soil? For the hysteric, walking has become, for example, a trampling on his mother's body, and in defense against the fulfillment of this wish his gait has become uncoordinated. Does this mean that plowing the soil does not, for the farmer, have the meaning of mutilating the maternal body? Folklore, customs, myths, etc., prove that these activities also have instinctual meaning for the person who carries them out undisturbed by neurotic symptoms. Yet the differences between the two are many. They range from those of quantity to those of ego-structure and ego-differentiation. Here I wish only to say that, for the hysteric, walking and aggression have come to have the same meaning, and he rejects walking in a way that is equivalent to what he would do if he were called upon to carry out the repulsive action in reality. In the farmer, we must assume, the aggressive imagery remains restricted to a territory outside of the ego, and instinctual energy, undisturbed, is discharged by the ego, which remains unimpaired by the impact of the forbidden imagery. The farmer's ego wants nothing more nor less than to cultivate the soil, although the unconscious representation of this action is still a forbidden one. It is right to speak here of aim-inhibited instinctual discharges, inasmuch as the ego has given up an original, instinctual aim, which is relegated to the unconscious and replaced in the ego with a new one that is divorced from the original. The poet, however, is in a peculiar situation. He shares, of course, in his unconscious the universal forbidden impulses, which in one way or another no mortal is spared from acquiring, but his ego has now actively to give form to them. He must give access to that forbidden imagery and not shut it out into the repressed part of the personality. If, of course, the imagery originating in the repressed part of the personality, or its derivatives, retained the same instinctual cathexis, creation would become hardly possible. The aim is now the new form that will be given to the original imagery.

Here the quantitative factor has to be considered. The forbidden imagery, or its derivatives, bursts highly charged into the ego's confines and is temporarily relieved of this charge by the created work. The ego has the capacity to turn the cathexis of the forbidden imagery to the ego-acceptable imagery of the created work.

Let us return to our initial question of whether or not the quality of the instinctual energy is changed when the process of aim-inhibition or aim-substitution takes place. Observation of the genius—as far as one can grasp him from the relics he left—makes me believe that it preserves its instinctual quality despite the profoundest change of aims.

For the following I wish to have it understood that I use the term "sublimation" as a change of instinctual aim and not as a transformation of energy.

Since it is posited that sublimated energy derives from instinctual energies, investigators have tried to check the validity of the psychoanalytic theory by correlating the extent of intellectual accomplishment with the extent of genital gratifications. They have postulated that one should find an inverse proportion if the theory of sublimation is correct (see 487, pp. 70–71; 521 (cited after 487). Dr. Anna Freud corrected this false assumption in a discussion in Worcester in 1949. Sublimated energies may derive from pregenital sources, and therefore extensive sublimatory processes are compatible with extensive genital activities and gratifications. This argument is undoubtedly correct. I should like to add two more suggestions. It is quite conceivable that a subject might be constitutionally and developmentally endowed with a particularly great supply of genital libido,[11] so that even extensive sublimation of genital libido would not interfere with a rich genital life.

Furthermore, I think we are still all too much bound by biological thinking in our discussion of certain problems of sexuality. The *number* of genital gratifications is not the decisive factor in an investigation of the correlation between sublimation and genital sexuality, but only the *quality* of such releases. One can observe clinically over and over again that a lack of psychological gratification in the genital activity predisposes towards an increase in biological potency. There are patients who, because of some neurosis that induces premature ejaculation, or because of depersonalization, or because of anxiety, do not reach a full orgasm. They are therefore capable of performing a large number of acts of

[11] The term genital libido is incorrect. It is an abbreviation for the more exact, but cumbersome: libido stemming from the genital, erogenous zone.

intercourse but they rarely achieve a satisfactory gratification. What appears like a particularly strong genitality is clinically the manifestation of a defect, namely, the incapacity for finding a true genital release.

To understand such clinical data one has to revert to Freud's early theories of the difference between psychoneuroses and actual neuroses. Freud demonstrated—and very much to the detriment of a sound psychosomatic medicine this viewpoint has been little used in the formation of psychoanalytic theories—that a biological release has to be psychologically integrated if it is really to decrease the total tension of the psychobiological unit. Otherwise biological releases become, on the contrary, a burden to the psychic apparatus. Therefore the number of genital releases is no reliable index in an investigation of the amount of genital libido at the disposal of the psychic apparatus for purposes of sublimation. In Goethe's instance the number seems to have been low. In Victor Hugo, if his claim can be trusted, it was enormous. Possibly this apparent contradiction of theory (if we assume that great creations require the sublimation of genital libido too) will be clarified once all the biographical data for this poet have been published. It is to be hoped that, somewhere in the midst of his vast correspondence and diaries, some remarks will be found from which it may be possible to reconstruct a true picture of what he actually felt during intercourse. The one remark we possess of Goethe's appears to indicate that the psychic echo, the mind's initial reverberation, to the impact of the genital release in Italy was not strong. In the course of his relationship with Christiane this resonance seems to have improved and simultaneously one notices the impact on the literary product. I can imagine that in the case of Victor Hugo a genital release had a stimulating rather than gratifying effect, that the unappeasable need for genital releases was not an index that genital energy was being drained away from creative processes but just the opposite. The full arousal of the genital craving in intercourse, and its nongratification despite the biological release, may have resulted in a constellation particularly propitious for an unending stream of creative processes.

In the course of my inquiry I have referred from time to time to Dr. Kris's eminent contribution to the psychology of art and creativity. One of the central themes of his disquisitions is the regression encountered in creative pursuits, a regression that is not, however, a sign of pathology but occurs in the service of the ego. It is a controlled regression, or at least it appears as if it were, for it does not lead to injury but to achievement. It is a concept equivalent to Plato's sacred madness. Yet regression and neutralized, indifferent energy—how do they go together? It is somewhat difficult to imagine that in a regressed state ego-functions operate with indifferent energy. Why would not the instincts, ever ready to use moments of relative weakness in the ego, also use these tempting opportunities to pounce upon the ego and disturb its primary purposes as they do while the ego is sleeping, by enforced dreams? I believe that precisely this concept of controlled ego-regression confirms the hypothesis that I proffer in this appendix. If a drive has been totally or almost totally integrated by the ego, if the drive has been so much tamed that it is ready to work for the ego how far soever the ego's new commands may lead the drive away from its original goal, then the ego can, as it were, take a nap and rely on the wisdom of the force of nature. In view of what I said earlier about drive-dependability, it all makes good sense that the drive, thus tamed, can now without the ego's supervision accomplish even better what the ego craves to accomplish than it can when the ego is given opportunity to interfere, burdened as it is with its desire to be perfect and its concomitant doubts. The ego, with all its wisdom and experience and memory and judgment, could not create artificially what can be created by abandonment to the free operation of tamed instinctual powers. Those forces that erstwhile endangered the growing ego are now the executors of its purpose. One is reminded here of the domestication of animals that once upon a time were the enemies of culture and—who knows how often —in their feral state annihilated its inceptive stages. Some of them were tamed, and their strength was harnessed to the growth and survival of civilization. But we do know for certain that they did not thereby change their animal state however much they may have changed appearance and behavior. In view of this speculation doubt has also to be cast on the propriety of applying the term "regression," even when qualified with the adjective "controlled," to states (such as inspiration and allied phenomena) that are observed on the genius's path towards the created work of art. To what states of its past is the ego regressing on such occasions? Ought we not rather look upon such "spells" as the highest form of progression, and may we not one day recognize in Plato's "sacred madness" the highest form of sanity?

Addendum, 1957

As an example of a biological process equivalent to what is observed in a genius, we may cite hypertrophy,[12] which is characterized by the fact that, while an innately pathological process, it may in certain circumstances lead to an improved functioning of the organism.[13] The genius quality rests proximately on a hypertrophy of certain ego-functions, and in saying this I am thinking not only of the quantitative factor but of the qualitative as well.

By and large one has to say that "genius hypertrophy" leads to improved functioning of the psychobiological organism, although the following two arguments may be raised against the statement: (1) The creations of the genius may arouse the objections of the community in which he lives and he may therefore be exposed to persecution that under certain aggravated conditions may lead to his annihilation. (2) The hypertrophied ego-functions may drain the energy of

---

[12] Cf. Robert Waelder (537), who speaks of the hypertrophy of certain tendencies in paranoid and creative thinking leading to hypergnosia.

[13] The evaluation of hypertrophy in pathology textbooks is not quite clear. My remark is liable to censure by the pathologist but will, I trust, be permissible by way of analogy.

other functions to such an extent that the whole organism may be endangered, suffer damage, possibly permanent disease or even death. Nevertheless, I believe the claim of improved functioning is not refuted by these observations. The genius organism must be viewed solely from the point of view of the creative production that makes him different from all other organisms. If the activation of the function impairs other functions, this alone does not prove pathology; only a demonstration that the impairment recoils upon and lowers the quality of a creation would justify a negative estimate. Even if it turned out that in a specific instance premature death was the concomitant of the creative achievement—as it possibly was with Mozart—one still would have to compare this with the well-known biological fact that the propagative function of certain species is organized in such a way that it regularly leads to the death of the males. There is no reason to call the male sexual function in such species pathological. In fulfilling their sexual function, those organisms prove their adequacy —whatever the outcome. Similarly the genius organism can be properly evaluated only in terms of the one function it is destined to serve.

The question I wish to scrutinize is whether anything can be said about the psychological prerequisites of genius hypertrophy. In organic hypertrophy it is practice, activation, use, of an organ that lead to hypertrophy, but the analogy with biological hypertrophy cannot be made to fit in this respect. The type of person who strives towards genius accomplishment and devotes all of his efforts loyally and consistently to this goal but fails, is well-known. To be sure, many geniuses go through long periods of great effort, practice, and exercise, but one cannot see in exercise the essence of genius.

Leaving aside the most important but still mysterious point of innate endowment, it seems that the evolvement of genius presupposes the formation of a certain personality structure. This structure is not of a kind that is open to inspection at all times; it may be accessible to observation sporadically or even be present constantly in only latent form. From the study of Goethe's life, at least, I got the very definite impression (and it can be only a matter of impressions at this stage of research into the psychology of genius) that his personality was set up in such a way as to permit—at least at times—the flow of his entire psychic energy towards one exclusive goal, creation, and to put his whole personality into the service of this one function. This feature may appear insignificant in comparison with the greatness of achievement it is supposed to explain, and at first glance far too frequent to be correlated with so rare an event as the occurrence of genius. However, before discussing these arguments I wish to say a few words about states in which the personality devotes itself to the achievement of one purpose. To be sure, regarded from a sufficient distance all organisms may be said constantly to be in such a state, since they serve the life process in all circumstances. But such general purposes are not meant here. Moreover, the life process has many aspects, some of which are even contradictory to one another. In the present context, I am concerned with states that are characterized by the subordination of all functions to one immediate purpose. These I shall call *unifunctional* (cf. 538; 539).

The state of dreamless sleep, for example, lives up to this requirement. It is brought about by the withdrawal of cathexis from the outer reality, from the superego, from the id as far as that is possible, and from the ego's periphery. Only the core of the archaic ego remains cathected, in the form of the wish to sleep; that is to say, the single-purposiveness of the state of sleep is achieved by a withdrawal of cathexis, by a paralysis of almost all other functions but the wish to sleep. The whole personality becomes subservient to this one goal. Under ordinary conditions some of the energy has also during sleep to remain at outposts of the ego for defensive purposes, in order to prevent the inroad of archaic impulses that have not complied with the general call for energic withdrawal, and then the sleep is no longer unifunctional. But after a prolonged period of physical exhaustion the ideal instance of a unifunctional state may be established and all energy present will subserve directly the sleeping process. The danger of any stimulus interfering with sleep has then been eliminated and the sleeper does not need any protection by the cathexis of outposts. All provinces of the personality cooperate faithfully with the sleep function under such conditions.

Another state in which the psychic apparatus as well as the personality of the adult is devoted to the achievement of a single purpose is orgasm. The distribution of energy is here quite different from and more complicated than in sleep. Cathexis is withdrawn from reality except for the pleasure-giving object, and even this may disappear in the event of a short-lasting void of consciousness at the peak; the ego-cathexis is greatly reduced and only those functions are cathected that are necessary for the gratification. The ego is totally subservient to the instinctual gratification; it is in a regressed state; sense organs are geared to the reception of pleasure; the body is overcathected, with an accumulation of cathexis of the sexual organs; the usually well-protected ego boundaries are fuzzy and the separation of the ego from the world of objects becomes unclear, rather as in the fusion of ego and reality in some phases of childhood development. A similar fuzziness occurs between ego and id. The drive takes almost full possession of the ego. Though, under healthy conditions, part of the superego may remain cathected and support the ego's concentration on instinctual gratification, we still must presume that those superego areas that are opposed or hostile to the drives must remain decathected or at least quarantined by countercathexis.

In this instance of orgasm, again, we notice that the unifunctional state is correlated with the decathexis of structures and with the concentration of energy on certain distinct sectors combined with a depletion of others.

In adult pregenital pursuits, only part of the personality becomes subservient to the gratification, as can best be seen in oral gratifications, which are commonly combined with complex and important social activities.

In other pursuits, such as work, vast areas of the personality have to stay decathected, or at least inhibited with regard to their usual manifestations. Pleasing as work may be, only rarely does it lend itself to extensive direct and full instinctual discharges. The preponderance of cathexis pertains to the super-ego and those parts of the ego that are necessary for the accomplishment. Untold variations and combinations of cathectic pictures are of course observable in the pursuit of work, even without taking pathology into consideration. In conjunction with work one may consider the possibility that states of high concentration are unifunctional, and this may be true of some instances. High concentration per se, however, does not prove the presence of a unifunctional state, for there are definitely two types of such concentration. In the one type, concentration works with a reliable and strong countercathexis against everything that may interfere with the thinking process (cf. 205, p. 121); in the other, the cathexis of the thought process may be so intense, and may so completely arrogate all available energy, that no stimulation can interfere with the course of exclusive attention: in this case no countercathexis is necessary. Only the latter type of concentration approximates the requirement of unifunctional states, for in the former enormous investments are dissipated in defensive functions that are not primarily related to the principal purpose. In concentration, only rarely, as I believe, is the total available energy expended and discharged in one function, but also then this requires the withdrawal of cathexis from other parts of the personality.

In psychopathology unifunctional states are encountered, perhaps even with greater frequency. In melancholia, for example, the enormous inflation of the superego absorbs all energic resources and imposes itself upon the rest of the personality. To be sure, this state also serves the purpose of defense and therefore an objection may be raised against its consideration as being unifunctional. But we know that the effect of the rank superego transgresses the subservient ego and infests the id. It would not be difficult to demonstrate how close schizophrenic conditions (such as delusional and acute hallucinatory states or the fantasy of impending world annihilation) come to being unifunctional. But in these instances also the unifunctional state is formed by extensive decathexis, as can be seen from the deep regressions that are prone to occur.

In normal life gratification and defense take place simultaneously. Gratification itself may be used for defensive purposes. The ego has to keep from its boundaries part of the influx of stimulation coming from reality and has to shield itself against the inroad of certain instinctual demands. The interplay of these functions is well-known although little understood. It militates against unifunctional states.

My thesis is that the creative act is in general a unifunctional state of the highest differentiation with minimal decathexes occurring. In order to advance this thesis I wish to digress into that branch of psychology that Dilthey called *Geisteswissenschaftliche Psychologie* (cultural science psychology), which may be defined roughly as a psychology which derives knowledge of man's psyche by the study of the works he creates. Freud devoted a book to such a purpose in his investigation of the psychology of jokes. The joke, in my estimation, is the smallest cultural unit by the study of which the problems of a *Geisteswissenschaftliche Psychologie* can be set forth (cf. 450). One may even say that every such psychology ought to start with the investigation of this unit because it represents, so to speak, a prestage of alloplastic cultural work. To a certain extent the joke may be called an autoplastic cultural unit when compared with other cultural elements. It is told, it passes, it is forgotten, it is valid only in specific situations. It is bound to the spoken word and therefore innately ephemeral. Just because the joke has not yet reached the full stage of artistic alloplasticity, that is to say, material concretization, we may be able to gain from the study of it some essential principle that can help in the investigation of more complicated cultural configurations.

I wish to set forth only that small part of Freud's investigation that is of relevance in this particular context. In reconstructing the psychic processes that occur in the mind of the person who makes a joke Freud sets forth a specific mechanism: thoughts, predominantly preconscious ones, must submerge for a moment into the unconscious and be subjected to the elaboration characteristic of that system before they can return to consciousness in the form of a joke. As a paradigm of that process I wish to repeat the first of many examples Freud analyzed in his treatise on *Jokes and Their Relation to the Unconscious* (1905). A man of very modest means boasts of his acquaintance with Rothschild, who treated him, as he says, like an equal—quite *famillionaire*.[14] The meaning of the joke is clear: the man wants to say he was treated in an informal or intimate way, as far as a millionaire is capable of so acting—an idea that is neither witty nor laugh-provoking. However, by the condensation of the two words *familiar* and *millionaire* and the creation of the substitutive formation *famillionaire,* a joke is produced.

This example is particularly instructive since the word *famillionaire* could occur in a dream, or as a slip of the tongue, as well as in a joke. The condensation and substitutive formation of words, that is, are processes that are characteristic of the unconscious[15] and quite familiar from the interpretation of dreams.[16] In the context for the sake of which I have brought up the example, the exact metapsychological description of the process that Freud described as the plunge of a thought into the unconscious [das Eintauchen ins Unbewusste] (161, p. 169) is of importance. In this area lies the key to the understanding of one group of problems that are germane to the psychology of crea-

[14] The example was taken by Freud from Heinrich Heine's *Die Bäder von Lucca.*

[15] This, of course, does not preclude the possibility that, once the principle has been set forth explicitly, someone may try to construct jokes consciously and in an organized way.

[16] As a matter of fact, Freud's attention was drawn toward the psychology of jokes by the observation that the interconnection between latent dream thoughts, and their connection in turn with the manifest dream content, all too often sounded like lame jokes.

tivity. Quite generally, I believe that in the formation of a joke we find in miniature many of the elements present in the creation of a work of art.

Here a brief remark about regression is necessary. In Freud's early formulation about the origin of dreams he considered only the last phase of dream-work as a regression, namely, the phase in which the latent dream thoughts, after they have been subjected to condensation and displacement, are pressed into visual images that finally form the manifest dream content. Therefore we find in Freud's book on jokes of 1905 a passage that says that the absence of regression in the formation of a joke constitutes the difference between the work that leads to the dream and that which leads to the joke, for the latter does not undergo the regression to representation by images (161, pp. 165–66). Later on, however, the concept of regression was extended by Freud, and the way the term has been used includes also the subjection of the latent dream thoughts to condensation and displacement prior to their regressive representation in images.[17] Therefore, one says today that the psychic work that leads to the formation of a joke, even though it is not reduced to presentation in images as in the dream, also uses a regressive mechanism, having reference to that moment of the submergence of thoughts in the unconscious where they are subjected to condensation and displacement. The recasting of thoughts is, however, quite different in the work of dreams from what takes place in the formation of the joke, as Freud very precisely stated. There is, so to speak, no limit to the extent to which condensation and displacement will go in the case of the dream. If there is any similarity at all, any kind of connection—remote as it may be—between elements, condensation and displacement will make full use of them. In the final product (the manifest dream content), the latent dream thoughts are then usually so profoundly distorted that the person who had the dream cannot trace them any more and remains ignorant of their existence. In the work of the joke, condensation and displacement work far more selectively. They do not proceed in the random fashion of dream-work, which aims at what is remotest, but have to find a specific solution, comparable to the solution we find to a riddle.

Hence it is that Kris speaks of a regression in the service of the ego. The regression that occurs in dream-work leads to the dream that interrupts sleep, though only for seconds; the regression in the parapraxia also interferes with the intentions of the ego; the same is true all the more of more serious states, such as a neurosis, and in a psychosis the whole fabric of the reality-adjusted personality goes partly or entirely to pieces. But by making a joke the person reaches an aim he has set up; he enriches a social situation by a valid and valuable entity that is perfectly adjusted to social reality; he creates a new social value that has never and nowhere existed before. In the formation of a joke condensation and displacement have to follow narrow rules and have to heed

[17] See 158, p. 548, for the paragraph added in 1914.

intelligibility. These archaic mechanisms are supposed to succeed in finding the one and only punch line that is possible and that has the capacity to arouse laughter. But all this shows definite traces of the secondary process. Indeed, we are confronted here with a situation that is in its essential structure not comparable to dream, parapraxia, or symptom. In the dream the ego is inherently passive. It says no to stimuli that wish to intrude upon its territory and passively lets them appear at its entrance after they have been disarmed, whitewashed, and almost sanctified. In the parapraxia it is ambushed, in the neurosis enslaved, and in the psychosis destroyed. It is always the loser, although in all these defeats there is something of a victory or an advantage. Without the dream it would wake up, without the parapraxia it might resort to an open aggression, without the neurosis it might develop a psychosis, and even the psychosis may protect it against something worse.

Despite these various concomitant advantages there can be no doubt that the ego is the loser in all these forms of psychopathology, and one cannot speak of a regression in the service of the ego in these instances. If, however, it is by means of regression that the ego gains the profit of joke formation, it may seem appropriate to speak of a regression in the service of the ego. Yet I doubt that the application of this concept to the specific phase in joke formation that I have set forth earlier, is really quite justified. It is not readily understandable how the ego's surrender of thoughts to an elaboration by the unconscious could lead to so precise and accurate a formation as is required in the creation of a joke. Of the many possible directions in which the primary process may go when thoughts are subjected to it, how could it select just the one and only one that fits into the structure of the respective joke? Freud proved, in 1900 and on later occasions, that the primary process as it is involved in dream-work is not capable of creating new solutions, or anything new for that matter. That which may appear in the dream as a solution to problems which a person has tried in vain to solve during waking hours, regularly turns out to be a composite of preconscious thoughts.

The question to be answered here is whether the *famillionaire* of the joke deserves the same evaluation as the identical formation in the dream. One difference is obvious. Almost all substitutive formations such as occur in dreams require the dreamer's associations in order to be explained. In the joke, the investigator can, without further resort to associations of the person who made the joke, deduce from the joke itself the elements that went into the substitutive formation. The substitution that is contained in a joke is not determined exclusively by subjective factors, as are the substitutions that result from dream-work, but also by the objective structure of the joke into which it is to fit. I express the same thought, only from a different viewpoint, when I say that the substitution in the joke must be understandable by another person or else what we would be dealing with would be nonsense, and not a joke. This leads me to believe that in the joke something new, let us say a new value, is actually created. To be sure, Freud demonstrated, by applying the method of retracing the joke to its original elements, that the actual ideas expressed by the joke are often none we would not have known before. In the example I have used this can easily be seen. That millionaires tend towards condescending behavior is no particularly witty thought. Thus many jokes depend on a formal quality, and their relative lack of new thought content itself recalls the dearth of newness in the manifest dream content.[18] I even believe that the joke character vanishes as soon as a new idea is actually conveyed by it. Still, because the joke does bring forth an original, unique, formal quality, it adds something new and must be considered creative. And because it is creative it cannot be equated with the unconscious elaboration of thoughts such as occurs in dreams.

From Dr. Anna Freud's work it is known that the primary process (condensation and displacement) can be put into the service of the ego for the purpose of defense. Processes that occurred in the id are now taken over by the unconscious part of the ego and work in the service of the ego against the inroad of the instincts. Something similar seems to take place in the formation of the joke, and in such instances we are wont to speak of a regression in the service of the ego. But is this really a regression? Does clinical observation really permit the assumption that thoughts are temporarily repressed, elaborated upon in the unconscious (id), and then again taken into the organized ego, to be used by it for its own reality-adjusted purpose? Even if we drop the idea of a temporary repression and assume that this process takes place where ego gradually changes over to id, as Freud intimated in his diagram in the *New Introductory Lectures* (210, p. 111), it is difficult to assume that the ego ever loses control over the vicissitude of those thoughts that are the ingredients of the joke to be created. To be sure, it cannot be a conscious control, but unconsciousness does not preclude control and organization, as can be observed in the huge number of automatisms that undoubtedly go to making organized ego behavior possible.

In my opinion the process that takes place in joke formation is the typical instance of an ego extension. It is difficult to decide which of the two following accounts is more appropriate: does the ego in such a moment spill over into the id, or does the ego let something of the id enter its own confines and use it for its own purpose? Perhaps these alternatives are to be correlated with two different ego–id processes. Clinical observation, I believe, does not permit speculation about such fine points. The main idea here is, at any rate, that such states as I

---

[18] Other noteworthy relations between the joke and the dream may be mentioned here. Both have a tendency towards brevity; both are autoplastic. One feels inclined to say that what the dream is in the visual sphere the joke is in the auditory. I believe the affinity of jokes to words has not been investigated sufficiently. An explanation of the fact that the dream is bound predominantly to the visual sphere and the joke to the auditory would lead to the deepest insight into the basic structure of the psychic apparatus. The modern comic strip is actually a synthesis of dream and joke.

am discussing at this point should not be regarded as regressive. In such states the ego or one of its functions is by no means drawn down to a condition of lessened differentiation. The ego, or the respective function that is involved, is actually in a state of higher differentiation, since it has become enriched by the contribution of the neighboring province and it imposes its own advanced aim upon a genetically more ancient part of the personality. If it had not obtained this additional succor it could not have achieved the formation of the joke; indeed, it might have risked being—in the long run—overwhelmed by an impulse which it is socially more appropriate to discharge in the joke, which is thus also a manifestation of the victory of the secondary process over the primary.

We must now turn towards another aspect of the problem, namely, differentiation. If the ego-states in question are undifferentiated, may this not be a sign that we are dealing with regressive states? Differentiation must be investigated in two different contexts. Cultural products are not created by random activity, as in the rumored method of a well-known painter of abstractions who, allegedly, with his back turned towards the canvas hurls paints without even seeing what parts of the canvas they cover. If true, this is unusual and atypical. In general, the product, before it takes on a material form, must be represented somehow in the creator's mind. To be sure, the ultimate form it will take does not need to coincide—and probably rarely does—with the mental representation that it had in the creative mind before it took on a material form. But this mental representation is already a differentiation.

Further, a function may be highly differentiated or it may be in a regressive state. In our present context, only the meaning of differentiation, in contrast to regression, is of importance.

Freud in his book on jokes demonstrated that the joke is working against a resistance, namely, the superego. The joke must circumvent the interdict of the superego, which objects, in most instances, to the hidden meaning of the joke but also to the seeming nonsense—the seeming illogicality. In other words, the joke does not include the superego. It can draw only a part of the id into the ego. I think the fact that Freud was able to deduce from a cultural product the pathway that the mental process leading to its production took in its creator establishes a principle of paramount theoretical importance. I wish to call this principle *the yardstick of the traveled pathway*. It says that the cultural product per se permits an estimate of the extent to which the provinces of the personality became involved in the production of human values. From the analysis of dreams Freud had learned to deduce the pathways that concordant and antagonistic psychic forces (cathexes) have to travel until the dream is finally produced. The reconstruction of this complex interplay was made possible by the study of the dreamer's associations. It is one of the most difficult tasks to use this principle wisely and adequately. The predominant opinion of many psychologists is that there exists an almost exact parallelism between the artistic product and the mind of the creative person. This is probably a fallacy. But that the finished work, the product, permits some deductions regarding mental processes in its creator has been proved by Freud in his book on jokes. From the heuristic point of view the most remarkable result is that Freud succeeded in reconstructing the variety of mental processes that had occurred in the person who formed a joke, *without* the use of any free associations or any other information concerning the subject but solely by the analysis of the end product (joke) itself. He thus proved that under favorable circumstances it is possible to draw from the cultural product per se reliable conclusions with regard to the dynamic constellation present at the time the cultural value was produced. This was possible because jokes have the function of producing a specific and well-defined emotion in the listener, are free of the ambiguity characteristic of most works of art, and do not require a specific medium to be concretized.

The taking apart of the joke permitted Freud to reconstruct the latent thoughts that must have been present in the person who made the joke, prior to his making it. We may call such reconstructions *content deductions*. It cannot be taken for granted that other cultural units will yield similarly specific conclusions. But Freud also reconstructed the metapsychology of the mental processes that led to the creation of a joke. These conclusions I wish to call *form deductions*. The field of form deductions is probably much broader and more promising than that of content deductions. If one applies the yardstick of the traveled pathway to the analysis of jokes, one finds that form deductions reveal that the pathway includes only the ego and the id, and these two, in most instances, only to a moderate extent. Yet within the cultural unit joke we can distinguish such as are closer to the id and such as are closer to the ego. Thus, the joke, the closer it comes on the one hand to the indecent or smutty, and on the other to the nonsensical or infantile, proportionately serves less the ego and more and more the id and hence shows the earmarks of the regressive, as can be noticed in the jokes that are made under the influence of alcohol or under the effect of group situations that also tend towards the effacement of individuality. These jokes no longer serve primarily the ego, but rather have to be regarded as the manifest inroad of the id upon the ego. A scale of gradations leads to those jokes we are prone to call witticisms, in which a highly differentiated ego imposes its aim upon the unconscious and uses it for its purposes. Here the function is to be assumed to be highly differentiated. An ego-function that would extend also to the superego and perhaps include even wider areas of the id than the joke would lead to more comprehensive cultural units and become even more differentiated.

In the creative act of the genius, it seems to me the following constellation is present. The ego boundaries are open towards the id and superego. Instinctual energy freely enters the ego; archaic imagery is highly cathected and must deliver the raw material out of which the final work will be formed. The superego is cathected. In my opinion it participates in the aesthetic and formal solutions that enter the final accomplishments. With the maximum fulfillment of the rules of art, with the accomplishment of new solutions superior to all preexisting ones, the superego achieves a triumph. In view of the sensuous quality inherent in the purely artistic aspect of the solution, the superego here works in harmony with the id, the repressed, and the ego (cf. 459). It supports the aims of the id without offending ethical standards, and thus lends valuable and indispensable assistance to the self's reaching its goal. Consequently, according to my construction, a cross section of a genius in the moment of the creative act will show all systems of the personality in a state of heightened, almost maximum, cathexis, or, in other words, all those parts that can contribute to the creation in question—and these may comprise the whole personality—will contribute their maximal share (see 82). Everything that may stand in the way of that goal will be completely impoverished of energy.

Yet, in view of the demand that is put on the personality in the moment when a genius masterwork is to be born, in view, further, of the almost unlimited resourcefulness necessary for such an act, one can hardly imagine that the activation of any area in the personality would militate against the quality of the end product. The drive at its maximum and reason at its maximum must meet and be synthesized if a genius accomplishment is to occur. If the ego is capable of drawing both together and of forming out of the antipodes a meaningful work of art, that is to say, of organizing out of contradictory extremes a unified, well-synthesized configuration in which the extreme contrariety of the inner sources is no longer recognizable or is presented in an aesthetically overtowering way, then a maximum achievement has been produced. Of course, one of the prerequisites is that those areas of id and superego that participate be far enough apart. The genius in art has the endurance and capacity to bear the tension created by the simultaneous demands put upon him by two far distant extremes, and has the talent to form out of them a unit of a higher order. One may safely say that the greater the disparity for which the aesthetic solution is found, the greater the accomplished work will be. Many a work of a talent perfect in its form has not reached the level to which we yield the characterization of genius, because it has not grown from a sufficiently large disparity in the originator.[19]

All the energy mobilized in the creative act is channelized into those ego-functions that are necessary for creation. The fact that these ego-functions have to carry an enormous amount of energy justifies the previous comparison with a hypertrophy.[20]

[19] Of the many examples of such works of talent one could cite I wish only to mention the plays of Edmond Rostand.

[20] Fairbairn (129; 130) has stated similar views. There is a difference of opinion mainly as to the particular relationship between ego, id, and superego in the creative movement. I disagree with his view that restitution is an indispensable part of the function of artistic creation. Be this as it may, his two papers were an important step forward in the psychoanalytic theory of art; yet it seems they have not been sufficiently appreciated in psychoanalytic literature. See also 441.

The description of the creative act as a unifunctional state of the highest differentiation stands definitely in contradiction with my previous view (in the text) that the manifest content of some of Goethe's dreams consisted of perfect poems. The state of sleep may be unifunctional, but it is not one of high differentiation, and undoubtedly belongs to the group of regressive states. As a matter of fact, in sleep we find a state which may no doubt properly be called a regression in the service of the ego. According to Freud, the ego wishes to sleep and therefore withdraws energy. It regresses to an archaic, undifferentiated state. In the joke, we have encountered the perfect blending of a limited, controlled, archaic mechanism and higher ego-functions. The two cooperate. One without the other could never achieve what they achieve together, and this blending actually results in the production of something new.[21] In the formation of the joke this blending requires not more than a moment when the unconscious does its work and the joke usually comes ready-made to one's mind like a flash (see 161, p. 167). When Goethe dreams a poem the *ebb of consciousness* is an extensive one, and we should now decide whether genius creation is reconcilable with an undifferentiated state, or is perhaps even favored by a state far from the highest degree of differentiation of which the genius is capable. When Goethe retires from company for weeks and writes *Werther,* in a state that may be compared perhaps with a fugue (or whatever its correct psychiatric designation may have been, but in which the state of consciousness was certainly reduced), we are not confronted with the same problem, for consciousness, despite its great usefulness, also harbors disadvantages that may reduce the effectiveness and differentiation of certain ego-functions. In creating a masterpiece, as stated before, extreme contrasts are to be synthesized into higher units. Consciousness, with its frequent tendency towards isolation, may stand in the way of the formation of comprehensive symbols, and the use of many other artistic means. When the preconscious system, in the formation of a great work of art, fulfills highly differentiated functions that are incompatible with the narrowness inherent in the system of consciousness, this is not to be interpreted as a sign of reduced differentiation but as just the opposite, namely, as a higher differentiation within a system that under ordinary circumstances operates on a lower level of differentiation.

This point of view will now be applied to Goethe's dreamed poems. Freud distinguished between the progredient course psychic life takes during waking hours, namely, from perception to action, and the retrograde course during sleep, from memory to perception (dream). In the famous *Autodidasker* dream

---

[21] However, this does not obviate the clinical fact that there are personality types in which a joke constitutes a symptom; the habitual joker, as he may cursorily be called, often belongs to the realm of psychopathology, and in such case the joke, when viewed within the total framework of the individual personality, may often appear as a regressive formation, but this must not be extended to the analysis of the species "joke."

he gave an example of how a dream looks when it does not follow the retrograde course but maintains the progredient direction (158, 4:298–302; 5:535, 542, 597). About Goethe's poem dreams we can say that they prove the preservation of the progredient direction of psychic energy preceding these particular dreams. This is rare, but clinical observation shows that it does take place. What is surprising, therefore, is only that this progredient course of energy should lead to a work of art, and not to words such as *Autodidasker* which are not understandable in themselves but require interpretation in order to make sense. The conclusion is that in Goethe's poem dreams, that is to say, also during sleep, the creative impulse of the ego won out over the archaic mode of dealing with disturbing stimuli. The pleasure derived from the play on words, symbolization, indirect presentation, all of which lead on the regressive level of dream-work to nonsense, sometimes led in Goethe's instance to the most beautiful poetry, which he was also capable of producing when the system of consciousness was fully cathected. All this permits the statement that even the wish to sleep (the biological momentum) was weaker than the wish to create, and that even when sleeping he maintained a state of high differentiation.

If Goethe had been capable of writing poems only when asleep this might possibly have constituted a serious objection to my thesis, but the fact that he was able to create poetry *also* in a state of sleep may indicate what high degree of differentiation the psychic apparatus had acquired in his instance. Even sleep could not efface the wish to create. The creative momentum apparently was so intense and the function so well integrated that the pattern of ego-functions necessary to form out of the preconscious thoughts and the infantile wish an ego-syntonic configuration was ineradicable, even when parts of the personality regressed. That is to say, despite the drag of the regressive, biological momentum, ego differentiation was maintained.

We have to consider also the possibility that parts of the final poem had already been formed preconsciously prior to the moment of falling asleep.[22] This possibility, however, does not detract from the achievement, whose significance lies in the fact that these preformed parts were immune to the dream-work, which under ordinary circumstances gnaws at the cohesion of preconscious thoughts. The preservation of the creative function during sleep is reminiscent of the sleep of a nursing mother or a wet nurse that remains geared selectively to the movements or sounds of the infant and is instantaneously discontinued when the infant becomes restless or cries (158, 4:222–23; 5:577). Here also we see that certain ego-functions remain selectively cathected. They do not regress. Thus I am inclined to say that sleep is the prototype of a regression in the service of the ego—certainly the most complete one known—and that in the selected

[22] Freud (161, p. 171) wrote about dream-work: "It cannot be disputed that portions of such indirect representation are already present in the dream's preconscious thoughts—for instance, representation by symbols or analogies—. . . ."

few in whom sleep does not discontinue the creative function, evidently some functions are resistant to regression and thus maintain their state of differentiation.[23]

It is my impression that the concept of regression in the service of the ego, as used at present, is based predominantly on the changes that occur in consciousness during the creative moment, spell, or period. However, the indices of consciousness are not a valid yardstick that could measure the degree of differentiation. Since the creative function in general requires an almost incredible ego extension and engulfs the whole personality, I feel inclined to liken it to a band of elastic material that is stretched beyond its natural measure. The details of that piece of material are then changed and usually become blurred. This happens also when the creative function is operating at its maximum. The fact that certain details of that function are then not observable does not prove that they are nonexistent.[24]

[23] It is a challenging task to compare dream, daydream, and work of art. Of the many facets involved I wish to mention only the following. The manifest dream reveals in exceptional instances id-contents almost without disguise. In general, however, the dream presents psychic reality in an unrecognizable, distorted fashion. The ego is in a relatively securer position when daydreaming than when sleeping and therefore the language of the daydream is usually much clearer than the language of the dream. The meaning of daydreams can often be established without the patient's associations, in contrast to the dream where this possibility is exceptional. The work of art also has an unconscious meaning which can be established to a certain extent on its own merit without reference to the author's biography, as Freud demonstrated in his analysis of Shakespeare's *Hamlet*. I surmise that such analysis of major works of literature will lead to three groups of interpretations: one that refers to contents commonly found in the repressed or more generally in the id; one referring to contents usually encountered in the superego; and one that contains a solution relevant to the ego or self. Whether these meanings are also relevant in terms of the author's life or the particular moment when the work of art is created must be examined in each instance anew. The necessity of concealing the various unconscious meanings, of making them palatable by presenting them in an aesthetically pleasing form, is not only enforced by consideration of the audience but primarily—as I think—also by the inner resistances of the creative person. The author's own ego would in most instances rebel just as much as the audience against the direct awareness of the crude raw material which can be discovered behind the manifest content of a created work. Here again I believe the factor of communication should be regarded as secondary. Matters of form have their primary relevance in terms of the needs of the creative artist's self.

[24] Except for the question of terminology, namely, my calling these processes progressions, I have, unless I am mistaken, only repeated what Kris has stated so admirably. See his *Psychoanalytic Explorations in Art* (346, p. 25 and *passim*). Whether the approach I suggest, namely, to see in this wide range of phenomena new forms of a higher synthesis, will prove productive to research remains to be seen. To clarify the difference of approach once more, I am referring to my earlier comparisons with the domestication of animals. At the time man introduced wild animals into his civilization this might have looked like cultural regression, after evolution had brought him to a level vastly superior to the kingdom of animals. To associate again with animals might at that point have looked like cultural regression (which it may well have been in some instances), but what looked like cultural regression turned out to be progress and facilitated further developments in other instances.

We have further to discuss here the standing of reality in the creative process.[25] It is twofold. The genius's conscious or preconscious motivation in the moment of creation may be closely related to his social environment, or, in the case of the rejected, so-called misunderstood genius, to that of the future that will acknowledge his merits. These motives, however, are no indispensable prerequisite and may be compared with the secondary gain that accrues to the neurotic patient from his disorder.[26] I include with the secondary gain also the function of communication, which plays such an important part in most contributions to the psychology of art and which I think has been greatly overrated, as has the secondary gain in the neurosis.[27] Fraiberg has convincingly presented an instance of artistic creation that is no longer motivated by an impulse for anything to be found or expected in the outer world (see 152).

More important is the aspect of reality that will find its representation in the final work of art. That part of reality is devoured by the genius, amalgamated with his own and partly archaic psychic reality, and then again spit out in the shape of the artistically formed work.[28] We see some works of art created when the genius is under the acute spell of reality, as happens in the state of being in love or in complete isolation in a seeming state of withdrawal, when the representations of past reality experiences are used for the creative process. The genius's extreme closeness to reality is a prerequisite of his producing. We have presented numerous examples of this closeness in Goethe's life, and have ascertained that the genius's way of experiencing the world is essentially different from that of the vast majority of others. In the genius's act of direct experience of the world there is already included this incredible closeness that later produces the overwhelming effect of the work created by him.

The act of creation, if a real masterpiece results, excludes ambivalence. It is not easy to achieve such absence of ambivalence. Therefore the genius often goes through long periods of hesitation, search, even bewilderment, until by good luck this absence of ambivalence occurs. It is a state that cannot be established by effort or planning but depends on imponderables. Furthermore, it is striking that the ambivalence of the genius's personality is in general considerable; it seems even to be of greater intensity than we are accustomed to encounter in the ordinary person. Is it possible that the stupendous effect that the temporary freedom from ambivalence has on the genius is also dependent on its contrast with the preceding heightened ambivalence? In view of the sometimes almost shattering conflicts of ambivalence that precede creative phases it would

---

[25] For an important connection between reality and creative (scientific) thinking see 432.

[26] Freud ended his twenty-third lecture with a short remark that refers to this secondary gain of the artist and how it fits into the course of artistic production. See 187, p. 328.

[27] For a unified theory of communication and primary gain achieved by the creation of literary works see 459; 462.

[28] This aspect is not in contradiction with Freud's integrating the three periods of time into a theory of causality and function of works of literature (166, p. 151).

be understandable that the poet feel ecstasy, or as if he were the trumpet of a superior power, when at last he obtains the bliss of freedom from ambivalence.[29]

I have tried in the foregoing to construct a model that may help in understanding one of the psychological prerequisites of the genius's creative spell. In practice all kinds of variations will be encountered, but it is my impression that this model covers fairly exactly a good many instances of Goethe's creative spells.

Of course, concomitantly with aging, much that depended earlier on imponderables may come closer to being routine. Creativity in the aging genius may ultimately become more an autonomous function, never, of course, acquiring that full autonomy which excludes imponderables completely. Thus it is questionable whether creating is in the aging genius a truly unifunctional state. (It is my impression that it was the effect of aging that drove Goethe to the regular intake of wine in his later years.)

In summarizing, I wish to state that the genius—at least in art (in science, I presume, despite some similarities the constellation is in general different)—becomes in the creative act the exceptional bearer of a unifunctional state without losing his differentiation; that is to say, without decathexis of relevant parts of the personality. If anything, he is then in a state of higher differentiation. All parts of his personality are in a state of heightened cathexis. Id and superego raise their demands; the most archaic and the most recent, the irrational and the rational—all are mobilized. It is the highest possible antinomic state simultaneously synthesized into a unifunctional one. Certain ego-functions become the last pathway of discharge for all these contradictory impulses, thoughts, emotions, and what not. The ego creates a solution in which the most antinomic becomes a unit of the highest order (see 130, p. 179) and thus provides all activated energy the maximum gratification of which this particular psychic apparatus is capable. It is quite understandable that a state in which the self has to cope with such inordinate quantities of energy also produces a painful sensation, but such a state may just as well be experienced in an ecstatic way.

If my reconstruction contains any truth I wonder whether it can be used to justify the introduction of a term that in the early stages of psychoanalysis held an important place in Freud's theories, but was later discarded by him. Even as late as 1917 (see 187, pp. 297–312), Freud divided the drives into ego drives and sexual drives, following the example of hunger (thirst) and love, certainly the

[29] If freedom or relative freedom from ambivalence is in a person a matter of course, it may have relevant consequences in terms of interpersonal relations, but I would not expect it to set a disposition towards a high artistic potential. The proper description and the understanding of ambivalence in the genius is one of the hardest tasks. In this context I stress the intensity of ambivalence and its relevance in the creative process, although at other places I stressed the strength of unambivalent attitudes. It seems that in order to reconcile these contradictory findings various layers or areas of the personality are to be considered. It is feasible that heightened ambivalence is significant in the more superficial parts of the personality and that the deeper we descend the less ambivalence is encountered. But such a view also is probably no more than a rough approximation and is not very satisfying.

two most basic drives in man. The former included the self-preservatory drives and the latter included all libidinal-sexual-erotic ones. This division is untenable for reasons not to be discussed here. At present there is agreement that all drives stem from the id, and that their division depends on the energy they consume and the goals that they pursue (eros and destruction). The division that Freud set up in the last phase of his investigation I do not intend to dispute, but I wish to suggest an additional one that may prove its clinical usefulness.

The instinctual energy that is generated in the id and does not change its character until it is brought to discharge can have, in the main, two vicissitudes: it can become chiefly or even exclusively attached to representations, imagery, and impulses that are in the repressed part of the id, or it may chiefly—never completely—enter the ego and cathect ego-functions as well as imagery-impulses that are part of the ego. I suggest calling the former *id-drives* and the latter *ego-drives*.[30] This nomenclature is based on a structural division that does not account for the origin, quality, or aim of the drives, but only for their degree of egosyntonicity. It is plain from my definition that this viewpoint does not permit a static classification of the drives but is variant in each individual instance. Hunger in one instance may be fully accepted by a person, that is to say, the hunger that generates in the id may have full access to the ego and be well integrated by it, with only a minimal simultaneous cathexis of archaic, repressed imagery. On the other hand, this energy may charge archaic, oral-sadistic imagery and be kept completely outside the confines of the ego. A patient who exhibits this constellation does not even feel hunger and must force himself in order to eat even the minimum amount of food. We then encounter clinically the syndrome of anorexia nervosa. In the one instance I would call hunger a pure ego-drive, in the other an id-drive.

I would have to go much further in order to expound the implications of this classification but wish only to add that, in the case of the genius, possibly a drive is formed that is quite different from what can be observed in others. There is a passionate necessity to create, a necessity that is felt with the same overpowering urgency, not suffering any delays or postponements, as we are accustomed to observe when purely physical instinctual demands impinge upon the psychic apparatus. The instinctual quality of this craving for creation is not to be disputed, as far as I can see. The remarkable thing about this urge is that it cannot be satiated by any physical gratification, that the aim of its demand is the creation of a new comprehensive value that replaces part of reality. After the gratification of that need, there takes place, at least in Goethe's instance, a return of the kind of temporary quietness and calm customarily observed after a physical gratification.

It seems that the creative urge in the genius absorbs all energy that can be mobilized in the id and is also fed from the superego, so that one is inclined to

[30] This would cover approximately what are called today egosyntonic (*ich-gerechte*) drives.

think in contrast to id- or ego-drives of organismic drives that originate in the whole personality (cf. 289; 290).

Another peculiarity of the psychic apparatus in the instance of genius must be mentioned. Alexander has called attention to the general law that with each of its differentiations the psychic apparatus loses the realization of a large number of others (6, p. 146). The child has the disposition to learn any language. But once a language has been learned by the child the potentialities for learning another one decrease. I do not know whether this law is generally correct. Though it is quite true that once the child has been introduced to the decimal system, it may be difficult for him to become proficient in another system of counting, it is still true that learning sets the disposition to learn more. Once addition is learned, the disposition to learn subtraction and then multiplication and so on up to the calculus is set. At any of these stations a plateau, of course, may set in and further differentiation may be replaced with repetition. Be this as it may, Alexander is right that there is a principle present, namely, the tendency to economize energy, which he calls the inertia principle.[31]

It is of interest to study phenomena that do not follow this principle. The genius does not appear to be subjected to it. Whereas instinctual gratifications have a tendency towards repetition, each creation of the genius sets the stimulus for new creations, and this demonstrates a principle of superabundance. This seems to be caused by the expansiveness of the creative (organismic) drive.

Despite the evolvement of a personal style that may be correlated with a manifestation of the inertia principle, there is the capacity for originality in the genius, reexpressed in each new creation and essentially different from the originality of the talent, difficult as it may be to define the difference between the two. Goethe's development from *Sturm und Drang* to classicism, to romanticism, and to high romanticism shows a capacity that requires special consideration. When an individual has evolved a line of success he pursues this line towards greater perfection, in accordance with the inertia principle, which can be studied so well in the creations, let us say, of the typical mystery-story writer. After a paragraph the author is identified and after a few pages, if not before, one is oriented about the further course of the plot. Such creations are variations on a theme, and development is hardly noticed if the complete works of a typical author are chronologically ordered. Yet only an expert or an extraordinarily acute ear will recognize the author of *Werther* in *Faust,* Part II. But, even if works nearer each other than these are taken, the *newness* of almost each creation is striking. If a comparison with the phenomenology of instinctual life is permitted, I would compare the newness of each of the genius's creations with the capacity of a man to experience each union with woman as if it were the first one.

---

[31] (6, p. 199). I presume Alexander refers here to what Freud had described as follows: "A general tendency of our mental apparatus, which can be traced back to the economic principle of saving expenditure [of energy] . . ." (172, p. 222).

Something of this kind is actually detectable in Goethe's life. Whenever he fell in love, even as an old man, he loved with surprise and despair, like an adolescent. In order to understand this capacity for an ever-repeating new beginning we have to assume the effect of a certain kind of regression that prevents an overhasty structurization of the psychic apparatus. A regression may in biology be degenerative or regenerative. Degenerative regression of cells takes place in certain diseases expressive of destructive or injurious effects. Similarly dreams, neuroses, or psychoses can be looked upon as the result of degenerative regressions. *Regenerative* regression, however, takes place when the supply of certain cells does not live up to the demands of the organism. The meaning of this regression becomes clear when it is considered that the cells of the organism in its initial developmental stage have the faculty of producing all types of cells; they are totipotential. With progressive differentiation they are capable of producing only certain types of cells: they have become multipotential. With the highest differentiation they are capable of producing only their own kind: they are unipotential. Under stress some unipotential cells regain part of their former capacity to produce another type of cell than their own kind. This regression serves the purpose of regeneration, distinctly different from degenerative regression. I compare the genius's capacity of multipotentiality with this regenerative regression. Goethe spoke of his repeated puberties. Puberty is comparable to a temporary dissolution of structure, a new lease given to find new objects of love. Thus I add to the biological characteristic of Goethe's, namely, the capacity for forming unifunctional, creative states without loss of differentiation, the capacity for preserving the multipotentiality of some ego-functions.[32] Yet Goethe's capacity to revert, from unipotentiality to multipotentiality and at some crucial turns of life almost to totipotentiality, strikes me as a final proof that the energy of his creative functions had never risen far off the instinctual level.

There is unclarity in my mind as to the extent to which I have in the foregoing mainly repeated in a different form what others have said and the extent to which I have struck off in a new direction. There is one paragraph in Freud's metapsychological writings that expresses by and large the essence of the position I am taking here. Freud wrote:

> Cooperation between a preconscious and an unconscious impulse, even when the latter is intensely repressed, may come about if there is a situation in which the unconscious impulse can act in the same sense as one of the dominant trends. The repression is removed in this instance, and the repressed activity is admitted as a reinforcement of the one intended by the ego. The unconscious becomes ego-syntonic in respect of this single conjunction without any change taking place in its repression apart from this.

[32] The true greatness of geniuses like Goethe can be divined when the large number of original and ever "new" creations are read in chronological order and there emerges, despite the vast difference from one creation to another, the personal style and the thread of development, which make, out of the diverse, a unit of the highest order.

In this cooperation the influence of the [unconscious] is unmistakable: the reinforced tendencies reveal themselves as being nevertheless different from the normal; they make specifically perfect functioning possible, and they manifest a resistance in the face of opposition which is similar to that offered, for instance, by obsessional symptoms. (183, pp. 194–95)

The kinship of my metapsychological hypotheses with the work of Kris (346) and Hartmann (276), despite deviations in respect to some issues, is evident. Yet in some respects the position I take is perhaps closer to the work of Robert Waelder (538). I was well acquainted with the work of these three psychoanalysts and kept abreast of their publications throughout the writing of these notes. The two papers by Fairbairn (129; 130), which I have cited only twice, despite some surprising similarity of views regarding some problems of the psychology of art, I read only after I had finished the manuscript.

Since this appendix was written, I have found two further items favorable to my thesis that no transformation of energy occurs in the creative process. One of them is merely an opinion, but when it is the opinion of a psychological genius such as Nietzsche it gives me welcome support. He wrote: "It is one and the same force that is expended in the conception of art and in the sexual act: there exists only one kind of force."[33]

The other item concerns a linguistic detail. Cicero praises the genius of the Latin language for having different terms for *being active* and for *suffering pain,* in contrast to Greek: "To these two things [toil and pain], our Greek friends, whose language is richer than ours, apply a single term, and accordingly they call diligent men devotees of, or rather lovers of, pain; we more aptly call them toilers, for toiling is one thing, feeling pain another." (88, Book II, Section XV, pp. 183, 185)

J. E. King, the editor and translator of the Loeb Classical Library, disputes Cicero on this score (88, p. 182, n. 4) but Kabza, the editor and translator of the German edition, supports Cicero, asserting in a note that the Greek word *philoponos* may mean either industrious or pain-loving (88, p. 74, n. 17).

I owe thanks to Professor Moses Hadas for confirming for me that Cicero was right. I first thought that perhaps Greeks identified activity with pain only in those instances in which activity was devoted to a kind of work for which they felt contempt, or which was not considered dignified. Yet Professor Hadas says (in a personal communication) that "the literary associations of *ponos* always suggest a favorable 'gentlemanly' sense. . . . In Homer it is used of strenuous fighting, in Pindar of the (admirable) training for competition in the games. *Philoponos* is therefore willingness to work hard for a noble end, not merely love of drudgery for its own sake."

---

[33] [Es ist ein und dieselbe Kraft, die man in der Kunst-Conception und die man im geschlechtlichen Actus ausgiebt: es giebt nur Eine Art Kraft.] (410, Book IV, #815)

It is of interest that Wilhelm von Humboldt (1795) held similar views.

There is no doubt that special terms are needed to distinguish between "active" and "pain-loving," but the fact that the Greek language did not differentiate the two may serve, in my opinion, as additional evidence that the two have something essential in common. In my view what they share is the instinctual factor.

Appendix V

Further Remarks Concerning Goethe's *Wilhelm Meister*

An UNDERSTANDING OF Goethe's life—which, as has several times been pointed out, it is not the goal of this study to attain, since this is mainly concerned with just one decade of it—would have to culminate in an understanding of *Wilhelm Meister,* that enigmatic novel which has rightly been called Goethe's "most personal piece of poetic writing."[1] What I will attempt here is to adduce several points of view of an auxiliary nature which may help to unravel the veil that shrouds this epic in prose. The points raised constitute only a preliminary approach and must remain isolated from one another until future, more penetrating research shall have discovered a common denominator for them.[2]

The first difficulty the researcher meets in his attempt at a psychological analysis of *Wilhelm Meister* is that it consists of three novels, two of which partly overlap, but each of which is a distinct entity. These three parts are: (1) *Wilhelm Meister's Theatrical Mission* [Wilhelm Meisters Theatralische Sendung], the "Ur-Meister" as it has also been called, the writing of which covered the years from 1777 to Goethe's departure for Italy in 1786, and the manuscript of which was found only in 1910, by chance. It consists of six books;[3] (2) *Wilhelm Meister's Apprenticeship* [Wilhelm Meisters Lehrjahre], consisting of eight books and written between 1793 and 1796. Although this contains

---

[1] [Goethes persönlichste Dichtung], quoted after Karl Heinemann in the introduction to *Wilhelm Meisters Lehrjahre* (258, 9:16).

[2] How difficult a critical analysis of *Wilhelm Meister* is can be seen from Goethe's own words to Eckermann (January 18, 1825) that this work "belongs to the most incalculable productions, to which I myself scarcely possess the key." [Es gehört dieses Werk übrigens zu den incalculabelsten Productionen, wozu mir fast selbst der Schlüssel fehlt.] (119, p. 112)

[3] Goethe brought Book VI to a close on November 11, 1785, and then started on the seventh. It is not known how far he got on this before leaving for Italy, for no traces of Book VII have been preserved.

extensive parts of the first version, so much of what gave that first its characteristic flavor was deleted or remodeled, and so much new was added, that it became a new novel clearly distinct in meaning, purpose, and artistic effect from its predecessor; (3) *Wilhelm Meister's Wanderings* [Wilhelm Meisters Wanderjahre], written between 1820 and 1829, and consisting of three books. This also contains a number of short stories, some of which had been written much earlier (around 1800) and were put into the novel without obvious connection with the main action or inner justification from the point of view of the meaning of the novel as a whole. The *Wanderjahre* is called Goethe's "novel of old age" [*Altersroman*]; on the one hand numerous flaws and inconsistencies have been discovered in it and it has been criticized for its pedantry; on the other it has been praised for its many poetic passages and the general philosophy it purports to convey.[4]

We are principally interested here in the biographical aspect, and in the text I have paid consistent attention to this aspect of only the original version (1). But what about the two subsequent Wilhelm Meisters, the apprentice and the wanderer? Whereas the early chapters of (1) sound like an almost undisguised presentation of Goethe's early childhood, as the work develops it seems to get further and further away from the realities of its originator. The Wilhelm Meister of (3) becomes a surgeon and emigrates to the United States with a group of like-minded people—the majority of the novel's principal characters—thus losing any obvious similarity to the experiences of the author. And yet Goethe spoke of Wilhelm Meister at times as his "dramatic likeness" or as a "pseudo-confession."[5] Indeed, when reading *Wilhelm Meister* one cannot escape the impression that the author constantly presented himself (not only in the principal character but also in some of the lesser ones) in the most intimate way, and in a far more personal way than necessarily happens when a great author writes a great novel. Of course, there are many episodes in *Wilhelm Meister* that permit an easy guess as to what events of Goethe's real life find their artistic presentation there. Yet this question is a secondary one when we want to understand the meaning of the novel.

In *Dichtung und Wahrheit* Goethe tried to write his autobiography, and he makes us acquainted with innumerable facts about his past; nevertheless, I venture to assert, he presents himself in a far more intimate way in *Wilhelm Meister* than in his autobiography. A decisive problem may be vaguely perceived here. What is the difference between a novel and a biography, as biography is

---

[4] Gundolf, by classifying it as a book of wisdom and warning against regarding it as a novel, destroys the whole psychological problem inherent in it. See 270, p. 716.

[5] To Charlotte von Stein he wrote on June 24, 1782, as quoted earlier, about "my beloved dramatic likeness" [meinem geliebten dramatischen Ebenbild]. This personal closeness was true not only of the original version but also of the final version, for in May, 1794, he wrote Herder that he had "to get the pseudo-confession off [his] heart and neck" [um . . . als eine Pseudo confession mir vom Herzen und Halse zu kommen]. (*Soph.* IV, *10*:158)

commonly written nowadays? On the face of it, it would appear that the one could easily be converted into the other, and it is fascinating to consider their relationship. One has only to assume when reading a novel that the events and dialogue occurred in reality, and, when reading a biography, that the author's references to real historical personages are only for the purpose of giving his hero-character a greater degree of plausibility.

And yet, if we turn to actual examples it seems that an abyss separates biography from novel. Take, as perhaps typical, M. André Maurois's recent biography of Victor Hugo (380). If I had read that book in the spirit in which a novel is read, I should have concluded that Maurois was a poor artist and a poor psychologist, because the events he tries to make the reader believe in are most improbable, never occur in reality, and therefore reveal his utter unfamiliarity with what man and his soul really are. And nevertheless I am sure that everything recorded by M. Maurois really happened. In turn, if I approach his book in the spirit appropriate to biography, I must admit that after reading it I know a score of facts about Victor Hugo's life of which I was ignorant before, but feel that I got no insight into Victor Hugo the man, the living being. Indeed, I must confess that if reading some of Victor Hugo's poetry and novels brought him close to me, he was now quite distant and a puzzle. What had the Victor Hugo of *Olympio* to do with the poems and novels assertedly written by a man who—by chance—had the same name? If a novelist left us in the same mood with regard to the principal character of his novel we should rightly say that he was a poor artist. Yet M. Maurois is an excellent biographer and had he gone beyond the limits he set for himself in that capacity we should be entitled to criticize him for having written, not a biography, as he set out to do, but a psychological, scientific study, or a novel. But M. Maurois stuck to his guns and wrote a biography and thus demonstrated again the woes of this craft, which is hopelessly caught in trivialities unless it relinquishes the restraints its legitimate definition imposes upon it, in favor of psychology or poetic art.

I consider this digression necessary in a biographical study of *Wilhelm Meister,* for the temptation is great to exhaust one's effort in revealing the innumerable threads that connect a large number of the novel's details with actual events of Goethe's life (a temptation I yield to in what follows, I trust, to no more than a reasonable measure). Yet any or all those threads will not uncover the secret of why we know—explicitly or implicitly—more about Goethe after having read *Wilhelm Meister* than we do about Victor Hugo after reading M. Maurois's *Olympio.*

As stated in the main text, the original version of *Wilhelm Meister* was written under the impact of Goethe's inexhaustible effort to acquire insight into his past. That insight would make it possible to overcome certain dysfunctions, which he had used most productively and creatively until then but which threatened to lead to gradual self-destruction after his genius had used their potentialities to the maximum. Goethe himself, as recorded earlier (see above, p. 261) marveled in later years at the distinctness and vividness with which the past had appeared in his mind during those earlier years. To be sure, being what he was, Goethe did not simply record the return of the past as it really was but blended it with the experiences of the present into a work of art. In accordance with the function that served this period of his life the result was a novel, in which what prevailed was the realistic, growing at times in an un-Goethe-like manner into the crude. It is just this aspect that fascinates the reader of the twentieth century, who has been conditioned by the great schools of the realistic psychological novel that developed during the nineteenth and early twentieth centuries, particularly in France and Russia.

The new *Wilhelm Meister* as presented in the *Lehrjahre* is different from its predecessor. As easy as it is to make oneself a picture of the psychological meaning of the first draft—(an elaboration and artistic working-through of the relentlessly intruding early childhood memories, and, furthermore, an artistic presentation of the main processes that were going on in the poet at the time of writing)—just so difficult it seems to be to find the key to this version. In attempting to deal with this problem I have reached a certain conclusion which I shall present in its final form without going through the chain of preliminary steps that led to it. When one compares Goethe as one knows him from his works and other biographical sources with the Wilhelm Meister of (2), one finds—despite all the kinship, similarity and at times almost identity between them—one, and, as I feel inclined to stress, only one, significant and decisive difference: Wilhelm Meister is a talented person, even an extremely talented person, but Goethe was a genius. The Wilhelm Meister of (2) is utterly lacking in this one superb quality. In all the great variety of situations in which he is presented one does not notice even a flicker of that quality, and he is kept consistently within the confines of a mere talent. This, I believe, is not the case in the original version, where a tragedy written by the hero is accepted by the audience as a masterpiece and at the end of the book the reader is entitled to assume that Wilhelm will have a career far above the average as a great author and stage manager, comparable to Shakespeare. How could it really be otherwise when a genius poet tries to present his dramatic likeness in a novel? In (2), though there also Wilhelm Meister does some writing, he is clearly presented as a poet of talent, devoid of the genius quality. What may have been the reason for this astounding discrepancy?

I conclude that the Wilhelm Meister of (2) was written out of a deep anxiety, out of the qualm produced by the very disquieting question which the genius Goethe evidently asked himself: "What would my life have been if I had been born without the genius quality, whose origin I do not know and the possession of which I must consider fortuitous? Should I have been able to survive if I had been born like so many others, very talented but not a genius?" Goethe knew that he was unique and that he possessed a concatenation of qualities that no one possessed before him and no one would possess after him. Every genius

possesses such a special concatenation and therefore he at times feels himself isolated and estranged, for he cannot meet his equal. I reported earlier (see above,
p. 1475) that passage in *Dichtung und Wahrheit* where Goethe alludes to the
awe and eeriness he at times felt about the coming and going of that spark that
made him so conspicuously different from others and whose appearance was beyond his will and command. The problem received only passing mention in his
autobiography, mainly, as I believe, because it found implicit elaboration and
final solution in *Wilhelm Meister*. The answer Goethe found in the novel was a
wholeheartedly positive one: "Without the genius quality I should have groped
around for many years, unable to settle down and to do productive work, but
finally I should have found a place in the community, contributed my share of
productive work and also found happiness in doing so." This answer, this great
reassurance which is expressed in the novel, must have allayed anxieties of no
minor intensity, since it made him partly independent of the mysterious power
that had chosen him to be a genius.

There are passages in *Wilhelm Meister* that even hint that Goethe believed
he would have been happier if he had not been a genius but only a man of talent.
My thesis may also help to explain a very essential difference between Goethe's
development and that which he attributed to Wilhelm Meister. At the dawn of
manhood Wilhelm establishes a very happy and adequate heterosexual relationship with Mariane, an actress, from whom he is forced abruptly to withdraw by
compelling though wrong circumstantial evidence of her unfaithfulness.[6] We
know for certain that Goethe did not as a young man accomplish this step,
which is of incomparable importance particularly in male development. In (2)—
it is questionable whether this was also planned when Goethe wrote (1)—Mariane dies in giving birth to their son, Felix, whom Wilhelm Meister later meets
and to whom his relationship becomes most important in the *Wanderjahre*.[7]

The importance of this difference between Goethe's life and Wilhelm Meister's cannot be overestimated. Wilhelm Meister, when he believes he has discovered that Mariane is unfaithful, falls into a grave illness, like Goethe's when he
was returning from Leipzig, where, according to all evidence, he failed to establish an adequate heterosexual relationship.[8] Since Mariane's early death in the
novel is not dictated by the necessities of plot construction, it requires a psychological interpretation. I believe that its underlying psychological meaning is of
a great consolation for the poet for having had to forgo so many pleasures that
the talent is permitted to indulge in. It may be expressed approximately like this:
"If I had been like other men endowed by nature with talent but not with genius, I should have fallen in love with a girl in my younger years and started a

---

[6] The fact that this object-relationship already appears in the first version of *Wilhelm
Meister* may be used as an argument against my thesis.

[7] Felix is a composite of Fritz von Stein and August, Goethe's illegitimate son.

[8] The illness which, in *Dichtung und Wahrheit,* he claims to have suffered from after
the break with Gretchen is, of course, to be considered here.

sexual relationship, just as I saw happen around me so often. But then I might easily have made the girl pregnant and she might have died giving birth to a child." Thus the life of the talented is presented as leading to evil whereas the genius, who fulfills his whole existence in the service of his mission, is spared a feeling of irreparable guilt.

This idea would confirm a thesis I have presented from time to time, but I must add in this particular context that when I speak of "irreparable guilt" I am referring to guilt incurred by an action criminal in reality. The genius too, of course, does not escape the feeling of guilt that arises from unconscious sources. Furthermore I wish to repeat that this thesis does not deny the existence of other factors in causing Goethe's retardation in heterosexual relationships, such as his excessive anxiety about being devoured by a beloved object, which forced him over and over again to turn away from the object towards his art. Goethe apparently knew of that anxiety and he alluded to it in one sentence of his *Wilhelm Meister*. The reader will recall that when Wilhelm is lying wounded on the battlefield he is rescued by a beautiful woman, whom he calls "the Amazon." He immediately falls in love with her and is thereafter almost constantly preoccupied with the imprint she has left on his memory. He fails to establish her identity and for a long time his relationship to her exhausts itself in the fantasies he is able to attach to details of the brief encounter. In version (2) he finally succeeds in meeting her. She is Natalie, whom he will later marry. Yet shortly after he encounters her again, Wilhelm is in a peculiar mood, which Goethe describes as follows:

> Restlessness still kept him awake for a while and he occupied himself with comparing the image of the Amazon with the image of his new present friend. They still did not want to fuse with each other; that one he had, so to speak, made for himself, and this one seemed almost to make *him* over.[9]
> [Goethe's italics]

Here, in the disguise of Wilhelm Meister, Goethe describes an anxiety that prevented him from ever entering into a full, adequate, heterosexual relationship, namely, the anxiety about being converted by the loved object into something not only new but evidently anticipated as unknown and ego-alien. The women for whom he expresses his love in his beautiful love songs were the Amazons whose images he "made for himself"; but the love for a real object might end the ego's absolute reign in its kingdom and thus make it into a vassal without identity.

In the relationship to Charlotte von Stein he temporarily abandoned this kingship because the ego needed reorganization towards a new identity, and

---

[9] [Die Unruhe hielt ihn noch eine Zeitlang wach, und er beschäftigte sich das Bild der Amazone mit dem Bilde seiner neuen gegenwärtigen Freundin zu vergleichen. Sie wollten noch nicht mit einander zusammenfliessen; jenes hatte er sich gleichsam geschaffen, und dieses schien fast *ihn* umschaffen zu wollen.] (*Soph.* I, 23:160)

transformation was at that time not so much the source of fear lest it threaten his life as it was a lifesaving goal. Wisely he abstained from a sexual tie to her, for if it had been linked by such a tie that which was destined to be transitory if it was to be useful might have become constant and therefore noxious. Christiane never became such a danger as Wilhelm sensed in Natalie. The difference between them was too great for sexual union with her to have had a long-lasting transforming effect upon his genius. It is noteworthy that in the last part of the epos, the *Wanderjahre,* Wilhelm does not spend any time in Natalie's company and when he emigrates to the United States Natalie is sent on ahead of her husband.

But if Wilhelm caused Mariane's early death and Goethe was spared this crime, Wilhelm saved the life of his beloved son Felix, whereas Goethe saw his own son gradually approaching annihilation. The *Wanderjahre,* and thus the whole epos, ends with the following scene. Wilhelm sees a young man on horseback falling down a cliff into the river. He is quickly brought to the shore but seems lifeless. Wilhelm, now an experienced surgeon, lets his blood, and the youth awakens to new life. It is Felix, who, regaining consciousness, exclaims to his father:

> "If I should live, then may it be with you." With these words he fell on his
> . . . rescuer's neck and wept bitterly. Thus they stood firmly embraced
> like Castor and Pollux, brethren, who meet each other on the vicissitudinous way from Orcus to light.[10]

And Wilhelm spreads a mantle over his son, who seems already fully recovered. Thus the difference between generations, their jealousies and rivalries, are eliminated. Father and son are Castor and Pollux, time-honored symbols of twin friendship. And as the father had once lain on a battlefield close to death and been rescued by a woman who spread a cloak over his wounded body, so now did the father do the same for his son, at last arrogating the female function to himself.

To the analyst there can be no doubt that a scene of birth is here enacted, in view of the significance of a dreamer's pulling a young man out of the water. Castrative impulses inevitably present in the aging father are effectively denied: the father makes the son bleed but only to resuscitate him to new life.

In this closing scene, forces irreconcilably in conflict in reality appear synthesized, and conscious harmony prevails where unconsciously relentless war had taken place. Man gives life to children; father and son are Castor and Pollux. Indeed, many a father succeeds in softening and even overcoming the deep ambivalence that separates the generation that is approaching death from that which is in full bloom of life. Goethe's father, I think, succeeded in that. Although many

[10] [Wenn ich leben soll, so sei es mit dir! Mit diesen Worten fiel er dem . . . Retter um den Hals und weinte bitterlich. So standen sie fest umschlungen, wie Kastor und Pollux, Brüder die sich auf dem Wechselwege vom Orcus zum Licht begegnen.] (*Soph.* I, 25:297)

discords and differences of temperament had often driven a wedge between father and son, the former had sacrificed professional success and independent existence to his son's welfare. The genius must never make this sacrifice, for to do so is to put an end to his creativity, and thus Goethe, despite his effort to the contrary, involuntarily pushed his son closer and closer to the abyss—into which August fatally fell shortly after his father had created the beautiful scene in which *Wilhelm Meister* found its conclusion.

Thus Wilhelm Meister is different from Goethe, and yet by letting us know this difference—by the negation, so to speak[11]—Goethe reveals himself in the most intimate and personal way possible, more intimately and personally than in *Dichtung und Wahrheit,* where he set out to let us know who he was. In this antinomy we again encounter one of those innumerable mysteries that are inherent in the human mind and that we are bound to stumble onto with particular alacrity and vehemence when we study man where he is at his very best—as an art-producing animal.

If, after having presented a few general viewpoints, which, unsatisfactory as they may be, still are indispensable in a psychological approach to *Wilhelm Meister,* I should turn to details, there would scarcely be an end to what could be said. The psychological richness of that novel is incredible and it constitutes a real treasure chest to anyone who is interested in psychology. Though I do not wish to yield to this temptation, I cannot let a commentary on *Wilhelm Meister* go without adding a few remarks, though they may appear picayune.

Wilhelm Meister's relationship to Mignon, Natalie and Philine could well be used to confirm statements made earlier about Goethe's relationship to his sister and about his sexual life. But this would be repetitive and I wish only to raise the following points:

(1) I reported earlier that Goethe, during one of his many separations from Christiane, asked her to send him one of her slippers worn out by dancing. This single instance is frequently used as an example of Goethe's alleged shoe fetishism. The great role that fetishism played in Goethe's life (and work) is unquestionable and has been discussed in the text at various places. *Wilhelm Meister* is a splendid source for further elaboration and enlargement on this topic. Nevertheless, I feel averse to an assumption that Goethe was a shoe fetishist. His request to Christiane was a solitary one, and this should have warned against overcertainty as to the existence of this perversion in Goethe's life. In *Wilhelm Meister* I think Goethe reveals what it was that really aroused his interest in shoes.

When Serlo, the actor and theatrical manager who is in love with Philine, praises her slippers, he adds what it is that really fascinates him in slippers. It is the sound (*klipp-klapp*) they make when worn by a girl rushing into his room.

[11] See 203, in which Freud describes the function of negation in letting a repressed content appear in consciousness.

The passage (Chapter 5 of Book V) is written with utter erotic charm and astounding freedom, at that, and it is inescapable to assume that Goethe was here revealing his own erotic feelings. The clip-clop sound of female slippers touching a hard floor apparently aroused him as the harbinger of things to come, as the churchgoer anticipates in the ringing of the bells the ensuing Mass.[12]

(2) In *Wilhelm Meister,* I believe, Goethe took occasion to permit a glimpse of many circumstances he generally held in secrecy. His predilection for the sound of female slippers is only one such. I have quoted earlier from Von den Steinen, who emphasized Goethe's seemingly not taking cognizance of one of the most important historical processes of his time, namely, the shift of Europe to the machine age. Indeed, scarcely any remarks by him on that topic can be found, despite Goethe's great historical astuteness. It is quite surprising to listen to the old seer as he very correctly predicts details of subsequent economic development, even the acquisition by the United States of the tract for the Panama Canal, and as he ardently wishes the English to come into possession of a canal at Suez.[13] Could a mind so superbly endowed with practical imagination really have been dead to the most conspicuous signs on the horizon? In 1790 Goethe had the opportunity to observe a steam engine at work, and in the last year of his life he received as a gift a small model of a railroad—just to cite two examples of his having in reality encountered modern technology.

In the *Wanderjahre* (Book III, Chapter 13), we find the explanation for the surprising fact of Goethe's seeming inattention to the technical revolution going on around him. It lies in the words of Susanne, one of the novel's characters who evidently again expressed the poet's own opinion. She is horrified by the threatened introduction of machines into the valley, where numerous weavers find breadwinning occupation without being estranged from the soil on which they grew up. Goethe has her say:

"The ever-spreading state of mechanization torments and frightens me; it rolls closer like a thunderstorm, slowly, slowly; but it has entered upon its course; it will come [to pass] and strike [its mark]. . . . One ponders upon it, one talks about it, but neither thinking nor talking will be of avail. And who would like to envision such horrors!"[14]

---

[12] Cf. the last line of the posthumously published Elegy I:
  Us delight the joys of the authentic, naked Amor
  And the endearing, creaking note of the rocked bed.
  [Uns ergötzen die Freuden des ächten nacketen Amors
  Und des geschauckelten Betts lieblicher knarrender Ton.] (*Soph.* I, 53:4)

[13] February 21, 1827 (119, pp. 475–76).

[14] [Das überhand nehmende Maschinenwesen quält und ängstigt mich, es wälzt sich heran wie ein Gewitter, langsam, langsam; aber es hat seine Richtung genommen, es wird kommen und treffen. . . . Man denkt daran, man spricht davon, und weder Denken noch Reden kann Hülfe bringen. Und wer möchte sich solche Schrecknisse gern vergegenwärtigen!] (*Soph.* I, 25:249)

Evidently it was an all too vivid image of what the world would look like, not an unawareness, that made Goethe silent upon this subject, and evidently he tried to keep his mind away from what he knew would inevitably happen most painfully and tragically despite any possible warning, feeling that man is powerless against the iron pace of history.

It is surprising (and not sufficiently known, for that matter) that in the novel Goethe strongly advocated emigration to the United States as a solution. Of course he did not foresee that this country would become the most highly industrialized in the world.[15] Also in the *Wanderjahre* he devised a program of education and political organization that must be called socialistic in nature. Aging evidently did not lead to mental regression in him and despite his actual integration in an aristocratic society he relentlessly went on to understand the signposts of his time and to replace with quite new and modern views those that he had most cherished for decades. Age did not prevent new reinterpretation of the world. In the *Wanderjahre* the aging Goethe presented his final views in the form of a Utopia. Such fantasies often serve the purpose of denying the existence of calamities. In Goethe's instance, however, the defensive function seems to have been minimal. He saw clearly the threat to individualism inherent in a socialistic scheme, and the struggle for maximum individualism despite a socialized system of raising children and of human cooperation forms the central point of his construction.

(3) The *Wanderjahre* is regarded as Goethe's "novel of old age" (*Altersroman*) in the sense that its shortcomings are laid to the account of the poet's partial weakening as a result of the aging process. I cannot enter here into the full proof that this view is wrong and that that which is commonly regarded as a deficiency in the novel is precisely what gives it its beauty. Of course Goethe wrote differently as an old man than he did as a young or middle-aged one. An exploration of the psychology of old age would be a necessary prerequisite to doing full justice to the book. The greatest obstacle to an adequate appreciation and critical analysis of its form and content has been the view that all changes that are brought about by aging are to be evaluated negatively. On this view the commonly encountered critical judgments of the *Wanderjahre* are correct. In any case, they are understandable, since most such commentaries are written by people who have not yet reached old age and who look askance at this period of life. However, such an outlook upon life as old age leads to is not deficient, but is as valid in its own way as that of the man between twenty and sixty. What are commonly regarded as deficiencies are elements that do not fit into the concepts, philosophy, and ideology of the next younger age group, and are therefore looked down upon. As soon as one stops automatically regarding them as faults and scrutinizes them to see if they have not indeed some positive value, they appear in a new light. Georg Simmel has expressed in the language of the phi-

---

[15] For Goethe's relationship to America, see 29; 529.

losopher and metaphysician the following thoughts about the works of great artists in their old age:

> Here creative life has become so sovereignly itself, so rich of itself, that it thrusts away any form that is shared with tradition or with others, so that its manifestation in art works is nothing else than its most own respective fate. As coherent and meaningful as the work may be in this aspect, just so shattered, disproportionate, as consisting of fragments, does it often appear from the point of view of the created forms. This is not senile incapacity to produce forms, no old-age infirmity, but old-age strength. The great artist is in this period of his perfection so purely himself that his work shows of form only that which the stream of his life produces of itself; as against him, form has lost its own special claims.[16]

The *Wanderjahre* is the sublime artistic expression of how the world appears to the aged, and, since Goethe almost never pretended in his art, old age too found its flawless, artistically superb presentation. The content of the novel very clearly demonstrates what the central conflict of Goethe was during that period of his life. Almost exactly in the middle of the *Wanderjahre* Goethe put the novelette *The Man of Fifty Years*. In that story a young girl is loved by both a man and his son, and the attempts of the father to conceal, if not undo, the ravages of age are described in detail. Yet aside from any problems concerning content—which can be solved with relative ease—the far more challenging task is the critical discussion of the formal elements: to find which formal elements are correlated with the aging process; to analyze the ideology of old age; and to establish the mode of etiological connection between the two.

(4) It is beyond my power of interpretation to explain why Goethe reverted to the image of the good mother in the final version of *Wilhelm Meister* after he had given such a forceful description of the bad mother in the original draft. At times he literally attributes to this new mother-image some of the good he had originally attributed to others, and conversely with the bad.

Could it have been that he came to believe that the stinging imprint a bad mother leaves in the adult is a prerequisite for the birth of a genius, and that a good mother suffices for the production of a man of mere talent?

(5) One of the most surprising subjects to find in the *Wanderjahre* is a de-

---

[16] [Hier ist das schöpferische Leben so souverain es selbst, so reich an sich selbst geworden, dass es jede Form, die irgendwie traditionell oder mit andern geteilt ist, abstösst, dass seine Äusserung im Kunstwerk nichts anderes ist, als sein jeweiliges eigenstes Verhängnis. So zusammenhängend und sinnvoll das Werk von diesem her sei, so erscheint es vom Standpunkt der hervorgebrachten Formen aus oft zersplittert, ungleichmässig, wie aus Fragmenten bestehend. Dieses ist nicht senile Unfähigkeit zur Gestaltung, keine Altersschwäche, sondern Altersstärke. Der grosse Künstler ist in dieser Epoche seiner Vollendung so rein er selbst, dass sein Werk nur das an Form noch zeigt, was die Strömung seines Lebens von selbst erzeugt; ihr Eigenrecht hat die Form ihm gegenüber verloren.] (498, p. 23)

tailed description of a homosexual experience in Wilhelm's early youth (Book II, Chapter 2). This is contained in a letter Wilhelm writes to Natalie, and since it is the last of the four letters to her scattered through the novel it acquires particular prominence. This is introduced by passages of some length, consisting of four parts broken up by asterisks. That breaking up, and the procrastination expressed in these passages, indicates that Wilhelm (Goethe) had to overcome an internal inhibition before he was able at last to come out with something that oppressed him very much.

Wilhelm describes a family outing—apparently the only one that took place in his youth—on the third day of Whitsuntide. Two visits had been arranged. At the first stop, the children pick flowers but the oldest boy of the village, the son of a fisherman, invites Wilhelm to go with him to the nearby river. This boy "had particularly attracted me right at his first appearance."[17]

They sit on the shore, the boy teaching Wilhelm how to fish. After a while the boy seems bored, steps down the bank, and swims around. Soon after, not being able to resist the boy's invitation, Wilhelm too takes off his clothes and steps into the water, although he does not know how to swim. The letter goes on:

> When he [the boy] came out and stood up to dry himself in the high sunshine, I thought my eyes blinded by a threefold sun, so beautiful was the human figure of which I had never had a conception. He seemed to regard me with equal attention. Quickly dressed, we stood facing each other still unveiled, our hearts attracted each other and with the most passionate kisses we swore an eternal friendship.[18]

Upon their return they join the others on their way to the second visit they are to make, to the bailiff's. Wilhelm wants to take his new friend along, but the impropriety of this (I assume because of the marked class difference between the two boys) is pointed out, and the fisherman's son is told that he should catch crawfish, which will be needed that evening. The boy leaves, but not before promising Wilhelm "with hand and mouth" [mit Hand und Mund] to wait for him that evening at the place where they parted.

When they reach the bailiff's house they have to wait for dinner and meanwhile Wilhelm is taken for a walk into the garden by the host's daughter, a girl younger than he.

[17] [der mich bei seinem ersten Auftreten gleich besonders angezogen hatte.] (*Soph.* I, 25:43)

[18] [. . . als er sich heraushob, sich aufrichtete im höheren Sonnenschein sich abzutrocknen, glaubt' ich meine Augen von einer dreifachen Sonne geblendet, so schön war die menschliche Gestalt von der ich nie einen Begriff gehabt. Er schien mich mit gleicher Aufmerksamkeit zu betrachten. Schnell angekleidet standen wir uns noch immer unverhüllt gegen einander, unsere Gemüther zogen sich an und unter den feurigsten Küssen schwuren wir eine ewige Freundschaft.] (*Soph.* I, 25:44–45)

My companion was pretty, blond, gentle, and we went together in friendly fashion; we took each other by the hand and seemed to wish nothing better.[19]

At this point Wilhelm's narration is interrupted by two paragraphs of general content, the first of which I wish to quote.

When I regard after so many years my situation of that day, then it appears to me really enviable. Unexpectedly, in that very moment, the presentiment of friendship and love seized me. For when I unwillingly took leave from the pretty child I was consoled by the thought of disclosing and confiding these emotions to my young friend and of enjoying his participation along with these recent sentiments.[20]

When Wilhelm returns to the arranged place he waits in vain for his friend:

I called, I felt anxious; he was not to be seen and he did not answer; I felt for the first time a passionate pain, double and manifold.

Already there was developing in me the immoderate demand of intimate attachment, already the urge was irresistible to set my mind free from the image of that fair-haired girl by chatting, to deliver my heart from the emotions she had excited in me.[21]

When he reached the village there was general excitement and lamentation. Screams were heard and it turned out that five children had been drowned. Wilhelm's friend had gone—as ordered—to catch the crawfish. Boys inexperienced in swimming joined him and tumbled into the water. He would have been able to save himself but the other boys dragged him to the depth. One youngster who stayed on shore collected the crawfish and ran to the village with the terrible news.

Wilhelm was thrown into a dreadful state. Furtively, through a window, he

---

[19] [Meine Begleiterin war schön, blond, sanftmüthig, wir gingen vertraulich zusammen, fassten uns bald bei der Hand und schienen nichts Besseres zu wünschen.] (*Soph.* I, 25:45–46)

[20] [Betracht' ich nach soviel Jahren meinen damaligen Zustand, so scheint er mir wirklich beneidenswerth. Unerwartet, in demselbigen Augenblick, ergriff mich das Vorgefühl von Freundschaft und Liebe. Denn als ich ungern Abschied nahm von dem schönen Kinde, tröstete mich der Gedanke, diese Gefühle meinem jungen Freunde zu eröffnen, zu vertrauen und seiner Theilnahme zugleich mit diesen frischen Empfindungen mich zu freuen.] (*Soph.* I, 25:46)

[21] [Ich rief, ich ängstigte mich; er war nicht zu sehen und antwortete nicht; ich empfand zum erstenmal einen leidenschaftlichen Schmerz, doppelt und vielfach.

Schon entwickelte sich in mir die unmässige Forderung vertraulicher Zuneigung, schon war es ein unwiderstehlich Bedürfniss meinen Geist von dem Bilde jener Blondine durch Plaudern zu befreien, mein Herz von den Gefühlen zu erlösen, die sie in mir aufgeregt hatte.] (*Soph.* I, 25:47–48)

penetrated into the hall where the corpses were laid out. There he saw the ill-fated bodies,

> nude, stretched out on straw, shining forth brightly white even by the gloomy lamplight. I threw myself upon the largest, upon my friend. I could not tell of my condition; I wept bitterly and flooded his broad chest with unending tears. I had heard something of rubbing which was supposed to be helpful in such a case; I rubbed in my tears and deceived myself with the warmth that I elicited. In my confusion I thought of blowing breath into him, but the pearl strings of his teeth were firmly closed; the lips on which the farewell kiss seemed still to rest refused even the softest sign of response. Despairing of human help I turned to prayer; I implored, I prayed; I felt as if in this moment I had to perform a miracle to roll forth the still indwelling soul, to lure in again the soul still hovering close by.[22]

I said at the outset that it is surprising to find in the *Wanderjahre* such an open description of an almost manifest homosexual experience. I have from time to time pointed out the great role homosexuality played in Goethe's life, as might easily be expected. Yet whereas in the course of his works quite a few episodes, or hints, can be found that permit at least tentative reconstruction of the main processes of his heterosexual development, the corresponding material regarding the homosexual development is extremely scarce. The hesitation with which Goethe has Wilhelm proceed in the letter, that hemming and hawing which is so marked before he starts his account of the episode, stems in my estimation from Goethe's own inner revulsion against referring to what must have been an actual experience that, in one way or another, underlay Wilhelm's story.

Why was Goethe able to write this story as an old man? In order to answer this question it is necessary to go again, if only to a bare minimum, into the psychology of old age. I agree with Gottfried Benn, who, at least in one place in his article (18),[23] seems to indicate that the works of art created by the aged genius do not have any characteristics in common that can be described in concrete terms. I believe the new—and often surprisingly new—that can be encountered in the productions of the aged genius varies from instance to instance, for it

[22] [auf Stroh, nackt, ausgestreckt, glänzendweisse Leiber, auch bei düsterm Lampenschein hervorleuchtend. Ich warf mich auf den grössten, auf meinen Freund, ich wüsste nicht von meinem Zustand zu sagen, ich weinte bitterlich und überschwemmte seine breite Brust mit unendlichen Thränen. Ich hatte etwas von Reiben gehört das in solchem Falle hülfreich sein sollte, ich rieb meine Thränen ein und belog mich mit der Wärme, die ich erregte. In der Verwirrung dacht' ich ihm Athem einzublasen, aber die Perlenreihen seiner Zähne waren fest verschlossen, die Lippen auf denen der Abschiedskuss noch zu ruhen schien, versagten auch das leiseste Zeichen der Erwiderung. An menschlicher Hülfe verzweifelnd wandt' ich mich zum Gebet, ich flehte, ich betete, es war mir als wenn ich in diesem Augenblicke Wunder thun müsste, die noch inwohnende Seele hervorzurufen, die noch in der Nähe schwebende wieder hineinzulocken.] (*Soph.* I, 25:49–50)

[23] The first thirteen pages of this article are a splendid epitome of possible approaches to this problem.

contains something with which the creative personality had struggled since it started to express itself by creating art. It seems to me that when the "surprising new" appears in the products of old age it is because old age has done away with an inhibition, a barrier, a repressive agent, and the effect of that removal is the appearance of that of which the creative mind may perhaps have known hazily or of which it was quite ignorant but which it had always felt the urge to search for, until it became possible to bring it to light when the closeness of death had removed the fear of anything worldly. But whether it is really this factor or some other that causes the final release of the repressed is a matter of speculation.

Be this as it may, in the episode of the five drowned boys Goethe was able to release a deeply repressed or suppressed content. Of course, he did not present it in its original form. The death of such a large number of youths in such dramatic circumstances would have been recorded somewhere and the large number of painstaking *Goetheforscher* would have unearthed the historical reports related thereto. At the end of July, 1774, Goethe wrote to Sophie von La Roche:

> My mind has not yet quite recovered since four boys were drowned yesterday night and none was rescued. Only in such moments does man feel how little he is and nothing is achieved with fervent arms and sweat and tears.[24]

This reality experience of the adult may easily have served as the outer garment in which to cloak a much earlier experience of comparable gruesomeness.

The trend which is brought forth in the story is unmistakable. It refers to the time of prepuberty or early puberty when the direct, sexual genital sensation was experienced for the first time under the kisses of an older boy. Whether or not ejaculation occurred on that occasion, whether or not he was genitally seduced by the older boy—all such details cannot, of course, be reconstructed. Neither are they of decisive importance. What is of interest is that Goethe juxtaposed Wilhelm's first infatuation with a girl. Again it is not probable that the two events actually occurred in such close sequence but that the correlation is between phases or mechanisms of libidinal development. Freud pointed out that certain elements in a delusion of a case of paranoia were "in reality nothing else than a concrete representation and external projection of libidinal cathexes" (173, p. 78). *Mutatis mutandis* an equivalent mechanism can be assumed in some elements of Goethe's story. The quick appearance of the blond girl represents the displacement of homosexual impulses upon the female, the flight taken from homosexuality to heterosexuality, the developmental progress from a rather narcissistic level to a more object-directed one. But the regressive force sets in quickly. One is even inclined to speculate that the sudden advance in heterosexuality may have been made possible only under the auspices of having

---

[24] [Mein Sinn hat sich noch nicht ganz erholt, wo vier Knaben gestern Nacht ertranken und keiner gerettet wurde. Nur in solchen Augenblicken fühlt der Mensch, wie wenig er ist, und mit heisen Armen und Schweiss und Thränen nichts würkt.] (*Soph.* IV, 2:181)

an older beloved friend to whose protection he could return at any moment for the sake of "enjoying his participation along with these recent sentiments," which may mean the security provided by the certainty of ridding oneself of the heterosexual danger by means of the homosexual contact.

Yet the story reports that this return to the homosexual love-object was blocked by the irretrievable loss of the object. It is indeed most noteworthy that death (or its euphemistic representation by injury or its equivalent) is twice found elsewhere again in connection with homosexuality. Both instances occurred during the occupation of Frankfurt by the French, when Goethe was ten years old, and both are related to the theater (*Dichtung und Wahrheit,* Book III). One refers to a duel with a friend whom Goethe called Derones, and in the other, which I have briefly referred to in Appendix I, an admired and envied boy dies after Goethe uses an ill-omened proverb. Homosexuality, in the sense applicable to puberty, was no doubt closely associated in Goethe's fantasy with death, that is to say, that period of life which usually is most important for the final putting into shape of direct sexual strivings stood under the sign of a horrible warning against homosexuality. We know that in some instances of genius manifest homosexuality does not interfere with creativity, but I said earlier that manifest homosexuality would have been a grave danger for the adult Goethe. We find here the reason for the ill effect a regression to homosexuality might have had on the adult poet. Since homosexuality and death were so closely associated in the pubescent boy, an actual homosexual experience in the adult would have aroused an unmanageable degree of panic and guilt, or, in other words, manifest homosexuality would have meant to the unconscious an act of killing.[25] Goethe, indeed, was well protected against manifest homosexuality. The reader may recall my account of Goethe's relationship to his younger sister as being one as to a twin, that is to say, Cornelia was his mirror-image and therefore an intensification of narcissism—regularly encountered in homosexuality—had to lead him towards the other sex.

However, the constellation is not quite transparent in Wilhelm's letter. Wilhelm's unconscious may have interpreted the catastrophe as a consequence of his unfaithfulness in falling in love with the girl. At least, the emphasis upon the urge to perform a miracle and to revive the dead sounds like the expression of a feeling of responsibility for the death of the friend. The correct interpretation would here be greatly facilitated if we knew the structure of the underlying reality experience. For it is quite possible that Goethe here indirectly expressed a fantasy containing a warning to himself never to fall back on homosexuality when confronted with a heterosexual conflict. This secondary factor in the struggle against homosexuality may have led to the construction of a frightening fantasy fulfilling the same function that anxiety has when the ego uses it

[25] See 214, p. 347, where Freud introduces the factor of a "spontaneous tendency to conflict" depending on "the intervention of an element of free aggressiveness" which will decide upon the degree of conflict aroused by homosexuality.

as a signal of warning (see 205). I am certain that notwithstanding the possible role of such a factor the unconscious meanings involved in the story go much deeper.[26]

It is noteworthy that in Wilhelm's account the pregenital and sadistic is emphasized in a fashion almost reminiscent of what I have called crude in the *Theatralische Sendung*. Anality appears already at the beginning. At the farm where the family visited, Wilhelm sees agricultural tools for the first time in a place where they are actually in use and he adds:

> Even the waste matter obnoxious to look at seemed to be the most indispensable thing in the whole area; it was gathered with care and preserved, so to speak, daintily.[27]

The switch to orality in the next sentence is significant. The sight of waste was quickly replaced, and

[26] How important homosexuality was in Goethe's personality becomes apparent at quite a surprising place in his work: the penultimate scene in *Faust*. As was pointed out before, the rationale of Mephisto's defeat is that Faust has found fulfillment and bliss, not, as Mephisto had anticipated, in sinful, physical pleasure, but in a socially constructive deed, and his soul is, therefore, not forfeit. But the actual concrete presentation explains Faust's escape on a quite different plane, as the result of Mephisto's being distracted at the crucial moment by the physical beauty of the angels. He becomes sexually aroused, and the angels take advantage of his momentary inattention to fly away with Faust's soul. Mephisto's love is undeniably homosexual. He addresses a particular angel, "the tall fellow" [langer Bursche], begging for a wanton look. He even, to the distress of some scholars, praises the charm of the angelic behinds (*Faust,* Part II, verses 11784–11800, *Soph.* I, *15*:324).

In its broadest significance, this episode strikes me as the acme of that irony that has held such an important place in Western literature since the time of the Greeks. More particularly, it also testifies to an unusual degree of expressive freedom and courage on Goethe's part. It is, of course, an especial challenge to the psychologically oriented biographer. However, it is beyond my powers to provide a psychological interpretation in the sense of suggesting a link with particular events in Goethe's life. I venture only some general remarks. Scholars agree that not only Faust but Mephisto as well are reflections or aspects of Goethe himself. Since Mephisto stands for evil, and he now, at the end of the play, discloses that his mode of sexuality is the homosexual, we may conclude that (1) homosexuality was for Goethe a real danger that he had to cope with; and (2) homosexuality was regarded by Goethe as in some way the very epitome of evilness. Many speculations could be added. It has its special piquancy that, once Faust is dead, enough homosexuality is released in Mephisto to make him lose sight for a moment of his main purpose; herein we may see how strong Mephisto's libidinal tie to Faust had really been. The seducer is in the end himself seduced and is tricked by his own passions. The episode also reveals Goethe's deep insight into the connection that exists (at least in our age and time) between unsublimated homosexuality, aggression, and general destructiveness, as against the socializing force inherent in heterosexual love. The apotheosis of the female with which *Faust* concludes derives its significance precisely from the contrast—for obvious reasons generally overlooked—with Mephisto's sudden access of homosexuality in his final scene.

[27] [. . . selbst der widrig anzuschauende Unrath schien das Unentbehrlichste im ganzen Kreise: sorgfältig war er gesammelt und gewissermassen zierlich aufbewahrt.] (*Soph.* I, *25*:42)

appetizing cake, fresh milk, and many another rustic delicacy were covetously taken into consideration by us.[28]

The oral element runs through the whole story, at times assuming a macabre quality. As will be remembered, the whole tragedy was indirectly caused by the fisherman's son's being asked to catch crawfish. The little boy who had not entered the water gathered up the crustaceans that his friends had caught before the drowning. Thus the family returned from the outing in the possession of this rare dish. Wilhelm's father objected to their being brought to the table, but Wilhelm's aunt became very much interested in them. She kept them alive by carefully feeding them and sent them piecemeal as gifts to a miserly person of great influence whom she thus bribed to win an appointment for an unworthy protégé of hers.

However, absurd consequences were not the only ones. Wilhelm's father, a community-spirited person, directed his interest towards the resuscitation of persons seemingly asphyxiated or who seemed dead from any other cause. In the course of the discussions on this topic Wilhelm heard that the boy victims had been treated in a way that was the opposite of that which ought to have been used, that they had been "in a way just murdered."[29] With the open introduction of the theme of murder a veritable hornet's nest is stirred up and we lose a reliable direction in the interpretative work. After all, Wilhelm had been with his friend in the same river that morning and he too did not know how to swim. Was it he that should have been murdered and was his friend only a scapegoat? Was it that, though both of them had indulged in the forbidden, only his friend, being the older, had to bear the severest punishment? Had Wilhelm murdered him by not insisting upon his joining him in the visit to the bailiff's? Here too many possibilities are opened to permit any hope of exactness. At any rate, the fantasy of murder proves anew the far-reaching implications contained in the story.

When Wilhelm also hears at this time that surgical bleeding might have saved the lives of the boys, he decides he will learn everything that is necessary to perform surgical bleeding. Thus the closing chapter of the novel, in which Wilhelm resuscitates Felix by bleeding him, contains the fulfillment of a youthful wish.[30]

A suggestion may be made regarding the reality experience underlying the homosexual episode. I surmise that it was experienced during the French occu-

[28] [. . . appetitliche Kuchen, frische Milch, und sonst mancher ländliche Leckerbissen ward von uns begierig in Betracht gezogen.]

[29] [ja sie gewissermassen erst ermordet.] (*Soph.* I, 25:55)

[30] It would be of interest to know whether it was Goethe's fantasy or a contemporary or earlier wrong belief that surgical bleeding was a remedy for asphyxiation. [I owe thanks to Dr. Paul Klemperer for having brought to my attention, in 1961, medical literature which leaves no doubt that in Goethe's time surgical bleeding was recommended and practiced for resuscitating drowned persons. See 85A. For further literature see 365A.]

pation when Goethe came into close contact with a transient French theater group. The clues I am able to present will perhaps not sound too convincing. I referred earlier to two homosexually colored incidents in connection with the French troupe (*Dichtung und Wahrheit*, Book III).

In the *Wanderjahre* Goethe introduces his ill-fated friend in a peculiar way. He writes that the boy attracted him with his first *Auftreten*, which I translated as "appearance." The noun *Auftreten* is derived from a verb which means literally "to step upon" and is used in various shades, one of the most common referring directly to the stage, i.e., "to tread the boards." One would use the word as Goethe did in the passage quoted—nowadays at least—only of someone making his appearance on the stage, and not on the occasion of meeting a person for the first time at a party.

Also, at the end of Wilhelm's account of the whole episode he reports how everyday life took possession of his attention and concludes:

> Meanwhile sensuousness, imagination, and mind were occupied excessively with the theater; how far I was here led and misled, I may not repeat.[31]

It is worth while to take notice what the—in my opinion—equivalent passage in *Dichtung und Wahrheit* has to say. There Goethe wrote the following about a detail of the French troupe:

> In a rather large, adjoining room that formerly served for games of cards, both sexes were for the most part together and seemed as little shy among themselves as before us children in so far as the putting on or changing of clothes did not always take place in the most decent manner. This kind of thing had never happened to me and nevertheless I soon found it quite natural through habituation at repeated visits.[3]

Evidently Goethe had the opportunity to gratify his sexual curiosity repeatedly on those occasions, to learn about a large range of sexual matters, and to become stimulated by an erotically and sexually uninhibited group. Did he witness homosexual activities also? Was he exposed to an attempt at

---

[31] [Indessen ward Sinnlichkeit, Einbildungskraft und Geist durch das Theater übermässig beschäftigt; wie weit ich hier geführt und verführt worden, darf ich nicht wiederholen.] (*Soph.* I, 25:55)

The word *Sinnlichkeit* in contemporary German means "sensuality," the word *verführen,* "to seduce." Goethe uses these words in the sense of "sensuousness" and "to mislead," but the latter term was also used in the sense of seducing in Goethe's time.

[32] [In einem ziemlich grossen Nebenzimmer, das ehedem zu Spielpartien gedient hatte waren nun beide Geschlechter meist beisammen und schienen sich so wenig untereinander selbst als vor uns Kindern zu scheuen, wenn es bei'm Anlegen oder Verändern der Kleidungsstücke nicht immer zum anständigsten herging. Mir war dergleichen niemals vorgekommen, und doch fand ich es bald durch Gewohnheit, bei wiederholtem Besuch, ganz natürlich.] (*Dichtung und Wahrheit,* Book III) (*Soph.* I, 26:144)

seduction; was he taken unawares and did he succumb? We do not know. But in comparing what the *Wanderjahre* lets us know about it with what is presented in *Dichtung und Wahrheit* we find out again how much more an author reveals when he intends to write about what he has *not* been, than when he tries to inform us about what he believes he *has* been.

Appendix W

Relevant Chronology of Goethe's Life*

Date	Event
July 31, 1710	Johann Kaspar Goethe (*father*) baptized.
February 13, 1731	Katharina Elisabeth Texstor (*mother*) baptized.
January 24, 1742	Charles VII (1697–1745), Roman Emperor (Elector of Bavaria), crowned in Frankfurt a.M. Remains in Frankfurt until April, 1743.
December 25, 1742	Charlotte von Schardt (later von Stein) born.
July, 1743–August, 1744	Charles VII again in Frankfurt.
August 20, 1748	Johann Kaspar Goethe and Katharina Elisabeth Texstor married.
August 28, 1749	JOHANN WOLFGANG GOETHE born in Frankfurt a.M.
December 7, 1750	Cornelia Friederike Christiane (*sister*) born.
Fall, 1752–Summer, 1755	Attends nursery school and kindergarten.
November 27, 1752	Hermann Jacob (*brother*) baptized.
Christmas, 1753	Puppet theater a gift of paternal grandmother.
March 28, 1754	Cornelia (*grandmother*) buried.
September 9, 1754	Katharina Elisabeth (*sister*) baptized.
April, 1755	Rebuilding of Goethe house.

* Most of the data given here have been taken from *Chronik von Goethes Leben* (260).

Date	*Event*
November 1, 1755	Earthquake in Lisbon.
January 22, 1756	Katharina Elisabeth (*sister*) buried.
April 1, 1756	Stillborn child (*brother*).
April–October, 1756	Suffers from smallpox.
November, 1760–February, 1761	Receives instruction in Latin and Greek.
1756–1763	Seven Years' War.
March 29, 1757	Johanna Maria (*sister*) baptized.
New Year's Day, 1757	Earliest known verses, poem for maternal grandparents.
February, 1758	Beginning of instruction in French.
1758	Execution in Frankfurt of Anna Maria Fröhlich for infanticide.
January 2, 1759	Frankfurt occupied by French.
January 13, 1759	Hermann Jacob (*brother*) buried.
August 11, 1759	Johanna Maria (*sister*) buried.
April 13, 1759	Battle at Bergen. Dangerous argument between Goethe's father and Count Thoranc.
June 15, 1760	Georg Adolf (*brother*) baptized.
1760	Instruction in penmanship.
February 18, 1761	Georg Adolf (*brother*) buried.
June, 1761	Count Thoranc leaves the Goethe house.
1760–1762	Instruction in Italian.
1762–1763	Instruction in English.
Summer, 1762	Instruction in Hebrew.
February, 1763	French quit Frankfurt.
Easter, 1763	Confirmation.
May, 1763	Beginning of instruction in piano.
April 3, 1764	Joseph II crowned in Frankfurt. End of Gretchen affair.

Date	Event
1765	Instruction in fencing and riding.
September 30, 1765	Departure for Leipzig.
October 3, 1765	Arrival in Leipzig.
Easter, 1766	Schlosser's arrival in Leipzig. Acquaintance with Anna Katharina Schönkopf.
October 13, 1767	Behrisch leaves Leipzig.
End of October, 1767	Fall from horse.
July, 1768	Pulmonary hemorrhage.
August 28, 1768	Departure from Leipzig.
December 7, 1768	Severe attack of colic; believed to be severely ill.
Late 1768–early 1769	Occupied with religion under the influence of Susanna Katharina von Klettenberg ("the beautiful soul").
April 1, 1770	Departure for Strassburg.
1770–1771	Attends University of Strassburg, taking courses in law, medicine and history.
May 7, 1770	The Dauphine Marie Antoinette enters Strassburg.
October, 1770	First visit at Sesenheim; meets Friederike Brion.
September, 1770–April, 1771	Herder in Strassburg.
June, 1771	Acquaintance with Jakob M. R. Lenz.
August 6, 1771	Graduates as Licentiate of Law.
August 7 (?), 1771	Farewell to Sesenheim.
August 14, 1771	Returns to Frankfurt.
August 28, 1771	Application for admittance as a lawyer in Frankfurt.
November–December, 1771	Writes first draft of *Götz von Berlichingen*.
December, 1771	Acquaintance with Johann Heinrich Merck.
January 14, 1772	Execution in Frankfurt of Susanna Margarete Brandt for infanticide.

Date	Event
March, 1772	In Darmstadt. Writes *Die Empfindsamen.*
May 23, 1772	Registers at Imperial Court of Chancery at Wetzlar.
June 9, 1772	Acquaintance with Charlotte Buff.
Sept. 11, 1772	Sudden departure from Wetzlar.
October 30, 1772	Jerusalem's suicide in Wetzlar.
November 6–10, 1772	With Schlosser in Wetzlar.
1773	First printing of *Götz von Berlichingen.*
April 4, 1773	Kestner and Charlotte Buff marry.
November 1, 1773	Cornelia marries Johann Georg Schlosser.
January 9, 1774	Brentano marries Maximiliane von La Roche.
January, 1774	Skates in his mother's fur coat.
February, 1774	Writes *Werther,* which is published in the same year.
June, 1774	Meets Lavater.
October, 1774	Klopstock visits Goethe in Frankfurt.
October 10, 1774	Writes "An Schwager Kronos."
December 11, 1774	Meets Karl August, Duke of Weimar.
December 13, 1774	Susanna von Klettenberg dies.
January, 1775	Acquaintance with Elise ("Lili") Schönemann.
January 26, 1775	First letter to Auguste, Countess von Stolberg.
April 20 (?), 1775	Engaged to Lili.
May 14, 1775	Begins first journey to Switzerland.
May 27–June 5, 1775	Visits Cornelia.
July, 1775	Acquaintance with Johann Georg Zimmermann, who shows him Charlotte von Stein's silhouette.
July 22, 1775	Returns to Frankfurt.
September 22, 1775	Invited to visit Weimar.
Autumn, 1775	Engagement to Lili severed.
October 3, 1775	Karl August marries Louise, Princess of Hessen-Darmstadt.

Date	Event
October 30, 1775	In Heidelberg, on his way to Italy, is overtaken by the Duke's messenger.
November 7, 1775	Arrives in Weimar.
November 11 (?), 1775	Acquaintance with Charlotte von Stein begins.
December 6, 1775	First visit at Kochberg with Charlotte von Stein.
1776	First printing of *Stella*.
March 25–April 4, 1776	Journey to Leipzig; invites Corona Schröter to Weimar.
April 3, 1776	Lenz arrives in Weimar.
April 21, 1776	Receives the Gartenhaus as a gift from the Duke; moves there on May 18.
May 21, 1776	Harsh letter to Klopstock, who had admonished him for his alleged way of living in Weimar.
June 11, 1776	Becomes a member of the Privy Council with a salary of 1200 *taler*.
July 18–August 14, 1776	In Ilmenau with the Duke; plan of opening the mines; subsequent beginning of geological and mineralogical studies.
November 14, 1776	Appointed Administrator of Mines.
November 16, 1776	Corona Schröter arrives in Weimar.
December 1, 1776	Lenz is dismissed from the Court of Weimar.
December 2, 1776	Second trip to Leipzig.
December 19, 1776	Third trip to Leipzig.
January 30, 1777	First performance of *Lila*.
June 8, 1777	Cornelia dies.
November 29–December 19, 1777	First journey to the Harz. First meeting with Plessing.
May 10, 1778	Fourth trip to Leipzig.
May 16, 1778	In Berlin.
June 1, 1778	Returns to Weimar.
September 24, 1778	Johanna Fahlmer and J. G. Schlosser married.

Date	Event
November 2, 1778	Promises F. Krafft support; provides for him until Krafft's death in 1785.
January, 1779	Assigned to the War Commission and as Director of Highway Construction.
February 3, 1779	Princess Louise born to the Duchess.
February, 1779	Begins the writing of *Iphigenia*.
February 28–March 12, 1779	Official trip to recruit soldiers and inspect highways.
April 6, 1779	First performance of *Iphigenia*.
August, 1779	Parodies Jacobi's *Woldemar*.
September 5, 1779	Appointed "Geheimer Rat."
September 12, 1779	Begins second journey to Switzerland.
September 19–22, 1779	At his parents' house in Frankfurt with the Duke.
September 25, 1779	Visits in Sesenheim.
September 26, 1779	Visits Lili in Strassburg.
September 27–28, 1779	Visits Schlosser; sees Cornelia's grave.
October 8–December 8, 1779	In Switzerland. Begins acquaintance with Marchioness Branconi.
December 30, 1779	In Frankfurt.
January 6–10, 1780	In Frankfurt.
January 14, 1780	Returns to Weimar.
April 23–25, 1780	Fifth trip to Leipzig.
August 18, 1780	First performance of *The Birds*.
August 26–27, 1780	Marchioness Branconi visits in Weimar.
September 6, 1780	Writes "Über allen Gipfeln."
January–May, 1781	The composer Kayser in Weimar.
February 15, 1781	Lessing dies.
March 7–15, 1781	With Karl August in Neunheiligen.
September 10, 1781	Dead daughter born to the Duchess.
September 21–30, 1781	Sixth trip to Leipzig.

Date	*Event*
November 14, 1781	Rents a house on the Frauenplan in Weimar.
March 29–April 18, 1782	Journey to Thuringia as the Duke's representative.
April 10, 1782	Nobilified.
May 8–18, 1782	Makes ambassadorial trip for Karl August.
May 25, 1782	Johann Kaspar Goethe (*father*) dies.
June 2, 1782	Moves into new house.
June 11, 1782	Appointed Secretary of the Treasury.
July 22, 1782	First performance of *Die Fischerin*.
December 25, 1782— January 4, 1783	Seventh trip to Leipzig.
February 2, 1783	Prince Karl Friedrich born to the Duchess.
May 25, 1783	Fritz von Stein moves into Goethe's house.
September 6–October 6, 1783	Second journey to the Harz, accompanied by Fritz von Stein.
November 12, 1783	Finishes Book IV of *Wilhelm Meisters theatralische Sendung*.
February 24, 1784	Makes a speech at the opening ceremonies for the mine in Ilmenau.
March 24, 1784	Princess Louise dies.
March 27, 1784	Discovers the *os intermaxillare*.
June 3, 1784	Travels to Eisenach for negotiations with the Diet.
July 6, 1784	Appointed Inspector of Revenue in Ilmenau.
July 19, 1784	Returns to Weimar.
August 16–September 1, 1784	Political journey to Brunswick with Karl August.
September 4, 1784	Third journey to the Harz; on the Brocken.
September 16, 1784	Returns to Weimar.
February 28, 1785	Dead son born to the Duchess.
March 18, 1785	Begins botanical studies.

Date	Event
June 23–August 21, 1785	Mountaineering. First journey to Karlsbad.
Autumn, 1785	The Diamond Necklace Affair.
September, 1785	Princess Gallitzin and Franz Hemsterhuis in Weimar.
July 18, 1786	Princess Caroline Louise born to the Duchess.
July 24, 1786	Departs for Karlsbad.
September 3, 1786	Secret departure from Karlsbad for Italy.
September 28–October 14, 1786	In Venice.
October 29, 1786	Arrives in Rome.
1787	First printings of: *Iphigenia; The Siblings; Triumph der Empfindsamkeit; The Birds.*
February 22, 1787	Departure for Naples.
April 1–18, 1787	In Palermo.
May 14–17, 1787	Returns to Naples.
June 7, 1787	Second Roman sojourn begins.
June 14, 1787	Ernst von Stein (Charlotte's second son) dies.
1788	First printing of *Egmont.*
April 11, 1788	Karl August grants Goethe's request to be relieved as Secretary of the Treasury.
April 23, 1788	Leaves Rome.
June 18, 1788	Arrives in Weimar. Freed from most of his governmental functions.
July 12, 1788	Begins relationship with Christiane Vulpius.
April 17, 1789	Son born to the Duchess, dies after birth.
June 8, 1789	Discontinues regular correspondence with Charlotte von Stein.
November, 1789	Moves from Frauenplan to Marienstrasse, where he lives until the summer of 1792.
December 25, 1789	Julius August Walther (*son*) born.
March 13–June 18, 1790	Second Italian journey.

Date	Event
July 26–October, 1790	Joins Karl August at maneuvers in Silesia.
September 2–11, 1790	Sees the first steam engine on the Continent. Visits mines in Eastern Europe.
January, 1791	Becomes director of ducal theater.
June 27, 1791	Merck's suicide.
October 14, 1791	Dead son born.
1792	Prince Bernhard born to the Duchess.
June 17, 1792	Moves to the house on the Frauenplan given to him by the Duke.
August 8, 1792	Leaves to join the Duke in the war against France.
August 12, 1792	Arrives in Frankfurt.
August 21, 1792	Leaves Frankfurt.
December 5, 1792	Second meeting with Plessing.
May 12, 1793	Leaves Weimar for the siege of Mainz.
May 17–26, 1793	In Frankfurt.
July 2–7, 1793	Last meeting with Schlosser.
July 9–19, 1793	In Frankfurt.
August 22, 1793	Returns to Weimar.
November 21, 1793	Caroline (*daughter*) born.
December 3, 1793	Caroline dies.
December 26, 1793	Josias von Stein (Charlotte's husband) dies.
July 20–23, 1794	Friendship with Schiller begins.
End of 1794 on	Frequent and prolonged visits in Jena.
1795	First printing of *Wilhelm Meisters Lehrjahre*.
May, 1795	Goethe's mother sells the house in Frankfurt.
October 30, 1795	Karl (*son*) born.
November 18, 1795	Karl dies.
October, 1796	*Xenien* are published.
October 22, 23, 1796	Ilmenau mine is inundated, work permanently stopped.

Date	*Event*
July 2–9, 1797	Burns his correspondence prior to 1792.
July 30, 1797	Departs on his third Swiss journey.
August 3, 1797	Arrives in Frankfurt; joined by Christiane and August, who leave on August 7. Last meeting with his mother.
August 25, 1797	Leaves Frankfurt.
November 20, 1797	Returns to Weimar.
March 8, 1798	Acquires a landed estate (Oberrossla).
October 17, 1799	Schlosser dies.
March 15, 1800	August (Goethe's *son*) legitimized by Duke's rescript.
January 2, 1801	Seriously ill, danger of suffocation.
December 16, 1802	Kathinka (*daughter*) born.
December 19, 1802	Kathinka dies.
1803	Sells his estate, Oberrossla.
April, 1803	Begins visiting the Frommann family where he meets Minchen Herzlieb.
September, 1803	Wilhelm Riemer becomes August's teacher and Goethe's secretary.
August 3, 1804	Prince Karl Friedrich marries Maria Paulowna.
May 9, 1805	Schiller dies.
October 14, 1806	French invasion of Weimar; Goethe is rescued by Christiane.
October 19, 1806	Marries Christiane.
March 23–April 12, 1807	Christiane is in Frankfurt with Goethe's mother.
1808	First printing of *Zur Farbenlehre,* Vol. I.
September 13, 1808	Goethe's mother dies.
October 2, 1808	First meeting with Napoleon.
October 10, 1808	Second meeting with Napoleon.
1809	First printing of *Die Wahlverwandtschaften.*
October 11, 1809	Begins his autobiography.

Date	*Event*
October 10, 1810	Asks Bettina von Arnim for a report on information his mother had given her.
1811	First printing of *Dichtung und Wahrheit,* Parts I–III.
August 4, 1814	Acquaintance with Marianne Jung (later Willemer).
February 4, 1815	Christiane falls ill.
September 26, 1815	Last meeting with Marianne Willemer.
June 6, 1816	Christiane dies.
July 20, 1816	Accident on a planned trip to Baden-Baden.
December 31, 1816	August engaged to Ottilie von Pogwisch.
April 13, 1817	Dismissed as director of the theater.
June 17, 1817	August marries.
April 9, 1818	Walther Wolfgang (*grandson*) born.
September 18, 1820	Wolfgang Maximilian (*grandson*) born.
1821	First publication of *Wilhelm Meisters Wanderjahre.*
Summer, 1821	Acquaintance with Ulrike von Levetzow in Marienbad.
November, 1821	Meets Felix Mendelssohn-Bartholdy in Weimar.
September 21, 1822	First visit of Frédéric Jean Soret.
June 10, 1823	First visit of Johann Peter Eckermann.
August, 1823	Mournful farewell from Ulrike von Levetzow.
January 6, 1827	Charlotte von Stein dies.
October 29, 1827	Alma (*granddaughter*) born.
June 14, 1828	Karl August dies.
February 14, 1830	Duchess Louise dies.
October 27, 1830	August dies in Rome.
November 25–26, 1830	Suffers pulmonary hemorrhage.
March 16, 1832	Beginning of final illness.
March 17, 1832	Last letter to Wilhelm von Humboldt.
March 22, 1832	Dies.

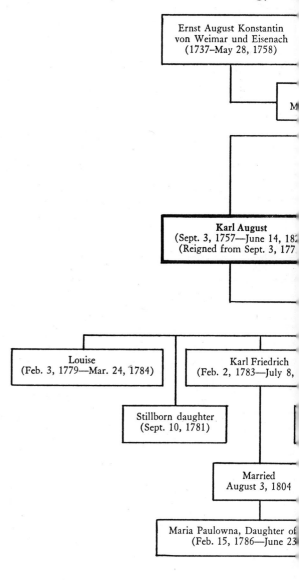

Ernst August Konstantin
von Weimar und Eisenach
(1737–May 28, 1758)

M

Karl August
(Sept. 3, 1757—June 14, 18.
(Reigned from Sept. 3, 177

Louise
(Feb. 3, 1779—Mar. 24, 1784)

Karl Friedrich
(Feb. 2, 1783—July 8,

Stillborn daughter
(Sept. 10, 1781)

Married
August 3, 1804

Maria Paulowna, Daughter of
(Feb. 15, 1786—June 23

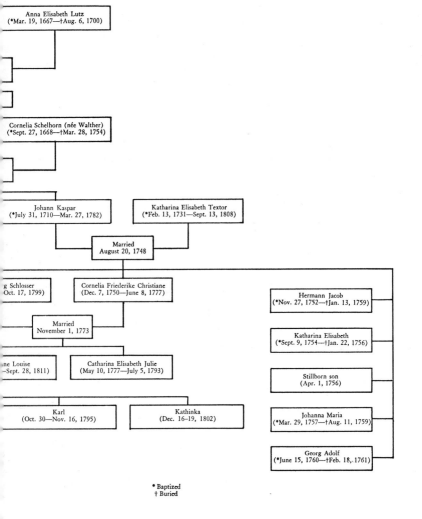

; Goethe

Anna Elisabeth Lutz
(*Mar. 19, 1667—†Aug. 6, 1700)

Cornelia Schelhorn (née Walther)
(*Sept. 27, 1668—†Mar. 28, 1754)

Johann Kaspar
(*July 31, 1710—Mar. 27, 1782)

Katharina Elisabeth Textor
(*Feb. 13, 1731—Sept. 13, 1808)

Married
August 20, 1748

g Schlosser
Oct. 17, 1799)

Cornelia Friederike Christiane
(Dec. 7, 1750—June 8, 1777)

Hermann Jacob
(*Nov. 27, 1752—†Jan. 13, 1759)

Married
November 1, 1773

Katharina Elisabeth
(*Sept. 9, 1754—†Jan. 22, 1756)

ne Louise
—Sept. 28, 1811)

Catharina Elisabeth Julie
(May 10, 1777—July 5, 1793)

Stillborn son
(Apr. 1, 1756)

Karl
(Oct. 30—Nov. 16, 1795)

Kathinka
(Dec. 16–19, 1802)

Johanna Maria
(*Mar. 29, 1757—†Aug. 11, 1759)

Georg Adolf
(*June 15, 1760—†Feb. 18, 1761)

* Baptized
† Buried

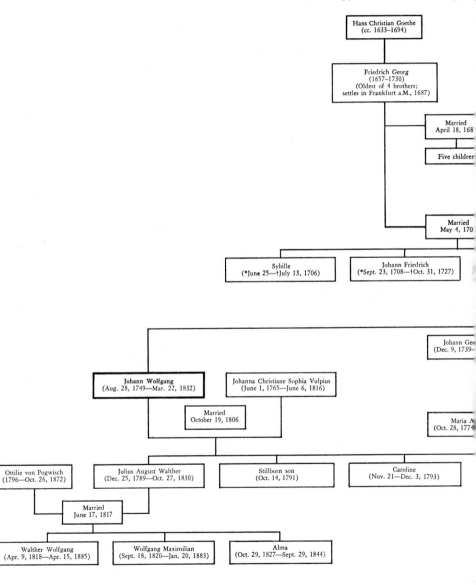

Hans Christian Goethe
(cc. 1633–1694)

Friedrich Georg
(1657–1730)
(Oldest of 4 brothers;
settles in Frankfurt a.M., 1687)

Married
April 18, 168

Five children

Married
May 4, 170

Sybille
(*June 25—†July 13, 1706)

Johann Friedrich
(*Sept. 23, 1708—†Oct. 31, 1727)

Johann Geo
(Dec. 9, 1739–

Johann Wolfgang
(Aug. 28, 1749—Mar. 22, 1832)

Johanna Christiane Sophia Vulpius
(June 1, 1765—June 6, 1816)

Married
October 19, 1806

Maria A
(Oct. 28, 1774

Ottilie von Pogwisch
(1796—Oct. 26, 1872)

Julius August Walther
(Dec. 25, 1789—Oct. 27, 1830)

Stillborn son
(Oct. 14, 1791)

Caroline
(Nov. 21—Dec. 3, 1793)

Married
June 17, 1817

Walther Wolfgang
(Apr. 9, 1818—Apr. 15, 1885)

Wolfgang Maximilian
(Sept. 18, 1820—Jan. 20, 1883)

Alma
(Oct. 29, 1827—Sept. 29, 1844)

arl August, Duke of Weimar

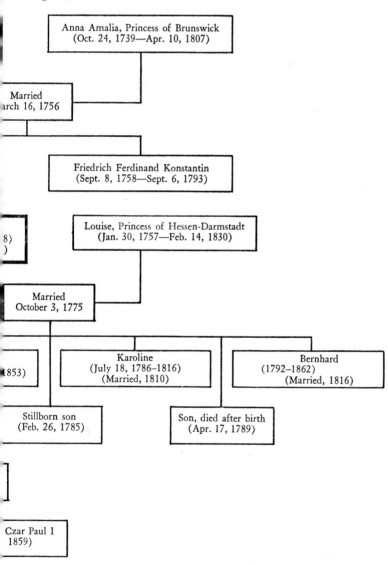

Anna Amalia, Princess of Brunswick
(Oct. 24, 1739—Apr. 10, 1807)

Married
arch 16, 1756

Friedrich Ferdinand Konstantin
(Sept. 8, 1758—Sept. 6, 1793)

Louise, Princess of Hessen-Darmstadt
(Jan. 30, 1757—Feb. 14, 1830)

8)
)

Married
October 3, 1775

853)

Karoline
(July 18, 1786–1816)
(Married, 1810)

Bernhard
(1792–1862)
(Married, 1816)

Stillborn son
(Feb. 26, 1785)

Son, died after birth
(Apr. 17, 1789)

Czar Paul I
1859)

Bibliography of Works Cited

Reference
Number

1   Abraham, Karl. Sollen wir die Patienten ihre Träume aufschreiben lassen? *Internationale Zeitschrift für Psychoanalyse, 1* (1913):194–96.

2   ———. [1924] A Short Study of the Development of the Libido Viewed in the Light of Mental Disorders. *Selected Papers of Karl Abraham,* pp. 418–501. London: Hogarth, 1948.

3   Aichhorn, August. [1925] *Wayward Youth.* New York: Viking, 1939.

4   Alexander, Bernard. Spinoza und die Psychoanalyse. *Almanach für das Jahr 1928,* pp. 94–103. Vienna: Internationaler Psychoanalytischer Verlag, 1928.

5   Alexander, Franz. [1927] The Neurotic Character. *International Journal of Psycho-Analysis, 11* (1930):292–311.

6   ———. *Our Age of Unreason.* Philadelphia: Lippincott, 1942.

7   ——— and Thomas Morton French. *Psychoanalytic Therapy.* New York: Ronald Press, 1946.

8   Allport, Gordon W. *The Use of Personal Documents in Psychological Science.* New York: Social Science Research Council, 1951.

9   Andreas, Willy. Sturm und Drang im Spiegel der Weimarer Hofkreise, II, Zu den Briefen der Gräfin Görtz. *Goethe* (N.F. des Jahrbuchs der Goethe-Gesellschaft), *8* (1943):232–52.

10   ———. *Carl August von Weimar. Ein Leben mit Goethe, 1757–1783.* Stuttgart: Klipper, 1953.

11   Arnim, Bettina von. [1835] *Goethes Briefwechsel mit einem Kinde.* Jonas Fränkel, ed. 3 vols. in 2. Jena: Diederichs, 1906.

12   Bateson, Gregory, and Margaret Mead. *Balinese Character: A Photographic Analysis.* New York: New York Academy of Sciences, 1942.

13   Baumgart, Hermann. *Goethes "Geheimnisse" und seine "Indischen Legenden."* Stuttgart: Cotta, 1895.

Reference
Number

14   Baumgart, Hermann. *Goethes lyrische Dichtung in ihrer Entwicklung und Bedeutung.* 2 vols. Heidelberg: Carl Winters Universitätsbuchhandlung, 1931, 1933.

    Beach, Frank A. *See* Clellan S. Ford.

15   Beaulieu-Marconnay, Carl von. *Anna Amalia, Carl August und der Minister von Fritsch.* Weimar: Böhlau, 1874.

16   Beck, Adolf. Der "Geist der Reinheit" und die "Idee des Reinen." *Goethe* (N.F. des Jahrbuchs der Goethe-Gesellschaft), *7* (1942):160–69; *8* (1943):19–57.

17   Benjamin, Walter. Die Aufgaben des Übersetzers. *Schriften, 1:*40–54. Frankfurt a.M.: Im Suhrkamp Verlag, 1955.

18   Benn, Gottfried. Artists and Old Age. *Partisan Review, 22* (1955):297–319.

19   Berger, Dorothea. Die Volksmärchen der Deutschen von Musäus, Ein Meisterwerk der Deutschen Rokokodichtung. *PMLA, 69* (1954):1200–12.

20   Bergler, Edmund. Can the Writer "Resign" from His Calling? *International Journal of Psycho-Analysis, 34* (1953):40–42.

21   Bergmann, Alfred. *Carl Augusts Begegnungen mit Zeitgenossen.* Weimar: Böhlau, 1933.

22   Bernfeld, Siegfried. Bemerkungen über "Sublimierung." *Imago, 8* (1922):333–43.

23   ———. Über eine typische Form der männlichen Pubertät. *Imago, 9* (1923):169–88.

24   ———. *Vom dichterischen Schaffen der Jugend.* Quellenschriften zur seelischen Entwicklung, vol. *3.* Leipzig, Vienna, Zurich: Internationaler Psychoanalytischer Verlag, 1924.

25   ———. Zur Sublimierungstheorie. *Imago 17* (1931):399–409.

26   ———. Trieb und Tradition im Jugendalter. *Beiheft 54 zur Zeitschrift für angewandte Psychologie.* Leipzig: Barth, 1931.

27   Bernhard, Walter. Freud und Spinoza. *Psychiatry, 9* (1946):99–108.

28   Beutler, Ernst. Die Kindesmörderin. *Essays um Goethe, 1:*100–16. Wiesbaden: Dietrich, 1948.

29   ———. Von der Ilm zum Susquehana (Goethe und Amerika in Ihren Wechselbeziehungen). *Ibid., 1:*462–520.

30   ———, editor. *Briefe aus dem Eltern-Haus.* Erster Ergänzungsband der *Goethe Gedenkausgabe,* Zurich: Artemis, 1960.

31   Bibring, Edward. Psychoanalysis and the Dynamic Psychotherapies. *Journal of the American Psychoanalytic Association, 2* (1954): 754–70.

32   Bidney, David. The Metapsychology of Spinoza. *The Psychology and Ethics of Spinoza,* pp. 386–407. New Haven: Yale University Press, 1940.

33   Bieber, Hugo. Plutarch. *Goethe-Handbuch, 3:*130. Julius Zeitler, ed. 3 vols. Stuttgart: Metzler, 1916–18.

34   Biedermann, Flodoard Frhr. von [Philologus]. *Intermezzi scandalosi aus Goethes Leben.* Berlin: Berthold, 1925.

Reference
Number

35   Biedermann, Woldemar Frhr. von. *Goethe und Leipzig.* 2 vols. Leipzig: Brockhaus, 1865.

36   ———. *Goethe-Forschungen.* Frankfurt a.M.: Rütten und Loening, 1879.

36A   ———. *Ibid., Neue Folge.* 1886.

37   Bleisch, P., editor. *Bilder aus Ilmenaus Vergangenheit.* Ilmenau: Schröter, 1910.

38   Bloch, Robert. Goethe, Idealistic Morphology and Science. *American Scientist, 40* (1952):313–22.

39   Boccaccio, Giovanni. *The Decameron.* London: Routledge, 1891.

40   Bode, Wilhelm, editor. *Stunden mit Goethe.* 10 vols. Berlin: Mittler, 1904–14.

41   ———. Charlotte von Stein in der Schilderung ihrer Verwandten. *Ibid., 4* (1908):217–20.

42   ———. Frau von Branconi. *Ibid., 5* (1909):14–59.

43   ———. Briefe der Frau von Stein an Knebel. *Ibid., 6* (1910):153–99.

44   ———. Frau von Stein als Figur im Werther. *Ibid., 6* (1910):215–19.

45   ———. *Amalie Herzogin von Weimar. Das vorgoethische Weimar.* Berlin: Mittler, 1908.

46   ———. *Goethe und die Tonkunst.* 2 vols. Berlin: Mittler, 1912.

47   ———. *Karl August von Weimar. Jugendjahre.* Berlin: Mittler, 1913.

48   ———. *Weib und Sittlichkeit in Goethes Leben und Denken.* Berlin: Mittler, 1916.

49   ———. *Charlotte von Stein.* Berlin: Mittler, 1917.

50   ———. *Goethes Sohn.* Berlin: Mittler, 1918.

51   ———, editor. *Goethe in vertraulichen Briefen seiner Zeitgenossen.* 3 vols. Berlin: Mittler, 1918–23.

52   ———. *Die Schicksale der Friederike Brion vor und nach ihrem Tode.* Berlin: Mittler, 1920.

53   ———. *Goethes Leben: Lehrjahre 1749–1771.* Berlin: Mittler, 1920.

54   ———. *Neues über Goethes Liebe.* Berlin: Mittler, 1921.

55   ———. *Goethes Schweizer Reisen.* Leipzig: Haessel, 1922.

56   Bojanowski, P. von. Johann Caspar Goethe in Venedig. *Weimars Festgrüsse,* pp. 3–54. Weimar: Böhlau, 1899.

57   Bolk, L. *Das Problem der Menschwerdung.* Jena: Fischer, 1926.

58   Bonaparte, Marie. [1939] Time and the Unconscious. *International Journal of Psycho-Analysis, 21* (1940):427–68.

59   ———. *The Life and Works of Edgar Allan Poe.* London: Imago, 1949.

60   Borcherdt, Hans-Heinrich, editor. *Briefwechsel zwischen Schiller und Goethe.* 2 vols. Berlin, Leipzig, Vienna, Stuttgart: Bong, 1914.

61   Bornhak, F. *Anna Amalia Herzogin von Sachsen-Weimar-Eisenach.* Berlin: Fontane, 1892.

62   Both, Rudolphine von. Unser Besuch bei Knebels. *Stunden mit Goethe, 3* (1907):262–78. Wilhelm Bode, ed. 10 vols. Berlin: Mittler, 1904–14.

63   Bradisch, Joseph A. von. *Goethe als Erbe seiner Ahnen.* Berlin, New York: B. Westermann, 1933.

Reference
Number

64   Bradisch, Joseph A. von. *Goethes Erhebung in den Reichsadelstand.* Leipzig: Lorentz, 1933.

65   ———. *Goethes Beamtenlaufbahn.* New York: B. Westermann, 1937.

66   ———. Goethe und Christiane. *The German Quarterly, 20* (March, 1947): 109–21.

67   Brauning-Oktavio, H. Juristischer Beruf Goethes. *Goethe-Handbuch,* 2:289–91. Julius Zeitler, ed. 3 vols. Stuttgart: Metzler, 1916–18.

68   Briefe Zimmermanns und Charlottens von Schiller an Charlotte und Friedrich von Stein. *Mitteilungen aus dem Literaturarchiv in Berlin,* 1897.

69   Brill, A. A. *Freud's Contribution to Psychiatry.* New York: Norton, 1944.

70   Brown, Thomas K., Jr. Goethe's "Lila" as a Fragment of the Great Confession. *Studies in Honour of John Albrecht Walz,* pp. 209–20. Lancaster, Pa.: Lancaster Press, 1941.

71   Brunswick, Ruth Mack. The Preoedipal Phase of the Libido Development. *Psychoanalytic Quarterly, 9* (1940):293–319.

72   Buckley, Theodore Alois, editor and translator. *The Tragedies of Aeschylus.* London: Bohn, 1849.

73   Buder, Hildegard. Goethes Traum vom Fasanenkahn. *Psyche, 3* (1949): 507–12.

74   Bühler, Charlotte. *Der Menschliche Lebenslauf als Psychologisches Problem.* Psychologische Monographien, vol. 4. Karl Bühler, ed. Leipzig: Hirzel, 1933.

75   Bühler, Karl. *The Mental Development of the Child.* London: Routledge, Kegan, Paul, 1949.

76   Burdach, Konrad. [1885] Die Sprache des jungen Goethe. *Goethe und sein Zeitalter,* pp. 61–72. Vol. 2 of *Vorspiel; gesammelte Schriften zur Geschichte des Deutschen Geistes.* Halle, Salle: Niemeyer, 1926.

77   ———. Faust und Moses. *Sitzungsberichte der Preussischen Akademie der Wissenschaften Philos.-hist. Klasse,* 1:358–403; 2:627–59; 3:736–89. Berlin, 1912.

78   Burkhardt, C. A. H. Jugend und Erziehung Karl Augusts von Weimar. *Westermanns Jahrbuch der Illustrierten Deutschen Monatshefte, 17* (1864–65):460–70.

79   Burlingham, Dorothy Tiffany. Die Einfühlung des Klein-Kindes in die Mutter. *Imago, 21* (1935):429–44.

80   ———. *Twins.* London: Imago, 1952.

81   Buxbaum, Edith. Freud's Dream Interpretations in the Light of His Letters to Fliess. *Bulletin, Menninger Clinic, 15* (1951):197–212.

82   Bychowski, Gustav. Metapsychology of Artistic Creation. *Psychoanalytic Quarterly, 20* (1951):592–602.

83   ———. From Catharsis to Work of Art: The Making of an Artist. *Psychoanalysis and Culture,* pp. 390–409. New York: International Universities Press, 1951.

84   Carletta. *Goethe a Roma.* Rome: Editrice Dante Alighieri, 1899.

Reference
Number

85   Carus, Carl Gustav. [1842] *Goethe*. Leipzig: Kroner, n.d.

85A   Cary, R. J. A Brief History of the Methods of Resuscitation of the Apparently Drowned. *Johns Hopkins Bulletin, 24* (1913): 243–51.

86   Cassirer, Ernst. Goethe und die mathematische Physik. *Idee und Gestalt*, pp. 27–76. Berlin: Bruno Cassirer, 1921.

87   Chekhov, Anton. *Three Plays*. Elisaveta Fen, ed. and trans. London, Baltimore, Melbourne: Penguin Books, 1951.

88   Cicero. [45 B.C.] *Tusculan Disputations*. J. E. King, ed. and trans. Loeb Classical Library. Cambridge: Harvard University Press, 1950.

89   ———. *Tuskulanische Gespräche*. (German edition of the above.) A. Kabza, ed. and trans. Munich: Goldmann, 1959.

90   Coleman, Rose W., Ernst Kris, and Sally Provence. The Study of Variations of Early Parental Attitudes. *Psychoanalytic Study of the Child, 8* (1953):20–47.

91   Daly, C. D. The Role of Menstruation in Human Phylogenesis and Ontogenesis. *International Journal of Psycho-Analysis, 24* (1943):151–70.

92   David, Frida. *Friedrich Heinrich Jacobis "Woldemar" in seinen verschiedenen Fassungen*. Leipzig: Voigtländer, 1930.

93   De Buisonjé, Johannes Cornelius. *Charlotte von Stein und Christiane Vulpius Spätere von Goethe in Goethes Lyrik*. Netherlands: C. A. J. Van Dishoeck Bussum, 1923.

94   Dechent [Hermann]. Die autobiographische Quelle der Bekenntnisse einer schönen Seele. *Berichte des Freien Deutschen Hochstiftes zu Frankfurt am Main, 13* (1897):10–59.

95   Deile, Gotthold. *Goethe als Freimaurer*. Berlin: Mittler, 1908.

96   Dennert, Friedrich. *Goethe und der Harz*. Quedlinburg: Verlag Harzer Meimatbücher, 1920.

97   Deri, Frances. On Sublimation. *Psychoanalytic Quarterly, 8* (1939):325–34.

98   Deutsch, Helene. Über Zufriedenheit, Glück und Ekstase. *Internationale Zeitschrift für Psychoanalyse, 13* (1927):410–19.

99   ———. *The Psychology of Women*. 2 vols. New York: Grune and Stratton, 1944–45.

100   Diderot, Denis. [1773] *Jacques le fataliste et son maître*. Paris: Delmas, 1948.

101   Diem, Carl. *Körpererziehung bei Goethe*. Frankfurt a.M.: Kramer, 1948.

102   Diezmann, August. *Aus Weimars Glanzzeit*. Leipzig: Hermann Hartung, 1855.

103   Dilthey, Wilhelm. [1894] Aus der Zeit der Spinozastudien Goethes. *Gesammelte Schriften, 2*:391–415. Leipzig: Teubner, 1921.

104   ———. [1905] *Das Erlebnis und die Dichtung*. Leipzig: Teubner, 1910.

105   Du Halde, Jean Baptiste. [1736] *The General History of China*. 3rd ed. 4 vols. London: J. Watts, 1741.

105A   Düntzer, Heinrich. *Frauenbilder aus Goethes Jugendzeit*. Stuttgart, Tübingen: Cotta, 1852.

Reference Number

106 Düntzer, Heinrich. *Aus Goethes Freundeskreise*. Braunschweig: Friedrich Vieweg, 1868.

107 ――. *Charlotte von Stein, Goethes Freundin*. 2 vols. Stuttgart: Cotta, 1874.

108 ――. *Charlotte von Stein und Corona Schröter. Eine Vertheidigung*. Stuttgart: Cotta, 1876.

109 ――. Goethes Gedichte auf dem Gickelhahn vom 2. und 3. September 1783. *Archiv für Literaturgeschichte, 8* (1879):491–503.

110 ――. Die Zuverlässigkeit von Goethes Angaben über seine eigenen Werke in "Dichtung und Wahrheit." *Goethe-Jahrbuch, 1* (1880): 140–54.

111 ――. *Goethes Eintritt in Weimar*. Leipzig: Wartig, 1883.

112 ――. Gretchen. *Abhandlungen zu Goethes Leben und Werken*, 1:32–65. 2 vols. Leipzig: Wartig, 1885.

113 ――. *Goethe und Karl August*. Leipzig: Dyk, 1888.

114 ――. *Freundesbilder aus Goethes Leben*. Leipzig: Dyk, n.d.

115 Dürler, Josef. *Die Bedeutung des Bergbaues bei Goethe*. Frauenfeld, Leipzig: Huber, 1936.

116 Dyck, Martin. Goethe's Views on Pure Mathematics. *The German Review*, 1956, pp. 49–69.

117 ――. Goethe's Thought in the Light of his Pronouncements on Applied and Misapplied Mathematics. *PMLA, 73* (1958):505–15.

118 Eberwein, Karl. Goethes Hausmusik. *Stunden mit Goethe, 7* (1911):276. Wilhelm Bode, ed. 10 vols. Berlin: Mittler, 1904–14.

119 Eckermann, Johann Peter. [1885] *Gespräche mit Goethe in den letzten Jahren seines Lebens*. H. H. Houben, ed. Leipzig: Brockhaus, 1910.

120 Edmonds, J. M., translator. *The Greek Bucolic Poets*. Loeb Classical Library. Cambridge: Harvard University Press, 1912.

121 ――, editor and translator. *Greek Elegy and Iambus with the Anacreontea*. 2 vols. Loeb Classical Library. Cambridge: Harvard University Press, 1954.

122 Ehrenberg, Rudolf. *Theoretische Biologie*. Berlin: Springer, 1923.

123 Eisler, Rudolf. *Philosophen-Lexikon*. Berlin: Mittler, 1912.

124 Eissler, K. R. On Hamlet. *Samiksa, 7* (1953):85–202. (Revised edition in preparation by International Universities Press, New York.)

125 Engel, J. J. *Herr Lorenz Stark. Ein Charaktergemälde*. 2nd ed. Berlin: Mylius, 1806.

126 Epstein, Paul. Goethe und die Mathematik. *Jahrbuch der Goethe-Gesellschaft, 10* (1924): 76–102.

127 Erikson, Erik Homburger. The Dream Specimen of Psychoanalysis. *Journal of the American Psychoanalytic Association, 2* (1954):5–56.

128 Ernst, Fritz. *Aus Goethes Freundeskreis. Studien um Peter im Baumgarten*. Erlenbach, Zurich: Rentsch, 1941.

129 Fairbairn, W. R. D. Prolegomena to a Psychology of Art. *British Journal of Psychology, 28* (1938):288–303.

Reference
Number

130   ——. The Ultimate Basis of Aesthetic Experience. *Ibid.*, *29* (1938): 167–81.

131   Fairley, Barker. *A Study of Goethe.* Oxford: Clarendon Press, 1947.

132   Falck, P. T. *Der Dichter Lenz in Livland.* Westfehling: Winterthur, 1878.

133   Fambach, Oscar. *Goethe und seine Kritiker.* Düsseldorf: Ehlermann, 1953.

134   Federn, Etta. *Christiane und Goethe.* Munich: Delphin, 1916.

135   Fenichel, Otto. *Hysterien und Zwangsneurosen.* Vienna: Internationaler Psychoanalytischer Verlag, 1931.

136   ——. [1934] Further Light upon the Pre-oedipal Phase in Girls. *Collected Papers,* 1st series, pp. 241–88. New York: Norton, 1953.

137   ——. [1937] The Concept of Trauma in Contemporary Psychoanalytical Theory. *Ibid.*, 2nd series, pp. 49–69. New York: Norton, 1954.

138   ——. [1939] The Counter-Phobic Attitude. *Ibid.*, 2nd series, pp. 163–73.

139   ——. *The Psychoanalytic Theory of Neuroses.* New York: Norton, 1945.

140   Ferenczi, Sandor. [1919] The Phenomena of Hysterical Materialization. *Further Contributions to the Theory and Technique of Psycho-Analysis,* pp. 89–105. International Psycho-Analytical Library, No. 11. London: Hogarth, 1950.

141   ——. [1923] On the Symbolism of the Head of Medusa. *Ibid.*, p. 360.

142   ——. [1926] The Problem of Acceptance of Unpleasant Ideas. *Ibid.*, pp. 366–79.

143   ——. Stages in the Development of the Sense of Reality. *Sex in Psychoanalysis,* pp. 213–39. New York: Robert Brunner, 1950.

144   Fielitz, Wilhelm. *Goethestudien.* Abhandlung zu dem Programm des Wittenberger Gymnasiums. Wittenberg: Löbcke, 1881.

145   Fischer, Hans. *Goethes Naturwissenschaft.* Zurich: Artemis, 1950.

146   Fischer, Paul. *Goethe-Wortschatz.* Leipzig: Rohmkopf, 1929.

147   Fischer-Lamberg, Hanna. Charlotte von Stein, ein Bildungserlebnis Goethes. *Deutsche Vierteljahrsschrift für Literaturwissenschaft und Geistesgeschichte, 15* (1937):385–402.

148   Flügel, J. C. Polyphallic Symbolism and the Castration Complex. *International Journal of Psycho-Analysis, 5* (1924): 155–96.

149   Ford, Clellan S., and Frank A. Beach. *Patterns of Sexual Behavior.* New York: Harper, 1951.

150   Forssmann, Julius. *J. K. Lavater und die religiösen Strömungen des 18. Jahrhunderts.* Riga: Ernst Plates, 1935.

151   Forster, J. G. *A Voyage Round the World.* London: B. White, 1777. (German edition: *Reise um die Welt.* 2 vols. Berlin: Haude und Speuer, 1778–80.)

152   Fraiberg, Selma. [1956] Kafka and the Dream. *Art and Psychoanalysis,* pp. 21–53. William Phillips, ed. New York: Criterion, 1957.

French, Thomas Morton. *See* Franz Alexander, 1927.

Reference
Number

153   Freud, Anna. [1936] *The Ego and the Mechanisms of Defense.* New York: International Universities Press, 1946.

154   ———. Asceticism at Puberty. *Ibid.,* pp. 167–72.

155   Freud, Sigmund. [1887–1902] *The Origins of Psycho-Analysis. Letters to Wilhelm Fliess, Drafts and Notes: 1887–1902.* Marie Bonaparte, Anna Freud, Ernst Kris, eds. New York: Basic Books, 1954.

156   ———. [1892] A Case of Successful Treatment by Hypnotism with Some Remarks on the Origin of Hysterical Symptoms through 'Counter-Will.' *Collected Papers,* 5:33–46. 5 vols. London: Hogarth Press and the Institute of Psycho-Analysis, 1924–50.

157   ———. [1899] Screen Memories. *Coll. Pap.,* 5:47–69.

158   ———. [1900] The Interpretations of Dreams. *Standard Edition of the Complete Psychological Works of Sigmund Freud,* vols. 4, 5. 24 vols. planned. London: Hogarth Press and the Institute of Psycho-Analysis, 1953– .

159   ———. [1901] The Psychopathology of Everyday Life. *Stand. Ed.,* vol. *6.*

160   ———. [1905] Fragment of an Analysis of a Case of Hysteria. *Stand. Ed.,* 7:7–122.

161   ———. [1905] Jokes and their Relation to the Unconscious. *Stand. Ed.,* vol. *8.*

162   ———. [1905] Psychical (or Mental) Treatment. *Stand. Ed.,* 7:283–302.

163   ———. [1905] Three Essays on the Theory of Sexuality. *Stand. Ed.,* 7: 130–243.

164   ———. [1908] Character and Anal Erotism. *Stand. Ed.,* 9:169–75.

165   ———. [1908] 'Civilized' Sexual Morality and Modern Nervous Illness. *Stand. Ed.,* 9:181–204.

166   ———. [1908] Creative Writers and Day-Dreaming. *Stand. Ed.,* 9:143–53.

167   ———. [1909] Analysis of a Phobia in a Five-Year-Old Boy. *Stand. Ed.,* 10:5–149.

168   ———. [1909] Family Romances. *Stand. Ed.,* 9:237–41.

169   ———. [1910] The Future Prospects of Psycho-Analytic Therapy. *Stand. Ed.,* 11:141–51.

170   ———. [1910] Leonardo da Vinci and a Memory of his Childhood. *Stand. Ed.,* 11:63–137.

171   ———. [1910] A Special Type of Choice of Object Made by Men. *Stand. Ed.,* 11:165–75.

172   ———. [1911] Formulations on the Two Principles of Mental Functioning. *Stand. Ed.,* 12:218–26.

173   ———. [1911] Psycho-Analytic Notes on an Autobiographical Account of a Case of Paranoia (Dementia Paranoides). *Stand. Ed.,* 12:9–82.

174   ———. [1912] The Handling of Dream Interpretation in Psycho-Analysis. *Stand. Ed.,* 12:91–96.

175   ———. [1913] The Claims of Psycho-Analysis to Scientific Interest. *Stand. Ed.,* 13:165–90.

Reference
Number

176 ———. [1913] The Disposition to Obsessional Neurosis. A Contribution to the Problem of Choice of Neurosis. *Stand. Ed.*, 12:317–26.

177 ———. [1913] The Theme of the Three Caskets. *Stand. Ed.*, 12:291–301.

178 ———. [1914] On Narcissism: An Introduction. *Stand. Ed.*, 14:73–102.

179 ———. [1915] Instincts and their Vicissitudes. *Stand. Ed.*, 14:117–40.

180 ———. [1915] Observations on Transference-Love. (Further Recommendations on the Technique of Psycho-Analysis, III.) *Stand. Ed.*, 12:159–71.

181 ———. [1915] Some Character-Types Met with in Psycho-Analytic Work, II. Those Wrecked by Success. *Stand. Ed.*, 14:316–31.

182 ———. [1915] Thoughts for the Times on War and Death. *Stand. Ed.*, 14:275–300.

183 ———. [1915] The Unconscious. Stand. Ed., 14:166–204.

184 ———. [1916] A Metapsychological Supplement to the Theory of Dreams. *Stand. Ed.*, 14:222–35.

185 ———. [1917] A Childhood Recollection from *Dichtung und Wahrheit*. *Stand. Ed.*, 17:147–56.

186 ———. [1917] Mourning and Melancholia. *Stand. Ed.*, 14:243–58.

187 ———. [1917] *A General Introduction to Psycho-Analysis*. New York: Garden City Publishing Co., 1938.

188 ———. [1918] From the History of an Infantile Neurosis. *Stand. Ed.*, 17:7–122.

189 ———. [1918] The Taboo of Virginity. (Contributions to the Psychology of Love, III.) *Stand. Ed.*, 11:193–208.

190 ———. [1919] The Uncanny. *Stand. Ed.*, 17:219–52.

191 ———. [1920] Beyond the Pleasure Principle. *Stand. Ed.*, 18:7–64.

192 ———. [1920] The Psychogenesis of a Case of Homosexuality in a Woman. *Stand. Ed.*, 18:147–72.

193 ———. [1921] Group Psychology and the Analysis of the Ego. *Stand. Ed.*, 18:69–143.

194 ———. [1922] Some Neurotic Mechanisms in Jealousy, Paranoia and Homosexuality. *Stand. Ed.*, 18:223–32.

195 ———. [1922] Dream and Telepathy. *Stand. Ed.*, 18:197–220.

196 ———. [1922] Medusa's Head. *Stand. Ed.*, 18:273–74.

197 ———. [1923] The Ego and the Id. *Stand. Ed.*, 19:12–66.

198 ———. [1923] The Infantile Genital Organization. (An interpolation into the Theory of Sexuality.) *Stand. Ed.*, 19:141–45.

199 ———. [1924] The Economic Problem of Masochism. *Stand. Ed.*, 19:159–70.

200 ———. [1924] The Loss of Reality in Neurosis and Psychosis. *Stand. Ed.*, 19:183–87.

201 ———. [1924] Neurosis and Psychosis. *Stand. Ed.*, 19:149–53.

202 ———. [1924] The Dissolution of the Oedipus Complex. *Stand. Ed.*, 19:173–79.

203 ———. [1925] Negation. *Stand. Ed.*, 19:235–39.

*Reference
Number*

204   Freud, Sigmund. [1925] Some Psychical Consequences of the Anatomical Distinction Between the Sexes. *Stand. Ed., 19*:243–58.

205   ———. [1926] Inhibitions, Symptoms and Anxiety. *Stand. Ed., 20*:87–172.

206   ———. [1927] Fetishism. *Stand. Ed., 21*:152–57.

207   ———. [1930] Address Delivered in the Goethe House at Frankfurt. *Stand. Ed., 21*:208–12.

208   ———. [1930] Civilization and Its Discontents. *Stand. Ed., 21*:64–145.

209   ———. [1931] Female Sexuality. *Stand. Ed., 21*:225–43.

210   ———. [1932] *New Introductory Lectures on Psycho-Analysis.* New York: Norton, 1933.

211   ———. [1932] The Acquisition of Power over Fire. *Coll. Pap., 5*:288–94.

212   ———. [1936] A Disturbance of Memory on the Acropolis. *Coll. Pap., 5*:302–12.

213   ———. [1936] Entwurf zu einem Brief an Thomas Mann. *Zeitschrift für Psychoanalyse und Imago. 26* (1941):217–19.

214   ———. [1937] Analysis Terminable and Interminable. *Coll. Pap., 5*: 316–57.

215   ———. [1938] Splitting of the Ego in the Defensive Process. *Coll. Pap., 5*:372–75.

216   ———. [1939] *Moses and Monotheism.* London: Hogarth, 1951.

217   ———. [1940] *An Outline of Psycho-Analysis.* New York: Norton, 1949.

218   Freye, Karl, and Wolfgang Stammler, editors. *Briefe von und an J. M. R. Lenz.* 2 vols. Leipzig: Wolff, 1918.

219   Fromm-Reichmann, Frieda. Das Jüdische Speiseritual. *Imago, 13* (1927): 235–46.

220   Fuchs, Eduard. *Illustrierte Sittengeschichte vom Mittelalter bis zur Gegenwart.* 3 vols in 6. Munich: Langen, 1909–12.

221   ———. *Geschichte der Erotischen Kunst.* 3 vols. Munich: Langen, n.d.

222   Fuchs, Johannes. *Advokat Goethe.* Weimar: Böhlau, 1932.

223   Funck, Heinrich. Die Wanderjahre der Frau von Branconi. *Westermanns Monatshefte, 79* (1895–96):172–84.

224   ———. Zehn Briefe von Susanna Katharina von Klettenberg an J. K. Lavater. *Goethe-Jahrbuch, 16* (1895):83–96.

225   ———, editor. *Goethe und Lavater. Briefe und Tagebücher.* Schriften der Goethe-Gesellschaft, vol. *16*. Weimar, 1901.

226   Gaedertz, Karl Theodor. *Bei Goethe zu Gaste.* Leipzig: Wigand, 1900.

227   Garraty, John A. The Interrelations of Psychology and Biography. *Psychological Bulletin, 51* (1954): 569–82.

228   Gebhardt, Martin. *Goethe als Physiker.* Berlin: Grote, 1932.

229   Geiger, Ludwig. Aus seltenen und vergessenen Büchern. *Goethe-Jahrbuch, 7* (1886):361–66.

230   Geitel, Max. *Entlegene Spuren Goethes.* Munich, Berlin: Oldenburg, 1911.

231   Gibb, John. Goethe's Friendship with Lavater. *The Hibbert Journal, 13* (1914–15):190–202.

Reference
Number

232   Glaser, Rudolf. *Goethes Vater.* Leipzig: Quelle and Meyer, 1929.

233   Gloël, Heinrich. *Goethes Wetzlarer Zeit.* Berlin: Mittler, 1911.

234   Glover, Edward. The Psycho-Analysis of Affects. *International Journal of Psycho-Analysis, 20* (1939):299–307.

235   Goedecke, Karl. Zu Goethe und Schiller. *Archiv für Literaturgeschichte, 8* (1879):101–10.

236   Goethe, Johann Kaspar. *Viaggio in Italia.* Arturo Farinelli, ed. 2 vols. Rome: Reale Accademia d'Italia, 1932–33.

237   Goethe, Johann Wolfgang. [1781] Nachricht von dem Ilmenauischen Bergwesen. *Schriften zur Geologie und Mineralogie, 1770–1810,* pp. 15–28. *Die Schriften zur Naturwissenschaft.* Erste Abteilung: Texte, vol. *1.* Günther Schmid, ed. Weimar: Deutsche Akademie der Naturforscher zur Halle, 1947.

238   ———. [1783] Nachricht von dem ehmaligen Bergbau bei Ilmenau. *Ibid.,* pp. 32–55.

239   ———. [1808] *Faust.* Georg Witkowski, ed. 10th ed. Leiden: Brill, 1950.

240   ———. [1826] *Maximen und Reflexionen.* Max Hecker, ed. Schriften der Goethe-Gesellschaft, vol. *21.* Weimar, 1907.

241   ———. *Briefe und Aufsätze von Goethe aus den Jahren 1766 bis 1786.* Adolf Schöll, ed. Weimar: Landes-Industrie-Comptoirs, 1846.

242   ———. *Goethes Briefe an Frau von Stein aus den Jahren 1776 bis 1826.* Adolf Schöll, ed. 3 vols. Weimar: Landes-Industrie-Comptoirs, 1848–51.

243   ———. *Ibid.* 2nd ed. Wilhelm Fielitz, ed. 2 vols. Frankfurt a.M.: Rütten and Loening, 1883–85.

244   ———. *Ibid.* 3rd ed. Julius Wahle, ed. 2 vols. Frankfurt a.M.: Rütten and Loening, 1899, 1900.

245   ———. *Briefwechsel zwischen Goethe und Knebel (1774–1832).* 2 vols. in 1. Leipzig: Brockhaus, 1851.

246   ———. [1870] *Unterhaltungen mit dem Kanzler Friedrich von Müller.* C. A. H. Burkhardt, ed. 3rd ed. Stuttgart, Berlin: Cotta, 1904.

247   ———. *Goethes Werke.* Herausgegeben im Auftrage der Grossherzogin Sophie von Sachsen. Sophienausgabe (referred to in the text as *Soph.*). Weimar: Böhlau, 1887–1918.

——— I. Goethes Werke. 55 vols. 1887–1918.

——— II. Goethes Naturwissenschaftliche Schriften. 13 vols. 1890–1904.

——— III. Goethes Tagebücher. 15 vols. 1887–1903.

——— IV. Goethes Briefe. 50 vols. 1887–1912.

248   ———. *Goethes Sämtliche Werke.* Jubiläums-Ausgabe. 40 vols. Eduard von der Hellen, *et al.,* eds. Stuttgart, Berlin: Cotta, 1902–07.

249   ———. *Goethes Briefe an Charlotte von Stein.* Jonas Fränkel, ed. 2 vols. Jena: Diederichs, 1908.

250   ———. *Goethes Gespräche.* Flodoard Frhr. von Biedermann, ed. 5 vols. Leipzig: Gesamtausgabe, 1909–11.

251   ———. *Der junge Goethe.* Max Morris, ed. 6 vols. Leipzig: Insel, 1909–12.

Number
Reference

252   Goethe, Johann Wolfgang. *Goethes Briefwechsel mit seiner Frau.* Hans
       Gerhard Gräf, ed. 2 vols. Frankfurt a.M.: Rütten and Loening, 1916.
253   ———. *Lyrische und epische Dichtungen. Goethes Gedichte in Zeitlicher
       Folge,* vol. *1.* Hans Gerhard Gräf, ed. Leipzig: Insel, 1916.
254   ———. *Goethes Briefe an Charlotte von Stein.* Julius Petersen, ed. 3 vols.
       in 2. Leipzig: Insel, 1923.
255   ———. *Goethe, Die Schriften zur Naturwissenschaft.* Weimar: Deutsche
       Akademie der Naturforscher zur Halle, 1947.
256   ———. *Johann Wolfgang Goethe. Gedenkausgabe der Werke, Briefe und
       Gespräche.* Artemis edition. 24 vols. Ernst Beutler, ed. Zurich, 1948–50.
257   ———. *Goethes Tätigkeit im Geheimen Consilium, 1776–1786. Goethes
       Amtliche Schriften,* vol. *1.* Willy Flach, ed. Weimar: Böhlau, 1950.
258   ———. *Goethes Werke.* Karl Heinemann, ed. 15 vols. Leipzig, Vienna:
       Bibliographisches Institut, n.d.
259   Gothein, Eberhard. *Johann Georg Schlosser als badischer Beamter.* Hei-
       delberg: Carl Winter, 1899.
260   Götting, Franz, editor. *Chronik von Goethes Leben.* Leipzig: Insel, 1949.
261   Gräf, Hans Gerhard. *Goethe über seine Dichtungen.* 9 vols. Frankfurt
       a.M.: Rütten and Loening, 1901–14.
262   ———, editor. *Johann Heinrich Mercks Briefe an die Herzogin-Mutter
       Anna Amalia und an den Herzog Carl August von Sachsen-Weimar.*
       Leipzig: Insel, 1911.
263   Gray, Ronald D. *Goethe the Alchemist.* New York: Cambridge Univer-
       sity Press, 1952.
264   Greenacre, Phyllis. Vision, Headache, and the Halo. *Psychoanalytic
       Quarterly, 16* (1947):1777–94.
265   ———. Certain Relationships between Fetishism and the Faulty Develop-
       ment of the Body Image. *Psychoanalytic Study of the Child, 8* (1953):
       74–98.
266   ———. The Childhood of the Artist. *Ibid., 12* (1957):47–72.
267   Greenson, Ralph R. Forepleasure: Its Use for Defensive Purposes. *Journal
       of the American Psychoanalytic Association, 3* (1955):244–54.
       Grolman, Adolf von. *See* Georg Simmel, 1918.
268   Grotefend, H. Zur Geschichte der Familie Goethe. *Mittheilungen an
       die Mitglieder des Vereins für Geschichte und Alterthumskunde in
       Frankfurt a.M., 6* (1881):225–37.
269   Gruppe, O. F. *Reinhold Lenz.* Berlin: A. Charisius, 1861.
270   Gundolf, Friedrich. [1916] *Goethe.* 2nd ed. Berlin: Bondi, 1917.
271   ———. *Caesar, Geschichte eines Ruhms.* Berlin: Bondi, 1924.
272   Gutman, James, editor. *Ethics of Benedict de Spinoza.* New York: Haf-
       ner, 1949.
273   Häcker, Valentin. Zwischenkiefer. *Goethes morphologische Arbeiten und
       die neuere Forschung,* pp. 5–16. Jena: Fischer, 1927.
274   Hárnik, Jenö. Psychoanalytisches aus und über Goethes Wahlverwandt-
       schaften. *Imago, 1* (1912):507–18.

Number
Reference

275   ———. Nachtrag zur Kenntnis der Rettungsphantasie bei Goethe. *Internationale Zeitschrift für Psychoanalyse*, 5 (1919):120–21.

276   Hartmann, Heinz. [1939] *Ego Psychology and the Problem of Adaptation*. David Rapaport, trans. Monograph Series No. 1, *Journal of the American Psychoanalytic Association*. New York: International Universities Press, 1958.

277   ———. On Rational and Irrational Action. *Psychoanalysis and the Social Sciences, 1* (1947):359–92.

278   ———, Ernst Kris and Rudolph M. Loewenstein. Comments on the Formation of Psychic Structure. *Psychoanalytic Study of the Child, 2* (1947):11–38.

279   ———. Contribution to the Metapsychology of Schizophrenia. *Ibid., 8* (1953):177–98.

280   ———. Notes on the Theory of Sublimation. *Ibid., 10* (1955):9–29.

281   Hartung, Fritz. Ein Gutachten über die Vereinfachung des Kanzleistils. Neue Mitteilungen aus Goethes amtlicher Tätigkeit, pp. 262–64. *Jahrbuch der Goethe-Gesellschaft, 6* (1919):252–82.

282   ———. *Das Grossherzogtum Sachsen unter der Regierung Carl Augusts 1775–1828.* Weimar: Böhlau, 1923.

283   Heinemann, Karl. *Goethes Mutter.* Leipzig: Seemann, 1893.

284   ———. *Goethe.* 2 vols. Leipzig: Seemann, 1895.

285   Heisenberg, Werner. The Teachings of Goethe and Newton on Colour in the Light of Modern Physics. *Philosophic Problems of Nuclear Science*, pp. 60–76. New York: Pantheon, 1952.

286   Hellen, Eduard von der. *Goethes Anteil an Lavaters Physiognomischen Fragmenten.* Frankfurt a.M.: Rütten and Loening, 1888.

287   ———, editor. *Das Journal von Tiefurt.* Introduction by Bernhard Suphan. Schriften der Goethe-Gesellschaft, vol. 7. Weimar, 1892.

288   Helmholtz, Hermann von. [1892] Goethes Vorahnungen kommender naturwissenschaftlicher Ideen. *Vorträge und Reden*, 2:335–361. 2 vols. Braunschweig: Vieweg, 1903.

289   Hendrick, Ives. Work and the Pleasure Principle. *Psychoanalytic Quarterly, 12* (1943): 311–29.

290   ———. The Discussion of the "Instinct to Master." *Ibid., 12* (1943): 561–65.

291   Henschele, Otto. *Herzogin Anna Amalia.* Munich: Bruckmann, 1949.

292   Hering, Robert. Herr Rat Goethe als Kläger vor dem Frankfurter Acker- und Schöffengericht. *Im Frankfurter Raum, 1*, No. 1 (1931): 33–38.

293   Héringer, Alexander. Goethe und Freud. *Psychoanalytische Bewegung, 3* (1931):19–31.

294   Hermann, Imre. Die Regression zum zeichnerischen Ausdruck bei Goethe. *Imago, 10* (1924):424–30.

295   Hildesheimer, Wolfgang. Aufzeichnungen über Mozart. *Merkur, 10* (1956):1033–53.

Number Reference	
296	Hiller, Ferdinand. *Goethes musikalisches Leben.* Cologne: DuMont-Schauberg, 1883.
297	Hirzel, Ludwig. Johann Georg Schlosser, Lavater, Goethe und Cornelia Goethe. *Im Neuen Reich, 1* (1879):273–85.
298	Hitschmann, Eduard. Psychoanalytisches zur Persönlichkeit Goethes. *Imago, 18* (1932):42–66.
299	———. [1932] The Personality of Goethe. *Great Men,* pp. 126–51. New York: International Universities Press, 1956.
300	——— [Multaretuli]. Goethe und die Psychoanalyse. *Psychoanalytische Bewegung, 4* (1932):386–92, 498–504.
301	Hoffer, Willie. Mouth, Hand and Ego-Integration. *Psychoanalytic Study of the Child, 3/4* (1949):49–56.
302	———. Development of the Body Ego. *Ibid., 5* (1950):18–23.
303	Hölderlin, [Friedrich]. *Sämtliche Werke.* 3rd ed. Berlin: Im Propyläen-Verlag, 1943.
304	Holt, Louisa P. Identification: A Crucial Concept for Sociology. *Bulletin, Menninger Clinic, 14* (1950):164–73.
305	Houben, H. H., editor. *Ottilie von Goethe, Erlebnisse und Geständnisse 1832–1857.* Leipzig: Klinkhardt and Biermann, 1923.
306	———. *J. P. Eckermann, Sein Leben für Goethe.* 2 vols. Leipzig: Haessel, 1925, 1928.
307	———, editor and translator. *Frederic Soret, Zehn Jahre bei Goethe.* Leipzig: Brockhaus, 1929.
308	———. *Goethes Eckermann. Die Lebensgeschichte eines bescheidenen Menschen.* Berlin, Vienna, Leipzig: Paul Zsolnay, 1934.
309	Humboldt, Wilhelm von. Über den Geschlechtsunterschied. Über die männliche und weibliche Form. *Neudrucke zur Psychologie, 1:*25–53. Fritz Giese, ed. Langensalza: Wendt und Klauwell, 1917.
310	Jacob, Heinrich Eduard. *Joseph Haydn, seine Kunst, seine Zeit, sein Ruhm.* Hamburg: Christian Wegner, 1952.
311	Jacobi, Friedrich Heinrich. *Wider Mendelssohns Beschuldigungen betreffend die Briefe über die Lehre des Spinoza.* Leipzig: Göschen, 1786.
312	Jacobs, Ed. Johann Friedrich Plessing. *Zeitschrift,* Harz-Verein für Geschichte und Altertumskunde, *20* (1887): 456–514.
313	Jacobson, Edith. Development of the Wish for a Child in Boys. *Psychoanalytic Study of the Child, 5* (1950):139–52.
314	Jaspers, Karl. *Strindberg und Van Gogh. Versuch einer pathographischen Analyse unter vergleichender Heranziehung von Swedenborg und Hölderlin.* Bremen: Storm, 1949.
315	Jekels, Ludwig. [1914] The Turning Point in the Life of Napoleon I. *Selected Papers,* pp. 1–73. New York: International Universities Press, 1952.
316	———. Shakespeare's "Macbeth." *Imago, 5* (1917–19):170–95.
317	Johnson, Adelaide M. Sanctions for Superego Lacunae of Adolescents.

Searchlights on Delinquency, pp. 225–45. K. R. Eissler, ed. New York: International Universities Press, 1949.

318   Jokl, Robert H. Psychic Determinism and Preservation of Sublimation in Classical Psychoanalytic Procedure. *Bulletin, Menninger Clinic, 14* (1950):207–19.

319   Jones, Ernest. [1914] The Madonna's Conception through the Ear. *Essays in Applied Psycho-Analysis, 2:*266–357. London: Hogarth, 1951.

320   ———. The Mantle Symbol. *International Journal of Psycho-Analysis, 8* (1927):63–65.

321   ———. *The Life and Work of Sigmund Freud.* 3 vols. New York: Basic Books, 1953–57.

322   Kantor, J. R. Goethe's Place in Modern Science. *Goethe Bicentennial Studies,* pp. 61–82. H. J. Meessen, ed. Bloomington: Indiana University Studies, 1950.

323   Kardiner, Abraham. *The Traumatic Neuroses of War.* Psychosomatic Medicine Monograph, 2/3. Washington: National Research Council, 1941.

324   Katan, M. Schreber's Hallucinations about the "Little Men." *International Journal of Psycho-Analysis, 31* (1950):32–35.

325   Kaufmann, Walter E. Goethe and the History of Ideas. *Journal of the History of Ideas, 10* (1949):503–16.

326   Kestner, A. *Goethe und Werther.* Stuttgart: Cotta, 1854.

327   Kielholz, A. Johann Georg Zimmermann zum zweihundertsten Geburtstag. *Imago, 15* (1929):243–62.

328   Kindermann, Heinz. *Das Goethebild des 20. Jahrhunderts.* Vienna, Stuttgart: Humboldt, 1952.

329   Kinsey, Alfred C., Wardell B. Pomeroy, and Clyde E. Martin. *Sexual Behavior in the Human Male.* Philadelphia, London: Saunders, 1948.

330   Klein, Melanie. [1932] *The Psycho-Analysis of Children.* London: Hogarth, 1954.

331   ———. [1946] Notes on Some Schizoid Mechanisms. *Developments in Psycho-Analysis,* pp. 292–320. Joan Riviere, ed. London: Hogarth, 1952.

332   Kleine, H. O. *Der Untergang der Goethe-Sippe.* Stuttgart: Enke, 1954.

333   Klopstock, Friedrich. *Gesammelte Werke.* Leipzig: Göschen, 1823.

334   Knetsch, Carl. Ahnentafel Johann Wolfgang von Goethes. *Ahnentafeln berühmter Deutscher.* N.F., No. 1, pp. 5–16. Leipzig: Zentralstelle für deutsche Personen und Familiengeschichte, 1932.

335   Kohlbrugge, Jacob H. F. *Historische-Kritische Studien über Goethe als Naturforscher.* Würzburg: Kobitz, 1913.

336   Kohut, Heinz, and Siegmund Levarie. On the Enjoyment of Listening to Music. *Psychoanalytic Quarterly, 19* (1950):64–87.

337   ———. The Psychological Significance of Musical Activity. *Music Therapy, 1* (1951):151–58.

338   Korff, H. A. *Geist der Goethezeit.* 5 vols. Leipzig: Koehler und Amelang, 1949–58.

Reference
Number

339   Korff, H. A. [1933] *Sturm und Drang. Ibid.,* vol. *1.*

340   Köster, Albert, editor. *Die Briefe der Frau Rath Goethe.* 2 vols. Leipzig: Insel, 1923.

341   Kretschmer, Ernst. *Geniale Menschen.* Berlin: Springer, 1929.

342   Krieg, Walter. Materialien zu einer Geschichte des Autorenhonorars vom 15. bis zum 20. Jahrhundert. *Das Antiquariat, 7* (1951):249–54, 302–06, 349–54; *8* (1952):4–6, 42.

343   Kriegk, G. L. *Die Brüder Senckenberg. Eine Biographische Darstellung.* Frankfurt a.M.: Sauerländer, 1869.

344   ———. Goethe als Rechtsanwalt 1771 bis 1775. *Deutsche Kulturbilder aus dem achtzehnten Jahrhundert,* pp. 263–517. Leipzig: Hirzel, 1874.

345   Kris, Ernst, and Otto Kurz. *Die Legende vom Künstler, ein geschicht-licher Versuch.* Vienna: Krystall, 1934.

346   ———. *Psychoanalytic Explorations in Art.* New York: International Universities Press, 1952.

346A   ———. [1932]The Art of the Insane. *Ibid.,* pp. 85–169.

347   ———. [1935] The Image of the Artist. *Ibid.,* pp. 64–84.

348   ———. [1935] The Psychology of Caricature. *Ibid.,* pp. 173–89.

349   ———. [1939] On Inspiration. *Ibid.,* pp. 291–302.

350   ———. [1941] Approaches to Art. *Ibid.,* pp. 13–63.

351   ———. [1950] On Preconscious Mental Processes. *Ibid.,* pp. 303–18.

352   ———. Neutralization and Sublimation. *Psychoanalytic Study of the Child, 10* (1955):30–46.

    ———. *See* Rose W. Coleman; Heinz Hartmann, 1947.

353   Kroeber, A. L. *Configurations of Culture Growth.* Berkeley: University of California Press, 1944.

354   Kühn, Paul. *Die Frauen um Goethe.* 2 vols. Leipzig: Klinkhardt und Biermann, 1912.

    Kurz, Otto. *See* Ernst Kris, 1934.

355   Laehr, Hans. *Die Heilung des Orest in Goethes Iphigenie.* Berlin: Reimer, 1902.

356   Lampl de Groot, Jeanne. The Pre-oedipal Phase in the Development of the Male Child. *Psychoanalytic Study of the Child, 2* (1946):75–83.

357   Lange-Eichbaum, Wilhelm. [1927] *Genie, Irrsin und Ruhm.* 4th ed., re-vised by Wolfram Kurth. Munich, Basel: Ernst Reinhardt, 1956.

358   Langer, Georg. Die jüdischen Gebetriemen. *Imago, 16* (1930):435–85.

359   Lantos, Barbara. On the Motivation of Human Relationships. *International Journal of Psycho-Analysis, 36* (1955):267–88.

360   Lappenberg, J. M. *Reliquien der Fräulein Susanna Catharina von Kletten-berg.* Hamburg: Rauhes Haus, 1849.

361   Lehman, Harvey C. The Creative Years in Science and Literature. *Scientific Monthly, 43* (1936):151–62.

362   ———. The Creative Years: "Best Books." *Ibid., 45* (1937):65–75.

363   Lenz, Jakob Mich[ael] Reinhold. *Ausgewählte Gedichte.* Erich Osterheld, ed. Leipzig: Eckardt, 1909.

Reference
Number

364 Leschnitzer, Adolf F. Faust and Moses. *American Imago, 6* (1949):229–43.

365 ———. Goethe und der Mythos. *Neue Schweizer Rundschau, 20* (1953): 549–57.

365A Lesky, Erna. *Österreichisches Gesundheitsweisen im Zeitalter des aufge-klärten Absolutismus.* Archiv für österreichische Geschichte, vol. *122,* part 1. Vienna: Österreichische Akademie der Wissenschaften, 1959.

366 Levarie, Siegmund. "Solitario bosco ombroso"—eine musikalische Kind-heitserinnerung Goethes. *Goethe* (N.F. des Jahrbuchs der Goethe-Gesellschaft), *19* (1957):196–202.
———. *See* Heinz Kohut, 1950.

367 Levy, Ernst. Goethes musik-theoretische Anschauungen. *Schweizerische Musik Zeitung, 52* (1952):7–15.

368 Lewin, Bertram D. Claustrophobia. *Psychoanalytic Quarterly, 4* (1935): 227–33.

369 ———. The Nature of Reality, the Meaning of Nothingness, with an Addendum on Concentration. *Ibid., 17* (1948):524–26.

370 ———. *The Psychoanalysis of Elation.* New York: Norton, 1950.

371 ———. Phobic Symptoms and Dream Interpretation. *Psychoanalytic Quarterly, 21* (1952):295–322.

372 Loening, Richard. *Die Hamlet-Tragödie.* Stuttgart: Cotta, 1893.
Loewenstein, Rudolph M. *See* Heinz Hartmann, 1947.

373 Lorand, Sandor. The Mantle Symbol. *International Journal of Psycho-Analysis, 10* (1929):98–100.

374 Lorey, Wilhelm. Goethes Stellung zur Mathematik. *Goethe als Seher und Forscher,* pp. 131–56. J. Walter, ed. Kaiserlich Leopoldinische Deutsche Akademie der Naturforscher zu Halle, 1930.

375 Lukács, Georg. *Goethe und seine Zeit.* Bern: Francke, 1947.

376 Maltzahn, Hellmuth von. *Karl Ludwig von Knebel.* Jena: Frommann, 1929.

377 Mann, Thomas. *Goethe als Repräsentant des Bürgerlichen Zeitalters.* Berlin: Fischer, 1932.

378 Markstrahler, Adolf. *Goethe und seine Züricher Freundin Barbara Schulthess in Konstanz.* With an appendix on "Goethe und die Ero-berung der Luft." Konstanz: Reuss und Itta, 1913.
Martin, Clyde C. *See* Alfred C. Kinsey.

379 Matthaei, Rupprecht. Über die Anfänge von Goethes Farbenlehre. *Goethe* (N.F. des Jahrbuchs der Goethe-Gesellschaft), *11* (1949):249–62.

380 Maurois, André. *Olympio.* New York: Harper, 1956.

381 Mauss, Marcel. Une Catégorie de l'Esprit Humain: La Notion de Per-sonne, celle de "Moi." *Sociologie et Anthropologie,* pp. 333–62. Paris: Bibliothèque de Sociologie Contemporaine, Presses Universitaires, 1950.

382 Mayer, Friedrich. *Verzeichnis einer Goethe-Bibliothek.* Leipzig: Dyk, 1908.

383 Mayer-Gross, W. Primäre Wahnerlebnisse. *Die Schizophrenie,* pp. 357–68.

Spezieller Teil, Part 5. *Handbuch der Geisteskrankheiten,* vol. *9.* Oswald Bumke, ed. Berlin: Springer, 1932.

384   Maync, Harry. [1906] *Geschichte der deutschen Goethe-Biographie.* Leipzig: Haessel, 1914.

    Mead, Margaret. *See* Gregory Bateson.

385   Meisner, J. *Goethe als Jurist.* Berlin: Kortkampf, 1885.

386   Menninger, Karl. Emotional Factors in Organic Gynecological Conditions. *Bulletin, Menninger Clinic, 7* (1943):47–55.

387   Mentzel, Elisabeth. Domenico Giovinazzi. *Goethe-Handbuch, 1:*718–19. Julius Zeitler, ed. 3 vols. Stuttgart: Metzler, 1916–18.

388   ———. Das Offenbacher Mädchen. *Ibid., 3:*57–58.

389   ———. *Aus Goethes Jugend.* Leipzig: Voigtlander, n.d.

390   Merker, Erna. Friedrich Constantin Freiherr von Stein (1772–1844). *Goethe-Handbuch, 3:*361–63. Julius Zeitler, ed. 3 vols. Stuttgart: Metzler, 1916–18.

391   Meyer, Heinrich. *Goethe. Das Leben im Werk.* Hamburg: Strom, 1949.

392   Meyer, Nicolaus. *Briefe von Goethes Frau an Nicolaus Meyer.* Strassburg: Trübner, 1887.

393   Meyer, Richard M. Studien zu Goethes Wortgebrauch. *Archiv für das Studium der neuern Sprachen und Litteraturen, 96* (1896):1–42.

394   ———. Das Gemeine. *Goethe-Handbuch, 1:*682–83. Julius Zeitler, ed. 3 vols. Stuttgart: Metzler, 1916–18.

395   Möbius, P. J. *Goethe.* 2 vols. Leipzig: Barth, 1909.

396   Mommsen, Wilhelm. *Die politischen Anschauungen Goethes.* Stuttgart: Deutsche Verlags-Anstalt, 1948.

397   Moreno, J. L. *Who Shall Survive?* New York: Beacon House, 1953.

398   Morris, Max. Prometheus und Hanswurst. *Goethe Studien, 1:*237–48. 2 vols. 2nd ed. Berlin: C. Skopnik, 1902.

399   ———. Herzogin Louise von Weimar in Goethes Dichtung. *Ibid., 2:*1–75.

400   ———. Christiane Vulpius in Goethes Dichtung. *Ibid., 2:*76–109.

401   Mozart, W. A. *Liebesbriefe ans Bäsle, an Aloysia und Konstanze.* Introduction by Elizabeth Soffé. Salzburg: Mirabell, n.d.

402   Müller, B. A. Schöne Seele. *Goethe-Handbuch, 3:*291–93. Julius Zeitler, ed. 3 vols. Stuttgart: Metzler, 1916–18.

    Multaretuli. *See* Eduard Hitschmann.

403   Münz, Ludwig. *Goethes Zeichnungen und Radierungen.* Vienna: Oster, 1949.

404   Musäus, J. K. A. *Volksmärchen der Deutschen.* Munich: Winkler, 1948.

405   Muschg, Walter. Dichtung als archaisches Erbe. *Imago, 19* (1933):99–112.

406   ———. *Tragische Literaturgeschichte.* Bern: Francke, 1948.

407   Muthesius, Karl. *Goethe ein Kinderfreund.* Berlin: Mittler, 1903.

408   ———. Johann Friedrich Krafft. *Goethe-Handbuch, 2:*390. Julius Zeitler, ed. 3 vols. Stuttgart: Metzler, 1916–18.

409   Neumann, W. *Johann Wolfgang Goethe.* Cassel: Ernest Balde, 1853.

Reference
Number

410   Nietzsche, Friedrich Wilhelm. [1884–88] *Der Wille zur Macht. Versuch einer Umwerthung aller Werthe. Gesammelte Werke,* 19:224–25. 23 vols. Munich: Musarion Verlag, 1920–29.

411   Nunberg, Herman. [1922] States of Depersonalization. *Practice and Theory of Psychoanalysis,* pp. 60–74. Nervous and Mental Disease Monographs, No. 74. New York, 1948.

412   ———. [1930] The Synthetic Function of the Ego. *Ibid.,* pp. 120–36.

413   ———. [1932] *Principles of Psychoanalysis.* New York: International Universities Press, 1955.

414   ———. *Problems of Bisexuality as Reflected in Circumcision.* London: Imago, 1949.

415   Oberhoffer, M. *Goethes Krankengeschichte.* Monograph 1, *Heilkunde und Geisteswelt.* Hannover: Schmorl und von Seefeld Nachf, 1949.

416   Olden, Christine. About the Fascinating Effect of the Narcissistic Personality. *American Imago,* 2 (1941):347–55.

417   Packe, Michael St. John. *The Life of John Stuart Mill.* New York: Macmillan, 1954.

418   Panofsky, Erwin. [1936] "Et in Arcadia Ego": Poussin and the Elegiac Condition. *Meaning in the Visual Arts,* pp. 295–320. New York: Doubleday, 1955.

419   Parr, Albert Eide. *Adaptiogenese und Phylogenese. Abhandlungen zur Theorie der Organischen Entwicklung,* Heft 1. H. Spemann, I. B. Freiburg, W. Vogt, B. Romeis, eds. Berlin: Springer, 1926.

Philologus. *See* Flodoard Frhr. von Biedermann.

420   Piers, Gerhard, and Milton B. Singer. *Shame and Guilt.* Springfield, Ill.: Thomas, 1953.

421   Piper, Paul, editor. *Joseph, Goethes erste grosse Jugenddichtung.* Hamburg: Gente, 1920.

422   Plato. *Dialogues.* Benjamin Jowett, trans. 2 vols. New York: Random House, 1937.

423   Plessing, F. V. Selbstschilderung des Professors Plessing. *Neue Berlinische Monatschrift,* 21 (1809):3–28.

424   Plutarch. *The Lives of the Noble Grecians and Romans.* Dryden translation. New York: Modern Library, 1932.

425   Pniower, O. Mütter. *Goethe-Handbuch,* 2:641–42. Julius Zeitler, ed. 3 vols. Stuttgart: Metzler, 1916–18.

426   ———. Proktophantasmist. *Ibid.,* 3:155–56.

Pomeroy, Wardell B. *See* Alfred C. Kinsey.

427   Ponsonby, Arthur. *English Diaries.* London: Methuen, 1923.

428   Popper, Josef [Lynkens]. [1899] Wovon sprechen Verliebte miteinander. *Phantasien eines Realisten,* pp. 174–82. Dresden: Carl Reissner, 1922.

429   Prang, Helmut. *Johann Heinrich Merck, ein Leben für Andere.* Leipzig: Insel, 1949.

Reference
Number

430   Preller, L. *Griechische Mythologie*. Berlin: Weidmannsche Buchhandlung, 1872.

431   *Priapeia; or the Sportive Epigrams of divers Poets on Priapus; the Latin text now for the first time Englished in Verse and Prose (the Metrical Version by "Outidanos" with Introduction, Notes Explanatory, and Excursus, by "Neaniskos")*. Cosmopoli, 1890. Privately printed.

        Provence, Sally. *See* Rose W. Coleman.

432   Rado, Sandor. [1922] The Paths of Natural Science in the Light of Psychoanalysis. *Psychoanalytic Quarterly, 1* (1932):683–700.

433   Rank, Otto. [1907] *Der Künstler*. 4th ed. Leipzig, Vienna, Zurich: Internationaler Psychoanalytischer Verlag, 1925.

434   ———. Belege zur Rettungsphantasie. *Ibid.*, pp. 134–57.

435   ———. *Das Inzest-Motiv in Dichtung und Sage*. Leipzig, Vienna: Deuticke, 1912.

436   ———. Die Nacktheit in Dichtung und Sage. *Imago, 2* (1913):267–301, 409–46.

437   ———. [1914] *Der Doppelgänger*. Leipzig, Vienna, Zurich: Internationaler Psychoanalytischer Verlag, 1925.

438   ———. Mythologie und Psychoanalyse. *Psychoanalytische Beiträge zur Mythenforschung*, pp. 1–20. Leipzig, Vienna, Zurich: Internationaler Psychoanalytischer Verlag, 1919.

439   Rapaport, David. Toward a Theory of Thinking. *Organization and Pathology of Thought*, pp. 689–730. New York: Columbia University Press, 1951.

440   Rausch, Georg. *Goethe und die Deutsche Sprache*. Leipzig, Berlin: Teubner, 1909.

441   Read, Herbert. Psycho-Analysis and the Problem of Aesthetic Value. *International Journal of Psycho-Analysis, 32* (1951):73–82.

442   Redslob, Edwin. Goethes Monodrama "Proserpina" als Totenklage für seine Schwester. *Goethe* (N.F. des Jahrbuchs der Goethe-Gesellschaft), *8* (1943):252–69.

443   Refardt, Edgar. *Der "Goethe-Kayser."* Zurich: Hug, 1950.

444   Reich, Annie. Narcissistic Object Choice in Women. *Journal of the American Psychoanalytic Association, 1* (1953):22–44.

445   ———. Early Identifications as Archaic Elements in the Superego. *Ibid.*, *2* (1954):218–38.

446   Reich, Willi. *Joseph Haydn, Leben-Briefe-Schaffen*. Lucerne: Josef Stocken, 1946.

447   Reik, Theodor. [1920] On the Dream Symbolism of the Cloak. *The Psychoanalytic Reader*, pp. 391–92. R. Fliess, ed. New York: International Universities Press, 1948.

448   ———. Psychologie und Depersonalisation. *Wie man Psychologe wird*, pp. 34–100. Vienna: Internationaler Psychoanalytischer Verlag, 1927.

449   ———. [1929] Goethe's Romance with Friederike. *Fragment of a Great Confession*, pp. 33–211. New York: Farrar, Straus, 1949.

Reference
Number

450 ——. Künstlerisches Schaffen und Witzarbeit. *Imago, 15* (1929):200–31.

451 Reinsch, Frank H. Johann Kaspar Goethe's Italian Journey. *The Modern Language Forum, 34* (1949):101–08.

452 Riemer, Friedrich Wilhelm. *Mittheilungen über Goethe.* 2 vols. Berlin: Duncker and Humblot, 1841.

452A ——. *Ibid.* New ed., Arthur Pollmer, ed. Leipzig: Insel, 1921.

453 Ries, John, editor. *Die Briefe der Elise von Türkheim.* Frankfurt a.M.: Englert und Schlosser, 1924.

454 Rimpau, W. Frau von Branconi. *Zeitschrift des Harz-Vereins für Geschichte und Altertumskunde, 33* (1900):1–176.

455 Roheim, Geza. Mond und Menstruation in Mondmythologie und Mondreligion. *Imago, 13* (1927):518–26.

456 ——. The Song of the Sirens. *Psychiatric Quarterly, 22* (1948):18–44.

457 Rosanow, M. N. *Jakob M. R. Lenz.* Leipzig: Schulz, 1909.

458 Ruland, C. Des Herrn Rath Haushaltungsbuch. *Weimars Festgrüsse,* pp. 55–92. Weimar: Böhlau, 1899.

459 Sachs, Hanns. Kunst und Persönlichkeit. *Imago, 15* (1929):1–14.

460 ——. Volentem ducunt fata, nolentem trahunt. *Die Psychoanalytische Bewegung, 4* (1932):143–50.

461 ——. The Delay of the Machine Age. *Psychoanalytic Quarterly, 2* (1933):404–24.

462 ——. [1934] The Community of Daydreams. *The Creative Unconscious,* pp. 11–54. Cambridge: Sci-Art Publications, 1942.

463 ——. *Freud, Master and Friend.* Cambridge: Harvard University Press, 1944.

464 Sarasin, Philipp. Goethes Mignon. *Imago, 15* (1929):349–99.

465 Schaefer, J. W. Goethe und Plessing. *Zur Deutschen Literaturgeschichte,* pp. 241–57. Bremen: Geisler, 1864.

466 Schapiro, Meyer. Leonardo and Freud: An Art-Historical Study. *Journal of the History of Ideas, 17* (1956):147–78.

467 Scherer, Carl. Carl Matthaei. *Goethe-Jahrbuch, 15* (1894):216–44.

468 Scherer, Wilhelm. Goethe und Adelaide. *Aufsätze über Goethe,* pp. 91–121. Berlin: Weidmann, 1886.

469 Scheumann, Karl H. Das Reich der Steine in Goethes Welt. *Goethe und die Wissenschaft,* pp. 119–51. Frankfurt a.M.: Vittorio Klostermann, 1951.

470 Schilder, Paul. [1925] The More Detailed Structure of the Ego-Ideal and of the Perceptive-Self. *Introduction to a Psychoanalytic Psychiatry,* pp. 13–20. New York: International Universities Press, 1951.

471 ——. *Gedanken zur Naturphilosophie.* Vienna: Springer, 1928.

472 ——. *Mind: Perception and Thought in Their Constructive Aspects.* New York: Columbia University Press, 1942.

473 Schmid, Günther. *Goethe und die Naturwissenschaften, eine Bibliographie.* Emil Abderhalden, ed. Halle, Salle: Kaiserlich Leopoldinisch-Carolinisch Deutsche Akademie der Naturforscher, 1940.

474   Schmidt, Erich. *Lenz und Klinger, zwei Dichter der Geniezeit.* Berlin:
       Weidmann, 1878.

475   Schnitzer, Manuel. *Goethes Josephbilder. Goethes Josephdichtung.* Ham-
       burg: Gente, 1921.

476   Schöll, Adolf. *Goethe.* Berlin: Hertz, 1882.

477   Schopenhauer, Arthur. *Sämtliche Werke.* Grossherzog Wilhelm Ernst
       Ausgabe. 5 vols. Leipzig: Insel, n.d.

478   ———. [1850] Vom Unterschiede der Lebensalter. Aphorismen zur
       Lebensweitsheit, pp. 557–80. *Parerga und Paralipomena,* pp. 371–580.
       Sämtliche Werke, vol. 4.

479   Schottländer, Johann-Wolfgang, editor. *Carl Friedrich Zelters Darstellung
       seines Lebens.* Schriften der Goethe-Gesellschaft, vol. 44. Weimar, 1931.

480   Schubart-Fikentscher, Gertrud. *Goethes sechsundfünfzig Strassburger
       Thesen vom 6. August 1771.* Weimar. Böhlau, 1949.

481   Schüddekopf, Carl, editor. *Goethes Parodie auf Fritz Jacobis "Woldemar."*
       Weimar: Gesellschaft der Bibliophilen, 1908.

482   ———, editor. *Briefe von Goethes Eltern.* Berlin: Deutsche Bibliothek,
       1912.

483   Schulenburg, Werner von der. *Johann Kaspar Goethe, Vater eines Genies.*
       Berlin: Metten, n.d.

484   Schultz-Gora, Oskar. Zur Geschichte des Ausdrucks Belle âme. *Archiv
       für das Studium der neueren Sprachen und Literaturen, 100* (1898):
       163–68.

485   Schwab, Gustav. *Die Deutschen Volksbücher.* Leipzig: Reclam, n.d.

486   Schweitzer, Albert. Goethe: His Personality and His Work. *Goethe and
       the Modern Age,* pp. 95–110. Arnold Bergstraesser, ed. Chicago:
       Regnery, 1950.

487   Sears, Robert R. *Survey of Objective Studies of Psychoanalytic Concepts.*
       Bulletin 51. New York: Social Science Research Council, 1943.

488   Secundus, Johannes. *Die Küsse und die feierlichen Elegien.* German trans-
       lation by F. Blei. Leipzig: Insel, 1907.

489   Seuffert, B. Merope und Elpenor. *Vierteljahrschrift für Literaturgeschichte,
       4* (1891):115–16.

490   Sharpe, Ella Freeman. [1946] From *King Lear* to *The Tempest. Collected
       Papers on Psycho-Analysis,* pp. 214–41. London: Hogarth Press and the
       Institute of Psycho-Analysis, 1950.

491   Silberer, Herbert. [1909] Report on a Method of Eliciting and Observing
       Certain Symbolic Hallucination-Phenomena. *Organization and Pathol-
       ogy of Thought,* pp. 195–207. David Rapaport, ed. New York: Colum-
       bia University Press, 1951.

492   ———. Symbolik des Erwachsenen und Schwellensymbolik überhaupt.
       *Jahrbuch für Psychoanalytische und Psychopathologische Forschungen,
       3* (1911–12):621–60.

493   ———. [1912] On Symbol-Formation. *Organization and Pathology of
       Thought,* pp. 208–33.

Reference
Number

494   ———. Zur Symbolbildung. *Jahrbuch für Psychoanalytische und Psychopathologische Forschungen, 4* (1912):607–83.

495   Silverberg, William V. On the Psychological Significance of *Du* and *Sie*. *Psychoanalytic Quarterly, 9* (1940):509–25.

496   Simmel, Georg. *Soziologie*. Leipzig: Duncker und Humblot, 1908.

497   ———. *Goethe*. Leipzig: Klinkhardt und Biermann, 1918.

498   ———. [1918] *Der Konflikt in der modernen Kultur*. Quoted in Adolf von Grolman. *Literarische Betrachtung*. Arbeiten zur Geistesgeschichte der Germanischen und Romanischen Völker, 6. Berlin: Junker und Dünnhaupt, 1930.

499   Simmons, Ernest J. *Leo Tolstoy*. Boston: Little, Brown, 1946.

500   Simon, Ernst. Religious Humanism. *Goethe and the Modern Age*, pp. 304–25. Arnold Bergstraesser, ed. Chicago: Regnery, 1950.

       Singer, Milton B. *See* Gerhard Piers.

501   Spitz, René. Authority and Masturbation. *Psychoanalytic Quarterly, 21* (1952):490–528.

502   Sprenger, Jacob. *Malleus Maleficarum*. Montagu Summers, trans. London: Pushkin Press, 1948.

503   Springer, Brunold. *Der Schlüssel zu Goethes Liebesleben*. Berlin: Verlag der Neuen Generation, 1926.

504   Staercke, August. *Psychoanalyse und Psychiatrie*. Leipzig, Vienna, Zurich: Internationaler Psychoanalytischer Verlag, 1921.

       Stammler, Wolfgang. *See* Karl Freye.

505   Steck, Rudolf. Goethe und Lavater. *Öffentliche Vorträge gehalten in der Schweiz*, vol. *8*. Basel: Benno Schwabe, 1884.

506   Steinen, Wolfram von den. *Das Zeitalter Goethes*. Bern: Francke, 1949.

507   Stekel, Wilhelm. Der Traum im Traume in Beiträge zur Traumdeutung, pp. 459–66. *Jahrbuch für Psychoanalytische und Psychopathologische Forschungen, 1* (1909):458–512.

508   Sterba, Editha, and Richard Sterba. *Beethoven and His Nephew*. New York: Pantheon, 1954.

509   Sterba, Richard. Aggression in the Rescue Fantasy. *Psychoanalytic Quarterly, 9* (1940):505–08.

510   ———. Some Psychological Factors in Negro Race Hatred and in Anti-Negro Riots. *Psychoanalysis and the Social Sciences, 1* (1947):411–21.

511   Sternfeld, Frederick W. *Goethe and Music*. New York: New York Public Library, 1954.

512   Stieda, Wilhelm. *Ilmenau und Stützerbach*. Leipzig: Seemann, 1902.

513   Straus, Erwin. *Vom Sinn der Sinne*. Berlin: Springer, 1935.

514   Strunz, Franz. *Goethe als Naturforscher*. Vienna: Urania, 1917.

515   Stümcke, Heinrich. *Corona Schröter*. Bielefeld, Leipzig: Velhagen und Klasing, 1926.

516   Suetonius. *The Lives of the Twelve Caesars*. Bohn Classical Library. London: Bell, 1909.

517   Suphan, Bernhard. Goethe und Spinoza (1783–86). *Festschrift zu der*

zweiten Saecularfeier des Friedrichs-Werderschen Gymnasiums zu Berlin. Berlin: Weidmann, 1881.

518 Suphan, Bernhard. Aus Weimar und Kochberg. *Preussische Jahrbücher, 50* (1882):495–504.

519 ———. Briefe von Goethe und Frau von Stein an Johann Georg Zimmermann. *Wartburgstimmen Halbmonatschrift für deutsche Kultur, 1* (May, 1904):171–83.

520 Susman, Margarethe. *Deutung einer grossen Liebe. Goethe und Charlotte von Stein.* Zurich: Artemis, 1951.

521 Taylor, W. S. A Critique of Sublimation in Males: A Study of Forty Superior Single Men. *Genetic Psychology Monographs, 13,* No. 1, 1933.

522 Teweles, Heinrich. *Goethe und die Juden.* Hamburg: Gente, 1925.

523 Thümen, F. *Die Iphigeniensage in antikem und modernem Gewande.* Berlin: Mayer und Müller, 1895.

524 Tornius, Valerian. *Die Empfindsamen in Darmstadt.* Leipzig: Klinkhardt and Biermann, 1910.

525 Traumann, Ernst. *Goethe der Strassburger Student.* Leipzig: Klinkhardt und Biermann, 1923.

526 Turner, Walter James. [1938] *Mozart.* New York: Doubleday, 1954.

527 Unger, Rudolf. [1921] Wandlungen des literarischen Goethebildes seit hundert Jahren. *Aufsätze zur Literatur und Geistesgeschichte,* pp. 220–32. *Gesammelte Studien,* vol. 2. Neue Forschung, Arbeiten zur Geistesgeschichte der Germanischen und Romanischen Völker. Berlin: Junker und Dünnhaupt, 1929.

528 Urlichs, Ludwig, editor. *Charlotte von Schiller und ihre Freunde.* 2 vols. Stuttgart: Cotta, 1861–62.

529 Urzidil, Johannes. *Das Glück der Gegenwart; Goethes Amerikabild.* Goethe-Schriften im Artemis Verlag, Heft 6. Zurich, 1958.

530 Viehoff, Heinrich. *Goethes Gedichte.* 2 vols. Stuttgart: Conradi, 1876.

531 Viëtor, Karl. *Goethe the Thinker.* Cambridge: Harvard University Press, 1950.

532 Voigt, Julius. *Goethe und Ilmenau.* Leipzig: Xenien, 1912.

533 Vorwahl, H. Zu Goethes Liebesleben. *Zeitschrift für Sexualwissenschaft und Sexualpolitik, 18* (1932):503–07.

534 Voss, Lena. *Goethes unsterbliche Freundin (Charlotte von Stein).* Leipzig: Klinkhardt und Biermann, 1922.

535 Vulpius, Walther. Die Familie Vulpius. *Stunden mit Goethe, 1* (1904): 85–196. Wilhelm Bode, ed. 10 vols. Berlin: Mittler, 1904–14.

536 Vulpius, Wolfgang. *Christiane.* Weimar: Kiepenheuer, 1953.

537 Waelder, Robert. Schizophrenic and Creative Thinking. *International Journal of Psycho-Analysis, 7* (1926):366–76.

538 ———. [1930] The Principle of Multiple Function: Observations in Overdetermination. *Psychoanalytic Quarterly, 5* (1936):45–63.

539 ———. [1934] The Problem of Freedom in Psychoanalysis and the Prob-

Reference
Number

lem of Reality-testing. *International Journal of Psycho-Analysis, 17* (1936):98–108.

540 Wagner, Karl, editor. *Briefe an und von Joh. Heinrich Merck.* Darmstadt: Diehl, 1838.

541 Wahl, Hans, editor. *Briefwechsel des Herzogs-Grossherzogs Carl August mit Goethe.* 3 vols. Berlin: Mittler, 1915–18.

542 ————. Carl Augusts Tagebuch. *Funde und Forschungen, Eine Festgabe für Julius Wahle,* pp. 180–92. Leipzig: Insel, 1921.

543 ————, editor. *Goethe. Aufzeichnungen des Freiherrn Carl von Stein-Kochberg.* Leipzig: Insel, 1924.

544 ————. Goethes geplante Biographie Bernhards von Weimar. *Goethe* (N.F. des Jahrbuchs der Goethe-Gesellschaft), *4* (1939):203–08.

545 ————. Ein unbekannter Brief Goethes an Charlotte von Stein. *Ibid., 7* (1942):220–26.

546 Waldmann, F. *Lenz in Briefen.* Zurich: Von Stern's literarischem Bulletin der Schweiz, 1894.

547 Warnecke, Friedrich. Goethes Harzreise im Winter. *Goethe-Jahrbuch, 33* (1912):113–27.

548 Watts, A. E., translator. *The Metamorphoses of Ovid.* Berkeley, Los Angeles: University of California Press, 1954.

549 Weber, Max. [1904] Askese und kapitalistischer Geist, pp. 163–206 in *Die protestantische Ethik und der Geist des Kapitalismus, Gesammelte Aufsätze zur Religionssoziologie, 1:*17–206. 4th ed. 3 vols. Tübingen: J. C. B. Mohr, 1947.

550 Weissel, Otto. *Der Advokat Goethe.* Vienna, Leipzig: Manz, 1927.

551 Winterstein, Alfred R. F. von. Zur Psychoanalyse des Reisens. *Imago, 1* (1912):489–506.

552 Witkowski, Georg. *Cornelia, die Schwester Goethes.* 1st ed. Frankfurt a.M.: Rütten and Loening, 1903.

553 ————. *Ibid.,* 2nd revised ed. 1924.

554 ————. *Goethe.* Leipzig: Seemann, 1912.

555 Wolff, Eugen. *Mignon.* Munich: Beck, 1909.

556 ————. Über allen Gipfeln. *Goethe-Handbuch, 3:*447. Julius Zeitler, ed. 3 vols. Stuttgart: Metzler, 1916–18.

557 Wollschlaeger, Landgerichtsdirektor. Goethe als Rechtsanwalt, *Deutsche Juristenzeitung, 4,* No. 17 (1899):344–47.

558 Wood, Alexander. Goethe's Elpenor. *American Journal of Philology, 12,* No. 4 (1891):458–80.

559 Zarncke, Friedrich. *Goetheschriften.* Leipzig: Avenarius, 1897.

560 Zeitler, Julius, editor. *Goethe-Handbuch.* 3 vols. Stuttgart: Metzler, 1916–18.

561 ————. Behrisch. *Ibid., 1:*179–80.

562 ————. Hanswursts Hochzeit. *Ibid., 2:*123–24.

Index

abasia, 1414
abgewöhnen, meaning, 431
Abraham, Karl, 1312
absolution, 200
absolutism,
  psychological, xxv
  and women, 52
abstinence, 893n, 1082
  in analytic treatment, 200
  in Goethe–von Stein relation, 201
  sexual, prolonged, 1030
accidents, 458
Ackermann, 860
acrophobia, 1216f
Acropolis, 1005, 1008
acting out,
  in analysis, 228, 1198
  in Goethe, 51, 404, 458, 555f, 1198
  initial, in analysis, 169
  in poets, 1018
  and repetition of own conception, 1043
  in schizophrenics, 236
  and traveling, 410
activity,
  as defense against passive wishes, 131
  and immortality, 1190
  and passivity, conflicts about, 458, 742ff,
    769, 892, 1284f
Acton, Lord, 1093
actor, Goethe as, 213, 262, 454, 556
adaptation, activity in, 1405
Adelheid (*Götz von Berlichingen*), 1090
adjustment, 680n
  good, 997
Adler, Alfred, 1197
adolescence,
  function of, 43

adolescence (*Continued*)
  protracted, and psychopathology, 1177
  turn against, 257
adolescents, and sexual fantasies, 611
Adonis, 372
Adramelech, 1204
adventure, 665
advising, 621f
Aeschylus, 334, 335
affectation, tendency to, 1177
Agamemnon, 335
  (*Iphigenia in Tauris*), 316f, 328
agate, 630ff
Agatha, St., 1278
age,
  biological conception of, 683
  coincidence with father's, at Goethe's first
    intercourse, 1034, 1039
aggression/aggressiveness
  in Goethe, 166, 175, 211, 517–18, 616,
    1366
  internal, in creative process, 867
  premature ejaculation as, 1061f
  and relation to father, 705
  and sublimation, 1407
aggressive-destructive strivings, 225
  and Goethe's drawing, 1221
aggressor, identification with, 281
aging,
  and creativity, 1432, 1448
  fear of, 389
  Goethe's, and *Wilhelm Meister,* 1447
agoraphobia, 157
Agostino di Giovanni, 1020
Ahnungsvolle, meaning, 707n
Ajax, 108
Alba (*Egmont*), 1041

1497

Albert (*Werther*), 86, 98ff, 112, 287, 290, 371–3, 417, 696, 790n, 820
albinos, 378
alcohol, Goethe's use of, 428
alcoholism
  of August von Goethe, 1309
  Christiane and, 1306n
Alexander the Great, 399, 1096n
Alexander, Franz, 665n, 1434
Alexis, St. 394f
Allegri, Gregorio, 1355
alloplasticity, 543–4, 545
Allport, Gordon W., 696n
Alsace, 129
Altenstein, Count (*Lila*), 240
Altenstein, interpretation of name, 240
Altersstil, 548
altruism,
  Goethe's early, 72, 1359
  sibling rivalry and, 205
Amazon, the (*Wilhelm Meister*), 902ff, 910, 913, 915, 916, 1443
Amazons, 318, 1210
ambitions for child, mother's failure to realize, 77
ambivalence,
  absent, in Goethe's mother, 77
  and anxiety, 587
  castration fantasy and decreased, 494
  and creativity, 710
  creation and absence of, 1431
  and Goethe's drawing, 1221
  effects of freedom from, 1432n
  in the genius, 1431f
  in Goethe, 448, 516, 585
    towards Charlotte von Stein, 315, 416, 474, 506, 816, 887, 962f
    towards Cornelia, 250f
    in reaction to Cornelia's death, 253
    towards father, 414, 821, 1051, 1362
    towards Duke Karl August, 490, 1317
    towards mother, 955
    towards music, 1247
  isolation of, 417
  and nature, 993
  and object-loss, 291
  overall effect of, 46
  in Goethe's poetry, 826f
  and replacement of deceased partner, 288
  and unconscious images, 1045
  women and, 587
  Zimmermann's, 252

Amelia (*Wilhelm Meister*), 724
amorousness, and repetition, 658f
Ampère, Jean Jacques Antoine, 569
Amphion (*Elpenor*), 784
Amyntas, 1302ff
Amyot, Jacques, 109
Anacreon, 416, 551
Anacreontea, 558n
Anacreontic poetry, Goethe's, 1175f
anality/anal functions
  and artistic creativity, 242
  and Goethe's relation to Charlotte von Stein, 298
  in Goethe's works, 1351
  and psychoanalysis, 241
  and satire, 280f
analysis, *see* psychoanalysis
analyst, meaning of, to patient, 184
  see also transference
anatomy, Goethe's study of, 992
Andrason (*Triumph of Sentimentality*), 254f, 257f, 284, 287, 288f
André, Johann, 1249
Andreas, Willy, 24n, 87n, 380, 383, 384n, 687n
androgyny, 757
Anekdote zu den Freuden Werthers, 280
animals,
  disgusting, 265
  domestication of, 1417, 1430n
animism, and animals, 265
anlage, Goethe's dream, 1356
Anna Amalia, Dowager Duchess of Weimar, 140, 143, 147, 158f, 381, 1014, 1246, 1346
  letter to Fritsch, 1211ff
Annette, *see* Schönkopf
Annette (volume of poems), 1342
anniversaries,
  and psychopathology, 1044
  and symptoms, 429
anorexia nervosa, 1433
anti-fetish, 908, 910
antinomy (-ies),
  freedom/contingency, 1161
  synthesis of, 594f
Antiochus, 914
Antiope (*Elpenor*), 784, 785f
anti-semitism, Goethe's, 1036n
Antonio (*Tasso*), 1157
anxiety, 609
  use of inherited, 658

aperçu, Goethe's idea of, 1116f
apes, 265ff
Apollo, 328, 335
Apuleius, 632
Arabian Nights, 488
Arbar (*Prometheus*), 477
Arcadia, 1052
Arcadian Society of Philandria, 1249n; *see
    also Arkadische Gesellschaft*
Ariadne, 1267f
aristocracy, Goethe and, 223, 511f; *see also*
    nobility; status
Aristophanes, 407, 420ff, 425n; *see also
    Birds, The*
Aristotle, 1147
Arkadische Gesellschaft zu Phylandria,
    835n; *see also* Arcadian Society
arm, as penis symbol, 312
Arnim, Bettina von, xxii, 71f, 74ff, 80,
    104–5, 267, 452, 672, 781, 1045,
    1228, 1355f
  letter to Goethe, 704
  letter to Goethe's mother, 267
Arnstein, 174
arrogance, in Goethe, 38f
art,
  automorphic element in, 566
  foreign, Goethe and, 640n
  Italian, 1277
  psychoanalysis and, xxiii ff
  psychopathology and, 69, 70
  and psychosis, 1097
Artemis, 328, 335
artist(s),
  and neurotic, difference, 1397
  relation to parents, and historical period,
    709n
  relation to work, 82
artistic creation, *see* creation; creativity
Askalaphus (*Proserpina*), 273ff
associations, free, *see* free associations
Athene, 335
Athens, 1008
Auerbach's Keller, 49
Auftreten, meaning, 1456
August, brother of Duke of Gotha, 1332n
Auguste, *see* Stolberg
Augustine, St., 590, 1311, 1337f, 1344
  See also De civitate Dei
Aurelia (*Wilhelm Meister*), 902, 908ff, 936
Aus meinem Leben, spätere Zeit, 79f
authority, Goethe's attitude to, 741

authorship, as vocation, 731
autobiography,
  in Goethe's work, 85
  as preparation for death, 710
  Wilhelm Meister as, 696ff
Autodidasker dream, 1428f
automorphism, 544ff, 556
  outside creative process, 572
  role-playing and, 560ff
autoplasticity, 543f
autosymbolic phenomena, 1281
awakening, 1376
awe, of persons of high birth, 616

Baden-Baden, 1215
Balaam, 1278
ballads, Goethe's, 1187f
balloons, 738f
Balsamo, Giuseppe, *see* Cagliostro
Balsazar, 41
Barchfeld, 599
barium sulphate, 1110n
Basedow, Johann Bernhard, 933
Bätely, 1218ff, *see also Jery and Bätely*
bathing, 605
Batty, George, 1241n
Baumgart, Hermann, 780n
Beaulieu-Marconnay, Henriette von, 1069
bed, retreat to, 733
'Bedeutende Förderniss durch ein Einziges
    geistreiches Wort,' 1156f
Beethoven, Ludwig van, 82, 537, 640, 1310f,
    1312f, 1353, 1372n, 1390
Behrisch, Ernst Wolfgang, 37, 38, 59ff, 192,
    237, 1064
  influence on Goethe, 49ff, 58, 119
  letters from Goethe to, 37, 44n, 51, 52, 53,
    56f, 60f, 69, 81, 112, 237, 674, 695,
    1022, 1064, 1148, 1177, 1367
'Bekenntnisse einer schönen Seele,' *see* 'Con-
    fessions of a Beautiful Soul'
Belinde, *see* Schönemann
Belleben, 4
Belsazar, 752f; *see also* Belshazzar
Belshazzar, 41, 94; *see also* Belsazar
Belvedere, 218, 496
Bendel (*Wilhelm Meister*), 728f, 751ff, 765
Bengel, 753
Benn, Gottfried, 1452
Bentham, Jeremy, 283
Berger, Dorothea, 806n
Bergler, Edmund, 1379n

Berlin, 298, 444

Bernardo (*Erwin und Elmire*), 1259

Bernfeld, Siegfried, 691n, 692, 693, 695, 697

Bernhard, Duke of Weimar, 410f, 570

Bernstorf, Countess, 497

Bertran de Born, 476n

Beschränkung, meaning, 623n

Bettina (Venetian girl juggler), 1348f

Beulwitz, Karoline von, 1374

Beutler, Ernst, 1016n

Bewusstsein, Goethe's use of word, 1360

Bible/bibliomancy, 296, 875

Bibring, Edward, 1078n

Bielchowsky, 1144

biography,
  and the novel, 1439f
  psychoanalytic, xix, xxi
  psychology and, xxiv f

biological processes, and psychic processes, relation, 1402, 1403

Biot, Jean Baptiste, 1136

Birds, The, 276n, 407, 420ff, 436f, 442, 443f, 446, 450, 736

Birsch valley, 371

birth, repetition of, and phobia, 1217

birthday,
  Christiane's, 1289
  official, of English sovereign, 750n
  see also Cornelia

birth fantasies, Goethe's, 123, 352, 393

bisexuality, 239, 351, 1403
  and Goethe's drawing, 1225

Bismann, Johann Andreas, 1249

bizarre, Goethe and the, 21

bleeding, surgical, 1455 and n

Blei, F., 1271f

blood imagery, 317ff, 330, 332
  see also menstruation

blood myth, 1209f

Boccaccio, Giovanni, 42, 196f

Bode, Wilhelm, xxiv, 37, 68, 146, 158n, 351n, 393n, 462, 781, 963ff, 974, 995n, 1024, 1029–30n, 1031, 1032f, 1053, 1139, 1152n, 1263, 1308

Bodmer, Johann Jakob, 423

Böhme, Johann Gottlieb, 597

Böhme, Maria Rosina, 599

Boisserée, 83

Bolk, L., 1392

Bologna, 1273, 1274, 1277
  Scientific Institute, 1278
  Second School of, 1277

Bologna stone, 1110n

Bonaparte, Marie, xix, 711, 872n

bookburning, 359

boredom,
  and genius, 1351
  and repetition, 662

Börne, 1310

Borneo, 1014

Bornstein, Bertha, 268n

Bottom, *see* Shakespeare, *Midsummer Night's Dream*

Botzen, 1002

bourgeoisie,
  and cultural renaissance, 160
  and women, 53

Bowdler, Thomas, 745n

Bradisch, J. A. von, 548, 670, 834n, 1340n

bragging, oral, 40

Branconi, Marchioness Maria Antonia von, 460ff, 466, 474f, 477, 479f, 481, 482, 816
  letter from Goethe to, 460f, 475n

Branconi, Pessina de, 460

breast, bad, symbol of, 267

breath, as fertilizing agent, 1225n

Brentano, Maximiliane, 87, 89ff

Brentano, Peter Anton, 89n, 90, 92

Breughel, 1348

briefs, law, Goethe's, 172ff

Brill, A. A., 941

Brion, Friederike, 13, 22, 27, 118, 119, 192, 375, 388, 390, 521, 806, 808, 1032, 1049, 1060, 1061, 1064, 1066ff, 1219
  letter from Goethe to, 521

Brocken, 3, 301ff, 313, 396, 1214

brother fixation, 252

brother, theme of rescuing, 327

brother-sister relationship, problems, 758

Brown, Thomas K., 239ff

Brühl, Count von, 234
  letter from Goethe to, 234

Brunswick, 3, 844

Brunswick, Duke of, *see* Karl Wilhelm Ferdinand

Brutus, 1129

Buder, Hildegard, 1277, 1280f, 1285n

Buff, Charlotte (later Kestner), 86, 87, 89, 91, 92, 93, 96, 102f, 104, 112, 118, 192, 584n, 633, 772, 1068

Buffon, Georges Louis Leclerc, Comte de, 359, 453, 1144

Bühler, Charlotte, 1142n

Buisonjé, Johannes Cornelius de, 302, 479, 550, 1371

Bürger, Gottfried August, 621
  letter from Goethe to, 621, 988f

Burlingham, Dorothy, 251

Büttner, Christian Wilhelm, 1120f, 1137

Buxbaum, Edith, xvi, 684n

Byron, Lord, 1158f

Cäcilie (*Stella*), 126f, 128

Caesar, Julius, 313

Cagliostro, Count Alexander, 644, 650, 982n

Calvin, Jean, 338

Campagne in Frankreich 1792, see *Campaign in France*

Campaign in France 1792, 4, 11, 12, 14, 15, 115, 1055
  quoted, 8, 9, 10, 11, 16, 1055f, 1115n

Camper, 1350

Canaan, 880

card-playing, 596ff, 654, 1215

Carl Wolfgang (illegitimate son of Duke Karl August), 1327n, 1329n

Carletta, 1012, 1020, 1047n

Carlin, 846

Carlsbad, 901, 953, 967, 994ff, 1059

Caroline, Landgravine of Hesse, *see* Henriette Christine Caroline

Carus, C. G., xxxi

cases and observations, analytic:
  university student, illustrating varying degree of participation in analysis, 282
  schizophrenic woman who experienced suspension in presence of nature, 398
  schizophrenic woman with daydreams recapitulating past, 697n
  schizophrenic woman who wrote novel regarding delusional character, 732
  paranoid schizophrenic with unimpaired intellectual gifts, 1178
  altruistic girl of 1½ years, 1359
  young artist who stimulated mother, 1360n

Cassel, 501, 816, 823

Castel Gandolfo, 1047

Castor and Pollux, 1444

castration, 756, 992, 1208, 1265, 1279
  complex, female, 145
  equivalent, 107, 293f, 325, 515

castration (*Continued*)
  fantasy, 494
  fears, 35, 62, 1301
  feelings, 295f
  Goethe's epigram and, 669, 675
  imagery, 293ff, 310n, 465, 482, 669, 1304f
  and incest tabu, 1206
  in *Iphigenia*, 1219
  in *New Melusine*, 802n
  symbols, 1276
  threat, 1284f; fetish and, 634
  in *Wilhelm Meister*, 905

catarrh, 409

catastrophes, 452, 492f

catatonia, 543

catharsis,
  art as, 70
  Werther as a, 578

Catullus, 1267, 1331

cemeteries, removal of, 4

Ceres, 274

Cervantes, 732

Cestius, Pyramid of, 1309

change, personality, structural and permanent, 666

changes, in poem, significance of, 312

charity, Goethe's, 356f, 621

Charlemagne, xxiii

Charles VII, Emperor, 75f, 269, 378n, 672f, 675n

Charlotte (*The Siblings*), 246, 476

cheek, swelling of, 293

Chekhov, Anton, 1396

child/children
  affinity to, 775n
  as barometers of others' opinion of us, 991
  desire to create, 81
  fantasy life of, 1388
  fear of having, 787
  form of address to, 825
  Goethe's attitude to, 774ff, 858
  Goethe's desire for, 584
  raising, 175
  and sexual excitement, 1382

childbearing,
  compensation for, 81
  and drawing, 1225
  envy of, 788; and cultural superiority, 1402
  infantile theories, 239

childbirth, Goethe's absence at times of, 1288

childhood,
  resistance to material from, in analysis, 403
  return to, 1005
child-penis equation, 906
child-work of art equation, 81
Christ, 1003
  comparison of Goethe with, 165
  Goethe's aversion for, 1347
  identification with, 67, 457, 536n, 1100, 1124, 1234f
  Lavater and, 646ff
  see also Jesus
Christiane, *see* Vulpius
Christianity, 420, 640f, 644, 739
Chromatology, 1114n, 1120, 1140, 1366, 1373, 1377, 1410n
  quoted, 1115n, 1120, 1121, 1129ff, 1136f
"Confession of the Author," in *Chromatology,* 1120, 1130
chronology, errors in, 114
Cicero, 1436
circumcision, xx, 1036n, 1206n, 1363
"city," defense of, 298f
clarification, 1078n
classicism, French, 21
Clauer, Balthasar Johann David, 101f, 1102
claustrophobia, 401, 1216
clitoris, orgasm and, 759
cloak, as penis symbol, 910f
clock, astronomical, 641f
clothes, Goethe and, in childhood, 704f
Clytemnestra, 316f, 323
coach, Goethe's, 172
Coalition War, First, 11
Coburg, 608, 616
coffee, 391, 1150
cohabitation, woman's attitude to, 935
Coleridge, S. T., 566
colic, 246
color optics, 831n, 1119f
  Goethe's theory, 1121n
comedy, 420, 425, 443
  depersonalization and, 426
comets, 626
comic strips, 1424n
"common, the," 439
communication, 199f, 1431
competition, between Goethe and Duke Karl August, 340, 512
composers, search for, 1247

compulsion,
  repetitious, 986, 1035, 1046n
  self-observation as, 432
compulsive traits, in Goethe, 111, 449, 818
concealment, 201
  and guilt feelings, 557
  need for, 745f
concentration, high, and unifunctionality, 1420
conception, re-enactment of own, 1043
condensation, 272f, 276
confession, 198, 199
  religious, 1098
"confession, grand," 68
"Confessions of a Beautiful Soul," 470, 471, 480; *see also Wilhelm Meister*
confidence, 179f
"configuration, own pure," 563
conflict(s),
  and adjustment to reality, 542
  artist's, not expressed in work, 699
  in Goethe's childhood, 261
  and Goethe's public work, 177
  with idealized woman, 480
  infantile and everyday life, 330
  internal, with father, 176
  and interpersonal relationships, 297
  from overvalued incidents in analysis, 227
  in patient, apart from main neurosis, 228
  in relatives and friends, 787
  spontaneous tendency to, 1380f
  and structural change, 1380
  variability of tendency towards, 46
conflict-free
  relationship, 1306
  sphere, 1294
conscience, 199
  see also Erinyes
consciousness, ebb of, 1428
constancy principle, 724, 1397
Constantin, Prince, *see* Konstantin
constipation, 241f, 246
content deductions, 1426
contrasts, reconciliation of, 418
Conversations with Eckermann, see Eckermann
Cook, James, 712
Copstein, Seymour A., 476n, 739n, 1252n, 1266n
copyright, 1310
coral, 1013
Corneille, 110

Cornelia (Goethe's sister),
Goethe's arrogance towards, 38ff
Goethe and her birthday, 300
death, 27, 28, 33, 248ff, 274ff, 281, 283ff,
700
in *Dichtung und Wahrheit,* 757f
frigidity, 761, 1103n
and *Iphigenia,* 326ff
Lenz and, 27, 28
marriage, 32, 91, 98, 214f
Mignon and, 757f, 761
as mirror-image of Goethe, 1347, 1358,
1453
as mother-substitute for Goethe, 102
pregnancy, 27, 85, 98, 102, 104, 211, 212,
245
projected novel about, 102
Goethe's relation to, 32ff, 54ff, 94, 97,
1088, 1358
and *The Siblings,* 207f, 211f
letters: from Goethe, 33f, 35, 38ff, 40f,
42, 43, 45, 48, 49, 55, 58, 63, 64f,
214, 1104, 1254; to Goethe, 244; to
Charlotte von Stein, 245, 251, 252n;
to Auguste Stolberg, 192n, 245
other references, 90, 92, 93, 101, 108,
111, 113, 114, 117, 118, 119, 123ff,
169, 181, 185, 189ff, 213ff, 224, 225,
286f, 311, 336, 390f, 447, 480, 514n,
708, 829, 1049, 1152, 1189, 1289f
correspondence, Goethe's, extent of, 1184
Corri, Domenico, 1252n
corset, 348, 373
cosmos, re-creation of, and genius, 1353f
Count, the (*Wilhelm Meister*), 836, 841
Countess, the (*Wilhelm Meister*) 841
cover memory, 1205
craving, unfulfilled, 1385
cream of tartar, 298
"creation, rejuvenated," prophecy of, 1145
creation,
artistic, shrinkage of ego in, 566
genitality and, 1181
intuitive, 1187ff
mental, and childbearing, 790
creativity,
gap in Goethe's, 568ff, 683
increased, in transference, 682
inhibition of, 1181
momentum of, in Goethe, 682
Goethe's mother and his, 78
phallic, 1405

creativity (*Continued*)
preservation of function in sleep, 1429
psychoanalysis and, 1095
psychology of, 70f, 545
psychosis and, 73, 1169ff
Goethe's, rhythm of, 1143
scientific, Goethe's, 1144f
subjective/objective elements in, 545
as triumph of ego, 114
and work, distinction, 171
Crete, 492
Creusa, 322
criticism, touchiness about, 191n
Cronos, 334
cruelty, in Goethe, 964
cultural products, and mental process of
creator, 1426
Cupid, 1034
Cupid and Psyche, 632f
cure,
causes of, 281ff
psychic, 234
Curialstil, 547ff, 566
curiosity,
Goethe's, 1058
oral, 262

daemon, Goethe's, 1414
dagger, 108, 113
Dalberg, Carl von, 1241n
Daly, C. D., 305n
Danaë, 371
Danaides, 121
dancing, 1071
Christiane and, 1307
see also egg-dance
danger, and rescue theme, 237
Dante, 1264, 1353
Darius, 752
Darsaintcourt, Mme., 818, 819
Darmstadt, 230, 231, 410n, 735, 825
Darmstadter Empfindsamen, 230f
dashes, use of, 536, 542
dating, errors of, 115, 241, 269, 956
David, Frida, 358, 359n, 360n
David and Goliath, 263
Day of Atonement, 28
daydreams,
active elements in, 85
recapitulating past, 697n
and work of art, compared, 1430n

death,
  and activity, 1190
  attitude to, Goethe's, 283, 474, 476f, 481,
    856f; eighteenth-century, 953
  aversion to word, 1206
  of beloved person, and release of libido,
    291
  of close relative, effect on patient's re-
    covery, 284
  escape from, and double, 271
  fear of, 296, 481
  and homosexuality, 1453
  meaning of, 113
  parapraxis as symbol of, 865
  and sexual intercourse, 478
  traveling and, 409
death wish, 204f
  against Charlotte von Stein, 474
Decalogue, 1035
Decameron, 42
decapitation, 310
deceased partner, replacement of, 288
December, depressions in, 300f, 811, 873,
    957, 959, 960
De Civitate Dei (St. Augustine), Annota-
    tions to, 1331, 1337ff, 1371
  translation, 1337ff
defective, Goethe's horror of, 706
defense(s),
  in analysis, 226
  Freud on, 299
  and gratification, 1420
  opposites as, 315
  sickness and, 409
defloration, 1268f
  symbolic, 863
Deianira, 322, 847
deification, 712f
  of human beings, 5
déjà vu, 1005n
dejection, and inhibition of creativity, 866
delinquency, 101, 1363f
  childhood, 1046f
delusional system, 1177, 1179ff
delusions,
  overvaluation of, 1120
  psychotic, 515, 543
democracy, and genius, 1312n
denial, 313, 629, 1206
Dennert, Friedrich, 303n
depersonalization, 279, 373, 426ff, 437ff,
    446, 456, 947f, 1005

depersonalization (*Continued*)
  in analysis, 185
  and masochism, 486
depression, 797, 876, 957
  annual, 1044
  see also December
deprivation, 205
  and love, 486
Derones, 1453
Descartes, 1376
despair, 1385
Dessau, 608
Dessau, Prince of, 674, 692
destructiveness,
  Goethe and, 1309n, 1312ff
  and psychopathy, 1391
detachment, Goethe's, from Charlotte von
    Stein, 952ff
Deutsch, Helene, 1404n
devaluation of surroundings, 609
devil, 366f
  genius and, 1169
Diamond Necklace, 31, 678, 982f, 1036n
diaries, Goethe's
  discontinuance of, 711
  history of, 690f
  Italian, 670n, 691, 1002, 1006, 1007,
    1008, 1025, 1274, 1280
  references and quotations, 15, 222, 223,
    241, 242n, 248f, 270, 289, 300, 319,
    344, 345f, 363, 368f, 380, 382f, 385,
    386, 389, 391f, 393, 408f, 417, 419f,
    424, 426, 427f, 429, 431f, 435, 436,
    438, 440, 442, 448, 457n, 462f, 489,
    493, 496f, 537f, 623, 678, 689ff, 783,
    1071, 1279
diary,
  and dream, compared, 696
  and letters, compared, 695
  as letter to oneself, 695
  motives for keeping, 692
  place of parents in, 695
Dichtung und Wahrheit,
  quotations, 50, 51, 83, 87, 89, 93, 94, 95,
    96, 106, 107, 108, 109, 118fn, 124,
    173, 175, 467n, 557, 566n, 596ff,
    607f, 671, 702, 704, 707, 723, 925f,
    931n, 933f, 936f, 940, 992, 1040,
    1060f, 1063, 1068, 1103, 1161f,
    1203ff, 1216, 1219, 1222, 1224,
    1229ff, 1250, 1251n, 1358n, 1360,
    1377n, 1456

Dichtung und Wahrheit (Continued)
 references, 49, 87, 92, 96, 105, 113n, 114,
  175, 213n, 259, 272, 375, 470n, 480,
  556, 568, 664, 677n, 706n, 722, 757f,
  763, 807, 924, 926, 932f, 950, 1016,
  1031n, 1032, 1047, 1066, 1102, 1201,
  1228, 1237, 1248, 1249f, 1363,
  1384n, 1439, 1442, 1453
Diderot, xxix, 428, 725n
Diede, Louise, 613, 614
differentiation,
 and jokes, 1425
 in sleep, 1429
Dilthey, Wilhelm, 932, 1368, 1420
Dionysus, image of, 1277
Dirce (*Elpenor*), 784
disbelief, suspension of, 566
discharge, arousal without, 1085f
disease, psychical effect of, 723
disguise, 1066f
displacement, 226n, 937f
 from below upwards, 1066
displeasure, Goethe's avoidance of, 175
Divine, man's relation to the, 794f
divorce, 1294n
Doctor, the (*Jest, Cunning and Vengeance*),
  1245f
doctorate dissertation, 172
Dodd, W., 63n
doll, 254f, 259, 266, 273
 see also puppets
Don Giovanni, see Ponte, L. da
Döring, Frau von, 145n, 166, 168, 1152n
Dostoevski, 357, 1382n
double,
 formation of, 271
 theme of, 255, 266f, 268, 271f, 1219
drawing,
 Goethe's, 468, 1221f; Goethe on his,
  1191f; failure in, 107f; lack of passion in, 1223; pigsty sketches, 415f
 and orality, 297f, 1224
dream(s),
 alterations in records of, 1275
 anxiety, 276
 and certainty, 577f
 changes in reported, 312
 and conflict solution, 1380
 conscious direction of, 1283n
 erotic, in *Werther*, 101
 function, in Goethe, 1355

dream(s) (*Continued*)
 incestuous, 313
 indifferent and important in, 276
 interpretation of, 1285n
 nonsense words in, 1119f
 overdetermined, 284
 overdistinct reality in, 482
 phenomenology of, 84n
 practice of writing down, 693n
 problem solution in, 1423
 as psychosis, 1097, 1375
 repetitive elaborations in, 511
 and wish-fulfillment, 1285n, 1375
 within dreams, 304, 311, 313
 and work of art, compared, 1430n
 see also poems
 Charlotte von Stein's:
  of lost cloak at communion, 910f
 Goethe's:
  automorphism in, 544
  of Charlotte von Stein in gown, 815
  incestuous, 313
  in infancy, 1356
  of Lotte, 93
  of marriage, 635
  of penis symbols, 60
  of pheasant, 1273ff
  of sack, 37, 56, 60ff, 80, 105
  of visit from Knebel and Charlotte von
   Stein, 493
dress, Christiane's, 1293
drive dependability, 1414
drives,
 ego and sexual, 1432
 egosyntonic, 1433
 in genius, 1433ff
 id- and ego-, 1433 and n
 not always irrational, 1413f
 organismic, 1434
Drusenheim, 1219
Dryden, John, 109
"Du,"
 use towards Charlotte von Stein, 506ff,
  513f, 522, 524, 532ff, 542, 550, 776,
  1033, 1226f, 1318
 use in letter to Charlotte sent to Herder,
  1033
 use in Goethe's time, 535
ducks, wild, 393
Duisburg, 7
dumpf, meaning, 195n

Düntzer, Heinrich, 4n, 7, 11, 13, 14, 96n, 102, 111, 207n, 343n, 348, 383, 412, 497n, 638n, 672, 678n, 779, 843, 856, 1228
Dürer, Albrecht, 419, 1279, 1348
Düsseldorf, 286
duty, 525

eating habits, and orality, 1071
Eckermann, Conversations with, quoted, 113, 177n, 262, 264, 332f, 347, 409, 568, 569f, 595n, 651, 745, 807, 835n, 859, 871, 939n, 991, 993, 1089, 1098, 1116, 1119, 1121f, 1123, 1125, 1145, 1156, 1186, 1187ff, 1191, 1247, 1264, 1369, 1372, 1438n
education of younger people, Goethe and, 780n
ἡγεμονικον, 429
egg-dance, 755, 764f
Egmont, 1040f, 1053
Egmont, 578, 579, 605n, 925, 926, 1039ff
ego,
    defense structure in, 299
    division of, 1161
    effect of creativity on, 682f
    and formation of double, 271
    modification by unusual external conditions, 483
    in orgasm, 1419
    secondary autonomy of, 1412
    and tamed drives, 1417
ego dissolution,
    balance with ego formation, 1179
    and Goethe's poetry, 1179
    recovery from threatened, 540
ego-functioning, adequate, in Goethe, 47
ego-ideal(s),
    displacement of, 572
    Duke Karl August as Goethe's, 1316
    revision of, 50
ego loss,
    fear of, 183
    and orgasm, 183
egosyntonic drives, 1433n
Ehrenberg, Rudolf, 683
Einsiedel, 552n
Einstein, Albert, 1128
Eisenach, 3, 140, 297, 608, 624, 636, 637, 842, 844, 882
Eisler, Rudolph, 4n

ejaculatio praecox, see ejaculation, premature
ejaculation, premature, 1058, 1061, 1064, 1270, 1280f, 1366
    imagery of, 1282
    quick, and potency, 1282
Elbingerode, 14
Elective Affinities, 239n, 1297n, 1298n, 1396
Electra (*Iphigenia in Delphi*), 1278
Elias, 457
Elisabeth (*Götz von Berlichingen*), 86
Elmire (*Erwin und Elmire*), 1259f
Elpenor, 783ff
Elsheimer, Adam, 459
embarrassment, 604, 607, 609ff
Emilie, 1060
Emmendingen, 124, 126, 128, 129, 244, 245, 327
emotion(s),
    anticipation of effect on others, 656f
    attempt to master, 430
    concreteness of, in genius, 1388
    denial of bearing of, 49
    effects on psyche, 665
    integrity of, 833ff
    Spinoza and the, 943
    and structure, 665
emotionality, Goethe's, 1058ff
emotional states, in analysis, 186
Empfindsamen, Die, see Sentimental Ones, The
end of the world, fantasy of, 1056n
endocrine changes, and genius, 1401
energy,
    indifferent, 1406ff; in Goethe, 1408ff
    instinctual, and thinking, 1408
    tendency to economize, 1434
Engel, Johann Jakob, 715n, 1238f
Engelhardt, Johann Christian Daniel, 855
Enlightenment, the, 4, 6, 49
"Entenfang," 393n
envy, 225, 1402f; *see also* penis envy; pregnancy
epigrams, 1371
epileptoid symptoms, 183
Epopeus (*Elpenor*), 784
Epops, 421, 425
Erasistratus, 914
Erfurt, 279, 608
Erikson, E., xvi
Erinyes (*Iphigenia*), 316, 320, 323ff

Ernst August, Duke of Sachsen-Weimar-
Eisenach, 140, 157f
Ernst August Konstantin, Duke of Sachsen-
Weimar-Eisenach, 158
error, psychology of, 1132
Erste Harzreise, 3
Erwin (*Erwin und Elmire*), 1259f
Erwin und Elmire, 1249, 1259f
erythroblastosis foetalis, 1287n
essays, Goethe's, 1340
eternity, man's, 412f
ethics, and artistic creativity, 893f
Etna, Mount, 451
Ettersburg, 359, 364, 450, 1240f
Eucharist, 266n
Euripides, 489
Evadne (*Elpenor*), 786
Everdingen, 508
evil, integration of, 453
"Exaltation of the Cross," 359
executions, 725, 726f
exhibitionism,
Goethe's, 605f, 940
and the theater, 721
and writing of poetry, 593
existence, reason for, 617f
experience, primal, 1127, 1129, 1134ff, 1377
"Experiment, The, as the Mediator between
Object and Subject," 1113
experiment(s), 1112ff
aversion to, 1114
eye, gesture of putting hand to, 56ff

Fabrice (*The Siblings*), 207, 209, 212, 215,
216, 220, 470
Fahlmer (later Schlosser), Johanna, 123,
124, 284, 286, 289f, 358, 363, 365
letters from Goethe to, 123, 124, 156n,
164, 216, 217f, 223, 285, 294, 295,
445, 459n, 1078
fairy-tales, xxii, 74, 1357
fainting, 183
Fairbairn, W. R. D., 1427n, 1436
falcon, 197
falsification, 364
fame, and death, 866
familiarity, confidential, 180, 185
family romance, Goethe's, xxiii, 378n, 671f,
677
fantasy(-ies),
archaic, 912
birth, *see* birth fantasies

fantasy(-ies) (*Continued*)
curing by fantasy, 236, 237
interpretation in analysis, 912
personified, 479, 488
splitting of, 272f
and writing of *Werther*, 257
See also birth fantasies; rescue fantasies
fantasy life,
artist's, 1387f
breaks in, 1388
in child and poet, 1390
Farinelli, 1012n
Fastnachtsspiel vom Pater Brey, Ein, 243
Fastnachtsspiele, 1261n
fate, immutability of, 182
father,
archaic, 782
dual position of, 412f
effects of loss of, 680
identification with, 754
inferiority/superiority to, 1008ff
maternal features in, 66
preoedipal, 781f
rebellion against, in Goethe's drawings,
1224
Goethe's, *see* Goethe, Johann Kaspar
father-figure,
aggression against, 390
Duke of Weimar as, 219
Frederick the Great as, 418
Fritsch as, 384, 386
Shakespeare as, 64
Thoas as, 326
father-substitutes, ambivalence towards, 639
fathers (of Goethe, Lenz, and Plessing), relation to sons, 18
Faust (*Faust*), 86, 696, 864f, 993
Faust, references and quotations, 49, 58f,
86, 239, 252, 253, 272, 303, 306ff,
366, 600, 601, 837, 859, 864f, 871,
1038, 1072, 1189, 1190, 1208, 1365,
1454n
Faustina, 1012, 1020, 1033ff, 1052, 1058,
1087, 1266, 1268f, 1290, 1346, 1371
fear,
Goethe and, 1057
Spinoza and, 943f
Fechner, Ludwig, 724
Federijo, 196f
Federn, Etta, 1306n
Felix (*Wilhelm Meister*), 239, 1442, 1444
fellatio, 1332

female genitality, acceptance of, 1007
female-lifeless equation, 262
female needs, understanding of, 1304
female psychology, Goethe's view of, 277
female superiority, denial of, 72
feminine component, warding off, 311, 312
femininity,
   Goethe's, 105, 788
   and production, 1188
Fenichel, Otto, 1215
Ferenczi, Sandor, 61, 1373n, 1383
Fernando (*Stella*), 126f
Ferrara, 1013, 1273
fertility rites, 1282n
Fesch, Willem de, 1252n
fetish,
   and aggression, 635
   ambivalence towards, 447
   double function of, 907
   as female penis, 905
   formation of, 905, 908
   gift as, 494
   ring as, 634
fetishism,
   Goethe's, 1445
   women and, 910
   see also shoes
fetus, identification with, 401
Fielitz, Wilhelm, 221, 223
finances, degeneration of State, 735
fire,
   Goethe's organization of fight against, 939
   at Gross Brembach, 450f
Fischer, Paul, 707n, 1210n, 1276n, 1360
Fisherwoman, The, 767f, 783
fixation, 1278, 1284
Flachsland, Caroline (Psyche), *see* Herder,
   Caroline
flash, mental, 1126f
Fliess, Wilhelm, xvi, 684n
flight, as escape mechanism, 176
flights, Goethe's, from beloved women, 94,
   97, 111, 123f, 998f
Florence, 1004
Flöricke, Karl Ludwig, 714n and f
fluorescence, 1111
flying machines, 738f
"fog, steaming," 469
food,
   Goethe and, 40, 43
   and love, equated, 355
   see also orality

food-giving woman, attraction of, 47
foramen incisivum, 1117
foreplay/forepleasure, 918n, 1266, 1282,
   1285
forgetting, symptomatic, 294
form deductions, 1426
forms, lack of respect for, 549
Forster, J. G., 712
Fraiberg, Selma, 1431
Fränkel, Jonas, 478n
Frankfurt, 37, 39, 75, 89, 90, 94, 95, 121,
   148, 171, 172, 190, 221, 222, 269,
   286, 375, 377, 386f, 409, 465, 511,
   579, 672, 677, 705, 838, 957f, 964,
   1245, 1363
Frankfurter Gelehrter Anzeiger, 88
Frankl-Hochwart, Ludwig August, 604
Frederick the Great, 49, 329, 341, 418f, 444,
   674, 843f
free associations, 502, 696, 1355
freedom, 1161
   lack of, in Goethe's pictorial art, 1224f
French, use in Goethe/Charlotte von Stein
   correspondence, 844f, 885f
Freud, Anna, 736, 1181, 1341n, 1356n,
   1361, 1415, 1424
Freud, Sigmund,
   on allo- and autoplasticity, 543
   on the artist, xxvii, 82n; on artist's sec-
     ondary gain, 1431n
   at Athens, 1005, 1008
   on attention and parapraxia, 1144n
   on being in love, 588
   on choice of names, 127
   on conflict of feeling and death, 710; on
     tendency to conflict, 46
   on cooperation of preconscious and un-
     conscious impulses, 1435f
   on defense, 299
   on delusional psychotics, 515
   discarded division of drives, 1432
   on disposition to obsessional neurosis, 1359
   on dreams, 276, 284, 1097; on conscious
     direction of dreams, 1283n; on
     dreams within dreams, 304; on over-
     determined dreams, 284; on dream
     and psychosis, 1375; first dream in-
     terpretation, 711
   on egoism and illness, 1181f
   on emotions and phylogenesis, 657
   on errors of dating, 115
   on fantasy of return to womb, 61f

Freud, Sigmund (*Continued*)
on function of fetish, 634
and Fliess, xvi, 684n
on Goethe, xix, 76f, 184n, 560n, 1357;
    parallels with Goethe's life, 1104n
on identification and object-relationship,
    42
on jokes, 1260, 1421
Joseph identification, 1104n
on Leonardo da Vinci, xxvii, 32, 691n,
    1114, 1410, 1413n
on loss of father, 678
on masochism, 458, 1381, 1383f
on mother-son relation, 77
on mourning, 658
on negation, 1445n
on obscenity, 1352
on oceanic feeling, 766
on Orestes' cure, 325n
on perceptual identity, 542n
on pleasure principle and analysis, 200
on preoedipal father, 781n
on Prometheus, 1382n
on psychoneuroses and actual neuroses,
    1416
on retrograde and progredient psychic life,
    1428
on rescue fantasies, 238n, 239, 750n
on schizophrenic speech and thinking, 564
on self-observation, 1160
and Spinoza, compared, 941
on splitting and fantasies in paranoia,
    272f
on three psychic principles, 1397
on transference love, 185
and transformation of instinctual energy,
    1406ff
traumatic infantile dream, 1043fn
on unconscious and time, 1043
other references, xvii, xviii, xix, xxiv, 80,
    176, 193n, 200 and n, 231n, 232,
    237, 265n, 268n, 297, 310n, 549,
    576n, 639n, 651, 709, 711, 724, 732,
    759, 775n, 827n, 872, 893n, 905n,
    907, 986, 990, 992n, 1015n, 1056n,
    1093, 1099, 1142n, 1163n, 1198,
    1200, 1219, 1224n, 1275n, 1361,
    1365, 1380, 1382, 1387 and n, 1395,
    1399n, 1412, 1425, 1429n, 1434n,
    1452, 1453n
Friederike, *see* Brion
Friederike (Swiss girl), 27

Friedrich (*Lila*), 244
friendship,
    and love, 359f, 362
    nobility and, 840f
    reasons favoring, 688
Fritsch, Jakob F. V., 381ff, 386f, 389, 404,
    692, 821f, 1211ff
    letters from Goethe to, 821, 857f, 978
    see also Anna Amalia
Fromm-Reichmann, Frieda, 514
Frommann, 1298n
frustration,
    and genius, 1351f
    Goethe's, in relation to Charlotte von
        Stein, 239, 293
    and rejection, 196
    use of, by Charlotte von Stein, 202
Fuchs, Eduard, 173, 174, 487
fugue, 1428
    hysterical, 861
fusion,
    with beloved, 113
    child/mother, 79n
    mouth/genital, 1075f
    with vacuum, 483
    with world, 374

"Gablidon," 650n
Galileo, 1116
Gallitzin, Adelheid Amalia, Fürstin von,
    970f, 1092n
gambling, 1215
games, Goethe's attitude to, 598
    see also card-playing
Ganymede, 1348
garden, sale of, 733
garden architecture, 275
Garraty, John A., xxiv
gastrointestinal disturbances, 241, 389, 390
Gauss, 639
Gay d'Oliva, Baronne, 311
Gebhardt, Martin, 1113n, 1117n, 1118
Geiger, Ludwig, 1020
Geitel, Max, 1145n
Gemeine, das, 439
genital activity, and genius, 1404
genital sexuality, and sublimation, 1415
genius, xxix, 744f
    analysis and, 1095n
    definition of, 1353
    distribution of, 1314
    Goethe's attitude to own, 1441f

genius (*Continued*)
  Goethe's, and parental influence, 1356
  as hypertrophy, 1417f
  morality of, 1308ff
  newness of creations, 1434f
  and object-relationships, 1367ff
  offspring of, 1309n
  paucity of, 1180
  and personality structure, 1418
  and psychopathology, xxxi f
  and routine, 439f
  self-evaluation of, 1119
  social response to, 1311f
  way of experiencing world, 1431
  in women, 1400f
George (innkeeper's son), 1066f
German language, Goethe and, 1263ff, 1350
Germany, cultural renaissance, 160
Geschwister, Die, see Siblings, The
gestures, interpretation by schizophrenic, 58
  see also eye
ghosts, disghosted, 290
Gibb, John, 652
Gickelhahn, 465, 466, 478, 481
Giovanna, 197
Giovinazzi, Domenico, 1249f, 1254
girls, education of, *see* school
Glaser, Rudolf, 270, 1050n
glass, overfilled, 111
Gluck, 1245
Glückliche Ereignis, 1113n
gnats, 375
God
  experience of time and, 882
  and guilt feelings, 420f
  unselfish love of, 935f, 984
Goethe, August von, 1151, 1287, 1305, 1306,
    1308f, 1313, 1328, 1361, 1372, 1445
  letters from Goethe to, 716f
Goethe, Caroline, 1287
Goethe, Cornelia Friederike Christiane (later
    Schlosser), *see* Cornelia
Goethe, Friedrich Georg, 1037
Goethe, Hans, junior, 1037
Goethe, Hans Christian, 1037
Goethe, Hermann Jakob, 757
Goethe, Johann Kaspar (Goethe's father),
    222, 327ff, 375f, 702ff, 925ff, 1203,
    1250f, *et passim*
  attitude to nobility, 177, 925
  attitude of Goethe to, 40, 171, 176ff, 416f,
    688ff, 1046ff

Goethe, Johann Kaspar (*Continued*)
  baptism and marriage, 1034
  and card-playing, 596
  circumcision, xx, 1036n, 1206n, 1363
  death, 269, 407, 412, 531, 678; effect of,
    on Goethe, 698
  and *Egmont,* 1040f
  identification with, *see* identification
  journey to Italy, 924, 1012ff, 1038
  as lawyer, 172f
  letter from Goethe to, 925f
  mentions of, in Goethe's letters, after his
    death, 714
  and Milanese girl, 1050
  premarital sex life, 1035
  sickness of, 270f, 410f, 629
  visit of Duke Karl August to, 1317fn
  work record of, 1201
Goethe, Johanna Maria von, 429
Goethe, Karl, 1287
Goethe, Katharina Elizabeth (née Textor)
    (Goethe's mother), 249, 250, 289,
    296, 429, 824, 1251
  attitude of Goethe to, 702ff, 713n, 971f
  family romance of, 672
  identification with, 480
  love-life of, 269, 511
  relationship to Christiane, 1295
  relationship with Goethe, 77f, 1357ff
  letters from Goethe to, 249, 284–5, 294,
    375–6, 581f, 677, 705, 873f, 1006
  letter to Goethe, 471, 473
  letter to Lavater, 472
  letter to Zimmermann, 252n
Goethe, Kathinka, 1287
Goethe, Ottilie von, 604
Goethe, Johann Wolfgang von,
  birth, 76, 272
  chairman of the Treasury, 444
  meets Charlotte von Stein, 148ff; relations
    with, *see* von Stein, Charlotte
  children, 1138, 1287
  as civil servant, 170, 194
  documentation of life, 1012
  family of, social ascent, 1037
  journey to Italy, 923ff
  as lawyer, 172ff
  letters, *see under names of recipients;*
    from Italy to friends in Weimar,
    1004, 1006, 1009, 1047, 1048, 1073
  life and works, relation, 82
  many-sidedness of, xxix f

Goethe, Johann Wolfgang von (*Continued*)
  marriage, 1288, 1299, 1327f; projected re-
    marriage, 1313n
  nobilitation, 670f
  offices held, 679f
  made Privy Councillor, 377
  psychological intuition, 12
  relation to his sister, 42ff, 54f, 65f, 71,
    97, *see also* Cornelia
  sexual life, 51ff *et passim*
  siblings, 5, 32, 104n
  thirtieth birthday, 389ff
  use of incognito, 15
  works, *see under individual titles*
  autobiography, *see Dichtung und Wahr-
    heit*
goiter, 401
"Golden Verses of the Pythagoreans," 480n
Görtz, Count, 146, 384n
Gospels, 740
gossip, *see* rumor
Gotha, 9, 349, 608, 609, 612f, 817
Gotha, Duchess of, 589
Gotha, Duke of, 895, 1027
  letter from Goethe to, 411n
Gotter, Friedrich Wilhelm, 555n
  letter from Goethe to, 81
Göttingen, 816
  University, 5
Götz von Berlichingen (character), 86,
    112f, 1319
Götz von Berlichingen, 25, 91, 112f, 122,
    169, 349, 628, 931, 1049, 1189, 1379
Goué, 88
Gräf, Hans Gerhard, 788n, 999n, 1288,
    1289, 1303
"Granite, On," 867ff, 985, 987, 1109
granite, 868ff
gratification(s),
  analysis and, 200
  genital and oral, 392
  minimization of, 200
  and love, 661
  oral, 428
Gray, R. D., 1147
greed, oral, 72, 355
Greenacre, Phyllis, xix n, 906, 908, 1353n
Gretchen (Goethe's sweetheart), 47, 94n,
    556f, 1071, 1221, 1228ff, 1364
Gretchen (*Faust*), 277, 309, 318, 727
Grimaldi, Francesco Maria, 1122, 1136f
Grimm, Friedrich Melchior, Baron von, 609

Gross Brembach, 450
group identity, and emotion, 721
group situation, and guilt feeling, 77
Gruppe, O. F., 22n
guilt,
  irreparable, genius and, 1443
  reality, in Goethe, 1375 and n
guilt feelings,
  in analysis, 282
  Christianity and, 420f
  and creativity, 70, 1181
  and erotic compositions, 553
  Goethe's, 71, 94, 192, 208, 226, 390, 395,
    430, 473, 491, 557, 689, 726, 1139,
    1223, 1366; and Christiane, 1295;
    towards Cornelia, 28, 65; and fa-
    ther's sickness, 270; and mother's
    storytelling, 78; orality of, 392; in
    relation to women, 253
  and idealized woman, 480
  and incorporation, 428
  and masturbation, 258, 264
  and menstruation, 333
  and mourning, 288
"guinea pig," use of patient as, 234
Günderode, Caroline von, 1236
Gundolf, Friedrich, 222n, 1169f, 1173,
    1177, 1439n
Günther, Johann Christian, 1170, 1177
Gustavus Adolphus, 411
Gustgen, *see* Stolberg, Auguste
Gutzkow, 11

Hadas, Moses, 558n, 1332ff, 1436
Hades, 274f
hair, as symbolic gift, 293
Halle, University, 5
hallucinations,
  and psychosis, 1376
  and words, 549
Hamann, J. Georg, 7, 736n
Hamlet, 320, 1159; *see also* Shakespeare
Hanswursts Hochzeit, 1345
harmony, basic, 523
Hárnik, Jenö, 239n, 1049n
harpist (*Wilhelm Meister*), 243, 696, 752
Hartmann, Heinz, 734n, 1294, 1376, 1378,
    1409n, 1412, 1436
Hartung, Fritz, 548
Harz mountains, 3, 295, 303, 816, 818,
    822ff
Hauch, 476n

Haydn, 1378n

health, mental, 1391n

Heidelberg, 222

Heine, Heinrich, 1182, 1421n

Heinemann, Karl, 91n, 127, 370, 780n, 808n, 1067, 1438n

Heinicke, Samuel, 1014

Heinz, W. C., 1215

Helena (*Faust*), 253

Hell, rescue from, 239

Hellen, Eduard von der, 301, 478n, 552n, 575n, 1128n

Helpful Wife, The, 242

hemorrhage, 37, 224, 722n, 1065

Hemsterhuis, Frans, 970, 1092n

Henriette Christine Caroline Louise, Landgravine of Hesse, 230

Henry IV of France, 1160n

Hercules, 322, 847

Herder, Caroline (formerly Flachsland), 230, 243, 455, 679, 990, 991, 993, 1320f

   letter from Goethe to, 835

Herder, Johann Gottfried von, 26, 99, 149, 243, 532, 597, 835, 885, 887, 953, 960, 967, 1033, 1163, 1299, 1316

   death, 1014

   on Goethe's offices, 679

   relationship with Goethe, 630, 847ff, 1318, 1393

   letters from Goethe to, 197f, 217, 697, 842, 849, 1001n, 1009, 1016, 1248, 1274, 1326, 1346f, 1371, 1439n

   letter from Knebel, 977

   letters to Hamann, 678f, 735n

Hering, Robert, 173f

Hermann, Imre, 107, 108, 297, 1221

Hermann und Dorothea, 1291n

hero, 114

   psychology of, 313n

Herodotus, xxi

heroism, and phobias, 1054f

Herr Lorenz Stark (J. J. Engel), 715

Herrnhuter, 471

Herschel, 639

Herzlieb, Christiane Friederike Wilhelmine, 1298

Hess, Friederike, 124n

Hesse, 230

Hessen-Darmstadt, 243

Hetzler, letter from Goethe to, 453n

Hildburghausen, 608

Himburg, Christian Friedrich, 940n

Hippolyta, 306; *see also* Shakespeare, *Midsummer Night's Dream*

"History of My Botanical Studies," 931

Hitschmann, Eduard, 1031n, 1042n, 1303

Hoffer, W., 1225

Hölderlin, 133, 256n, 1169

holiday, creation of personal, 750

Holland, 1022n, 1023

Holtei, K. von, 604

homeopathy, 265

Homer, 29, 235, 680, 1129, 1336n, 1436

   Odyssey, 231, 680

homosexual

   love-object, function of, 50

   rivalry, 513

   tension, in Goethe, 59ff, 350

homosexuality, 1329f, 1347f

   and attitude to fellow men, 629

   and death, 1453

   decrease of unconscious, 655

   in *Faust,* 1454n

   Goethe on, 917f

   Goethe's, Karl August as object of, 1317f; modification of, in Italy, 1319; vicissitudes of, 630ff

   in Italy, 1024

   manifest, 1391n

   projection on woman, 936

   sublimated, 492

   and Switzerland, 370, 373

   in *Werther* letters, 374

   in *Wilhelm Meister,* 1449

   see also politics

homosexuals,

   imitation of women in, 105

   penis pride in, 736

Hopewell (*The Birds*), 421f, 424f, 427, 443f

Hör-, Schreib- und Druckfehler, 992n

Horace, 862, 1390, 1399n

Horae, 1187

horseman, Latin, 1067

hostility, of asylum patient, and external calamity to object of hostility, 282

Houben, H. H., 569, 570, 859f

house, quarrel with father about, 1046

Hufeland, Christoph Wilhelm, 855n, 1077

Hugo, Victor, 1416, 1440

human figure, inhibition in drawing, 1224

Humanus (*Die Geheimnisse*), 888ff, 896

Humboldt, C. W. von, 602, 780, 1436n
  letter from Goethe to, 602
Hyacinth, 320, 321
Hydra, 175
Hyginus, 784
hyperactivity, 315
hypertrophy, 1417f
hypochondriasis, 1098, 1159
hypomania, 516, 612, 985ff
hysteria,
  conversion, in Charlotte von Stein, 1086
  condensation in, 272
hysterical attacks, autoplasticity and, 543

ibex, 378
Ibsen, Henrik, 1370–1n
iconography, Christian, 1278f
id,
  and ego, in joke-formation, 1424f
  process, and diaries, 696
  and time, 1043f
  and wish-fulfillment in dream, 1283f
idealization, and sexual eroticism, 514
identification(s), 171, 177f, 356
  acting out, 66
  and castration, 515
  with child, 455
  with deserted women, 517
  effect on ego, 1017
  female, and creativity, 1391
  Goethe's, with Charlotte von Stein, 168;
    with Duke Karl August, 387; with
    Cornelia, 42; with father, 71, 80,
    176ff, 418f, 480, 548, 754, 892, 928,
    1011, 1037f, 1142, 1199, 1289; with
    mother, 80, 480; feminine, 105, 113,
    246, 311f; in lyric poetry, 1176;
    with historical characters, 1100;
    homosexual, 402; with ideal struc-
    ture, 573; with Jews, 940; in Lenz,
    21; manifestations of, 1017; and
    masochism, 454, 482; mechanism of,
    1180; poets and, 1017f; with preg-
    nant mother, 876; psychopathology
    of, 1199; with puppets, 264; with
    totem animal, 514; *see also* aggressor
identity,
  changed, and orgasm, 183
  insecurity of, 448f
  perceptual, 542n
ideological clashes, 577

ideology,
  basis of, 235
  and mental health, 278
  reorganization, in analysis, 278
  vicissitudes of, 277ff
idolatry, 5
illegitimate births, punishment for, 1139
illness, Goethe's, in 1777, 293
Ilmenau, 196, 455, 553, 608, 827, 858ff,
    881, 982n, 984, 1365
Ilten, Karoline von, 489n, 819
imagery,
  erotic, in sleep, 1281
  visual, relation to words, 1173f
images, parent, *see* parent images
imagination, in child and poet, 1389
Imbaumgarten, Peter, 357
Imhoff, Amalie von, 1291n
imitation,
  dangers of, 23
  literary and psychological senses, 21
immediacy, 1281
immorality, and creativity, 1311f
immortality, 253
  and creativity, 1190
  of love-object, 619
impediment, sexual, Goethe's, 1053ff
  causes of cure, 1076ff
"impossible," the, 681f
impotence, 1061
  psychic, 1053
  and return to womb, 61
incest taboo, in primitives, 190
incestuous dream, Goethe's, 313
incestuous feelings, Goethe's,
  for Charlotte von Stein, 182–3n
  for Cornelia, 32, 45, 46, 116, 207
  in *Werther,* 101
  see also poems, Goethe's
incestuous relationships, unconscious, in art-
    ists, 32
incorporation, oral, 266, 428
independence, financial, Goethe's request for,
    271
individuality,
  regret for, 458
  and social function, 998
inertia principle, 1434
inferiority feelings, 39, 670
inflation, of ego, and creation, 1181
infusoria, 993

inhibition(s), 1411
  artistic, in Goethe, 698f
  and efficiency of ego-functions, 1412
  in poet, 308
  regressed, 392
  selective, 41
  self-mastery as, 299
  visual, 1027
initials, on Goethe's ring, 447
Innsbruck, 1014
insanity, Goethe's view of, 992
insincerity, in Goethe's letters to Charlotte
  von Stein, 964
inspiration, 1395f, 1397
instinctual cravings, relation of object to, 268
instinctualization, of ego functions, 1412
institutions, and psychotherapy, 1098
integration, 601, 617
  of ego-alien, 937
intellectualization, 226, 948
intercourse,
  and erotic poetry, 1343
  Goethe and, xxiv, 52, 1019ff, 1342;
    Goethe's first, 1034, 1362
  fear of, 395n
  observation of, 708
  sadistic concept of, 310
  and sexual desire, 1053
  substitute for, 863
intermaxillary bone, 768n, 849ff, 1109,
  1116, 1127, 1163
Intermezzi Scandalosi aus Goethes Leben,
  537
"internal, the," 441f
internalization, 228f
interpersonal relations, and psychotherapy,
  1098f
interpretation, 226, 1077, 1078f
interviews, staggering of, 202
intimacy, in Goethe–von Stein relation, 200f
introversion, 10
"inventive day," 431, 432
invulnerability, 588
Iphigenia, 315ff, 327
Iphigenia in Delphi, 1278ff
Iphigenia (Iphigenie auf Tauris), 255, 292,
  315ff, 339, 346, 367, 423, 562, 787,
  992, 1209f, 1218, 1258f
  quotations from, 319ff, 1209
  rewritings, 336
  writing of, 329, 340
irony, 1454n

Isakower, Otto, 1044n, 1131
isolation, 790ff, 794, 885f, 1114f
Italian Journey/Voyage, 239n, 956n, 1015,
  1034, 1039f, 1047, 1052, 1183, 1246,
  1273f, 1275ff, 1280
Italy, 111, 222, 231n, 311, 408, 666, 879f,
  901, 994ff
  first idea of journey to, 999
  Goethe's attitude on second visit, 1016
  parallels with father's experiences in,
    1014f
  reasons for journey to, 999
ivy, 1302f

Jacob, Heinrich Eduard, 1378n
Jacobi, Betty, 90, 895
  letter from Goethe to, 90
Jacobi, Friedrich Heinrich, 212, 285 and n,
  286, 358ff, 368, 741f, 895f, 933
  Eduard Allwills Papiere, 360n, 363
  Friendship and Love, 360f
  Woldemar, 359f, 362ff, 368, 446
  letters from Goethe to, 212, 741f, 769,
    792, 794, 797, 854, 865n, 932, 957,
    971, 979f, 987f, 1074
Jacobs, Edward, 4n, 6
Jacobson, Edith, 1208n
Jagemann, Caroline, 346, 1327n
Jahrmarktsfest zu Plundersweilen, Das, 243
Jarno (*Wilhelm Meister*), 839
Jason, 322
Jaspers, Karl, 1180n
jealousy, 67f, 80, 97, 118, 225, 516, 655
  Goethe's, of Lenz, 212, 227
  projected, 80
Jena, 637, 817, 849, 852f, 961, 963, 966,
  1288, 1294, 1295
  Battle of, 1327, 1330
  University, 159
Jerusalem, Johann Friedrich Wilhelm, 88n
Jerusalem, K. W., 87ff, 90, 104, 560n
Jery, 1218f
Jery und Bätely, 1218f, 1245
Jest, Cunning, and Vengeance, 1245f, 1261
Jesus, 239
  Lavater and, 577f
  see also Christ
Jewish quarter, fire in, 939f
Jews, 433f
  Goethe's attitude to, 940, 1036n
Joannes Eremita, 628
Jöchhausen, 437, 450

John, St., Apostle, 29
  Gospel of, 188
jokes, 1421ff
  and dreams, relation, 1424n
  as symptom, 1428n
Jokl, Robert H., 1095n
Jonathan, 720
Jones, Ernest, 905n, 1044n, 1142n, 1225n, 1382n
Joseph, identification with, 1099ff
Joseph II, Emperor, 671n, 1232
Jove, 274
joy, 944f
judgments, moral, variation in, 776
jugglers, 1348
Jung, C. G., 273, 1277, 1285n
Jussuph (*Westöstlicher Divan*), 1104n

Kabza, A., 1436
Kahn, meaning, 1273
Kalb, Johann August Alexander, 435f, 679, 692, 736
Kanne, Christian Karl, 44n
Kant, xxx, 639
Karl August, Duke of Sachsen-Weimar, 3, 26, 137, 146, 147, 158ff, 216, 221, 233, 339, 370, 400f, 408, 426f, 459, 488f, 511, 550, 606, 655, 737, 791, 820, 827, 828, 843 and n, 848, 925, 957, 977ff, 1022ff, 1262, 1299
  response to Christiane, 1327
  and Corona, 344ff
  and Countess von Werthern-Neuenheiligen, 499ff
  dietary system, 490f
  First Coalition War, 11
  and *The Birds,* 443f
  Goethe's influence on/relation to, 161, 219, 348ff, 377ff, 383ff, 418, 490f, 629, 636ff, 1315ff
  identification with Goethe, 688
  Napoleon and, 1330
  political ambitions, 1318
  letters from Goethe to, 156n, 340, 348f, 526, 610, 622, 957f, 999f, 1001, 1003, 1004, 1016, 1022, 1023, 1025ff, 1028, 1042, 1134, 1240ff, 1321f, 1324, 1325, 1327f
  letter to Goethe, 637
  letter to Merck, 687, 793
  letters to Knebel, 348, 638n
Karl Friedrich, Prince, 814

Karl Wilhelm Ferdinand, Duke of Brunswick, 460, 1022n
Karlsbad, 523
Karlsruhe, 92
Karsch, Anna Luise,
  letter from Goethe to, 327n
Kästner, 779
Kaufmann, Walter E., 82n
Kayser, Philipp Christoph, 1217, 1244ff, 1261ff
  letters from Goethe to, 879f, 1255, 1262, 1264
Kestner, A., 87, 88, 89, 92, 93, 96, 97, 98, 103, 110, 112n, 116, 192
  letters from Goethe to, 86, 88, 92, 93, 103, 113, 418, 584, 716, 789n, 795
Kestner, Lotte, *see* Buff, Charlotte
keys, 606
"keystone" feeling, 766ff, 1361n
Kieser, D. G., 861
kinesthetic stimulation, 763
Kindermann, Heinz, xxv n
King, J. E., 1436
Kinsey, A. C., 1036
kissing, 1058, 1060ff, 1070, 1222, 1266ff
Klärchen (*Egmont*), 1041
Klein, Melanie, 782
Kleine, H. O., 1287n
Klemperer, Paul, 1455n
Klettenberg, Susanna Katharina von, 470ff, 480, 653, 953, 1087
  letter from Goethe to, 471, 653f
Klinger, Friedrich Maximilian, 933, 1379
Klopstock, G. F., 26, 292n, 415n, 416, 423, 445, 640, 825, 888, 1129, 1171, 1173, 1177, 1203, 1309n
Knebel, Karl Ludwig von, 81, 83, 138, 147 and n., 329, 348, 353, 354f, 454, 456, 457, 478, 493, 623n, 641ff, 722n, 818, 885, 961, 966, 1320, 1321
  letters from Goethe to, 81, 83, 541, 583, 595, 618, 623 and n, 625, 630, 734, 736, 790f, 792, 794, 842, 854, 857, 959, 960, 966f, 977, 981, 985f, 1009f, 1122, 1164, 1326
  letters from Duke Karl August to, 348, 638n
  letters from Charlotte von Stein to, 423n, 796, 814, 854f, 953, 955, 974f
Knebel, Frau, 1305, 1321
knowledge, of others, unconscious, 1079

Kochberg, 143, 153, 202, 203, 207, 210, 218, 224, 248, 368f, 451n, 456, 457, 608, 968, 970, 1091
Koenig, Louise, 124n
Koetschau, 454
Kohlbrugge, Jacob H. F., 849n, 1144f
Kohut, Heinz, 1256, 1258
Konfliktneigung, 787
Königsberg, 18
Konstantin, Prince, 147n, 387n, 457, 472n, 489, 816, 817, 819f
Korff, H. A., 1379
Körner, 533
Köster, Albert, 275, 421n
Krabskrälligkeit, 1288
Krafft, 355–7, 386
  letters from Goethe to, 355, 356, 525
Kramer, Paul, 1404
Kraus, Georg Melchior, 249, 496, 512, 856n
Kreutzburg, 608
Kriegk, G. L., 173, 1229
Kris, Ernst, xx, xxii, xxiii f, 364n, 587, 699, 734n, 1099n, 1387n, 1407n, 1416, 1422, 1430n, 1436
Kurz, Otto, **xxii**

lactation, Goethe's, **267f**
La Lune, 1055
Lamarck, 639
Lamotte-Valois, Countess, **311n**
landscape, beauty of, **195**
Langer, Georg, 515
language,
  archaic and sublime functions, 1175
  foreign, Goethe and, **44, 68**
  function in schizophrenia, 564
  legal, simplification of, 547ff
  orality in Goethe's, 1073
la Roche, Maximiliane, *see* Brentano, Maximiliane
la Roche, Sophie von, 90, 472
  letters from Goethe to, 90, 472, 1452
Lassberg, Christiane von, 333
Latin, Goethe's use of, 1341
Lauterbrunn, 395
Lavater, Johann Kaspar, 12, 29, 85n, 96n, 125, 130, 146, 149, 162, 182n, 250, 370, 376, 384f, 387f, 401f, 425, 463, 575ff, 639ff, 659, 672n, 678, 689, 738, 739ff, 933, 980, 983, 1127, 1246, 1320

Lavater, Johann Kaspar (*Continued*)
  letters from Goethe to, 182n, 216, 217, 366, 419, 463, 464, 482n, 491, 492, 524, 526, 595, 642, 644, 645, 647f, 649, 650, 664, 739, 740, 747, 777f, 891, 1389, 1403
  letters to Goethe, 641, 643, 644, 645, 649, 739
  letter from Katharine Elisabeth Goethe, 472
  letter to Zimmermann, 283n
Pilatus, 575, 740
law practice, Goethe's, 172
Lear, King, Freud on, 272n
leeches, 308f
Lehman, H. C., 1142n
Leichtsinn, 937n
Leipzig, 25, 35, 37ff, 49f, 59, 88, 192, 213, 288, 299, 341, 414, 506, 600, 608, 1046, 1078
  Goethe's letters from, 64n, 1022
  University of, 172
Leipziger Theater, 1768, 341
Lengfeld, Lotte (later Schiller)
  letter from Charlotte von Stein to, 953
Lenz, Jakob Michael Reinhold, 16ff, 38, 124, 131, 187f, 218, 219, 224f, 228, 241, 277, 288, 351n, 352, 353, 519, 621, 678, 933, 1289n, 1379
  causes of failure, 25
  comparison with Goethe, 25f
  pathology, 22ff, 27f
  relations with Goethe, 26ff
  Charlotte von Stein and, 187f, 202f, 207, 212, 220, 227, 507
Der Engländer, 29
Der Hofmeister, 20, 25
Pandaemonium Germanicum, 25f, 28, 29
"Tantalus," 30
Leonardo da Vinci, xxvii, 32, 690n, 738, 792n, 1114, 1353, 1410, 1413n
  diary of, 691n, 693n
Lessing, Gotthold Ephraim, 26, 639, 731
letter writing, difficulties in, 502
letters, Goethe's, *see under names of recipients*
Letters from Switzerland, 370ff, 432
Leuchtsenring, Franz Michael, 243
Levarie, Siegmund, 1252n, 1256, 1258
Lewin, Kurt, 61, 401, 482
L'Hermite, Daniel, 628

libido,
  and aggression, in Goethe, 1180, 1221
  genital, and sublimation, 1415
  sudden release by death of beloved, 291
  transformation of, 1406
  two contradictory properties of, 1413
libretti, Goethe's desire to write, 1244ff
Lida (name for Charlotte von Stein), 240,
  351
life expectancy, 874
light, 483
  meaning of, to Goethe, 1135
  polarization of, 1136
Lila (*Lila*), 232, 238, 271, 320
Lila, 230ff, 245, 248, 255ff, 265, 268, 317,
  1217n
  and *The Siblings,* compared, 244f
Lila (L. H. F. von Zeigler), 230, 242
Lili, *see* Schönemann
limitations, Goethe's reaction to his, 1248
Limprecht, Johann Christian, 653
  letter from Goethe to, 653
Lindenau, Count of, 37n, 60
Lindenbrog, 1334
Linnaeus, Carolus, 930f
lion, as food, 265
Lisbon earthquake, 452
literary art, functions of, 1117f
Livonia, 17
Loder, Justus Christian, 849n
Leoning, Richard, 929
London, riots in, 451
looking, aggressive, 314
Lothario (*Wilhelm Meister*), 208n, 909
Lotte (*Werther*), 86, 100f, 112, 215, 287,
  362, 557n, 573, 818f
  see also Buff, Charlotte
Louis XVI, 1036n
Louise, Duchess of Weimar, 23, 216ff, 230f,
  233, 339, 813
  Goethe's relationship with, 218f, 227f,
  339, 513, 1315f
  stillbirth, 551, 783
Louise Auguste Amalie, Princess, 339
love,
  and death, 703
  heavenly and profane, 187
  and physical gratification, 661
  transference, 185
love-life, division of Goethe's, 1084ff
love-objects, choice of, 1306

love poetry
  functions of, 565f
  Goethe's, 1170
love relation,
  repetitiveness in, 185
  and transference, 185
loyalty, to father, 1051
Lucinda, 1060f
Luden, Heinrich, 411
  letter from Goethe to, 411
Ludwig IX, 735
Ludwig X, 735
Lukács, Georg, 999
Lupton, Harry, 94, 114, 115
Luther, 367
Lützen, Battle of, 411
Lützendorf, 1241
Lycus (*Elpenor*), 784, 785f

machine age, rise of, 1145
madness,
  Orestes', 320f, 323f
  Plato on, 1395, 1416, 1417
Maeder, A., 1380n
Magi, three, 825
magic,
  oral, 266
  power of words, in schizophrenia, 564f
  see also words
magnetism, 333
Mainz, 472
Mambre, 669f
man, and the universe, 603
"Man of Fifty Years, The," 768, 1448
Manasseh, 1101
Mandandane (*Triumph of Sentimentality*),
  254f, 258, 266, 271, 273, 287
Mann, Thomas, 1196
Manon Lescaut, see Prévost
mantle, as penis symbol, 905
"Mara," *see* Schmehling, G. E.
Marcus Aurelius, 503
Maria (*Götz von Berlichingen*), 1090
Mariane (*Wilhelm Meister*) 720f, 755, 1442
Marianne (*Lila*), 244
Marianne (*The Siblings*), 207ff, 215, 219ff,
  244, 246
Marie Antionette, Queen, 311, 678, 982,
  1036n
Marienstrasse, 1138
Markus (*Die Geheimnisse*), 888ff

marriage,
  by capture, 275
  exogamous, 1101f
Marseillaise, 484
Martinswand, 1006
martyr, 1399n
Mary, Mother of Jesus, 1038
Mary Magdalene, 311
masochism, 277
  and depersonalization, 486
  and drives, 1413
  female, 145
  gambling and, 1215
  and genius, 1381f
  in Goethe, 188f, 195, 395, 453f, 485ff,
    588, 619, 1085f, 1384n
  moral, 1381, 1384
  sublimation of, 195
masonry, 821, 835n
masturbation, 255ff, 264, 268, 279, 289,
    290f, 969, 1031, 1080
  music and, 1255
  struggle against, 279
maternal quality, in Goethe, 386
mathematicians, personality of, 1143, 1144
mathematics, Goethe and, 1145f
Mather, K.,
  letter from Goethe to, 378n
Matthaei, Rupprecht, 1135n
Matthei, Karl, 396
Matthew, Gospel of St., 457n
Matthisson, F. von, 418n
maturation, incomplete, and the artist, 1392
Maupassant, Guy de, 1169
Maurois, André, 1440
Maximen und Reflectionen, 1159, 1162
Maximilian, Emperor, 1006
Mayer, Friedrich, xx
Maync, Harry, xxv
mechanization, 1446f
Medea, 322
medicine, dehumanization of, 1112n
medievalism, effect on Goethe, 1147
Medon, 81
Medusa, 309, 310
Meerkatze, 772n
Meiningen, 608
Meissel, Gottlieb, 1291
melancholia, 1420
Melina (*Wilhelm Meister*), 728, 751ff, 831
Melina, Madame (*Wilhelm Meister*), 728f
Melusine, 798, 801ff

memory,
  repressed childhood, 313
  vividness of, 261, 264
Mendelssohn, Moses, 640, 807n, 940, 979
Menninger, Karl, 409
Menschenklauberei, 330
menstruation, 310, 799ff, 1207f, 1210
  effect on children, 332, 809
  and genius in women, 1401
  memory of, 313
  and traveling, 409
mental disorder, Goethe's treatment of, 235f
Mephistopheles, 51, 58, 308f, 310, 1372,
    1454n
Mercien, Louis Sebastian, 20
Merck, Johann Heinrich, 30, 50, 90 and n,
    95, 96, 230, 243, 376n, 384, 385,
    443, 444n, 459n, 581, 630ff, 655,
    687, 688, 735f, 793, 895, 1015, 1016
  letters from Goethe to, 216, 410, 411n,
    444, 445, 453, 594f, 852f, 1144
Mercury, 1028n
Merry-Andrew's Wedding, 1345f
metaphors,
  oral, 1073
  use of, 609
Metastasio, Pietro, 1252n
metempsychosis, 182, 183
meter, and rhythm, 1173
Meyer, Heinrich, 350n, 718n, 1320
Meyer, Johann Heinrich, 370, 1215
Meyer, Nicolaus, 1300
Meyer, Professor, 1296, 1300, 1303
Meyer, Richard M., 1067n, 1158
Meyer, Wilhelm, 1053
Michelangelo, 1118, 1353
Midas, 436, 1370f
Mieding, Johann Martin, 348, 828
Mignon (*Wilhelm Meister*), 52, 253, 258n,
    696, 728, 751, 755ff, 828f, 902, 919
"Milanese, Beautiful," *see* Riggi, M.
Milder-Hauptmann, Pauline Anna, 1257
Mill, John Stuart, 1030n
Minchen, *see* Herzlieb
mineralogical studies, Goethe's, 493
mining, bureau for, 382
Minotaur, 1267f
Mira (*Prometheus*), 477
mirror-image, Goethe's potential, 31
  see also Cornelia
Mirza, 487
misogyny, 756, 916n

"Mistakes of Hearing, Writing, and Printing," 992n
Möbius, P. J., 37, 44, 1143
moderation, 442
Molière, xxix, 345, 420, 671
Möller, Johann Philipp (pseudonym of Goethe), 930
moly, 490n
monodramas, 255 and n, 276
Montgolfier brothers, 739n
moon, 183, 246n, 475
    and menstruation, 306
moonlight, 475
morality,
    and the artist, 87
    and genius, 1308ff
Morris, Max, 310, 808, 1140, 1261, 1346
Moscow, 24
Moser, Carl Friedrich, 735f
Moses, 880, 1073, 1262
mother
    bad, 267, 268, 269, 272, 290; and good, 1448
    devaluation of, 917
    Goethe's, and early childhood, 71; his relationship with, 66f, 268n, 269, 272, 916
    identification with giving, 355
    and keystone feeling, 768
    negligent, 197
    preoedipal, 781, 828n, 872f
    quarrelsome, 311
    return into, 1280n
    as storyteller, 73f
    threatening, 80
    see also Goethe, Katharine Elisabeth
mother-son relationship, ambivalence and, 77
mother-transference, 210, 227
"Mothers, the," 272, 871f
mourning, 288, 291, 391, 658ff, 858
    and contradiction in external reality, 700
    Freud and, 658
    and personality change, 666f
    phases in, 662n
    and regression, 291
    superego and, 700n
mouse, red, 307f, 309, 310, 1208
mouth-hand relationship, genetic importance, 1225
Mozart, xxix, xxxi, 82, 639, 1096n, 1263, 1312, 1345, 1353, 1355f, 1390, 1395, 1398, 1418

Müller (painter), 526
Müller, Friedrich von, xxv, 265, 267, 917, 1021n, 1155, 1329, 1404n
Multaretuli, 993
multipotentiality, of genius, 1435
Münster (Switzerland), 341, 397, 399, 401
Münz, Ludwig, 469
murder,
    and blood, 332
    impulse to, 59
Musäus, 805n
Muschg, Walter, 1097n, 1117, 1381, 1382f
mushrooms, 1048, 1049
music, Goethe and, 1244ff
mutilation, of letter from Goethe to Charlotte von Stein, 539f
mystery stories, 1434
mysticism, 644
myth, Greek, 334, 336
mythology, Goethe and, 336f

names,
    changing of, 730n
    choice of, 127
Naples, 1008, 1010, 1011
Napoleon, 49, 113f, 1012, 1046, 1327, 1330
narcissism, 354, 417, 515, 703
narcissistic gratification, excessive, 38
Narcissus, 372, 732
narrowness, 396f, 399
Natalie (*Wilhelm Meister*), 1443, 1444
    see also Amazon, The
National Theatre, German, 262
nature,
    Goethe's attitude to, 1325
    consistency in, 985f
    cruelty of, 452
    desire for experience of, 373f
    and homosexuality, 374f
    reproduction of, and Goethe's drawings, 1224
Naturphilosophie, 867
Nausicaa, 231
negation, 1445
Nero, 110
Neue Lieder, 1171
Neue Mallerei und graphische Kunste, 459n
Neuenheiligen, 497
Neumann, W., 862
neurosis,
    actual, and psychoneurosis, 1416
    compulsive, 543, 867

neurosis (*Continued*)
obsessional/obsessive, 189, 1053; disposition to, 1359
transference, 886
traumatic, and emotions, 665
neurotic symptoms, in Goethe, 1054, 1363f
neutralization, 1178n, 1377f, 1407
New Melusine, The, 801, 804ff
newness,
experience of familiar as, 1005
loss of ability to experience, 663, 667
"new one, my," 519, 520f
Newton, Sir Issac, 1113, 1115n, 1117, 1120ff, 1127ff, 1135f, 1347
Goethe's character sketch of, 1128
New Year's Day, 588f
Nicias, 1302
Nicolai, Christoph Friedrich, 280f, 308
Nicolai auf Werthers Grab, 280
Niederland, William G., 708n
Nietzsche, Friedrich, xxiii n, 1169, 1436
nightmares, 36, 37, 393, 544, 1223, 1375
see also dreams, Goethe's
nobility,
Goethe's attitude to, 350, 378, 835ff, 839ff
Goethe's elevation to, 670, 834ff
and women, 52f
see also aristocracy; status
noblemen, and work, 1194ff
nosebleed, 490f, 495n, 1075
notebooks, Goethe's, 308
nudity, Goethe's attitude to, 371ff, 1027, 1349
numerical relations, 523
Nunberg, Hermann, 665n
Nycteus, 784

obedience,
deferred, 639
revenge by, 608
Oberon, see Titania; Shakespeare, *Midsummer Night's Dream*
object, concentration on single, 434
object-choice, flexibility of, 291
object-loss,
and ambivalence, 291
and mourning, 658
object-related tendencies, concentration of, 192
object-relationship
concealment of, 54f
in genius, 1367, 1385

object-relationship (*Continued*)
Goethe's sexual dysfunction and, 1373
and identification, simultaneous, 42, 43
in psychoanalysis, 43
and transference relation, compared, 293
volition and, 947
object-representation, 574
obscenity, Goethe's indulgence in, 1345f
observation, Goethe and, 1111f
obsessional thought, in Goethe, 189
oceanic feeling, 766f
O'Donnell, Countess Josephine,
letter from Goethe to, 502n
odor, effect on child, 332f
oedipal/Oedipus
complex, and creativity, 1391f; Joseph and, 1101; pheasant dream and, 1279
conflict, 593, 621, 705, 706; dissolution, 1039
fantasies, 190
fears, 384
problem, in *Balsazar* play, 752; in *Wilhelm Meister,* 753
Oeser, 811, 812
letter from Goethe to, 812
Offenbach, 94n, 1070, 1228n
Old Vic company, 305n
Oliva, St., 311
Olla Potrida, 232, 233
omnipotence, 766; and activity/passivity, 746; belief in mother's, 272; magic, 98; transference and, 681
Onanie, 279n
opera buffa, 1256
operettas, 230n
opposites, psychic, 315
coincidence in unconscious, 379n, 515
oracles, 107f, 110f, 112, 288f, 636, 643
see also bibliomancy
oral curiosity, see curiosity
oral deprivation, 427f
oral greed, see greed, oral
oral magic, 266
oral zone, hypercathexis of, 1068
orality, 197, 389, 431
compulsiveness regarding, 490
and drawing, 297f, 1221f
and genitality, relation, 1074
Goethe's, 1073ff
and language, in Goethe, 1073f
see also eating habits; regression, oral
Orestes, 335, 993

Orestes (*Iphigenia in Tauris*), 316f, 319ff, 328, 330, 340n, 346, 1209
Orestes (*Iphigenia in Delphi*), 1278
orgasm,
    absorption of world in, 768
    description of, in *Wilhelm Meister,* 760f
    and ego loss, 183
    Goethe on, 1028, 1065
    unifunctionality of, 1419
orgastic experiences, childhood, 758ff
Oronaro (*Triumph of Sentimentality*), 254, 256, 258, 267, 279, 287, 288f, 291
os intermaxillare, see intermaxillary bone
Ossian, 29, 98, 112
Otho, Emperor, 108–10
overdetermination,
    in dream interpretation, 284
    of works of art, 284
overestimation, 946f
overinterpretation, 965n
overstimulation, visual, in childhood, 906
overvaluation,
    of love-object, 574
    sexual, 827n
Ovid, 273f, 276, 305, 321, 1331

Packe, Michael St. J., 1030
pain,
    endurance of, 206, 770
    and genius, 1381
    see also masochism
painting(s)
    given to Duke Karl August, 459
    Goethe's failure in, 107
Palermo, 1083
Panama canal, 1446
Pandora, 477
Panofsky, 1052
paramnesias,
    Goethe's, 91, 96, 97
    multimotivated, 96
paranoia, fantasies in, 272
paranoid attacks, 37, 58, 59, 60, 67, 68
paranoid ideas, in Goethe, 537
paranoid symptoms, and parody, 363f
parapraxias, 493f, 495, 507n, 517, 605f, 613, 861ff
    and attention, 1144
    Goethe's views, 992n
    regression and, 1422ff

parents,
    Goethe's, his relation to, 1360f; *see also individual names*
    resentment at idea of, in schizophrenics, 750
parent image(s),
    discord between, 351
    united, 782
parental attitudes, and genius, 1356f
Paris, 147
Parnassus, Mount, 322
parody, 363f
    of Jacobi, Goethe's, 364f, 368, 369f
Parr, A. E., 1405
parrot, 421f
parrot tails, 34f, 913
passion,
    absence of, in nongenius, 1410f
    and change in ego, 183
passivity, 396, 398, 399
    and activity, in Goethe, 243, 337
    in neurotic and poet, 1395f
    see also activity
past and present, bringing together, 331
pathway, yardstick of traveled, 1425
patient-analyst situation, 153, 184
Pausias, 1287n
peak of life, Goethe's, 1142
pen, given to Goethe by Charlotte von Stein, 494f
penis
    conflict, and fetishism, 635
    envy, 145, 1402
    erect, and creativity, 1282
    fantasies, Goethe's, 35
    overestimation of, 1208
    symbols, 60, 312, 1275f, 1281
penknife, 106, 110
perception,
    overacuteness, 58
    place in Goethe's personality, 1115n, 1117
    psychic apparatus and, 1376
perfection, artistic, 82
periodicity, in Goethe's correspondence, 801
personality,
    artist's, in relation to work, 565f
    and ideology, 235
    structure, and genius, 1418
pessimism, 453
Pestalozzi, 639
Petersen, Julius, 478n, 1185
petrifaction, 1144

Pfuiteufelchen, 1288
Phaëton, 320, 321
phallus, female, 312, 1208
Pharaohs, 766, 1101
pheasants, 1273f
phenomenology, clinical, classification, xxxii
Phidias, 1312
Philaenis, 1344
Philine (*Wilhelm Meister*), 752, 757, 830, 902, 934, 1041
Philoponos, 1436
phimosis, 1036n, 1206n
phobias, Goethe's, 1094, 1216ff
phobic attacks, 393f, 401
phylacteries, 509, 510, 514, 515
phylogenesis, and emotions, 657
Physiognomische Fragmente, 12
physiognomy,
  and character, 130
  expression of psyche in, 12
  Goethe's interest in, 672n
physique, Goethe's, after Italian visit, 928, 1011
piano lessons, 1248f
Pietism, 4
  Lenz and, 19
pigsty, 414, 1221
pigtail-cutting, 635
Pindar, 1436
pique, 1078
pirating, of Goethe's works, 939, 940, 1310
pity, flight from, 291
Platen, 693n
Plato, 425, 566, 871, 1416
  Phaedrus, 1395
play,
  Goethe's attitude to, 598f
  within play, 275
pleasure,
  genius and, 1400
  and repetition, 762
pleasure principle, 724, 1397f
  in analysis, 200
  means of overcoming, 937
  science and, 546n
Plessing, Friedrich Victor Lebrecht, 3ff, 17, 131, 237, 295
  psychiatric commentary, 7
  relations with Goethe, 7ff, 31, 357, 742f, 746
  letters from Goethe, 15, 742
  letters to Goethe, 3, 7, 8

Plessing, Johann Friedrich, 4
Pliny, 1287n
Plutarch, 108f, 748, 871
Pluto, 274
plutonic theory, 871
Plutonicus, Joh. Prätorius Anthropodamus, 308
Plymouth Brethren, 471
Pniower, 1218
Poe, Edgar Allan, 872n
poems, Goethe's,
  conditions necessary for writing, 484
  dreaming, 69, 84, 544f, 546, 1428f
  incestuous element in, 182f
  involuntary creation of, 83, 938
  and relationship with Annette, 68
  written in Leipzig, 1169ff
  titles and first lines:
    Amyntas, 1301ff
    Ballad, 1187 and n
    Bliss of Love, The, 1170n
    Butterfly, The, 1170n
    Cupid, loose, self-willed boy . . . , 1034
    Den Einzigen, Lotte [Lida] . . . 587, 609
    Diary, The, 553, 1346n
    Divine, The, 794
    Einer Einzigen angehören . . . , 351
    Erlkönig, 768n, 780f
    Four Seasons, The, 955
    Frech und Froh, 311
    From the Greek, 415n, 416, 491, 551, 558n
    Futile Prattle, 895
    Ganymede, 413, 782, 794
    Gehab dich wohl . . . , 349
    Geheimnisse, Die, 883ff
    Goblet, The, 415, 416n, 550f, 555, 558n, 559, 567, 608
    Harzreise in Winter, 396, 399
    Holde Lili warst so lang . . . , 349
    Ilmenau, 825f, 828
    Inconstancy, 1170n
    Kennst du das Land . . . , 756, 803
    King of the Elves, *see* Erlkönig
    Lilli's Park, 487n
    Limitations of Mankind, 412ff, 794
    Morning Complaints, 1371
    My Goddess, 479, 488
    Neue Pausias, Der, 1287n
    New Saint, 311

poems, Goethe's (*Continued*)

Night, The, 1170n, 1171ff

Night Thoughts, 416n, 550f, 552n, 555, 558n, 567

Nicht allein meine Liebe verreist . . . , 575

On the death of Mieding, 828

Pariah, The, 561ff

Pilgrim's Morning Song, 231

Poetical Thoughts about Jesus Christ's Descent to Hell, 239, 470

Prometheus, 413, 477

Secrets, The, 883ff

Sixteenth Birthday, On his, 39

Soldatentrost, 311

Song of the Spirits over the Waters, 395f, 399, 483

Tagebuch, Das, 553, 1346n

To the Cicada, 558, 559

To Driver Cronus, 825ff

To the Locust, 558n, 559

To the Moon, 1170n

To Sleep, 58

To the Spirit of Janus Secundus, 1270

Triumph of Virtue, The, 1342f

True Enjoyment, The, 674

Über allen Gipfeln . . . , 466ff, 476ff, 480, 481ff, 1398

Visit, The, 1371

Von mehr als einer Seite verwaist . . . , 698, 700

Wahre Genuss, Der, 674

Wandrers Nachtlied, *see* Über allen Gipfeln . . .

Warning, 311, 312

Wedding Song, 1170n

What pleasure, God! . . . , 1064f

What volupty . . . , 52f, 256, 1269

Wie einst Titania . . . , 301f

You are serious . . . , 315

Your fate, O Midas . . . , 1370

Zwischen beiden Welten . . . , 351, 634n

poetry, incestuous root in, 182n

Pogwisch, Ottilie von, 1306, 1309

politics, and homosexuality, 629

Polycrates, 436

polyglottism, Goethe's, 44

Polymetis (*Elpenor*), 786

Polyphemus, 1302

pomegranate, 274, 275, 276

Ponte, Lorenzo da, 1247

Poppaea, 110

Popper, Josef, 659n

porcelain, 940

pornography, 1386

Portia, 1204

Potiphar, 1100f

Potiphera, 1101

Pound, Ezra, 476n

Powis, J. M., 1101n

practicality, Goethe's, 541

preconscious processes, artistic structuration of, 84

pregenital pleasures, 52, 1349

pregenitality, in geniuses, 1390f

pregnancy,

envy of, 211

feelings of disgust about, 401

imagery in, 398ff

rationalization of, 905

traumatic effects on Goethe, 104, 339

premonitions, 204

preoedipal phase, 872

present, *see* past

presumptuousness, Goethe's, 79

Prevost, Abbé, 1234ff

Priapeia, 1331ff; Annotations to, 1331ff, 1371

translation, 1332ff

Priapus, 1332ff, 1343ff

primal experience, *see* experience

primal scene, 763f

primary scene, 261

primary process

and artistic creation, 1258n

and defense, 1424

in dream work, 1423

music and, 1256

and secondary process, 651, 1096

primates, sex role interchange among, 351

princes, and disgust, 265

principle, fourth, 1398f

probability, and the unconscious, xxi

problems, solution of, in sleep, 84

Probst, Mina, 345

process, *see* primary process

procreation fantasies, 701

production, Goethe's techniques of, 1186ff

productivity, 1116

professional work, attitude to, 175

profit, from poetry, Goethe's attitude to, 939

progeny, genius and, 1372

projection, 536, 572, 626ff
Prometheus, 70f, 417, 451, 477, 1223, 1382n
Prometheus, 477, 762, 1223f, 1346
propagation, symbols of, 708
Propertius, 1269
Proserpina (*Proserpina*), 273ff, 283, 287, 318
Proserpina, 255, 273ff, 305n, 317, 1247
prostitutes, 1347
Proverbial, 1160
Prussia, 977
Psyche, 230, 630f
  see also Cupid
psychiatry, integration into modern life, 1098
psychoanalysis, 993
  and art, xxiii ff
  awareness of sexual and aggressive strivings in, 225
  case (university student) illustrating varying degree of participation in, 282
  circumstances bringing patient to, 228
  cornerstones of, 198
  counteraction of, 201
  dependence on, 878f
  effect of trivial events on, 226f
  Goethe's possession of essentials of, 990
  and gratification, 200
  heightened sensitivity to unconscious in, 711
  ideologies and, 277f
  improvement in patient at beginning of, 157
  influence of outside events on, 281ff
  interpretation in, 226
  relation between everyday life and childhood problems in, 330
  situation in, 153f
  transference in, 184, 515n
  transmogrification of, 1163n
  see also transference
psychology,
  cultural science, 1420
  Freud on origin of, 710
  Goethe's antipathy to, 571, 991
  instruction in, and analysis, 226
psychopathology, 992
  annual recurrence, 1044
  and art, 69, 70
  and the artist, 1391
  and creativity, 1095
  Goethe and, xxxii

psychopathology (*Continued*)
  Goethe's, 1054, 1363; in Leipzig, 1176ff
  four modes of, 1363
  unifunctionality in, 1420
psychosis (-es), 1375ff
  and artistic creativity, 70, 73, 1169ff
  dynamics of, 1133
  effect on personality, 24
  genius and, 1097
  paranoid, 787
  partial, 1126 and n, 1130, 1142, 1148
  possible temporary paranoid, in Goethe, 37, 58ff, 67, 516, 1373
  sublimation of, 1377f
  symptoms of, in Goethe, 1176f
  treatment of fantasy in, 237
psychosomatic medicine, 389
psychotherapy, Goethe and, 235, 245n
psychotic,
  re-creation of cosmos by, 1354
  see also delusions
puberties, Goethe's repeated, 1435
puberty,
  conflict of, in Goethe, 48
  tubercular disease at, 37
punishment,
  fear of, 372n
  see also wish-fulfillment
puppets, 259ff, 701, 708f
puritanism, 943
purity, Goethe's desire for, 392f, 495
Pygmalion, 732, 1004
"Pylades," 1229, 1232n
Pyramus, 305f, 1207
  see also Shakespeare, *Midsummer Night's Dream*
Pyrmont, 145

questioning, psychology of, 448n

Radegiki (original name for Oronaro, q.v.), 290
Raimund, 801f
Rameau, 1129
Rank, Otto, 32, 232, 1219
Raphael, 1278, 1279
rats, 501, 505
reaction-formation, 147
reading public, Goethe and the, 422, 423, 437
realism, in *Wilhelm Meister*, 698

reality,
  and creative process, 1431
  internal, 627
  negative and overdistinct, 482f
  quality of, in dream, 61
  science and, 546
reality principle, 212, 627, 1376, 1397f
  and pleasure principle, reconciliation, 138
  in Goethe's life, 1200
  science and, 545
  work and, 171, 175
rebellion, and guilt feelings, 71
rebirth, 954, 1001, 1003
recruiter, Goethe as, 329f, 331, 340, 625n
Redcoat (*Neue Melusine*), 805n
Redslob, Edwin, 274
Regeln für Schauspieler, 262n
regression, 62, 80, 190, 297, 505, 1085n
  and artistic creation, 699
  in creative pursuits, 1416
  degenerative and regenerative, 1435
  in dreams and jokes, 1422
  and indifferent energy, 1416
  masturbation and, 291
  and mourning, 291, 703
  oral, 40, 392, 481
  partial, 50
  to preoedipal level, 689f
  in service of ego, 1422f, 1429f
Reichard, H. A. O., 232n
Reichardt, Heinrich August, 1263
Reichardt, Johann Friedrich, 1122, 1217n,
    1244
  letter from Goethe to, 1122
Reik, Theodor, xxii, 97n, 430, 432, 804n,
    805, 806f, 1053, 1057, 1060, 1061f,
    1066f, 1219
Reinhard, Countess Christine, 1301
Reinhard, Count Karl Friedrich, 561, 1301,
    1396n
  letter from Goethe to, 561
Reinsch, F. H., 1012n, 1050n
rejuvenation, 1290
relationships,
  artist's, 469
  interpersonal, 1158
relativism, psychological, xxv
religion,
  Goethe's attitude to, 653f
  healing power of, 747
  and mental health, 278n
religiosity, secular, 983

Rembrandt, 1353, 1368
reminiscence, historical, 881
remorse, 944
renunciation, 438n
  of sexual gratification, 770
repentance, 944
repetition, 1233
  of emotional expression, 657
  and love, 185, 659
  in science and art, 545
repose, 397ff
repression, 629, 1411
  and home environment, 410
  second, 1164
rescue fantasies, 238n, 239, 750n
rescue theme,
  in Goethe's work, 238f, 753
  in *Lila,* 237f, 245
  in religious mythology, 239n
resignation, 188, 189, 201
  total, 937f
resistance(s),
  in analysis, 201f, 402f
  analysis of, 199, 202, 1198
  Goethe's, and Charlotte von Stein, 202
restitution, 1427n
restlessness, 295
Reti, Madame (*Wilhelm Meister*), 728f,
    751ff
reverie, masochistic, in Prevost, 1236
rhinoceros, 853
Rhone valley, 393
"rhyming," 63
rhythm, and meter, 1173
ribbon, gift from Charlotte von Stein, 514,
    515
Rice, Hugh S., 475n
riddance, 28f
Riemer, Friedrich Wilhelm, 12, 476, 598,
    599, 917, 918, 1297, 1299n, 1300
Riese, 40, 47
  letters from Goethe to, 40, 47
Riggi, Maddalena, 1047ff and n
ring,
  Charlotte von Stein's, sent to Goethe,
    446ff, 465, 543, 1042
  "Psyche" signet, 631ff
rites de passage, 111
ritual, compulsive, 108
rivalry, in twins, 251
  see also sibling

Rochlitz,
  letter from Goethe to, 1161
Rode, 632
Roediger, Max, 276
role-playing, 555ff, 608
Rolland, Romain, 766
Rolli, Paolo, 1252n
Roman Elegies, 533, 1012, 1019ff, 1024n,
  1042, 1052, 1053n, 1058, 1072,
  1266ff, 1325f, 1343, 1346, 1371
  quoted, 1266n, 1267ff, 1446n
Romans, and technology, 990
Rome, 1001n, 1003ff, 1025f
  Goethe's sexual experience in, 1019ff,
  1266
  meaning for Goethe, 1007, 1042
Roos, Johann Heinrich, 1191
Rorschach card, 542; test, 130
Rosanow, 21
Rostand, Edmond, 1427n
Rouget de Lisle, Claude Joseph, 484
Rousillon, Henriette von (Urania), 230, 231
Rousseau, Jean-Jacques, 170, 255, 257, 277,
  639, 1119n, 1373
routine, creative genius and, 439ff
Rovigo, 1038
ruling family, significance of birth in, 812f
rumor, and fantasy, 445
Rumpf, Josefine, 104n
Runckel, 42, 46

Sachs, Hanns, 990, 1114n
Sachsen-Meiningen, Dukes of, 616, 621
sack, 37, 56, 60f, 394, 609
  see also dreams, Goethe's
sacrifice, 107, 316
  substitute, 335
sadism, 277, 505
  in Charlotte von Stein, 1086, 1087
  infantile, in Goethe, 727
  and tragedy, 726f
  and vision, 725
St. Gotthard, 924
Saint-Martin, Claude Marquis de, 591
St. Petersburg, 24
Salzmann, Johann Daniel, 119, 192, 597
Sarasin, Philipp, 755n, 756, 757, 759, 761n,
  764, 780, 828, 1047n, 1104n
satire, 280, 363f, 446
  Lenz and, 21, 23
  see also parody
Scaliger, Joseph Justus, 1331n

scapegoat, 28, 271, 328, 457, 491
Scapin and Scapine (*Jest, Cunning, and
  Vengeance*), 1245f
Schaefer, J. W., 13
Schapiro, Meyer, xxviii, 709n
Schardt, Johann Wilhelm Christian von,
  140f
Schardt, Konkordia von, 140f
  renunciation to God, 1411
Schardt, Sophie von, 855n, 1374
Schelver, Friedrich Josef, 919
Scherer, Wilhelm, 286
*Scherz, List und Rache, see Jest, Cunning
  and Vengeance*
Scheumann, Karl H., 1111
Schilder, Paul, 564, 986n
Schiller, Charlotte, 151
Schiller, Ernst Friedrich Wilhelm, 1287n
Schiller, Friedrich, 87, 370, 373, 533, 640,
  961, 1113, 1117, 1187, 1189, 1293,
  1295, 1299, 1365, 1382
  review of *Egmont,* 1040n
  letters from Goethe to, 87, 746, 787f,
  1192, 1215, 1287 and n, 1296
  letter to Goethe, 788
schizophrenia, 1127n, 1148, 1177ff
  and originality, 1180
  and unifunctionality, 1420
schizophrenic(s), 23, 30
  acting out of delusions and, 236
  activity/passivity problem, 744
  artistic potential in, 70
  and interest in children, 775n
  interpretation of gestures by, 58
  "middle register" missing in, 205
  speech and thought of, Freud on, 564
  and splitting, 273
  and struggle with drives, 1378
Schlegel, J. E.,
  Canut, 213
Schlosser, Cornelia, *see* Cornelia
Schlosser, H. P., 173
Schlosser, I. F. H., 87
  letters from Goethe to, 87, 838
Schlosser, Johann Georg, 24, 26, 32, 44, 47,
  50, 85n, 86f, 92, 93ff, 110, 123ff,
  170, 172, 173, 177, 212ff, 220, 245,
  249, 275, 283, 284, 286, 288f, 358,
  678, 714n, 723, 1198
  as ideal model for Goethe, 213
  letters from Goethe to, 174
Schlosser, Johanna, *see* Fahlmer

Schmehling, Gertrud Elizabeth, 341
Schmerz, *see* Weh
Schmid, Gunther, xx
Schmidt, Erich, 26n, 393n
Schmidt, Johann Christoph, 1321
Schnauss, 692
Schneeberg, 994, 1042
Schöll, Adolf, 209n
Schönborn, 177n
Schönemann, Anna Elisabeth (Lili), 94, 111,
    117, 118ff, 124, 126ff, 155, 156, 161,
    192, 197, 222, 224, 251, 327, 349f,
    358, 374, 388f, 391, 925, 1037n,
    1068ff
Schönkopf, Anna Katharina (Annette, Käth-
    chen), 44, 47, 49, 55, 58, 62f, 116,
    119, 224, 1064, 1065, 1367
  letters from Goethe to, 116
school for girls, 65, 251
Schopenhauer, xxx f
Schoppe, Caspar, 1331n, 1340
Schreiber, Carl, 689n
Schröter, Corona, 119, 219, 242, 339, 341ff,
    352, 379ff, 404, 447f, 463, 585f, 828
  letter from Goethe to, 379f
Schuhu (*Birds*), 421f
Schulenberg, Werner von der, 172n, 1035n,
    1201n
Schulthess, Barbara, 652f, 755n
Scipio, 1129
Schwab, Gustav, 801
Schwalbenstein, 329
scientific discovery, psychology of, 545
scientist, creativity of, 1382n
science, Goethe's interest in, 989f, 1109f,
    1144ff, 1163, 1326
Scioppius, *see* Schoppe
screen memory, 260, 262
Seckendorf, Count von, 1015
Seckendorf, Karl Siegmund, 335n, 1217
secondary process, and artistic production,
    826
  see also primary process
secret, 208, 215ff
secretary, J. C. Goethe's, 1357
Secundus, Johannes (Janus), 1270, 1271
seduction, 258n, 322
seductiveness, in Charlotte von Stein, 1086
Seekatz, Johann Konrad, 608
Seidel, 400, 875n, 997, 1002, 1218
  letters from Goethe to, 1002, 1003, 1027
Seleucus, 914

self-annihilation, 67
self-awareness, denial of, 485
self-conception, 1043, 1362
self-consciousness, 615
self-criticism, 1159
self-cure, 325
self-destructiveness,
  and creativity, 866
  of Goethe's relations to women, 224
self-discernment, 1162
self-evaluation
  in analysis, 277f
  erroneous, 737
  Goethe's, as poet and scientist, 1119
self-knowledge, 1155ff
  resistance to, in analysis, 402
self-observation, 293, 430, 432, 942, 1156f
self-preservation, 1366
self-punishment,
  illness as, 293
  for oedipal desires, 417
self-redemption, 726
self-revelation, 434
Selke de Sanchez, Angela, 416n, 462n
Senckenberg, Johann Christian von, 1035n,
    1229n
Sentimental Ones, The (*Empfindsamen,
    Die*), 290
separation,
  happiness before, 590
  toleration of, 401
separation anxiety, 535, 723
Serlo (*Wilhelm Meister*), 902, 908ff, 1445
serpent, brazen, 433f
Sesenheim, 97, 1066, 1069
Seven Years' War, 158, 159
sex role, interchange of, 351
sexual
  confessions, Goethe's, to Karl August,
    1324
  demand, and repetition in love, 660
  development, Goethe's, phases, 1031
  gratification, and art, mutual exclusive-
    ness, 1386n
  intercourse, *see* intercourse
  patterns, and parental influence, 1036;
    and social ascent, 1036
  play, 36; *see also* forepleasure
  strivings, 225
sexuality
  and artistic creation, 893
  as ego-function, 1412

sexuality (*Continued*)
  and guilt feelings, 421
  infantile, and relation to parents, 709
sexualization, of ego-functions, 1411f, 1414
Shaftesbury, 932
Shakespeare, xvii, xix, 29, 55, 61, 63, 64, 82,
    351, 352, 420, 745, 929, 931, 1118,
    1141, 1164, 1260, 1314, 1353, 1393
  As You Like It, 63
  Hamlet, 902, 920ff, 927ff, 957, 1040n,
    1430n
  Midsummer Night's Dream, 301, 304ff,
    310, 312, 314, 1207ff
"Shakespeare and No End!," 931, 1164n
shame, and guilt, 1066
"share," meaning of, to Goethe, 1276n
sheep, 1191
shoes, and fetishism, 1445f
shyness, 315
siblings,
  and sexual conflicts, 101
  Goethe's memory of his, 702f
  incestuous relationship, 251
sibling rivalry, 73, 378, 621
Siblings, The (Die Geschwister), 155,
    207ff, 225, 227, 246, 252, 255
  quotations, 209, 211, 213
  and *Lila,* compared, 244f
Sicily, 1008ff, 1042, 1085
sickness
  Goethe's attitude to, 664
  Goethe's (of 1768), 875f
  and traveling, 409f
signal, and referent, identification, 564f
Silberer, Herbert, 271, 1281
Silesia, 1346
silhouettes, 129f, 149, 252, 1389
Simmel, Georg, 964, 998, 1447f
sin, Spinoza's view, 943
Singspiele, Goethe's, 1249ff
  psychological meaning, 1259ff
Sion, 400
sister-conflict, in *Lila,* 244
skating,
  in men's clothing, 104f, 939
  rink, 104, 112, 113
skins,
  Goethe's use of imagery of, 1036n, 1164
  stripping off, 609
sleep, 1375
  defense against, 485
  dream and wish to, 1283

sleep (*Continued*)
  dreamless, 1419
  psychology of, 965f
  as regressive state, 1428
  thought processes during, 84
slippers, *see* shoe fetishism
smell,
  of human activities, 363
  see also odor
snake(s), 33, 913n
social criticism, 623ff
society, response of genius to, 1311f
Socrates, 425n
sodomy, 1332
soldiers, phobic, 1054
"solitario bosco ombroso," 1252f
Sömmering, Samuel Thomas von, 283
  letter from Goethe to, 1110f
somnambulism, 83, 114
son, Goethe's first, 1138f, 1142
"son religion," 652
songs, 1256
Sophocles, 1089
Soret, 283, 300, 332, 859f, 1125
  letter from Goethe to, 1125
"soul, beautiful," 470f, 473f, 475
specters, terrifying, 612
speech,
  direct, use of, 563n
  Goethe's interrupted, at Ilmenau, 859ff
spermatogenesis, 1402
Spinoza, 930ff, 984
Spitz, René, 256n
splitting, 272, 277
Springer, Brunold, 32
spurts, in Goethe's creativity, 1143
Staercke, August, 284
staircase, 1046 and n
Stapfer, Philipp Albert, 569n
starfish, 1013
status,
  and personality, 350
  role in Goethe's life, 39, 350, 378f, 669ff
  social, of Goethe's sweethearts, 1071
  see also aristocracy; nobility
Staubbach, 395f
Stein, Charlotte von,
  appearance, 146
  attitude to sexuality, 144f
  character, 1086ff
  and Christiane, comparison, 1307
  as "confessor" of Goethe, 199f

Stein, Charlotte von (*Continued*)
  and Goethe's creativity/productivity, 682, 1189
  and *Egmont,* 1041
  family and life, 140ff
  and kissing, 1070, 1270
  and *Lila,* 239ff
  marriage, 143
  personality, 142ff
  relation to her mother, 188
  Goethe's relationship to, and psychoanalysis, compared, 1093f, 1099n
  Goethe's relationship with, 138f, 140ff, 176, 179ff, 210, 224, 292ff, 325ff, 367, 388, 434f, 495, 570ff, 731, 750, 815ff, 881ff, 945ff, 952ff, 972, 1077ff, 1084f, 1088, 1097ff
  as representing reality principle, 1200
  Goethe's resistance to, 201f
  Rino, 1084n
  selfishness of, 1199
  sexual relationship with Goethe, question of, 200f, 519ff, 551, 776f, 963
  and *The Siblings,* 209ff, 470
  separation from, 1149ff
  silhouette of, 129f, 149, 252
  and Spinoza, 933
  as superego representative, 690
  letters from Goethe, *see table on pp. 1535ff. below;* general comments, 180ff, 461f, 965n; missing, 956; frequency distribution, 1183ff; use of 'Du' in, *see* 'Du'
  letter to Goethe, 535
  letter to Frau von Döring, 166
  letters to Fritz von Stein, 143f, 928
  letters to Herder, 532f, 910f, 1033
  letters to Knebel, *see* Knebel
  letters to Zimmermann, 160, 161, 162, 163, 164, 165, 166, 167, 168, 169, 187, 507
  other references, 23, 26, 119, 129f, 140ff, 209ff, 251f, 257, 281, 283, 292ff, 311, 313, 315, 327, 343ff, 351ff, 361ff, 368f, 388f, 402f, 407f, 417, 428f, 446ff, 464, 473f, 478ff, 487f, 497, 505f, 513, 515f, 522f, 524f, 544, 552ff, 558, 583, 610, 614, 617, 652f, 655, 659, 662f, 667, 698, 769, 771, 793, 797, 807, 810, 819ff, 833, 847, 851f, 919, 950, 976, 998f, 1031,

Stein, Charlotte von (*Continued*)
  1070, 1083ff, 1155, 1163f, 1198, 1230ff, 1236, 1317ff, 1443
Stein, Ernst von, 554, 599, 771f, 774, 952ff
Stein, Fritz von,
  correspondence with Goethe's mother, 877
  as mother substitute, 776
  Goethe's letters to, 1010, 1094
  other references, 143f, 283, 302, 455, 519, 532, 539, 554, 588, 609, 634, 771ff, 786, 817, 822ff, 828, 829, 845, 874f, 968, 971, 972f, 1074, 1150, 1184, 1290
Stein, Baron Gottlob Ernst Josias Friedrich von, 143, 145, 147, 489, 591f
Stein, Heinrich Friedrich Karl vom und zu, 496
Stein, Karl von, 605, 771f, 773, 1184, 1290
Steinen, Wolfram von den, 1145, 1446
Steiner, 419
Stekel, Wilhelm, 304
Stella (*Stella*), 126f
Stella, 126ff, 358
Sterba, Editha and Richard, 1310, 1312, 1313, 1372n, 1390
Sternberg, Count K. von,
  letter from Goethe to, 440
Sterne, Laurence, 1026
Sternfeld, Frederick W., xix, 1256
Sternthal, interpretation of name, 239f
Sternthal, Baron (*Lila*), 232, 239f, 242f, 246
Stickfluss, 854
Stieler, Karl, 1228
Stolberg, Counts, 370, 373, 848
Stolberg, Auguste, Countess of, 119ff, 128, 190ff, 201, 245, 250, 253, 1089
  letters from Goethe to, 120, 121, 122, 123, 191, 192f, 217, 250, 536f, 676n, 988
Stolberg, Friedrich Leopold, 988
stone-eater, 427, 433
stories, make-believe, 566n
Storm and Stress, *see* Sturm und Drang
storytelling, 74f, 77f; *see also* fairy tales
Strassburg, 19, 23, 97, 119n, 129, 148, 172, 192, 375, 597, 630, 654, 1060, 1066, 1216
Stratonice, 914, 915
straw, wisps of, 34f
Strecke, Johann Philipp, 1015f
structure, personality, accretion of, 667
Strümcke, Heinrich, 344

Sturm und Drang, 6, 16f, 19, 22, 105, 160, 177, 257, 268, 277, 279f, 281, 358, 374, 386, 488, 606, 649, 651, 652, 828, 885, 933, 945, 1096, 1311, 1315, 1379f, 1393
Stützerbach, 293, 458, 488, 1029n
style, function of, 549
Styria, 1014
subjectivation of objective, 644
subjectivity, and reaction to works of art, 82
sublimation, 188, 1178n, 1406ff, 1415f
  capacity for, and creativity, 70
  Freud and, 1406ff
  and group membership, 1037n
  of homosexuality, 629
  male, 1404
  phallic, 1405
  of pregenital instinctual energy, 297
  of psychosis, 1377f
  and works of art, 1378
sublime, experience of the, 397
substitutes, for love-object, 733
Suetonius, 109f
Suez, 1446
suffering, and creativity, 1382f
suicide, 29, 88, 202, 208ff, 224
sun, sign for, 300, 461
superego, 176, 324f, 741
  aggrandizement and inflation, 797
  beloved woman as, 495
  and cultural products, 1426f
  development of, in Goethe, 79n, 392, 480
  dissolution of parts of, 50
  and father identification, 1011
  Goethe's "Divine" and, 794
  Duke Karl August as representing, 638
  lacunae in, 1393f
  and oedipal vicissitudes, 268n
  in orgasm, 1419
  and reality testing, 700n
  reorganization of Goethe's, 972
  representatives, Goethe's, 1322
  resistance to jokes, 1425
  Barbara Schulthess as, 653
  structure of, in genius, 1392
Suphan, Bernhard, 933, 1033
surgery and analysis, comparison, 281f
Susanne (*Wilhelm Meister*), 1446
sutura incisiva, 1117
swallowing, pain in, 428f
Swedenborg, 644

Swift, Jonathan, 127
Switzerland, 24, 28, 129, 368ff
  Goethe's second journey to, 1214ff
  meaning of, to Goethe, 370, 756
symbol(s),
  change of, and reality, 538, 542
  dream, interpretation of, 1276f
  masculine, 434n
symptoms,
  and creativity, 866f
  disappearance in analysis, 157, 435
  first appearance, in patient, 227f
  neurotic, Goethe's, 1054, 1363ff
  psychotic, and works of art, 1375
  transformation into character traits, 1378
syphilis, 37, 1036n
Szymanowska, Marie, 1257f

Tagebücher, 111; *see also* diaries
"Tag- und Jahreshefte," 254f, 570, 1135
talent,
  and genius, comparison, 1379; relation, 1403f; in *Wilhelm Meister,* 1441f
  in women, 1401
  in young, and future genius, 1314
talion, 306
talisman, 611f
Talleyrand, 842
Tantalides, 1035
Tantalus, 274, 1073
tapeworms, 438
Tasso, 218, 338, 431n, 519, 569, 588, 1018, 1157, 1261, 1316, 1325, 1326
Tasso (*Tasso*), 696
Tasso, Torquato, 123, 1013, 1264
Tauris, see *Iphigenia in Tauris*
Tchao chi cou ell, 784
teasing, 1088
technical terms, Goethe and, 440
technology, modern, Goethe and, 1446
teilen, 1276n
telepathy, 1219f
tension,
  in Goethe's poems, 1172
  level of, and art, 273
Textor, Anna Christine, 214
theater,
  Goethe and the, 262, 719ff
  status of, 341
theft, 811
Theocritus, 1302
Therese (*Wilhelm Meister*), 208n

theses, Goethe's, 172

Theseus, 1267f; *see also* Shakespeare, *Midsummer Night's Dream*

thinking,
  in analytic patient, 198
  inefficiency of, 1187
  source of energy used for, 1407

Thisbe, 305f, 1207; *see also* Shakespeare, *Midsummer Night's Dream*

Thoas, 316f, 326, 1209

Thomas (*Jery und Bätely*), 1218

Thoranc, Count, 607, 1046, 1102, 1363

Thorn, Goethe's letter to, 1177n

"thralldom," 584f, 603

"throttling," 1065

thrusting, 107f

Thuringia, 606, 867

Tibullus, 1331

tide, as symbol, 1283

Tiefenort, 608

Tiefurt, 300, 429, 431

Tiefurter Journal, 415, 551f, 553, 555f, 558f, 794

time,
  archaic, 1045
  and diary keeping, 693
  experience of, Goethe's, 490; in love and worship, 882
  preoccupation with, 462
  splitting and condensing, 490, 617
  subjective and objective, 1190f
  unconscious and, 1043
  various forms of, 1043f

Tischbein, Johann Heinrich Wilhelm, 778, 893, 1027, 1246

Titania, 301, 303ff, 310, 311ff, 916; *see also* Shakespeare, *Midsummer Night's Dream*

Titus, 1129

Tobler, Georg Christoph, 443n, 649n, 788f

tolerance, 525f, 979

Tolstoi, L. N., 1017n, 1312n

touching, 326

tower, suspended, 1279

traditional characters, identification with, 1100

tragedy, 425, 724
  Greek, 1192

transference, 184ff, 220, 226, 293, 367, 516n, 527, 572f, 879
  defense against, 169
  discovery of generality in, 186n

transference (*Continued*)
  dissolution of, 945
  effect of analysis of, 331
  limitations of, 683 and n
  "madness" in, 523f
  patient's reaction to, 184
  peak of, 680ff
  struggle for means to overcome, 879
  see also mother-transference

transference love, 515 and n

transformation, of poet's ego, 314f

transition periods, mechanisms in, 36

transmigration of souls, 182

transsubstantiation, 338

Trapp,
  letter from Goethe to, 598

traumata,
  "benign," 665n
  and repetition of emotions, 657

traveling,
  and death, 409
  Goethe's attitude to, 370, 409, 663, 911f, 1214ff
  and menstruation, 409f
  and sickness, 409f

Trebra, Friedrich Wilhelm, 866

tree-pruning, simile, 292f

triangle situation, 127, 192, 228, 261

Trinity, 1140n

Tristram Shandy, see Sterne

Triumph of Sentimentality, 254ff, 267, 272, 273, 274, 276, 277, 278, 284, 288, 317, 1080, 1247

"Triumph of Virtue" (poems), 1342

troubadours, 600

Truefriend (*The Birds*), 421f, 425, 437, 444, 446, 736

truth, psychological, 626

tuberculosis, 37, 759, 1148, 1178

Türckheim, Lili, 534, 1068
  letter from Goethe to, 534
  see also Schoenemann, Lili

twins, 251

Tydeus, 1336

Ubald (*Tasso*), 123

"Über den Granit," *see* "Granite, On"

Ulrich, Caroline Wilhelmina Johanne (later Riemer), 1299

Ulysses, 232

uncanniness, 180, 249

unconscious, 237, 403
  contradictions in, xxi
  and creative thinking, 1187n
  images in, 1045
  impact on present, 331
  and time relations, 1043ff
  timelessness of, xxii, 693
unfaithfulness, in transference, 221
Unger, Rudolf, 527
Ungleichen Hausgenossen, Die, 1261, 1263
unifunctional states, 1419
  in the genius, 1432
United States, 118, 1446, 1447
"Universe," Goethe's unwritten novel about
  the, 684
Unterhaltungen deutscher Ausgewanderter,
  809
"Untheilnehmung," 410
Unzelmann, Karl Wilhelm Ferdinand, 269
Urania, 230
Urfaust, 472n
Utopia, 1447

vacuum, 482, 483
vagina dentata, 1280n
van Gogh, Vincent, 1169
Varro, Marcus Terentius, 1337
Veit, D. J., 261n
venereal disease,
  Goethe's fear of, 1024, 1053n, 1269, 1347,
  1350
  Duke of Weimar and, 1323f
  see also syphilis
Venetian Epigrams, 1163, 1325f, 1346ff,
  1371
Venice, 1014, 1016, 1346
Venus, sign for, 496
Verazio, Dr. (*Lila*), 232, 234, 236ff, 240,
  242ff
verbalization, and luck, 500n
Verleugnung, 438
Verona, 1003
versatility, of Goethe, 1019
*Versuch (Der) als Vermittler von Objekt
  und Subjekt,* 1113
*Versuch über die Metamorphose der Pflan-
  zen,* 919
vertigo, *see* acrophobia
Vicenza, 1025
Vienna, 1245
vision, and sadism, 725
visualization, of images, 1173f

Vogel, Christian Georg Karl, 755n
void, meaning of, 482
Voight, C. S.,
  letter from Goethe to, 1291n
Voigt, C. G., 714, 859
Voltaire, 669, 843
Voss, Johann Heinrich, 145, 160f, 352n
voyeurism, 231f, 374, 511, 607f, 721, 1148
Vulpius, Dr., 678n, 1183
Vulpius, Christian August, 1286, 1287, 1289
Vulpius, Christiane, 34n, 72, 465, 806n, 808,
  837, 962, 1012, 1020, 1022, 1041,
  1061, 1085n, 1096, 1139f, 1149,
  1151f, 1236n, 1271, 1286ff, 1370f,
  1372, 1416, 1444, 1445
  biographical data, 1286f
  character of correspondence with Goethe,
  1292
  comportment, 1298
  Duke Karl August's attitude to, 1327,
  1329
  Goethe's image of, 1300ff
  marriage to Goethe, 1299
  personality type, 1306f
  pregnancy of, 1374
  relation to Goethe, 1290ff
  reasons for Goethe's not marrying, 1294
  saves Goethe's life, 1327, 1330
  letters to Goethe, 1288, 1291ff, 1295,
  1296, 1298, 1305
  letters from Goethe to, 838, 1293, 1296,
  1297, 1298, 1299, 1302
Vulpius, Johann Friedrich, 1286
Vulpius, Juliane, 1287
Vulpius, Sophie Ernestine Louise, 1287, 1289
Vulpius, Wolfgang, 1216, 1286n, 1287n

Waelder, Robert, xxvi, 1181, 1407n, 1417n,
  1436
Wagner, Heinrich Leopold, 933, 1310n,
  1379
Wahl, Julius, 478n
waistcoat, gift from Charlotte von Stein, 514
Waldner-Freundstein, Luise Adelaide, 855
Walpurgis-night, 303, 306f, 310; *see also
  Faust*
Walther von der Vogelweide, 1170
Wanderer, The (nickname of Goethe), 231
Warnecke, Friedrich, 31n
Wartensleben, Countess, 601n
waterfall, 395, 396
Weber (alias of Goethe), 3, 15

Wedel, Otto Joachim Moriz von, 400, 501

Weh and *Schmerz,* 206

Weimar, 3, 9, 11, 17, 23, 26, 123, 137ff, 148, 149, 222, 286, 347f, 384, 434, 445, 460, 465, 523, 555, 606, 677, 925, 958, 984, 996, 1245, 1246, *et passim*
  court behavior at, 241, 489, 606
  history, 157ff
  sack of, 1327

Weininger, Otto, 1354

Weislingen (*Götz von Berlichingen*), 1049, 1090

Weiss, Christian Samuel, 1146

Welt, 502n

Weltschmerz, 206

Wenden, 18

Werner (*Wilhelm Meister*), 722f

Wernigerode, 3, 4, 5, 9, 14, 15

Werther, 7, 25, 29, 47, 81f, 85f, 90f, 95, 98ff, 112f, 115, 117f, 129, 148n, 150f, 211n, 221, 227, 246, 255, 257, 264, 268, 274, 277, 280f, 283, 360, 362, 417, 540f, 560f, 563ff, 577f, 628, 714, 790n, 810, 818ff, 869, 881, 995, 1049ff, 1055, 1192, 1253, 1260f, 1369, 1396, 1428

Werthern, Countess of, 996, 1318

Werthern-Frohndorf, Emilie, Countess von, 454n, 455

Werthern-Neuenheiligen, Count von, 495ff

Werthern-Neuenheiligen, Countess von, 380n, 420, 446, 454n, 495ff, 508, 512f, 516f, 593

Wertherstimmung, 540

West-östlcher Diwan, 573, 1104n, 1362

Wetzlar, 86, 88, 93ff, 111, 156, 192, 286, 633, 636

wholeness, 1081

Wilhelm Meister (*Wilhelm Meister*), 239, 259, 262f, 271, 696, 831ff, 839, 901ff, 914ff

Wilhelm Meister, 269, 270, 273, 329, 435, 570, 678, 694ff, 701ff, 750, 751ff, 826, 883, 901ff, 928, 959f, 992, 1094, 1118, 1164, 1261, 1265, 1323, 1438ff
  quotations, 253, 259f, 262, 702, 706, 709, 718ff, 723, 725, 754, 759f, 764f, 829ff, 834, 836, 840f, 903f, 909, 915, 920, 921, 928f, 1193ff, 1443, 1444, 1446, 1449ff, 1454ff

Wilhelm Meisters Lehrjahre, 208n, 235, 470f, 512, 1220, 1438ff; *see also* "Confessions of a Beautiful Soul"

Wilhelm Meister's Theatrical Mission, 259, 261f, 264, 266f, 494n, 556, 690, 694n, 701ff

Wilhelm Meisters Wanderjahre, 239, 804, 1439, 1447f

Wiederfinden, 1115

Wieland, 90, 159, 164, 182, 348, 358, 382, 384, 390, 443, 444n, 679f, 731, 774, 854, 1077, 1310n
  letter from Goethe to, 182
  letter to Merck, 523

Wiesbaden, 33

Wilbrand, Johann Bernhard, 1124

Wilhelmsthal, 608

Willemer, Marianne von, 573, 1072, 1216n

William (*The Siblings*), 207ff, 219ff, 246

Winckelmann, 321, 984

wine, red, avoidance of, 1065f

Winterstein, A. R. F. von, 1042n

wish-fulfillment, 208, 369, 475
  and dreams, 1285n
  hallucinatory, 297
  in *Lila,* 240, 242
  and pheasant dream, 1284
  and punishment, 314

witches, 1061

withdrawal, from infantile love-objects, 662

Witkowski, Georg, 64n, 69, 123n, 163, 834n

Wittenberg, university, 5

Wolff, Christian, 1014

Wolff, Eugen, 478n, 759

Wolff, Oskar Ludwig Bernhard, 1300

Wollschlaeger, 176n

Wolzogen, Matherine von, 151

woman (women)
  and absolutism, 52
  arrogance towards, in Goethe, 166
  and bourgeoisie, 53
  as castrated being, 312
  distressed, helping, 343
  elevation of, 334
  genius and talent in, 1400f
  happy, rare in Goethe's work, 935n
  and nobility, 52f
  phallic, 1208
  unconscious desire to debase, 1345

womb, fantasy of return to, 61

Wood, Alexander, 786n

"Word about the Author of Pilatus, A,"
737f
words,
  and breath, 1225
  meaning of, for Goethe, 547, 564
  magic of, 549, 564f, 1222
work,
  child's, 1189
  and creativity, distinction, 171
  Goethe's attitude to, 601f, 1186ff
  Goethe's father and, 1201
  inability to, meaning of, 1200
  and instinctual discharge, 1420
  psychotherapy and, 1197f
work-disturbance, Goethe's, 171
"world," 502
world, artist builds his own, 549
wrestling, Swiss, 1218
Württemberg, Duke of, 170

Xenien, 1116, 1158

Yorick, 1040

Zahn, Johann Karl Wilhelm, 1020f
Zelter, Carl Friedrich, 476, 715, 1244
  letters from Goethe to, 467n, 476, 714f,
    912, 930, 997f, 1082, 1123, 1146,
    1216, 1257, 1262, 1369
Zethus (*Elpenor*), 784
Zeus, 71, 412
Ziegler, Louise Henriette Friederike von
  (Lila), 230, 231
Zimmermann, Johann Georg, 130n, 145,
  148ff, 160, 162, 203, 245, 251, 252,
  283n, 445, 512, 1152n
  letters, to Charlotte von Stein, 149, 150
  letters, from Katharine Elisabeth Goethe,
    252n
  letter, to Lavater, 146
  see also Stein, Charlotte von
Zurich, 387, 423, 641ff, 1245, 1246

References to Goethe's Letters
to Charlotte von Stein
(chronologically arranged)

1776, undated	199f, 217, 647, 771	Sep. 14	297, 1223n
Jan. 8	155	Oct. 30	298, 390
Jan. 9	155	Oct. 31	273
Jan. 27	772	Nov. 7	294f
Feb. 12	187, 772	Nov. 8	292, 441
Feb. 23	179	Dec. 4	14
Feb. 24	179	Dec. 6	14f
Mar. 19	774, 1077	Dec. 9	295f, 366, 875
Mar. 20	1078	Dec. 10	302
Mar. 25	342, 506f	Dec. 27	15
Mar. 26	342		
Mar. 31	343	1778, Jan. 1	293
Apr. 5	772	Jan. 19	334
Apr. 14	180f	May 10	298
May 1	188	May 17	298
May 2	366	May 19	298f, 444
May 20(?)	189f	May 28	298
May 24	192f	Jun. 1	414f
Jun. 22	194	Jun. 2	337
Jul. 5	218	Jun. 4	415
Jul. 16	195, 773	Aug. 27	462f
Jul. 22	468	Sep. 13	1091
Aug. 8	196	Nov. 11	474n
Aug. 10	198	Dec. 10	301
Sep. 10	202f	Dec. 11	301
Sep. 11	204		
Sep. 12	203, 205, 218	1779, Feb. 14	329n, 1259
Sep. 16	205	Feb. 22	1259n
Oct. 7	210	Mar. 1	330
Nov. 3	279	Mar. 2	337f
Nov. 8	294	Mar. 7	401f
		Apr. 19	353
1777, Jan. 3	240	Apr. 20	354
Jun. 12	292	May 7	354
Sep. 6	293, 1075	May 12	396
Sep. 12	290	May 13	355

1779,	Aug. 21	516	Mar. 3	493
	Sep. 1	389	Mar. 7	497, 498
	Sep. 7	514	Mar. 8	498f, 514
	Sep. 26	391	Mar. 10	499f
	Sep. 28	388f, 390	Mar. 11	501ff, 507ff
	Oct. 3	397f	Mar. 12	508ff, 514
	Oct. 14	400	Mar. 13	517f, 777
	Oct. 23	460	Mar. 22	518
	Nov. 2	1214n	Mar. 23	518f, 522
	Nov. 5	377f	Mar. 25	519, 520
	Nov. 11	393ff	Mar. 26	585
	Nov. 24	640	Mar. 27	522, 586
	Nov. 30	425f	Mar. 28	663
			Apr. 4	591
1780,	Jan. 3	1218	Apr. 22	588
	Mar. 1	1074	Apr. 27	636
	Mar. 26	429	May 3	567f
	Apr. 4	431	May 7	601
	May 1	412, 414, 446	May 21	668
	May 3	427	May 27	637
	May 5	427f, 433	May 28	593
	Jun. 5	433, 435	May 30	600f, 652
	Jun. 14	439, 441, 446, 447, 1092	Jun. 6	668
	Jun. 24	436	Jul. 1	594
	Jun. 26	450	Jul. 5	554
	Jun. 28	454	Jul. 8	553
	Jun. 30	433, 434, 436f, 455, 458	Jul. 12	664
	Jul. 3	452	Aug. 28	584
	Sep. 6	466, 467f	Sep. 13	587
	Sep. 8	453, 478f, 490, 670	Sep. 20	551, 552f
	Sep. 10	488	Sep. 21	551
	Sep. 11	489	Oct. 1	555, 777
	Sep. 12	485, 487f, 489	Oct. 9	574, 587, 609
	Sep. 18	454	Oct. 19	588
	Sep. 19	485	Oct. 27	588
	Sep. 21	485	Oct. 29	1232
	Sep. 24	1389	Nov. 7	492
	Oct. 10	456, 857	Nov. 12	664n
	Oct. 14	485	Nov. 14	650
	Oct. 20	632	Nov. 18	670
	Oct. 25	631f	Nov. 27	631, 634
	Oct. 29	457, 536, 588, 632	Dec. 2	634f
	Nov. 2	455	Dec. 4	599
	Nov. 24	526f	Dec. 7	662, 684
	Dec. 12	525, 1075n	Dec. 9	610f, 664
	Dec. 24	494	Dec. 10	591, 599f, 612, 637f
			Dec. 12	538, 542, 550, 612
1781,	Jan. 15	493	Dec. 19	590, 712
	Feb. 6	495	Dec. 20	712
	Feb. 8	490f, 1075	Dec. 29	538f, 659n
	Feb. 20	639		
	Mar. 1	493	1782, Jan. 1	588f

1782, Jan. 2	589	Dec. 24	811
Jan. 20	623	Dec. 25	811
Jan. 27	662	Dec. 27	670
Feb. 18	611f, 668	Dec. 29	811f
Mar. 14	589		
Mar. 17	590, 828	1783, Jan. 13	800
Mar. 20	587, 656	Feb. 1	813
Mar. 21	676	Feb. 3	814
Mar. 22	601, 618	Feb. 7	814
Mar. 24	636	Feb. 8	815
Mar. 29	606	Mar. 1	815
Mar. 30	613	Apr. 14	817
Mar. 31	613f	Apr. 19	818
Apr. 2	614, 624, 670	May 4	815f
Apr. 3	625	May 28	817
Apr. 5	625, 627	Jun. 14	817
Apr. 6	541, 615, 650	Jun. 16	817
Apr. 9	618, 619, 620	Jun. 24	819
Apr. 10	601, 611, 689	Sep. 9	807f, 822f
Apr. 12	592, 615, 621f, 626, 669, 671, 674nf	Sep. 11	823
		Sep. 20	816, 823
Apr. 17	625f	Sep. 28	823
May ?	778	Oct. 2	824
May 7/8	590	Oct. 7	824
May 12	616f	Nov. 19	794
May 13	622, 676	Nov. 23	946
May 15	617, 676	Nov. 26	880
Jun. 21	693f	Dec. 6	873
Jun. 24	694, 1439n	Dec. 8(?)	880f
Jul. 8	732	Dec. 14	880
Aug. 9	732		
Aug. 10	729	1784, Feb. 21	862
Aug. 23	722n	Mar. 24	854
Aug. 26	734	Mar. 27	849ff
Aug. 27	734, 737	May 6/7	846f, 882
Aug. 28	747f	Jun. 3	847f
Sep. 8	733	Jun. 5	843f
Sep. 9	733	Jun. 7	843
Sep. 17	743	Jun. 10	616
Sep. 18	767, 808n	Jun. 14	846, 882f
Oct. 2	748	Jun. 24	877
Oct. 18	722n	Jun. 25	877
Oct. 21	800	Jun. 28	877f
Nov. 7	748, 880	Jul. 24	883
Nov. 8	749	Aug. 13	885
Nov. 16	797	Aug. 18	844f
Nov. 17	797ff	Aug. 19	628, 773f
Nov. 23	802f	Aug. 22	885
Dec. 1	810	Aug. 30	886f
Dec. 5	810f	Sep. 28	846
Dec. 8	811	Nov. 9	1092
Dec. 16	800	Nov. 22	963

1784, Dec. 5	957	May 21	960
Dec. 12	959	May 23	960
		Jun. 15	987
1785, Jan. 11	961	Jun. 25	995
Feb. 19	961	Jul. 9	985, 996
Mar. 9	961f	Jul. 21	980f
Mar. 10	962	Aug. 16	994, 1042
Mar. 15	946, 965	Aug. 22	99
Apr. 20	966f	Aug. 23	994
May 24	978	Sep. 1	99
Jun. 27	967	Dec. 29	1008, 1274
Aug. 8	967f		
Sep. 5	990	1787, Jan. 17	1009, 1366
Sep. 8	968	Jan. 20	1081f
Sep. 11	968	Feb. 2	1009
Sep. 17	968	Feb. 21	922
Oct. 1	969f	Apr. 18	1010, 1083
Oct. 3	973	May 25	1079
Oct. 6	971, 973	Jun. 8	1080f
Nov. 11	983		
Nov. 13	973f	1789, Jun. 1	1149f
Dec. 26	976	Jun. 8	1150f, 1374
Dec. 27	976	Sep. 7	1151
1786, Jan. 26	1263	1826, Aug. 29	1153

This book was edited by Esther E. Jacoby and Georgiana W. Strickland. The book was designed by Richard Kinney. The type face used for the text is Granjon based on a design by Claude Garamond and redesigned under the supervision of George W. Jones for the Linotype Corporation. Bodoni, designed by Giambattista Bodoni in about 1788, is used for the display type.

The book is printed on Warren's Olde Style Antique white wove paper. The binding is Columbia Mills' Riverside Linen, and Minerva Vellum. The slipcase is also covered with Minerva Vellum. Manufactured in the United States of America.